Rosemarie Lamlee
784-2830

Child Development M-W 12:30

DEVELOPMENTAL PSYCHOLOGY TODAY

FOURTH EDITION

ACKNOWLEDGEMENTS

We would like to acknowledge several people whose contributions to an earlier edition of this book are reflected in this fourth edition. Dr. Robert B. McCall of Boys Town Center for the Study of Youth Development was the original author of the chapters on prenatal development and the newborn; Dr. Sandra Scarr of Yale University was the original author of the three introductory chapters; and Dr. Bert Moore of the University of Texas at Dallas, Dr. Joy Moore of the University of Texas at Dallas, and Dr. Bill Underwood of the University of Texas were the original authors of the personality chapters.

Dr. Dan I. Slobin of the University of California at Berkeley was the author of the language chapters in an earlier edition, and he also reviewed the chapters for this edition. Dr. Margaret Reedy of the University of Southern California was the original author of the three chapters on adulthood and provided a draft on the final chapter on the end of life; she also contributed revisions for these chapters in the present edition.

We are also grateful to the following individuals. Their ideas, comments, and suggestions were of great help to us as we revised this edition:

Frank R. Ascione, *Utah State University at Logan*
Nancy Bedford, *Germanna Community College*
Elizabeth Brown, *University of Maryland*
Robert B. Cairns, *University of North Carolina at Chapel Hill*
Vera Cull, *University of Alabama in Birmingham*
Marvin W. Daehler, *University of Massachusetts at Amherst*
Polly Gillette, *Northern Virginia Community College*
James Gingles, *Washington State University*
Bernard S. Gorman, *Nassau Community College*
Mark T. Greenberg, *University of Washington at Seattle*
Jonas Langer, *University of California at Berkeley*
Cynthia Rae Margolin, *San Jose State University*
Cynthia Marshall, *Skyline College*
Trevor McKee, *Brigham Young University*
Alexandra Muller, *Indiana University*
Douglas Muller, *University of New Mexico*
Nora Newcombe, *Pennsylvania State University*
Michael Newton, *Prentice Women's Hospital and Maternity Care Center*
Niles Newton, *Northwestern University Medical School*
Ned W. Schultz, *Texas Tech University*
William P. Smotherman, *Oregon State University*
R. Brent Thompson, *University of Maine at Orono*
I. David Welch, *University of Northern Colorado*
Georgia Witkin-Lanoil, *Westchester Community College*
Lenisa White, *Brooklyn College of the City University of New York*

Our special thanks again go to Katie and Scott, and to Robby, who helped make everything worthwhile and easier by their patient caring.

Robert E. Schell
Elizabeth Hall

FOURTH EDITION

DEVELOPMENTAL PSYCHOLOGY TODAY

ROBERT E. SCHELL
lecturer
San Diego State University
University of California at San Diego
ELIZABETH HALL

Fourth Edition
987654321

Library of Congress Cataloging in Publication Data

Schell, Robert E.
Developmental psychology today.

Bibliography: p.
Includes index.
1. Developmental psychology. I. Hall, Elizabeth, 1929– . II. Title.
BF713.D48 1982 155 82-5198
ISBN 0-394-32577-X AACR2

Cover art: Sculpture, G. Charpentier, "Les Jumelles"/Courtesy, Galerie Felix Vercel. Photograph © Suzanne Kaufman/L. Speier 1982.

Text design: Dana Kasarsky Design

Manufactured in the United States of America by R.R. Donnelley & Sons, Co. Willard, OH.

Photo Research: Lynn Goldberg

Photo credits: 4—© Leonard Speier 1979; 25—© Eric Kroll/Taurus Photo; 52—A.K. Moon/Stock, Boston; 80—Roberts/Rugh; 106—© Steve Meltzer 1978/West Stock, Inc.; 132—Rogier Gregoire; 154—© Leonard Speier 1981; 178—© Paul Damien; 1981/Click, Chicago; 206—Jeffrey Foxx/Woodfin Camp & Assoc.; 236—© Mical Heron/Monkmeyer Press Photo; 258—©Leonard Speier 1982; 282—© B. Ullmann/Taurus Photo; 304—© Leonard Speier 1982; 334—Rogier Gregoire; 362—Doug Wilson/Black Star; 390—Peter Hudson; 414—© Joe Gordon 1980; 434—© Mark Antman 1982; 462—© Daily Telegraph Magazine by Dave Waterman/Woodfin Camp & Assoc.; 486—© Leonard Speier 1982; 510—© Leonard Speier 1982; 532—© Leonard Speier 1979.

Figure credits: P. 33. Fig. 2–2: From Minnesota Symposia on Child Psychology, Volume 8, edited by Anne D. Pick, University of Minnesota Press, Copyright © 1974 by the University of Minnesota.

P. 63. Fig. 3–1: Reprinted from *Childhood and Society,* 2nd Edition. Revised, by Erik H. Erikson, by permission of W. W. Norton & Company, Inc. Copyright © 1950, © 1963 by W. W. Norton & Company, Inc.

P. 73. Fig. 3–2: From Luria, A. R. *Cognitive Development: Its Cultural and Social Foundations.* Harvard University Press, 1976. Reprinted by permission.

P. 93. Fig. 4–3: Models indicating the position of the fetus during passage through the birth canal. (Reproduced, with permission, from the *Birth Atlas,* published by Maternity Center Association, New York).

P. 158. Fig. 7–1: Adapted from Fagen, J. W., "Stimulus Preference, Reinforcer Effectiveness, and Relational Responding in Infants," *Child Development,* 51 (1980), 374. Copyright by the Society for Research in Child Development, Inc.

P. 163. Fig. 7–2: Adapted from "The Origin of Form Perception" by Robert L. Fantz, May 1961. Copyright © 1961 by Scientific American, Inc. All rights reserved.

P. 165. Fig. 7–3: From Hainline, L. "Developmental Changes in Visual Scanning of Face and Nonface Patterns by Infants," *Journal of Experimental Child Psychology,* 25 (1978), 90–115. Reprinted by permission.

P. 195. Fig. 8–2: From *Human Nature,* September 1978, accompanying the article "Learning the Mother Tongue" by Jerome S. Bruner. Copyright © 1978 by Human Nature, Inc. Reprinted by permission of the publisher.

P. 239. Fig. 10–1: Adapted from Hutt, Corinne (1966) "Exploration and Play in Children." *Symposium Zoological Society London.* No. 18:61–81.

P. 248. Fig. 10–2: From P.K. Smith and S. Dutton. "Play and Training in Direct and Innovative Problem Solving," *Child Development,* 50 (1978), 830–836. Copyright by the Society for Research in Child Development, Inc.

P. 255. Fig. 10–3: From B.B. Whiting and J.W.M. Whiting, *Children of Six Cultures: A Psycho-Cultural Analysis.* Harvard University Press, 1975, p. 48. Reprinted by permission.

P. 269. Fig. 11–4: From M.W. Daehler and M.P. O'Connor. "Recognition Memory for Objects in Very Young Children: The Effect of Shape and Label Similarity on Preference from Novel Stimuli," *Journal of Experimental Child Psychology,* 29 (1980), 312. Reprinted by permission.

P. 274. Fig. 11–5: Adapted from Flavell, J.H., S.G. Shipstead, and K. Croft. "Young Children's Knowledge about Visual Perception: Hiding Objects from Others," *Child Development,* 49 (1978), p. 1209. Copyright by the Society for Research in Child Development, Inc.

P. 292. Fig. 12–2: From J.L. Miscione, R.S. Marvin, R.G. O'Brien, and M.T. Greenberg. "A Developmental Study of Preschool Children's Understanding of the Words 'Know' and 'Guess,'" *Child Development,* 49 (1978), 1111. Copyright by the Society for Research in Child Development, Inc.

P. 376. Fig. 15–1: Adapted from B.B. Keller and R.Q. Bell. "Child Effects on Adult's Method of Eliciting Altruistic Behavior," *Child Development,* 50 (1979), p. 1007. Copyright by the Society for Research in Child Development, Inc.

P. 387. Fig. 15–3: Adapted from L.D. Eron, L.R. Heusmann, M.M. Lefkowitz, and L.O. Walder. "Does Television Violence Cause Aggression?" *American Psychologist,* 29 (1972), 257. Copyright © 1972 by the American Psychological Association. Reprinted/Adapted by permission of the author.

P. 457. Fig. 18–2: From *The Adolescent: A Psychological Self-Portrait* by Daniel Offer, Eric Ostrov, and Kenneth I. Howard. Copyright © 1981 by Basic Books, Inc., Publishers, New York.

P. 471. Fig. 19–1: After Frieze. I.H., J.E. Parsons, P.B. Johnson, D.N. Ruble, and G.L. Zellman. *Women and Sex Roles.* New York: Norton, 1978, p. 317.

P. 474. Fig. 19–2: Based on Cerella, Poon, and Williams, in Poon (Ed.), *Aging in the 1980's.* Copyright © 1974 by the American Psychological Association. Reprinted/Adapted by permission of the author.

P. 489. Fig. 20–1: Condensed from "Age Norms, Age Constraints, and Adult Socialization," *American Journal of Sociology* by B. Neugarten, J.W. Moore, and J.C. Lowe. Reprinted by permission of The University of Chicago Press. Copyright © 1965, 710–717.

P. 500. Fig. 20–2: Based on B.C. Rollins and H. Feldman, "Marital Satisfaction Over the Family Life Cycle," *Journal of Marriage and the Family,* 32 (1970), 20–28.

P. 520. Fig. 21–1: From J.L. Fozard, "The Time for Remembering," in L.W. Poon (ed.), *Aging in the 1980's.* Copyright © 1980 by the American Psychological Association. Reprinted/Adapted by permission of the publisher and author.

P. 526. Fig. 21–2: Based on J.P. Clayton, J.A. Halikes, and W.L. Maurice. "The Bereavement of the Widowed," *Diseases of the Nervous System,* 32 (1971), 597–604. Permission granted by Physicians Postgraduate Press Inc.

PREFACE

DEVELOPMENTAL PSYCHOLOGY TODAY first appeared in 1971. Published by CRM, the book division of PSYCHOLOGY TODAY MAGAZINE, it was the first text to approach developmental psychology from a lifespan perspective. We were part of a large team of contributors—Robert Schell was one of thirty eminent psychologists who wrote draft chapters, and Elizabeth Hall was one of several professional writers who turned the academics' writing style into accessible prose. Students seemed to find the book both interesting and readable. However, we felt that it would have more appeal to instructors if the research that underlay the findings were more thoroughly covered. Therefore, the second edition was completely revised and became virtually a new book. Experts, including Robert McCall, Sandra Scarr, and Dan Slobin, were called upon to provide new drafts for many chapters. At the same time, our roles were greatly expanded—Schell served as coordinator and chief advisor, and Hall rewrote the entire text to ensure evenness of style. Both classical and current research studies were cited, and the more important studies were discussed at length and in terms students could understand. The second edition seemed to be well received by both instructors and students, and after Random House purchased CRM in 1974 we were asked to co-author a revision of the book, building the third edition on the solid foundation of the second.

As before, the accent of this fourth edition is on change. Our guiding theme is that development involves interdependent changes in all areas of behavior. Our major aim in this edition continues to be a respect for this interdependence in development, while presenting an up-to-date and balanced overview of information, topics, viewpoints, and issues in developmental psychology.

Once again we emphasize the cognitive underpinnings of language, personality, and social development. In addition, we have continued to integrate theory and research, so that coverage is not tied to a single theory or theorist. This approach gives instructors the freedom to emphasize particular theoretical positions as they see fit—either through supplementary lectures, assigned readings, or other means.

In revising this book, our objective was to make it as usable as possible by the student and instructor. Specifically, we attempted to increase student interest and understanding, enhance readability, capture important developments in the field, and illustrate the value of applied as well as basic research.

Instructors familiar with previous editions will note both major and minor changes. In the introductory unit of the book, we have placed the discussion of determinants of development (Chapter 2) before the discussion of theories of development (Chapter 3). This move was made because we believe students will find that a grounding in influences on development makes the theoretical explanations more meaningful.

In addition, each of the three chapters in this introductory unit has been restructured and rewritten. The chapter on theory, for example, contains new sections on information-processing theories and on dialectical theories of development.

We have heavily revised our coverage of physical development. Physical development during infancy and childhood is now concentrated in Chapter 6, which has been rewritten and reorganized so that it not only considers physical development in infancy but also points ahead, noting major changes that can occur in childhood.

In place of the chapter on physical development during early childhood in the previous edition, we have added a new chapter on play (Chapter 10). Instead of discussing play at various points in both personality and cognitive chapters, as in earlier editions, we have gathered all aspects of play into an integrated chapter with greatly expanded coverage in all areas, including theory, cross-cultural work, and therapy. Although the chapter focuses on early childhood, it looks back at infancy and ahead to later childhood and early adolescence. The chapter also provides some supplemental coverage of physical development with sections on rough-and-tumble play, as well as motor skills development, practice, and instruction. This chapter is one of two places (the other being Chapter 16, Morality: From Rules to Conduct) where we felt it worthwhile to stop and take a topical/chronological approach toward an important facet of development.

The cognitive chapters (7, 11, 14) have been completely reorganized and rewritten. They now consider Piagetian, information-processing, and dialectical approaches to cognitive development. Chapter 7 (on infancy) includes a new section on learning and memory, and its concentration on sensorimotor thought has been expanded with a discussion of Piaget's six substages of the sensorimotor period. Chapter 11 (cognition in early childhood) focuses on preoperational thought, with extensive coverage of causality, the number concept, and egocentrism, both in terms of Piaget's position and in relation to later research that clarifies or modifies his work. Memory development is also discussed from the viewpoint of Piaget, information-processing, and dialectical psychology. Chapter 14 (cognition in later childhood) now focuses on concrete-operational thought, reserving a consideration of formal thought for the unit on adolescence. In Chapter 14 are extensive discussions of such topics as conservation, transitivity, class-inclusion, and causal reasoning.

The two language chapters (8, 12) have been heavily revised, updated, and rewritten. They continue to stress the relation of language to cognitive development and the acquisition of syntax, but they now reflect the recent outpouring of research on the pragmatic bases of language development, as well as new research on semantics.

The chapters on personality development (9, 13, 15) have undergone considerable revision. Chapter 9 (infancy) has been restructured so that stages of attachment are more fully covered. Also, all three chapters have new content on self-concept, gender identity, understanding others (empathy and social cognition), peers and siblings, sex roles, parent-child relationships, changes in family organization, and the effects of television.

Chapters in the adolescent unit have been heavily reorganized. Physical development and sexuality are the concern of Chapter 17. Cognitive and personality development in adolescence have been combined to form a single chapter (18) in this edition. This reorganization helps to eliminate the scatter of information and discussion that came from presenting first a personal and then a social view of adolescence.

A new look for this edition is provided by the boxed inserts in most chapters. These inserts highlight areas not generally covered in the text or show how research can be applied to social or personal situations.

Throughout the book, we have tried to convey gracefully and grammatically the development of both sexes. To that end we have eliminated all "sexist" language, especially in regard to pronouns and to the use of "man" or "mankind" to denote the human species. And we have continued our practice of using the first names of investigators when describing research, in order to convey quietly the extent of women's contributions to developmental psychology.

Because this book covers the entire life span, it can be used in courses on child development or child psychology, on child and adolescent development or psychology, or on human development. Although the book is organized in an age-period, life-span way, it has a topic/process organization within each section. It can be used in either manner, depending upon an instructor's preference.

CONTENTS

DEVELOPMENTAL PSYCHOLOGY TODAY

FOURTH EDITION

UNIT ONE

THE MEANING OF DEVELOPMENT

Confronted with twenty newborn infants in a hospital nursery, no one would be able to distinguish the future bank president from the future robber, the physician from the murderer, the priest from the atheist, the college professor from the dishwasher, the loving spouse from the sexual adventurer. Although the tiny infants are alike in many ways, there are vast differences among them. Heredity has already started each out on a different path, and culture and experience will complete the task, interacting with genetic inheritance to produce twenty unique individuals. Explaining how these babies develop into adults and why their developmental path takes one turning and not another is the province of developmental psychology. Yet it is general rules of development and not the precise prediction of any one person's life course that is the goal. As you will discover in reading this unit, several different explanations of human development have been put forth, and although each has increased our understanding, none has by itself adequately described the progression from cradle to grave.

1 THE CONCEPT OF DEVELOPMENT

The development of a human being may seem mysterious—even magical. Can we possibly explain how a one-cell fertilized egg develops into a fully human newborn, a linguistically accomplished kindergartner, a budding engineer, a competent parent, and an involved citizen? Understanding changes across the life cycle is the aim of developmental psychology. This branch of psychology explores how human physical growth and intellectual and social behavior change over time, and it seeks to find how growth and behavior relate to each other.

Developmental psychology sees human behavior as a changing system that includes both biological and cultural determinants, which work together to produce behavioral development. At no time is a person without an environment or without biological systems that affect behavior. Rather, a developing person is the product of biological and environmental forces that act together in an organized way. That integration changes over time and poses some of the most basic questions that can be asked about the nature of humanity.

In this chapter we will examine the various views of human beings that have influenced our ideas about human development. We will trace the emergence of the concepts of childhood and adolescence and the realization that adulthood itself is not a monolithic stage. We will discover that the social and economic views of a society shape the way its members view the life span. We will find that developmental psychology describes behavioral change over the life span by gathering various types of information and applying insights from other disciplines. Although research allows us to describe average development, such descriptions, we will discover, do not predict the behavior of all individuals. We will learn that development is an orderly, ever-increasing and ever more complex change in a consistent direction. In addition, we will find that it is helpful to regard behavior as proceeding through phases of development. When you have finished reading this book, you may find yourself looking at your own behavior—and the behavior of those around you—in a different way.

EARLY PHILOSOPHICAL VIEWS

Although our knowledge of human development has increased vastly over the centuries, today's developmental psychologists are concerned with the same issues that have fascinated philosophers for centuries: the existence of inborn differences among people, how much people change in response to the environment, the role human beings play in their own development, the natural goodness or evil in humanity, and the relationship of child to adult behavior.

Three centuries before the birth of Christ, Plato focused on innate differences in human aptitude and contended that these individual differences should be used in rearing and educating children. Aristotle, who was Plato's pupil and Alexander the Great's tutor, believed that all people were alike at birth because the mind of the newborn was a blank slate. However, Aristotle agreed with his mentor that each person had natural inclinations and that these individual differences should be the basis of education and vocational training.

During the Middle Ages, which lasted for a thousand years, stress was on the moral nature of humanity; human beings were believed to be born sinful and corrupt. As a result, they required harsh training to correct their depraved nature.

By the seventeenth century, human nature had been rehabilitated. Human beings were regarded as born innocent and primitive, only to be corrupted by society. For this reason, moral education would lead children to become trustworthy, disciplined, and rational adults.

A different view arose in the latter part of the seventeenth century, when John Locke (1690), a British philosopher, proposed that all newborn infants have the same innate human tendencies and abilities. Since, like Aristotle, Locke saw the human mind as a blank slate, he contended that training or experience is required to instill ideas, concepts, and other human qualities.

In the meantime, the idea that human beings are inherently wicked was revived, and Jean Jacques Rousseau (1762), a French philosopher, resisted the current view by again proposing that human beings are born peaceful and compassionate, and then corrupted by an evil society. If inborn propensities were allowed expression and were given slight guidance, healthy development would follow.

Despite the appearance of new ways of looking at human beings, old assumptions have never disappeared. Many of the issues in developmental psychology arise from these different views of humanity as they are applied to an understanding of psychological development.

DIVIDING THE LIFE SPAN

As ideas about human nature changed, so did the way society divided the life span. Although many people assume that life has always been divided into the prenatal period, infancy, childhood, adolescence, and adulthood, this view of the life cycle is peculiar to the technological societies of the twentieth century.

Philippe Ariès (1962) has examined the concept of the life cycle as it has been seen from the Middle Ages to the present and has concluded that in the Middle Ages even the concept of childhood as we think of it was virtually unknown. There was a clearly admitted infancy, which lasted until a child was about seven years old. But thereafter, people whom we would consider children were simply assimilated into the adult world. In both the art and the social documents of the Middle Ages, children and adults are mingled in one unified community, wearing the same clothes, and performing the same functions. Society made no distinction among them on the basis of age or phase of psychological development. The vast majority of children—and adults—were, of course, totally unschooled. But even those who obtained the minimal schooling required to become priests or clerks learned in ungraded schools where children, adolescents, and adults were taught together.

During the seventeenth century, when Velasquez painted this scene, childhood was just beginning to emerge as a separate period of life. Children still dressed and were treated like miniature adults. ***(Scala/EPA)***

The Concept of Childhood

Only in the seventeenth and eighteenth centuries did concern with childhood as a separate stage of life slowly begin to appear in Europe and North America. As Rousseau popularized a sentimental view of childhood, theories of education became concerned with promoting children's moral and intellectual development, protecting them from the evils and corruptions of adult society, and preserving their virtues. Schools became increasingly graded by age, and a larger proportion of children between the ages of six and fourteen were deliberately segregated into schools. Both the average length of schooling and the number of children who received formal education increased.

From historical evidence, it seems clear that this change had economic as well as philosophical roots. Childhood became a separate stage of life only when large numbers of people entered the middle class, the amount of leisure time increased, and the rate of infant mortality decreased. As the middle class prospered, there was less need for children to work in order to ensure the family's economic survival. The lowered rate of childhood mortality meant that more children would live to reach puberty; therefore, parents could devote themselves less cautiously to each child. And the new mercantile capitalism required that a larger portion of the citizenry be literate and fluent with numbers; thus, economic demands also led more children to go to schools.

This economic and philosophical analysis of the way childhood gradually emerged over the centuries has influenced our understanding of the relationship between social and cultural change and psychological development. Ariès spoke about changing concepts of childhood, but the experience of being a child also changed over the years. For centuries, infanticide was common; babies with birth defects, girl babies, and illegitimate infants were often killed or allowed to die (deMause, 1975). Among the survivors, many died before the age of six. The rest were apprenticed out or put to work. Both parents and masters often treated these children harshly, and showed little evidence of tenderness, protectiveness, attention, or care. Parents rarely seem to have been emotionally involved with their children; nor were children spoken of as precious beings who were to be cherished and protected.

As the concept of a state of childhood began to emerge, the segregation of children into schools increasingly sheltered the young from the demands of adult work. For the first time, children were able to play and to explore the world, a freedom that gave them the opportunity to develop social and technical skills. With the introduction of universal primary education in this century, the experience of childhood was extended to the working and lower classes, and

Because we are accustomed to a long period of adolescence, when physically mature human beings do not participate in the functioning of society, it is difficult to realize that for centuries children worked as hard as adults. Not until the twentieth century were most children in the working and lower classes free from long hours of drudgery. ***(Photograph by Lewis W. Hine, 1912. George Eastman House Collection)***

childhood became entirely separate from the rest of the lifespan in developed Western societies. Over a period of four hundred years, childhood has undergone profound change, as society moved from a time when this phase of life was not recognized to a time when it is protected by schools, law, and custom.

The Concept of Adolescence

The concept of adolescence as we think of it emerged only in the nineteenth and twentieth centuries. Although puberty in the sense of biological maturation occurs in all societies, it seemed to go largely unmarked in early Western societies. When children are considered neither innocent nor different from adults in important ways, puberty represents neither a fall from innocence nor a change in status, and it therefore has little special meaning.

In previous centuries many men and women passed through what would now be recognized as an adolescent experience, but a postpubertal stage of life was first noted in the eighteenth century, and not until this century did the modern concept of adolescence appear. Three important changes have shaped the contemporary view of adolescence. First, adolescence as a stage of life has been socially recognized and acknowledged. Second, society has begun to sanction and support adolescence, increasingly buttressing it with educational, familial, institutional, and economic resources. Third, these new resources, coupled with other changes in society, have given an ever-larger proportion of young people the possibility of continuing psychological growth during the years from thirteen to eighteen. This opportunity arose when society granted them protection from adult responsibilities, created educational institutions to fill their duty-free time, and developed a positive image of a postchildhood, preadulthood stage of life: adolescence.

As with the recognition of childhood, the emergence of adolescence is closely related to social, economic, and historical changes. Increasing industrialization has freed most young people past the age of puberty from farm and factory labor. In fact, present standards of economic productivity make the adolescent almost impossible to employ. The new attitudes toward adolescence are expressed in laws that make full-time employment before the age of sixteen or eighteen illegal. The growth in affluence has provided most families and the larger society with the wealth needed to support these economically unproductive adolescents in school. And all these changes have happened, on a mass scale, almost within living memory; even our child labor laws were passed only in the twentieth century. However, the extension of adolescence as a stage of psychological growth is far from complete. Descriptions of the general society necessarily ignore pockets of poverty, where the middle- and working-class adolescent experience is not possible. One such group is found in the inner city, where the absence of jobs for young people whose parents cannot afford to keep

Because social and economic changes have freed young people past the age of puberty from the demands of farm and factory labor, the period of adolescence has emerged in Western societies. *(© Paul Fusco/Magnum Photos)*

them in school has resulted in large numbers of the young with nothing to do, no income, and bleak prospects. A second group is made up of migratory farm laborers, where because family survival requires all members to contribute, children and adolescents must work illegally.

Our images of adolescence continue to be fluid and changing. For example, the media alternate between portrayals of the adolescent as awkward, acned, and anguished or deviant, wild, and uncontrolled; as an idealistic and accurate critic of society or as a person interested only in professional and personal gain (Dragastin and Elder, 1975).

Adulthood

Not too many years ago, an adult was considered a person who had completed the course of human development. In recent years our concept of adulthood has changed, and today we realize that development does not stop at adolescence but continues throughout life. People face new tasks, new challenges; and as these tasks are met and as experiences accumulate, individuals change. The forty-five-year-old with a responsible job, with children in college, perhaps with grandchildren is different in many ways from the twenty-five-year-old who has just become self-supporting or is anticipating the birth of a first child.

The realization of this continuing development has led to a further division of this phase of life into young adulthood, middle adulthood, and late adulthood. During early adulthood, people generally become independent, select their life's work, and establish a family. As the passage from young to middle adulthood takes

More and more Americans are living into later adulthood, a period of life when people are generally more capable than younger members of society realize. *(Ken Heyman)*

place, life changes, and a realistic acceptance of these changes leads to maturity. Although middle adulthood is a fairly stable period, when people are expanding their authority and responsibility, it is also a time when they must adapt to changes in body appearance and health. It is during this period that people first come to terms with the realization that their own lives will end.

Until this century most people died before they reached the age of seventy, so that little attention was paid to the period of late adulthood. Today a substantial number of people live into their eighties, well past the time when their active participation as wage earners has ceased. In some societies, such older adults are seen as wise, experienced advisers; but in the United States, they are often regarded as irrelevant. Because older adults acquired their experiences during an era that no longer exists, the young tend to regard the old as passé and perhaps as uncomfortable reminders of their own fate. Like children and adolescents, older adults sometimes are segregated into special institutions that keep them out of view and out of the minds of younger people. This experience creates many problems for older adults.

Markers of Life's Phases

Today we take the periods of childhood, adolescence, adulthood, and late adulthood for granted and divide development into phases that are marked by social events, biological changes, cultural traditions, or economic structure. Social events include the beginning of meaningful speech (the end of infancy and the start of childhood, at about the age of two) or the achievement of adult roles in employment, marriage, and reproduction (the end of adolescence and the start of adulthood, in the early twenties for many people), or even the loss of roles (retirement from work). Among the biological markers we attach to the life span are birth (the end of the prenatal period and the start of infancy) and reproductive maturity at puberty (the end of childhood and the start of adolescence).

We are not consistent in choosing markers for periods in the life span, and our markers are by no means universal. Other contemporary societies divide life into three periods—such as infancy, childhood, and adulthood—or only two—infancy and adulthood (Mead, 1968). Hindus divide the life cycle into four phases, beginning with school age, or what we would consider middle childhood. According to Sudhir Kakar (1978), this religious view does not explicitly consider infancy and early childhood as part of the life cycle. The first phase of the cycle combines middle childhood and adolescence. Adulthood is further divided into stages that correspond to young adulthood, adulthood, and old age. Each of these stages is considered separate and as having its own developmental tasks.

The way in which people in a society view the life span depends largely on its social and economic system. If the preparation for adult roles is gradual and continuous from early childhood and if the necessary technology can be acquired by apprenticeship, then adulthood is likely to begin shortly after a person reaches reproductive maturity. On the other hand, if full participation in the economic system depends on years of technical education, a period of adolescence is likely to be recognized. Toward the end of the life span, when participation in the economic system becomes less active, older adults may be forced to retire from their jobs, creating a period that some call "old age." Older adults are, of course, still adults, but the loss of social and economic roles can drastically change the experience of later adulthood.

THE FIELD OF DEVELOPMENTAL PSYCHOLOGY

Developmental psychology has only recently emerged as a separate branch of general psychology. General psychology was founded in Germany in the last quarter of the nineteenth century and then introduced in the United States. Its purpose was to study normal behavior—mainly that of adults—and to discover what mental processes accompanied or led to behavior.

During the first several decades of this century, psychology broadened its goals, its methods, and its technology. As psychologists began to investigate other aspects of human and animal behavior, the range and amount of information increased rapidly, as did the development of new research methods. Specialization became inevitable, and the field eventually divided into different branches. Some of the first branches to split away were physiological, clinical, experimental, social, and child psychology. Other branches, like community, environmental, and organizational psychology emerged later.

Developmental psychology has grown out of the field of child psychology although it includes material from all the other branches. G. Stanley Hall is acknowledged as the founder of child and adolescent development as fields of study. His approach was to make broad generalizations about human development and functioning and to support those generalizations by collecting information through questionnaires. Because he viewed development as being primarily determined by genetic and biological factors until adolescence, he suggested that efforts to curb the natural unruliness of children would be ineffectual until they were about twelve. By then, children would have matured and their characters could be changed by training (Hall, 1904).

Two of Hall's students had a lasting effect on the course of developmental psychology. The first, Arnold Gesell, was a careful and precise researcher. His observations of children were systematically planned and carried out, and always recorded in detailed form. He analyzed still pictures from filmed observations of children to discover patterns of infant behavior (1928). The developmental standards he constructed for motor, visual, language, and personal-social behavior at different ages are still used to describe sequences of development.

Lewis Terman, the second of Hall's students, pioneered mental testing in this country. He studied one thousand children, ranging in age from three to eighteen, and provided standards for mental development during childhood and adolescence. Terman also began a study of gifted children in 1921. The people in his study have been followed for more than fifty years (Sears, 1977; Terman and Oden, 1959), and his information on the social development, personality, education, and achievement of these gifted individuals has become a lasting part of psychological knowledge.

The testing movement and the work of Gesell, Terman, and others reached its high point in the late 1940s. By that time there had been an outpouring of descriptive information on child

Developmental psychologists have moved from studying infants and children to examining the entire lifespan of human beings. Studies of older people have disproved many stereotypical ideas of aging. *(Scala/EPA)*

development, but many psychologists had become disenchanted with collecting descriptive information and had moved to testing their theories of development by controlling the environmental experiences of children.

The emergence of developmental psychology in this country has been greatly influenced by social and political change. For example, interest in developmental questions increased sharply when child-guidance and psychological clinics began to be founded around the turn of the century (Sears, 1975). Such clinics represented popular acceptance of the idea that children should be helped with their emotional and intellectual problems in order to enable them to lead constructive lives.

Other historical events have also shaped the course and content of developmental psychology. One of the first child-development research centers was established by Gesell at Yale in 1911, and in 1917, another was set up in Iowa. During the 1920s and 1930s, other centers were established at major universities across the country. These institutes investigated all aspects of children's development and welfare, and their shared goal was to acquire a comprehensive understanding of development that could be used to help children and those who care for them.

Many of these institutes are still active, and much of the progress in developmental psychology rests on their findings.

As life-cycle research added information on the development of young adults, other researchers became interested in the latter years of the life span. The realization that development does not stop at age eighteen or twenty-one, together with the fact that as people live longer, women have fewer children, and members of the baby boom get older, an increasing percentage of the population would be over sixty-five, led to the establishment of centers to study the effects of aging and the developmental tasks faced by older people. At the University of Chicago, for example, Bernice Neugarten (1971) has supervised a study of middle-aged and aging adults, following more than 2,000 adults since the late 1950s. Her research has helped destroy the stereotype of the unhappy old person whose remaining years are spent in a rocking chair.

Developmental psychology today is much like the field of general psychology just before it split into various branches. The field covers perceptual, motivational, intellectual, social, and neuropsychological issues and problems, and uses various methods to study them. Until recently, the developmental psychologist was a generalist who had acquired knowledge in a large number of areas. Today the field covers an even broader range of topics and attempts to integrate them across the human life span. Many developmental psychologists find that, while they are generalists, they must also specialize in some aspect of the field. The amount of information on human development is now too great for any individual to master. In the past twenty-five years, there has been a decided shift in the emphasis of developmental psychologists. They have moved from describing what people do at specific periods in life to emphasizing how circumstances affect what they do at different periods and what kind of sequence takes place in development. Along with this shift has come an increased interest in the intellectual aspects of development and a greater appreciation of differences among individuals.

STUDYING DEVELOPMENTAL PSYCHOLOGY

The concerns of developmental psychology cut across content areas to *describe* and to *explain* changes in human behavior across the years of the life span. The first step toward an understanding of development is an accurate and detailed description of those changes. The second step, or series of steps, concerns explanations for the observed changes. Psychologists can probe the competencies, motivations, and emotions of children and adults through the study of **behavior,** which is an observable act that can be described or measured reliably. **Reliability** means that two or more observations of the same act will produce the same information. Behavior can be measured in many ways, sometimes simply by watching and at other times by using instruments of various kinds, such as recordings of heart rates, questionnaires, and films of children's interactions. Developmental psychologists do not pick any behavior at random to measure and describe; nor do they attempt to study all possible behavior of human beings. Instead, psychologists select for detailed study behavior that is theoretically or practically important.

The Use of Theory

The explanation of behavior depends upon *theories,* sets of logically related statements about the nature of development. These statements are usually set forth in abstract terms, with no direct reference to the actual behavior on which they are based. For example, according to Erik Erikson's (1963) theory of psychosocial development the growing individual faces a crisis at each stage of development, and the way the person resolves that crisis will affect how he or she approaches the next stage. One of the logically related statements of Erikson's theory is the claim that young children around the ages of two to four need to develop **autonomy,** a feeling of self-control and self-determination. Autonomy is an invisible quality, but if Erikson's prediction is correct, the two-year-old should show some visible evidence of the need to direct his or her own behavior. When we look at two-year-olds, we find a consistent tendency to say "No" to any parental request, to rebuff offers of help with a short, "Me do it," and sometimes to throw a temper tantrum when an immediate goal is thwarted. Erikson's theoretical statement about autonomy explains a number of observations, and it predicts the child's behavior.

Theories should lead to testable **hypotheses** or predictions about observable behavior. If the statements of a theory successfully predict a great deal of human behavior, then we say that the theory is a useful explanation of human development. Thus far, no theory has satisfactorily covered all aspects of human development. Rather, as Chapter 3 shows, theories tend to be restricted to some part of development, such as social behavior or intellectual development or language acquisition.

When testing hypotheses derived from theories, developmental psychologists use scientific methods that can be described so that other investigators can apply them. If the studies are to be considered useful, they must lead to results that others can repeat and confirm. However appealing children and adolescents may be, no anecdotal description of their actions adequately explains their behavior.

If theories lead to valid predictions, they can be used to *control* behavior. For example, the control of behavior through rewards and punishments is of theoretical importance to psychologists and of practical importance to parents, teachers, and other adults who have responsibility for rearing children.

Because developmental psychologists are interested in development across the life span, information on behavioral changes in all periods is important. However, theories tend to guide research, and many developmental theories focus on what happens to a person from infancy through adolescence, paying scant attention to the adult phases of the life cycle. In addition, during the early years, development is rapid and changes can be measured in a relatively short period of time. During adulthood, change is slow and often difficult to measure. Partly for these reasons, researchers have collected more information on babies and children than on adults. But practical considerations have also affected the kind of information that is gathered. It is extremely difficult to set up properly controlled experiments when people are scattered about and living in widely varied circumstances. Because maternity hospitals and schools gather people of similar ages together, they provide excellent opportunities for psychologists to investigate human development. Finally, social problems may also play a part in directing research, since funds are more likely to be available when a problem becomes pressing. During the 1960s, for example, compensatory education programs, such as Head Start, gave researchers a chance to work with preschool children. And more recently, concern over the growing proportion of older adults has led to the availability of funds for the study of late adulthood.

The Contributions of Other Disciplines

The description and explanation of human behavior is also a concern of other scientific fields: biology, sociology, and anthropology. Developmental psychologists depend on information on the individual's biological history and maturation, on social organization, and on cultural influences, which comes from these other disciplines. They need such information to explain behavior because psychologists see the developing person as a changing system that integrates biological factors and experience. The kinds of experiences we have in growing up depend largely on what kind of family and society we live in (for example, whether we live with one parent or two, whether we have brothers or sisters, whether our parents are strict or indulgent, whether our society is agricultural or technological) and on cultural values that distinguish right from wrong, good from bad. What we learn in the sociocultural context depends on both our readiness to learn and the availability of materials and ideas. In the case of children, maturational level has a profound influence on what they notice in the world around them; the environment determines what is available for the child to learn.

Take language, for example. The ability to learn a language is an evolved human characteristic. All normal members of the species learn to speak. But developmentalists know that children must reach a certain level of neurological development before they can talk (Lenneberg, 1967): No six-month-old speaks in sentences. At the same time, a child living in a relatively unstimulating, unresponsive environment begins to speak later than a child reared in a stimulating home. In the first case, the child is not biologically ready to speak; in the second, the child's world does not offer adequate speech models to learn from. The time and rate at which language develops in a particular child are the result of the child's level of maturity and previous experience in vocalizing, in listening to language, and in being rewarded for its use. The language children learn to speak fluently is that of their cultural group.

Each discipline makes its own contribution to developmental psychology. Evolutionary biologists have given insightful accounts of humanity's evolutionary history, which have set the stage for understanding individual development. All children have more in common with one another than any one of them has with any other species. Despite individual differences, that commonality is reflected in development.

Developmental biologists have provided detailed descriptions of embryological development that can serve as a model for understanding all development. The complex integration of genetic and environmental influences across the life span, and from the level of the single cell to that of the whole organism, has made psychologists aware of the need to consider both classes of influences on human behavioral development.

Sociologists and cultural anthropologists have emphasized the importance of understanding development within a sociocultural context. A person is always a member of a human group: a family, a neighborhood group, a school class, and so forth. This setting influences most behavior, either through immediate circumstances or through long-range membership in various groups. As indicated earlier, the ways in which a culture interprets the life span can have profound influences on the expectations that others have for a person's behavior at different time periods in life.

EXPLANATIONS OF HUMAN DEVELOPMENT

Developmental psychology adds to basic psychological principles information drawn from other fields. In using such material to explain human behavior, however, we must be careful to adopt a level of explanation that is appropriate for that behavior.

Levels of Explanation

Human development is determined by interacting causes that operate at many levels of influence: biological, psychological, sociological, and anthropological. Biological principles sometimes appear to explain behavior, but by themselves they are inadequate. A study that explained behavioral differences between males and females only in terms of parental treatment, for example, would be criticized as simplistic, that is, as having reduced the complex causes of human behavior to a single, falsely simple, explanation. The different ways in which parents treat daughters and sons undoubtedly contributes to sex differences in behavior, but by itself it cannot explain most observed differences. Factors that do not involve parental responses—such as teachers, television, peers, and hormones—may also play important roles in shaping sex differences in behavior. To explain the differences we observe, we must consider the effects of parental responses along with hormones and other prenatal and postnatal differences in environment. In this example, parental treatment is only one component in the behavioral system.

It would be just as erroneous, of course, to say that nursery-school teachers, hormones, or even rewards for appropriate behavior are by themselves responsible for sex differences in be-

THE CONDITIONS THAT FOSTER CHILD ABUSE

Each year more than 600,000 children are neglected or abused in this country. A number of developmental psychologists have been searching for ways to combat the problem, and all are agreed that child abuse has no single cause. Researchers have discovered a number of major factors: personality characteristics of the parents and whether they were abused as children, physical and personality characteristics of the child, patterns of family interaction, socioeconomic strains on the family, the family's isolation from the rest of the community, and the culture's acceptance of violence (Starr, 1979). Interfering in this interlocking web at any point could rearrange the strands and reduce the chances of abuse. For example, if a parent, predisposed to abuse a child, and a child, with the personality characteristics that appear to evoke abuse, are kept out of an environment that increases the likelihood of abuse, violence may never occur.

Studies by James Garbarino and his associates (Garbarino, 1976; Garbarino and Crouter, 1978) show that under certain socioeconomic conditions, the incidence of child abuse increases sharply. Working in New York and Nebraska, Garbarino found that abuse was high in neighborhoods where income and educational levels were low, mothers tended to head the household, the neighborhood was unstable, and no day care was available. Apparently, the combination of economic stress, continuous child care, lack of support from friends, and ignorance of where help might be obtained can set up a situation in which a child's crying, whining, or aggressiveness can provoke vicious, even deadly, blows from an overwhelmed parent.

Yet in some poor neighborhoods little child abuse exists. With Deborah Sherman, Garbarino (Garbarino and Sherman, 1980) compared two neighborhoods of similar socioeconomic make-up. According to statistical patterns, each area should have had between 65 and 75 cases of child abuse each year. Yet 130 children were abused in one of these neighborhoods whereas only 16 were abused in the other. Intensive studies in both areas showed clear differences between them.

In the low-risk neighborhood, there was not a single "latchkey" child, that is, a child who regularly

havior. When we focus on any one type of influence, we lose sight of the context in which all children lead their lives and of the fact that development is determined by interaction among all levels of influence. The accompanying box on the conditions fostering child abuse demonstrates the importance of understanding such interactions.

Similarly, when we try to understand the baby's early experiences in the family, we cannot rely simply on studies of babies with their mothers or fathers. Instead, as Jay Belsky (1981) stresses, we must also look at the marriage relationship. Developmental psychologists have studied the effect of the parents on the baby, and some have studied the effect of the baby on the parents. But for a complete understanding of the baby's early experiences, information about the effect of the baby on the marriage relationship must be added, and for such information we must also rely on the work of other researchers, such as sociologists. As Belsky points out, the marriage relationship undoubtedly affects the way parents act toward their babies.

In short, if we expect to explain behavior, we need to draw on findings from fields other than psychology, but we must be careful to integrate this information into our picture of human development at the level at which behavior is influenced.

Although economic stress is sometimes an important factor in child abuse, prosperous parents may also abuse their children. *(© David R. White 1980/Woodfin Camp & Assoc.)*

carries a front-door key in order to get into the family's empty apartment. A parent was generally present when the child came home from school. Although families felt responsible for their own children, they exchanged assistance and child supervision with neighbors. Neighborhood children customarily played together. People kept up their houses. Families tended to use preventive and recreational agencies, such as the Boy Scouts.

In the high-risk neighborhood, where the rate of child abuse was eight times as high, 13 percent of the children came home to an empty house, and only one child out of four was greeted by a parent. Families tended to be social isolates. Less than half the neighborhood children played together. There was no exchange of aid or child supervision, and mothers believed that no one was interested in their children's welfare. Houses were allowed to become dilapidated. Families tended to be involved with treatment agencies, such as the Family Service Association. In addition, the high-risk neighborhood tended to attract families that already were functioning poorly. The negative conditions in the neighborhood made family problems worse, further increasing the chances of child abuse.

Garbarino's work indicates that child abuse breeds in *socially* impoverished neighborhoods, areas in which people with great needs are congregated and must struggle to meet those needs. In such neighborhoods, the family's problems are compounded, and life is threatened both from within and without.

Types of Information

Most developmental psychologists gather information on (1) behavior at different ages; (2) behavioral changes as people grow older; (3) environmental events that influence behavior; and (4) variations among individuals in their development. These four kinds of information make up most of the knowledge in developmental psychology.

Before researchers can evaluate explanations and theories, they must first gather descriptions of behavior. The development of handedness has been extensively described by Douglas Ramsay (1980; Ramsay, Campos, and Fenson, 1979). Between the ages of six and nine months, most babies use the right hand when reaching for an object that is placed in front of them (Type I information). By the time they are fifteen months old, if a toy hammer is put into their left hands, they will transfer it to the right in order to use it (Type II information). Studies of hand preference among toddlers whose right hands have been immobilized for several weeks or months because of injuries would help us to assess the role of learning in handedness (Type III information). Finally, not all babies show hand preference at the same age, and about a quarter of the eight-and-nine-month olds in some studies prefer to use their left hands in reaching for objects (Type IV information). The four types of knowledge are complementary and valuable, each in its own way. No explanation of behavior could be complete unless it took all of them into account.

Two additional kinds of information play a role in the field of developmental psychology: case histories of individuals and research on other species. Case histories of unusual patterns of development can sometimes give us insights about normal development. For example, Dorothy Baruch's (1964) case history of a boy who developed extreme fears illustrates how early parent-child relations affect later development. Around the turn of the century, a number of ardent parents kept diaries that described every change in their infants' behavior over the early years. Psychologists found these baby biographies useful in describing sequences and individual differences in development. Although the diaries were not objective, scientific descriptions, they provided a basis for further scientific study. Case histories by scientific observers, such as Jean Piaget's (1926) observations of his own three children, have provided a rich source of ideas for further investigation.

For ethical reasons, some theoretically interesting ideas about development cannot easily be tested with human beings. Therefore, research on nonhuman species has a long history in psychology, and studies of chimpanzees and rhesus monkeys have provided valuable information about human development. For example, no psychologist would isolate a human baby in a laboratory to observe the effects of deprivation. But Harry Harlow and his associates (Harlow and Harlow, 1966; Harlow and Zimmermann, 1959) have conducted just such research with monkeys. Their results, which are discussed in Chapters 9 and 13, demonstrate the importance of contact comfort for the normal social development of monkeys. Because monkey and human babies have similar periods of close infant-mother relationships, these results suggest that human babies who are deprived of close contact with a caregiver might also show distorted social development. Indeed, when hypotheses derived from research on other primates have been tested against the experiences of babies reared in large, impersonal institutions and against occasional case histories of infants isolated by neglectful mothers, the inference of distorted social development has been supported (L. Yarrow, 1961).

Individual Variation

When explaining human development, psychologists are aware that the conclusions about behavior or developmental change that come from their research do not apply to all individuals. These conclusions are general statements summarizing what was found to be true for the largest number of subjects or for the "average" subject in an experiment. But the behavior or development of some subjects may have been different from that of the majority. For example, William Rohwer's (1971) study of children's learning showed that categorically organized materials are easier to remember than randomly ordered lists. That is, the list "car, boat, plane; chair, table, bed" is easier to remember than the list "car, bed, table; plane, chair, boat." Most elementary-school children will look at the first list and think "three things to ride in, three furnitures," which helps them recall the individual items. Some children, however, do not use categories to help them remember and thus recall as few items from the first list as from the second.

In this case, we can say that elementary-school children are likely to use categories to help them remember lists of items, even if all children do not use that strategy. Individual exceptions exist in all areas of development. A developmental psychologist may say that young adolescents generally become self-conscious about their appearances without being proved wrong by the example of an adolescent who remained slovenly and paid no attention to his appearance until he was eighteen.

Individual variations in behavior can provide clues about the many possible ways of behaving in the same situation. Children who learn to read successfully in the first grade seem to do so in a variety of ways. Choosing a single

Human beings are similar in many ways, but each is also unique, and the closer one looks the more differences one finds. These variations mean that research findings that apply to most people rarely describe everyone. *(© Charles Gatewood)*

method to teach reading to less successful readers has been nearly impossible because no one method has been successful with all children who have reading problems. Studies indicate that some children learn more quickly with a phonic approach, whereas others learn best using a sight, or look-say, method (Chall, 1967). Individual differences in aptitudes for reading are only one example of normal variation.

The fact of individual differences in almost all behavior does not keep developmental psychologists from testing general hypotheses about development or from making general statements about their results. General statements are often useful practically as well as theoretically. We know, for example, that excellent day care does not harm most children (Belsky and Steinberg, 1978). Although some day-care placements are not good and some children are more upset than others about leaving their mothers, research has shown that the development of young children in such situations is as normal on the average as the development of children at home with their mothers. That statement has obvious practical implications.

On the other hand, a researcher might study a day-care center that was itself an exception. It might be that by chance, a large number of unhappy children were enrolled in the center. On the basis of studying this single center, a researcher might conclude—incorrectly—that day-care centers and unhappy children go together. The best safeguard against accepting such a chance variation as typical is to have other investigators study other children in other day-care centers in the same way to see if they get the same results. This is called a **replication** study. Because so many factors can influence a study of behavior—including the investigator's own bias (R. Rosenthal, 1968)—it is important that others who do not have exactly the same ideas be able to repeat the results.

THE NATURE OF DEVELOPMENT

Normal infants grow first into children and then into adults, and this progression implies several characteristics about development: (1) development is orderly change; (2) it is directional; (3) it is cumulative to a large extent; and (4) it is characterized by increasing differentiation and complex organization.

Sequences

The notion of sequences of development pervades developmental psychology. Most theorists have acknowledged that behavioral development proceeds in an orderly fashion, and many have pointed to the increasing differentiation and complex organization of behavior at later ages. But before explaining the development of any behavior, we must be able to specify the exact nature of its sequence.

There is an orderly sequence to behavioral development, whether we talk about language acquisition, play, or moral judgment. Each kind of behavior can be described in a series of developmental steps. For example, the sequence of language development is orderly, directional, and predictable. All children begin by babbling, then around eleven to fourteen months of age, start to use single words. Toward the end of the second year, they can put two words together, and about the time they are three, most children can deliver an account of their activities in complex sentences.

The same sort of orderly development occurs in play. Symbolic play, which thrives during the preschool years, does not suddenly appear. At first babies simply manipulate their toys, mouthing, poking, squeezing, and shaking them. About the time they are a year old, infants begin to show some sense of function in their play; they might put a lid on a toy teapot. Within a month or so, they pretend to drink from the toy cup, and during the second year, they not only pretend to drink tea but can pretend that another object, such as a seashell, is a cup. Such simple substitutions pave the way for the young child's elaborate games of make believe (Belsky and Most, 1981). The sequence is the same for all children.

These sequences of development often proceed from simpler, more global behaviors to increasingly differentiated but integrated sets of behavior. For example, moral judgments of young children are often based on global concepts of "right" and "wrong." Their ideas of rightness and wrongness depend more on the outcome of an act than on the intentions of the actor. A child of four or five may feel that a boy who steals a cake because he is greedy is no worse than another who steals a cake to give to a hungry man. In both cases the boy stole the cake. But most older children and adults would separate the two cases and base their moral judgments on the boys' intentions. Older children also differentiate shades of wrongdoing. Many adolescents and adults base specific moral judgments on complex ideals that they have abstracted from experience in concrete situations. The development of moral judgment closely parallels other changes in children's thinking, which becomes more hypothetical from childhood to maturity.

Phases

This book uses the concept of phases to describe periods of the life span. As we have already noted, the ways in which periods of life have been conceived of in the past and in other cultures differ considerably. In talking about development, however, it is convenient to use five chronological periods or phases that roughly correspond to our cultural usage.

There are as many ways to divide the human lifespan as there are theorists. This popular nineteenth-century division of woman's life "from the cradle to the grave" rests on both social and biological markers. ***(The Life and Age of Woman, lithograph by N. Currier, 1850. Museum of the City of New York)***

The **prenatal** phase begins at conception and ends at birth. It is the least arbitrary and the easiest to define because its beginning and end are clearly marked. **Infancy** begins at birth and continues until approximately age two. By the end of the second year, most children have begun to acquire language and symbolic thought. In addition, most adults think of two-year-olds as children rather than as infants, which corresponds to the developmental shift from nonlinguistic to linguistic communication. Of course, other important changes occur in social and emotional behavior from infancy to childhood.

The third phase, **childhood,** begins around age two and continues through late childhood at around age twelve. Puberty is usually accepted as the end of childhood and the beginning of adolescence. **Adolescence,** the fourth phase, is a less definite period because its end is not defined as well as the end of other phases of development. Adolescents are generally accepted as adults when they acquire adult economic and social roles. **Adulthood,** the fifth phase, generally begins in the late teens or early twenties and continues until death. This is clearly the longest phase, spanning early adulthood, the middle

Phase	Biological Marker	Age	Psychosocial Marker
Conception		−9 months	
	PRENATAL	↓	
Birth		0 1 Month	
	INFANCY	↓	Forming attachments
Walking Talking		2 years	
	CHILDHOOD **Early**	↓	
		6 Years	Mastering basic skills
	Later	↓	
Puberty		11 Years	
	ADOLESCENCE	↓	Building personal and sexual identity
Physical Maturity		20 Years	
	ADULTHOOD **Early**	↓	Establishing personal and economic independence
		40 Years	
Menopause (in Women)	**Middle**	↓	Expanding personal and social involvement and responsibility
		60 Years	
	Later	↓	Reformulating social roles and personal goals
Death			

FIGURE 1.1 Since the phases of human development are based on cultural views of the life span, they vary from one society to another. Each phase of development used in this book is marked by particular biological or psychosocial events.

years, and late adulthood. There are many social and biological changes in adulthood, although the rate of development is much slower than in the earlier years.

Although dividing development into phases makes it easier to discuss behavioral changes that accompany one another, it is important to remember that development is continuous. Despite periods of relatively rapid or slow development, each person's life shows a continuity from conception to death.

THE USES OF DEVELOPMENTAL PSYCHOLOGY

When students enroll in a course on developmental psychology, they may first want to know *when* people develop certain skills and abilities. They may want a description of *what* behavior is typical of children and adults at different ages. Most students think of developmental psychology as a source of data about average development: When should children know their colors? When does the adolescent growth spurt begin? What differences are there in the IQ scores of people from different ethnic and socioeconomic backgrounds? Does intelligence really decline as people age? These students are partially right; developmental psychology does answer many questions about when development occurs. But more interesting than descriptive questions are questions that ask *how* and *why* development occurs as it does. Why do most children know primary-color names by kindergarten? (Why not earlier or later?) Why does the adolescent growth spurt show the same pattern in a majority of young people? Why do people differ in IQ scores? And so forth.

Information about the hows and whys of development have provided a sound basis for describing and explaining much about development. This book relies heavily on the results of scientific studies of development, and it interprets these results in terms of various theoretical positions. But it is neither a narrative of changes in behavior across the life span nor an exposition

EVALUATING PROJECT HEAD START

When social programs are proposed in Congress, the results of research in developmental psychology often are used to decide where to spend tax dollars. Project Head Start, which was designed to help disadvantaged children resist the effects of their early environment, is an example of a program that involved psychologists in all its phases. Some Head Start programs took place in day-care centers, some were carried on at home; some programs worked only with children, others focused on the parents. In one program, for example, children were placed in an enriched day-care environment and coached in language development (Caldwell, 1970). In another, mothers were taught to carry out at home activities designed to stimulate intellectual growth (Guinagh and Gordon, 1976).

Early results were promising. Instead of showing the steady decline in their IQ scores common among disadvantaged preschoolers, those who attended the intervention programs did significantly better on IQ tests than did other disadvantaged children. But when children were followed into their school years, the hopes raised by these early studies were dashed. The gains that made the programs so attractive seemed to fade over the years until, four years after a project's close, most of the gains had disappeared. In fact, the results based on IQ scores were so grim that an evaluation of the program in 1969 by the Westinghouse Learning Corporation almost led to the end of Project Head Start (Zigler and Trickett, 1978). Apparently, the effects of a child's natural environment were so strong that intervening for a few hours each day had little lasting effect.

But many psychologists protested the use of IQ scores as the sole evaluation of the programs. If one looked at children's social competence instead of merely at their IQ scores, said Edward Zigler and Penelope Trickett (1978), benefits from the program would become apparent. In order to measure social competence, these psychologists suggested, the children should be rated on physical health, school achievement, school attendance, rate of juvenile delinquency, and a number of motivational and emotional factors, in addition to IQ.

It appears that Zigler and Trickett may have been right. When Richard Darlington and his associates (1980) followed nearly 1,600 Head Start graduates from eight separate preschool programs, they found evidence of the project's success. True, IQ scores declined, just as earlier evaluations had indicated. But Head Start graduates, when compared with children from the same area who had not attended such programs, were significantly less likely to suffer failure in school. Whereas 45 percent of comparable children were either held back at least one grade or placed in special-education classes, only 24 percent of the Head Start children were held back or placed in special classes. Had Zigler and Trickett's other measures of competence also been used, the benefits of Head Start programs might have appeared even more impressive.

on how to rear children or how to lead "the good life." As scientists, psychologists learned long ago that their primary mission is to provide sound and useful sets of information for consumers to evaluate, rather than an arbitrary set of rules for them to follow. Psychologists are always interested in and alert to the applications of psychological data and theories. They are more likely, however, to discuss the effects of praise on a person's behavior than to tell employers that they must compliment their employees.

Studying developmental psychology often provides a new way of looking at the development of human behavior. It is easy to view lower organisms with detachment, for their behavior is removed from anything human beings have experienced. It is more difficult, at first, to look at the behavior of a human being in a similarly objective fashion. But a major message of psychology is that human behavior has its antecedents and its consequences, that there is a regularity and a degree of lawfulness in development. With appropriate analysis and objective study you should be able to discover why certain types of behavior occur and how conditions may influence later behavior. After reading this book you should no longer be content, for example, to ascribe aggressive behavior to meanness, but you should demand (and should be able to begin to formulate) a more penetrating analysis of why a person so often fights with others.

Almost every social question that involves children or adults is under study by developmental psychologists, from the effects of television advertising on preschoolers to ways to improve memory among eighty-year-olds. Information generated by such research is useful to students, parents, teachers, pediatricians, social workers, government planners, and others who need to understand how people's development can be enhanced or improved by life circumstances, how best to plan programs for the citizenry, young and old, and how to improve everyone's chances for optimum development. Parents face problems in the management and rearing of their own children. Teachers are confronted with difficulties in instructing their students. Pediatricians are more aware today of the relationship of behavior to physical problems in their young patients. Social workers must make decisions that affect the future success of people in their charge. Government planners need to know what kinds of programs will best serve young children in day care, teen-agers in work-study programs, older adults in nursing care, and so forth. For example, in the 1960s the government relied on developmental psychologists in planning, carrying out, and evaluating Project Head Start, a program devised to help overcome some of the negative effects of poverty on early development (see box on page 23).

Some questions about human development cannot be answered at present, but there is enough sound information and incisive theory for developmental psychology to offer exciting possibilities to anyone interested in understanding and influencing the development of human behavior.

SUMMARY

1. Many of the issues in developmental psychology spring from the problems that have fascinated philosophers for centuries: inborn differences, how much people change in response to the environment, the role human beings play in their own development, the natural goodness or evil in humanity, and the relationship of child to adult behavior.
2. In the twentieth century, we generally divide the life span into the prenatal period, infancy, childhood, adolescence, and adulthood. But societies with other kinds of social and economic systems have viewed the life span differently. The concept of a separate childhood emerged with the rise of the middle class, and adolescence with the onset of industrialization. The recognition that development continues throughout adulthood grew as life expectancy increased.
3. Developmental psychology grew out of child psychology, but developmental psychologists emphasize how circumstances affect what people do at different periods and the kinds of developmental sequences that take place.
4. Developmental psychologists attempt to describe, understand, and explain changes in human behavior across the life span. Their theories of human behavior are constructed using information from psychology, biology, sociology, and anthropology.

5. Developmental psychologists are careful to use an appropriate level of explanation to explain a given behavior. They search for explanations by studying behavior at different ages, behavioral changes as people grow older, environmental events that influence behavior, and variations among individuals, as well as by conducting research on nonhuman species and studying case histories of individuals. Replication studies are the best safeguard against accepting a chance finding as typical.

6. Development from infancy to adulthood involves orderly change that is directional, is largely cumulative, and involves increasing complexity and organization. Several concepts have been used to explain the relationship among developmental changes in behavior: sequences indicate that some behaviors precede others in a meaningfully related way; phases indicate that development is continuous across the life span and that the divisions are culturally determined.

7. Developmental psychologists' questions about the hows and whys of human development have led to much useful information about its regularity and lawfulness. Although some questions about human development cannot yet be answered, what is known offers insight into and understanding of many facets of human development.

2 DETERMINANTS OF DEVELOPMENT

If a child in the second grade has difficulty learning to read, her teacher may say that she has poor eyesight, or that her parents tried to teach her reading too early, or that she is lazy, or that she is of low intelligence. The teacher seldom considers that all four factors could have been involved and that each one could have contributed to the child's reading disability. When it comes to explaining behavior, even those of us who pride ourselves on our ability to understand the complexities of life often search for a single answer. However, few facets of behavior and development can be understood by looking at the relationship between a single developmental effect and a single cause.

In this chapter, we will explore some of the different causes of human behavior and the ways that developmental psychologists set about studying them. We will see that heredity and environment always work together to shape behavior and that maturation plays an important part in the process. We will discover that genetic research with animals can help us to understand heredity in human beings, and we will discuss some of the ways that researchers go about exploring genetic influences on individual differences. We will look at environments and observe how they influence the developing person. We will note that developmental psychologists use different kinds of studies and that each type gives them a different amount of control over the investigation of various biological or environmental determinants. We will find that no one type of study can supply all the necessary information about development and that all kinds of investigation are needed for a full account.

CLASSES OF DETERMINANTS

In order to understand human development, it is necessary to explore and document the way many causes interact. Yet before considering the interaction of causes, it is necessary to separate them and talk about different *classes* of causes. So we shall speak of hereditary influences (genetic and biological) on behavior, even though heredity cannot operate in isolation from the environment. The physical environment—whether the mother's uterus in the prenatal period or the chemically contaminated Love Canal area in New York State—is another class of developmental determinants. The social environment also affects the behavior of children and adults. The same environmental influences, however, may work differently on persons of different body types, different skin colors, different ages, and different generations.

Because developmental psychologists generally study change across time, they are especially aware that behavior depends on both the person and the environment—on *nature* as well as on *nurture.* Although both play necessary roles in development, some theorists stress one influence or the other.

When exploring the genetic-biological and the environmental aspects of development, researchers ask two questions:

"How?" and "How much?" The question "How?" refers to the ways in which heredity and environment combine to produce development. For example, how do **genes,** the microscopic elements that carry the blueprints of heredity, combine with environmental factors, such as nutrition, to produce growth? Answers to the question "How?" come from studies of people in general. The question "How much?" refers to the sources of differences among individuals. How much of the differences in height among members of the New York Philharmonic is due to nutritional differences while the musicians were growing up (environmental effects) and how much to each musician's own heredity (genetic effects)? Answers to the question "How much?" come from studies of the ways that individuals differ in their development.

BIOLOGICAL DETERMINANTS

Our heredity is of two kinds: the general inheritance of our species that makes us into that peculiar primate, *Homo sapiens,* and our specific inheritance from our parents and grandparents and great-grandparents that makes each of us visibly and temperamentally different from other members of our species. Both inheritances are biological determinants, and they begin working on us at the moment of conception and continue their work until we die. Heredity determines gender, the color of a child's hair, the fact that all of us have two eyes and that they perceive various wavelengths of light, and our susceptibility to various diseases, such as diabetes.

Answers to questions about genetic influence on behavior and development are difficult to obtain. Researchers cannot experimentally manipulate a human being's genetic structure. Nor can they select two people, ask them to mate and produce a child, and subject their offspring to one environment or another in order to determine the kinds of behavior that might be attributed to genetic differences or to experience. How, then, do we know about the contributions of genetics to human behavior?

Genetic Studies with Animals

One way to study human genetics is to derive a set of general principles from research on lower animals, in which nearly ideal genetic research can be performed. One type of experiment involves breeding genetically related animals until pure strains are produced. A variant of this technique involves breeding animals for a selected trait. For example, R. C. Tryon (1940) tested a group of rats on their ability to learn the path through a maze and interbred those rats that learned quickly. This process was repeated with the offspring, generation after generation, until a group of rats were at last born that were almost "purebreds" for superior performance in mazes. Studies applying these breeding techniques to mice and rats have shown that genetic differences can affect aggressiveness, maze-learning ability, hoarding, exploratory behavior, sex drive, alcohol preference, and a variety of other traits (McClearn, 1970).

Such experiments indicate that different strains of animals do not always respond to the same experience with the same kind of behavior. Therefore, it is impossible to predict the outcome of a particular learning experience unless the genetic make-up of the organism is specified.

For example, Daniel Freedman (1958) found unexpected genetic influences when he tested the effects that indulging or disciplining a puppy during its early weeks of life would produce on its self-control. He selected dogs from each of four different breeds: Basenji, Shetland sheepdog, wirehaired fox terrier, and beagle. The caretakers indulged some of the dogs from each breed between the third and eighth weeks of their lives by encouraging them to play, to be aggressive, and to engage in rough-and-tumble activities. Other dogs from each breed were disciplined by restraining them, teaching them to sit, stay, come on command, and so forth. After this training, each dog was tested. When it was hungry, its caretaker took it into a room containing a bowl of meat. For three minutes the caretaker prevented the animal from eating by hitting it on the rump with a rolled newspaper and shouting "No" every time the dog approached the food. Then the handler left the room, and an experimenter recorded the length of time that elapsed before the dog began to eat the meat.

Some theories of development might lead to the conclusion that an overindulged dog will not be able to inhibit its impulse to eat in such a test. But the results of eight days of testing indicate that such a prediction is not valid for dogs. In two breeds, the terriers and the beagles, the indulged animals waited longer before approaching the food than their disciplined companions. Neither the indulged nor the disciplined Shetlands ever ate the food, and all the Basenjis dug right into the meal. Although this experiment tells us nothing specific about human beings, it warns us to be cautious about dismissing genetic influences. It is clear that we cannot predict the effect of early indulgence versus discipline on a dog unless we first specify its genetic make-up or breed.

Just as both the genetic make-up of an organism and its environmental circumstances affect the development of any behavior, momentary environmental circumstances also affect the way that behavior is expressed or whether it appears at all. In many cases, hereditary behavior patterns appear only in the presence of a releasing stimulus, that is, an event that regularly evokes certain behavior in all members of a species.

For example, the male stickleback fish will attack an intruding male stickleback only if the stranger shows by its red belly that it is ready to mate (Tinbergen, 1951). The battle looks natural, and each fish seems to be behaving flexibly, but the fish protecting its nest is merely imitating the marauder's moves. When the stranger threatens, the defender threatens; when the stranger bites, the defender bites. The red belly of the strange fish releases the defender's attack, and each of the stranger's moves in the subsequent battle releases a response identical to the stimulus. To an observer, the fight is adaptive, natural, and flexible, but the components of the battle are fixed action patterns released by specific stimuli from the stranger. In this case, genetic behavior requires the appropriate environmental stimuli or it will not appear.

Human beings are less predictable than stickleback fish, but ethologists have pointed out the existence of releasers in humanity. Long ago, Charles Darwin (1872) suggested that the baby's smile helps to ensure an infant's survival because it evokes a feeling of joy in the caregiver. Even blind babies smile in response to human touch or voice, so it appears that the smile is as "natural" as walking (Freedman, 1974). Blind babies have no model of a smiling caregiver to imitate; hence their smiles are unlearned. This social smile, apparently part of our evolutionary heritage, can be seen as a releaser that helps forge an emotional bond.

Human Genetics

Principles derived from animal studies have guided research into the effects of genes on human development. However, with our present knowledge, we cannot answer questions that ask *how* genes affect the development of behavior. There are at least 250,000 pairs of genes in the developing human embryo, and many genes contribute to the development of most behavioral characteristics. For example, hundreds of them affect brain development. This estimate is probably low and is based on the knowledge that

150 independent genes can cause different forms of mental retardation. We know that several hundred more genes are probably required to develop a normal brain, because the causes of many forms of retardation have not yet been identified. But we do not know how these hundreds of genes act together to produce a normal brain or normal intelligence.

Genes exert their influences throughout the life span. The timing of growth and aging and the sequence of development are related to gene action. Genes are "turned on" at some but not other points in development. The "turned on" genes are active in producing substances within the body that create new structures, regulate their functions, or maintain their state. Genes are carried on beadlike strings called **chromosomes,** which will be discussed in Chapter 4. The appearance of enlarged segments of chromosomes, called puffs, is related to genetic activity. Puffs appear on different segments of different chromosomes throughout life, suggesting that genetic activity continues to help determine how development proceeds. Lissy Jarvik and Donna Cohen (1973) have shown that breaks in chromosomes and unusual numbers of chromosomes are increasingly found in people's cells as they grow older. Aging may somehow be related to, among other things, gradual deteriorations in the genetic code.

Questions that ask *how much* genetic differences affect the development of individual differences are easier to answer. Still, we have conclusive answers only for some abnormal physical traits that are caused by single genes, and no one has yet shown any normal behavior for which a single gene accounts for a considerable amount of the differences among people (Freedman, 1974). (In Chapter 4 we will see how single-gene traits are transmitted from parent to child.) In the case of normal traits, such as height, we get some idea of whether genetic factors are involved by comparing the trait among related and unrelated people. The more closely these people are related and the more similar the trait, the more likely it is that genetic factors have influenced the trait. Appearance is obviously influenced by genetic differences, because genetically related people resemble each other more than unrelated people do, whether they grow up together or not. Thus, taller parents tend to have taller children than shorter parents do.

TABLE 2.1
CORRELATIONS OF INTELLIGENCE TEST SCORES

Correlations Between	*Median Value*
Unrelated persons	
Children reared apart	−.01
Children reared together	+.20
*Collaterals**	
Second cousins	+.16
First cousins	+.28
Uncle (or aunt) and nephew (or niece)	+.34
Siblings, reared apart	+.46
Siblings, reared together	+.52
Fraternal twins, different sex	+.49
Fraternal twins, same sex	+.56
Identical twins, reared apart	+.75
Identical twins, reared together	+.87
Direct line	
Grandparent and grandchild	+.30
Parent (as adult) and child	+.50
Parent (as child) and child	+.56

*Descended from the same stock, but different lines.
Source: Based on estimates reported in John C. Loehlin, Gardner Lindzey, and J. N. Spuhler, *Race Differences in Intelligence,* San Francisco: W. H. Freeman, 1975; and in Arthur Jensen, "How Much Can We Boost IQ and Scholastic Achievement?" *Harvard Educational Review,* 39 (1969), 49.

The intellectual skills that are sampled by IQ tests also appear to be influenced by heredity, as a comparison of parents' and children's IQ scores shows. This tendency shows clearly in Table 2.1, which presents the correlations between the IQ scores of pairs of individuals who bear different degrees of genetic similarity to one another.

To understand this table one must know something about **correlation coefficients.** A correlation is a numerical expression of how closely two sets of measurements correspond. A correlation of .00 represents no direct relationship at all. For example, in Table 2.1 the correlation between the IQ scores of two children who are unrelated and reared apart is −.01, essentially .00. This number implies that knowing the IQ score of one child tells you nothing about the IQ score of the unrelated child. If a correlation coefficient were +1.00, then the correspondence between pairs of individuals would be perfect. In this case, knowing that Matt had the highest IQ score in his group would indicate that Richard also had the highest IQ score in his group (but not necessarily the *same* IQ score). If the correlation were −1.00, then if Matt had the highest score in his group, Richard had the lowest score in his group. In psychological research, correlations are rarely exactly .00 or +1.00 or −1.00. Rather, they fall at various places in between. The larger the coefficient, the more closely two measures correspond and the better one score can predict the other. When the correlation is high and the sign is positive, a high score in one member of the pair predicts a high score in the other; but when the correlation is high and the sign is negative, a high score in one predicts a low score in the other.

As the relatedness between two people increases, the correlation between their IQ scores also increases. Notice that in Table 2.1 the correlations for siblings (brothers or sisters) are not very different from the correlations for fraternal twins (twins developed from two separate egg cells). This is to be expected, because on the average both siblings and fraternal twins share half their genes. But identical twins (twins developed from a split single female egg cell) have identical genetic make-ups, and their IQs show much higher correlations. Both the mother and the father also share half their genes with their children, so that the correlation for parents and children is about the same as for siblings and fraternal twins. Therefore, it can be said that IQ scores appear to be directly related to the degree of genetic relatedness.

However, such evidence does not allow us to say that genetic make-up is the primary determinant of a person's intellectual ability. As relatedness between individuals increases, so does the similarity of the environment in which they live. Unrelated children reared apart share no common environment, and the correlation of their IQ scores is essentially .00. Brothers and sisters share some of their environment, but because they are born at different times and because each is subjected to some unique life experiences, their environments are not identical. In addition, because identical twins look alike, parents are more likely to treat them alike than if they were fraternal. As a result, it is possible to interpret the evidence presented in Table 2.1 as simply indicating that the IQ scores of two people are similar to each other when their environments are similar.

Another way of trying to discover how much genetic differences affect intellectual ability is to compare the IQ scores of related individuals, some of whom live in the same environment and the rest of whom live in different environments. For example, it is possible to compare the IQ scores of adopted children with the IQ scores of both their biological parents and the parents who reared them. Researchers who have studied this problem (Honzik, 1957; Scarr-Salapatek, 1975; Skodak and Skeels, 1949) have discovered that correlation coefficients between the IQ scores of adopted children and their biological parents are greater (approximately +.35) than between those same adopted children and their rearing parents (.00 in some studies; from +.09 to +.16 in others).

In fact, there is little difference between the correlations for adopted children and their biological parents and the correlations for children reared by their own parents (Figure 2.1). This result presumably argues for a genetic component in intelligence.

However, a look at the *average* IQ score of these children reveals that this score is closer to the average IQ score of their upper-middle-class foster mothers than to the average IQ score of their impoverished biological mothers. In one study the average IQ score of the biological mothers was 86, but the average IQ score for the children was 106, a score near the estimated IQ of the parents who reared them. This evidence argues for an environmental component of intellectual ability and suggests that IQ scores can be improved if people subsequently are placed in a rich environment.

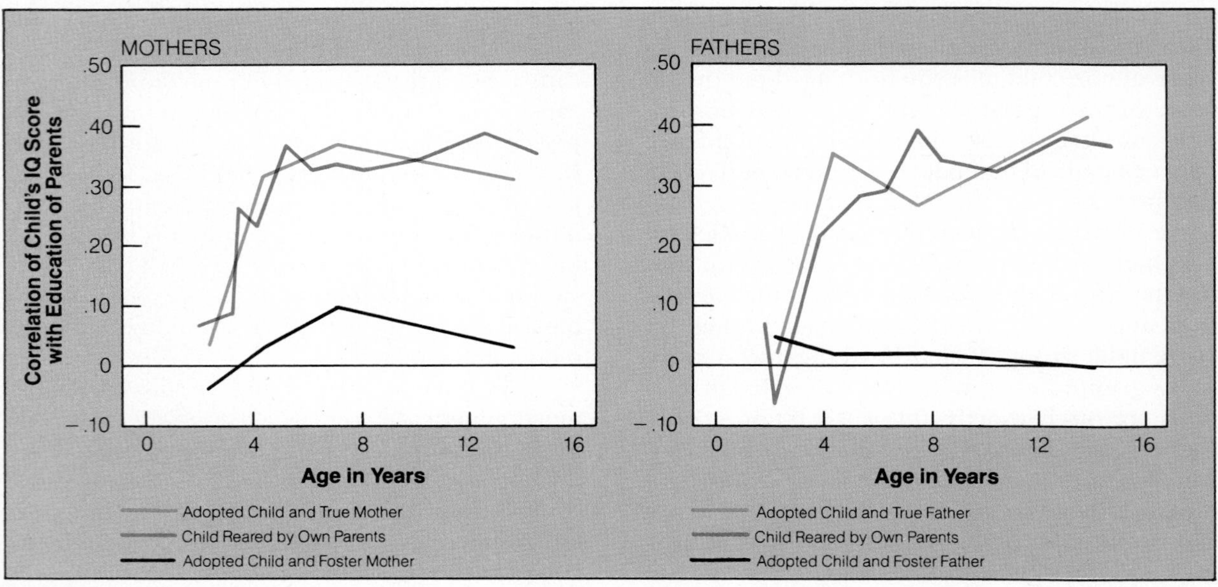

FIGURE 2.1 Correlations between children's IQ scores and the estimated IQ scores of their parents (based on the parents' educational level) show that as children get older, their scores correlate more closely with their biological parents' scores, but that there is little change in the low correlation between the scores of adopted children and those of their foster parents. ***(Adapted from Skodak and Skeels, 1949; after Honzik, 1957)***

More recently, Sandra Scarr and Richard Weinberg (1976) tested the idea that an enriched environment can raise IQ test scores by studying more than one hundred poor black children who were adopted by middle-class white families, in which most of the parents were college graduates. They found that when such black children are adopted early in life into such white families, their average IQ score is above the national average of both black and white children, indicating that environment has a profound effect on IQ scores.

Results like these illustrate a crucial concept for understanding genetic influences: the **reaction range.** The genetic make-up of each person has a unique range of possible responses to the environments that he or she may encounter. In other words, there are some limits on how each of us can respond to good and poor environmental conditions. In the case of height, good nutrition will make all of us taller than poor nutrition will, but in both kinds of environments some of us will be taller than others, as Figure 2.2 indicates. Genes do not specify a particular height for anyone. They do specify a pattern of growth that varies depending on nutrition and other environmental factors. The final height we achieve depends on both genetic and environmental factors.

The development of intellectual skills that are sampled by IQ tests also has a reaction range. No matter how stimulating the environment, few people become Albert Einsteins or Leonardo da Vincis. And in other than very deprived circumstances, most people do not become mentally retarded. Each person has a range of at least twenty-five IQ points in which his or her IQ score will tend to fall, depending on rearing conditions (Scarr-Salapatek, 1975).

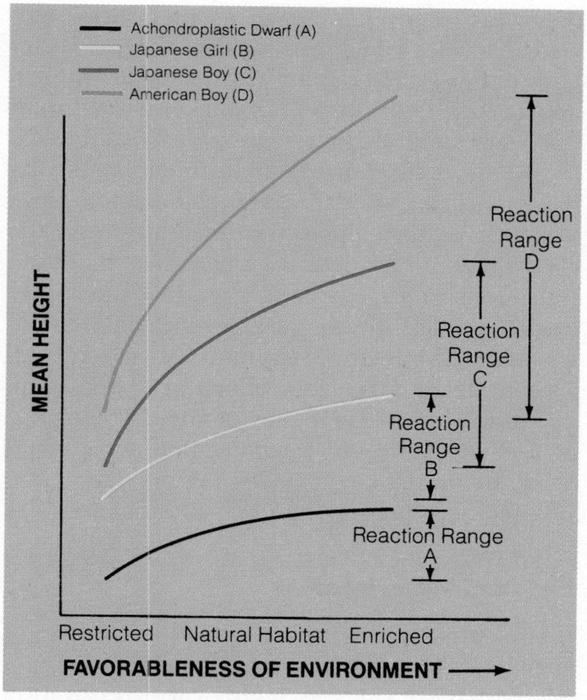

Achondroplastic Dwarf (A)
Japanese Girl (B)
Japanese Boy (C)
American Boy (D)
Reaction Range D
Reaction Range C
Reaction Range B
Reaction Range A
MEAN HEIGHT
Restricted Natural Habitat Enriched
FAVORABLENESS OF ENVIRONMENT →

FIGURE 2.2 When the heights of adolescents with four different genetic make-ups are compared, it becomes clear that environment and genes combine to produce development. The Japanese boy (Genetic make-up C) who had grown up in an optimum environment would be taller than the American boy (Genetic Make-up D) who had grown up in a severely restricted environment. But if both environments were natural, severely restricted, or optimum, the American boy would be taller. Under no circumstances could the dwarf (Genetic Make-up A) be as tall as any of the other three. ***(From Gottesman, 1974)***

Heritability

Exploring another important genetic concept may make it easier to understand the influence of genes on IQ scores or any other trait. We know that individuals in any group have different genetic compositions as well as different life experiences. But how much of the differences in their temperament or height or IQ scores is associated with differences in their genetic make-up and how much with differences in their lives? The relative contribution of genetics to any trait is the **heritability** of the trait in a particular group.

Heritability is only an estimate based on the number of cases in a particular group; it may or may not represent the heritability of the trait in the general population. Suppose it were possible to find a group of people with identical genetic make-up. If these individuals were randomly placed in various environments and then given an IQ test, none of the differences in their IQ scores could be attributed to differences in their genetic composition. The heritability would be .00. On the other hand, if it were possible to rear a group of individuals with totally different genetic dispositions in the same environment, then all the differences in their IQ test scores would be associated with differences in their genetic make-up. Heritability would be 1.00.

These examples demonstrate that heritability is a relative measure that depends on the specific research sample. Many estimates of the heritability of IQ came from research with white, upper-middle-class groups living in environments that permit traits to develop in the upper part of the reaction range. Such groups probably do not represent the full range of genetic make-up or environments among the population of a country—or a race or a social group (Loehlin, Lindzey, and Spuhler, 1975).

The heritability for a trait can even change from year to year. This is possible because heritability depends on the specific characteristics of the group. If either the group or the factors that produce the trait change, the heritability will also shift. A century ago, the bacillus for tuberculosis was so prevalent that almost everyone came into contact with it. Since every person was exposed to TB, all had the same environment for this factor, and the primary determinant for the development of tuberculosis was a person's inborn biochemical susceptibility to the bacillus. The heritability for TB was high. Today, the TB bacillus has been eliminated except in extremely unsanitary places. As a result, exposure to the bacillus has become the primary determinant for the disease's development, because most people who have a biochemical susceptibility to the bacillus never come into contact with it. Therefore, the heritability for TB is now quite low.

The cause of TB, however, has not changed: the invasion of the TB bacillus in an individual with a biochemical susceptibility to that bacillus. But the heritability for TB has changed because whether one gets the disease is now more closely associated with where one lives than with genetic predisposition. Therefore, the fact that a trait has high heritability does not mean that genes cause it, nor does low heritability mean that environmental circumstances cause a trait to appear. Instead, its appearance is a function of both kinds of determinants.

There is an old expression that genes set limits on development while environments determine what actually develops. This is *not* true. Environments are equally implicated in setting limits on development by providing only certain opportunities and stimuli for a person to develop a particular characteristic or behavior. Genes are equally responsible for determining the level of development by responding to given environments in unique ways. Individual differences among people, then, are caused by genetic differences in their reaction ranges *and* by specific differences in their environments.

ENVIRONMENTAL DETERMINANTS

Environmental determinants play a powerful role in the development of the growing child, as the most radical of biologically oriented theorists would agree. But the term "environment" is too broad to have much scientific usefulness. One must always specify which features of the environment affect any particular behavior. To explain why a number of children achieve low scores on IQ tests, for example, some environmentalists merely point to the obvious disparities between advantaged and disadvantaged homes, schools, and neighborhoods, claiming that (somehow) all of the noticeable differences determine differences in IQ scores. However, there are various ways of defining the environment and of explaining how experience influences development. For example, Urie Bronfenbrenner (1979) has highlighted an **ecological** approach to development that takes into account the interaction among various environmental levels: the child's immediate setting (e.g., the living room), the child's other customary settings (the rest of the house, the neighborhood, the classroom), other settings that affect the child (the place where the child's mother and father work, an older brother's classroom), and the environmental influences of the larger society. All ways of defining the environment can be useful, depending upon the behavior that is being explained; and the more factors that are considered, the more likely we are to understand environmental influence.

Physical Determinants

It is obvious that all organisms must have sufficient air, water, food, and light to maintain life. Without these there is biological deterioration and even death. What is not so obvious is the extent to which other features of the physical environment affect the course of development. For example, the environment of the mother's uterus is critical to the survival and development of the fetus, which requires an efficient exchange of oxygen and nutrients and the elimination of wastes. If the maternal environment is deficient in nutrients such as calcium or protein, the infant's development will be stunted. The relative spaciousness of the maternal environment is also a factor: short mothers have small and premature babies more often than tall mothers do, and twins are often so crowded that they are born prematurely. As Chapter 4 will explain, the maternal physical environment also has other important effects on fetal development.

At later ages of the developmental process, physical environments provide a metaphorical rather than the literal capsule the uterus does. Each of us develops in a physical context that has limiting and determining effects on our development. For example, life in a nomad's tent and life in an apartment have different influences on a growing child. Similarly, Roger Barker and Herbert Wright (1951) have described the interplay

Going swimming in the neighborhood pool may be casual to a suburban child, but not to a city boy or girl. Although there are many similarities between contemporary environments, elements that make an environment unique also affect the lives of children growing up in it. *(© Richard Kalvar/Magnum Photos)*

between one boy and his Kansas town, where he could dig, jump, run, explore fields, and engage in a variety of activities in a physical environment that was very different from the concrete and asphalt surroundings of an inner-city child in Detroit.

When a young city boy wants to dig, for example, getting him to dirt or sand is a major project for his parents, who must take him down in an elevator and then walk him through city traffic to a park. In addition, the noise and visual stimulation of the traffic and the sidewalks crowded with pedestrians provide a completely different experience from that of the suburban child who merely walks out the back door to his sandbox. All children develop in a physical context that offers some kinds of experiences and limits others.

The physical design of buildings can also have a profound effect on the people who live in them. For example, when low-income families move from smaller buildings into high-rise apartments, they feel isolated and regimented. They fail to develop the community identification that is generally found in city neighborhoods composed of smaller buildings. As Oscar Newman (1973) has pointed out, many of these high-rise apartment buildings are designed so that the corridors and entries cannot be supervised, thereby encouraging crime and vandalism, which breeds fear and suspicion among the inhabitants.

The role physical context can play in children's development is also illustrated in a study by Sheldon Cohen, David Glass, and Jerome E. Singer (1973) that explored the effects of long-term exposure to loud noise. The investigators found in Manhattan a thirty-two story apartment building that was located over an expressway: inside the building, the lower floors were filled with the sounds of traffic, but noise levels dropped with the height of the building so that apartments on the higher floors were relatively quiet. When Cohen and his associates tested the children who lived in the building, they found that those who had lived at least four years on the lower, noisier floors were less able to pick up the subtle sound contrasts of speech, such as "gear-bear" or "cope-coke," than children who lived on the higher, quieter floors. Nor did children who lived on the lower floors read as well as those who lived on the higher floors. Thus, noise levels in the apartments and the length of time children had lived in them were closely related to reading ability and auditory discrimination. Other factors could also have been involved in the children's ability to hear or read well, but the study appears to indicate that the physical environment can have important effects on physical and mental abilities.

Physical factors in the environment can also have an impact on social behavior, at least among preschool children. In one study, Peter K. Smith (1974) found that when little play equipment was available, children shared their toys and apparatus and tended to form large play groups. On the other hand, when many toys and equipment were available, children tended to keep the toys to themselves, playing either in small groups or alone. Even the kind of equipment affected the children's behavior. Some were given only apparatus, such as chairs, tables, and a ladder, to play with, while others were given only toys, such as puzzles, dress-up clothes, tea sets, and blocks. The children who had only apparatus to play with increased their verbal and physical contacts, played more in cooperative groups, smiled and laughed more, and devised new and creative uses for the apparatus. It seems that when the physical environment has few resources, people can cooperate and invent creative ways to use the available material.

When the influence of the family on the growing child is mentioned, one assumes that the reference is to the nuclear family, made up of father, mother, and one or more children. *(Hubbell/Woodfin Camp & Assoc.)*

Social Determinants

Among the social determinants are all the influences that people and social institutions have on the developing person. The effect of people is reflected in families, peer groups, and neighborhoods; social institutions wield their influence through schools, group attitudes, values and beliefs, and the media.

Family From sex roles to intellectual skills, the family affects most aspects of behavioral development. A person's self concept, social skills, ideas of masculinity and femininity, as well as intellectual development all show heavy family influence. For example, fathers appear to play an important part in the young boy's development of a traditionally masculine sex role. This influence showed clearly when E. Mavis Hetherington and Jan Deur (1972) studied young adolescent boys who had lost their fathers. Boys who had lost their fathers before they were five years old showed less traditionally masculine competitiveness and rough-and-tumble play. But as the boys reached adolescence, the effects of a fatherless boyhood tended to decrease. Boys who had lost their fathers later in life were no different from boys who had grown up with fathers present. On the other hand, another study (Hetherington, 1972) indicated that the early loss of a father had no apparent effects on girls until they reached puberty. Then the adolescent girls behaved inappropriately around males. This research, although limited to lower-class and lower-middle-class girls, indicates that girls may acquire from their fathers the social skills needed to interact with the opposite sex.

The age and sex of one's siblings also help determine sex-role development. Boys with older sisters show a weaker preference for the traditional masculine sex role than boys with older brothers or boys who lack older siblings (H. Koch, 1966; Sutton-Smith and Rosenberg, 1970). Girls with older brothers behave in more traditionally masculine ways than do girls with older sisters or no older siblings. Because older siblings tend to act like parents toward younger children in the family, especially if there is a large age difference, it is not surprising to find that older siblings appear to affect the sex-role development of younger children.

Families also provide a context for intellectual development. The opportunities that are available to children and the way that the parents respond to their curiosity affect what children learn and how rapidly they learn it. If there are many children in the family, their intellectual skills tend to be less well developed than those of children in smaller families. Birth order also has an effect: first-born children and those early in birth rank tend to have higher IQ scores than children born later. The effects of family size and birth order seem to come about because parents

Not all children live in the traditional nuclear family. The single-parent family, generally with a mother at the head, has become increasingly common. *(Tim Eagan/Woodfin Camp & Assoc.)*

pay less attention to any one child when there are many and to later-born children in general (Belmont and Marolla, 1973). The dilution of parental attention may also be responsible for the lower IQ scores of twins as compared to those of single children. When there are twins to care for, the amount or quality of attention that parents can give seems to diminish.

Peers The influence of peers is first felt when a child goes off to day care, nursery school, or kindergarten. Thus most children in today's society come under the influence of other children much earlier than did their grandparents, who may not have had any organized peer contact before the first grade. In the environment of the peer group, children enter a world with its own values and rules of behavior, which may differ radically from those of the family.

The environment of the group affects even small children, as Lawrence Sherman (1975) found when he investigated sociability among young children. He wanted to discover the factors that seem to trigger and maintain an atmosphere of glee among children. Sherman defined glee as a raucous, happy event that consists of laughter, yelling, and animated physical expression. By studying many videotapes of preschool groups, he found that gleeful episodes were more likely to occur when lessons included props and movement (e.g., drums and dancing) as compared to lessons requiring individual activity (e.g., simple construction). In more than 70 percent of the episodes, the children's glee began as a reaction to some triggering event, such as a call for volunteers. Once it started, glee in one child stimulated it in another, until the laughter and animated activity had spread through the group.

In middle childhood and adolescence, the peer group provides an important personal testing ground. Because a person cannot go through life being "Mama's boy" or "Daddy's girl," he or she establishes other identifications and goals. Adolescent peers are decidedly important in the development of a sense of identity (Erikson, 1968). Because peers share the problems of establishing independence and identity, they provide positive support in the often painful process of becoming an adult.

In later years peers continue to influence behavior. They are friends, consultants on problems, people to compete with and emulate. Although little research has been done on the effects of peer groups in adulthood, young parents often consult other young parents on questions about child rearing. Older adults share common experiences and gain support from peers in their increasingly difficult problems of

The rules and values of the peer group may be radically different from those of the family and provide children with a testing ground where they can establish their identities. *(Constantine Manos/Magnum Photos)*

adjustment to adult children, retirement, and changing physical status.

Neighborhoods Over the years it has been found that many features of a neighborhood influence its structure and function, thereby affecting the development and behavior of the people who live there. For example, in close-knit, active neighborhoods, children use the sidewalks to get acquainted, to meet their friends, and to play. They provide a setting that encourages contacts. But if street traffic is dense and rapid, the sidewalks cannot be used as social areas and the neighborhood is less likely to be friendly.

Age segregation, such as the predominantly youthful composition of college neighborhoods or the elderly composition of retirement communities, also affects the activities and atmosphere of an area. Size is another factor. The social world of a small Iowa town, for example, is very different from that of a large city. A girl who grows up in Iowa knows everyone in her town and feels comfortable walking its streets after dark. As she strolls down a street, she greets the people she passes. She is unacquainted with the burglaries, violence, and street-corner drug dealing that are commonplace in some large cities. Walking down a city street, the girl would soon discover that—except for responding to requests for directions—residents rebuff the rare social overture and avert their gaze to avoid eye contact when passing strangers. In some parts of the city, a lone pedestrian would not venture out after dark.

When a country is in a state of war or revolution, a walk down a neighborhood street may become a trip into violence and danger, as it could for this child in Northern Ireland. *(© Jim Anderson 1981/Woodfin Camp & Assoc.)*

The relationship between a neighborhood and its people runs both ways; we have seen the effect of the neighborhood on human development and activity, but the people who live in a neighborhood also shape its activity. Because this is so, whenever the residents in a neighborhood change, changes in neighborhood life follow. If the age, interests, life style, or ethnic background of residents shifts, accompanying changes soon appear in friendship patterns and neighborhood projects or events. "Old-time" residents often resent and fight such changes, but gradually the reshaping of the neighborhood by its newer residents results in a different but stable pattern of developmental influences and experiences for both children and adults.

Schools Schools socialize children in many of the same ways that families and peer groups do, but there are also great differences. When children enter school, they face new demands that they support their peers, reduce their pleasures, find satisfaction in the completion of tasks, and become industrious (Gump, 1978).

Such aspects of the school environment as the type of program (open or traditional), or the size of the school can affect children differently. For example, because fewer students are available in small high schools for extracurricular activities (sports, journalism, drama, band, etc.), attending such a school leads to greater pressure for students to participate in these activities. Additionally, there is wider assumption of responsible positions, greater satisfaction, and increased feelings of responsibility among the students, as compared with those attending large schools (Gump, 1980). The effect is especially pronounced among academically marginal students, who participate as much as other students in small schools but, feeling almost no responsibility, participate infrequently in large schools.

At all levels, the standards of conduct and values set by school staffs often are different from those of the children's families and friends. Notable problems have arisen when the school represents an alien middle-class white world in the middle of a culturally different neighborhood. Some Hispanics and blacks have demanded more control over what their children are taught in school, because they believe that the established curriculum (and perhaps the staff) is irrelevant. Most parents believe that schools have profound effects on their children's future success. They believe that getting along with teachers, earning good grades, and scoring well on standardized tests are related to opportunities for further education and entrance into prestigious occupations.

Indeed, studies of nations where education is not available to all children suggest that schools do affect the intellectual achievements of children (e.g., Cole, 1978). At the very least, schoolchildren learn new ways to apply their cognitive skills to problems that the society says are important (and therefore puts in the school curriculum). The effects of schools are not limited to the intellectual realm. Schools also influence social skills, psychological growth, and children's feelings about the rules and regulations of society.

Media All media affect behavior, for good and for bad. But the most pervasive medium today is television, and it is virtually impossible for a child to grow up without being exposed to heavy doses of it. Surveys indicate that 99 percent of all families with children own television sets, and most children spend from one-fifth to one-third of their waking hours before the flickering screen (Murray and Kippax, 1979). Children who spend a good deal of their free time watching television go to bed later than other children and spend less time reading.

Television can have both good and bad effects on children. But in families where a flickering parade of cartoons, commercials, and game shows substitutes for maternal care, its value is questionable. *(Ken Heyman)*

The effects of showing aggression on television have been hotly debated, and Chapter 15 will explore research that applies to the controversy. In general, watching violence on television does not seem to trigger aggressive behavior in most children, but some violence-prone youngsters appear to be influenced toward more aggression by watching aggressive models (Bandura, 1973).

Questions have also been raised about nonviolent programs. Educational series such as "Sesame Street" and "The Electric Company," which have been designed to teach specific academic skills to disadvantaged children, have been a success: the more often the children watch, the greater the improvement in their skills (Lesser, 1974). But middle-class children also watch these programs, and they seem to benefit as much as or more than the disadvantaged children for whom the programs were designed. This means that widespread watching of educational television is not likely to close the academic gap between advantaged and disadvantaged children.

Each culture provides a different kind of environment for children. This small boy, growing up in an extended family in Germany, probably will be reared as much by grandparents as by parents. *(Thomas Hopker/Woodfin Camp & Assoc.)*

Culture Culture is a powerful but generally unnoticed influence on development. Differences among cultures in dress, language, customs, and history are taken for granted by children, but many adults are unaware that culture also affects personality, values, the way people express emotion, how they think, move, and solve problems (Hall, 1976). Even the experience of being male or female varies widely among cultures.

Each culture has its own ideas, practices, technologies, institutions, and so on that influence each of its members. There are, for example, cultures in which mothers or fathers have little to do with the rearing of their children; cultural practices and beliefs are passed on by brothers or sisters or by older unrelated children or adults who have been given the child-rearing function.

Within cultures there are also subcultural variations that are related to ethnic background, social class, and economic influences, each of which has a profound influence on how a person develops. We will discuss some of these distinctions in later chapters, but we can note one or two here. In the United States, for example, ethnic and social-class differences in wealth, education, and IQ test scores have developed in such a way that the three often go together (Hess,

Social class may have a profound influence on the developing child; these children, crowded into an urban apartment, will never have many advantages taken for granted among the middle class. *(Bruce Davidson/Magnum Photos)*

1970). Because of the effects this sort of status has on individual opportunity, children in middle- or upper-class families are more likely to feel that they have the chance and ability to shape their own futures. On the other hand, lower-class children and adolescents may be wiser than middle- or upper-class children in other respects and better able to survive, should they suddenly be cast on their own resources.

STUDYING DETERMINANTS

Obviously the social environment strongly influences the development of behavior. But how do these influences really work? The first step in identifying various determinants and their effects on human development is to design a study in which appropriate information can be gathered. Psychologists can use several different methods, and the distinctions among them depend on how much *control* the investigator has. A researcher may or may not have control over (1) the selection of subjects for study, (2) the experience they have in the study, and (3) the possible responses they can give to that experience. At one extreme of control is the simple, **naturalistic observation** of behavior without any interference from the investigator. At the other extreme is **experimentation,** where the experimenter can control all three aspects of the study. Between the two extremes are numerous types of **field studies** and **clinical studies,** where some but not other types of control are possible.

Each type of study has its advantages and disadvantages, and the investigator's purpose as well as specific circumstances will determine which type is chosen. No one study, however, will ever answer all relevant questions. A soundly designed and executed study can, at best, support our subjective judgment that a conclusion is correct or show that it is wrong.

In psychology, there has probably never been a truly crucial study that provided a clear basis for choosing between two opposed theories. Such investigations are rare in any science. As noted in Chapter 1, the final test is replication. A scientific finding becomes established when it has been found in several investigations (and the more, the better) conducted by different researchers in different places but using the same basic methods.

Naturalistic Observation

In naturalistic observation, the investigator carefully records the behavior of people going about their daily activities. The major advantage of this type of study is its closeness to what happens in everyday life, so that there are few problems in generalizing the results of observations to actual situations. If such a study is well conducted, valuable information can be gained about the everyday effects of environmental **variables,** or factors, on human behavior. But in order for

CHILD ADVOCACY

Many developmental psychologists feel their efforts on behalf of children should include helping to define and guarantee the rights of children and adolescents. Since 1948, the courts have held that rights guaranteed to adults also apply to children, but defining the narrow ground between the sometimes conflicting rights of parents and their offspring is difficult. The developmental aspect of this issue concerns determining the ways that children differ from adults and, then, deciding whether special protection is needed to ensure whatever rights are involved in those differences (Shore, 1979).

According to Milton Shore (1979), the historically recent evolution of the concepts of childhood and adolescence has led people to resist the idea that children and young people are separate and autonomous individuals. This resistance has gone hand-in-hand with such cultural beliefs as government should not interfere in family life and parents should have the right to control their children and to determine what is best for them. As Shore points out, politics is the major force for social change in this country. Since children cannot vote, politicians have no incentive to protect children's rights.

Sometimes the rights of parents and children clash. Some researchers have suggested, for example, that a divorced parent who fails to win custody of his or her child should not be allowed to insist on visitation rights against the child's wishes (Goldstein, Freud, and Solnit, 1979). Less obvious examples involve other aspects of the child's right to grow up psychologically and physically healthy. There is, for example, the question of whether a parent's decision to withhold medical treatment or education from a child on religious grounds should be a matter for state intervention. Or the question of the point at which parents' beliefs, preferences, and life style may harm their children.

The movement to define and guarantee the rights of children and adolescents is called **child advocacy.** Psychologists interested in child advocacy sometimes serve as expert witnesses in court cases or supply information and testimony to legislative committees drafting legislation. Child advocates have even suggested that all legislation should be systematically reviewed to determine its possible impact upon children, youth, and families (Shore, 1979).

naturalistic observation to be successful, there must be explicit rules for categorizing and recording what the observer sees.

For example, when psychologists wanted to find out whether the structure of a nursery-school program affected the way children play in their free periods, they observed children in a traditional nursery school and in a school with a discovery-based program meant to encourage the development of logical thought. Before James Johnson, Joan Ershler, and Colleen Bell (1980) could begin their study, they had to have clear definitions of the variables they were concerned with. They agreed on how long children would have to play for it to be considered an episode, they agreed how each type of play was to be defined, and they devised guidelines so that two observers watching a child at the same time could make comparable observations.

In this study, each child was observed twenty times over an eleven-week period, for one minute at a time. Observers counted three kinds of social play (how the children played) and three kinds of cognitive play (the content of their play), and noted when the observed child was not playing but watching others or simply doing nothing. After analyzing their observations, Johnson and his associates found no difference in social play between the two groups; but they found large differences in cognitive play, indicating that a nursery school's program may indeed influence the content of a young child's free play.

The major problem that may plague an observational study is the possibility of unknown factors—factors that researchers cannot control—influencing the results. Thus one task of inves-

TABLE 2.2
THE ADVANTAGES AND DISADVANTAGES OF VARIOUS RESEARCH METHODS

Method	*Advantages*	*Disadvantages*
Naturalistic observation	Situation close to everyday life	No control over selection of participants, or over their experience and responses Difficult to duplicate Unknown and uncontrolled factors may influence results Observer may affect responses Observations may be unreliable Often expensive and time-consuming
Field study	Situation close to everyday life Some control over experience and responses of participants	No control over selection of subjects. Unknown and uncontrolled factors may influence results Observations may be unreliable Often expensive and time-consuming
Clinical study	Situation close to everyday life Some control over selection of participants Experience and responses of participants may be standardized	Unknown and uncontrolled factors may influence results Observations may be unreliable
Experiment	Unwanted factors may be controlled or eliminated Generally most efficient in terms of time and money expended	Situation may be far removed from everyday life
Cross-sectional design	May take any of the above forms with its advantages	May be flawed by cohort effects May take any of the above forms with its disadvantages May not show pattern of individual change
Longitudinal design	May take any of the above forms with its advantages May be the only valid way to study developmental change	May take any of the above forms with its disadvantages Repeated observations may distort behavior of participants Generally expensive and time-consuming
Single-subject design	Advantages of experimental method	Results may not generalize to other people

tigators is to determine which of the many uncontrolled variables might have an important effect on the results of the study. Sometimes the presence of such factors may go unnoticed, only to be discovered when another group of researchers attempts to replicate the study and finds that their results are not the same.

Among other difficulties in observational

studies is the effect of the watching psychologist on a child's behavior. Children may behave differently if they know they are being watched. When children are studied in a laboratory, psychologists can watch them through a one-way mirror; but outside the laboratory it often involves trying to be inconspicuous, or becoming so familiar to the child that one's presence is ignored.

Finally, the observations in such studies are sometimes unreliable, and often such studies are expensive and time-consuming. For example, the nursery-school study discussed here required the time of several observers over an eleven-week period. In contrast, an experiment may be completed in an hour or so.

Field Study

Field studies also take place in natural social settings, but they differ from naturalistic observations in that the investigator introduces some factor into the natural situation that changes it. Field studies are not true experiments because the researcher can control only some aspects of the situation, although a field study is often more closely controlled than either observational or clinical studies.

Field studies allow investigators to study important phenomena that cannot be brought into the laboratory, and to study them under real instead of artificial conditions. For example, students in a talent show at Ohio State University became the subjects in a field study that explored stage fright. Each act consisted of from one to ten performers, and Jeffrey Jackson and Bibb Latané (1981) wanted to find out whether the size of the performing group had any effect on the amount of stage fright a performer experienced. Before show time, all of the students completed a questionnaire that explored their present nervousness, how nervous they expected to be during the show, and how well they expected to do. As each act came off stage, the performers were asked how nervous they actually had been and how well they thought they had done.

Students in the study consistently expected to feel more nervous than they actually felt during the performance, and the larger the group, the less stage fright the students experienced. Jackson and Latané suggest that since the audience divides its attention among the performers, students who perform in large groups attract less attention individually and hence suffer less stage fright. Should the performance go badly, responsibility for failure is divided. In addition, coperformers provide social support in the form of smiles, hugs, or praise.

Field studies have their own problems. The investigators may not have complete control over the experience the subjects undergo or the possible responses they can give. Because investigators generally cannot assign subjects randomly to one group or another, they must be aware of ways in which the comparison groups differ. Because the researcher can never prove that all differences between the two groups have been found, the results of field studies are often less certain than those of true experiments. In addition, field studies are expensive; they are often time-consuming; and they sometimes fall victim to erroneous observations.

Clinical Study

In clinical studies, investigators conduct in-depth interviews, often supplemented by observation and questionnaire. Because the same methods can be applied in a standardized way to each subject, the clinical study gives a psychologist some degree of control. When clinical studies are carefully designed, they can provide important data. For example, Hetherington's (1972) studies of father loss used in-depth interviews and observation of adolescent girls and their mothers.

Extensive clinical studies have been used by investigators to establish the effectiveness of different styles of coping with the stress that accompanies such events as the diagnosis of cancer or the death of a spouse (Horowitz and Wilmer, 1980). In addition to conducting clinical interviews, researchers developed standardized questionnaires that explored the impact of the events and the methods used to cope with them. These studies have discovered some methods of coping that seem helpful no matter what the stressful events and other methods that are much more helpful to cancer patients than to people who have been fired or who have lost a loved one. By exploring patterns of coping, such investigations may establish which methods are most effective in meeting crises in various periods of life.

In a controlled clinical study, the procedures must be clearly and precisely defined; the investigator can improvise only in such matters as introducing the subject to the clinical situation or maintaining the subject's cooperation. Unless these activities are explicitly stated and controlled, they may bias the results. As with the two previous types of studies, clinical study can be flawed by unknown and uncontrolled factors or by unreliable observation.

Experimentation

An experiment gives the investigator the greatest amount of control over the situation, which can be constructed to eliminate influences that might be present in natural settings. In an experiment, researchers examine the effect of selected variables on behavior. All the precautions of objectivity, clarity, reliability, and replicability required of controlled clinical and observational study are necessary when using the experimental method. It is often much easier to attain these goals through an experiment, however, because the investigator is better able to control and manipulate the variables under study.

Studying behavior through the experimental method has been used successfully in thousands of psychological studies. In a typical experiment, Arthur Jensen and William Rohwer (1965) designed a study to show developmental changes in children's learning. Their subjects were children from kindergarten through the twelfth grade. Jensen and Rohwer showed the children pairs of pictures of common objects. Half of the children at each age level were asked to name each picture, and the other half were asked to construct a sentence that related each pair of pictures. Afterward, all the children were shown the pairs of pictures and were asked to learn the members of each pair well enough so that when one picture was shown, they could recall the other. From the second grade, children who made sentences learned the material much faster. This experiment illustrates the powerful effects of relating objects in a meaningful manner and thus adds to psychologists' knowledge of learning in children. It is doubtful that this information could have been obtained so efficiently or so convincingly had the researchers relied on other methods such as naturalistic observation or clinical or field studies.

Even experimental studies are not perfect. Because experiments are often conducted in laboratories, subjects may not respond as they would to the same situation in a natural setting. At one time, for example, it was widely believed that, when they were about eight months old, all babies developed a fear of strangers. Later it was discovered that they might indeed fear strangers in the unfamiliar surrounding of a laboratory, but that most babies showed little or no fear when encountering a stranger in their own homes (Tracy, Lamb, and Ainsworth, 1976). In this case, the variable the researchers were changing in order to study infants' reactions (the stranger) had less influence on their subjects than the variable that remained constant (the laboratory itself).

The second pitfall in experimental studies comes from the rigid control that is also their virtue. Because the researcher designs the experiment so that he or she can control as many variables as possible, the situation may have no counterpart in the subject's world, as when memory is studied through the memorization of nonsense syllables. Therefore, the results, valid within the confines of the experiment, may have little reference to people's natural behavior.

Experimental Design

After a researcher has chosen a method of study, the next step is to choose the design. Although most research is either cross-sectional or longitudinal, experiments can also involve only a single subject.

SIX WAYS TO STUDY A DETERMINANT

Suppose that six psychologists intending to study the effects of racial integration (the determinant) on social behavior visit a recently integrated neighborhood. Each designs a different study, exploiting one of the ways of collecting information that have been discussed in the text.

Psychologist Number One chooses naturalistic observation. At predetermined intervals, his team observes residents in the area, counting the number of people engaged in social interaction with members of their own or of the other group. The researchers decide to use physical nearness as the primary measure of social interaction and to divide the behavior they record into aggressive, dependent, dominant, and egalitarian categories. Using the same techniques, they also observe a segregated neighborhood at the same socioeconomic level and compare the results of the two observations.

Psychologist Number Two decides to do a field study. She believes that a person's participation in integrated activities will depend upon his or her degree of bigotry. To test her idea, she gives residents a survey that taps their attitudes toward new experiences, assuming that people with closed minds will be bigoted whereas people with open minds will be ready for integrated activities. Scorers in the top (most bigoted) and bottom (least bigoted) 25 percent are invited to a neighborhood dance, where instructors from a dance studio give free lessons in the latest disco steps. Her team records how many people agree to come to the neighborhood dance and whether those who attend will accept a partner from the other ethnic group.

Psychologist Number Three believes that clinical studies reveal the most about people's attitudes and behavior. He designs an hour-long in-depth interview that probes the interviewee's prejudices about ethnic groups. Half of the people are interviewed by a member of their own ethnic group; the other half by a member of the other ethnic group.

Psychologist Number Four opts for an experimental study. She designs a training program of ten one-hour sessions centering around a graduated set of experiences with ethnically mixed groups. Each member is assigned a task that requires cooperation with members of the other ethnic group if an immediate problem is to be solved or a goal reached.

Psychologist Number Five uses a cross-sectional design in a field study. He believes that younger children will be more willing than older children or adolescents to interact with children from another ethnic group. He selects samples of different ages and sets up both mixed- and like-group activities. Each child has an opportunity to participate in both kinds of activities, and the behavior of the different age groups is compared.

Psychologist Number Six believes that the effects of integration become apparent gradually, and school attendance may be a powerful force in its acceptance. Only a longitudinally designed field study, she contends, can accurately measure the effects of the one on the other. She selects a group of four-year-olds who have never been to nursery school, studies their behavior and attitudes in an integrated situation, then studies them again, twice a year for five years.

Single-Subject Design Researchers who use the single-subject design believe that direct manipulation of conditions that may affect a particular person is the best way to study the possible determinants of his or her behavior. In a typical **single-subject experiment,** the investigator first measures the behavior that is to be studied without attempting to change it in any way. This is called establishing a **baseline.** As the person's experience is altered by the introduction of a new condition, his or her behavior continues to be recorded. The baseline serves as a control condition. By comparing a person's behavior under the control condition with his or her behavior under the experimental condition, the effect of the experimental condition often becomes clear.

Social behavior is the commonest area for the use of the single-subject design, and the method has been extremely effective in pinpointing the effect of various social interactions on behavior. The design is also applied to the study of attitudes and intellectual skills. It has been used, for example, to determine the effectiveness of various kinds of teaching aids commonly used in arithmetic classes (Lovitt et al., 1974). A basic disadvantage of the single-subject design is its possible lack of generalization. A second person, for example, might react to experimental conditions more (or less) promptly and positively than did the first subject.

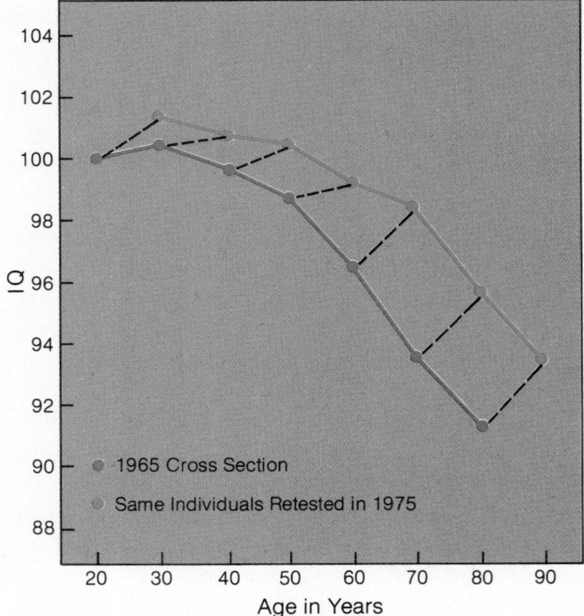

FIGURE 2.3 In this hypothetical example, eight groups of people were tested in 1965; the results of this cross-sectional study, shown by the lower dashed line, indicate that IQ declines with age. However, when the same samples were retested a decade later, the longitudinal results (shown by the solid lines) show a rise in IQ for each age group. Apparently, cohort differences, not aging, are responsible for the downward trend.

Longitudinal and Cross-Sectional Designs

Studies that compare different age groups, called **cross-sectional studies,** provide most of the information we have about development. When interpreting the results, the researcher often assumes that whatever differences appear among such groups are the result of developmental change. Yet unless the samples of people at various ages are selected carefully, the cross-sectional design can have two major flaws: different age groups may be affected by experience peculiar to their **cohorts** (age-group members), and age-group changes may be different from individual patterns of growth. For example, a cross-sectional study of the decline of IQ scores in later life might show a curve like that in Figure 2.3. IQ scores appear to decline with increasing age. But an inspection of the graph reminds us that people studied at age eighty in 1975 were born in 1895, whereas those studied at age twenty in 1975 were born in 1955. In the time between those birthdates, the cultural and social environment changed in many ways, and the resulting sociocultural influences may have affected the development and maintenance of intellectual skills. Longer education and mass communications may be responsible for the fact that, as a nation, each new generation scores higher on IQ tests, presumably because these forces expose more people to the information required to score well on such tests (Baltes and Schaie, 1974). Although older cohorts score lower on IQ tests than younger cohorts do at the same age, the apparent dramatic decline in IQ scores over age is in part an effect of the lower scores for older groups throughout their lives. Cross-sectional studies cannot detect cohort changes.

Cohort effects do not flaw all cross-sectional studies. When differences appear between groups that are close in age, such as three- and four-year-olds or six- and ten-year-olds, the changes are unlikely to be due to cohort membership. Since the sociocultural environment al-

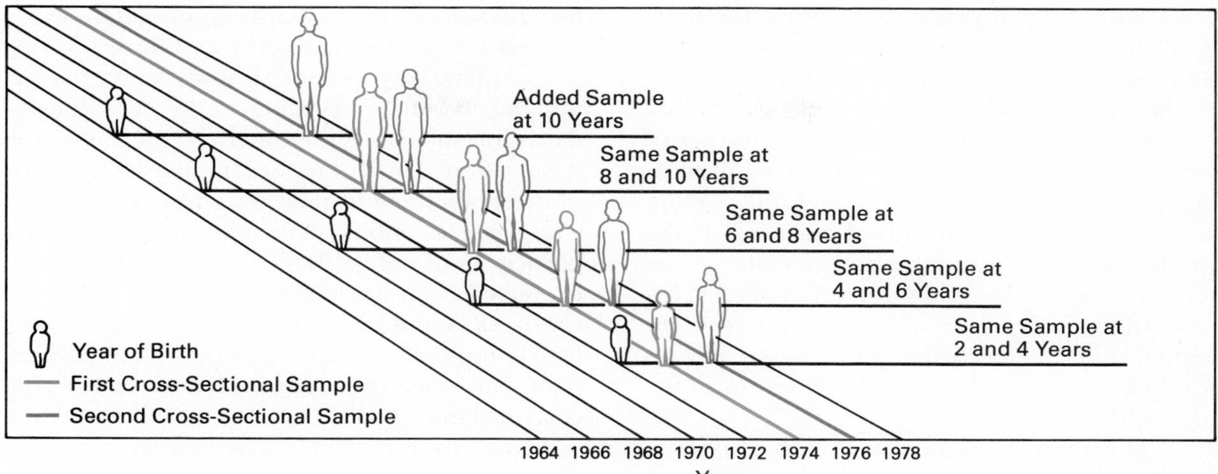

FIGURE 2.4 A research design that combines cross-sectional and longitudinal research. First, samples of children at each of four ages (two, four, six, and eight) are selected and studied. Two years later the same samples of children are studied again, and another sample of ten-year-olds is included. Using both methods on the same group of children offsets the weaknesses inherent in each type of study.

ters relatively slowly, differences between close age groups are likely to be due to development.

Cross-sectional groups also may not show the actual pattern of individual change, especially for a developmental shift that occurs rapidly. At puberty the growth of any one individual accelerates and decelerates rapidly, but because different individuals begin and end their growth at different times, graphs of group averages will show a smooth curve of growth for the entire cohort. Cross-sectional data alone would not reveal the pubescent growth spurt.

Studies that follow the same subjects over time, **longitudinal studies,** may seem to answer all problems in developmental studies. The same people can be compared with themselves at ages twenty and eighty. But there are problems here, too. The fact that the same people have been studied repeatedly over many years may have affected their development, and the long-term changes that appear in their behavior may be a response to sociocultural shifts as well as evidence of developmental changes. In just the past few decades, for example, our sociocultural environment has been profoundly affected by scientific developments (television, space probes, computers), an altered physical environment (pollution, the energy shortage), and social and political upheavals (the civil rights movement, the resignation of a President). These shifts in our environment may have had profound effects on some aspects of our development.

Neither cross-sectional nor longitudinal studies alone can provide the basic data for developmental studies. Because of this, K. Warner Schaie (1965) has proposed that the two designs be combined to provide controls over the biases in each design. He suggests that researchers sample subjects cross-sectionally and then follow them longitudinally until the samples overlap in age. For example, initial samples drawn at ages two, four, six, and eight can be followed for two years until the two-year-olds are four, the four-year-olds are six, and so forth. A final cross-sectional sample can be drawn at age ten to compare to the longitudinal eight-year-olds, who would then be ten. The effects of repeated testing, if any, will appear as differences between the starting scores for four-year-olds and the ending scores for the two-year-olds at age four. If the whole design is repeated some years later to detect shifts in the sociocultural environment, cohort effects will appear. If important environmental shifts had occurred, the scores at all ages would be higher or lower than the scores in the first study.

The desirability of using both cross-sectional and longitudinal designs becomes clear if we consider linear growth. Height measurements of a cross-sectional sample would indicate that people grow until middle adolescence and then begin to shrink. The "shrinkage" would be due to cohort effects. People born a number of years ago are shorter on the average than people born more recently, and they were always shorter. A longitudinal study of people now in their seventies would show that they grew until late adolescence and then maintained their heights until late adulthood, when they may actually have shrunk a bit. A longitudinal study of a younger cohort would find them reaching maximum growth at an earlier age; because of better nutrition, they are both taller and earlier maturing. In the case of height, it is necessary to separate the truth about development from long-term changes in the sociocultural environment. In the case of other factors, it is important to separate developmental change from the effects of repeated measurements.

ETHICAL CONSIDERATIONS

In the past few years there has been increased awareness that research on human beings can lead to invasion of privacy and sometimes to social, physical, and psychological risks. As a result, the federal government, as well as most major scientific and professional organizations have formulated sets of standards and regulations to protect the people who serve as subjects.

Today, any proposed study must pass a number of tests. According to the ethical standards formulated by the American Psychological Association (1972), for example, researchers must obtain the informed consent of individuals who serve as subjects. People must be free to participate or not, as they see fit. And all must be protected from harmful psychological or physical stress. Should the procedures used in a study lead to undesirable consequences for any participant, the researcher is expected to detect and correct them.

The study must be carried out in an atmosphere of openness and honesty. The investigator is expected to tell the participants about all aspects of the research that might affect their readiness to take part and to answer all their questions so they can understand the consequences of their participation. When the study is complete, the investigator is required to tell the participants about the purpose and uses of the research and to clarify any misconceptions that may have come up. All information about participants must remain confidential and anonymous.

Adherence to high ethical standards is especially important in the case of children, adolescents, the infirm, the indigent, and the elderly. They are generally less likely to be fully informed about their civil and human rights and less able to take action to protect themselves. In research with babies, for example, the parent must give full consent, and when children are studied, informed consent must be obtained from both child and parent. When necessary, the informed consent of those who serve in a parentlike role (e.g., teacher, principal) must be obtained.

Given the subtleties involved in ethical decisions, no guidelines can cover every possible case. Therefore, most institutions that engage in or sponsor research have established ethics advisory committees to evaluate proposed research, and to monitor studies once they are under way. The job of such a committee is to make sure that the rights of each participant are safeguarded. Although human research is intended to produce new knowledge about human beings, unethical practices do occur, and ethical research sometimes has unforeseen consequences. Ignorance, faulty thinking, or mixed motives can distress or harm the people who participate in studies. By establishing standards, researchers hope to protect participants while ensuring the discovery of knowledge that will help future generations.

SUMMARY

1. Human development is the result of multiple interacting causes operating through heredity—the person's nature—and through environment—the person's nurture. Questions arise over "how" and "how much" each contributes to development.
2. In studying the role of heredity, researchers frequently have studied animal genetics. Such studies help establish general principles and provide important information on the effects of genetic and genetic-environmental interactions. However, they cannot provide specific details about the way these interactions affect human development. The study of individuals of various degrees of relatedness has provided some insight into the way that genetic differences affect the development of human beings. An important concept in understanding research on the effects of genetic factors on human beings is the concept of reaction range, which refers to the limits set by genetic conditions on an individual's possible behavior.
3. The term heritability refers to the relative contribution of genetics to a trait or behavior. As an estimate, it varies with who is studied and when. Heritability does not indicate that either genes or environment "cause" the trait or behavior. Instead, the appearance of a trait is a function of both genetic and environmental determinants.
4. Environmental determinants of human development include physical and social factors. Physical factors include those ecological features that maintain life—air, water, food, and light—and those features—life in a tent or apartment—that create different responses.
5. Social determinants include all those effects that cultures have on people and people have on one another in families, peer groups, social institutions, and the media. From birth to death, these influences direct, limit, and enhance the development of the individual.
6. In studying the determinants of human development, different methods have different advantages and disadvantages in terms of their reliability, efficiency, and representativeness. Most of these advantages and disadvantages are associated with a method's degree of control over who is studied, the setting or circumstances, and the behavior that can occur. At one extreme is naturalistic observation and at the other is experimentation, with many types of field and clinical studies in between. Longitudinal and cross-sectional designs, in which the same or different individuals are studied at various ages, provide some of the information needed to investigate different developmental determinants.
7. The growing awareness that research on human beings can lead to invasion of privacy and sometimes to social, physical, and psychological risks has led to the establishment of ethical standards to protect the subjects of studies. These standards are now basic to any research design.

3
THEORIES OF DEVELOPMENT

A couple is waiting in line to buy tickets to a concert when two adolescents push in front of them. "I'd like to talk to the parents of those kids," says the man, "and tell them how to raise children"; "What can their parents do?" the woman responds, "Boys are like that."

Each of us has a personal theory of how and why people behave as they do. Unfortunately, we rarely agree in our explanations, and there is no easy way to decide which of us (if any) is correct. Private theories of development are derived from our personal experiences (which may be radically different from the experiences of others), the books and magazines we read, the motion pictures and television programs we watch, and the common assumptions of our culture, which may be contradictory as well as different from the assumptions of other cultures. Our private, naive "theories" of development are not really theories in a formal sense. They are often internally inconsistent, and, as with the statement "Boys are like that," they are seldom specified clearly enough to generate testable propositions.

In this chapter we will explore five major types of developmental theories and discover that each set is based on different assumptions about human beings and generates testable hypotheses about the development of behavior. Each set, we will find, has looked at different areas of behavior, used different methods, and studied different age groups. Mechanistic theories assume that the environment is all-powerful. Psychodynamic theories spring from Sigmund Freud's insights into human motivation. Adaptation theories consider the evolutionary history of the human species to be dominant factor in development. Organismic theories see the biological organism as the active creator of reality. And dialectical theories see development as profoundly altered by historical and cultural influences. After considering each set of theories, we will investigate the idea of stages in development and discover that although no one group of theories can explain the development of all human behavior, each can make a useful contribution.

MECHANISTIC THEORIES

In the mechanistic world view, human beings are often likened to machines. The human mind, for example, is seen as a computer. During the course of development, the passive individual receives stimulation from the environment but without filtering any part of it. Since a person does not construct the world, what he or she perceives is a copy of the real world, which exists independently of the perceiver. As people develop, their knowledge accumulates, but there is no major change in the structure of their minds. As a result of experience, thought and behavior change in quantity, but not in quality. Learning theories are the major example of mechanistic theories, but cognitive psychologists who follow an information-processing view share some of their assumptions.

The Behavior-Learning Approach

In the behavior-learning approach to development, human beings are regarded as organisms that have learned to behave in uniquely human ways. Newborn babies are prepared to react to stimulation of the environment but have few organizing properties of their own. Thus experience or learning is responsible for most of what babies become, and learning begins before the child leaves the uterus. The notion that the infant is a malleable recipient of environmental stimulation echoes the idea of the blank slate proposed by Aristotle and Locke, but not until this century was the proposition embodied in formal theories of learning.

Then, in the 1920s the subjective-mentalistic view of psychology was effectively challenged by behaviorism. John B. Watson (1913; 1924), who led the attack, argued that psychologists should study the relationship between stimuli in the environment and behavior, not mental events. The way to do this, he said, was not by asking people what they thought, but by watching what they did. Although Watson later became less certain about some of his sweeping early claims, as when he had offered to take a group of infants and produce any kind of adult his critics specified, his work left an indelible mark on American psychology. It was interpreted by many to mean that human behavior could be molded in almost limitless ways, and that human beings could be improved in any desired direction.

Watson's views on the control of behavior did not please everyone. Critics pointed out that, assuming such control was possible, there was no guarantee that it would be used for desirable ends. Aldous Huxley's novel *Brave New World* (1932) was an imaginative warning that extreme behavioral control could dehumanize people and turn them into robots.

Conditioning Over the years, adherents of learning theories have agreed that classical and operant conditioning are important in understanding how people learn. Traditional learning theorists believe that conditioning can explain all learning, from how children acquire language to what makes people attend a ballet, cherish free speech, or go to war.

Studies of classical, or respondent, conditioning grew out of the work of Ivan Pavlov (1927) in Russia. Pavlov demonstrated that certain behaviors, which he called **reflexes,** were responses to external stimuli. There are two kinds of reflexes: unconditioned reflexes and conditioned reflexes. **Unconditioned reflexes** are responses that—before any learning takes place—a person naturally pairs with a specific stimulus, such as blinking one's eye when a puff of air strikes the eyeball or salivating when food is placed in one's mouth. **Conditioned reflexes** are established when one associates a neutral stimulus, such as a bell or light, with an unconditioned stimulus. If the conditioned stimulus occurs repeatedly just before the unconditioned stimulus, a person comes to respond to the conditioned stimulus much as he or she originally did only to the unconditioned stimulus. This process is known as **classical conditioning.**

Emotions are particularly subject to classical conditioning. Parents have noticed the process of classical conditioning at work in their children and commonly observe that, by the time their baby is a year old, he or she begins to cry at the sight of a nurse who has previously been paired with painful injections. A child who has been bitten by a dog may come to fear the house or the whole city block in which the attack occurred. Moreover the fear may become generalized. For example, the infant who has been given injections by the nurse may come to fear all people in white coats or all rooms that look like an examining room. The child bitten by a dog may come to fear all four-legged creatures.

Classical conditioning ignores the consequences of a person's responses, which are a central concern of the second form of conditioning. The learning process that describes the effects of rewards and punishment is called **operant conditioning,** or instrumental conditioning. In this basic kind of learning, which is associated with B. F. Skinner (1938), the frequency of a response changes as a result of **reinforcement.** Reinforcers can be concrete rewards, such as money, toys, or candy, or they can be intangible, such as affection, praise, attention, or the satisfaction that comes with the completion of a difficult task. For example, when a boy receives a reward like candy or social approval immediately after he responds in a certain way, he is likely to repeat that response. The candy or praise acts as reinforcement. If the child gets no reward, or if he is punished, he will not repeat the response so often. Responses that are not reinforced decrease in frequency or may even be eliminated **(extinguished).**

Skinner emphasized the effects of such consequences on behavior, saying that any person's behavior at any time can be explained by his or her genetic endowment, past history, and the present situation (Hall, 1972). Although Skinner never presented a theory of development himself, Sidney Bijou and Donald Baer (1961, 1965) used his approach, seeing the developing child as an "interrelated cluster of responses and stimuli." Because the child and the environment are interacting continuously, the child's development consists of progressive changes in the ways of interaction, changes that are the result of opportunities and circumstances. When children start school, for example, the environment is so different from the home that their ways of interacting shift, sometimes dramatically (Bijou, 1976).

The application of operant principles has been remarkably successful in changing many kinds of behavior, such as overeating or disrupting the classroom, and in teaching students to read. Developmental psychologists who wish to use this technique search for the relationships that exist between responses and stimuli (including reinforcers). Investigators also concentrate on how various ways of providing reinforcement change the frequency of a child's responses.

These timetables for reinforcing behavior are called **schedules of reinforcement.** A person at first may be reinforced for each correct response; but once a behavior is established, such a schedule is not necessary. Numerous studies have shown that responses can be maintained just as effectively by reinforcing a person for the first response after a specified time has passed, or by providing reinforcement only after he or she has responded a certain number of times. Comparable situations in daily life would be workers who come to work each day and are paid at the end of the week and those who work each day but are paid only after they have finished making a certain number of shirts.

Operant principles can also be used to develop new behavior. When they are applied in this way, the new behavior is shaped by rewarding **successive approximations,** or behavior that resembles more and more closely the desired response. This method has been used successfully in a wide variety of situations, from toilet training young children and coaching athletic teams to teaching social and cognitive skills (Semb, 1972) and persuading a shy six-year-old who could not utter a word in the classroom to talk normally (Richards and Siegel, 1978).

Social Learning Some psychologists considered the behavior-learning approach too narrow and inflexible. They believed that not all learning could be explained as the result of classical and operant conditioning. Instead, they developed **social-learning theory,** which grew out of earlier behavior-learning views but which

ALBERT BANDURA (1925-)

(Courtesy Dr. Albert Bandura)

Albert Bandura received his doctorate in clinical psychology from Iowa State University in 1952; after completing a post-doctoral internship, he accepted a position at Stanford University, where he is professor of psychology. His research and writing on personality and social development reflect his background in clinical psychology and his strong interest in child development. Over the past few years, his theories have had a major influence on the thought of developmental psychologists.

Early in his career, Bandura became dissatisfied with the gaps that existed between the concepts of clinical psychology and those of general psychology. He also believed that behavior-learning views, including social learning, were too narrow to account for socialization and the development of behavior.

To overcome the deficiencies, Bandura developed a broad, integrated sociobehavioral approach to human behavior. According to his view, direct experience is not the only teacher; human beings learn from infancy by simply observing what other people do and noticing what happens to them. Other symbolic models are provided by way of television, books, or magazines, and such models may teach unacceptable as well as acceptable behavior. Bandura emphasizes the importance of distinguishing between learning and performance. He stresses that although people learn to do many things, they are most likely to do the things that they or others consider acceptable or rewarding.

Bandura's work stresses the links between cognitive processes, learning, and performance. Thus, cognitive skills, information, and rules strongly affect what an individual does. And because people can think about what happened to them or what may happen to them, their behavior cannot be manipulated simply by reinforcement. Bandura sees people as freer to choose and to make changes in their lives than did the original behavior-learning theorists.

stressed that a good deal of human behavior is learned, not through shaping and reinforcement, but by watching others.

With observational learning given such prominence, the process of **imitation** came to play a key role in most social-learning accounts of human development. Many studies have demonstrated the increasing resemblance of the child's social behavior to that of adult models. Some researchers have discovered that if a child is rewarded for imitating a model, the child will tend to imitate the model even when not rewarded (Bandura, 1969b).

Over the years there have been several different but supplementary social-learning interpretations regarding the role and importance of imitation. Some time ago Neal Miller and John Dollard (1941) proposed that nurturance from parents becomes the motivating force for a child's imitations. That is, as parents satisfy the child's needs for food, warmth, and affection, they become associated with the satisfaction of those needs and take on reinforcing properties themselves. Because the parents' behaviors are reinforcing, the child imitates them to reward him- or herself. Subsequently, Jerome Kagan (1958) and John Whiting (1960) pointed out that parents also have more power and control more possessions than the child does and that the child envies their status and therefore copies them in the hope that the imitations will give the child their influence and status. More recently, Albert Bandura and Richard Walters (1963) have stressed that children can learn new responses from merely watching a model and that they also are likely to imitate behavior that they see rewarded.

In the past few years, the gradual but radical shift in social-learning theory has continued. The work of Bandura and his colleagues is representative of this shift, and Bandura (1977) has restated many aspects of human learning and motivation in terms of **cognition,** that is, the processes we use to gain knowledge about the world, such as perception, learning, memory, or thinking. According to Bandura, cognitive processes play a central role in regulating what children attend to, how they describe or think about what they see and hear, and whether they repeat it to themselves and lodge it in memory. Short-lived everyday experiences can leave lasting effects because they are retained in memory in symbolic form. Learning from a model is not simply a matter of imitation. As children and adults watch others, they form concepts about possible behavior that will later guide their own actions. As they then observe their actions and the consequences, they can change their concepts and act in different ways.

Children tend to copy a model's complete pattern of behavior, instead of slowly learning bits of a pattern in response to reinforcement. When watching a model, children can learn entirely new behavior, although they may not immediately show it. A 10-year old girl might, for example, watch a television program in which one child helped another who was in trouble. Although there is no observable change in the watching girl, she may go out of her way a week or two later to offer assistance when she sees a child in need of aid. Children may also either behave or refrain from behaving in ways they have already learned, refusing to play with a forbidden toy or playing with it despite prohibitions. Or children may behave in ways they learned earlier but have just been reminded of by the model's actions.

In this new view, the idea of stimuli as purely external physical events that control behavior has been replaced with the view that stimuli serve as signals that help people decide what to do. The person's conception of a stimulus, not the stimulus itself, regulates behavior.

Cognitive social-learning theorists stress that people process and synthesize information from their experiences over long periods of time, which means that they are not bound by what takes place in the immediate situation. On the basis of their past experiences, they decide what behavior may be effective. As human beings develop, they construct and reconstruct expectations about future events. They estimate possible positive and negative consequences of various actions. In doing this, people set their own standards, which they use to evaluate their performance, to reward their actions, and to provide their motivation.

The new social-learning theorists have moved a long way from other behavior-learning viewpoints. They give human thought and knowledge central importance in explaining the development of human behavior, and see people as approaching, exploring, and dealing with things that they perceive are within their range of abilities. They tend to avoid things that seem stressful or beyond their capabilities. Others play a primary role in development. What they do and say, and the way they behave, become sources of information that developing human beings use in making judgments and creating expectations about themselves and their world.

The Information-Processing Approach

Psychologists who use the information-processing approach are interested primarily in thought processes, or cognition. They see human beings as information-gathering, information-processing systems. The mind functions like a computer, receiving stimulation from the environment, which it encodes, modifies, stores, and when requested, produces (Chaplin and Krawiec, 1974). This human computer consists of hardware, which is the basic storage system itself, and software, the programs or sets of instructions used to code, analyze, and retrieve information and to make decisions. Looking at the development of information processing in children, psychologists find little evidence of significant change in cognitive hardware after the first two years of life. For example, when special strategies are not required to remember information, four-year-olds do about as well as adults in a memory task (Brown, 1975). Software, on the other hand, continues to develop and change.

Processing begins when stimulation from the environment is encoded. This first perceptual encoding of what a five-year-old sees or hears appears to be no different from the adult's first encoding, either qualitatively or quantitatively (Kail and Siegel, 1977). But as children acquire concepts and knowledge, the information they code for later retrieval acquires more sophisticated forms. As children develop, the speed with which they process information also increases, and they show a greater selectivity in the environmental stimuli to which they attend. The strategies children use to make information available for later recall also change radically. The very young child appears to have few, if any, strategies available, whereas the adolescent and adult have a whole array of them, which they can use to encode new information or to recall information that has been stored.

Some psychologists have written computer programs that simulate cognitive functioning. David Klahr and J. G. Wallace (1976), for example, have developed a program that describes children's thought processes when trying to decide whether a lump of clay squeezed into a ball contains the same amount of clay as a ball of the same size stretched into a long, narrow strip. Such programs do not, however, deal with the emotions and their influence on a person's thought processes.

Cognitive psychologists do not always keep the analogy between mind and computer so literal. Many simply study one or more of the processes involved in information processing, tracing its development or examining its emergence among children and adolescents. Some study perception, which involves the reception and coding of information; some study memory, which involves the storage and retrieval of information. Some study thought itself, examining how people form and test hypotheses, and still others study people's ability to assess their own thinking (Ault, 1977).

PSYCHODYNAMIC THEORIES

Most psychodynamic theories discuss and analyze human development in terms of various confrontations between the growing individual and the demands of the social world. They stress how the individual must accommodate to society while gratifying basic human drives. Most also emphasize that the child gradually develops a sense of self, an identity against which to judge his or her own behavior.

As a group, psychodynamic theorists have centered their attention on personality development. Their concern has been to understand and explain the development of both rational and irrational feelings and behavior. To some extent, all psychodynamic theories have tried to account for human development by looking for early experiences, usually emotional, that may influence later behavior.

Psychodynamic theories are generally concerned with inner development and view human beings as motivated by various internal and external forces. These forces in turn are considered to be determining factors in human behavior. Some psychodynamic theories view the internal forces as benign or positive growth forces that can be either impeded or facilitated by environmental events. In other psychodynamic theories, the internal forces are irrational or nongrowth forces, which must be controlled by various socialization practices and cultural standards.

The idea that there is a "me" or a "self" intuitively makes sense to most people. In most psychodynamic theories, the concept of a self is a major construct. It manages to capture each person's feeling of realness and uniqueness as well as to bring together, and seemingly to explain, a number of observations about a person that might otherwise appear meaningless.

Because there are many psychodynamic theories, this section will discuss only two major theories—those of Sigmund Freud and Erik Erikson—in detail.

Freud's Psychosexual Theory

Sigmund Freud (1905) is the father of psychodynamic theories and the founder of psychoanalysis, a form of psychotherapy. Whether or not one accepts his theory of human development,

SIGMUND FREUD (1856–1939)

(Photo by Edmund Engelman, from *Berggasse 19*)

Sigmund Freud's theories reflect his training in the biological sciences and his clinical experience. He specialized in physiology, received his M.D. degree in Vienna in 1881, and began lecturing and doing research in neuropathology. A grant enabled him to go to Paris and study under the famous neurologist Jean Martin Charcot, who was using hypnosis to treat hysteria.

Later, as Freud treated his patients, he developed the therapeutic methods of free association and dream interpretation. He found that his adult neurotic patients had repressed their memories of early childhood emotional experiences, which generally involved sex, aggression, or jealousy. Because these experiences were unpleasant, Freud proposed that they became lost to awareness because they were pushed into an unreachable area of the mind, the unconscious.

In his theory of psychosexual development, he interpreted what he learned from treating his patients in the light of embryology and physics. He proposed that the emergence of psychosexual stages was primarily determined by maturation and that mental life followed the law of conservation of energy, which states that energy cannot be created or destroyed, only transformed. People's mental and emotional lives, he believed, show a comparable transformation of psychic energy (libido) from one stage to the next. This energy motivates people's thinking, their perceptions, and their memories, and it remains constant even though it becomes associated with different regions of the body during development.

his influence on psychology, the arts, and literature has been enormous. In a prim Victorian age, he put forth a bold, new theory of unconscious motivation, human sexuality, and instinctual aggression.

As Freud saw it, from earliest infancy human beings are motivated by irrational urges toward pleasure. Rational behavior develops out of conflict between social demands and the young child's instincts, which are **sublimated** (altered in socially acceptable ways) in the course of the child's adaptation to the environment. In his theory, intelligence or adaptation is given much less importance than a sensuality that has become socialized.

Freud proposed three conflicting aspects of human personality: the id, the ego, and the superego. In the **id** reside all of the **unconscious** impulses (the person is unaware of these forces). The newborn baby is pure id. The **superego** is the conscience, which develops in early childhood as a child internalizes parental values and standards of conduct. The **ego** guides a person's realistic coping behavior and mediates the eternal conflicts between what one wants to do (the province of the id) and what one must or must not do (the province of the superego).

Freud's view of human development is in part an evolutionary one. Our biological urges are part of our evolved animal nature, and development proceeds through interaction with external reality, which transforms us. With further maturation, we continue to interact with reality, which again transforms us, and so forth. Almost inevitably, the cost of our coming to terms with rational behavior is a loss of contact with our basic impulses and a denial of their direct gratification. As a consequence, most civilized adults are anxious. In contrast, infants are not anxious until they begin to differentiate themselves from the caretaking environment and begin to cope with the demands of reality.

Freud believed that development is an unfolding of genetic stages in which instinctual impulses become attached to various pleasure centers of the body. He described the human life cycle in psychosexual terms, tying psychological development to the resolution of the conflicts that characterize each stage of life. Current psychodynamic theories are elaborations and modifications of Freud's thought or reactions to it. Unless the growing child successfully navigates a stage, Freud believed, he or she will become *fixated* at that stage and as an adult will have an immature personality in which the characteristic traits of the stage predominate.

The first year of the child's life is spent in the **oral stage,** when the lips and mouth are the focus of sensual pleasure. A baby busily sucking at a pacifier or thumb, breast or bottle, may not be hungry but simply enjoying the pleasurable feelings that arise when the mouth is stimulated. Although during the first few months babies lack the coordination to pick up an object and deliberately insert it into their mouths, whatever brushes cheek or lips goes in. Babies actively seek oral stimulation.

At about their first birthdays, babies enter the second stage of psychosexual development, the **anal stage.** During this period, which lasts until they are about three, pleasurable feelings center around the rectum. The delights of oral stimulation do not fade completely, but children now enjoy both expelling and retaining feces. Toilet training may become a battle over control, in which children learn to use their sensual pleasures as a weapon against their parents.

The third, highly critical, period includes the years from three to five or six. During this **phallic stage,** the genitals become the focus, and children learn to derive pleasure from fondling them. Boys are said to fall in love with their mothers and girls with their fathers. Powerless to push the rival parent out of the way, both boys and girls resolve this Oedipal conflict by identifying with the parent of the same sex, boys assuming their fathers' masculine characteristics and girls their mothers' feminine characteristics.

After the stormy phallic period, Freud believed, sexual feelings become less obvious in children. From about six until they reach puberty, children are in the **latency period.** Tenderness predominates over sexual feelings, and children learn to feel shame and guilt. With the mastery of the Oedipal conflict, they have developed a superego. During the latency period, they also discover moral and aesthetic interests.

The final period of psychosexual development, the **genital stage,** emerges with puberty. Among children who successfully navigate all the stages, primary sensual pleasure transfers to mature sexual relationships with members of the opposite sex.

Once Freud's theories found their way into academic and popular thinking, the field of human development was changed.

Erikson's Psychosocial Theory

Erik Erikson (1963), one modifier of Freud's psychoanalytic theory, has developed an elaborate stage theory. Erikson describes emotional development across the life span, which makes his theory particularly important.

In Erikson's psychosocial theory, personality develops according to steps predetermined by the human organism's readiness to be driven toward, to be aware of, and to interact with a widening social world, a world that begins with a dim image of mother and ends with an image of humanity. Erikson saw development as consisting of the progressive resolution of conflicts between needs and social demands. At each of eight stages, conflicts must be resolved, at least partially, before progress can be made on the next set of problems. The failure to resolve problems at any stage can result in psychological disorders that affect the rest of the life span.

From Trust to Industry Babies need to develop a relationship in which they can get what they require from a person who is ready and able to provide it—almost always a mother. They need to develop feelings of comfort with their mothers and need to know that a consistent caregiver will be there when they need one. Constant, reliable care promotes the baby's sense of *trust.* This consistency in care enables babies to learn to tolerate frustrations and to delay immediate gratifications, because they know that

ERIK ERIKSON (1902–   )

(Olive R. Pierce/Black Star)

Erik Erikson was born in Germany of Danish parents. He graduated from art school and went to Florence, Italy, intending to become an art teacher. In Vienna, where he had gone to teach children of American families, he met Freud and other analysts, and soon entered psychoanalytic training.

When Hitler came to power in Germany, Erikson emigrated to America. He held a series of positions in child-guidance clinics and major universities while maintaining a private practice. During an appointment at Harvard University, Erikson developed an interest in anthropology and studied the Sioux and Yurok Indians. During a subsequent appointment at the University of California, Berkeley, he studied adolescents, using a technique in which the way young people played with dolls revealed their unconscious thoughts and feelings.

Erikson is one of the few theorists to describe emotional development across the life span. In his theory, personality develops through eight stages, from infancy to the final stage of life. As a person interacts with a widening social world, he or she moves from a universe of self and mother to an image of humankind. Each stage has its own conflict to be resolved, and the failure to resolve any of these conflicts can lead to psychological disorders. Erikson's psychodynamic theory is important because, unlike Freud, he believes neuroses can develop at any stage during life, and that they are not necessarily the result of problems in infancy or early childhood.

adults around them care and can be trusted to meet their needs. If the baby's needs are not consistently met, he or she may develop a sense of mistrust and react to frustration with anxiety and upset.

After infants begin to walk and to exercise some self-direction, they run into social restraints. During this second stage, they increasingly demand to determine their own behavior ("Me do it!"), but because they have little judgment about their actual capabilities, they need to be gently protected from excesses while granted *autonomy* in those matters that they can handle. It is particularly important at this stage, Erikson suggests, that parents not shame a child into feeling that he or she is incompetent. Shame can be a devastating experience for anyone, and it is particularly difficult for young children who are struggling for autonomy and who are not yet sure that they can develop any degree of competent self-regulation.

After children have gained a relatively secure sense of autonomy, they enter the third stage of development and are ready to take the initiative in planning their own activities. As Erikson sees it, *initiative* adds to autonomy the quality of undertaking, planning, and attacking a task for the sake of being active and on the move. In the preceding stage, self-will often inspired acts of defiance. In the third stage, children are ready for positive, constructive activities under their own initiative. The potential problem at this period is guilt; children may come to feel that their intrusiveness and activity have evil consequences. This is the period of sexual attraction to the opposite-sex parent: of seductive behavior by little girls toward their fathers and of assertive, manly behavior of little boys toward their mothers. As children resolve these hopeless attractions, they identify with the same-sex parent and develop a conscience. Harsh parental responses to a child's sexual overtures and other

In Erik Erikson's psychosocial theory, the baby's first task in emotional development is to develop a sense of trust. *(© Mark Haven/Magnum Photos)*

initiatives, however, can lead to an overdeveloped, harsh conscience that may always plague the person with guilt.

Erikson theorizes that, once children have come to terms with their families by identifying with the same-sex parent, they enter the fourth stage and are ready to move into the larger world. About this time, in our culture, they go to school. Before children can become adults in any society, they must become workers; they learn that they will gain recognition by producing things *(industry).* The child, therefore, wants to learn the technical skills that characterize adults —be they literacy or hunting or herding. The potential problem in this period lies in a sense of inadequacy and inferiority, which can develop if children are not praised for their accomplishments. In Erikson's theory, this is a decisive stage, for the child must prepare for effective adult roles.

From Identity to Ego Integrity In the fifth stage, adolescents question all of their previous resolutions to problems of trust, autonomy, initiative, and industry. Rapid body growth and genital maturity create a "physiological revolution" within them at the time that they face adult life. According to Erikson, adolescents search for continuity and sameness within themselves—a sense of *identity*—and in their search they have to refight the battles of earlier years, usually casting their parents in the role of adversaries. They try and discard roles and ways of behaving, then reformulate them and try them again. The potential problem at this period is that an adolescent's identity will fail to become consistent and that he or she will have a sense of personal diffusion. Some adolescents cannot seem to develop a sense of who they are as people, as sexual beings, as adult workers, as potential parents. People in whom a sense of role diffusion lasts into adulthood may never be able to make consistent decisions about who they are and where they are going in life.

Young adults, emerging from the search for identity, are eager and willing to fuse their identities with those of others. In terms of Erikson's sixth stage, they are ready for **intimacy,** for relationships with others in which they are strong enough to make sacrifices for another's welfare without losing themselves in another's identity. It is at this point that true sexual love can emerge. The young adult has the job of putting work and love together. The potential problem at this period is isolation from others, a failure to commit oneself to loving relationships because of competition or fear.

Generativity characterizes the seventh stage and refers to the adult's concern with establishing and guiding the next generation. According to Erikson, productivity in work and creativity in one's life are important concepts in this period. Having a sense of accomplishment in adult life depends on giving loving care to others

Erikson's Stages of Development								
Stage	1	2	3	4	5	6	7	8
Maturity								Ego Integrity vs. Despair
Adulthood							Generativity vs. Stagnation	
Young Adulthood						Intimacy vs. Isolation		
Puberty and Adolescence					Identity vs. Diffusion			
Latency				Industry vs. Inferiority				
Locomotor/ Genital			Initiative vs. Guilt					
Muscular/ Anal		Autonomy vs. Shame						
Oral/ Sensory	Trust vs. Mistrust							

FIGURE 3.1 Erikson's proposed sequence of psychosocial stages of development and the types of possible outcomes often associated with each stage. Beginning with the oral/sensory stage, Erikson's first four stages are, respectively, extensions of Freud's oral, anal, phallic, and latency stages. In the remaining four stages, Erikson has elaborated on Freud's approach by adding dimensions of interpersonal relationships. *(Adapted from E. H. Erikson,* **Childhood and Society,** *2nd rev. ed., copyright © 1963 by W. W. Norton & Company, Inc.)*

and regarding one's own contributions to society as valuable. Merely producing children does not give a person a sense of generativity; adults must see the role of rearing children as a contribution to humankind and the larger society. The possible dangers of this period are self-absorption and a sense of stagnation, a sense of going nowhere, doing nothing important.

In Erikson's theory, the final stage of the life cycle should result in a sense of wholeness, of purposes accomplished and a life well lived. If a person "had it to do over again," he or she would change little about the choices made, about the way life has been lived. In such a final consolidation of life's stages, death loses its sting. The potential problem in the final stage is regret and despair over wasted chances and unfortunate choices. A person in this stage who feels despair fears death in an ironic way that those with **ego integrity** do not. The despairing person, while expressing disgust over life, continues to yearn for another chance. The person with integrity accepts death as the end of a meaningful trip.

Freud and Erikson, as well as other psychodynamic theorists whose work will appear in later discussions of personality and identity, make important statements about the developmental course of human drives to become a complete person. Complete human beings not only have fulfilled their needs, but they cope, resolve conflicts, give support to others, and contribute to their societies as well. It is this wholeness in ego functions that all these theorists have stressed.

ADAPTATION THEORIES

A growing group of dedicated naturalists who have sought to observe development in its real-life settings have become an emerging force in developmental psychology. These new ethologists translate biological evolutionary concepts into behavioral terms to study human development. The trend toward ethological-genetic thinking is increasing at a rapid rate. As we will see at various points throughout this book, observational techniques, so rigorously developed by ethologists, are gaining favor in many areas of developmental psychology.

Like all species, human beings evolved in various environments, and the nature of humanity cannot be understood unless these evolutionary contexts are also understood. Because human beings could not survive unless they were in harmony with their environment, ethologists who study human behavior regard development as a form of adaptation. In their view, social behavior is related to such problems as the cohesiveness of the group, the competition for mates, and the survival of the young. Intelligence, which allows us to modify our behavior on the basis of inferences from evidence, enabled our ancestors to adapt (Humphrey, 1978). During the course of human evolution, only those individuals who solved the problems they encountered were likely to leave offspring for the next generation.

When seen from the ethological viewpoint, human behavior is best understood by examining the way it enables babies, children, or adults to survive and flourish in an environment similar to the one in which our species evolved. The bond between infant and mother, for example, is regarded as part of a behavioral system that evolved to protect the developing organism. Because human infants are helpless for so long, their survival depends on protection from mature members of the species, and the attachment of babies to their caregivers generally keeps the pair in close proximity. Although attachment is expressed in varying ways in different cultures, some variety of bond between infant and caregiver has been present in every society studied.

Jerome Bruner (1972) has speculated on the uses of the long period of immaturity in human development. Human educability is a prime species characteristic. The baby and child are easily taught many skills, and they yearn to explore and to learn. Play is an important way in which the young practice skills without suffering adult consequences, as when they play house or doctor or soldier or any adult role. Evolution has guaranteed that during the years between birth and adulthood, children will want to learn the many skills required of adults if they are to survive and leave offspring. According to Bruner, language, playfulness, curiosity, and the need to master one's environment appear to be evolved characteristics that make human development what it is.

Ethologists have also noted remarkable similarities in the social behavior of human beings and their nearest primate relatives (N. Blurton-Jones, 1972). Some observers have remarked that children's play groups have "dominance hierarchies" much like troops of macaques or chimpanzees. Children climb the dominance ladder by means of physical attack, threats, or struggles over objects. Even in preschool play groups, most children know which child belongs on each rung of the ladder (Strayer and Strayer, 1976). Usually the children agree on who is "toughest," who is "smartest," and so forth, and roles of leaders and followers are solidly established. Studies of how dominance is established and maintained among young children throw light on power relations in groups and on individual responses to those relations. As Janet Strayer (1977) found in a study of several preschool play groups, the most aggressive child in a group rarely is the child at the top of the dominance hierarchy, and the child who winds up as scapegoat is the one who does not keep on the appropriate rung. Scapegoats either do not understand the group's structure, or else they know it and deliberately violate it.

One major ethological notion is that of **releasing stimuli,** which was discussed in Chapter 2. Such stimuli can explain regularities in

THE SOCIOBIOLOGICAL WAR

With the publication of Edward O. Wilson's *Sociobiology* (1975a), the ethological examination of human development became highly politicized. **Sociobiology** is the systematic study of the biological basis of all social behavior. By combining ethology with ecology and genetics, sociobiologists hope to discover some general principles about the biological nature of entire societies (Wilson, 1978). Human traits are seen as having evolved from the struggle to pass along as many genes as possible to the next generation. Because the traits were adaptive at the time the species evolved, they spread throughout populations. Since human nature is composed of these traits, stable societies evolve within a range that is compatible with them.

According to Wilson, genes probably influence emotional responses—determining the range of forms they take as well as their intensity. Genes may also predispose people to learn such things as the sounds of human language or such relationships as sexual pair-bonding, which perpetuate the species. Sociobiologists have concentrated their explorations on general areas: competition, cooperation, altruism, sex roles, the socialization of children, territoriality, and aggression. Because of their genetic determinism, they have been accused of encouraging the sort of thinking that provides "a genetic justification of the *status quo* and of existing privileges for certain groups according to class, race or sex" (Allen et al., 1975). For example, Wilson's position that temperamental differences between the sexes are probably responsible for male dominance and are the basis of the sexual division of labor has led to charges of sexism. Strong evidence for his position is lacking. No one has ever demonstrated any genetic basis to male dominance. Although there may indeed be some genetic connection between gender and temperament, it does not appear to be especially potent.

Wilson has always stressed the power of learning and social conditioning, however, and has pointed out on more than one occasion (1975b, 1978) that demonstrating a genetic bias toward a certain kind of behavior does not justify its perpetuation in society. The present human environment is so different from the environment in which a good part of our genetic evolution occurred that to follow a practice because it was genetically influenced would be not only bad biology, but disastrous for the species as well. The tendency toward warfare could now lead to global suicide; the tendency toward rearing the maximum number of offspring could mean environmental disaster.

It will probably take years before the dust of battle has settled and the proposals of Wilson and others can be examined in a less contentious atmosphere. Despite the acrimony over sociobiology, the trend toward using the ethologists' observational techniques and the move away from a totally environmental approach to child development continue.

mating patterns, aggression, appeasement, and some other kinds of typical behavior. For example, no matter where they live, most human beings respond to cuteness in babies and baby animals by wanting to pick them up and cuddle them. What makes baby forms of a species "cute"? Young animals are cute because they have relatively large heads, particularly foreheads, and foreshortened facial features. The toy industry takes advantage of this to make cute dolls with very small features embedded in large heads and small bodies. The baby's smile is considered a social releaser. Perhaps cuteness is a releasing stimulus for human caregiving, and perhaps human beings have evolved the response to cuteness because it improves the chances of adequate infant care and survival (Lorenz, 1943).

Courtship and greeting also show apparently universal ritualized aspects of behavior. Irenäus Eibl-Eibesfeldt (1970) has studied such behavior extensively in groups around the world. He has discovered amazing similarities in human facial expressions. For example, in flirtatious greetings by females, the eyebrows go up, the head tilts, the gaze lowers, and the eyelids drop. No matter which cultural tradition a woman comes from, she seems to display this form of greeting to the opposite sex. In greeting other people, both sexes usually employ the eyes and the eyebrows.

In general, then, adaptation theories suggest that behavior is partially the product of our evolutionary history. The structure of behavior is inherent in genetic-biological development and that behavior develops in interaction with the environment.

ORGANISMIC THEORIES

The evolutionary perspective has also influenced organismic theories, but organismic theorists do not interpret development in terms of its evolutionary function. They believe that human beings have evolved to behave in uniquely human ways. Just as the internal organs and the external limbs have evolved to certain forms, so our behavior has characteristic patterns.

Organismic theories regard the child as a spontaneously active organism that actively constructs his or her knowledge of the world. Development is not a series of cumulative changes. Instead, as the child develops, the mind undergoes a series of reorganizations. With each reorganization, the child moves into a higher level of psychological functioning. In this view, a child's behavior cannot be understood apart from its goal. Breaking up behavior into bits and studying it apart from its context, therefore, serves no purpose.

The two theorists discussed in this section, Heinz Werner (1948, 1957) and Jean Piaget (1952b, 1970b), shared common influences. They were familiar with each other's work and were trained in the biological and natural sciences. This training and interest in biology led both to emphasize the adaptive functions of behavior in maintaining an equilibrium between the individual and the environment. Each emphasized that genetic maturation and experience together determine development: as the two interact, they produce and regulate changes in behavior and functioning.

Werner and Piaget viewed cognition as a biological system. The function and characteristics of thought were like those of digestion or respiration—taking in, modifying, and using whatever elements were needed.

Both stressed that human behavior could not develop if people were not born with a set of specifically human functional systems (sensorimotor systems) that allowed them to interact with the environment and to incorporate experience and stimulation. From birth, human beings actively engage and use their environment, and they construct their own understanding of it.

Werner and Piaget also stressed the developing child's shift from egocentrism to perspectivism. At first, infants are **egocentric;** they make no distinction between themselves and the external world, or among feeling, thought, and the external world, so that feeling and thinking are fused. Gradually, children acquire **perspectivism,** a sense of themselves as people who are separate from the world, with objectively based concepts that they share with others.

Werner and Piaget studied development at an everyday level, intervening in everyday situations and studying the effect of the experimental manipulations on a child's behavior. This approach was consistent with their opposition to fragmenting natural patterns of behavior.

Piaget's Theory

Piaget's theory has had more influence in recent years than other organismic theories. It gives

JEAN PIAGET (1896–1980)

(Yves de Braine/Black Star)

Jean Piaget was born and reared in Switzerland. As a boy he was a keen observer of animal behavior and, when he was only fifteen, published a paper on shells in a scientific journal. He came by his interest in knowledge and knowing (epistemology) as a result of studying philosophy and logic. Whereas most American psychologists have been influenced by the evolutionary theories of Charles Darwin, Piaget was influenced by the creative evolution of Henri Bergson, who saw a divine agency instead of chance as the force behind evolution.

After receiving his doctorate in biological science at the University of Lausanne in 1918, he became interested in psychology. In order to pursue his interest in abnormal psychology, he went to Paris and, while studying at the Sorbonne, secured a position in Alfred Binet's laboratory. During his work there, he began to pay more attention to children's wrong answers than to their right ones, realizing that the wrong answers provided invaluable clues to the nature of their thinking.

Piaget's interests in children's mental processes shifted and deepened when, in 1929, he began observing his own children. As he kept detailed records of their behavior, he worked at tracing the origins of children's thought to their behavior as babies. Later, he became interested in the thought of adolescents. Piaget's primary method was to present problems in a standardized way to children of different ages. He then asked each child to explain his answers and probed these explanations with a series of carefully phrased questions.

Soon after completing his work in Paris, Piaget accepted an appointment as director of research at the Jean Jacques Rousseau Institute in Geneva. He lived in Geneva until his death, conducting research and writing on cognitive development as professor of experimental psychology and genetic epistemology at the University of Geneva.

meaningful continuity to the development of human understanding, and it has strongly influenced research in the field of perceptual and intellectual development. Piaget called his approach **genetic epistemology.** Epistemology is the study of knowledge—how we know what we know. The term "genetic" here means developmental. Piaget's theory covers the development of intelligence (ways of knowing) over the life span.

For Piaget, all knowledge comes from action. For example, babies act on objects around them—feel, turn, bang, mouth them—and grow in their knowledge of those objects through structuring their experiences. The baby's knowledge grows neither from the objects themselves nor from the baby but from the interaction of the two and the consequent links between actions and objects.

Schemes Piaget saw a child's understanding of the world (as opposed to the mere recording of it) as arising from the coordination of actions and the interrelationships of objects: The infant is a **constructionist.** Both relationships—of actions and of objects—are the baby's constructions of reality, not something given by the actions or the objects alone. For example, infants can shake a rattle or throw it; they can apply those same actions to a small stuffed bear. When the rattle is shaken, it makes a noise; when it is thrown, it lands with a sharp clatter. But the tiny bear is noiseless when shaken and makes only a soft thud when thrown. Yet the bear can be squeezed, whereas the rattle resists the pressure of their fingers. From such apparently ordinary and simple actions on objects, infants come to know some effects of their actions and some properties of objects. They also learn to coordinate their actions—they cannot throw and roll the same object simultaneously, but they can finger it first and then throw or roll it. Action patterns, which Piaget called **schemes,** are built up and coordinated throughout development. In the infant, they are like concepts without words.

Older children and adults have more internalized action schemes, which they use to gain and structure their knowledge. Later schemes can be mental actions. Although the actions of thinking are internal, they derive from earlier concrete experiments that the infant performs on the world. Mental arithmetic replaces the physical act of counting; logical sequences of thought, such as "If . . . then" statements, replace the younger child's concrete manipulations of cause-effect relations. An older person need no longer literally try out the solution to every problem.

For example, most adults have come to understand the principle of gravity: When released from an elevated position, objects fall. But a ten-month-old baby explores gravity by dropping toys over the side of the crib and watching as they hit the floor. Blocks, stuffed animals, cups, teething rings, every object the baby can reach is dropped, and all fall satisfactorily to the floor. Before long the baby's scheme of dropping objects in space becomes coordinated with many objects, so that the carpet around the crib is not always littered with toys. And since a toy that is dropped cannot be played with, the baby eventually realizes that manipulating objects and dropping them are not compatible schemes.

Assimilation and Accommodation In Piaget's theory, children's thinking develops through two processes: assimilation and accommodation. **Assimilation** refers to the incorporation of new knowledge through the use of existing schemes. For example, a child can bang a large variety of objects and assimilate to an existing scheme whether or not "banging" is a primary attribute of each object. Some objects make loud noises, others, soft; some break, others squeak; and so forth. **Accommodation** refers to the modification of the child's existing schemes to incorporate new knowledge that does not fit them.

The processes of assimilation and accommodation always work together in complementary fashion. To assimilate is to use what one already knows how to do; to accommodate is to acquire a new way of doing something. Both processes continue to function throughout the life span. For example, in the United States we are being asked to convert our thinking to the metric system. In essence, we are being asked to restructure our existing schemes (accommodation). After we have learned the metric units of weight, volume, and linear measure, we will have to assimilate much of what we knew under the old scheme to the new one. Is a man who weighs 140 kilograms too fat? (Yes.) Is $1.00 per liter a cheap price for gasoline? (No.) Is 6¼ kilometers too far for a daily jog? (Not if you're in top condition.) In other words, any new way of acquiring knowledge will have to be applied to what we have already learned in a different way under other schemes.

At any given time, the developing person can change his or her cognitive structures only to a limited extent. There must always be some continuity. The balance, or equilibrium, between assimilation and accommodation changes over the life span in the direction of greater balance. **Equilibration** is the most general developmental principle in Piaget's theory; it states that the organism always tends toward biological and psychological balance and that development is a progressive approximation to an ideal state of equilibrium that it never fully achieves. A child's equilibrium at any one stage may be upset by external events, such as new information he or she cannot readily assimilate, or by internal processes that bring the child to a new "readiness" to accommodate. In both cases, the child's previous temporary equilibrium is upset, and development advances to a new, higher level of organization.

In Piaget's view, to obtain the toy this baby first tries a familiar grasping scheme (assimilation) and then alters it with new knowledge (accommodation) to get the toy through the bars. *(George S. Zimbel/Monkmeyer Press)*

Stages According to Piaget, intellectual development goes through a series of stages, and the organization of behavior is qualitatively different at each stage. The two essential points of Piaget's stage theory are (1) that stages emerge in a constant order of succession, and (2) that neither heredity nor environment independently explains the progressive development of mental structures.

Piaget proposed three major stages of intellectual development: a **sensorimotor** period (divided into six subperiods); a period of **representational** thought (subdivided into **preoperational** and **concrete-operational** periods), and a **formal-operational,** or propositional, period. The sensorimotor period, which is discussed in Chapter 7, begins at birth and extends through the first two years of life. The period of representational thought begins around the age of two with the preoperational stage, when children start to record experiences symbolically. This period is discussed in Chapter 11. Beginning at about seven or eight, children enter the concrete-operational period, discussed in Chapter 14, when they attain logical thought but only in respect to concrete objects. They now understand new kinds of logical operations involving reversible transformations. By eleven or twelve, young adolescents begin to develop a formal logic that consists of propositions ("If . . . then" statements). At this time they enter the formal-operational period, the culmination of cognitive development, which is discussed in Chapter 18. The ages given for each stage are, of course, approximate. For example, although the concrete-operational stage begins at about seven, many five- and six-year-olds have already entered it.

Werner's Theory

Like Piaget, Heinz Werner emphasized the interaction of genetic maturation and environmental experience. Werner believed that psychological development resembled the development of the embryo: all normal children pass through the same milestones of development in the same

HEINZ WERNER (1890–1964)

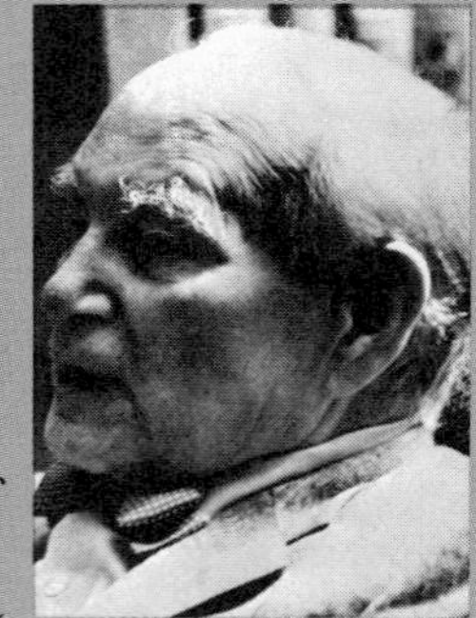
(Courtesy International Universities Press)

Heinz Werner was interested in formulating a comprehensive theory of cognitive development. He adopted principles and concepts from embryology, biology, and other natural sciences and applied them to mental development. Werner considered learning views of development wrong, because he believed development was much more than a gradual and continuous process of acquiring bits of behavior.

Because he was interested in explaining mental life, his approach was broad, eclectic, and comparative. He wanted his theory to explain the course of cognitive development over the life span and to account for differences in thought among species, among cultures, and among abnormal groups.

He stressed that the development of human beings shows both change and stability. People go through an ordered sequence of stages, which are characterized by different organizations of cognitive structure and functioning. Each stage involves both adaptive change and organizational stability. Adaptive change means that with maturation there is a progressive development of specific, separate ways of doing and seeing things, and that these more advanced ways take precedence over early, simple forms. Organizational stability means that, even though changes occur, a person retains an essential and basic organization.

Werner showed that even as infants, human beings are organized and have some degree of competence, and this inborn organization is the basis for adaptive behavior and learning. Although movement, vision, thinking, and so on are always organized, they undergo progressive changes in a patterned order.

order. Like Piaget, Werner was a stage theorist, but he neither presented his stages as a single system nor attached specific ages to each stage.

The major theme of his developmental theory is the **orthogenetic principle** (Werner, 1948). In physical, psychological, and social development, the child moves from a global, undifferentiated state to one of high differentiation and integration. Responses and skills are increasingly organized into hierarchies, a trend Werner called **hierarchic integration.** This progression is easy to see in the physical area, where the baby develops hierarchic patterns of movement that bring each separate motor capability into the service of others in a highly organized way. When babies first learn to drink from a cup, for example, they combine and integrate a series of simple skills. First, they must be able to sit up and fix their eyes on the cup. Then, they must be able to use visual information to reach out, find the cup, grasp it, and hold it upright. Next, they must combine visual information with kinesthetic information about the position of the head and mouth, arms and hands, in order to bring the cup to the mouth, tilt it at the correct angle, stop tilting it before it spills, and swallow. When young babies drink from a cup, they combine and integrate all these skills so smoothly that their mothers never consider the number of simple abilities that are involved.

As infants become able to integrate perception and thought into hierarchies, they learn to distinguish parts from the whole, see relationships, and understand the difference between relevant and irrelevant qualities. They come to understand, for example, that Father is still the same person, even though he has shaved off his beard. Gradually, their higher mental functions control the lower ones. They begin to use language to direct their behavior, and by the time they are seven, they are less bound by immediate situations and increasingly able to plan and to tolerate delay.

Although Werner has not been as dominant a figure as Piaget, his ideas about differentiation and hierarchic integration have been incorporated into a number of theories in developmental psychology.

DIALECTICAL THEORIES

In the dialectical view, human development cannot be understood without considering how historical-social changes affect behavior and its development. Knowledge is seen as social, created by society and transmitted to the individual. Neither child nor adult, therefore, processes stimuli as simple reflections of the real world. Instead, both apply internalized historical and cultural factors to their sensations. When development is approached from this viewpoint, major cultural changes, such as computers and television, are seen as perhaps altering how we perceive the world, categorize it, think, and organize our inner consciousness.

Organismic psychologists come close to the dialectical view, for they see development as arising out of the child's active operations on the environment. But according to Klaus Riegel (1975a), their theories fall short because they fail to consider social interaction. Piaget, for example, seemed to view the environment as a collection of things without activity or history. In addition, his focus on equilibrium led him to emphasize stability at the expense of change.

The dialectical view has its roots in the philosophy of G. W. F. Hegel and Karl Marx and regards development as a dialectic process. In a **dialectic,** each idea is seen as a thesis, which interacts with its antithesis, or opposite, to form a synthesis on a new level. The synthesis becomes a new thesis, and the process begins again. Similarly, a person in each stage of development interacts with society to reach a new level of functioning. Dialectical psychology first became prominent when Soviet psychologists were searching for an approach that would fit comfortably within the Marxist framework. In recent years, American psychologists have reevaluated the theoretical views and methods of Soviet psychology. As a result, a number of them have come to regard dialectics as a helpful tool instead of as a dogmatic straitjacket.

The Russian Dialectical View

Shortly after the Russian Revolution, Lev S. Vygotsky proposed a way of looking at human development that viewed mental activities as taking shape in a matrix of social history. Society, he believed, was essential to human development. Concepts, language, voluntary attention, logical memory—everything that distinguishes the human mind from that of the chimpanzee—comes from the culture and begins between the child and another person. Each of these functions appears twice in a child's development—first shared between the child and an adult (an interpersonal process) and then inside the child (an intrapersonal process) (Vygotsky, 1978).

As children reconstruct a process, according to Vygotsky, they move through a series of spiral stages, passing through the same point at each new reconstruction, but on a higher level. With each new level, they gain more and more control of the regulation of their behavior. Development is neither an accumulation of small changes in behavior nor a single upward line. In each succeeding stage, new responses are carried out in new ways under the influence of different psychological processes.

But Vygotsky did not regard maturation as the primary source of the child's intellectual development. He saw children as active organizers who used the tools and language of the culture in a continual interaction with the social world, thereby affecting both the world and themselves. Vygotsky was especially interested in language, for he believed that once the child developed inner speech (thought), the nature of development changed. As he explained it, the young

LEV SEMANOVICH VYGOTSKY (1896–1934)

The Russian, Lev S. Vygotsky, was a contemporary of Piaget and Werner. Graduated from Moscow University in 1917, until 1923, he taught both literature and psychology in Gomel. In 1924, just after Soviet psychology had officially adopted "reactology"—an approach to psychology that depended upon behavioral reactions in a Marxist framework (Cole and Scribner, 1978)—Vygotsky returned to Moscow to work at the Institute of Psychology. His views did not coincide with the major European approaches to psychology, which were either introspective or behavioristic (as was reactology). Nor did Vygotsky find the Gestalt psychologists' attempts to study behavior and experience as wholes a very satisfactory solution.

Vygotsky believed that the study of psychology was the study of changing processes, for as people respond to a situation, they alter it. One of his complaints about Piaget's theory was that the Swiss psychologist did not give enough weight to the influence of the environment on the developing child. Vygotsky believed that the internalization of social and cultural activities was the key to human development and that internalization distinguished human beings from animals.

In some respects, today we might regard Vygotsky as a psychologist who was interested in human cognition, for his primary areas of interest were thought, language, memory, and play. At the end of his life, he worked on the problems of education. But Vygotsky was also trained as a physician and advocated the combination of neurology and physiology with experimental studies of thought processes. Just before his death from tuberculosis in 1934, he had been asked to head the department of psychology in the All-Union Institute of Experimental Medicine.

Vygotsky died at thirty-eight, but his influence on Soviet psychology continued through his students, who hold major positions throughout the Soviet Union. For years after his death, Vygotsky had no influence in this country; but in 1962, *Thought and Language* was translated, and his ideas entered the American psychological community. With each passing year, his notions about the relation of thought and language, and the nature and uses of play, have received more attention. In 1978, his essays, *Mind in Society,* were translated and published.

child thinks by remembering, but the adolescent remembers by thinking (Luria, 1976).

Vygotsky's views influenced most Soviet psychologists, and one of his best-known followers was Alexander Luria. Luria's primary fields of interest were the brain and the workings of the mind. He was especially interested in neuropsychology, child development, language, and mental retardation. In 1931, he set out for Uzbekistan and Kirghizia, remote rural areas of the Soviet Union, where people were just beginning to be affected by education and technology. Luria hoped to discover whether—and how—mental functioning changed as these peasants were incorporated into modern life. Many of the adults he studied were illiterate, others were workers on collective farms who had attended school briefly and had been given practical courses in farm management. Still others were women students in a school for teachers. In controlled interviews, he presented these adults with objects to sort and simple problems to solve.

Luria discovered that adults without schooling had trouble with abstract classifications, such as "tools" or "weapons." Instead, they tended to group by function. Given a ham-

	Number of Subjects	Functional Grouping	Mixed Grouping	Abstract Grouping
Illiterate peasants from remote villages	26	21 (80%)	4 (16%)	1 (4%)
Collective-farm workers (barely literate)	10	0	3 (30%)	7 (70%)
Students in school for teachers	12	0	0	12 (100%)

FIGURE 3.2 ***(From Luria, A.R. Cognitive Development: Its Cultural and Social Foundations. Harvard University Press, 1976)***

mer, saw, hatchet, and log, for example, they would classify the log with the saw because one cuts the log with it. Asked to solve problems, they were unable to abstract the problems from life. Told that cotton can grow only where it is hot and dry and that it is cold and damp in England, they refused to say whether cotton would grow in that country. As one peasant said, "I don't know. I've only been in the Kashgar country." Adults with only a few years schooling had no trouble with any of the problems (Luria, 1976).

Luria's research, unpublished in the Soviet Union for forty years, was banned because it could be interpreted as an insult to the peasants studied. Yet the research indicates that culture does affect mental functioning. Although it does not change basic capacities, it teaches new mental strategies and how and when to apply them.

The American Dialectical View

Among American psychologists, Klaus Riegel (1976) has been the most enthusiastic proponent of dialectical psychology. He saw this approach as concerned with the way children, adults, and groups recognize challenges and ask questions. He was, therefore, opposed to a child-centered developmental psychology, for he believed that development and change were constant features of life. Like Vygotsky, Riegel believed that all psychology is developmental psychology.

He suggested (Riegel, 1975b) that development progresses along several interdependent dimensions: biological, sociological, psychological, and physical. When one dimension is out of phase with the rest, a developmental crisis occurs. Once the dimensions are again synchronized, the child or adult makes a developmental leap. Without such crises, there would be no change—in either the individual or society.

The existence of these crises and contradictions led Riegel (1975a) to propose that we add a fifth and final stage to Piaget's stages of cognitive development—the stage of dialectical operations. In this stage, a person does not require equilibrium but can accept contradiction as the basis of all thought. Such a person realizes that contradiction is both essential and constructive.

Many psychologists who do not consider themselves dialectical psychologists conduct research that meets the requirements of dialectical psychology. For example, Jerome Bruner's (1978) research into prelinguistic games and dialogues between mother and child can be interpreted as studies of social dialectics, in which development arises out of social interaction.

THE CONCEPT OF STAGES

Stage theories make assumptions about the nature and course of development that stem in part from biology, but that apply to cognition as well as to other psychological aspects of development. The concept of stages is basic to the theories of Werner, Piaget, Freud, and Erikson, but is absent from mechanistic theories.

In stage theories, development and change always take place in a given sequence. As development proceeds, new forms of functioning emerge that are not a combination of earlier forms, but represent a new organization. Although people never give up earlier forms of functioning, as when a woman uses sensorimotor thought in playing the piano or when a man who long ago gave up his childhood belief that objects have feelings angrily kicks a car that refuses to start on a winter morning, their development makes it impossible for them to return completely to an earlier stage.

Stage theorists believe that both continuity and discontinuity characterize human development. A stage theorist would agree with a proponent of behavior-learning theory that a change in amount, frequency, strength, or duration of a behavior shows continuity. But when ways of behaving that have an inherently new organization emerge, the stage theorist would point to discontinuity in development. This discontinuity indicates qualitative changes in behavior and functioning and in their underlying processes.

Although Werner and Piaget, whose theories were primarily about cognitive development, believed that emphasis on either the continuous or discontinuous aspects of behavior would lead to a distorted view of development, the idea that discontinuity is one characteristic of cognitive development has been closely tied to their views.

As an individual develops, he or she goes through the stages in a fixed order, without skipping any. Movement from one stage to another is gradual, and individual differences in development appear because people move through the stages at different rates and because some may stop developing before they reach the most advanced stage.

Few psychologists have had a theory of stage development more firmly based on biological development than Freud. Biological changes and discontinuities play a much larger part in Freud's theory of development than in that of any of the other theorists discussed. Erikson's stages are less tied to biology; instead they grow out of conflicts between the developing person's needs and social demands—and their resolution.

Although stage concepts and theories have been useful, they have also come under criticism. For example, in a strict stage theory, a stage must represent qualitative changes in behavior from that of earlier periods. Quantitative changes, or changes in amounts, occur throughout the life span and give no evidence for stages.

The evidence for qualitative changes in behavior is mixed. Often a closer look at an earlier "stage" will reveal antecedents of behavior that seemed to pop up, full-blown. In number concepts, for example, Rochel Gelman (1972; 1977) has shown that three- and four-year-olds possess many parts of later skills. Indeed, when small numbers are used, preschoolers can count accurately, and they are not fooled by changes in the length of an array of three to five chips. Although most children do not easily manipulate large numbers until they are in the early school grades, preschool children already have many of the component skills. What appears to be a dramatic qualitative shift to a new "stage" of logical reasoning probably involves some important quantitative changes as well.

OVERVIEW

Despite the fact that the theories we have explored may appear to inhabit different worlds, some common themes run through them all. Human growth and development, they agree, is regular; behavior is at least potentially predictable. Yet various groups of theorists focus on different kinds of behavior, although they may call it by the same name. "Learning," for example, means one thing to a learning theorist and something different to an adaptation theorist. In addition, different groups of theorists frequently explain different aspects of development.

When they look at the same process, they tend to discuss it in different ways. The relationship between baby and caregiver, called attachment, for example, is regarded by psychoanalytic theorists as an outgrowth of the caregiver's satisfying the infant's need to suck that characterizes the oral period. Learning theorists see attachment as the result of conditioning: the primary caregiver both satisfies the infant's basic needs and provides interesting and satisfying stimulation. And as noted earlier, ethological theorists view attachment as an evolved response that increases the likelihood of the infant's—and therefore the species'—survival.

On the other hand, the various viewpoints appear to be converging and may one day approach a common theoretical framework. All groups have a common concern with identifying the processes involved in human growth and development. They share the goal of synthesizing observations and experimental findings to explain how and why behavior originates and develops. They are concerned with looking at human development over the entire life span. In recent years, as we have seen, many theorists have begun to modify the early, narrow positions and to use insights from other viewpoints to expand their explanations of human behavior and development.

As you read this book, you will notice that different sections stress different theories. Work that implements cognitive theories will be discussed most heavily in chapters on language and intellectual development; psychodynamic theories will appear most often in the discussions of personality. Because behavior-learning theories regard all behavior as learned and because their techniques of study are used by psychologists of all persuasions, behavior-learning work or methods will appear throughout the book. Theories developed by the new ethologists, whose evolutionary approach is exciting, if unfulfilled, will appear wherever they seem to contribute to an explanation of human development.

In the chapters of this first unit, we have explored the concept of development, the determinants that affect a developing organism, the methods that researchers use to study them, and some of the theories that have evolved to explain development. Our theme now changes from general principles to the individual, and the rest of the book will trace the way a person develops, from the union of two cells at conception to the ending of a long life.

SUMMARY

1. Mechanistic theories see development as primarily the result of experience. In behavior-learning theories, there are two major types of learning: classical conditioning and operant conditioning. Social learning, which emphasizes the role of observation and imitation, has expanded behavior-learning to include in development the role of human thought and knowledge. Information-processing theorists, while not sharing all assumptions of mechanistic theories, view human beings as information-gathering, information-processing systems and believe the mind functions like a computer.

2. Psychodynamic theories see human behavior as motivated by various internal and external forces. For Freud, the unconscious forces of the id are tempered and sublimated by the ego and the superego. For Erikson, personality develops according to steps predetermined by the organism's readiness to interact with the external world. In general, psychodynamic theories stress that the development of how one feels about oneself is of great importance and that the individual follows a developmental course toward becoming an active, complete person.

3. Adaptation theories observe human be-

havior from an evolutionary perspective, stressing the way it enables human beings to survive and flourish in an environment such as that in which our species evolved. Adaptation theorists believe that the structure of behavior is inherent in genetic-biological development and that behavior develops in interaction with the environment.

4. Organismic theories view cognition as a biological system, stressing that people are born with a set of specifically human functional systems that allow them to interact with the environment and to incorporate experience and stimulation. In organismic theories, development progresses by stages. Piaget's theory, one example of such a view, sees the child as constructing an understanding of the world, and suggests the notion of schemes with which the child assimilates and accommodates new knowledge, thus maintaining equilibrium between internal schemes and the outside world. Intellectually, the child progresses through the sensorimotor, the representational, and the formal-operational stages. In Werner's theory, the child moves from a global, undifferentiated state to one of high differentiation and integration.

5. Dialectical theories stress that historical and social changes have profound effects on behavior and its development. Dialectical theories see knowledge as social, created by society and transmitted to the individual; development is seen as arising out the child's interactions with the environment.

6. Stages are central to the developmental theories of Werner, Piaget, Erikson, Freud, and Vygotsky. In stage theories, developmental change takes place in a given sequence, with each new stage representing a higher form of functioning. Stage theories have been criticized for failing to meet certain proposed scientific requirements.

7. Although they focus on different aspects of the developmental process, the five groups of theories discussed in this chapter are largely complementary, and all can be useful in different ways.

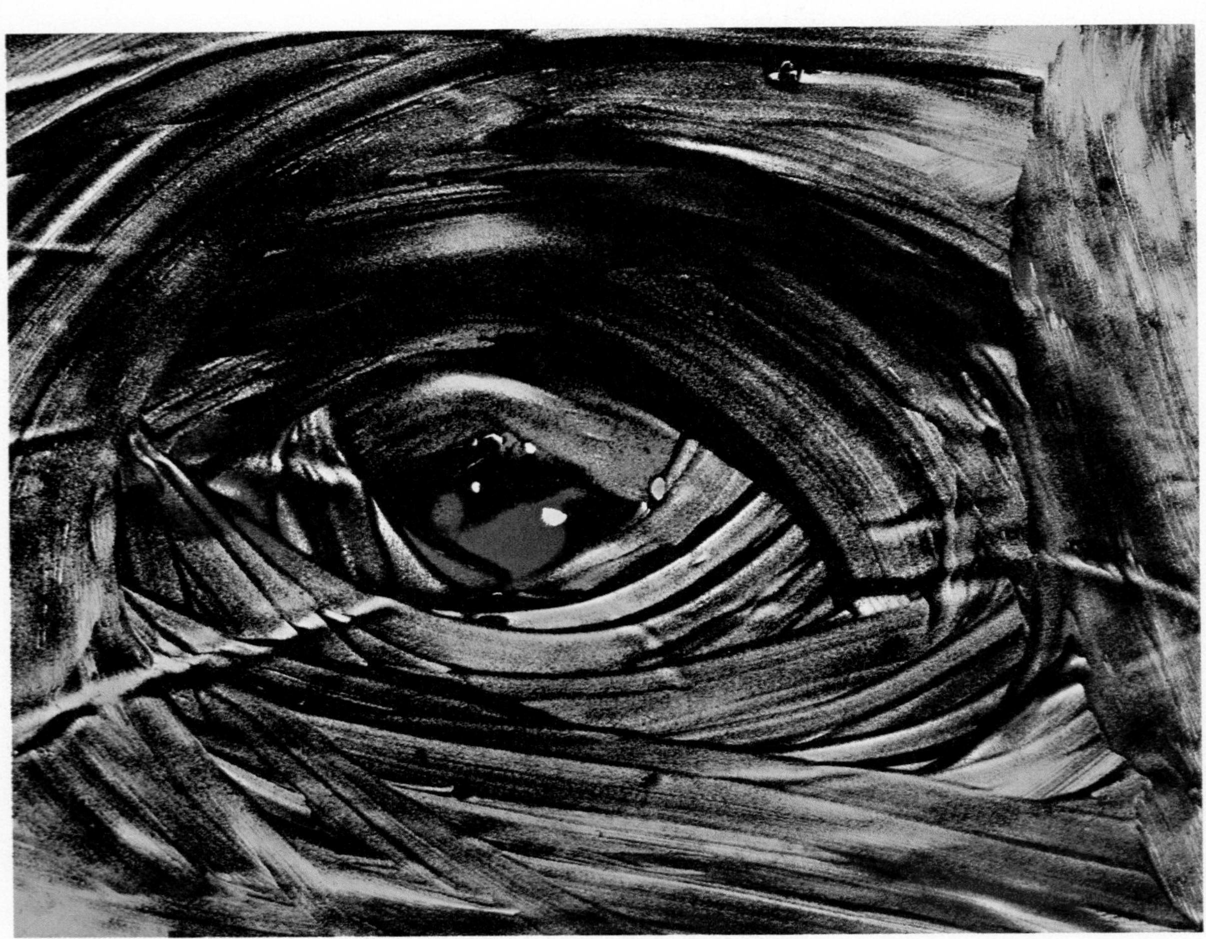

UNIT TWO

THE BEGINNING OF LIFE

When a baby is born, a new, independent life begins. In thirty-eight weeks, a baby grows from an undifferentiated cluster of cells to an individual capable of unassisted life. During those weeks within the uterus, the developing organism is utterly dependent upon the mother's body. With birth, infants must rely on their own mouths for sustenance, their own lungs for air, and their own eyes and ears to tell them about the world. Although newborns are helpless in many ways, they come into the world prepared to gather information. As their bodies grow, their nervous systems mature, their experiences deepen, and they gradually become capable of handling their own needs. This unit describes how development within the uterus prepares the newborn for this radically changed existence and how the new human being progresses during the first four weeks of life.

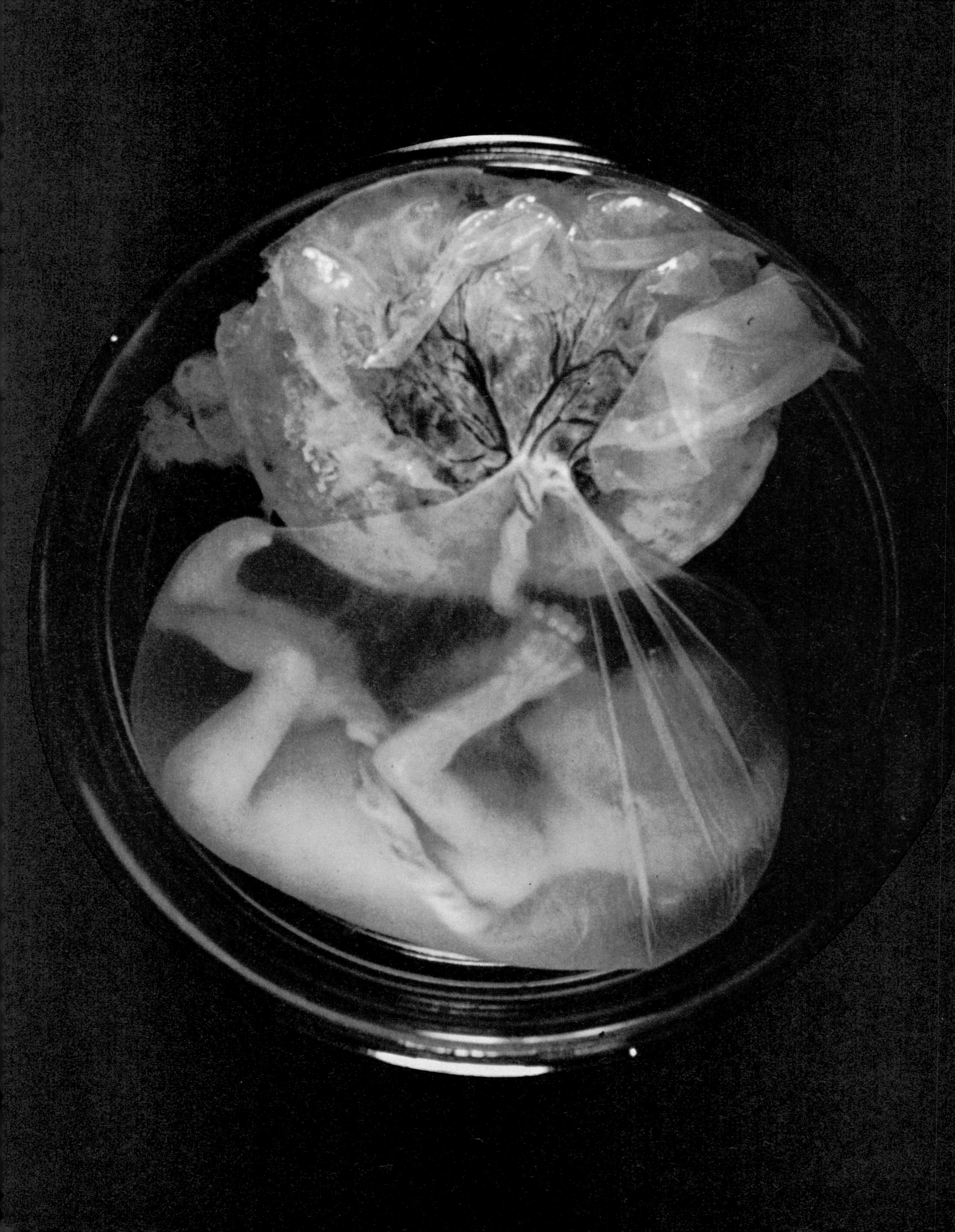

4 PRENATAL DEVELOPMENT

Development begins when two cells unite in the mother's body. At that instant, the inheritance of the new individual is established in the form of a unique physical appearance and a disposition toward certain personality characteristics and mental abilities. But this genetic composition is expressed only in an environmental context, and the two together determine how a person looks and behaves. Perhaps the oldest debate in psychology is how much influence inheritance or environment has in producing any given trait. Further, when a characteristic is "inherited," what does that fact tell us about how the trait will develop and about the possibility of changing that characteristic through life experiences?

When we consider that thirty-eight weeks after two tiny cells come together a viable and behaving human being emerges, it is clear that more growth and development take place during the prenatal period than during any comparable segment of life history. The structures and functions that emerge during this time form the basis of the new individual's body and behavior for the rest of life.

In this chapter we will follow the development of the fertilized egg into a healthy, normal baby who is ready for independent life outside the mother's womb. We will study the transmission of specific traits from parent to child, a subject that was introduced in Chapter 2. The behavior and capabilities of the growing fetus will become apparent, and the problems that can arise in the course of development will be spelled out. We will look at the link between the mother and her unborn child and will discover the importance of maternal health, diet, habits, and emotions.

HOW LIFE BEGINS

During the course of history, people have held a variety of beliefs and superstitions about the beginnings of a human life. Until the middle of the eighteenth century, it was commonly believed that life began with a completely formed and functioning miniature human being. During the prenatal period this miniature person simply became larger.

A major debate of this period raged over the source of this preformed fetus (Needham, 1959). Some biologists held that it was somehow contained in the mother's egg and that the father's sperm merely stimulated the growth of the already-formed baby. Other scientists claimed that the preformed infant existed in the head of the father's sperm and that the mother's womb simply served as an incubator. Anton van Leeuwenhoek, the inventor of the compound microscope, observed semen with his new instrument and in 1677 claimed that he saw in the sperm little animals of both sexes who copulated and produced new animals. Other scientists reported being able to tell the difference between the semen of donkeys and horses because the animals in the sperm of donkeys had longer ears.

In 1759, Kaspar Wolff asserted that both parents contributed equally to the beginning of life and that an embryo began as a cluster of globules. This assertion had major implications. It contended that the very young organism lacked the organ systems and structures that it would possess at birth. This meant that prenatal development had to consist of the appearance and growth of new cells, structures, and functions, not simply enlargement of a preformed individual. More than fifty years later, Karl von Baer (1827) substantiated this theory when he discovered the mammalian egg cell under his microscope, and the science of embryology began.

Conception

The development of each person begins at the moment of conception, when the sperm cell, or **spermatozoon,** from the father unites with the egg, or **ovum,** of the mother. The ovum is the largest cell in the human body, and it can sometimes be seen without a microscope. The eggs mature in the female's ovaries, and one egg is released approximately every twenty-eight days during the woman's fertile years. The freed egg, which probably can be fertilized for less than twenty-four hours, travels down the **Fallopian tube** toward the uterus (see Figure 4.2).

All the eggs that a woman will ever produce are present in immature form in the ovaries at the beginning of her fertile years, but a man continually produces new spermatozoa. During normal intercourse, the male releases approximately 400 million spermatozoa, which may survive in the female genital tract for as long as seven days, although they probably are capable of fertilizing the egg for no more than forty-eight hours.

From one standpoint, it is a wonder that sperm and egg ever get together. First, the egg can be fertilized for only three of the twenty-eight days in a **menstrual cycle.** Second, only a small percentage of the sperm manage to pass through the cervical canal, the small opening in the **cervix,** or lower part of the uterus. Third, the sperm must be able to reach the Fallopian tube by their own motions and/or with the aid of the muscular action of the uterus. Fourth, the egg must be able to enter the Fallopian tube. Fifth, the egg must travel down the Fallopian tube fast enough to meet the sperm while both cells are alive. Such a variety of circumstances must be met before conception can take place that, some physicians estimate, one couple in ten is unable to conceive. On the other hand, it takes only one of those 400 million spermatozoa to fertilize an ovum, and some couples achieve conception after one act of sexual intercourse.

Chromosomes and Genes

The traits and dispositions that parents transmit to their offspring are coded in twenty-three pairs of chromosomes, which are present in every cell of the body. The chromosomes are composed of beadlike strings of genes, microscopic entities containing the codes that produce inherited physical traits and behavioral dispositions. These genetic codes are embodied in a complex chemical called **deoxyribonucleic acid,** or DNA. Whatever one passes on to one's offspring is contained in approximately 250,000 genes composed principally of DNA molecules, which contain a chemical code that guides the development of bones and eyes, brain and fingernails, as *(top)* **Living, active human spermatazoa, highly magnified. The waving tail propels the sperm to ovum, and the head contains the nucleus, which carries the chromosomes.** *(bottom)* **A living human ovum magnified. The human egg is smaller than one of the periods on this page. Unlike many other vertebrate ova the human egg lacks large amounts of yolk, and the fetus must get its nourishment through the placenta.** *(From Rugh and Shettles, 1971)*

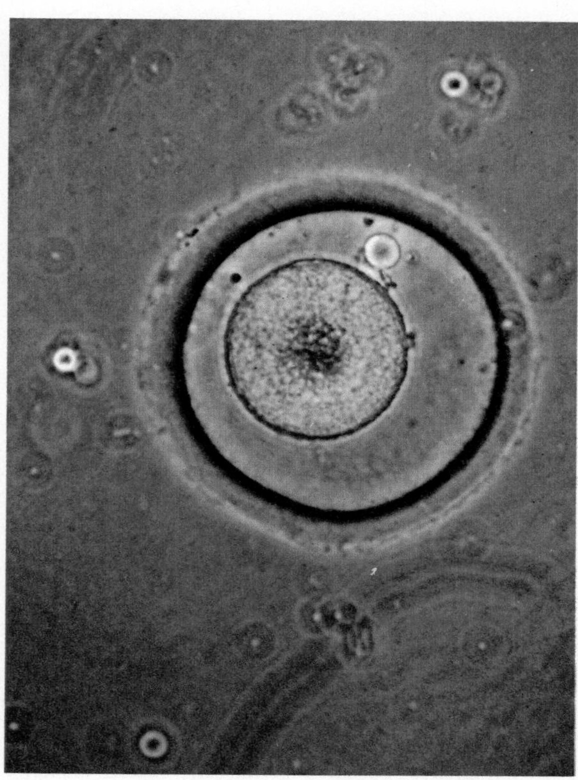

Part of the set of forty-six human chromosomes, magnified and stained. The chromosomes assume this form as they prepare to divide. *(Courtesy Leonard Hayflick. Copyright © the President and Fellows of Harvard College)*

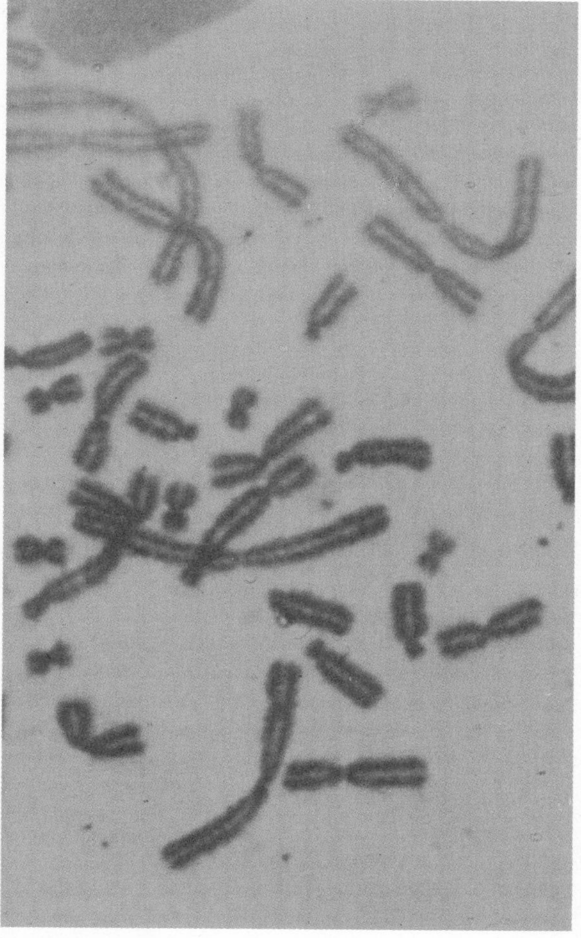

well as disposes the offspring toward certain behavioral patterns. All that information is contained in a fertilized cell smaller than the period that ends this sentence.

The Production of Sex Cells

Most cells of the human body contain twenty-three pairs of chromosomes, direct copies of the original twenty-three pairs with which each person begins life. There is one major exception, however, and that occurs in the ova and spermatozoa, that is, the **gametes.** At puberty the gametes begin to form by a special kind of cell division called **meiosis.** During meiosis, a normal cell containing twenty-three pairs of chromosomes divides and divides again to produce four cells that contain one of each type of chromosome. The process begins when chromosomes of the same type pair up within the nucleus of a cell. The members of each chromosomal pair divide and gravitate to opposite ends of the cell, which then splits into two cells each containing twenty-three *single* chromosomes rather than twenty-three *pairs.* These cells then reproduce themselves, producing four cells each having a set of twenty-three *single* chromosomes. At conception, when a sperm unites with an egg, the result is a single cell having twenty-three pairs of chromosomes. Figure 4.1A illustrates meiosis in two pairs of chromosomes.

The Transmission of Genes

Children sometimes resemble their parents in certain physical characteristics and sometimes do not. For example, a mother and father may both have brown hair, but one of their three children may be blond. How are physical characteristics passed on from parent to child?

Although hair color is a common and easily observed characteristic, its transmission is complicated. It is simpler to explain genetic transmission by examining a characteristic that depends on a single pair of genes. Consider **phenylketonuria,** or PKU, an inherited inability to metabolize phenylalanine, a component of some foods. If this metabolic abnormality is left untreated, the afflicted child will have fair skin and hair, a small head in proportion to body size, eczema, agitated and restless behavior, a stiff gait, and moderate to severe mental retardation.

In order to understand how PKU occurs, let *N* symbolize the gene corresponding to normal metabolic ability and *p* represent the gene for PKU. The related genes, *N* and *p,* are called **alleles.** Now look at Figure 4.1B, which illustrates the alleles in only one pair of chromosomes. The parent cells in the figure contain the alleles of interest, labeled *N* and *p.* In this example, the mother's and father's cells have a gene for both *N* and *p.* When the parent cells divide to form gametes, half of the father's sperm cells and half of the mother's ova will contain a gene for PKU *(p)* and half will contain a gene for the normal metabolic condition *(N).* During conception, one of four possible combinations of these gametes will result. Depending on which male gamete unites with which female gamete, the new baby will have a genetic inheritance of *NN, Np* (which is the same as *pN*), or *pp;* these are shown in Figure 4.1B. If the selection process were perfectly random, one-fourth of the offspring of these parents would have the combina-

FIGURE 4.1 (A) The production of sex cells. Sex cells divide in a pattern of cell division called meiosis to produce gametes—ova and sperm—that have only half the number of chromosomes of the parent cells. For simplicity, only two of the twenty-three pairs of chromosomes are shown here. In meiosis, first the members of each pair split up (First Division), and then the chromosomes themselves split in half. In a subsequent step, they regenerate their missing halves (next line). At conception, the union of the gametes results in a zygote that has the full number of chromosomes, half from the mother and half from the father.
(B) Transmission of alleles in the inheritance of PKU. The chromosomes in this pair carry the alleles N and p. Both parents have both forms of the gene, and therefore they produce gametes with chromosomes bearing either the *N* or the *p* gene in equal numbers. Depending on which gametes happen to unite in conception, the new cell may have the alleles *NN, Np, pN,* or *pp.* Because *p* is a recessive gene, only babies with *pp* will have PKU.

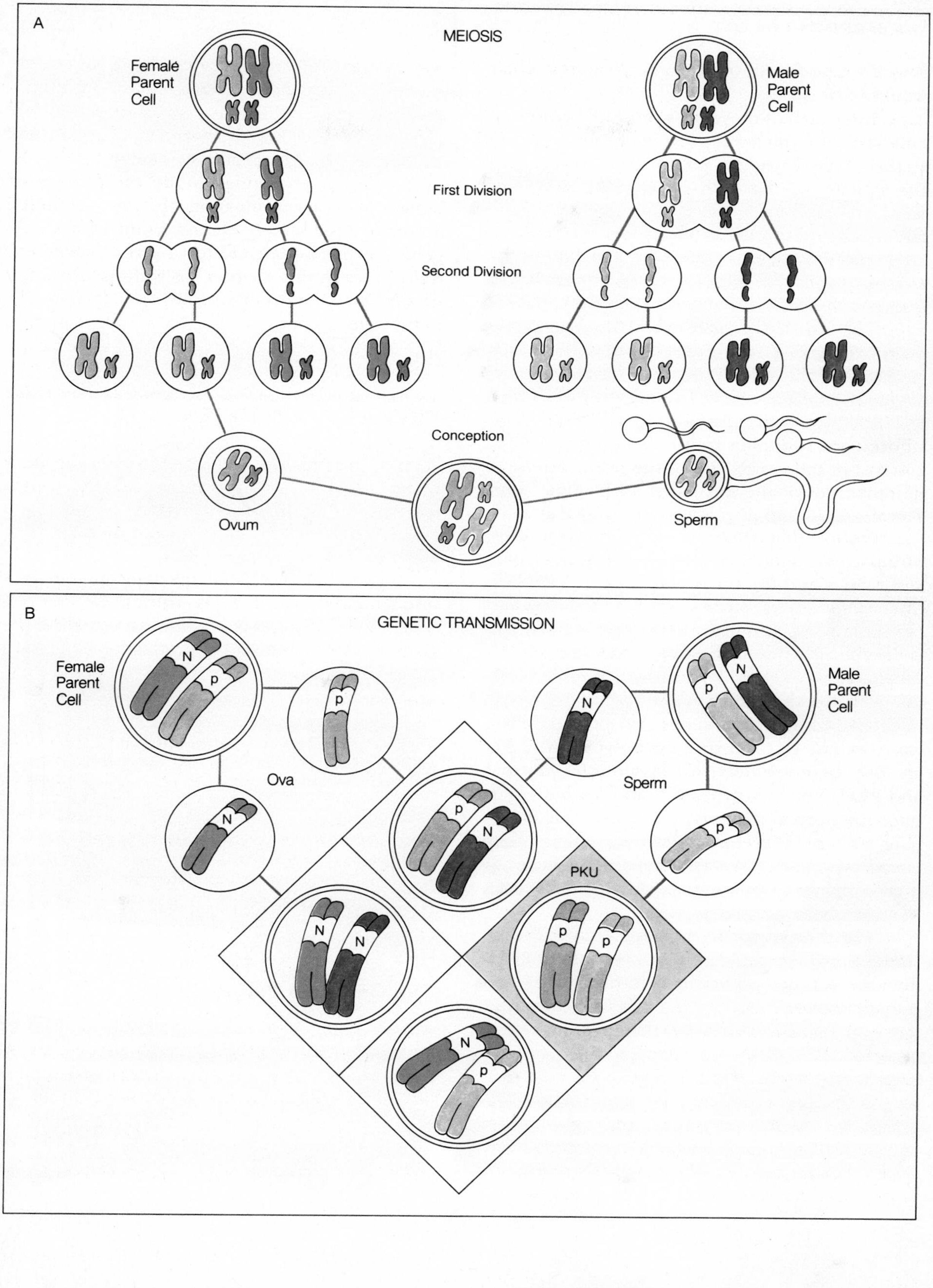

A

MEIOSIS

Female Parent Cell

Male Parent Cell

First Division

Second Division

Conception

Ovum

Sperm

B

GENETIC TRANSMISSION

Female Parent Cell

Male Parent Cell

p

N

Ova

Sperm

N

p

N

p

PKU

N

N

p

p

N

p

tion *NN,* one-fourth would have *pp,* and one-half would have *Np.*

But which of these offspring will be normal children, and which will show symptoms of PKU? In this example, the *NN* baby will be normal, and the *pp* baby will have PKU. These offspring are **homozygous,** which means that their cells have matching genes for this characteristic. But an *Np* baby is **heterozygous,** meaning that his or her cells have different genes for the same trait. Are these *Np* babies normal, or do they have PKU?

The answer depends on which gene is **dominant** and which is **recessive.** A dominant gene is one whose corresponding trait appears in the individual even when that gene is paired with a different gene for the trait. The paired gene whose corresponding trait fails to appear is recessive. In the case of PKU, the normal gene is dominant over the recessive PKU gene, and therefore *Np* individuals will be normal.

Notice that there is not a perfect one-to-one correspondence between the genes a person carries and the traits that appear. This lack of correspondence illustrates the difference between **genotype** and **phenotype.** The genotype is the specific combination of alleles that characterize one's genetic make-up, whereas the phenotype is the nature of the trait as it appears in the individual. The genes that produce PKU can combine to form three genotypes: *NN, Np, pp.* But there are only two phenotypes: normal and PKU. The genotypes *NN* and *Np* both produce the normal phenotype because *N* is dominant over *p.* Therefore, there are some differences between one's genetic make-up (genotype) and what one actually looks like and how one behaves (phenotype).

For a variety of reasons, genetic transmission is rarely as simple as it is in the case of PKU. First, most traits, especially behavioral ones, are **polygenic,** which means that several genes have an equal and cumulative effect in producing the trait. In other cases, some genes in the combination have more influence than others on the phenotype. Second, dominance is not always all-or-none. That is, there appear to be gradations of dominance, so that one allele for a trait is not totally dominant. The result may be somewhat of an "average" of two extremes. Third, one allele may not express itself unless an allele of quite a different characteristic is also present. Consequently, it is possible to carry a "dominant" gene that does not affect one's phenotype.

The more scientists study the process of human genetic transmission, the more complex it seems. One simply cannot point to a single gene that is responsible for a given behavioral trait. Later in this chapter we will discuss some of the issues and complexities involved in genetic transmission.

PRENATAL GROWTH

As soon as a sperm and an egg unite, development begins and progresses at a rapid rate. In approximately thirty-eight weeks, the organism goes from one tiny cell to a living, functioning, and behaving newborn baby.

The course of prenatal development falls into roughly three periods. During the first two weeks after conception, called the **germinal period,** the fertilized egg is primarily engaged in cell division. In the next six weeks, the **embryonic period,** the organism begins to take shape, and its various organ systems begin to form. Thereafter, from approximately eight weeks after conception to birth, the developing organism is called a **fetus.** The total **gestation period** usually lasts about 266 days (thirty-eight weeks) from conception or 280 days (forty weeks or nine calendar months) from the beginning of the mother's last normal menstruation. The **menstrual age** is the age of the fetus, when calculated in the latter way.

The Germinal Period

Almost immediately after fertilization, the egg begins the process of cell division that will eventually produce a human body made up of many billions of cells. Although the cells of an adult are highly differentiated according to their location and function in the body (for example, nerve cells are quite different in form and function

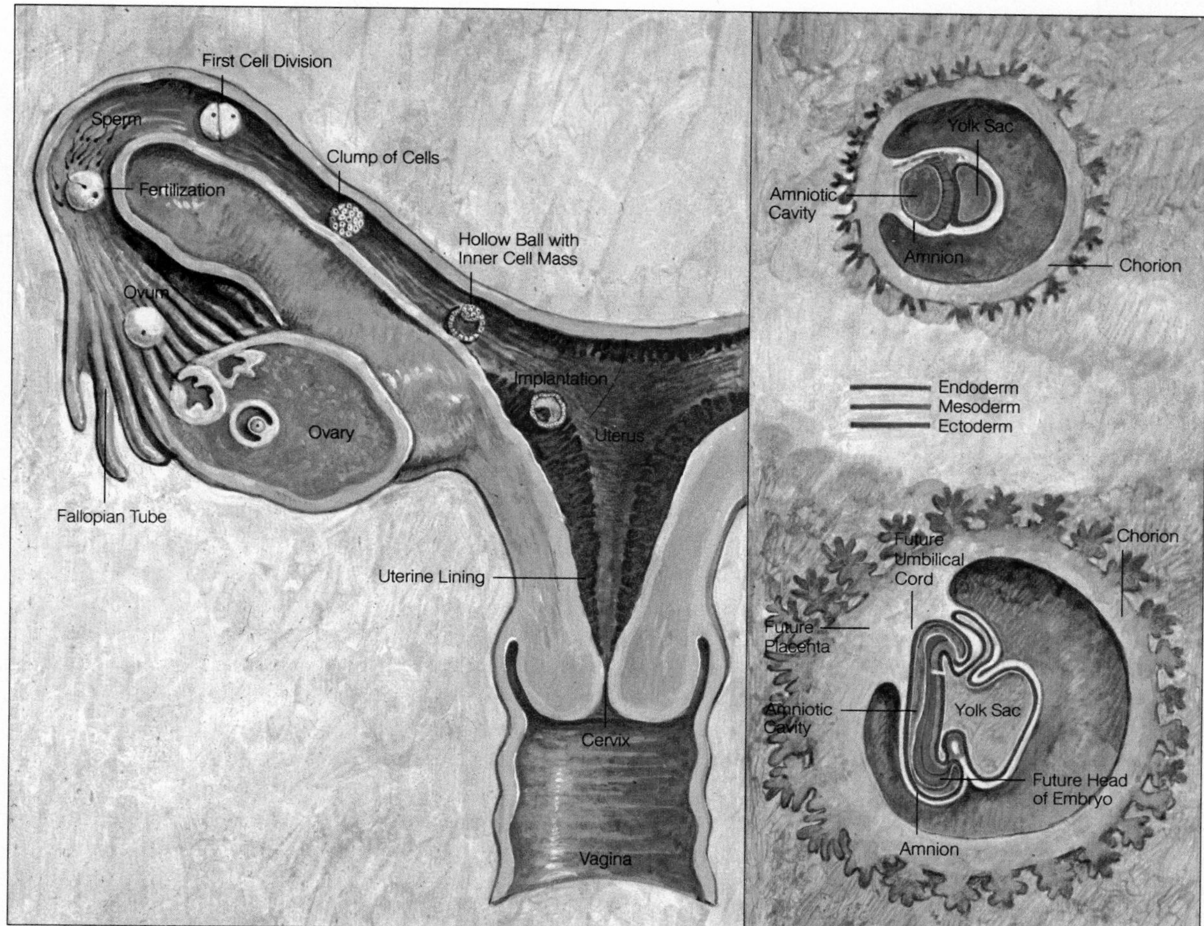

FIGURE 4.2 The early development of the human embryo. Fertilization occurs at the upper end of the Fallopian tube. By the time the fertilized ovum reaches the uterus, it has already divided many times. Within seven or eight days, it is securely implanted in the uterine wall, where the process of prenatal development continues.

from muscle cells), the cells at this point in development are all identical.

It is estimated that the fertilized ovum takes approximately three days to progress through the Fallopian tube to the uterus, where it floats freely for another four or five days before becoming implanted in the uterine wall. By the end of the first two weeks, the cells have multiplied greatly in number and have begun to differentiate themselves. An outer membrane **(chorion)** and an inner membrane **(amnion)** form a sac that surrounds and protects the developing organism. In addition, the microscope can distinguish the **placenta,** which transmits nourishment and wastes between the mother and the fetus, and three primary layers of cells. These layers are the **ectoderm,** which is the source of future cells composing the skin, sense organs, and nervous system; the **mesoderm,** from which the muscular, circulatory, and skeletal systems will develop; and the **endoderm,** which will give rise to the lining of the intestinal tract and to related organs such as the liver, pancreas, and thyroid.

One phenomenon that needs explanation is how cells become differentiated into nerve, muscle, fat, and blood. Genes may reprogram the embryonic cells, and some scientists have speculated that newly produced cells are essentially neutral, or undifferentiated. Somehow, these neutral cells are attracted to locations that need them, and then by some means, probably chemical, they are altered to serve the purpose required at that location.

For example, suppose that you cut your hand. Neutral cells are sent to the wound, where they are transformed into specialized skin cells by chemicals apparently released by layers of tissue immediately below the skin. If the wound is not too deep, the cell differentiation is almost perfect, and there is no scar. However, if the cut is deep enough to destroy the layers that produce the differentiating chemicals, the body's repair job is incomplete, and a scar forms. It is possible that the fetus develops by similarly transforming neutral cells.

By the end of the germinal period, the two-week-old organism is already anchored to the lining of the uterus, which maternal hormones have prepared for the developing egg. With both the organism and its host ready for development, life is on its way.

The Embryonic Period

Within four weeks after conception, the organism is already about one-fifth of an inch long, 10,000 times larger than the original fertilized egg. In addition, its heart is beating to pump blood through microscopic veins and arteries, and there are the beginnings of a brain, kidneys, liver, and digestive tract and discernible indentations that will eventually become jaws, eyes, and ears.

Organs along the central axis of the body develop first; the extremities develop later. Thus, in the early weeks the organism is literally all head and heart. Later, the lower part of the body begins to enlarge and to assume its newborn proportion and size.

By the end of the embryonic period, the organism is almost an inch long, and it is clearly human. What look like the gill slits of a fish are really rudimentary forms of structures in the neck and lower face. What seems to be a primitive tail eventually becomes the tip of the adult spine; the tail reaches its maximum length at about six weeks and then slowly recedes. The head is clearly distinct from the rounded, skin-covered body and accounts for about half the embryo's total size. The eyes have come forward from the sides of the head, and eyelids have begun to form. The face clearly contains ears, nose, lips, tongue, and even the buds of teeth. The knobs that will be arms and legs grow, and in a matter of weeks, they differentiate into hands and feet and then into fingers and toes.

In this early period, the brain sends out impulses that coordinate the functioning of other organ systems. The heart beats sturdily, the stomach produces minute quantities of some digestive juices, the liver manufactures blood cells, and the kidneys purify the blood. One can distinguish testes or ovaries, and the endocrine system has begun to produce hormones. However, all these organ systems are in a primitive form, and it will be several months before they can be considered fully functional (Pritchard and MacDonald, 1976).

The Fetal Period

Approximately eight weeks past conception, when bone cells begin to develop, the developing organism is known as a fetus. Within twelve weeks it has begun to stretch out a little from its C-like posture, and the head is more erect. The limbs are nicely molded, and folds for fingernails and toenails are present. An external inspection could readily determine the sex of the fetus. The lips become separate from the jaws, beginnings of teeth are apparent, the nasal passages of the nose have formed, the lungs have acquired their definitive shape, the brain has attained its general structure, the eye is organized, and the retina is becoming layered. The pancreas secretes

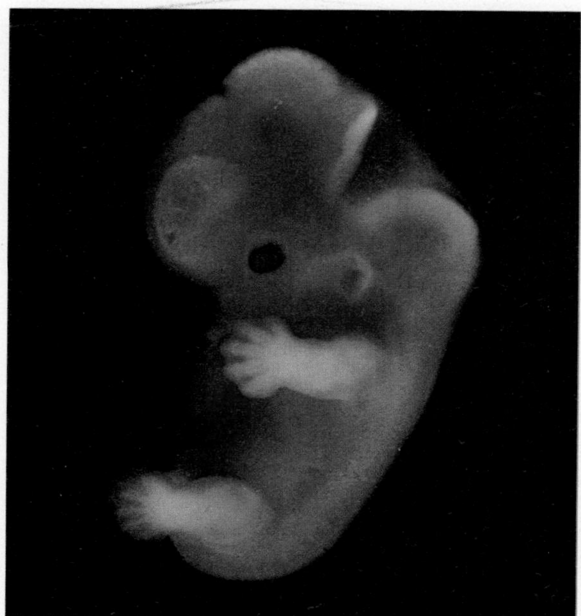

Normal fetus at forty days. Note the rudimentary brain, eye, ear, fingers, and toes. ***(From Rugh and Shettles, 1971)***

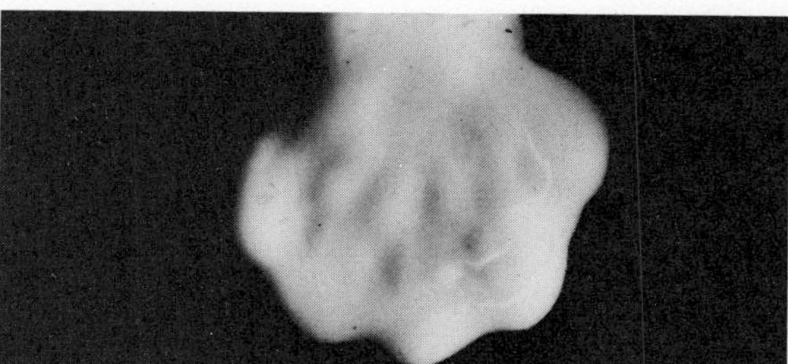

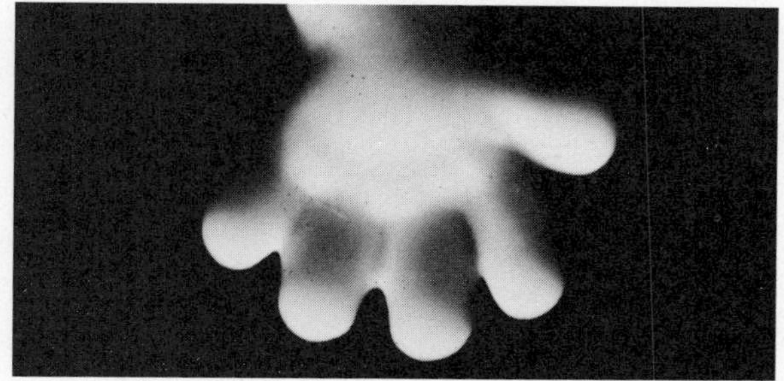

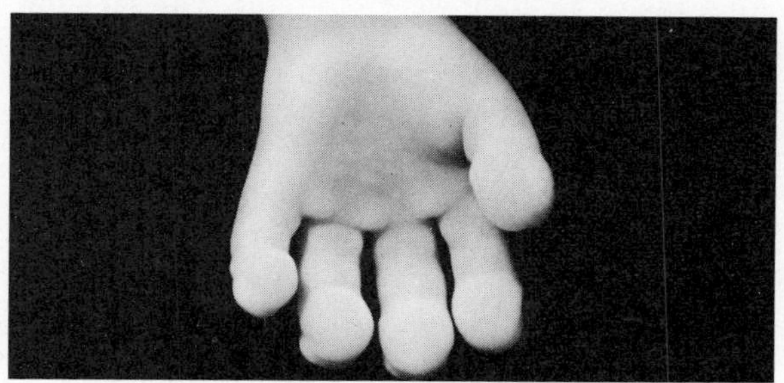

In the fifth week, hands are a "molding plate" with finger ridges. In the sixth week, finger buds form. In the seventh and eighth weeks, the fingers, thumbs, and fingerprints form, and the touch pads are prominent. ***(Courtesy Carnegie Institution of Washington)***

bile, and the bone marrow has begun to produce blood. At this time the fetus weighs about an ounce and is approximately three inches long.

By sixteen weeks the fetus is approximately six to seven inches long and weighs about four ounces. Until now, its head has been enormous in relation to the rest of its body, but by sixteen weeks the lower part of the body has grown until the head is only about one-fourth of the total body size. The sixteen-week-old fetus looks like a miniature baby. Its face looks "human," hair may appear on the head, bones can be distinguished throughout the body, and the sense organs approximate their final appearance. All major internal organs have attained their typical shape and plan. Although the fetus could not survive if it were delivered at this point, its development has progressed so far that almost all basic systems and physical characteristics are present, down to hair on the head and sweat glands.

Although most basic systems are present in rudimentary form by sixteen weeks, certain functions necessary for survival outside the uterus are not yet fully developed. One of these functions is the ability to breathe. A necessary component in this process is the liquid **surfactin,** which coats the air sacs of the lungs and permits them to transmit oxygen from the air to the blood. Around the age of twenty-three weeks, the fetus develops a way to produce and maintain surfactin, but if it is born at this time, it often

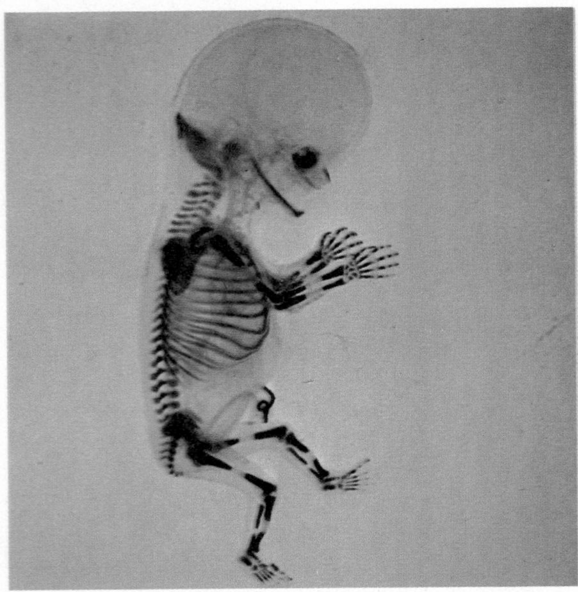

An x-ray of an eight-week-old fetus. The skeleton has developed and the advanced bone formations appear as darkened regions.

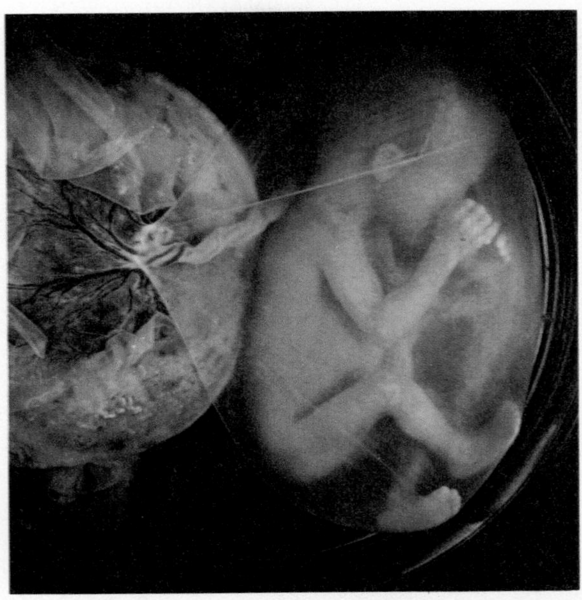

Human fetus at twelve weeks, with the placenta attached. The placenta provides for the exchange of gases, nutrients, and metabolic wastes between the developing fetus and the mother. ***(From Rugh and Shettles, 1971)***

cannot maintain the necessary surfactin levels and may develop **respiratory distress syndrome** (formally called hyaline membrane disease of the lungs) and die. However, by about thirty-five weeks (sometimes earlier), the fetus develops a new system for maintaining surfactin, and this new method will allow it to live outside the uterus (Gluck and Kulovich, 1973).

Generally speaking, 175 days (twenty-five weeks or just under six months) is regarded as the minimum possible age at which a fetus may survive. Babies have been born and survived from as early as 175 to as late as 334 days after conception, although the normal term of pregnancy is 266 days from conception. If born much before term, the fetus must be placed in an incubator, which helps regulate the baby's body temperature, facilitate breathing, maintain the acidity-alkalinity balance of the blood, and so forth. Fetuses born after 252 days of gestation (thirty-six weeks) are considered to be of normal term, although unusual circumstances may still make special care necessary for the first few days or weeks of life. A fetus that remains in the uterus much after term may require oxygen and nourishment immediately upon delivery because as the placenta ages, supplies to the fetus may become so reduced as to cause actual weight loss.

During the final period of prenatal development, at a time when the fetus could survive on its own, its organs step up their activity, and its heart rate becomes quite rapid. Fat forms over its entire body, smoothing out the wrinkled skin and rounding out contours. The fetus usually gains about one-half pound a week during the last eight or nine weeks in the uterus. At birth the average full-term baby is about twenty inches long and weighs a little more than seven pounds, although weight may vary from less than five to

SPINA BIFIDA: A PUZZLING DEFECT

Of every thousand babies born in this country, two have neural tube defects. Early in pregnancy, as the tube that forms the brain and spinal column develops, it sometimes fails to close—either at the top or along the spine. The defect occurs in all population groups, and no one knows why it happens in one pregnancy and not another, but the results are always serious.

When the tube fails to close at the top, babies are born without a brain—or with an incomplete one. If they are alive at birth, they die within a few days.

When the opening is along the spinal column, the babies have a condition known as *spina bifida:* a bundle of nerves protrudes through an opening in the spinal column. These babies generally live, although many are retarded or paralyzed below the waist. In some, fluid does not drain properly from the skull, so that they also have *hydrocephaly* (water on the brain).

The lot of babies with spina bifida can be improved by surgery. The opening in the spinal column can be surgically closed and a permanent device implanted that drains excess fluid from the brain. Babies with hydrocephaly, even if it is treated, often are mentally retarded, and many of them die before they are two years old. Among babies without hydrocephaly (one-third of those with spina bifida), 83 to 90 percent are not mentally impaired (Kolata, 1980). They will wear braces or use wheelchairs, and they will have no bowel or bladder control, but they can become contributing members of society.

An inexpensive test has now been developed that can detect a fetus with neural tube defects (Kolata, 1980). In such pregnancies, the fetal liver produces excessive amounts of alpha-fetoprotein (AFP), which passes into the amniotic fluid and from there to the maternal bloodstream. Mothers whose blood shows high levels of AFP can be tested by ultrasound and amniocentesis (see page 101), which are efficient at picking out the cases of neural tube defects from those in which other conditions of pregnancy, such as the presence of twins or an incorrect estimate of fetal age, have led to high AFP levels.

more than twelve pounds, and length may vary from less than seventeen to more than twenty-two inches.

DEVELOPMENT OF THE BRAIN

The development of the central nervous system (brain and spinal cord) is both intricate and extremely fast. It starts out as a cluster of cells. As these cells continue to differentiate and multiply, they form a tubelike structure, which bends over at one end as it develops. This end eventually becomes the brain. By the end of the first four weeks of life, the embryo has a spinal cord and a recognizable brain with two lobes; by the sixteenth week the brain's major structures and shape resemble those of an adult. By the sixteenth week, too, the cortex—a mantle of neural cells covering the cerebral hemispheres—has grown back over the lower parts of the brain.

Although the lower parts of the brain are primarily responsible for sustaining life, coordinating reflexes, and other primitive behavior, their development is not sufficient to maintain life outside the womb much before twenty-eight weeks. By thirty-two to thirty-six weeks, the cortical areas for motor and sensory behaviors are reasonably mature, as are parts of the primary audition areas. But at birth the remaining and larger mass of the cortex is still very immature.

During the prenatal period, two major events mark cell growth in the brain (Dobbing and Smart, 1974). The first is the development of all the neural cells, or **neurons,** that make up the adult brain. Many more neurons form than the brain needs, and those that do not make contact with other neurons die during the developmental stage (Cowan, 1979). Neurobiologists estimate that the average adult brain has 100 billion neurons. Research indicates that these cells begin to develop when the fetus is about ten weeks old and that all 100 billion are developed by about sixteen to twenty weeks.

The second major event involves the continuing growth of these neurons and the growth of other supporting and connecting cells in the brain. The other cells, called **glial cells,** seem to play an essential role in the nourishment of the neurons and in the development around each neuron of a sheath of **myelin,** a fatty substance that keeps nerve impulses channeled along the neural fibers and reduces the random spread of impulses from one fiber to another. This development begins at about twenty weeks and accelerates until the fetus is about twenty-eight to thirty-two weeks old. The glial cells continue to multiply until about the second year after birth. Myelination continues in most areas until about the fourth year, although some parts of the brain are not fully myelinated until adolescence. As neurons move from the depth of the developing brain, where they form, to their final position, they appear to migrate along a path charted by special glial cells, whose excessively long fibers extend to the outer surfaces of the brain (Cowan, 1979).

The fetal brain remains immature in other respects. For one thing, the adult cortex is composed of nine types of neurons arranged in six different layers. Not all these cells reach a mature form in the fetal cortex, nor are the cells distributed in the neat, layered arrangement of the mature cortex. Further, according to best estimates, each of the 100 billion neurons in the adult brain has an average of 10 thousand connections with other cells. In comparison, the fibers that extend from neurons in the fetal brain are short and stumpy, and as the cells mature, many will be retracted (Cowan, 1979). Although, as we will see in the next chapter, the newborn infant has many capabilities, it will take time for the almost unbelievably massive and rich interconnection to develop among the neurons. As the nerve circuits form, it is likely to be in a precise order and according to a rigid timetable (Hirsch and Jacobson, 1975).

PRENATAL BEHAVIORAL DEVELOPMENT

How early in its life can the fetus respond to stimuli, what kinds of responses does it make, and what kinds of spontaneous behavior does it show? The major behavior that characterizes the fetus is movement. Although most mothers say they first feel the fetus move at about sixteen weeks, it has in fact been able to move its muscles for approximately eight weeks.

Fetal behavior is difficult to study within the uterus, but thirty years ago Davenport Hooker (1952) had the opportunity to observe the spontaneous behavior and reactions of embryos and fetuses that were delivered by Caesarean section. They were too immature to survive, but their movements were recorded on film for later study. Hooker discovered that by twelve weeks the fetus can kick its legs, turn its feet, close its fingers, bend its wrists, turn its head, squint, frown, open and close its mouth, and respond to touch.

By twenty-three weeks the fetus often moves spontaneously. It sleeps and wakes as a newborn does, but it also undergoes sluggish periods not found in the newborn. The fetus even has a favorite position for its naps. By twenty-four weeks it can cry, open and close its eyes, and look up, down, and sideways. By this time it has also developed a grasp reflex and will soon be strong enough to support its weight with one hand. It may hiccup. During the final eight or nine weeks, the fetus is quite active, although its actions become limited by the increasingly snug fit of the uterus.

Behavioral development in the prenatal organism corresponds to the development of its nervous system and of the muscles of its body. The earliest responses found in embryos appear at about seven and one-half weeks. When the area of the mouth is stroked with a fine hair, the fetus responds in a general manner, moving its upper trunk and neck. By nine weeks, the fetus will bend its fingers when the palm of its hand is touched and either curl or straighten its toes in response to a touch on the sole of the foot. By eleven weeks, the fetus can swallow. As the organism develops, more and more of its body becomes sensitive to stimulation, and the response eventually narrows to the area stimulated. Thus, when one touches the mouth, only reflexes about the mouth appear. Within the last few months before birth, the fetus behaves essentially as it does at birth, with grasping, sucking, kicking, and other typical infant reflexes.

Although a fetus can learn, it is a rudimentary sort of learning. Two studies, neither of which has ever been repeated, suggest the sort of learning that is capable within the uterus. Lester Sontag experimented by making a loud noise near a pregnant woman's abdomen. At first the sound produced a large change in fetal heart rate, but after frequent repetitions of the noise on successive days, the fetus no longer reacted. Apparently, it had adapted to the sound—it had "learned" it in a sense (Sontag and Newbery, 1940). David Spelt (1948) showed that a fetus twenty-eight weeks old or more who responds to very loud noises can also learn to respond to the neutral stimulus of a vibrator applied to the maternal abdomen. Thus, the fetus seems capable of remembering sounds.

THE BIRTH PROCESS

As the time for birth approaches, the fetus generally lies head down in the uterus, which resembles a large sack with its opening into the vagina constricted by the cervix. Researchers have not determined the exact mechanisms that begin labor. They may involve changes in hormone levels in both mother and fetus. On the mother's side, her pituitary gland releases the hormone *oxytocin,* her uterus stretches, the relationship of other hormones within her uterus changes, and her body releases a substance that causes the uterus to contract. When the fetus is ready to be born, its adrenal gland produces cortisol and its pituitary produces oxytocin. Although some researchers believe that the production of fetal oxytocin is the signal that begins birth, they have yet to establish the direct transfer of the hormone through the placenta (Kumaresan et al., 1975).

FIGURE 4.3 Models indicating the position of the fetus during passage through the birth canal. ***(Reproduced, with permission, from the* Birth Atlas, *published by Maternity Center Association, New York)***

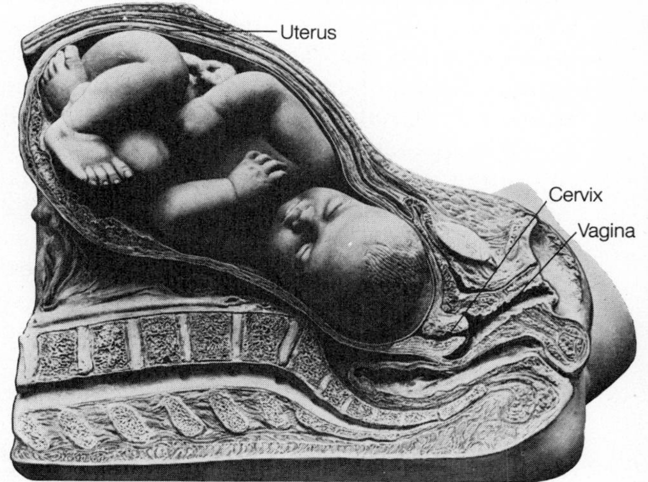

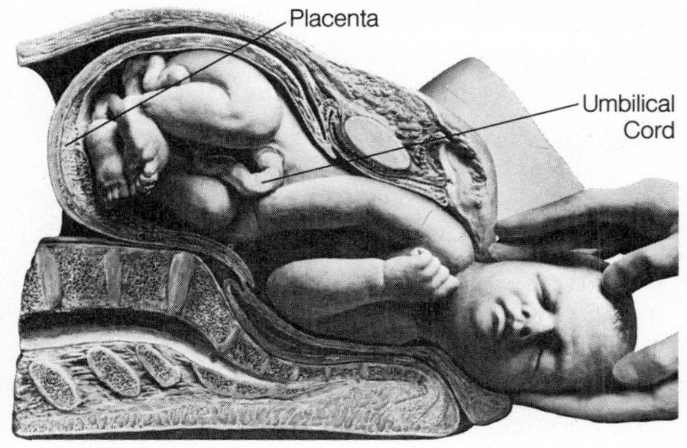

Labor and Delivery

When the birth process begins, the upper portion of the uterus contracts at regular and progressively shorter intervals while the lower part of the uterus thins out and the cervix dilates to permit the fetus to pass through the birth canal. Later the mother's abdominal muscles also contract in a bearing-down motion. Unless drugs deaden sensations, she usually pushes hard to get the baby out. This entire process is called labor. For first-born infants, labor often lasts thirteen to fifteen hours, although its actual length varies greatly from mother to mother and is markedly less for later-born children.

The first stage of labor lasts until the cervix is completely dilated. It usually begins with faint contractions that grow stronger and more frequent. In the second stage of labor, the fetus passes head first through the birth canal and is born, a process that lasts approximately eighty minutes for first-born children. After birth the attendant cleans the baby's nose and mouth with a suction apparatus to make breathing easier and to prevent substances from entering the lungs. Then the umbilical cord is tied and cut. In the final stage of labor, uterine contractions expel the **afterbirth**—the placenta, its membranes, and the rest of the umbilical cord. This process lasts approximately five to twenty minutes, and the afterbirth is immediately examined by the attendant to determine whether it is complete and normal.

Not all deliveries proceed in this normal fashion. In a breech delivery, the baby's buttocks appear first, then the legs, and finally the head. Such deliveries can be dangerous because the baby may suffocate before the head emerges. If the mother's pelvis is too small to permit her baby to pass through, the baby must be delivered surgically, by Caesarean section.

The newborn baby is assessed for appearance (color), heart rate, reflex irritability, activity, muscle tone, and respiratory effort to determine whether further medical help is needed. A much-used and practical scoring system for assessing these attributes is known as the **Apgar score** (Apgar and James, 1962). Each of the characteristics is rated 0, 1, or 2 (2 being best), and these scores are added to constitute the baby's Apgar score, which may vary from 0 to 10. Most normal newborns achieve a score of 8 to 10 one minute after birth (Self and Horowitz, 1980).

Another widely used measure is the Brazelton Neonatal Behavioral Assessment Scale (Brazelton, 1973), which consists of approximately thirty tests that score the baby on twenty reflexes and twenty-seven kinds of behavior, including alertness, cuddliness, motor maturity, and responses to stress and to environmental stimuli. The Brazelton scale is more complicated than the Apgar and is not routinely administered, but it allows researchers to measure behavior within the first days of life that previously could not be assessed until babies were older.

Methods of Childbirth

Over the past few decades, American methods of childbirth have undergone dramatic change. At one time all labors were considered difficult and painful. In most American hospitals, drugs were routinely given, and episiotomies (surgical incisions to enlarge the vaginal orifice) and forceps were used to speed the birth process. Such practices were considered the best possible way to care for mothers and babies. But a growing number of parents and medical personnel began to question these procedures (Hahn and Paige, 1980), and their dissatisfaction seemed to be supported by evidence from other cultures.

Anthropologists reported that childbirth varied dramatically around the world and that in cultures that regarded birth as something to be hidden, women often had prolonged and difficult labors. On the other hand, in cultures that regarded birth as an open, easy process, women generally had short, uncomplicated labors (Mead and Newton, 1967).

Grantly Dick-Read (1944), a British physician who had noticed that some of his patients found childbirth a relatively peaceful, painless experience, believed fear generated a tension that produced pain among most women. His urging of what he called "natural childbirth" met with some success, and his techniques, combined

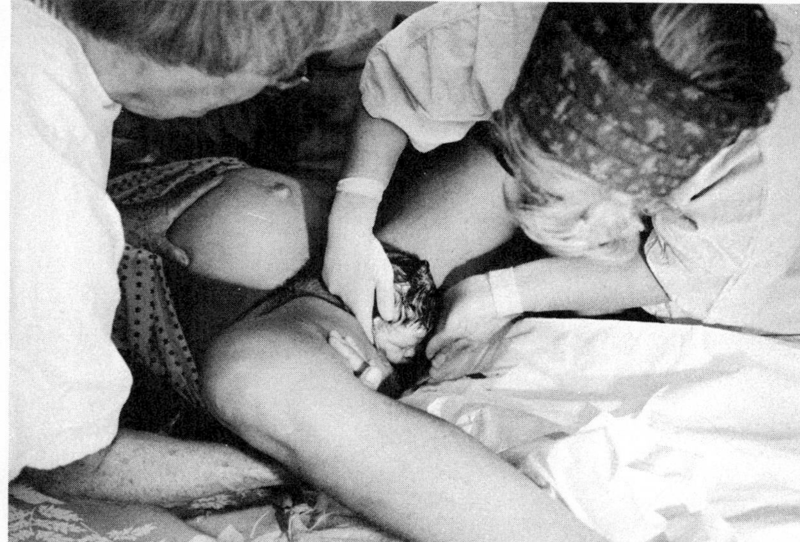

Many young mothers, convinced that a hospital atmosphere is impersonal and unnatural, are having their babies at home. A trained midwife delivers this baby, a custom that is common in the Netherlands, where about half of all babies are born at home. *(© Joel Gordon)*

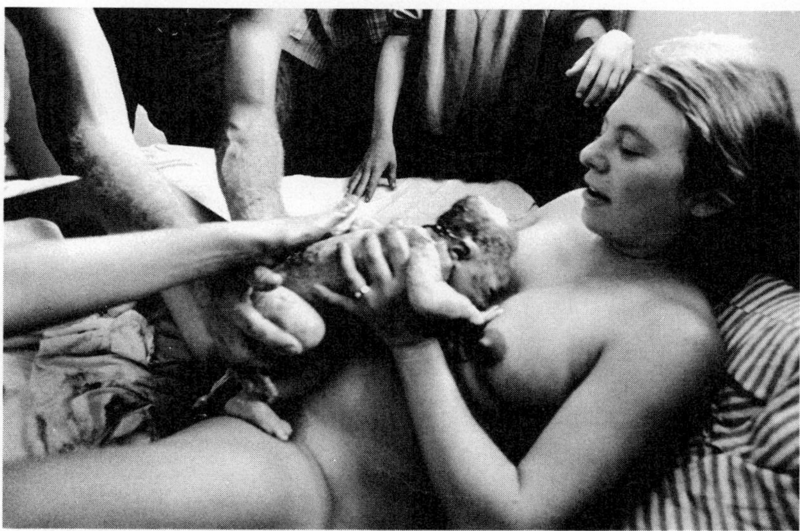

In this home birth, the newborn infant is placed in the mother's arms before the umbilical cord is cut. *(Suzanne Arms/Jeroboam)*

with the more recently introduced Lamaze method, have brought about changes in the way many obstetricians handle childbirth. In the Lamaze method, women learn to substitute new responses for learned responses of pain and, by concentrating on breathing, try to inhibit painful sensations (Chabon, 1966). Another feature of this method is a "coach," whose presence during labor provides psychological encouragement.

The rising popularity of the Lamaze method has gradually led many American hospitals to change their procedures. In most cities, a husband may accompany his wife into the delivery room, where he can offer her emotional support and can participate in the birth process. Further, some of the routine hospital customs, from

In the Lamaze method of childbirth, women learn exercises meant to help them have a more natural and less painful delivery. *(© Michael Weisbrot & Family)*

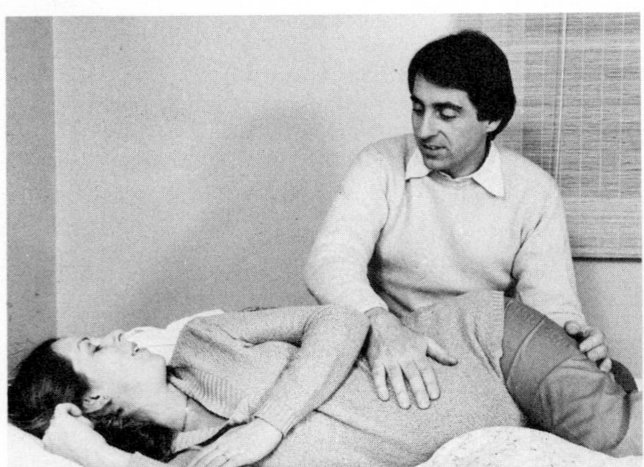

Many fathers are taking an active role in the births of their children. This woman, who is in the early stage of labor, will receive encouragement and emotional support from her husband throughout labor and delivery. *(© Karen Keeney 1981/Woodfin Camp & Assoc.)*

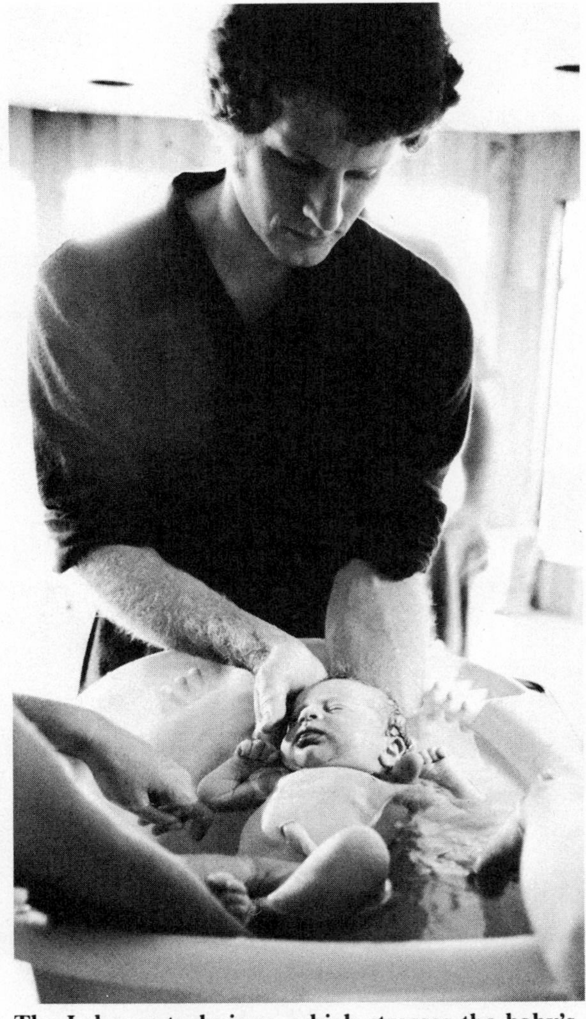

The Leboyer technique, which stresses the baby's emotional wellbeing, calls for an immediate bath in warm water, which is like the amniotic fluid of the uterine environment. *(Suzanne Arms/Jeroboam)*

automatic medication to episiotomy, that tend to make birth an abnormal and unpleasant procedure, have been eliminated for normal deliveries in a number of hospitals. The medical profession has come to realize that all family members benefit from sharing the experience of childbirth and has urged a more homelike hospital atmosphere, the presence of the father, a bed that allows the mother to be placed in a semisitting position, an opportunity for mother, father and infant to be together after delivery, and the encouragement of breast feeding (Interprofessional Task Force, 1978).

Frederick Leboyer (1975), a French obstetrician, has taken the psychological approach to childbirth a step further. He focuses on the emotions and sensations of the baby, urging peace and quiet, dim lights, delay in severing the umbilical cord, body contact for newborns, and an immediate bath in warm water that approximates the conditions within the womb. Leboyer contrasts the traditional picture of a screaming newborn held upside down by its ankles with the smiling, bright-eyed, contented infants delivered by his method.

FETAL ABNORMALITIES AND BIRTH COMPLICATIONS

Most pregnancies follow a normal course of development and most babies are normal and healthy. On occasion, however, a genetic abnormality or an environmental factor will affect the developing fetus. Some of the resulting defects are minor, some respond to medical or surgical intervention, and others are so serious that they threaten the life of the baby. By using the techniques described in the accompanying box, many serious abnormalities can be discovered before birth.

Chromosomal Abnormalities

When a cell divides to form a gamete, the process may go wrong. During meiosis, a pair of chromosomes may fail to separate, so that one of the gametes has one chromosome too many and the other lacks a chromosome. If the missing chromosome is a sex chromosome, the fertilized egg may live to develop into a baby that suffers from **Turner's syndrome.** Such girls tend to have short stature, a webbing or shortening of the neck, a broad-bridged nose, low-set ears, and short, chubby fingers. They generally lack secondary sex characteristics and may have mild to moderate mental retardation.

The cell with an extra chromosome may produce a person with an abnormal number of chromosomes in all his or her cells. Each of the twenty-three pairs of chromosomes has been numbered by researchers. If the fertilized egg has an extra Chromosome 21 (three instead of two), the egg will develop into a baby who suffers from **Down's syndrome** (formerly called mongolism). These children tend to be short and stocky and to have a broad nose bridge, a large, protruding tongue, an open mouth, square-shaped ears, a broad, short neck with extra, loose skin over the nape, and large folds of skin above the eyes that give the child an "oriental" appearance. These children frequently have congenital heart disease and other problems and often do not live past the teens. They have moderate to severe mental retardation, although the extent of retardation varies considerably from case to case.

Although Down's syndrome is generally caused by an extra chromosome, sometimes it is not. In these cases, which are extremely rare, the disorder develops when extra material from Chromosome 21 becomes attached to another chromosome. This tendency is inherited. Most cases of Down's syndrome arise when an error in cell division produces an offspring with an extra Chromosome 21, a genetic make-up unlike that of either parent. This tendency is not inherited. It had always been assumed that the extra chromosome came from a faulty cell division within the egg. But today it is possible to stain and compare chromosomes. And when such comparisons between parents and children have been made, about one-fourth of the cases of Down's syndrome have been traced to faulty cell division in the sperm (Holmes, 1978). The presumption that a defective egg was always responsible may be due to the fact that the likelihood of producing children with Down's syndrome through an error in cell division increases as the mother ages.

Some studies show that the risk of producing a child with Down's syndrome is only about 1 in 2,500 for mothers less than twenty years old, 1 in 1,900 for mothers twenty-five to twenty-nine years old, and 1 in 1,000 for mothers thirty to thirty-four years of age; but the ratio rises to about 1 in 100 for mothers forty to forty-four years old and 1 in 50 for forty-five-year-old mothers (Frias, 1975). But older mothers are generally married to older men, and older men may produce faulty sperm. Other abnormalities also occur more frequently in children born to older parents, which is the reason most geneticists encourage parents to have their children before the mother reaches forty.

Prematurity

A historical problem in dealing with the subject of the premature baby is the definition of that term. Years ago, "premature" simply referred to the baby that was born before **term,** a **gestational age** of 266 days from conception. This definition proved to be inadequate, because some early babies were of normal weight and health. Moreover, some babies born late had serious weight deficiencies and reduced abilities to survive. As a result, the definition of prematurity came to be made in terms of birth weight. Newborn babies who weighed less than about 5½ pounds at birth, regardless of their gestational age, were simply labeled "low birth weight" and considered premature. This criterion has also proved to be inadequate, because some newborns who weigh less than five and one-half pounds may be less than full term but may otherwise be perfectly normal.

Some babies are simply born small. For example, a baby may weigh only two pounds. If this baby was born substantially before term, the young gestational age would explain the small size. Given proper premature infant care, the baby may show an accelerated "catch-up growth" once the weight of five pounds is reached. (Catch-up growth is discussed in greater detail in Chapter 6.) By three years of

The life-support system of a premature infant.
(© David Hurn/Magnum)

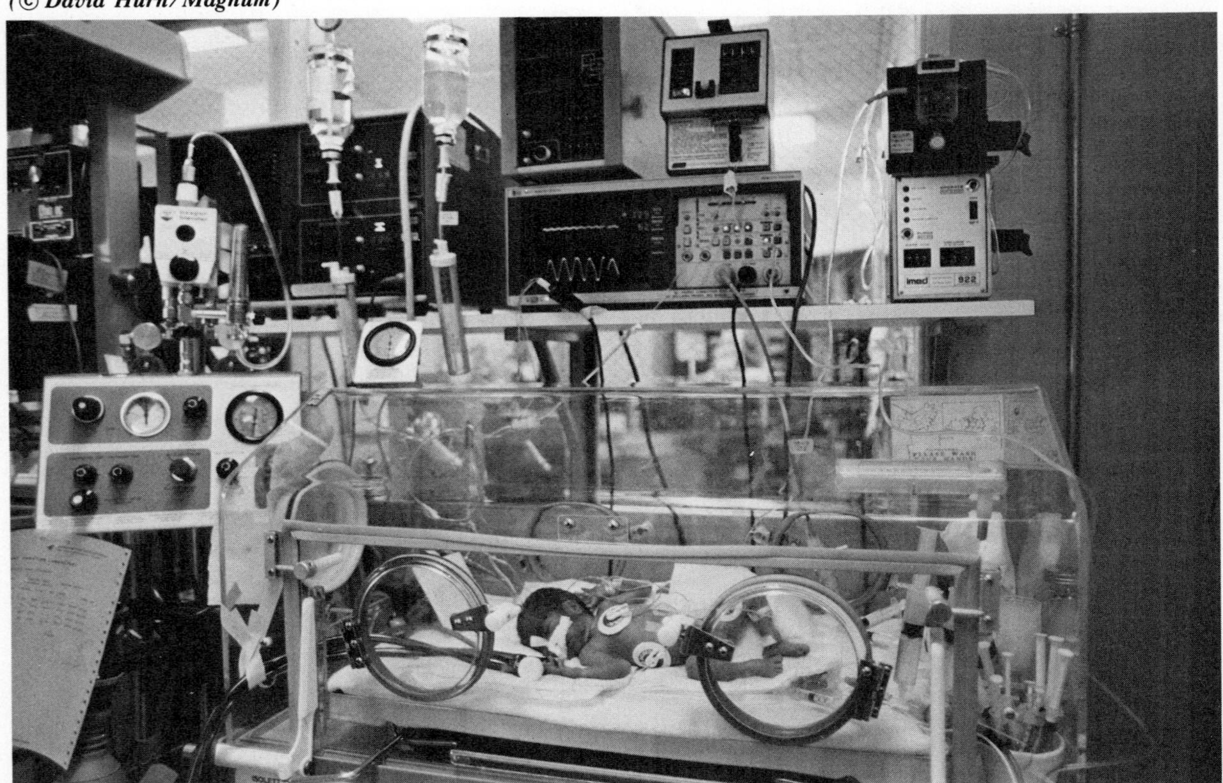

age, this child may be at average height and weight. In contrast, consider a baby who has spent the full 266 days in the womb but weighs only two pounds at birth. Such a baby, who is underweight for gestational age, is called **small-for-dates.** It is likely that some aspect of development has gone awry and has inhibited fetal growth. Also this baby is likely to have physical problems. Whatever circumstance kept him or her from gaining weight as a fetus seems to inhibit catch-up growth. A small-for-dates infant often grows into a relatively short and light preschooler (Cruise, 1973).

Maternal Health

Although the environment within the uterus is usually stable, it is not immune to agents that can alter or kill the developing organism (see Table 4.1). Such agents are called **teratogens,** and they cause physical defects ranging from minor abnormalities such as stained tooth enamel (caused by the antibiotic tetracycline) to gross deformities or even death (caused by the sedative thalidomide). When the mother is exposed to excessive X-rays or other radiation, especially in the first few months of pregnancy, the fetus may be in danger of malformation. Deficient secretion of certain hormones from the mother's endocrine glands may affect fetal development, and the incompatibility of an inherited blood substance (the Rh factor) between mother and child can, if not detected, result in premature labor, mental retardation, or heart defects. Medication taken by the mother, her consumption of food contaminated by lead or mercury, and nutrition are among the factors that can affect the fetus.

Even when the extent of fetal exposure to a destructive influence is known, however, there is no way to predict the influence it will have on the developing fetus. Timing is apparently a crucial factor in determining whether an environmental influence will produce an abnormality. If some destructive agent is introduced at the time an organ is forming, that organ may never develop properly. However, the agent may have less serious effects—or no effect at all—on organs already formed or on those that are not yet ready to make their appearance. Most of the basic organ systems develop in the first third, or **trimester,** of pregnancy, so that problems in maternal health are likely to have a greater impact on the fetus at this time than later. In addition to timing and dosage, the genetic susceptibility of the fetus and the mother's physical condition can reduce or exaggerate the likelihood of malformation (Tuchman-Duplessis, 1975).

Disease If a pregnant woman contracts **rubella** (German measles) during the first trimester, the disease may cause such abnormalities in the developing fetus as blindness, deafness, brain damage, and heart disease. Fortunately, not all babies born to mothers who have suffered from rubella are abnormal, but the earlier the mother catches the disease, the more likely it is that her baby will be affected. A study by Richard Michaels and Gilbert Mellin (1960) indicates that 47 percent of the babies born to mothers who had rubella during the first month of pregnancy were abnormal, whereas 22 percent of babies whose mothers had the disease in the second month and 7 percent of those whose mothers contracted it in the third month were seriously affected.

Other diseases in the mother can also have unfortunate consequences for the fetus. Two that are approaching epidemic proportions in the American adult population are **syphilis** and **gonorrhea.** Although the placenta manages to screen a good many of the organisms that cause syphilis, some make their way from the mother's blood through the placenta, transmitting the disease to the fetus. Therefore, if a pregnant woman is in only the first or second stage of syphilis, with symptoms of chancres, rash, or fever, and if she receives treatment, her baby is likely to be born without ill effects. But if she remains untreated or if she is in a more severe stage of the disease, the baby may be born with congenital syphilis. If the mother has a mild case of the disease, her baby may have a rash, anemia, jaundice, or other mild problems, but if she is seriously infected, her baby may suffer a wide variety of debilitating and severe abnormalities.

TABLE 4.1
SOME SUBSTANCES THAT MAY HARM THE FETUS*

Danger Established	*Danger Suspected*	*Possible Danger*
(Definite evidence of harm)	*(Appear to increase the chances of death or disability)*	*(Animal data are suggestive, but human data are limited)*
Alcohol	Anesthetic gases	Caffeine
Antibiotics (some)	Narcotics	Carbon disulfide
Antitumor drugs	Appetite depressants that work on the nervous system	Chlordane
Cadmium	Anticonvulsive drugs (Dilatin)	Insulin
DES	Quinine	Lithium
Lead	Drugs for heart disease or high blood pressure (thiazides, reserpine)	Aspirin
Mercury		Tranquilizers (Valium, Librium, Meprobamate, phenothyazines)
Oral contraceptives		
Cigarettes		
Thalidomide		

*This sampling from the growing list of harmful substances reinforces the wisdom of the obstetrician's advice to take as little medication during pregnancy as possible.

Adapted from S. G. Babson, M. L. Pernoll, G. I. Benda, and K. Simpson, *Diagnosis and Management of the Fetus and Neonate at Risk: A Guide for Team Care,* 4th ed. (St. Louis: C.V. Mosby, 1980), pp. 26–27.

As the fetus moves down the birth canal, it can come into contact with the **gonococcus,** the bacterium that produces gonorrhea. A number of years ago, many babies became blind when their eyes were infected during the birth process. Because many women have gonorrhea without showing any symptoms, it has become common practice to place drops of silver nitrate or penicillin in the eyes of all newborn babies. The practice has almost wiped out this kind of blindness.

The prospects are less hopeful for a **genital herpes simplex** infection, which represents a real danger for a fetus that picks up the virus while moving down the birth canal. Since the incubation period for this virus is from four to twenty-one days, infected babies may not show any symptoms until after they go home from the hospital. Up to half the babies born to mothers with a genital herpes infection contract the disease, and only about half of them survive it (Babson et al., 1980).

Maternal Sensitization Human blood comes in many types. Most are not compatible, which is why a doctor who administers a transfusion always makes sure that a person receives blood that matches his or her own. Generally, no serious incompatibility exists between a mother and her baby, because blood types are transmitted according to the genetic principles discussed earlier. However, in about 1 in 200 births, there will be a crucial difference in the Rh factor of the blood of the mother and her baby.

If the mother is Rh negative and the father is Rh positive, their child may be born with the dominant Rh-positive factor. Because the mother's and baby's blood circulations are kept separate by the placental barrier, only slight mixing occurs during pregnancy, and the first baby is born without problem. But during birth, when the membranes of the placenta are ruptured, there is an increased mingling of blood, and the mother may become sensitized to the Rh-positive factor in the baby's blood. If this couple has another baby and that baby is also Rh positive, it may suffer serious complications. In less than 10 percent of such cases, the fetus develops what is called **erythroblastosis.** In these pregnancies, when fetal red blood cells enter the mother's circulation, her sensitized immune system produces substances that cross the placenta, enter the baby's circulatory system, and begin destroy-

DETECTING COMPLICATIONS

Many factors, from drugs taken by the mother during pregnancy to chromosomal abnormalities, can affect the normal development of the fetus. Some years ago, it was not until a child was born that abnormalities or potentially fatal diseases could be detected, and by that time it was too late to take preventive action. However, gross abnormalities in fetal development can now be discovered early in pregnancy by the use of ultrasound.

In an ultrasound examination, sound is bounced off the fetus, and the echoes are transformed into thousands of dots that appear on a screen. The dots form a picture, called a **sonogram,** which shows details of the fetus, the amniotic fluid, and the placenta. Sonograms can find visible abnormalities, resolve confusion over the age of the fetus, and discover such conditions as a placenta that is blocking the birth canal or the presence of more than one fetus.

Ultrasound is often used as a guide in performing another procedure that detects chromosomal abnormalities. In this procedure, which is called **amniocentesis,** the physician inserts a hollow needle through the maternal abdomen and draws out a sample of amniotic fluid. Amniocentesis should be done sometime between the fourteenth and sixteenth week after conception.

The fetus sheds cells into the amniotic fluid, and if the fetal cells in the sample of this fluid are grown in a culture, technicians can perform chromosomal analyses that will detect abnormalities such as Down's syndrome, Turner's syndrome, and others. The chemical composition of the amniotic fluid also frequently provides clues to other diseases and reveals whether the fetus can produce enough surfactin to avoid respiratory distress when it is born. In addition, tests can detect the blood group and sex of the fetus. However, the process carries a slight risk for the fetus and is not used routinely.

ing its developing red blood cells, causing it to become anemic and lack oxygen and nutritional supplies. Sometimes the baby is stillborn. If it survives, such a baby may become mentally retarded or have cerebral palsy. This condition can occur in a first pregnancy if the mother has been sensitized to the Rh-positive factor by a previous transfusion of Rh-positive blood.

At one time, it was necessary to monitor the Rh-negative mother's blood throughout pregnancy and, if she began to show signs of incompatibility, to be prepared to exchange completely the newborn baby's blood by means of massive transfusions. Fortunately, there is now a relatively simple treatment for Rh incompatibility. The Rh-negative mother is given an injection soon after the delivery of each Rh-positive child, stopping the formation of immune substances in her blood and making her body safe for the development of her next Rh-positive baby (Freda et al., 1975). Similar injections must be given after an abortion when there is Rh incompatibility.

Should the injection be omitted, the presence of erythroblastosis can be detected by amniocentesis, a procedure described in the accompanying box. In such cases, blood compatible with that of the mother can be transfused into the umbilical vein of the fetus, which generally results in the delivery of a living but probably very sick baby.

Nutrition Almost all vitamins, minerals, and nutrients are transported to the fetus through the placenta. The fetus stores none of these necessary substances against the time of its independent existence except iron. Consequently, the nutritional state of the mother, especially during the first trimester, appears to be important for normal development.

Severely deficient maternal diets are associated with increased rates of abnormality (Robinson and Robinson, 1965). Diets deficient in calcium, phosphorus, and vitamins B, C, and D are associated with higher frequencies of malformed fetuses. During the German occupation of the Netherlands in the 1940s, when food became extremely scarce, the rate of stillbirths and premature births increased among Dutch women, and the birth weight and birth length of their babies decreased. After the war, when food again became plentiful, these rates returned to normal (C. Smith, 1947). Additional data supporting the importance of adequate prenatal nutrition for fetal development come from depressed areas of the United States and from other countries where individuals customarily exist on relatively poor diets. In these regions, dietary supplements (both protein and calories) have led to improved maternal health, higher infant birth weight, and reduced levels of disease and death among infants (Pitkin, 1976).

A review of the findings on maternal nutrition clearly shows that a poor maternal diet can be dangerous to normal prenatal development, but it is less clear how serious and widespread the effects of minor deficiencies in the mother's diet are on the developing fetus. However, there are many indications that maternal and fetal well-being may be affected by less than adequate nutrition.

Drugs and Smoking A golden rule of obstetric practice has been to advise women to take as little medication during pregnancy as possible. Even aspirin has become suspect, and some authorities (e.g., Babson et al., 1980) believe it can lengthen pregnancy and lead to bleeding in the newborn infant.

Sometimes drugs given to maintain a pregnancy can affect the developing fetus. Diethylstilbestrol (DES), for example, a synthetic hormone that was widely prescribed from the 1940s until about 1970, has been associated with vaginal cancer in women whose mothers received the drug. And prednisone, a drug prescribed for infertility, for the subsequent maintenance of pregnancy, and for such unrelated conditions as asthma or arthritis, has been associated with significantly reduced birth weights in full-term babies (Reinisch et al., 1979).

Heroin use creates an added problem. The newborn infant of a heroin or methadone user must often go through withdrawal, because both drugs pass through the placenta. Such babies have sharply increased reflex responses and tremors; they are irritable, their sleep is disturbed, and they cry a great deal. Many of them are also small-for-dates; they eat voraciously but do not gain weight. When they are older, many are restless, find it difficult to sit still, and have short attention spans (Kolata, 1978).

Several years ago a small group of pediatricians in the United States and Europe noticed that babies born to alcoholic mothers often suffered from what has become known as **fetal alcohol syndrome.** Studies in many countries have shown that babies born to alcoholic mothers may be small-for-dates, have an odd, conical-shaped head and characteristic facial features, and be mentally retarded. Occasionally these infants have cleft palates, heart murmurs, hernias, kidney damage, and eye or skeletal defects (Streissguth et al., 1980). But a mother need not be an alcoholic for her baby to be affected. Infants born to heavy social drinkers may be small-for-dates, have abnormal heart rates, low Apgar scores, suck weakly, and perform poorly on tests of newborn behavior. Heavy drinkers also have about three times as many stillbirths as light drinkers. Not all these effects may be the result of alcohol by itself, because heavy drinkers often smoke, use both prescription and nonprescription drugs, and eat unwisely. As yet, no adverse effects have been found among women who take less than two drinks each day, but animal research indicates that even moderate consumption of alcohol may result in malformation (Chernoff, 1977).

The smoking of cigarettes can also affect the fetus. In pregnant women who normally do not smoke, it produces an increase in fetal heart rate. Nicotine, tar, and carbon monoxide appear to be the noxious influences, and smoking seems to reduce the capacity of the blood to carry oxygen. Heavy smokers tend to miscarry more often than nonsmokers, to have smaller, lighter babies, and to have significantly more low-birth-weight babies (Babson et al., 1980).

Some physicians have become reluctant to administer pain-relieving drugs to women in labor because a number of studies have found that such medication can produce lingering effects on babies' behavior. Yvonne Brackbill's (1979) review of more than thirty studies revealed that in twenty of them, drugs had substantial effects on a baby's behavior, in nine there were significant but less substantial effects, and in only two did the effects seem negligible. In most of these studies, the drugged babies performed poorly on standard tests of infant behavior as compared with babies whose mothers received no drugs.

Emotional Condition Because stress alters maternal hormone production, it also alters the fetal environment. Thus, it is not far-fetched to suspect that a woman who is pregnant and under considerable emotional stress is likely to produce a newborn baby that is in some way affected by her emotional situation. The effect of maternal emotions has often been a subject of folklore.

Some scientific investigations have suggested that the mother's emotional state can indeed influence her offspring. A number of researchers have demonstrated that stressful experiences in human and rat mothers during pregnancy affect the activity level, birth weight, heart rate, motor development, and emotionality of their offspring (Joffe, 1965; Thompson, 1957). When mothers are under intense, brief emotional stress, their babies' movements increase for only a short time, but when mothers undergo long-standing emotional stress, their babies' activity is greatly prolonged and may reach ten times the normal level (Sontag, 1966).

Abortion Sometimes pregnancies are terminated, and the developing organism is expelled or removed from the uterus. If this happens spontaneously and without deliberate interference on the part of the mother or a physician, it is called a **miscarriage** or **spontaneous abortion** when the fetus is less than twenty weeks old and a **premature delivery** if the fetus is older. It has long been believed that miscarriages and spontaneous abortions are nature's way of eliminating an abnormal fetus, and that such an event, although sad, should be viewed as a blessing. Science supports this notion; examinations of spontaneously aborted fetuses indicate a much higher rate of abnormalities than are found among normal, live births.

There is some evidence that male fetuses are spontaneously aborted more often than female fetuses. Although it is difficult to make such estimates, it is believed that approximately 130 to 150 males are conceived for every 100 females, but only about 106 males are born for every 100 females (Beatty and Gluecksohn-Waelsch, 1972). Consequently, it would appear that the prenatal death rate is higher for males than for females, a proposition that squares with the fact that following birth, females resist infection better, survive the infancy period more often, and live longer than males do (Fryer and Ashford, 1972).

Since the United States Supreme Court upheld the right of abortion, legal **induced abortions** have been more frequent. Physicians prefer to abort a fetus before it is twelve weeks old, because it is then a relatively simple procedure involving the use of suction to remove the embryo or fetus, together with the uterine lining that sloughs off during a normal menstrual period. From twelve to twenty weeks, an abortion usually requires injecting a substance into the amniotic fluid surrounding the fetus so as to make the uterus contract. This is a more difficult procedure and carries a greater risk to the mother. After twenty weeks, induced abortion is no longer advisable because there is a chance of delivering a baby who has a remote possibility of surviving.

The decision to have an abortion, especially when the life or health of the mother is in no danger, often presents complicated legal, psychological, social, and moral problems. From society's point of view, one important legal question is whether a fetus has a right to be born, and if so, at what point in its development this right begins. Another important question is whether a woman has the right to determine how many children she will bear and when she will bear them. These issues are the focus of passionate debate and personal conflict.

In spite of all the possible complications of

the prenatal period set forth in this chapter, most babies come into the world as normal individuals. As a baby emerges from the dark of the uterus, the most intimate human relationship ends. Within the womb, a child is completely dependent on the mother for the automatic satisfaction of every need. At birth, the baby starts life as a separate individual. In the next chapter, we will look at the beginnings of independent life—the world of the newborn child.

SUMMARY

1. A person's development begins at the moment of conception, when the father's sperm cell, or spermatozoon, unites with the mother's egg, or ovum. These gametes each have twenty-three single chromosomes composed of genes, which make possible the genetic transmission of traits and predispositions from parents to their offspring.

2. The complex processes of genetic combination determine the offspring's genotype, the unique combination of genes that the child carries. The phenotype, or physical expression of those genes, is often different from the genotype because some genes are dominant and some are recessive. The inherited metabolic abnormality called PKU appears when two genes for the trait are paired. When only one PKU gene is present, the dominant normal gene masks the recessive gene for PKU.

3. During a 266-day gestation period, the organism rapidly progresses from a fertilized egg engaged in cell division (germinal period) to an embryo with organ systems beginning to take shape (embryonic period) to a fetus that increasingly resembles a human being (fetal period).

3. The central nervous system starts as a cluster of cells; it develops rapidly, and by twenty weeks all the neurons that make up the adult brain have formed. Behavioral development corresponds to development of the fetal nervous system and muscles. At eight weeks, the fetus is capable of movement; and by twenty-eight weeks, a rudimentary kind of learning. Twenty-five weeks is the minimum possible age at which a fetus may be able to survive outside the uterus.

4. Birth begins with labor, in which strong uterine contractions push the infant and the afterbirth through the birth canal. The attendant then evaluates the baby's appearance and functioning. The experience of childbirth varies dramatically around the world; the popularity of natural methods of childbirth has led to changes in the way American hospitals manage birth.

6. Complications occasionally occur in prenatal development and birth. Chromosomal abnormalities that occur during meiosis (detectable by a process called amniocentesis) can result in a missing or extra chromosome, which often creates physical abnormalities. In prematurity, the small-for-dates baby, who at birth is underweight for gestational age, is the potential problem baby.

7. Maternal health problems—including diseases, poor nutrition, use of drugs, and emotional stress—can also complicate prenatal development, depending on timing, dosage, and genetic susceptibility. Pregnancies are sometimes terminated through the natural process of miscarriage (spontaneous abortion) or by a legal induced abortion—a topic that has become the focus of heated debate.

5 THE NEWBORN'S WORLD

A newborn baby is a curious mixture of competence and incapacity. All vital organs are formed and functional. Unlike the newborn kitten or puppy, a baby's eyes are open. Babies can see and hear and smell; they can cry and feed and move their limbs. The evolution of the species, the genetic mixture presented by their parents, and experiences in the womb have already begun to shape infant development and behavior.

Yet until recently, other ideas dominated thought about the human newborn. One was championed by John Locke (1690), who proposed that a newborn baby comes into the world nearly devoid of behavioral dispositions and that the child accumulates all mental abilities and personality through learning and experience. Many years later, the American psychologist William James (1890) supposed that the world must appear terribly chaotic to such a naive baby, "assailed by eyes, ears, nose, skin, and entrails at once, [who] feels it all as one great booming, buzzing confusion. . . ." These scholars emphasized the helplessness of the human newborn, who in their view possessed almost no structure or functions to deal with a new environment and waited passively for the environment to fill an unmarked psychological notebook with the marks of social and mental experiences.

In the last two decades there has been considerable scientific interest in the psychological world of the human newborn. The evidence suggests that Locke and James were wrong. In this chapter we will see that babies enter the world possessing a variety of functions and skills to cope with their environment and sample its character. It will become plain that newborns are not passive sponges that soak up the events taking place around them; instead, they are active, searching, dynamic forces who seem to create much of their own experience.

We will discover that although newborn babies spend most of their time asleep, their bodies are remarkably prepared for life outside the womb. We will find that many of their basic body functions, such as sleeping and waking, hunger and thirst, sucking, and body temperature, are kept in balance according to rhythmic biological schedules. Various studies will demonstrate their possession of a set of reflexes, many of which they will lose in a few weeks, that help them accomplish the tasks of feeding and coping with this strange environment. We will look at newborns' sense organs and find that most of them are functional, or soon will be, and that they use them in an active and selective search of their environment. As we will discover, newborn babies are capable of learning, and each possesses the rudiments of a unique personality and temperament. Finally, we will see how the way they look and listen or the way they quiet when upset may provide the roots for their differing social development.

The technical term for a newborn baby is **neonate,** a word derived from Greek and Latin terms meaning newborn. Although some researchers would limit the neonatal period to the first week of life and others would limit it to the first two weeks, most agree that we can refer to a baby as a neonate until the end of his or her first month of independent life (Pratt, 1954).

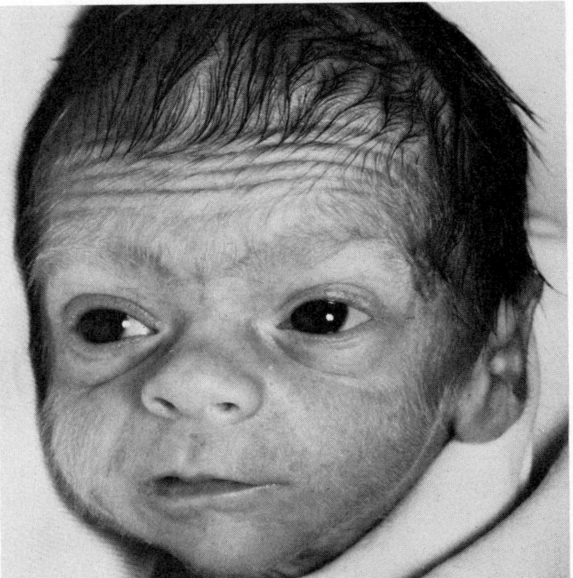

A normal premature baby, showing lanugo hair on the face and illustrating the shape and proportion of facial features characteristic of most newborns. ***(A. K. Tunstill)***

THE NEWBORN

To most of us, the thought of a little baby brings to mind images of a warm, roly-poly, cuddly, cooing bundle of softness and joy. Although this characterization will be apt in a few weeks, the sight of the newborn baby sometimes disappoints, if not shocks, parents. Although most parents regard their own babies as beautiful, outsiders often disagree. One of America's earliest child psychologists, G. Stanley Hall (1891), described the neonate as arriving with its "monotonous and dismal cry, with its red, shriveled, parboiled skin . . . , squinting, cross eyed, pot bellied, and bow legged. . . ." Others have likened the physical appearance of newborns to that of a defeated prize fighter—swollen eyelids, puffy bluish-red skin, a broad, flat nose, ears matted back at weird angles, and so forth. Of course, if one considers the wet, cramped quarters of the uterus and the violent thrusting necessary for the baby's delivery, this ragged appearance is not surprising.

At the moment of birth, newborns emerge blotched with their mother's blood and covered with a white greasy material called **vernix,** which has lubricated them for passage through the birth canal. Their puffy, wrinkled appearance derives in part from the presence of fluid and small pads of fat under the skin. Some newborns have fine hair, called **lanugo,** over parts of their body. When the baby emerges, the lanugo appears pasted to the skin by the greasy vernix, but after the infant is cleaned and dried, he or she may look quite furry for a few weeks until the lanugo disappears.

A newborn baby often looks somewhat battered. For example, the head may be oddly shaped or even peaked, a condition made possible by the fact that the "bones" of the skull are not yet hard and consist of overlapping pieces of

HELPING THE HIGH-RISK INFANT

Three to four out of every hundred babies are considered high-risk infants by physicians. More than half of these babies are either born long before their time and weigh less than three pounds five ounces, or they have severe respiratory distress (Babson et al., 1980). The two conditions often go together. These babies require intensive care in modern nurseries, where blood pressure, temperature, respiration, and heart rate can be continously monitored and where they can receive intravenous feedings of water and milk.

Many babies recover completely from such unpromising beginnings, but high-risk babies do face hazards of development. They are likely to be behind normal babies in mental and motor development. Although, by the time they are four years old, such babies may catch up with their peers, some continue to have problems with language and to show signs of neurological disability. In fact, about 15 percent of babies with birth weights of less than three pounds, five ounces suffer intellectual impairment (Kopp and Parmalee, 1979).

Part of the problem for very small babies may be lack of stimulation, and Susan Rose and her associates (1980) set out to see if remedying this situation would help close the behavioral gap between such babies and normal babies. For two weeks, Rose and her associates massaged tiny babies, spending twenty minutes, three times each day, stimulating a baby's head, shoulders, back, arms, hands, legs, and feet. Once the babies were strong enough to be removed from the incubators, the investigators changed the method of stimulation, holding the infants while rocking in a rocking chair. In addition to the physical stimulation, the investigators also talked to the babies and made eye-to-eye contact with them.

Just before the babies were discharged from the hospital, they—along with another group of babies of the same size and with similar medical histories—were tested after a midmorning feeding. The babies who had been massaged and rocked reacted more like a control group of normal babies, showing sharp accelerations in heart rate when suddenly touched on the abdomen during active sleep. The babies who had not been massaged showed little reaction when touched. The massaged babies also displayed greater behavioral responsiveness and responded more noticeably to sounds than did the babies who had not been massaged. What is more, on tests given six months later, the babies who had been massaged were better at recognizing stimuli they had previously seen than were the babies who had not been massaged.

Rose and her associates say that although sensory enrichment in the nursery improved the sensory functioning of these babies, it is not clear just how the improvement came about. Some cells in the central nervous system require environmental stimulation to develop, and Rose and her associates speculate that perhaps their intervention helped those neurons to develop. But whatever the mechanism, the extra stimulation and attention apparently helped the babies shake off part of the disadvantage that high-risk infants must overcome.

cartilage. This condition allows the head to compress so that the baby can emerge through the mother's pelvis. As a result, the head may be lumpy: hard in some places and soft in others. The soft areas at the crown of the head that lack cartilage frequently pulsate up and down as the blood supply is pumped about the brain. At the other end of the body, the legs are often bowed, and the feet may be pigeon-toed or even cocked at strange angles because the legs were tucked around the baby in the cramped quarters of the uterus.

Newborn babies may also sound strange. In the womb, they were suspended in liquid, and they arrive with nasal and oral passages filled with amniotic fluid and mucus. In Western hospitals, the physician cleans these passages with a suction bulb as soon as the baby's head has emerged from the uterus so that the newborn does not inhale this liquid into the lungs with the first gasping breath.

After the umbilical cord has been tied and cut, a nurse drops silver nitrate or penicillin into the newborn's eyes to prevent infection, makes simple tests for certain diseases and then swaddles the baby and allows the infant to sleep.

Although newborns will occasionally jerk or cough up mucus, their first sleep is usually quite deep. They are difficult to arouse, and even a loud sound may fail to elicit any obvious response. During this sleep, the body is preparing to function on its own. In the womb, the placenta linked the circulatory, digestive, temperature regulation, and excretory systems with those of the mother; but now the baby's own physiological equipment must take over these necessary functions. While these systems are being balanced and tuned, a baby frequently does not eat. Stores of fats and fluids tide the infant over until the first nourishment, which may take place within several hours of birth or may not occur for several days. As a result of this delay in feeding, most newborns lose weight during the first few days of life.

BASIC FUNCTIONS AND RHYTHMS

Fortunately, newborns are not thrust into the world without some mechanisms to keep their body systems in balance. A certain pattern or rhythm does characterize many of these basic body functions.

Temperature Regulation

The human being is a warm-blooded animal, which means that the body takes steps to keep its temperature within a certain range. In the newborn, temperature regulation is important because the functions performed by most cells and organs are governed by enzymes that can act only within a narrow range of temperature. If the baby's temperature is much lower than the optimum, several body functions might slow to dangerous levels. For example, the metabolic rate might decline so much that the infant dies. If body temperature is too high, the baby's physiological activity might be too rapid, triggering a mechanism that tends to shut down enzyme activity. Moreover, when newborns are too hot, they tend to breathe more rapidly, their blood becomes too acid, and several other biochemical and physiological systems are thrown out of balance. Consequently, it is essential that babies maintain a relatively constant temperature.

When adults become overheated, their metabolism slows, their blood vessels dilate so that more blood can go to the body surface, where heat is dissipated into the air, they sweat and lose heat through evaporation, and they pant and release heat by exhalation. Conversely, when adults are too cold, they conserve heat by shunting blood away from the surface of the body, where it would cool, and they may move around or shiver, thus generating heat.

The newborn baby, in contrast, has a problem. In proportion to body weight, the newborn has more surface area exposed to cool air and less insulating fat than an adult. Together these factors mean that a newborn loses heat almost four times as fast as an adult does (Brück, 1961). The newborn rapidly develops mechanisms to deal with this problem. Within fifteen minutes of birth, premature and full-term babies will respond to cold by constricting surface blood vessels and increasing their heat production. Two or three hours later, the newborn baby's metabolic response to cold is nearly as good as that of the adult, relative to the baby's body weight if not to body surface area. The problem is not that the newborn lacks the equipment to regulate body temperature but that the task is so great.

The efficiency of the newborn's temperature control is quickly put to the test in the first encounter with the hospital environment. The uterus generally remains at a constant 98.6°F., but the gaseous environment that greets the newborn is invariably colder: rarely over 80°F. and sometimes as low as 60°. Because babies are born wet, they lose considerable heat through

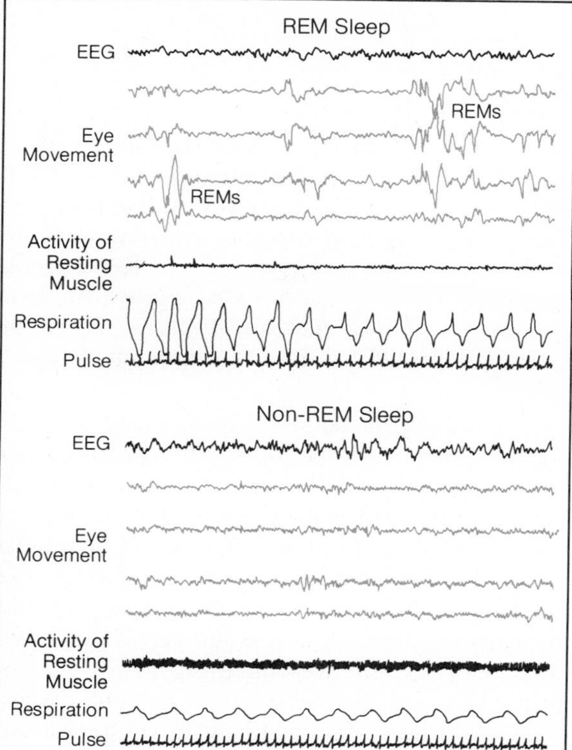

FIGURE 5.1 ***(top)*** **This baby is in a stabilimeter crib, which measures his muscular activity. The belt around his abdomen measures respiration, and the electrodes on his chest produce electrocardiographic records. When electroencephalographic recordings are made, electrodes are placed on the head and at the outer corners of the eyes. Although cumbersome, the apparatus is not uncomfortable for the baby.** ***(bottom)*** **Recordings showing the differences between thirty seconds of REM sleep and non-REM sleep in a newborn. Besides the heightened eye activity during REM sleep, note the absence of muscle activity, the rapid respiratory rate, and the changing respiratory amplitude.** ***(Photograph by Jason Lauré; chart after Roffwarg, Dement, and Fisher, 1967)***

evaporation and exposure of their skin to cool air. In fact, the drop in temperature may be so steep and rapid that the baby would have to produce twice as much heat energy per unit of body weight as the adult does in order to offset these conditions (Adamsons, 1966). Although many hospitals try to minimize this shock, life in the uterus remains considerably warmer than life in the delivery room or hospital nursery, and newborns need to be able to regulate their temperature to handle the transition. This is one reason that very small neonates often require a stay in the incubator.

Sleep Patterns

Newborn infants sleep a lot—approximately sixteen out of each twenty-four hours. Unfortunately for parents, most newborns package this sleep into seven or eight naps per day, with their longest single sleep averaging about four and one-half hours. Consequently, newborns are roughly on a four-hour sleep/wake cycle, sleeping a little less than three hours in each four. However, by six weeks, the naps have become longer, and babies take only two to four of them each day. Even the newborn sleeps a little more at night than during the day, and by approximately twenty-eight weeks most children sleep through the night without waking.

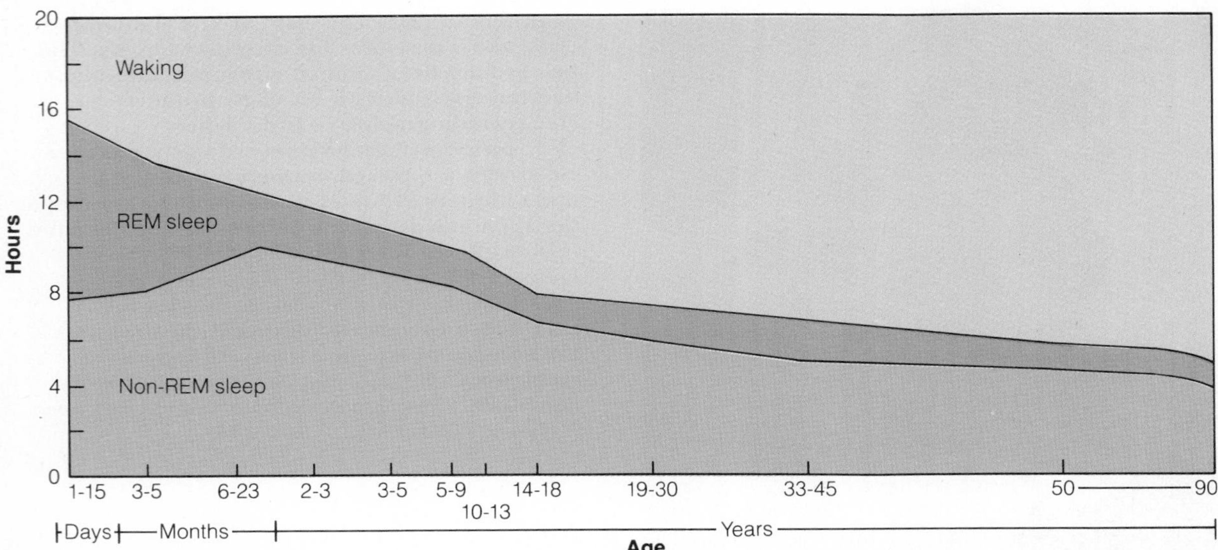

FIGURE 5.2 Proportion of REM/non-REM sleep over the life span. The proportion of REM sleep tends to decrease until about the age of five and then remains relatively constant. The proportion of non-REM sleep tends to increase during the first two years of life and then gradually decreases, in part because of the ongoing steady increase in waking time. The age scale used here is not proportionately true, and derived, approximate values are used for the age intervals. ***(After Roffwarg, Muzio, and Dement, 1966)***

In addition to differences in the amount and phases of sleep, the quality of the newborn's sleep is also different from that of the adult. There are two general kinds of sleep, distinguished principally by whether **rapid eye movement** (REM) occurs. During REM, or *active,* sleep, eye movements are accompanied by more rapid and changeable respiration, less muscular activity, and a more even pattern of brain waves. In Figure 5.1, the tube around the baby's stomach expands and contracts with each breath, the electrodes on the chest detect heart rate, and the stabilimeter that the baby lies on detects body movements. In addition, electrodes placed near the eyes detect eye movements, and other electrodes placed on the head record brain waves on an electroencephalograph (EEG). The minute electrical changes that accompany muscular movements are amplified and written by a polygraph on a continuously flowing sheet of paper.

Figure 5.2 shows that newborns spend almost half of their sixteen hours of sleep in REM sleep. Not until children are almost five years old does this proportion drop to approximately 20 percent, which is the adult average. The amount of non-REM, or *quiet,* sleep changes little over the childhood years, indicating that much of the newborn's extra sleep is composed of REM sleep.

What do the rapid eye movements of REM sleep signify? Adults awakened during REM sleep often report that they have been dreaming. Consequently, some people have supposed that newborn babies (and perhaps one's pet dog) dream during REM sleep. Physiologically, the REM sleep of neonates is nearly identical to that of dreaming adults, but it is unlikely that a newborn baby experiences anything like the integrated series of clear images that most adults do, especially when one considers the limited visual capability and experience of the newborn. But one cannot say that the neurological activity of REM sleep serves no purpose or is irrelevant to dreaming. Most adults whose REM sleep is interrupted become nervous and anxious, and have trouble concentrating (Dement, 1960), and they make up for the loss of REM sleep by showing a higher percentage of it in subsequent sleep periods. Some scientists have suggested that the brain requires periodic neural activity, either from external or internal sources, and that REM sleep signifies self-generated activity in the absence of any external stimulus (Roffwarg, Muzio, and Dement, 1966). Others suggest that REM sleep in newborns reflects either a high metabolic rate or neural immaturity (Berg and Berg, 1979). Because newborns sleep so much and have less opportunity to respond to events in the world around them, they may require more of this neurological self-stimulation. In one study, neonates who spent a good deal of their waking time looking attentively at stimuli afterward showed a temporary decrease in REM sleep (Boismier, 1977). Premature babies show even higher percentages of REM sleep than full-term infants do. It is possible that such activity is necessary before birth if neurological development is to occur. Therefore, the first function of REM sleep may be as an internal stimulus to neurological development; later it will carry the visual patterns and integrated experiences that constitute the dreams of older children and adults (Roffwarg, Muzio, and Dement, 1966).

Feeding Schedules

The newborn's sleep/wake cycle is closely tied to the need for nourishment. The typical neonate sleeps, wakes up hungry, eats, remains quietly alert for a short time, becomes drowsy, and then falls back to sleep.

Books advising parents often suggest a four-hour feeding schedule. The four-hour schedule may have emerged from a study in 1900 of three newborns who were fed a barium-milk solution and were X-rayed periodically after they swallowed it. The study showed that within four hours the stomach had emptied (Frank, 1966). Some years ago it was common practice to feed young babies on a strict schedule regardless of whether they appeared to be hungry. Parents even waked sleeping babies to feed them. Yet when babies are allowed to choose their own schedules, a regimen called self-demand feeding, they vary widely in the size and timing of their meals. When unrestricted breast feeding is practiced, in which babies are given the breast if they cry or fuss and allowed no other nourishment, they are likely to eat ten or more times a day in the first few weeks (Newton, 1979).

Unrestricted breast feeding is not common; most breastfed babies are given water, sweetened solutions, juices, and sometimes supplementary formula or baby foods. Infants who are fed this way and those who are entirely bottlefed generally eat less often. Anderson Aldrich and Edith Hewitt (1947) studied one hundred such babies who were allowed to establish their own feeding schedules during the first twelve months of life, and the resulting schedules are shown in Figure 5.3. At every age different babies demanded different numbers of meals. For example, during the first month of life, 60 percent of the babies ate every three hours, 26 percent ate every four hours, and approximately 10 percent demanded a feeding every two hours. Most newborns begin by putting themselves on a three-hour schedule and reach three meals a day by the time they are ten months old. Although all babies show some rhythm in their feeding patterns and all require progressively fewer daily feedings as they grow older, there are marked differences among babies in the frequency of their meals. Because of studies like this, parents are now encouraged to feed their babies whenever they are hungry while working toward fewer and fewer feedings as their babies grow.

Sucking Patterns

A basic rhythmical behavior that has been studied in great detail is the newborn's sucking. Being able to suck effectively is the foundation of feeding and therefore of survival. Consequently, it is one behavior that the newborn must perform competently and precisely.

The young baby sucks rhythmically, in bursts separated by pauses. On the average, a baby will put together approximately five to twenty-four sucks in a single burst, sucking at a rate of approximately one to two and one-half times each second, and then take a brief rest. Although a baby's hunger, age, health, and level of arousal influence the pattern of sucking, individual babies also have their own characteristic patterns of sucking. Whether particular sucking patterns are innate is unknown, because sucking at birth is affected by drugs that pass through the placenta during labor. Several days later, when these drugs have worn off, sucking patterns may already have been affected by the behavior of the baby's mother (Crook, 1979).

The neonate's feeding performance may be a little ragged during the first few days of life, but a baby quickly develops a fairly smooth coordination between sucking, swallowing, and breathing. The fact that a newborn can swallow almost three times faster than an adult and can suck at the same time he or she takes in air aids in the accomplishment of this feat. Adults who sucked in a liquid and breathed at the same time would probably choke. Babies can manage simultaneous sucking and breathing because they extract milk from the nipple by pressing the nipple against the roof of the mouth instead of by inhaling it.

REFLEXES

The reflexes of the newborn attracted the attention of neurophysiologists and pediatricians quite early, and their studies have provided us with an extensive catalog of reflexive behavior. The newborn comes equipped with a set of reflexes that are elicited by specific stimuli. Some are adaptive and may help the new baby feed or avoid danger. Others appear to be vestiges of the past, left over from our nonhuman ancestors. Still others are simple manifestations of neurological circuitry in the baby that will later come under voluntary control or will be integrated in more useful patterns of behavior. Most of these reflexes disappear within a few weeks or months, primarily as the result of neurological development, especially in the cortex of the brain (Minkowski, 1967). When these reflexes fail to drop out, it may be a sign of abnormal neurological development.

A number of the newborn's reflexes apparently played a role in the survival of the species. Babies close their eyes to bright light and twist their bodies or move their limbs away from sources of pain. A hungry baby whose palms are pressed will respond by sucking.

The Rooting Reflex

All babies have a rooting reflex—a tendency to turn the head and mouth in the direction of any object that gently stimulates the corner of the mouth. Babies are most likely to show this at about a week or two of age when they are quietly awake with their eyes open, especially if the infants are somewhat hungry. If one strokes the corner of the baby's mouth with an index finger, moving sideways from the mouth toward the cheek, the newborn may move tongue, mouth, or even the whole head toward the stimulated side. At first this reflex appears even when one strokes the cheek a long way from the mouth. As the baby gets older, the reflex appears only when the stimulation is at the mouth, and only the baby's mouth will respond. This reflex has obvious adaptive significance because it helps the baby place the nipple in the mouth. Babies sometimes learn to suck their thumbs while rooting.

Grasping and the Moro Reflex

A baby in the first few weeks of life has a strong **grasping reflex.** If one places a one-week-old baby on his or her back and inserts a finger into the baby's hand, the infant is likely to grasp it sturdily. Sometimes a grasping newborn can literally hang by one hand.

Ernst Moro (1918) first described the **Moro reflex,** which consists of a thrusting out of the arms in an embracelike movement when a baby suddenly loses support for both neck and head. It is easily seen after the first week when the baby

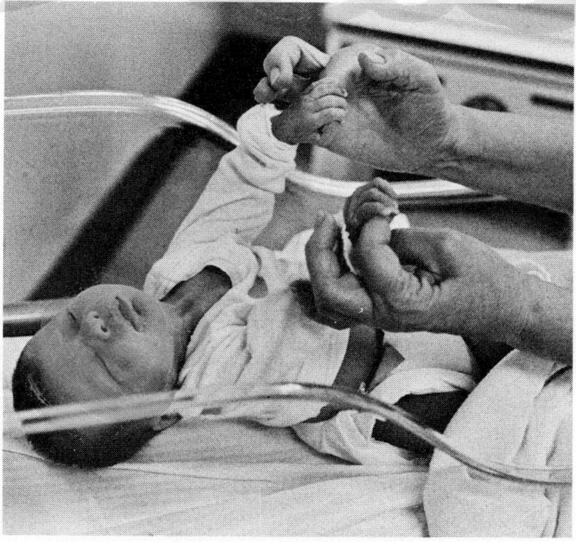

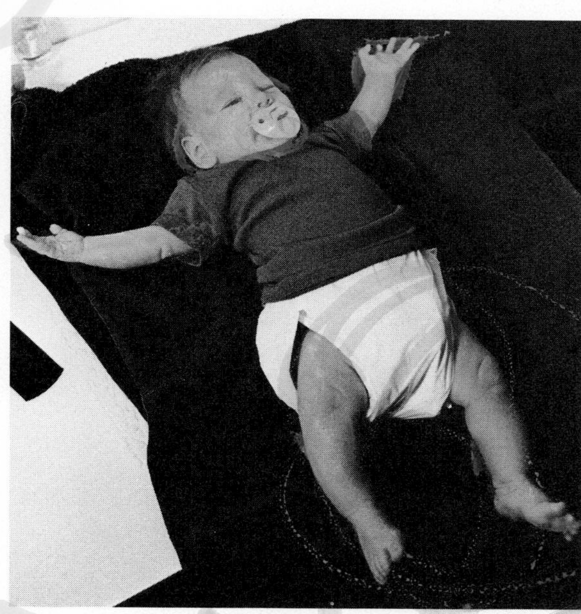

(left)* The grasping reflex. *(William MacDonald)
(right)* The Moro reflex. *(© Lawrence Frank 1981)

is alert with open or barely closed eyes. It can be elicited by holding the baby with one hand under the head and the other in the small of the back and then rapidly lowering one's hands, especially the hand holding the head, and then bringing them to an abrupt halt. A second way to obtain the Moro reflex is to lay the baby on his or her back with the head facing straight up and then slap the mattress behind the head with enough force to jerk the head and neck slightly. Typically, the arms shoot out and upward and the hands curl slightly as if preparing to grab something. In fact, if your finger is in a baby's hand when somebody else provides the stimulus for the Moro, you can feel the baby suddenly tighten the grip on your finger. The Moro reflex decreases as the baby gets older; it is difficult to elicit after the baby is three months old, and it is almost always gone by five or six months.

The meaning and purpose of the grasping and Moro reflexes are not clear. It has been suggested that this behavior is an inheritance from our animal ancestors. Because monkeys carry their young on their backs or stomachs, a loss of support is less likely to produce a fall if the youngster reaches out and grasps its mother's fur or skin (Prechtl, 1965).

Walking Movements

A one- or two-week-old baby may show behavior that resembles the movements required in walking. One of these is a **stepping** motion that can be elicited by holding the baby under the arms while gently lowering him or her to a surface until both feet touch it and the knees bend. If one slowly bounces the baby lightly up and down, he or she may straighten out both legs at the knees and hip as if to stand. Then if moved forward, the baby may try stepping motions, as if walking.

The second walking motion, a **placing** response, is simply the baby's propensity to lift his or her feet onto a surface. If held up and moved toward a table until the top part of the foot touches the edge, the baby is likely to lift up a foot and place it on the table.

Such behavior has relatively little practical utility in itself, because the one- or two-week-old

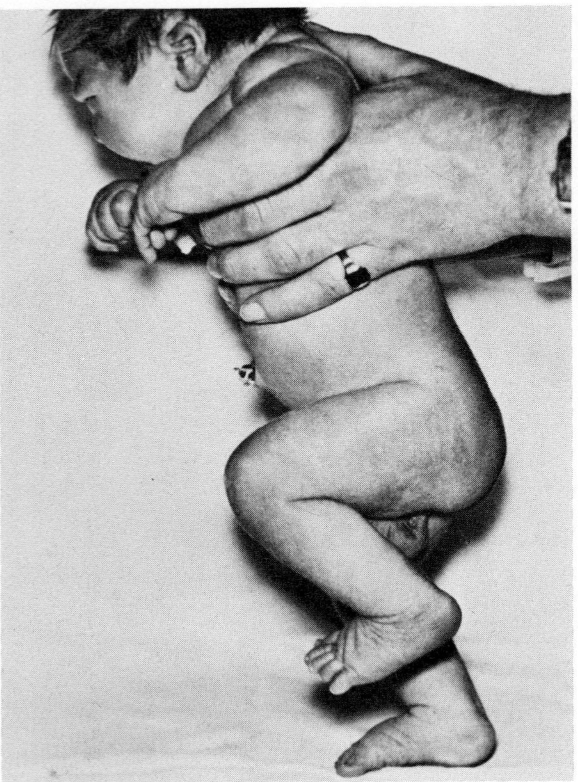

The stepping reflex.

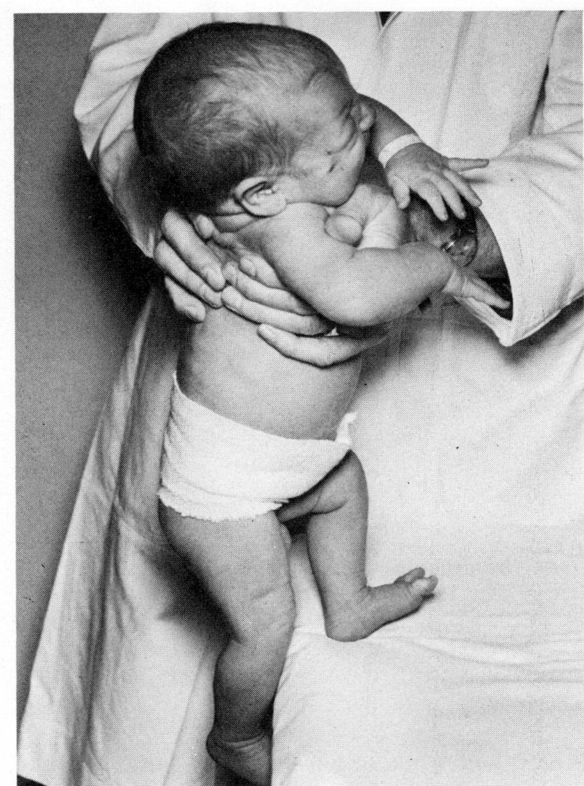

The placing reflex. *(A. K. Tunstill)*

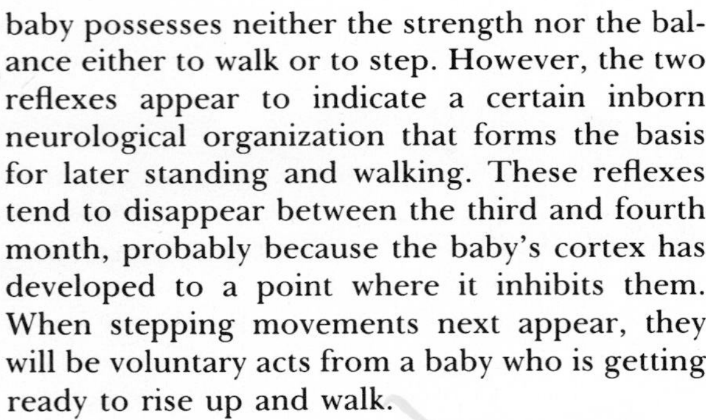

baby possesses neither the strength nor the balance either to walk or to step. However, the two reflexes appear to indicate a certain inborn neurological organization that forms the basis for later standing and walking. These reflexes tend to disappear between the third and fourth month, probably because the baby's cortex has developed to a point where it inhibits them. When stepping movements next appear, they will be voluntary acts from a baby who is getting ready to rise up and walk.

SENSORY CAPABILITIES

Some years ago, many people believed that the newborn baby could not sense the physical energies in the environment. It was held that the baby could not see clearly, smell, or taste and could feel only pain, cold, and hunger. However, research has established that neonates' senses, although not as precise as those of adults, do inform them about their surroundings. Since the ability to think, to learn, and to become a social being depends upon one's perceptions of the world, it is important to know about the state of newborns' sensory capabilities. If we know what newborn babies can see, hear, smell, and taste, we can discover which events in the environment might influence them.

Seeing

If you hold one finger a few inches from your nose and another at arm's length, you can quickly alternate your focus from one to the other, an ability called **visual accommodation.**

The newborn does not possess this capability but is instead like a fixed-focus camera: only objects that are about nine inches from the eyes will be in focus. Focal distance varies from baby to baby, ranging from seven to fifteen inches. By the age of six weeks, babies' ability to accommodate appears to improve markedly, but they will not be as skilled as an adult until they are approximately four months old (Haynes, White, and Held, 1965). You can begin to appreciate the staggering limits this places on the young baby's visual experience by focusing on your finger, held about nine inches from your nose, and then attempting to concentrate on other objects in the room. This limited focus is one mechanism that minimizes the baby's "booming, buzzing confusion"; it sharply reduces the amount of distinctive visual stimulation that gets through. The newborn's peripheral vision is also quite limited. An adult's field of vision covers 180 degrees, whereas the newborn's is only 60 degrees, shutting out two-thirds of the available stimulation and further minimizing possible confusion.

When adults look at an object, they focus both eyes on it. Each eye sees a slightly different image, and by a mechanism called **convergence,** the two images come together until only a single object appears. If you hold your finger at arm's length, focus on it, and then move it toward the tip of your nose, you can feel the muscles of your eyes perform this function. The newborn does not possess this ability until the age of about seven or eight weeks. If, therefore, one holds two objects nine inches in front of a young baby's face, it is possible that the right eye will look at the right object and the left eye will look at the left one (Wickelgren, 1967).

Because the normal newborn's eyes are not usually aligned toward the same point, the baby often looks walleyed (a condition called **strabismus**) for the first month or so. Given their limited muscular ability, newborns are lucky if they move both eyes in the same direction half the time, let alone keep both of them trained on the same object. Even without convergence, however, newborns have some sense of depth perception (Yonas and Pick, 1975). Using only one eye, a newborn can tell whether an object appears to have moved nearer or farther by relying on the cues of changing size and clarity. Thus when a relatively small and blurred image that is projected on the eye becomes larger and clearer, the baby detects and responds to the implied difference in depth.

Visual **acuity** refers to the ability to see objects clearly and to resolve detail. If a newborn could change focus and thus resolve distant detail, then the week-old baby would have approximately 20/600 vision. In terms of adult standards, this means that at a distance of twenty feet from an object, the newborn sees it about as well as the average adult would at a distance of 600 feet, which constitutes legal blindness. However, vision improves rapidly, and by six months, most babies can see as clearly as the average adult (Banks and Salapatek, 1981).

For almost a century, scientists have been trying to determine whether newborn babies can see color. Babies easily tell the difference between objects that differ in brightness, but no one has yet been able to separate brightness and hue in such a way as to test newborns for color vision (Maurer, 1975). On the basis of physiological evidence, it appears that the color-sensitive cells in the eyes of newborns are few in number and barely developed in structure. This suggests that for at least the first several weeks of life the newborn is likely to be color-blind.

Hearing

There is no question that newborn babies hear. Their ears operate four months before they are born, the basic neurology that enables them to discriminate between different tones and intensities is probably ready two months before birth, and approximately one month before birth they are prepared to direct their attention toward a sound. At first, the sounds reaching a neonate may be somewhat dampened, because for the first few days of life the middle-ear passages are filled with amniotic fluid. However, all normal newborns can hear, and some can hear very well. Most newborns will turn their heads in the direction of a shaking rattle (Muir and Field, 1979), and one study suggests that the faintest sound that a baby can detect is about as soft as the faintest sound heard by the average adult (Eisenberg, 1970). Although the newborn can hear a sound as opposed to no sound, babies have difficulty in discriminating between one sound and another. For example, the average newborn can only detect the difference between tones of 200 and 1,000 cycles per second, which is roughly comparable to the difference between a foghorn and a clarinet (Leventhal and Lipsitt, 1964). On the other hand, some exceptional infants have responded to tones that differ as little as 60 cycles per second, which is roughly equivalent to one step on a musical scale (Bridger, 1961).

Tasting

Like many of the newborn's other abilities, the sensitivity to taste is much more highly developed than was believed only a few years ago. When drops of various concentrated solutions are placed on their tongues, newborn babies respond with facial expressions much like those of adults. Jacob Steiner (1979) tested 175 full-term babies and found that an extremely sweet liquid brought forth smiles, followed by an eager licking and sucking. When they tasted a sour solution, most babies pursed their lips, wrinkled their noses, and blinked their eyes. When a bitter fluid was dripped into their mouths, they stuck out their tongues and spat. Some even tried to vomit. Yet when Steiner placed distilled water on their tongues, the babies simply swallowed, showing no expression at all. A group of twenty premature newborns, given plain water and a sour solution, responded just as the full-term infants had done.

Within several days after birth a baby's taste sensitivity becomes even more developed (Johnson and Salisbury, 1975). For example, fed solutions of salt water, sterile water, artificial milk, or breast milk, a baby is likely to show a distinctly different pattern of sucking, swallowing, and breathing for each solution. Charles Crook and Lewis Lipsitt (1976) studied the newborn's sensitivity to solutions varying in their degree of sweetness. They found that babies suck more slowly and their heart rates increase with sweeter solutions. These results appear contradictory, because one might expect a baby to suck more vigorously when given a solution that tastes good. In an attempt to resolve this paradox, Crook and Lipsitt suggest that because babies savor the taste of the sweeter solutions, they slow down to enjoy them, and that pleasurable excitement causes their hearts to speed up.

Smelling

Newborns definitely react to strong odors. Babies less than twelve hours old reacted in a recognizable manner to synthetic odors of various foods (Steiner, 1979). When a cotton swab saturated with the odor of rotten eggs or concentrated shrimp was waved beneath their noses, the infants responded as babies in Steiner's previous experiment had responded to bitter tastes. To the aromas of butter, bananas, vanilla, chocolate, strawberry, and honey, the babies responded with expressions of enjoyment and satisfaction.

In earlier experiments (Engen and Lipsitt, 1965), newborns quickly turned away from the smell of ammonia or vinegar. Within two or three days, newborns also recognize for a time a strong odor they have smelled before. When first presented with the odor of anise oil, for example, a baby's activity increases and his or her heart rate and breathing pattern change. If the odor continues, the baby gradually stops responding to it. At this point, if a new odor, such as phenyl alcohol, reaches the baby's nose, the infant again becomes more active and shows a changed heart rate and breathing pattern.

The keenness of the newborn's sense of smell may be further illustrated by the research of Aidan Macfarlane (1977) at Oxford University. He had noticed that when placed next to the mother's breast, a typical newborn turns his or her face toward it before seeing it or touching the nipple. Macfarlane wondered if this was because the baby could smell the milk beginning to drip from the nipple. To test this notion, he performed two simple and ingenious experiments. First, he collected breast pads that mothers had used to absorb the small amount of milk that leaks between feedings. For the first experiment, he simply placed the mother's breast pad on one side of a baby's head and a clean pad on the other side next to the cheek. Because many babies prefer one side or the other, usually the right, care was taken to alternate the pads' placement. Babies spent more time with their heads turned toward their own mothers' milk-scented pads than toward the clean pads. But the babies' noses were sharper than Macfarlane expected. In the second experiment, he substituted a milk-scented pad from another mother for the clean pad and compared the baby's reaction. He found that babies turned their heads toward both pads for about the same amount of time during the first two days, but that by the time they were six to ten days old, they turned most of the time toward their own mothers' pads.

PERCEPTION AND ATTENTION

If newborns were simply passive recipients of anything that the environment presented, they would not attend to or respond to some stimuli and ignore others. However, this is just what they do. They look at some things and not at others, which indicates that they are actively selecting and filtering those aspects of their world that they will notice and learn about.

Visual Attention

As we will see in Chapter 7, the two-month-old baby notices brightness, movement, and pattern. But does the neonate respond to these aspects of the world? As far as brightness goes, objects that are too bright or too dim will not capture the newborn's gaze. Maurice Hershenson (1964) found that a baby who is two or three days old will look longer at objects of moderate brightness than at those that are too bright or not bright enough. This research confirms the experience of parents, who often report that their newborns shut their eyes and turn away from bright lights, especially sunlight.

Babies respond early to movement. A five-day-old newborn who is sucking on a pacifier will stop this rhythmical sucking if a light moves across the visual field (Haith, 1966). Despite the fact that their right and left eyes do not always look at the same thing, newborns briefly pursue a slowly moving object with a smooth eye movement, but the movement soon becomes jerky (Kremnitzer et al., 1979). Not until babies are about three to six weeks old does their visual pursuit become coordinated and smooth. This suggests that if the movement is not too rapid, even newborns will be more attracted to a moving object than to a stationary one.

A great deal of research has been devoted to a baby's attention to pattern. As early as 1944, Fritz Stirnimann found that babies only one day old would look longer at a patterned surface than at a plain one. Robert Fantz (1965) performed some of the first modern experiments on the baby's attention to different forms. He used a "looking chamber" to study babies between two days and six months old. Fantz placed the baby in a drawerlike carriage and slid the carriage into the looking chamber, where stimuli were placed directly above the baby. When Fantz used this procedure, he also found that newborns attend more to patterns than to homogeneous gray stimuli. As the babies reached two or three months, they preferred more complex, three-dimensional stimuli and bull's-eye patterns.

Contrast When babies look at a visual pattern, what aspect of it attracts their attention? In order to find out, William Kessen, Marshall Haith, and Philip Salapatek developed a device that records a baby's eye movements. The shifting gaze of six different babies can be seen in Figure 5.3. Notice that the newborn tended to look at the edges of a triangle, especially at the vertex, where black-white contrast is highest. These newborns did not systematically scan the entire shape; instead, they concentrated their attention on a corner and perhaps on the sides forming that corner (Salapatek and Kessen, 1966).

The conclusion seems to be that newborn babies do not look in a random fashion; instead, their attention is attracted to and maintained by points of high contrast. Moreover, once neonates find such a point of contrast, they are not

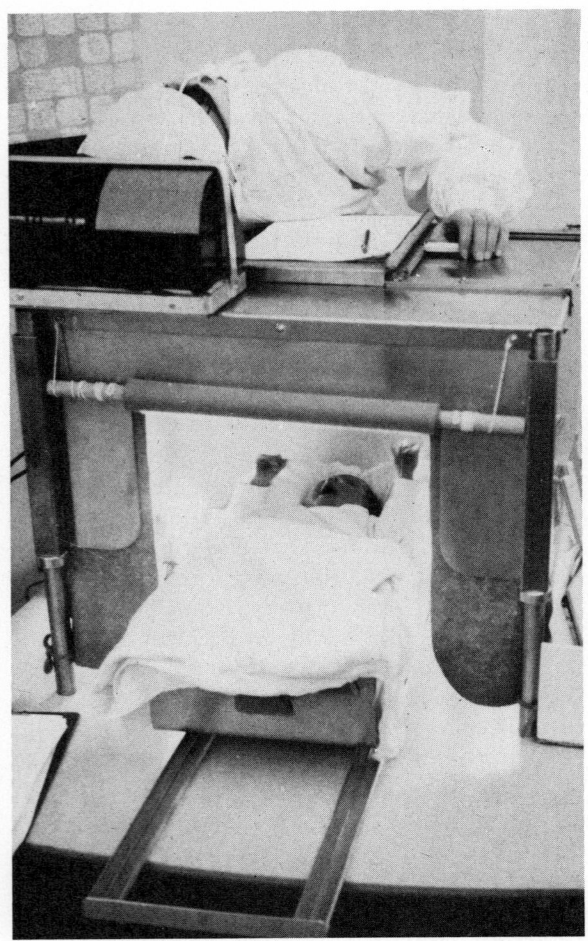

"Looking chamber" used in Fantz's studies of perceptual development in babies. The baby lies on her back looking up at two panels. Contrasting visual stimuli—for example, an outline of a human face and a half-white, half-black oval figure—are placed on the panels, and the baby's eye movements are observed and recorded to determine which of the two panels she looks at more often and for a longer period of time. ***(Courtesy Dr. Robert L. Fantz)***

likely to search the figure for another. That development must wait until they are a few weeks older (Banks and Salapatek, 1981).

Search Strategy The newborn does not scan an object in detail but does possess some simpler visual strategies. When newborns wake up in a totally dark room, they are more likely to open their eyes and scan the environment in a horizontal direction than in a vertical one. In addition, there is a certain rhythm to their scanning (approximately two scans per second), roughly the same as their sucking rate. In short, the rule appears to be: If there is no light, search systematically with a predominantly horizontal, rhythmical eye movement (Haith, 1980).

If light is available, newborns search, not for the source of light, but for edges or points of high black-and-white contrast in the visual field. Because their scanning strategy is mostly horizontal, they are more likely to encounter a vertical line or a black-white edge than a horizontal one (Kessen, Haith, and Salapatek, 1970). Moreover, some research suggests that the brighter the contrast between the light and the dark areas of the object, the more likely the baby is to look at it. As Chapter 7 shows, the scanning strategies of the older baby are much more sophisticated.

Auditory Attention

Is the neonate a selective listener to sounds as well as a selective viewer of sights? The answer to questions of auditory attention are difficult to obtain. For one thing, it is relatively easy for scientists to determine when a baby looks at something or what part of an object he or she focuses on, by observing where the baby's eyes are turned. But it is much harder to tell whether an infant listens and even more problematical to tell what aspect of an auditory stimulus the baby listens to. Some information has been gained by monitoring the heart rates, respiration rates, brain waves, and sucking patterns of babies when they are exposed to various sounds.

Babies do respond differently to sounds of contrasting frequencies or pitch. Low tones tend to quiet babies who are upset, whereas high fre-

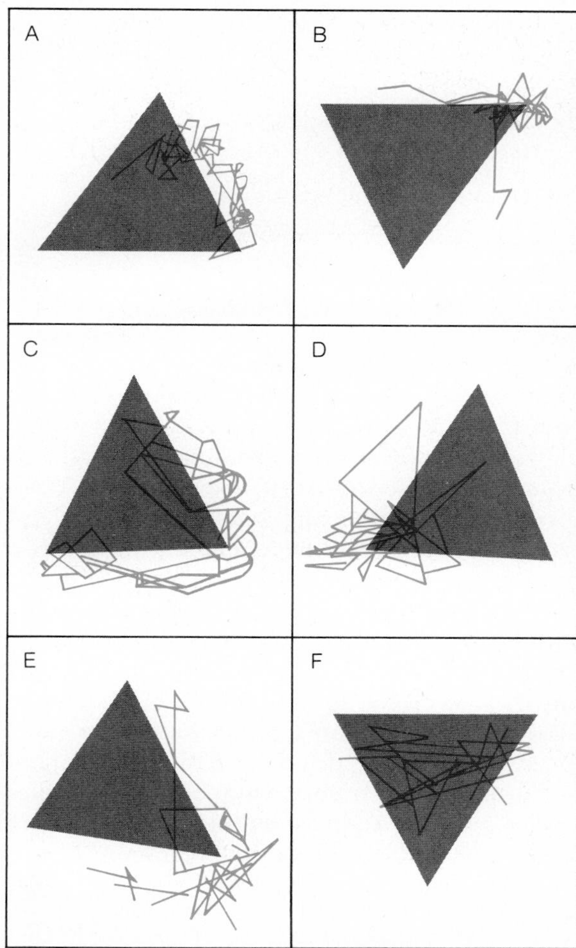

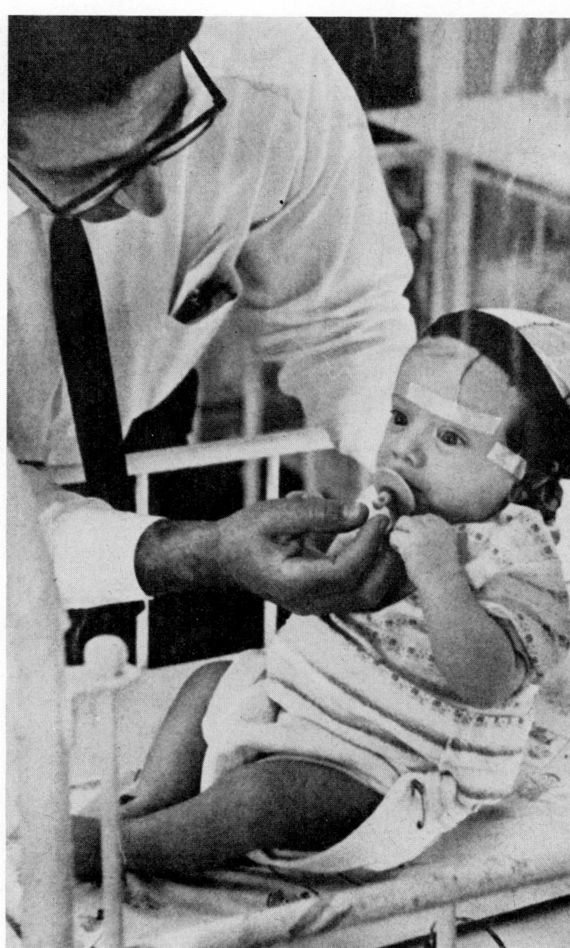

FIGURE 5.3 In this perception experiment, newborn babies were shown a large black triangle on a white field. ***(left)*** **Infrared marker lights were placed behind the triangle and reflected in the baby's pupil, permitting the baby's eye movements to be traced and photographed.** ***(right)*** **Besides showing that the infants looked more toward the corners of the triangle, the six tracings illustrate the wide variation in patterns of scanning that occurs among babies.** ***(Photograph courtesy Dr. William Kessen; data from Salapatek and Kessen, 1966)***

quencies are likely to distress them and may even produce a kind of freezing reaction (Eisenberg et al., 1964). Some scientists have called attention to the parallel between the newborn's response to these sounds and the tendency among adults to use sounds of different frequencies to convey feelings of distress or calm. For example, the acoustical properties of musical instruments, alarm systems, and even some words used to describe our reactions to certain events use high frequencies to alert and convey excitement or disturbance and low frequencies to communicate relative calm (Eisenberg, 1970).

There is also some indication that newborns are especially responsive to sounds in the frequency of the human voice (200 to 500 cycles per second) and to sounds of moderate length, approximately five to fifteen seconds in duration (Eisenberg, 1970). In one study, three-day-old babies clearly showed a preference for their own mothers' voices over that of a strange woman (DeCasper and Fifer, 1980). Chapter 8 describes how this response to the human voice plays a role in the development of language.

It should be clear from these examples of visual and auditory attention that the newborn's perceptual world is somewhat less confusing than psychologists once thought. Although the newborn's sensory systems do function, the ability to detect stimuli or to discriminate among them is seriously limited, and a considerable amount of the visual environment is simply not accessible. Some babies are quite good at discriminating between one kind of sound and another, but the average newborn perceives many sounds as the same that adults would perceive as different. Finally, newborn babies are selective about what stimuli will attract their attention or increase their responses: they tune some things in and tune other things out. As a result, the newborn neither detects nor pays attention to much of what adults perceive. The newborn's perceptual world is probably simpler and more orderly than we might guess.

ADAPTING TO THE WORLD

Given that babies have many ways of sensing events in the outside world and certain coordinated patterns of behavior for meeting situations that might arise, what are the mechanisms by which they adapt to the environment? How does the newborn come to know more about the world?

The neonate can learn—at least some things under some circumstances. For example, they learn to integrate sucking and breathing into an efficient feeding process, and they can learn to modify this behavior to fit the circumstances at hand. In addition, they are able to form crude memories of certain stimuli, to remember those stimuli for five to ten seconds, and then to detect whether a subsequent stimulus is different from that memory.

Memory and Perceptual Analysis

The newborn baby spends most of the time either asleep, fussing and crying because of hunger, or feeding. In fact, the average newborn probably is quietly alert only about thirty minutes in every four hours. Many parents are fond of putting mobiles and other objects in the crib with their newborn. Is it possible that a young baby, who is alert for such short periods, can become familiar with such objects—that is, can form a memory of them, retain that memory, and recognize an old mobile as familiar or detect a new one as strange?

Steven Friedman explored this possibility with babies from one to four days old (Friedman, 1972; Friedman, Bruno, and Vietze, 1974). One of the checkerboards pictured in Figure 5.4 was shown to a baby for sixty seconds at a time. Friedman presented the stimulus again and again until on two successive occasions babies looked a total of eight seconds less than they had looked the first two times they had seen the object. When this happened, the infant had **habituated.** The process of habituation is roughly analogous to becoming bored with a stimulus, which implies that the baby has learned and remembered something about it. Such a decline in looking after repeated exposure may signify that the baby has formed a memory of that stimulus. On the other hand, the baby may simply be tired or fussy; perhaps the infant does not remember the stimulus at all. To find out whether the baby was showing memory or fatigue, Friedman changed the stimulus on a later test. If the baby looked longer at the new stimulus than the last time he or she saw the familiar one, the baby must have had a memory for the familiar one that signaled that the new stimulus was different from the old. Figure 5.4 shows one neonate's pattern of looking at the repeated sight of a given stimulus and at the introduction of a new one. Notice that during the familiarization phase this neo-

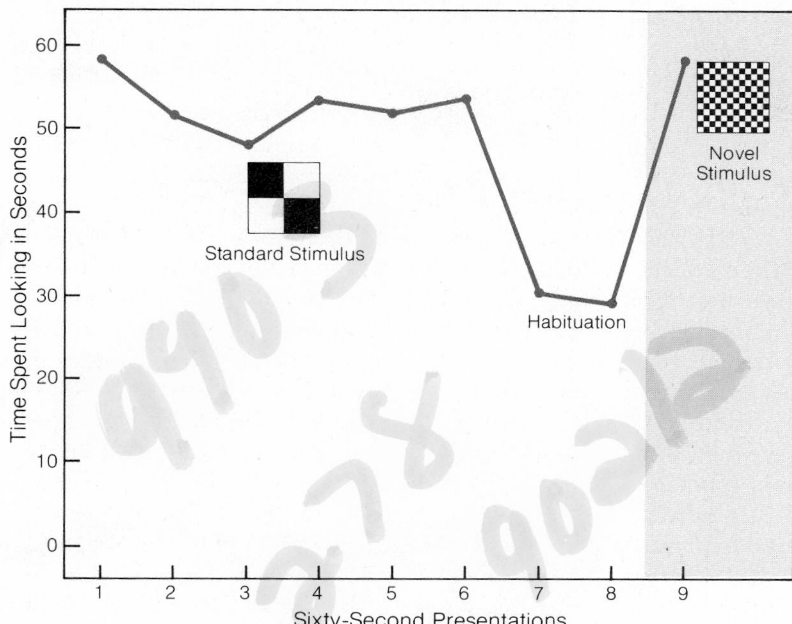

FIGURE 5.4 One newborn's response to familiar and unfamiliar checkerboard stimuli. After seven sixty-second exposures to the standard (familiar) stimulus, the baby became habituated. When the baby was then exposed to a novel (unfamiliar) stimulus on the ninth presentation, however, he immediately looked at it for an extended time. ***(After Friedman, 1972)***

nate looked for about the same length of time again and again until suddenly the looking time dropped sharply on two successive occasions. When Friedman introduced a new stimulus, the baby looked a long time (almost the entire sixty seconds), indicating that the infant detected the new stimulus as being different from an earlier memory.

Given the stimuli used in this study, it was also possible to ask whether a newborn looked longer at a new stimulus that was radically different from the familiar stimulus than at one that was only slightly different. The results suggest that the length of time the babies looked at the novel stimulus depended on how different it was from the familiar one. It appears that newborns perform a crude perceptual analysis of the difference between the new stimulus and their memory of the familiar one.

On the basis of such research, we can conclude that newborns can form a memory of a stimulus, retain that memory for five to ten seconds, retrieve it, and make some kind of analysis of the relationship between the memory and the new stimulus.

Conditions for Learning

It is clear that human newborns can learn. However, just how much they actually do learn in their natural environment is another question. We have seen that newborns work under certain handicaps and that their environment may not satisfy the stringent requirements necessary before they can sense, perceive, attend, and perhaps learn.

One requirement of the learning situation appears to be *timing.* In experimental studies, it has been found that there can be almost no delay of reward for the newborn; the baby who does not receive reinforcement within one second is unlikely to learn (Millar, 1972). Another requirement is *repetition;* a stimulus must be presented over and over again with only short delays between each presentation in order for the young baby to form a memory of it (Lewis, 1969). However, as a baby grows older, learning proceeds even when there are greater delays between the infant's response and the reward or between the presentation of one stimulus and another.

Although the scientist can construct a situation that satisfies the newborn's requirement for close timing, the baby's natural environment does not always meet that rigid standard. The delay between the baby's actions and their effects on the people and objects nearby will often be longer than a second, making learning unlikely. Even when the condition of timing is met, the condition of repetition may not be. For example, a push of the baby's hand may immediately remove a blanket that has fallen across the face, but he or she may not have an immediate opportunity to push away another blanket. In a sense, then, there may be a period of "natural deprivation" (J. S. Watson, 1966), in which the baby is capable of learning but the environmental conditions provide no opportunity to learn.

Other studies (Fitzgerald and Brackbill, 1976) have discovered additional limits on the young baby's ability to learn. For example, even among very young babies, there are individual differences in the ability to learn. Some newborns can learn tasks that are difficult or impossible for other babies of the same age. It also matters whether the response to be learned is a voluntary or an involuntary one. An involuntary response, such as the blink of an eye at the sound of a buzzer, may be extremely difficult for a neonate to learn, whereas a voluntary response, such as learning to turn toward the buzzer, may be relatively easy.

PERSONALITY AND SOCIAL RELATIONS

It is difficult to talk about the personality of a newborn. Adults think of personality in terms of verbal, cognitive, and emotional behavior displayed in a social context. But a neonate cannot express personality in this way. However, newborn babies do differ in their behavior, and they do engage in primitive social relations.

Temperament

Temperamental differences among babies can be detected in the first few days of life and may be categorized as differences in motor activity, irritability, and responsiveness. Some newborns are more *active* than others. They frequently thrash about with their legs and arms or later bang toys and shake rattles with considerable gusto; other babies are more placid, moving more slowly and with less exaggeration. Mothers are sometimes aware of this kind of difference even before their babies are born: some fetuses kick and move about more than others, and there is some relationship between such fetal kicking and differences in behavior among children for at least two years (C. E. Walters, 1965).

Newborns also differ in general *irritability.* Some cry a lot, others do not. Certain babies are restless sleepers and tend to have fits of irritability during sleep or wakefulness. When a group of such babies were followed for more than two years, they continued to cry more often than their peers and to have more irregular sleep patterns (Snow, Jacklin, and Maccoby, 1980). There is also some evidence that irritable or fitful sleepers may have different personalities as young children from babies who do not show such restless sleep (Thomas, Chess, and Birch, 1970).

Newborn babies also differ in *responsiveness.* Some babies are cuddlers. They are soft and snuggly and seem to enjoy being cuddled, kissed, and rolled about in one's arms. In contrast, other babies resist such affectionate play by stiffening their bodies when they are handled (Schaffer, 1971). It is easy to understand how such a rudimentary social response might have a substantial impact on parents who had been looking forward to the opportunity to hug and kiss their newborn and who find themselves parents to a noncuddler. They may falsely infer that their baby dislikes them or that they are inadequate parents, forming negative attitudes that could color the way they subsequently interact with their child.

Many studies have documented early personality differences among babies. An important early study by Margaret Fries (1954), in which she carefully observed the amount and vigor of

Affectionate babies elicit loving responses from adults and other children. *(© Elizabeth Crews)*

neonate activity, led her to classify newborns into three activity types: the active, the moderately active, and the quiet. Other newborn predispositions that may be important to a child's personality have been identified and described by Alexander Thomas and his colleagues (1963). These researchers decided that the intimate knowledge mothers gain in the constant care of their babies would be a source of meaningful data. Using carefully formulated interviews, they conducted an extensive study that disclosed four major behavioral characteristics that seem important for personality: activity level; approach-withdrawal behavior, as seen in the baby's characteristic first reaction to any new stimulus; threshold of responsiveness, or the amount of stimulation required to evoke a visible or audible response; and general quality of mood, such as friendly, unfriendly, joyful, or angry.

Of course, child and adult personality are much more complex than these simple categories would imply. A child's personality is a developing and evolving set of tendencies to behave in various ways. Nevertheless, it is easy to see how the general tone of social interaction within the family could be influenced by the baby's characteristic activity, irritability, and social responsiveness. Parents often interpret the smallest behavior as revealing their newborn's personality, and by the time their infant is two weeks old, mothers may develop both a style of relating to their baby and an opinion of his or her personality (Osofsky and Connors, 1979).

Social Relations

Social relations in the newborn are primitive by adult standards, yet they exist. Whenever there is communication between individuals, there is a social relation, and newborns and their parents certainly carry on a rudimentary sort of nonverbal communication.

Historically, the way in which a newborn was fed was thought to have major consequences for the child's developing social relations and personality. Such ideas stemmed from Freudian theory, which placed great emphasis on the possible impact of events early in the child's life. Because the newborn spends most of his or her waking hours feeding, it made good sense to assume that social relations began in the feeding situation. The design of the human body ensures that nursing neonate and mother are placed in a situation that facilitates communication. When a mother first breast-feeds her newborn baby, the infant is cradled in her arm with the small face about nine inches from hers—the distance at which the baby's eyes can most easily focus.

Recent research by Kenneth Kaye and Anne Wells (1980) indicates that the feeding period may contain the seeds of turn-taking, a skill that is essential to language and social development. Mothers, whether breast- or bottle-feeding, tend either to jiggle the nipple in the baby's mouth or to stroke the baby about the mouth whenever sucking stops. But the baby does not resume sucking until the mother stops jiggling. It appears that the infant's normal sucking routine of bursts and pauses fits naturally into the turn-taking of human dialogue and that mothers use their child's natural feeding rhythm as a basis for early social communication.

THE FIRST BOND

The first few hours of an infant's life may be a sensitive period, when new parents find it easiest to become attached to their baby. When her infant is placed by her side in the delivery room, a new mother generally touches the baby's skin and establishes eye-to-eye contact, behavior that may initiate the maternal bond. John Kennell, Diana Voos, and Marshall Klaus (1979) have noted that when babies are born very ill or small-for-dates and must be given intensive care, the mother-baby relationship may suffer. Such babies, they say, show a higher-than-average incidence of neglect or child abuse. They speculate that early separation of mother and infant may disrupt or weaken the bonding process, pointing out that ten studies have shown that early contact affects the development of the bond.

In a Swedish study (DeChateau, 1976), mothers who held their naked newborns for the first thirty minutes after birth breast-fed their babies longer than mothers in a control group (six months as compared with three and a half months), found adaptation to their babies easier, and displayed more affection during an observation period. The babies of the mothers with extended early contact also cried less and smiled more than did the babies of mothers in a control group. Early contact also appears to strengthen the bond between baby and father. Swedish fathers who undressed their infants twice during the first three days and established eye-to-eye contact for an extended period on each occasion spent more time in caring for their babies during the first three months than did fathers who lacked this experience (Lind, Vuorenkoski, and Wasz-Höckert, 1973).

Among a group of poor, [inner-city,] mothers, those who were given extended contact with their babies in the hospital were less likely to let their month-old infants cry and were more reluctant to leave them with a sitter than were mothers who had had no extended contact (Kennell et al., 1974). Mothers with extended contact were also more likely to fondle their infants and to gaze into their faces while feeding them. When the babies were a year old, these mothers spent more time near their babies during a physical examination and more time soothing them when they cried than mothers without extended contact.

Results are not always so dramatic. Sven Carlsson and his associates (Carlsson et al., 1979; Schaller, Carlsson, and Larsson, 1979) also found clear differences in maternal behavior between mothers who had extensive contact with their babies immediately after birth and while they were in the hospital and mothers who saw their babies only at feeding times. By the time the babies were six weeks old, however, the differences between the two groups had disappeared. The researchers point out that mothers in this study were well-educated women living in stable socioeconomic conditions, whereas the mothers described by Kennell were unskilled, mostly unmarried, poor women. It may be that a middle-class environment sets up expectations for the maternal role that make maternal attachment relatively easy, even when mothers see their newborns only at feeding time.

None of these studies, however, took physical condition into account. A heavily sedated mother will find it difficult to take an interest in her newborn, and a baby born to such a mother may be drowsy, sluggish, and slow to respond to her overtures. The tone of the pair's relationship may be set by the first few hours or days in the hospital. Herbert Birch (1968) has pointed out that a mother responds to her baby's actions, and her responses stimulate the baby to act again, perhaps affecting the baby's rate of development. A drugged or undernourished baby may lead to an unresponsive mother, with unhappy consequences for their relationship. English babies studied by Martin Richards (1975) showed such a trend. The babies were sleepy and unresponsive, and during the first week after they were born, their mothers had to work to keep them awake and sucking at feeding time. A year later, these babies spent more time sucking their thumbs and less time in social exchange with their mothers than did babies who had not come into contact with drugs during birth.

Without realizing they are doing it, parents also tend to structure their interactions to fit their babies' capacities. According to Hanuš Papoušek and Mechthild Papoušek (1978), analyses of films and video recordings reveal that mothers use the position of their babies' hands, small tests of muscle tone, and eye contact as cues to the type and amount of stimulation they give their babies, thereby tailoring their own behavior to their baby's state.

Perhaps the most obvious method that the newborn uses to communicate with the social environment is crying. Generally speaking, a baby cries as if to say "Help me," and even quite young babies display different cries depending on whether the crying is stimulated by hunger, pain, or anger. Each cry can be distinguished by the pattern of pauses between bursts of crying, by the duration of the cry, and by its tonal characteristics. The baby's crying appears to be a wired-in, autonomous activity. If earphones are placed on the crying newborn's head and sounds are played, the crying pattern shows no interruption, even though such competing stimulation would disrupt the speech of an adult (P. Wolff, 1967).

Fathers respond to an infant's wail just as mothers do. As Ann Frodi and her colleagues (1978) discovered, there is no detectable difference in the physiological reaction of mothers and fathers to a crying baby: in each blood pressure rises and skin conductance increases. This arousal is accompanied by feelings of annoyance, irritation, and distress. So when a parent picks up a wailing baby, it is apparently as much to stop the aversive sound as to relieve the baby's distress.

Are differences in babies' cries detectable by parents or only by scientists armed with complex technical instruments? The answer is that complex instruments are superfluous. Most mothers can recognize the cries of their own babies before the babies are a week old (Morsbach and Bunting, 1979). When a mother responds to the hunger cry of her baby, it may be with more than a simple verbal statement that her child is hungry. In fact, mothers respond physiologically and prepare to breast-feed; the increased flow of blood and milk raise the surface heat of the breasts (Lind, 1971). Many a lactating mother can relate occasions when her baby has given a hunger cry and she has discovered milk gushing from her breasts in response.

But social communication is necessarily a two-way street, and Judith Bernal (1972) discovered that whether a mother picked up and fed her crying newborn depended primarily on the context of the cry. Among the English mothers she studied, unless three hours had passed since the last feeding, most left their babies to cry, perhaps communicating to the baby the news that crying had little effect.

It appears that almost from the moment of birth, the neonate detects some social dimension to crying and responds emotionally. Marvin Simner (1971) found, for example, that two- to three-day-old babies start to cry much more frequently when they hear another newborn crying than when they hear nonhuman sounds of equal range and volume. People working in hospital nurseries have made similar observations, noting that when one baby starts to cry, other babies in the nursery soon join in. Abraham Sagi and Martin Hoffman (1976) at the University of Michigan have confirmed this finding and suggest that it may be an inborn, early precursor to later forms of human empathy.

Communication also occurs when a parent responds to a crying baby. There are several ways to quiet a crying baby besides feeding him or her. One is to stabilize the baby's temperature and keep something in contact with the infant's skin. Perhaps it is for this reason that babies throughout history have been swaddled.

Movement also quiets a crying baby, but certain types of movement are better than others. One psychologist developed a rocking machine to determine the kind of rocking that would quiet a baby best. The result: one rock per second, approximately 2-¾ inches in depth, will calm a baby within fifteen seconds. Further, the baby will remain quiet even after the rocking stops (A. Ambrose, 1969).

Auditory stimulation, especially pulsating sounds, also appears to quiet an infant. In an early experiment, babies who listened to sounds

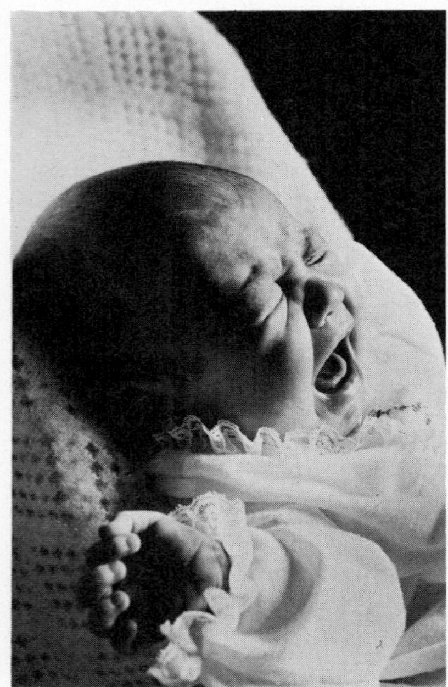

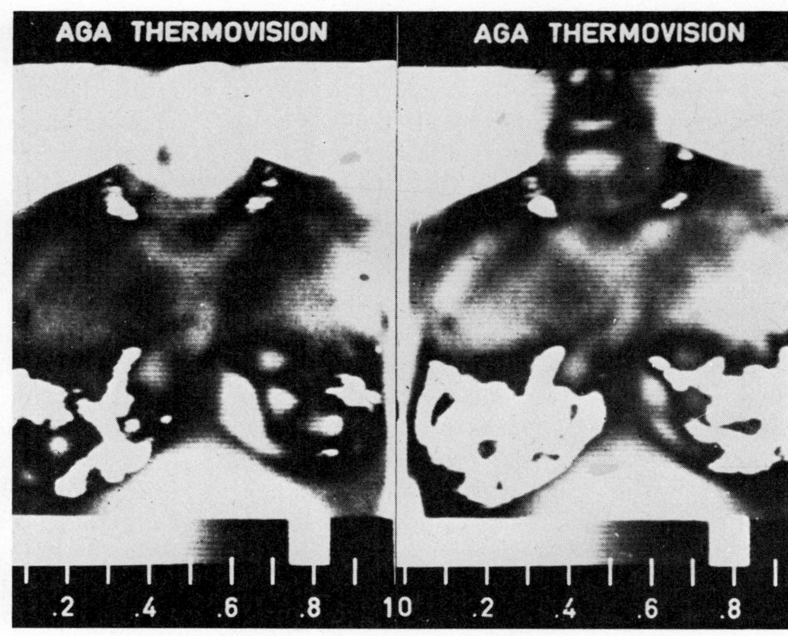

In response to her baby's hunger cry, a mother physiologically prepares to breast-feed, as shown by thermographs of changes in the surface heat of her breasts, generated by the increased flow of blood and milk. *(Steve McCarroll; Professor John Lind)*

roughly comparable to human heartbeats for four days cried less and gained more weight than babies who did not hear the sounds. This result prompted the researchers to conclude that the baby was conditioned while in the womb to the mother's heartbeat and that heartbeats therefore have special importance throughout human life (Salk, 1962). However, subsequent research has indicated that heartbeat sounds, the beats of a metronome, and even a lullaby are equally effective in quieting a newborn infant, and any of these is better than no sound at all. In fact, continuous sounds, sights, or pitching and rocking movements have calming effects on one-month-old babies, and the more of these different stimuli that are applied at a time, the more effectively the infant's distress is reduced (Brackbill, 1971). Consequently, almost any stimulus, but especially moderately varied stimuli, will quiet a baby.

From the first moment of independent life, babies are different. They differ in their need for sleep, food, and stimulation. Some want to be cuddled, others do not like to be held. Some are placid; some are fussy. With such a wide span of individual differences at birth, it is no wonder that—given the additional influence of widely different environments—no two children or adults are alike. From the time babies draw their first breath, the differences become more and more pronounced. But despite wide individual differences, there are common themes in human development, tasks and challenges that each child will meet in his or her own way. Already in these first weeks, babies communicate with others. They may not yet realize why their cries are followed by dry diapers and warm milk; nevertheless, newborns are influencing the people around them.

SUMMARY

1. Newly arrived from complete dependence on the uterine environment, the newborn, or neonate, undergoes a period of remarkable development.
2. The newborn quickly begins to function with patterns or rhythms: body temperature becomes regulated soon after birth; sleep, composed of both REM and non-REM patterns, evolves into a four-hour sleep/wake cycle for many newborns; feeding, left to self-demand, occurs every three or four hours for many newborns, although breast-fed neonates may eat ten or more times a day.
3. From birth, the newborn is equipped with a set of reflexive behaviors that may be elicited by specific stimuli. These include the rooting reflex, the grasping reflex, the Moro reflex, and stepping and placing responses.
4. The sensory capabilities of newborns keep them in touch with their environment. Although they may be color-blind for the first several weeks, they become capable of accommodation, or focus; of convergence, or seeing one image with both eyes; and of acuity, or seeing detail. Their auditory sense allows newborns to discriminate loudness and pitch, and their sense of taste and smell become increasingly acute.
5. Newborns actively select and filter the visual and auditory stimuli around them. They direct their visual attention to objects according to brightness, movement, pattern, and contrast, and according to certain search strategies. Auditory attention is similarly selective.
6. In adapting to the world, the neonate forms short-term memories of certain stimuli and then compares new stimuli to them. This learning depends on such conditions as the timing of reinforcement and repetition of the stimulus.
7. Newborn babies differ in temperament, and these temperamental predispositions influence the tone of the baby's social relationships, which may in turn affect later personality development. Feeding experiences and responses to their crying offer newborns their first chances for social interaction.

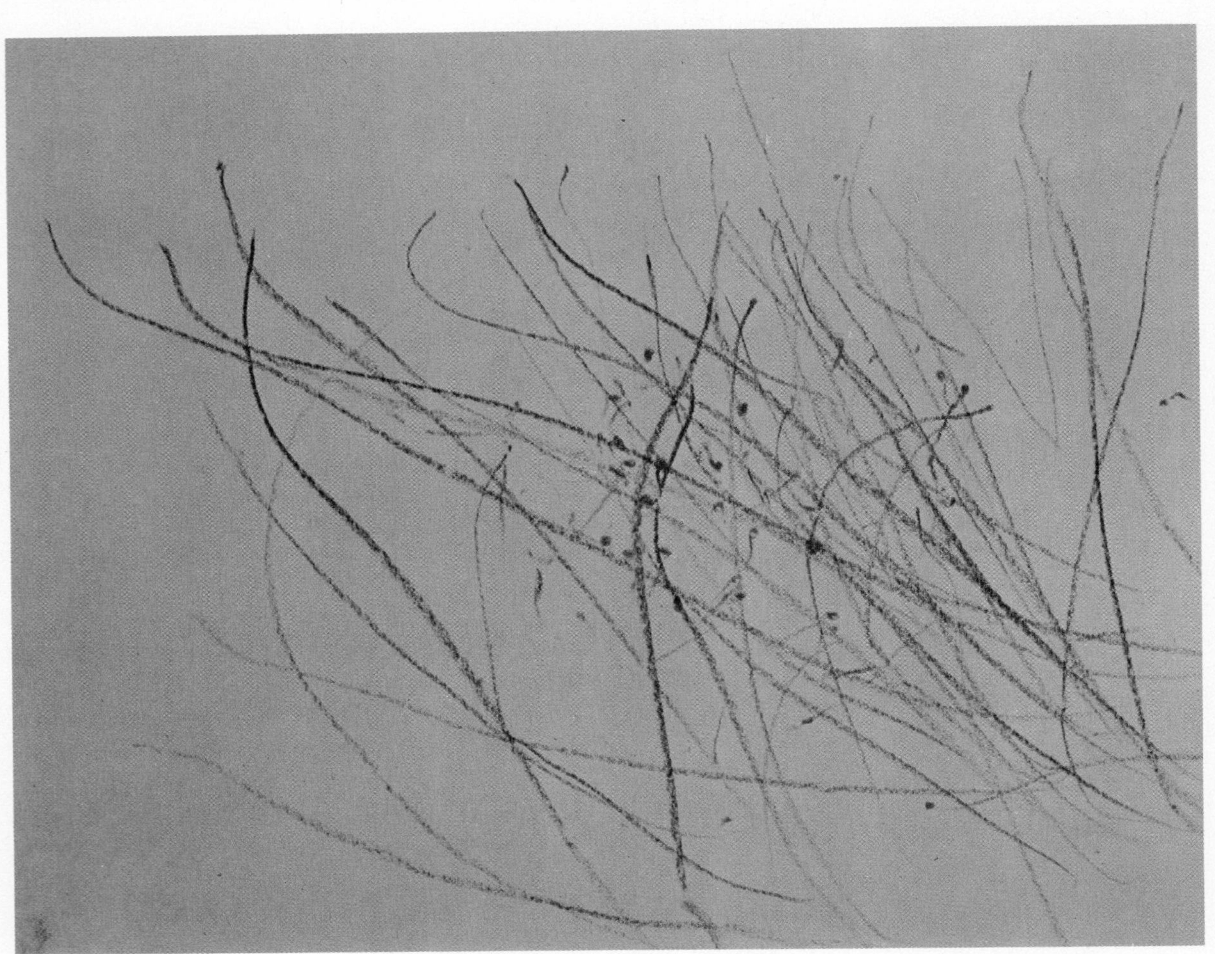

UNIT THREE

INFANCY: THE DAWN OF AWARENESS

In the course of the first two years of life, normal infants develop the ability to communicate with parents and other people and to understand what they say. They gain some twenty pounds in weight and a foot or two in height. They change from sensory beings who may only partially understand the world to thinkers who not only perceive the world in detail and act effectively on it but who also remember the past and plot future actions. By the time a child is two, the hand that held a rattle clutches a fat crayon and produces scribbles that appear to bring the young artist pleasure. With the beginning of language, children's social capabilities expand far beyond the smile and coo that they brought into the world. The early attachment to mother expands, and the independent toddler makes friends with other children. This unit is about how and why these developmental changes take place.

6 PHYSICAL GROWTH: FUNDAMENTALS

Lauren, who is eleven months old, has just learned to stand up. Each time her mother places her on the floor, she creeps to the nearest piece of furniture and pulls herself to her feet. Then she wails loudly for help because she cannot walk and she is afraid to let go. She has learned to keep her knees stiff and support her weight, but she cannot keep her balance. As soon as her mother sets her back down on the floor, Lauren creeps to another part of the room and repeats the scene. It will be several weeks before she learns to slide back to a sitting position or to let go and simply sit down.

Lauren's physical development follows the norm, but some babies her age have been walking for several months and others will not stand for another three or four months. The first thing an observer notices about a group of infants of the same age is how different each appears. Marked structural differences have existed among them since soon after conception. Newborn infants differ in such physical variables as height (length), weight, muscularity, hairiness, dental development, and a host of other measurable characteristics. As the child grows, these physical differences persist. Some, such as height and weight, may become more pronounced; others, such as hairiness, less noticeable.

Growth results from interaction between infant and environment. During the growth process, as babies rapidly become larger, their bodies develop an increasingly complex structure and function, and their size, organs, and body build change in the direction of adult conformations. They will never again grow so rapidly; after infancy the rate of physical change slows and will never again be as fast—not even during the adolescent growth spurt. The study of physical change can provide some understanding of the relations between inherited factors and factors in the child's environment, and can identify the conditions that lower a child's efficiency or hinder normal development. If we can understand these interactions, we have some hope of controlling unwanted deviations from the normal patterns of growth.

In this chapter we will follow the baby's physical development until the age of two. Basing our discussion on some of the basic principles that govern all physical growth, we will outline some of the ways in which psychologists have tried to summarize growth, the measures they have used, and the descriptions they have compiled of the average infant. We will develop a general picture of the growth that takes place and the motor abilities that appear in the first two years of life. The environment, we will discover, exerts a powerful influence on the rate and quality of a child's physical development; diet, illness, socioeconomic class, and emotional stress can all affect its progress. Since each person's environment and heredity are unique, we will consider how physical development may differ from one child to the next. We will see how such differences can affect a child's personality and social behavior and how the motor changes of infancy influence the baby's intellectual and perceptual growth, broadening his or her world in many ways.

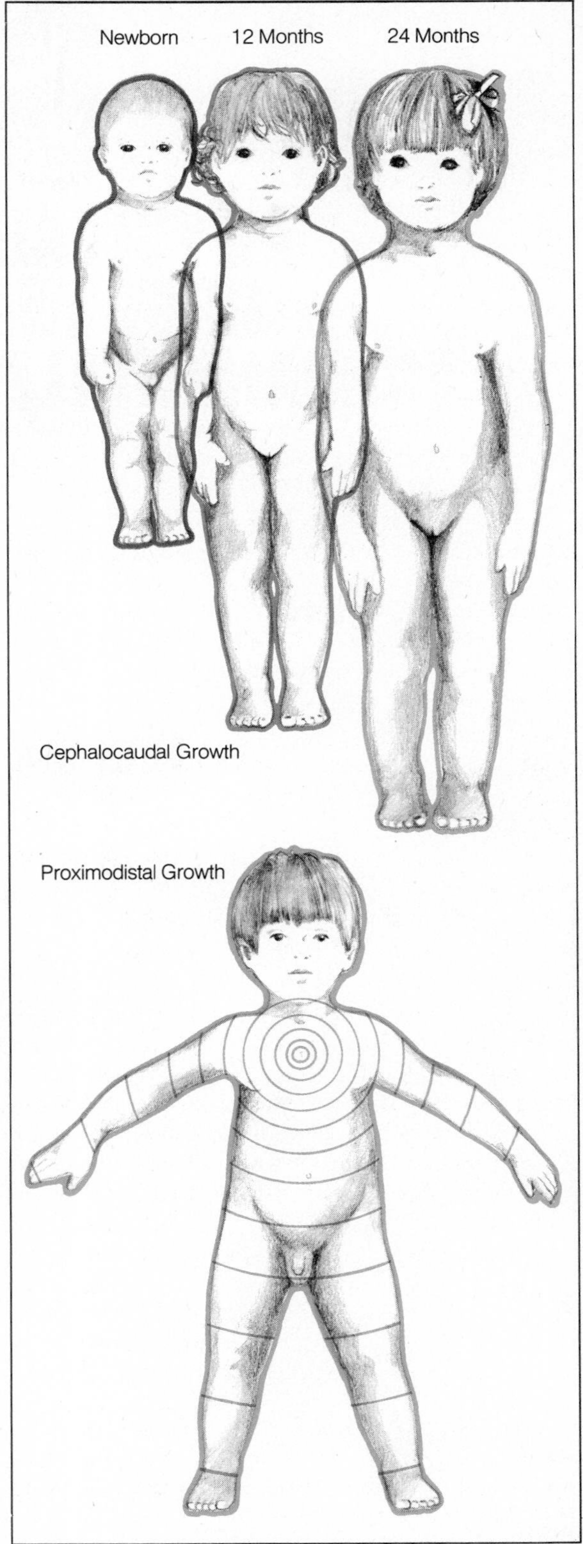

GROWTH PRINCIPLES

Three basic principles underlie the growth and development of all body systems: cephalocaudal development, proximodistal development, and differentiation and hierarchic integration.

Cephalocaudal growth refers to the direction of the body's physical growth, and the word "cephalocaudal" comes from the Greek word for head and the Latin word for tail. The body displays cephalocaudal growth in both the order in which its various parts become larger and the order in which its functions and structures become more complex. Thus growth progresses from head to foot; the head is the first to develop and grow. Only after head growth is established do torso, arms, and legs join the process, a pattern that seems to reflect the fact that the most rapid embryological development occurs in or near those cells destined to become parts of the brain and nervous system (Debakan, 1959).

Yet the head has the least amount of growing to do. At birth, it is closer to its adult size than any other part of the body. Although an infant's head will double in size by adulthood, the trunk will triple in size, the arms and legs grow to four times their length, and the legs and feet increase five times in size. During childhood, the largest increase in height takes place in the growth of the legs. Because of this pattern, the head contributes proportionately less to body length as the child grows, shrinking from one-quarter of the total at birth to one-twelfth at maturity (Bayley, 1956). These changes in body proportions are shown in Figure 6.1.

The same head-to-toe progression is reflected in the control and complexity of movement and motor ability. First, babies gain control over the muscles of the head and neck, then the arms and abdomen, and finally the legs. Babies learn to hold up their heads before they learn to sit; they learn to sit before they can walk. Long before they can walk steadily, they can make complicated, controlled movements of their arms and fingers, even being able to pick up tiny specks of lint.

The second principle of growth, **proximodistal development,** refers to the fact that physical growth and motor development progress from the center of the body toward the periphery. Babies learn to control the movements of their shoulders before they can direct their arms or fingers. They use their hands as a unit before they can control the finer movements of their fingers. In general, control over movement seems to travel down the arm; that is, the baby becomes increasingly accurate and sophisticated in attempts to reach for and grasp objects. In the same manner, babies gain control over their upper legs before they can manage the lower leg or foot.

FIGURE 6.1 ***(opposite)*** **Physical growth and motor abilities develop in two directions simultaneously: from top to bottom (cephalocaudal) and from center to periphery (proximodistal).**

The third principle of growth and development is differentiation and integration. **Differentiation** refers to the increasingly distinct nature of the infant's abilities. For example, a young baby's reaction to a shoe that pinches may be a wiggling and thrashing of the entire body, accompanied by wails of distress. When older, the infant's movements of distress become more specific, and only the offending foot is thrashed about. Eventually, the child learns to make specific and complex responses, saying, for example, "Foot hurt." Sensory stimulation from the foot travels to the brain, where it is interpreted; this interpretation influences the form the infant's language takes to describe it.

In order to make complex responses the infant must combine and integrate increasingly specific, distinct, and differentiated skills. The trend toward combining simple, differentiated skills into more complex skills was called hierarchic integration by Heinz Werner (1948) (see Chapter 3). For example, after a baby has mastered the use of the arms as levers, the muscles of the abdomen as lifters of the upper body, and the neck muscles to control the head, he or she develops hierarchic patterns of movement that bring each separate motor capability into the service of the others in a highly organized way. Finally, after each of the simpler movements has been developed, the baby puts them all together and soon can sit up.

Sitting and later standing require more than the integration of muscle action. Babies also integrate visual information to keep themselves from toppling over. The use of visual feedback in standing was demonstrated when David Lee and Eric Aronson (1974) placed infants with limited walking experience in a room with moving walls. The room's floor was stationary, but the walls and ceiling moved together on a track so that the flow of visual information gave the babies the impression they were swaying backward. As the room moved, the majority of them swayed, staggered, or fell to the carpet, as their compensatory movements threw them off balance. Because this reaction also occurred when the room's end wall moved away from the infants, the investigators feel confident that the babies' response was

Drinking from a cup requires the integration of specific skills and actions. This year-old infant uses and adjusts her grasping and sucking skills as she learns to drink from a cup. ***(Tom Suzuki)***

to visual feedback about their own posture and not an attempt to avoid a wall that loomed toward them. Later research (Butterworth and Hicks, 1977) indicates that the same sort of visual information helps younger babies maintain their upright position while seated.

NORMS

The principles we have just discussed describe growth and development at a general level. Psychologists interested in the normal course of development have compiled detailed, specific descriptions of individual events in the infant's growth process. A number of investigators (Bayley, 1956; Cattell, 1940; Gesell, 1925; Griffiths, 1954; Lenneberg, 1967) have analyzed the sequence in which physical characteristics and motor, language, and social skills emerge. Their investigations have produced **norms,** or typical patterns that describe how important attributes and skills develop and the approximate ages at which they appear.

Growth Patterns

These norms allow us to summarize patterns of infant growth and development. In the first year of life, babies show extensive growth changes; body length increases more than one-third, and weight almost triples. A baby boy who was twenty inches long and weighed seven and one-half pounds at birth will probably be twenty-eight or twenty-nine inches long and will weigh approximately twenty-two pounds by the time she or he is one year old. The head grows more slowly than the trunk and limbs, so that by the time the child is two, the proportions will assume more adultlike dimensions. In addition, the facial skeleton will become relatively larger, so that the cranium is no longer so out of proportion with the face (see Figure 6.2).

Boys and girls grow at different rates, and the difference begins before birth. By the time they are halfway through the fetal period, girls' skeletal development is three weeks ahead of boys', and by the time they are born, girls have outstripped boys by four to six weeks in skeletal maturity, although not in size (Tanner, 1978). Also, some organ systems are more developed at birth in girls, and this may help explain why more girls than boys survive the process.

According to an old rule, children reach half their adult height by the end of their second year. However, differences discovered in the

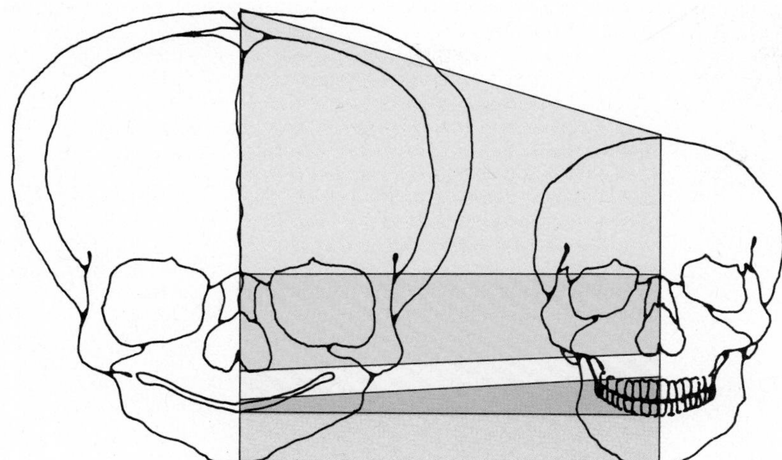

FIGURE 6.2 Changes in proportions of facial features and skull with growth. The skull at the left is that of a newborn, whereas the skull at the right is that of a mature adult; in each case, the relative proportions are based on the length of the nose. ***(Adapted from Jackson, 1923)***

growth patterns of boys and girls make this old rule unreliable for girls. Boys grow faster than girls during the first few months, but girls outstrip boys from seven months until they are about four years old. Since girls mature earlier than boys, they reach the halfway mark sooner: at about eighteen months. The old rule remains fairly reliable for boys.

Motor Development

By carefully observing many children, scientists have described and charted hundreds of small but important motor developments that occur in the first two years of life, and norms for some of the major milestones are presented in Figure 6.3. Each of these milestones emerges in small steps over a period of weeks or months; and within the development of a single ability—such as grasping or walking—it is possible to outline further steps. Drawing on these detailed descriptions, we can develop portraits of the infant at different periods.

In the first three months, infants spend a great deal of time sleeping, eating, and crying. During these weeks, parents see small but steady changes in their baby's behavior that indicate the infant is seeing, hearing, and noticing the world. About the third month, infants begin to show an increased visual involvement in the world around them. They respond more to repetition and show more signs of boredom (or habituation) when they see the same scene or objects over and over again. At this time, their first appreciation of a three-dimensional world appears.

During the period from four to seven months, many developmental changes occur. Perhaps the most important of these is improved eye-hand coordination, which allows the baby to reach for and grasp objects accurately. Although the newborn infant could reach for an object, this eye-hand coordination disappears by the end of the first month. Not until infants are about five months old do they again make eye-guided, purposeful reaches for objects. Now that they can control their hands, most objects end up in their mouths, regardless of size, shape, or sanitary condition.

By the time they are six months old, most infants can roll over completely, both from back to stomach and from stomach to back. At this age they discover their own feet and become fascinated by them, for infants still have little muscular control over their feet and may regard them as objects that pass unexpectedly in and out of the visual field. Infants now respond warmly to people and events, smiling, cooing, and wiggling.

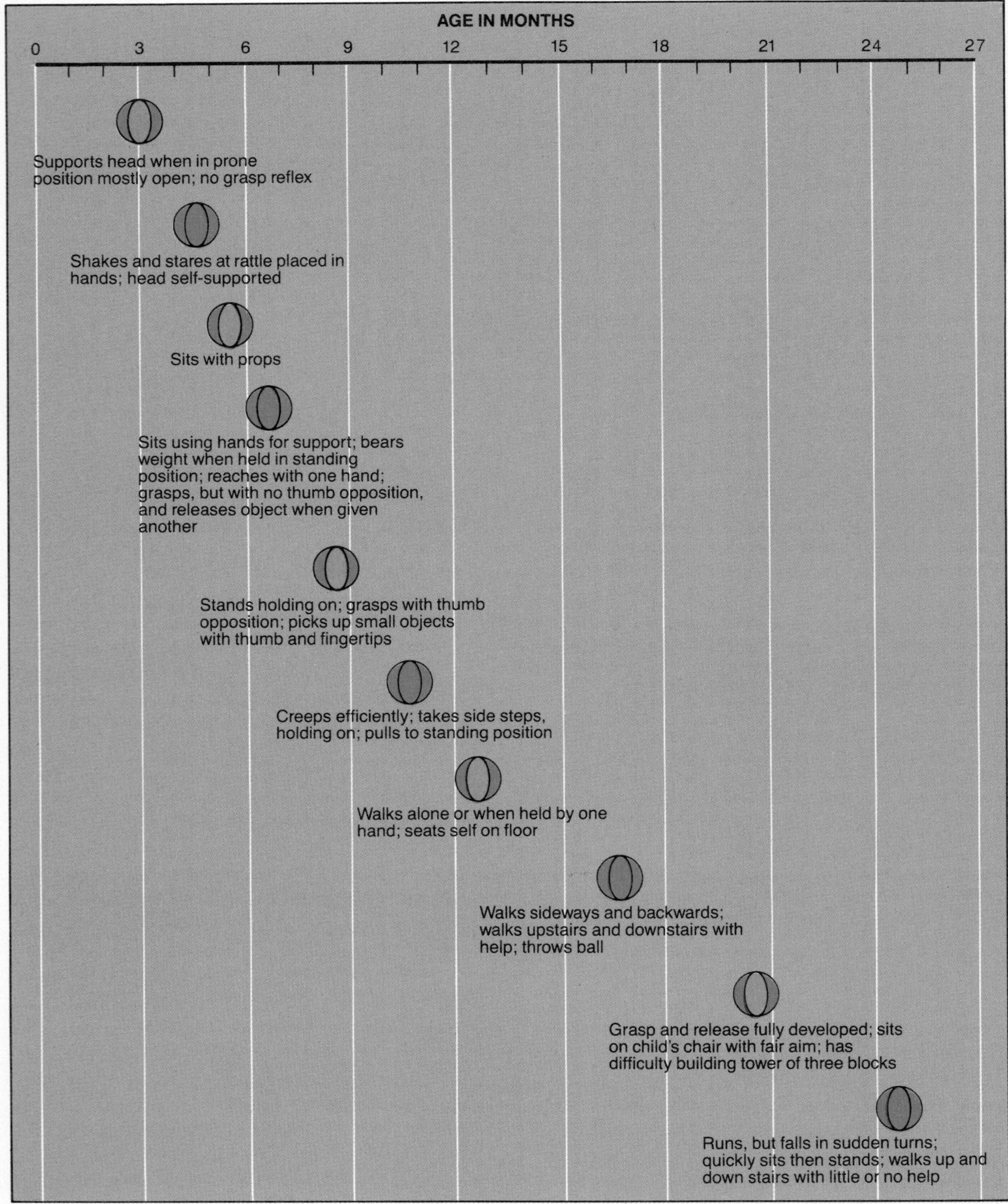
AGE IN MONTHS
0
3
6
9
12
15
18
21
24
27
Supports head when in prone position mostly open; no grasp reflex
Shakes and stares at rattle placed in hands; head self-supported
Sits with props
Sits using hands for support; bears weight when held in standing position; reaches with one hand; grasps, but with no thumb opposition, and releases object when given another
Stands holding on; grasps with thumb opposition; picks up small objects with thumb and fingertips
Creeps efficiently; takes side steps, holding on; pulls to standing position
Walks alone or when held by one hand; seats self on floor
Walks sideways and backwards; walks upstairs and downstairs with help; throws ball
Grasp and release fully developed; sits on child's chair with fair aim; has difficulty building tower of three blocks
Runs, but falls in sudden turns; quickly sits then stands; walks up and down stairs with little or no help

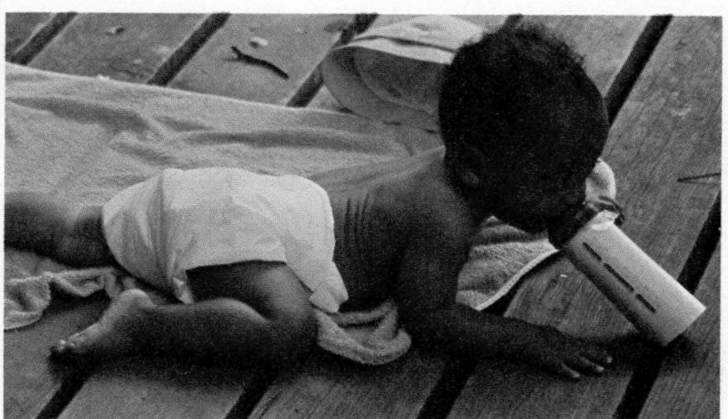

Babies begin to explore the environment with their eyes. As their eye-hand coordination develops, they can grasp and manipulate objects. At eight or nine months, their improved coordination allows them to crawl.
(Clockwise: ***Suzanne Szasz; Bill Stanton/Magnum Photos; Frostie/Woodfin Camp & Assoc.*****)**

At about seven months, babies may sit up without help and at about eight or nine months, they may begin to crawl, scooting about on their bellies while dragging their feet along behind them. In another month, many will creep about on their hands and knees. Some babies neither creep nor crawl, but one day simply get up on their feet and walk.

Soon after their first birthday, most infants take their first steps (Falkner, 1966). The consequences of this development for both child and parent are incalculable. By now, the majority of infants respond to simple commands and may also be able to express their desires in one- or two-word utterances, lessening the precariousness of their position.

By eighteen months, most infants can run, if somewhat clumsily and can drag or push a toy along as they propel themselves through the environment. Their range of physical capabilities continues to expand during the next six months,

FIGURE 6.3 Some of the major milestones in motor development that occur over the first two years of life. Each dot indicates the approximate average age of occurrence. Individual infants may demonstrate these skills somewhat earlier or later than the average indicated. ***(After Lenneberg, 1967, and Bayley, 1969)***

and by the time they are two, most can walk proficiently and run reasonably well, if incautiously. They may be able to use 200 different words, point to the parts of the body, and play alone for short periods of time. In short, they are no longer infants or babies, but children.

The Concept of Norms

If we are to use norms to study child development, we must understand that they are based on simple mathematical calculations that reflect average growth tendencies. They do not explain growth or development, they merely describe it, indicating what is most likely to appear in the development of children at various ages.

For most infants, norms can be useful in describing how they develop. They can help in assessing the effects of environmental changes on behavior, such as the effect of separating children from their mothers, or they can be useful in studying cross-cultural and subcultural variations. They have also been used to examine the effects of institutionalization, of gender, and of birth order on a child's development. And they have been helpful in studies of prematurity and of early pathology (Kessen, Haith, and Salapatek, 1970).

The value of norms as a diagnostic tool for the individual child is, however, limited, because in every aspect of growth, normal children vary widely on each side of a norm. The range within which growth is still considered normal shows clearly in a study Howard Meredith (1963) conducted among Iowa males. At the age of eighteen, the lightest boy in his study weighed no more than the heaviest boy had weighed when he was eight. The boy who was lightest at eight weighed about the same as the heaviest boy when he was two.

The age at which normal children master motor skills also shows great variability. We have noted that some children never creep or crawl but go directly from sitting to taking their first steps. The normal range for the onset of walking is itself large, from as early as eight months to as late as twenty.

Individual Growth Patterns

A child's growth pattern, or individual rate of growth, may also show great differences from the norm. Healthy children may mature much more slowly or more quickly than the mythical average infant described by norms. It is possible to measure the distance a child has progressed toward physiological maturity by the rate at which teeth erupt and bones approach mature shape and position or—much later—by the time at which puberty occurs. Maturation rates seem to be related to body build. That is, the child who is broadly built, large, and strong is likely to grow rapidly, whereas a slender, long-legged, but small, lightly muscled child is likely to grow more slowly (Bayley, 1956).

The confusion created by the great differences in growth can be eliminated by looking at an individual's growth only in relation to his or her own growth curve. Data taken at intervals over long periods of time allow us to make statements about the child's growth relative to him- or herself. For example, data on a child's height, weight, the closure of bones in the hand, etc. become the standard against which to compare the same child's status at other times. Individual children's growth patterns can then be compared with relevant norms, in order to discover any relative precocity or slowness.

Although individual growth patterns are relatively stable, they can be temporarily disrupted by severe dietary deficiencies or stress. When the condition responsible for retarded growth is eliminated, a child often goes through a period of "catch-up" growth. J. M. Tanner (1978) calls this temporary deviation from the normal growth curve, and the subsequent return, the **canalization** of growth. He argues that each child's growth curve is genetically determined and self-stabilizing. Although illness or malnutrition can deflect a child's growth from this natural curve, as a stream may be temporarily diverted from its normal course by an obstruction, once the environment becomes normal, the child catches up.

Newborn babies show catch-up growth in both weight and height. From birth to six months or so, smaller babies gain more weight than do larger ones (Tanner, 1978). This explains the fact that small women often bear babies who become large adults. Such newborn catch-up growth is usually completed by the end of the third year.

BRAIN DEVELOPMENT

Motor abilities and physiological growth develop at the same pace. In early infancy, for example, ability to perform motor functions and muscular development are highly correlated. The repeated observation of such correlations has led researchers to look at brain development as internal growth that may be related to both physical growth and motor development.

Brain Growth

At birth, the baby's brain has reached about 25 percent of its adult weight and size. Within two years, it will attain up to 80 percent of that size. The increased growth is due in part to increases in the size and shape of supporting glial cells (Bullock, Orkand, and Grinnell, 1977). And in part it is due to development within individual neurons, where protein is being synthesized and small, fibrous structures appear. The increased number and complexity of connections among neurons also add to brain growth, as does the continued formation of myelin around the neural fibers.

The course of this growth is genetically fixed, and it proceeds in an orderly and patterned way. The major pathways that connect parts of the nervous system and brain and are responsible for the sustenance of life are fully functional at birth. As other neural circuits develop, the cells show a great variety in shape and size, and their conducting fibers are relatively small and short. In keeping with nature's blueprint, each region of the brain eventually becomes characterized by specific types of cells arranged in specific patterns. As the connecting fibers spread, the distance between the cells of the infant's **cortex**—the surface layers of the brain that make up 99 percent of the two cerebral hemispheres—increases, and the enlarged surface of the cortex continues to fold and become increasingly wrinkled (Rose, 1973).

Perhaps because of its extensive, rapid growth during infancy, the baby's central nervous system is more plastic than it will be later in life. It has been found that if an infant is born with a maldeveloped major brain tract, the nervous system may be capable of correcting for it, possibly by developing the same function in a different area. In addition, when an infant's brain is damaged, it is likely to recover quickly and the baby may show no apparent aftereffects (Searleman, 1977). If, for example, the part of the brain that controls language function should be injured, the baby will probably develop normal language functions anyway.

At birth, when babies are awake or asleep, the electrical activity of the brain shows characteristic wave patterns, some of which were mentioned in Chapter 5. When babies are two or three months old, they begin each sleep period with quiet sleep instead of going immediately into REM sleep, as they did at birth. Other regular changes in electrical activity, including a typical pattern that occurs during the transition from wakefulness to sleep, appear during the last half of the first year. Robert Emde and his colleagues (1976) have been trying to establish a connection between the development of infant wave forms and the appearance of certain types of emotional expression, but their data show no close relationships. The brain's electrical activity reflects events in the world, and investigators have found that when babies see a new sight or hear a new sound, they respond with increasingly complex patterns of wave forms in various areas of the brain (Cobb and Mozocitti, 1967; Hoffman, 1978). The size and speed of these forms show maturational changes throughout childhood.

Cortical Control

The human cortex has been of special interest to developmental psychologists because it is the seat of language, attention, memory, spatial un-

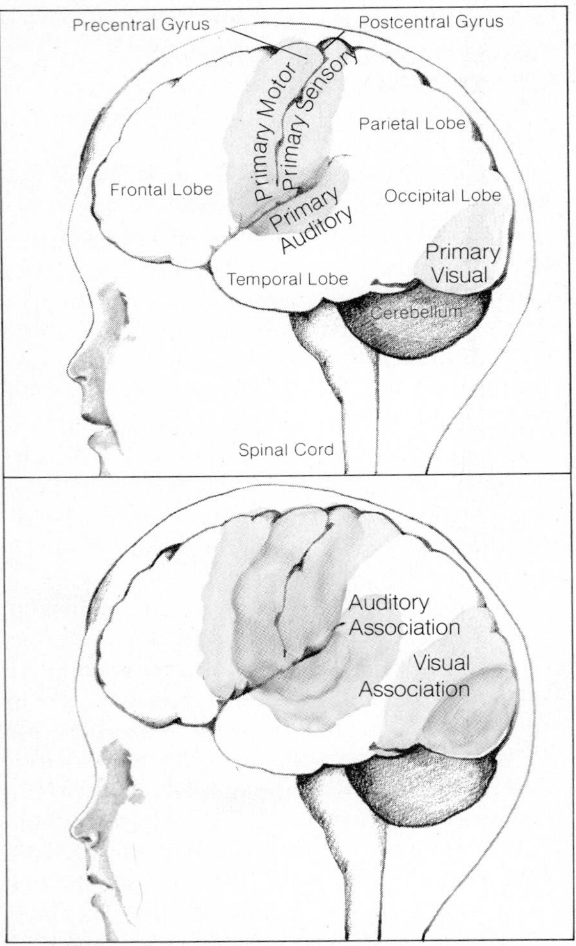

FIGURE 6.4 ***(top)*** **Drawing of the human brain, showing some of its major structures and their location and indicating the location of those primary sensory and motor areas of the cerebral cortex discussed in the text.** ***(bottom)*** **Similar drawing, showing location of later-developing association areas of the cerebral cortex, as discussed in the text.**

derstanding, and motor skills. Jesse Le Roy Conel's pioneer studies (1939–1963) of postnatal development in the cerebral cortex helped demonstrate a basis in the central nervous system for the orderly development of infant sensory and motor functions. Such work showed that certain areas of the brain control particular sensory and motor functions, and that these areas develop at different rates. As soon as a specific area in the cortex develops, the corresponding function appears in the infant's development.

Postnatal development of the cortex can be followed in two ways. One is the order in which the functional areas of the brain develop; the second is the advancement of body functions within each of these areas (Minkowski, 1967). The early stages of development are characterized by an orderly sequence in which the primary areas of the cortex begin to function efficiently. First, the primary motor area in the precentral gyrus develops, then the primary sensory area in the postcentral gyrus (see Figure 6.4). Next, the primary visual area, at the back of the head in the occipital lobe, develops, followed by the primary auditory area at the side of the head in the temporal lobe. At first, these primary areas function at a simple level. For example, newborn babies can control some of their basic body movements, and they can hear and see. During the early months, the cortical association areas, which must develop before babies can integrate and interpret the stimuli they encounter, lag behind the corresponding primary areas.

The cortical control of behavior develops sequentially (Wittrock, 1980). Most of the cerebral cortex thickens during the baby's first three months, but the primary motor area develops more rapidly than the rest. Again, the cephalocaudal and proximodistal developmental patterns hold true; cortical control of the head, upper trunk, and arms appears before that of the legs, and cortical control of arm movements appears before infants can use their hands skillfully. Other primary cortical areas develop in sequence, and the infant is then capable of controlled movement and simple auditory and visual functions. During this period, a sheath of myelin, which speeds the transmission of nerve impulses, rapidly develops around the cells of the motor and sensory areas.

When the baby reaches the age of six months, the primary motor and sensory areas are still the most advanced, but other areas of the cortex are beginning to catch up. There is marked growth in the cortical motor areas that

The baby gains control over the hands, arms, and upper trunk well before control over the legs develops. *(Jan Lukas/Photo Researchers, Inc.)*

control the hands, upper trunk, head, and legs. Between six and fifteen months, growth of these motor areas slows down. By then, infants can control their hands and arms, but control over the legs is not nearly so well developed. In fact, some children still do not walk at fifteen months. During this same period, the visual association areas of the cortex are more advanced than the auditory association areas. By the time the child is two, all primary motor and sensory cortical areas are well advanced, and the cortical association areas have developed further. This continued development enables two-year-olds to integrate the information they get from their own movements as well as from the environment into complex patterns of behavior.

The growth of particular cortical areas and the development of motor functions is correlational. As noted earlier, correlations do not tell us what is cause and what is effect. Some researchers have argued, therefore, that the baby's use of the body and nervous system causes the growth of appropriate brain areas, instead of brain growth leading to increased physical and mental control. Steven Rose (1973) is among those who suggest that the barrage of sensory information that assails newborns when they emerge from the uterus leads the cortex to grow and neural connections to develop. In support of this position, we can point to studies of animals, which have shown that without stimulation, parts of the nervous system atrophy (Cummins et al., 1979; Rosenzweig and Bennett, 1976; Wiesel and Hubel, 1963). Yet studies of premature human babies show that they reach various motor milestones at the same age as full-term babies—if the premature babies' age is calculated from the moment of conception, rather than from the time of birth. So although premature babies have received an extra month or two of external stimulation, this is not reflected in speeded motor development (Douglas, 1956).

GROWTH AND ENVIRONMENT

No one is sure how or why environmental factors influence growth during infancy and childhood. The internal mechanism that regulates growth appears to be affected by hormonal and chemical factors, and nutrition, illness, and stress may

BREAST OR BOTTLE?

Since the composition of human milk evolved along with the species, it apparently contains the correct balance of nutrients for the developing infant. Yet babies can also thrive on the milk of cows or goats or on artificial formulas. A health problem that surfaced in the past decade came from the trend toward formula feeding in developing nations. In preindustrialized countries, breast-fed babies traditionally received an adequate, clean food supply during their early months (Thomson, 1968). But as more mothers began to use the "modern" method of formula feeding, babies suffered. Contaminated milk prepared under unsanitary conditions and placed in dirty bottles led to infant deaths from diarrhea. At the same time, inadequate nutrition, when family poverty led mothers to dilute the formula, caused babies to waste away. In East Africa, such babies are said to suffer from chupa-itis, or "inflammation of the bottle" (Jelliffe and Jelliffe, 1978). The situation became so serious that the World Health Organization voted to urge a global ban on the promotion of infant formulas (Campbell, 1981).

In deciding whether a baby should receive breast milk or formula, both the physiological and the psychological aspects of nursing need to be considered. From the medical standpoint, human milk—and especially colostrum, the fluid that is secreted for a few days after childbirth, before regular milk production begins—provides the baby with the mother's immunity to diseases and helps prevent allergies. Breast-fed babies appear to be less likely to develop asthma and allergic skin rashes than bottle-fed babies. Also, breast-fed babies are less likely to show deficiencies in folic acid (vitamin B_{12}), since breast milk contains a factor that greatly increases the body's absorption of folic acid, an element whose deficiency leads to impaired body growth and central nervous system development in the first year of life (Colman, Hettiarachchy, and Herbert, 1981).

However, breast-feeding has its negative aspects, too. Drugs and alcohol ingested by mothers pass into the breast milk and affect their babies. And when mothers live in contaminated areas, chemicals, such as the carcinogen PCB, concentrate in their milk. But a mother can refrain from drugs and alcohol during the months she nurses her baby; and if she fears her milk is contaminated, it can be tested.

Because mothers who choose to breast-feed and those who choose to use the bottle generally have different values and perhaps different personalities, it is difficult to measure the psychological effects of various feeding methods. Researchers (e.g., Newton, 1971) have found that mothers who choose to bottle-feed generally give such reasons as, "It doesn't tie me down." Mothers who choose breast-feeding tend to say "It's much better for the baby."

Charlotte Modahl and Niles Newton (1979) studied a group of mothers who alternately used breast- and bottle-feeding with their infants. The same mothers were tested while they were breast-feeding, while they were bottle-feeding, or when they were not feeding their babies. When the mothers were tested during bottle-feeding, they showed significantly more anxiety, stress, depression, fatigue, and guilt than when they were tested under either of the other conditions. The investigators suggest that since mothers spend a good deal of time feeding their new babies, a mother's consistent moods during that time might affect the tone of their relationship, perhaps even altering the quality of the bond between the pair.

Bottle-feeding generally means less cuddling from the mother. Studies have shown that mothers who choose to breast-feed tend to spend more time holding their newborns than do other mothers, and breast-feeding mothers are more likely to rock their babies and to sleep with them (Newton et al., 1975; Newton, 1979). As bottle-fed babies get older, mothers tend to put them down with the bottle instead of holding them as a breast-feeding mother must do. Whether this affects either the bond between mother and child or the baby's later personality is unknown. Bottle-feeding does, however, give the father a chance to join in the early feeding process, thereby associating himself with whatever bonding properties it may have. Since there are pros and cons to each method, a couple's decision to breast- or bottle-feed their baby will depend on the specific situation.

affect the composition and production of these chemicals (Tanner, 1978).

Socioeconomic background, illness, and stress may influence growth in part through their indirect effect on nutrition. Children who are ill or extremely upset may not eat as much or as well as healthy, contented children. Children from lower socioeconomic classes may have parents who cannot afford to provide proper nutrition and medical care or who do not understand how to provide sufficient proteins, vitamins, and minerals on limited budgets by using inexpensive but unfamiliar high-protein food such as soybean flour.

Nutrition and Health

Because nutrition is a central environmental determinant of normal physical growth, dietary deficiencies are often responsible for abnormal growth patterns during infancy. In some instances, the choice of early feeding methods may have important effects on development, as the accompanying box indicates.

General malnutrition, in which children simply do not get enough to eat, is marked by a lack of calories as well as a lack of protein, vitamins, and minerals. This near-starvation is most prevalent in developing countries (Waterlow and Payne, 1975). As the number of calories available to a young child drops dangerously near the level required for maintenance and growth, the child becomes listless and ceases to play or to explore the environment. When calorie intake drops below the minimum level, growth ceases.

The importance of nutrition is also reflected in the growth records of infants and children who have been exposed to wartime famine. These children show delayed growth during such periods; but if the episode of malnutrition is neither too severe nor too long, the effects of acute malnourishment can usually be overcome through catch-up growth. Studies of children who were subjected to severe wartime malnutrition in Europe and Asia indicate that once these children return to a normal diet, they catch up with their peers by adolescence (Wolff, 1935; Acheson, 1960). In Figure 6.5, the growth of a little girl who suffered from two periods of malnutrition in infancy and early childhood shows how dramatically catch-up growth functions.

Still, a child who is chronically undernourished will suffer permanent effects. Such children generally grow to be smaller adults than they would have been had they eaten an adequate diet. Nevin Scrimshaw and John Gordon (1968) have discussed the probable effects of severe malnutrition on the human nervous system. They point out that, although head circumference shows no relationship to intelligence among normal children, it is a reasonably good indicator of brain size. They then cite the reports of researchers in Mexico, Guatemala, Peru, Uganda, and other developing countries, which show that children who have had severely deficient diets from birth show smaller head circumference than children of the same ethnic group who have always been well-fed. However, a later study of Guatemalan infants indicates that during the first two years of life an infant's height and weight are better guides as to the effects of malnutrition than is head circumference (Lasky et al., 1981). Both height and weight were good predictors of performance on mental and motor tests among these infants; and when height and weight were controlled for, head circumference failed to account for any significant difference in test performance.

Deficiencies of specific nutrients can affect growth in specific ways. For example, a serious, often fatal disease, called **kwashiorkor,** develops from severe, prolonged protein deficiency. This ailment is prevalent among infants in developing countries who go off breast milk and on to a low-protein substitute when they are weaned (Scrimshaw, 1969; Waterlow, 1973). Such infants have a scaly skin, profound apathy, diarrhea, swollen limbs and abdomen, and liver degeneration. When they begin to eat adequate protein, victims of kwashiorkor grow rapidly but never catch up with normal children of their own age (Eichenwald and Fry, 1969). If the disease is allowed to go untreated for a lengthy period, the infants may be severely retarded (Cravioto and DeLicardie, 1970).

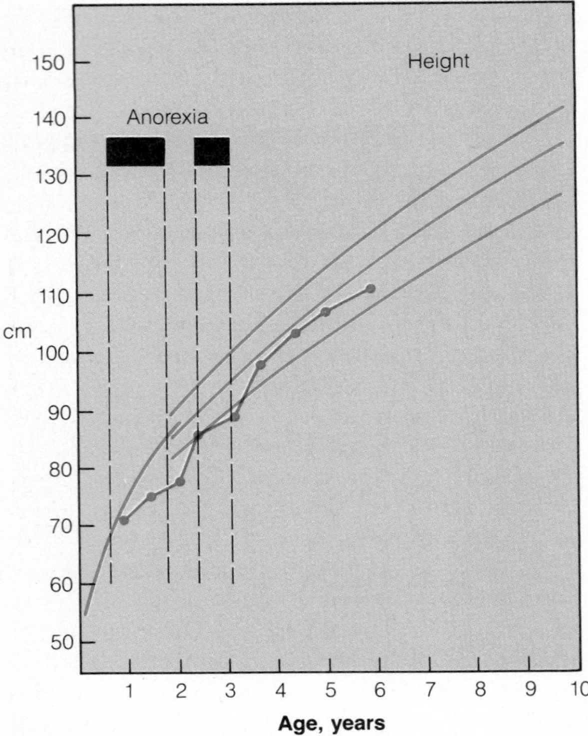

FIGURE 6.5 Each time this little girl went through a period of near starvation, her growth slowed and her recorded height fell below her individual growth curve. But the catch-up growth that accompanied adequate nutrition eventually returned her to her own growth curve. *(J.M. Tanner.* **Fetus into Man** *Harvard University Press, 1978. Redrawn from Prader, Tanner, and von Harnack, 1963 page 155)*

Too much food can also upset normal growth patterns and result in obese, or excessively fat, children. Studies (e.g., Bronstein et al., 1942; Bruch, 1957) have shown that childhood obesity can almost always be traced to overfeeding; malfunctioning glands are rarely to blame. Such overfeeding is common in affluent Western nations, especially when mothers provide an oversupply of nutritious food in a determination to have healthy children. However, excessive food can produce unhappy and socially maladjusted children who generally grow up to be fat adults. It has been proposed that overnutrition in infancy may lead to a multiplication of extra-large fat cells (Dwyer and Mayer, 1973). In comparison with muscle cells, fat cells have tiny nuclei, but each cell expands to an enormous size by storing fat. Once formed, fat cells never disappear, so that when extra fat cells develop in infancy, a person remains susceptible to obesity throughout life. The danger of establishing obesity extends past infancy. Forcing food on a two- or three-year-old whose growth rate has settled into the childhood plateau can also result in an obese child.

Not all obese children are so because their parents overfeed them. There may be some sort of perceptual difference that makes food more appealing to certain people, leading them to overeat. When babies of overweight parents were compared with those of normal-weight parents, two striking differences appeared. First, babies whose mothers and fathers were overweight had a sweet tooth; after sucking a sweet sugar solution, they were more likely to reject plain water than were babies whose mothers and fathers were of normal weight. Second, babies of overweight parents showed a heightened response to visual patterns, shifting their gaze more rapidly and making larger visual shifts than did babies of normal-weight parents (Milstein, 1980). A similar heightened responsiveness to environmental cues has appeared in many studies of obese children and adults (Rodin, 1981).

Other research indicates that some people may become overweight because their bodies burn calories more slowly than most people's do (Harvard Medical School, 1981). It appears that the red blood cells in certain individuals use considerably less energy than might be expected. Yet, in such cases, the basic problem of calories is the same; obesity is still the result of consuming more calories than the body needs to have.

Illness can also affect growth patterns. Short illnesses, especially the communicable diseases common among children from two to six, have little effect. When illness is severe, however, certain aspects of growth tend to slow. During an extended illness a child's growth rate may slow slightly, but in most cases catch-up growth compensates for the slowdown. For example, Roy Acheson (1960) found that one year of severe, confining illness resulted in a height loss of only about one-fourth inch. When serious and protracted illness results in permanent underdevelopment, the cause is not simply the sickness but the loss of periods of reasonably steady growth needed for adequate development.

Being poor during infancy and/or childhood often means not getting enough of the nutritionally right foods to eat. *(© Nick Sapieha/Stock, Boston)*

Social and Psychological Factors

Among children of the lower socioeconomic classes, setbacks to growth are common. In such circumstances, inadequate nutrition often has undramatic but insidious effects. Sluggish children whose interest is hard to arouse may reflect the low energy levels that accompany poor diets. Diseases of the eyes and skin and the respiratory and gastrointestinal tracts may be prevalent because undernourished children are more vulnerable to infection. Nagging ailments, including badly decayed teeth, may result because of a lack of regular medical care.

Among children two to four and a half years old, growth differences between those whose fathers are in highly skilled occupations and those with fathers in less skilled occupations become steadily larger. Also, children in the upper socioeconomic classes seem to grow more rapidly. Research in both England and Scotland supports this conclusion (E. Scott, Illsby, and Thomson, 1956), as do studies conducted in the United States (Hamill, Johnston, and Lemeshow, 1972). These studies indicate that children of higher socioeconomic background tend to be larger at all ages. Part of the differences in childhood stature is probably a result of the fact that children in the wealthier classes generally have faster growth rates, reaching puberty earlier. As the slowly developing children mature, however, they do not make up all the height difference, which means that there are socioeconomic differences in adult height.

Nutrition and medical care may provide only a part of the explanation for these differences. Class differences in sleep and exercise habits, and in general home life, may contribute to the effect. Meager resources and large families may combine to diminish the quality of maternal care, leading to retarded growth rates. No matter what the cause, children from poor homes suffer more illnesses, encounter more accidents and disasters, and undergo more physical trauma than do middle-class children (R. Hess, 1970).

Severe emotional stress can also retard growth, apparently by affecting the body's secretion of hormones. Several hormones have important roles in the regulation of growth, but the growth hormone (GH) itself is one of the most important. At one time, children who lacked GH became midgets, perfectly proportioned adults about 4 feet tall. Today, such children receive injections of GH, taken from human pituitary glands, which stimulates catch-up growth and enables the children to grow tall enough to fall within the normal height range.

So far as is known, the level of GH rises in the blood only a few times each day—about an hour or so after children go to sleep, after they exercise, or when they are anxious. GH stimulates the liver to produce somatomedin, a hormone that acts on the growing cartilage cells at the ends of bones and probably on muscle cells as well. A single dose of GH keeps somatomedin blood levels high for at least twenty-four hours (Tanner, 1978).

In some children, severe psychological stress stops the production of GH. Like children whose bodies do not produce the hormone, they fail to grow. The onset of the condition, called "deprivation dwarfism" or "psychosocial dwarfism," is associated with severe emotional distress in young children (Powell, Brasel, and Blizzard, 1967). Indeed, if affected children are removed from their disturbed environment, they show rapid catch-up growth.

The rate of growth can also be disrupted by less severe stress, perhaps indicating a reduced secretion of GH. This phenomenon may explain the report that children in an orphanage run by a severe, punitive administrator grew more slowly than children in a less harsh orphanage, whose diet even had 20 percent fewer calories (Widdowson, 1951). Similarly, boys in boarding schools have been known to grow more slowly during the school term than when they were home for the holidays (Tanner, 1978). However, the everyday stresses of a child's life have little impact on growth; only severe stress will slow the rate of growth.

THE DEVELOPMENT OF MOTOR ABILITIES

Environment also affects the development of motor skills, and some quite simple sequences depend on an intricate interplay between maturational changes and experience. An especially puzzling aspect of motor development is handedness.

Handedness

Among the world's adult population, only 5 to 10 percent are left-handed, although 15 percent of preschoolers favor their left hands, suggesting a partially experiential basis for handedness. Heredity may also be implicated, for the frequency of left-handedness in both identical and fraternal twins is significantly higher than it is among single births (Hicks and Kinsbourne, 1976), and left-handed parents are the most likely to have left-handed children (Carter-Saltzman, 1980). But the genetic or constitutional basis for handedness is unknown (Hardyck and Petrinovich, 1977), and it is possible that living with left-handed parents increases a child's tendency to use that hand.

One possible explanation for the predominance of right-handed people has to do with **cerebral dominance.** That is, the left side of the brain controls the voluntary muscles of the right side of the body, and the right side of the brain controls the voluntary muscles of the left side of the body. In most people, the left hemisphere becomes dominant; but whether most of us are right-handed because we are left-brained or left-brained because we are right-handed is uncertain (Hécaen and Ajuriaguerra, 1964).

Handedness begins to become evident in the latter part of the first year. Almost as soon as infants can use their two hands independently, most prefer the right. Several findings suggest that this preference develops according to a timetable. Immediately after birth, most babies show a tendency to turn their heads to the right (Kinsbourne and Swanson, 1979), and the direction in which a newborn turns the head significantly predicts later handedness (Michel, 1981). In addition, when young babies turn their heads, they automatically extend an arm in the direction the head is turned. Because the arm they extend reflexively is likely to be that of the dominant side, this posture (called the tonic neck reflex) predicts which hand they will later prefer. By about three months, most infants hold a toy longer when it is placed in their right hand than when it is placed in their left, and between six and nine months, most babies use their right hands when they reach for an object that is directly in front of them.

Because in nearly all adult right-handers and some left-handers the left side of the brain

HANDS, EARS, AND EYES—AN EXPLORATION OF DOMINANCE

Dominance of ear and eye—that is, whether the left or right predominates—often accompanies the establishment of cerebral dominance and the development of handedness. To establish which ear is dominant, researchers generally use a **dichotic** listening technique, in which different stimuli are presented at the same time, one to each ear. Because an individual is more likely to report hearing the stimulus in the dominant ear, and because what is heard in each ear is transmitted to the opposite hemisphere for processing, the results of a dichotic listening test reveal both which ear is dominant and which hemisphere processes spoken communication. Studies using this technique indicate that right-ear superiority becomes established quite early in a majority of children. For nouns such as "ball," "cup," and "dog," most children show right-ear preference by the time they are three years old, the youngest age tested (Ingram, 1975b).

Developmental research on sighting dominance suggests that the right or the left eye may become dominant earlier than the ear or hand. In studies of sighting dominance, Stanley Coren (1974) noted which eye suddenly stopped converging, or diverged, when a light shining from directly between and in front of the eyes was gradually brought toward the face. The eye that reacted was the dominant eye. Coren found that when children were tested in this manner, a majority of year-old infants showed sighting dominance and the incidence of right-eye dominance did not change among older children. But not all right-handed adults are right-eyed; only about 65 percent of right-handed people show right-eye dominance (Dziadosz and Schaller, 1977).

A large minority of children and adults show no expected associations among handedness, eye or ear preference, and cerebral dominance. In one study of three- to five-year-old right-handed children, Merrill Hiscock and Marcel Kinsbourne (1977) found that only 60 percent showed a right-ear dominance when listening to numbers. In another study of three- to five-year-old right-handers, Dianna Ingram (1975b) discovered no relation between ear preference and the hand children gestured with during speech. Mixed patterns of dominance occur frequently among normal children and adults—and may even be associated with superior abilities in processing various types of information (Kershner, 1974; Corballis, 1980). Clearly, interaction between the two hemispheres and the rest of the body is more complicated than it might seem at first.

is primarily responsible for the production and comprehension of language, several investigators have suggested that both the onset of handedness and the beginnings of speech may be due to the establishment of the left hemisphere's dominance in the control of motor functions. That handedness and speech may be connected is suggested by the fact that somewhere between twelve and fifteen months most infants begin using their hands in coordination, adopting a consistent right-left strategy when faced with a task that requires both hands (Ramsay, Campos, and Fenson, 1979). In exploring toys with movable parts, right-handed babies generally hold the base of the toy in the left hand and manipulate its movable parts with the right. This strategy appears either at the same time as or just before babies first put together dissimilar syllables to form words (such as "daddy," "baby," and "pretty") (Ramsay, 1980).

If handedness is indeed connected with speech, the basis for right- or left-hand preference may be laid down before birth, because studies of newborns have found the left side of the brain is already more active than the right in processing speech. Dennis Molfese and Victoria Molfese (1979) played speech syllables to sleeping newborns and recorded the electrical activity

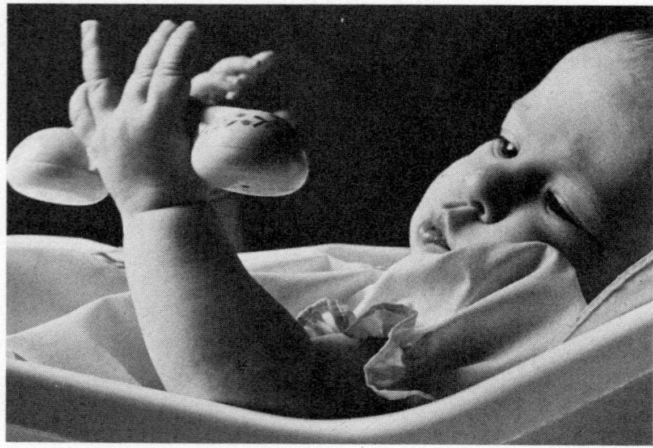

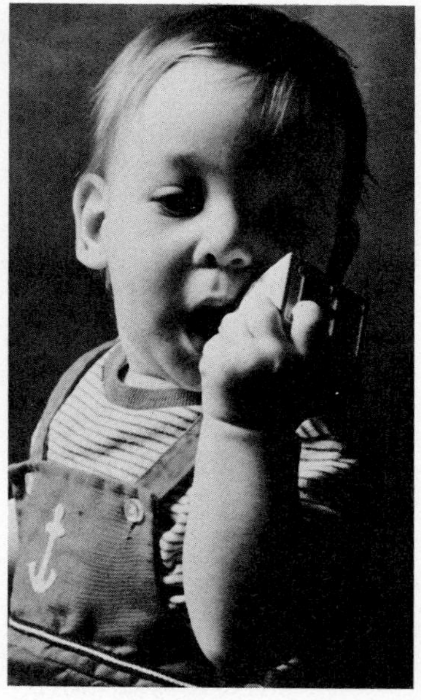

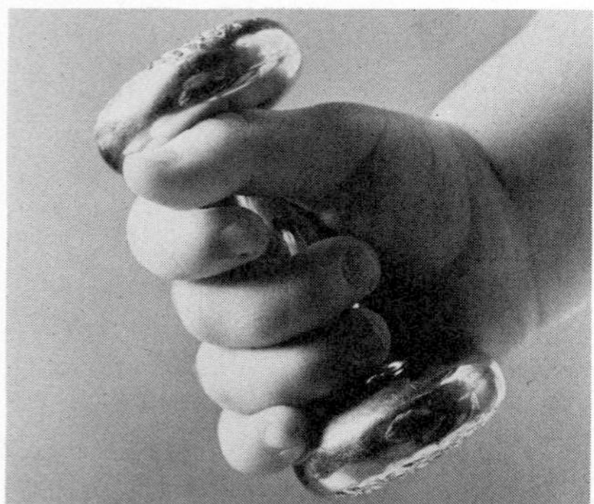

(top left) **At twenty weeks, infants hold objects without firmly grasping them.** ***(top right)*** **By twenty-eight weeks, they can use their palms to close in on and pick up an object.** ***(bottom left)*** **By forty weeks, they use the thumb and forefinger in opposition, grasping much as an adult does.** *(Steve McCarroll)*

from each hemisphere. They found that although both hemispheres registered the sounds, the left was faster than the right. In fact, it was the only hemisphere to register some types of sounds, suggesting the presence of special mechanisms in the left hemisphere that detect and analyze the sounds of human speech.

Differences between the way the brain processes speech and other sounds are apparent among somewhat older babies (Molfese, Freeman, and Palermo, 1975). When slightly older infants hear consonant-vowel sounds or extended passages of speech, their brain-wave recordings reveal greater cortical activity in the left than in the right hemisphere. When they hear musical chords or passages of music, the right hemisphere shows increased cortical activity compared with the left. Such differences do not indicate that only one hemisphere can handle certain tasks, such as language, but that each hemisphere is more proficient at processing certain kinds of material.

Maturation and Experience

In the development of certain skills such as stepping or reaching for objects, there may be a sequence in which early, more primitive coordinations disappear and then reappear later in more advanced forms (Bever, 1981). The causes of this sequence are unknown, but they may be due to developmental changes in brain and nervous sys-

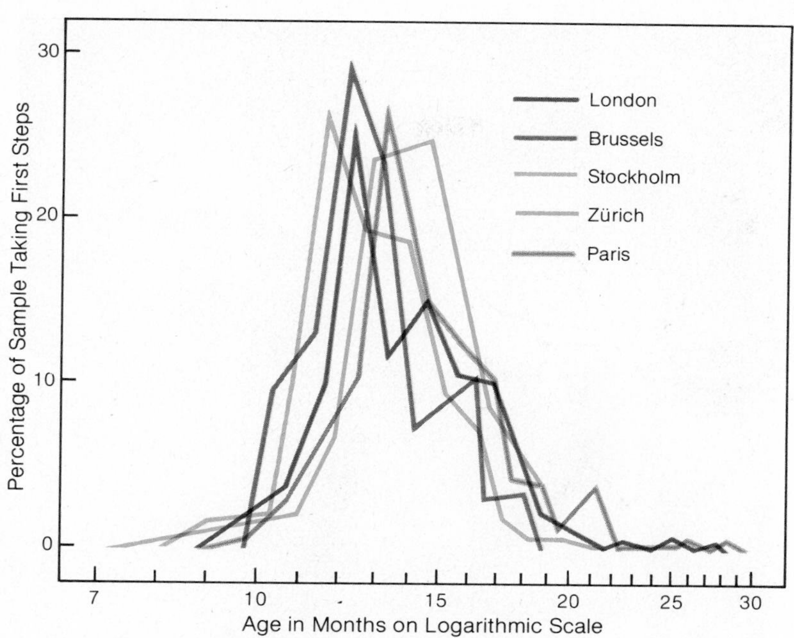

FIGURE 6.6 Ages in months at which infants in several cities took their first steps. ***(Adapted from Hindley et al., 1966)***

tem organization. Perhaps when control shifts to the developing cortex, a previously reflexive action must be relearned as a skill. In some instances, the changes can be influenced by stimulation. If, for example, babies are given practice in the stepping reflex for about ten minutes each day from two weeks until they are eight weeks old, they are likely to walk a bit earlier than the average baby (Zelazo, Zelazo, and Kolb, 1972).

Yet studies of infants in different cultures indicate that in spite of widely different opportunities to practice the skill, children walk at roughly the same time in all cultures. For example, although Hopi Indian infants spend their first year bound to cradleboards (see photo on page 152), they walk at about the same time as infants in other cultures, who have had more practice in muscular coordination (Dennis and Dennis, 1940). In addition, despite the fact that child-rearing methods differ across Europe, so that infants in some areas receive more encouragement to walk, most infants in five of Europe's largest cities take their first steps within a few months of one another (see Figure 6.6).

The relative contributions of maturation and experience have also been assessed by using **co-twin control,** in which the researcher gives one of a pair of twins some experiences believed to be important in learning a skill and withholds or delays those same experiences for the other twin. In Myrtle McGraw's (1935, 1939) classic co-twin control study, one twin received practice in crawling and standing and the other was kept from all opportunities. Despite the difference in their experience, both twins crawled and walked at the same age. But practice did make a difference in the way the twins developed individualistic skills, such as swimming and skating.

One means of evaluating the roles of maturation and experience is to deliberately restrict a child's movement. For example, Wayne Dennis (1941) left a pair of female twins on their backs from birth to nine months, never allowing them to sit or to stand. Yet the sitting and standing of both twins emerged fully developed, with little or no practice. It should be noted that except for the experimental restriction, both girls had a fairly normal environment.

Although Hopi infants spend much of their first year bound to cradleboards, which limit motor activity and practice, they begin to walk at about the same time as most infants in other cultures. ***(Marcia Keegan)***

When children grow up in an environment that is both socially and physically impoverished, the development of motor skills may lag severely. In a series of studies conducted in institutions with such environments, Dennis and his associates (Dennis, 1960; Dennis and Najarian, 1957; Dennis and Sayegh, 1965) found that children who were ignored by adults and surrounded by an unstimulating environment showed retarded motor development from the time they were two months old.

Yet the effect of such deprivation can be overcome. In one study, Dennis and Yvonne Sayegh (1965) worked with infants in The Creche, a foundling home in Lebanon. In that institution infants spent most of their first year lying on their backs in cribs. Some of the infants in their study who were more than one year old could not sit up. The infants in the experimental group were propped into a sitting position and were allowed to play with such simple attractive objects as fresh flowers, pieces of colored sponge, and colored plastic disks strung on a chain for as little as an hour each day. This seemingly small amount of stimulation caused the babies' developmental age to jump dramatically.

In a related study, Burton White and Richard Held (1966) investigated the effect of enriched stimulation on the development of grasping. They concluded that appropriate extra stimulation could accelerate the baby's acquisition of grasping. However, more detailed studies have suggested (B. White, 1971, 1975) that stimulation must be appropriate to both the age of a baby and his or her abilities. Too much stimulation, for example, may irritate or confuse the baby, at least temporarily, and fail to accelerate the development of motor skills.

Thus although a motor development may not require any practice beyond normal freedom for spontaneous activity, some environments promote development, whereas others retard it.

SUMMARY

1. Three basic principles underlie the growth and development of all body systems: cephalocaudal growth, which refers to the progression of growth from head to foot; proximodistal development, which refers to the progression of growth from the center of the body toward the periphery; and differentiation and integration, which refers to the fact that skills become increasingly specific and combined into more complex skills.

2. Norms are typical patterns that describe the way important attributes and skills develop and the approximate ages at which they appear. An individual's growth may be quite different from the norm, and maturation rates seem related to body build. Should severe dietary deficiency or stress disrupt growth, the child generally shows a later period of rapid, or catch-up, growth that returns growth to the normal curve, a pattern called canalization.

3. The primary motor and sensory areas of the cortex develop rapidly, with body functions advancing with the growth of corresponding areas of the brain. Development in the association areas, where stimuli are integrated and interpreted, is relatively slow. Although studies indicate that stimulation is necessary for the development of the central nervous system, maturation is also important, as indicated by the fact that premature babies reach various levels of motor development at the appropriate age calculated from conception—not birth.

4. Environmental factors, such as nutrition, illness, stress, and the quality of maternal care can either promote or impede a child's growth. Children in upper socioeconomic classes grow more rapidly and mature earlier than children in lower socioeconomic classes, perhaps because of differences in nutrition, although class differences in sleep, exercise habits, and maternal care may also play a part.

5. The cause of handedness is not known, and it is probably influenced by both genetic and experiential factors. Handedness and speech appear to be connected, because infants often begin using a consistent strategy for exploration (for example, holding an object in the left hand and manipulating it with the right) at about the time they form words from unlike syllables ("daddy," "baby").

6. Psychologists have studied the relative roles of maturation and experience by comparing the age at which infants in different cultures acquire certain skills, by providing only one of a pair of twins with some experience considered necessary in learning a skill, and by assessing the effects of restrictions in a child's experience. Although only minimal normal practice appears to be necessary for the development of most skills, some environments promote development and some do not.

7 COGNITION: FROM SENSING TO KNOWING

David, who is fifteen months old, has discovered his mother's pen, which was lying open on the coffee table. When his mother comes to check on her quiet son, she finds ink on his mouth, on his hands, and on his clothes. She takes away the pen, puts it on a high shelf and, when David protests, picks him up for a moment. As soon as she puts him down, he toddles over to the shelf, stretches out his arm, opens and closes his fingers, and says "Day-boo"—his word for himself—to indicate he wants the pen. Although he cannot see the pen, he knows that it is lying on the shelf. David has not always been so persistent. When he was eight months old, he forgot about forbidden playthings when his mother distracted him. But now that he is older, his memory has developed and he has a mental image of the forbidden toy.

David has taken the first steps on the long and challenging journey called cognitive development. In order to understand the demands of the journey, it is important to realize what is involved in the development of the human mind.

The adult mind is organized. Healthy adults clearly distinguish between what is within them—their thoughts, feelings, and dreams—and what is outside them—the physical world of objects and the social world of people. Things in the world are related. Some are related by being members of the same category: the banana, potato, and pork chop are all foods; the hammer, knife, and saw are all tools. Other things are related in terms of action and its effects. The light switch on the wall is related to the physically dissimilar and spatially remote light on the ceiling. The pressing of a key on the typewriter is related to the letter that appears on the blank page.

Adults recognize that some things that appear to be dissimilar are in fact similar. The water that pours from the tap is the same substance that escapes as steam from the teakettle spout or that clinks as ice in a glass of lemonade. Adults accept such transformations as maintaining the identity of the object that has been transformed. They accept certain different things as equivalent to one another, such as A and a. Other transformations surprise people and demand explanation. If someone covers an object with a handkerchief and it has disappeared when he or she removes the handkerchief, adults are puzzled. Their expectations about the behavior of the world are violated.

All these features of adults' orientation to the world seem so natural that it is hard to believe that human beings do anything other than passively observe the way things are. It is hard to believe that this commonplace organization of things into categories and into cause-and-effect relationships is, in fact, the product of years of maturation and experience.

In this chapter, we will follow the development of the child's mind during infancy, the first two years of life. We will see the baby's senses become proficient as he or she begins to organize perceptions. We will discover what infant studies allow us to infer about the development of attention and the increasing ability to learn from experience. We will discuss the stages of cognitive growth in infancy, tracing the baby's separation of self from the world. Finally, we will examine the development of the understanding that objects continue to exist even when they are out of sight.

COGNITION

The term "cognition" refers to the manner in which each of us comes to know about our world and to what we know about it. Cognition includes processes such as sensing, perceiving, using symbols, thinking, planning, reasoning, and fantasizing. The lengthy story of cognitive development is the story of how children progress from the limited and dissociated store of knowledge and intellectual skills they possess at birth to the concept-rich, well-ordered store of knowledge that most adults use so well.

By the time we complete our tale of the first two years, we will have seen babies as remarkably active organisms, curious about the world and themselves and eager to make sense of them both, constructing from their varied experiences new hypotheses—about how its parts fit and mesh and about which of their actions are permissible and which forbidden. We will see them as architects of time, space, and objects, and as designers and users of symbols. Cognition is the vehicle by which infants become intellectually accomplished adults.

Cognitive progress results from the interaction of biological maturation and cumulative experience. In order for experiences to make their mark on the infant they must first register on the baby's sensory receptors. Infants are biologically constructed so as to be able to pick up certain aspects of the physical world; in other words they are capable of **sensation,** of receiving stimulation or information from the external world. It is important, however, to distinguish between sensitivity to a certain physical or chemical property of the universe and the act and experience of seeing, hearing, smelling, tasting, and touching.

This higher level of knowing about the world is reflected in the infant's **perceptions** of that world. Perceptions go beyond sensation and involve awareness. How infants organize and interpret the sensations they receive at their sense receptors determines what those perceptions will be. And their interpretations are affected both by their previous experiences and by the innate characteristics of their nervous systems.

Cognition, in turn, includes more than just sensation and perception. We adults are much less bound in our thinking to concrete experience than young children and infants are. Most of our concepts and beliefs have been translated into symbols, such as words and pictures. This ability to represent our knowledge of the world with symbols and to use those symbols to imagine new combinations and transformations of reality is one of the great cognitive achievements of the human species (Flavell, 1977).

Because infants are incapable of using language to tell us what they know or believe about the world, we must infer their knowledge from what they do and from when and how frequently they do it. In making such inferences about their ideas and perceptions, we must be careful not to assume that infants perceive and conceptualize things and events as we do.

It is also important to realize that infants may perceive or know certain things that they cannot easily convey to us because of inability, fatigue, lack of interest, or unwillingness to behave in a way that would reveal this knowledge. Indeed, a considerable amount of the methodological ingenuity of infant research derives from attempts to get around this problem. Consider a concrete example. If one shows a five-month-old a toy, he or she will reach out and pick it up. If, however, one drops a cloth over the toy before it has been picked up, the infant will sit quietly and will make no attempt to remove the cloth and get the toy. The five-month-old's failure to look for the hidden toy could be due to any of several reasons. Perhaps out of sight means out of mind, so that the vanished object no longer exists for the baby. Or possibly, he or she simply lacks the motor skills necessary to remove the cloth and get the toy. Or the baby may have the motor skills but have lost interest in the toy.

The difference among these three interpretations is not trivial. It is important that we be able to distinguish lack of conceptual skill from lack of motor skill and both from lack of interest. The extensive use in infancy research of autonomic responses such as changes in heart rate and in galvanic skin response and of simple-to-execute motor movements such as slight head turns, foot kicks, eye fixations, and eye movements is a way of getting at what the infant knows without requiring that she or he use any difficult motor skill to inform us. Similarly, making sure that the infant is not too hungry, too sleepy, or too full can minimize "lack of interest" factors as reasons for any failure to respond to tasks or situations that test the baby's knowledge (Kessen, Haith, and Salapatek, 1970).

PERCEPTUAL FUNCTIONING

Before they can investigate the baby's cognitive processes, researchers must know how well the baby's senses function. It is through the senses that a baby transforms the raw material of stimulation into information, relying on eyes, ears, mouth, hands, nose, and skin to extract information about the pains and pressures, the sounds and sights, and the tastes and smells in the world.

Seeing

During the third month of life, significant changes occur in the visual world of the infant (Kessen, Haith, and Salapatek, 1970). For one thing, as babies' ability to discriminate improves, they begin to watch strange objects in preference to familiar ones. For example, Joseph Fagan (1971) showed infants of five, seven, and ten weeks of age visual stimuli, some that were already familiar to the babies and others that were new to them, and studied their responses. He found that seven-week-olds preferred the familiar stimulus, whereas the ten-week-olds preferred the novel one. Fagan, Robert Fantz, and Simon Miranda (1971) were interested in knowing whether biological maturation of the visual system played a role in these preference changes. They conducted the same familiar-versus-novel test using one group of infants born four weeks before they were due and another group born at full-term. When they compared the results, they found that eleven-week-old premature babies did not behave like eleven-week-old full-term infants. In fact, the premature babies did not behave like eleven-week-old full-term babies until they were fifteen weeks old. In other words, four additional weeks of visual experience did not affect the visual preference of premature babies. Before they could respond to the familiar-novel dimension of visual information, their visual systems needed to reach a certain level of biological maturation, enabling them to remember that an object had been seen before.

By the time babies are four months old, they perceive color as hues like red, blue, green, and yellow (Bornstein, 1975, 1976). These categories and babies' perceptions of them tend to correspond to the apparently universal and nonarbitrary psychological color categories used by older children and adults in all cultures,

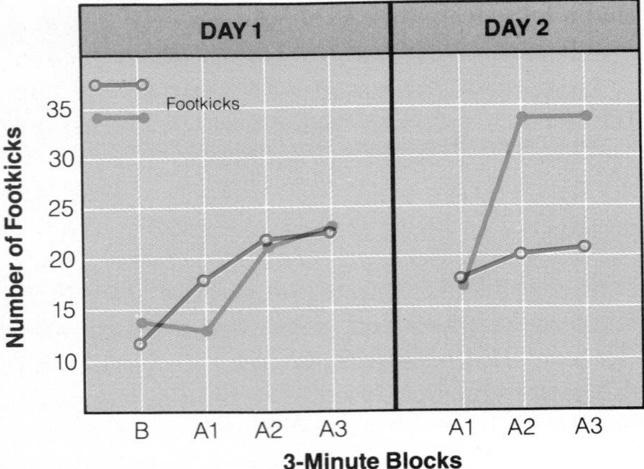

FIGURE 7.1 Babies seem to prefer blue to green, as shown by their operation of colored mobiles, powered by kicking their feet. On the first day babies kicked as often to run the green as the blue mobile, but on the second day, when the blue mobile seemed even more fascinating, the green mobile seemed to lose its charm. When on the third day the colors of the mobiles were switched, babies who now had a green mobile were so upset that eight of the infants began crying and had to be taken out of the experiment. *(Adapted from: Fagen, J. W., "Stimulus Preference, Reinforcer Effectiveness, and Relational Responding in Infants, Child Development, 51 (1980), 374)*

whether or not the culture has a name for them (e.g., Heider, 1972). What the sight means to babies, of course, is very different from the meaning the same sight will convey several years later (Haber and Hershenson, 1973). Even a four-month-old prefers one color to another, and most babies look longer at blue objects than at green ones (Bornstein, 1975). When a group of babies were given a chance to operate a mobile by kicking their feet, they kicked more often when the shapes that made up the mobile were blue than when they were green (Fagan, 1980). On the third day of the study, all of the babies were shifted to a mobile of a different color. Those who were switched from green to blue kicked to operate the new mobile, but most babies who were switched from blue to green began crying after a few minutes and had to be taken out of the experiment.

Vision may be the baby's most important source of information about the environment in the early months of life, and the visual system develops rapidly. Six-month-old babies can probably see as well as adults, especially if objects are directly in front of them. At birth, babies cannot detect objects that are more than 30 degrees to the side; but by the time they are seven weeks old, their peripheral vision has developed enough for them to pick up objects as far as 45 degrees to one side (Macfarlane, Harris, and Barnes, 1976). At this point, a baby's visual field is half that of an adult's. But detecting an object is not enough to recognize it; for that, a seven-week-old infant would have to turn his or her head. A study by Daphne Maurer and Terri Lewis (1979) showed that three-month-old babies can distinguish between radically different objects when they are 30 degrees to the side, but that objects which are only slightly different can be no farther off center than 10 degrees for the baby to discriminate between them. By six months, the peripheral system is mature, but no one is certain how well it interacts with central vision (Cohen, DeLoache, and Strauss, 1979). Once the two systems are interacting smoothly, the baby will use peripheral vision to guide his or her eye movements and to decide what to look at directly.

Just how early babies can recognize the shape of an object when it shifts to cast a different image on the retina is uncertain. A common example of this is the way we see a coin or a hoop as round even when it is rolling on its edge and casting an oval image on the retina. Babies appear to develop this ability some time after they are two months old. Using habituation (which was discussed in Chapter 5 as decreased responsiveness to a stimulus after prolonged or repeated exposure to it), Michael Cook and his associates (1978) found that three-month-old babies could tell the difference between a cube and an L-shaped block, but not between a cube and a wedge. If the ability is beginning to emerge at three months, it seems established by five. Eleanor Gibson and her associates (1978) discovered that five-month-old babies recognized a foam-rubber disk whether it rotated directly or at an angle. When an experimenter distorted the disk by squeezing it so that it had a rippled surface, however, babies reacted as if it were a new object. Apparently, they expected the disk to be rigid in all conditions—constant in texture as well as in shape.

No matter what an object's shape, the baby's ability to judge its distance develops gradually, and the closer an object is, the easier it may be for the infant to make the judgment. Early studies (Bower, 1966) indicated that even a two-month-old baby had developed this ability; but later research (McKenzie and Day, 1972) failed to find it among babies as old as four months. In a more recent experiment, B. E. McKenzie, H. E. Tootell, and R. H. Day (1980) showed colored models of a woman's head to babies of various ages. One model was life-sized, a second was reduced in size by half. The investigators showed each baby the life-sized head at a distance of 2 feet until the infant had habituated, then showed either the life-sized model once again or the reduced model, placing them at either 1 or 2 feet from the baby. At 1 foot, the small head produced the same sized image on the baby's retina as the life-sized head at 2 feet. The only basis for discrimination in this test was the distance of the two objects. If the baby exhibited renewed interest in the half-sized head, it would indicate he or she could tell them apart. Six-month-old babies could tell the two heads apart, but four-month-olds could not.

Distance and depth perception seem to emerge at about the same time, with depth perception appearing between three and six months. Albert Yonas and his colleagues (1978) projected a solid object so that it appeared to come directly at three-and-a-half- and five-month-old babies. All babies watched the object intently, their eyes converging on the illusory missile that seemed ready to strike them. But only the five-month-old infants either reached out toward the object or blinked and withdrew their heads as it appeared to draw near.

It is one thing to perceive relative shape, distance, and depth, and quite another to use these visual cues as warnings about such dangers as falling off tables or chairs. Eleanor Gibson and Richard Walk (1960) studied this sort of depth perception by placing eight- to twelve-month-old infants on the edge of a "visual cliff," which consisted of a patterned platform covered with plexiglass and lighted so that it seemed to have a shallow and a deep side. Most babies who had begun to crawl refused to cross over the deep side of the cliff, even to reach their mothers. And when restricted to using only one eye, infants avoided the deep side of the cliff just as the babies with normal vision did, showing that binocular differences are not required to perceive the apparent danger. Because the youngest infant in this study was eight months old, Gibson and Walk could not determine whether the refusal to venture over the edge of the cliff was due to the maturation of vision or whether learning played a central role. In a later study using the visual cliff, Sandra Scarr and Philip Salapatek (1970) found that, when placed on the deep side, babies younger than seven months old showed no fear and that babies avoided the edge of the cliff only if they already were crawling. It seems, then, that some crawling experience is necessary before the infant can learn that visual cues of depth may signify danger. Recent research supports this finding, indicating that the fear of depth emerges just after the baby develops the ability to move around (Campos et al., 1978). Without that experience, a baby may sense the difference yet show no fear. When two-month-old babies are placed on the deep side of the cliff, their hearts slow down, suggesting they make some sort of discrimination related to depth. When nine-month-olds are placed on the deep side, however, their hearts speed up, suggesting they are afraid (Campos, 1976).

Yet these studies do not account for the behavior of some babies. Although most infants who can crawl refuse to cross the deep side of the cliff, in every experiment at least 10 percent of the crawlers do cross it. The determining factor appears to be the age at which a baby begins to

Visual-cliff apparatus. An infant who can crawl (about six to seven months) may cross the glass surface over the "shallow" side to reach his mother, but he is likely to refuse to venture out over an edge that appears to be a sudden drop or to cross over to the surface on the "deep" side, even if his mother is on the other side urging him to join her. *(Steve McCarroll)*

crawl. Using babies with about two months' crawling experience, John Richards and Nancy Rader (1981) discovered that infants who begin crawling before they are six and a half months old will cross the cliff, but babies who start after that time will not. Richards and Rader speculate that early crawlers use tactile information to direct their crawling (the feel of a solid surface beneath their fingers) and do not depend upon visual input, noting that early crawlers often do not look at the surface ahead of them as they move about. Babies who begin crawling later appear to depend upon visual information to guide them, perhaps because of the maturation of visual-motor coordination.

Hearing

Babies are incredibly sensitive to sound, which is a primary source of environmental information. For example, babies between three and five months old not only are responsive to pitch but can imitate it. In a study by William Kessen and his associates (1979), mothers coaxed their babies to vocalize, then responded to their vocalizations with a musical note. Before long, the babies were imitating the notes their mothers sang. When trained musicians listened to the tape-recorded sessions, they said that all the babies did well and were generally within a quarter tone of the notes they copied. Kessen's group suggests that the ability to match a pitch is natural and that as children acquire language, the ability is often eroded or lost.

Auditory perception is important in learning to understand and speak language and in determining the location of people or events. Shortly after birth, young babies prefer their mothers' voices to those of strangers (DeCasper and Fifer, 1980), and older babies seem to recognize familiar word patterns before they say their first words. Jerome Kagan and his colleagues (1971) tested eight-month-old boys, reading four sentences to each baby in the study. Two of the sentences were meaningful statements and included such words as "smile" and "daddy" that parents often use in talking to their babies.

The other two sentences were nonsensical. When they heard the meaningful sentences with familiar words, babies babbled more than they did when hearing the nonsensical ones. This was true even when the sentences were read by a male stranger.

As they approach the first birthday, infants show a considerable increase in their auditory capabilities. Added to their early sensitivity to frequency, duration, and intensity of sound is a sensitivity to differences among combinations of words. Infants now recognize certain words and are on the threshold of language acquisition, which will progress rapidly during the second year of life.

Touch

In their explorations of the world, babies also learn a great deal through the sense of touch. They grasp objects and try to suck them, not just for the pleasure of sucking but for the information about the form, texture, hardness, and taste of the object that they get from the touch and taste receptors of the mouth and its parts. When babies are not sucking objects, they may run their fingers over their surfaces and through the crevices. If objects are squeezable, they will be squeezed; if crushable, crushed; and if throwable, thrown.

Before they are a year old, babies can recognize objects they have touched but never seen. Sherri Soroka, Carl Corter, and Rona Abramovitch (1979) placed ten-month-old babies in a dark room and gave them either wooden rings or wooden crosses to play with. After the babies had handled them for two minutes, the objects were removed. Now the babies, still in the dark, were handed another object. Half received the shape they had already handled; the other half received the shape they had not yet handled. Babies who were given the shape they had explored earlier handled it for a significantly shorter period than babies who were given the strange shape. Apparently, many of the babies recognized the object they had previously explored with their hands and mouths.

Sensory and Sensorimotor Coordination

The senses of the healthy infant do not function in isolation; instead, senses and motor abilities work together (Gibson, 1969). Babies are tireless reachers, graspers, and handlers of objects, which they study with their eyes and their fingers. As Jean Piaget (1954) has shown, by the latter part of the first year, the infant will construct notions of objects in terms of their combined touchable, tastable, smellable, hearable, seeable, graspable, and reachable characteristics. Because most events or objects provide multiple kinds of stimulation, infants discover that one kind of sensation signals that sensations of other kinds are probably near them in space or in time. For example, infants learn that when they hear a sound, it pays to look because they may see some interesting sight.

Babies seem born prepared to learn about the relations between sights and sounds. This was the conclusion of Morton Mendelson and Marshall Haith (1976), who studied the visual reaction of newborn infants to sounds. The researchers reflected infrared lights on the pupils of the babies' eyes and measured any change in their glances. At the sound of a male voice, the infants opened their eyes wide, increased their eye control, looked at the center of their visual fields, and scanned it with smaller eye movements, as if the voice had alerted them to a source of possible visual stimulation. When the babies heard a tape recording, on which the same excerpt from a children's poem was played repeatedly, the infants at first looked in the direction of the voice, but as the poem continued, their gazes drifted away from the sound.

Very young babies turn their eyes toward the source of a sound that is outside the field of vision, but at two months many babies do not search for the sound. Jeffrey Field and his associates (1980) conducted a longitudinal study, in which they followed babies from the third day of life until they were three months old, testing the infants by shaking a bottle filled with popcorn. Most infants turned their heads toward the source of the sound during the first four weeks of life; but at two months, a number of them failed to respond. Within another month, however, they were again responding to the sound of shaking popcorn, leaving the investigators to speculate that although babies may "listen, look, and see" at birth, at about three months, they begin to listen and then "look to see," associating the visual and auditory characteristics of objects.

By the time babies are three or four months old, they not only connect sights with sounds, but connect them with appropriate sounds. Elizabeth Spelke (1979) gave four-month-old babies the choice of watching two movies: a continuous game of peekaboo or a woman's hands playing toy percussion instruments. Although babies looked from one film to the other, whenever the accompanying soundtrack carried the music of the toy band, their gaze switched to the percussion instruments.

Another important coordination that develops in the first half year is that between the eyes and the hands. We take it for granted that our hands will reach out the proper distance to touch or grasp objects that appear in our line of sight. But it is not until they are four and one-half months old that half of all infants will be able to touch a cube that is placed in front of them on a table, and not until six months are virtually all infants that skilled. The importance of this coordination will become plain in our later discussion of the emergence of intelligence from sensorimotor experiences.

By the time they are eight months old, babies can transfer information from touch to sight. Peter Bryant (1972) and his colleagues demonstrated this ability with a pair of semiround objects that were identical except for a small square notch in the end of one. When activated, either of the objects could make a "bleep." Both objects were shown to babies while they sat in their mothers' laps, then were taken away. Without a baby's being able to see the objects, one of them was placed in his or her hand and, while the infant held it, it was made to bleep. After the hidden object was removed, both objects were shown again to the infant. About two-thirds of the babies, who ranged in age from six to twelve months, reached without hesitation for the object they had just touched, indicating their ability to translate information from a tactual to a visual mode.

It takes six months for most babies to develop the coordination between eyes and hands that enables them to grasp and explore the objects before them. *(Tom Myers/Taurus Photos)*

Some of the intersensory and sensorimotor coordinations that emerge during the first year of life clearly reflect the infant's experiences. For example, infants learn that they must fully extend the arm to reach a stuffed animal one foot away, because in the past they have been unable to grab a toy at that distance without reaching for it. Their visually directed grasp for the animal was made possible, however, by the maturation of visual and motor functions in the central nervous system. All coordinations improve during the second year of life because infants have greater opportunity to use them on a diversity of objects and events.

ATTENTION

It is impossible for us to attend to all the stimuli in the world about us. Attending to some things and not to others begins almost at birth, and a number of factors determine why a baby attends to one stimulus rather than to another. For example, certain absolute features of stimuli may determine attention. Robert Fantz (1961) showed infants ranging in age from one to six months a set of six flat disks. Three of the disks were patterned; the other three had no patterns but were brightly colored. At all age levels, infants looked longer at the patterns than at the brightly colored but unpatterned disks. Fantz proposed that the ability to recognize a pattern, particularly that of the human face, has played a more significant role in infant survival over the course of human evolution than has color recognition. If so, it suggests that human infants are constructed so that when patterns and colors are presented simultaneously, the patterns are more likely to attract their attention.

As infants get older, the relationship between a given stimulus and their previous experiences with related stimuli plays an increasing role in determining what will attract their attention. They are said to build up an expectancy for certain stimuli, and violations of this expectancy make them attend. In general it has been found that stimuli that are **discrepant** (that is, related to but somewhat different from those the baby has previously encountered) will be particularly attractive (J. Kagan, 1978). Such expectancy showed clearly in a study by Charles Super and his colleagues (1972), who allowed babies to look at mobiles every day for three weeks. The mobiles were of three different kinds: some almost identical with, some moderately different from, and some totally unlike a standard mobile, which the babies were shown after their three weeks' exposure to the first mobiles. Babies whose first mobiles were only moderately different from the standard paid most attention to the standard; the babies who had earlier seen the nearly identical mobile and those who had earlier seen a completely different mobile showed much less interest in the standard mobile.

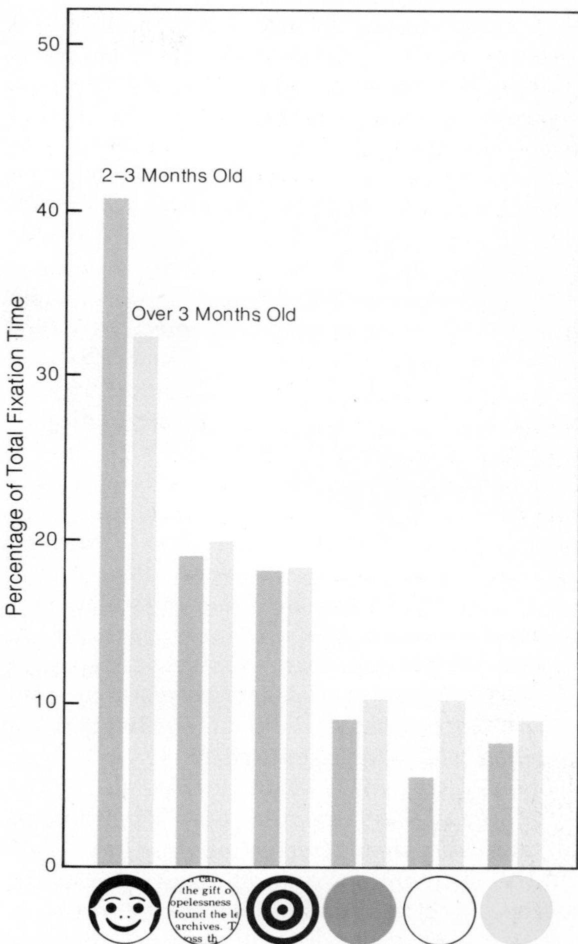

FIGURE 7.2 In Fantz's experiment, disks were shown to infants in a looking chamber. Fixation-time percentages indicate that, whether the infants were younger or older than three months, they looked at pattern longer than at color or brightness. *(Adapted from Robert L. Fantz, "The Origin of Form Perception," copyright © 1961 by Scientific American, Inc. All rights reserved)*

A concept closely related to deviations from expectancy is **novelty.** Novelty and discrepancy are not identical, although it is not always easy to separate the two. All discrepant stimuli have an element of novelty, but a totally novel stimulus is not discrepant because discrepant stimuli are related in some way to a previous expectancy. Hildy Ross, Harriet Rheingold, and Carol Eckerman (1972) studied the attractiveness of novel objects to one-year-old infants. They gave babies an opportunity to explore one of two rooms and to play with one of two toys that differed in their novelty. The infants chose to explore the more novel of the rooms and to play with the more novel of the toys. Another study by Meyer Parry (1972) suggests that the strength of novelty's pull on attention may be reduced if a baby encounters a novel situation or object in an unfamiliar setting.

By the time babies are three or four months old, novelty or discrepancy have become just as powerful in seizing attention as the contour and movement that catch the attention of two-month olds. Apparently, as a baby's cognitive abilities develop, the informational properties of an event (such as discrepancy or novelty) become as important as physical properties (such as contour, movement, and number of elements) in catching and holding attention (e.g., Cohen, 1976; Cornell, 1975; Kagan, 1976).

Stimuli that attract the attention of infants begin to bore them after a while, and babies will shift their attention to another stimulus or fall asleep. Such habituation and the response to novel stimuli are basic to the infant's ability to learn. Unless the infant can remember a stimulus, there can be no conditioning, no adaptation, no learning of any sort (McCall, 1971).

Learning to attend can occur in the earliest weeks of life, and as a child grows past infancy, such learning plays an increasingly important role in intellectual development. A baby's selective attention is an instance of learning and often results from some "payoff" the infant receives for attending to one aspect of a situation rather than to another. For example, although babies initially prefer form to color, if they are rewarded with a smile, a tickle, or some other pleasant consequence for looking at color and get no reward for looking at form, they may learn to shift their attention to color, the feature they originally preferred less.

Attention is important because of the intellectual processing that goes along with it. As mentioned earlier, sensation underlies perception, which in turn underlies cognition. To investigate the cognitive aspects of attention, some researchers have studied the baby's response to a human face. In one such study, Daphne Maurer and Philip Salapatek (1976) showed faces to young babies. One-month-olds tended to inspect details along the edge of the face, such as the chin or the ear, but two-month-olds gazed at features within the face, such as the nose, the mouth, or an eye. Other studies (Hainline, 1978) have also found increased attention to internal facial features among two-month-old babies and discovered that the eyes seem to hold special interest. Eyes draw the attention of babies this age under all conditions—whether the face remains still, moves slightly from side to side, or talks. Not even the mouth movements involved in speech draw a baby's attention away from the eyes (Haith, Berman, and Moore, 1977).

It may be that babies are attracted from the periphery of the face to the eyes because, as they mature, they come to see the face as a meaningful entity instead of simply as a collection of features. By this time, the eyes may have taken on social meaning and babies may have learned that when a face is accompanied by speech, fixing their attention on the eyes keeps the sound of the human voice going. Throughout the first year, the infant's perception of the face appears to rest on a gradual discovery of its invariant features and an integration of its parts into a meaningful configuration (Fagan, 1976; Haaf, 1977).

The cognitive aspects of attention also can be seen in babies' attention to number. In a study by Prentice Starkey and Robert G. Cooper, Jr. (1980), four- to seven-month-old babies detected the difference between displays of two and three dots, paying increased attention to a two-dot display after habituating to a three-dot display, and vice versa. But the babies could not discriminate between four- and six-dot displays, continuing to show boredom when the displays switched back and forth between the larger arrays of dots. Starkey and Cooper speculate that babies are able to detect differences between

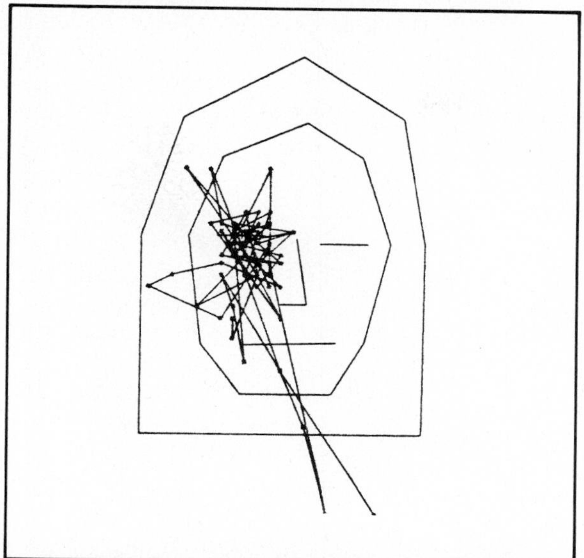

FIGURE 7.3 This computer generated pattern reflects the eye movements of an eight-week-old infant when shown a color photograph of a human face; notice the concentration of gaze in the region of the eye, indicating increased attention to internal features of the face. *(Adapted from Hainline, L. "Developmental Changes in Visual Scanning of Face and Nonface Patterns by Infants,"* **Journal of Experimental Child Psychology,** *25 1978, 99)*

very small numbers by an inborn perceptual mechanism that allows them to apprehend number directly and that this mechanism serves as the basis for later counting skills.

LEARNING

The term "environmentally induced developmental change" corresponds roughly to what most psychologists call learning. Babies learn, and their behavior is modified by either classical or operant conditioning, processes that were described in Chapter 3. The question of whether boys and girls learn differently is explored in the box on page 166.

Conditioning

One of the most important and powerful unconditioned reflexes is the baby's sucking reflex, which is elicited by the presence of the mother's nipple in the baby's mouth. Shortly after birth, the sight, smell, sound, and feel of mother as she prepares to nurse the baby will be enough to elicit sucking. By the process of classical conditioning, these previously neutral stimuli become associated with the unconditioned stimulus "nipple-in-the-mouth," thereby acquiring the ability to influence the infant's sucking. Researchers have classically conditioned numerous other reflexes of the infant and have conditioned them to a wide variety of previously neutral stimuli. But, as Hanuš Papoušek (1967) has shown, stable classical conditioning occurs more readily in older infants than in younger ones, and it appears that biological maturation is an important factor in the changing capacity of the infant to respond to classical conditioning.

As early as the first week of life, however, a baby's behavior is subject to operant conditioning, as the studies in Chapter 5 show. In one study by Harriet Rheingold, Jacob Gewirtz, and Helen Ross (1959), four-month-old infants who were tickled and smiled at when they babbled tended to increase their rate of babbling. Researchers have operantly conditioned sucking, smiling, crying, head turning, looking, and many other kinds of behavior by arranging for the baby to get some reward only if the behavior occurs (Lancioni, 1980). The rewards that have proved effective are quite varied; one of them is the privilege to see a sharply focused pattern. Einar Siqueland and Clement Delucia (1969) designed a special pacifier that controlled the focus of a pattern on a television screen. When the infant sucked the pacifier vigorously, the pattern was in focus. But if sucking slowed, the picture blurred. When this effect was linked to his or her behavior, a baby tended to suck energetically as shown in Figure 7.4 on page 167.

By experimenting, infants learn which of their actions are most effective in getting the world to do their bidding and in what circumstances the desired results are produced. John S.

DO BOYS AND GIRLS LEARN DIFFERENTLY?

Study after study has shown that girls are generally better than boys in reading, writing, and spelling—all skills that are based on verbal ability. Boys, on the other hand, tend to be better at tasks requiring the visualization of three-dimensional objects. A study by John Watson and his associates (1980) discovered a possible biological basis upon which years of learning might build these differences. Three-month-old boys and girls appear to respond to lights and sounds in a markedly different way.

The investigators placed babies in bassinets beneath a black ceiling in which two white translucent circles were set. Then they taught infants to fix their gaze on one of the circles. When they looked at the right circle, half the babies were rewarded with sound, the other half with the appearance of a red light within the circle. The sound and the light varied in intensity.

During the experiment, the babies had three periods of conditioning, each followed by an extinction period when there was no reward, no matter where the baby looked. In the second and third periods, there was no difference between boys and girls; both did well. But during the first period, the differences were striking. Baby boys did best when rewarded with a red light; baby girls did best when rewarded with a low tone. The boys did worst when the reward was a low tone; the girls did worst when the reward was either a faint light or a very loud tone.

It is plain from this experiment that boys and girls both learn, whether the reward is sound or light; but clearly, the boys learned fastest through sight and the girls through soft sounds. The investigators point out that most home environments are characterized by low to moderate intensities of stimulation. Under such conditions, sights may initially be more rewarding for boys, while sounds may initially be more rewarding for girls. If babies do find more success or more pleasure in responding to certain kinds of stimulation, that may increase their tendency to seek out the same sort of stimulation in the future. One might also speculate that after years of such possibly different experiences, girls could become more verbally fluent than boys, while boys could become more adept at spatial tasks.

Watson (1971) has suggested that the responsiveness of the environment is of primary importance to the development of a baby's behavior and perhaps plays a greater role than the amount of stimulation the child receives. He placed automated mobiles over the cribs of two-month-old infants for ten minutes a day over a period of two weeks. Babies who were able to control the mobile, switching it off and on with a turn of the head, benefited more from this experience, as measured by a learning test given six weeks later, than did babies who simply watched the moving mobile but could not control it.

Even in the first months of life infants will master complex learning tasks purely for the joy of solving a problem. Hanuš Papoušek (1967) reinforced babies when they turned their heads twice to the right, three times to the left, and once to the right again. The reinforcement was a seconds-long burst of white light. But the babies barely glanced at the light; they apparently used it only to prove to themselves that they had solved the problem. These six-month-old infants enjoyed the challenge of a puzzle.

Babies are highly adaptive and can overcome many deficiencies in their early experience. Nevertheless, because their perceptions and cognitions come from their experiences, infants reared in a bland, restricted, and nonresponsive environment are less likely to be intellectually competent than babies brought up in a diversified, responsive world. Children cannot know

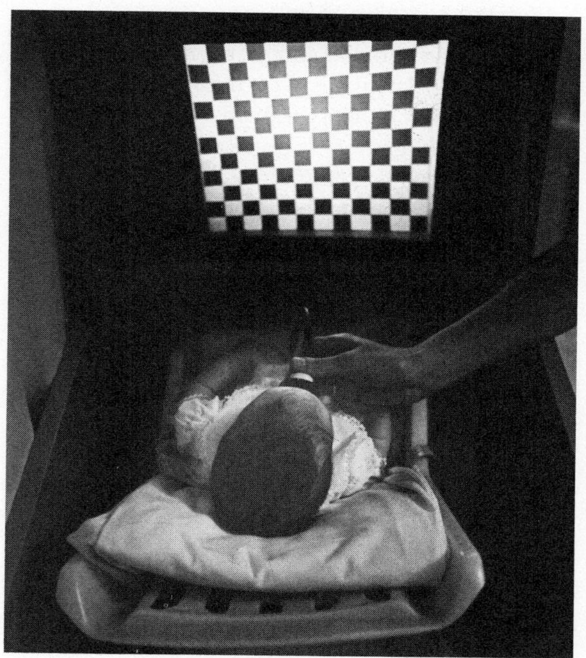

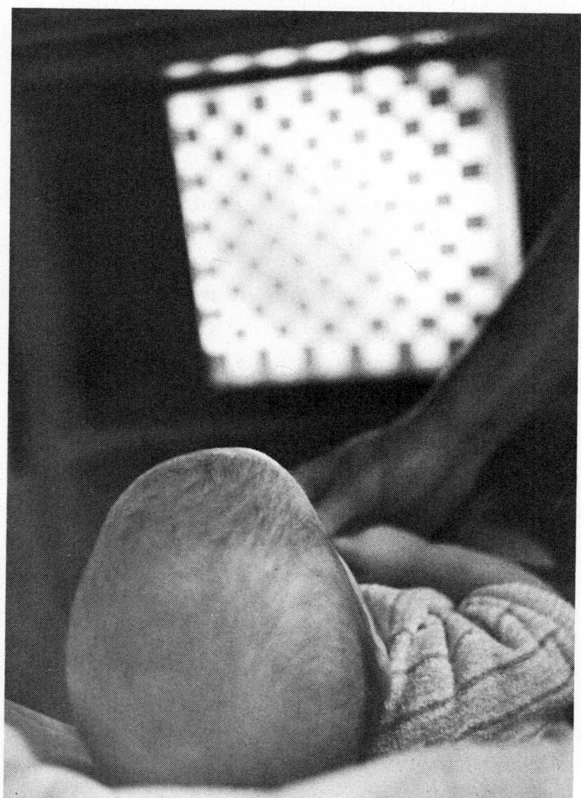

In Siqueland and Delucia's study of learning in young babies, the four-month-old infant is shown a pattern on a televisionlike screen. ***(top)*** **He can keep the pattern in sharp focus by sucking on a pacifier connected to the projector. For a while he will suck with great energy and interest to keep the picture in sharp focus.** ***(bottom)*** **Like most babies, he eventually becomes bored, slows his sucking, and the picture fades. When a different picture appears before him, he will again suck vigorously.** ***(Jason Lauré)***

about places and things if they have not dealt with them, and the more varied and frequent their dealings, the more they know. A concept of a ball based exclusively on having seen one is "poorer" than a concept derived from learning as well how the ball feels and what happens when the infant bends or bites or rolls it. And, as we will see in Chapter 9, the broader and more responsive the social environment, the more the infant will understand about how different people think, act, and feel.

Memory

If learning is to be stable, reinforcement must be almost immediate. Experiments have repeatedly shown that if there is a delay of as little as three seconds between a baby's response and its apparent effect on the world, six- to eight-month-old babies are unlikely to connect the two (Ramey and Ourth, 1971; Millar and Watson, 1979). Apparently, they fail to make the connection because in such situations their ability to process information becomes overloaded and the connection does not get transferred into memory.

When required only to recognize an object, a newborn infant, as noted in Chapter 5, can remember a stimulus for five to ten seconds and can detect a difference between that memory and another stimulus. As babies grow, it takes them less time to register sights in their memory, so when they are allowed to look at a pattern or some other stimulus for a specified length of time, they show gradual improvements with age in their ability to retain a memory. But when they are allowed to look at an object until they lose interest, even two-month-old babies remember the sight as well as older babies do. This finding suggests that although there are age differences among babies in processing visual information, once it is processed, retention does not differ.

Babies begin forgetting immediately, probably within fifteen seconds, but traces of a memory may remain for weeks (Werner and Perlmutter, 1979). Although two-month-old babies may recognize stimuli they have seen the day before (Martin, 1975), in other studies (Millar and Watson, 1979), babies younger than eight months old had great trouble in retrieving experiences from memory. More recent research helps explain this discrepancy by indicating that when babies recognize events after delays of days or even weeks, the world has probably supplied them with cues to help them locate the event in memory. Carolyn Rovee-Collier and her associates (1980) allowed three-month-olds to see (but not operate) a mobile the infant had learned to power several weeks earlier by kicking their feet. The next day, given the opportunity, they immediately began kicking to set the mobile in motion. But babies who had not been reminded of the mobile by seeing it again the day before the test showed little recognition and had to learn how to operate it again. Such reencounters may explain the persistence of memories in young babies. By the time they are ten to twelve months old, however, babies can hold events longer in memory, need fewer cues to recall past events, and more easily compare present events with stored knowledge of the past.

Most research with infants indicates that they can recognize objects they have seen before, but little experimental evidence exists to indicate that they can remember an object that is not present. Some evidence of this kind of memory has been found in the daily lives of infants by Daniel Ashmead and Marion Perlmutter (1980), who asked parents of seven- to eleven-month-old infants to record any incidents showing such memory. Most of the babies remembered where household items, such as a bottle of baby lotion, belonged and showed surprise when an item was not in its regular place. The infants searched for people or objects, and they remembered the routines of such games as peekaboo. Since these memories were demonstrated in their own homes, the infants probably were using environmental cues in order to help them retrieve the information.

When meaningfulness is added to the cues of a familiar environment, the memory of older infants shows clearly, as Judy DeLoache (1980) found when she had mothers play hide-and-seek at home with their eighteen-month-old infants. The mothers hid a stuffed Big Bird toy while the infants watched, then set a kitchen timer, telling the infants that they could go find the toy when the bell rang. In nearly 70 percent of the cases, the infants immediately jumped up and got the coveted toy as soon as the bell sounded.

SENSORIMOTOR THOUGHT

The most comprehensive account of cognitive development is that provided by Jean Piaget, whose theory was discussed in Chapter 3. Newborn infants cannot distinguish between their own bodies and objects and people in the world around them, so a major task of the first two years is that of separating themselves from the world. While this process is going on, babies move from reflexive, self-centered creatures to symbol-using individuals who act purposefully on the world. That development is the result of the child's spontaneous activity, and Piaget's conceptualization of the period is summed up in the title of one of his books on infancy: *The Construction of Reality in the Child* (1954).

The child's principal tools in this period are assimilation and accommodation. When three-month-old babies are offered their first chance to drink from a cup, for example, they first try to assimilate the cup to their current mouth-using skills, sucking at its edge as they would suck at a nipple. When this does not work, the infant modifies, or accommodates, those mouth-using skills so that they are as effective with the hard rim of the cup as they were with the soft rubber of a nipple. As babies grow, they continue to use old responses on new objects and then to modify these old responses, thus learning to adapt to a widening world.

Stages of Sensorimotor Thought

Piaget divided the period of sensorimotor thought into six substages, each representing an advance in cognitive development, and each reflecting the contents of the infant's mind in his or her behavior. The ages for each substage are approximate.

Stage 1—Reflex Acts The first substage covers the neonatal period (0–1 month), when the baby's actions are primarily based on the reflexes with which he or she enters the world. Babies suck reflexively when their mouths or cheeks are stimulated, their lips working even when their mouths are empty. They respond to sights and sounds, but they are not purposeful, active investigators of their world. Much of their behavior is a response to internal stimulation, and their actions are rigid and inflexible—although they can be affected by experience. Newborns learn to regulate sucking, for example, and will accommodate their sucking to the type of nipple, the flow of liquid through it, and its flavor. During this first substage, the baby's primitive reflexes tend to disappear, and the adaptive reflexes, such as vocalizing, grasping, and sucking, stabilize and become more efficient.

Stage 2—Primary Circular Reactions During this second substage (1–4 months), the reflexive schemes of the baby become sensorimotor schemes that incorporate experience. Babies intentionally look at and listen to the sights and sounds around them. They are beginning to coordinate their senses and will use their eyes to direct their grasp. As yet, they cannot distinguish their actions from the world and the objects in it, but they have begun a rudimentary form of imitation. The hallmark of this stage is what Piaget called **primary circular reactions.** These reactions refer to any behavior the baby does repeatedly because of the stimulation the action provides. This grasping, sucking, looking, or vocalizing is different from the reflexive action of the first stage because the baby intentionally repeats it. For example, Piaget (1962) described the manner in which his eight-week-old daughter, Lucienne, imitated him. Piaget had observed Lucienne moving her head spontaneously from side to side. The next day he moved his head quickly in the same way while the baby watched. As soon as he had finished, Lucienne moved her head in the same way three times. Piaget waited, then repeated his head movement. Again Lucienne copied him. However, at this stage, Lucienne, like all babies her age, could imitate only those actions that were already in her repertoire of behavior.

Stage 3—Secondary Circular Reactions Instead of behaving in ways that are primarily based on the capabilities they brought into the world, babies in this third substage (4–8 months) are busy with actions they have learned. This development is possible in part because of improved sensorimotor coordination and increased proficiency at grabbing attractive objects. Piaget called the major activity of this period **secondary circular reactions;** they are learned, as opposed to the repetition of unlearned behavior in primary circular reactions. Although Piaget (Piaget and Inhelder, 1969) would not have agreed, secondary circular reactions look to the observer much like the result of operant conditioning. A six-month-old shakes a rattle or bangs a cup on the high-chair tray. These actions were at first accidental, but the infant now repeats them because he or she finds them reinforcing. The action schemes are now meant to prolong events that interest the baby.

Perceptions and actions are still so intertwined at this age that babies find it hard to separate them. The infant presumably has no mental image of objects as separate things; instead he or she represents objects through motor responses.

When such a young baby "talks" to an adult, the imitation must be an action already in her repertoire. *(© Linda Ferrer 1980/Woofin Camp & Assoc.)*

For example, if the rattle drops, the baby will keep shaking his or her hand, as if expecting these actions to bring back the toy. Robert McCall (1979b) describes this cognitive view as "the world is what I do with it."

Stage 4—Coordination of Secondary Schemes
In the latter part of their first year (8–12 months), babies are active learners. They can now imitate behavior that is not ordinarily part of their own actions, which means they no longer have to stumble accidentally onto some new action but can learn by watching others. (Although some studies have reported the presence of imitation in younger babies, such research has not been replicated, as the accompanying box indicates.) Babies still engage in secondary circular reactions, but they are now coordinating their action schemes into purposeful, larger schemes. For by now, a sense of causality has emerged. Instead of simply prolonging interesting events, babies use their schemes to obtain a goal. For example, when his son, Laurent, was nine months old, Piaget (1954) swung him by pulling a cord that was attached to his infant swing. When Piaget stopped the swinging, Laurent grasped his father's hand and pressed it against the cord.

Stage 5—Tertiary Circular Reactions Babies in this stage of sensorimotor thought (12–18 months) are beginning to distinguish between themselves and the world. Objects and events are now seen as independent from an infant's action, another big step in cognitive development. It is at this time that Piaget (1968) de-

THE TROUBLE WITH INFANT IMITATORS

A few years ago, researchers announced that babies of two, three, or six weeks of age would imitate adults. Some investigators (e.g., Maratos, 1973) found that six-week-old infants would stick out their tongues in response to the protrusion of an adult tongue. Andrew Meltzoff and Keith Moore (1977) took the research a step farther. They reported that twelve- to twenty-one-day-old babies would not only stick out their tongues but protrude their lips, open their mouths, and open or close their fists in mimicry of an adult's actions. Moreover, their observations of babies as young as an hour old led them to propose that the capacity is innate, requiring neither maturation nor learning.

These findings, if replicated, would require a serious rethinking of infant cognitive development. As indicated in the text, babies of eight weeks or so will imitate an adult who has first imitated a habitual response of the baby's, but this has been regarded as pseudo-imitation. Not until the latter part of the first year were infants supposed to be able to imitate actions they could neither see nor hear themselves perform, such as opening and closing their eyes or mimicking facial expressions.

Meltzoff and Moore argued that when infants stuck out their tongues or opened and closed their hands, they were somehow mentally representing visual information and sensory information from their mouths, lips, tongues, and fingers; matching the two and imitating the gestures they had seen. Since then Sandra Jacobson (1979; Jacobson and Kagan, 1979) has found that the picture is not quite so simple. Jacobson discovered that six-week-old babies indeed tended to stick out their tongues in "imitation" of an adult, but that they would do the same if a small white ball or a black felt-tip pen was moved toward their mouths, held there for three seconds, and then moved away. The babies would also open and close their hands in response to investigators' hand movements, but they would do the same if an orange plastic ring was placed near their hands.

Jacobson contends that what Meltzoff and Moore documented was a releasing mechanism, an unconditioned response that babies automatically tend to make whenever anything moves toward the mouth or hands. Sticking out one's tongue, suggests Jacobson, might serve an adaptive function relating to feeding, but it is not the selective imitation of a facial expression.

The question is not resolved and probably will not be for some years. The issues raised also show that even carefully controlled studies often fail to settle developmental questions, especially when the child subjects are too young to talk.

scribes the infant's behavior as "intelligent"; but it is a practical intelligence, one based on perceptions and movements rather than on words and concepts. The infant's schemes have become **tertiary circular reactions.** They differ from secondary circular reactions in that they are intentional adaptations to specific situations. Faced with a problem, babies now set about solving it through the process of trial and error. They cannot predict the results of a new action but must first try it out. Babies may seem to vary their schemes simply to see what will happen, as if they are working away at understanding the world. At fifteen months, for example, Piaget's daughter Jacqueline showed her awareness of the relation between her actions and external objects. Instead of simply jerking hard at her dress when it caught on a nail, she stepped back and detached her skirt from it (Piaget, 1954).

Stage 6—Beginning of Symbolic Thought

This final stage of sensorimotor thought (18–24 months) is really a transitional period between the sensorimotor and preoperational stages. Babies in this substage can mentally represent objects, visualizing both their own actions and events involving others. Once this happens, infancy rapidly draws to a close, for the baby can set about acquiring language. In the baby's daily life, two important changes now show up. First, because babies can visualize their own actions, they are able to solve problems in their heads, working out a solution with mental combinations and then applying it. They no longer must go through an obligatory trial-and-error process. Second, babies can now defer their imitations. They can now imitate on Wednesday the actions they saw their parents perform on Monday or Tuesday. Along with the ability to form mental images comes the capacity for symbolic play. Although a baby in the fifth substage might drink pretend tea from a cup, a baby in the sixth substage can pretend to eat and drink without the presence of food or utensils, or even use an empty box in place of the doll's teacup.

The Object Concept

You believe that objects remain the same, even though they may move from one place to another or undergo transformations that do not affect their basic identity. If at the same time you see two objects with identical features, you assume that they are separate objects. And if you see an object on Tuesday and an object with identical features on Wednesday afternoon, you assume that you have either seen the same object twice or two separate objects at two different times. If you find out that you have seen two separate objects, you usually believe that the first object still exists somewhere, even though it is now out of sight.

These interrelated ideas about the identity and permanence of objects and about their potential for movement or for disappearing from view and reappearing are not present at birth. Babies devote a good part of their first two years to building this intricate conceptual network of objects, movement, time, space, and causality. They acquire these ideas as a result of their sensory, perceptual, and motor interactions with the environment. Our understanding of the infant's gradual acquisition of beliefs about reality comes in part from Piaget's observations (1952b, 1954) of his own three children and from subsequent studies inspired by his reports.

Out of Sight, Out of Existence When an object being watched by a baby of less than four months disappears from sight, the baby either keeps gazing at the spot where it was last visible or acts as if the object had never been in view. The baby does not actively search for the object, but behaves as though it exists only when it is within sight.

During the next four months or so, however, the baby in Stage 3 often searches for an object that disappears from view—but it is only a visual search. For example, if a cup falls from the high chair while he or she is looking at it, the six-month-old may lean toward the floor to see where it went instead of just staring at the spot where it was. Even though the cup is out of sight, the infant now acts as though expecting it to be somewhere else. But this occurs only when the baby sees it starting to move away. If the cup were suddenly covered by a towel or a napkin, he or she would not try to pick up the covering to get it, even though physically quite able to do so. At this point in the development of the object concept, an object seems to exist for them only as long as they can continue looking at it. If one covers the infant's hand while an object is grasped in it, the baby will either simply withdraw the hand or keep holding the object but behave as if unaware it is still in the hand.

Several experimenters have supplemented Piaget's early observations with analyses of the responses of young infants to different types of movements, disappearances, and features of objects. In one such study, Alastair Mundy-Castle and Jeremy Anglin (1969) placed babies where they could watch an object appear on their right side and rise up out of sight. After the object disappeared, a second, identical object dropped on the infants' left side and fell down out of sight; then the object on the right again rose into view. After watching this cycle occur several times, infants who were less than four months old began looking from one side to the other as

This experimental set-up shows how the mother actually disappears and how her disappearance probably appears to the baby. *(Steve McCarroll)*

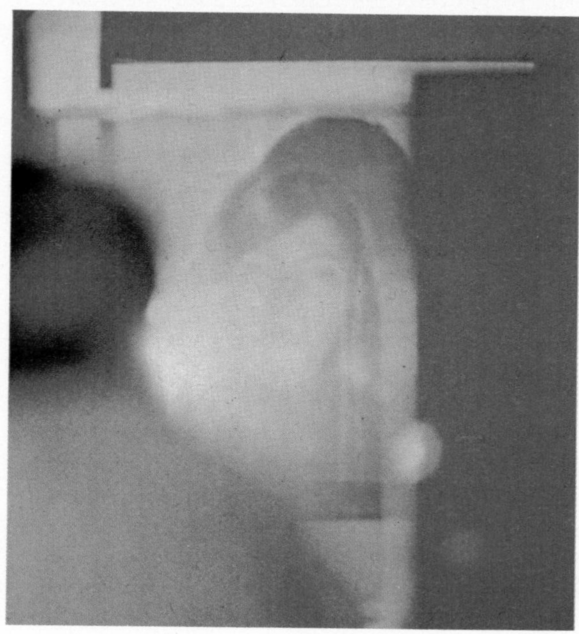

the objects appeared. Four-month-olds, however, assumed that they had been watching a single object that was traveling on a circular trajectory, and their eyes followed the path that such an object would take. Although the object was out of view, it continued to exist for the four-month-olds. In addition, the four-month-olds looked back to the right if the vanished object did not reappear on the left—something the younger babies did not do.

Object Permanence Undoubtedly the most important object for the infant is his or her mother. But if she no longer exists for young infants when they are not looking at her, then her sudden disappearance should not surprise them. Using mirrors and special lighting to show babies an image of their own mothers, Thomas Bower (1971) tested this deduction, making the image gradually dissolve into nothingness. Infants under twenty-four weeks watched their mothers fade away and disappear with no evidence of upset. However, infants older than twenty-four weeks reacted to the dissolution of their mothers with considerable upset and appeared to search for them. This behavior of the older babies seems to indicate a conceptual advance, a belief that regardless of what they have just seen, mother must exist somewhere.

Babies extend this belief in the permanence of their mothers to other human beings and indeed to other objects. But judging from the way babies search for vanished objects, it will be many months before their notion of object permanence is like that of an adult.

In observations of his own children, Piaget (1952b, 1954) found that during the last four months of their first year, they searched, but in a limited fashion, for objects that they saw him place behind a screen. For example, Piaget moved a toy behind a screen while one of his children was observing him. The child retrieved

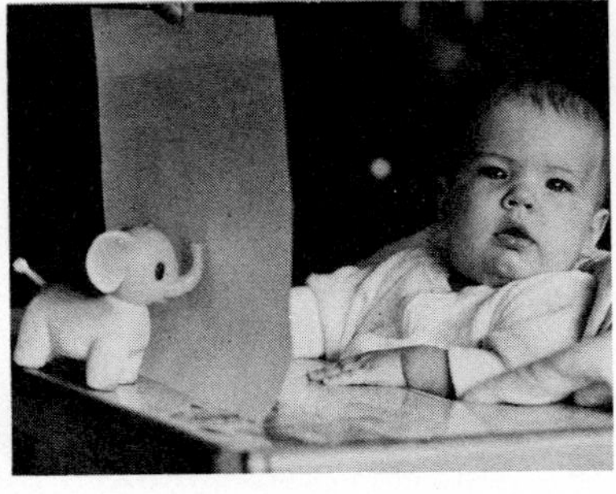

(top) **This infant of about six months has not yet developed a concept of object permanence.** *(left)* **She looks intently at a toy elephant that is in front of her** *(right),* **but when the elephant is blocked from view, she gives no indication that she understands the toy is still there.** *(George Zimbel/Monkmeyer Press)*

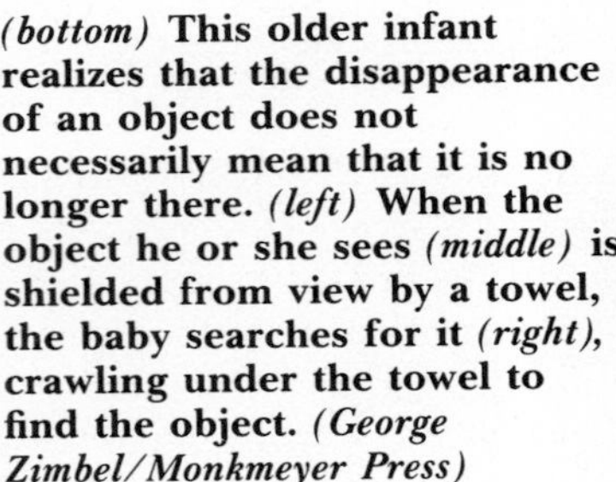

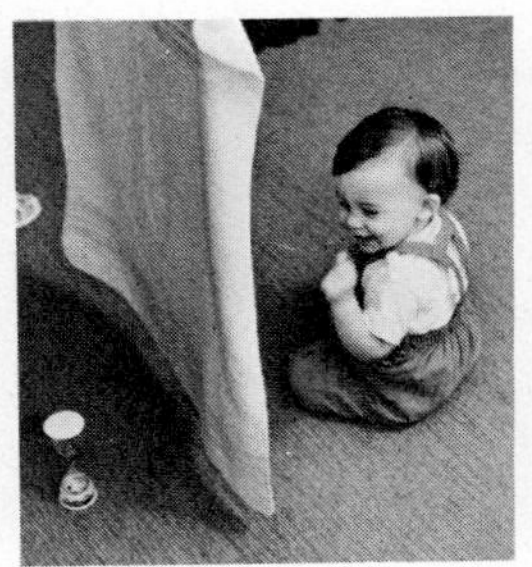

(bottom) **This older infant realizes that the disappearance of an object does not necessarily mean that it is no longer there.** *(left)* **When the object he or she sees** *(middle)* **is shielded from view by a towel, the baby searches for it** *(right),* **crawling under the towel to find the object.** *(George Zimbel/Monkmeyer Press)*

it. Piaget hid the toy again, and the child again recovered the toy. This sequence was repeated several more times. Then, with his child watching, Piaget hid the toy behind a screen located in a different place. Surprising as it may seem, the child insisted on searching for the toy in the original location. Piaget concluded that the baby's concept of space is based on a failure to dissociate the objects of the world from the infant's own actions on them, and that babies remember a place by recalling the movement they made when first retrieving the toy. John Flavell (1977) suggests that at this level of development, babies are not so much searching for a specific object as seeking to reinstate an action pattern that previously brought them pleasure.

Because this reaction by the baby is essential to understanding the development of the infant mind, researchers have conducted many similar experiments in an attempt to explain the baby's error. They have found that babies continue to reach toward Point A even when the toy remains plainly visible at Point B (Butterworth, 1977; Harris, 1974), and also when a toy different from the one hidden at A is hidden at B (Evans and Gratch, 1972). It may be that babies simply learn that Point A is the "toy place" (Gratch, 1975). But the error may depend in part on memory, because babies rarely make it if they already are reaching for the toy as it is being hidden or if they are allowed to reach for it immediately after it has been hidden at B (Gratch et al., 1974).

J. G. Bremner and Peter Bryant (1977) designed an experiment to test whether the error was due to infants' simply making the same response that earlier brought them the toy or whether they remembered where the toy was first hidden. After hiding the toy at Point B, Bremner and Bryant either moved the baby to the opposite side of the table or rotated the table half-way round. If the baby remembered the place, he or she would have to make a different movement to get the toy. Nine-month-old infants most often responded just as they had before the table was rotated, indicating they remembered the response and not the place.

Bremner and Bryant conclude that their results support Piaget's interpretation and that the baby's reliance on movement instead of place may develop because the first nine months of life are relatively nonmobile. Before babies can move about freely on their own, objects remain static. The baby stays in the same place in relation to them, and once he or she locates a toy visually, does not need visual information to relocate it; simply repeating the previous reach will gain the toy. Once babies begin to crawl, however, their relations to an object in space vary as they move, so that they now must use visual information to guide their actions.

Bremner and Bryant point out that a general **egocentrism,** or the infant's inability to differentiate the self from the world, can also explain the error: the infant's frame of reference for spatial relations is him- or herself, and babies repeat a reach because that is the side where the toy was in relation to their bodies. Studies by Linda Acredolo (e.g., Acredolo and Evans, 1980) indicate that most nine-month-old babies do rely on their bodies as a frame of reference. However, if given some striking marker—such as blinking lights and garish stripes—they will switch from an egocentric viewpoint to using the landmark. Tested at home, however, a crawling nine-month-old appears to use familiar surroundings as landmarks, doing as well on tests as sixteen-month-olds do in the laboratory (Acredolo, 1979).

The explanation of the reaching error could be even simpler. As Bremner and Bryant note, babies may know the toy is not at Point B but lack the control that allows them to inhibit an established response.

When Piaget followed up his observations of his children during the first half of their second year, he found that they still reached for the toy at Point A unless they had watched him move the toy behind the screen to Point B. By the second half of the second year, Piaget's children were able to infer not only a single invisible displacement of objects, but several. When Piaget successively hid the object enclosed in his hand first at Point A, then at B, then C, and so forth, the children systematically searched his hand and all these locations. They inferred that the object had to be somewhere that Piaget had been, even though they did not actually see him move it. They had now developed an understanding about the permanence and existence of objects independent of their own activity with respect to the objects. They had also developed the ability to represent objects mentally and to hold the image in working memory while they searched for it.

Most theorists agree that babies acquire their concepts of object identity and permanence, and their knowledge of the distinctive features of objects, by their active involvement in the world of objects. By looking at, listening to, smelling, tasting, grasping, sucking, throwing, and moving all kinds of things frequently and repeatedly, they learn which objects are small or large, rough or smooth, squeezable or hard, bitter or sweet, and which produce loud or soft noises when struck. As they get older, they notice specific features of objects, and their definition of objects becomes more differentiated. In a similar manner, infants derive their ideas about space, time, and physical causality from their observation and manipulation of people, things, and events.

Individual Differences

There is no lockstep in cognitive development. As Piaget believed, although children pass through the same sequence of stages, they attain the various levels of sensorimotor thought at different ages. Research studies of large groups of infants generally corroborate Piaget's view (Gouin-Décarie, 1965; Uzgiris, 1976). For example, one child might show evidence of deferred imitation at fifteen months, another at twenty. However, all children who live in natural human environments will, unless they suffer from serious birth defects, attain each of the skills described by Piaget (Scarr-Salapatek, 1976).

Various scales of infant development, some based directly on Piaget's theories, are used to assess the level of a baby's cognitive functioning. But these early ratings often bear little resemblance to later scores on intelligence tests given in childhood. In a longitudinal study of forty-one

A baby's mouth and hands are important tools in explorations of the world. While mouthing an object, the infant discovers its form, texture, solidity, and taste. *(Linda Rogers/Woodfin Camp & Assoc.)*

children, for example, babies who scored low on tests given early in their first year tended, by the end of the year, to catch up with babies who had made high scores (Bayley, 1955). In general, the abilities measured by infant scales—such as alertness, reaction to stimuli, sensorimotor coordination, vocalizations, and the recognition of differences—tend to be poor predictors of later cognitive development.

As our discussion of norms in Chapter 6 indicated, such tests or standards can detect babies who need extra attention because of birth complications, and they are quite effective at picking out babies who are severely retarded. As Robert McCall (1979a) indicates, a physician who weighs a six-month-old baby does not try to guess the infant's adult weight but uses the measure in deciding whether the baby needs some kind of medical attention.

There is also little question, as Sandra Scarr-Salapatek (1976) has pointed out, that sensorimotor intelligence is radically different in quality from later intelligence. In her analysis, Scarr-Salapatek proposes that the sensorimotor skills of the preverbal child evolved much earlier in human history than did later cognitive skills, that learning processes in human infants and chimpanzees are very similar, and that the only requirement for the development of sensorimotor intelligence may be the opportunity to explore and to learn.

As this chapter has made clear, babies become active explorers who use all their senses to investigate their surroundings. During their development, they use old responses on new objects and then modify these responses, assimilating and accommodating their skills as they learn to adapt to a widening world.

SUMMARY

1. Babies are active and curious. During the first two years, they organize and reorganize their understanding of the world and the people, objects, and events that fill it. Increases in understanding come from the interaction of biological maturation and cumulative experiences, and experiences affect the infant through the conversion of sensation, or received stimulation, to perception, or organized and interpreted stimulation.

2. By the end of the first year, infants can judge shape, distance, and depth, discriminate familiar from unfamiliar objects, and use visual cues as warnings. Their hearing becomes sensitive to combinations of sounds, so that they recognize certain words and attach meanings to them. Most important, all the infants' senses working together, and combined with their motor skills, provide them with extensive knowledge of the environment.

3. Selective attention to stimuli continues from the moment of birth. Previous experience as well as certain physical features of objects appear to determine what infants usually attend to. Stimuli that violate an expectancy or that are novel are most likely to attract an infant's attention. Human faces appear to hold a unique fascination, partly because infants come to see the face as meaningful. Babies also appear to apprehend number directly, an ability that may be responsible for early counting skills.

4. Both the responsiveness of the environment and the joy of solving a problem appear to spur learning in babies, and much of their learning is the result of conditioning, as babies come to associate an action with its consequences. If learning is to be stable, however, reinforcement must come swiftly—within three seconds. Although a baby begins forgetting within fifteen seconds, traces of a memory may last for weeks, especially if the world supplies the infant with cues.

5. In Jean Piaget's theory of cognitive development, the first two years of life are the sensorimotor period, which is divided into six substages, each representing an advance in cognitive development and each reflecting the contents of the infant mind in behavior. By the time infants reach the sixth and final substage, they can mentally represent objects, an ability that allows them to solve problems with mental combinations and to defer imitations. The baby's realization that objects continue to exist when out of sight is not usually complete until the second half of the second year. At this time, babies can hold an image of the missing object in working memory while they search for it.

8 LANGUAGE: BEGINNINGS

Lauren is nearly a year old and her mother is playing with her, making various cooing noises. Among the noises comes something like "givemommyakisssweetie . . . givemommyakiss." At the same time, Mommy expectantly puts her cheek near Lauren's lips. Lauren does not know much about language, but she senses that she is supposed to do something. She also senses that this particular set of noises that her mother is making sounds somehow different from the cooing, and the specially accented noise "kiss" reverberates in her ears. Another time Daddy says "lookatthedoggy" when a small furry animal comes into sight. Lauren is ready to learn to talk. What does she have to do? What does she have to know?

Without language, it would be difficult to grow up and to function in any human society. Children would be able to learn only what they saw others do. There would be some things, of course, that they could learn or figure out by themselves; not all thinking is verbal. Words are not necessary for the use and enjoyment of sounds, images, and spatial relationships. But imagine trying to learn history or how our society works without being able to understand or speak a language.

The importance of language for development is expressed in the word "infant," for it comes from the Latin word for being without language. If an "infant" is one who does not possess language, then human beings are infants throughout most of their second year. For although babies may communicate, until they begin to put words together, they do not have command of the structure of their language.

In this chapter, we will discuss some of the early achievements of children in deciphering their native language, pointing out the task that lies before them and setting forth the level of cognitive development that must precede the baby's first words. After examining various theories that attempt to explain language acquisition, we will look at some of the ways in which very young babies respond to speech sounds, the first sounds that babies

Long before babies can say "bow-wow" or "doggie," they have mastered some of the rules that govern discourse. *(Suzanne Szasz)*

make themselves, and the distinction between babbling and talking. We will discover that language grows out of social interaction and that communication actually precedes the infant's intent to communicate. Long before babies say their first words, we will see them mastering some of the basic rules that govern human discourse. We will find that context is essential to an understanding of babies' first words and that infants overextend and then shrink the meanings of many words, so that "bow-wow," for example, changes in meaning from "dog" to "animal" and back to "dog" again. We will discover the significance of the universal progress from one- to two-word utterances and the way infants master the basic grammatical machinery of their language. Basically, it is during the first two years that infants tune up their cognitive and linguistic abilities until they become speaking human beings. This tuning is the result of a complex interplay of cognitive and linguistic development, paced by neurological maturation.

DEFINING HUMAN LANGUAGE

Human beings are not the only species that communicates. A vervet monkey has a vocabulary of at least five sounds that not only warn its fellows of danger but specify whether the source is a snake, a leopard, or an eagle and how close the predator is (Wilson, 1975a). The honeybee has a special waggle dance, whose pattern tells the other worker bees how far and in which direction to fly for a new source of nectar (Von Frisch, 1967). Communication may also take place between two different species. A cat meows to get in or out of the house or pushes its head beneath a hand for a caress. And, even more impressive, a chimpanzee may learn to use its hands, plastic chips, or a computer to answer a question or to ask for a drink. Yet, as the accompanying box indicates, even this last example falls short of language as most theorists view it.

The Properties of Language

Human language, suggests Roger Brown (1973), is set off from the communication systems of animals by three important properties: semanticity, productivity, and displacement. All human languages, whether English, Russian, Chinese, or Urdu, possess these properties.

Semanticity, or meaningfulness, means that the symbols of human language represent an enormous variety of people, objects, events, and ideas. A mynah bird may mimic human speech perfectly, but it does not use these sounds in any meaningful way, and so it does not possess language. Although the honeybee's dance or a vervet monkey's cries can communicate limited meanings, the number of things these animals can talk about is quite small.

The second property of language is **productivity,** the ability to combine individual words into an unlimited number of sentences. Except for common clichés, such as "How are you?" or "Have a nice day," almost every sentence we hear or speak is brand new (Chomsky, 1972). According to one estimate, uttering all

THE CHATTER OF CHIMPANZEES

The accomplishment of chimpanzees who communicate with sign language, with plastic chips, or through computers is impressive, but how close have these clever primates come to meeting the criteria for language: semanticity, productivity, and displacement?

Washoe, who learned 132 signs from American Sign Language (ASL), the language of hand signs used by deaf Americans, combined her signs into strings such as "Please sweet drink" (Gardner and Gardner, 1969). Her use of words showed the overextension found in human children's language, but she paid no attention to word order, and her signs lacked the productivity that syntax gives to language (Klima and Bellugi, 1973). (This lack is not inherent to ASL. When used by human beings, ASL is a highly productive silent language that meets all the stated criteria.)

Sarah, a chimpanzee who communicated by placing plastic symbols on a board, followed a regular word order in her communications. She understood compound sentences and could pass a test with an experimenter who did not know her language and therefore could give her no cues (Premack, 1976). Her communications included displacement. Given the written instruction, "brown color of chocolate," to introduce the color brown, then told to "take brown," Sarah correctly chose the brown disc from a group of four.

Lana, who learned to strike computer keys to produce a series of geometric signs on a lighted display, also used correct word order. She learned stock sentences, into which she could insert appropriate nouns or verbs, and once even asked the computer to tell her the name of a strange object so she could ask for it (Rumbaugh and Gill, 1976).

These accomplishments made it appear as if chimpanzees were on the brink of true language. But an analysis of research with Nim Chimpsky, who learned 125 signs in ASL, caused Herbert Terrace (1979) to question the primate's progress. A close look at Nim's videotapes showed that the chimpanzee was not a speaker but an imitator. He never got past the two-word stage. Although he piled up strings of signs, they turned out to be merely a grab bag of every sign that might be associated with a desired object. Nim rarely expanded upon what his trainers said, as children do, and he did not understand turn-taking, an essential part of language that children learn before they can talk.

Further analysis by the team that taught Lana essentially agrees with Terrace's criticisms (Savage-Rumbaugh, Rumbaugh, and Boysen, 1980). Chimpanzees, these investigators say, have reached the linguistic level of a nine- or ten-month-old. They can use symbols to request things and to control the behavior of their trainers, but the words appear to be simply replacements for the natural gestural systems they use in the wild. They do not comment on events, which children in the two-word stage habitually do, nor is it certain that they truly understand their symbols. It may be that chimpanzees have been conditioned to associate certain symbols with certain events, as pigeons learn to peck keys in sequence to get corn. In fact, using a similar but much simpler system than Lana's, pigeons have learned to carry on a spontaneous conversation about hidden colors (Epstein, Lanza, and Skinner, 1980).

The arguments of the critics are powerful. Chimpanzees clearly have demonstrated displacement, however. And in a study involving Lana and two new chimpanzees, the new animals appear to have met the criterion of semanticity—categorizing unfamiliar objects correctly as either food or tools, something Lana could not do (Savage-Rumbaugh, Rumbaugh, Smith, and Lawson, 1980). Although no chimpanzee has yet demonstrated productivity, that goal may one day be reached.

the twenty-word sentences possible in English would require a person to talk for 10,000,000,000,000 years (Farb, 1974). Productivity appears to be a property limited strictly to the communication systems of human beings, for none of the chimpanzees who have learned to use symbols can pass such a test of their ability to communicate.

The last essential property of language, according to Brown, is **displacement,** the ability to communicate information about objects in another place or another time, such as the flat tire on the car in the garage or last Sunday's episode of *Masterpiece Theater.* Displacement is the property that allows us to transmit information from one generation to another so that we do not have to rediscover all knowledge every thirty years or so. The bee's dance uses displacement in denoting the location of nectar, but because it lacks the properties of semanticity and productivity, the dance is not true language.

Ways of Studying Language

Since human language uses semanticity, productivity, and displacement within a system of social communication based on sound, there are several possible ways to look at language. Thus in studying language acquisition, developmental psychologists have generally focused on one of four aspects: phonology, semantics, syntax, or pragmatics.

Phonology, which is the study of speech sounds, focuses on the sound patterns of language. Each language combines vowels and consonants in some ways but not in others and uses stress, tone, and intonation to affect meaning. In English, the intonation pattern is important; ending an utterance on a rising note, for example, indicates that the speaker is asking a question. In Chinese, however, the tone of the word determines its meaning; in the national dialect, five different tones can be used to change the meaning of a monosyllable, so that "Ma ma ma ma ma," given proper tonal qualities, can mean "Has Mother scolded the horse?" (Burgess, 1975). Research developed along the phonological path focuses on the way the child deciphers the streams of human sound and learns to produce similar noises.

The sounds of speech have meaning, and **semantics,** which reflects Brown's first essential property of language, concentrates on the content of language and the meaning of words. Researchers who study semantic development are interested in the way children form concepts, learning to map the word "bird," for example, onto the variety of feathered creatures they see flying about, so that when they hear the word they immediately know that it refers to black birds and bluebirds, to big birds and little ones, to caged birds and wild ones, but not to bats, butterflies, or airplanes. Research in semantics also encompasses such topics as how a child learns to distinguish between such words as "tall" and "short," whether children understand more than they can say, and how adults' and children's meanings of words may differ.

The second essential property of language, productivity, is reflected in **syntax,** or the structural principles that determine the form of sentences. The syntax of a language is what makes it productive, for it is part of grammar—and sets forth the rules for combining words.

These rules vary from language to language. In English, "Mommy kisses baby" and "Baby kisses Mommy" have different meanings because the order of the words is different in the two utterances. But in Russian, the equivalent of "Mommy kisses baby," with the three words in that order, could mean either that Mommy gets kissed or that baby gets kissed, depending on whether it is "Mommy" or "baby" that has a particular sound on the end. So a Russian one-year-old must learn to pay special attention to the sounds that come at the end of words, but an American one-year-old must learn to pay special attention to word order.

Researchers who focus on syntax study the child's gradual grasp of grammar. They may be interested in how a child forms the past tense, in a child's understanding of passive sentences, or in the first use of questions involving auxiliary verbs ("Can he skate?").

Pragmatics, which is the study of language's social purposes, examines the way language is used to get things done. When language is used for communication, each utterance is a social act, and the words are chosen because of the assumptions and intentions of the speaker. The act can be judged successful if the utterance has a desired effect on the listener. The effect can be as simple as getting a stamp for a letter or as complicated as persuading a politician to change a vote on a critical bill.

Research in pragmatics centers on social interaction, examining the context of speech to see how the immediate situation affects both the expression and understanding of language. Much recent research in pragmatics has focused on infants, tracing the emergence of language from earlier methods of communication, such as touching, pointing, and gazing.

Although these approaches cover the major aspects of language, it is virtually impossible to study sound, meaning, structure, or function in isolation from each other. And when explaining the acquisition of language, they must be considered together.

ACQUIRING LANGUAGE

Somehow, over their first few years, children master the system of spoken communication they hear around them; the problem is to discover just how they do it. Learning a second language is difficult enough for most people, yet they already have a linguistic system of reference. They can learn that *arbol* means "tree," or that *pas ce soir* means "not tonight," or that in German the verb often moves to the end of the sentence. Yet without this aid and without any direct teaching, children crack a verbal code, deriving meaning from the sounds they hear about them, developing a fluent command of their native tongue.

As we will see, several explanations have been advanced to show the way children acquire language, each of them focusing on a different aspect of the process. Cognition is obviously important; until babies have developed a certain understanding of the world, they cannot talk. Maturation is also important; before a certain age, language acquisition appears to be impossible. And social interaction plays a vital role; without the society of other human beings, a child will not learn to speak.

The Infant's Task

If infants are to communicate meanings and understand what people are saying, they must actively figure out the ways in which speech is structured in their native language. No baby knows, to begin with, what particular native language she or he is acquiring, yet all children manage to acquire their native language with amazing ease and rapidity. This leads us to believe that human beings are in some way endowed with specialized information-processing abilities that make it possible for them to figure out the structure of their own language, just as they are able to figure out the structures of the other sights and sounds and smells and feelings that are necessary in order to function as thinking and feeling human beings in society.

But infants who are figuring out language cannot depend on isolated words; they must learn enough about meanings in the nonlinguistic world to discover how the two systems are related. Babies learn something about this relationship before they begin to speak. In fact, some children who, because of physical handicaps, cannot speak at all come to understand language. Eric Lenneberg (1962) studied one such child and tested him in several ways for language comprehension. The boy, who was then eight, was told a short story and questioned in complex grammatical constructions about its contents. From his responses, there was no doubt that the boy had learned to understand English, his native language. Such cases make it clear that having knowledge of a language is not identical with speaking. Because such knowledge may develop in people who cannot speak, knowledge must be fundamental, and the ability to speak, accessory.

Language and Cognition

The basis for the child's ability to understand and speak a language is an understanding of the world. Clearly, a child who remained at the intellectual level of the human newborn, whose actions are primarily reflexive, would never learn to speak, and a child who regarded the world as an extension of him- or herself would have little to talk about. Before children can use words meaningfully, they must have some notion that there is a world of enduring objects and people and that people can act on objects. As we saw in Chapter 7, these notions of object permanence, object identity, and causality develop during the first year of life.

One aspect of causality, a child's understanding of tools, was related to the emergence of language among American and Italian babies studied toward the end of their first year by Elizabeth Bates (1979) and her associates. Infants who tugged at a supporting cloth in order to get an object they wanted, or who used sticks as tools to reach a desired toy, generally had larger vocabularies than babies who did not understand the use of tools to obtain a goal.

About the time babies begin to play symbolically, as this one is doing, they are also acquiring their first words. *(©Barbara Alper, 1982)*

An infant's use of language could also be predicted by imitation. Most twelve-month-olds imitate events long after they have occurred, convincing evidence of their ability to represent objects and events mentally. Jean Piaget (1951) reported many instances of the imitation of past experiences among one-year-olds. For example, at the age of sixteen months, his daughter Lucienne, who was taking a bath, imitated her sister Jacqueline. She picked up a towel, rolled it into a ball, wiped her mouth with it, and tucked it under her chin, as her sister often did. At seventeen months, when her sister was away, Lucienne rocked her doll in her arms, in imitation of her older sister. Since Lucienne did not imitate her big sister at the time she watched the two actions, she must have stored some representation of the event in her mind, acting it out in imitation much later. Just as one-year-olds can imitate events some time after they have experienced them, so they can use words some time after they have heard them. The abilities to imitate and to store internal images of sights and sounds are necessary prerequisites for the development of any language.

An infant's first words also emerge about the same time the baby begins to use symbolic gestures and to engage in make-believe play. A baby girl who pushes a building block along the floor, pretending that it is a car, or runs her hands through her hair, pretending she is combing it, has demonstrated symbolic play. Such play, as well as the sort of manipulative play in which a baby builds towers of blocks or stacks wooden rings on a stick, is closely related to both his or her use of words and comprehension of others' speech (Bates, 1979).

Tool use, imitation, and symbolic and manipulative play are connected with the emergence of language. There is some evidence that when these capacities are absent, infants do not acquire language (Bates, 1979). Apparently, the same underlying capacities are necessary for any complex symbolic behavior to develop. In words, gestures, play, and the use of tools, infants reflect the level of their understanding of the world, and this symbolic behavior helps them refine and organize their thoughts and feelings.

EXPLANATIONS OF LANGUAGE ACQUISITION

Although, as has been indicated, several explanations have been advanced to describe the way that children acquire language, none has satisfactorily accounted for all facets of its development. These explanations, which derive from various assumptions about child development, can be divided into biological, mechanistic, and functional theories of language acquisition.

Biological Approaches

In biological approaches language development is seen as primarily a matter of maturation because, according to linguist Noam Chomsky (1975, 1979), the structure of language is laid down in our genes. All human languages, despite their surface differences, share an underlying deep structure, which he calls a universal grammar. This grammar consists of principles, conditions, and rules of sound, meaning, and structure. Since biological constraints characterize the grammar children will construct, they take the bits and pieces of language they hear, analyze them, and fit them to the universal grammar. Only in this way, says Chomsky, can we explain how children in a given community—each having entirely different, and mostly fragmentary, language experience—come up with the same rich, complex language system. In this view, language is partly predetermined, in the same way that genes determine the pattern of sexual maturation, and—given experience—children will inevitably acquire language.

When maturation is considered the determining factor in language acquisition, the reference is to maturation of the brain. Eric Lenneberg (1967), convinced that it was the key to language acquisition, proposed that there is a sensitive period in human development when language can be learned, a period that begins when children are about two years old and lasts until they reach sexual maturity. At that time the ability to learn a language declines, and by the late teens it is difficult—or even impossible—to acquire a first language. The end of the sensitive period, said Lenneberg (1973), coincides with the maturation of the brain; once brain tissue is fully differentiated, it loses plasticity and can no longer make the adjustments that the acquisition of language requires.

There is some evidence to support this view. Until they are sexually mature, most children with damage to the brain's left hemisphere recover the ability to talk, but adolescents and adults who receive similar injuries do not. Since, as noted in Chapter 6, language is located in the left hemisphere for most people, this phenomenon points to maturation as a critical factor in its development. In children, Lenneberg said, even though the left hemisphere handles most language functions, the right is still involved in speech, and because brain tissue is still plastic, the right hemisphere can assume the function in the event that the left hemisphere is damaged.

Recent studies have led some researchers to question the concept of a sensitive period for language development. Some evidence indicates that brain lateralization is complete by the time children are five (Carter and Kinsbourne, 1979), and other research indicates that a child is born with the left hemisphere more proficient than the right at processing language (Molfese and Molfese, 1979).

If a sensitive period for language learning exists, it does not apply to the acquisition of a second language. A strict interpretation of Lenneberg's theory suggests that children under twelve should find it easy to acquire a second language and their parents and adolescent siblings should find it extremely difficult. Folklore keeps this idea current, but a study by Catherine Snow and Marian Hoefnagel-Höhle (1978) among English-speaking families that had moved to the Netherlands failed to support it. Adolescents learned Dutch the fastest, and three- to five-year-olds (who should have been the star pupils) were the slowest to learn, falling far behind their parents' fluency in Dutch. In fact, learning the new language caused the preschoolers' fluency in English to drop sharply.

But the sensitive period may still exist if it applies only to the acquisition of a first language. The case of Genie, a California girl who grew up in almost total isolation, indicates that language can be acquired after sexual maturity, but that the language will not be the rich, fluent system spoken by other members of the speech community (Curtiss, 1977). Genie was discovered when she was nearly fourteen, and her social experiences had been limited to spoon feeding by her almost blind mother. No one spoke to her, and whenever she made a noise, her father beat her. Although Genie was severely disturbed and had no language, she subsequently acquired English. The acquisition was difficult, however, and Genie's language is abnormal. Although she understands normal language, she does not produce many of its basic structures, especially those that require a rearrangement of normal word order, such as questions beginning with "what," "where," or "why," and passive sentences. Her speech is rule-governed and productive, however, and she also is able to speak of people and objects that are not present. Genie's case, therefore, supports a weak version of Lenneberg's theory, indicating that acquiring a first language after the brain is mature is difficult but not impossible.

In both mechanistic and functional theories, face-to-face interaction between mother and baby plays an important role in the acquisition of language. *(Suzanne Szasz)*

Mechanistic Approaches

When language acquisition is explained by strict learning theorists, among them B. F. Skinner (1957) and Sidney Bijou and Donald Baer (1965), it is simply vocal behavior reinforced by the action of another person. Because mothers generally talk to babies while they care for them, using words to express affection, a mother's speech becomes reinforcing. Babies can also reinforce themselves by listening to their own vocalizations. As they mature and gain control over their speech apparatus, babies begin to direct the sounds they produce, and the more closely their babbling resembles their mother's speech, the more reinforcing their vocalizations become. When babies babble, their mothers often reward them with attention, adding further reinforcement.

When babies begin to label the objects in the world, their parents reinforce them with attention or approval. The reinforcement is for the sound itself, but the child soon responds to the sight of the object (ball, sock, doll) with the label. Other words are learned because the child receives tangible rewards for producing them, as when the words "cookie" or "bottle" are followed by the objects they represent.

Social-learning theorists would add that imitation plays a major role in the acquisition of speech. Parents serve as models for their children, who imitate the speech they hear. As noted in Chapter 3, imitation does not have to be immediate. A child can learn by observing and imitate the forms of adult speech when a later occasion warrants it. Both comprehension and speech, says Albert Bandura (1977), are based on observational learning.

Although reinforcement and imitation undoubtedly contribute to the acquisition of individual words, mechanistic theories of language acquisition have been challenged on the ground that children learn more than words. They develop rules that allow them to produce and interpret an endless variety of novel sentences. Children produce sentences that are different from the sentences they hear. When children say "All-gone sticky" after washing their hands or "I seed two mouses," they are not imitating forms they have heard others use. Indeed, the latter sentence shows an attempt to force on language a rule-governed regularity it does not possess.

Social-learning theorists maintain, however, that children do imitate the structures they hear. Such sentences as "I seed two mouses," says Bandura (1977), simply indicate that children "model too well." Delayed selective imitation, argue Grover Whitehurst and Ross Vastra (1975), explains children's acquisition of language. In fact, by reinforcing four-year-olds each time the children indicated their understanding of sentences with both direct and indirect objects (e.g., "The boy gives the puppy the bone"), Whitehurst (1974) was able to get them to use similar constructions in their own speech.

Functional Approaches

The functional approach to language acquisition agrees with the biological approach that maturation is vital and that until they reach a certain cognitive level, children cannot acquire language. It also agrees with mechanistic approaches that social interaction is the place to look for the emergence of language. But it maintains that innate mechanisms cannot, by themselves, explain the child's grasp of language, and that the basis for linguistic competence goes beyond conditioning and observational learning to include nonlinguistic aspects of human interaction: turn-taking, mutual gaze, joint attention, context, assumptions, and cultural conventions. The forms of language are acquired in order to carry out communicative functions (Bates, 1979). Investigators with these functional views see pragmatics as the key to language development in a child.

The nonlinguistic aspects of interaction provide the prespeech bases of language and send children a long way along the path of human communication before they say their first words. Instead of the unfolding of preprogrammed behavior, language becomes the product of the child's active interaction with an environment provided by other human beings (Gleason and Weintraub, 1978). These other human beings are tuned to the child's linguistic needs, and their speech meshes precisely with those needs. As Jean Berko Gleason and Sandra Weintraub (1978) point out, cognitive development can result from interaction with the physical world, but children cannot acquire language merely through simple exposure to it as passive listeners.

Jerome Bruner (1980a) suggests that children may begin their language acquisition by using the context of a situation to figure out what speakers are trying to accomplish. In this view, language competence grows out of familiar situations, such as seeking help and establishing joint attention, situations that provide a framework in which children learn to make their own intentions plain and to interpret those of others. Perhaps, suggests Bruner, this interaction with adults acts as a primer that cues a preadapted, innate process, instead of simply being a preformed set of structures for language.

Each of these theories has contributed to our knowledge of language acquisition, and we will encounter research based on all of them. In this chapter, research based on functional theories will receive emphasis, since such studies pay special attention to the way language emerges from the communication that precedes speech.

SOUND

Before they can acquire language, babies must separate speech from the other noise in the environment. Indeed, they seem born prepared to do just that, for babies only a few days old prefer human voices to other sounds, as Earl Butterfield and Gary Siperstein (1974) discovered when they gave newborns a chance to hear music. By sucking on a pacifier, the babies could turn on tape-recorded music. The babies sucked to get musical reinforcement; but they sucked more to hear voices singing with music than to hear melodies without accompanying voices. These babies were actively selecting sound over silence and human sounds over nonhuman.

Listening to Sounds

Human sounds have a special significance for babies only a few weeks old (Menyuk, 1971). A crying baby will fall silent at the sound of a person talking but keep wailing if a bell is rung or a rattle is shaken. The first specific sounds an infant notices may be those words that receive the heaviest emphasis and that often occur at the ends of utterances. By six or seven weeks, an infant can detect the difference between syllables pronounced with rising and falling inflections. Very soon, these differences in adult stress and intonation can affect a baby's emotional states and behavior. Long before babies understand the words they hear, they sense when an adult is playful or angry, attempting to initiate or end behavior, and so on, on the basis of such cues as the rate, volume, and melody of adult speech.

Just as significant for language development as the response to intonation is evidence that a tiny baby can make fine distinctions between speech sounds. In a series of experiments, Peter Eimas and his colleagues (Eimas and Tartter, 1979) discovered that one-month-old babies can hear the difference between the sounds "ba" and "pa," and that by two months they can distinguish between "ma" and "na," and between "dae" and "gae." Other investigators have found that six-week-old infants can tell the difference between "bad" and "bag" (Jusczyk, 1977). Such studies suggest that babies come into the world prepared to make precisely those perceptual discriminations that are necessary if they are to acquire human language.

Young babies cannot, however, make all the sound discriminations necessary for language. Rebecca Eilers, Wesley Wilson, and J. W. Moore (1977) found, for example, that a three-month-old seems not to hear the difference between "s" and "z" at the ends of syllables, or between "sa" and "za." In addition, babies may lose their ability to detect differences that do not appear in the language about them (Eimas and Tartter, 1979). In one study, seven-month-old infants from an English-speaking culture could tell the difference between a contrasting pair of sounds that change the meaning of words in Hindi but not in English; to adult English speakers, the sounds sounded the same (Werker et al., 1981). These two trends indicate that experience and the heredity of the species both play a role in the decoding of speech sounds.

Detecting sound differences when they are connected to meaning takes longer than when they are heard in isolation, as Olga Garnica (1973) found in a study of eighteen-month-old infants. She gave the children colored blocks with features pasted on them, naming each block with a nonsense syllable such as "bok" or "pok." When asked to put the "pok" under the blanket, few of the infants seemed to discriminate between the "b" and "p" sounds that newborns notice. After several training sessions, however, three times as many children made the distinction between "bok" and "pok," indicating that children can learn to pay attention to such sound differences.

Long before the baby can understand any words, the infant will be able to detect a father's mood by relying on the stress and intonation of his speech. *(©George Malave 1976/Stock, Boston)*

Producing Sounds

Although babies can discriminate early among the sounds they hear, most are at least a year old before they can produce sounds that can be identified as words. It is much easier to perceive auditory discriminations than to acquire motor control over the various muscles and organs involved in producing speech (McCarthy, 1954). The progress from crying to babbling to speech follows the same sequence in most infants, but many pass through the various linguistic developments shown in Figure 8.1 earlier or later than the suggested ages.

From Cries to Babbles A baby's first sounds are cries. After about three weeks, his or her vocalizations gradually increase in frequency and variety. Some sounds are only physical and digestive mouthings and gurglings, but by the second month babies invent new noises, from squeals to Bronx cheers, and repeat them again and again in a circular fashion (P. Wolff, 1969). Sounds of joy, called cooing, also may appear at this time, usually when babies seem happy: after eating, while watching a smiling face, when listening to singing, and while looking at or handling objects.

Because crying is part of a child's social interaction, infants in institutions with few adults around make fewer spontaneous noises and may not even cry as much as other babies. If no one comes to answer a cry, crying becomes a useless noise. When adults respond to the sounds a baby makes in play, however, their frequency increases. In a series of experiments with institu-

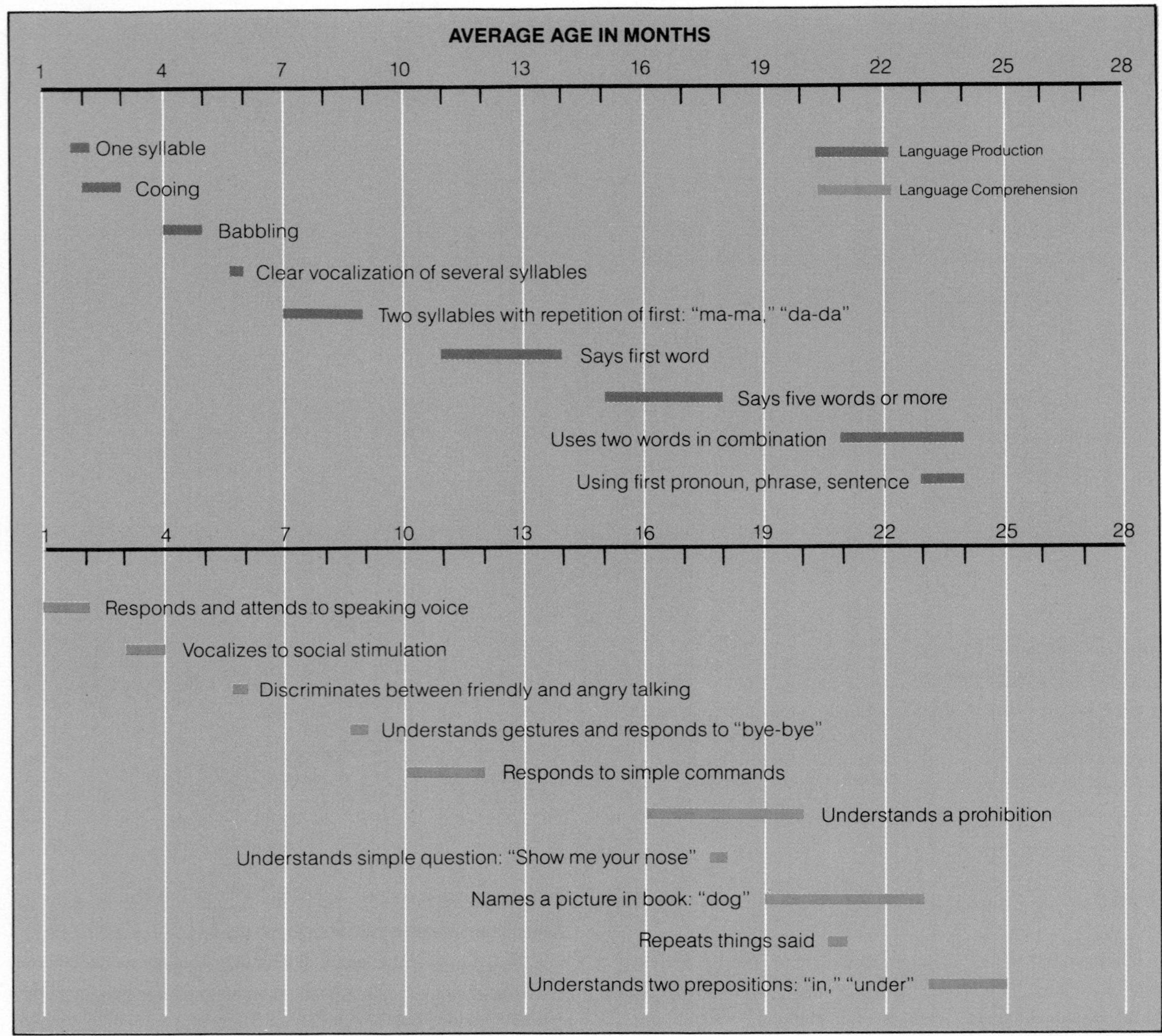

FIGURE 8.1 Highlights of language development during the first two years of life. The ages shown are approximate, and the length of the bars reflects the age range that researchers have reported for the appearance of a particular linguistic advance. ***(Adapted from Lenneberg, 1967; McCarthy, 1954; Bayley, 1969).***

tionalized babies, Harriet Rheingold, Jacob Gewirtz, and Helen Ross (1959) used the sort of simultaneous smiles, sounds, and light touches to the abdomen commonly found in adult-infant play to condition babies' vocalizations. They did not reinforce coughs, whistles, squeals, snorts,

Crying is a part of the baby's first social interactions. *(©Terry Evans/Magnum)*

fusses, or cries of protest. The reinforcement quickly doubled the babies' responses.

Around the age of five or six months, babies begin to babble, producing strings of alternating vowels and consonants, such as "babababa." These sound sequences give the impression that the baby is uttering a string of syllables. Such repetitions indicate a greatly improved control over the muscles that govern speech. This control, together with the coordination of speech production with the perception of sound, is probably the primary function of babbling. When babies feel certain patterns of motor activity involving throat, tongue, and lip muscles, they associate those movements with the sounds they hear themselves making. And as they gain motor control, their babbling develops in accordance with the same rules and constraints that will later govern the development of words (deVilliers and deVilliers, 1978).

Early babbling appears to be primarily motor play, as indicated by the fact that deaf babies babble as much as babies who can hear. But because the babbling of normal six-month-old babies shows a greater diversity of sound than the babbling of deaf infants, we can suppose that hearing speech sounds stimulates the baby. Soon after six months, deaf infants stop babbling, whereas hearing infants go on to greater diversity and experimentation in their speech play (Lenneberg, 1967).

But babbling may not be directly related to the acquisition of any particular native language (McNeill, 1970a). Babbling includes many sounds that adults do not make and that the baby may be unable to make a year later. Moreover, the babblings of children from different language communities cannot be distinguished from one another.

Near the end of the first year, however, intonational variations begin to appear in the child's vocalizations. Now the rising and falling pitch of the utterances becomes more and more like adult speech, and the babbling of an English baby sounds like English, while the babbling of a Russian baby sounds like Russian. Infants often produce long, complex sequences of meaningless sounds with the pitch contour of adult sentences. These sequences may appear in situations where language is appropriate, as when a child "talks" to a doll.

First Words The range of sounds in a baby's first words is sharply limited, and many babies are unable to imitate sounds they made earlier in playful babbling. First words tend to be short, of one or two syllables, and each syllable generally consists of a consonant followed by a vowel. The first syllable may occur when infants simply release their lips while vocalizing, producing sounds such as "ma" or "ba." The first distinction between consonants that infants make is often between a sound such as "ma," which they produce by releasing air through the nose with the lips together and then opening the mouth, and "ba," which they produce by suddenly letting the air out between their lips. Once they have reached this point, they may be able to say "mama" and "ba" as distinct words and are ready to build a vocabulary.

Nor is the pronunciation of first words stable. If a baby's first word is something like "ba" for "ball," its pronunciation will vary from "bee" to "bow," and the consonant will also vary, being sometimes "p," "v," "d," or "th" (Ferguson and Farwell, 1975). Because a listener may expect to hear the sound "ball," she or he may believe that the baby has a stable pronunciation of it. In fact, although babies can perceive the difference among sounds in adult speech, it takes a great deal of effort on their part to figure out how to produce the complex of sounds that correspond to adult words.

Because infants have few consonants at their command during the second year, their store of syllables is small and they often repeat them. For example, they may say "pa-pa" or "bi-bi" or "car-car." They may also utter words that have different meanings but sound the same because their small collection of syllables offers few possibilities for different word forms. Thus a baby boy may say "ba" to imitate the words "ball," "bird," and "flower." The first time he says "ba," his mother or father will probably say "ball" if a ball is nearby or "bird" if a bird flies by. Such auditory reinforcement helps the infant to shape his "ba" until at last he does say both "ball" and "bird" (McCarthy, 1954).

The work of decoding and reproducing the sounds of speech does not end with the child's first words. As we will see in Chapter 12, children continue to work at the task after they enter the stage of grammatical speech.

THE IMPORTANCE OF SOCIAL INTERACTION

If children are to be competent speakers, they must be able to get things done with words. In fact, words can be seen as "meaningful social behavior" (Bruner, 1976). Viewing language as a social act, in which the speaker is trying to accomplish something, leads researchers to look at the emergence of intent in the baby's actions, at the social interaction between baby and caregiver, and at the context in which language is used. As Alastair Mundy-Castle (1980) points out, the language-learning process begins at birth, not with a child's first words. Long before children speak, they learn to manipulate the context of their actions according to rules they have acquired in activity with their caregivers.

The Emergence of Intent

Although newborn babies communicate successfully, their messages are sent without *intent.* Despite this lack of intent, their cries tell their parents the babies are hungry, wet, uncomfortable, or in pain, and hence the howls often succeed in remedying the problem. Milk, dry diapers, or cuddling arrives in response to the cries; but the baby's message was not, "Give me milk!" but simply a signal of distress.

Babies clearly develop intentions before they try to communicate them to others. At about two or three months, for example, a baby girl who sees an attractive object dangled before her shows her eagerness to grasp it. She opens and closes her mouth, moves her head, and wiggles her body, behaving as she would if she had the object. Within another month or so, if a toy is dangled before her, she will reach for it. In neither case, however, does the baby make an attempt to get assistance from an adult. Similarly, when given a toy that requires adult assistance, the baby will hit at the toy, push it, or throw it instead of indicating a need for help.

About the age of nine or ten months, however, babies undergo a great change in their behavior in this respect (Bretherton and Bates, 1979). Now, if babies want a toy that is out of reach, they will look at a nearby adult, then at the toy, then back at the adult. If there is no response, they may fuss loudly to attract attention. Very soon thereafter, the grasp toward the elusive toy becomes an intentional signal, perhaps a repetitive opening and shutting of the hand, and the fussing sound becomes short, regular noises that change in volume and insistence depending upon whether or not the adult responds. This is a great moment, says Elizabeth Bates (1979), in the dawn of language. It shows the child's intent to communicate as well as his or her realization that there are mutually agreed on signals, such as pointing, that can be used for mutually agreed on purposes. Earlier, the infant may have wanted to communicate but lacked any shared notion of conventional ways to express intention. The way is now open for the baby's first words.

Seeking help is only one of the intentions that govern infants' communication at this early age. They also use sounds, looks, and gestures to persuade adults to look at something with them (thereby achieving and regulating joint attention), to increase affiliation (enjoying the exchange of gestures, sounds, and facial expressions), and to induce others to join them in their make-believe play. These four intentions, says Jerome Bruner (1980a), encompass most infant communication during the early phases of language acquisition and, as we will see, they develop in a social context with the caregiver playing an active role.

The Caregiver's Role

If babies are to be successful with a language, they must have the background knowledge assumed by all its speakers. They must know the cultural conventions that surround communication: how to maintain joint attention, how to refer, how to take turns, how to reverse roles, and so forth. This knowledge begins in the interaction of baby and caregiver.

Almost from the beginning, parents interact with their babies by responding to movements and sounds as if they were meaningful and intentional, and by encouraging the babies to "take their turn" in conversation. Language conventions are learned in these dialogues between caregiver and infant, with the caregiver at first supplying both sides of the conversation. As a result, even though young babies may not be trying to communicate, they are learning something about the nature of human conversation. For example:

INFANT: (smiles)
MOTHER: Oh, what a nice little smile! Yes, isn't that nice? There. That's a nice little smile.
INFANT: (burps)
MOTHER: What a nice wind as well! Yes, that's better, isn't it? Yes. Yes.
INFANT: (vocalizes)
MOTHER: Yes! There's a nice noise (C. E. Snow, 1977).

As such exchanges progress, parents pay close attention to the baby's reactions, and as the infant's competence increases, the conversations change. More and more participation is demanded from the baby—first in the form of babbling, then in words. Later, the parent may repeat a question until the infant supplies an answer.

Carrying on a conversation requires infants to master other conventions as well: they must learn to take turns, speaking at the proper time and not interrupting their partners; they must learn to make eye contact and to indicate that they are paying attention. These turn-taking and other nonverbal conversational skills grow out of early games, such as peekaboo, in which baby and adult share experiences and exchange roles in ritualized ways. For example, the earliest give-and-take games always begin at the caregiver's initiation. Gradually the baby begins to start the games and, as Figure 8.2 on page 195 shows, before children are a year old, they play leader a major part of the time (Bruner, 1978).

Joint attention becomes easier at about six or seven months, as babies seem to learn that certain signals in adult speech mean that something the adult is attending to is worth looking at (Bruner, 1980a). Shortly thereafter, the baby learns to follow the adult's gaze to find the object. In a study with Michael Scaife, Bruner (1975) found that between eight and ten months, two-thirds of the babies would follow an adult's gaze and look intently at whatever was the focus of adult attention. By the time they were a year old, all babies did this. Such shared gaze is soon followed by pointing at interesting objects (Leung and Rheingold, 1981) and paves the way to shared linguistic reference and the acquisition of words.

Parents also speak in special ways to their babies. This altered manner of speaking at first consists of exaggerated pitch, loudness, and intensity, exaggerated facial expression, extension of vowel length, and emphasis on certain words

As babies grow older, they initate many games and in the process master such conventions of language as turn-taking. *(© William Hubbell 1981/ Woodfin Camp & Assoc.)*

(Stern, 1977). At about ten months, just when the baby shows an intent to communicate, parents shift to a kind of speech that has been called baby talk or "motherese" (Gleason and Weintraub, 1978). When they switch to baby talk, adults speak more slowly and use simple sentences, inserting pauses into their words. They use very short sentences, replace difficult consonants with easy ones, substitute nouns for pronouns, and repeat words, phrases, or whole sentences. As in the earliest speech to infants, pitch and tone change, as the adult seems to be both conveying affection and capturing the child's attention for the task at hand. Baby talk appears in societies around the world; its presence has been documented in at least fifteen cultures, and it is used by parents, strange adults, and older children alike (Ferguson, 1977).

Adults also talk to infants primarily about the here and now. They comment on what they are doing, or what the infant is doing or is about to do. They limit their vocabularies, and they select words that are most useful for the infant, words that relate to what babies are interested in. As Roger Brown (1977) put it, the adult is trying "to keep two minds focused on the same topic."

The result of baby talk is, however, anything but babyish. The content and the intonation of the communication is childish, but the dialogue pattern is strictly adult (Bruner, 1978). Without baby talk, infants might never become competent speakers, for evidence suggests that young children will not acquire language through simple exposure to normal adult speech. This conclusion could be drawn from J. S. Sachs and M. Johnson's (1976) study of the hearing child of deaf parents. Although the boy heard a good deal of adult speech on television, his parents used only sign language with him, and when he was four, his language lagged far

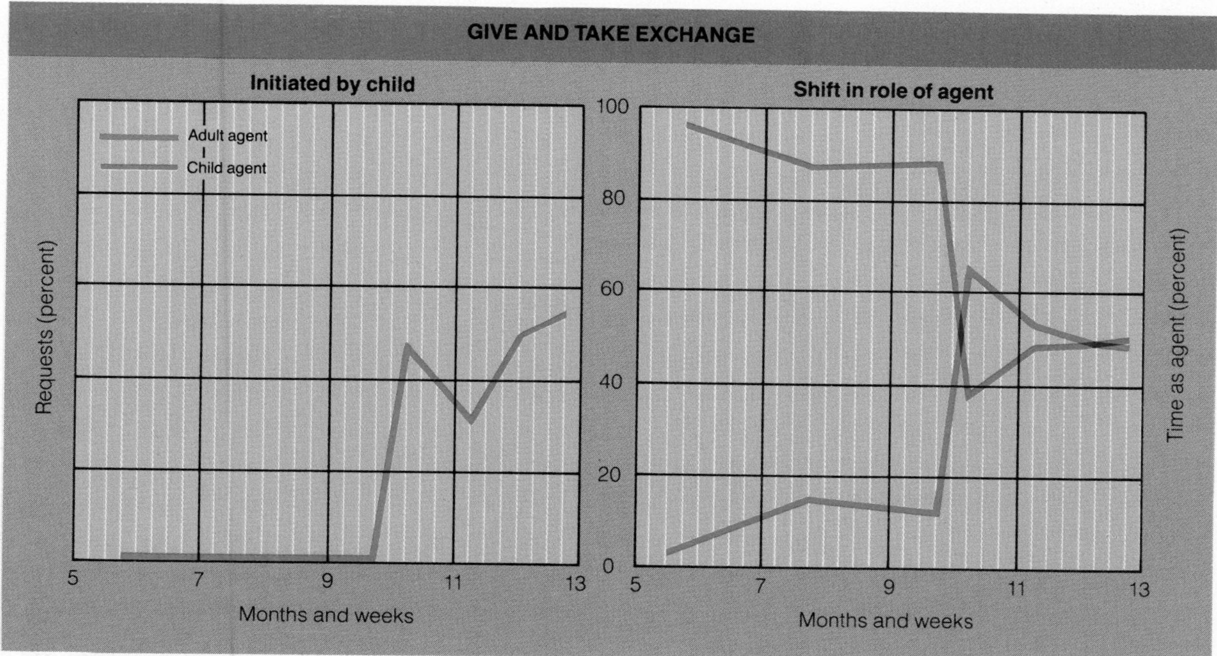

FIGURE 8.2 During the infant's first year, control of games passes from caregiver to baby, with the baby gradually becoming the iniator in most games of give-and-take. In the process, the infant learns about sharing and taking turns, conventions that are basic to conversation. *(Bruner, 1978).*

behind that of other children. His vocabulary was quite small, probably learned from playmates and from television jingles. Other research has discovered that children who watch television programs in a language other than their own do not seem to acquire the second language (Snow et al., 1976). Such speech is probably too rapid for children to follow, it is not aimed at a child's immediate situation, and, it pays no attention to the child's reactions.

Accounting for Context

It is natural that babies' first words carry on the patterns of behavior and intent they have developed during the prespeech period. For some time, they have been using speechlike sounds, intonation patterns, and gestures to express several basic functions of communication, and the first words act in the same way. They refer to objects and events, express mood states, and command adults to carry out actions that the infant desires.

Before babies accomplish these acts with the aid of labels attached to objects and actions in their world, they pass through a phase when a single sound performs many functions at once. For example, one little girl, whose first words are shown in Table 8.1, might say, "uh," and point to a bottle on the kitchen table. With a single undifferentiated utterance, she can simultaneously refer to the bottle, express her hunger, and request that the bottle of milk be given to her. As we will see, once a child can combine several words in one utterance, these functions will become differentiated in speech.

TABLE 8.1
THE FIRST SEVEN "WORDS" IN ONE CHILD'S LINGUISTIC DEVELOPMENT

Utterance	*Age in Months*	*Meanings*
uh?	8	An interjection. Also demonstrative, "addressed" to persons, distant objects, and "escaped toys."
dididi	9	Disapproval (loud). Comfort (soft).
mama	10	Refers vaguely to food. Also means "tastes good" and "hungry."
nenene	10	Scolding.
tt!	10	Used to call squirrels.
piti	10	Always used with a gesture, and always whispered. Seems to mean "interest(-ed), (-ing)."
deh	10	An interjection. Also demonstrative. Used with the same gesture as above.

Source: Adapted from David McNeill, *The Acquisition of Language: The Study of Developmental Psycholinguistics* (New York: Harper & Row, 1970), p. 22; based on material from Werner F. Leopold, *Grammar and General Problems in the First Two Years,* Speech Development of a Bilingual Child: A Linguist's Record, Vol. 3 (Evanston, Ill.: Northwestern University Press, 1949), p. 6.

A toddler who says the single word "door" can be understood only in context. The word might mean "Open the door," "Close the door," or any of several other statements. ***(Sybil Shelton/ Monkmeyer Press)***

Most infants are nearly two before they can say more than one word at a time, and during this period they often rely on intonation to communicate the intent behind a single word. Figure 8.3 shows the intonation patterns of the word "door" as spoken by an infant on three different occasions. Paula Menyuk and Nancy Bernholtz (1969) tape-recorded these utterances and played them for listeners, who agreed when the child's use of "door" was a declaration, a question, or an emphatic statement. Clearly the infant was not using the word "door" simply to label an object. When the word was spoken with a falling pitch (frequency contour), listeners judged the utterance as referring to a door. When the same word was uttered with a rising intonation, listeners interpreted it as a question, and when the intonation rose sharply and then fell, it was heard as an emphatic assertion or demand. Thus, the single word "door" could mean: "That's a door" or "Is that a door?" or "Are you going to open the door?" or "Open the door!" or "Close the door!"

Simple utterances—early one-word utterances and later two- and three-word utterances—can be fully understood only in context. Context includes the beliefs and assumptions of the speaker concerning the setting of his or her remarks; it includes the prior, present, and future actions and remarks of both speaker and listener, and it includes the knowledge and intentions of everyone involved (Ochs, 1979). For example, on hearing a recording of the word "door" spoken with an emphatic intonation, we could not decide whether the infant speaker wanted the door opened or closed or merely wanted attention paid to the door. But if we were watching a toddler stand in front of a closed door and knew that on the other side of the door her mother was baking cookies, we would know immediately that the emphatic word meant that we had been asked to open it.

At these early stages the child's communication succeeds because adults are good at guessing children's intentions. Like adults, children give clues to their intentions in intonation and gesture. In addition, because children's communicative needs are always embedded in an ongoing context of activity, it is generally possible to figure out what they are trying to say. To some degree the process works in both directions. Children also assess a communication in terms of its context. However, as words become increasingly important to the toddler, they can sometimes overpower the nonverbal context in which they are set, as the box on page 198 indicates.

As children begin to share the presuppositions that surround the use of language, and as their vocabulary and grammar develop, they will be able to talk about objects and people that are not present, about things they did yesterday or want to do tomorrow. Immediate physical context, although still important, will become less vital, and true conversation will become possible for them.

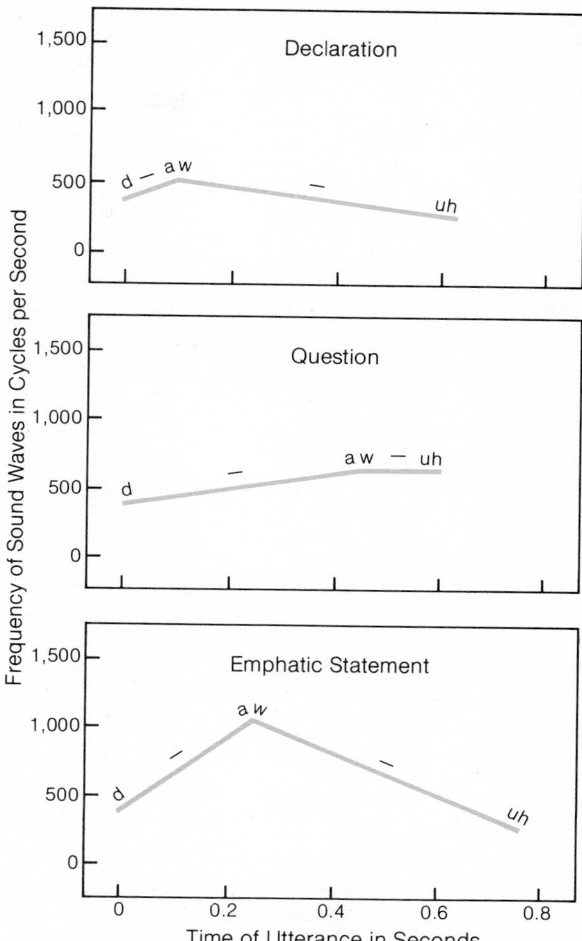

FIGURE 8.3 Three intonation patterns for the word "door" spoken by an infant at the one-word stage. *(After Menyuk, 1971)*

THE DEVELOPMENT OF MEANING

Although some babies begin to use a variety of single words toward the end of their first year, most will pass their first birthday with a vocabulary of no more than three words. Language ability develops similarly in boys and girls during the first eighteen months, although some studies have shown a slight edge for girls and still others have found that newborn girls vocalize more than boys (McCarthy, 1954).

Meanings of First Words

The first words of infants generally are names of objects and indicate the baby's recognition, first, that objects are worth talking about and, second, that they have names (Nelson and Nelson, 1978).

THE POWER OF THE WORD

Infants in the one- and two-word stages respond both to speech and to nonverbal methods of communication—such as gesture, tone of voice, and facial expression. At this early stage of language acquisition, which is more powerful? Despite the fact that children less than two years old are not fluent speakers and might be expected to rely on gestures and facial expressions, it seems they pay more attention to words.

In their discovery of the power of the spoken word, Fred Volkmar, Lawrence Hoder, and Alberta Siegel (1980) gave young children a series of commands, in four different ways. In the first command, the child heard and saw consistent messages, that is, the verbal and nonverbal messages were the same. In the second, the child only heard the command given. In the third, the child only saw the command given. And in the fourth, the child heard and saw conflicting messages. During the experiment, one of the investigators entered the room where an infant and mother were sitting. He either asked the child to come over to him or told the child to stay away, and he systematically varied his message so that the child received the command in every possible combination. When children did toddle over to him, he allowed them to stick a colorful plastic flower onto a balloon he held.

A few of the children approached only when the verbal and nonverbal messages were both positive, that is, when the investigator smiled, beckoned, and said "Come here" in a warm voice. But for a majority of the children, the words overpowered facial expression and gesture. When either the words alone or the gesture and expression by themselves sent a message, whether "Come here" or "Stay away," children obeyed it. When the two messages conflicted, as when the investigator smiled and beckoned but said in a cold voice "Stay away," or when he frowned and motioned the child away but spoke a warm "Come here," the child obeyed the verbal message. In these cases, the investigators point out, the behavior of the gesturing adult was bizarre and meaningless, and observing it, an adult might have thought she or he had stumbled onto a psychotic. Yet the children responded to the words.

Volkmar and his associates believe that the children neither denied nor discounted any of the messages they received. Instead, they appear to have perceived and interpreted all the messages correctly; but when they integrated the information received from visual and auditory channels, they gave greater weight to the words they heard than to the sights they saw.

The interests of infants and of those around them determine the exact content of early vocabularies, but the first words usually express the same basic notions (Nelson, 1973). Most babies begin by naming movers, common objects that can move on their own and can manipulate other things, such as people, vehicles, and animals. Infants also refer frequently to movables, objects that can be moved and manipulated but cannot move independently, such as toys, food, articles of clothing, and household items. Such things as locations and objects used as tools (such as spoons) are less common early words. The form of these early words allows us to infer quite a bit about the way infants perceive and arrange their world (Clark and Clark, 1977), and as we will see in Chapter 11, the infant's attention to the movement and use of objects may play an important role in the development of concepts.

When children first learn a word, its meaning may be very different from the conventional meaning attributed to it by adults. They often extend the meaning of a word to cover other objects or actions for which they have no words, a process called **overextension.** For example,

When "reading" to the stuffed bear, this baby may use a single word to refer to many related objects or actions. ***(Emily Siroka 1980/Woodfin Camp & Assoc.)***

one child used a single word to refer to the sound of a train, music, cars, trains, a chair pushed across the floor, a toy wheelbarrow, and pictures of cars (Leopold, 1949). In this case, the word was extended from the sound of a moving object to include anything that could move, including in its meaning all the related events and experiences for which the child had no separate names. Overextension is a fairly common practice. Analyses of parental diaries and observation of young children indicate that from 20 to 34 percent of a child's early words are extended in this fashion (Nelson et al., 1978).

After examining diaries of language acquisition kept in various languages by linguist and psychologist parents, Eve Clark (1973) has concluded that when an infant extends a word, it is usually possible to find some perceived similarity of form or function among the objects and events it includes. She gives six examples of major categories that various infants have used to sort out their world: *movement,* in which "titi" was extended from animals to all things that could move; *shape,* in which "mooi" was extended from the moon to all round objects; *size,* in which "fly" was extended from a specific insect to specks of dirt, dust, all small insects, the infant's own toes, crumbs of bread, and a toad; *sound,* in which "koko," a Yugoslav infant's word for a crowing cock, was extended to all music and even to a merry-go-round; *taste,* in which "candy" was extended to mean cherries and then to refer to anything sweet; and *texture,* in which "bow-wow" was extended from a real dog to a toy dog, then to a fur piece with an animal head, and finally to all fur pieces.

As new words enter young children's vocabularies and as new experiences refine their concepts, they restructure and reorganize their early word meanings. Clark charts this development for a single word, showing its course in a young boy's experiences with the word "bow-wow." He first applies "bow-wow" to dogs, but soon uses it to refer to many animals—dogs, cows, horses, sheep, and cats—perhaps basing his meaning of the word on shape and movement. When he learns the word "moo," the little boy distinguishes cow from other animals, apparently dividing the animal kingdom into two categories: cows ("moo") and other animals ("bow-wow"). As the boy learns more animal names, he keeps subdividing the general class "bow-wow," so that eventually he has separate names for dogs, cows, horses, sheep, and cats.

At each step, the available animal names take on more precise meaning, based on those features that the youngster uses to distinguish animals. For example, at one step, the category "bow-wow" may include the feature of small size, because "bow-wow" refers only to fairly small animals like dogs, cats, and sheep, whereas the words for horse and cow may include large size among their features. In this process, the global meaning of infants' first words narrow as they acquire new words and begin to attend to new features of objects and events. Each time they learn to notice and apply a new feature to the world, such as small, living, soft, and so forth, they may restructure a number of words (McNeill, 1970a).

Children's overextensions may not always signify a true confusion of meaning, for those who overextend words in speaking often understand them in a much more restricted fashion. Janice Gruendel (1977) has found that youngsters who refer to all animals as "bow-wow," for example, when asked to point to the "bow-wow" will always pick a dog from a group of animals and never point to a cat or a sheep, even though they themselves use the term to refer to those animals. It is as if, she says, in comprehension a word denotes a single concept (such as dog), while in production it denotes the entire category of which the concept is a member (animals). In addition, instances of overextension may not always be examples of naming. Sometimes it appears as if the child is focusing attention on similarities, as when a youngster calls a grapefruit a moon (roundness). If the child's grasp of language were firmer, she or he might say "It's like a moon" or "It's round."

FIGURE 8.4 A hypothetical example of how an infant overextends and restructures the meaning of the word "bow-wow," as discussed in the text. *(Adapted from E. Clark, 1973)*

Deciding What to Talk About

Infants who are limited to one-word utterances often have more than one word in their vocabularies that applies to a situation. If a baby girl is playing with a toy airplane, swooping it through the air as she sits in her highchair, how does she decide which of her words is the appropriate comment on the situation? Informativeness is the criterion by which a child selects his or her comments, believes Patricia Greenfield (1979), whose analysis generally predicts infants' choices of words during this level of development. Information they regard as certain is not mentioned; whatever they cannot take for granted will be the topic of conversation. "Certain" information is information that is certain to the child, not the adult, for children at this level of development assume that adults share their perceptions. In the above example, the baby's comment would not be "plane," because the airplane, being in her possession, is certain and can be taken for granted. She is likely to direct her comment at the plane's action, saying "bzzz," or whatever word she uses to denote the sound of an airplane at this point.

Should the plane slip from her grasp, the baby would say "plane," because the airplane has suddenly become uncertain. But once she has mentioned the plane, it becomes old information and therefore certain. Now she is free to comment on her elusive toy and may say "down" or "fall" or "gone." When commenting on a person's actions, young children take the person for granted and talk about the action. Sitting on the living-room floor and wishing to comment on the fact that her mother is reading a book, the baby would say "book" and not "Mommy." But if her mother leaves the room, she becomes un-

Because babies do not waste their comments on "certain" information, this little girl will not use her word for the stroller unless it slips away from her. *(Suzanne Szasz)*

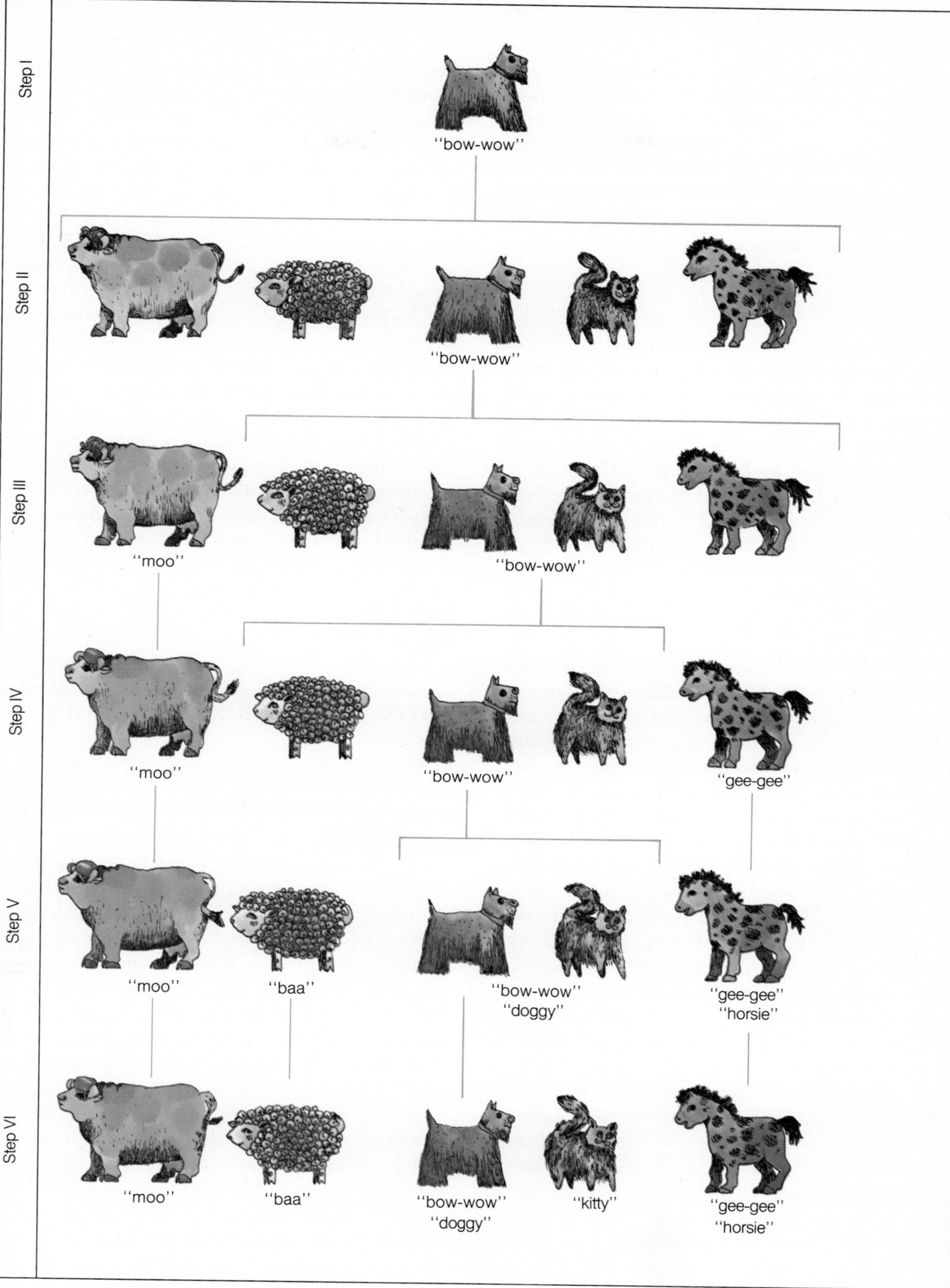
Step I
"bow-wow"
Step II
"bow-wow"
Step III
"moo"
"bow-wow"
Step IV
"moo"
"bow-wow"
"gee-gee"
Step V
"moo"
"baa"
"bow-wow"
"doggy"
"gee-gee"
"horsie"
Step VI
"moo"
"baa"
"bow-wow"
"doggy"
"kitty"
"gee-gee"
"horsie"

certain in the baby's scheme of things and the comment would be "Mommy," no matter how interested she was in her mother's action. Since, as Greenfield points out, adults and children appear to analyze a situation similarly, the baby's mother understands her daughter's comments during play and responds appropriately, making communication possible.

First Sentences

Toward the end of the one-word period, infants make sequences of separate one-word utterances that seem to relate to a larger meaning, even though they speak each word separately, with its own falling intonation. For example, a one-year-old girl described by Lois Bloom (1973) struggled to put a button into her pocket. She said "button" and then "pocket" but could not join the two words together in a single utterance. A month or two later, the same girl could say "button pocket" with no pause between the words and with a falling intonation that spread over the whole utterance.

The emergence of the two-word stage seems to be the result of some increase in neurological capacity that allows the young child to plan and to produce a two-word utterance before running out of working memory. Once a child can process two words at a time, more information can be fitted into an utterance. The concepts that children express with their two words were, however, already present in their one-word utterances. For example, Ronald Scollan (1979) reports an eighteen-month-old girl who said such things as "finger" and then "touch," as she reached out to touch the microphone connected to his tape recorder. Within two months, she was firmly in the two-word stage, saying such things as "wash clothes" and "Brenda here," with no pause between the words.

The two-word stage is significant because it represents a striking advance in children's ability to code their understanding in linguistic terms and to project their ideas into the world of human interaction. At this stage, children mean more than they can say in one utterance. For example, a small boy who wants his mother to give him a cookie cannot express the entire thought in a single statement. He can say "Mommy give," "Give cookie," and "Mommy cookie," yet he cannot say "Mommy give cookie." As they did in the one-word stage, youngsters may string together two-word utterances to express a longer thought, like the little girl in Scollan's experiment who said such things as "My turn. Do it." and "Scary monster. Read dat."

The meanings expressed in these two-word utterances reflect the level of understanding of a child about two years old. Early language development has been studied in many different cultures, and the picture is always the same (Slobin, 1972). Somewhere around their second birthday, children start to put two words together to express the same universal range of basic concepts that form the core of human language. Indeed, a large part of later language development is primarily a matter of elaborating and refining the basic notions that are already present at this early age.

FROM TWO WORDS TO SYNTAX

In the next several years, children develop a command of grammar, the rules that all of us know implicitly and use to organize our words into sentences. It is this knowledge of inflections, prepositions, word order, and so on that makes it possible for us to produce and understand sentences outside of any immediate physical context. The development of this grammatical knowledge actively occupies the child's mind from two to five, as we will see in Chapter 12.

When linguists first began to analyze the speech of children at the two-word stage, they concentrated on the formal grammatical rules that govern the distribution of word classes, such as nouns and verbs, in children's sentences. It soon became apparent that such analysis of two-word utterances was of little use because it treated a sentence like "Baby chair" as being the same, no matter how it was used (Bloom, 1970). But a two-year-old boy may say "Baby chair" and mean "Baby is sitting in her high chair," or he may say "Baby chair" and mean "That is baby's high chair." In both cases, he is using two nouns, yet in the first he is indicating the baby's location, in the second, her possession of the chair.

Despite the resistance of children's early two-word utterances to such analysis, the rudiments of grammar do appear in speech near the end of this stage. These first grammatical devices are the basic tools of human language: intonation, word order, and inflection.

Intonation

We have already discussed the important role that intonation plays in earlier periods of language development, when a baby can indicate a request with a rising tone or a demand with a loud, insistent tone. Intonation continues to be used to differentiate a statement from a question. For example, "Daddy book" spoken without a rising tone may mean "This is Daddy's book," whereas "Daddy book?" with the rising tone means "Is this Daddy's book?" or "Will Daddy read a book?" Toward the end of the two-word stage, the child begins to use another intonational device, *stress.* In the example of "Baby chair," an English-speaking child may emphasize the first word, saying "BABY chair" to indicate possession ("That is baby's chair"), or emphasize the second word, saying "Baby CHAIR" to indicate location ("Baby is in the chair") or destination ("Put baby in the chair").

Word Order

In English and in many other languages, the order in which words are spoken partly determines the meaning of word combinations. The typical English sentence follows a subject-verb-object sequence, and as soon as children understand this basic rule, they can distinguish between the meanings of "Kiss baby" and "Baby kiss," because English speakers place the verb before the object. In Germany, however, children follow the rules of German word order and consistently place the object before the verb in two-word utterances (Roeper, 1973).

Instead of using the two-word limit in any order to produce a random collection of words (Brown, 1973), children use their knowledge of word order grammatically to distinguish the meanings of word combinations. For example, children who want Daddy to throw a ball will use some two-word combinations ("Daddy throw," "Daddy ball," "Throw ball") but not others ("ball Daddy," "ball throw," "throw Daddy").

Children also use word order to understand the speech of others. Asked to act out simple sentences (such as "The cat kissed the dog"), in which word order is the only cue to meaning, children who can only speak sentences of two words will correctly portray the sentence (deVilliers and deVilliers, 1973). Similarly, linguists, parents, and other children use their own knowledge of word order to decipher the speech of children in the two-word stage.

Individual differences appear in speech when children first combine two words to express meaning. According to Martin Braine (1976), as children enter the two-word stage they discover different patterns of word order. One child may communicate the idea that an object is at a particular location by naming the object first and the place second ("Baby chair"); another may discover a pattern in which the place comes first ("Here baby," "There book"). Some children at first prefer to combine two content words, as in "play bed" and "doggie bark"; others begin by combining content words with pronouns in most of their utterances, as in "I finish" (Bloom, Lightbown, and Hood, 1975). Katherine Nelson (1981) suggests that this latter difference, between children who use many nouns and those who tend to use pronouns, is primarily due to the language environment provided by parents. She has found that young children who use many nouns generally have mothers who teach through questioning, so that the youngsters have come to regard language as basically an informative, cognitive medium. Children who rely on pronouns also tend to include many social routines (such as "stop it," or "I want it") in their vocabularies; they usually have mothers who use language to tell the youngsters what to do, language that is centered around the child's activities. As a result, these children regard language as a pragmatic medium, good for social control and social exchange.

Inflection

Grammatical markers, such as the possessive *-'s* and the past tense *-ed,* that are added to words to change their meanings are called **inflections.** Compared with some languages, English uses few inflections, and children begin to learn them quite early. Their mastery of the plural and the possessive, for example, soon makes it possible for them to indicate the difference between "Baby's toy" and "Baby toys." Some languages use different word endings (inflections) to express contrasts in meaning, such as the Russian example of "Mommy kisses baby" that appeared early in the chapter. Children at the two-word stage who learn highly inflected languages are quick to acquire the word endings that express the notions implicit in speech, such as direct and indirect object and location. The direct-object inflection is one of the first endings that children pick up in learning such languages as Russian, Serbo-Croatian, Latvian, Hungarian, Finnish, and Turkish (Slobin, 1973).

Much of the basic grammatical machinery children need to acquire a particular language is present in their speech by the time they reach the end of the two-word stage. These basic rules of intonation, word order, and inflection occur, in varying degrees, in all languages of the world. As a result, all languages are about equally easy for children to learn, and all children are ready to go on to more complex grammatical rules by the time they are about two and a half years old.

SUMMARY

1. Human language has three important properties: semanticity (meaningfulness), productivity (the ability to combine words into an unlimited number of sentences), and displacement (the ability to communicate about objects in another place or time). By this definition, no other species has true language, although most communicate with their fellows. The four aspects of language studied by developmental psychologists are phonology (the study of speech sounds), semantics (the study of meaning), syntax (the study of structural principles), and pragmatics (the study of language's social purposes). In order to explain the acquisition of language, all must be considered together.

2. Since children acquire a language without direct teaching, human beings are apparently endowed with information-processing abilities that make it possible for them to figure out their own language. Before children can acquire language, they must know that there is a world of enduring objects and people. In addition, tool use, imitation, and symbolic and manipulative play are connected with the emergence of language. These capacities reflect the infant's understanding of the world, and in their absence, language does not develop.

3. Biological theories of language acquisition, such as that proposed by Noam Chomsky, assert that language development is largely a matter of brain maturation and that biological constraints characterize the universal grammar that underlies all languages. Mechanistic theories, such as that proposed by B. F. Skinner, assert that language is simply vocal behavior reinforced by the actions of others. Social-learning theorists believe that in addition to reinforcement, observational learning and imitation are important. Functional theories, such as that proposed by Jerome Bruner, believe that maturation is important, but that the nonlinguistic aspects of human interaction provide a prespeech basis for language, which does

not develop in the absence of interaction with fluent speakers.

4. Babies seem born prepared to respond to speech, and within the first month of life human sounds have a special significance for them. Small babies can make fine distinctions between speech sounds, an ability they lose if the distinctions are not used in the language they hear about them. Babies progress from crying to babbling to speech, and until intonational differences appear near the end of the first year, the vocalizations of children from all language communities sound alike. The pronunciation of first words is not stable, but gradually becomes so as a result of auditory reinforcement.

5. When a child is about nine or ten months old, the intent to communicate appears, indicating the baby's realization that mutually agreed-on signals can be used for mutually agreed-on purposes. Interaction with caregivers teaches babies language conventions, such as turn-taking, that are necessary for language. With their infants, caregivers use a special speech, called baby talk, which makes language acquisition easier. The baby's early speech cannot be comprehended out of its context.

6. When children first learn a word, they may overextend it, using the word to cover other objects or meanings for which they have no words. Overextension may occur only in production and not in comprehension. The two-word stage represents a striking advance in children's ability to code their understanding in linguistic terms.

7. Children in the two-word stage use three basic grammatical devices common to all languages: intonation, word-order, and inflection. All languages are equally easy for children to learn, and all children are ready to advance to complex grammatical rules by the time they are about two and a half years old.

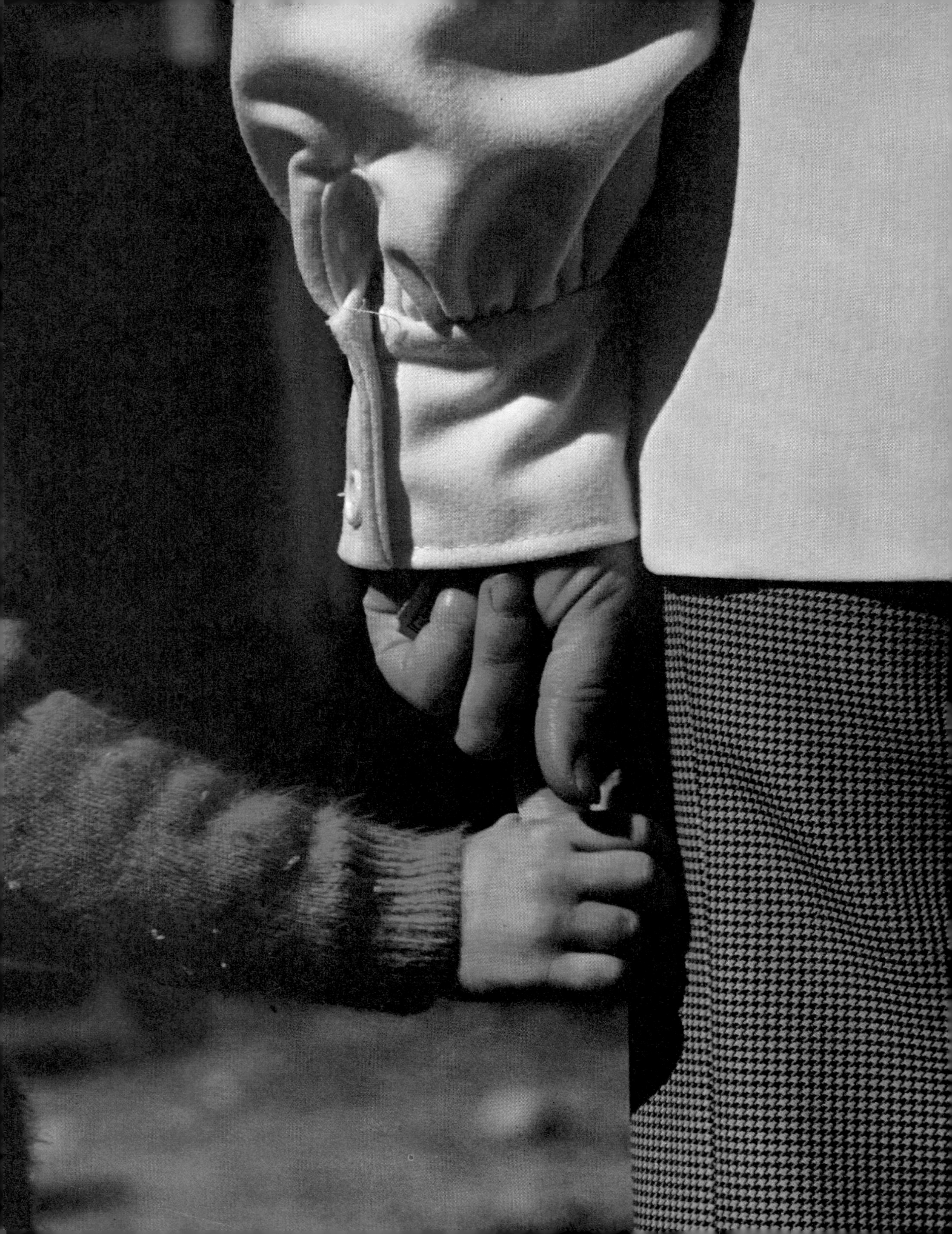

9 INFANCY: THE DAWN OF AWARENESS

"She's not a playmate—she can't do nothin'," Matt said, regarding the new baby with disgust. The baby's eyes opened, seemed to wander uncoordinated, and then came to rest on the happy-face button that Matt was wearing. "Hey, she's looking at my button!" cried Matt, snatching it off his shirt and moving it back and forth in front of baby Susan's eyes. His sister briefly followed the button with slow, jerky movements of her eyes; she even turned her head to follow it to one side. A fleeting upturn of the corners of her mouth evoked a response from her brother: "She's smiling, look, she's smiling!" In his excitement, Matt slipped and fell heavily against the bassinet. The baby startled and reacted with her whole body: flailing arms and legs, screwed-up red face, and imperative screams. Matt ran to get his father. After his father rocked Susan and soothed her, he placed her back in the bassinet. Matt, who had been observing quietly, headed outdoors to play. As he walked out of the room, he looked back and said, "She's nothin' but a cryer and a wetter."

From these unpromising beginnings, Matt's new sister will develop into a complex, unique, social individual. Susan will pursue numerous goals in life; relate to people in a variety of ways; be angered, frightened, and elated; and have beliefs, attitudes, and values that in part reflect her upbringing and in part are unique to her.

This chapter traces the beginnings of that development. In it we will see how early experiences, which begin at the moment of birth, contribute to a baby's developing personality. We will look at a baby's first social bond with primary caregivers and discover that there are wide differences in the form that this attachment takes. We will find that attachment plays an important role in the baby's developing trust in the world and in the growing sense of self. We will examine the effect of the bond on development of the infant's autonomy and note the influences of peers and siblings on personality. By the end of the chapter, we will have examined a number of ways in which the important lessons of the infant's first two years of life lay the groundwork for the person that the baby will eventually become.

THE EFFECTS OF EARLY EXPERIENCE

The proposal that experience in infancy and early childhood can have enduring effects became widely adopted through the influence of Sigmund Freud (1917). His belief that early experiences are crucial for personality development has been accepted by developmental psychologists with widely different theoretical outlooks.

Social Deprivation in Animals

Evidence that establishes the effects of early experience comes primarily from studies of animals. Among various species, deprivation or severe restriction during early infancy has marked effects on their behavior, and these effects on social and emotional development often persist into later periods of life (Greenough, 1976; Hunt, 1979; Riesen, 1975). For example, puppies who spend their first few months in complete isolation, seeing neither human beings nor other dogs, show "bizarre postures" and tend to be unresponsive to playthings, people, and other puppies (J. Scott, 1967). A puppy less extremely deprived tends to behave in a normal fashion but may have an intense fear of strange people and strange situations. Similarly, chimpanzees raised in a restricted environment are timid, especially in unfamiliar situations (Menzel, Davenport, and Rogers, 1963).

If an impoverished early environment can have such striking effects, we might expect that an enriched early environment would also have a major impact on infant animals. This appears to be the case. Although restriction often results in fearful animals, extra stimulation at an early age often produces animals that are bolder than normal (Weinberg and Levine, 1977), even when the extra stimulation consists of mild electric shocks (Pfeifer et al., 1976). Boldness is not the only effect of early enrichment; animals raised in such environments also tend to be curious in new situations (Rosenzweig and Bennett, 1976). This sort of evidence suggests that in some species, early experiences have important, enduring effects on the way animals respond to the world.

Limiting Factors

Despite the pervasive effects early learning seems to have on later development, other research suggests that the connection is more complicated than it appears. As noted in Chapter 5, newborn infants show differences in temperament, and such differences as irritability and activity level appear to be at least in part genetically based (Goldsmith and Gottesman, 1981). Such constitutional differences can limit the effect of specific experiences; as a brief consideration of imprinting in animals and the development of fear and laughter in human babies indicates, there are other strong constraints on such effects.

Sensitive Periods Animals of many species form strong, long-lasting social attachments to their mothers, but research has led many investigators to conclude that such attachments can develop only during a sharply restricted period of life, called a **sensitive period** (Columbo, 1982). In some species of birds, this attachment, called **imprinting,** forms when a newly hatched bird sees and follows a moving object. In the normal course of events, the first thing a bird sees is its mother, so that the bird becomes imprinted to her, but birds have also become imprinted to human beings, rubber balls, and other objects. A bird overcomes substantial obstacles in order to follow this object (or others like it) and shows great distress when it is out of sight (E. Hess, 1973). A young bird will try to feed the object to which it is imprinted and may even use it as a model for a suitable mate. But imprinting occurs only during a sensitive period shortly after birth, and the attachment can be changed. Ducklings that were imprinted to human beings have changed their attachment to mature ducks

Imprinting. A few hours after they were hatched, these baby geese saw ethologist Konrad Lorenz instead of a mother goose. Thereafter the goslings followed Lorenz around as if he were their mother. *(Thomas McAvoy/Time-Life Picture Agency, © Time, Inc.)*

(E. Hess, 1972), and a young monkey even shifted its attachment from another monkey to a dog (Mason and Kenny, 1974).

Some theorists have suggested that the bond between human babies and their mothers develops in the same way that baby birds or goats or sheep become imprinted to their mothers. If this were true, it would have significant implications for child rearing. But as we will see, human attachment is far more complicated and diverse than animal bonding. The importance of the imprinting phenomenon lies in two implications: first, that sensitive periods might exist in human beings during which certain kinds of learning, such as language acquisition, must occur if they are to take place at all; and second, that experiences during infancy can have enduring effects on a child's later development, as Freud maintained. As we trace the development of babies, it will become clear that early experiences are important but that they do not irrevocably determine the way a child develops.

Learning and Emotions Emotions may affect human learning, but an emotion cannot develop in the absence of learning. The development of fear, for example, involves complex relationships. When Matt stumbled against the bassinet and Susan responded with wails of distress, she was not truly afraid. Although sudden loud noises, unexpected events, and physical pain may produce crying, distress, and avoidance reactions in newborns and very young babies, their responses are not fear in the sense that we use the term.

True fear requires a sophisticated level of cognitive development. To be afraid, the baby must be able to hold the feared object or situation in memory, and the sight of the object must call up the perceptual and emotional experiences that were connected with it in the past. Later, the mere mention of the object will be enough to evoke fear.

The increasing importance of cognitive development in the nature of children's fears was shown in early studies by Arthur Jersild and Frances Holmes (1935) (see Figure 9.1). For example, no children less than two years old were afraid of physical harm and few were afraid of the dark, being alone in the dark, or imaginary creatures, but a significant percentage of four- to six-year-olds feared these things. These fears, in contrast to "fear" of sudden loud noises, seem to require imaginative constructions based on past experience.

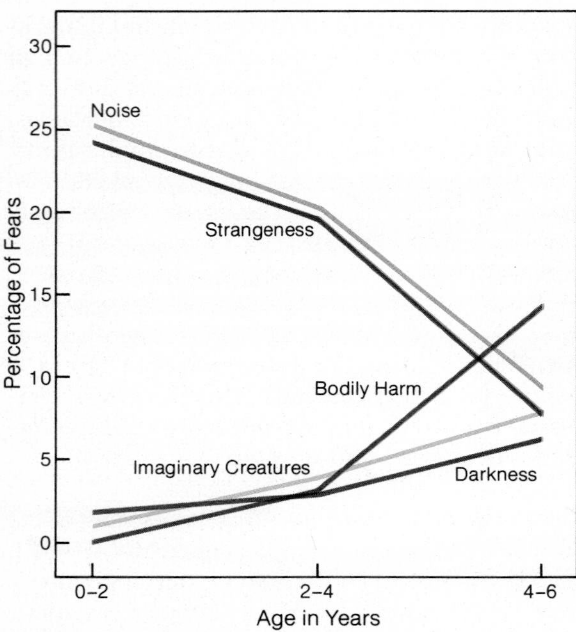

FIGURE 9.1 Developmental changes in the nature of children's fears as indicated by their responses to a few different objects and situations. *(Adapted from Jersild and Holmes, 1935)*

Similar developmental trends were reported by Sandra Scarr and Philip Salapatek (1970). Among the infants in their study, the fear of strangers, of a grotesque mask, and of heights (as measured by the visual-cliff technique described in Chapter 7) increased between the ages of five and eighteen months. These fears could develop only after the infants learned about the familiar and safe aspects of their environments. During the same period, there was no increase in the babies' fear of loud noises or of a jack-in-the-box that suddenly popped up at them.

Suppose that when Susan was six months old Matt suddenly thrust his head over the side of her crib and made a grotesque face. Would she scream with fear? She might laugh at Matt's face but scream at the same behavior in a stranger. Laughter and fear both seem to occur in response to a stimulus that is unfamiliar or incongruous in comparison with a familiar standard of reference.

This conclusion is supported by Alan Sroufe and Jane Wunsch's (1972) study of the development of laughter during the first year of life. They found that laughter, not fear, was the response to being confronted with a mask. The discrepancy between the infants' responses was the result of an important difference in the studies: The mask that elicited laughter in the Sroufe and Wunsch study was human-looking and was worn by the baby's mother; the mask that elicited fear in the Scarr and Salapatek study was nonhuman and was worn by the experimenter. Sroufe and Wunsch speculated that an incongruous event arouses tension that, depending on the circumstances, will either lead to crying and avoidance or be released in laughter.

Findings such as these on fear and laughter suggest additional limitations to the notion that early learning experiences automatically establish enduring personality dispositions. They indicate, just as the imprinting data do, that an infant or a child is not always open to the same learning experiences. They also suggest that the same experience may produce different effects, depending on an infant's maturational state, cognitive growth, past experiences, and present surroundings.

THE DEVELOPMENT OF ATTACHMENT

Human babies are born prepared by millions of years of primate evolution to respond to the sights and sounds of people and to behave in ways that elicit responses from them. Developmentalists who take an ethological view, among them John Bowlby (1969) and Mary Ainsworth (Ainsworth et al., 1978), have argued that the baby's inborn tendencies, such as crying or fussing when distressed, play an active role in ensuring survival by keeping adults nearby. Adults, in turn, are seen as having been prepared by evolution to respond to the baby's signals, providing care and giving the infant opportunities for social interaction.

These tendencies are considered the foundation of complex systems of social behavior that begin in the family. In most cultures, mothers and infants are involved for a time in a close symbiotic relationship in which the child is almost an extension of the mother's being. For this reason, many investigators have concentrated on the development of **attachment,** the special bond between infant and caregiver.

Our understanding of the development and consequences of attachment is heavily indebted to research with animals, and such research has dispelled some early assumptions about the nature of the bond. For many years, psychoanalysts and learning theorists assumed that babies develop close bonds with their caregivers because the caregiver satisfies the baby's physical needs. J. P. Scott has noted that this assumption leads to an unromantic conclusion: Infants love us only because we feed them. Research with monkeys has demonstrated, however, that there is more to attachment than being fed. In one series of studies by Harry F. Harlow and Margaret Harlow (1966, 1969), infant monkeys were raised in cages with two surrogate mothers. One mother substitute was covered with soft terry cloth; the other, equipped with a feeding mechanism, was made of hard wire mesh. If feeding were the major factor in attachment, the infant monkeys would have become attached to the wire mother, which fed them. But the monkeys spent much more time clinging to the cloth mother, which gave them no nourishment at all.

The monkeys seemed genuinely attached to the cloth mother. Given a choice of things to observe in a machine that allowed them to see various objects, they looked at the cloth mother

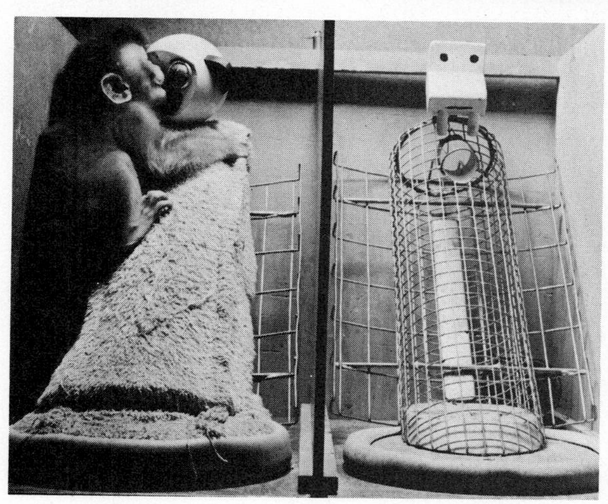

(*top*) When a large and frightening toy was placed near a baby monkey in the Harlow experiments (*middle*), it ran to the cloth-covered surrogate mother for comfort. Later it ventures out to explore the bear. Monkeys with only a wire mother (*bottom*) to cling to remained afraid of the toy. (*Harry F. Harlow, University of Wisconsin Primate Laboratory*)

much more often than at the wire mother. When monkeys raised with these artificial mothers were put in a strange place or when frightening objects were placed near them, they ran to the security of the cloth, but not the wire, mother. At first, the baby monkeys seemed terrified, but when allowed to cling to their cloth mother, they soon calmed down. Eventually, the monkeys used the cloth mother as a base for exploring the world, leaving to manipulate strange objects but often returning to cling to their soft, snuggly mother, as monkeys raised with real mothers do. The wire mothers were never used in this way.

Baby monkeys may have become attached to the terry-cloth mother because contact is important to the formation of attachment in monkeys. At birth young monkeys cling to their mothers; it seems to be as natural to them as scanning and vocalizing are to human babies. A soft terry-cloth mother encourages clinging, but a cold, hard mesh mother does not; and the difference leads to lasting effects. After a year's separation, a monkey will run to embrace its soft terry-cloth mother, holding on passionately to its soft form. But after a similar separation from wire mothers, monkeys show no affection at all when they are reunited.

The Stages of Attachment

Although attachment in human beings and in monkeys follows a similar pattern, the response of the human baby to his or her mother develops more slowly than the monkey's attachment to its mother. In human beings the bond takes months to appear, requires a complex intermeshing of behavior between infant and caregiver, and assumes widely varied forms.

Attachment in human babies refers to the early love relationship between the baby and the caregiver (usually one or both parents), and developmental psychologists study the bond by examining the behavior associated with such a relationship. Signs of attachment include smiling and joyous greeting when the caregiver appears and crying when he or she leaves. A crucial aspect of the bond is that such behavior is directed toward some people and not toward others.

A baby's earliest responses to people are indiscriminate and do not reflect attachment. This initial, indiscriminate stage of responsiveness lasts for about the first two months of life. During this time the baby's cries bring milk, dry diapers, an end to physical discomfort, and the pleasure of close human contact. Such aid and comfort are accepted from anyone. Toward the end of this period, social smiles and babbling generally appear, but they are directed toward anyone, suggesting that their onset is controlled primarily by maturation.

During the next stage of attachment, until they are about seven months old, babies begin to discriminate among the people around them. At five months, they may smile at familiar faces as often as or even more frequently than they did earlier, but the smiling at strange faces that was so prevalent at about two or three months drops off or even disappears. Harriet Rheingold (1969) has suggested that the talking, smiling human face, with its changing expressions and movements, interests and attracts a young baby. Gradually, through a variety of experiences, the faces of principal caregivers come both to elicit positive emotional and social responses in the baby and to reinforce them. Although at this stage babies may respond in special ways to specific people, they are unlikely to have developed a true attachment to a caregiver. For example, if a parent leaves a five-month-old baby with a sitter, the baby is unlikely to protest.

By the time they are eight months old, most babies have developed the intense bond that signifies true attachment. This third stage generally begins at about seven months and lasts until the infant is two or two and a half years old. Basic to the emergence of true attachment appears to be the infant's realization not only that the same people react to his or her needs in the same predictable ways, but that people continue to exist after they disappear from view. Most babies studied by Silvia Bell (1970) were aware of their mothers as objects who continue to exist when out of sight slightly before the babies showed a similar awareness of the existence of physical objects. Although person permanence may not develop before object permanence in all situations

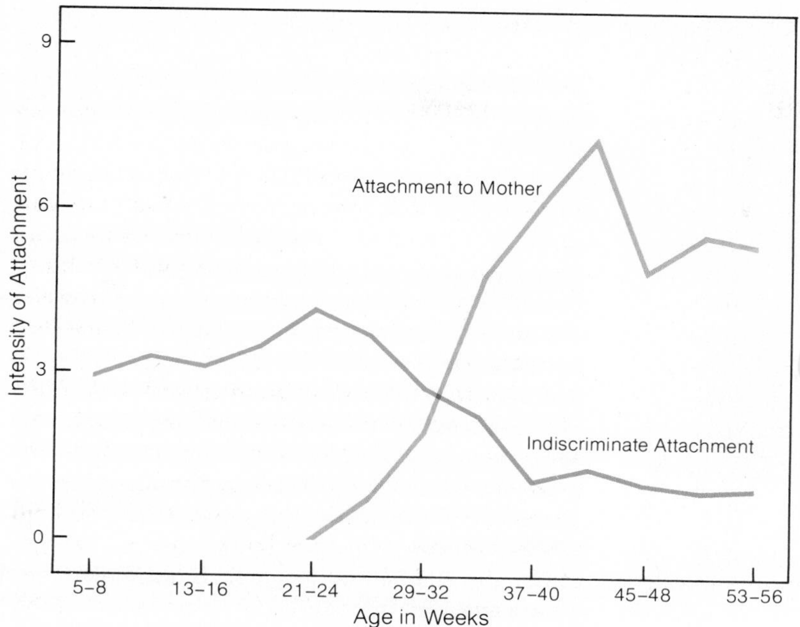

FIGURE 9.2 During the early weeks of life, most infants prefer not to be separated from the person they are with regardless of who that person is. Such "indiscriminate attachments" begin to decline at about the same time that the infant starts to show preferences for specific persons, such as his mother. *(Adapted from Schaffer and Emerson, 1964)*

(Jackson, Campos, and Fischer, 1978), the comings and goings of the human caregiver, related as they are to the satisfactions of the baby's needs, may induce the baby to pay special attention to the location of this very important "object." In her study, Bell also found that babies with stable attachments to their mothers were aware of their mothers as permanent objects earlier than babies with less stable attachments. In addition, when babies developed the concept of person permanence early they also developed the concept of physical object permanence early, suggesting that understanding in the social realm influences understanding in the physical realm.

Separation Distress

When a mother leaves her ten-month-old baby in an unfamiliar place, the baby is likely to cry and stop playing. The baby may also reach out for her when she leaves and, if able, may crawl in pursuit of her. Such a negative reaction to the departure of an attachment figure is called **separation distress.** Although the basic function of attachment is to keep the infant alive, the bond also provides the baby with emotional security. Because an attachment figure acts as a security base for the baby, the figure's presence prevents or reduces any fear the baby may experience when confronted with an unusual situation.

Separation distress first appears at different ages in different cultures, but it seems to be a universal phenomenon. When separated from their mothers, Ugandan babies begin to protest as early as six months (Ainsworth, 1967). Separation distress among Guatemalan babies, on the other hand, emerges a bit later and shows a developmental pattern similar to that of North American babies (Lester et al., 1974). Distress begins to appear at about eight or nine months, reaches a peak at around twelve months, then declines.

When they find themselves in a strange situation, most nine- to twelve-month-old babies become concerned if their primary caregivers are not nearby. For example, Mary Ainsworth and Barbara Wittig (1969) found that babies in a

When baby's primary caregiver left her in a strange place, she was overcome by fear and began to cry, a response known as separation distress. *(Cour. by Laszlo Hege)*

strange situation first establish contact with their caregivers. Somewhat later, the babies venture out on short forays to explore the strange environment, but they always return to their caregivers between expeditions.

This tendency can be observed when a mother brings her infant or toddler on a first visit to a friend's home; the young child clings to (indeed, hides behind) the parent. Only after the child becomes accustomed to the new setting is she or he likely to let go of the parent's leg. This reaction is similar to the way both cloth-surrogate reared and normally reared young monkeys behaved in a strange environment.

On the other hand, Harriet Rheingold and Carol Eckerman (1970) saw no distress in a similar separation-and-return pattern among infants placed in a novel situation. The infants they studied seemed to share their joy and excitement with attachment figures. Babies apparently use attachment figures both to reduce their fear and to share in the pleasures of life, and the same general pattern of behavior seemingly serves both purposes.

Wariness of Strangers

The baby's wariness of strangers usually develops a month or two after specific attachments appear. This wariness appears to be a natural reaction that complements attachment and helps the baby avoid situations, people, or objects that might endanger life. Babies' reactions to strangers appear to pass through four phases. At first babies do not discriminate between strange and familiar persons. Later they respond positively to strangers, although not as positively as they do to familiar people. Then they go through a period of reacting uneasily to strangers; if an attachment figure is present, they look back and forth between the stranger and the caregiver as though comparing the strange person with the familiar one. At this time, babies merely become sober and stare at the stranger. It is not until they are around eight months old that some babies respond to strangers with fear and withdrawal, looking away, frowning, whimpering, or even crying. This reaction is particularly intense when the baby's attachment figure is absent (Ainsworth, 1967).

The calming effect of a caregiver's presence showed clearly when George Morgan and Henry Ricciuti (1969) studied the development of wariness in the presence of strangers. At four and six months, babies respond positively to the approach of a stranger, whether they are on their mothers' laps or several feet from them. But at eight, ten, and especially at twelve months, babies are more likely to be upset by a stranger's approach when they are several feet from their mothers than when they are seated on their mothers' laps. When seated on a caregiver's lap, babies may continue to respond positively to a stranger's approach.

The way a stranger approaches them also influences babies' reactions. Most babies become fearful if a stranger arrives and reaches for them, touches them, or picks them up (Sroufe, 1977). When babies are given time to evaluate the stranger, however, many show little distress. As Mary Anne Trause (1977) found, if a stranger pauses before walking up to a year-old baby, the baby is more likely to smile and less likely to

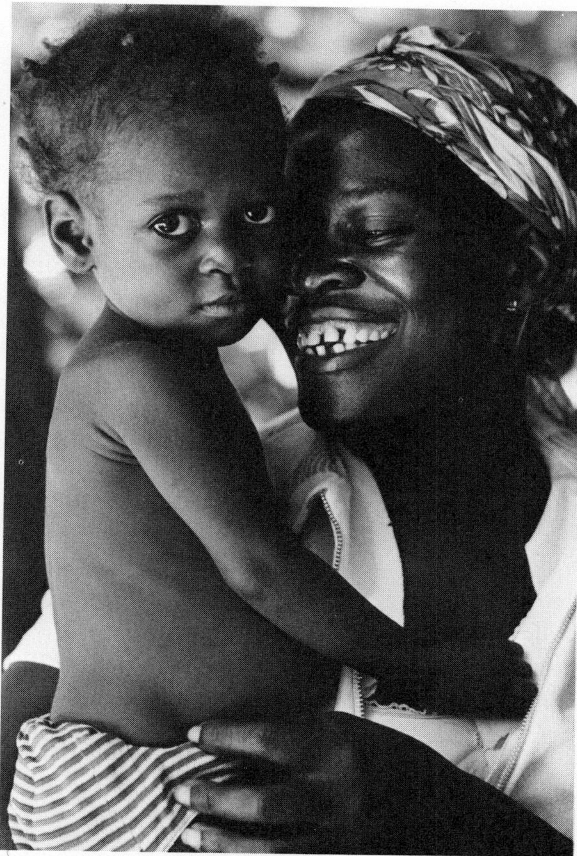

This Haitian baby has already formed an attachment relationship, and will show distress when separated from the mother. *(©Ann Chwatsky 1979)*

show distress than if the stranger walks rapidly over to the infant. A slower approach is less provocative, apparently because it gives babies time to judge whether a stranger may be a danger.

The characteristics of the stranger can be another source of influence on babies' reactions. Alison Clarke-Stewart (1978) has noted that the situation is one of social interaction, and the stranger's sex, appearance, and manner influence the infant's reactions. Consequently, in laboratory experiment where strangers act out a rigid script, babies show more wariness or fear than they do when an experiment allows strangers to interact naturally with them.

Because babies' memories have developed by the time they are nine months old, the effect of their past experiences also may change their responses from simple wariness toward strangers to fear, or from fear to wariness (Bronson, 1978). In her study, for example, Trause found that babies were less friendly toward a stranger on a second visit, suggesting that the babies connected the appearance of the stranger with the separation from their mothers that had accompanied the stranger's earlier approach.

Other research indicates that the quality of a baby's attachment may also affect his or her responses to a stranger. In a study by Mary Ainsworth and Barbara Wittig (1969), year-old infants with a secure attachment to their mothers were not distressed by the presence of a stranger, but infants who seemed to have insecure attachments were apparently upset by the stranger's appearance.

Like separation distress, wariness of strangers is most apparent when the baby is in an unfamiliar setting. Babies are much less likely to show wariness in their own homes than when they are observed in a laboratory. Russel Tracy, Michael Lamb, and Mary Ainsworth (1976) studied babies in their own homes from the time they were three weeks old until they were more than a year old, observing them for four hours every three weeks. The investigators found that once babies began to crawl, they tended to follow their mothers from place to place and to play comfortably in the presence of strangers. Although no baby at any age ever followed a stranger, few cried or showed other distress at a stranger's approach. Babies also explore more and vocalize more at home than they do in the strange and perhaps frightening surroundings of the psychologist's laboratory.

VARIATIONS IN ATTACHMENT

The emotions involved in the parent-child relationship run both ways; just as the infant becomes attached to the caregiver, so the caregiver develops an attachment to the baby. Given the parent's love for the baby and the baby's love for the parent, each affects the development of the other's emotion and the fears or anxieties that may accompany it. One way to make this circular relationship clear is to look at it from each side.

Mothers

Whether mother-infant interaction consists primarily of caregiving activity or social play, the attachment that develops seems equally strong (Schaffer and Emerson, 1964a). It appears that the crucial factor in the relationship is the baby's development of a mental representation of the mother as a distinct person, a step facilitated by increased exposure to her.

Yet strong attachments are not all alike, and the quality of the bond may be linked with the way mothers interact with their infants. After extensive studies of mothers and their babies in strange situations, Mary Ainsworth and her colleagues (1978) discerned three major kinds of attachment: secure, avoidant, and ambivalent. After a separation from their mothers and a meeting with a stranger, *securely attached* infants actively seek out their mothers when they return, and a baby's contact with his or her mother quickly ends the distress. Less securely attached infants fall into two major groups: *avoidant* infants, who shun contact with their mothers upon being reunited, and *ambivalent* infants, who alternate between seeking contact with their mothers and angrily squirming to get away from them.

A consistent connection appears between the quality of a year-old baby's attachment and a mother's style of caring for her baby, a connection that is supported by a recent study showing a low proportion of securely attached infants among a group of twelve-month-olds that had been abused or neglected (Egeland and Sroufe, 1981). Securely attached babies have mothers who respond quickly to their infants' cries, smiles, and other signals. These mothers hold their babies tenderly and are flexible in their interactions with them. They show affection freely and cooperate with their babies' efforts.

Avoidant babies have mothers who are insensitive to their signals. The mothers do not hold their babies closely, are rigid in interacting with them, and rarely express affection. Instead, these mothers often show anger and irritation.

Ambivalent babies have mothers who are relatively insensitive to their babies' signals. Such mothers hold their babies closely but do so in an awkward manner. They rarely play with their babies, picking them up primarily to care for them.

Variations in a mother's emotional warmth, support, sensitivity, predictability, and reliability are reflected in the baby's socialization. Securely attached babies are more likely than either avoidant or ambivalent babies to cooperate with their mothers, to cry infrequently, to show affection, and to be neither spoiled nor overdependent. Indeed, they show a balance between independence and cooperative interaction (Ainsworth, Bell, and Stayton, 1974).

If secure attachment to a mother has important effects on a baby's socialization, we might expect to find lasting influences on their development. Some investigators have found such a connection, indicating that babies with secure attachments become competent, independent toddlers. For example, Leah Matas, Richard Arend, and Alan Sroufe (1978) gave two-year-olds a series of increasingly difficult problems. Children who had been rated as securely attached at both twelve and eighteen months attacked the problems with an enthusiasm not often displayed by children who earlier had been rated as having ambivalent or avoidant attachments. When they reached the final problem, which was too difficult for them to solve, securely attached children were less likely to throw tantrums and more likely to accept help from their mothers than were children with insecure attachments.

But the effects of the attachment bond do not act in isolation; babies continue to be affected by the daily behavior of their mothers. In this study, when their two-year-olds faced the difficult problem, mothers of securely attached children generally offered hints that allowed the children to feel they had solved the problem themselves. Mothers of insecurely attached children, on the other hand, tended to allow their toddlers to become frustrated before they offered help, and then the mothers often solved the problem themselves.

Fathers

In traditional two-parent families, fathers are likely to spend little time with their young babies. So for a long while, fathers were regarded as relatively unimportant in their children's early social development. It is now clear, however, that infants become attached to both parents at about the same time, and that a father may have an important social function (Parke, 1981).

Studies show that a father's attachment to his baby is just as deep as that of a mother. Fathers make nurturant, competent caregivers, and they become intensely involved with their babies. When Ross Parke and Douglas Sawin (1976) observed parents in the hospital with their newborn infants, they found that middle-class fathers and mothers spent an equal amount of time with their babies. Both parents looked and smiled at their babies, talked to and kissed them, explored their bodies, and gave them their bottles. Given the opportunity, lower-class fathers also were nurturant and competent with their newborn babies. When, for example, their baby became distressed during a feeding, both father and mother showed their sensitivity in the same way; they stopped the feeding, looked at the baby, and patted the infant solicitously.

Equal attachments do not, however, lead to identical behavior on the part of each parent. Fathers interact with their babies in a different manner from the pattern shown by mothers (Lamb, 1977). Most of the time, mothers pick up their babies to care for them; when fathers pick them up, it is generally to play. Mothers play traditional games like peekaboo and pat-a-cake; fathers engage in rough-and-tumble play with babies, regardless of the infant's sex (Lamb, 1976b). Nor is the quality of attachment always the same with both parents. Some infants are securely attached to one parent and insecurely attached to the other, and the secure attachment is as likely to be with the father as with the mother (Main and Weston, 1981).

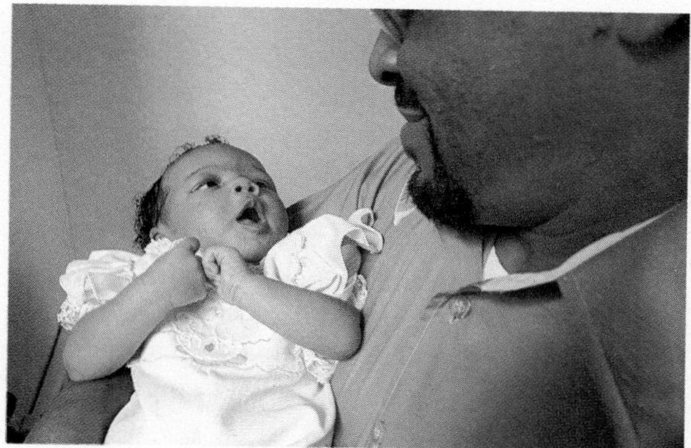

Although most primary caregivers are mothers, fathers are nurturant and competent with their babies. Fathers and mothers generally interact in different ways with infants. *(© William Hubbell 1981/Woodfin Camp & Assoc.)*

Increasing numbers of fathers are assuming the responsibility of infant care. In an attempt to discover whether fathers who play the traditional maternal role behave differently from other fathers, Tiffany Field (1978) compared twelve fathers who were primary caregivers with twelve traditional mothers and twelve fathers who were traditional secondary caregivers. All the parents were white, middle-class, and college-educated. The parents brought their four-month-old babies to a laboratory, where the baby sat in an infant seat opposite the parent. Field asked each parent to pretend the pair were at home, playing together at the kitchen table. Then the parent was left to entertain the baby while video cameras taped their interactions.

Field found that in some ways all parents acted alike. The mothers and both groups of fathers talked the same amount, wiped their babies' noses, mopped up their burps, and attended to their needs. But being a primary caregiver did affect a father's actions. Primary caregivers—whether father or mother—laughed less and smiled more than did the fathers who were secondary caregivers. They also imitated their babies' grimaces more often and mimicked their vocalizations in the high-pitched style that is characteristic of baby talk. Field points out that such similarities between primary caretakers, which transcend gender, suggest that many observed father-mother differences may be the result of different amounts of experience mothers and fathers traditionally have with their infants. Parents who spend a good deal of time with their babies imitate them more simply because they have learned that babies enjoy being imitated. They also imitate a baby's grimaces instead of laughs because grimaces are characteristic of a four-month-old infant.

Despite the new role of some fathers, male-female differences remained. Fathers—whether primary or secondary caregivers—played more games and poked at their babies more than did mothers. Fathers also held the babies' arms and legs less than did mothers. And fathers of sons played more games and did more high-pitched mimicking than did fathers of daughters.

In Sweden, where legislation has made it financially possible for parents to share caregiving responsibilities, there is increased opportunity to observe fathers as caregivers. Here, too, fathers and mothers show consistent differences in the way they behave with their babies, as Michael Lamb and his associates (1982) found in their study of fifty-two middle-class Swedish families, half of whom were traditional and half of whom shared or reversed the responsibility for child care. In order to see if attitudes affected parental behavior, the investigators interviewed parents shortly before the birth of their baby and found that the parents fell neatly into two groups: In traditional families, the fathers found work more fulfilling and parenthood less fulfilling than did their wives, and these fathers planned little involvement in baby care. In the nontraditional families, fathers found work less fulfilling and parenthood more fulfilling than did their wives, and these fathers planned extensive involvement in child care.

When the babies were three months old, the investigators observed each parent alone with his or her baby for an hour. Despite the difference in attitudes, the fathers' behavior in both types of family tended to be alike, and both groups of fathers behaved differently from mothers. They touched, tickled, kissed, and tended their babies less than the mothers did. They also smiled and talked to the infant less. The reason for the different behavior of fathers in the two studies is unclear, but it could be the result of different cultural expectations, or it could reflect the fact that not all the Swedish nontraditional fathers were primary caregivers.

Perhaps in response to differences in the way fathers and mothers behave with babies, when infants from twelve to eighteen months old are with both parents in a stressful situation, they will go to their mothers (Lamb, 1976a). But in other situations, babies either show no preference or prefer their fathers. When observed in their homes, baby girls may prefer either parent, but baby boys generally prefer their fathers (Lamb, 1976c). Alone with either parent, however, a baby is likely to smile at him or her and to vocalize more frequently than when both parents are in the room.

Infant Responsiveness

For a long time, the effect of an infant's characteristics on a caregiver were overlooked (Lewis and Rosenblum, 1974; Bell and Harper, 1977). But a baby's reactions—or lack of them—clearly influence the tone of the parent-infant relationship. If, for example, a baby happens to be unresponsive and poor at nursing, and in appearance falls short of the mother's expectations, the quality of attachment that develops may be marginal (Blehar, Lieberman, and Ainsworth, 1977).

In addition, babies who actively resist cuddling tend to develop attachments later than cuddlers do. After studying the effect of the baby's temperament on the mother-infant relationship, Rudolf Schaffer and Peggy Emerson (1964b) concluded that for some infants, "contact is not comforting." Cuddlers have a more intense attachment to their caregivers throughout the first year of life than noncuddlers do, but this difference seems to disappear during the second year, apparently as the infant and mother adapt to each other's style. In Schaffer and Emer-

A father's time with his infant is mostly devoted to play; perhaps for this reason many babies—especially boys—prefer their fathers in stress free situations. *(Michael Weisbrot & Family)*

son's study, babies who actively resisted contact did not necessarily prevent social interaction with their parents. Instead, each baby and the parents gradually evolved a system of interaction that did not depend on physical contact. The intensity of the noncuddlers' attachments bore no relation to feeding, weaning, or toilet-training practices. Once again, maternal responsiveness and the amount of social interaction were related to the quality of attachment; but Schaffer and Emerson stress the *quantity* of interaction, whereas Ainsworth's group found that the *quality* of interaction was the factor that determined the quality of attachment.

Because the distress and comfort of infants and their parents are likely to be reciprocal, a fussy baby can be especially difficult for parents. As noted in Chapter 5, mothers and fathers both respond to a baby's cry with feelings of annoyance, irritation, and distress. Despite the aversiveness of the cries, parents of babies who fuss frequently generally wait longer before responding to those cries than do parents of babies who fuss infrequently (Dunn, 1977). This may be analogous to the tale of the boy who cried wolf; parents of fussy babies may interpret their signals of distress as being simply bids for attention, or, if the babies do not quiet easily, the parents may decide that since responding has little effect, they may as well ignore the cries until they become intolerable. Babies who quiet easily, on the other hand, are likely to reinforce their parents' attention and make them feel more secure as caregivers. In this connection, Susan Goldberg (1977) notes that because parents need to feel they can respond to their baby's signals and satisfy his or her needs, the baby whose signs are easy to read enhances the parents' feelings of competence. Thus the baby whose signals say clearly, "I'm hungry," "I'm bored," or "I'm wet," who sucks vigorously and smiles freely is also the one who is most likely to make parents feel successful and important.

As infants continue to develop, the baby who walks early, say at nine or ten months, but does not learn to respond to commands until fourteen or fifteen months is likely to require more parental patience, to provoke more irritation, to need more physical restraint, and generally to get into more trouble than the child who walks later. The infant who walks late may, however, provoke parental anxiety and concern in other ways. The parents may frequently pull their baby upright, encourage the infant, even drag him or her along. Or the parents may view the baby's relative slowness as a reflection of their own failure and therefore ignore the infant.

With increased skills and abilities, infants can have major effects on their parents' personal lives (Harper, 1975). As babies become more mobile and inquisitive, parents are likely to increase their protective supervision, admonishing the baby not to touch hot appliances, covering open wall sockets, removing and storing breakable or dangerous objects. If there are no playmates in the immediate neighborhood, some parents of a two-year-old may even move to another area in order to accommodate their child's social needs.

Maternal Deprivation

Loss or lack of mothering presents a serious challenge to an infant's well-being, but assessing its effects has proved difficult. Michael Rutter

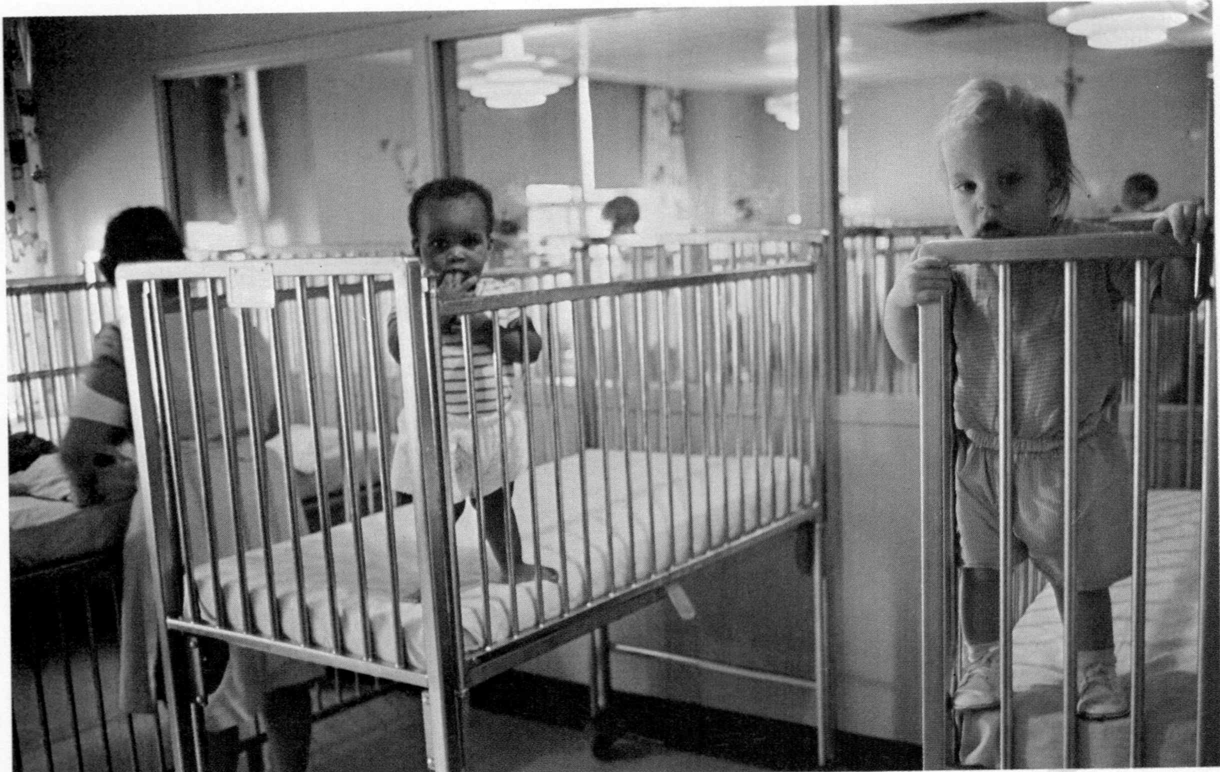

Children reared in institutions require stable relationships with caregivers and a stimulating environment if they are to thrive. *(Elliott Erwitt/Magnum Photos)*

(1979), who has reviewed research on maternal deprivation, suggests that the concept is really a catchall term for a variety of early experiences. Before it is possible to investigate the lasting emotional effects of such an experience, the nature of caregiving arrangements and the kinds of stimulation that babies receive must be specified.

As yet, researchers have not shown that a single primary caregiver is absolutely necessary for normal development. Although early studies of children reared in institutions found devastating effects on their social and intellectual development, it is now clear that these children suffered from a general lack of the stimulation necessary for social and cognitive growth as well as from the absence of a single stable caregiver. The babies in Lebanese institutions, who were described in Chapter 6, showed gains in both cognitive and physical development when introduced to interesting objects for only a few minutes each day. Indeed, studies of children reared from their first few months in institutions and of children separated from their parents at an early age because of war, death, parental neglect, or economic disaster show that when their environmental circumstances are radically improved, such children respond, apparently recovering from the most extreme psychosocial adversity (Clarke and Clarke, 1977). However, the attachments formed by children reared in institutions are not as strong as those formed by home-reared children, and institutionally reared children tend to be less successful in their social relations (Rutter, 1979).

Research with monkeys suggests that development can follow a relatively normal course in the absence of a parental relationship. Monkeys raised without mothers or mother surrogates but with other baby monkeys for company were more normal in their adult social and sexual behavior than were monkeys raised with a surrogate mother but without peer contact. These findings support Lawrence Kohlberg's (1969) suggestion that it is the opportunity for pleasurable social interaction that is important to the infant's social-emotional development, not a specific tie to a caregiver.

Not all infants who suffer maternal deprivation are able to cope with their loss. An infant who finds his or her attachment to a primary caregiver ruptured may develop depression, or an extreme sadness. The British child psychiatrist John Bowlby (1973; 1980) observed what he regarded as depression in fifteen- to thirty-month-old healthy infants after they had been separated from their families and placed in a hospital or other resident institution. After an initial phase of active protest and crying, these infants fell into a phase of despair. They became withdrawn and inactive, made no demands on the environment, cried intermittently though without specific cause, and seemed to feel increasing hopelessness and sadness. Later, the depressed infants gradually moved into a phase of increased emotional distance. They began to interact in a pleasant but shallow manner with institutional caregivers, and when their parents visited, they responded in an aloof and detached way.

If a separation is only temporary, when children return home they may continue for a time either to treat their parents as strangers or to cling to them excessively and refuse to be left alone (Schaffer, 1977). But temporary ruptures of the attachment relationship rarely appear to have long-lasting effects. Bowlby and his associates (1973) found, for example, that boys and girls in middle childhood who had been hospitalized for long periods during their first two years showed no obvious signs of impaired relationships with their parents.

THE EFFECTS OF CLASS AND CULTURE

All young children become attached to their caregivers, but the nature of the parent-infant relationship varies widely across classes and cultures. Different values and different styles of life are bound to make their mark on the growing infant (see the box on page 222).

Socioeconomic Differences

The influence of social class on maternal attitudes and behavior showed in Jerome Kagan and Steven Tulkin's (1971) study of ten-month-old middle- and lower-class babies. Although mothers in both groups held, tickled, kissed, and bounced their babies, other maternal behavior differed between classes. A middle-class mother was more likely than a lower-class mother to vocalize within two feet of her baby, to imitate the baby's sounds, to have long bouts of social interaction, to reward her baby with words, and to encourage her baby to walk. About two-thirds of the lower-class mothers used food to soothe their babies, but less than a third of the middle-class mothers solved problems with food.

When Kagan and Tulkin tested these babies in the laboratory, they found no class differences in the levels of babies' reactions to speech, whether words or meaningless sounds. But middle-class babies quieted more dramatically to highly inflected, highly meaningful speech than to other stimuli. They were also more likely than lower-class babies to look at a stranger after they heard such speech. In addition, middle-class infants quieted more to their mothers' voices than to strangers' voices, and they vocalized more than lower-class infants did after listening to recordings of their mothers' voices. Similar class differences in language have appeared in other studies (Lewis and Freedle, 1973; Golden and Birns, 1976).

GROWING UP IN A COMMUNE

In the late 1960s, Americans began experimenting with variations on the traditional nuclear-family theme, and some young people chose to join communes that serve as extended families. A study by Bernice Eiduson (1979) and her associates found that communes of any type can provide a nurturant atmosphere for a child.

In Christian religious communes, children were regarded as future evangelists and their development was supervised with that goal in mind. As babies, they were often left with caregivers while their parents went on religious missions. Although caregivers changed frequently, babies were expected to take the changes in stride. By the time they were two or three, the children were given responsibilities. Discipline consisted of spanking followed by hugging, and the punishment was done with religious sanction and without parental guilt. The Christian communes were not egalitarian; parents and children were both expected to adhere to sexual stereotypes.

In communes that centered around Eastern religions, parents were expected to rear their own children. The commune provided an outline for life, but the parents were supposed to translate it into child-rearing practices. The father's role did not differ from that in the traditional nuclear family; fathers appeared at mealtime and in the evening but spent their days working for the religious order. Child care was left to the mother, although commune members sometimes baby-sat. Commune practices steered children into stereotyped sex-roles.

In "families" that centered about a charismatic leader, children were reared in radical ways. A family's child-rearing philosophy was likely to be experimental and erratic, and few caregivers were trained. The nursery in which children lived sometimes concentrated on intellectual stimulation, sometimes on hedonism, and sometimes on destroying the special bond between parent and child on the ground that it makes children too dependent. Eiduson suggests that in this last sort of family, close ties between parent and child are seen as weakening the child's tie to the group.

In agricultural families that were part of the back-to-nature trend, children had the freedom typically found on farms. Their lives were regulated by the demands of farm life, and the children participated in many of their parents' activities. Adults in these communes had strong inner discipline; they were efficient, conscientious, and determined, and they worked hard. They carried those same qualities over into their child-rearing practices.

The communal families that had sprung up in cities were informal and relaxed. Child rearing was casual, spontaneous, and impulsive, and there were few demands on young children to conform. Infants and young children slept either in their parents' rooms or in a nursery. In most families, they were in day care or in a nursery group, or they had a baby-sitter; the idea was to free the mother for other activities.

In all the communes she studied, Eiduson found that the children developed normally through the first year of life, and no aspects of intellectual or social development sharply distinguished any family type. The children were average in both motor and mental skills, and there was no difference between them and a control group of children from traditional nuclear families. Even when the commune's official policy was one of shared caregiving, Eiduson found, the mother-child unit remained basic. The biological and psychological needs of the baby took precedence over the social rules of the organization.

On mental tests, babies with several caregivers tended to make higher scores than babies with only a single caregiver. When the father or other women helped in child care, scores on physical tests tended to be high. Breast feeding was also related to high scores on motor tests; significantly more bottle- than breast-fed babies scored in the lowest 25 percent on such tests.

As Eiduson's study makes clear, children can be successfully socialized in a wide variety of living arrangements.

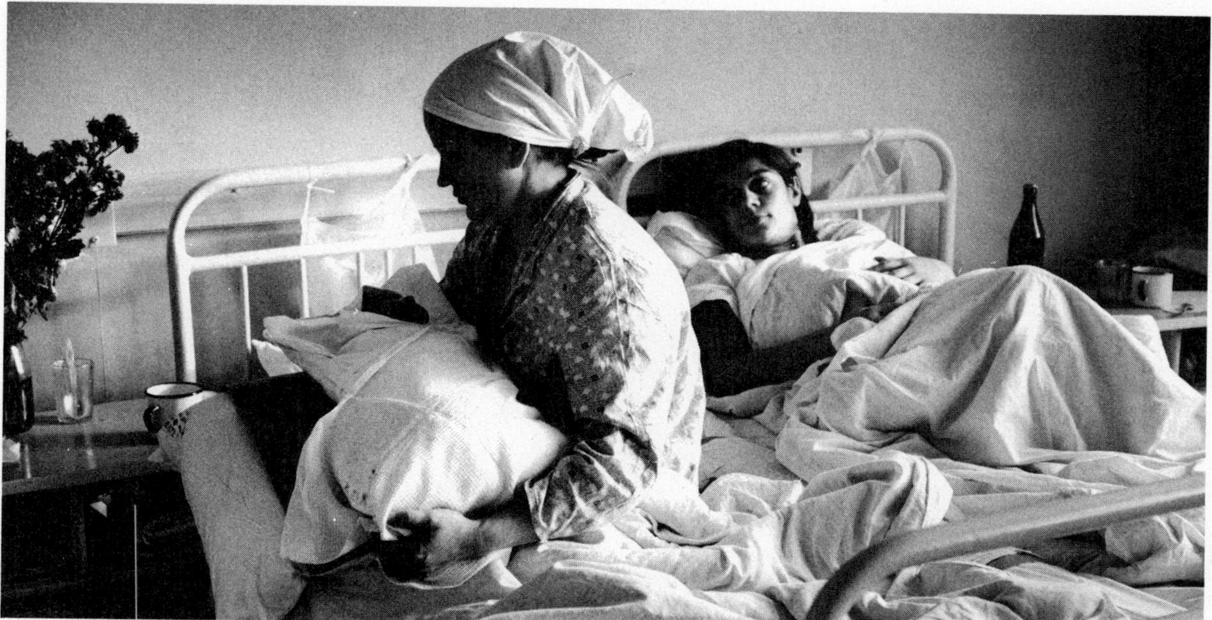

This Russian newborn will get more kissing, hugging, and cuddling than an American baby, but will also be held more tightly and have less freedom of movement. *(Martine Franck/VIVA/Woodfin Camp & Assoc.)*

Cultural Differences

Parent-infant relationships also vary across societies. Research with Ugandan infants (Ainsworth, 1967), whose mothers generally interact more extensively with them than Western mothers do, supports the notion that experiences with the caregiver speed the development of attachment, for these babies form specific attachments somewhat earlier than the Scottish babies studied by Schaffer and Emerson. Similarly, close human contact is a prominent feature of early life among the !Kung San, a much-studied band of hunter-gatherers who live a nomadic life in Africa's Kalahari Desert under conditions that may be like those of our early ancestors. !Kung-San babies spend most of their first year or so either on their mothers' laps or carried in a sling on the mothers' hips. The babies have continual access to the breast and nurse frequently. When they cry, their mothers respond immediately, and the babies' whims are gratified. Yet when these "indulged" babies are two to five years old, they do not hang onto their mothers, as observers from our own society might expect. Far from being spoiled or dependent, they show considerable independence, interacting less with their mothers and more with other children than English children of the same age (Konner, 1977). This suggests that in an environment like the one in which humanity may have evolved, a sensitive, immediately responsive caregiver is part of child rearing.

Wide variations exist also in the child-rearing practices of Western industrialized societies. Urie Bronfenbrenner (1970) has described some of the differences between the Soviet Union and the United States in the parent-infant relationship and the socialization of children. These differences can be traced to the contrast between a

THE EFFECTS OF DAYCARE

From 1969 to 1977, as more women joined the American labor force, the number of children enrolled in day care increased 23 percent (Connell, Layzer, and Goodson, 1979). During the same period, the number of children under two years old in day care jumped 32 percent. These nearly 900,000 children represent only a small portion of the infants and young children who are cared for by someone other than their mothers. Nursery schools and day-care centers together account for only 11 percent of the infants and children in substitute care. About 26 percent of youngsters in substitute care have a babysitter other than a relative come into their home, and another 16 percent are taken to someone else's home (National Childcare Consumer Study, 1975). At present, little is known about the quality or effects of this kind of care, although a large study recently conducted in England indicates that children who are taken to a sitter's home fare less well than children in day-care centers, and that one-third of the children who spend their day in a sitter's home become withdrawn and passive (Bruner, 1980b).

Not much is known about the effects of nursery schools and day-care centers, either. When Jay Belsky and Laurence Steinberg (1978) reviewed the research that had been done to date, they concluded:

> To even say that the jury is still out on day care would be in our view both premature and naively optimistic. The fact of the matter is, quite frankly, that the majority of evidence has yet to be presented, much less subpoenaed.

As Belsky and Steinberg point out, present research has been largely confined to high-quality care in centers connected with universities. These day-care centers offer enriched programs and are not simply custodial institutions. The daily program is designed to foster emotional and social as well as cognitive development.

In these high-quality programs, infants and young children seem to develop normally (Kilmer, 1979). Their attachment to their mothers remains strong, and they get along better with their peers than do home-reared children. They also may be more aggressive and impulsive than other young children and less cooperative with adults (Schwartz, Strickland, and Krolick, 1974). The only study that has followed such children into adolescence, how-

family-centered and a collective-centered system of child rearing.

Russian babies are handled significantly more than their American counterparts. Russian babies are almost always breast-fed, and even when not fed spend most of their time in someone's arms. Russian babies get much more hugging, kissing, and cuddling than American babies do, but at the same time they are held much more tightly and are allowed little freedom of movement. Russian mothers are generally much more solicitous and protective, and are so eager to protect the baby from discomfort, illness, or injury that they curtail the baby's mobility and initiative. Bronfenbrenner speculates that such child-rearing practices may in the end produce dependent individuals who readily conform to social standards.

Multiple Caregiving

In today's world, multiple caregiving is a frequent form of infant care, even among babies who are not in institutions. The lack of a central caregiver in such surroundings has shown no ill-effects on the children. A review of research by Michael Rutter (1971) indicates that when the main attachment figure shares caregiving with other people, as when mothers work or when the baby is part of an extended family, children ever, found that boys who were enrolled in day care before they were five years old were high in sociability and liked by their peers (Moore, 1975).

In the area of cognitive development, there appear to be no lasting effects upon most children. Intellectual gains stimulated by the highly enriched curricula appear to vanish soon after a child leaves the program. But disadvantaged children do appear to profit from these programs; they do not show the decline in IQ scores during early childhood that is characteristic of poor children (Etaugh, 1980).

A study by Jerome Kagan, Richard Kearsley, and Philip Zelazo (1978) concluded that attendance at a high-quality day-care center has little or no effect on middle- or working-class infants, whether Chinese or Caucasian. Ethnic and class differences were much larger in this study than were differences between young children who attended the center and those who were at home. Kagan's group recommends that babies should be enrolled in a center either before they are seven-months-old or after they are fifteen to eighteen-months-old. In this way, babies enter substitute care either before they develop separation distress or after it has waned.

A second recommendation to come out of the Kagan study is that each caregiver be responsible for no more than three infants or toddlers. In the survey cited earlier, the average number of children per staff member in day-care centers in this country is 3.9 for infants under seventeen months and 5.9 for toddlers from eighteen to twenty-four months. In fact, some licensed centers have as many as ten infants or fourteen toddlers assigned to each caregiver.

The effects of day care under such conditions are just beginning to be explored, and it appears that the involvement of the substitute caregiver is especially important. Christine Anderson and her associates (1981) studied youngsters between the ages of nineteen and forty-two months who were enrolled in day-care centers with no university connections. The ratio of staff to children in these centers was 1 to 12; half the centers were considered high-quality in terms of equipment, program, and encouragement of individual activities, and half were considered low quality. When nursery-school caregivers were highly involved with the children in their charge, the youngsters displayed an attachment to these caregivers and used them as bases for exploring the environment. But when the caregivers were uninvolved with the children in their charge, the youngsters showed no evidence of attachment and seemed to prefer strangers to their substitute caregivers. This was true whether the day-care center had been rated as high- or low-quality. Apparently the quality of interaction provided children in substitute care is more important than the quality of the centers themselves.

thrive as long as other caregivers provide stable relationships.

Children reared in the original Israeli *kibbutzim* also show normal social and emotional development. Infants in the early kibbutzim were reared communally in residential nurseries and saw their parents for only a few hours a day or on weekends. The kibbutz caregiver, or *metapelet,* took care of the infant's daily needs and training, and parents primarily provided emotional gratification (Beit-Hallahmi and Rabin, 1977). Babies became equally attached to their mothers and to the *metapelet* (Fox, 1977), suggesting that parents may be absent for significant amounts of time without radically influencing attachment patterns, as long as someone who cares is indeed present.

There is little evidence that infants reared by multiple caregivers will develop differently from those reared by a single caregiver. Although in the African country of Kenya infants are reared by multiple caregivers, infant development follows a course similar to that of infants reared by a single caregiver (Leiderman and Leiderman, 1977).

Studies of infants in day care also have failed to find any evidence that such care interfered with the development of attachment to their mothers or other primary caregivers (see box). In one such study, Jerome Kagan, Richard

Kearsley, and Philip Zelazo (1978) followed day-care and home-reared infants from the time they were three and a half months until they were twenty-nine months old. The babies were from white and Chinese-American families, who were both working- and middle-class. Separation distress was the same in both groups, peaking at around nine and again at around thirteen months. Furthermore, there was no difference in the amount of separation distress shown by day-care and home-reared infants.

THE DEVELOPMENT OF SOCIABILITY

As infants grow, their significant relationships broaden beyond the important attachment to parents. Susan will have to contend with Matt as a potential threat or aid to her well-being, just as she will have to contend with Matt's playmates, her playpen peers, and possibly her younger siblings. It is within the first two years of life that we find the rudimentary development of personality usually called sociability. As we have seen, the early experiences of infants and young children dispose them in varying degrees to regard and to approach other human beings with warmth, positive expectations, and trust.

Attachment and Sociability

The results of studies showing the importance of the social-emotional bond between infants and their caregivers are in harmony with Erik Erikson's (1963) theory of personality development. The child's first task is to resolve the conflict between trust and mistrust in interpersonal situations. Babies who have developed secure attachments will show evidence of basic trust. Although trust is assumed to be an inner attitude, it reflects a system of interaction with the social world. As infants grow, a rudimentary sense of personal identity emerges, a sense that depends on the recognition that their memories and anticipated sensations and images are firmly linked with familiar and predictable things and people. This comfortable certainty about the world and their place in it allows babies to venture into new realms of experience.

Once their initial wariness of strange situations and people is overcome, infants display a natural disposition toward affiliative and exploratory behavior. Their natural inclination to affiliate with others encourages them to interact with other people, promoting their social development—a necessity in a social species like humanity. Babies' natural inclination to explore encourages them to find out about the world and promotes their sense of competence. Just as attachment may reduce wariness in infants, so may it enhance affiliation and exploration. If an infant's attachment figure is missing or unreliable, the child is likely to become wary and refuse to investigate new situations, making it difficult for a sense of competence, autonomy, and sociability to develop.

Self-Concept

From their early experiences, infants appear to develop a first crude sense of "me" and "not me." These experiences begin in the first hours of life, for detailed studies of interactions of babies and their mothers reveal that a baby is a social creature from birth (Sander, 1977; H. R. Schaffer, 1977). Although the mothers may not be aware of their own changing responses, most mothers quickly learn to read their babies' cues and adjust their own behavior so that the baby takes the lead in their interactions. During these turn-taking experiences, babies control the rate, level, and nature of their experiences (Stern, 1977), not unlike the way one adult interacts with another (Cappella, 1981).

The infant's sense of self forms an increasingly noticeable and integral part of sociability from the latter part of the first year. As a result of cognitive development, infants become conscious of themselves as separate and distinct persons. This blossoming self-awareness in turn influences their interest in others and how they relate to those others.

The baby's developing sense of self has been explored in a series of studies by Michael

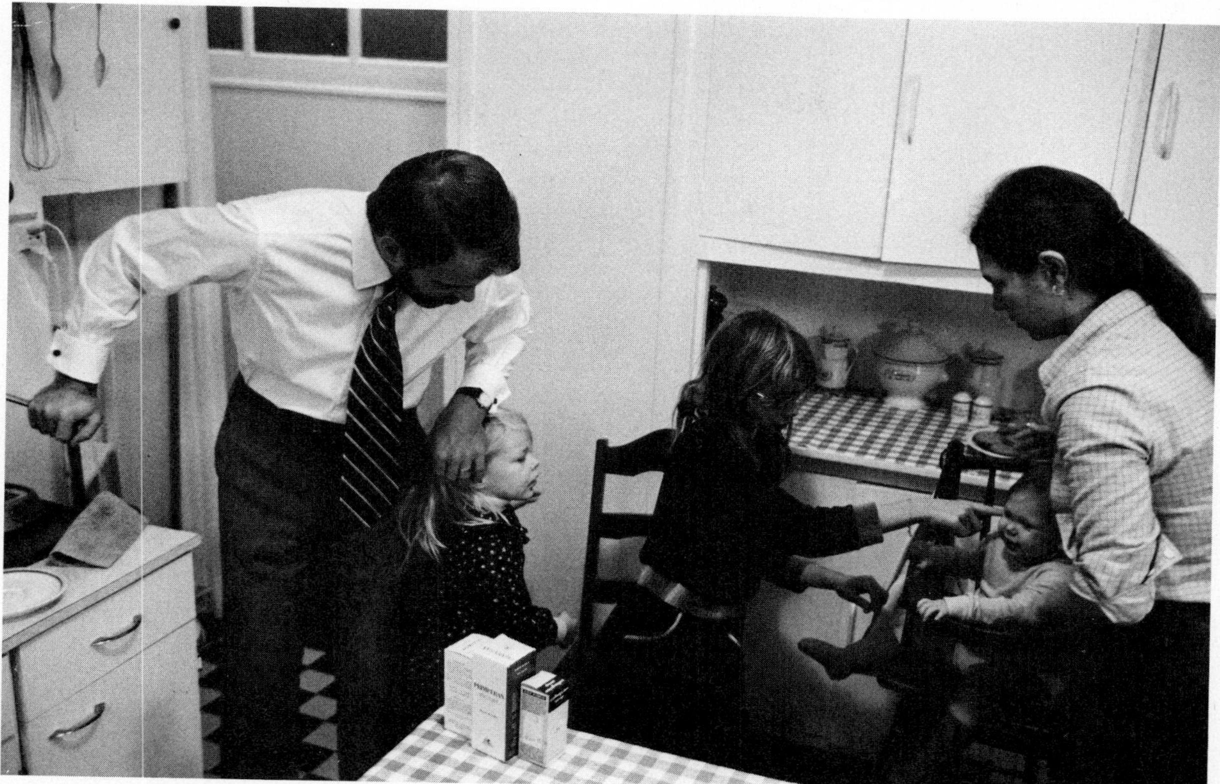

Sociability has its roots in the interactions of baby, parents, and siblings; these early experiences will either encourage or deter the baby's tendency to approach human beings. ***(© Richard Kalvar/Magnum)***

Lewis and Jeanne Brooks (Brooks and Lewis, 1976; Lewis and Brooks-Gunn, 1979a, 1979b). They found that by twenty to twenty-four months, babies have developed a self-concept and readily recognize themselves. The babies identify themselves and other people, reacting in terms of the gender, age, familiarity, height, and facial features of others. In one experiment, infants as young as seven months stared with apparent surprise at a midget. Their eyes widened, their eyebrows arched, and their mouths rounded, as if they expected a small body to have a child's face.

In order to test infants' recognition of themselves, Lewis and Brooks placed babies before a mirror after first surreptitiously dabbing rouge on their noses. No babies under a year seemed to recognize that the smudged nose in the mirror belonged to them, but among babies from fifteen to eighteen months, 25 percent immediately touched their noses, and by twenty-four months, 75 percent grabbed for their noses as soon as they looked in the mirror.

This gradual development in babies' ability to recognize themselves appears to be related to their development of the concept of object permanence. Bennett Bertenthal and Kurt Fischer (1978) found a high correlation (.84) between

Babies begin to develop a self-concept early, and by twenty-four months it is established; they recognized themselves and identify both themselves and other people. *(©George Zimbel/Monkmeyer Press)*

babies' self-recognition and awareness of object permanence, although sometimes object permanence ran ahead of self-recognition and sometimes the two were equally advanced. There would seem to be good reason for the parallel development of the two concepts. Without an awareness that objects and other people continue to exist, babies could not develop a sense of their own continuing identities.

The development of self-concept also shows in the reactions of infants as they look at pictures or videotapes of themselves and others. Lewis and Brooks found that babies looked longer and smiled more at their own pictures than at any others and that they reacted most to videotapes of themselves. They vocalized and imitated themselves twice as much as they imitated strange babies, blinking, waving, and sticking out their tongues. It appears that infants as young as nine months can recognize and react with pleasure to themselves, and that they are especially responsive to those people who are most "like me."

Infants' increasing sense of self and their understanding that others are separate from them may be linked to their development of empathy. Martin Hoffman (1979; 1981) believes that even year-old infants can empathize with others, and he has proposed that children go through several stages in the development of empathy. He describes an eleven-month-old girl who saw another child fall and begin to cry. The baby girl, looking as if she were about to cry herself, put her thumb in her mouth and buried her face in her mother's lap—her customary reaction to her own distress or injury.

Competence and Autonomy

Once infants can sit, their hands are freed for exploration and they can both experience the world tactually and reach out to initiate physical contact. Crawling and walking give them further opportunities to satisfy their curiosity and to initiate and sustain social interactions. Each time children's physical abilities increase and their perceptual world widens, the potential for learning more about the social world increases. They learn what people do, how they feel, and what they like and do not like. They learn that touching brings a smile, tugging gets attention, and hitting brings a reprimand. They learn whom to seek out and whom to avoid.

As their competence develops, babies find increasing satisfaction in exploring the social world. Harriet Rheingold and Carol Eckerman (1970) point out that although infants show distress at being left by their parents, they show no distress when they themselves leave their attachment figures to explore. When Eckerman and Rheingold (1974) placed ten-month-old babies in an unfamiliar place and gave each the opportunity to approach and touch a strange toy or

As this baby boy begins to detach himself from his mother, novelty, complexity, or change draws him away. He wants to touch, take apart, put together, and figure out everything in his world. *(Linda Ferrer Rogers/Woodfin Camp & Assoc.)*

person, babies promptly approached the toys and played with them. They rarely made physical contact with the strangers; instead they looked at them and smiled, suggesting that looking and smiling serve the same sort of exploratory function as touching and manipulating.

The studies by Rheingold and Eckerman also suggest that early exploratory behavior depends on age, not gender. They recorded children's forays from their mothers, placing forty-eight children between one and five years old in an L-shaped yard, arranged so a child could wander out of his or her mother's sight. How far a boy or girl would travel from his or her mother could be predicted by knowing only the age of the child; sex was not a factor.

Records of infant explorations indicate that during the second year of life, the infant's need for physical contact declines, apparently spurred by the desire to be competent, to know the social and object world, and to evoke smiles and attention from new people. Novelty, complexity, and change draw infants away from the comfortable familiarity of attachment figures.

The infant's new independence does not signal the end of attachment. The desire to be close to familiar and loved people and the desire to try out new experiences and expand competence appear to coexist throughout an individual's life. Infants with secure attachments feel safe to explore and to develop a sense of self as an independent agent (Clarke-Stewart and Hevey, 1981). From their explorations, they bring back new knowledge and abilities that they may incorporate into increasingly complex, interesting interactions with the people they love.

Toward the end of the second year, infants display the first concentrated push toward autonomy. At this time, they enter a period of social development that can make family life difficult. No matter what parents suggest, no matter what they ask, the consistent response is "No!"

This "negativistic crisis" develops as the infant becomes aware of the distinction between self and others, and between the infant's own will and the will of others. Until now, infants have depended on caregivers for the satisfaction of their needs, in what David Ausubel (1958) has called **executive dependence:** the parent acting as an executive arm, instrumental to the infant's needs. As infants become more aware of their competence and their effects on the world, they strive for **executive independence,** or autonomy. They want to do things for themselves. The infant whose invariable response is "no" is trying to discover the limits of his or her center of activity and initiative: the self. Parents frequently note that the clash of wills seems to have no practical point; the infant is concerned not with an issue but with a principle.

This developing sense of competence and autonomy will be important throughout life. It appears to underlie what will later become their **locus of control,** the degree to which children believe that they or others control their fates.

As a infant's competence increases, she becomes more aware of her intentions, needs, and desires—and expresses them. She also becomes less dependent on others for their fulfillment. ***(Suzanne Szasz)***

People with an internal locus of control generally believe that they are in control of what they do and of what happens to them. People with an external locus of control generally believe that what they do makes little difference and that other forces, such as luck, fate, or powerful other people, determine what happens to them.

Boy or Girl

Before infants learn whether they are girls or boys, they must discover what a "girl" or "boy" is. The voyage to this discovery begins before they are aware they have embarked on it, for parents treat boys and girls differently right from the start (Falbo, 1980). Babies are wrapped in pink or blue blankets in the hospital nursery and surrounded with sex-typed clothes and toys at home. Their gender may even affect the way they are fed, for one study (Lewis, 1971) found that middle-class mothers were more likely to breast-feed a daughter than a son.

If parents treat their own infants as they do the young infants of other people, gender affects interactions with their babies in subtle ways. In a study by Caroline Smith and Barbara Lloyd (1978), when mothers of firstborn babies played with a strange six-month-old, adult behavior changed as investigators changed their identification of the baby. Told the baby was a boy, mothers encouraged "him" with words to crawl, walk, and behave vigorously. Told the baby was a girl, they never encouraged motor activity and never chose a hammer as a plaything for the "girl." Similar differences turned up when Hannah Frisch (1977) changed gender labels on fourteen-month-old infants. But in Frisch's study, adults who were sympathetic to feminism often urged a "girl" to ride a tricycle or play with blocks, but never encouraged "boys" to play with a doll or a baby bottle.

It is possible that when adults play with strange babies they act on the only available information: age and gender. After reviewing the research, Eleanor Maccoby and Carol Jacklin (1974) concluded that mothers and fathers treat their own infants individually, encouraging motor activity in girls who have shown they like it and talking quietly to boys who prefer that. Maccoby and Jacklin found that the choice of sex-typed toys was the only difference in parents' treatment of daughters and sons.

But young children show sex-typed differences in behavior before they are two, and the differences are too pervasive to be the simple consequence of toy selection. Other studies have found differences in parental behavior that could account for a good deal of gender differences. For example, Susan Goldberg and Michael Lewis (1969) found that mothers of thirteen-month-old infants discouraged their sons from touching them and suggested that the little boys play with toys that lay across the room. But mothers of girls allowed their daughters to play near them and to touch them. The boys and girls also played differently. Boys played more roughly than girls did; they manipulated light switches and doorknobs and, when separated from their mothers by a picket fence, tried to get around it. Girls played quietly with toys; they stayed near their mothers and, when separated from them by the fence, cried.

In another study (Clarke-Stewart and Hevey, 1981), which followed infants over time, mothers were almost twice as likely to initiate physical contact with twelve-month-old sons as with daughters. By the time the children were eighteen months old, mothers were more likely to touch their daughters. Infants followed the same gender- and age-related pattern in seeking physical contact with their mothers. In both mothers and offspring, however, the change over time consisted solely of a drop in mother-son contact; mother-daughter contact remained steady.

Additional differences in parental behavior turned up in a study by Beverly Fagot (1978a), who observed families with an only child that was just under two years old. She discovered that parents often rewarded or punished sons and daughters differently for the same behavior. Girls were never encouraged when they played with blocks, and only girls tended to be discouraged when they manipulated objects. As a result, boys explored the physical world freely, but girls often got criticized for it. Girls were also encouraged to be helpers and to ask for assistance when they tried to do things. The parents were unaware that they were training their daughters to be dependent and their sons to be independent.

For their part, infants begin to learn gender labels and to apply them to others at about eighteen months, generally relying on hair and clothes as cues. By the time they are two, most can identify females in pictures as "girl" or "mommy" even when the pictured models have short hair or wear long pants. But, as Spencer Thompson (1975) found, most two-year-olds are not sure of their own sex. Although they can sort pictures of stereotypical males and females correctly by gender, they cannot always do the same

When looking at themselves in a mirror, two-year old girls do not always identify the image they see reflected back as that of a girl.
(Susan Meiselas/Magnum)

with pictures of themselves, nor do they always answer correctly when asked, "Are you a girl?" or "Are you a boy?" A rudimentary realization that one is a girl or a boy often develops around two, however, and it may be crucial to the child's later understanding and acceptance of her or his own gender.

Peers and Siblings

In the past, investigators simply did not look for social interaction between infants, perhaps because of the general belief that young babies are too egocentric for such sociability. Ask any park-bench mother, however, and she will report that infants as young as nine months who meet regularly play give-and-take the toy or peekaboo, or simply crawl after each other in follow-the-leader fashion.

At this age, the familiarity of peers seems to increase social interaction. When Jacqueline Becker (1977) observed pairs of nine-month-olds in their homes, she found that babies who were with each other for ten play sessions paid more attention to each other than to toys or to their mothers. The babies reached toward and followed each other, they passed toys, and they looked at each other far more often than did infants who played together for only two sessions. In addition, when Becker subsequently placed each infant in a play situation with an unfamiliar baby, infants who had previously played with a peer for ten sessions played more with the strange baby than did those who had played with a peer for only two sessions.

As babies near the end of the first year, they take increased enjoyment in their peers. A one-year-old may give another infant a toy and display obvious pleasure when the other child takes it. That same toy can become the source of a squabble, however, and the loser will scream in distress. In fact, such assertive acts, in which infants take toys from peers, strike them, or issue negative commands, account for about half of all peer interactions (Holmberg, 1980). One-year-olds also stimulate each other to begin play. For example, one baby begins to bang on a table or to take toys out of the toy box, and the others join in. As each object is pulled from the box, the infants all smile.

Once they have resolved their conflicts over play materials, babies attend positively to peers. Among eighteen- to twenty-four-month-olds, play objects and playmates are more successfully integrated, and social interactions begin to predominate, so that by twenty-four months, positive interactions are twice as prevalent as assertive actions (Holmberg, 1980). Infants of this age modify their behavior to their playmates' activity, as Judith Rubenstein and Carollee Howes (1976) found when they studied seventeen- to twenty-month-old playmates who met regularly in their own homes. The babies not only played freely and made few demands on adults, but they also seldom squabbled over toys. Play between a pair of playmates was more intricate and constructive than solitary play by either member of the pair or play by one of the babies with his or her mother.

Peer interaction is one example of the great social expansion that takes place in the second year of life. It allows young children to try their skills and to explore their differentiating sense of self, as they learn to take turns and enjoy each other's actions. Some understanding of others' feelings can usually be seen at this time. Many children start to form real attachments with specific peers and squeal with delight on spying them. An infant of one and one-half to two years may appear to comfort peers in distress, or at least to observe them with concern.

Peer interactions change considerably during the first two years of life. From minimal interactions during the first nine months, a baby goes through a period characterized by fighting for toys, then during the second year develops cooperative, satisfying, enjoyable patterns of social play. *(William MacDonald)*

Although little research has focused on the interaction of infants and their siblings, a pair of studies by Michael Lamb (1978a, 1978b) indicates that preschool brothers and sisters are active models and teachers, and can have a decided impact on their younger siblings' development. Lamb observed babies with their preschool siblings, first when the babies were twelve months old, then again six months later. On both occasions, the infants carefully watched their older brothers and sisters, often taking over toys they had abandoned and imitating them. The older children, in turn, talked to their baby brothers and sisters and offered them toys. Although the boys touched their young siblings more than the girls did, the girls were more sociable and paid more attention to the infants—essentially playing mother.

Preschoolers were more likely to hit an infant brother or sister than the infant was to strike them, suggesting that infants with older siblings learn quickly who is more powerful. This reluctance to hit or strike back was reaffirmed in another study, in which eighteen-month-old infants without older siblings were more likely than babies with siblings to grab toys from peers and to squabble with them (Easterbrooks and Lamb, 1979).

Although Lamb's studies took place in a laboratory, a study done in the home by Rona Abramovitch, Carl Corter, and Bella Lando (1979) also found older siblings exercising a strong influence over infants. Older boys, for example, hit, kicked, bit, and pinched their infant siblings more than older girls did; but the girls were just as likely to tussle over a toy, tease, threaten, or tell their mothers about their younger brothers' and sisters' misbehavior. The older girls again played the nurturant little mother. Abramovitch also found that infants did most of the imitating, but she pointed out that older children did 20 percent of it, banging Play Dough on the table, blowing cake crumbs, or dancing around in imitation of their infant brothers and sisters.

SUMMARY

1. Although early experiences can have enduring effects on later development, studies suggest that there are strong constraints on the effects of early experience. These constraints may involve sensitive periods in development as well as maturational state, cognitive growth, and previous experience.
2. The attachment bond between infant and primary caregiver is a close relationship in which the child is almost an extension of the mother's being. Studies of monkeys and human infants have illustrated the complex nature of this relationship. In human babies, the relationship takes months to develop, requires extensive meshing of infant and caregiver behavior, and is subject to much variation. The baby moves from a stage of indiscriminate responsiveness into a stage of discrimination without attachment, and finally, at about eight months, develops an intense attachment.
4. Once the infant develops a primary attachment, separation distress and wariness of strangers may appear. The form these reactions take appears to depend on the quality of the attachment bond and the situation itself.
5. The three major kinds of attachment are secure, avoidant, and ambivalent, and the quality of a baby's attachment is connected with the mother's style of caring for her baby. Fathers become as deeply attached to their infants as mothers do; however, they interact with their infants differently.
6. A baby's reactions—or lack of them—influence the tone of the parent-infant relationship. The baby's temperament and speed of development can make parents feel successful as caregivers or incompetent and anxious.
7. Research has not shown that a single primary caregiver is absolutely necessary for normal development; when the main attachment figure shares caregiving with other people, children thrive as long as other caregivers provide stable relationships.
8. The baby is a social creature from birth, and early personality and sociability are largely a product of interaction with parents. As a sense of self develops and the infant becomes motivated by a desire for competence, she or he generally begins to show increased autonomy. Parents and other adults treat boys and girls differently, however, so that boys are encouraged to be autonomous and girls to be dependent. Play and interaction with peers increasingly become sources of enjoyment.

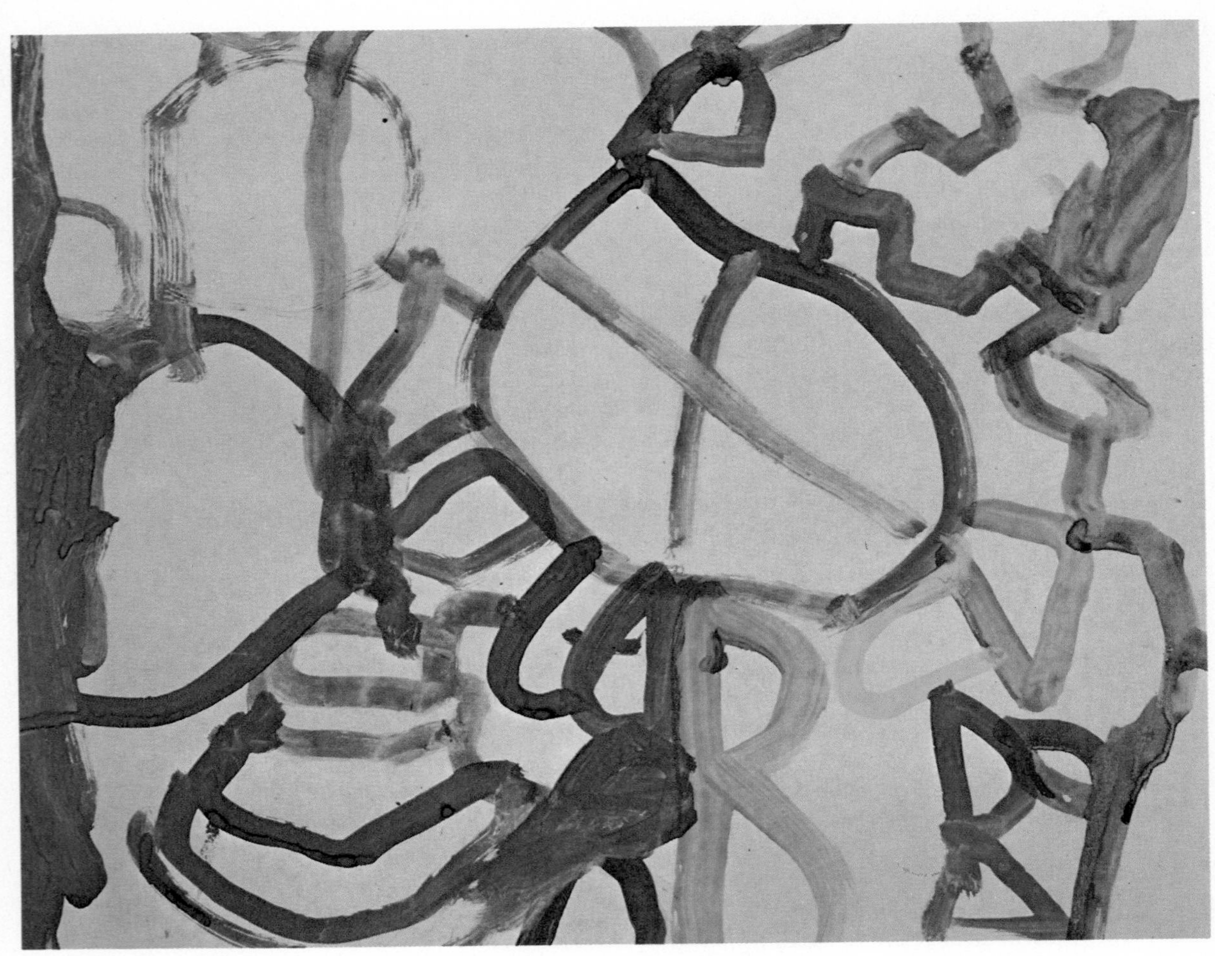

UNIT FOUR

EARLY CHILDHOOD: THE FORMATIVE YEARS

Between the ages of two and six, the toddler becomes a child. The chubby body begins to slim, and the sometimes awkward attempts at the games of childhood become smooth and skilled. As a child uses more sophisticated techniques to explore the environment, increased experiences and rapidly developing understanding allow the youngster to enter a wider world. Although parents retain the strongest influence on development, other children and adults begin to play an increasingly important role. Society further strengthens its influence on the growing child by transmitting cultural values and by holding the youngster to what it considers appropriate behavior for one of his or her sex. When you finish this unit, you will see that there are many ways in which the continuous interaction of child and society affects development.

10 PLAY: ITS DEVELOPMENT AND FUNCTION

Scott is chasing David through the nursery-school yard. He catches up with his friend and with a loud yell, wrestles him to the ground. After a momentary scuffle, Scott jumps up and runs off laughing. David dashes after him, reaches his side as Scott rounds the corner of the sandbox, and draws back his open hand as if to strike Scott. But the blow does not actually land. Instead, David throws Scott onto the soft sand and falls down beside him. Both boys laugh. Adults watching such rough-and-tumble play might believe that a fight was in progress; but the laughter, the expression on the faces of the youngsters involved, the wrestling, and the jumping tell ethologists and children alike that the struggle is not aggressive and that no hostility is involved. According to Nicholas Blurton-Jones (1976), such play is similar to play among young rhesus monkeys, where it is important in the development of the monkeys' social and sexual behavior.

Some developmental psychologists have looked at play and its relation to children's cognition; others at its effect on a child's physical or social development. In this chapter we will do all three. After defining play, we will discuss its function in the development of the child. We will examine the physical aspects of play, paying attention to the importance of motor skills and the phenomenon of rough-and-tumble play. Next, we will look at the stages of play, from the practice play of the two-month-old infant, to the symbolic play of the preschooler, to the structured games of the schoolchild. We will explore the influence of play on later problem solving and the appearance and development of play with language. We will see that play helps socialize a child and that some cultures actively discourage imaginative play among children. Finally, we will find that play can be used to help children work through problems of personal and social development.

THE MANY FACES OF PLAY

Developmental psychologists generally agree that play has an important role in children's development but find its definition hard to specify (Chance, 1979; Sutton-Smith, 1980). One reason is that the same behavior can be play in one instance and work in another. Members of a professional football team are not playing when they go out on the gridiron on Sunday afternoon, but ten-year-olds engrossed in a game of touch football are. Skipping a stone across the water is play; throwing the same stone with intent to harm is not.

What Is Play?

A good definition of play for our purposes is that offered by Catherine Garvey (1977), who proposes that play must meet four conditions: it must be pleasurable; it must be an end in itself, not a means to some goal; it must be spontaneous and freely chosen by the player; and it must involve some active engagement on the part of the player.

Most definitions of play are similar to Garvey's, either adding to or subtracting from her list. Jean Piaget (1951), however, believed that all the conditions of play were included in his own simple definition, that play is primarily assimilation. The pleasure involved is simply the emotional expression of that assimilation, in which the child responds to the "whims of the ego" instead of accommodating to the demands of the world.

Piaget's belief that play is mainly a matter of assimilation is supported by the results of Corinne Hutt's (1976) research. She brought thirty nursery-school children, one at a time, into a small, familiar room. In the room was a red metal box on four brass legs. Protruding from the box was a lever topped with a blue wooden ball, and there were four counters that registered the lever's movements, as well as a bell and a buzzer. Left alone with the box, children began by exploring the strange object, and Hutt discovered that their exploration did not appear to be play. Instead, they seemed to be trying to answer the question, "What does this object do?" Only after a child had learned all that he or she could about the way the object worked was it incorporated into play. When this occurred, the child's facial expression, which had been intent during exploration, relaxed, and the question became, "What can I do with this object?"

The Functions of Play

As Garvey (1977) points out, play has been linked with many cognitive and social activities, among them creativity, problem solving, language learning, and the development of social roles. Although most research that involves play attempts to specify the link between it and one of these areas of development, there is general agreement that play serves several complementary functions.

Through play, children develop an increasing knowledge of the physical world, a growing competence in managing it, and an expanding mastery over it, making play seem essential to development. This increased competence and mastery grows out of incidental learning that takes place after a child's initial curiosity about new objects has been satisfied. Although learning about the object has ceased to be a matter of concern, playing with it reveals new properties and uses (McGhee, 1979; Garvey, 1977). In such play, children can practice and perfect action schemes that can later be put together in different ways to solve problems.

Play is also a route to learning about society. Children at play respond to the world and discover how it responds to them, learning about its structures, its rules, its rewards, and its punishments. Because play minimizes the consequences of the child's actions, as Jerome Bruner (1972) notes, it allows learning to take place under circumstances of minimum risk. This function is especially obvious in various forms of social play, and it was made clear decades ago in Meyer Fortes's (1938) observations of boys among the Tale, an African society. These boys practiced shooting barbless arrows at cornstalks, pieces of wood, and small birds—a safe prepara-

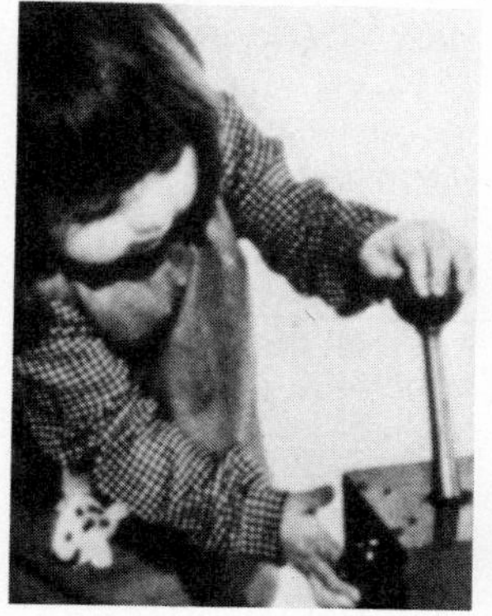

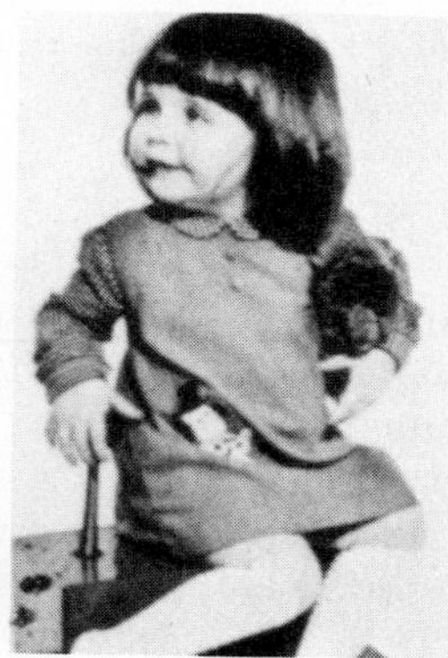

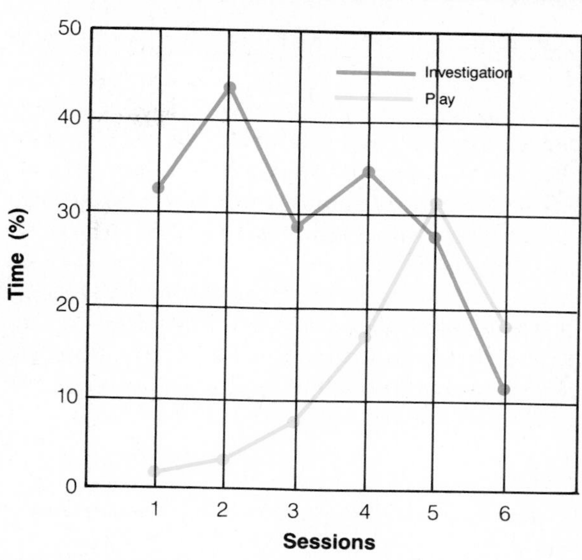

FIGURE 10.1 When nursery school children were left alone with a strange object on six different occasions, the first few sessions were devoted primarily to exploring the object. Only after children had discovered the object's functions did they begin to play with it, supporting the idea that play is mainly a matter of assimilation. *(Adapted from Hutt, in Bruner, Jolly, and Sylva, 1976)*

tion for the hunting with barbed and poisonous arrows that would be part of their adult responsibilities. Similarly, when young children in Western societies practice the skills of doctoring, driving, cooking, war making, parenthood, and marriage, they are playing at adult social roles without any of the physical, emotional, or economic consequences that accompany mistakes made when engaging in the real thing.

Another important function of play is its provision of opportunities to experiment with new kinds of behavior that would, under the pressure of daily life, never be tried (Bruner, 1972). Make-believe play, for example, allows the child to manipulate reality, trying out possibilities, concepts, and new ways of thinking about the world.

Yet another function of play is its role in the development of sociability and personal competence. From infancy, play with peers reflects children's growing conception of themselves and others. Through their social play, children learn that others may see things differently or prefer to carry out activities in another manner. They learn how to resolve squabbles, share, cooperate, hold a conversation, and make and keep friends—all in the course of playing with other children.

This emphasis on the cognitive and social aspects of play should not obscure the purely physical functions of play in children's development. Play that allows children to manipulate small objects may be of great importance in developing dexterity, and play that involves vigorous exercise contributes to general physical health. In addition, Corinne Hutt (1979) suggests that free play may serve an even more basic physiological function. She notes that children at play show greater fluctuations in heart rate than do children who are solving puzzles. Since it is generally accepted that concentration is accompanied by a steady heart rate and relaxation by a varied rate, Hutt conjectures that free play allows the nervous system to "idle," temporarily suspending information-processing functions and allowing it to recuperate. She likens the role of play in the awake child to that of REM-sleep in the sleeping youngster, and calls play a "time-out" for the consolidation of information the child has acquired while exploring, learning, or solving problems.

Playing at being a fireman is a safe way for a child to try out this adult role. *(©Leonard Speier 1982)*

THE PHYSICAL ASPECTS OF PLAY

A baby's first play is purely physical, the repetition of movement solely for the pleasure it brings. This same pleasure of repeated movement also dominates the running, jumping, and physical exuberance of young children, and it will continue into adulthood. The child who swings or who rolls down a hill, luxuriating in the sensation, becomes the adult who skis, dances, or becomes involved in gymnastics. With maturation, practice, and the imposition of rules, physical play also becomes hopscotch or soccer among schoolchildren and rock climbing or tennis among adults. The development of motor skills thus becomes important in understanding physical play and its effects on the growing child.

Developing Motor Skills

A child's skill at running, jumping, manipulating objects, or competing with peers in games depends on several physiologically based factors: strength, speed, and coordination. Between the ages of three and eleven, children's strength tends to double, becoming more important in the play of boys than of girls because individual differences in strength are often a factor in boys' play. At around the age of three, boys become more proficient than girls at play that requires strength, such as throwing a ball for distance, although girls of this age are more skillful in activities that do not demand such power. Strength remains the only difference between the sexes. Among the ten-year-old children in one study (Govatos, 1959), boys were more proficient than girls in play that required superior strength in the arms and legs, such as kicking a soccer ball or throwing a baseball for distance. But in events as diverse as jumping, reaching, the standing broadjump, the twenty-five-yard dash, and throwing a ball for accuracy, girls did as well as boys.

Speed also becomes important in the play of children. A major factor in speed is **reaction time,** the interval of time that elapses between the instant a stimulus is presented and the individual's reaction to it. Speed can also be a measure of the absolute time it takes a child to perform a given activity. With increasing age and practice, children learn to use their speed in games that require fast reactions by their minds and bodies, and for some children, the faster they can do something the more exciting and enjoyable it becomes.

Coordination, which includes the child's accuracy of movement, poise, smoothness, rhythm, and ease, is the basis of almost all play skills. Since it involves far more than strength or speed, it is a better index for determining a child's ability and agility at physical play. A child acquires coordination more slowly than strength or speed, because coordination requires the interplay of sensory and motor skills that often depend on the maturation of small muscles and on practice. Children themselves are usually extremely conscious of their own and their playmates' degree of coordination, so their mastery —or lack of it—in games and sports that require coordination often influences their feelings of self-sufficiency and self-confidence.

Regardless of the skill they are trying to master, until they develop the required coordination, children's movements at play tend to be inaccurate, undifferentiated, and unrefined. As a result, adults may get the impression that children's play is less directed and purposeful than it actually is (Millar, 1968).

Swinging on the bars requires the development of coordination, which involves a sophisticated interplay of previously developed sensory and motor skills. *(©Alice J. Garik)*

Practice and Instruction

There are, of course, large individual differences in the ages at which children are able to do various things, as well as differences in the degree of their skill and coordination in each activity. Although maturation of muscles and bones plays a large part in the emergence of running, jumping, and skipping, the opportunity to practice and the encouragement of others helps to guarantee smooth, speedy, confident mastery and refinement of such abilities.

For simple movement patterns, as Caroline Sinclair (1973) points out, instruction and coaching are not necessary. Given time, space, equipment, and encouragement, children will develop these patterns on their own. More complicated skills, however, may require formal instruction. Many children are exposed to such skills as swimming, skating, skiing, and tennis during early childhood, and such early exposure and practice tends to give them an advantage in their performance. For example, in Myrtle McGraw's (1935) co-twin study, which was discussed in Chapter 6, early training in swimming was extremely effective. Researchers began training one little boy to swim when he was eight months old; by the time he had reached seventeen months, he could swim up to fifteen feet without help. McGraw was also successful in teaching this twin diving and skating. Other studies have demonstrated that a child who watches others and listens to instructions improves in throwing and catching a ball; and naturally, play activities that require fine motor skills, such as drawing or painting, improve with instruction.

Children sometimes profit from help in the mastery of recreational and play skills, and Bryant Cratty (1967) has developed a set of guidelines for teaching them. He suggests that any skilled performance can be divided into three phases—pretask, task, and posttask—and that instruction is most effective when it varies with each phase. Pretask instruction should be kept to a minimum; it should describe the basic mechanical principles of the skill and tell the child about the task's extent, intensity, duration, and difficulty. During the task, instruction should not interfere with the child's performance, whether it is swimming, skiing, batting, or serving a tennis ball. At this time, the child finds visual demonstrations and manual guidance helpful. Posttask instruction should give the child immediate and clear feedback about his or her success or failure.

Generally, Cratty points out, directions should emphasize what a child should do, rather than what he or she should not do. If speed is important, it should be emphasized early. Cratty notes that repeatedly slowing down a child's performance on a skill that requires speed is often detrimental to the child's ultimate mastery of it.

Rough and tumble play is more culturally common among boys than girls, although both sexes show equally vigorous play in other situations. *(©Leonard Speier 1982)*

Rough-and-Tumble Play

Rough-and-tumble play is always social, for it requires a partner. It is more common among boys than among girls, at least in the United States, in Great Britain, and among the !Kung hunter-gatherers of Africa (Blurton-Jones and Konner, 1973). Such play appears in children as young as eighteen months, and Nicholas Blurton-Jones (1976) believes that those who do not begin it early may never engage in it.

Analysis indicates that episodes of rough-and-tumble play, as when Scott chased David in the beginning of this chapter, combine seven movement patterns that occur together but not in combination with other movements (Blurton-Jones, 1976). Children run, chase and flee, wrestle, jump up and down with feet together, beat at each other with open hands (but do not actually land blows), laugh, and fall down. In addition, children engaged in such play exhibit a typical facial expression—an open-mouthed smile with the lips covering the teeth. During real hostilities, children beat with closed fists, frown, and fix their gaze on each other. Such actions are never a part of rough-and-tumble play. When children begin rough-and-tumble play, it either continues until they are exhausted or turns abruptly into a game that requires rules, such as tag or cowboys and Indians.

Although players engaged in rough-and-tumble play show no hostility to each other, a child's reaction to the play may change in midstream. A small boy who is fleeing, for example, may speed up his flight; then suddenly his eyebrows may go up, his smile disappear, and his shrieks of laughter turn into a continuous scream—a sound, Blurton-Jones notes, resembling the noise children sometimes make when they find a large, slightly ominous bug scuttling about on the playground. For this child, the aggression has become real and the game is no longer fun.

Part of the significant gender difference in rough-and-tumble play may derive from the fact that young girls seem to perceive as a threatening advance the same action that young boys interpret as an invitation to roughhouse. In a group of preschoolers studied by Janet DiPietro (1981), girls showed just as much vigorous activity on the trampoline as boys, but the attempts to take a toy from another child that often turned into rough-and-tumble play among boys were seen as bids for dominance among girls.

The effects of rough-and-tumble play appear to be positive. Children who engage in it generally stay together after the game ends and tend to play together on subsequent occasions. Although no one knows all the functions of rough-and-tumble play, Peter Smith (1977) suggests that the formation and consolidation of friendships is one of its basic purposes, and others (e.g., Suomi, 1977) have suggested that it provides a safe way to practice aggressive behavior. Blurton-Jones (1976) also points out that because children consistently give the same signals (the typical facial expression, laughter, etc.) to indicate its lack of hostility, rough-and-tumble play may have had an important role in the evolution of human beings.

PLAY AND COGNITION

Whether most learning takes place during exploration or during the play itself, the links between

CHOOSING TOYS FOR CHILDREN

Manufacturers produce a bewildering array of toys, and a trip through the pages of a toy catalog or the aisles of a toy store leaves parents, grandparents, aunts, and uncles more perplexed than confident. When selecting a toy, an adult would do well to consider the cognitive level of the child, and as the following examples indicate, research can sometimes guide the choice.

Since mastery over the environment is one of the pleasures of play, toys that have obvious effects are good choices for babies. Research by John S. Watson (1972) reported in the text showed the pleasure of two-month-olds who found they could control a mobile by turning their heads. Such an arrangement is beyond the capabilities of most parents, but tying yarn loosely around a baby's wrist or foot so that any waves or kicks make the mobile move has the same effect. Such opportunities to exert mastery teach the baby that actions have consequences, and they delight the infant.

Many "educational" toys are almost formless—smoothly sanded but featureless blocks of wood with wheels, for example, are meant to be toy cars. Although such toys work well with older preschoolers, children under two find them difficult to play with, as might be expected from Joy Elder and David Pederson's (1978) research, which was reported in the text. When a roundtable of psychologists met to discuss play (Chance, 1979), there was general agreement that young children have trouble playing with unrealistic toys. Children under three, they suggested, might get along better with a toy with specific features—a car with license plates, windows, headlights, a hood ornament, and even a driver painted in the window. As children grow older, however, the lack of specificity that made play difficult for the toddler makes a toy more flexible. Now the child's imagination can turn the featureless vehicle into an ambulance, a fire truck, a racing car—even a boat or a haywagon drawn by a team of horses.

Imagination also has a role in the kind of toys children like. Highly imaginative five-year-olds, for example, like to play with clay, blocks, and fingerpaints—play materials that are unstructured and allow free range to the imagination. Less imaginative children prefer dolls, trucks, and teasets, which tell the child exactly what to do with the objects in play. Using unstructured toys, such as blocks of various shapes, children play longer, more elaborate games than when they play with structured toys. Yet when they first see a collection of toys, they may indicate a preference for the structured, highly detailed toys.

Other research presented at the roundtable indicated that children's imagination may be freed when they play with unusual combinations of toys. In one study, children played either with toys that went together (a shovel, a rake, and a watering can) or with toys that did not go together (a shovel, a boat, and a telephone). After children had played with the toys, they were shown a shovel and asked to tell the investigator all the things it could be used for. The children who had played with the mismatched set of toys came up with more original uses for the shovel than did children who had played with the neatly combined toys. Thinking of uncommon uses for familiar objects is, in fact, one test that psychologists use to measure creativity, suggesting that children who are forced to improvise in play may find their imagination spurred.

a child's cognitive level and his or her play are strong (Fein, 1981). As children's thought develops, their play changes and different forms predominate—from the thoughtless repetitions of motor movements seen in the young baby to the intricate, challenging games of the older child and adolescent. But the cognitive connection can be even closer: the freedom to play can produce efficiency in problem solving. In addition, as children develop, their play with language shows an increasing appreciation of ambiguity and subtlety.

The baby's sense of play develops during the early months. But not until the second year will an infant begin to initiate games. ***(©Jay Lurie/ West Stock, Inc.)***

Stages of Play

The earliest play is, of course, sensorimotor. As noted in Chapter 7, babies often repeat movements because of the stimulation provided by the action. Piaget (1951) placed the beginnings of play in the primary circular reactions of the sensorimotor period, and he described this sort of activity as **practice play.** Piaget noted, however, that it is difficult to distinguish between adaptive reactions, when the baby is accommodating schemes to incorporate new knowledge, and practice play, when the baby is assimilating actions to existing schemes. Indeed, Martin Bax (1977) has suggested that the distinction may be so difficult to make that it might be best to exclude most of these early actions from the category of play.

The pleasure and satisfaction that babies feel when they repeat familiar behavior is obvious to the casual observer. A baby boy, for example, "repeats his behavior not in a further effort to learn or to investigate, but for the mere joy of mastering it and of showing off to himself his own power of subduing reality" (Piaget, 1951). Thus babies bang the side of the crib, shake rattles, or swing their arms back and forth in front of their faces. From Piaget's perspective, this early practice play is thoughtless, devoid of any social reference, and intrinsically pleasing.

As play develops during the early months, the baby regards the world as "what I do with it" (McCall, 1979b) and, using circular reactions, acts upon it. After analyzing babies' early games, John S. Watson (1972) concluded that their importance to the baby lay in the sense of mastery over the environment they provide (similar to Piaget's suggestion that they show off the baby's power of subduing reality). Watson found that two-month-old babies who could control the movements of a mobile by pressing their heads against a pillow began cooing and smiling on about the third day of "the game," just as babies of the same age respond in social games. An increase in vigorous smiling and cooing failed to appear among infants who watched a colorful display they could not control.

This idea of mastery through play is supported by psychodynamic theorists. Erik Erikson (1963), for example, writes that such play "is the infantile form of the human ability to deal with experience by creating model situations and to master reality by experiment and planning."

At about seven months, a baby may begin to separate the object from the action and increasingly imitate actions. But not until the second year, when, in Piaget's words, babies become capable of tertiary circular reactions, do they gain a full sense of mastery over the environment. It is in this period, says Robert McCall (1979b), that babies understand they can influence other people from a distance. With this realization, babies act, then wait, anticipating that their parents or playmates will respond (Ross and Kay, 1980).

The development of play from sheer sensorimotor activity to symbolic social action can be seen in a study by Larry Fenson, Jerome Kagan, and their associates (1976). They observed infants from seven to twenty months as the babies played with a toy metal teaset. At seven months, most of the babies were content merely to mouth, chew, or bang a cup or spoon. At nine months, most of them spent their time using two pieces of the teaset together, perhaps tapping the teapot with the spoon. At thirteen months, all the infants used two pieces together in an appropriate way, such as putting the lid on the pot or a spoon in the cup. About half of them engaged in at least one symbolic activity, such as pretending to drink, pour, or stir a cup of tea. By twenty months, all the infants engaged in such symbolic activities.

In another study, Fenson and Douglas Ramsay (1980) found that nineteen- and twenty-four-month-old infants were increasingly likely to pretend they were pouring or stirring substances, to feed a doll from a bottle, or to put the bottle in the doll's hand so it could feed itself. In addition, they found that by twenty-four months, infants consistently combined more than one scheme in their play, for example, putting a toy soldier on a platform and then pulling it around the room, or combing their mother's hair and then holding a mirror so she could see their handiwork.

Infants in a third study (Fenson and Ramsay, 1981) imitated schemes they did not produce spontaneously, suggesting that children's understanding is more advanced than their spontaneous behavior would indicate. Some twelve-month-olds and most fifteen-month-olds imitated a single activity from a sequence they had seen modeled, and some fifteen-month-olds and a majority of nineteen-month-olds imitated a combination of actions.

Some time during the second year, then, symbolic relations begin (Fein, 1981). Children are acquiring language and can represent objects in thought, which means that they can transfer relationships they observe to new contexts. It is now that **symbolic play,** which Piaget proposed as the second kind of play, begins. Thus, for example, the child pours imaginary coffee for a Snoopy doll, then holds the cup to the doll's mouth. Children are leaving infancy behind and are launched on the preoperational period, during which imaginative, make-believe play flowers. This symbolic play is, according to Piaget, assimilation at its height.

As children develop concrete-operational thought, symbolic play often declines. Children now prefer **games,** Piaget's third form of play, with their intricate rules that everybody accepts. Although dramatic play continues in a formal, structured way (as in plays put on for parents and friends or in neighborhood games of cops and robbers), the spontaneous activity of playfully transforming reality in order to act out personal desires increasingly becomes interior dialogue, fantasy, and daydreams. As Lev Vygotsky (1978) put it, imagination in schoolchildren and adolescents is "play without action."

Make-Believe and Fantasy

Play incorporates the child's increasing ability to symbolize and imagine, so that it may include elements that are not present ("Pretend like we have horses") or material that is not factual ("You be the mommy"). Vygotsky (1978) suggested that symbolic play provides a transition between the tight constraints of the young child's mind and the adult's ability to abstract thought completely from context. In this view, imaginative play helps children free themselves from situational constraints and allows them to separate meaning from action. For example, when a child stamps the ground and pretends she is riding a horse, she has detached the meaning of her action from a real action (an actual horseback ride). Vygotsky pointed out that in the earliest symbolic play children must use props that resemble real objects. That is, they can pretend that a stick is a horse, but they cannot imagine a postcard as one. Because adults make conscious use of symbols, they find it easy to pretend a postcard is a horse.

A study of play among children between sixteen and twenty-three months supports Vygotsky's developmental description but finds the ability to use dissimilar objects in imaginative play emerging earlier than Vygotsky would have supposed. None of the youngest children observed by Elaine Jackowitz and Malcolm Watson (1980) could imagine without some kind of prop, but 46 percent of the sixteen-month-olds and more than 60 percent of the twenty-three-month-olds could pretend that a toy car was a telephone or a cup of tea. In one case, when a little boy was left without a prop and asked to imitate a researcher who drank tea from a cup, the child searched the carpet until he found a piece of lint, then pretended to drink from it.

PEOPLE OR OBJECTS?

Studies of play report what most children do: how they play, what they play with, how rapidly they pass through various stages. In every study, however, some children behave differently from the rest. They find different objects interesting, they play for shorter or longer spans of time with a toy, they move into symbolic play sooner (or later) than other children. Recently, investigators have noticed that not all children follow the same course into symbolic play; nor do all children show the same delight in making believe.

Howard Gardner and his associates (Shotwell, Wolf, and Gardner, 1979) have been following the development of a group of first-born, middle-class children since they were a year old and have found that the children divide into two types: patterners and dramatists. *Patterners* are fascinated with the relations between objects, and they begin to classify objects early, attending to sizes and shapes. *Dramatists* focus on people and are interested in dramatic play.

These different cognitive approaches show in the games the children play. At fourteen months, dramatists play peekaboo, but patterners prefer a game centering on the exchange of small objects. A patterner of this age who is given a teaset and dolls finds stacking the plates and nesting the cups more interesting than pretending to drink a cup of tea. One little girl who was a consistent patterner momentarily interrupted her stacking to smack her lips and hold a spoon toward an adult, but this symbolic play soon gave way to more stacking and restacking. Provided with a box of objects, the patterner takes out similar objects, one at a time, and studies them. The dramatist takes out objects indiscriminately and gives each to his or her mother.

At two years, patterners generally divide blocks by sizes and shapes, but dramatists are likely to pretend a block is a glass of milk or a bowl of applesauce, or that the block on top of a tower is a hat; or they may make believe that blocks are people and enact some event with them. When it comes to word play, patterners are the first to produce metaphors, an ability that typically appears at this age. Asked to rename blocks, the young patterner can see the block in different ways—as a wall, a car, a train. And when slightly older, the patterner can see letters in the shape of tree twigs. Although dramatists use blocks in symbolic play, in the metaphor game they have trouble coming up with visual metaphors; they prefer that someone else rename objects.

Although by the time they are three, the patterners develop some of the symbolic, interpersonal skills of the dramatist, and the dramatists begin to classify and sort out the object world, both continue to approach the world primarily in terms of their dominant stance.

Gardner and his associates are not sure what determines a child's style of play. They suggest that it could be a hereditary disposition to see the world in a certain way; or the result of modeling, as the infant watches brothers, sisters, or parents play or use objects in certain ways; or the result of an interaction between a baby's predispositions and the parents' responses to them. While they continue to follow the first group of children, Gardner and his associates have added another group of children to their study in the hope of learning more about the differences between patterners and dramatists.

Since the children have been followed for only three years, the significance of the different styles has not been determined. It may be that the patterner is oriented toward form and the dramatist toward verbal symbolism; but it is possible that the patterner is inclined to the inward-looking style of the introvert and the dramatist to the outgoing style of the extrovert.

In contrast, a study of slightly older children found that many of them had trouble using dissimilar objects in imaginative play. Among the children studied by Joy Elder and David Pederson (1978), two-and-a-half-year-olds could pretend with similar objects, imagining that a flat piece of wood was a comb and that a box was a pitcher, but could not pretend that a rubber ball was a comb, a hairbrush, or a pitcher. Asked to pretend that a small car was a shovel, children of this age might drive the car back and forth across the table or say, "I can't. It's a car." But among children a year older, few had trouble using dissimilar objects in their play. They happily combed their hair with a rubber ball, poured pretend liquids from the hairbrush, and made digging motions with the car.

Most children, say Jerome L. Singer and Dorothy Singer (1981), engage in "let's pretend" by the time they are three or so, and more than half the preschoolers they studied had imaginary playmates. Boys were likely to choose animals as their imaginary companions, while girls chose people—often selecting a person of the opposite sex, something boys rarely did. Only children were more likely than children with siblings to have an imaginary friend.

The age of five, say Singer and Singer (1979), is the "golden age" of make-believe. Children can become so involved in their fantasy play that they may react with fear to a playmate who has been assigned a terrifying role. Their delighted shrieks at the approach of a lumbering playmate who is pretending to be a Frankenstein monster may be tinged with a touch of real fear.

Using their increasing role-taking ability, young children also engage in a great deal of fantasy play that mingles elements from the roles they see enacted around them ("I'm Daddy getting the baby dressed for bed"), from television ("We're on a ship, and there are sharks around us"), and from seemingly pure fantasy ("This is the time I learned how to fly"). Any available prop seems to generate a string of associations, which children weave into play that is sometimes infinitely flexible ("We can all walk on water") and sometimes extremely rigid ("You can't be a fireman because you don't have a hat on").

According to the Singers, youngsters who pretend are likely to be happy children—if smiles, laughter, and similar indications of mood are used as a measure of happiness. What is more, fantasy appears to benefit children in other ways. Highly imaginative children seem to be able to wait longer, entertain themselves more, resist temptation better, and remember and report details better than unimaginative children. One of the reasons this may be so, say the Singers, is that in the course of make-believe play children can try out alternative environments and test novel words and phrases, perhaps learning more about the world around them than children whose play lacks the element of fantasy.

Children who show imagination in their play seem to be both happy and emotionally mature for their age. *(©Michael Weisbrot & Family)*

If imaginative play is to flourish and expand after a child is four or five years old, however, it seems to require some kind of social nurturance (Singer and Singer, 1979). Unless parents are tolerant of fantasy, imagine along with their children, or provide them with specific opportunities for make-believe, the amount of fantasy play is likely to decline—or even disappear. Children between the ages of nine and thirteen still enjoy make-believe activities and fantasy games, but their interest may be suppressed. Because our culture tends to discourage what it regards as nonutilitarian thought, parents and teachers—without realizing it—may signal their disapproval of fantasy (Pulaski, 1974).

Learning to Solve Problems

Free play experiences can help children learn to solve problems. The advantages that play gives

	Play	Training	Control Group
Solution time in minutes			
Task 1	3.44	3.58	5.13
Task 2	1.70	3.98	6.53
Number of hints required			
Task 1	1.92	2.25	3.78
Task 2	.42	2.03	4.22

FIGURE 10.2 When young children played freely with materials that were later used to solve a problem, they solved the problem as rapidly as children with training in the use of the materials and much faster than children who had had no experience with the materials. In addition, the children who played with the materials required fewer hints. ***(From Smith and Dutton, 1979 p. 833)***

children in a problem-solving situation were evident in a study by Kathy Sylva, Jerome Bruner, and Paul Genova (1976), who asked preschoolers to discover a way to retrieve a piece of chalk from a box without getting up from their seats at a low table. The box, whose lid fastened with a hook, rested across the table from the child, too far to be reached by stretching or with one of the sticks that lay on the table. In order to reach the chalk, children had to clamp together three pieces of wood with two "C" clamps that lay on the table, nudge the hook open, and insert the end of the stick in the box.

Children who were allowed to play freely with ten sticks and seven clamps before they were given the problem were just as likely to solve it as children who watched an adult demonstrate how to clamp the sticks together to extend their length. The playing children were not simply exploring the materials, because they did such things as use the sticks to form letters or to construct a house with the aid of the clamps. It was not the act of playing itself that led to the children's solutions, suggest the investigators, but the self-initiation that is a part of free play—and an essential part of problem solving. Playing with the materials also gave the children a chance to practice flexibility and reduced the amount of stress they might otherwise have felt when presented with the problem.

In a similar study, Peter Smith and Susan Dutton (1979) asked four-year-olds to get a marble out of a box under conditions much like those in the previous experiment. This time, instead of using clamps to join the sticks, children had to insert the sticks into holes bored in the face of wooden blocks. Reaching the box required the joining of only two sticks. As in the previous experiment, children who played freely with the materials and those who were given training in joining sticks both solved the problem faster than children in a control group. But Smith and Dutton pushed the children further, by moving the box so far away that they had to join several sticks in order to reach it. In this new situation, those who had simply "played" with the materials solved the problem significantly faster than children who had been given training, and far fewer of them required hints. Most children in the control group showed little interest in solving the new problem, and they needed many hints in order to find a solution. In this case, play allowed the children to approach the problem in a flexible manner, as Bruner (1972) has proposed, for the playing children were much more adept than any of the others at combining old routines to solve new problems.

The pleasure that comes when one finally solves a difficult problem may also become a form of play. Placed in a psychologist's laboratory and given two buttons to press, for example, children have little trouble discovering that one button delivers M&Ms more often than the other. Even rats can figure out which button pays off more often with pellets of food. If children were like rats, they would always press the button that produced the bigger payoff, but they are not. Once children catch on to the fact that the button on one side pays off 70 percent of the time and the one on the other side pays off 30 percent of the time, they generally switch from trying to get more candy to trying to outguess the machine (Lewis, 1979). They begin to play, enjoying the challenge of figuring out when the 30 percent side is most likely to pay off.

Play with Language

Language play is closely related to cognitive development. The verbal humor of preschoolers is spontaneous, original, and often rambling (McGhee, 1979). At this age, children explore the sound of words, chanting or singing a word or phrase while changing its stress or syllabic division. Catherine Garvey (1977) describes a three-year-old boy who chanted "dune buggy" over and over, becoming so absorbed in his word play that he forgot the small model of a dune buggy that had initiated his game. Since preschoolers are interested in the appearance and sound of objects and events, their verbal humor often simply exaggerates or distorts these qualities. They may, for example, pretend that a dog miaows like a cat, or call one child by the name of another. They play with word structure and with nonsense syllables, slightly changing a word's initial sound (sunny, funny, bunny, hunny) or assigning funny names (dool, peepah, diarrhea, Mrs. Fingernail,) to themselves, to their playmates, or to imaginary people.

Riddles are another favorite form of word play, becoming popular about the time children start school. This rapid development in riddle appreciation may derive in part, says Paul McGhee (1979), from the emphasis placed in school on having the right answers. Children's earliest riddles fail to meet adult standards, for they usually are simply descriptive questions, such as "What's yellow? A banana." Five- and six-year-olds often repeat such questions over and over, reveling in the capacity of language to refer to things in the world (Kirschenblatt-Gimblett, 1979). Most children at this age see riddles as questions with arbitrary answers. For that reason, their riddles often baffle adults: "Why did the monkey throw the ball? Because the mouse was yellow!"

Many riddles and jokes are based on the fact that words and phrases have more than one meaning. Children, in order to appreciate such humor, must be aware of the multiple meanings of a word or phrase and see how an unanticipated meaning resolves the ambiguity. In Thomas Shultz's (1974) analysis, a riddle is a misleading question followed by an incongruous answer. The listener must figure out how the incongruity makes sense; the pleasure comes when the listener resolves the problem by explaining the incongruous answer.

This kind of appreciation is beyond the capacity of children in the preoperational stage. For example, a four-year-old, when told that his mother could not watch him swing because "she was all tied up," asked solemnly, "What kind of rope did they use?" A child who is unable to resolve linguistic ambiguities in a spoken riddle may, however, find the same riddle funny if it is presented as a series of simplified cartoons (Pien and Rothbart, 1976). Long before children are able to resolve the incongruities in riddles, they memorize and repeat them, laughing each time they hear the now familiar riddles.

In his study of riddles, Shultz systematically analyzed children's appreciation at the ages of six, eight, ten, and twelve. The children heard a series of riddles, each having three possible answers. For example:

Why did the farmer name his hog Ink?
1. Because he kept running out of the pen.
2. Because he kept getting away.
3. Because he was black.

In variation 3, the incongruity is removed: The hog was named Ink because he was black. In variation 2, the incongruity remains but is unresolved: The answer is arbitrary and pure nonsense. In variation 1, however, the incongruity is resolved in a way that plays on words. A clear change in children's appreciation of humor appeared between the ages of six and eight. Six-year-olds found the arbitrary, nonsensical answer humorous, whereas eight-year-olds, who have moved into the concrete-operational stage, appreciated the resolution of ambiguity based on word play. Other studies (e.g., Shultz, 1976; McGhee, 1971) have found that the cognitive skills of the concrete-operational period, which we will discuss in the next chapter, are strongly related to changes in children's appreciation of humor.

Daniel Yalisove (1978) extended Shultz's approach, testing riddle comprehension and liking among nearly 600 schoolchildren in grades one through ten. He discovered that first graders prefer reality riddles, that is, riddles that involve neither word play nor absurdity but are based on conceptual tricks. For example, "How many balls of string would it take to reach the moon? One, but it would have to be a big one," tricks the listener, who at first assumes he or she is being asked to consider normal-sized balls of string. As in Shultz's study, riddles based on language ambiguity were most popular in the fifth grade. But seventh, eighth, and ninth graders preferred absurd riddles, such as "How can you fit five horses on a bicycle? Three in the basket and two on the handle bars."

Yalisove suggests three stages in the comprehension of riddles. In the first, strongest among first graders and lingering among a number of third graders, the child interprets the riddle as a test of his or her ability to tell the difference between the sensible and the silly. In the second stage, which is strongest among third graders, children focus on the reasonableness of the answer and attempt to explain away the incongruity of the riddle. They seem unable to tolerate the idea of the absurd, the illogical, or the implausible. In the third stage, which begins in the sixth grade and becomes increasingly prominent, children acknowledge the incongruity and then justify it on the basis of a special rule.

For children in this third stage, simple linguistic ambiguity has become boring, and the riddles that eight-year-olds love they find too easy. As McGhee (1979) points out, for full appreciation, the riddle must be complicated enough so that one does not immediately see the point yet easy enough so that one does not have to think too laboriously about it. Older children prefer jokes to riddles. Instead of memorizing misleading questions with incongruous answers, they trade anecdotes in which the humor is based on the behavioral expectations of others or illogical behavior and events.

PLAY AND SOCIALIZATION

It is through play with others that babies begin to develop personal competence and sociability (Ross and Kay, 1980). The early social play between babies and their caretakers, for example, provides the foundation for later, more complex interactions with others. As noted in Chapter 8, this social play usually takes the form of a game between baby and mother, which is, as Jerome Bruner (1975) points out, essentially a dialogue in action. In the give-and-take game, which begins at about three months, the mother "gives" a toy to her baby and the baby "takes" it by having it pushed into a hand. By six months, the baby reaches actively for the toy when the mother offers it. And by one year, the baby gives the toy as well as takes it—getting real pleasure from the exchange itself. Over the months, the baby has gradually learned what mother's signals mean, how to signal her, and—in playing the game—how to get things done with another person.

Peers

Play with peers serves a similarly important role in the development of sociability and personal competence (Mueller and Vandell, 1979). It was once assumed that all infants begin with solitary play, then move on to parallel play, in which two children play side by side, each intent on his or her own toy and each keeping up a running monologue that amounts to "thinking out loud." Not until later was group play thought to develop. This sequence of development was proposed when investigators concentrated on egocentrism in young children to the exclusion of their rudimentary ability to empathize with others. But recent investigations suggest that these assumptions may be too simple.

When Peter Smith (1978) studied preschoolers, observing them at play for a period of nine months, he found that parallel play is not always an inevitable step in the development of social play. Many children went directly from playing alone to playing in a group. This pattern of behavior was especially typical of three- and four-year-olds. Two-year-olds, however, often did go through a period of parallel play before they ventured into group play. Although parallel play decreases with age, says Smith, where it exists it continues through the preschool period. Other researchers (Bakeman and Brownlee, 1980) suggest that parallel play should be regarded as a strategy, not as a developmental step. They note that the preschoolers they observed seemed to use it as a means of bringing themselves into group play.

When youngsters play with their regular playmates, play's socializing effects become apparent. Anna-Beth Doyle, Jennifer Connolly, and Louis-Paul Rivest (1980) found, for example, that when children had opportunities to play with familiar peers, nearly every aspect of play changed. When playmates were strangers, children tended simply to watch each other or to engage in parallel play; but when playmates were friends, play became cooperative, with a sharp increase in the exchange of toys and conversation. Friends were generally more sociable and more competent than strangers and behaved on a higher cognitive level.

Similarly, Catherine Garvey (1977) found that young children who are familiar with one another function on a higher level of sophistication when playing than at other times. Three-year-olds at play with familiar peers sustain conversations, pay attention to each other's play, and are responsive to their friends' requests. For example, Garvey's (1979) recordings of preschoolers at play captured one three-year-old girl playing at being a baby, while directing a small boy in his role as parent. The little girl deftly switched from baby to stage director and back, talking to the boy in his two roles as playmate and parent, always keeping all the roles straight.

When children play with their friends, the level of play is more sophisticated than when playmates are strangers. *(©Alan Carey/Image Works)*

As indicated earlier, children who are playing parent, doctor, bus driver, or any adult role are indoctrinating themselves into the culture, testing what they have learned about social roles and the way society works. And, as we will see in Chapter 13, children also use social pressure to steer their playmates into what they consider appropriate sex roles. When a boy plays with dolls or a girl pretends to be a carpenter, for example, preschoolers usually stop playing with the offender and five- to seven-year-olds often directly attempt to change the offender's behavior.

Pressure from peers often makes it hard for a child to play with objects traditionally associated with the opposite sex. *(©Sepp Seitz/Woodfin Camp & Assoc.)*

As children practice a variety of roles and deal with the inevitable conflicts that arise, their skill in role-taking increases (Rubin, 1980). They begin to understand the effects of their actions on others and increasingly come to see their playmates as individuals rather than as objects of play. As they discover more about different children, their specific attachments increase, and they form friendships that may be remarkably durable.

During social play, children can try out various kinds of peer interactions, creating rules for games or developing ways to cooperate or share (Bruner, Jolly, and Sylva, 1976). This interaction gives them the opportunity to experience the results of certain social behavior within a limited setting. They may also incorporate modeling into their social play. An imaginary superhero may provide a model of generosity and helping. Or a child may learn these same skills by watching other children cooperate—for example, in a play kitchen, sharing the cooking pots and pans.

Games

The socializing function of play shows clearly in children's games, which center on shared rules. Children spend a great deal of time making these rules and usually insist that they be followed, no matter how silly they may appear to adults. Younger children consider their rules to be absolutely binding, but in later childhood they come to understand them as conventions, agreed upon for specific purposes and therefore open to modification by common consent (Piaget, 1932).

Although a leader may break a rule, children with low group status usually find themselves under tremendous pressure to conform. If they fail to do so, they often are expelled from the group and not allowed to return until they promise to abide by the game's rules. This slavish attention to detail probably serves children in several ways. They learn that social commerce must be regulated in order to sustain interaction. (At a younger age, if they do not like the rules they merely drift away from their peers.) They learn that once a formal structure has been set up, they can relax, enjoying themselves within its confines without worrying about being rejected. And rules provide a means by which new arrivals may rapidly find their place in a group.

Children's games also allow them to succeed in various ways: by decision-making ability in games of strategy, such as checkers and chess; by speed and power in games of physical skill, such as relays and baseball; and by luck in games of chance, such as cards. Children learn to compete, but within a safe world that minimizes the penalties associated with failure. Preschoolers attach little significance to who wins or loses;

For children, the playing of games tests out adult skills such as the ability to plan strategy. *(©Leonard Speier 1982)*

Although older children enjoy winning competitive games, the outcome is secondary; their primary enjoyment comes from playing the game. *(©Sylvia Johnson 1980/Woodfin Camp & Assoc.)*

they do not worry about prizes and show little concern if a game is not finished. Even among older children, where competition is strong and the desire to win high, children like games that restart almost immediately so that everyone gets a new chance. In contrast to adults, they often get most of their enjoyment from experiencing, not from winning.

In the course of games, children can also discover their own capacities and worth. Many games of prowess allow children to test their physical abilities, both against their own standards and in comparison with the abilities of others. Such games seem designed to let children explore the capabilities of their own bodies for personal satisfaction, so that follow-the-leader, skating, tag, and hopscotch represent competition with the self as much as with peers. Older children who set out on an expedition to no-where-in-particular may climb a fence, walk along a narrow board over a ditch, swing on a rope, jump a gulley, crawl through a drainpipe, and jump off a high ledge—all to exercise their physical powers and to share the excitement with their companions.

Some of the excitement in games reflects experiences from the world around children that are frightening or beyond the child's comprehension or control. For example, Fritz Redl (1959) cites themes that run through children's games and finds that racing, chasing, attacking, seducing, capturing, harassing, searching, and rescuing appear repeatedly. Within the world of the game, children experience excitement and tension. Playing hide-and-seek in the dark, the child feels the terror of waiting to be pounced on. The fun of such games seems to depend on being frightened in the context of safety. They provide quick reversals of tension within a limited and structured period.

PLAY AROUND THE WORLD

Some familiar aspects of play can be found in most societies: hide-and-seek, tag, tug of war, and riddles and other types of language play turn up again and again in the observations of anthropologists. There is great variation, however, in what a society considers play and in how much time children spend playing. For example, dancing is a form of play for most people in Western

Children around the world play similar games; the circle game that absorbs these Chinese children closely resembles a game found on most primary school playgrounds in America. ***(©René Burri/Magnum)***

societies, but in Bali dancing is "sacred work," a part of the religion (Kirschenblatt-Gimblett, 1979). Similarly, lacrosse is considered a game by most youngsters, but it is a religious ritual among Cherokee Indians.

Time for play also varies widely. When Bernice Whiting and John Whiting (1975) analyzed observations of children from six different cultures, they found that the amount of playtime ranged from 17 percent among the Nyansongo, a farming community in western Kenya, to 76 percent among the children of Taira, a farming village on the coast of Okinawa. One reason for this marked difference in playtime is the amount of work expected from children. In Nyansongo, for example, over half of the three- and four-year-olds worked at carrying wood and water, preparing food, gardening, cleaning, and taking care of animals. In Taira, although three-year-olds cleaned and swept, not until they were of school age did most children take care of animals or carry wood and water, and most children neither gardened nor cooked. A six-year-old in Taira also learned to combine fun with work—playing with peers while caring for a younger sibling who was strapped to his or her back (Maretzki and Maretzki, 1963).

As noted earlier, enacting adult roles is familiar play in most societies. In many African communities, for example, boys and girls "play house" by building and thatching small huts and making their own versions of the clay pots, grass mats and baskets, axes, spears, and bow and arrows used by their elders (Leacock, 1976).

Symbolic play is not, however, encouraged in all societies. In Nyansongo and in areas of rural Egypt, for example, children not only lack conditions for play but also are kept from playing by adults (Levine and Levine, 1963; Ammar, 1954). Dina Feitelson (1972) found that Middle Eastern mothers neither modeled play for their children nor provided play objects. In addition, they seemed to feel threatened, and interfered actively, whenever imaginative elements entered a play situation.

Besides the *atmosphere* provided by adults, Feitelson (1977) notes three other factors are likely to affect the amount of imaginative play found in a society: space, time, and toys. *Space* is important; when children are prevented from using whatever space is available, play cannot flourish. Among Kurdish immigrants to Israel, for example, children have nowhere to play and are literally expected to be seen but not heard. Even in good-sized homes, their play space is limited to a bedroom, while the ornamental garden and other rooms are reserved for adults. Under these conditions, two- and three-year-olds are quietly passive.

In some societies, as we have seen, children may not have *time* to play. The busy children of Nyansongo, for example, spend 41 percent of their time working (Whiting and Whiting, 1975). As a result, children can be so incorporated into adult society that even six- and seven-year-olds find their days filled with chores, baby tending, and errands.

Finally, although children do not require elaborate toys, they do need *play materials.* Some children grow up in areas where the country's aridity makes natural play objects such as leaves, sticks, and cones scarce or unavailable. In undeveloped societies, household objects may be so scarce that none can be spared for children's play.

These four factors interact so that the amount of symbolic play varies widely from cul-

CHILDREN'S ACTIVITIES						
Activity	**Simpler Cultures**			**Complex Cultures**		
	Nyansongo (Kenya)	Juxtlahuaca (Mexico)	Tarong (Philippines)	Taira (Okinawa)	Khalapur (India)	Orchard Town (U.S.A.)
Play	17%	49%	48%	76%	31%	52%
Casual social interaction	43%	37%	31%	11%	46%	30%
Work	41%	8%	14%	9%	11%	2%
Learning	0%	6%	7%	4%	9%	16%

FIGURE 10.3 The amount of time children spend playing varies from culture to culture, with some societies demanding a great deal of work from very young children. These proportions were based on the observations of anthropologists in each culture. ***(From Whiting and Whiting, 1975)***

ture to culture. Among the Nyansongo, for example, observers saw only two instances of make-believe play in the two years they spent observing children in that culture (Levine and Levine, 1963).

Since atmosphere, space, time, and toys are affected by the child's immediate situation, it might be expected that socioeconomic level would be as important as culture in determining imaginative play. In a study comparing white South African preschoolers with Israeli preschoolers, Orlee Udwin and Diana Shmukler (1981) found that socioeconomic level was indeed the primary factor affecting levels of imaginative play, but that culture also played a part. In this case, the effect was due not to a lack of space, time, or play materials among the preschoolers but to the atmosphere provided by the parents. The low levels of imaginative play among lower-class children in both societies were attributed to the lack of direct teaching and modeling by adults that help youngsters to relate their experiences and to use them in solving problems. Among the middle-class children, the Israeli children showed much higher levels of imaginative play than the South African children, a difference that was attributed to the high levels of peer interaction among Israeli children and to the South African mother's tendency to step in and organize her children's activities. Although some researchers (e.g., Murphy, 1972) have suggested that low-income American children show few instances of make-believe play, a study of black, low-income preschoolers found fantasy play levels similar to those noted among white, middle-income children (McLoyd, 1980).

Play also indoctrinates children into the values of a culture. Children in Western industrialized societies play a game to win; but among the Tangu of New Guinea, the original game of *taketak* was not over until everybody had the same score (Burridge, 1976). In fact, skill at *taketak,* a game that involves spinning a top into a mass of palm spines that had been stuck in the ground, required a player who was ahead to spin the top among the spines *without* bringing down any spines that belonged to the opponent. In recent years, however, the rules of *taketak* have changed. After extensive contact with Western societies, a new form of the game has emerged. In today's *taketak,* two teams compete and the goal is to knock over all the spines belonging to the other team. Apparently, as a culture's values change, so may the rules of its games.

PLAY AS THERAPY

While many psychologists were treating play, in Susanne Millar's (1968) words, as a "linguistic wastebasket" for behavior that looked voluntary but seemed to have no obvious function, therapists were using it with their young patients to discover the sources of emotional problems and to help troubled children work through their difficulties. Such a use of play is in harmony with Piaget's (1951) analysis, in which he described symbolic play as essentially egocentric and as transforming the real into the desired. Piaget wrote:

> In most cases, indeed, the doll only serves as an opportunity for the child to re-live symbolically her own life in order to assimilate more easily its various aspects as well as to resolve daily conflicts and realize unsatisfied answers. (p. 107)

Piaget pointed out that during play, children can relive past experiences, deliberately recalling fears but in a situation where they can control them. The symbolism that appears in children's play, said Piaget, can be as revealing as the symbolism of dreams.

Psychodynamic theorists have agreed. For example, Melanie Klein (1932), who devised the Play Technique, provided children with small toys—especially dolls that could stand for family members. The toys were regarded as a vocabulary through which the child could express both thoughts and feelings. Klein believed that by interpreting the child's play as if it were a dream, the therapist could begin to understand the child's problems. In a more directed situation, Erik Erikson (1963) gave small toys to ten- to twelve-year-olds and asked them to "construct an exciting scene out of an imaginary moving picture." He found that the instructions had the same effect as the psychoanalyst's request that an adult patient "associate freely"; themes that appeared in the children's play were often intimately related to their past experiences.

It is often difficult for children, especially small ones, to tell a therapist what is troubling them; but their play may express their thoughts and feelings. So therapists often provide family dolls, a doll house, small animals, blocks, sand, clay, paint, etc., that allow children to express specific emotions—for example, guns, darts, toy soldiers, or punching dolls to express aggression.

Some therapists believe that the play of a troubled child is more than a way of expressing problems; play can also heal. Playing in a therapist's office may be more therapeutic than playing at home, because part of the child's problems may be connected with feelings of hatred, fear, or guilt toward parents or other family members. Play at home then becomes insecure and liable to be interrupted by a marauding sibling or a nagging parent. Erikson (1963) proposes that the child who today needs the safety of the therapist's office for play might, a few generations ago, have played in the safe harbor of grandmother's or a favorite aunt's home.

Many therapists take the position that once children have a good relationship with a therapist, they can resolve their own problems through play in the secure conditions of the therapist's office. The therapist may help children clarify their feelings about events in their lives, but it is the child's own play in the context of the positive relationship that works the therapy. The play need not center around dolls or other representational toys; conflicts can be worked out during the course of, say, a game of checkers. In fact, Virginia Axline (1969) describes the case of a twelve-year-old boy who suddenly turned a checker game into a dramatization of his problems regarding his divorced parents.

Sometimes drawing is also used, as in the "squiggle technique" invented by Donald Winnicott (1971). First the therapist, then the child, makes a squiggle on a piece of paper, which the other turns into a simple drawing. As the therapy session progresses and a series of squiggles have been passed back and forth, the child conveys his or her feelings and may, with the aid of the therapist, develop self-understanding and a way to deal with a problem.

As we have seen, play has many faces and serves many functions in the development of the child. As we turn to the changes that take place in children's thinking during the preschool years, it would be well to remember that much of the experience that brings about those changes comes when the child is at play.

SUMMARY

1. The same behavior can be play in one instance and not in another. To be considered play, an activity must be pleasurable, an end in itself, and spontaneously and freely chosen, and it must involve some active engagement by the player. Piaget believed that play was primarily assimilation, a proposal supported by research showing that children first explore a strange object, then play with it. Play serves many functions; it allows children to develop increased competence and mastery of the physical world, to gain knowledge about society and their future roles in it, to experiment with behavior that could not otherwise be tried, to develop sociability, to achieve dexterity, and to increase their general health.

2. A baby's first play is purely physical, and the pleasure of repeated movement will continue into adulthood. Children's skill at physical games depends upon strength, speed, and coordination. Some skills emerge naturally with maturation and practice, but others may require formal instruction. Rough-and-tumble play is always social and is more common among boys than among girls. Its basic purpose may be the formation and consolidation of friendships, although it also provides a safe way to practice aggressive behavior.

3. Play develops through three stages: practice play, which is the repetition of physical movements that help an infant gain a sense of mastery over the world; symbolic play, in which children use imagination; and games, which are structured by rules. The earliest symbolic play requires the use of objects that are similar to the real thing; but by the time children are nearly four, they find it easy to use dissimilar objects when making believe. Imaginative children tend to be happier and to be able to wait longer, resist temptation better, and remember details more than unimaginative children. After children are about five years old, symbolic play declines or disappears unless parents encourage it.

4. Free play experiences can help children learn to solve problems, teaching them to approach a problem in a flexible manner. Language play is closely related to cognitive development, and it moves from the spontaneous, rambling humor of the preschooler to the appreciation of multiple word meanings and the resolution of ambiguity that characterize the humor of older children.

5. Play with peers serves an important role in the development of sociability and personal competence. Although it was once assumed that parallel play was a necessary stage between solitary and group play, research indicates that not all children engage in parallel play and that it may be a strategy and not a step in development. Games center on shared rules and teach children that social commerce must be regulated to sustain interaction. Games also allow children to succeed through decision-making ability, speed and power, or luck, permitting them to compete in a situation that minimizes the penalties of failure.

6. Some types of play are found in most societies, but there is great variation in what a society considers play. Some societies discourage symbolic play; for it to flourish, children require an encouraging adult atmosphere, time to play, space to play in, and toys. Socioeconomic level can be as important as culture in determining the level of imaginative play. Play indoctrinates children into the values of a culture, and as a culture's values change, so may the rules of its games.

7. Piaget and psychodynamic theorists agree that play can be used both to help children express their problems and to work through them. Dramatic play in a therapist's office has been widely used in therapy with children, as have games and drawings.

11 COGNITION: CHANGES IN THINKING

Brian and his father are having a heart-to-heart talk. With all the seriousness of his four years, Brian begins to speak about getting married when he grows up. "I'll move into a different house," he says, "then I won't be your son anymore." One of the attributes that defined Brian's concept of "son" is living in the same house as his father. Because in Brian's experience the father of the child referred to as "son" has either been present or clearly known to be living at home, Brian's understanding of the concept is not illogical. Yet his definition does not correspond to the one accepted by the culture, and he will have to modify it to remove the notion that residence is one of the concept's defining attributes.

Redefinition of concepts is only one of the intellectual tasks that face the young child. In this chapter we will look at the cognitive changes that occur during early childhood and find that they are considerable. We will discover that what children's senses pick up helps determine their concepts of the world. We will see that the young child uses self-generated as well as culturally transmitted symbols, and we will look at the way burgeoning linguistic capabilities mesh with intellectual skills. We will see the child as artist and learn that children's drawings can be exercises in problem solving. By examining children's attention, memory, and problem-solving skills, we will see that the young child's thought changes both in quality and in quantity, and that meaningful context increases a child's understanding of the world. We will find that children gradually come to realize that another person may not experience the world as they do and that as their knowledge of the objective world increases, their understanding of causality becomes more realistic. Finally, we will discover that through their interactions with others, children gradually refine concepts in the direction of their adult use. Throughout these early years, one characteristic remains fairly constant: the child's basic curiosity about the environment and the quest for meaning.

REPRESENTATIONAL SKILLS

During the second year of life, infants begin to use symbols, and this development helps free them from the constraints of the immediate world of experience. Young children use symbols to represent an ever-widening range of objects and events, but most of their information is stored in images, not words. In the last chapter, we saw an increasing use of representational skills in play and the role of play as a tool in the child's understanding of the world. Children use imitation, language, and graphic symbols in the same way, and all these representational skills become closely linked to their learning, reasoning, and acquisition of concepts.

Concepts

All concepts are symbols, but a concept can be applied to many related examples. For instance, the word "teddy bear," which is the symbol three-year-old Lauren uses as a mental representation of stuffed bears, applies to all the stuffed bears Lauren sees, no matter where she goes. However, the symbol "Pooh" stands for only her own teddy bear. In order to develop concepts, children must be able to separate a symbol from a particular example (Lauren's own teddy bear), and they must understand that the symbol's independent characteristics (ears, button eyes, furry coat, softness, and squeak) describe many different teddy bears. On a relatively simple level, children learn about the visible properties of specific objects. They know, for example, that the trucks called fire engines are red and have long hoses and sirens, and that animals known as elephants are massive and have long trunks and tusks.

Young children tend to form their concepts around both the perceptual qualities and the function of objects, and function often seems to predominate. For example, when preschoolers are asked to respond to a word with the first word they can think of, a four-year-old will reply to "bed" with "sleep." When Katherine Nelson (1978) asked preschoolers to define an apple, ten out of the fourteen said "eat." Three children replied with such perceptual qualities as skin and seeds, but it was the apple's edibility—its function from the standpoint of the child—that seemed most important. Given the same task, an older child might reply to the word "apple" with "fruit," its semantic class, or with "pear," another member of the same class.

It may be, as Jeremy Anglin (1977) speculates, that the first example in a group a child hears named provides a visual basis for the concept. For example, the child's concept of car is probably based on the appearance of the family compact car. Later, the child adds to this image the attributes that determine the group. For the concept "car," these attributes are likely to include both perceptual attributes (four wheels, doors, headlights, engine sounds) and function (needs gas, goes fast, transports people, carries groceries). The way the child first visualizes the concept remains part of the later representation, but the initial image is enriched with more specific as well as more general referents. Both appearance and function are important in concept formation; the debate is over which aspect is dominant.

Symbol use develops extensively during early childhood, but the young child continues to be an active explorer of the concrete, real world. The use of symbols to represent reality does not replace the child's natural curiosity about and exploration of the physical universe but supplements it. In fact, precisely because many of the concepts that young children acquire about people, events, and objects derive from their own experience, the concepts are often imperfect by adult definitions (Anglin, 1979).

For example, if Lauren's parents do not tell her explicitly that "food" refers to all edible things, she may err in using the term until she discovers for herself the common attribute of fruits, vegetables, fish, meat, and poultry: edibility. Until Lauren has abstracted the property of edibility, she may refer to some nonfoods as food, and may fail to include in the category some of the things she eats that she has never heard others call food, such as lollipops—a tendency we will explore in the next chapter. Because adults tend to provide young children with few verbal definitions of concepts, the child relies extensively on his or her own powers of discovery and abstraction in figuring out adult concepts. These powers may not always be equal to the challenge (Ausubel, 1968), and one important function of formal schooling is to remove some of the guesswork in concept learning. Teachers and books supplement the child's self-discovery method with systematically presented verbal and nonverbal definitions and examples of concepts.

Imitation

Babies' ability to imitate what they see and hear advances markedly at the beginning of the second year. These imitations are primitive symbols and provide evidence for the existence of other symbols, in picture or in sound, within the child's mind. These mental symbols, of course, cannot be observed, but adults can infer their presence from the child's actions.

When four-year-old David watches his father read a book and himself takes up a book, turns the pages, and pretends to read, his behavior stands for the actions of another. This kind of direct and immediate imitation of an action is on the same cognitive level as an imitation by an eight-month-old. However, if David picks up a book the next day and imitates his father reading, then in addition to viewing his behavior as a symbol of reading at the level of action, we can infer that David has created a mental image of his father in the act of reading. This memory is a condensed, internal imitation, in thought rather than in action, and it allows the child to imitate some behavior long after the event. Deferred imitation, which develops in the last half of the second year, is common among young children.

Drawing, which is discussed later in this section, is another form of imitation. In this case, the imitation is reduced to a graphic, schematic representation. The child depicts only certain features of a scene, and the drawing's resemblance to the original scene of father reading is less a "copy" than was his physical imitation of the act. The symbolic nature of imitation makes it a milestone in intellectual development, because it forms the basis for human civilization: for language, mathematics, science, and the arts (Piaget, 1951).

Language

Language is the supreme representational skill, and the relationship between language and thinking is close. Because we use verbal symbols for things and actions, we can reason rapidly and efficiently, figuring out, for example, how many miles a car gets from each gallon in a tank of gas. We use language to refer not only to concrete entities and simple actions performed on them, but to complex events and intangible relationships as well. It is only because we possess well-developed symbol systems that we are able to reason about things at complex, abstract levels. We can reason about unicorns and time travel—about purely imaginary or hypothetical situations that never have occurred and probably never will.

Investigators have used a variety of approaches to look at the developmental relationship between language and thought in children. John Flavell, David Beach, and Jack Chinsky (1966) were interested in finding whether five-year-olds spontaneously use language to help them solve a simple memory problem. They showed children pictures of familiar objects, pointing to some of them, and later asked the children to point to the same pictures in the same order. The five-year-olds remembered fewer pictures than the eight-year-olds. It appears that the children's difference in performance on this task related to differences in their use of language. A majority of the eight-year-old children repeated the names of the pictures that they had to remember. However, almost none of the five-year-olds did this, indicating that young children do not automatically use the language at their command in all cases where it would be helpful.

When told to use language as an aid in observational learning, however, they are capable of using it effectively, as Brian Coates and Willard Hartup (1969) discovered. They showed preschoolers a movie of a man doing such things as building a tower of blocks and whirling a hula hoop, telling the children they would later have to act out what they saw. Four-year-olds who followed the investigators' suggestion and described the model's actions as he performed them could later act out more of these actions than children in a control group who watched the model passively.

Some investigators (Kendler, 1972) believe that language is critical to concept formation, and Marion Blank and Wagner Bridger (1964) have found at least one instance in which it is essential. They discovered that young children could not discriminate between one and two flashes of light unless they could attach verbal labels to them. When the experimenters told a child to "pick the one that goes like this," and pointed to the light flashing once, but "don't pick the one that goes like this," and pointed to the light flashing twice, a young child could not master the task. But a child of the same age who was told to pick the light that flashes one time but not the light that flashes two times easily learned to follow the experimenters' instructions.

Although five-year-olds may not use language on their own as an aid to memory, they do use it extensively to guide their behavior and to help them plan their actions. For example, young children often talk to themselves as they play. Indeed, a small boy may actually engage in a dialogue with himself as he draws a picture or builds a tower of blocks: "First I'll put this block over here and it will be the fence . . . no, put it there. OK . . . now this one goes here . . . and this one on top. Oh-oh, it's going to fall down . . . so put it next to the fence where it won't fall." In this case, the child's language is "thinking out loud."

The relationship between language and cognitive development has been studied by Hans Furth, who has conducted research on the intellectual abilities of deaf children. Most children who are born deaf or who become deaf in infancy learn to speak their native language haltingly, if at all. However, intellectual development proceeds even among those who never learn a spoken language. According to Furth (1964, 1969), the thinking processes of deaf, linguistically deficient, elementary-school-aged children are generally similar to those of children who hear and are linguistically competent. On some types of cognitive tests, young deaf children do not perform as well as young hearing children, but Furth attributes this difference to the restricted experience and training of the very young deaf child, which becomes a less important factor when he or she enters school. On the basis of research with the deaf, Furth (1969) agrees with Piaget (1967) that intellectual development is considerably less dependent on linguistic ability than most people assume.

Language is only one of several symbol systems. The deaf themselves frequently use sign language, and human beings also use visual imagery, pictorial representation, and written notational systems (such as the symbols of music or complex electronic circuits) to depict the world. People often think with these tools. However, some intelligent behavior can be acquired without any symbol system at all. Indeed, infants acquire a substantial set of intelligent behavior before they begin to use verbal symbols. It is safe to say, however, that language development and cognitive development continually interact, and that both are primary tools for bringing order to the world.

Using Graphic Symbols

During these early years, the young child also begins to use artistic media, representing objects, animals, and people with crayons, pencils, paints, and clay. Many investigators have noted a three-step sequence in young children's drawings of a person. At first the child tends to make a circular figure with few or no differentiating parts, such as the various organs and limbs. Somewhat later the drawings assume the shape of a tadpole: The head and limbs are attached directly, but the body has no trunk. Finally, the child draws a complete person with head, trunk, and attached limbs.

Claire Golomb (1973) wondered if a child's early imperfect drawings reflected limited cognitive competence or simply inexperience with graphic media. So she asked 105 children, rang-

FIGURE 11.1 Two examples of the scoring criteria used by Golomb to assess children's cognitive competence from the way they produce human figures using different media. ***(From Golomb, 1973)***

ing in age from three to seven years, to produce the human body in a variety of media. Older children produced more differentiated and better-organized figures than younger children did, no matter what the medium. But both the medium used and the investigator's instructions had a definite effect on the nature of the figure the children constructed. Golomb therefore sees the young child as an inventor of symbols rather than as a confused and incompetent copier of what he or she sees, and believes that the inferior performance of younger children may be due in part to inexperience in using artistic media and a more playful attitude toward the symbols they create.

The charm and playfulness of children's art may keep us from realizing that all features of their drawings are aspects of problem solving. In a series of studies, Jacqueline Goodnow (1977) discovered that young children follow rules in their drawings. When they leave out part of the human figure, for example, the omission may be due to a reluctance to use space that they regard as "psychologically unavailable," since they seem to follow a principle Goodnow calls "to each its own space." For this reason, young children are unlikely to draw both hair and arms on the circle that represents a head.

In one study, Goodnow gave children uncompleted drawings consisting of a rectangle with two circles filling most of the space beneath it. This was a train, Goodnow told children, but it needed two more wheels, and their task was to finish the drawing. Some children put wheels on top of the train, some on the side, some squeezed in tiny wheels beneath the train, some simply extended the drawing to give them room for additional wheels. But out of a hundred chil-

When watching a child draw a crude human figure, it is easy to forget that all children's drawings are aspects of problem solving. *(© Jeffrey Foxx/Woodfin Camp & Assoc.)*

dren, only one drew wheels that overlapped the ones already in the drawing, thus violating the "to each its own space" rule.

As children's drawings become more complex, one can trace the course of cognitive development in them. As Goodnow points out, "graphic work is truly 'visible thinking.' "

INFORMATION PROCESSING

During the preschool years, children's thought appears to change in both quality and quantity; their store of information increases and their understanding of it deepens. In information-processing terms, the various cognitive processes, such as perception, attention, and memory, function more rapidly and efficiently. As a result, children can handle complex information and can process more of it.

Perceptual Advances

As their perceptual skills develop, young children isolate and abstract more of the distinctive features of their environment. They glean more precise information from sensory stimulation, and they pick up the information more efficiently, learning to filter out what is irrelevant and to attend to important elements. According to Eleanor Gibson (1974), as children develop they respond to different aspects of what they see. One-year-olds can discriminate the features of the human face and thus can tell one face from another; by the time they are six, many children are already adept readers, readily differentiating the features that distinguish the various letters of the alphabet.

Between the ages of three and six, there is a dramatic improvement in the child's ability to transfer information from one sense to another. This advance shows clearly in tasks of intersensory recognition (Blank and Bridger, 1964; Zaporozhets, 1965). In one study (Zaporozhets, 1965), V. P. Zinshensko and A. G. Ruzskaya gave children of three, four, five, and six abstract forms that they were permitted to explore by touch but could not see. The researchers then tested the children to find out if they could recognize at sight objects they had explored with their fingers. At about age five, there was a sharp jump in performance. This improvement in intersensory coordination probably develops because, as five- and six-year-olds are exposed to objects and sophisticated methods of exploration, their mental images become increasingly detailed and precise.

Another kind of intersensory coordination, in this case the relationship between visual and auditory perception, has been investigated by Alice Vlietstra and John Wright (1971), who wondered if learning to tell differences between sound intensities makes it easier for youngsters to tell differences between intensities of visual stimuli. If young children come to understand that the quality "stimulus intensity" can be perceived by any of their sense organs, then their experience with intensity in one sense, such as hearing, should transfer to a different sense, such as vision. However, if experience with intensity does not transfer from one sense to another, children would find their experience with sound of no help when they tried to discriminate between the intensity of two visual stimuli, such as two lights of varying brightness. When Vlietstra and Wright tested children who had learned to discriminate the intensity of sounds, they found that the skill indeed transferred; the children found it easier to discriminate differences in visual intensity provided that the same general levels of intensity were considered correct in both tasks. Transfer of this sort helps children coordinate the information they gather through their separate senses into increasingly complex perceptions of the world.

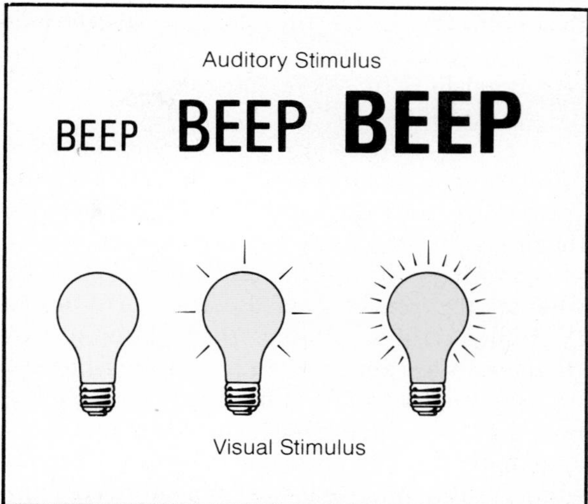

FIGURE 11.2 After learning to discriminate among different intensities of sound, young children found it easier to discriminate among comparable differences in intensities of light, indicating transfer of experience from one sense to another, as discussed in the text.

Attention

Children's concepts of the world depend on which characteristics of it get their attention. As their thought processes become increasingly sophisticated, they look at objects more systematically and their ability to focus their attention also increases.

Scanning The way children look at things and the things they notice suggest a developmental sequence. When four-year-olds look at a picture, for example, their attention is first caught by the center of interest and they scan downward from that point. From the time they are about five, however, children scan a picture from top to bottom regardless of where the center of interest lies (Day, 1975).

Young children also glance randomly from point to point in a display, and they tend to stop scanning before they have all the information they need. In one study, children looked at simple drawings of houses and tried to decide whether the houses were the same or different (Vurpillot, 1968). When they differed, the changes always appeared in one of the windows, where curtains, blinds, a birdcage, or a window box might be added. Five-year-olds scanned unsystematically, and they failed to inspect every window. But nine-year-olds began at the top, compared each pair of windows in turn, and examined every window in the drawing. Such differences in scanning patterns indicate that changes in attention continue into later childhood, as children develop techniques for acquiring visual information and learn what aspects of the environment it pays to notice.

Two- and three-year olds tend to sort objects by color; by the time they are four most will pay more attention to the form of objects. *(© Frostie/Woodfin Camp & Assoc.*

Focused Attention Young children are most likely to look only at what interests them, and this preference plays an important role in their learning to discriminate among objects and events. For example, most children between the ages of four and six tend to pay greater attention to the form of objects than to their color, whereas those between two and three generally prefer color to form (Stevenson, 1972). If young children are required to sort objects of various colors according to their shapes, those who initially attend to shape will find this task fairly easy, but those who first attend to color will find the task more difficult.

These color and form preferences can be changed, as Joan Gusinow and Louis Price (1972) discovered in a study of four- to six-year-olds. The researchers first determined which dimension children preferred, by asking them to match blocks. Then the children were allowed to earn toys by matching blocks on the basis of the other dimension, so that the ones who matched blocks by shape had to match by color to get a toy, and vice versa. When these children were later given another matching test, a large proportion of them voluntarily switched preferences, with many who had originally preferred color matching by shape, and many who had originally preferred shape matching by color. In addition, Gusinow and Price found that children who were also required to name their unpreferred dimension (color or shape) to earn toys were more likely to switch their preferences on later tests than children who were not required to name it. Appropriate rewards and the use of language apparently are effective in altering children's preferences. As other studies have shown, reinforcement seems to focus a child's attention, making it probable that he or she will

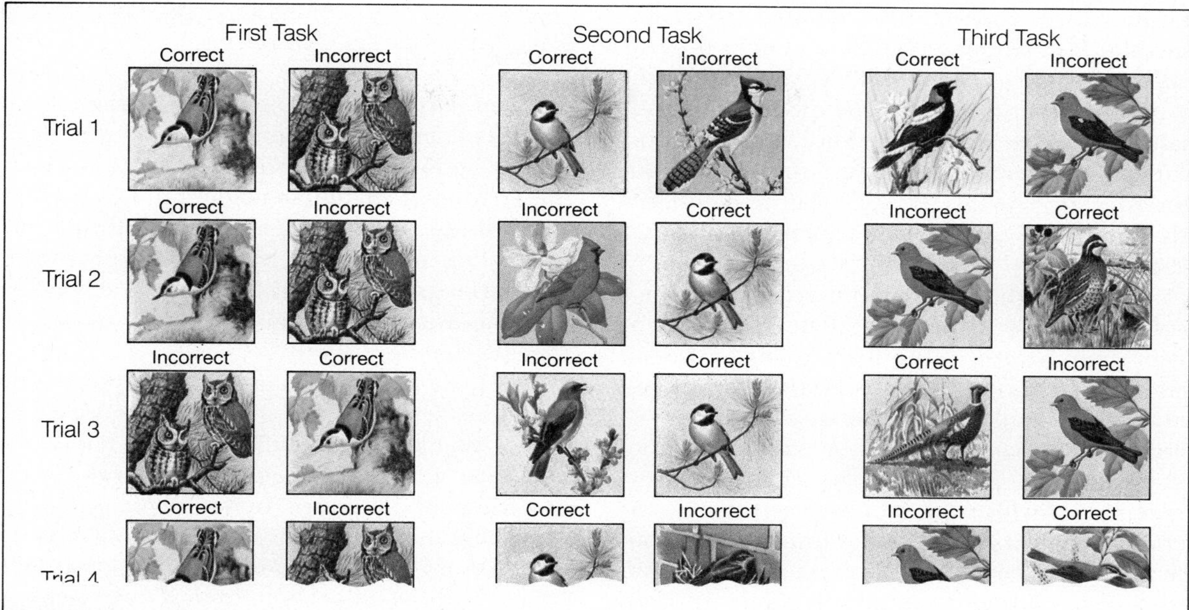

FIGURE 11.3 These pictures are similar to those used in White's experiment on the discrimination learning of younger and older children. ***(Adapted from S. White, 1965)***

indeed pay attention to the important features of a task (Pick, Frankel, and Hess, 1975).

When confronted with a problem that requires sustained attention to one or two properties or dimensions and deliberate ignoring of other, irrelevant information, the four- or six-year-old is usually less effective than the eight-year-old in solving the problem (Osler and Kofsky, 1965). Younger children tend to respond to irrelevant cues, which of course hinders their performance. They also are not as proficient as eight-year-olds in classifying information into categories that are relevant to the task.

This developmental difference showed clearly in an experiment by Sheldon White (1966). Young children were compared with nine- and ten-year-olds on three discrimination-learning tasks. White presented each child with pairs of bird pictures, giving the child a marble or a piece of candy every time he or she chose the right picture. In the first task, the child saw the same pair of bird pictures on every trial; the same picture was always correct, but the position of the pictures changed. In the second task, the same bird picture was always correct, but the wrong picture changed from trial to trial. In the third task, the wrong picture remained the same throughout, but the correct picture was different on each trial. Eight- and nine-year-olds learned all three discriminations at the same speed, but young children were hampered by White's procedure of varying the cues on the second and third tasks. They learned which picture was correct much faster in the first problem. Although younger children had greater difficulty than older children did, they still solved the problems; it simply took them longer.

The young child's less efficient attending does not mean that he or she has a "short attention span." Many youngsters spend long periods of time exploring objects that interest them. Their dedicated perseverance at a task may even bewilder their parents. For example, after the fourth or fifth reading of a picture book, Lauren may say, "Daddy, read it to me again," although by that time her father may be quite bored and inattentive to the simple plot with its limited vocabulary and sentence structure. Obviously, attention span depends as much on the nature of the material as on the intellectual level of the person.

John Wright and Alice Vlietstra (1975) believe that between the ages of three and six a major shift occurs in the features that control children's attention. Before children are three, they are primarily explorers; their attention is motivated by curiosity and is caught by the prominence of a stimulus. As children grow older, this playful exploration gives way to systematic search, a goal-oriented strategy based on the relevance and informativeness of stimuli rather than on their prominence. Exploration is playful and involves rapid, impulsive responding, whereas searching is focused, task-oriented, and slower. Exploration is controlled primarily by features in the environment, whereas searching is guided mostly by logic and the need for information. Despite the impulsive nature of exploration, some tasks are more appropriately handled by its use. Tasks requiring imagination or novel solutions are best handled by curiosity and exploration, say Wright and Vlietstra, but tasks that have a logical solution require a searching strategy. A child's cognitive competence, they believe, depends to a large degree on the ability to bring attentional processes under the control of internal goals, so that the child is not continually distracted by objects and events in the environment.

Memory

The young child's memory develops steadily from babyhood, and researchers have systematically investigated various aspects of its development, studying how children acquire, store, and retrieve information; how well they retain it; and how well they understand the workings of memory (Ornstein and Corsale, 1979). As children get older, they become more skillful at **encoding** (registering information) and **retrieval** (getting information back again).

Theoretical Views Researchers who study memory from Piaget's perspective believe that it cannot be looked at in isolation but can only be understood in relation to cognition. Researchers who study memory from an information-processing perspective believe that once they grasp the processes involved when a person remembers, they will begin to understand cognition (Perlmutter, 1980).

Those who take an information-processing view look at memory in one of two ways. Some (e.g., Atkinson and Shiffrin, 1968) apply the computer analogy by seeing the memory system as a series of structures. In this *multistore* model, information is stored in three ways: in **sensory registers,** where information begins to disappear in about three seconds; in **short-term store,** a temporary working memory, where active information is held; and in **long-term store,** where information is stored indefinitely. Improvements in memory as children get older come about as they develop control over the memory processes and can keep information moving through the system and in and out of long-term storage.

Other information-processing theorists (e.g., Cermak and Craik, 1979) focus on the stages of information processing, describing it as involving *levels of processing.* Information is analyzed at increasingly deeper levels, from the initial perceptual level to deeper levels of meaning. Information that is not analyzed at deeper levels is soon forgotten, so that memory is a by-product of interaction with information (Ornstein and Corsale, 1979). In the levels-of-processing view, improvements in memory with age develop as children grow more expert at encoding and analyzing material at deeper levels.

In the dialectical approach to memory, information is processed at various levels, but memory improves with age as the result of interaction—not simply between techniques and information but between the child's memory, understanding, and role-taking ability as well. In order to understand memory, dialectical psychologists examine it in the context of the child's situation, his or her goals and personal history, and the history of the society (Meacham, 1977).

No matter what their theoretical view, psychologists believe that memory can be demonstrated by recognition, by reconstruction, or by recall.

Recognition Recognition is the simplest form of memory. As we saw in Chapter 7, even young infants can recognize something they have seen before. From Piaget's point of view, recognition is simple because it is based on perception and on sensorimotor schemes. From an information-processing point of view, recognition is simple because it requires a child merely to match a present perception with a representation in memory.

Young children readily show their recognition skills. In a typical experiment, Marvin Daehler and Mary O'Connor (1980) tested recognition in two- and three-year-olds by showing them pairs of common objects. Later the youngsters looked at different pairs of objects, each of which included an object they had previously seen. In both groups, children strongly preferred to look at the objects they had never seen, indicating that they recognized the old objects. In another study, two-year-olds did as well as four-year-olds in recognizing that an object was strange to them, but the older children were better at recognizing familiar objects, suggesting that the ability to represent objects in memory improves during early childhood (Myers and Perlmutter, 1978).

Five-year-olds are quite good at recognizing simple objects, but their skills at scanning and selecting relevant information are still undeveloped and they lack experience. Although they can recognize pictures of familiar objects as accurately as adults, adults do much better with pictures of strange or unusual objects (Nelson and Kosslyn, 1976). Once information is processed, however, a preschooler can remember it about as well as an adult.

Reconstruction Reconstructive memory involves reproducing something that has been seen or heard, and young children are often quite good at it. The tasks used to show reconstruction typically require children to manipulate concrete objects and to repeat a natural order of events. As a result, in Piaget's terms, the child's action schemes are called into play and he or she intentionally reproduces the action. In some studies where children use sticks or matches to reconstruct models they have seen earlier, their models are more accurate than their drawings from memory (Piaget and Inhelder, 1973).

Even children as young as two or three are capable of reconstructive memory. In one experiment, when young children had to reconstruct a display of toys by putting each small toy in the same compartment of a plain wooden box that it

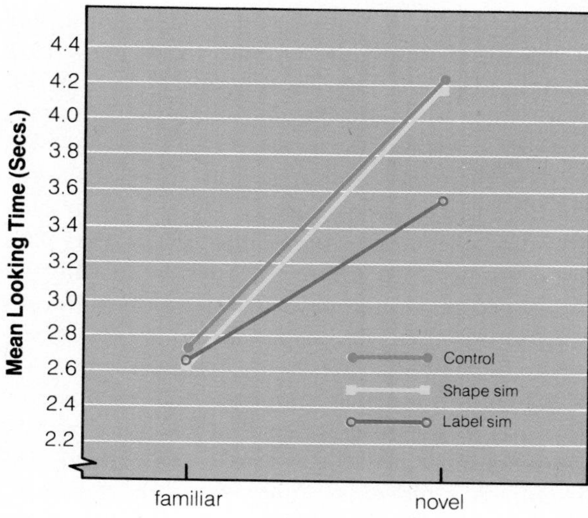

FIGURE 11.4 The recognition memory of two- and three-year-olds was tested by showing them pairs of common objects, each of which included an object the children had previously seen. The members of each pair either had similar labels (e. g., a small round bottle and a tall, thin bottle), similar shapes (e.g., three black buttons and three pennies), or were completely dissimilar (e.g., a flag and a guitar). In every condition the youngsters looked longer at the unfamiliar object in the pair. ***(From Daehler and O'Connor, 1980)***

had previously occupied, the average youngster managed to remember where six of eight toys belonged (Cohen, Perlmutter, and Myers, 1977). But when an eight-room dollhouse was substituted for the plain wooden box two-year-olds fell in their performance, but three-year-olds found the job even easier. The two-year-olds were so fascinated by the dollhouse that they paid little attention to where the toys went, whereas the three-year-olds may have used the different locations in the dollhouse as an aid in remembering (e.g., the block goes in the bedroom).

Some evidence suggests that reconstructive memory is not passive, that it is not a faithful representation of an original perception. Instead, as children's comprehension develops, their memories may change to conform to their new understanding (Inhelder, 1976). Consequently, as time passes, a child's reconstructions may get either farther away from or closer to the model as the child originally perceived it.

Plays and pageants at Sunday School and kindergarten give youngsters a chance to show off their ability to recall information they have memorized. *(© Michael Weisbrot & Family)*

Recall Recall is more complex than other forms of memory. Unlike recognition, it takes place in the absence of the object or information to be remembered, and unlike reconstruction, there are no physical objects to act as cues. According to Piaget, recall is impossible in babies less than a year old because it requires the use of internalized images to reinstitute a memory (Piaget and Inhelder, 1973). From an information-processing point of view, recall requires children to generate information internally.

By the time they are three or four years old, children are capable of accurate recall. Almost all preschoolers sing advertising jingles and nursery rhymes, and their recall of parental promises seems almost perfect. And when studied in their homes, three- and four-year-olds have been able to recall a good deal of information about their experiences (Todd and Perlmutter, 1980). Their recollections were both spontaneous and in response to a researcher's question. Most of the episodes they remembered were social, involving themselves or other people, although they recalled some incidents involving objects or cartoon characters. Almost half the events the children recalled had taken place within the preceding month, although a third of them had happened more than three months before. In their spontaneous recall, four-year-olds produced more recollections than three-year-olds, and the events they remembered were likely to be unusual ones. Three-year-olds, on the other hand, tended to be able to remember everyday occurrences.

Perhaps because they are rarely required to engage in deliberate memorization of the sort demanded by laboratory studies, preschoolers do poorly on traditional tests of recall. When asked to remember a list of objects, for example, they may recall only two to four out of a short list. According to Marion Perlmutter (1980), there are several good reasons for the inefficiency of the preschooler's recall. Young children seem unaware of the techniques used by their elders to register information in memory. They use inappropriate search techniques when trying to retrieve information, and—even when they have the information—their limited verbal ability makes it difficult for them to produce it. There is some evidence that children's mood affects their memory (see the accompanying box).

There is also evidence that the young

DO HAPPY CHILDREN HAVE BETTER MEMORIES?

A recent study indicates that a child's emotional state may affect his or her ability to remember. James Bartlett and John Santrock (1979) studied five-year-old middle-class children in an attempt to see how mood influences memory. Each child heard three stories, which were either sad stories or happy ones. The stories always began alike but ended very differently, and embedded in each was a series of words that the investigators planned to use as a test of the children's memory. The children were not told they would be expected to remember anything, therefore they had no reason to try and fix any of the details they heard in memory.

After one woman had told the children the stories (always acting either sad or happy herself, depending upon which set of stories she was telling), she left the room and another woman came in. This woman—acting either sad or happy—showed each child a series of pictures that matched her own mood, then asked if the child could tell her "the stories like the other lady told them to you." After the child had recalled the stories, he or she was reminded about the main characters and about the sort of objects, such as toys, that had been planned as the primary test of memory. This further probing showed the investigators how much more the child could remember with the assistance of outside cues.

Children who heard happy stories from a happy storyteller and then were asked about the stories by a happy person could recall many more of the stories' details than any of the other children. Children who did the worst in free recall were those who heard happy stories but were asked about them in a sad situation by an obviously unhappy person. This striking effect appeared only during free recall. When the questioner gave the children hints about the content of the stories, mood seemed to have little effect on memory. Apparently, the mood change made it much more difficult for the children to retrieve information from long-term storage when they had to generate all the cues themselves.

Results were similar but not nearly so clear among children who heard sad stories, with a change in mood—that is, being asked about the stories by a happy person in a happy situation—reducing the number of details children recalled freely. It may be that the happy stories did a better job of making children happy than the sad stories did in making them sad.

Studies with adults have shown that drugs—such as alcohol, marijuana, amphetamines, and barbiturates—can have similar effects on memory (e.g., Eich et al., 1975). Adults who learn material when under the influence of a mood-altering drug have great difficulty in recalling the information unless they go back into the drug state. The same effect has been found among children who take mood-altering drugs to control hyperactivity, a condition in which children are extremely restless and cannot sustain attention long enough to complete tasks (Swanson and Kinsbourne, 1979). Bartlett and Santrock's study, which has been supported by similar studies of adults' memory for word lists, stories, and childhood events (Bower, 1981), suggests that this phenomenon, *state-dependent learning,* can be created by mood alone—without using drugs.

child's memory is enhanced when information is presented in a meaningful context. For example, Ann Brown (1976) showed three- and four-year-olds sets of four pictures. Some of the sets depicted a sequence of events; others showed unrelated pictures. Half the sequences were presented in a scrambled order. The children easily remembered, whether immediately or after a delay, the sequences that had been presented in order. They also could recall the scrambled sequences immediately, but they had some trouble remembering them after a delay, suggesting that they could not store scrambled sequences as well as they stored ordered ones. The kind of errors they made in recalling scrambled sequences indicated, further, that they found it difficult to ignore the inherent order that could be found in such sequences, for many of the children tended to recall scrambled items in an ordered sequence.

Although some studies (e.g., Piaget, 1959) have found that young children are likely to mix the order of events when they retell a story, other researchers (e.g., Wimmer, 1980) report that if the story has an obvious structure, four-year-olds have no trouble recalling the events in their correct order.

Young children are unaware of the techniques older children employ to help them remember, but sometimes they inadvertently use a memory technique. In the study of recall in the home, for example, three- and four-year-olds often discussed events with their parents, a procedure that helped them encode the material so that it could be remembered. But their use of this technique was not intentional (Todd and Perlmutter, 1980).

Three-year-olds do show a glimmer of **metamemory**—understanding of the way the memory system works—and once this understanding develops, they begin to make conscious use of memory aids. Even at this early age, told to remember where a toy is hidden, three-year-olds are likely to look at or touch the hiding place and in some way make that place distinctive from every other place. They may know that noise makes it hard to remember and that it is easier to remember a few items than to remember a lot of them (Wellman, 1977). Youngsters are better at remembering where a toy is hidden than memorizing a list of items. When the only goal is recall, as with a list of items, three- or four-year-olds may not realize that memorizing requires them to do something special with words or objects and that their job is to do something now that will be of questionable use later (Flavell and Wellman, 1977). By the time they are five, however, they often overestimate their ability and many believe that with effort they can remember almost anything (Wellman, Collins, and Glieberman, 1981).

Problem Solving

Preschoolers appear to solve problems in a different manner from that used by older children. Some psychologists have proposed that most young children learn by forming direct associations between the stimuli in the world and their responses. Not until about the time they begin school do they start to learn in a different manner, applying symbolic information they already have stored to the problem before them. Tracy Kendler (1979), who has suggested such an explanation for the apparent change in children's problem-solving ability, points out that young children seem to learn by a gradual strengthening of their tendency to choose behavior that previously has been reinforced. Faced with a problem, they find it extremely difficult to attempt a solution that requires them to behave in ways that have never been rewarded. When they do solve a problem in a new way, it is not because they have devised a hypothesis and are now testing it, but because they have simply stumbled onto the solution.

There is evidence, however, that some five-year-olds and most six-year-olds can be taught to use hypothesis testing. In one experiment, for example, Joan Cantor and Charles Spiker (1979) found that when given a problem, only about a quarter of the five-year-olds and about a third of the six-year-olds they studied devised a hypothesis themselves, then tested it. But when given direct instruction, over a third of the five-year-olds and about three-quarters of the six-year-olds used hypothesis testing to solve a problem.

Other psychologists believe that perceptual advances, an increase in the child's scanning and focusing skills, or some combination of these developments with Kendler's explanation is responsible for children's new skill. For example, Barry Gholson (1980), who has attempted to weave together information-processing and Pi-

This preschooler will find the next piece for her puzzle, not by formulating a hypothesis about its shape, but by acting in a way that has already been reinforced. *(© Suzanne Szasz)*

agetian theory, suggests that the reason young children tackle problems in such an inefficient manner can be traced to the limitations of the preoperational mind. That is, young children may be unable to organize and integrate their cognitive processes so that they can systematically test new solutions. In the next section, we will see how the organization of the preoperational child's mind might set certain limits to the way young children approach problems.

PREOPERATIONAL THOUGHT

Adults often are amused by young children's words and actions, and most of the charming stories that fond parents relate are based on the exploits of children between the ages of two and six or seven. According to Piaget, certain general features that characterize early ways of thinking about the physical and social environment are responsible for these aspects of the young child's behavior.

Egocentrism

A baby first "defines" or knows objects in terms of his or her own activity upon them and somewhat later differentiates him- or herself from the objects of the world. This differentiation is not yet complete in early childhood. Although at the sensorimotor and perceptual level very young children distinguish themselves from the rest of the world, they may be egocentric in other ways. They appear to think that another person sees things the way they see them and experiences the same behavior and the same thoughts and feelings about things as themselves. For example, when a three-year-old boy talks on the phone to his grandmother, he assumes she can see everything he does, and he cannot understand why she asks about something that is in plain sight.

Most evidence for the young child's egocentrism comes from tasks in which children have to describe abstract forms or objects for a blindfolded person or in a way that someone in a different position might see them. In one such study, Lynn Liben (1978) asked young children to look at a white card with her. Either the child, Liben, or both wore colored glasses as they inspected the card. The child's glasses had yellow lenses; the lenses in Liben's glasses were green. About half the three-year-olds Liben tested gave egocentric responses, indicating their belief that the experimenter saw the card as they did. They said, for example, that Liben saw a yellow card when they wore yellow glasses or a white card when they took off their glasses, and they paid no attention to whether or not Liben was wearing her green glasses. When children this age are shown a three-dimensional model of a landscape, then asked to pick a card showing the model as it would look from various locations, they do even worse (Laurendeau and Pinard, 1970). Four-year-olds do not appear to understand the problem, and even many schoolchildren give egocentric answers, choosing the card that shows the display as they see it.

Other factors that make children appear egocentric in such situations include their lack of information, their inadequate memory, and their still-developing language skills, which are simply not up to describing the situation. When children are given tasks that fit their cognitive skills, their level of egocentrism appears to drop sharply. In a study by John Flavell, Susan Shipstead, and Karen Croft (1978), for example, even two-and-a-half-year-olds could hide a Snoopy doll behind a tabletop screen so that the experimenter could not see Snoopy from where she sat. Flavell's group is convinced that in this instance young children could distinguish what they saw from what another person might see, could think about what the other person saw, and could both produce and recognize some physical situations in which another person could not see some object they could see.

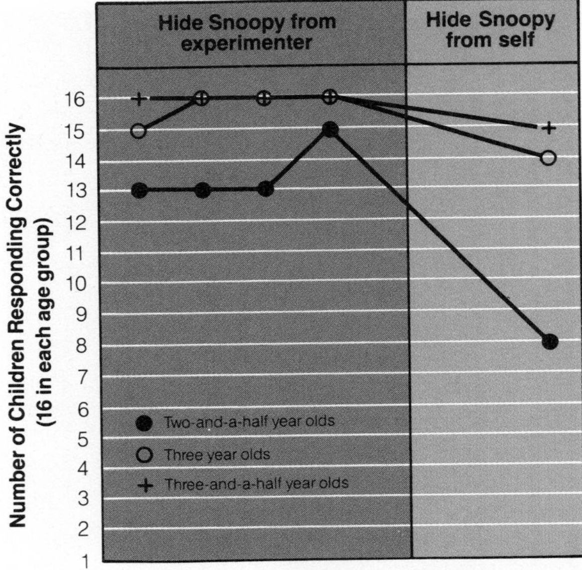

FIGURE 11.5 When young children were asked on four occasions to hide Snoopy doll so the experimenter could not see it, even two-and-a-half year olds did well; but when asked to hide Snoopy from themselves, the youngest children's performance dropped sharply. ***(Adapted from Flavell, Shipstead, and Croft, 1978)***

In another study, young children demonstrated a realization that people differ in skills and abilities. Ellen Markman (1973) asked five-year-olds about their memory and motor skills and about those of two-year-olds and of teen-agers, putting such questions to them as how many pictures they could remember or how far they could jump. The children's predictions showed they realized that two-year-olds cannot do as well as four-year-olds, but that teen-agers can do much better. In addition, the children indicated that although they thought that two-year-olds had a fair degree of motor skill, they doubted that two-year-olds could remember much, if anything. The five-year-olds were correct; the motor skills of two-year-olds are more advanced than their cognitive skills.

Both the Snoopy problem and the motor-skills problem are much simpler than many of the tests on which young children have seemed so egocentric. Perhaps because the simpler problems are closely connected with what young children see and do in daily life, they place less strain on the child's information-processing capacities. In the landscape display problem that is a standard test of egocentrism, a child must look at a series of mountains spread out on a table and — without changing position—tell the investigator how the display would look to a person who stood on another side of the table. To solve this problem, a child must be able to code the entire display, then hold both it and the hypothetical viewer's position in working memory, while comparing them with possible solutions shown on cards (Huttenlocher and Presson, 1979). Faced with a task beyond their capacities, youngsters may simply fall back on what they see before them. As these capacities develop, children seem to go through a sequence in their understanding of what others can see, first realizing that another person sees something, then what the other person sees, and finally, how it appears from the other person's perspective (Shantz, 1975).

Causality

Related to the young child's egocentrism is an apparent tendency to ascribe thoughts, feelings, and life itself to inanimate objects. This aspect of children's thought is reflected in their notions about the causes, purposes, and activities of such things as dreams; night and day; the sun, moon, and clouds; and mountains and rivers. Because the sun and moon appear to follow him around, a young child like David may believe that they do. And because he tends to think that other people see things the way he does, he may believe that others also perceive the sun and moon as following him around. The young child may also believe that the "purpose" of mountains and other worldly objects is their utility to him and to the world he knows. Thus although children are not egocentric when they recognize mountains as distinct physical objects, they seem to fall into egocentrism when it comes to ascribing meaning to objects in their world.

This level of thought affects the young child's view of reality. For example, Monique Laurendeau and Adrien Pinard (1962) investigated the ideas that children had about dreams. There was a clear difference in the kinds of answers given by preschoolers on the one hand and seven-year-olds on the other. About half of the four-year-olds believed that dreams originate from some external source and that they take place in front of the dreamer, on the wall or on the pillow. Quite "logically," they often believed that their eyes were open while they dreamed, because one could not see a dream with one's eyes closed. But almost none of the seven-year-olds described dreams in this way. Their overwhelming response was that dreams both originate and occur inside the individual and cannot be seen by anyone else. Thus most four-year-olds failed to differentiate the objective things they saw when awake from the subjective visions they saw in their dreams, but seven-year-olds easily made this distinction by substituting a new, realistic understanding for an old belief. Some children, particularly six-year-olds, were in a transitional stage. Their explanations included both internal and external viewpoints about their dreams, even though at a logical level the two explanations were contradictory.

This kind of reasoning Piaget called **precausal:** the child maintains that some events are either completely or partly caused by psychological, subjective factors, because the child cannot differentiate between psychological and physical causes. For example, children may believe that they have good dreams because the dreams themselves want to entertain them and that nightmares come because the nightmares themselves want to punish them. But even in this precausal state, children are quite concerned with cause-effect relationships. They search for a cause to explain every minor occurrence. Preschoolers simply do not believe in accidents, and when two events occur together, the young child assumes that one has caused the other.

Since nothing is accidental, young children believe that everything in the world has been built either by human beings or by some human-like divine being. As Piaget (1967) put it, "mountains 'grow' because stones have been manufactured and then planted; lakes have been hollowed out, and for a long time the child believes that cities are built before the lakes adjacent to them." (p. 28)

As children develop, they gradually acquire naturalistic explanations, which, said Piaget, grow out of their interactions with machines. As they try to make their toys function, produce physical effects, or overcome physical resistance in objects, they begin to learn about the nature of physical causality. It is no wonder, then, that children resort to animistic answers when asked about complex natural phenomena. Asking preschoolers what causes the wind and rain, why rivers flow, how bicycles and other machines work is asking them to talk about things they have had little experience with (Gelman, 1978). Since they lack the knowledge, they make up animistic but plausible answers. When Michael Berzonsky (1971) questioned children about remote events, asking "Why does the moon change shape?", they generally gave precausal answers. When asked about familiar events, such as a tire going flat or flying kites, however, they usually gave physical, mechanical answers.

Young children's experience in the world help them to acquire naturalistic explanations for everyday phenomena, but when asked what causes snow, they will give an animistic explanation. *(© Marion Bernstein)*

Similarly, Rochel Gelman (1978) and Merry Bullock found that when they asked four- and five-year-olds to explain a physical event, they got physical answers. In front of the children was a box with two handles on the sides; one handle started a ball rolling down an incline; the other switched on a series of flashing lights that made it appear as if a single light were moving down the incline. The children watched the ball and light move down the incline together and disappear into a second box. Three seconds later, a jumping jack popped out of this box. Given a chance "to make the jack jump," the children chose to start the ball instead of the light. When trying to account for actions, preschoolers tend to choose a reasonable cause (a rolling ball causes physical impact) over an unreasonable one.

When it comes to less technical aspects of life, such as their relations with parents and pets, even younger children understand causality. Shown pictures of a boy pulling a dog's tail, a dog biting a boy, and a boy crying, for example, three-year-olds can correctly choose which picture represents the cause of the dog's actions, understanding that the dog bit the boy because its tail was pulled—not because the boy was crying (Kun, 1978).

Although most young children appear to take a nonchalant attitude toward logical contradictions that arise from their conflicting explanations for a single event, proper exploitation of these contradictions can spur their intellectual development. Such logical inconsistencies may be fundamental to cognitive growth, because cognitive conflict can motivate a child to seek new information and to reorganize the old, thereby clarifying his or her understanding of the world, reducing tension, and producing a new state of cognitive integration.

Identity

The concept of identity, which gradually emerges during the preoperational period, is the conceptual equivalent of object permanence, which developed in the sensorimotor period. The child who slowly learned that objects continue to exist when they are out of sight must now learn that objects and people remain the same, even if there are irrelevant changes in their appearance.

As we will see in Chapter 13, young children tend to believe that being male or female is not necessarily a permanent state of affairs, that a girl might become a boy or vice versa. Children are not even sure that cats must remain cats. Rheta DeVries (1969) showed a black cat to children whose ages ranged from three to six. One at a time, she told the children to keep watching the cat. She screened the cat's head from sight and placed on it a realistic mask resembling either a dog or a rabbit, then turned the cat around and asked the children once more to identify the animal. Three-year-olds called the cat by whatever species its mask resembled. Children a little older generally said the cat would remain a cat even if DeVries put a dog's mask over its head; but once the transformation was completed, they changed their minds. The sight of the dog's head on a cat's body—even though the animal's body never left their field of vision—overwhelmed their earlier assertion that its species would remain unchanged. Only the five- and six-year-olds could not be fooled. They had developed the concept of identity and stoutly maintained that a cat was a cat, no matter how it looked.

Preschool children do accept the identity of their own bodies; they realize that despite their increase in size, pictures of their younger selves are "still me" and that when they are big enough to go to school, the schoolchild will also be "me." But in the case of a plant, they will say "it grew, but it isn't the same any more; here it's a little plant and there it's a big plant, it's not the same plant" (Piaget, 1968). Not until they are about seven will they admit to the identity of the seedling and the mature plant.

Halloween can be an anxiety-filled occasion for young preschoolers who believe that donning a mask literally changes a person's identity. *(© Leonard Speier 1981)*

Number

Young children do not understand the concept of number as Piaget defines it, although they may be efficient counters. Piaget (1965) was not interested in whether children could count, add, or multiply; his definition of the number concept required that children be able to reason about number *without* counting. That is, they must be able to understand that changing the way a line of checkers looks—by spreading it out, squeezing it together, or completely scrambling it—does not change the number of checkers. This approach to number is an example of conservation, a concept that will be discussed at length in Chapter 14.

Rochel Gelman and C. R. Gallistel (1978) have traced the development of number and have found the beginnings of the concept among two-year-olds. They found that two-year-olds have started to count, even though many of them can count only as far as two. They count, even if they do not know their language's words for number. They may use letters to count, or they may invent their own words. Or they may borrow number words but invent their own sequence, counting, for example, "one, six, eleven, ten," but always using their number words in the same way. In this instance, "six" always stands for "two," "eleven," for "three," and "ten" for "four." Before they are three, children point at objects they are counting or touch them, saying their number words aloud. When they are a little older, they will count to themselves, announcing only the total. But if a five-year-old is asked to count a good many objects, he or she will count them aloud.

COGNITION AND EXPERIENCE

What kinds of experiences encourage the development of intellectual competence in preschoolers? Although neither social class nor culture appears to noticeably affect intellectual development during the first two years of life, an increasing gap develops between the test scores of lower- and middle-class children during the preschool years (Golden and Birns, 1976). Parents and educators alike have wondered to what extent class differences contribute to this gap, and a number of experiments have suggested that differences in the use of language are an important factor (e.g., Lewis and Freedle, 1973). Until recently, however, no one had systematically observed children in their daily activities over an appreciable length of time, in order to see exactly what kinds of experiences were connected with rapid intellectual development.

Now Jean Carew (1980) has completed a pair of longitudinal studies, one following a group of children in their homes and another following a group of children in day care, observing them frequently and testing them repeatedly on infant mental scales, intelligence tests, and tests of spatial and language ability. The crucial role of language was confirmed. Carew found that the role of the caregiver in providing intellectual experiences—especially experiences with language—during the second and third years of the child's life was extremely important and that it predicted performance on tests of intellectual ability at age three. In fact, language mastery experiences with caregivers before thirty months predicted both spatial and language skills at age three, but spatial experiences predicted neither. This was true whether the caregiver was the child's mother, as in the first study, or the teacher, as in the second.

For example, in a typical language mastery experience at nursery school, the teacher pulled up a little boy's zipper, saying, "That's your zipper, Mark. It keeps your pants on you." Her words both labeled the zipper and defined its function. In this case, the child merely listened; in other cases, there was interaction between the adult and child. Not all language experience with adults contributed to cognitive growth. Time with caregivers that was devoted to routine talk ("Feeling good today?" or "I'm going to make the bed now") correlated negatively with test scores at age three.

Carew is not certain as to how her results should be interpreted. Since the caregiver effect shows up at nursery school, it is not simply a matter of intelligent mothers teaching intelligent babies. And since the same nursery-school teachers do not interact with all children the same way, there must be some quality in the child that evokes the intense caregiver interaction that leads to early intellectual competence. Perhaps, Carew suggests, mothers and nursery-school teachers—without knowing it—react to qualities in the child, judging when a child is ready for intellectual stimulation. Or perhaps some children know how to listen to adults, thereby leading the adult on to further interaction.

Although Carew does not apply her research directly to socioeconomic differences, her findings fit comfortably with other research that has found class differences in language. It may be that middle-class mothers, aware of the importance of education, are especially responsive to a child's readiness to learn, expressions of interest in the world, or mastery of the art of listening.

Four- and five-year-olds, say Gelman and Gallistel, are beginning to understand the principles that govern counting. Given a group of objects to count, they can begin with any of the objects and they can count them in several ways, starting with a different object each time. They can figure out whether one set of objects is equal to another, and that a set remains the same even if altered in appearance. They can add and subtract. But they can do all these things only with very small groups of objects, and they must always count them. They will not understand number according to Piaget's definition until they begin to reason about numerical relations, as opposed to number itself.

COGNITION AND SOCIAL INTERACTION

As young David interacts with his family and his friends, he is exposed to different outlooks, and these experiences affect his intellectual development. Often children learn that they have misunderstood a concept when others correct them by refusing to accept their views. They may engage in vehement debates, as each pits his or her personal understanding against that of peers. Such debates spur reflection and—through cognitive conflict—ultimately modify a child's understanding. In Piaget's terms, the child's cognitive equilibrium is disturbed and the child searches for answers that restore equilibrium at a more advanced level.

For example, two five-year-old boys were arguing over whether cave men are real. The young believer said, "My father's father's father's father's father was a cave man." The other remained skeptical. The believer retorted, "You go home and ask your father, and he will tell you that they are real!" In view of the seriousness and vehemence attending the dispute, the skeptic probably asked his father and either modified or clarified his understanding. Were it not for the social interaction, the boy may never have questioned his belief that cave men are imaginary. But his argument probably led to a more differentiated concept: Cave men were real long ago, but they are no longer real today.

Social interaction also appears to affect a young child's comprehension of the rules that govern children's games. Some time ago, Piaget (1932) found that young children tended to believe that the rules of a game of marbles were fixed and absolute, rather than conventions for play that could be changed by mutual consent of the players. The children in this study lived in homes where the parent-child relationship was one-sided and authoritarian. Children were not asked for their views, nor did they receive explanations when they were told how to behave. As they got older, the children interacted more with peers and less with parents, and they played marbles according to more flexible rules. Interaction with other children gave them opportunities to assert their own points of view, to have them challenged, and to hear diverse opinions. The younger children's rigid interpretation of rules may have been due, in part, to the limited and one-sided nature of their social interactions, whereas the more flexible and realistic rules of the older children may have been affected by the cooperative nature of their social interactions. Apparently, social interactions can affect cognitive development in many ways, as the accompanying box indicates.

SUMMARY:

1. Children tend to form their concepts around both the perceptual qualities and the function of objects, and function often predominates. As children construct conceptual networks of interrelated ideas about objects and events, they rely on the cognitive skills involved in limitation, language, and graphic representation. Symbolizing and imagining supplement rather than replace a child's natural curiosity and exploration of the real world. Advances in representational skills are closely linked to advances in a child's ability to learn, reason, and acquire concepts.
2. As young children's perceptual skills develop, they isolate and relate more of the distinctive features of objects and events. As a result

of experience, more sophisticated ways of exploring, and changes in cognitive understanding, children's ability to coordinate the information they receive through their senses improves dramatically.

3. Children's concepts of the world continue to depend upon which aspects of it get their attention. As in infancy, previous experience as well as certain physical features of objects and events generally determine what a given child will attend to. The focusing and shifting of attention are likely to vary with the complexity of a task, its rewards, and the effectiveness of instructions.

4. Recognition, the simplest form of memory, is quite good among young children, as is reconstruction, which provides concrete objects as cues in children's attempts to repeat the order of events. Preschoolers do poorly on tests of recall, perhaps because of inefficient search techniques and limited verbal ability, but their recall in natural situations is much better. Young children are inefficient problem solvers, and some psychologists have proposed that the reason lies in the child's tendency to learn by forming direct associations. Other psychologists suggest that young children perform poorly because they are unable to organize and integrate their cognitive processes, rendering a systematic test of solutions impossible.

5. Although young children have distinguished themselves from the rest of the world, they remain egocentric in that they appear to think that other people see and experience things just as they do. The degree of egocentrism a child displays varies according to the situation. Related to egocentrism is young children's belief that inanimate objects are alive and their precausal reasoning—the belief that there are no accidents and that events can be caused by psychological as well as physical factors.

6. The concept of identity develops slowly in early childhood, as children come to realize that objects and people remain the same, even if their appearances change. The concept of number (as opposed to numerical relations) also develops in the years between two and six. Two-year-olds can count small numbers, and four- and five-year-olds are beginning to understand the principles that underlie counting.

7. Social interaction has a strong effect on children's cognitive development. Through their interactions with family members and age-mates, children are exposed to different viewpoints that often change their own understanding.

12

LANGUAGE: UNDERSTANDING AND USE

One spring day, six-year-old Connie and her grandmother decided to walk back to Connie's house after visiting a neighbor. After they had gone about a block, Connie looked back over her shoulder and saw that her mother and father, who had also been at the neighbor's house, had started the family car and were pulling out of the driveway. "Hurry, Grammy, hurry!" she cried. "They're gaining on us. They're gaining on us." Then she stopped, looked up at her grandmother and said, "What does 'gaining on us' mean?" Although most people assume that children mean exactly what they say, even children who have mastered the basic structure of their native language do not always understand the meaning of the words or forms they use.

Between the ages of one and a half and four years, normal children all over the world master the basic grammar of one or more of the world's thousands of different languages. Although each child hears a personally unique set of sentences from the adults and children that he or she interacts with, all children exposed to a language learn to understand other speakers and end up with the same pronunciation, grammar, and vocabulary as the rest of their speech community. This means that each child in a speech community arrives at the same basic rules.

In Chapter 8, we brought children to the threshold of grammatical development. In this chapter, we will try to understand how the child who could speak in only two-word utterances rapidly becomes a competent master of a complicated language. We will find that young children tend to impose regularities on language beyond those that exist, and that children use various strategies, such as word order, for figuring out complicated sentences. As we will see, children learn the meaning of a word gradually, at first attributing to it only part of the meaning the word has for adults. When discussing the problems preschoolers sometimes have in articulating sounds, we will discover that their reliance on context sometimes keeps them from hearing their own mispronunciations. We will explore the role of context in a child's comprehension of language and will find that conversations with adults continue to play a major role in the child's acquisition. We will see the child switching language as he or she switches roles, talking one way with parents, another with peers, and yet another as he or she adopts the role of teacher to a younger child. Finally, we will examine the influence of socioeconomic and ethnic differences on language development.

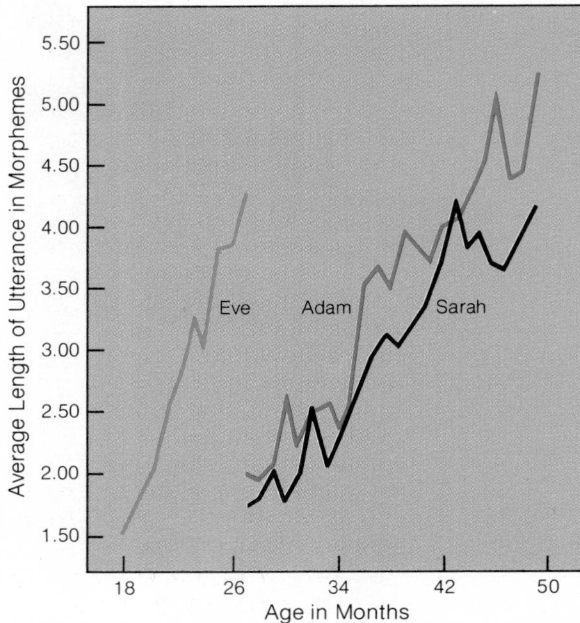

FIGURE 12.1 As Eve, Adam, and Sarah grew, the average length of their utterances increased. Morphemes are small linguistic units of speech that have definable meanings. ***(Adapted from Brown, 1973)***

UNDERSTANDING SYNTAX

Near the end of the second year, children convey their intentions by applying the syntactic devices of intonation, inflection, and word order to their store of words. In extending their grasp of language structure, they apply these devices with increasing sophistication, and as their command of the language expands, they reveal their comprehension of it by the kinds of errors in their speech.

Developing Rules

Developmental psychologists use various methods to study children's knowledge of grammar. Some set up situations in which children must either show by their actions that they understand certain linguistic constructions or else produce the forms themselves. Others simply listen to children, recording their natural speech and noting the errors and omissions as well as the correct forms produced by the child.

Demonstrating Rules A child's knowledge of language rules must be inferred by indirect evidence. Each time children correct their own speech, for example, they show that they believe certain combinations of words are incorrect, thereby revealing they have a sense of grammatical norms (W. Miller and Ervin, 1970). A small child, returning from a walk along the shore, was heard to say, "Down sand beach I been . . . I been down sand beach." Such revealing instances are relatively rare, but they are the first signs of a child's ability to think about the form of language; they begin to appear about the time children are two years old (E. Clark, 1978).

In a major longitudinal study of language development, Roger Brown, Courtney Cazden, and Ursula Bellugi-Klima (1968) observed three children, whom they called Adam, Eve, and Sarah, over a period of several years. Brown and his colleagues selected these children because they were just beginning to combine two words in their utterances and because their speech was clear and easy to understand. The researchers visited the children regularly, recording everything they said and all that was said to them.

The recorded dialogues demonstrate the children's gradual understanding of English syntax. For example, in a single dialogue between two-year-old Eve and her mother, both participants made requests, formulated positive and negative statements, and asked questions. However, interesting differences appeared between the speech of the adult and that of the child. Certain elements that were systematically missing from Eve's speech were present in her mother's sentences. Eve's mother used auxiliary verbs (such as the forms of "to be") wherever English syntax required them. These grammatical elements were not present in Eve's speech. Eve, for example, said "It time," whereas her mother said "It's time." Although the child's speech lacked the required auxiliary verb, it was understandable.

Within three months, Eve's language showed a dramatic change. She was using auxiliary verbs in negatives, questions, and statements. Her sentences were longer and more complex, and she was joing simple sentences together with words like "when" and "and." She still made errors, of course, and some of these errors revealed that she was beginning to figure out the rules of English. For example, she said, "Then Fraser won't hear her too," whereas an adult would say, "Then Fraser won't hear her either." There is an odd rule in English that changes "too" to "either" in negative sentences (it is correct to say "Fraser will hear her too"). Eve had not figured out this rule for negative statements, but her use of "too" indicated that she understood the general function carried out by both "too" and "either."

Figuring Out Rules After examining children's acquisition of language in many cultures, Dan Slobin (1973) concluded that they approach language with expectations and a set of strategies that they apply to the words they hear. These strategies, which Slobin called **operating principles,** may determine what sort of linguistic constructions will be easiest for children to learn. The first principle is *Pay attention to the ends of words.* In the languages Slobin studied, children learned suffixes (such as -ed, -ing, -s, in English) more rapidly than they learned prefixes. This device is essential in languages like Russian, and it also plays a role in English. The existence of this principle was demonstrated when Stan Kuczaj (1979) tested preschool children with a nonsense syllable, which he alternately placed at the beginning and end of words. For example, some children heard "The boy drove the ip-car," while others heard, "The boy drove the car-ip." With some children, the syllable "ip" always meant "big"; with others, it always meant "red." Whether "ip" meant "big" or "red," children who heard the syllable as a suffix found its meaning easier to learn than children who heard it as a prefix. Either children process word endings better than initial sounds, or they pay attention to endings because paying attention has paid off in the past.

Another of Slobin's operating principles was also involved in Kuczaj's study, one that states *The phonological forms of words can be systematically modified,* or, the sounds of words change in a regular way to indicate changes in meaning. In this study, the same suffix was systematically added to nouns and most children found the changed words comprehensible.

The remaining operating principles are *Pay attention to the order of words, Avoid interruptions or rearrangement of linguistic units, Mark underlying semantic relations clearly* (for example, add "-ed" to indicate past actions), *Avoid exceptions,* and *The use of grammatical markers should make semantic sense.* This last principle, which states that there should be a sensible reason for the way words fit into the linguistic structure, shows itself most clearly, Slobin believes, when it is violated. In some languages, for example, the gender of nouns has no meaning but is purely arbitrary. This convention is not used in English, because English uses the neuter designation for inanimate objects and does not require the ending of adjectives to conform to the gender of nouns. But some languages do use this rule. In French, for example, it is *une petite tourte* (a small pie), but *un petit gâteau* (a small cake). Children apparently have more difficulty learning these linguistic markers (adjectival endings) than they do learning meaningful inflections, such as those indicating that a noun is a direct object, because children can see no reason to attribute gender to any inanimate objects.

Not all of Slobin's operating principles have been tested in experimental situations, so they may not always apply in all situations. But the principles provide a helpful framework for examining the development of grammar.

The Tendency to Overregularize

Children's adherence to the operating principle, *Avoid exceptions,* discloses their control of certain language rules, and many of the errors they make in speech appear to be attempts to make the language more systematic than it actually is. For example, Eve's use of "too" in both positive and negative utterances was a regularization of English, in which negative statements are an exception to the general rule. Overregularization in English shows most clearly in children's errors in the past tense of verbs, the plural form of nouns, and to a lesser degree, the asking of questions.

Verbs The regular way to form the past tense for English verbs is to add "-ed": "walk," "walked"; "ask," "asked." However, many common verbs form their past tense in an irregular manner: "go," "went"; "come," "came"; "drive," "drove"; "break," "broke." Investigators in the field of child language have found that children often learn a number of these irregular past forms as separate words at an early age and produce correct sentences: "It broke"; "Daddy went out"; "I fell." After using these correct past tense forms for many months, they discover the rule for forming regular past tenses, and the irregular forms may disappear from their speech and be replaced by overregularized forms. The child of three or four now may say, "It breaked"; "Daddy goed out"; "I falled."

As children get older, a curious pattern of redundant usage develops. Five- and six-year-olds begin to drop forms like "eated," "goed," and "maked," and in their place may use a doubled past form, like "ated," "wented," and "maded" (Kuczaj, 1978). By the time children are seven, they will have nothing to do with the redundant form; most have ceased to overregularize the verb in any way.

What looks like regression in the younger children is actually a sign of progress in the child's analysis of language. Clearly, children have not heard the overregularized forms from their parents; instead, they construct the forms to conform with the regularities they have noticed in the speech of others. And so a change from "went" to "goed" indicates that children have, on their own, discovered a regular pattern in English. In order to *avoid exceptions,* they are indicating the idea of the past in a regular way in their speech. Similarly, their insistence on adding the "-ed" to irregular past forms clarifies the past status of the verb, showing the application of another of Slobin's operating principles: *Mark underlying semantic relations clearly* (Kuczaj, 1978).

When children overregularize their speech it often seems impervious to gentle efforts at correction, as the following conversation reported by Jean Berko Gleason (1967) shows:

CHILD: My teacher holded the baby rabbits and we patted them.
MOTHER: Did you say your teacher held the baby rabbits?
CHILD: Yes.
MOTHER: What did you say she did?
CHILD: She holded the baby rabbits and we patted them.
MOTHER: Did you say she held them tightly?
CHILD: No, she holded them loosely.

Although his mother substituted the correct form of the verb twice in this short dialogue, the little boy persisted in repeating "held" as "holded," tenaciously clinging to his own linguistic structure. Apparently, regularity is more powerful in its influence on children than is previous practice, reinforcement, or immediate imitation of adult forms. The child at this level of development seeks regularity and is deaf to exceptions (Bellugi, 1970).

As children gradually become aware of their overregularization errors, the correct forms seem to filter in and out of consciousness. Slobin (1978) reports a conversation with his young daughter, who was in a transitional phase. Slobin asked her if the baby-sitter had read a book the previous night, and Heida replied, using first the correct past tense "read," then switching to "readed." During the exchange, Slobin said, "That's the book she readed, huh?" His own overregularization alerted Heida to the correct form and she replied in an annoyed tone, "Yeah . . . *read!*", following up with the comment, "Dum-dum!" Although Heida was shifting back to "read," she may still have been saying "goed" or "maked," because children eliminate their overregularization errors slowly. They must learn, one by one, that only a single past tense form exists for each irregular verb (Kuczaj, 1978).

Plurals The formation of plurals is another area in which children tend to overregularize. The English language has several ways to indicate whether a speaker is talking about one or more objects. The English plural has three regular phonetic forms: "-s" (as in "roots," "books"), "-z" (as in "barns," "bees"), and "-ez" (as in "horses," "matches"), and a child must learn that the rules for using these three endings depend on the final sound of the singular noun.

A child's knowledge of these rules may be tested in a manner devised by Jean Berko (1958). In this test, an investigator shows a child some object for which there is no name. (The large stuffed toys of unfamiliar shape used in one test are shown in the accompanying photograph.) The investigator names these objects with possible but nonexistent English words. She presents the child with one object and says, for example, "Here is a wug." Then she puts down another, similar object next to it and says, "Now there is another wug. There are two ———?" The child

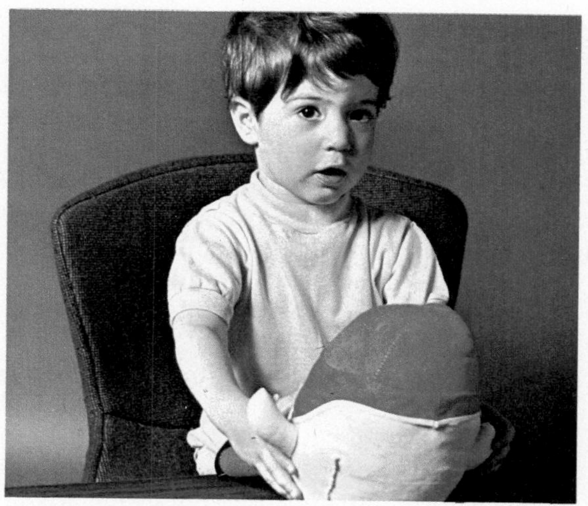

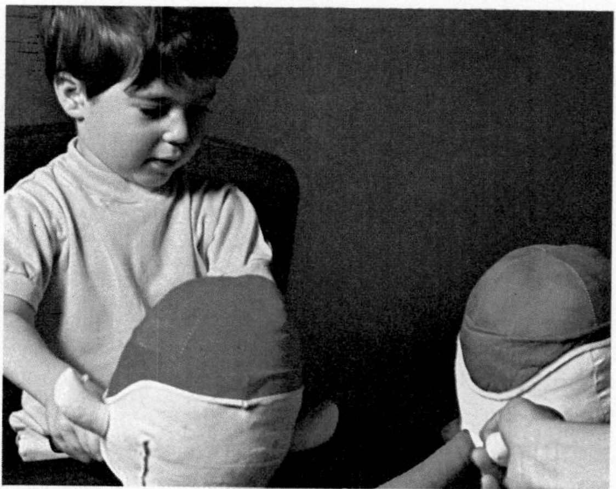

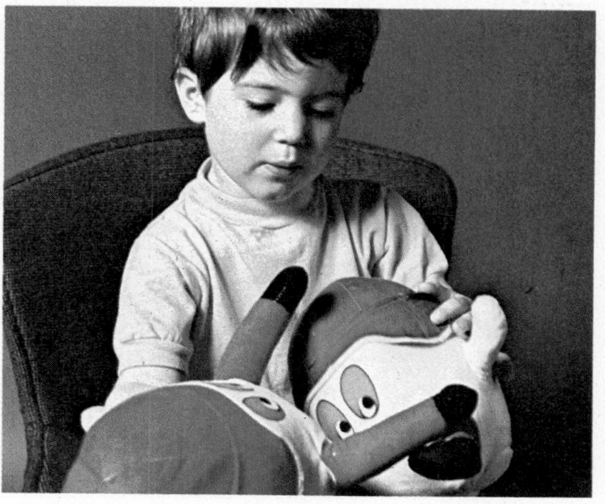

In this singular-plural test, *(top)* the child is handed an object for which he has no name and is told, "Here is a wug." *(middle)* Then another object is put down, and the child is asked to finish the sentence, "Now there are two———." *(bottom)* If the child knows the rule for forming plurals, he responds with "wugs." *(William MacDonald)*

obligingly fills in the nonexistent word, "wugs," pronouncing it "wugz" if he or she knows the appropriate rule for forming plurals in English.

English also has some irregular plural forms, many of them common words: "feet," "mice," "men," "children." These irregular forms, like irregular verb past-tense forms, must be learned as separate vocabulary items. Researchers have found that the child who has been correctly using irregular plural forms ("feet," "men," "mice") may, for a time, overgeneralize the newly discovered rules of formation and say "foots," "mans," "mouses"—another example of the kind of regularization that appears in the child's use of verbs. A child may even learn the irregular form but apply the plural rule anyway, saying the redundant "feets," "mens," "mices."

Asking "Wh-" Questions Children discover a great deal by asking questions that begin with "who," "what," "where," "when," "why," "how," and "how come." Except for "how come," each of these words immediately precedes the auxiliary form of the verb in a question. For example, if the child follows the English grammatical rule, he or she must ask, "Why is David crying?" or "When will Santa Claus come?" or "Who can fix this?" But in the case of "how come," the auxiliary moves behind the subject, as in "How come Lauren is laughing?"

In learning to ask these questions, children begin by placing the auxiliary after the first noun, saying such things as "What he can ride in?" Next, children begin to use the correct form with "what" or "where" but fail to apply it to other "wh-" questions. Apparently they do not learn a general rule, but begin by learning specific applications of the rule. Once they grasp it, however, they generalize the rule to all "wh-" questions, forcing "how come" questions into the same form, so that children produce the overregularized "How come can the dog sleep on the couch?" (Kuczaj and Brannick, 1979).

Understanding Complex Constructions

The simple rules children develop for figuring out the meaning of sentences can sometimes betray them, leading a youngster to misinterpret sentences that do not follow the rule, such as those using passive constructions. Children hear many simple declarative sentences, each containing an actor, an action, and the object of that action: "Daddy is cooking hamburgers"; "James feeds his teddy bear"; "Jenny filled the glasses." In each of these sentences, the relationship between the actor (Jenny), action (filled), and object of the action (glasses) is expressed by word order. In passive constructions, however, the word order is reversed, and in the sentence "The glasses were filled by Jenny," the object of the action ("glasses") is the first noun in the sentence and the actor ("Jenny"), the last.

Children's comprehension of sentences can be revealed by giving them objects to manipulate and asking them to act out the statements they hear. For example, the investigator may ask the child to act out "The truck follows the car." Using a toy truck and a toy car, most two- and three-year-olds can act out such declarative sentences. But asked to demonstrate a passive sentence, such as "The truck is followed by the car," even four-year-olds are seldom correct. In fact, most four-year-olds carry out the opposite action each time, relying on word order.

Children apparently go through several strategies before they arrive at the complex rules of English grammar. Their changing understanding showed clearly in a study devised by Thomas Bever (1970). He gave children between the ages of two and four a toy horse and a toy cow and asked them to act out sentences such as the following:

1. The cow kisses the horse.
2. It's the cow that kisses the horse.
3. It's the horse that the cow kisses.
4. The horse is kissed by the cow.

Two-year-olds acted out the first three sentence types correctly, but their performance was random on the fourth (passive) sentence. They were equally likely to have the horse kiss the cow and the cow kiss the horse. Bever suggests that when two-year-olds hear a noun and a verb in a row, such as "cow kisses," they assume that the

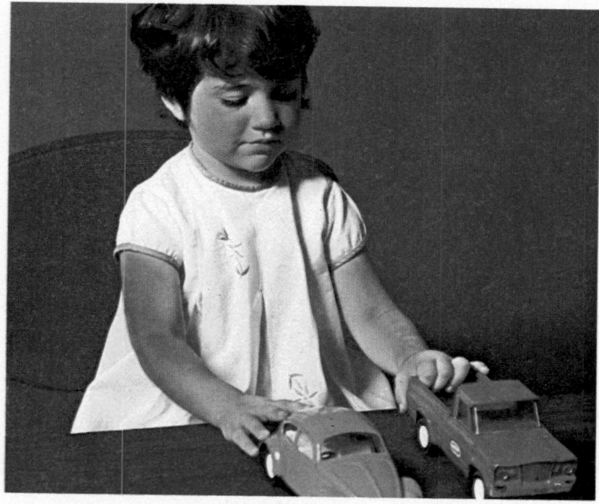

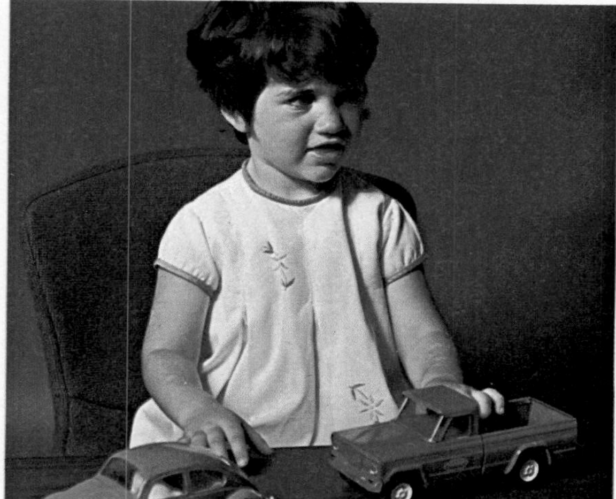

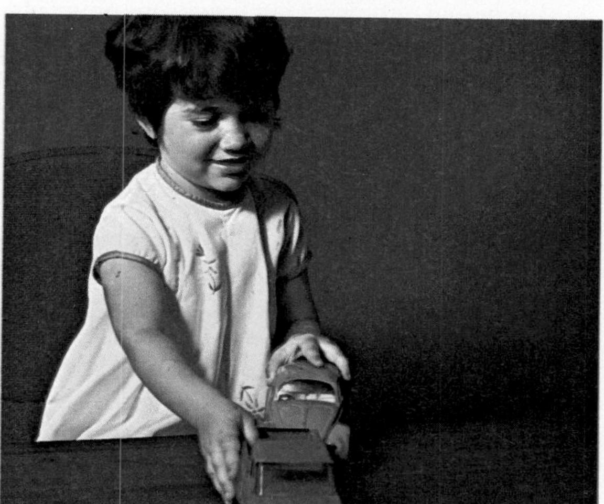

To test a young child's comprehension of active/passive sentences, *(top)* a car and a truck are placed before her. *(middle)* When told, "Show me 'the truck follows the car,' " she correctly demonstrates the active sentence. *(bottom)* The vehicles are replaced and she is told, "Show me 'the car is followed by the truck.' " This time her enactment of the passive sentence is incorrect. *(William MacDonald)*

noun is the actor. This noun-verb sequence is heard as a single perceptual unit meaning "actor-action." But if another word (or words) interrupts this simple sequence, as in passive sentence 4, the strategy fails and the children make a random choice of actor.

Four-year-olds, according to Bever, have developed a different strategy, one in which they hear the first noun in a sentence as the actor and the noun following the verb as the object of the action. This strategy leads them astray on sentences like "It's the horse the cow kisses," so in Bever's study they did worse than two-year-olds in this situation, generally picking the horse as the actor. In following their strategy, four-year-olds process a passive sentence as if it were an active sentence with some extra, uninterpretable parts. Thus in the study they consistently reversed the interpretations of passive sentences and acted out sentence 4 by having the horse kiss the cow.

Word order may not be the only cue children employ. Henrietta Lempert (1978) found that young children also use the animacy of the nouns involved to judge the meaning of passive sentences. When subject and object are both animate or both inanimate, the question does not arise; but when the sentence mixes animate and inanimate forms ("The ball is hit by Mickey Mouse"), three- and four-year-olds systematically choose the inanimate noun as the subject (acting out the sentence as "The ball hits Mickey Mouse," but correctly acting out "Mickey Mouse is hit by the ball"). The five-year-olds in her study had given up this strategy, generally giving correct demonstrations of passive sentences. Other studies indicate that not until the school years do children understand the passive construction when the verb involved is not an action verb ("Donald Duck was liked by Goofy") (Maratsos et al., 1979).

Passive sentences are not the only construction that gives children trouble. When active sentences are complicated, even nine-year-olds may resort to word order, interpreting the noun that most closely precedes the verb as the subject (C. Chomsky, 1969). For example, they interpret "Karen promised Father to mow the lawn" as meaning that Father mowed the lawn.

Children do not proceed directly toward adult grammar but instead construct and discard a variety of provisional grammars as they go along. As a result of these changing strategies, sentences that are correctly interpreted at one age may be misinterpreted later. The rapidity with which children acquire language, developing and discarding rules as they go, indicates that human beings are born prepared to learn language, but that extensive experience is needed for its acquisition.

THE EXTENSION OF MEANING

At the same time that children are grasping the rules that govern language, they are expanding their vocabularies and their understanding of the world. Children learn words at an amazing speed; the best guesses of researchers put the rate of increase among children of average intelligence at more than twenty words a day (G. Miller, 1978).

The Structure of Meaning

The way that children go about structuring word meaning remains a puzzle. In Chapter 11, we saw that investigators are uncertain as to whether function or perceptual qualities dominate in the formation of meaning (see the accompanying box). Clues to children's semantic knowledge often can be found in the errors they make, and researchers generally assume that these errors indicate the child's lack of knowledge or inability to retrieve a word from memory (Bowerman, 1978). However, Melissa Bowerman believes that errors are sometimes made by knowledgeable children through slips of the tongue. She recorded the speech of her preschool daughters and found that the girls began to use words incorrectly weeks or even months after they had been using them properly. When Christy was four, for example, she said when sent to her room for being naughty, "I wish you didn't *let* me go in my room," confusing "let" and "make"; and two-year-old Eva, on forgetting to bring home a book from the sitter's house said, "I didn't *put* it home," confusing "put" and "bring."

The girls were insensitive to the errors they made, never tried to correct them, and sometimes used the same word correctly only a few minutes after they had used it improperly. They rarely confused nouns; most of their errors were confined to verbs, prepositions, and adjectives that bore some relation in meaning, such as "behind" and "after" or "take" and "put." Bowerman suggests that children learn individual words without recognizing their similarity of meaning, and that errors do not appear until youngsters become aware of the similarity. As previously unrelated words move together in the organization of the child's vocabulary, they may put a strain on children's ability to plan and monitor speech. Thus, in searching for a word, a child may make the wrong choice among available words in the same semantic neighborhood.

Another clue to the way children structure word meanings is a feature that is just the opposite of the very young child's tendency to overextend meanings, which we examined in Chapter 8. Older children tend to **underextend** meanings, applying to a term only part of the meaning it has for adults. In the case of nouns, a child may know the word "food" perfectly well, for example, and asked what it means, say in the functional sort of definition that is prevalent among children, "Food is to eat." Yet asked if a cookie or a lollipop or catsup is food, the child will say no (T. White, 1982). The child probably has never heard anyone refer to catsup, cookies, and lol-

A JIGGY THAT ZIMBOS

Opinion varies among developmental psychologists as to whether children rely more on the function of objects or on their perceptual qualities when establishing mental representations of nouns. In a study designed to discover which plays the major role, Dedre Gentner (1978) reported mixed and somewhat surprising results. Gentner brought adults and children of all ages into a laboratory, one at a time. In the first room, she showed them a "jiggy," a blue and yellow wooden box with a pink plastic face on one side. The jiggy had a small hole in its bottom and a lever that caused its nose and eyes to move, changing the jiggy's expression. The adult or child was encouraged to manipulate the toy. In the second room, each person was shown a "zimbo," a plastic sphere filled with jelly beans and mounted on a red base. It, too, had a small hole in the bottom and a lever, but the zimbo's lever made jelly beans pop out of the hole. Again, the child or adult was encouraged to manipulate the zimbo and eat the jelly beans.

Next, Gentner showed each person a new object. This time it looked like a jiggy but acted like a zimbo, producing jelly beans instead of a changed expression when its lever was moved. After making sure that each person recalled the previous objects, Gentner asked them what this new object should be called. No one was allowed to use a hybrid word, such as "jiggy-zimbo" or "ziggy"; instead, each was forced to select one of the two previous names. If concepts are formed primarily on appearance, the new object should be a jiggy; if they are formed on function, it should be a zimbo.

Most three- to five-year-olds elected to call the hybrid a jiggy, choosing appearance as the dominant factor. So did adults. But more than half the five- to nine-year-olds and three-fourths of the nine- to eleven-year-olds called it a zimbo, relying on function. Although the consistent switch to function in middle childhood is unexplained, Gentner believes that she has clearly established the dominance of perceptual features in the establishment of meaning among preschoolers. She points out that children found zimbo much easier to learn than jiggy and that they played more with the jelly-bean-producing zimbo than with the jiggy, yet they persisted in naming the jelly-bean-producing jiggy a "jiggy."

lipops as food, and may have established a central meaning for the term different from that held by adults. Food might mean, for example, "things to eat that are good for you," or "fruits, vegetables, meat, and cereal." Therefore, proposes Jeremy Anglin (1977), these underextensions are not perceptual but conceptual, and they arise when children come upon poor examples of a concept—items like "catsup" that are a long way from the central meaning of "food."

Understanding Verbs

As children increase their vocabularies, verbs are added more slowly than nouns. Such a trend should not be surprising, for nouns are often concrete and their meaning is bounded by their physical nature. In contrast, verbs express relations that depend upon abstract concepts; learning the meaning of a verb requires a child to understand the abstract relations involved (Gentner, 1978). In the sentence, "Mark gave Susan some candy," for example, a child can see Mark or the candy or Susan, but must abstract the relationship between Mark's initial possession of the candy, Susan's final possession of it, and the way the candy passed from one to the other (freely? by coercion?) and so forth.

According to Dedre Gentner (1978), children learn verbs in the order of their complexity and, until they know the meaning of a complex verb, will underextend its meaning, representing just those aspects of it with which they are familiar. To test this proposal, she asked children between the ages of three and eight to act out sentences such as "Make Ernie buy a car from Bert," using dolls, toy cars, and play money. The youngest children could act out the meaning of "give" and "take"; children who were a little older could act out "pay" and "trade"; but only the oldest children could act out "buy," "sell," or "spend money." Younger children most frequently acted out "buy" as "take" and "sell" as "give." As Genter points out, children have acquired enough of the meaning of "buy" and "sell" to know that objects change hands in a certain direction, but they are unaware of the monetary nature of the transactions.

This sort of development could be traced in another study, in which John Miscione and his associates (1978) tested three- to seven-year-olds on their knowledge of "know" and "guess." Most three-year-olds have no knowledge of the words' meanings. They use "know" and "guess" indiscriminately and, say the investigators, either randomly choose one or else use the one that has been more common or regarded as more desirable in their experience. After four, the words begin to separate in meaning, and children use "know" to mean both "know" and "guess successfully," while using "guess" to mean "guess unsuccessfully." Next they go through a phase in which "guess successfully" is added to the meaning of "guess" but not applied consistently. Finally, around five or even later, they always use both words correctly. This development shows how language and cognition are linked, say the investigators, for in order to use "guess" correctly, children must be aware of the "nonperceivable aspects of the world," so that external appearance and physical outcome (the success or failure of a guess) no longer dominate their thoughts and their interpretations of words.

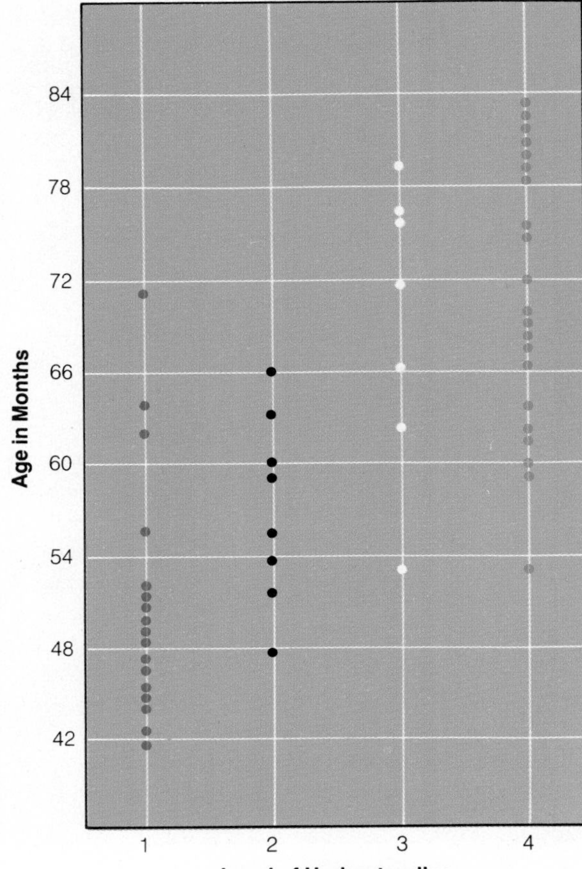

FIGURE 12.2 Children's understanding of the verbs "know" and "guess" develops gradually through four phases. In phase 1, children use either word indiscriminately; in phase 2, "know" means both "know" and "guess successfully," while "guess" means "guess unsuccessfully"; phase 3 is a transitional phase in which the words receive their correct meanings sporadically; in phase 4, both words are always used correctly. ***(From Miscione, Marvin, O'Brien, and Greenberg, 1978)***

STRUGGLING WITH SOUNDS

Although seemingly attuned to the sounds of speech at birth, many preschool children and some young schoolchildren have trouble articulating certain sounds. A common problem in English, for example, is the confusion between "r" and "w" sounds, so that children consistently say "west" instead of "rest" when it is naptime at nursery school.

Some children apparently do not notice

any difference between the sounds they confuse, but they are in the minority. Only about a third of the three- to six-year-olds who made this speech error agreed with John Locke (1979) that a picture of a common garden implement was indeed a "wake." The rest of the children had no trouble distinguishing between the sounds when an adult pronounced them and denied that a rake was a "wake," although in their speech adults perceive them as saying exactly that.

Quite a few children who make speech errors respond in this way, often becoming indignant if adults substitute the child's sounds in their own speech. That response is embodied in a conversation between mother and child reported by D. W. J. Corcoran (1971):

CHILD: I thing in thcool.
MOTHER: Do you thing every day?
CHILD: Not "thing." *Thing!*

In some cases, the child's exasperation can be explained by the fact that children are making a distinction in their speech that adults do not detect. When Judith Kornfeld (1971) subjected children's speech to spectographic analysis, she found that two-year-olds who seemed to be saying "gwass" for both "glass" and "grass" were not producing a real "w" and that the sounds they made for "l" and "r" were consistently different when analyzed by machine instead of by human ear.

Despite this actual difference in the child's production, subsequent tests have shown that when most children hear their own recorded speech, they seem to perceive it as adults do. In another study, Locke (Locke and Kutz, 1975) showed five-year-olds pictures of a wing, a ring, and a king, and asked them to point to the correct picture and label it when they heard the experimenter say the names. Later the children heard their own naming of the objects played back and again pointed to the picture as they heard the label. All children could point to the correct picture when they heard the experimenter say the label, and children who customarily made the "l-r" distinction in their own speech could identify the pictures from their own recorded labels. But children who confused the sounds in their own speech pointed to the wing whether their taped voices were ostensibly saying "wing" or "ring." In other studies, Locke (1979) has found that children who say "wing" for "ring" when looking at a picture of a ring, if asked immediately, "Did you say 'wing'?" will reply "No."

Children who confuse such sounds during production but who seem to comprehend their meaning may fail to process their own speech sounds. However, Locke thinks it more probable that the children do process their own speech sounds but pay little attention to the auditory and kinesthetic feedback from them, relying instead on their knowledge of their own intentions and on the context of the situation.

LANGUAGE IN SOCIAL SITUATIONS

As we saw in Chapter 8, babies discover that language is good for getting people's attention, that words can refer to objects in the world around them, and that using words can cause things to happen. Through their experience in social situations, they discover what can be accomplished with language. Although young children use words in rule-governed utterances, for some time their interpretation of what they hear relies heavily on context.

Context and Comprehension

If children are to comprehend the language they hear about them, they must be alert to the social, or pragmatic, meaning of others' words and often disregard their literal meaning. For example, if David's mother wants him to hang up his jacket, she could be direct and say, "Hang up your jacket." But it is highly possible that she would use an indirect way of getting her purpose accomplished, saying, "Can you hang up your jacket?" or "Your jacket is on the table." If David attended only to the literal meaning of his mother's words, he would hear nothing in either utterance that required him to do anything about his jacket. But David has learned the social con-

These girls are skilled speakers of English and have no trouble understanding each other's pragmatic meanings. An apparent insult, delivered with an affectionate grin, will be interpreted as a gesture of friendship. *(© Jeffry W. Myers/West Stock Inc.)*

ventions of English and knows that his mother is simply using a less overtly authoritarian way of phrasing her request.

Children seem to understand such indirect utterances very early. It may be that very young children do not process an entire utterance but only its core, hearing and acting on "hang up your jacket" in the question directed to their ability and "jacket" in the assertion; or it may be that they have learned to interpret such forms as "Can you" or "I wish" or "Would you mind" or "Why not" as being commands to do whatever is specified (deVilliers and deVilliers, 1978).

It may be that in many situations very young children ignore the syntax and meaning of language that is addressed to them and simply carry out whatever action seems appropriate in the immediate social context. If the context is ambiguous, they assume that language demands action. Such a proposal seemed to describe the behavior of two-year-olds studied by Marilyn Shatz (1978), who tested their comprehension with commands, questions, and simple declarative sentences spoken in a neutral fashion. She found that whether she said, for example, "Fit the ball into the truck" or "Can you fit the ball into the truck?" or "The ball fits into the truck," most children responded by putting the ball into the truck.

When she manipulated the context by setting up a situation that clearly demanded information from them, however, the children responded appropriately. For example, using a toy telephone, she either steered the child toward action (saying such things as "Push the button" and "Ring the bell") or toward information (saying such things as "Who talks on the telephone at your house?" and "Can Daddy talk on the telephone?"). Asked the test question, "Can you talk on the telephone?", children in the action setting generally responded by talking on the play phone. Children in the information setting generally said "Yes" and left it at that, or else they said "Yes" and then proceeded to demonstrate their ability. Thus, in the first situation, "Can you talk on the telephone?" was interpreted as a command; in the second situation, it was interpreted as a request for information. When words and actions work together to make simple action inappropriate and the giving of information appropriate, children will provide the needed information.

A child's interpretation of another's utterance may also depend upon his or her status in relation to the speaker. When the words come from a parent, a teacher, or another adult, five-year-olds are likely to treat simple declarative statements or ambiguous questions about their ability to carry out an act as indirect commands. By the time they are in the second grade, however, they pay more attention to the form of an

No matter what sort of scene this little girl finds in her magazine, her comments are likely to be limited to identifying the objects she sees. *(© Joel Gordon)*

utterance and respond to requests, commands, ambiguous questions, and statements in different ways (Olson, 1980).

Context continues to guide children in other ways. Five-year-olds are attentive to the implicit information in others' remarks and use it to frame their own utterances. Younger children, however, generally ignore such information. This difference appeared in a study of three- to five-year-old Canadian children conducted by Verne Bacharach and Mary Luszcz (1979). Before showing the children a series of pictures, the investigators commented in a manner meant to define the children's responses to the command, "Tell me about the picture." Showing the picture of a horse pulling a wagon, for example, the investigator sometimes prefaced the command with "Did you know horses can do a lot of different things? Horses can run. Horses can eat hay." At other times, the investigator said such things as "Did you know there are a lot of different animals? A cow is an animal. A rabbit is an animal."

Young children generally ignored the content of the remarks, responding in both situations with "Horse" or "It's a horse" or "Wagon." But the five-year-olds structured their remarks around the content of the prefacing comments, in the first instance saying such things as "It's pulling a wagon," and in the second, "That's a horse." The reason for the younger children's disregard of the implicit directions is unclear. They may lack the linguistic ability to use such information; the information may already have slipped from working memory by the time they respond; they may be biased toward identifying objects in all conditions; or they may simply fail to pay attention to the investigator's remarks.

Using Conversation

Until children begin school their conversations with their caregivers continue to be the major influence on their acquisition of language. From the games and interactions of infancy, children have learned the way a conversation is structured; they have mastered the arts of turn-taking, joint attention, and signaling their intentions. Once they begin putting several words together, their side of the conversational exchange grows. No longer restricted to such replies as "Uh huh" or "Dere" or "Daddy coat," they can make suggestions and introduce new topics.

Sometimes a conversation goes well, and a two-year-old maintains his or her side of the talk over twenty or more turns, always responding appropriately. At other times, conversation breaks down and the child either lapses into silence, resorts to repeatedly saying "huh?" or makes an irrelevant comment, as when one thirty-month-old boy replied to "Which is your ball?" with "Drink copee" (Brown, 1980). After studying the transcripts of conversations between twenty-one young children and a pair of developmental psychologists, Brown concluded that the content of adult-child conversations is their least important aspect. As he points out, when an adult says, "What's this, Susan?" and Susan replies, "A rabbit," the adult has learned nothing about the picture book they are sharing, but a good deal about Susan's assumptions and linguistic knowledge.

When a child's responses are relevant, the adult conversational partner is reassured that the pair share certain cultural beliefs that form the background of the conversation (Pickert and Furth, 1980). The child's contributions reveal his or her linguistic competence and knowledge, so that, as Brown points out, adults use these conversations as a running check on the child's progress. Research has shown that most parents are good at predicting their preschoolers' level of linguistic proficiency (Gleason and Weintraub, 1978).

When conversation does break down, adults are alerted to gaps in the child's understanding and adjust their own conversation to compensate (Brown, 1980). If the missing part is small (suppose Susan had identified the rabbit as "A mouse"), they try to help by filling in whatever information the child needs. But if the breakdown is due to a more general problem of understanding, as in the small boy's irrelevant "Drink copee," the adult holds back but tries the same sort of situation again later. Instead of launching into lengthy tutorial sessions, says Brown, adults use small efforts spread over long periods of time.

Although parents often correct gross errors in a child's choice of words or pronunciation, they are usually more interested in the truth of an utterance than in its syntax (Brown, Cazden, and Bellugi-Klima, 1968). For example, in the longitudinal study of Adam, Eve, and Sarah, when Eve wanted to indicate that her mother was a girl and said "He a girl," her mother replied "That's right." But when Adam said, using acceptable grammar, "Walt Disney comes on on Tuesday," his mother corrected him because the Disney program appeared on Sunday.

As a result of their experiences with adults, children become more skillful at adjusting their speech to conventional usage. As Susan Ervin-Tripp (1976) points out, they learn to stay on the topic by using expressions like "and" or "because." They learn to soften their requests, adding "please." They learn to time their speech so it does not overlap with or disrupt what their partner says, and to keep the conversation focused on the matter at hand by planning what to say next. Gradually, they learn the convention that when they change the topic, they are supposed to indicate the shift. By about the age of eight or nine, they are likely to signal a change by saying something like, "Oh yeah, that reminds me. . . ."

Role-Switching

Just as adults change their way of talking when interacting with children, so children quickly learn to adapt their speech to the audience. When Rochel Gelman and Marilyn Shatz (1977) asked four-year-olds to explain the workings of a toy to two-year-olds, they found that the older preschoolers modified their speech much as adults would. One four-year-old, explaining the way a dumping station with trucks and marbles worked, said:

> I gave you it. You want to have something funny? Put the marbles in here. Put the marbles in here. I'll give you the marbles. Now pour them in here. Go up here. And pour them in here. Now we have to dump it. Dump it. No, not in here. Pour it in here. Pour it in here, OK? That's funny. No, not like that. I'll do it. See, Sara? (p. 43)

Like this child, the four-year-olds used repetition and simple, short sentences, adapting their speech to the limited capabilities of their pupils. They also used a "show and tell" technique, describing and demonstrating what the younger children were to do. Four-year-olds without younger brothers or sisters were as skillful in modifying their speech as four-year-olds with younger siblings, indicating that the switch to teacher does not come from practicing the role at home.

Children switch to a special style of language among themselves, sprinkling their speech with code words, such as "yukk." *(© René Burri/Magnum Photos)*

Other research has shown that children also use a particular style when talking to their peers. They use certain expressive code words, such as "yukk," "blech," or "gross"; they use chants and rhymes and often use first names; and they copy one another's utterances (Gleason and Weintraub, 1978).

Children talk differently to parents and to teachers, to peers and to younger siblings, to the policeman on the street corner and to their grandmothers. By the time youngsters are in school, their grammar and vocabulary have become flexible enough for them to understand that different listeners have different needs, to distinguish between more and less polite styles of speech, to detect whether an interchange requires a polite or a colloquial manner, and to choose from their various speech styles the appropriate code for the situation (deVilliers and deVilliers, 1978).

Both ethnic and socioeconomic influences on speech are likely to affect the success of these Hispanic children in formal education. *(© Hazel Hankin/Stock, Boston)*

SOCIAL FACTORS AND LANGUAGE DEVELOPMENT

Because language is acquired in the family, a child's speech inevitably reflects the influence of social class and ethnic group (Laosa, 1981). Although differences are not deficits, these influences may lead to difficulties when children start school.

Socioeconomic Differences

The attitudes of parents toward language, the richness of their vocabularies, their responses to a child's attempts at speech, and the amount and kind of conversation that takes place in a home are likely to affect children's attitudes toward speech and to influence their success in formal education. Language style, vocabulary size, and ease of expression may all show evidence of socioeconomic class. Studies that compare the language use of various children indicate that children from the more advantaged sections of society score higher on tests of pronunciation, vocabulary, and sentence structure than do children from lower socioeconomic groups (R. Hess, 1970), since the language of the school is fairly close to the language of the middle-class home. Such tests do not, however, show that middle-class children use superior sentence structure or grammatical patterns in their regular speech.

Children from different social classes also show differences in their expressive language. Early studies led researchers to believe that individuals in lower socioeconomic groups tend to express themselves with gestures in situations where those in higher socioeconomic groups use words (Miller and Swanson, 1966). Related language differences appeared in a series of studies by Basil Bernstein (1962, 1966). Bernstein analyzed the speech of sixteen-year-old boys from English lower and middle classes who were matched for intelligence. He discovered that the middle-class boys produced more elaborate descriptions, used a wider vocabulary with more nouns, and spoke fluently, making short pauses in their utterances. The boys from the lower socioeconomic class made fewer distinctions, used more common words—especially pronouns—and paused longer in their speech. As a result, the descriptions by the middle-class boys were

MAKING DEAF CHILDREN COMPETENT COMMUNICATORS

More than nine out of ten deaf children are born to hearing parents (Schein and Delt, 1974), and it is often late in infancy before deafness is diagnosed. Since hearing parents do not acquire a gestural language until after the diagnosis is made, most deaf children are unlikely to have the same richness of early symbolic interaction with their caregivers as hearing children do.

More than half the deaf preschoolers in this country are now being trained in both sign and spoken language. But until recently, deaf children were discouraged from using sign language on the grounds that they would rely on it and would never learn to speak properly or get along in a hearing world (Lane, 1980). Some educators still believe that spoken language should be primary and that sign language should be considered a last resort.

Indications that such a policy may have negative consequences for deaf children appeared in a study of deaf preschoolers by Mark Greenberg (1980). Greenberg studied deaf, but otherwise normal, three- to five-year-olds with hearing parents, dividing them into children who used both manual and oral communication with their mothers and those who used only speech. Through a one-way mirror he videotaped the youngsters in both a play situation and an instructional situation with their mothers. Regardless of their method of communication, the fluent communicators in each group behaved similarly in regard to language—asking questions, stating information, discussing their own actions, and discussing absent objects, people, or events significantly more than children who were not competent communicators. The only difference between the oral and manual groups on language measures was the greater tendency of children in the manual group to use both hands and speech to communicate or to initiate exchanges with their mothers.

When Greenberg observed other aspects of social interaction, however, he found large differences in the patterning and quality. Children who used both methods of communication were more sociable and cooperative; they were less likely to avert their gaze from their mothers and more likely to touch them than were children who were confined to speech. Mothers of the dual communicators laughed more often than did the mothers of the group who only spoke. Finally, each interaction between dual communicators and their mothers tended to be longer and more complex than was each interaction between the children who were confined to speech and their mothers.

Other studies indicate that deaf children show a higher incidence of behavior problems than hearing children, tend to be egocentric and impulsive, and have problems in school (Schlesinger and Meadow, 1972; Meadow, 1975; Levine, 1960). Since teaching oral language to deaf children involves both struggle and heavy repetition, Greenberg suggests that the ease that seems to accompany the dual method of communication provides a more accepting atmosphere for the child than does insistence on speech, and that it may lead to swifter communication gains and better social adjustment. In addition, since deaf children generally acquire language more slowly than hearing children, the high incidence of spontaneous communication among children who used both oral and manual methods might also presage a more rapid acquisition of language.

less tied to context than those by the lower-class boys and made fewer assumptions about the listener's knowledge.

This sort of difference appears to vary with such factors as the topic boys are asked to talk about, the setting, and the purpose (Higgins, 1976). For example, when an inner-city black child of eight was interviewed in a test situation, the boy answered in monosyllables, his replies consisting largely of reluctant "Nope's" and

"Hmm-m's." But when he was seen in a less formal setting, where the researcher sat on the floor, passed around potato chips, introduced taboo words to indicate it was safe to say anything, and asked another child to join the conversation, the boy's utterances lengthened, he used complex grammatical constructions, and he was an eager participant in the conversation (Labov, 1969b).

Dialect Differences

When societies are made up of many ethnic groups, language dialects vary from region to region. Substantial segments of the U.S. population are either Hispanic or black, and children who speak Spanish or Black English at home may find themselves suddenly faced with problems when they enter the school system. The Hispanic problem is straightforward; most teachers recognize Spanish as a legitimate language and see their role as introducing the Spanish-speaking child to a second language that she or he will need to succeed in the larger society. But for many years, teachers and some researchers regarded Black English as a debased form of Standard English, calling it "not merely an underdeveloped version of English, but . . . a basically non-logical mode of expressive behavior" (Bereiter et al., 1966). Analyses of Black English have shown that such a view is simply wrong.

In linguistic terms, Black and Standard English are minor variants of the same English language; in developmental terms, acquisition of the two dialects follows similar patterns. For example, studies by Dan Slobin and Claudia Mitchell-Kernan (Slobin, 1975) of black children in the Oakland, California, ghetto show no difference between the basic pattern of language development in ghetto children and in the middle-class children studied by Roger Brown at Harvard. The Oakland children spend most of their time learning language from older siblings and playmates, who watch over them during the day. This situation is common in cultures around the world, however, and seems to have no effect on the basic rate at which a child acquires syntax. The two dialects are especially close at the preschool period and are roughly equivalent on functional and grammatical grounds, as shown in the examples in Table 12.1.

TABLE 12.1
DIALECT DIFFERENCES IN NEGATIVE UTTERANCES OF PRESCHOOL-AGE CHILDREN

Oakland Children	*Harvard Children*
That's not no bathroom.	It wasn't no chicken.
I'm not doing nothing.	I wasn't doing nothing.
I don't get no whipping.	I don't want no milk.
Nobody wasn't scared.	But nobody wasn't gonna know it.
Why bears can't talk.	Why I can't put them on?
But Renée or nobody wouldn't peel me no kinda orange.	Nobody won't recognize me.
Why she won't sit up?	Why we didn't?
	Why it's not working?
Nobody wouldn't help me.	No one didn't took it.
I don't have no suitcase.	It don't have no wings.
Never I don't get no whipping.	I never won't get it.

Source: The Oakland examples are drawn from unpublished data of Claudia Mitchell-Kernan, and the Harvard examples from unpublished data of Roger Brown.

During later childhood, the dialects diverge; but even at the adult level, the difference is only superficial, as William Labov (1973) has pointed out. Schoolteachers often criticize Black English because it apparently lacks the verb "to be." Labov (1969a) has shown, however, that the verb occurs in many places in Black English and that its omission follows a strict rule. Speakers of Standard English often contract "to be" to a simple "-'s" in the present tense ("She's tough" rather than "She is tough"). Wherever Standard English can contract, Black English can—but does not always—omit the verb ("She tough"). Such an omission does not indicate that Black English lacks an important part of English grammar. Wherever it is impossible to contract "to be" in Standard English, it is impossible to delete "to be" in Black English, as shown in Table

TABLE 12.2
EXAMPLES OF *BE* IN TWO DIALECTS OF AMERICAN ENGLISH

Black English	*Standard English*
Deletion	*Contraction*
She the first one.	She's the first one.
But he wild.	But he's wild.
You out of the game.	You're out of the game.
We on tape.	We're on tape.
He always complainin'.	He's always complaining.
He gon' try to get up.	He's gonna try to get up.
Nondeletion	*Nondeletion*
I was small.	I was small.
You got to be good.	You've got to be good.
Be cool, brothers!	Be cool, brothers!
He *is* an expert.	He *is* an expert.
Is he dead?	Is he dead?
Are you down?	Are you down?
Is that a shock or is it not?	Is that a shock or is it not?
I don't care what you are.	I don't care what you are.
Do you see where that person is?	Do you see where that person is?

Source: Adapted from William Labov, "Contraction, Deletion, and Inherent Variability of the English Copula," *Language*, 45 (1969), 715–762. The Black English examples are drawn from Labov (with some abbreviation), and the Standard English equivalents have been supplied for the purposes of this comparative table.

Although Black English is only superficially different from Standard English, its use outside the black community may prove an obstacle to a child's social and economic advancement. ***(Barbara Young/Photo Researchers, Inc.)***

12.2. When speakers of Standard English want to emphasize a statement, they put heavy stress on the verb ("She IS tough"). In this situation, "is" also appears in Black English, and the Black form is the same as the Standard.

Given differences as subtle and superficial as these, it is difficult to believe that the use of Black English indicates anything more than a difference in sociocultural background. However, the vocabulary, pronunciation, and style of Black English tend to label the child speaker in the eyes of the middle-class speaker of Standard English. Sometimes communication even breaks down. If a black child tells his teacher, "Dey ain't like dat," the teacher assumes that the boy has said "They aren't like that." Instead, the message the child intended was "They didn't like that." When this happens, the teacher often decides that because the child's speech is unintelligible, he is unintelligent. A vicious circle may begin. Since the teacher expects the boy to do poorly, the child fulfills her expectations and fails.

One way to break the circle is to instruct teachers in Black English so that they can understand their students. (This suggestion, of course, also applies to teachers of Hispanic students; it applies to the teachers of any students who in their homes speak a language or dialect other than Standard English.) Despite its richness as a language, Black English has an uneasy relationship with success in American society. Unless its young speakers can use the Standard dialect as well, they will lack a basic tool for social and economic advancement.

Compensating for Differences

Social environments differ in regard to how closely they match the school environment. As we have seen, speakers of Black English are at a disadvantage when compared with middle-class children, whose socioeconomic background has led them to acquire the motivations, habits, speech forms, vocabulary, and pronunciation demanded by the school system. The mismatch between home and school that has been observed among social groups in various countries is not based on purely linguistic factors; it is also related to other environmental features.

Studies of Norwegian children show that different social settings can affect cognitive development in different ways. Marida Hollos and Philip Cowan (1973) compared isolated Norwegian farm children with the children of families of similar size and educational background in a small village and in a medium-sized town in Norway. The farm children spent most of their time watching others or playing alone. They had few toys. Their mothers neither prompted nor encouraged them to talk, and there was no storytelling or discussion. The children interacted with adults only at mealtimes and in the evenings, which were largely devoted to television.

Yet the basic language development among these isolated farm children was similar to that of village and town children, although the latter groups had many more opportunities for verbal interaction. The greater language experience of the village and town children put them ahead of the farm children in one area: they were more advanced in their ability to take a viewpoint other than their own. But the farm children were superior to the town and village children in their ability to think logically about physical properties and their relationships. Both abilities are important for schooling and necessary for the process of development.

Because the verbal environment affects only some aspects of cognitive development, thinking which supposes that "cultural deprivation" or poverty results in language deficits, and that deficient language delays or blocks full cognitive development, needs to be reexamined. Such premises have been the basis for many compensatory education programs for lower-class minority children in the United States (Bereiter and Engelmann, 1966). Most studies indicate that all children learn the basic rules of language equally well, according to universal patterns of development. In this sense, there is no such thing as a "language deficit" in child development, only a "language difference" (Laosa, 1981).

The problem of schooling, therefore, is neither one of teaching the child to think nor of teaching the child to speak. Instead, it is a matter of finding out which aspects of cognition need stimulation for a particular child or group of children and then devising appropriate means (not necessarily verbal) to foster those facets of intellectual growth.

In the past few years, specific programs for developing language skills have been developed. Some have used learning-based procedures, including instructions, adult modeling, social approval, and other rewards. The results indicate that such programs can improve specific language skills, increasing the rate of children's spontaneous speech and its correctness, teaching them to time their conversation appropriately, and improving their storytelling skills and their descriptions of their own behavior. But it should be noted that these programs do not need to focus on teaching the basic structure of a language.

SUMMARY

1. Children appear to approach language with expectations and a set of strategies, called operating principles, that make some linguistic constructions easier to learn than others. In

observing young children's natural speech and noting their omissions, errors, and well-formed utterances, researchers have found that children simplify language by avoiding exceptions to grammatical rules, thus overregularizing their speech. In English, overregularization shows most clearly in the past tense of verbs ("breaked") and in the plural form of nouns ("foots").

2. Children's strategies sometimes lead them to misinterpret sentences, especially when the grammatical construction is complex. Over time, children appear to construct and discard a variety of provisional rules correctly interpreting a certain kind of sentence, such as a passive one, at one age but not at another.

3. Errors of meaning found in young children may indicate not a lack of knowledge but a growing awareness that two words have similar meanings. Older children frequently underextend meanings, applying only a part of the meaning a word has for adults; the underextension is not perceptual but occurs when items are poor examples of a concept.

4. Verbs are added more slowly to children's vocabularies than are nouns, since nouns are often concrete whereas verbs generally involve abstract relations. Until children know the meaning of a verb, they will underextend its meaning, representing only those aspects with which they are familiar.

5. Children who confuse sounds in their own production of sentences do not confuse them in comprehending the speech of others. [illegible] be that such children pay little attention to feedback from their own speech sounds but instead rely on their intentions and on context.

6. Young children may decode the language they hear according to social context, not syntax. Preschoolers treat adults' declarative statements and ambiguous questions as indirect commands, but seven-year-olds distinguish among requests, commands, ambiguous questions, and statements. In addition, preschoolers ignore implicit information in the remarks of others, but five-year-olds are attentive to such information. Children quickly learn to adapt their speech to a particular audience, switching their speech style when talking to parents, peers, or younger children.

7. Various socioeconomic and ethnic backgrounds result in differences in language style, vocabulary, and ease of expression, with middle-class children having an advantage in school because the language of their homes matches the language of the school. However, none of these backgrounds leads to major differences in the acquisition of the basic grammar of a language. Dialectical differences in language, such as that found in speakers of Black English, reflect no difference in the knowledge of English syntax. Nevertheless, the use of dialects affects the degree of success in society, so youngsters need to be able to use the Standard dialect fluently.

13 PERSONALITY: ESTABLISHING SOCIAL INTERACTION

When David was eighteen months old, his big sister once amused herself by dressing him like a girl. She draped a cloth around him like a dress, put a woman's hat on his head and a pair of their mother's shoes on his feet, decked him with jewelry, and carefully painted his lips and rouged his cheeks. David thought it was fun, and staggered through the house in high heels, showing himself off to the family. David is now four; last week his older sister tried to dress him in girls' clothes and he objected violently. "Boys don't dress like that!" he said indignantly. David has accomplished one of the social tasks of early childhood; he has established his identity as a male.

The years from two to six are the magic years of childhood. Probably at no other time do children experience so much that is new, exciting, and pleasurable. And at no other time in their lives do they confront so many challenges, conflicts, anxieties, and fears. During these formative years, children turn away from caregivers and expand their world to include other children, other adults, and an ever-widening environment. By learning from their parents, by imitating their brothers and sisters, by observing other children and adults in person and on television, youngsters come to behave as those around them do.

In this chapter, as in Chapter 9, we will consider the development of personality as a function of socialization. We will see how children's contacts with their parents, their peers, and their culture affect their personalities. After discussing the general process of socialization, we will look at the process of identification, a major mechanism of socialization. We will examine the development of sex roles and of self-concept as significant aspects of personality. One by one, we will consider various sources of socialization: parents, peers, teachers, and television—paying special attention to sex-role development and to methods of socialization: reinforcement, punishment, and modeling. When we consider television, we will examine what children watch and when they act upon the positive social messages they receive from the omnipresent medium.

THE PROCESS OF SOCIALIZATION

Socialization is the process of absorbing the attitudes, values, and customs of a society. Through pressures from parents, peers, teachers, other adults, and the media, acceptable behavior is encouraged and undesirable behavior discouraged. As a result, children learn to behave in culturally approved ways, paying at least lip service to the dominant values, ideals, and motivations of the groups that include them.

Although the specific elements of socialization differ across cultures, many psychologists believe that in all of them the same individual and social mechanisms operate: (1) the desire to obtain affection, regard, acceptance, and recognition; (2) the wish to avoid the unpleasant feelings that follow rejection or punishment; (3) the tendency to imitate the actions of others; and (4) the desire to be like specific people whom the child has grown to respect, admire, or love—a process called **identification.**

Although the concept of identification is central to Freudian theory as well as to social-learning and cognitive approaches to personality development, each group ascribes a different role and function to it. Sigmund Freud (1917) saw identification as the process by which children take on the characteristics and match the behavior of the parent of the opposite sex. He believed that the process plays an important role in the development of moral standards, sex roles, and social attitudes. Freud proposed that identification resulted from children's psychosexual conflicts with, and attachment to, their parents. When children identify with the parent of the same sex, their personality undergoes structural changes. The social-learning view, represented by Walter Mischel (1968), sees identification as part of the general process of learning, acquired by observing parents and imitating their behavior. Since parents are powerful models, identification is important in the acquisition of complex behavior. The cognitive-developmental view, represented by Lawrence Kohlberg (1963), sees identification as an aspect of a particular phase of cognitive development, arising once children understand their gender is permanent. It is a way for children to enhance their competence by sharing the skills of others.

Despite these differences in their views of the origin and functioning of identification, all three groups hold in common: (1) the central place of identification in the socialization process; (2) the child's development of new, complex behavior by matching the behavior of parents; and (3) the particular significance of this mechanism in the development of sex roles.

SEX-ROLE DEVELOPMENT

Matt and Susan were not born male and female —psychologically. They became so by being socialized into adopting the behavior and qualities that their society considers appropriate and desirable for people of their gender. Cultures make many distinctions between the social roles of the sexes, and these **sex roles,** or outer manifestations of gender—such as speech, dress, and actions—encompass behavior that has little to do with the reproductive and erotic differences dictated by biological equipment (Tavris and Offir, 1977).

But children must also develop **gender identity,** an invisible role that consists of the inner experience of gender, the unchanging sense of self as male or female (Money and Ehrhardt, 1972). In the discussion of self-appraisal in the next section, we will see how children acquire a sense of gender identity, and how gender identity overlaps with sex role. Gender identity has generally received less attention from researchers than sex-roles have, because society places enormous importance on appropriate male and female behavior.

The Cultural Bases of Sex Roles

Cultural conceptions of masculine and feminine behavior have important influences on the kind of person that a child will become, and every culture establishes its own patterns of behavior and psychological standards for each gender, im-

PERSONALITY IN EARLY CHILDHOOD

PSYCHODYNAMIC VIEW

Sigmund Freud emphasized the notion that early childhood is critical in the socialization of the individual. During these years, the child's sensual pleasure is focused on the genitals, and the child develops an incestuous desire for the parent of the opposite sex, along with a wish to do away with the parent of the same sex. Whether the opposite-sex parent responds with warmth and affection to the child, thereby indirectly satisfying the child's desires, affects personality development. According to Freud, the oedipal conflict is resolved when the child gives up sexual rivalry and instead identifies with the parent of the same sex. This identification forms the basis for appropriate sex-role development, with the parent also becoming the model for the values that will be part of the child's adult personality.

Erik Erikson concurs with the view that peer and parental responses are important factors in socialization during early childhood. Appropriate sex-role behavior develops when a child identifies with the same-sex parent and assimilates the parent's behavior into the child's own personal identity. Parental support and encouragement when the child first attempts to acquire appropriate male or female behavior can help the child achieve a positive self-image and a strong personal identity. But parents are not the only people who fill this role; members of the child's peer group are also important.

COGNITIVE-DEVELOPMENTAL VIEW

Lawrence Kohlberg emphasizes cognitive development as the most important factor in socialization. Identification with the same-sex parent develops only after a child acquires a sense of gender identity. Thus once girls or boys begin to think of themselves as girls or boys, they want to talk, think, and act as others of their sex do. In the process, they come to identify with their parents. In this view, although parents, peers, and other adults are important in socialization because they provide models and approval, children basically socialize themselves as they discover how to behave in competent, acceptable ways.

SOCIAL-LEARNING VIEW

Walter Mischel, a social-learning theorist, has concentrated on the development of personality, and sees the process of socialization as continuous from infancy through childhood. By interacting with their environment, children learn to behave in increasingly complex ways and discover the consequences of their actions. Sex-role development involves learning appropriate behavior, which—in turn—is modified by the consequences that follow when the child performs it. Parents act as models; they—as well as the child's peers and other adults—shape the child's behavior by the nature of their response to his or her actions.

posing these standards at an early age (E. Werner, 1979). Sex roles are inevitably interwoven with the status that society attaches to each role. Male dominance was one of the earliest bases of discrimination among human beings, presumably because survival among hunting and gathering tribes depended on the ability to move about unencumbered by childbearing and nursing. The burden of advanced pregnancy or of carrying a small child would make it impos-

Every culture establishes its own standards of behavior for each gender; in the culture of these children a boy can care for a younger sibling and still feel masculine. *(© Leonard Speier 1980)*

sible for a woman to throw a spear accurately or to run after game (Friedl, 1978).

Male children have always been valued, and many cultures regularly killed excess female babies at birth (deMause, 1974). Over succeeding generations, the superior position of the male was incorporated into customs, laws, and socialization patterns. According to a cross-cultural survey of tribal societies by Herbert Barry, Margaret Bacon, and Irvin Child (1957), the more its economy requires physical strength, the more strongly a society emphasizes sex differences in socialization. In most societies, the prestige of a task determines whether it is assigned to males or females, with women often treated as if they were members of an inferior group.

Children learn these status differences early. For example, three-year-olds in a university nursery school firmly believed that boys would grow up to be boss and that girls would grow up to clean the house and be nurses or teachers (Kuhn, Nash, and Brucken, 1978). As children get a little older, the status differences seem to become more deeply ingrained in boys than in girls. When nearly sixty kindergarten children were asked what the most important job in the world was, both boys and girls mentioned policeman, fireman, and doctor. Girls added teacher to the list. But when asked whether they could fill "the most important job" when they grew up, less than half the girls but two-thirds of the boys believed they could. And while more than three-fourths of the girls agreed that boys could handle the most important job, only about a fifth of the boys said a girl could do it (Tavris and Offir, 1977).

Although changes in the roles of women and men in this society have been going on for at least two decades, the traditional responsibilities of the sexes remain as they have been. Despite the large increase in the number of working women, any major shift in their responsibility for home and children is unlikely to come about soon (Frieze et al., 1978). As a girl grows, she discovers that society has defined her role as spouse and parent as primary and her vocational role as secondary; the reverse is true for a boy. To fulfill these social roles, girls are likely to be reared to nurture others and boys to achieve. Thus as soon as children enter early childhood, almost all societies foster obedience, nurturance, and responsibility in girls, and achievement and self-reliance in boys.

The differences between male and female roles go beyond prescribed sex-role behavior, extending into **sex-role stereotypes**—simplified, fixed concepts about the behavior and traits typical of each sex. Learning their society's stereotypes is a major developmental step for young children, and their exaggeration of sex roles makes the acquisition easier. By the time they are five or six, children have sex-typed the virtues (Kohlberg, 1966). Most girls come to perceive that feminine competence and status are based on being attractive and good rather than on being powerful, aggressive, or fearless. Most boys come to perceive that they should be aggressive when attacked, independent, and able to suppress the display of emotions. In studying sex roles, psychologists have shown a particular interest in the development of aggression and dependence—two sex-related traits that are magnified in sex-role stereotypes.

Assertion and Aggression

Children around the world bicker, hurl epithets, shove, kick, hit, fight, and break things. All cultures have rules for socializing aggressive behavior, teaching youngsters acceptable ways of managing their hostility and anger. These feelings arise in situations that appear either to jeopardize an individual's physical well-being or to threaten important goals and values. The immediate emotional response is anger at the threatening person or object; the adaptive response involves taking effective action to avert the threat.

The concept of aggressiveness has become tangled with assertiveness in our thinking, particularly with respect to competition and striving for success. We tend to describe behavior in ourselves as assertive that we would label as aggressive in anyone else. And because this culture values gentleness in women, an assertive girl is likely to be called aggressive; her behavior violates the female sex-role stereotype. One way to avoid this dilemma is to define **assertiveness** as goal-directed verbal or physical behavior that is appropriate and harms no one, and **aggressiveness** as goal-directed verbal or physical behavior that is inappropriate or injures someone. Confusion between the concepts can have disastrous consequences, for attempts to stamp out all aggressive behavior in children may also inhibit legitimate self-assertion. In the healthy socialization of aggression, children learn effective ways to stand up for themselves without injuring others.

There is a good deal of evidence that in this society it is difficult for females to be either assertive or aggressive. Studies (Cosentino and Heilbrun, 1964) have found more anxiety and conflict about aggression in females than in males. Women who feel angry tend to feel guilty about it and to cope with their anger in ineffectual ways, with indirect displays of hostility, with sudden hostile outbursts, or simply by avoiding the situation.

Data gathered by developmental psychologists consistently show that aggressive behavior has been considered appropriate only for boys (Maccoby and Jacklin, 1974), with what appears to be an inevitable consequence. In a study that followed eighty-nine children from early childhood to young adulthood, Jerome Kagan and Howard Moss (1962) found that aggressiveness tended to be stable in males over the years but declined in females. Since we tolerate aggressive behavior in boys, the aggression they show in early childhood is unlikely to be the target of systematic efforts toward change.

Other investigators have reported that boys as young as two are more physically aggressive and more negativistic than girls. By the time they are in nursery school, boys are selective in the targets of their physical assaults, usually picking as victims other boys, particularly those who give in (Maccoby, 1976). Rarely is a girl the target of assault.

The consistency of the finding that males are, on the average, more physically aggressive than females suggests biological contributions to such behavior, and in their survey of more than 1,400 studies of sex differences, Eleanor Maccoby and Carol Jacklin (1974; 1980) concluded that there appears to be some biological predisposition to aggression among males. But a child's behavior is the product of continuous interaction between constitutional factors and the child's environment. As Seymour Feshbach (1970) has suggested, males may not be predisposed to aggressiveness but may have different social experiences because of their greater physical strength and more vigorous motor impulses. For example, boys are more successful than girls in getting what they want by hitting. Also, parents more often frustrate a boy's impulsive acts, thereby stimulating his aggressive reactions.

Regardless of predisposing constitutional factors, the social environment can overwhelm-

Although American society has traditionally inhibited aggression in girls, today a girl is often encouraged to be assertive. *(© Michael Weisbrot & Family)*

ingly influence the way aggression is expressed. Physical aggressiveness is the hallmark of masculinity in many societies, but cultural patterns of aggression for each sex vary widely (B. Whiting, 1963). The link between biology and sex roles may have to do with the relative ease with which children learn whatever sex-role behavior their culture considers appropriate. Facilitating aggression in boys and inhibiting it in girls while channeling it into desired forms in both sexes may require that socializing agents devote more effort to children of one sex than to the other (Eron, 1980).

As a result of cultural stereotypes, fathers and mothers expect more physical aggression from boys than from girls (Maccoby, 1976), and they may praise or otherwise reinforce their sons' aggression when it is directed not at them but at other children. In addition, most parents are inclined to overlook mild physical aggression in their sons and punish only extreme acts. By doing so, they teach their sons that aggression is acceptable in some situations.

As several researchers have indicated (Feshbach, 1970; Feshbach and Fraczek, 1979), the form aggression takes, a factor that is influenced by society, is important in considering sex differences in overt aggression. A variety of studies have shown that boys are likely to express aggression physically, but girls are likely to scold or argue or to use such indirect forms of aggression as gossip, resistance to demands, and subtle forms of rejection.

Although girls and boys may differ in the extent to which they find aggression a useful and accepted way to solve problems, girls are just as capable of aggression and under certain circumstances express it as much as boys do (Franzini, Litrownik, and Blanchard, 1978). The situation does not change as they grow up. When Ann Frodi, Jacqueline Macauly, and Pauline Thome (1977) reviewed numerous studies on aggression, they found that in some circumstances women are as aggressive as men. In face-to-face encounters with another adult, women are less likely than men to engage in verbal or physical aggression. In situations where aggression is justified, however, or when they can remain anonymous, women tend to be as aggressive as men.

Dependence and Independence

As we saw in Chapter 9, when infants attach themselves to someone, they attend to that person, demand attention from him or her, derive pleasure from interacting with the person, show distress when separated, and seek physical contact with the attachment figure in strange or threatening situations. As children venture into the world of playmates and adults, these manifestations of attachment fade; instead, three- or four-year-olds display a less intense behavior that psychologists have described as **dependence behavior.**

Most developmental psychologists distinguish between two kinds of dependence: emotional, referring to the child's relations with people; and instrumental, referring to the child's relations with the environment. In **emotional dependence,** children's aims are affection and support; they find contact with people rewarding and satisfying. In **instrumental dependence,** children seek help and comfort as a means to other ends, as when they ask adults to help them perform tasks or to aid them in conflicts with their playmates.

Several factors influence the way dependence is shown by young children. In situations that evoke anxiety or stress, or when deprived of social contact, they are likely to show increased emotional dependence (Hartup, 1964b). In very early childhood, there is a high correlation between emotional and instrumental dependence, but as the child gets older they become less related. Thus, a four- or five-year-old who shows extreme instrumental dependence may show little emotional dependence (Emmerich, 1966).

By the time boys and girls are six or seven, they show relatively stable and well-defined gender differences in dependence (Mischel, 1970), differences that arise in part from past parental practices. Parents are likely to encourage independence earlier in their sons than in their daughters. Beverly Fagot (1974) found that mothers discouraged their toddler sons from following them around the house but encouraged their daughters to stay near them. Other studies show that boys are allowed to investigate wider areas of the community without asking for parental permission (Saegert and Hart, 1976) and that they are expected to run errands at an earlier age. When mothers of four-year-olds were asked at what age they thought children should be permitted various independent activities, mothers of boys listed younger ages, compared with mothers of girls, for such behavior as crossing the street alone, using sharp tools, and going off to play without telling a parent their destination (Callard, 1964). As a result, boys tend to check with their mothers less often and to become more independent, exploratory, and assertive. Girls tend to continue checking frequently with their mothers, to be less assertive and more dependent, and to stay in secure surroundings. The stable pattern of dependence in girls generally continues into adulthood, probably because the cultural sex-role stereotype supports such behavior in women.

This young boy is displaying emotional dependence, seeking affection and support in a stressful situation. *(Burk Uzzle/Magnum)*

As sex-role stereotypes in contemporary American society change, and traditional conceptions of masculine and feminine behavior become more fluid, more and more husbands share careers, housekeeping, and child-care responsibilities. Such parents are less likely than conventional parents to model rigid sex-role differences and less likely to expect them from their children. They are more likely to encourage their children to develop a combination of feminine

UNDERSTANDING GENDER			
	Percent Answering Correctly		
Task	24 months	30 months	36 months
Identify own picture	82	100	100
Apply gender labels to stereotypical pictures of people	76	83	90
Stereotype objects and clothes by gender	61	78	86
Answer gender questions about self	44	70	79

FIGURE 13.1 In a group of sixty-six two- and three-year-olds who were tested on their knowledge of gender, an understanding of the concept increased with age, although 21 percent of the three-year-olds still could not decide whether they were boys or girls. ***(Adapted from Thompson, 1975)***

and masculine attitudes and behavior that allows them to be flexible adults who match their behavior to the situation. As we will see, however, even preschoolers with feminist parents generally adhere to sex-role stereotypes.

SELF-CONCEPT

Throughout early childhood, children increasingly come to perceive themselves and others in terms of categories that consist primarily of concrete attributes such as sex, age, appearance, activities, and possessions. Although these aspects of a child's self may seem superficial to an adult, they have great meaning for the child and form a basic part of his or her sense of being. They are closely tied to experiences with other people and the environment children live in.

Because young children take such a strong present-oriented view of themselves, their self-concepts necessarily reflect this here-and-now quality. Asked to describe themselves, they reply in terms of those attributes: "I'm Sharon" (name), "I'm four" (age), "I have a brother" (kinship), "I'm pretty" (physical appearance), "I play dolls" (activities), "I like ice cream" (likes), "I'm little" (size), "I have a kitty" (possession), "I sit and watch TV" (habitual actions), "I wash my hair myself" (acts of competence), and "I help Mommy" (helpful acts) (Keller, Ford, and Meacham, 1978).

Self-Appraisal

An important element of a child's self-concept is his or her sense of gender identity, and many developmental psychologists believe that gender identity is not secure until a child feels comfortable in his or her sex role. Thus a child's degree of masculinity or femininity would be indicated by the amount of satisfaction he or she derives from being male or female (Lamb and Urberg, 1978). Other psychologists (Kohlberg, 1966) believe that satisfaction has nothing to do with gender identity; the concept is intellectual, limited to the understanding of one's gender. When gender identity is defined in this way, children or adults who accept their gender but do not feel comfortable with it are still seen as having acquired gender identity.

Among two-year-olds, less than half know their own gender, but within six months nearly three-quarters of them will answer gender questions about themselves (Thompson, 1975). When they reach their third birthdays, a fifth of them still have trouble with such questions. This small group does not realize that they—and all other people—are either male or female.

Yet this elementary sense of gender identity is only the first step, according to Lawrence

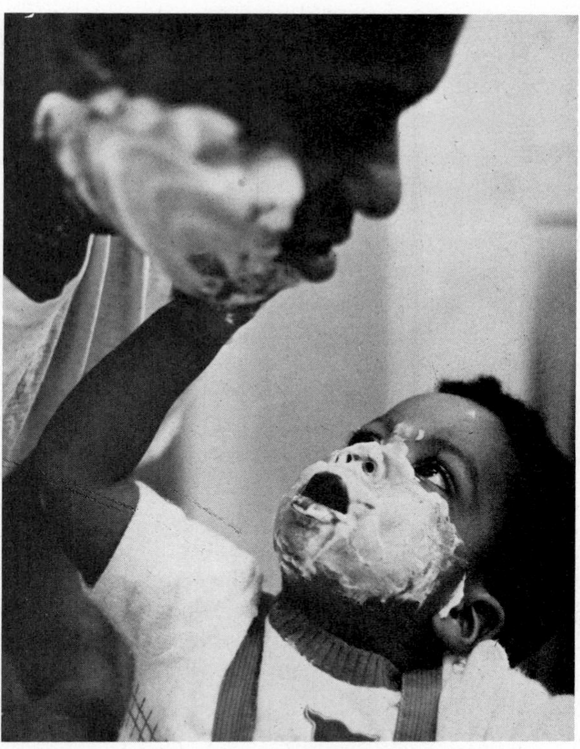

Learning sex-roles begins almost at birth, and by the preschool years even children of liberated parents are likely to have embraced sex-role stereotypes. *(© Burk Uzzle/Magnum Photos)*

Kohlberg (1966). He believes the process is not complete until the child acquires **gender constancy,** believing that boys always become men and girls always become women, and that maleness and femaleness cannot be changed. When Kohlberg asked children if a girl could become a boy, most four-year-olds said she could—if she cut her hair and put on boys' clothes. Even experience with unclothed people did not appear to speed the development of gender constancy; four- to seven-year-olds who could describe exactly "how you could tell (naked) boys from girls" were no more advanced in their understanding of gender constancy than were children with no knowledge of anatomical differences.

Some children appear to develop a sense of gender constancy earlier than Kohlberg proposes. Ronald Slaby and Karin Frey (1975) found children as young as three who understood that boys always become men and girls always become women, and children as young as three and a half who understood that gender can never be changed. Among two- to five-year-olds, 25 percent understood the "always become" concept and another 40 percent understood the "never change" standard. But gender constancy may not be necessary for a child to acquire a sense of gender identity (Martin and Halverson, 1981). The simple realization that one is a girl or a boy, a knowledge that, as we saw in Chapter 9, often develops around the age of two, may be the critical step, although the meaning that knowledge has for a child will change over the years.

Once children know their own gender is permanent, they decide they are happy with it, believing the positive things they hear about their own gender and the negative things they hear about the opposite sex. They identify with the parent of their own sex and seek out the behavior and attitudes that go along with their own gender. Now sex roles and gender identity become almost identical, and children begin to imitate others who seem to provide good examples of their own sex roles.

With the flowering of gender identity, children decide that complying with sex-role stereotypes is good and breaking them is bad. Whether they are middle-class or lower-class, white or black, have traditional or liberated parents, most children adhere to this judgment. So despite differences in adult behavior, children behave in a stereotypical boy or girl fashion, and such behavior may help the child to establish his or her self-concept (Martin and Halverson, 1981).

Although preschool children do not understand all the implications of gender, research suggests that they do recognize the importance of attractiveness and that the recognition affects their behavior and their self-concepts. Young boys and girls prefer attractive peers as potential friends and expect them to be friendly and nice, but they reject unattractive peers and expect them to be unfriendly and mean (Dion, 1973). Judith Langlois and Cookie Stephan (1977) found that kindergarten children hold the same views. In this study, black, Anglo, and Hispanic children saw attractive peers, regardless of their race, as being more likable, smarter, friendlier, and more generous than unattractive peers. Attractive Anglo children reaped the most benefit from these shared social sterotypes, since they were likely to be perceived by children of all groups as the smartest, kindest, and happiest, and as doing the best in school. The social advantage this gives to Anglo children may enable them to maintain or develop a more positive self-concept than children from other groups.

By establishing how they are like others and how they differ from them, youngsters develop a sense of who they are. To this end, preschoolers actively engage in social comparison. They compare their possessions ("My spaceship is higher than yours"), their activities ("I hope I'm ahead of you"), their abilities ("I can run faster than you"), their attitudes ("Brown is my favorite color"), and their status ("I'm 4½; you're 4") (Mosatche and Bragonier, 1981).

The formation of self-concept also relies on the process of identification. It is traditional to emphasize the importance of the child's identification with the same-sex parent, but children also may identify with older siblings or with others whom they admire and respect. The more children believe they can be like the admired person, the more strongly they identify with him or her. In the process, children come to include in their self-concepts the degree to which their personal attributes match those exhibited by the other person.

In striving to be independent, competent, and autonomous, children look for ways that meet with approval, especially the approval of the people they admire. By discovering what these people expect of them and by learning to match their behavior to these expectancies, children acquire many of their basic concepts about themselves. To the extent that their social experiences communicate that they are competent, admirable, and acceptable, children are likely to develop **self-esteem,** regarding themselves with pride, satisfaction, and approval.

Self-Regulation

All societies expect young children to assume increasing responsibility for themselves. From the time they are toilet-trained, children in this culture are expected to show increasing self-control and self-reliance, and most four- or five-year-olds can take care of their personal needs and have learned to tolerate some delay when they must wait for something they want.

Self-Control Learning self-control obviously takes time. Most parents recognize this and adjust their standards to their children's changing abilities. Although most young children want what they want immediately, research indicates that three- and four-year-olds are capable of delaying gratification. Whether they do so varies with such factors as their mood and what they do while waiting.

The way children's moods affect their ability to delay gratification became clear when Bert Moore, Andrea Clyburn, and Bill Underwood (1976) asked three- to five-year-olds to talk and think about things that made them sad or to talk and think about things that made them happy. Afterward, each child was allowed to choose between the immediate reward of a round pretzel (a less-valued treat) or a small lollipop (a more-valued treat) several hours later. Children who talked and thought about sad things more often chose the pretzel, but those who talked and thought about happy things more often chose the lollipop, suggesting that negative moods may increase children's impulsiveness but that positive moods may increase their patience.

What children do while they wait also affects how long they will delay gratification. Most children will wait longer for a treat if they distract themselves by singing, whistling, talking to themselves, playing games with their hands or feet, and so on. The way children think about the delayed treat can also play a part in the length of time they will wait. Walter Mischel and Nancy Baker (1975) gave children the choice of eating one pretzel or marshmallow immediately or getting two pretzels or marshmallows if they waited. Children who thought about the pretzel sticks in front of them as being "little brown logs" or "crayons" or who thought about marshmallows as being "cotton balls" or "clouds" managed to wait for a relatively long time—an average of fourteen minutes. But when they thought about the "crunchy, salty, toasty taste" of pretzels or the "chewy, sweet, soft taste" of marshmallows, they gave up and took their single pretzel or marshmallow after an average wait of less than five minutes.

Locus of Control Children's reactions to the world depend on what they perceive as the cause of their behavior (Lefcourt, 1976). If they have an internal locus of control, believing they get along with their friends or play games well because of their own ability and effort, they are likely to take pride in those accomplishments. If they have an external locus of control, believing that such results are due to outside factors over which they have little control, they are likely to take small satisfaction in whatever they do.

Most children with an internal locus of control have been encouraged to be self-reliant at an early age. Such children generally stay away from home overnight or are left to do things on their own by the time they are four years old. Children who have an external locus of control generally get no such encouragement until they are older (V. Crandall, 1973; Wichern and Nowicki, 1976).

By the time they are in kindergarten, most children show a consistency in their explanations, and both socioeconomic level and intelligence affect the kind of explanation they choose. In one study, Toni Falbo (1975) found that five-year-old middle-class children were more likely than working-class children to stress the effect of a person's effort on success or failure. (As we will see in a later section, this socioeconomic effect is probably the result of parental influence.) In addition, children who were bright generally explained success as the result of personal ability, and failure as the result of the task's difficulty. Less bright children tended to explain success as being due to the ease of the task but used lack of personal ability to explain failure. Falbo points out that the bright children's explanations encourage them to perceive themselves as responsible for success ("I'm smart") and not responsible for failure ("It was too hard"). In contrast, less bright children's explanations encourage them to perceive themselves as responsible for failure ("I'm dumb") and as deserving no credit for their success ("It was just easy").

In judging their own performance, many four- to six-year-olds pay no attention to their own success or failure as compared with that of their peers when it comes to situations involving achievement. In a series of experiments, Diane Ruble and her associates (1976; 1980) found that despite preschoolers' active use of social comparison in other situations, children do not allow such information to affect their judgments about themselves. Perhaps youngsters ignore this information because they are aware of their own limited abilities and relative lack of coordination. At this age, their concern is in making sure that they get their fair share of any rewards. By the time they are six, children's evaluations of their own performance generally vary according to the situation and the activity, probably because they better understand their own assets and liabilities. Lauren, for example, may regard herself as being very attractive but only average in physical skill, whereas Susan may regard herself as being physically skillful, about average in academic skills, and not very attractive.

Understanding Others

Young children see others, as they see themselves, in terms of concrete attributes. Asked to describe their peers, they list the attributes that they and another have in common, such as sex, age, or personal appearance. They also describe friends in terms of shared activities ("She sits with me"); a friend is someone they see a lot or someone with whom they play or share possessions (Damon, 1977; Youniss and Volpe, 1978; Youniss, 1980).

Although children at this age appreciate the abilities and limitations of other people, their feelings of empathy make no allowances for individual differences. They infer others' emotions almost exclusively from the situation, assuming that all people react the same way to the same event. For example, Frederick Gove and Daniel Keating (1979) gave four- to six-year-olds pairs of pictures and asked them to describe the feelings of the children in each one. Although the event was the same in both pictures, the emotions of the children were radically different. In one, for example, a little girl was delighted to have a new puppy; in the other, a little boy with a new puppy was obviously frightened. Gove and Keating found that four-year-olds either said the children's emotions were the same in both pictures or else they changed the situation so that it was different for the two children, perhaps saying the girl is happy because "her dog does not have teeth." Four-year-olds seemed unable to imagine that others could feel differently unless the situation itself was different. Most six-year-olds understood that two children could react differently to the same situation.

In a related study, Melda Brandt (1978) told children stories accompanied by pictures, then asked each child to answer questions from the point of view of someone who lacked information she had given the child. In one story, for example, after a boy had been warned to confine his fingerpainting to the kitchen, the family dog blundered into the paint and wagged his paint-covered tail against the living-room door. Only the children in the study knew of the dog's role. Four-year-olds generally assumed that the boy's parents would surely know how the paint got on the door, despite the fact that the parents never received the information. Brandt suggests that four-year-olds may be unable to store the information they have been given and then retrieve it to answer questions about the story. Again, six-year-olds could allow for differences in information; two-thirds of them correctly predicted the reaction of the "ignorant" parent.

Young children's level of understanding, coupled with their limited first-hand experience, also gives them a distorted view of society, as Hans Furth (1980) found when interviewing British school children. Five-year-olds had no glimmering of the role of money; they believed that shopkeepers gave people whatever they wanted and that change from purchases was an additional gift to the purchaser as well as the source of money. These children also believed that garbagemen get no pay but live on presents they get at Christmas and that firemen pay for the fire engine with money they earn when the conductor pays them for riding on the bus. Children who saw society this way also could not distinguish between personal and social roles. One five-year-old, asked if a mother could be a teacher, replied, "No. If teachers are teachers, they can't be mothers, or if big ladies go to school, that means they're teachers."

PARENTAL INFLUENCE

During the first few years of life, the family is the major agent of socialization. By encouraging some behavior and discouraging other, parents transmit the culture's standards. In addition, the way they provide for their child's physical needs and meet the child's psychological need for attention and affection affects the child's behavior, exerting a strong influence on the kind of person he or she becomes.

HOW A NEW BABY AFFECTS THE MOTHER-CHILD RELATIONSHIP

Most studies of parents and young children focus on the relationship as if parents had only a single child. But when infants become toddlers, many of them find themselves transformed into big brothers and sisters, as a new baby comes along to occupy parental attention. In England, Carol Kendrick and Judy Dunn (1980) studied the effect of a new baby on the relationship between forty toddlers and their mothers and found two major effects: an increase in confrontations between the toddler and his or her mother, and a decrease in playfulness between the pair.

Kendrick and Dunn visited the toddlers' homes several weeks before the new baby was due and again several weeks after the mother had come home from the hospital with her new infant. On the first visit, they observed the pair both when the mother was busy with housework and when she was relaxed. On their second visit, they also made sure to be there when the mother was feeding the new baby in the presence of the toddler.

After a baby's birth, toddlers and their mothers spent less time in joint games and in looking at things together. It seems that just when youngsters are having to learn to share their mothers with a new sibling, they lose out on another score—when mothers are away from the new baby, they pay less attention to the toddler than they did before the baby's arrival. The decrease in attention did not appear to be due to the mother's preoccupation with the new baby, because when she was holding the infant, she did not ignore the toddler. Instead, she and her older child looked at each other more and shared attention more at these times than when the new baby was not around. On the other hand, when the baby was in the mother's arms, confrontations between toddler and mother—marked by childish incidents of naughtiness and maternal "no's" and "don't touch that's"—also increased.

The feeding session itself was not an occasion of conflict among mothers who breast-fed their babies; but among the mothers who used bottle feeding, it did increase their confrontations with toddlers. This difference in interaction did not extend to occasions when the mother was merely holding the baby or when the baby was in another room.

In trying to account for the difference in the feeding situation, Kendrick and Dunn found that mothers who breast-fed were more skilled at distracting their toddlers during the feeding and more willing to interrupt the feeding to help the toddler. The reason for the difference in maternal actions is unclear, but the researchers doubt that the difference was due to the contrasting personalities of mothers in the two groups. However, mothers who breast-fed spent more time holding their toddlers before the new baby arrived than did mothers who chose bottle feeding.

As additional siblings are born, the nature of the parental relationship may change (see accompanying box). Nevertheless, the attachment bond established between infant and caregiver continues to affect personal and social development during early childhood. In one study (Waters, Wippman, and Sroufe, 1979), children who had been rated on the quality of their attachments at fifteen months were observed at play in nursery school when they were three and a half. Preschoolers who had earlier been rated as having secure attachments were less hesitant and withdrawn than children with ambivalent or avoidant attachments. They were also more likely to be leaders, to suggest play activities, to have their company sought by other children, and to be sympathetic to the distress of others. Striking differences in personal competence and other aspects of their self-concept also set the children apart. Those who had been rated as securely attached were more self-directed, displayed greater curiosity about new things, showed greater enjoyment in learning new skills, and pursued their goals more forcefully than children who had earlier been rated as insecurely attached.

Child-Rearing Practices

Discipline begins in parental attempts to make family life possible. The aim is to instill a sense of responsibility in children that will guard them from danger, protect parental possessions from destruction, and teach the children to fit into family routines (Sears, Maccoby, and Levin, 1957). Some parents use harsh methods to accomplish their goal, intending to stamp out their children's hidden urges. Others make no attempt to discipline their children, in the belief that giving children freedom for self-actualization will allow their natural goodness to unfold. Although few parents fit neatly into either group, most fall nearer one pole than the other. (See the box on the following page about various styles of parenting.)

The aim of most parents, believes Diana Baumrind, is to produce *instrumentally competent* children—children who are "self-assertive, friendly with peers, and not intrusive with adults" (Lamb and Baumrind, 1978). She found that parents who rear such children exert firm control, enforcing necessary rules, resisting unreasonable demands, and providing necessary guidance. These parents punished their children often, using a variety of methods: scolding, social isolation, withholding expected rewards, and the withdrawal of affection. Although most punishment was not physical, the parents did include corporal punishment (spankings, not beatings) in their disciplinary techniques.

Whether a parent is affectionate, sensitive, and caring ("warm") or not caring ("cold") also plays a part in determining the effectiveness of child-rearing practices. Baumrind's studies also found that when firm control is associated with warmth, it is most likely to produce socially mature children. Some years ago, in another large study, Robert Sears and his associates (Sears, Maccoby, and Levin, 1957) also found that although most warm mothers rarely used physical punishment, those who did claimed it worked. Relatively cold mothers who used physical punishment were much less likely to say that it was effective.

Research has shown that to be most effective, punishment should come soon after the child misbehaves and that the child should know exactly why he or she is being punished. If, for example, four-year-old Susan is spanked or sent to her room when her mother catches her with a cookie in each hand and a broken cookie jar on the floor, she should be told clearly that the punishment is for taking a forbidden cookie just before dinner, not for breaking the cookie jar. Such discipline should also be consistent; to punish for taking the cookie one day and ignore it the following week only confuses a child.

As most parents find, physical punishment works and is often effective in controlling a child's behavior. However, such punishment can produce other, undesirable results (Walters and Grusec, 1977). A child is likely to respond to it with fear or anger, negative feelings that he or she may come to associate with parents or with the situation. In addition, the parent who hits a child is serving as a model of physical aggression. The parent demonstrates that when one disapproves of another's behavior, the appropriate way to react is to hit that person.

Punishment is not the only way that parents affect their children's behavior. They reward them as well. Even parents who do not give concrete rewards generally show their pleasure at good behavior with praise, smiles, hugs, or tone of voice. In the study by Sears and his associates (Sears, Maccoby, and Levin, 1957), for example, warm mothers were especially likely to use lots of praise and tangible rewards with their children.

Another strong influence on children's behavior is what they see their parents do. Observational learning is powerful, and parents are permanent models for their growing children. They dispense rewards and punishment, and when they are warm and nurturant as well, they are precisely the kind of model that researchers have found to be most effective. When parents

PARENTAL STYLES

No two sets of parents approach the responsibility of child rearing in exactly the same way, and because a child's development is affected by so many different factors, it is impossible to single out precisely the parental traits that lead to competent children and to prescribe them—like daily doses of vitamins. According to Diana Baumrind (e.g., 1968, 1972, 1975, Lamb and Baumrind, 1978), who has been studying the interaction of parents and children for twenty years, the styles of most parents fall into one of four patterns. Parents are authoritarian, authoritative, permissive, or nonconformist; and each style has a particular effect on the growing child.

The *authoritarian* parent sees obedience as a virtue. When the child's actions or beliefs conflict with the parent's view of proper conduct, the child is punished forcefully. Respect for authority, work, and the preservation of order are important, and the child is expected to accept without question the parent's word on matters of right and wrong.

The *authoritative* parent agrees that control is necessary but uses reason as well as power to achieve it. When directing their child's activities, authoritative parents use a rational, issue-oriented method and encourage a verbal give-and-take that the authoritarian parent does not tolerate. The aim is the child's responsible conformity to group standards without the loss of his or her independence.

The *permissive* parent avoids outright physical control, relying on reason alone and consulting with the child about matters of policy. Permissive parents are nonpunitive, accepting, and affirmative, making few demands that their child take on household responsibilities or behave in an orderly fashion. The child regulates his or her own activities and is not pushed to obey standards set up by others. The *nonconformist* parent, like the permissive parent, is against authority and authoritarianism but exerts more outright control and may demand high performance in some areas.

Daughters and sons fare differently under these various regimes. As preschoolers, the children of both permissive and authoritarian parents turn out similarly: girls tend to set low goals for themselves and to withdraw in the face of frustration; boys tend to be hostile. Baumrind speculates that the children of permissive and authoritarian parents are so much alike because both kinds of parents tend to shield their children from stress, inhibiting the development of assertiveness and the ability to tolerate frustration. As she sees it, both passive permissiveness and overprotection produce dependent children.

Rearing by nonconformist parents also has quite different effects on preschool boys and girls. Girls are like the daughters of permissive and authoritarian parents: they are dependent, set low goals for themselves, and cope with frustration by withdrawing. Boys, however, are much more independent than the sons of permissive and authoritarian parents; and they tend to set higher goals.

Daughters of authoritative parents tend to be independent and socially responsible; sons are also socially responsible, but no more independent than average. According to Baumrind, these preschoolers develop social responsibility because their parents impose clearly communicated, realistic demands on them.

These results are clearest among preschoolers. However, as children come under outside influences, some of the differences narrow. Thus by the time children are nine years old, the children of authoritative parents no longer hold such a commanding lead in social competence.

encourage their children's identification with them and approve of their children's attempts to imitate them, their modeling may become even more effective.

Class and Culture

Differences among social classes and ethnic groups within a single society, as well as differ-

Through socialization these Amish children will adopt certain values that would differ from those found among children in California, Texas, or New York City. *(© Cary Wolinsky/Stock, Boston)*

ences among cultures, further complicate attempts to make pronouncements about the effect of socialization of children (LeVine, 1980). The values adhered to by a child's parents depend upon the social class and culture to which they belong. In the Soviet Union, where obedience and discipline are highly valued, parents use a combination of reason and praise, backed up by the withdrawal of love, to instill these qualities in their children. According to Urie Bronfenbrenner (1970), the differences between American and Russian discipline lie in the way emotions are used in parent-child relationships. Russians are more demonstrative than Americans and are quick to withdraw affection when a child misbehaves. As a result, the child feels that he or she is ungrateful and has betrayed the parent.

As noted earlier, the United States has a variety of regional, religious, ethnic, and economic subcultures, which vary greatly in social structure and values. Ethnic differences may, for example, lead parents to stress different values. Spencer Kagan and Millard Madsen (1971) studied cooperation and competition among children from Mexican, Mexican-American, and Anglo-American backgrounds. When pairs of children played a game that offered a choice between cooperation and competition, rural Mexican children were the most likely to cooperate in order to win the game. Mexican-Americans were the next most cooperative, and urban Anglo-Americans were the most competitive. This study made it seem as if competition was dominant among Anglo-Americans. However, a subsequent study (Knight, Kagan, and Buriel, 1981) that used more discriminating measures indicates that individualism (or maximizing one's own gains), not competition (which concentrates on getting more than the other person) characterizes Anglo-American behavioral norms.

Social-Class Differences Middle-class parents generally have different expectations for their children than lower-class parents. Asked to predict their four-year-olds' performance on four tasks, for example, middle-class parents consistently expected their children would do at least as well as the average child, but lower-class parents expected their children would do less well than the average (Marcus and Corsini, 1978). When children attempted the tasks, both groups of children made similar scores. Perhaps their parents' low expectations are one reason that lower-class children often do poorly in school.

Parents at all social-class levels say they want their children to be honest, happy, considerate, obedient, and dependable. But when it comes to autonomy, the classes diverge. Parents in higher social classes also want their children to be responsible, self-controlled, and interested in how and why things happen; but parents in lower social classes want their children to be neat, clean, and good students. The effect is to encourage autonomy in one social class and conformity in the other (Kohn, 1979).

This difference in values is encouraged by the way parents treat their children. Working-

Although all parents want their children to be honest, happy, and considerate, these middle-class parents will probably encourage autonomy in situations where lower-class parents might encourage conformity. *(© Greg Brull/West Stock Inc.)*

class mothers talk less to their toddlers than do middle-class mothers, intrude more into their activities, and tend not to explain their punishments or prohibitions. In a study of first-born Caucasian children, Jerome Kagan (1978) and his associates found that lower-class mothers issued twice as many "no's" and "don't touch that's" as did middle-class mothers.

Lower-class parents tend also to punish their children on the basis of the consequences of the child's behavior, probably as a result of their emphasis on conformity, whereas middle-class parents generally punish on the basis of the child's intent, in line with their value of autonomy (Kohn, 1979). Working-class parents who punish for fighting, for example, may not punish brothers and sisters for arguing. Middle-class parents, however, are likely to treat both situations similarly.

By the time children enter nursery school, they have learned their lessons in conformity or autonomy. As we saw earlier, middle-class children generally believe that they have some control over what happens to them, indicating an internal locus of control, but lower-class children tend to believe their efforts will have little effect, indicating an external locus of control (Stephens and Delys, 1973).

Inner-City Black Families Many children in black families face stresses that are not considered in studies of white middle-class families but that may have a profound impact on their personal and social development. Black children are more likely to live in the central city, to be poor, to have both parents working at low-paying, precarious jobs, and to be illegitimate; and they are less likely to be living with both parents or to have a father at home. To all these burdens must be added that of racism.

Despite these obstacles, most black families are healthy, cope effectively with their problems, and rear competent children. Robert Hill (1971) has found a number of strengths that enable black families to overcome negative social and economic conditions. Kinship bonds are likely to be especially strong, with the extended family providing money, advice, and services in times of trouble and accepting child and adult relatives into the family. Both the husband and the wife are likely to have a strong work orientation, and both participate in decision making. Members of the black family are characterized by a strong desire to achieve—to get a better education, better job, more income—although they are not convinced that such improvement is possible. Finally, black families tend to rely on the church, which helps maintain the values of respectability, perseverance, and achievement.

In a study of black families in Washington, D.C., Albert McQueen (1979) looked for ways in which these strengths showed themselves and for the characteristics that distinguished families that coped successfully. All the families he studied were poor or near poor, but some, whom he called the *troubled poor,* had difficulty in feeding and clothing their children and in paying the rent. The *future-oriented poor* seemed able to handle their economic problems. Both types aimed at improving their economic lot, wanted to rear their children well, and wanted good family relations, but the future-oriented were more likely to believe their children could finish college or obtain upper-level white-collar jobs.

The most important difference, McQueen found, was that future-oriented families devoted more of their resources to family goals. Despite their near poverty, a third of these families were buying their own homes and a quarter had savings. None of the troubled poor had savings, and among them only one family was buying its own home. The future-oriented families turned less to the extended family than did the troubled poor. When they ran out of money, they simply "made do," whereas most troubled poor turned to kin. (Future-oriented families had as many social contacts with the extended family as did the troubled poor, but apparently these upward-striving families drew the line at financial transactions.) Because future-oriented families neither borrowed from kin nor loaned to them, they were better able to achieve their goals. The borrowing and lending patterns of the troubled poor kept them insolvent, affecting their own and their children's expectations.

When these baby monkeys were taken away from their mothers and raised with only peers for company, some strange, but temporary, patterns of behavior developed, such as this "choo-choo train" clinging. ***(Harry F. Harlow, University of Wisconsin Primate Laboratory)***

PEER INFLUENCE

The influence of a child's peers can be extremely important in shaping development. About a third of all three- and four-year-olds meet their peers in regular, organized contact in nursery school, where they practice within the peer group what they have learned about the world (Rubin, 1980). Within the group, peers provide emotional security, set norms for behavior, instruct one another in cognitive, motor, and social skills, stimulate and encourage play, and help children adjust to life (Asher, 1978). As a result, a child's dependence on adults often decreases while dependence on peers increases. Most well-adjusted youngsters have a comfortable reliance on their peers (Emmerich, 1966).

These peer relations are colored by the relationships established earlier between young children and their parents. Alicia Lieberman (1977) found, for example, that three-year-olds who were securely attached to their caregivers played more positively with their peers than did youngsters with insecure attachments, being less likely to throw toys, fight, leave the room, or cry, and more likely to share toys, point out objects of interest, and laugh together. On the basis of these results, Lieberman speculates that mothers who foster secure attachments also encourage their children to play with others and lead them to have a positive attitude toward their peers.

Peer Socialization Among Primates

The importance of peer contact in socialization is not limited to the human species. Early interaction with peers is apparently necessary for the normal development of many primates, and studies of primate social interaction have provided insights into the role of peers in the socialization of the human child.

In many primate species, young animals spend much of their time in a play group consisting of other infants and juveniles. Within this group, young primates practice the behavior they will later be expected to perform as adults. It is here that primates perfect the intricate patterns of facial gestures and social threat. And it is here, by approach and mounting during play, that young primates learn adult sexual behavior. Rough-and-tumble play within the peer group also develops the aggressiveness that primates use to maintain status and to defend the group against predators.

The role of peers in socialization has been demonstrated by the animal research of Harry Harlow and Margaret Harlow (1969) and their associates. Infant monkeys raised in total isolation never learned to play the usual monkey games, and they had no opportunity to acquire the social roles that they would need in later life. After six to twelve months of such isolation, these monkeys found it almost impossible to fit within a group when, as adolescents, they were introduced to others of their kind. They tended to remain isolated from the rest of the group; they rarely engaged in social play; and when they did, it was with other isolates. Even individual play was infrequent among monkeys that had been isolated for twelve months.

The isolated monkeys encountered great difficulties when they became sexually mature. Males did not know how to approach young females (or even that it was females they should approach), and the females did not know how to entice and yield to the males. Both males and females were abnormally aggressive. They attacked and bit young monkeys, which normally reared animals almost never do. They also launched attacks against the largest and most dominant adult males, an extraordinarily maladaptive action for an adolescent.

Clearly, these monkeys had severe social problems (Suomi and Harlow, 1975). To try to pinpoint the cause of the problems, researchers raised more monkeys, but each group was raised in a different manner. Some monkeys spent the first few months of their lives with their mothers but had no contact with any other monkeys. Another group of monkeys spent the first few months of life entirely with other infant monkeys. The infants raised with only their mothers behaved in a far less abnormal manner than did the monkeys raised in isolation. They were, however, less affectionate with peers and more aggressive than monkeys raised in a normal manner. The longer the baby monkeys were isolated with their mothers, the more abnormal was their behavior.

Researchers had suspected that the peer-raised animals would show severe social problems, and their suspicions were correct. For the first few days, the infants simply clung together in a "choo-choo" pattern, as shown in the accompanying photograph. Although this pattern eventually broke up and the monkeys established play with strange monkeys, the later development of peer-raised monkeys was not completely normal (Suomi, 1979). They continued to show closer ties with their early companions than with other monkeys, and their play patterns tended to be brief and took primitive forms. As adolescents and young adults, the monkeys showed excessive reactions to stressful stimuli and generally responded by clinging to another monkey—a reaction seldom seen in monkeys of this age.

Such results seem to indicate that although peers teach certain personal and social skills that the young do not—or cannot—learn from their parents, the early influence of adult caregivers is also necessary for normal development among rhesus monkeys. Peers provide one another with necessary stimulation; but because peers lack the social skills found in mature monkeys, young monkeys have no opportunity to observe such skills, hence do not develop them.

Reinforcement by Peers

Whether children praise another child's behavior, join in the activity, imitate the first child, comply with his or her requests, or simply watch attentively, the first child has been reinforced, and the likelihood that he or she will eventually repeat that behavior has increased. However, events that reinforce an activity like aggression are not likely to reinforce an activity like sharing, and because of varied past experiences, one child may respond to a sort of encouragement that has little or no effect on another. Nevertheless, praise and affection reinforce most children in most situations.

The way young children initiate social interaction with their peers helps determine whether their social overtures will be reinforced (Leiter, 1977). Children who whine, beg, or cry when making requests generally get ignored. But when youngsters approach others in a friendly manner, smiling or pleasantly suggesting an activity, most other children agree. If they use demands or coercion, compliance drops sharply. Aggressive children may have friends, but those whose blows and verbal abuse seem inappropriate to their peers are disliked (Moore, 1967).

Popular youngsters tend to dispense praise and approval generously. In addition to providing such direct reinforcement, they are lavish with indirect reinforcement (attention and conversation), approaching others in a friendly manner. As a result, they receive a good deal of reinforcement in return (Masters and Furman, 1981). Yet young children perform better at simple tasks when they dislike the child who praises their performance than when they like the youngster. This connection between dislike and approval showed when Willard Hartup (1964a) had children carry out a task that required them to drop marbles through holes. Periodically, either the child's best friend or a child whom the marble-dropper disliked expressed approval. Children dropped marbles faster when the disliked children applauded their skill than when the praise came from their friend.

The effectiveness of approval from a disliked child may have something to do with expectations. Joanne Floyd (1965) found that children who received unexpectedly large or small rewards in a sharing task changed their patterns of sharing more radically than children who got rewards they had more or less expected. If a child expects disliked children to disapprove of his or her actions, approval from such children exceeds expectations and can have a powerful influence on performance. On the other hand, the effect may simply be due to rivalry: the marble-dropper may be showing the disliked children what a wonder job he or she can do.

Peers use reinforcement and punishment to enforce appropriate behavior; among these girls a good kicker will be praised, not criticized. *(© Ann Chwatsky)*

Children's playmates can also affect a peer's aggressiveness, and Gerald Patterson, Richard Littman, and William Bricker (1967) have described how the process works in a nursery school. When attacked, children either become passive, cry, or assume a defensive posture, or else they tell the teacher, retrieve their own property, or retaliate with their own aggressive act. When a physical attack is followed by passiveness, crying, or defensiveness, the young attacker is likely to mount another foray against the original victim. Counteraggression, on the other hand, often changes the attacker's behavior. The young offender is likely to act in a changed manner toward the former victim, to pick a different victim, or both. In many cases, however, a child who successfully counterattacks later becomes an aggressor, attacking a third child.

Peers also use systematic punishment to enforce appropriate behavior for each sex, pressuring one another to conform to the stereotypes. For example, three- to four-year-old boys who played with dolls or played dress-up were criticized by their nursery-school peers (Fagot, 1977). Boys who consistently engaged in such play were criticized five or six times as often as other children, no matter what they did. Girls who played with boys' toys escaped criticism, but were generally ignored by the other children; as a result, they were allowed to continue their play.

The way young children punish peers who violate sex-role stereotypes tends to change as they get older. Michael Lamb and his associates (Lamb and Roopnarine, 1979; Lamb, Easterbrooks, and Holden, 1980) found that three-year-olds are likely to stop playing with a boy who plays with a doll or a girl who begins hammering—perhaps simply indicating a lack of interest. By the time they are five, however, children make direct attempts to change the offending children's behavior. They criticize the children, ask them to stop their behavior, divert them with another toy, stop playing with them, complain loudly, or physically intervene to stop the play. Regardless of the kind of punishment they receive, children stop cross-gender play almost immediately. Even when children are rewarded with attention, praise, or encouragement for cross-gender play, they drop the activity much sooner than when they are engaged in gender-appropriate play, indicating their own knowledge of their transgression.

Peer reinforcement is as powerful as punishment, and when it disappears, children's behavior changes. For example, Robert Wahler (1967) selected five nursery-school children whose behavior was somehow related to encouragement from their peers. He then enlisted the aid of the children's friends, asking them to ignore their friend when he or she acted in a certain way. Within a few days, the selected behavior—whether talking, shouting, fighting, or cooperating—decreased. When Wahler told the children's friends to resume their usual treatment, the five children went back to behaving just as they had before the experiment began. Studies such as this one indicate that, by being alert to established patterns of peer reinforcement, parents and teachers may be able to use the peer group to help solve its own problems.

Modeling of Peers

When some action is modeled by peers, the effect on the watching child's behavior is often as powerful as that of reinforcement or punishment. By observing another child, children may learn how to do something they either could not do (such as working a computer) or would not have thought of doing (such as walking a fence rail). They may learn what happens when one acts in a certain way (biting others gets children into trouble). Or a model may suggest how a child can behave in a strange situation (one child begins throwing water at other children on the playground and the watcher immediately joins the game).

Children act as models for one another and when a popular child devises a new way to play space invader, his friends are likely to adopt his variation on their game. *(© Paul Fusco/Magnum)*

Immediate imitation of a peer model is most prevalent among preschoolers, and it declines sharply as children reach school years. In a study by Rona Abramovitch and Joan Grusec (1978), when children did imitate immediately, the more a child was watched by other children, the more he or she was imitated. Children imitated most were those high in the dominance hierarchy, but these children also imitated others. Immediate imitation, say the investigators, may be a good method of establishing and maintaining social influence.

A model's words can establish a situation that encourages compliance or disobedience, as Thomas Wolf (1972) found when he told young boys not to play with an attractive toy and then had another boy comment about the prohibition.

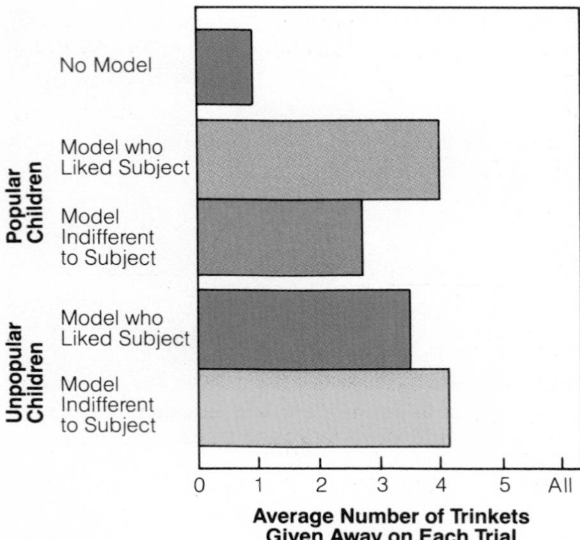

FIGURE 13.2 The results of Hartup and Coates' study of children's altruistic behavior. Children had six trinkets that they could give away in each trial. In all four of the experimental conditions, children saw an altruistic model, and in each case they shared more trinkets in comparison to the children in the control group, who saw no model. In addition, popular children gave away more trinkets when the model they saw was a child who usually reinforced them, whereas unpopular children tended to give away more trinkets when the model they saw was a child who had never before shown them attention or approval. *(After Hartup and Coates, 1967)*

Some children heard the boy say that he expected most boys would not play with the toys, and others heard him say that he expected most children would play with the forbidden toy. The model's statements about playing with the toy apparently established the appropriate course of behavior, for children who heard the model say he expected disobedience disobeyed more often than the others.

Additional research (Walters, Leat, and Mezéi, 1963) has shown that the consequences received by the model affect watching children as if they had received those rewards or punishments themselves. If a model is reinforced, as when an aggressive child gets to keep a toy he has grabbed, the other children are likely to imitate the model, grabbing another child's toy at the first opportunity. But if the model is punished, as when the grabber is scolded and made to return the toy, the watching children are unlikely to grab a toy themselves.

Peer models can encourage altruism as well as aggression or disobedience. In a study by Willard Hartup and Brian Coates (1967), while four- and five-year-olds watched, one of their classmates solved a series of maze-drawing problems and then shared the prizes he received with a mythical child from another class. The model was actually the experimenter's confederate and had been coached to give away most of the trinkets. After the altruistic model had left the room, the experimenter asked the watching children to complete the same maze-drawing task, rewarding their solutions with trinkets and giving them an opportunity to divide them with the "other child." As Figure 13.2 shows, children who watched the altruistic model gave away many more trinkets than did children in a control group who had not seen the model, providing straightforward evidence that peer models can influence socially approved activities.

The effectiveness of a model varies, and in the Hartup and Coates study, two factors seemed to influence a model's effectiveness: the nature of a child's previous experience with the model and the nature of the child's interactions with the entire peer group. Popular children (who are accustomed to receiving reinforcement) were more likely to imitate a child who had previously reinforced them than a child who had never given them attention or approval. But unpopular children (who are rarely reinforced) were readier to imitate a child who had never paid them any attention than a child who had reinforced them in the past.

The kind of behavior modeled also affects the likelihood that children will imitate it. David Hicks (1971) had young girls judge a model's behavior as either "awful" or "nice." Two months later the girls imitated behavior they had rated "nice" much more frequently than behav-

This policewoman serves as a role model and may have a strong influence on the attitudes and career choices of the children she encounters. *(© Hazel Hankin 1981)*

ior they had rated "awful." Although modeling often establishes the appropriateness of actions children are unsure about, this study indicates that when children regard behavior as inappropriate, they are unlikely to imitate it despite seeing a peer model it. Imitation seems most likely to occur when the modeled actions are so clearly "good" or "bad" in the eyes of watching children that they are unlikely to confuse them with other behavior.

Since both adults and peers can serve as models, we might wonder which model a child is likely to follow when the examples conflict. Hartup (1964b) has noted that children who imitate models tend to do so whether the model is an adult or another child. But when it comes to learning new ways to express aggression, young children are more likely to imitate other children than adults (Hicks, 1965).

INFLUENCES FROM THE WIDER WORLD

The world beyond the child's family increasingly impinges on his or her development. Peers are not the only outside influence; once children venture outside the family, other adults—especially nursery-school teachers—have strong effects on children's attitudes and behavior. Perhaps the most pervasive outside influence is one that has been present since birth—the television set.

Teachers

Teachers seem to be as active as children's peers in establishing sex-typed behavior among their young charges. For example, Lisa Serbin and her associates (1973) found that nursery-school teachers help shape traditional sex roles by prompting and reinforcing independent, assertive behavior in boys and dependent, passive behavior in girls. In one classroom, children were making party baskets, a task that required them to staple a paper handle in place. Teachers provided the boys with instructions, allowing them to manipulate the staple gun and attach the handle. But teachers often took the basket from a girl, stapled the handle, and handed it back. The investigators point out that most teachers do not realize that they demonstrate and explain more to boys than to girls and that they give boys more directions that require them to accomplish things on their own. As a result, the investigators conclude, most girls learn to be submissive, to remain near an adult, and to be rewarded with affectionate hugs, whereas most boys learn to be assertive and to reap their praise for being independent problem solvers.

Most teachers claim that they permit no more physical aggression from boys than from girls, but studies show that even at the nursery-school level, teachers respond to physical aggression in ways that are consistent with traditional sex-role development (Lee and Voivodas, 1977). Their reactions indicate that they expect boys to fight, and they pay strong attention to them when they do, inadvertently reinforcing aggression in young boys. In another study, Paul Brown and Rogers Elliot (1965) found that when nursery-school teachers ignored boys' aggression and at the same time paid attention to their cooperative acts and praised them, aggression dramatically decreased. When the teachers stopped reinforcing cooperation, verbal aggression remained low but the boys' physical aggression increased. As soon as the teachers went back to ignoring aggression and praising cooperation, physical aggression again dropped.

Teachers tend to perpetuate stereotypes even in nursery schools dedicated to avoiding sex-typing. In one such school, teachers complimented girls on their dresses but not on their pants, and they praised boys for being "brave little men" and for defending themselves (Tavris and Offir, 1977). When nursery-school children engage in cross-gender play, teachers may join peers in making them feel uncomfortable (Fagot, 1977). Teachers tend to criticize boys who dress up or girls who play outside in the sandbox. But when girls dress up or boys hammer or play blocks, the teacher often joins in, suggesting additional kinds of activities or making favorable comments.

In one area, however, teachers reinforce cross-gender play, and the more experienced the teacher, the stronger the pressure he or she puts on boys (Fagot, 1978b). Experienced teachers reinforce boys more than 80 percent of the time for art activities and looking at books, tasks that are overwhelmingly favored by girls. Teachers without experience reinforce boys equally for the active play they prefer and the literary and artistic play teachers wish they liked. This potential mismatch between the early school curriculum and boys' inclinations may help explain why girls make better students early in their academic careers—and why more little boys than little girls dislike school.

Television

The influence of television on children's personal and social development continues to be controversial (Rubenstein, 1978). Most researchers agree that television is a powerful source of persuasion, information, and instruction; but disagreement flares over its content, programming methods, and effects. Friends of television have pointed out that it increases children's knowledge of the world and teaches them personal and academic skills. Critics have charged that television presents a distorted view of the world, stifles children's imagination, increases their apathy and cynicism, and fosters the development of aggression and selfishness. As yet, research can show us only what children watch on television, how they watch it, when they watch it, and what they may learn from it.

Most children do not begin to follow a television program systematically until they are about two-and-a-half years old (Anderson, 1979). Before then, the flickering screen appears to capture their attention for only a minute or two, and they soon return to play or to interacting with their mothers. Until they are well over two, children seem to lack the cognitive ability to grasp the meaning of related images and sounds.

Preschool children generally play with their toys while they watch television, frequently glancing at the screen. In fact, children who have toys to play with watch the screen only half as much as children who do not, but they remember just as much of the program's content (Lorch, Anderson, and Levin, 1979). Whether a child pays attention to the screen depends upon the sound, camera techniques, and program content. Studies show that the voices of children or women, peculiar voices, sound effects, applause, laughter, and a change in sound quality attract a preschooler's attention from toys to the screen. Such sounds tell children that the program is changing or that the content will interest them. But they do not look up when a man's voice accompanies the picture, perhaps because adult male voices indicate that the program is abstract or of interest only to adults.

Camera techniques also affect whether children watch. Elizabeth Susman (1978) found, for example, that four-year-olds stop watching when the camera zooms in for a closeup, and she suggests that the zoom removes the focused material from the visual flow of events, so that young children can no longer follow the program. Switching from one segment to another (as in *Sesame Street*) does not interfere with children's viewing; and once they start watching a program, the longer children watch the more probable it is that they will continue to do so (Anderson et al., 1980).

Young children often develop personal bonds with the fantasy figures in commercials aimed at them (Atkin, Reeves, and Hocking, 1979). They trust Ronald McDonald, Fred Flintstone, and Cap'n Crunch, and believe they tell the truth about their fries, shakes, and sugared cereals. Most also believe that the characters know whether children eat their products. In addition, even many five- to seven-year-olds continue to believe that if they were to eat competing products, their fantasy friends would feel badly; some further believe the characters would be angry.

Young children often develop personal bonds with the fantasy figures they see on television and even believe that a character knows whether or not they buy the products advertised. *(© Ruth Silverman/Stock, Boston)*

The messages embodied in programs are generally understood by children when they watch television designed for them (Kelly and Gardner, 1981). In one study (Roberts et al., 1974), children who saw four episodes of *Big, Blue Marble* changed their attitudes toward other children in the world. After watching the episodes, they perceived children in other countries as more like themselves and were less likely to agree with ethnocentric statements. In another study (Columbia Broadcasting System, 1974), 90 percent of the children who watched an episode of *Fat Albert* recalled at least one positive social message from the program.

Recalling a message does not necessarily mean that children allow it to influence their behavior. Aleta Stein and Lynette Friedrich (1975) showed four episodes of *Mr. Rogers' Neighborhood* to kindergarten children. The programs attempted to teach children empathy and altruism. After viewing each episode, some of the children heard a story that covered the material in the program, explicitly labeling it, and then they answered questions; others replayed the story they had seen with hand puppets. All children learned from what they had seen on the screen—even a group who watched the episodes and then carried out unrelated activities; they knew more about the embedded social themes than did children who had seen neutral films. When placed with a child who needed assistance, however, most children were no more helpful than children in a control group who had seen neutral films. Only children who replayed with hand puppets the story they had seen were likely to translate their learning into action.

In another study (Rubenstein et al., 1974), preschool children saw an episode from a commercial television program, such as *I Love Lucy* or *Lassie,* every day for four weeks. Half the children saw episodes that were high in positive social themes and low in aggression; the other half saw neutral episodes. Children who watched the positive episodes helped one another significantly more than children who saw neutral films. Boys were more willing to put aside attractive toys to help another child, and both boys and girls cooperated more with other children. These preschoolers saw five times as many programs as children in the Stein and Friedrich study, so their greater exposure to the positive themes may have been responsible for the heightened effects.

SUMMARY

1. The process of absorbing the attitudes, values, and customs of a society is called socialization. Among the major mechanisms in socialization and personality development are the desire for affection, the wish to avoid the unpleasantness that accompanies rejection, the tendency to imitate others, and the desire to be like admired people (identification).
2. Becoming psychologically male or female involves the acquisition of sex roles (the outer manifestations of gender, such as dress, speech, and actions) and gender identity (the inner sense that one is male or female). Sex-role stereotypes—simplified, fixed concepts about the behavior and traits typical of each gender—are established early. By the time they are five or six, children are strongly influenced by such sex-typed virtues as aggressiveness and independence for boys and attractiveness and dependence for girls.
3. Gender identity, physical appearance, social comparison, identification, and the establishment of self-control contribute to the development of young children's self-concepts. In addition, what children perceive as the cause of their behavior—their locus of control—will have an important effect on their reactions to the world.
4. Young children assume that all people react the same way to the same event, so that their feelings of empathy make no allowances for individual differences. Because of their cognitive level and their limited experience, preschoolers have a distorted view of society and cannot distinguish between personal and social roles.
5. As the earliest and most durable source of socialization, parents remain the strongest influence in a child's personal and social development. Thus, the way that parents reward and punish their children's behavior has a potent effect on the development of such characteristics as independence, assertiveness, aggressiveness, and the development of sex roles.
6. Children's personality and behavior reflect the values of the culture or subculture in which they are reared. Lower-class families encourage their children toward conformity; middle-class families encourage autonomy. Black families have hidden strengths that enable them to overcome the additional social and economic obstacles most face.
7. The role of peers as agents of socialization becomes more pervasive during early childhood. Children increasingly learn from other

children the attitudes and behavior involved in various roles. Within the peer group, they practice the roles they will perform in later years. Much of what children learn from interacting with their peers depends on what they have observed other children doing (modeling) and whether those actions were encouraged or discouraged (rewarded or punished).

8. Teachers and television provide additional influences on children's socialization and personality. Teachers are often unwitting shapers of stereotypical males and females, encouraging dependent, passive behavior in girls and independent, assertive behavior in boys. Until they are about two-and-a-half years old, few children follow television programs systematically. Older youngsters generally understand the positive social messages embedded in the programs they see, but that knowledge is not generally translated into action.

UNIT FIVE

LATER CHILDHOOD: GROWING UP

In later childhood, the developing boy or girl comes under further direct control of society in the form of school, which has the official task of presenting formal education. Childrens' cognitive structure evolves and stabilizes, they develop new and more realistic ways to categorize the world, to operate in it competently, and to perceive its parts and the logical and causal relationships among them. At the same time, through games and social experiences, they develop social skills that help them to understand how others think and feel. During this period, the differences between appropriate male and female behavior sharpen, and each child tends to play primarily with peers of his or her own sex. Now they lay down friendships and patterns of social behavior that may last throughout life. A sense of right and wrong continues to evolve; the child who began life as an amoral infant becomes a being with a sense of guilt that plagues the youngster when he or she violates a personal moral code. As a reminder that development is cumulative and continuous, this unit looks at the development of morality over the life span.

14 COGNITION: ADVANCES IN THINKING

When David was four, he was given a red and blue Superman costume. With great excitement he put on the suit, waited impatiently for his mother to tie the red cape around his neck, crouched down, tensed his muscles—and tried to fly. When his feet remained on the ground, he was surprised and disappointed. The innocence and gullibility of young children like David is a frequent theme in literature. Just as many children are sure that a man in a red suit drives a team of reindeer through the sky to bring them presents, many do not realize that the claims presented in television advertisements for breakfast cereals may not be true. The young child may think of truth as relevant only to his or her own statements and perhaps to those of close friends, family, and neighbors.

Now that David is ten, he readily understands that truth applies to the statements of people he meets and to the media, and he may also use the concept to evaluate books that he reads. Most developmental psychologists would agree that the ten-year-old's understanding of concepts tends to be more general and inclusive than the young child's. However, the ten-year-old probably does not think of truth as a general concept that can be applied to any statements ever made about any subject by any person at any time in history. By the time David is fifteen, he will understand this and will be able to apply the abstract definition of truth, "something that is the case," to an infinite number of events or statements.

In this chapter, we will follow the growing child's cognitive advances and find an increased sensitivity to language reflected in a changing appreciation of metaphor and an increased understanding of stories. We will see that reading instruction lends new importance to perceptual skills, including the child's ability to scan efficiently and to focus attention on the task at hand. We will learn that obvious improvements in memory come from the child's discovery of strategies that enable efficient coding of information and its quick recovery from storage, a discovery based on the child's new awareness of the way memory works. We will see that during the school years, the strategies a child uses to solve problems become more systematic, more thorough, and more often based on deduction. Our examination of thought during this period of concrete operations will show that children can now mentally reverse transformations in appearance, understanding that the quantity of a substance does not change when its shape is altered. We will explore the child's ability to comprehend and to deal more efficiently with relational concepts, and the growing ability to understand natural phenomena. We will find that the child develops an increased ability to imagine the viewpoint of another person. Finally, we will examine the concept of intelligence and the use and abuses of tests that have been developed to measure it.

ADVANCES IN REPRESENTATIONAL SKILLS

During the years from six to twelve, the growing human being becomes an even more skillful user of symbols. These increasingly sophisticated representational skills provide evidence for the cognitive advances of later childhood.

Imitation

Imitation can be external action or internal image. As we saw in Chapter 11, it can be immediate or delayed, and it can vary in its degree of correspondence with the imitated action. Children become more skillful at imitation, and they can use it to learn complex actions, watching another person and then trying to imitate that behavior. So Lynn McLaughlin and Joseph Brinley (1973) found when they set up an experiment to discover whether children would learn to solve problems more efficiently if they first observed a model solve them. Children from seven through twelve were asked to sort fifteen blocks into four groups. The blocks could be sorted according to their shape, their color, or their proportions. McLaughlin and Brinley told each child that although there were several possible ways to sort, only one would be considered correct. The correct solution was to classify the blocks on the basis of multiple attributes. Regardless of age, children who first watched a model sort the blocks sorted them better than children who neither saw a model nor had a chance to practice sorting before the test.

In a second sorting task, the same children were asked to sort fifteen animal pictures into four groups. The animals differed in kind, number, and the presence or absence of faces and/or cage bars. Only the eleven- and twelve-year-olds were able to abstract the general principles that guided the block-sorting problem and transfer them to the animal picture task. It seems, therefore, that children as young as seven can imitate the problem-solving performance of a model—but only if the task is identical to the one they watch. Even more promising is the practical prospect of using filmed, televised, and live models to teach children problem-solving and abstraction skills, a method that has proved successful in a number of studies (Denney, Denney, and Ziobrowski, 1973; T. Rosenthal and Zimmerman, 1978).

Language

As we saw in Chapter 12, by the time children are four or five, they have mastered a good part of the complex structure of their native language. Much of this development seems intimately related to changes in the child's thought. Children cannot understand the increasingly complex meaning of the sentences they hear if the concepts expressed in those sentences are beyond their intellectual grasp. After all, in order for a symbol to be meaningful, the symbol user must first comprehend the object, event, or relationship for which it stands. Advanced language use and comprehension probably depend more on cognition than cognition depends on language, although language is undoubtedly important for certain kinds of intellectual skills and makes concept learning easier and concept use more flexible.

As children grow they become more skillful at imitation; after watching another person they will try to repeat the performance—whether it is modeling a clay figure or hanging by the knees from a trapeze. *(© Paul Fusco/Magnum Photos)*

Jean Piaget (1972) argued that the emphasis should be on cognition, for he believed that children learn new concepts and rules best by working extensively with concrete materials. According to Piaget, concepts and rules can be derived more readily from active play, exploration, and investigation than from listening to or reading about them. He believed that verbal formulations tend to bore or frustrate the child. Piaget's emphasis on the fundamental importance of concrete over verbal experience is not universally accepted (Ausubel, 1968), and he himself focused on the role of language in formal concept learning, in everyday reasoning, and in a systematic approach to solving complex kinds of problems.

Understanding Metaphors The child's increasing ability to deal with abstractions shows clearly in developmental changes in the capacity to understand metaphor, an ability that depends on the child's perception of relationships between different objects or qualities.

When Howard Gardner and Ellen Winner (1979) asked children to explain metaphors, they found a developmental change in understanding, from concrete to conceptual to psychological resemblances. Five- to seven-year-olds tended to explain the metaphor "After many years of working at the jail, the prison guard had become a hard rock that could not be moved" by saying that a magician changed the guard into a rock or that the guard piled hard rocks all day

FIGURE 14.1 Adjective pairs (Column A) and related pairs of phrases (Column B) like those used by Gardner in his study of the development of the appreciation of metaphor, as discussed in the text. *(After Gardner, 1974)*

Column A	Column B
Sad—Happy	Hearing the phrase "A cloudy afternoon"— Hearing the phrase "A bright morning"
Warm—Cold	Seeing the color red— Seeing the color blue
Hard—Soft	Seeing a photograph of a frowning face— Seeing a photograph of a smiling face
Loud—Quiet	Seeing thick line drawings— Seeing thin line drawings
Dark—Light	Touching a piece of abrasive sandpaper— Touching a piece of mild sandpaper

long. They avoided a psychological explanation. Children of eight or nine no longer tried to impose a physical relationship on the metaphor. They recognized that a psychological meaning was intended, but they were likely to say that the metaphor meant that the guard was "fussy" or "angry." Not until children were about eleven did they explain the metaphor in terms of the guard's lack of feeling.

In another study, Gardner (1974) presented children with phrases that described sights, sounds, and sensations, such as "a cloudy afternoon" or "a bright morning," and asked them to match the phrases with the appropriate adjectives (such as "sad" or "happy"). This time even three- and four-year-olds made many correct matches. The ability to detect metaphors increased as children grew, until they were eleven years old. There the improvement stopped: eleven-year-olds did as well as college students.

Even when metaphors are presented in the form of pictures, the use of language appears to make their detection easier. Nathan Kogan and his associates (1980) showed children groups of three pictures and asked them to indicate the pair that "go together best" and to explain their choice. For example, one set of pictures portrayed an old man in a wheelchair, a candle that had nearly burned out, and a smoking pipe. The older the children, the better they were at picking up the metaphors. But when the investigators labeled the pictures, the children's scores soared, perhaps because the words called their attention to the metaphorical connection (describing a river as "winding" enabled nine-year-olds to make a metaphorical connection to a snake).

Understanding Stories As children pass through elementary school, their understanding of story structure also increases. In order to relate a story, children must remember what it was that caused the main character's action, what the character did, and what the results of the action were (Stein and Glenn, 1979). Steven Yussen and his associates (1980) found that second graders do not appear to appreciate that these parts of the story are necessary if one is to tell it to a friend. Their choice of these key elements never exceeded chance; second graders appeared to choose at random what they regarded as critical elements in the stories. But by the time children were ten years old, they were likely to home in on the critical elements, indicating that they grasped the basis of the story's structure.

If children are simply asked to retell a story, however, the picture changes. Jean Mandler and her associates (1980) compared the ability of Liberian children who had never gone to school with that of American schoolchildren and found that the Liberian children did about as well as American children in retelling a story. Both the six- to eleven-year-old Liberians and the American first and fourth graders tended to forget and remember similar elements from the story. Older children remembered more of the story than younger children did, but the pattern of recall was similar. Children in both cultures were most likely to remember critical items: the initiating event and the results of the character's actions. They were least likely to recall the character's emotional response to the initial event, the character's final feelings, and the story's moral. Mandler and her colleagues suggest that the tightly structured story form they used helps to increase recall, and that telling the complete story instead of choosing the essential points helps six-year-olds to remember the critical elements in the story.

ADVANCES IN INFORMATION PROCESSING

As their representational skills develop, children also learn new, more efficient ways of processing information. The methods they employ to pick up the information, the strategies they use to make sure it can be retrieved when they need it, and their knowledge of their own thinking processes all improve.

Attention

Childhood changes when children go to school. Learning to read and to think about events and problems that are removed from everyday life requires a different use of their skills, and studying the process can help us understand cognitive development. For example, when children learn to read, they must discriminate among letter forms, paying close attention to the shapes of letters and to their sequence but ignoring the shading of the print and the size of the letters. Once the letters have been discriminated, children must use them in combination to gain immediate access to meaning—as immediate as the sight of a medium-sized, four-footed animal with a wagging tail calls forth the concept "dog" (Gibson, 1974). As the box on the following page indicates, when information processing is slowed, reading problems can develop.

One way to follow the development of attention during childhood is to look at the way it affects the reading process.

Scanning As children develop, their scanning patterns continue to reflect their interests, their expectations about the visual world, and their strategies for acquiring information (Day, 1975). In contrast with five-year-olds, older children are likely to scan more exhaustively and systematically, scanning downward from the top of a picture, page, or pattern. They also can scan without being as distracted by irrelevant information as younger children are, and once they have the information they need, instead of continuing to scan—as younger children often do—they stop. In addition, older children usually have learned to scan more rapidly than they did as preschoolers, either because they are processing the information they pick up faster, because they are integrating information across glances, or because each fixation of their eyes picks up information from a wider field (Day, 1975).

In order to see if children use meaning to help them in their search, Eleanor Gibson and her associates (Gibson, Tenney, and Zaslow, 1971) asked children to scan a list of words in search of a particular animal or a part of the

In school, children must pay sustained, formal attention to relevant material while ignoring irrelevant parts. For example, shapes and order of letters are important but style or size of script is not. *(© Leonard Speier 1982; Ken Heyman)*

body. They found that placing other words from the same category in the list had no effect on the rate at which the children scanned, suggesting that meaning plays a minor role in scanning. Children scan for words faster than they do for single letters, and Gibson (1974) believes that the increased speed comes about because in a search for letters, each single letter must be scanned, whereas in a search for a particular word it is not necessary to look at each letter. Apparently, says Gibson, children learn to process information in the largest possible units that are appropriate to the task at hand.

Selective Attention As scanning studies indicate, children learn to focus their attention on whatever information they need and to ignore information that is irrelevant or distracting. Some research suggests that as they begin to read more proficiently, children may rely more heavily on visual information. In a study (Golinkoff, 1974) that asked children to decide which of two nonsense words (e.g., TARB, RBAT) was most like a "real word," first graders did poorly whether they looked at the words or heard them pronounced. But when they looked at the words while they heard them pronounced, they were right 72 percent of the time. Second graders did no better than first graders when they both saw and heard the word; but when they simply saw the word, their scores increased significantly. Being more experienced readers, they apparently relied more on visual information and found hearing the word pronounced a distraction.

Developmental changes in selective attention also appeared when John Hagen and Gordon Hale (1973) asked seven- to thirteen-year-old children to remember the *location* of some pictures they would see. Each child looked at a row of picture cards. On each card were two pictures, one of a common household object, such as a television set or a lamp, and one of an animal, such as a camel or a cat. The experimenter then turned the cards face down and showed the child a "cue card" with either an animal or an object on it. The child was asked to point to the one card in the set that lay face down that pictured the same animal or object. The number of correct matches measured the child's **central learning.** After having been tested on picture location, which was the specified task, the child was asked if he or she remembered which

CHILDREN WHO CANNOT READ

Many children who have extreme difficulty in learning to read, write, or spell are considered to have **developmental dyslexia.** Most of these children are boys, and their problem is not any lack of intelligence, for they can talk, recognize numbers, and understand mathematics, science, and history as well as other children. But they seem to have trouble connecting the written symbols they see with the sounds these symbols stand for. For this reason, they often have great difficulty sounding out a word from its letters and may have to learn to read each word separately (Gardner, 1975). Some dyslexic children persist in trying to read from right to left instead of from left to right. And some confuse letters that are similarly constructed but differ in their orientation (such as *d, b, q,* and *p*).

Studies of dyslexic children indicate that they may process information more slowly than normal children do. Sylvia Farnham-Diggory (1978), who has reviewed the research on dyslexia, reports that this slowness has shown up in studies of visual and auditory perception, in memory, and in the coordination of information. For example, in order to identify a single letter, normal children typically need to see it for only 50 microseconds, but dyslexic children usually need to see it for 65 microseconds. It appears that these children pick out letters in a line of print so slowly that before the first letter can be recognized, the next one has pushed it out of their working memory.

Part of the problem in connecting sight and sound may lie in the speed with which these children process sounds. Some—but not all—dyslexic children cannot discriminate speech sounds unless they are artificially slowed. These children, suggests Farnham-Diggory, may never have registered, learned, and stored portions of syllables. They therefore may not be able to tell the teacher the first sound of "cup" because they have never heard it in a way that allows them to separate it from the rest of the syllable.

In a study by Carl Spring and Carolyn Capps (1974), dyslexic boys were much slower at naming pictures of familiar objects, patches of color, and digits than were normal children. Apparently, they took longer to extract the labels from memory. Spring and Capps also found that although almost all normal readers they tested rehearsed a group of number cards they were asked to memorize, only half of the dyslexic boys did so. Children who do not use rehearsal, as was indicated in the text, have much poorer memories than children who use this strategy. It may be that because it takes dyslexic children longer to recall stored information, they simply have no time to rehearse. Farnham-Diggory's own studies show that dyslexic children also take longer to process sounds than sights, which means that as they try to read, their attention moves on to the next word or letter before they retrieve the sound of the first from memory.

As Farnham-Diggory points out, many dyslexic children can do all the tasks that are connected with reading; they simply seem to take longer than customary reading instruction allows. Paul Rozin (1976) and Lila Glietman have tried to overcome the difficulty of connecting sight and sound by devising a system of reading that begins with pictures. In this system, children first learn to interpret pictures, then read regular drawings that depict each word (a tin can for the word "can," for example). After learning to build words with picture syllables, they graduate to letters. Using this method, Rozin has successfully taught reading to children who were failing in normal classrooms.

objects had been paired with which animals on the cards. The correct recall of the pairings measured a child's **incidental learning.**

Children who scored high on incidental learning must have paid attention to features that were irrelevant to the task described to

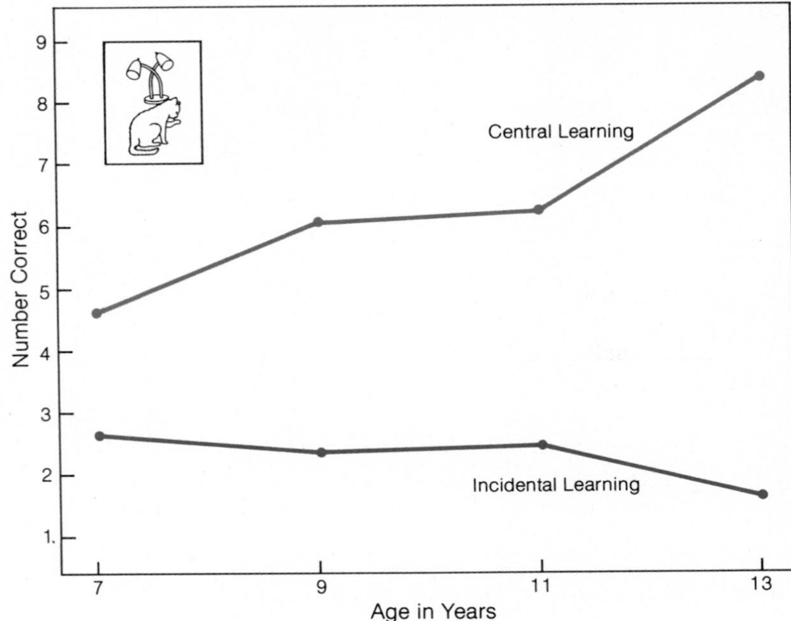

FIGURE 14.2 In Hagen and Hale's study of childrens' attention and learning, there was an increase with age in the average number of pictures identified correctly on the basis of their location (central-learning task). The inset *(top left)* is a sample of the cards used in the study. The average number of pictured pairings of animals and objects remained relatively constant until age thirteen, when it dropped sharply (incidental learning). At about age twelve, a child's selective attention becomes so powerful that he seems to exclude extraneous material. *(Adapted from Hagen, 1967)*

them. Conversely, children who scored low on incidental learning must have paid little attention to the irrelevant aspects. It is reasonable to infer that children who scored high on central learning and low on incidental learning were more selective in their attention, because if they had not concentrated exclusively on the specified task they would have learned more about the pairings.

As Figure 14.2 shows, children's performances on the central-learning task improved with age in a very straightforward way. The older the child, the higher his or her location score. Although seven- to eleven-year-olds scored lower on incidental- than on central-learning tasks, there was no significant change with age. Among the twelve- and thirteen-year-olds, however, the incidental-learning scores dropped, suggesting that they focused their attention more selectively than the younger children did.

The character of incidental information, however, can affect the way both children and adults focus their attention, as Linda Anooshian and Lisa Prilop (1980) found when they asked fourth graders and adults to learn a list of twelve words. The words were read aloud, and each target word had both a synonym and a rhyming word associated with it. Thus, the word "gun" was accompanied by the rhyme "sun" and the synonym "rifle." Adults learned about as many words as they had on an earlier test that included neither rhymes nor synonyms, but fourth graders did so much better than they had on the earlier test that the difference between their scores and those of the adults was not significant.

Apparently the presence of synonyms and rhymes helped the fourth graders to encode the target words more efficiently, whether by sound, by meaning, or both. When it came to incidental learning, the children remembered the synonyms and rhymes equally well, recognizing about half of those they were tested on. Although adults recognized fewer rhymes than the children did, they recognized more synonyms, suggesting that when incidental information has a meaningful (i.e., semantic) relationship to central information, it is more likely to attract the attention of adults than of ten-year-olds.

Because incidental learning does not increase with age, it appears that as a child grows older, he or she becomes more competent at selective attention, focusing primarily on the relevant features of a clearly defined task. At about the age of twelve, however, selective attention may become so powerful that the child excludes irrelevant material from consciousness.

In clearly defined situations, this procedure is valuable; but many of life's situations are ambiguous, and a person cannot know in advance which features can be safely ignored. Placed in such a position, a person would do well to use broad and nonselective attention at first in order to find out, by sampling from the range of possibilities and by searching memory, which components are relevant and which are not. There is some evidence that eight-year-old children are superior to five-year-olds in using this sample-and-search strategy and are even as competent as twelve-year-olds (Hale and Morgan, 1973). Thus as people mature, their past experiences lead them to concentrate on what they expect will be the relevant aspects of a situation.

Memory

Memory improves throughout childhood—not because of any change in its basic structure but primarily because children gradually develop increasingly sophisticated strategies for putting information into memory and getting it back out again. Children begin to use such strategies as they become aware of their own memory processes and come to understand that in certain situations—such as in the classroom—a deliberate strategy is necessary if the material is later to be recalled. Another influence on the development of memory is the child's increasing knowledge of the world (Lindberg, 1980). Material that is meaningful is more easily remembered. Thus with increased experience, more events can be related to what children already know and be encoded without the use of deliberate strategies. As memory and representational skills improve, children also become proficient at making their way through the world away from home (see the accompanying box).

Strategies A formal memory task, such as recalling a list of words, is a problem-solving situation. Strategies can be viewed as a means to the goal of remembering specified information, and those strategies most studied by developmental psychologists are the techniques of rehearsal, imagery, and organization.

Rehearsal involves repeating material that is to be remembered, and a child may rehearse silently or aloud. In Chapter 11, we saw that children who repeated the names of pictures they were required to remember did a better job of recalling them than children who did not. Simply because a child does not use verbal rehearsal does not mean that he or she cannot use it. When younger children are instructed to repeat the names of items they are to remember, their performance shows a marked improvement. Given a similar memory task, however, and allowed to memorize the material in any way they like, children who are successful when told to rehearse generally fail to use it with a new list of items, and their recall falls to its original level (Keeney, Cannizzo, and Flavell, 1967).

When they recall names of words from a list of items, children of almost any age are most likely to recall the last item they have seen or heard. This effect is probably because the test comes so soon after the list is presented that the last item may still be lodged in short-term storage. Older children, however, are also likely to recall the first item they saw, which indicates that they have been rehearsing the list.

As they become more skilled, children tend to use their rehearsal time differently. Older children are likely to be aware of the value of rehearsal time and they generally make good use of it (Waters, 1982). If allowed to take as much time as they like, they generally spend more of it studying than younger children. They also often test themselves, deliberately looking away from the material to be remembered and repeating it to themselves.

When children use **imagery,** they visually associate two or more things they are supposed to remember. Sometimes they are asked to memorize a list of paired words, such as "dog/piano," so that when they hear the first word of the pair, they recall the second. Children who put the two

LEARNING TO GET TO SCHOOL

Every morning, thousands of six-year-olds pick up their lunch boxes and set off for school. Somehow they have learned to get from one part of their neighborhood to another, and developmental psychologists have become extremely interested in this type of cognitive development. Studies indicate that children apparently learn their way to school by establishing landmarks (Evans, 1980). When Lauren began first grade, for example, she learned that to get from her house to school she must walk toward the big oak tree in Mrs. Smith's yard; once there, she turned and walked in the direction of the traffic light beside the red brick house with white awnings; another turn and she was within sight of the school building. It seems that her navigation of this rudimentary "cognitive map" is a process of visually recognizing each landmark in turn and bearing toward it.

In this early development of cognitive maps, each pair of landmarks and its link is considered separate from the rest of the route (Piaget, Inhelder, and Szeminska, 1960). If asked to draw a map of the way to school, six- and seven-year-olds will draw the objects themselves—their own home, the oak tree, the brick house and the traffic light, and the school—without fitting them into any general map of the neighborhood. Piaget suggested that young children use topological relations in thinking about spatial relations—a method that relies on landmarks and not on precise distances.

Once children have established landmarks, they gradually develop routes, perhaps visualizing the routes in a linear representation similar to that used in solving the problem of transitivity described in the text (Siegel, Allen, and Kirasic, 1979). As they get older, children become less dependent on landmarks, because they begin to code spatial relations in terms of distance. By now they have developed a series of routes—one from home to school, another from school to the local Burger King, another from school to the library, and yet another from home to the corner grocery store. But these clusters of routes are not yet integrated into a large-scale cognitive map of the area. That development must wait for the child to form some kind of objective frame of reference that allows the organization of routes into systems in space (Siegel and White, 1975). Such a frame of reference requires the same sort of perspective-taking ability as do the landscape display problems discussed in Chapter 11.

Children's experience of moving about in the wider world can affect the speed with which they develop cognitive maps. Dennis Norman's (1980) study of ten-year-olds showed that working-class boys and girls who lived in rural Appalachia, a region characterized by hilly terrain and sparse settlement, did much better on drawing maps of a miniature landscape than did ten-year-olds from suburban Connecticut or urban Massachusetts. The maps drawn by the middle-class suburban children and the working-class urban children were at the same developmental level, and they were less advanced than the maps drawn by the rural children—in showing correct proportions, in demonstrating perspective, and in using symbols to convey meaning to a third person who tried to use the map.

words together in a visual image, imagining a dog playing a piano, for example, find the second word easier to recall than children who do not. When instructed to use imagery, children show a marked improvement in memory from about the age of nine. In a study with six-year-olds, Michael Pressley and Joel Levin (1980) found that youngsters who were simply told to use imagery at the time they heard the paired words did little better than those who were given no instruction. But when six-year-olds were reminded at the time of recall to try to remember the images, they remembered many more words. Studies in which investigators supply the images for children, showing them pictures that connect the words so that they do not have to create their own images, have found that even five-year-olds show some improvement (Reese, 1977).

Imagery may be effective because pairing words with pictures enables the child to code information in both images and symbols, the double coding increasing the chances a child will remember it. Or perhaps the image places the information in a meaningful context, a situation that seems automatically to increase the amount that children remember.

Clustering, or grouping items to be remembered around some common element, is one of the most effective aids to memory. Children who use such **organization** (for example, grouping all the animals, all the toys, and all the furniture in a word list to be recalled) remember many more of the words than children who do not. Despite the fact that their memory is aided by semantically organized material, research shows that five-year-olds do not deliberately use this strategy as a memory aid, although they have no trouble sorting items into categories (Moely, 1977). When asked to recall material by category, however, they will remember items they did not recall spontaneously. And eight-year-olds who do not spontaneously sort items by category are aware that such organization makes recall easier (Corsale and Ornstein, 1980).

The way children organize material to be remembered appears to change with age. Six-year-olds are more likely to group by relationship (saw/wood, or hammer/nails) than by category (saw/hammer); but by the time they are nine years old, an increasing number of them will be using categories to organize their recall. Some nine-year-olds may use a story line and organize their recall along the story's theme. No matter what the method of organization is, however, the older the child the more likely he or she is to use it.

Like any of us, children may sometimes know more than they can recall. Asked to produce an answer in class, they find that the information they memorized is stuck in long-term storage. Later, in the school cafeteria, it surfaces when they no longer need it. There are, however, a number of strategies that aid retrieval, and they can be as simple as the continued search for an item or as complex as the planned use of an encoding strategy.

Reading music is a skill that requires attention and the application of memory strategies; when the child begins to play a carefully rehearsed piece, the notes on the sheet music act as external retrieval cues. *(© Leonard Speier 1982)*

One simple retrieval strategy is an *external cue,* such as a shopping list or a landmark. Simple retrieval cues can sharply increase the efficiency of children's memories. When James Hall and his associates (1979) cued children's recall by offering associated words as cues, both second and fifth graders remembered many additional words from a memorized list. To cue the recall of the word "water," for example, the investigator said "thirsty." The cues were more helpful to fifth graders than to second graders. The older children recalled 71 percent of the remaining words, as compared with the younger children's recall of 52 percent of them. When children got no cues, the fifth graders did as poorly as the second graders—they recalled less than 5 percent of the remaining words.

Retrieval strategies are not always external. They can also be *internal cues,* generated by the person who is trying to remember the information. For example, if information has been organized, remembering the label for a group increases recall of the group members. Younger children almost never attempt this strategy on their own, although when instructed in its use, a few six-year-olds can adopt it. By the time they are nine, many children can employ internal cues. However, the strategy is not likely to become common until later in life (Kobasigawa, 1977).

Metamemory Unless children have some understanding of the way memory works, they are unlikely to make deliberate use of any strategy. By the time they are in kindergarten or first grade, most children know what it means to learn and something about the process of remembering and forgetting. The extent of their knowledge was revealed in a study of metamemory by Mary Anne Kreutzer, Catherine Leonard, and John Flavell (1975), who interviewed kindergarten, first-, third-, and fifth-grade children. Most of the youngest children were aware that events that happened a long time ago were hard to recall, that meaningless strings of items such as telephone numbers are quickly forgotten, and that once something is learned, it is easier to relearn the same material than to learn something new. Kindergartners and first graders also seemed to know that having to learn a lot of things is harder than having to learn only a few things. These young learners realized that they could plan their study time to help their memory and even proposed deliberate schemes, such as careful inspection of the items to be learned. They also suggested and understood the use of external memory aids such as other people, tape recordings, written notes, or a string on the finger to help them remember.

Third and fifth graders were firmer than younger children about what they knew and had acquired additional information about memory. They not only recognized that time affects memory, but they also understood that more study time helps recall and having to learn more items will hinder it. They realized that these two factors interact, so that a short study of a short list leads to better recall than long study of a long list.

According to Flavell (1977), a main developmental difference between younger and older children is the ability to plan. Older children are better at forming and maintaining a memory goal and at using strategies to help them reach it. But memory is more than knowing about strategies. As children learn more about the workings of the memory system, they are also learning more about the world. That stored knowledge can influence the way they handle new material, making it probable that they will integrate the new and old knowledge meaningfully, processing it so that it is easier to retrieve when needed (Cavanaugh and Perlmutter, 1980).

Reconstruction Children's cognition may interact with their ability to code and retrieve information, so that their memories neither remain the same nor deteriorate, but improve as time passes. Such an interaction appeared when Jean Piaget and Bärbel Inhelder (1968) showed children a group of ten sticks of various lengths and asked them to draw the arrangement from memory. After six months, the same children, asked to redraw the sticks, often produced copies that were closer to the original display than were their first drawings. Apparently, memory is not simply a faithful copy of original perceptions. Instead, as children's comprehension develops, their memories change to conform to their new understanding. Piaget and Inhelder (1973) maintain that memory cannot be separated from intelligence, because memory borrows schemes from intelligence to structure stored information actively and selectively.

Other studies have supported this explanation. In one experiment, Hans Furth, Bruce

Ross, and James Youniss (1974) showed children ranging in age from five through nine years a picture of a glass tilted from the horizontal base to a 45-degree angle, as in Choice A of Figure 14.3. The children were told: "This is a glass with cola in it. It is tilted and on a table. Now draw this picture on your paper, just the way you see it here."

Many children do not realize that the level of the liquid remains horizontal with respect to the table even though the glass is tilted. They have not yet acquired this particular understanding of spatial transformations, even though they have seen numerous tilted glasses of milk, water, orange juice, and so forth.

At varying intervals, the same children again drew the tilted glass. Furth found that the oldest children always did better than the others at reproducing the drawing. In sessions held six months later, however, 20 out of the 116 children drew more accurate pictures than they had drawn shortly after they saw the picture of the glass. Only 17 percent of the children showed this improved memory, but the finding goes against one's expectations that recollections either remain the same or deteriorate. Furth maintains that, during the six-month interval, these children had acquired a more sophisticated understanding of what happens to the level of contained liquids and that this knowledge affected the way that they remembered the picture. Thus the child's memory of a perception is not a static photograph but the product of an active process in which advances in cognitive maturity modify the information that the child stored earlier.

Changes in understanding may not, however, always affect memory in the way Piaget and Inhelder suggest. In more recent studies, Lynn Liben (1977) has found that changes in understanding are not always reflected in improved drawings, nor are improved drawings always accompanied by changes in understanding. Some children who do poorly on tests of understanding may reproduce the models accurately. Although most researchers would agree that children do reconstruct their memories of past events, it seems clear that the way understanding and memory interact is not yet understood.

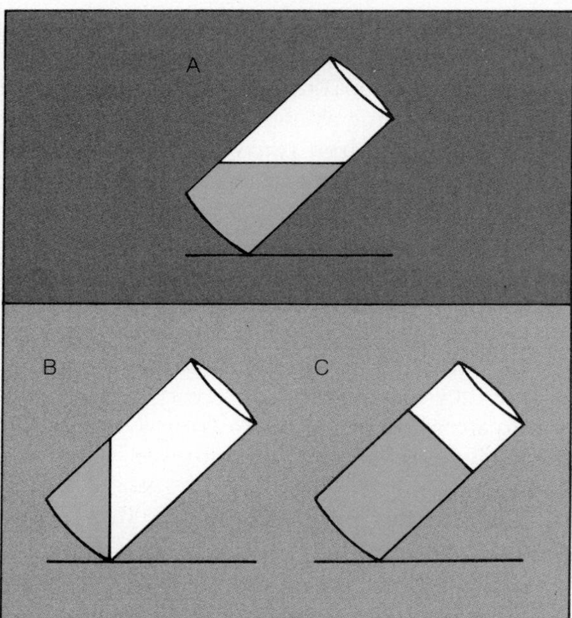

FIGURE 14.3 A tilted-glass experiment like that carried out by Furth, Ross, and Youniss. (*A*) Depiction of the actual angle of the level of liquid in a tilted glass. (*B* and *C*) Depiction of the angle reproduced by two children. *(Adapted from Furth, Ross, and Youniss, 1974)*

Problem Solving

During later childhood, children tend to become increasingly proficient at solving problems. Given a problem, instead of trying one response, then another, at random, and finally blundering onto the solution, they begin to form hypotheses and test them.

Studies that probe the way children solve problems often present a child with two geometric figures, say a large blue circle and a small white square, and ask the child to choose between them. When a child finally learns that the large blue circle is correct, the experimenter moves on to the real problem.

Now, faced with a large blue square and a small white circle, the child must choose again. The task is to decide just what element is now correct. It could be size (the larger or smaller figure), color (the white figure or the blue one), shape (the circle or the square), or simply position (the figure on the left or the one on the right). By changing the figures and watching the pattern of the children's answers, it is possible to discover whether they are actually testing hypotheses (such as "stay with your choice if you win, switch if you lose"), thus responding in terms of what has been correct before, or responding at random. As it turns out, five-year-olds often simply choose by position. They either select the figure on the same side each time or else they switch sides after every answer, paying no attention to success or failure. They show no inclination to test hypotheses (Gholson, 1980).

By the time children are in the second grade, their behavior is likely to have changed. They no longer stick to a position or a shape, ignoring the consequences of their choice. They are now able to formulate a plan and carry it through to a solution, but they must test one dimension at a time. For example, they may make several guesses based on the hypothesis that blue is the correct cue but ignore any information that affects the other dimensions—size and shape. If their color hypothesis proves wrong, they may switch to size and try that dimension.

For most children, this method of approaching the problem persists throughout later childhood. Few ever arrive at the most effective form of testing, in which if the large blue circle is correct, the child immediately rejects small, white, and square as possible cues (Gholson, 1980). Only about 15 percent of sixth graders use the most efficient form of hypothesis testing, in which they eliminate all disconfirmed dimensions with each guess. The way that six- to twelve-year-olds test one dimension at a time, ignoring other relevant information, reflects the thinking of a child in Piaget's concrete-operational stage.

There is some evidence, however, that younger children who cling to position and fail to test hypotheses concerning even a single dimension can learn to do so. Anita Tumblin and her associates (1979) found that when a model solved such problems for six-year-olds, explaining what she was doing and announcing on each try which hypothesis she was testing, most of the children switched to hypothesis testing by their third problem.

From an information-processing point of view, the differences in the way five- and twelve-year-olds solve problems develop from the increased speed and efficiency of the various cognitive processes (such as perception, attention, and memory) among older children. From a broader perspective, the change can be viewed as evidence that children have moved from the kind of problem solving that is explained by strict learning theory to the kind of mental operations that fit comfortably into either an organismic or a social-learning point of view.

CONCRETE-OPERATIONAL THOUGHT

About the time children start school, said Piaget (Piaget and Inhelder, 1969), they reach a decisive turning point in cognitive development—the concrete-operational period. Now capable of logical thought, they can apply it only to tangible objects. The logical thought of the school years does not suddenly spring out of nowhere; it is based on concepts that have developed during earlier years—for example, the concept of object permanence, which developed during the sensorimotor period, and the concept of identity, which developed sometime during the preoperational period.

Conservation

Once children understand that an object continues to exist when out of sight, and that superficial alterations in its appearance do not change its basic identity, they are ready to grasp the principle of **conservation.** Children who are "conservers" understand that irrelevant changes in the external appearance of an object have no effect on the object's quantity—its weight, length, mass, or volume.

In the best-known test of conservation, children watch an experimenter fill two glasses of the same size and shape to an equal level with colored water. The children are asked whether the two glasses contain the same amount of water. When the children assert that the amounts are the same, the researcher pours the water from one of the glasses into a shorter, broader glass, so that the levels of colored water in the two glasses differ. A nonconserver, when asked whether each glass now contains the same amount of water, will say, "No! This one has more water in it because it is higher."

But seven-year-old Larry is not fooled. He points out that although the squat glass is shorter, it is also broader; he understands the concept of conservation of quantity. He knows that if he pours the water back into the tall glass, the level will be just where it was before. Larry has acquired what Piaget called the concrete operation of **reversibility.** Having acquired reversibility, Larry can prove to himself that the amount of water has remained the same by mentally returning the liquid to its previous state, that is, by reversing the procedure in his mind.

At one time, many developmental psychologists believed that children who gave erroneous replies in the experiment with the glasses of colored water had clearly demonstrated that they did not understand the conservation of quantity. But researchers have begun to question this conclusion. For one thing, when children are allowed to pour the colored water themselves, more of them solve the problem correctly. For another, as Margaret Donaldson (1979) has pointed out, the conditions of the experiment push the children toward the wrong answer. When the experimenter pours the water, he or she generally says, "Now watch what I do," indicating to the child that the change is important and will affect whatever follows.

The influence of the experimenter appeared when Susan Rose and Marion Blank (1974) conducted a version of the conservation experiment in which they did not ask the child about the quantity of the two items *before* they manipulated their appearance. They suspected that asking the same question both before and after the manipulation might suggest to children that they should change their answer. When they tested six-year-olds with only the final question, they found that the children not only made fewer errors on the task at hand but also scored much higher a week later when tested in the manner devised by Piaget.

It appears that changing the way a test is presented may allow additional children to demonstrate their grasp of conservation. In Piaget's view, however, not even the most skillful teacher can teach a preoperational child that pouring water into a short, squat glass does not change the amount of water, or that twisting a necklace into a curve does not affect its length. Although he agreed that learning takes place during cognitive development, Piaget maintained that all a child can do is apply cognitive structures he or she already has acquired to new cognitive content (Brainerd, 1978). Yet a number of investigators (for example, Brainerd, 1977; Rosenthal and Zimmerman, 1978) have been able to teach three- and four-year-old children to pass conservation tests.

There may be an explanation that reconciles the two views. Preschoolers who appear to understand conservation may not be mentally reversing the change in appearance but simply maintaining their belief in the object's identity (Acredolo and Acredolo, 1979). Such an explanation squares with the results of a study by Gilbert Botvin and Frank Murray (1975), which showed how children who fail to conserve weight, mass, and number on standard tests learn the concept from other children. Botvin and Murray put first-grade children in groups of five, each made up of three nonconservers and two conservers. A researcher first asked each child to answer questions about weight and mass conservation. The group then talked over their explanations and agreed on an answer to the conservation problems. After they had reached an agreement, the researcher questioned each child.

Most of the nonconservers learned to conserve mass, weight, and number. During the earlier group discussions, original conservers tended to explain conservation by talking about

In this conservation experiment the child is shown two rows of seven checkers, evenly spaced, and asked which row has more checkers. Most children reply that they have the same number. Then the checkers in one row are bunched together. Young children now say that the other row contains more checkers, but children who understand conservation say that both rows still have the same number of checkers. *(William MacDonald)*

the reversibility of the change, whereas the new conservers tended to give "identity" explanations, noting that nothing had been added to or subtracted from the original amount, or that the change had been irrelevant. Botvin and Murray interpret the change as the result of modeling, suggesting that when the models gave correct answers, they produced mental conflicts, which prodded the other children into reorganizing their thinking. In this case, the first grasp of conservation seemed to rely on an understanding of identity, not on the concept of reversibility, which may be the way most children develop their comprehension.

Piaget's experiments (Piaget and Inhelder, 1969) on children's notions of conservation reveal an interesting phenomenon. Although seven-year-olds realize that the mass of an object, such as a piece of clay, does not change when the clay is stretched or compressed, they may fail to realize that its weight and volume also remain unchanged. Piaget found that children always acquire the various kinds of conservation in the same order. First a child like Larry understands conservation of quantity; then, at about the age of nine or ten, he grasps the notion of conservation of weight; and finally, at about ten or eleven, he realizes that there is also conservation of volume, in the sense that the amount of water displaced by an object is not affected if its shape is changed (Piaget and Inhelder, 1941). Other researchers have confirmed Piaget's basic findings about the sequence of these acquisitions (Sigel and Mermelstein, 1966; Uzgiris, 1964).

Developmental psychologists are still far from understanding exactly how children acquire conservation concepts or why they seem to acquire them in a particular order. Conservation is an extremely complex cognitive skill, which Susan Carey (1974) sees as developing from two sources. First, as the nervous system matures, children's ability to process information increases (that is, they can handle more bits of information simultaneously, they can process the information more rapidly, etc.). Second, children acquire the pieces of knowledge that allow them to understand and solve problems of conservation. Once information-processing abilities have matured somewhat, children can be taught by practice or observation, as were the children in Botvin and Murray's study.

Even without formal schooling, children constantly experience the heaviness or lightness of objects they lift, push, or pull. They "know" from their handling of them—although they may not realize that they know—that things do not get heavier or lighter if their shape or color changes. Many children conserve weight in the sense of knowing to maintain constant muscular pressure in lifting a ball of clay that has just been elongated, even though, if asked, they would state that its weight had changed. Thus they may demonstrate a working knowledge of conservation, just as they daily demonstrate their fluency as speakers of language. But they cannot explain that knowledge, just as they cannot explain the rules of syntax they use each time they speak.

Relational Concepts

Many concepts are challenging to learn because they involve fairly complex relations between things and events. Jean Piaget (1952a) studied several of these concepts and believed that the mastery of them is an indication of concrete-operational thought.

Transitivity One relational concept is that of **transitivity.** Told that David is older than Larry and Larry is older than Susan, concrete-operational children infer that David must be older than Susan. This deduction requires the joining together of two instances of the relational concept "older than." According to Piaget, this concept is rarely found in children younger than seven. He tested children's grasp of the concept in the following manner:

> We present two sticks to a child, stick A being smaller than stick B. Then we hide stick A and show him stick B together with a larger stick C. Then we ask him how A and C compare. Preoperational children will say that they do not know because they have not seen them together—they have not been able to compare them. On the other hand, operational children . . . will say right away that C is bigger than A, since C is bigger than B and B is bigger than A (Piaget, 1970a, p. 30).

When transitivity is tested in this way, young children generally fail the test, perhaps because it also measures such factors as language ability and memory, in addition to testing transitivity (Brainerd, 1978). Piaget required that children not only give the correct answer but also explain each inference logically, a skill that may be beyond the scope of some who would otherwise pass the test. The factor of memory may be even more critical. Young children may fail to infer the proper relationship between sticks *A* and *C* because, by the time they reach the third (inferential) step of the experiment, they have forgotten the information given during the first two steps.

Peter Bryant and Tom Trabasso (1971) used a version of Piaget's test to find out if memory plays a part in children's failures to make correct inferences. Instead of asking children about the relationship between three sticks, they used five. Bryant and Trabasso constructed four one-step comparisons (*A* and *B, B* and *C, C* and *D,* and *D* and *E*) in which three of the sticks occur as both the larger and smaller members of pairs. This precaution ensured that a child could not pass the test simply by recalling that "bigger" was the only quality connected with the larger stick in most comparisons.

In an initial training period, the children learned and remembered the four direct comparisons. Later, when asked to compare *B* and *D* in their heads, 78 percent of the four-year-olds, 88 percent of the five-year-olds, and 92 percent of the six-year-olds made the correct inference, indicating that memory is indeed crucial to the task. This result seemed inconsistent with Piaget's belief that children cannot grasp the concept of transitivity until they have reached the concrete-operational stage.

In subsequent research, Trabasso (1977) studied children to find out how they processed the knowledge needed to solve the problem. He discovered that children (and adults) do not store the information the way they learn it—as four separate pairs. Instead, they recode it, constructing an internal representation of the entire group of sticks, perhaps as a list, perhaps as a visual image. When asked to compare two sticks, they "read" off the answer from their representation. If children stored the information by pairs, as they learned it, they would be fastest at retrieving the comparisons they had memorized *(B* is longer than *C),* but they are not. The farther the sticks are separated in the array, the faster the children can answer questions about them. They can, for example, report the relationship between *B* and *D* (an inference) faster than they can report the relationship between *B* and *C,* which they memorized.

John Flavell (1977) agrees that children solve problems of transitivity earlier than has been commonly believed and by using a different cognitive process than has been supposed. He points out that if children (and adults) are simply reading off the answers from a mental image, they are solving the problem without using inference. Piaget, therefore, may have been wrong about the young child's ability to solve the stick problem but correct in maintaining that young children cannot reach such conclusions when inference rather than internal visualization seems to be required.

Class Inclusion Lauren, who is seven, has eight lemon drops and five licorice drops. She knows (1) that lemon drops are candy, (2) that licorice drops are candy, and (3) that she has more candy than licorice drops. She has mastered the concept of class inclusion, another concrete operation, and realizes that if *A* includes both *B* and *C,* as in Figure 14.3, then *A* must be greater than *B* alone or *C* alone.

Although younger children know perfectly well that lemon drops and licorice drops are both candy, they will stoutly maintain that they have more lemon drops than candy. Piaget (1952a) explained this by saying that young children cannot think of both an entire class and a subclass at the same time; therefore, they cannot compare them. Presented this way, the problem is even more difficult than Piaget supposed. Some investigators (e.g., Winer, 1980) have discovered that many children are at least ten years old—not seven—before they can solve traditional class-inclusion problems.

A variation on the lemon and licorice drops experiment indicates that part of the children's problem may lie in language, not in concept. James McGarrigle (see Donaldson, 1979) tested forty-eight children, who were about six years old, with four toy cows. Three of the cows were black and one was white. McGarrigle placed all the cows on their sides and told the children they were sleeping. When he asked the standard Piagetian question "Are there more black cows or more cows?" only 25 percent of the children correctly answered "More cows." But when he asked "Are there more black cows or more sleeping cows?" 48 percent of the children correctly said "More sleeping cows." The inclusion of an adjective that encompassed the entire class enabled many more children to compare class with subclass. Using collective nouns instead of class nouns also makes a class-inclusion problem easier to solve. When Ellen Markman and J. Seibert (1976) used collective nouns (forest, band, crowd, pile) instead of class nouns (trees, musicians, people, bricks), the number of children who answered class-inclusion questions correctly jumped from 45 to 70 percent.

The way children encode information about the objects strongly determines whether they can answer the questions. Children can encode a display of five plastic horses and three cows only as animals (the entire class), as cows and horses (the two subclasses), or as both animals *and* cows and horses (hierarchically). Unless children use this last type of coding, they cannot solve the problem (Trabasso et al., 1978). The finding that encoding plays a major role supports Piaget's analysis, since only with hierarchical coding can children think of the objects as both class members and subclass members.

Causal Reasoning

A child does not shift from precausal to causal thought in all areas at the same time. One kind of precausal thinking that plays a gradually declining role in the beliefs of children is **artificialism,** which refers to the explanation that either God or man has built everything in the world. The child's God bears little resemblance to the adult's concept of a Creator; instead, children see God as a giant or a magician. In the following discussion with a nine-year-old child, the explanations of night move from a physical explanation (clouds) to an artificial one (Jesus as artisan):

ADULT: Why is it dark at night?
CHILD: The clouds make it dark.
ADULT: Where does the dark come from at night?
CHILD: From the sky.
ADULT: Where do these clouds come from?
CHILD: From the sky.
ADULT: How does the sky make these clouds, with what does it make them?
CHILD: It's good Jesus. He makes them and hangs them in the sky. He makes them alone, with nothing. (Laurendeau and Pinard, 1962)

If the child had meant this picture of Jesus hanging up clouds as a poetic description, Monique Laurendeau and Adrien Pinard (1962) would not have considered it a precausal, artificial explanation. But the child apparently shifted from a physical to an artificial explanation because the youngster considered the latter to be more intellectually sound.

A twelve-year-old deals with these same questions in an entirely different manner, showing causal thinking:

ADULT: Why is it dark at night?
CHILD: Because the sun is down and it's the sun which projects light during the day.
ADULT: Where does the dark come from at night? What makes it night?
CHILD: It comes from nowhere, it's the color of the sky. In the daytime, it's the sun which makes it blue, and when the sun is gone it becomes dark. (Laurendeau and Pinard, 1962, p. 178)

Laurendeau and Pinard found that the transition in thinking from artificialism to notions of strict physical causality takes place gradually during the years from six to twelve. But, as was pointed out in Chapter 11, children tend to give physical explanations on matters with which they have had experience, resorting to artificial explanations in matters that are remote. Among the children these researchers studied, 74 percent of the seven-year-olds attempted to explain night by at least a partial appeal to either human or divine creation, but only 10 percent of the twelve-year-olds resorted to this level of reasoning. By adolescence, most children have abandoned artificialism.

Using familiar toys, Piaget (1978) further explored the child's growing awareness of causality. In one study, he gave children a small sailboat equipped with rudder and square sail, a large bowl of water, and a hairdryer to create wind, and asked them to sail the boat in various directions. He found that as six-year-olds begin the transition to concrete operations, they connect the relation of the rudder or sail to the boat's path, but cannot figure out how the angle of rudder or sail affects the small vessel's course. Eight- and nine-year-olds, who are concrete-operational, begin to grasp the relationship, but

FIGURE 14.4 The way that children order and understand the physical world typically becomes less egocentric, magical, and precausal during the later childhood years. These excerpts are from an illustrated children's book by Etienne Delessert, *How the Mouse Was Hit on the Head by a Stone and So Discovered the World,* produced with the assistance of Piaget, which describes the world through the eyes of five- and six-year-old children. The book tells of a mouse who never left his home beneath the ground until the day he discovered the world while digging a tunnel. *(top)* The mouse discovers the sky and clouds. *(bottom)* He talks to the moon.

only after a period of trial and error. They manage to steer the ship by rudder or by sail but cannot coordinate the two influences. As they near the end of the concrete-operational period, ten- to eleven-year-olds can coordinate the effects of sail and rudder but cannot understand the causes. Only the twelve- and thirteen-year-olds can explain the respective effects of sail and rudder, a sign, Piaget concluded, that they have entered the stage of formal operations.

COGNITION AND SOCIAL INTERACTION

As earlier chapters noted, young children may assume that other people see things just as they do and be unaware that other perspectives exist. This apparent egocentrism can interfere with a child's attempt to communicate, leading young children to leave out essential details, so that their messages are sometimes meaningless.

In an attempt to find out how long this tendency persists, John Flavell (1966) conducted a series of studies that examined the effect of egocentrism on communication. In one study, Flavell showed children aged from seven to sixteen a set of seven pictures that, like a comic strip, illustrated a story when "read" in the proper order.

For example, one set of pictures told the following story:

1. Boy is walking.
2. Boy sees dog.
3. Dog chases boy.
4. Boy sees apple tree.
5. Boy climbs apple tree to escape from dog.
6. Boy watches dog depart.
7. Boy eats apple.

As the child looked at the pictures, he or she narrated the story. Afterward, the experimenter removed three of the pictures, leaving only four, which told quite a different story:

1. Boy is walking.
4. Boy sees apple tree.
6. Boy sits in apple tree with dog in background.
7. Boy eats apple.

At this point, a second person entered the room, and the child was told that this person was seeing the pictures for the first time. The child's task was to predict the story that the new person would tell after seeing the four pictures.

Many of the seven- and eight-year-olds in the study found it difficult to separate their predictions about the story that the newcomer would tell from the initial story. Some of them simply restated the seven-picture story; others at first predicted a story that stuck to the four pictures but, when questioned, reverted to information about the dog that only they had seen. Children who were nine or older had little difficulty in separating what the newcomer saw from their prior knowledge, confining themselves to the details in the abbreviated story.

Other studies have produced conflicting results, indicating that in some circumstances, even preschoolers realize that others cannot see what they see and give verbal descriptions that show a high sensitivity to the plight of their listener (Maratsos, 1973). Maureen Landry and Karlen Lyons-Ruth (1980) have offered an explanation for this apparent difference in evidences of egocentrism. There are, they suggest, two levels of perspective taking. In the first, a child can think about another person's thinking about an objective event. Hence young children can empathize with the problems of another. But the second level, in which a child must think about another person's thoughts about a third person's thoughts about an objective event (as when the child must understand what the newcomer knows about what the boy in the story knows), requires advanced cognitive ability. In their study, few five-year-olds but most eight-year-olds were capable of perspective taking at the second level.

As they become more experienced and skillful, the way children themselves judge communication changes. When a message is ambiguous, five-year-olds blame the listener for not understanding it; but by the time they are seven, children blame the sender for the confusion.

This developmental change appeared when E. J. Robinson and W. P. Robinson (1977) asked children to listen to Mickey Mouse and Donald Duck dolls exchange messages that were supposed to help each other select the correct card from those in front of them. Whether the message was precise or ambiguous, the doll who heard it answered correctly half the time. The children's job was to decide whether each message's success or failure was the responsibility of the sender or the receiver. Five- and six-year-olds generally blamed the receiver when the answers were wrong, maintaining that all the messages were good, even when essential information was clearly missing. Seven- and eight-year-olds spread the responsibility according to the content of the communication, judging precise messages as good and ambiguous ones as bad.

Other experiments have found that children judge messages from peers and adults according to different standards (Sonnenschein and Whitehurst, 1980). When adults send ambiguous or uninformative messages, six-year-olds judge the messages as being good; but when peers are ambiguous or uninformative, six-year-olds are quick to say so. The experience of judging messages in a situation similar to that used by Robinson and Robinson often helps a child learn to communicate. Susan Sonnenschein and Grover Whitehurst found that whether the good senders were adults or peers, children copied the style of their messages. The children did not copy the bad senders, but they sometimes learned from them. After hearing peers deliver uninformative messages, children's own messages became more informative. But uninformative messages from adults had no effect. As the two researchers point out, children learn what is desirable from those who do it well and what is undesirable from those who do it poorly.

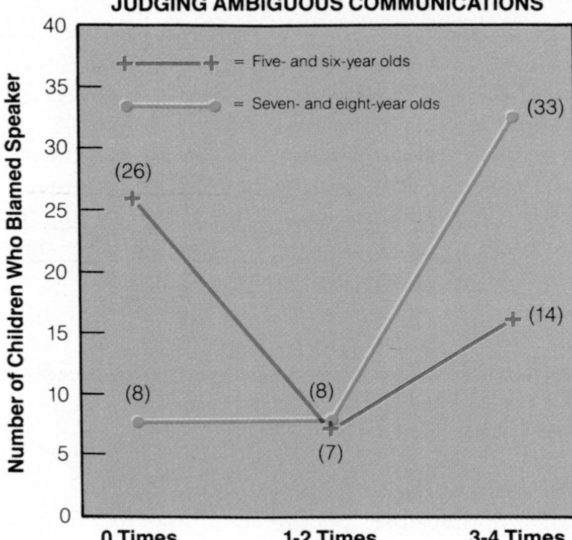

FIGURE 14.5 Children younger than seven tend to blame the listener for failing to understand an ambiguous communication; by the time they are seven, however, they generally blame the speaker and point out that the message was bad. ***(Adapted from Robinson and Robinson, 1977)***

INTELLIGENCE

When Piaget spoke of intelligence, he referred to cognitive functions shared by the entire species. In this view, we have been exploring the development of intelligence throughout this chapter. During the twentieth century, however, attempts to measure individual differences in intellectual development have led to the widespread use of IQ tests that both reflect a child's educational progress and affect the future course of the child's education.

Concepts of Intelligence

Intelligence is best and most broadly defined as the disposition to behave adaptively when faced with the demands of the environment. As such, intelligence is spread throughout the animal kingdom, and the intelligence level of any species is the result of its evolutionary history. Simply knowing the species of an organism reveals its relative level of intelligence and indicates what sort of adaptive behavior one might expect it to display. A dog, for example, is more intelligent than a rat or a hen, but seems incredibly stupid when compared with a chimpanzee. And as D. O. Hebb (1949) has pointed out, even the dullest human being who can earn a living is far more intelligent than a genius among chimpanzees. When we consider intelligence levels across species, differences among members of the same species fade into insignificance.

Many developmental psychologists are interested primarily in the analysis of the structures that underlie intelligence, and they approach the subject without a particular concern for individual differences. As Piaget (1953) has said, the purpose is to "discover the actual operational mechanisms that govern such behavior and not simply to measure it." Studies of cognitive structures, however, invariably show that children do not attain various levels of development in lockstep. In a group of six-year-olds, for example, some will be firmly preoperational, some will be in a transitory stage, and others will be well launched into the concrete-operational period.

From an information-processing point of view, individual differences in intelligence arise from differences in the speed and efficiency with which people process information. Children and adults differ, for example, in how rapidly they can manipulate information in working memory, how fast they can retrieve information from their long-term memory, and how efficiently they can shift information from one form of memory to another (Hunt, 1976).

Around the turn of the century, psychologists interested in the possibility of measuring individual differences in intelligence took a very different approach to the concept of intelligence. Instead of theorizing about its nature, they attempted to measure intelligence, working toward the construction of tests that would identify those children whose level of cognitive functioning made it impossible for them to learn in the average classroom. Soon, these early developmentalists concerned themselves with plotting changes in mental age as chronological age increased. Put simply, the standard, or normal, mental age for a child would be that which was typical or usual for most other children of that age. In order to determine whether a given child deviated from the typical and if so, by how much, investigators used standard testing procedures to devise behavioral norms for each age. In order to assess intelligence, they developed the convention of IQ—a quotient that represents a child's performance relative to the performance of numerous other children who have previously been tested under the same conditions. Given the way that intelligence tests are constructed and standardized, the IQ score provides no more than a descriptive statistic relating a child's present performance to that of other children of the same chronological age.

Measuring Intelligence

The early association of the psychological measurement of intellectual ability with a program measuring various physical attributes caused many people to suppose that tests of intelligence produced scores that were as accurate and immutable as physical measurements. But studies that have repeatedly measured people's intelligence over many years have led psychologists to reject this idea. IQ scores often fluctuate; the scores of approximately 20 percent of American children change by at least fifteen IQ points between the ages of six and ten, and some children's scores, although not many, change by as many as fifty points. Many factors determine a child's intellectual performance, among them biological change, general education, life experience, motivation, and personality. External influences at the time of the examination, including the manner of the examiner and the attitude of the child, can also affect test performance. Thus a child who made an average score on a standardized test of intelligence at one age can score considerably higher—or lower—several years later. Because of these multiple influences, we should be wary of making important decisions about the future of an individual based on only one or even just a few assessments of his or her intellectual abilities (McCall, Appelbaum, and Hogarty, 1973).

For many years psychologists thought that

Although an IQ test will measure how deeply this child has absorbed the dominant culture and will also predict his probable grades in school, it will not measure some of the basic processes that contribute to intelligence. *(Photos by John Olderkamp with permission of the Houghton Mifflin Company from Terman and Merrill Stanford Binet Intelligence Scale)*

an IQ score measured practically everything of importance in cognitive development. Performance on an IQ test was taken as an index of creative abilities, productive thinking, and problem-solving abilities. Along with this faith in the IQ test went a belief that it was not possible to train mental capacities.

Evidence and experience have modified these ideas about IQ, and the concept of what IQ really measures is being redefined. Today psychologists know that a person's IQ score is not a measure of his or her total intelligence and that intelligence is not a single, unitary entity. Rather, intelligence includes a wide range of abilities that are not measured by tests. On any test, the majority of the questions measure a skill or a segment of knowledge that a child already possesses, not his or her ability to learn something new. Thus the IQ test does not measure some of the basic processes that most people acknowledge as contributing heavily to intelligence.

Modifying Intelligence

Most psychologists agree that intelligence is based on the ability to benefit from experience and the ease with which one learns a new idea or new behavior. It is generally assumed that each person has a ceiling, a point above which he will not be able to profit from experience in a specific activity, and that this ceiling is governed by environmental and hereditary factors.

Heredity The discussion of hereditary influences on intellectual ability in Chapter 2 indicated the difficulty of separating genetic and environmental effects. Yet the debate about the genetic contribution to tested IQ performance refuses to die.

Arthur Jensen (1969) fathered the modern controversy by arguing that 80 percent of the differences among the IQ scores of individuals can be traced to differences in their genetic backgrounds. Others have suggested that a close examination of these data reveals so many problems in untangling genetic and environmental influences that there is little evidence for a genetic component to IQ (Kamin, 1973; Schwartz and Schwartz, 1974).

It is instructive to try to interpret Jensen's claim that the heritability for IQ is .80, in light of the earlier discussion. First, the statement implies that in a group of individuals, approximately 80 percent of the *difference* in their scores is associated with differences in their genetic make-up—not 80 percent of the entire scores. No one has claimed that 80 percent of an individual's entire IQ score is "determined" by genetics and 20 percent by environment, as if eighty of the one hundred points in an average child's IQ score were contributed by his genes. Most behavioral geneticists agree that it is impossible to put a number on the proportion of behavior that is inherited (Scarr and Weinberg, 1978). A complex and interdependent set of genetic and environmental circumstances that scientists are only beginning to understand causes the child's test performance.

Second, the heritability of .80 depends on the nature of the samples used to calculate it. Heritability may not be the same among blacks as among whites, among upper-middle-class individuals as among the poor, among individuals tested in the 1930s as among those tested in the 1970s or 1980s.

Third, because of the way genetic research must be done with human beings, often involving variation in both hereditary and environmental influences, the accuracy of that estimate of .80 heritability, even in the specific samples tested, is questionable.

Fourth, even if human heritability for IQ were .80, this finding does not suggest that all attempts to stimulate or improve intellectual functioning would be fruitless. It may be difficult to change intellectual ability or it may not, depending on whether we can discover which experiences are most important for its development.

Environment Differences in intelligence attributable to environment can come from differing levels of nutrition or sanitation, from the nature of the child's physical surroundings, the quality of the parent-child relationship, or an interaction of all these factors. For example, up to 75 percent of children with fetal alcohol syndrome are mentally retarded (Jones et al., 1974). But children of middle-class alcoholic mothers are unlikely to show the severe retardation found among children of lower-class mothers. This difference shows the strong effect of environment on the development of intelligence, even when physical factors work against the child.

Tests consistently show differences of ten to fifteen IQ points between middle- and lower-class children. Studies of home environments also turn up consistent differences. During infancy, for example, lower-class infants are likely to be confined in playpens, whereas middle-class infants generally are allowed to explore their environments freely (Tulkin and Kagan, 1972). In addition, various factors that may affect intellectual development—including the toys, books, magazines, mobiles, and other items that provide visual, tactual, and aural stimulation—are abundant in most middle-class homes and often scarce in lower-class homes.

Major class differences in parent-child interaction center around language—the principal component of many IQ tests. Middle-class mothers of young children generally differ from lower-class mothers in several ways: they use more complex, explicit language; they explain more; they ask their children more questions; and they respond more often to their children's questions (Rossman et al., 1973).

Other class differences also affect IQ scores. If children are strongly motivated to improve the quality of their intellectual skills and have high standards for intellectual mastery, they are likely to score higher on tests than children who are not highly motivated or who have low standards. Because middle-class children are more consistently encouraged than lower-class children to learn to read, spell, add, and write, a child's IQ, social class, and school grades all should be positively related to each other. This is generally the case. In addition, the personality attributes of children who do well in school (persistence, lack of aggression, and responsible behavior) are similar to the characteristics of children from middle-class homes.

The Use and Abuse of IQ Tests

When properly used, the IQ score is an efficient way of summarizing the degree to which a child has learned the concepts and rules of middle-class Western society. The IQ score is useful because it predicts school success, indicating fairly well, for example, how easily a child of eleven will master the elements of calculus or history when he or she enters college. However, the questions that are asked on an intelligence test have been specifically chosen to make such predictions possible. Questions that predict school success are kept; those that do not are thrown out. Because of the test's specific purpose, children are asked to define "shilling" rather than "peso." They are asked to state the similarity between a fly and a tree rather than the similarity between "fuzz" and "Uncle Tom." They are asked to compare abstract figures rather than to defend themselves against the neighborhood bully.

Over the years, the misuse of IQ tests has created a host of social, political, and legal problems. Such tests have been used to excuse bad education for minority groups; they have caused children who lacked exposure to middle-class culture to be saddled with a "retarded" label (Mercer, 1972); and they have caused self-fulfilling prophecies to be set up, convincing teachers that some children could not profit from instruction (R. Rosenthal, 1973). Despite all these problems, there are good things to say about the proper use of IQ tests: they have saved many children from being placed in classes for the retarded; they have discovered gifted children who would otherwise have lost out on extra educational opportunities; and they have provided children from disadvantaged families with an opportunity to move out of poverty (Hyman, 1979).

There is no reason to discard present IQ tests because they are biased toward measuring skills that upper- and middle-class white Americans value and teach. But the parent and teacher should appreciate the arbitrary content of the test. If one's primary objective is to predict the child's success in school subjects, then the IQ test is the best instrument psychologists have devised so far.

Realization of the problems and deficiencies of present IQ tests has led researchers to devise other ways of measuring intelligence. In California, Canada, and Great Britain, psychologists are working on intelligence tests based on Piaget's experiments with children, in the hope that tests grounded in a comprehensive theory of intellectual development will allow them to assess a child's cognitive level without comparing him or her to other children (Tyler, 1976).

If we are to devise more efficient tests, psychologists will need more exact knowledge about the separate cognitive functions and how they are combined in thought. If we are to use tests properly, we will have to realize that the behavior of a child in a test situation depends as much on the child's motives, fears, and expectations as it does on the quality of mental structures.

SUMMARY

1. As children's representational skills improve, they become more adept at imitation, so that seven-year-olds can imitate problem solving when the task before them is identical to the one they have watched. By the time children are about eleven, they can abstract general principles from a model's performance and apply them. An increasing ability to deal with abstractions shows in the understanding of metaphor, which moves from concrete to conceptual to psychological resemblances. By the time children are eleven, their ability to detect metaphors has developed fully, and by the age of ten, they appear to grasp the critical elements in a story's structure.

2. Schoolchildren scan rapidly, exhaustively, and systematically, and they are less distracted by irrelevant information than they once were.

Meaning appears to play a minor role in scanning, and children learn to process information in the largest units appropriate to the task. Selective attention becomes increasingly powerful, until—at about the age of twelve—children exclude irrelevant information from consciousness.

3. As children become aware of their own memory processes, they begin to form and maintain memory goals, using strategies to help them reach their goals. Among their encoding strategies are rehearsal, imagery, and organization; decoding strategies include external and internal cues.

4. As perception, attention, and memory become more efficient, children begin to solve problems by testing hypotheses. Thus children move from the kind of problem solving explained by strict learning theory to the kind of mental operations that fit comfortably into either an organismic or a social-learning point of view.

5. As children enter what Piaget called the concrete-operational period, they grasp the concept of conservation, understanding that relevant changes in the external appearance of an object have no effect on the object's weight, length, mass, or volume. Children's initial understanding of conservation appears based on identity; but for a complete understanding of conservation to develop, children must grasp the idea of reversibility, so that they mentally reverse changes in appearance.

6. The ability to solve problems involving transitivity, a concept that requires children to make inferences about the relationship of several objects, appears to develop earlier than Piaget supposed, but children seem to solve the problems using less complex forms of cognition than he believed were required. Traditional solutions to class-inclusion problems, which require children to think of both an entire class and a subclass at one time, may not develop until children are about ten, and their solution depends upon the child's ability to encode objects as being both class members and subclass members. Precausal thinking becomes less apparent during the concrete-operational period, as children more often attempt to understand, examine, and explain things in causal terms.

7. Social interaction continues to have a strong influence on cognitive development. Through interactions with others, children begin to show marked advances in role-taking, conceptual skills, and communication.

8. Intelligence is best defined as the disposition to behave adaptively when faced with the demands of the environment. Because intelligence tests do not measure many important cognitive abilities, they do not present a complete picture of intelligence. IQ scores are primarily an indication of a child's performance relative to the performance of other children. Class differences in IQ scores are due in part to class differences in nutrition, sanitation, home environment, and parent-child interaction. Still, although IQ tests have often been misused, they remain the best predictor of school performance.

15 PERSONALITY: EXPANDING SOCIAL INTERACTION

Eleven-year-old Matt watched the other boys jump off the end of the pier, bob to the top, and swim away. He took a hesitant step forward, then stopped and stared. His friends began calling to him: "Come on!" "Jump!" Matt could only dog paddle; the ten feet between him and the water seemed like a hundred. "What's the matter, sissie," yelled another boy, "are you scared?" The demands of his friends overcame his fear. Matt shut his eyes and jumped into the deep water.

During the later years of childhood, the influence of children's peer groups can be extremely important in shaping their development. At the same time, children learn what the adult society expects. They learn to meet some of these expectations in the classroom—from books and pictures, and from teachers who tell them what is good and bad, what they can do, must do, and dare not do. But most of what a child learns at school takes place on the playground. Thus, Matt may learn from playing basketball with his peers that cheating is not tolerated, or he may learn from playground intrigues that a person should stand up for his close friends.

In this chapter, we will examine some of the changes in the child's world as his or her personality develops throughout later childhood. We will focus on aspects of personality, such as sex roles, aggression, and self-concept, that were discussed in Chapter 13 and will broaden our discussion to consider the development of generosity and helpfulness. We will look at the effects of parents on achievement and what happens to children when mothers work or fathers are missing. We will note the decline in parental influence as compared with the increase in peer influence. Finally, we will consider the growing impact of school and television on the child.

THE ACQUISITION OF ROLES

As children are socialized, they take on additional roles: girl or boy, friend, leader, follower, schoolchild, and so on. A look at sex roles and peer roles will show that each has its effect on the growing child.

Sex Roles

Children's sex roles build on the stereotypical behavior adopted in the preschool years. Some neighborhood play may continue in mixed-sex groups; but at school, children generally segregate into same-sex groups, and these segregated groups endure until the romantic interests of adolescence draw children out of them (Fine, 1981). Each sex professes a contempt for the other, with girls talking about "yukky boys" and boys complaining about "dumb girls." There is a good deal of continuity between some of girls' play activities and traditional female roles (home maintenance and child care) but in this culture much less between boys' play and adult male roles. Boys seem to have a great need to assert their masculinity—perhaps to distinguish themselves from the primarily female influence at home and at school. Calling a boy a "sissy" is a strong weapon of behavioral control, and this fear of being linked with cross-gender behavior makes boys reluctant to take part in girls' activities, although girls often engage in activities stereotyped for boys.

The channeling of children's inclinations along traditionally sex-appropriate lines can restrict a child's potential. This stifling influence appeared in a study by Aletha Stein, Sheila Pohly, and Edward Mueller (1971), who gave gender labels to neutral tasks to see if the label affected the way sixth-grade children performed them. Boys did best on "masculine" tasks, worst on "feminine" tasks, and somewhere in between on tasks labeled as appropriate for both sexes. Girls did as well on "equally appropriate" tasks as they did on "feminine" tasks but performed worst on tasks labeled "masculine."

This girl has absorbed her culturally prescribed sex role; she imitates the stereotypical behavior she has seen in adult role models. *(© Suzanne Szasz)*

The emotional conditioning associated with sex roles so pervades the child's social environment that it is practically invisible to later, rational inspection. Because individuals cannot consciously recover the experiences that conditioned their attitudes toward sex roles, they often tend to believe that their own attitudes are inborn, genetic accompaniments of their sex organs, rather than the accumulation of years of learning.

Peer Roles

During later childhood, organization creeps into children's relationships, and two kinds of patterns characteristically develop. The first is the sense of belonging to a group that is supported by special activities and rituals and the exclusion of outsiders. Children come to define their own special qualities and behavior by comparing them to the way group members act or by contrasting themselves with outsiders. Since group organization is not rigid, cliques break up and re-form, sometimes allowing arbitrarily excluded children to slip into the fold. The second

PERSONALITY IN LATER CHILDHOOD

PSYCHODYNAMIC VIEW

Sigmund Freud considered later childhood to be a calm period of sexual latency after the stormy phallic period of early childhood. During later childhood, the repression (or exclusion from conscious thought) of children's sexuality permits them to form relationships with children of the same sex and to assume the role of either leader or follower. According to Freud, the influence both of children's peers and of the authority figures in their world (parents and teachers) continues to affect personality, especially by strengthening the child's self-image or by causing the child further to repress sexual urges.

Erik Erikson places great emphasis on the influence of others in role development during later childhood. The child's learning takes place in the context of school and society, and Erikson suggests that popularity and the potential for leadership are a function of the child's relative success in learning to exert control over the environment. Successful control enables children to make positive contributions to those around them. Children acquire positive self-concepts from their ability to be productive, self-directing, and accepted.

SOCIAL-LEARNING VIEW

Walter Mischel sees peer-group pressure and the impact of the school as two significant forces shaping the child's behavior. From observation and participation, the child learns to conform to the demands and expectations of peers as well as to those of parents and other adults; in the process, the child learns both positive and negative behavior. From observing what behavior meets with social approval and what is punished, children learn to behave in ways that enable them to become popular or to assume positions of leadership. Through interacting with an expanded environment and through assessing their own behavior in relation to its consequences, children develop a clear and more complete self-concept.

pattern of group interaction is the elaboration of hierarchies that developed in the nursery-school years. Any child in a fifth-grade classroom can rattle off an ordered list of the smartest, the most athletic, and the most popular, and classmates show surprising agreement. The roles children take in peer-group play train them for their later assumption of adult social roles, and the ranking of children in their dominance hierarchies seems to predict general social competence (Hartup, 1979).

Competence is related to popularity, perhaps because, as noted in Chapter 13, the child who emerges from secure and rewarding relationships at home tends to be trusting, confident, and able both to initiate rewarding interactions and to receive overtures from others. These characteristics correlate with a child's popularity as measured by **sociometric analysis,** a method that charts how often a child is chosen by peers as a preferred friend or companion (Campbell and Yarrow, 1961).

Yet popularity is not solely a matter of social competence (Putallaz and Gottman, 1981). Children's expectations, their behavior, and the responses of others form an interlacing web, so that it is difficult to say which comes first. In addition, factors outside a child's control may affect the responses of others. Research has shown, for example, that physique is likely to

The child who is considered a leader in a group of peers is generally popular as well as skillful in the specific activities demanded by the club, team, or gang. *(Jane Bown)*

influence a child's popularity. Among six- to ten-year-old boys studied by Robert Staffieri (1967), muscular boys were more popular than skinny or plump boys, and most boys wished for a muscular build that corresponded with the masculine stereotype.

Although popular children tend to become leaders, the peer group is generally discriminating in its assignment of these roles. When children organize a baseball game, they listen to an athletically skilled child; when they stage a play, they turn to an imaginative child. Thus in a study of leadership among six- to eleven-year-olds, Wade Harrison, James Rawls, and Donna Rawls (1971) found that leaders tended to be more competent than other children in a specific area of development. Leaders also tended to be more intelligent, active, aggressive, achieving, and socially adept than children who rarely led.

The personal and social consequences of popularity show up in other ways, as Herbert Harari and John McDavid (1969) found when they recruited both a popular and an unpopular child and had them carry out prohibited acts, such as stealing money from the teacher. The other children in the class, who had watched, later were called into the principal's office and asked what had happened. Half the children came in by themselves; the rest were accompanied by another child.

The principal questioned all the children, insisting that they inform on the culprit. When children were interrogated alone, all identified the guilty child; but when they were questioned in pairs, they refused to tell on the popular child but without hesitation told on the unpopular one. Children apparently realize that their actions in the presence of another are likely to get back to their peers. Informing on a popular child could lead to their own rejection, whereas informing on an unpopular child is unlikely to have personal consequences.

PERSONAL AND SOCIAL DEVELOPMENT

As growing children try out a variety of roles, they learn to work with other people and to allow for their needs. By looking at the development of altruism, we can see how children learn to consider others; by examining aggression, we can see where consideration of others breaks down.

Altruism

Altruism, as described by Paul Mussen and Nancy Eisenberg-Berg (1977), is action intended to benefit another person and taken without any anticipation of external reward. Often the action involves some risk or sacrifice on the part of the helper. The term covers a variety of positive actions, ranging from the simple sharing of candy or toys to springing to the aid of a child who is being bullied (Underwood and Moove, 1982). Although there is some evidence that helping others is an adaptive action that has been selected for in the course of evolution, it is not apparent at birth. No matter what its source—

genetic predisposition, learning, increased cognitive understanding or a combination of these factors—a child's readiness to help others increases with age.

Empathy Without empathy, which is the vicarious identification with another's emotions, altruism would probably be impossible (M. Hoffman, 1981). Although a child may develop empathic responses without becoming altruistic, a child is unlikely to be altruistic unless she or he first develops empathy (Mussen and Eisenberg-Berg, 1977). A child may be generous or helpful without being altruistic (Rushton, 1980; Staub, 1979), of course, since generous or helpful acts done for reward or to conform to a rule are not, by definition, altruistic.

Many developmental psychologists believe that empathy develops through conditioning, as the child comes to associate another's pain or distress with his or her own painful past experiences. Other psychologists agree but stress the importance of changes in children's understanding as necessary for the development of an empathy that goes beyond the immediate situation (M. Hoffman, 1979, 1981).

In order to condition empathy, similar emotions must be aroused in both the child and the other person—and almost at the same time. In addition, the child's action must either give the other person pleasure or end the distress. As James Bryan (1975) explains it, once empathy is established, the act that makes the other person joyful creates joy in the child and either reinforces the child's altruistic acts or motivates him or her to perform them. With Elizabeth Midlarsky, for example, Bryan (Midlarksy and Bryan, 1967) conditioned primary-school-aged girls by having a female experimenter express joy and hug them when prizes were donated, on the supposition that the girls would feel happy themselves and come to empathize with the experimenter's obvious pleasure. Girls who were hugged by a joyful experimenter were more likely than girls who were not hugged to sacrifice their own prizes—even after the experimenter stopped hugging them and expressing joy. What is more, these girls later made larger anonymous donations to poor children than did other girls. Girls who were hugged but by an experimenter who did not express joy were no more likely to sacrifice prizes or donate to the poor than were girls who were never hugged.

Sex differences in socialization may help explain why girls often are regarded as more empathic, more nurturant, and more generous than boys (Edwards and Whiting, 1980; M. Hoffman, 1977b). Girls are more likely than boys to be taught to express their emotions, to be sensitive to the feelings and needs of others, and to be assigned responsibility for caring for other children. Girls are also more likely than boys to experience nurturance and help from others.

Generosity Indeed, when it comes to generosity, girls seem to benefit from cultural expectations. In a study (Shigetomi, Hartmann, and Gelfand, 1981) of fifth- and sixth-grade children, although both teachers and pupils regarded the girls as more helpful, generous, and friendly, girls were more generous only with their time and effort. Boys were more generous when asked to donate material objects, and the sexes were the same when asked to give money to charity.

Older children are usually more willing than youngsters to share candy, toys, or money with others. This increase in generosity with age develops for several reasons (Staub and Noerenberg, 1981). First, older children often find it easier to part with possessions simply because they do not seem quite so valuable. For example, a three-year-old regards a nickel as a huge sum and is reluctant to part with it. In contrast, a ten-year-old sees a nickel as such an inconsequential amount that it can easily be given to help others.

Second, older children have had more opportunities to learn that people are supposed to help others. They may have seen their parents donate to charities or do volunteer work in hospitals. They may have rung doorbells on Halloween to collect money for UNICEF. They may have heard people say that "it is better to give than to receive." Such experiences make it clear to children that society places a premium on helping other people.

Third, as children grow, they become less egocentric—as we noted in the last chapter. Many have learned to take the perspective of others and to empathize with people who need help. The connection between diminished egocentrism and generosity appeared when Kenneth Rubin and Frank Schneider (1973) measured the egocentrism of seven-year-olds, then gave them an opportunity to donate candy to poor children and to help a younger child complete a task. Children who were better able to see things from another's viewpoint were more likely than other children both to donate candy and to assist the youngster.

Consistent individual differences in generosity also appear among children. Some children help others in most situations, whereas others are likely to help little or not at all (Mussen and Eisenberg-Berg, 1977). Children with solidly established positive social views tend to donate regardless of the immediate situation, but children with weaker views toward positive social action generally donate only when the situation makes it the easiest thing to do.

Various sorts of experiences lead to these individual differences. Seeing another act in a generous manner increases generosity, and a nurturant model seems to be most effective. In one study, Marian Yarrow, Phyllis Scott, and Carolyn Waxler (1973) found that although any adult model could affect children's immediate generosity, children who saw a warm, nurturant model were still generous two weeks after they watched the generous adult. Models who have strong, lasting effects on children are likely to be those who have close, rewarding relationships with them—such as their parents. In the absence of such a relationship, the example of a model is likely to have only a fleeting effect.

In another study, Joan Grusec and Sandra Skubiski (1970) found that children who watched an adult donate to charity gave more themselves; but when the adult simply said that the children should share their money with charity, donations dropped. Exhortations to give had strong effects only among girls who previously had a warm relationship with the adult who urged generous behavior.

Although exhortations do not generally affect children's generosity, they do increase children's statements that people should be altruistic, as Philippe Rushton (1980) and other investigators have noted. The lesson from these studies seems clear. If we want children to talk altruistically, we should talk that way ourselves; but if we want them to behave altruistically, we should act as altruists.

Reinforcement for altruistic acts is also effective. Children respond to verbal praise with increased generosity, giving more of their prizes, whether the praise is for their act ("That was a helpful thing to do") or for themselves ("You are a very nice and helpful person"), as Joan Grusec and Erica Redler (1980) discovered. But whereas praise that attributes generosity to their own character leads most eight-year-olds to transfer their generosity to other situations several weeks later, praise that simply applauds the act has no effect on later behavior. Ten-year-olds do not make this distinction. Perhaps because they are more flexible at interpreting rules, they tend to transfer their generosity whether their character or their act is singled out for praise.

Giving Aid Generosity is usually clearly defined, but the circumstances in which giving aid, a second form of altruism, is appropriate are usually confusing. It may be unclear that an emergency exists, that responsibility for help rests on the child, or even that the child is competent to help. This kind of altruistic behavior, therefore, follows a different developmental course from that taken by generosity.

Although offering aid at first increases among children as they grow older, the tendency often reverses itself and declines in later childhood. In a series of studies, Ervin Staub (1979) left children alone in a room for a few minutes; while they waited, each child heard a crash from the next room, followed by the sound of a crying child. Staub found that children's tendency to enter the room, presumably to give assistance or to tell the experimenter about the sounds of distress, first increased with age and then decreased. He suggests that because they are less able to empathize with others, few young chil-

Through conditioning and cognitive development, children develop empathy, which helps them come to the aid of someone in distress. *(© Fredrik D. Bodin/Stock, Boston)*

dren assist a child in distress. As they get older, children become more capable of putting themselves in another's place and so are more likely to help in an emergency. In later childhood, however, children also become more sensitive to criticism, which makes them reluctant to help for fear of incurring adult disapproval.

In a subsequent investigation, Staub strengthened this interpretation, finding that under similar circumstances, children who had a warm relationship with the adult investigator were more likely to help than those who lacked this relationship. He proposes that, because children believe that a warm, nurturant adult is unlikely to criticize them, the principal barrier that keeps older children from giving aid is removed.

In this study, Staub also found that seeing an adult give aid increases the number of children who help, and he speculates that this effect occurs because the model's example reassures the child that leaving the room to go to the aid of another will not lead to criticism. In the case of generosity, the influence of adult models is different, as we saw; models apparently show a child that generous behavior is correct. But even young children are unlikely to need adult guidance to tell them they should help someone who is hurt.

Aggression

Altruism strengthens human relationships, but aggression can destroy them. Although psychologists have never demonstrated whether human beings have an inherent drive toward aggression, children often respond aggressively when frustrated or threatened. One of the earliest forms of peer interaction is shoving another child to get a desirable toy. Although children experience restraints on aggression at home, they increasingly come to see that controlled aggression, such as that on the football field or in the fight ring, is valued by society. Their task is to learn where, when, and how to express aggressiveness in order to maximize gain and minimize punishment.

As children get older, the way in which they express aggression shifts. Since they increasingly encounter punishment for aggressive acts, they become more discriminating about when and where they commit them. For this reason, the development of aggression is not uniform. David, who gets away with aggression toward his siblings and his neighborhood playmates, is a model of decorum in the classroom and a ferocious fighter on the playground. Matt, whose parents punish him severely for aggressive acts, is docile at home and a terror at school.

The aim of overt aggression changes as children grow older. Willard Hartup (1974) has charted the development as an increase in **hostile aggression,** which aims at hurting another person, and a decrease in **instrumental aggression,** which aims at retrieving or acquiring an object, territory, or privilege.

Two early studies (Dawe, 1934; Goodenough, 1931) found that young children tend to engage in instrumental aggression and that the proportion of hostile acts increases with age. More specifically, Dawe found that 78 percent of the conflicts between eighteen-month-old infants centered on the possession of toys or other objects, but that five- or six-year-olds quarreled over possession only about 38 percent of the time.

This change in the way that children express aggression coincides with a development in cognitive skills. Children under six often find it difficult to imagine another viewpoint or to make inferences about other people (Flavell et al., 1968). If hostile aggression depends on attributing negative intentions to the person who frustrates them, then younger children should be less likely than older children to show this kind of aggression.

Using this rationale, Hartup (1974) tested the earlier findings of Goodenough and Dawe. He observed children at play over a ten-week period and found that older children (from six to eight years) showed less total aggression than younger children (four to six years) and that this difference was due primarily to the preponderance of instrumental aggression among younger children. As he had expected, older children showed a higher proportion of hostile aggression. Hartup also found, as had Goodenough, that children shifted from physical to verbal aggression as they got older, confirming that both the form and the amount of aggression change as children develop. As they get older and their acts of physical aggression are punished, children find more subtle ways of expressing aggression.

The same socializing influences that lead children to be generous or helpful also teach them to behave aggressively. In Chapter 13 we found that watching someone behave in a violent or aggressive manner tends to make children behave aggressively, but that watching such aggression does not always lead them to imitate the aggressor. The situation itself helps decide whether a child will imitate such a model, as Marian Martin, Donna Gelfand, and Donald Hartmann (1971) found in a study of one hundred children. The children watched a model go through a series of aggressive acts. During a later play period, children were most aggressive when a peer of the same sex was present. When an adult was present, a child at first showed little aggression, but if the adult failed to disapprove of the child's aggressive acts, the child became more and more aggressive. Apparently, the presence of an adult tends to inhibit aggression, but the inhibition disappears if children become aware that their aggressive acts are acceptable, or at least neutral, in adult eyes.

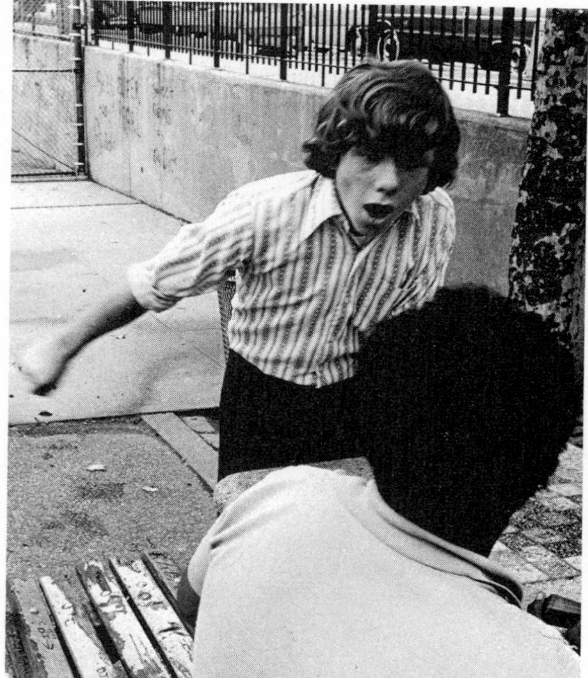

Children often respond to frustration or thwarting with aggression. As they grow older their aggression is more likely to be verbal than physical. *(Alex Webb/Magnum Photos)*

Adult demands for obedience can overcome a child's inhibitions about aggression. When Jordanian children were told that they were teachers in a learning experiment and that the learner (actually a confederate of the experimenters) must get a shock of increasing intensity each time he made a mistake, 73 percent of the children obeyed, delivering what they thought were shocks until the highest level was reached —even though the children believed the shocks were harmful (Shanab and Yahya, 1977). Although neither the sex nor the age of the children, who ranged from six to sixteen, made a difference in their behavior, girls were more likely than boys to say that they gave the shocks in order to obey the experimenter. Before condemning the children for obediently following the unethical demands of the experimenter, consider that Stanley Milgram (1974) surprised the psychological community in 1964 when he demonstrated that as many as 65 percent of the adults he studied would administer what they thought were severe, even lethal, shocks to an innocent person simply because an authority ordered them to do so in the course of an experiment. Clearly, under special conditions, people will behave in ways they ordinarily would reject.

Such conditions are rare. In ordinary situations, children consider the consequences before responding to the demands of others. Their past experiences and their developing self-concepts affect their decisions.

SELF-CONCEPT

In an individualistic and competitive society like our own, children are almost inescapably drawn into comparing themselves with their friends and peers in school and at play. Through these comparisons, children deepen and sometimes alter their self-concepts.

Self-Appraisal

In their view of themselves, children remain primarily present-oriented; but in later childhood they begin to see themselves in terms of what they were like in the past and what they might be like in the future. Asked to describe themselves, they tend to reply in terms of where they live ("I'm an American," "I live on Date Street in Aberdeen, Ohio"), body image ("I'm fat"), memberships ("I'm a Scout"), or even abstract terms ("I'm a person"). Personal qualities also begin to enter their self-descriptions, and a child might say "I'm shy" or "I'm a hard worker."

The reliance on external attributes in self-descriptions declines over the school years, as Don Mohr (1978) found when he asked children to distinguish between themselves and others ("What would you have to change about yourself for you to become your best friend?"). He also got children to think about the stability of their self-concepts by inquiring about their future selves ("What will [will not] change about yourself when you grow up?") and their past selves ("What has [has not] changed about yourself since you were a baby?"). Six-year-olds relied primarily on external attributes in their answers to all questions; eight-year-olds divided their responses between external attributes and behavior; and eleven-year-olds had almost given up referring to external attributes, responding mostly in terms of their behavior. Only eleven-year-olds gave many answers that referred to internal states (feelings, thoughts, knowledge), and those replies came mostly in response to questions about the stability of their self-concepts.

Just as their physical appearance creates expectations in others, so do children's names. Like other attributes, a child's name is likely to influence both how others perceive the child, affecting popularity, and how the child perceives him- or herself, affecting self-concept. An attractive first name is an asset in both instances; an unattractive first name appears to be a liability (McDavid and Harari, 1966). Children with attractive first names, such as John or Karen, are more likely to be popular with their peers than children with unattractive names, such as Horace or Adelle. In another study, sixth-grade boys with desirable names had a more positive view of themselves, their abilities, and their interpersonal relations than boys with undesirable names (Garwood, 1976). Boys with desirable names also believed they could do better work and get along better with others, and they also made significantly higher scores on a standardized achievement test.

Gender constancy continues to influence self-concept, and a firm sense of gender constancy appears linked to an understanding of conservation, which was discussed in Chapter 11. Just as children come to understand that the amount of clay remains constant, whether it is squeezed into a lump or rolled into a long string, so they come to understand that gender does not change, by dress or by magic. The connection appeared when Dale Marcus and Willis Overton (1978) tested five- to eight-year-olds with standard Piagetian conservation tasks involving clay of various shapes and the transfer of soybeans from a squat to a narrow container. Each child's understanding of gender constancy was determined on another test, in which the child looked at pictures of girls and boys and was asked whether the pictured children's gender remained constant as their clothes and hair styles changed. Most children understood gender constancy somewhat later than they understood conservation, and bright children understood that gender was constant earlier than did other children. The older the child, the firmer his or her sense of gender constancy.

A firm sense of gender constancy may well give children enough confidence about their sex roles to loosen the hold of stereotypes, allowing them to be less strict about adhering rigidly to sex-typed activities. Among six-year-olds who lack gender constancy, D. Z. Ulian (1976) found that many believed their own gender might change if they did not stick to activities prescribed for their own sex. Eight-year-olds, on the other hand, had an unshakable sense of gender constancy and believed it was all right for males and females to carry out activities considered the province of the opposite sex.

Self-Regulation

As they get older, children are expected to show increased patience and self-restraint. They continue to use methods they discovered earlier to make waiting easier, but when placed in situations requiring self-control, seven- and eight-year-olds often show a shift in their strategies for postponing pleasure. For example, Brian Yates and Walter Mischel (1979) found that kindergarten children, given a choice, prefer to look at actual rewards while they wait, a decision that makes the waiting difficult. Second graders have learned to look at pictures or objects that have no connection with the promised rewards, indicating that they have come to understand how frustrating the sight of the delayed reward can be.

Through these years, children continue to develop their locus of control, and parents' expectations and behavior can encourage its increasing internal or external direction. When fourth- and fifth-grade boys worked on a task, parents of sons with an external sense of control more often intruded in the task and became highly directive, whereas parents of sons with an internal sense of control were more likely to support their sons' efforts and give less direction (Loeb, 1975).

Once children start school, they may find it necessary to revise their expectations of themselves, depending upon their academic performance and how it is evaluated (Entwisle and Hayduk, 1978). Some children experience repeated disappointments and frustrations that lower their expectations; others encounter success that raises their expectations. For most children, the biggest change is that for the first time, they are evaluated in terms of how well they do in comparison with other children instead of with their own previous performance. This change in standards eventually affects children's judgments about themselves, as they rely increasingly on comparisons with others. Although six-year-olds do not feel bad when they fail and pay little attention to how their performance compares with that of their peers, eight-year-olds are distressed at failure and pay close attention to information about the way they measure up to the level of their peers (Ruble et al., 1976; 1980).

During this period, children's beliefs about locus of control tend to become increasingly related to their behavior and attitudes. This seems particularly true in regard to school achievement (Buriel, 1981). Research consistently shows that children with an internal locus of control perform better in school than children whose locus of control is external (Uguroglu and Walberg, 1979). Children who do well in school generally attribute their success to ability ("I succeed because I'm smart") and their failures to effort ("I didn't work hard enough"). Because effort is a matter of personal control and can be changed, they perceive themselves as being able to overcome failure.

Children who do poorly in school are likely to develop a different pattern of perceiving cau-

If this girl attributes her temporary disappointment to an inherent lack of ability, she may cease to try, but if she attributes it to a lack of effort she is likely to work harder next time. *(© Walter Hodges/West Stock Inc.)*

sation, attributing their successes to external events such as difficulty ("It was an easy test") or chance ("I was just lucky"). They also are likely to attribute their failures to ability ("I failed 'cause I'm dumb"). Since ability is a stable, internal characteristic, they are likely to see no reason to try harder on future occasions.

These different attribution patterns are generally linked with other differences in children's self-concepts (Coopersmith, 1967; Nakamura and Finck, 1980). Children who perceive themselves as successful are likely to have a positive self-concept; they feel confident about themselves and their abilities. Children who perceive themselves as unsuccessful are likely to have a negative self-concept; they lack confidence in themselves and their abilities, and feel unworthy (Dweck, 1981).

But it is not success or failure itself that determines attitudes; it is the way children explain the success or failure to themselves. When children believe that their consistent lack of success is due to external factors and that they cannot change things, they will cease to try—even in situations where they can succeed. This inability to see any hope of success easily leads to what has been called **learned helplessness** (Seligman, 1975). When children learn to be helpless, they no longer try to deal with their problems, because repeated experience has taught them that what happens to them is independent of what they do. As we will see in the section on teacher influence, many girls fall victim to learned helplessness in the classroom.

Understanding Others

In later childhood, as children are less likely to believe that others think and feel exactly as they do, their descriptions of others generally move from concrete attributes to personal qualities. An eight-year-old's description of a friend is full of comments that either do not distinguish between the child and the friend ("We play together") or describe things they have in common ("He goes to camp; me too") (Honess, 1980). By the time children are eleven, such descriptions decline and there is a sharp increase in statements that compare personal qualities ("She knows more than I do"; "He doesn't get mad like me"). Descriptions of friends now tend to focus on the relationship itself, placing emphasis on ideas of equality ("We feel the same"), reciprocity ("We help each other"), and trust ("She never lets you down") (Youniss, 1980).

The trend from describing people's surface appearance toward describing their inner qualities, as Carolyn Shantz (1975) has suggested, resembles the developmental course of conservation. Clothing, hair styles, and possessions may change, as the level of cola changes when poured from a tall into a squat glass, but other people's values, beliefs, and inner qualities are seen as remaining steady despite surface alterations.

Along with this change, children gain increased social experience and understanding, so that their empathic skills are more refined and less situation-bound. They can better understand how an event may affect another person and that others react differently to the same event. At the same time, they become increasingly able to infer another's responses by taking that person's role, mentally putting themselves in the other's place—a skill many children develop by the age of nine (Kurdek, 1977).

The mastery of this skill does not automatically make children empathic. In an experiment in which Ronald Iannotti (1978) had children assume the roles of characters in a story, he found that the ability to take another's role did not affect children's empathy. For example, six- to nine-year-olds acted out the behavior of children who have found a billfold bulging with money. Afterward they answered questions that encouraged role-taking ("Why did you do what you did?" "Why do you feel that way?"). Compared with a control group, these children had an improved ability to take another's role; but when asked to describe the feelings of characters in a story, they were no more empathic than children in the control group.

How well children understand what motivates people in different situations also tends to vary with their breadth of experience, as the developmental change in assessing others' motives indicates. In one study, five-year-olds generally took the view that when someone helps another and is given a material reward, he or she wanted to help more than did a person who got nothing for the aid (Cohen, Gelfand, and Hartmann, 1981). That is, they saw people who are later paid as having a stronger altruistic motive than people who are not. But eleven- and twelve-year-olds, like adults, generally discount someone's altruistic motives if some plausible external reason for their action is present. That is, they see people who are later rewarded as having a weaker desire to help others than people who get no reward.

Children's understanding of the larger social world also changes during later childhood. Seven- or eight-year-olds are likely to understand interactions and transactions they have observed or experienced, so they usually understand the difference between paying for an item in the store and giving money as change. Despite their understanding of the function of change, they often believe that merchandise is free to the shopkeeper and that the money paid to him for various items is then given to the blind or the poor (Furth, 1980). Ten- or eleven-year-olds usually have grasped the entire transaction, and their ideas tend to approximate those of adults. They understand that shopkeepers sell goods for more than they pay for them and that selling is how they make their living.

Although seven- and eight-year-olds may distinguish between personal and social roles, understanding that a teacher can also be a parent, they may resort to fanciful constructions when asked about roles with which they have had little contact. Asked how the school got there, Angela spun a tale that identified the construction of the building with the creation of the school system: "One day a lady came along and she thought of having a school where people learn things, and so she got lots of men together and learned them to be builders, and they built lots and lots of schools, and then when we were born, the people who were born made the schools for others, and when they died, other people became them, and so on and so on" (Furth, 1980, p. 137). Ten- and eleven-year-olds generally have a more complete understanding of personal and social roles, and they are also aware of personal motivations and individual differences. Asked if a particular job requires a certain kind of person, a ten-year-old may remark that a teacher of small children needs "patience."

A rich store of previous experiences helps children understand not only the people they encounter in daily life but those they see on television as well (Collins, 1981). Andrew Newcomb and Andrew Collins (1979) showed edited episodes from network comedies to middle- and lower-class black and white children. One centered around a middle-class white suburban family; the other episode featured a working-class black family living in a housing project. Children's comprehension of the program got progressively better with age, and their ethnic background had no effect on their understanding. Among ten- and thirteen-year-olds, social class also did not affect their understanding of either episode. But among seven-year-olds, social class had a strong effect. Middle-class children understood the episode about the middle-class family much better than the lower-class children did, also doing significantly better at inferring an actor's feelings and the cause for his or her behavior. The situation was reversed for the working-class episode, with lower-class children understanding it much better than middle-class children and doing significantly better at inferring feelings and causes of behavior. As Newcomb and Collins suggest, when younger children's previous experiences bear some relation to a program's content, their understanding of all aspects of the program is improved.

Parental influence remains strong in childhood; the value placed by these parents on reading has clearly had a strong effect on their children. (© *Hazel Hankin 1982*)

PARENTAL INFLUENCE

In later childhood, parents continue to exert a strong influence on socialization. Children still depend on their parents for material needs and for attention, affection, physical contact, and assistance. Because the manner in which parents fulfill children's needs affects the children's behavior, parental control remains strong.

Effect of the Child's Characteristics

Children's own characteristics undoubtedly play an important part in how parents (and other adults) treat them, so that whether a child is responsive, for example, may affect the kind of discipline parents use. In a novel study, Barbara Keller and Richard Bell (1979) found that by coaching children to act in specific ways, they could evoke specific disciplinary techniques. Keller and Bell trained nine-year-old girls to behave in two different ways. In the "person-oriented" style, the girls looked at the person's face, smiled, and answered questions promptly. In the "object-oriented" style, the girls kept their attention on the material that had been placed before them and counted silently to five before responding to comments or questions.

The researchers then asked women college students to interact with the girls and to attempt to get them to show some consideration for others—for example, to make a pillow for a handicapped child. In order to give the women power over the girls, each student was supplied with a stack of poker chips, which could be exchanged for toys or books. The student could give a girl chips or take away chips the girl already had. Before interacting with a girl, the student

ADULT'S STATEMENTS						
		References (Number per child)				
Child's Behavior	Power Assertions	Tokens	Commands	Feelings	Consequences
Person Oriented	25%	2.8	3.7	4.5	6.4
Object Oriented	56%	6.2	2.2	3.4	2.0

FIGURE 15.1 When girls impeded the altruistic tasks set for them, a girl's style of interaction affected the way an adult responded. Girls who were person-oriented tended to hear appeals based on reason (references to the consequences of their actions and the feelings of the receipient), whereas girls who were object-oriented heard more references to power (tokens that could be taken away). *(Adapted from Keller Bell, 1979)*

watched through a one-way mirror as the child behaved in either the person- or object-oriented style. The student then had a period of interaction with the girl, and the girl (carrying out instructions) impeded whatever helpful task for others the student urged her to do.

The way a girl behaved had a strong effect on the way she was treated and perceived. With a girl who behaved in a person-oriented manner, students relied on reason, often referring to the consequences of the child's behavior. With a girl who behaved in an object-oriented manner, they fell back on the only power they had, referring to the poker chips. Students' impressions of the girls also were affected by the girls' behavior. They rated a girl as significantly more attractive, responsive, cheerful, intelligent, and physically active when she behaved in a person-oriented manner than when she responded in an object-oriented manner. Such results suggest that children themselves may help determine the disciplinary techniques their parents use.

Learning to Achieve

In subtle ways, parents may teach their children how to behave without being aware of their actions or their effect, as we saw in the discussion of sex-role development in Chapter 9. When Jeanne Block and her colleagues (1978) watched as parents taught their children the same task, they found that mothers behaved similarly, whether their child was a girl or a boy. But fathers behaved differently toward sons and daughters. When teaching a son, fathers tended to emphasize achievement; when teaching a daughter, they indicated that achievement was not the most important aspect of the task and seemed more interested in the interpersonal aspects of the situation.

Some years earlier, Marian Winterbottom (1958) found clear differences between mothers of boys with strong achievement motivation and mothers of boys whose achievement motivation was weak. Compared to the latter, mothers of boys with strong achievement motivation made more demands on their sons before they were eight years old and placed more restrictions on them before they were seven—but the demands made were greater than the restrictions imposed. At an early age, the boys were expected to do such things as hang up their clothes, make their beds, do well in competition, attempt difficult tasks without asking for help, make their own friends, and select their own clothes. These mothers also evaluated their sons' accomplishments higher and rewarded them more profusely than did mothers of boys with low achievement

MOM, YOU'RE THE GREATEST

When researchers study the relationship between parents and children, they often focus on reinforcements, punishment, and modeling. A Mother's Day newspaper contest gave John Weisz (1980) an opportunity to see how children view the relationship. An upstate New York newspaper offered free dinners at a local restaurant for the best letters telling "Why my Mom is the greatest." The children who entered the contest were self-selected, so their responses cannot be applied to all children. Nevertheless, the content of their letters provides an interesting check on the theories of developmental psychologists.

More girls than boys wrote letters to the newspaper, and as children got older, girls wrote proportionately more of them. Among children of nine or under, the sexes divided equally, but among children from ten to seventeen, girls rose to 77 percent of the correspondents. Without a Father's Day contest for comparison, there is no way to tell whether girls write more letters than boys or whether children are more likely to write about parents of the same sex, with whom they presumably have identified.

Children paid little attention to praise or reward—only 6 of the 249 letter writers mentioned it, indicating that although children respond to reinforcement, they do not appear to be consciously aware of it. In other respects, the letters read like a confirmation of developmental research.

Although modeling was mentioned infrequently, when comments such as "She teaches us to love and respect other people" were included, they were likely to be in letters written by girls. This finding supports the view that a child tends to select the same-sex parent as a model.

References to affection and to physical nurturance were common and may explain why rewards were rarely mentioned. The chocolate cakes, the kisses, and the new clothes could all be considered reinforcement. As a seven-year-old girl wrote, "She cooks the best chili and kisses me every day on the nose." With age, references to physical nurturance faded somewhat (although they never disappeared) in favor of psychological nurturance ("When I have troubles she talks them over with me"). Such references support a research finding that as children get older, they become more aware of inner qualities. Older children were also the ones who appreciated when others could take their perspective ("She always seems to know how I feel") and the ones who valued their mothers for "just being there."

Younger children prized their mothers for allowing them to have control over their own actions ("She lets us do most anything"; "She let me have my ears pierced"), whereas older children had often come to value their mothers for saying no ("She teaches me right from wrong even though it may hurt"; "She makes us eat fruit and vegetables"). Again, the letters support psychologists who propose that as children begin to recognize the intent behind their parents' actions, they begin to appreciate the value of limits.

motivation. In general, these mothers' expectations for their sons indicated that they trained them for both independence and achievement, and a connection between doing well and doing things by oneself seems obvious.

A bit later, Bernard Rosen and Roy D'Andrade (1959) reported that the parents (mothers and fathers) of boys with high achievement motivation had high aspirations for their sons, expected them to do well, believed they were competent problem solvers, and were interested in and concerned about their sons' performance. These parents also tended to be competitive and involved, and to enjoy problem solving themselves. They showed more affection for their sons than did the parents of boys with weak achievement motivation, and they rewarded successful performance with warmth and approval.

Boys with high achievement motivation generally have warm parents who encourage them to excel. *(© Leonard Speier 1982)*

The crucial role of affection also appeared in another study: Robert Sears (1970) found that twelve-year-old boys whose early years were marked by warm parents and nondominant fathers had high self-concepts and a high level of school achievement in both reading and arithmetic. For girls, there was no relation between father dominance and self-concept, but school achievement was linked to parental warmth.

On the basis of their reviews of the research, Lois Hoffman (1972) and Janet Spence and Robert Helmreich (1978) agree that boys' and girls' tendency to be achievers depends on their parents' warmth, guidance, and the encouragement of such behavior. They also note that when boys and girls show comparable levels of achievement, the achievement-related behavior of boys is generally due to an internalized sense of achievement motivation, but the achievement-related behavior of girls is generally based on social comparison and concern over personal relationships, a difference that parallels the different socialization practices parents use with sons and daughters.

Maternal Employment

The way American children are socialized may be changing, as increasing numbers of mothers work outside the home. In a study of more than two hundred ten-year-olds that examined the cumulative effects of maternal employment, Dolores Gold and David Andres (1978) found what they considered to be mixed effects. Most children of working mothers were less bound by sex-role stereotypes than children of mothers who did not work, with the children of working mothers seeing much greater similarity between men and women in personality traits, behavior, jobs, and authority. The effect was strongest among girls. Working-class boys whose mothers worked, although less rigid in their attitudes than working-class sons whose mothers had never been employed, were much less egalitarian than other children of employed mothers. The way the mothers themselves felt may have had some bearing on these attitudes, for the more content the mother was with working, the more egalitarian her child—and working-class mothers of sons were not at all content at being employed.

When it came to achievement in school, the sons of middle-class employed mothers did the worst of any group; the daughters of middle-class employed mothers did best, but only slightly better than the daughters of middle-class mothers who did not work. Although the sons of working-class employed mothers had the highest achievement scores of any boys, they disliked school the most.

In general, a mother's employment had no effect on her child's adjustment. As a group, children of employed and unemployed mothers did not differ. The father's involvement with his children, however, appeared to be a key to their school success. When mothers worked and fathers were involved with their children, both the children's grades and their educational aspirations tended to be high.

Father Absence

A father's attention seems important to school success, but up to half of all children live for some time in a single-parent home, and in 90 percent of the cases the missing parent is a father (Glick and Norton, 1978). Researchers who have explored the effect of a father's absence have found consistent differences between children reared with and without fathers, but factors other than the absence of the male parent may be responsible.

Girls appear to recover from the immediate effects of divorce in about two years, but boys—although they improve markedly during that period—tend to have more problems at school, at home, and with peers than do girls in divorced families or children in intact homes (Hetherington, 1979). Despite this finding, living in a home filled with marital discord leads to more disturbance in both boys and girls than does the long-term effect of divorce (Rutter, 1979).

Boys who grow up without fathers do not seem to do as well in junior high school as other boys, even when investigators control for any difference in IQ (Shelton, 1969). Girls, on the other hand, do not seem to be as affected. Some studies that have reported detrimental effects on school performance may be reflecting the immediate impact of a father's departure, not the lasting influence.

The permanent loss of a father after a boy is six years old has little effect on his independence, his dependency on adults, his aggression, or his sex-role preferences, according to a study that looked at first-born, lower-class boys—both black and white (Hetherington, 1966). But boys who lose their fathers before they are four are not aggressive and tend to make feminine scores on a sex-role test. On the basis of a review of research, Henry Biller (1976) concurs with these findings; early father absence does appear to weaken or retard (but not prevent) the acquisition of the male sex role. There is no firm evidence to indicate that boys who grow up in fatherless homes will become men with an inadequate masculine identity (Herzog and Sudia, 1973).

Evidence showing that the absence of a father affects a girl's sex-role development is scant. According to Biller's review, some studies indicate that girls are less affected than boys by the absence, but others find that girls from broken homes tend to reject the role of wife and mother or have difficulties in achieving satisfactory sexual relationships. The father's early departure may affect girls as it does boys, but the influence does not show until girls reach adolescence. Mavis Hetherington (1972) found, for example, that working-class adolescent girls who had lost their fathers before they were five seemed uncertain about their actions around males. When taking part in an interview, they were either painfully shy (if their fathers had died) or excessively seductive (if their parents had divorced). But college women who have lost their fathers before they were five do not show the same inappropriate responses to males (Hainline and Feig, 1978). So either middle-class girls have wider opportunities than working-class girls to learn how to behave with the opposite sex, or else practice in socialization during high school helps most girls overcome the problem.

Some studies have found that boys without fathers run the added risk of becoming juvenile delinquents, but other studies have found no connection. Elizabeth Herzog and Cecelia Sudia (1973), after reviewing the research, conclude that the available data are simply too confused to permit one to say with any certainty that children in fatherless homes are more likely than other children to become delinquent. They suggest that father absence is probably less important than the climate and tone of the home and the kind of supervision the child receives.

Growing up without a father obviously leaves some mark on a child, but no one can say exactly what the effects are or how long they last. Myriad other factors can heighten or ameliorate the impact of his absence. So many factors are linked together—the age of the child at the father's departure; the length of his absence; the presence or absence of siblings and whether they are older or younger, of the same or different sex; the presence or absence of a stepfather; the socioeconomic level of the home; the mother's reactions to the departure and her ability to exercise supervision; and community standards—that it is impossible to define the precise effects of father absence on socialization.

PEER INFLUENCE

During the school years, the peer group becomes larger and more important. A wider group of acquaintances, however, does not necessarily lead to an increase in the number of close friends (Rubin, 1980). Friendships in later childhood increase in intensity rather than in number, and with this increased intensity comes stronger peer influence.

Popularity

Children's skill in relating to their peers plays a major role in determining their friendships and their acceptance or rejection by others. As Steven Asher (1978) has pointed out, a child must be able to initiate new relationships and then maintain them. When popular children first meet a strange child, they are likely to greet the newcomer, give or request information, and invite him or her to join in games and activities (Gottman, Gonso, and Rasmussen, 1975). If the first meeting with a strange child goes badly, children who believe the rebuff is due to a misunderstanding are likely to try again when they encounter new children (Dweck and Goetz, 1977). But children who believe they simply do not know how to make friends are likely to avoid a new encounter. Children who get along well with their peers generally help them in socially accepted ways (Nakamura and Finck, 1980). Children who suggest highly unusual ways of helping their peers tend to be rejected and disliked (Ladd and Oden, 1979).

When children are asked to name their friends, about 10 percent of the members in any group are not named at all (Asher and Renshaw, 1981). Not all of these ignored children are shy, withdrawn, or aggressive, but their neglect tends to pen them into a state of social isolation. In many cases an isolated child possesses the social skills required to get along with others but for one reason or another does not use them. Such children tend to disagree with their peers, to criticize others without giving a reason, and to call attention to themselves instead of entering into the group's activity (Putallaz and Gottman, 1981). Some children have not developed the necessary skills, but as the accompanying box shows, they can readily acquire them.

Conformity

The strong influence that peers can have on a child's behavior was clearly demonstrated in a study by Philip Costanzo and Marvin Shaw (1966), who asked children to compare the lengths of a pair of lines. One line was obviously longer than the other, but all except one of the children were confederates of the investigators, and they chose the incorrect line. If the child denied the evidence of his or her senses and agreed with the obviously incorrect judgment of the group, the child had altered a personal judgment to conform to that of peers. As Figure 15.2 on page 382 shows, a child's susceptibility to this form of peer influence increased with age, reached its peak during the preadolescent years, and then gradually declined.

A more recent study, by Thomas Berndt (1979), supports Costanzo and Shaw's finding. Berndt discovered that while antisocial conformity to pressure from peers increased sharply during the years from eight to fourteen, conformity to parents' wishes decreased. Among eight-year-olds, parents' wishes still outweighed those of peers; where there was conflict, the chil-

Children's social skills play a major role in determining their acceptance by the peer group. *(© Jay Lurie/West Stock Inc.)*

dren generally conformed to their parents' desires. Although peer influence increased among eleven-year-olds, there seemed no conflict between family standards and those of the peer group; the children apparently lived in two separate worlds, each with its own standards. Peer pressure peaked among fourteen-year-olds, and conflict between the standards of peer group and parents became sharp, with the children feeling compelled to conform to peers' wishes. Such results indicate that peers exert a very strong influence during later childhood and early adolescence.

Willard Hartup's (1970) descriptions of peer influence help explain this rise and subsequent decline. He believes that peer influence increases as the growing child's ability to see things from the perspective of another grows; the later decline can be explained by children's ability to reinforce themselves. By self-reinforcement, Hartup means that as children interact with their peers, they begin to internalize the statements other children make about their behavior as well as the effects of peers' responses to them. By internalizing the judgments of others, children develop the ability to evaluate their own actions.

Immediate imitation of a peer begins to drop sharply among six- and seven-year-olds (Abramovitch and Grusec, 1978), and it becomes

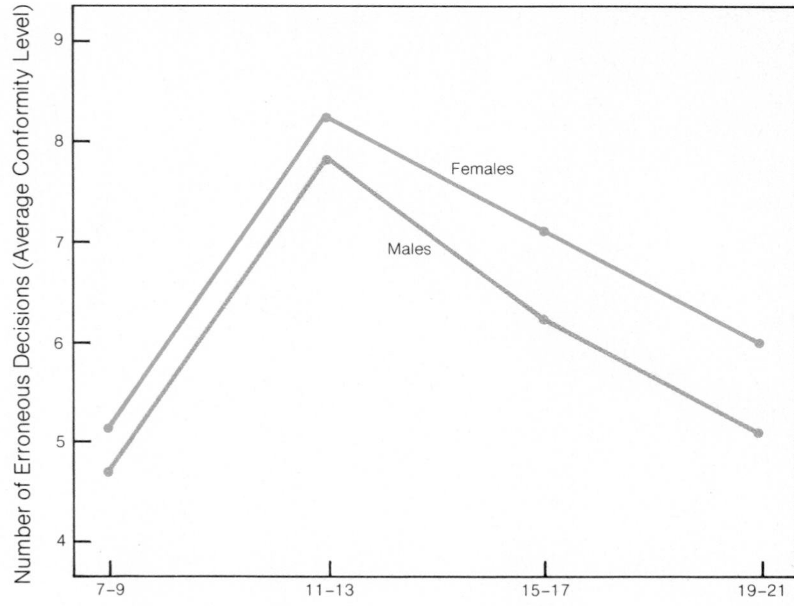

FIGURE 15.2 Children's conformity to the judgments of a peer group. Both females and males show increased susceptibility to peer influence with age, until early adolescence; then it gradually declines. ***(After Costanzo and Shaw, 1966)***

increasingly rare among nine- to eleven-year-olds. When it does occur, it is likely to involve the immediate imitation of a child who is often watched by other children and who ranks high in the peer hierarchy. Imitation of peer models by older children may be much more frequent than Abramovitch and Grusec found, however, since children often learn a new response and save it for an appropriate occasion. In addition, storing a response for later use helps avoid the label of "copycat," which is no compliment among schoolchildren.

The Peer Group

Once in school, the child spends more time under the influence of the peer group, a formally structured collection of peers that seems to be an inevitable part of socialization. When Muzafer Sherif and Carolyn Sherif (1953, 1964) divided boys into two groups, they found that a hierarchical structure always formed among the boys in each group. The most popular boys did not automatically become leaders, nor were leaders always the most talented or the toughest.

No matter what status children hold in a group, its solidarity exercises a great deal of in-

Eleven year olds seem to live in two separate worlds; they adhere to parental or peer standards, depending upon which group they are with at the moment. *(© Leonard Speier 1979)*

TEACHING SOCIAL SKILLS

Children who are ignored or rejected by their peers are a special concern of teachers and parents. In recent years, several promising techniques have been developed to help bring these social isolates into the group. The methods are based on the premise that many isolated children simply lack the social skills required to initiate and maintain friendships.

Sometimes modeling techniques are used with withdrawn or shy children. At first, children watch filmed models who approach peers at play and join in their activities. Afterward the children are led through role-playing experiences in which they rehearse the social skills they have seen in the film. Children who receive such training show an increase in successful social interaction with their peers. In one study (Evers and Schwartz, 1973), when investigators checked back a month later, the children were still interacting with others at a high level.

When a training program combines modeling techniques with reinforcement, the effects of the two combined may be more powerful and longer lasting than when modeling alone is involved. In such a program, Mark Weinrott, John Corson, and Marc Wilchesky (1979) added peer reinforcement and group rewards to individual rewards for withdrawn children. By the end of the training period, formerly isolated six- to nine-year-olds were involved in as much social interaction as other children. In addition, the children's activities had extended to lunchroom and playground contacts, and they had begun to visit friends and invite them to their own homes.

Another effective approach to teaching social skills involves coaching or directly instructing the children in such skills. For example, Sherri Oden and Steven Asher (1977) taught socially unskilled eight- and nine-year-olds how to start playing a game; to pay attention; to take turns; to share materials; and to reward others by looking at them, smiling, and offering help or encouragement. The children practiced the skills in play sessions with peers. Then they met again with the coaches and went over the skills they had learned. By the end of a six-week program, the children were more accepted by their peers; a follow-up one year later showed that their acceptance had increased even further.

---

fluence on their behavior. Competition within a group may decrease solidarity (French et al., 1977; Jensen and Moore, 1977), but balanced competition *between* groups promotes it (Johnson et al., 1981; Sherif and Sherif, 1953). Group members generally become much closer during a competition, although occasional rancor may appear just after a competitive defeat. In a study of unbalanced competition, when one group consistently lost, the losing group threatened to collapse in disharmony (Sherif and Sherif, 1953). Apparently, the constant unpleasantness generated by defeat overcomes any tendency for group members to cooperate.

Any kind of competition produced extreme friction between the groups studied by the Sherifs. Boys in one group looked down on members of the other, and the situation eventually exploded into open hostility. Hostility between the groups further strengthened group solidarity and increased the influence of the group over the behavior of its members, so that boys who were not normally hostile participated in intensely aggressive acts for the sake of the group. In such cases, the structured group can overpower children's tendencies toward self-judgment and lead them to engage in behavior they would normally avoid.

Competition for a starring role would decrease the solidarity of this peer group, but the members appearance together as a corps de ballet would increase the group's cohesion. *(© Lawrence Frank 1981)*

INFLUENCES FROM THE WIDER WORLD

In a rapidly changing society, the experiences of children may vary dramatically from one generation to the next. A generation ago, even eight- to ten-year-olds were expected to have some kind of part-time job (delivering papers, cutting grass, helping clean house) to supplement their meager allowances. Household chores were commonplace, as were large homework assignments for even very young children. And lacking the instant entrée into the adult world that television now offers so pervasively, yesterday's children knew considerably less about the world than today's children do.

Television

Parents are still the single most important determiner of the normal child's attitudes toward the world, but the programs a child watches on television convey messages about values, attitudes, and beliefs. Although parents cannot blame their offspring's misbehavior on television, the medium's content and approach surely have some effect on the growing child.

Television and Sex Roles For the most part, television has been a purveyor of sex-role stereotypes. As Carol Tavris and Carole Offir (1977) have pointed out, when Wonder Woman was not saving the world, she worked as a secretary, and the Bionic Woman taught school. In addition, most television heroines, from Charlie's Angels to Police Woman, unmask villains by luck or accident. In children's programs, men are aggressive, constructive, and helpful; their activities bring them tangible rewards. But women tend to be deferential, passive, and ignored; if they are too active, they are punished (Sternglanz and Serbin, 1974).

Although women sometimes get to be heroines in the programs themselves, few commercials shatter sex-role stereotypes and most teach women to be dependent and submissive (Geis et al., 1979). Some now feature female bank managers or traveling sales representatives, but the women in most of them are mothers, housewives, or sex objects, who defer to men's needs, wishes, and preferences. It is the authoritative male who confronts women shoppers with twelve-hour cold capsules, corrects their choice of detergent, convinces them their husbands prefer stuffing to potatoes, and delivers the smooth, authoritative, voice-over commentary in most commercials.

Since the average child watches more than 20,000 television commercials each year, the results of a recent study come as no surprise. Terry Frueh and Paul McGhee (1975) found that heavy television viewers (children who watch more than twenty-five hours each week) have significantly more stereotypical notions about sex roles than children who watch ten hours or less each week. And the older the child, the more ingrained the stereotype.

Television and Violence There has been continuing concern about the possible effects of television violence on the developing child. Even when parents regulate their children's viewing habits, the network news and the Saturday morning cartoons deliver a steady diet of murder and mayhem, presenting models who not only transmit new behavior but may also reduce the inhibitions on antisocial behavior children have already learned.

Numerous experiments have been conducted to assess the effects of television violence on children. In an investigation of children's emotional reactions to programs, D. Keith Osborn and Richard Endsley (1971) found that violent films, whether cartoon or live action, produced the most emotional reactions. Children remembered details of the violent films best; they found the human violence the scariest; and they preferred the nonviolent cartoons. It seems that watching television violence evokes emotional responses in children and influences them to remember the details of depicted violence.

Moving closer to the central question of whether television violence affects the way that children behave, the Office of the Surgeon General (1972) commissioned an exhaustive study of the effects of television violence but failed to reach any definitive conclusions. However, various investigations give some clues as to how television may affect behavior.

Studies have shown that children can learn new ways to express aggression from television (Bandura, 1973), and Robert Liebert and Robert Baron (1972) found that watching televised aggression can make children more willing to hurt another child. Liebert and Baron showed brief excerpts taken directly from regular television shows to boys and girls from five to nine years old. The excerpts were either violent and aggressive (a fist fight or a shooting) or exciting but nonaggressive (a tennis match). After they saw one of these programs, children were told that pushing one button on a panel before them would help another child (who was not actually present) to win a prize but that pushing the other button would hurt the child. They were also told that the longer they pressed either button, the more the other child would be helped or hurt.

Despite their brief exposure to these television shows, children who had watched the violent program hurt the other child for a significantly longer time than those who had watched nonaggressive scenes. Apparently, watching one kind of aggression can lead to aggression of a very different sort. In addition, violent television programs may remove or reduce some children's inhibitions against committing violence—at least

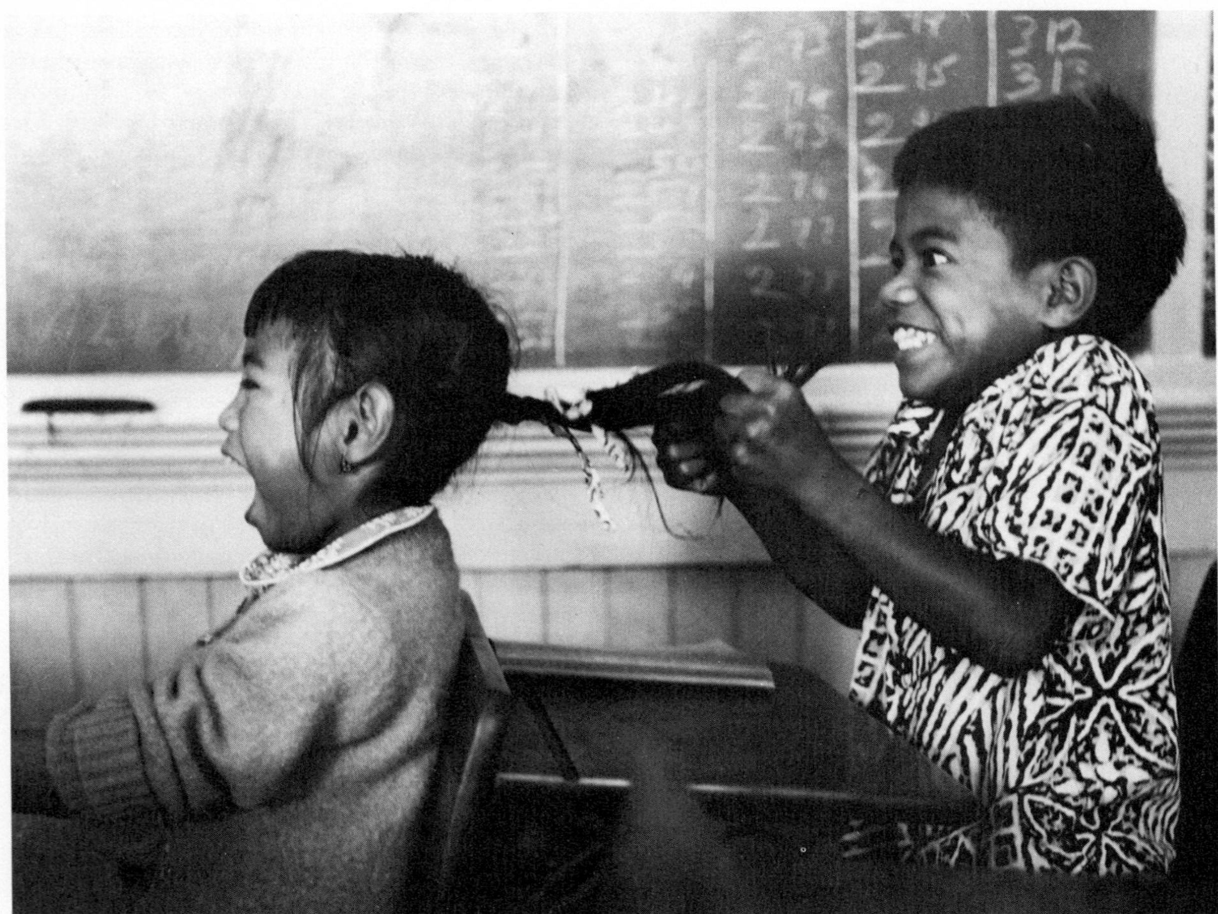

Children learn new ways to express aggression from television and may put their learning into action when the appropriate occasion arises. (© *David S. Strickler/The Picture Cube*)

immediately after a child has seen the program. Additional studies support this position (Watt and Krull, 1977).

Television violence showed up in the classroom in a study by Monroe Lefkowitz and his colleagues (1977; Eron, 1980). They found a significant relationship between the amount of television violence that third-grade boys watched and their classroom aggression as rated by their peers. Even more impressive is their finding of a relationship between the amount of television violence that boys watched in the third grade and their aggression at age nineteen. The investigators concluded that it was not that children who commit aggressive acts watch more television violence, but that those who have watched television violence steadily are later judged to be aggressive.

These studies indicate that television violence may both teach new forms of aggressive

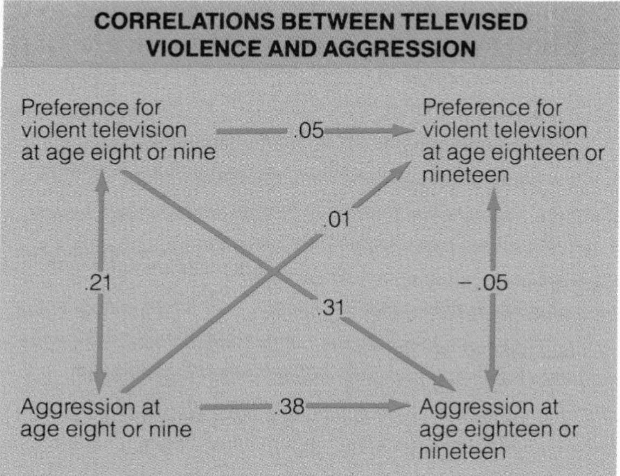

FIGURE 15.3 When 211 boys who were studied as eight- and nine-year-olds were restudied after a lapse of ten years, their preference for violent television programs as youngsters correlated positively with the amount of aggression they displayed as eighteen or nineteen year olds. Although correlation does not indicate causation, the relative strength of this correlation is impressive. ***(Adapted from Eron, Huesmann, Lefkowitz, and Walder, 1972)***

behavior (such as attempts at kung-fu) and relax inhibitions against its expression. But the factors controlling overt aggression are complex, and other research indicates that the long-term effect of heavy television watching may be less violence, not more. When George Gerbner and Larry Gross (1976) compared viewing habits with perceptions of the world, they found that people who watched four or more hours of television each day tended to be significantly more suspicious of others and afraid of being involved in violence themselves than people who watched television two hours or less each day. They also discovered that nearly half the twelve-year-olds they studied watched at least six hours of television each day. Gerbner and Gross believe that heavy television viewing may teach people to play the role of victim and to become passive in the face of aggression. Similarly, a national survey (Zill, 1977) found that children who are heavy viewers of television are significantly more likely than other children to be fearful about life in general.

Television opens children to vast worlds of experience that are otherwise unavailable. It educates, and it illustrates things that remained abstractions to preceding generations. It may also induce children to spend hours in front of a television set that they would otherwise have spent interacting with their peers. Thus the electronic box affects children's knowledge of the world, their activities, their heroes, the time spent with their peers, and a variety of other facets of life (Comstock et al., 1978). Our experiences affect our behavior and attitudes, and television is a form of experience.

Teachers

Teachers serve children as models—models who are not as powerful as parents, but with a definite influence of their own. A pair of studies by David Perry and Kay Bussey (1979) show that children respond to adult models who are not related to them as if they were averaging their performance, judging appropriate behavior by watching a number of models. In the first study, eight- and nine-year-old children watched a group of male and female models choose between pairs of items that had no connection with gender—between a plastic cow and a plastic horse, for example. Afterward the children were given a chance to choose between the items themselves, and the more models of their own gender who had selected an item, the more likely the children were to choose it. In the second study, children watched adult models whom they had previously seen make choices between items that were connected with gender. Afterward both boys and girls imitated the adult models of their own sex who had earlier made gender-appropriate choices, and they also imitated models of the opposite sex who had earlier made choices that were inappropriate for their gender. For example, boys tended to imitate the choices of a woman whose earlier selections consistently were the same as those of men.

Teachers are more than models; their actions can affect children in various ways. For example, they are as biased against children with unattractive first names as are a child's peers. Herbert Harari and John McDavid (1973) randomly assigned attractive names (e.g., David or Lisa) or unattractive names (e.g., Herbert or Bertha) to a group of fifth-grade essays of similar quality. When teachers graded the essays, those with attractive names attached received marks that were a full letter grade higher than essays that carried unattractive names.

Individual characteristics of teachers can influence children's attitudes toward learning and their sense of autonomy, and some research has shown that the effect becomes established within the first six weeks of the school year. In a study of fourth-, fifth-, and sixth-grade classrooms, Edward Deci, John Nezlek, and Louise Sheinman (1981) found that when teachers ran their classrooms with strict control, the students tended to be extrinsically motivated: they worked primarily for grades, showed little curiosity, and disliked challenges. The children also perceived themselves as not very competent. When teachers ran their classrooms in an autonomous manner, encouraging children to take responsibility and to consider all aspects of a situation, the students tended to be intrinsically motivated: they worked primarily in order to master a skill or concept, showed curiosity, and preferred challenges. These children also perceived themselves as competent. Since children stay in a classroom for only a year, one teacher's push toward control may be countered the next year by another's encouragement of autonomy. A series of teachers with similar attitudes, however, could have a lasting effect on a child's sense of autonomy and self-worth.

Teachers can have an additional effect on the girls in their classes, and may promote in some of them a sense of learned helplessness (Dweck and Bush, 1976). In elementary school, girls do as well as boys on tests of math achievement, yet by the time they reach junior high or high school, they often fall behind boys on math tests (Meece, et al., 1982). Carol Dweck and her colleagues believe that this consistent result has nothing to do with gender but a good deal to do with how teachers treat boys and girls in the classroom. When boys fail at a task, teachers generally attribute the failure to lack of effort, a failure to follow instructions, or the messiness of the work. This criticism tends to ascribe any shortcomings to motivational factors, so that boys tend to attribute their classroom failures to lack of effort. In contrast, when girls fail, teachers almost always ascribe their failure to errors in the work itself, and they may accompany their criticism with praise for the girls' motivation and effort. This kind of criticism attributes the shortcomings to lack of ability, so that girls may decide they are incapable of academic success. As a result, boys who experience frequent classroom failure can continue to perceive themselves as capable, but girls who experience frequent failure may develop a sense of learned helplessness.

To find out if teachers' reactions to their schoolwork was indeed a factor in the girls' problem, Dweck and her colleagues (1978) divided fifth-grade boys and girls into groups that received either "boy" or "girl" criticisms for mistakes in solving anagrams. Children who got "boy" criticism heard negative remarks that were devoted half the time to the inaccuracy of their solutions and the rest of the time to their lack of neatness. Children who got "girl" criticism heard critical comments devoted exclusively to the inaccuracy of their answers. After they had been criticized, the children were asked to fill out a slip on which they checked the reason for their failure ("I did not try hard enough"; "The man was too fussy"; "I am not very good at it"). So they would not end the experiment on a note of failure, all the children worked additional problems, for which they received much praise.

Sure enough, few of the boys and girls who received "boy" criticism thought their own ability had anything to do with their mistakes. Eighty percent of the girls and 50 percent of the boys said they had not tried hard enough; 20 percent of the boys said the man was too fussy. Boys as well as girls reacted to "girl" criticism in a way that promoted learned helplessness. Most attributed their failure to lack of ability; only a few thought they had failed because they had not tried hard enough. None blamed the experimenter.

If girls take criticism as the indication of a general lack of ability, the effect may extend beyond the classroom. Girls may develop the stereotypical expectation that males are the ones who are supposed to solve problems and that females are naturally helpless.

SUMMARY

1. During later childhood, parents, peers, and society continue to influence socialization and personality development. As peer relations become organized, peer roles become more important, and peer groups tend to choose leaders who are competent in specific areas of development.
2. Altruism grows out of empathy and may require both conditioning and increased cognitive understanding if it is to develop. As children grow, their aggressive acts tend to shift from instrumental aggression, which aims at acquiring something, to hostile aggression, which aims at hurting someone; the change coincides with cognitive development.
Whether children regularly engage in altruistic or aggressive actions depends on a number of factors, including social and situational effects and the influence of models.
3. Among the attributes that affect a child's self-concept is the attractiveness of his or her name. A firm sense of gender constancy may give children enough confidence to allow them to escape some sex-role stereotypes. Beliefs about locus of control may be influenced by academic performance and are related to children's behavior and attitudes.
4. With increased experience and cognitive development, children become skilled at placing themselves in another's place and are better able to understand that the other person's reaction to an event may be different from their own. The understanding of society increases, and children are able to distinguish between a person's personal and social roles.
5. Parents continue to influence their children's development by giving or withholding attention, affection, and material resources, and by acting as models. However, children's own characteristics may affect the way their parents treat them. Parental warmth, guidance, and encouragement are linked with children's achievement motivation.
6. When working mothers enjoy their employment, their children are less bound by sex-role stereotypes. When, in addition, the fathers are involved with their children, the children do well in school. Father absence leaves a mark on a growing child, but the exact effect is hard to separate from other factors. The absence of a father affects boys more than girls, but both boys and girls are better off living in a single-parent home than amid marital discord.
7. During later childhood, the peer group usually increases in size and relative influence. Contacts with friends and acquaintances and participation in structured peer groups generally become more frequent and intense. Peer influence, especially in regard to antisocial actions, increases during late childhood, peaking in early adolescence and then declining.
8. Television conveys messages to the child about values, attitudes, and beliefs, and appears to increase stereotypical notions about sex roles. Television can—but does not necessarily—teach new forms of aggressive behavior and relax inhibitions against it.
9. Teachers also serve as models. By their attitudes they influence children toward autonomy or obedience and convince a child that he or she is competent or inept. Girls seem more vulnerable than boys to classroom indications that they are incompetent.

16
MORALITY: FROM RULES TO CONDUCT

On August 9, 1974, Richard M. Nixon resigned as president of the United States—the only president in American history to take such a drastic step. His resignation, made when it had become virtually certain that he would be impeached and probably removed from office, was the culmination of a striking example of public immorality, the loosely connected events including burglary, wiretapping, and perjury gathered together under the label of Watergate. When the transcripts of presidential conversations had been made public, philosophers, ministers, journalists, judges, and average citizens asked how supposedly moral men could have participated in immoral acts.

Perhaps the most tempting, and certainly the easiest, explanation of people's moral conduct is simply that some people are scrupulously moral, whereas others are less so. Observers of the national scene have consistently applied this type of explanation to the men involved in the Watergate affair. Yet most of these men were described by their neighbors as warm and helpful human beings, pillars of their communities. Many had strong religious convictions. How could their daily behavior have appeared so impeccably moral to friends and neighbors while they were involved in political immorality and illegality of such astonishing magnitude? This question should arouse our suspicions of easy explanations of morality. Therefore, an examination of contemporary findings on the way that moral conduct develops should help to explain how apparently moral men can behave in immoral ways.

Human behavior is complicated, with intellectual, social, and emotional factors generally combining to influence any act. In this chapter, we take a particular kind of conduct, moral conduct, and consider how it involves intellectual, social, and emotional factors and how it develops from early childhood to adolescence. We will look at how moral thought, feeling, and action vary from one situation to another, tracing developmental changes in thinking about moral problems and noting that opportunities to take the roles of others may change the way a child perceives and thinks about moral issues. We will discover that how individual children or adolescents feel when they remember or anticipate a transgression affects the way that they regulate their own behavior. After discussing the effect of discipline, we will examine the influence of modeling on moral development and moral conduct. Finally, we will discuss the complexities of judging the behavior of other persons.

THE COURSE OF MORAL DEVELOPMENT

For many generations, morality was the central category for defining social relationships and development, and the social sciences were called "the moral sciences." In the last few decades, morality has slipped in and out of focus as a central interest in developmental psychology. The important work of Hugh Hartshorne and Mark May in the late 1920s on children's moral conduct and that of Jean Piaget in the 1930s on moral judgment were followed by two decades of relative inactivity. In the 1930s and 1940s, thought about moral character concentrated on discussions of social adjustment, and specific concerns about moral development focused on discussions of socialization processes.

In the past decade or so, thoughtful psychologists and laymen have become acutely aware of the inadequacies of dealing with moral issues in terms of mental health or group adjustment. Mental-health labels are not scientific; they simply make value judgments about people in terms of social norms. And neither mental-health nor social-adjustment terms define the norms and values that represent universal moral principles. The atrocities of the socially conforming members of the Nazi system and the crimes committed by politicians have made people acutely aware of the fact that adjustment to the group is no substitute for moral maturity.

In order to understand the moral conduct of groups, it is necessary to understand the development of moral conduct in the individual. Moral conduct, like any complex behavior, is determined by the interplay of many factors. When a member of Congress is offered a bribe or a preadolescent is tempted to cheat on an examination, his or her conduct does not take place in a vacuum. Past experiences affect present actions, and moral conduct changes greatly between infancy and adulthood. It is generally agreed that (1) babies come into the world as amoral beings; (2) they are active learners; (3) they acquire their first personal moral values and standards from their parents; (4) early moral edicts are tied to specific situations; (5) a child's early moral concepts and understandings differ from those of adults; and (6) moral concepts and understanding change with increasing cognitive sophistication and social experience.

By the time they start school, most children still have literal conceptions of right and wrong. They are likely to show consistency between their thoughts, feelings, and actions, to the degree that they have learned to do so at home. But as they interact with new schoolmates, most soon show some discrepancy in the way they think, act, and feel. Some quickly learn, by example and direct experience, to be more devious in what they say and do (Furman and Masters, 1980). Others may become more consistent, as they follow the precepts and ideas of peers, teachers, and others.

As children develop toward adolescence, their ways of thinking and acting are likely to change. For example, the older child and the adolescent think in more sophisticated ways, can move from a specific situation to a more general ethical rule, and are more likely to consider the needs and views of others. As we will see, these changes, along with increased self-regulation and wider learning experiences, usually result in a more complex form of moral conduct.

INCONSISTENCY IN MORAL CONDUCT

Although people continue to talk about moral conduct as a class of reactions that go together and are governed by some central controlling process such as conscience, it is plain that most people behave inconsistently in situations involving moral problems. After surveying the research, Douglas Graham (1972) concluded that people are likely to show highly consistent moral conduct only when the range of situations that confront them is restricted or when a high level of abstract thinking allows them to apply general principles over many varied situations.

More than fifty years ago, Hartshorne and May (1928) conducted a landmark study of consistency in moral conduct and disappointed all those who would like to divide the world into moral and immoral people. In the course of their research, Hartshorne and May tested thousands of children for many types of moral conduct (such as cheating, lying, and stealing) in different contexts (such as tests, games, and contests) in widely varied settings (such as home, church, and playground). They found that children's moral opinions and judgments as expressed on a questionnaire remained consistent, provided that the two questionnaires were administered in the same setting. When the setting was moved, for example, from a church to a clubhouse, the correlations between the scores on the two tests dropped drastically, making it appear that the children's basic moral codes changed when the situation changed.

The children's moral behavior was even less consistent than their statements about morality. Hartshorne and May found that almost all children cheat some of the time and that knowing a child has cheated in one situation does not make it possible to predict whether the same child will cheat in another. Expediency appeared to determine a child's decision to cheat. When it seemed safe and easy to cheat or when it appeared that other children cheated or approved of cheating, a child was more likely to cheat. In some classrooms, for example, many children cheated, whereas in others, almost no one cheated. It also appeared that the child who cheats in the classroom is not necessarily the same child who tells lies there, nor is the child who lies to the teacher the same child who lies to peers. Finally, the relationship between children's statements about morality and their actual behavior was virtually nonexistent. Their results convinced Hartshorne and May that it was foolish to try to categorize children or adults as moral or immoral. The question was not whether an individual would behave morally or immorally but rather when he or she would do so.

The children studied by Hartshorne and May did not cheat at random. According to Roger Burton (1976), who reanalyzed these classic studies, the investigators did find the existence of individual predispositions to be honest or dishonest. Burton believes that children's learning experiences lead some of them to be relatively consistent in their honesty or dishonesty and others to be relatively inconsistent. However, whether a child develops a generalized tendency to resist or to succumb to temptation, the conditions surrounding each moral choice will have quite a strong effect on the child's final decision.

Other research has not challenged these basic conclusions. For example, Robert Sears, Lucy Rau, and Richard Alpert (1965) compared six different tests of children's resistance to temptation in play settings. Almost all the resulting correlations were positive, but none indicated a very great degree of consistency, even though all were administered in the context of a play situation. A similar study of moral consistency led Wesley Allinsmith (1960) to conclude that a person with a truly generalized conscience is a statistical rarity.

The connection between moral reasoning and behavior is also tenuous. When researchers have found a relationship between the two, it has generally been of the modest variety reported earlier by Hartshorne and May. Walter and Harriet Mischel (1976) surveyed the existing research and concluded that it is difficult to justify claims of strong links between moral reasoning and individual action. They suggest that knowing people's moral reasoning allows one to predict only 10 percent of the variation in their behavior in different situations. It is often possible to be able to predict moral behavior just as accurately from a person's need for achievement or need for affiliation as from his or her level of moral reasoning.

Inconsistency in moral conduct should not be surprising. Moral situations involve strong

Circumstances influence a child's behavior. For some children, the chance of getting caught will determine whether they will steal. *(© Sepp Seitz/Woodfin Camp & Assoc.)*

and conflicting pressures (Gerson and Damon, 1978), and only a slight change in these pressures may shift the proposed situation from moral to immoral in a person's judgment. Different circumstances may also influence different people. For one person, the chances of getting caught may determine behavior. For another, the magnitude of the payoff may be the determining factor; a third person's behavior may depend on the amount of effort involved (Farrington, 1979). Although moral reasoning may become increasingly consistent as a person develops, his or her behavior often depends on situational constraints. Moreover, resistance to temptation is a kind of behavior pattern different from the donation of money to a charity. Both may be examples of moral behavior, but they are not necessarily governed by the same processes nor do they necessarily manifest themselves in a consistent fashion across individuals (Nelsen, Grinder, and Flack, 1980).

THE DEVELOPMENT OF MORAL REASONING

The ways in which people come to think, act, and feel morally depend partly on developmental changes in their understanding, and the development of moral reasoning can be seen as a specific case of general cognitive development. Thus we would expect the same factors that are important in general cognitive development to be important in moral development. The dominant figures in developing theories of moral thought have been Jean Piaget and Lawrence Kohlberg.

Moral Judgment

Jean Piaget (1932) proposed that children's moral judgments fall into two major and overlapping stages. In the first, sometimes called **objective morality,** virtuous conduct is based on obedience to authority. Judgments are marked by the belief that rules are given and unchangeable; transgressions are defined in terms of what is forbidden; and punishment is inevitable—a concept known as **immanent justice.** In the second stage, sometimes called **subjective morality,** morality develops out of cooperative peer relationships. Judgments are marked by the understanding that rules are agreed on, relative, and changeable; transgressions are defined in terms of what is expected, fair, or just; and the intentions of the transgressor are more important than the consequences of his or her action.

Piaget realized that both of these moralities could exist side by side, that a child might apply objective morality to one action and subjective morality to another, but he believed that as children grew older, they tended increasingly to judge in terms of subjective morality.

When Piaget studied moral judgment, one of his techniques was to have children listen to a pair of stories and judge the actors. In one story, for example, a child accidentally broke fifteen cups while opening a door and in the other a child accidentally broke a single cup while getting into a cookie jar. Young children generally consider the child who did the most damage naughtier and deserving of more punishment. On the basis of such results, Piaget concluded that although children as young as three or four might be able to distinguish between accidental and intended acts, they were unlikely to use such information in making a moral judgment, and instead were likely to use the consequences of an act as the basis of their decision. According to Piaget, young children believe that transgressions deserve punishment, and because their parents punish transgressions that do great wrong most severely, young children follow the same standards.

Recent research indicates that Piaget's results and interpretations are correct in some respects but not in others (Lickona, 1976; Karniol, 1980; Shultz, 1980). Cognitive immaturity does appear to be the source of the young child's idea that rules are inflexible; as children grow older, they do increasingly judge by the intentions of the actor. The belief in immanent justice does decline sharply between the ages of five and ten, and fifth graders simply do not believe in it (e.g., Suls and Kalle, 1979). But Piaget's belief that subjective morality develops out of cooperative peer relationships has not been substantiated (Hogan and Emler, 1978); children appear to be less consistent in judging acts by one of the two stages of morality than Piaget had expected (Lickona, 1976); and judgments appear to depend more upon children's understanding of causality than on their sense of justice (Karniol, 1980).

In addition, the traditional pairs of stories used by Piaget are unlikely to provide a fair test of young children's understanding of a culprit's intent or their use of it in making a judgment. The stories require a child to remember and then compare two intents and two outcomes; but the intentions of the actors are not stated clearly or explicitly, and the outcome is always stated last. When the stories are simplified so that only one intent and one outcome have to be considered at a time (e.g., Berg-Cross, 1975), and both intent and outcome are explicitly stated or illustrated and systematically varied (e.g., Gottlieb, Taylor, and Ruderman, 1977; Nelson, 1980), young children may show much more advanced moral reasoning than Piaget found. In such cases, young children not only can distinguish between accidental and intended actions, and between good and bad intentions, but they can also weigh both intention and consequence in making moral judgments (Surber, 1977). Moreover, they are likely to distinguish between harm to human beings and other types of damage, and to judge the former more harshly (Elkind and Dabek, 1977).

As Piaget found, however, young children—even when they are fully aware of the intentions behind an action—may base their moral judgments primarily on the result of an act (Brandt and Strattner-Gregory, 1980). Rachel Karniol (1978) suggests that young children appear to learn, first, that acts based on bad intentions are naughty regardless of their outcome and therefore deserve punishment. But when young children must decide between a well-intentioned act that results in great harm and an act with bad intentions that results in little harm, they may say the well-intentioned act is naughtier because they focus on the harmful consequences and give them greater weight in making their decisions. This interpretation, according to Karniol, is consistent with common socialization experiences of young children. That is, parents are more likely to punish consequences than to reward good intentions, so children are likely to learn early what others consider wrong; they learn to distinguish good behavior later and more slowly.

Variations in Moral Reasoning

Lawrence Kohlberg (1963; 1969) has proposed a provocative and appealing approach to moral thinking that is in part an elaboration and refinement of Piaget's ideas about the nature and development of moral reasoning. Kohlberg's approach is based on children's and adults' responses to a number of moral dilemmas, such as the following:

> In Europe, a woman was near death from cancer. One drug might save her, a form of radium that a druggist in the same town had recently discovered.

Principled

Stage 6

This is a stage of fully internalized principles that the person holds as universally valid. He or she believes them personally and has not adopted them because they have been laid down by authority. For example, the only soldier who refused to obey orders at the My Lai massacre during the Vietnam War had reached this stage. A person at Stage 6 believes that an act is right if it follows from self-chosen principles, principles that may demand deviating from rules. The universal ethical principles of Stage 6 are based on a deeply balanced sense of the relationship among human beings, and emphasize justice and respect. A person at the highest level might say, "Laws that destroy the dignity of human life should be broken."

Pro If you don't steal the drug and your wife dies, you will always condemn yourself for it afterward. You would have lived up to the law, but you wouldn't have lived up to your own standards of conscience.

Con If you stole the drug, you'd condemn yourself because you would have violated your own standards of honesty.

Stage 5

The person at this stage recognizes that for the sake of agreement, rules or expectations must contain an arbitrary element. Rules are social contracts made for a purpose, and specific social purposes can change. The essential obligation is the contract, not the content of a specific rule, and majority will and welfare are extremely important. This stage represents a loosening of commitment to the expectations of others and the conventional order and an emphasis on personal standards of social responsibility. The Stage 5 person recognizes these standards as valid even when special circumstances might justify deviation. A person at this stage might say, "The end doesn't justify the means."

Pro If you let your wife die, it would be out of fear of the consequences. The social contract was never meant to cause another's death, so the theft would not violate its spirit.

Con If you stole the drug, you would violate the law regarding personal property, a basic part of the social contract. You'd lose respect for yourself if you were carried away by emotion and forgot the long-range point of view.

Conventional

Stage 4

People at this stage base their thinking on the dictates of established authority. Examples of this stage are numerous because many people never get beyond it.
Confronted with a moral choice, a person in Stage 4 is likely to say, "Because he is the President" "Because the Bible says so" or "A rule is a rule." They see value in rules and obligations because they see them as necessary for a stable society. Stage 4 people do their duty and show respect for authority.

Pro When you married your wife, you swore to love and cherish her, so you shouldn't let her die because you're afraid to do the only thing that will save her. If you don't do your duty to her, you'll always feel guilty because you caused her death.

Con Stealing is against the law, and if everybody stole, society would break down. If you steal the drug, you'll always feel guilty over your dishonesty and law breaking.

Stage 3

People at this stage internalize the values of others. They make up their minds about a moral dilemma on the basis of how they believe parents, peer group, or small group would behave or would want them to behave in the situation. The law-and-order mentality of the Archie Bunker type, which is concerned with "people like us" as opposed to the larger society, is typical, as is the morality of people who want to please and help others, thereby gaining their approval ("You're a nice boy/nice girl"). At this stage, people try to visualize themselves in the situation of others and "do right" because they care for others. Such a person might say, "Do unto others as you would have them do unto you."

Pro If you don't steal the drug, your family will think that you're an inhuman husband, and if your wife dies, you'll never be able to look anyone in the face again. Besides, if you were in the same situation, you'd want someone to steal the drug for you.

Con It isn't just the druggist who will think you're a criminal, everyone else will too. After you steal it, you'll feel bad thinking how you've brought dishonor on your family and yourself; you won't be able to face anyone again.

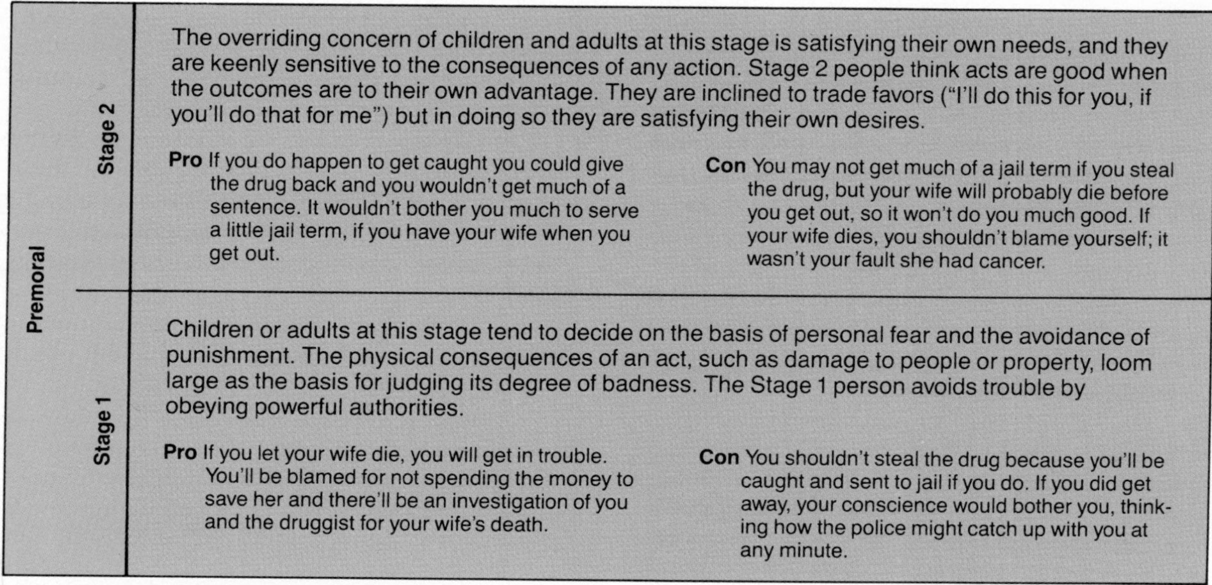

FIGURE 16.1 Kohlberg's proposed order of progression in the development of moral reasoning. The reasoning characterizing each stage and level is illustrated by examples showing possible responses to Heinz's dilemma. *(After Kohlberg, 1963)*

The druggist was charging $2,000, ten times what the drug cost him to make. The sick woman's husband, Heinz, went to everyone he knew to borrow the money, but he could only get together about half of what it cost. He told the druggist that his wife was dying and asked him to sell it cheaper or let him pay later. But the druggist said, "No." The husband got desperate and broke into the man's store to steal the drug for his wife. Should the husband have done that? Why? (1969, page 379)

Using the responses to such dilemmas, as well as interviews that probe the reasoning behind them, investigators attempt to ascertain the nature of a person's moral reasoning. This method assumes that moral judgments are largely the result of moral thought confronted with a moral dilemma like the one faced by Heinz; for in such a dilemma, any action a person takes—even choosing to do nothing—the choice breaks at least one rule.

Drawing on studies that have used this method, Kohlberg has proposed a progressive series of six developmental stages of moral reasoning, as illustrated in Figure 16.1. Notice that the stages differ in the reasons that a person is likely to give for making a decision and in the type of concerns indicated for self, authority, and society. As can be seen, it is not the decision to steal or not to steal but its justification that identifies a person's stage of reasoning. A person at any stage may decide either way in a given situation.

Each succeeding stage consists of a more complex and balanced way of looking at the moral-social world. Children presumably advance through the stages in sequence; they must understand the reasoning typical of one stage before they can begin to understand the greater complexities of the next. As they move to a new stage of understanding, people must reorganize their thoughts and feelings and not just add new ones. Thus as a child advances through the stages, old moral-social relationships between the child and other people, and between people in general, acquire a new look.

As Figure 16.1 shows, the proposed six stages form three basic developmental levels of moral reasoning, distinguished by what defines right or moral action. The first two stages form what is called the **premoral level,** because value is placed not in persons or social standards but in physical acts and needs. The next two stages form the **conventional level,** with value placed in maintaining the conventional social order and the expectations of others. The final two stages form the **principled level,** where value resides in self-chosen principles and standards that have a universal logical validity and that therefore can be shared. Because the distinctness of each stage remains uncertain (Kurtines and Greif, 1974), we will focus on the levels of moral reasoning.

Developmental Changes

There is at least suggestive evidence that the levels of moral reasoning are related to age. For example, Figure 16.2 shows that among children aged seven to sixteen, older children tend to be at more advanced levels. Moral statements that reflect the premoral level decrease with age. Those at the conventional level appear to increase until about age thirteen and then stabilize. Those that reflect the principled level appear to increase slowly after age thirteen, although they still constitute only a limited proportion of the judgments among sixteen-year-olds.

In general, the speed with which children move from one level to the next also appears to vary with their intellectual ability. Higher-level moral concepts and attitudes are acquired only in late childhood or in adolescence; apparently they require an extensive foundation of cognitive growth and social experience. Nor do people appear to skip a level when advancing to a higher level of reasoning (Kohlberg and Kramer, 1969). In addition, children and adolescents appear to rate moral reasoning that is below their own level as inferior and that above their own level as better. However, they recall moral reasoning that is below their own level more accurately than they recall reasoning that is above it (Rest, 1973; Rest, Turiel, and Kohlberg, 1969).

Although a certain level of intellectual ability seems to be necessary for a given level of moral reasoning, intellectual ability in itself does not guarantee the development of higher levels of moral reasoning. Thus children who are

FIGURE 16.2 Variations with age in the proportions of different levels of moral reasoning in a sample of American boys. *(After Kohlberg, 1963)*

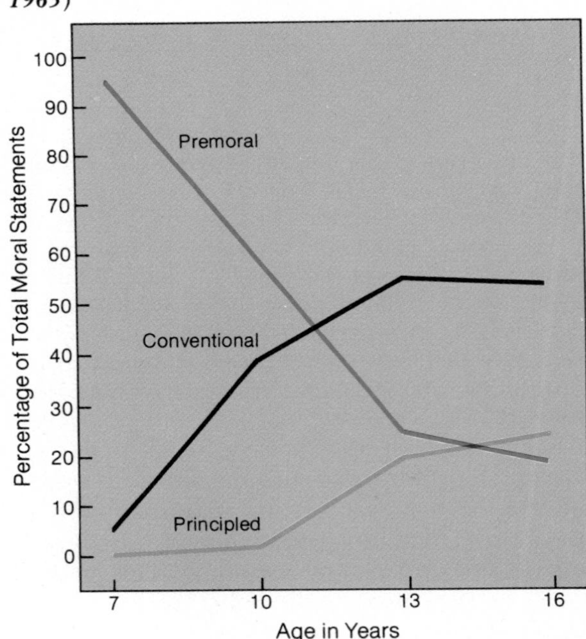

Although moral reasoning at the principled level increases slowly during adolescence, only a limited proportion of sixteen-year-olds judge moral dilemmas at this level. *(© Leonard Speier 1979)*

above average in intellectual ability are as likely as other children to vary in their level of moral reasoning. However, a child's relative brightness and level of moral reasoning can combine to produce unexpected results. In a study by Richard Krebs (1968), for example, it was found that, among children who were at an opportunistic, premoral level of reasoning, those who were bright and attentive enough to see that they could cheat jumped at the chance. Among those children who were at a rule-oriented, conventional level of moral reasoning, however, the ones who cheated seemed to be those who were not bright or attentive enough to succeed by understanding and following the rules.

Critical appraisals of Kohlberg's theory and research have pointed out several problems with his system (e.g., Kurtines and Greif, 1974; Baumrind, 1978; M. Hoffman, 1979; 1980). The responses to his moral dilemmas are difficult to score. The stages within a level are difficult to distinguish. All people do not appear to pass through the six stages in their given order. The separate stages are not associated with distinctive patterns of behavior. The theory neglects the motivation of people faced with a moral dilemma; and the theory is biased toward males.

In response to these criticisms, Kohlberg (1976; 1978; 1981) and his associates (Colby, 1978) have revised the scoring method to make it more objective and easier to use, and other researchers have employed Kohlberg's dilemmas to develop a more objective and simpler test (e.g., Rest, 1976). In his revisions, Kohlberg has proposed the existence of two types of reasoning (A and B) at each stage of development. Each type is presumed to reflect a different orientation to moral-social issues: Type A reasoning stresses literal interpretations; Type B emphasizes the intent of a rule, norm, or standard. Of the two, Type B is rated as the more advanced, as it is considered to be more balanced and developed. Stage 6 is no longer considered a separate stage by Kohlberg, because studies have generally failed to confirm its existence; it is now viewed as an extension of Type B reasoning at the fifth stage.

Kohlberg also has changed the rating of "Archie Bunker" law-and-order reasoning, originally considered Stage 4 morality, to Stage 3, because Bunker is more concerned with the small group than with society (Muson, 1979). According to Kohlberg, this shift of Archie Bunker type thought from Stage 4 to Stage 3 should end the results that typically place more men than women in Stage 4.

Such a shift may eliminate part of the sex-related bias in the system, but evidence suggests that the male bias remains built into Kohlberg's sequence of stages. Females do not show the expected pattern of movement through the stages (Gilligan, 1977; Holstein, 1976)—a difference that may be the result of socialization. The values of compassion, responsibility, and obligation are more likely to be stressed in the socialization of females than in that of males, but because Kohlberg has assigned these values to the conventional level of moral reasoning, females who base their reasoning on these values are automatically classified at a lower level of moral development.

Other investigators, including Elizabeth Simpson (1974) and Sarah Harkness (1980), have pointed out that Kohlberg's theory also appears culturally biased, and hence not universal, because it is based on a social organization and values that fit only Western culture. Simpson argues that because Kohlberg's approach focuses on issues of equality, rights, and justice, moral reasoning at a principled level fits only a constitutional democracy. In addition, the abstract thinking involved at this level is probably beyond most of the people in the world. It may be that like formal, abstract reasoning, principled moral reasoning requires formal education for its development. This conjecture is supported by the data summarized in Figure 16.3, which show that, although moral reasoning may develop in a similar way in various cultures, principled reasoning appears primarily in the American sample. In a later study of Bahamian children and adolescents, not a single one reached the principled level of reasoning (White, Bushnell, and Regnemer, 1978).

ROLE-TAKING AND SOCIAL INTERACTION

The process of role-taking, which was discussed in Chapters 13 and 15, appears to play a critical role in moral development generally and in moral reasoning in particular. During childhood, boys and girls participate in many social situations and, through practice, become increasingly able to take the position of another. This ability enables them to restructure their perceptions and thoughts about moral-social issues.

This development means that young children first see standards of morality as something given and as external to themselves. At this level of reasoning, they are unlikely to adopt the viewpoint of others, and they may perceive moral matters solely in terms of personal consequences —whether their actions are rewarded or punished. When they reach the conventional level of reasoning, their moral standards become more general and internal, based on ideas of cooperation, respect, and conformity, and they consider the views of others when contemplating a course of action. Should they reach the principled level,

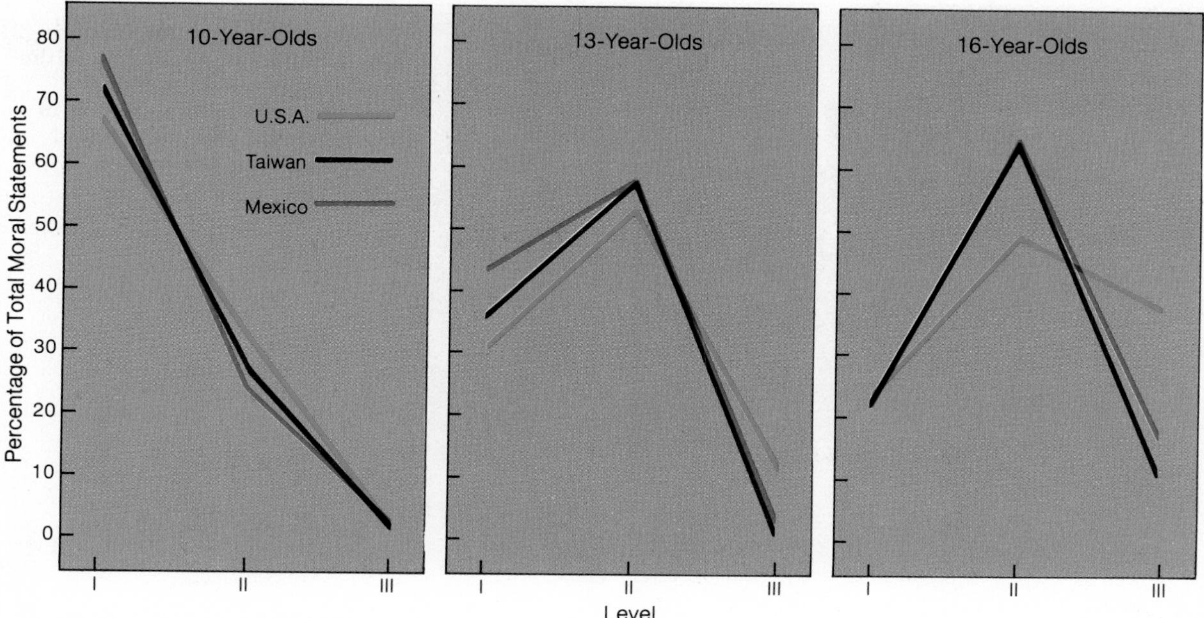

FIGURE 16.3 Variations with age in the proportions of different levels of moral reasoning in three cultures: the United States, Taiwan, and Mexico. The sample from each culture consists of middle-class urban boys. Levels I, II, and III indicate, respectively, premoral, conventional, and principled levels. *(After Kohlberg, 1968)*

their moral standards will become even more general and largely internal, based on more fully developed ideas of mutual respect, trust, fairness, and justice. Before acting, they will consider the viewpoints and needs of other people and of society in general.

In this process, children's social interactions with peers, which stimulate role-taking abilities, seem to be important. For example, Charles Keasey (1971) found that fifth- and sixth-grade children who took an active part in social interaction were more likely than children who did not to show a conventional level of moral reasoning. Apparently, if children are to reach a conventional level, they must be able to see that their actions can affect the way another person reacts. This connection was illustrated in a study by Robert Selman (1971), who found a significant relationship between the ability to take the role of another and the attainment of conventional moral reasoning among eight-, nine-, and ten-year-olds. Among children who were deficient in role-taking skills, some later acquired the skills without developing conventional reasoning, but none developed conventional reasoning without also developing proficiency in role-taking. Later research suggests, however, that some children do attain conventional reasoning without developing proficiency in role-taking (Kurdek, 1978).

The family provides opportunities to take another's role in a way that influences the development of moral reasoning. One study found that a child's moral understanding was related to participation in family activities, confidences, and decisions, and being trusted with responsi-

Families influence the development of moral reasoning. The chances are that none of the Hatfields (shown here) or the McCoys saw anything wrong in the feud that nearly destroyed both families. ***(The Bettman Archive)***

bility (Peck and Havighurst, 1960). In later research, Constance Holstein (1972) and Bindu Parikh (1980) found that parents who take their child's opinions on moral issues seriously and discuss them (providing a role-taking model as well as opportunities to practice role-taking) are more likely to have children who reason at a conventional level than parents who do not do so. In addition, Holstein found that mothers who show a principled level of moral reasoning are more likely than those who show a conventional level to have children who reason at the higher of the two conventional stages. This finding suggests that mothers at the principled level are more likely to be skilled in role-taking and to value opportunities for role-taking and provide them for their children.

Given their superior role-taking skills, parents and other adults generally adjust their own moral reasoning and actions to fit a child's level of understanding (Olejnik, 1980). For example, with small children they are likely to key their words to direct rewards or punishment, whereas with older children they are likely to talk about personal, interpersonal, or perhaps even abstract social consequences. Thus parents are unlikely to talk to a three-year-old about property rights or justice. Instead, they will admonish the child in concrete terms: "Don't touch that, it'll break" or "Don't do that, or you'll get spanked." Parents of an older child tend to emphasize social consequences and personal intentions and, as the child nears puberty, to justify moral action in terms of abstract principles. An eight-year-old may be told, "The lady broke the law only to help somebody else," whereas a fifteen-year-old may hear, "Laws that discriminate against women are unjust."

Socioeconomic status also appears to influence the development of moral reasoning (Kohlberg and Kramer, 1969). Whether they are middle-class or working-class, adolescents and young adults seem to go through the same levels of moral reasoning, but those in the middle class seem to advance faster and further, as shown in Figure 16.4. It may be that growing up in the middle class provides a wider range of opportunities and more stimulation for role-taking and social participation, so that middle-class adolescents and young adults begin to see themselves and others from more general, organized, and flexible perspectives.

Differences in role-taking skills are not the only factors that account for the differences in

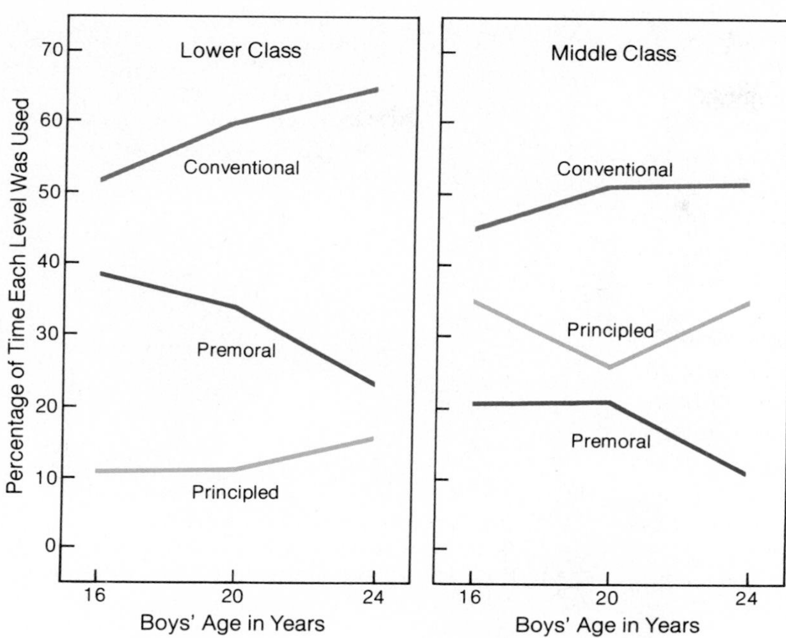

FIGURE 16.4 Variations with age in the proportions of different levels of moral reasoning in samples of boys from two social classes. *(Adapted from Kohlberg, 1968)*

moral reasoning between, for example, a university professor and a preadolescent gang member. Cognitive ability plays its part, but social-learning factors are also important (Jurkovic, 1980). The professor's peer group is likely to approve and reward the use of abstract principles in reasoning, whereas the preadolescent's peer group is likely to approve and reward on a concrete basis. Such differences in group orientation reflect the primary interests of each group and are likely to have a strong influence on the moral reasoning of its members.

GUILT AND SELF-REGULATION

The language of morality is full of terms that relate to feelings, and most people regard the emotions of guilt, shame, anxiety, and indignation as important influences on their behavior. In fact, without resorting to the notion that it would make them "feel bad," it is difficult to understand why people do not more often engage in immoral thoughts and actions. When people speak of conscience, they are not referring to a voice that quotes the Golden Rule or to possible consequences of their actions. Instead, they think of their feelings when they remember or anticipate some transgression. As this section makes clear, how people come to feel about their actions is a critical factor in the development of moral conduct.

When most people talk about a child's moral conduct, they refer to the youngster's ability to inhibit a desire (not taking a toy from another child) or to resist temptation (not cheating on a test or taking a piece of pie that a sister was saving). A good deal of the research on moral development, therefore, has looked at factors that affect the development of guilt and self-regulation.

Establishing Guilt and Self-Regulation

Although there have been many theories as to how guilt and self-regulation are established, most of them agree with social-learning positions—that through conditioning people gradually develop a sense of guilt that helps them regulate their conduct. Young children begin by trying to do things their parents approve of and not do things their parents consider wrong. Youngsters soon discover that doing or saying things their parents applaud generally brings them affection, and through conditioning this affection becomes coupled with their feelings of self-approval.

Children also quickly discover that when they do things their parents disapprove of, the parents often withdraw their affection or administer some other kind of punishment. Through conditioning, this punishment becomes coupled with their feelings of guilt. As a result of such learning, children eventually may behave morally even when their parents or others are not present. Gradually, youngsters' thoughts and feelings replace rewards and punishments administered by others, and they come to regulate their own conduct.

Studies have shown that the nature of the parental relationship, the explanation of the reasons for discipline, and the timing of punishment are all important factors in the establishment of moral conduct and the feelings that accompany it (Shaffer and Brody, 1981).

One way to help a child internalize moral standards is to reason with him and point out the effects of his wrongdoings on others. (© *Suzanne Szasz*)

Love and Reasoning One of the clearest ways in which parents and others promote the development of guilt and self-regulation is by disciplining a child for transgressions. As we saw in Chapter 13, discipline goes beyond spanking and includes the withdrawal of affection, verbal reprimands, and social isolation. Mild physical punishment, coupled with a mild withdrawal of love, appears to establish guilt and self-regulation much more efficiently than severe physical punishment does (M. Hoffman, 1977a). A child can always avoid the brief unpleasantness of physical punishment merely by avoiding the punisher, but if a normally loving parent also withdraws his or her love, the punishment lasts until the love is restored. Children disciplined by severe and unexplained punishment rarely develop an effective sense of guilt or self-regulation; instead they learn to behave so that they will not get caught.

It was first thought that withdrawing love might be the most important factor in establishing guilt feelings and self-control. For example, Robert Sears, Eleanor Maccoby, and Harry Levin (1957) found that children who are disciplined by the withdrawal of love and by reasoning develop stronger self-control and are more susceptible to guilt than children who are disciplined by physical punishment. But this was true only if the children had "warm" mothers. Children of "cold" mothers who relied on the withdrawal of love were unlikely to develop strong self-control or guilt. Later studies suggest that reasoning with children and pointing out the effects of their wrongdoing are just as effective as withdrawing love (e.g., M. Hoffman and Saltzstein, 1967; Aronfreed, 1969), and as the accompanying box indicates, the emotional tone of the parent's explanation is also important.

Verbal explanations and reasoning do two things: they encourage youngsters to take the

Because this child's punishment comes after her transgression, she is likely to feel shame (a reaction to disapproval) instead of guilt (a sense that she has deviated from personal standards). *(© William Hubbell/Woodfin Camp & Assoc.)*

role of others, and they help children to internalize moral standards by providing thoughts they can associate with their feelings and with any rewards or punishment they receive (Hoffman, 1980). Thus as children come to understand how their behavior affects others and how others' behavior affects them, and as they come to adopt the moral thoughts and attitudes of their parents, they begin to respond with self-approval to what are now their own correct thoughts and actions. They learn to use self-instruction and self-praise. Thus when faced with a temptation, such as a dazzling display of dials and push buttons on a color television set, a child may regulate her conduct by telling herself, "No. Don't touch. That's a good girl. I'm a good girl for not touching."

Timing of Discipline Whether physical punishment or other techniques are more effective in promoting self-adherence to moral standards is still a matter of debate (La Voie, 1974). However, the timing of discipline appears to be especially important in the development of guilt and self-regulation. For example, in studies by Richard Walters, Ross Parke, and Valerie Cane (1965), children were punished either just as they were about to play with a forbidden object or after they had begun to play with it. Afterward, they were placed in a situation in which the same forbidden object tempted them. Children who were punished early generally showed greater resistance to temptation than children who were punished later.

The explanation for such results is that when children are punished early, the form of anxiety that we call guilt becomes associated with the anticipation of doing something wrong. However, when children are punished *after* they have disobeyed, doing something forbidden is followed by the fear that is generated when one is caught and punished. This distinction is often characterized as the difference between guilt and shame: **Guilt** stems from deviation from one's own internalized moral standards; **shame** is a reaction to the disapproval of others. Thus one five-year-old may feel guilt when she contemplates pulling her sister's hair and resist the act, whereas another five-year-old may pull her sister's hair and then feel afraid because her father might catch her.

It is often impossible to punish a child just before or just as the youngster begins to do something that is forbidden. However, psychologists (e.g., Verne, 1977) have also found, as have parents before them, that delayed punishment can be effective if the situation that led to a transgression is re-created as fully as possible by talking with the child and describing the forbidden action at the time the child is disciplined. By using this sort of approach, Donald Meichenbaum and Joseph Goodman (1971) have been able to teach impulsive children with a history of getting into trouble to talk to themselves when they are tempted to do something forbidden. Using such self-regulation, the children end up modifying their own behavior.

Reasoning and Guilt

The importance of cognitive understanding and reasoning in the development of guilt and self-regulation is also shown in other ways. For example, over the years, the basic feelings that a person attaches to moral actions may be the same, but his or her *interpretation* of these feelings appears to change with cognitive development (Kohlberg, 1969). Thus anxiety over deviating from moral standards may register in the pit of the stomach for children and adults alike. But a young child is likely to perceive the physical sensation as a dread of external punishment. A five-year-old boy resists the impulse to take a quarter from his mother's purse because he thinks that his parents may be watching or that God will punish him (M. Hoffman, 1978). Older children and adults, on the other hand, generally perceive the same physical sensation as a dread of their own self-judgment and want to avoid feeling guilty for violating a principle.

Reasoning, feeling, and self-regulation are interrelated in other ways in moral conduct; a violation of what a child or an adult considers just or moral often elicits a strong feeling of indignation or even moral outrage. For example, Kohlberg describes his son's first expression of moral reaction, which occurred at age four. At that time his son joined the pacifist and vegetarian movement and refused to eat meat because, as the child said, "It's bad to kill animals." In spite of lengthy parental arguments about the differences between justified and unjustified killing, the boy remained a vegetarian for six months. However, his principles recognized occasions of just or legitimate killing. Kohlberg recounts how, one night when he was reading aloud a book that described an Eskimo seal-killing expedition, his son got angry and said, "You know, there is one kind of meat I would eat, Eskimo meat. It's bad to kill animals so it's all right to eat *them.*" It seems likely that the boy's attitude toward killing was not an internalization of the cultural rule "Thou shalt not kill" but a response based on his immediate empathy for other living beings and that his punitiveness was based on the primitive principle by which one bad act deserves another.

There is some evidence that girls may be more naturally empathic, and thus more susceptible to the development of guilt, than boys. Traditional socialization practices that emphasize emotional sensitivity and expressiveness for girls may reinforce this tendency (M. Hoffman, 1977a; Barnett et al., 1980). When involved in a transgression, boys are more likely to feel fear where girls would feel guilt; this disparity of feeling may also stem from socialization pressures on boys to achieve and to succeed—to the extent that concern with doing well overrides any concern about being honest or doing what is right.

Reactions to Guilt

Because guilt is unpleasant, children generally learn how to avoid or reduce it, and this learning takes many forms during the development of moral conduct. As children's cognitive ability increases and as they gain additional social experience, they learn new ways to manage guilt (Thompson and M. Hoffman, 1980). And although individual differences in this aspect of moral development are large, most children appear to develop somewhat similar ways of managing their guilt (McMichael and Grinder, 1966).

One of the most obvious ways to avoid guilt, as we have seen, is through self-control. For example, children can resist temptation and refuse to do something that is forbidden. If, however, they believe that they might succumb to temptation, they may learn to avoid guilt by not thinking about forbidden things, because the thoughts themselves provoke guilt feelings.

As their cognitive sophistication increases, most children learn even more elegant ways of avoiding guilt. For example, if Matt hurts another person, he may define his actions in benevolent terms, saying, "I just did it for his own good." Or he may learn to avoid guilt and self-condemnation by telling himself that the other person is a "tattletale" or a "cheater." Other learned ways of reducing the unpleasantness of guilt appear equally effective. Matt may instead learn to confess his transgressions or to apologize for what he says or does. Or he may learn to reduce his guilt by saying that his misbehavior was only half as bad as it could have been or as what others have done.

Some of these ways in which children and adults learn to handle their feelings of guilt and responsibility appear strikingly similar to what has been called the "just world hypothesis" (M. J. Lerner, 1980). In general, people want to see the world as working in a consistent and just fashion, so that evil is punished and good is rewarded, and among children the need to punish evil may be the stronger, as the box on page 408 indicates. Adopting the just world perspective allows people to see themselves as caring, and concerned, no matter what happens to others. They have, therefore, a way to escape feelings of guilt or responsibility when someone else is the victim of an obvious wrong; if the world is just, the person must have deserved it.

These young smokers have learned to avoid any guilt over breaking their parents' prohibitions against smoking, perhaps by saying that their misbehavior is trivial compared with drinking or taking drugs. *(© Richard Kalver/Magnum Photos)*

MORAL CONDUCT AND MODELING

Modeling also affects the development of moral conduct because as children watch others, they learn new behavior, discover the possible consequences of an action, and find out whether certain acts are acceptable. By watching, children learn how to do whatever a model does, whether the model is generous or selfish, aggressive or helpful, honest or hypocritical (Rushton, 1979) —although they may not always copy the specific behavior.

If models are warm, powerful, and competent (and to a young child that is just how parents are likely to seem), a child may well copy their behavior (Eisenberg-Berg and Geisheker, 1979). But as pointed out in Chapter 15, what happens to the models they see also affects the probability that the child will imitate them. If the model is rewarded, the child is likely to copy the model and to expect a reward for behaving similarly. If the model is punished, the child is not likely to copy the behavior because she or he would expect to receive similar punishment. And if a model resists moderate temptation—especially if the model explains why she or he resisted—children will forgo temptation, even when it means that they have to keep working on a boring task (Grusec et al., 1979).

Changes in Anticipated Consequences

One of the most important findings to come out of research on observational learning in moral conduct is that an unpunished transgression appears to have the same effect on the watching child as a transgression followed by rewards. An early study indicated that children who see peers playing with forbidden toys are more likely to play with the toys than children who see no such transgression (Grosser, Polansky, and Lippitt, 1951). Apparently, when a child sees other children break a prohibition and get away with it, the consequences anticipated by the child for violating the prohibition change.

A later experiment, by Richard Walters and Ross Parke (1964), supported the idea that the absence of expected punishment may act as a reward. They showed films of a model playing with forbidden toys to several groups of children. Some of the children saw the model rewarded, some saw the model punished, others saw that nothing—either good or bad—happened to the young transgressor. When the chil-

PERPETRATORS AND VICTIMS

Children are more concerned that transgressors be punished than that their victims be compensated. This preoccupation with punishment at the expense of relieving the victim showed clearly in a study of six- to eleven-year-old Canadian children. Dale Miller and Douglass McCann (1980) told these children stories about such juvenile misdeeds as hitting another child with a ball, riding another child's bicycle through broken glass and flattening the tires, and pushing down a child carrying a bag of groceries. Sometimes the injustices were intentional and sometimes they were accidental.

Children of all ages judged all situations similarly. They believed that intentional acts were worse than accidental ones, that victims of accidental injuries deserved less compensation (in dimes) than victims of intentional injury, and that when perpetrators had already received some punishment (a spanking), their victims deserved less compensation.

Especially clear was the children's preference for punishing the perpetrator over aiding the victim. If they had to choose between catching a boy who had pushed another to the ground (so that the victim's groceries scattered, his pants were torn, and his knee scraped) and helping the innocent victim, children of all ages would leave the victim to fend for himself and run after the young vandal.

As Miller and McCann point out, Jean Piaget (1932) found that young children regard punishment as having an almost magical capacity to put things right. But in this study there were no age differences. Eleven-year-olds were as adamant as younger children in their preference for punishment over playing Good Samaritan.

The investigators, therefore, propose two other explanations that might have affected children's judgments. First, in the course of children's socialization, they learn that society is more concerned with badness than with goodness. Allowing perpetrators to go unpunished can disrupt society, for the perpetrator may attack another victim, and others may copy the action if they think they can get away with it. The second explanation is connected with the "just world hypothesis," which is discussed in the text. Both victim and perpetrator, say Miller and McCann, threaten the belief in a just world—victims because they indicate that bad things can happen to good people, and perpetrators because they indicate that bad things do not always happen to bad people. But perpetrators pose the greater threat to a child's belief in a just world, because an unpunished perpetrator makes children fear they might become victims themselves.

dren were later placed in a situation like that depicted in the film, both those who had seen the transgression rewarded and those who had seen it go unpunished were more likely to play with forbidden toys than children who had seen the model's actions punished or those in a control group who saw no film.

All the children who viewed the films learned the model's behavior, for when the experimenter indicated that no one would be punished for playing with the forbidden toys, children who had seen any of the films were more likely to play with the toys than children who had not seen the films. Apparently, those who had not copied the model's transgression earlier were trying to avoid expected punishment.

Subsequently, Walters, Parke, and Cane (1965) found that in certain conditions, only the prospect of punishment may keep a child from transgressing. Once again, they showed children films of a model playing with forbidden toys, but this time the toys were so enticing that even many of the control children who saw no film at all succumbed to temptation and played with them. In a situation of great temptation, punishing the model was the only consequence that affected children's transgressions; the rest—children who saw the model rewarded, those who saw nothing happen to the model, and those who saw no film—could not resist the tempting toys.

When children watch a model go unpunished, two things happen. First, the punishment-free transgression suggests to them that the usual negative sanction does not apply in this situation, and they modify their own thinking accordingly. Second, the children then copy the model's violations because transgression is safe and because playing with the forbidden toys is rewarding. Consequences to a model can also affect other aspects of moral conduct. When children see a model go unrewarded for moral behavior, such as altruism, they fail to copy him or her (Staub, 1975). Thus, paradoxically, seeing moral behavior go unrewarded may decrease the rate at which children behave morally, just as if the behavior were actually immoral and therefore punished.

The Guardian Angels, who roam the New York subways in the hope of reducing crime, serve as models for many children. Whether the Angels are applauded or condemned for their unofficial acts will affect the chances that a child will imitate them. *(© Leonard Speier 1980)*

Verbal Modeling

Although many gaps exist in our knowledge about the way moral reasoning and conduct develop, clearly, the verbal modeling of parents and others has a strong instructional influence during the course of moral development (Mussen and Eisenberg-Berg, 1977; Harvey and Liebert, 1979; Shaffer and Brody, 1981). There is at least suggestive evidence that one of the ways others influence moral reasoning in a child is by changing the factors that he or she takes into consideration in arriving at moral judgments. For example, Albert Bandura and Frederick McDonald (1963) found that by having an adult consider a character's intentions or fail to consider them in making moral judgments about stories, they could get children to shift their reasoning in either direction.

Using a method similar to those parents use in reasoning with their offspring, Moshe Blatt and Lawrence Kohlberg (1975) also found it possible to change children's moral reasoning. As children discussed moral dilemmas in the classroom, teachers supported and clarified arguments that indicated a conventional level of moral reasoning but challenged those based on premoral reasoning. This procedure led to eventual changes in the children's levels of reasoning; what is more, a year later the differences between these children and others who had not heard premoral arguments challenged still existed.

Although it seems clear that verbal modeling can change children's moral reasoning, no evidence indicates that these changes are automatically reflected in their behavior. As we saw in Chapter 15, actions influence children more strongly than words, and children tend to copy what is done rather than what is said (La Voie et al., 1981). In a study by James Bryan and Nancy Walbek (1970) the superior power of actions showed clearly. A model either kept gift certificates won in a game or donated them to charity, accompanying the action by saying either that people should be generous or that they should be selfish, or by making neutral statements.

Later, children who had watched the model played the game and had their own opportunity to donate the winnings to charity. Children who had watched a generous model donated more than children who had watched a selfish model. Most important, however, no matter what the model had said, the words had no significant effect on the children's generosity. Other research shows that the way children perceive their own behavior also affects their generosity (Grusec and Redler, 1980). Children are more likely to be generous if they believe they are donating out of altruistic motives than because they have been told to give (e.g., Grusec et al., 1978).

When President Ford pardoned Richard Nixon for any crimes he might have committed while president, Ford set off a controversy over the morality of his own action. *(United Press International)*

For many people, moral reasoning, behavior, guilt, and self-regulation come together in a relatively cohesive way during the course of development, and parental influence often has a lasting effect on the result. For example, people who are less likely than most to lie, possibly less likely to steal or cheat, and more likely to respect the rights of others and to give them a second chance are people who trust others. And according to Julian Rotter (1980), people who trust others and are trustworthy themselves often have learned that trust from parents. In other studies, researchers have found that children with nurturant parents, who have seen their parents react with helpfulness in situations of both love and distress, are themselves likely to be more helpful and consistently altruistic in later situations (Rushton, 1980). Another demonstration of lasting parental influence was shown by David Rosenhan (1970), who points out that people who engage in dramatic social action, such as those who went to the South to work in the civil rights movement, are more likely to have parents who do not merely advocate positive social action but engage in it themselves.

CONSISTENCY IN MORAL DEVELOPMENT

Just thirty days after Gerald R. Ford became president of the United States, he pardoned Richard M. Nixon, whom he had replaced, for any crime Nixon may have committed while President. By doing so, Ford set off a storm of controversy. The explanations offered in justification of that act of pardon covered every imaginable argument at every conceivable level of moral reasoning. No matter what President Ford's reasons actually were, most people saw his moral conduct as fairly consistent with his own life history and with some particular level of morality. From the developmental perspective taken in this chapter, however, it should be clear that there are no easy answers to many of the questions that have been raised about the moral conduct of either Ford or Nixon. When applied to an individual case, such questions are often unanswerable, because the kind of reliable and relevant developmental information required to answer them is unavailable.

As this chapter has indicated, a person's consistency in moral conduct depends on the way that intellectual, social, and emotional factors combine during the course of moral development. At present, there is no way to predict the consistency of moral thought, feelings, and action in any individual or group.

In general, compared with those who behave inconsistently, children and adolescents who show consistent moral conduct usually are less influenced by immediate situational pressures, depend more heavily on internal guidance in their moral reasoning, and demonstrate a more mature sense of guilt and self-regulation across situations. This consistency can probably be traced to cognitive sophistication, varied role-taking experiences, and learning influences that emphasize consistency in both word and deed.

SUMMARY

1. Moral conduct is determined by the interplay of many factors. The amoral infant is an active learner who acquires the first moral standards from parents in specific situations. The child's early moral concepts are different from those of adults, and change as a result of increasing cognitive sophistication and social experience.
2. Although moral conduct is often viewed as a group of related reactions governed by some central process such as conscience, research indicates that people are inconsistent in what they say, do, and feel. Despite this general tendency, the experiences of some children lead them to be relatively consistent in their honesty or dishonesty. Conflicting pressures, the nature of the situation, and the kind of moral behavior being tested also affect their actions.
3. According to Piaget, children first develop objective morality, which is based on obedience to authority and in which punishment is inevitable (immanent justice). Only later do they develop subjective morality, which grows out of cooperative peer relationships and in which intentions are more important than consequences. In Lawrence Kohlberg's approach, moral reasoning develops through a progressive series of stages that form three basic developmental levels: premoral, conventional, and principled. This full course of development, which has been studied by assessing people's reactions to posed moral dilemmas, appears to be related to age, to gender, to education, and to a constitutional democracy.
4. The process of role-taking seems to be crucial to moral reasoning and conduct. Research suggests that social interaction not only stimulates the development of role-taking skills but also influences the level of moral understanding that is reached.
5. Guilt and self-regulation develop gradually and become more general in their effects. However, studies indicate that the process depends on such considerations as the nature of the parental relationship, the explanation of the reasons for discipline, and the timing of punishment. As a result of cognitive development, a child may come to experience strong moral feelings produced by his or her own reasoning and learn increasingly sophisticated ways of avoiding guilt. Many children adopt the "just world hypothesis," in which evil is punished and good is rewarded.
6. What parents, peers, and other people who serve as models say, feel, and do has a strong influence on moral development. As children watch others, they learn new ways of behaving, find out what is acceptable, and discover the consequences of various actions. Although verbal modeling by others is likely to influence the development of moral reasoning, it does not necessarily lead to changes in behavior.
7. It is impossible to predict consistency in any person's moral conduct. People who behave in a relatively consistent manner are likely to show higher levels of cognitive sophistication and to have a background of varied role-taking experiences and learning influences that emphasized consistency in word and deed.

UNIT SIX

ADOLESCENCE: BUILDING AN IDENTITY

The major physical changes of adolescence turn the child into the adult man or woman. Sexual development obviously has wide psychological and social consequences. When the adolescent attempts to find sexual gratification and to discover love and security outside the home, the personality that developed and established itself in late childhood faces an inevitable test: biological maturation forces sexual opportunities; the disappearance of the childhood home requires the construction of another. Life's joys as well as its pains arise from this confrontation between a still-developing personality and the rigor of biological and psychological development. Out of the confrontation comes the adolescent's sense of identity and self-esteem. This unit shows how boys and girls react to the transformations of adolescence and how cultural changes affect the range of choices that society presents to them.

17 PHYSICAL AND SEXUAL MATURATION

As youngsters go through the transition from childhood to adolescence, the changes and interactions that characterize their development are more pronounced than at any time since infancy. There are large qualitative and quantitative changes in their bodies, primarily involving the sex organs and the secondary sex characteristics that differentiate man from woman. It is during adolescence that the adult emerges from the child.

One of the reasons that adolescence is seen as such an important phase of development is that, for the first time, the individual is truly aware of the physical changes that occur. Neither a girl nor a boy can remain oblivious to the significance of the many events taking place in their bodies. The teenager sees, feels, and experiences body changes that are quite different from the sensations of childhood. An adolescent may experience these changes, especially those involving sexual maturity, as exciting, gratifying, embarrassing, wonderful, or frightening.

In this chapter we will discuss the physical and maturational changes that characterize adolescence and the impact of these changes on youngsters' psychological and social development. We will look first at the adolescent growth spurt, then at sexual maturity and its impact on other areas of development. We will discuss individual reactions to the physical developments of adolescence, focusing on those changes that arouse the most concern in each sex. Next, we will consider sexual behavior among adolescents, discovering that during the past twenty years, changes in sexual attitudes and behavior have led to a trend toward mutually satisfying, equalitarian relationships.

GROWTH CHARACTERISTICS

In the beginning, adolescence is a biological phenomenon, and sexual maturation is its central theme. Long before emotional considerations and social conflicts become important in the course of adolescent growth, hormonal

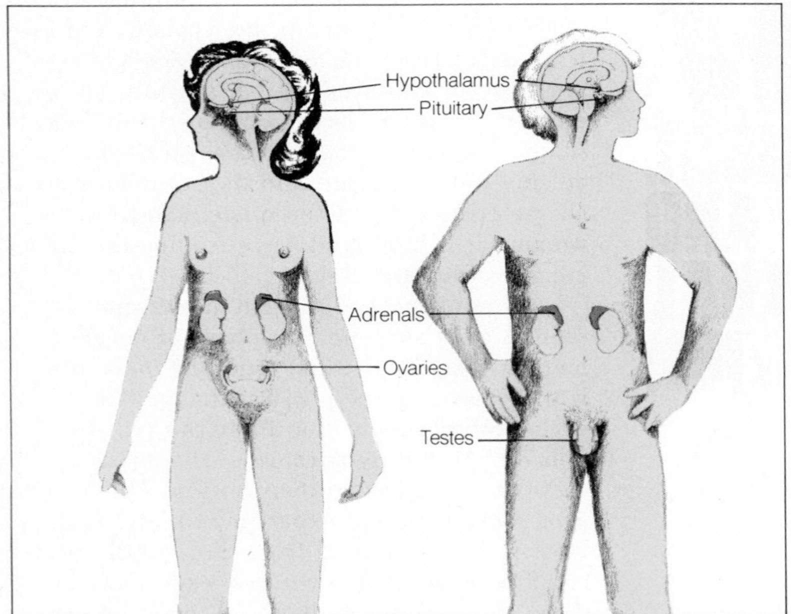

FIGURE 17.1 The endocrine system, showing only the major glands involved in pubertal changes. The hypothalamus (a part of the brain with neural and endocrine functions) signals the pituitary gland, which in turn stimulates hormonal secretions from other endocrine glands, resulting in many of the changes typifying adolescent physical and pubertal development.

changes begin to affect the body (Petersen and Taylor, 1980). The main biological event of adolescence is **puberty,** which is characterized by the attainment of biological sexual maturity. During puberty the reproductive glands first release ova and sperm. These glands are the **ovaries** in girls and the **testes** in boys. With the release of ova or sperm, the individual is, for the first time, capable of reproduction.

Both boys and girls produce male hormones **(androgens)** as well as female hormones **(estrogens)** in relatively equal amounts throughout their childhood. As Chapter 6 noted, hormones help to regulate growth at all ages, but it is only when a child reaches puberty that the hypothalamus of the brain signals the pituitary gland to begin the hormonal production found in adult men and women. The pituitary gland stimulates other endocrine glands, the adrenals, ovaries, and testes (shown in Figure 17.1) to secrete hormones directly into the bloodstream, creating a balance that includes more androgens in boys and more estrogens in girls. These hormonal changes lead directly to the physical developments that emerge during puberty (Tanner, 1978).

During puberty, the ovaries and testes produce enough hormones to cause accelerated growth of the genitals and the appearance of secondary sex characteristics. In girls, a cyclic excretion of estrogens anticipates the rhythm of the menstrual cycle well before **menarche,** or the first incidence of menstruation (Meredith, 1967).

Body Growth

The velocity of growth curves takes on great significance during adolescence. At that time, the plateau period of childhood growth ends, and the adolescent growth spurt begins. Adolescence is virtually the only time in a person's life that this curve accelerates. Once the adolescent reaches the maximum point of growth velocity (in the case of stature, "peak height velocity"), deceleration again occurs until the annual growth increment is zero and growth ceases (see Figure 17.2).

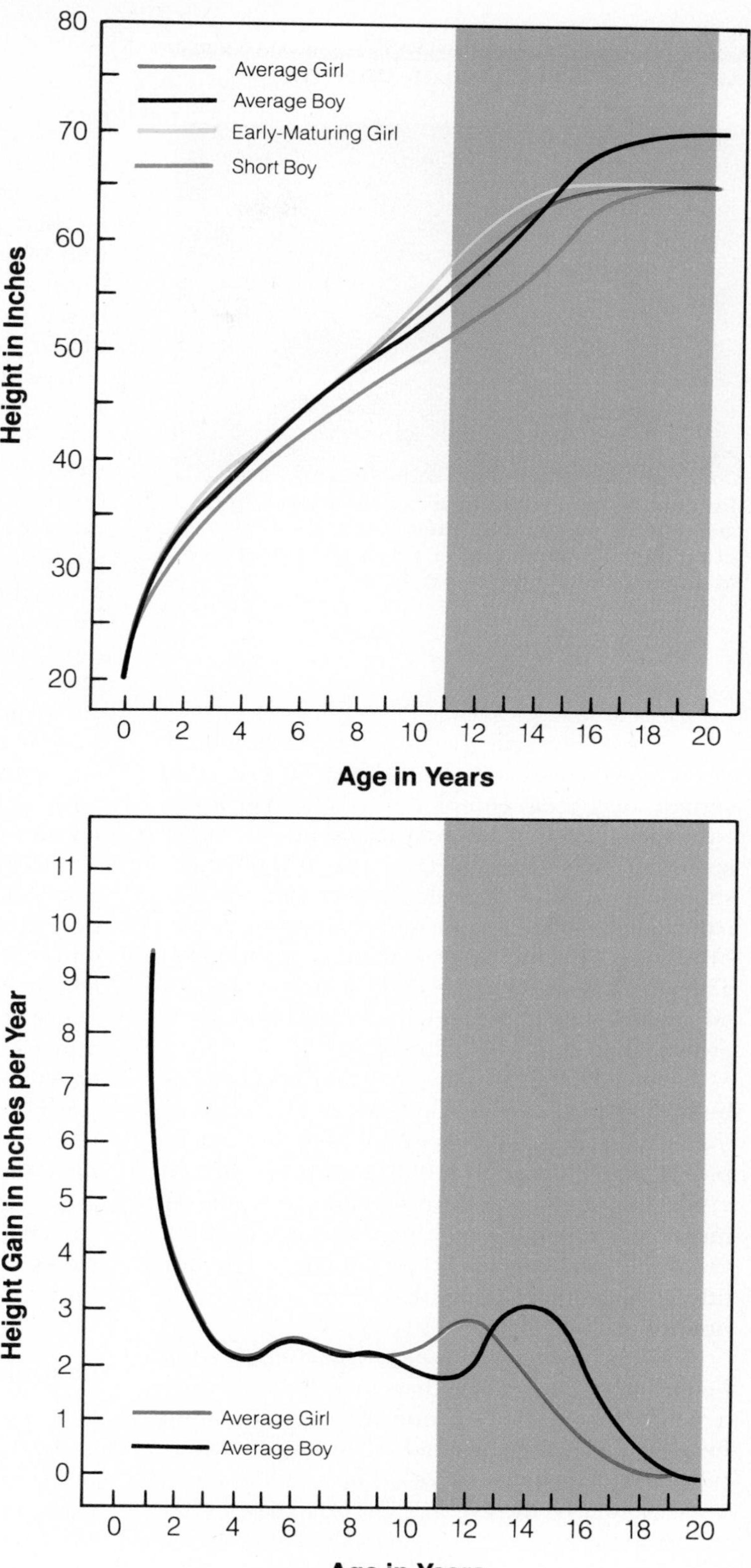

FIGURE 17.2 Sample growth curves for adolescents eleven to twenty years of age (shaded area). ***(top)*** **Notice that the early-maturing girl's rate of growth levels off by thirteen years of age, whereas the short boy continues to grow until approximately seventeen years of age. Individual variability is also reflected in the fact that the early-maturing girl reaches the average height for females, although the boy will be shorter than average.** ***(bottom)*** **Averaged and smoothed growth curves for boys and girls, showing inches gained in height per year. After the relatively stable period of gain in height during later childhood, the adolescent growth spurt starts, with its onset and end occurring earlier for girls than for boys.** ***(Adapted from Bayley, 1956)***

Because today's adolescents are heavier, taller, and mature earlier than their forebears, they often develop much higher levels of competence in athletic skills. *(© Suzanne Szasz)*

The adolescent growth spurt in height is often spectacular and, to the boy or girl concerned, may seem completely erratic. Yet it occurs within certain boundaries, some of which are relatively stable. On the basis of their measurement of boys, Donald Broverman and his colleagues (1964) found more variation at the beginning of pubertal growth than at the end. Thus the boy who has the earliest start in pubertal growth has a potentially longer period of growth than one with a late start.

Boys and girls today are taller and heavier before, during, and at the end of adolescence than they were some generations ago. For example, Howard Meredith (1963) points out that in 1955 American boys were five and one-quarter inches taller than boys of their same age in 1870. Over the same period, the average weight for fifteen-year-old boys increased by thirty-three pounds.

Both sexes now reach their final adult height at an earlier age than they did a century ago. The average boy now reaches his adult height at eighteen instead of at twenty-three, twenty-four, or twenty-five, as he would have in 1880. Similarly, the average girl now reaches her full height at about sixteen instead of at eighteen or nineteen.

Although individual height varies widely, a child's size at the beginning of adolescence predicts a great deal about his or her size at the end. Herbert and Lois Stolz (1951) found a correlation of more than + .80 between height at the onset and at the end of the pubertal period (not based on chronological age). Shifts in relative height do occur, but a boy who is taller than others at the beginning of his pubertal growth cycle is also likely to be taller at the end of it.

Both sexes experience a growth characteristic called **asynchrony.** Asynchrony refers to the fact that different body parts mature at different rates. This means that at any given time during adolescent growth, certain body parts may be disproportionately large or small in relation to the rest of the body. This disproportion becomes most pronounced with puberty (Dwyer and Mayer, 1968–1969). For example, a girl may complain that her hands and feet are too big, and a boy may object that his nose seems large or that his jaw is too prominent. As growth progresses, body proportions usually become much more harmonious.

The dramatic character of an adolescent's physical growth immediately provokes the question of where the energy to maintain such intense growth comes from. The answer is, of course, from calories. Some vigorous adolescent males at peak height velocity need a daily caloric intake comparable to that of a large adult doing heavy manual work, about 6,000 calories a day. (Little wonder that some adolescents always seem to be hungry and to spend time at the local hamburger stand indulging in carbohydrate orgies.) After an adolescent reaches peak height velocity, the extra energy needed for growth declines until the individual reaches the daily caloric intake that adult maintenance requires.

Sexual Maturation in Girls

The female growth spurt typically begins at around age ten, peaks at twelve, and continues until about fifteen, representing a trend toward earlier onset of puberty that has lasted for more than a century, but that appears to have slowed or stopped. In 1840 the average girl's first men-

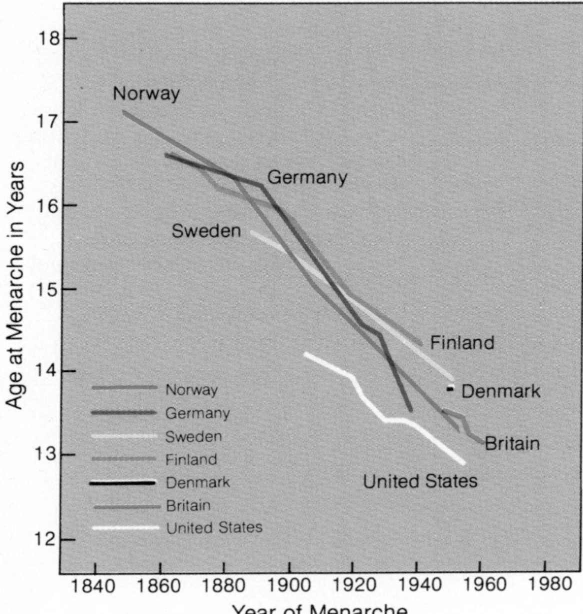

FIGURE 17.3 Over the last century, the average age of menarche (onset of menstruation) has declined in the United States and in various European countries. *(After Tanner, 1962).*

struation occurred at the age of seventeen; each decade since, menarche has tended to occur about four months earlier. In 1960 the average age of menarche in the United States was about thirteen, and by 1970 the average age had dropped to slightly less than thirteen (Muuss, 1970).

The appearance of secondary sex characteristics signals the onset of puberty in girls. For example, the "breast bud" develops (Douvan and Gold, 1966), and pigmented pubic hair appears. Breast enlargement begins around the middle of the tenth year and continues for about three years until full size is reached. As the entire breast enlarges, other changes occur. The areas around the nipples grow larger, more conical in form, and darker in color. At the same time that her breasts develop, a girl's vagina and uterus also begin to mature and her voice lowers.

Pubic hair usually appears when a girl is about eleven, but averages mean little in talking about an individual adolescent. Puberty varies so widely in its onset that such developments can occur at any time between the ages of eight and thirteen (Tanner, 1978).

Parents and adolescents often regard menarche as the true indicator of puberty, but this event occurs relatively late in the pubertal sequence. Nevertheless, because menarche is easily identified, it is often used as a basis for making normative comparisons of sexual maturity among girls. The norms for adolescent development suggest that the average American girl is likely to have her first menstrual period between the ages of ten and seventeen (Tanner, 1978). It is rare for a girl whose glands function normally to experience menarche before she is nine or after she is eighteen. Most girls have their first period when they are about twelve.

The relationship of menstruation to fertility is not well understood. One popular misconception is that menarche signals the attainment of full reproductive functioning. Although menarche does signal an advanced stage of uterine growth, the adolescent girl often remains infertile for as long as twelve to eighteen months after menarche (Tanner, 1961). This period of infertility is shorter if a girl's first menstruation occurs later than average. Even four to six years after menarche, a girl is somewhat less likely to conceive than she will be later in life. Full sexual maturity and fertility is generally reached sometime in the early or middle twenties.

Sexual Maturation in Boys

The adolescent growth spurt generally occurs about two years later in boys than in girls and peaks at about the age of fourteen. Although data concerning the onset of puberty in boys are not as complete as those for girls, the trend toward earlier male maturation has been apparent at least since the beginning of this century. Today, the onset of puberty typically occurs at about twelve, and as with girls, puberty includes more than one event. The appearance of live spermatozoa in the urine marks the onset of pu-

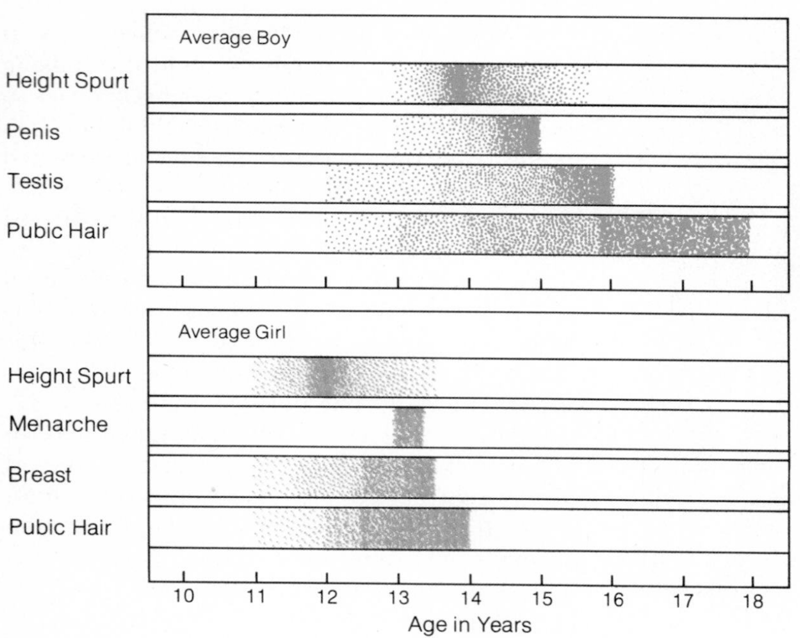

FIGURE 17.4 The pubertal development of an average boy and girl. Shaded areas represent the range of years during which such development usually occurs, with the darker shading indicating the period of most rapid growth or change. Although individual growth and change patterns may vary widely from these norms, girls generally start and end such development earlier than boys. ***(Adapted from Tanner, 1962)***

berty, but because this event can be detected only by clinical tests, more observable changes are often used. These include accelerated growth of the testes and scrotum, the pubertal height spurt, and nocturnal emissions. Secondary sex characteristics in boys include pubic hair, which may appear at the beginning of puberty or within the following year, a deepened voice, and the appearance of facial hair.

The penis and scrotum usually begin their accelerated growth when a boy is around twelve, but there are wide individual variations, and the growth may begin as early as ten and one-half or as late as fourteen and one-half. Maturation and development of the penis continue for about five years, and the scrotum reaches maturity in about seven years (Meredith, 1967). Although the external genitalia of girls change little, in boys the changes in the penis, testes, and scrotum are substantial. The shaft of the penis lengthens, and its head enlarges; the scrotum and testes grow larger and become pendulous. A boy is able to ejaculate semen about one and one-half years after accelerated penis growth begins (Tanner, 1972).

During adolescence, the larynx enlarges, and the vocal cords lengthen. This change leads to the gradual deepening of the male voice and sometimes to the embarrassing cracking of the adolescent boy's voice into a squeaky falsetto.

The appearance of facial hair is a final and significant event for the adolescent male. The downy hair on his upper lip, especially at the corners, becomes longer, coarser, and darker. Next, long down appears at the sides of his face in front of the ears. Later, coarse hair appears on his chin and lower cheeks. However, this culture's ultimate symbol of masculinity, a hairy chest, does not develop until a male reaches later adolescence or even his early twenties.

Brain Maturation

In the past, it was generally believed that maturational changes in the brain were probably complete before adolescence. Today, several lines of evidence suggest this is not the case (Galin et al., 1979; Geschwind, 1979). For one thing, continued myelination has been observed in the reticular system—the core of tissue that runs through the brain stem and filters incoming stimuli—and in some parts of the cortex as late as the third decade of life.

Recordings of brain waves (EEGs) indicate that maturational changes in the structure and functioning of the brain may occur just before or around the time of puberty. For example, although characteristic wave patterns associated with drowsiness and arousal from sleep appear during infancy, they continue to change during childhood and apparently do not assume an adult form until a child is nine to ten years old (Gibbs and Gibbs, 1964). As noted in Chapter 6, the wave patterns recorded from the brain during sleep and wakefulness also change gradually during childhood, and it is not until a child is between eleven and fourteen that the typical adult patterns emerge (S. Rose, 1973). Alpha rhythm appears to follow a similar course of gradual change, assuming an adult form when a child is between ten and fifteen years old. In addition to these changes, Robert Dustman and Edward Beck (1966) found evidence of a further maturational change in the magnitude of the brain's electrical response to visual stimulation at about fifteen years of age.

There is some evidence that brain development differs in boys and girls. Jesse LeRoy Conel (1963) found that neural tissue grows and matures earlier in a girl's left hemisphere and a boy's right hemisphere. Other work (Hutt, 1972; Taylor, 1969) suggests that the female brain matures more rapidly and that in most girls the left hemisphere becomes dominant earlier than in the male brain. Support for this position comes from the knowledge that language is generally processed in the left hemisphere and that girls are consistently superior on all tests of verbal ability.

However, research with both children and adults indicates that despite earlier maturity, females show *less* hemisphere dominance than males and that they use both hemispheres to process all kinds of information (Springer and Deutsch, 1981). For example, in a study by Sandra Witelson (1976), boys who were asked to identify objects they had explored only by touch found it easier to identify those they had explored with their left hands, indicating a right-hemisphere dominance in processing spatial information. Girls, however, identified shapes equally well, no matter which hand they used, indicating an involvement of both hemispheres in the task, up to age thirteen—the most advanced age tested in the study. On the basis of these findings, Witelson concluded that girls use both hemispheres to process spatial information at least until adolescence.

Evidence of a connection between brain maturation and puberty appeared in a study by Deborah Waber (1976; 1977). She found that regardless of sex, adolescents who reached puberty early performed better on verbal than on spatial tasks, whereas those who reached sexual maturity late performed better on spatial than on verbal tasks. Although boys and girls who reached puberty late were better at spatial tasks than those who matured early, the reverse was not true. Early maturers did not have an advantage over late maturers on tests of verbal ability. Waber proposes that the differences she found are due to differences in the rate of sexual maturation. Girls generally mature earlier than boys, and Waber suggests that the effects of sex hormones on the brain at puberty, instead of biological differences at birth, may account for general male superiority on spatial tasks. If she is right, it would mean that whatever neural structures are responsible for hemisphere dominance must be especially sensitive to sex hormones.

If reported differences in hemisphere dominance between the sexes are biologically based, can they be modified by experience? Studies have found that on visual-spatial tasks, which are generally processed more efficiently by the right than by the left hemisphere, training improves performance among girls but not among boys (Connor, Serbin, and Shackman, 1977). This suggests that any biological differences in cerebral organization are likely to be influenced in a very complicated manner by experience. It also suggests that although right-hemisphere tasks may not come as easily to girls as they do to boys, girls may be as capable as boys of acquiring them. As some investigators (e.g., Wittig and Petersen, 1979) have recently emphasized, most sex-based differences in cognitive performance and brain function—although measurable—are neither large nor impressive.

REACTIONS TO PHYSICAL CHANGE

Physical changes of the magnitude experienced by adolescents have a significant effect on how both sexes feel about themselves. Three factors appear to affect adolescents' concern about their developing bodies: the reaction of parents and others to these physical changes; the adolescent's own personality; and cultural standards of attractiveness (Petersen and Taylor, 1980).

The mythical **body ideal,** the body type defined by the culture as "attractive" and sex-appropriate, is an important influence. The individual learns these ideal characteristics from peer and family expectations and from the mass media. William Schonfeld (1963) has pointed out that movies, television, advertising, and the worship of sports heroes perpetuate the reverence for the ideal body and encourage the disparagement of those whose bodies do not conform to the ideal.

Cultural body standards may also influence a person's image of his or her own body. Stanley Schonbuch and Robert Schell (1967) asked male college students to select photographs that most nearly resembled themselves from a group of ten pictures. Males who were fifteen or more pounds overweight tended to overestimate their size, selecting photographs that portrayed fatter men. Schonbuch and Schell speculated that the negative comments and reactions of others may lead fat adolescents to regard their body differences as greater than they actually are.

Body image appears to affect the way adolescents feel about themselves (Hamburg, 1974). All studies have found a strong correlation between the way college-aged students view their bodies (body concept) and the way they judge themselves as people (self-concept) (Lerner and Spanier, 1980). Adolescents of both sexes are especially sensitive to any body characteristic that might be interpreted as sex-inappropriate. During childhood, boys and girls learn which physical attributes are feminine and which are masculine, and they show deep concern over any deviations from any of those stereotypes (Schonfeld, 1964).

This concern with body image may be heightened in the United States, for some cross-cultural data suggest that adolescents in other societies may not share the American adolescent's concern with body image. For example, Canadian high-school students seem to place more value on academic performance and less on athletic prowess, popularity, and good looks than their American age-mates do (Friesen, 1968). Among Japanese high-school students no link appears between body concept and self-concept, but among college students the link is as strong as it is in the United States (Lerner et al., 1980).

The adolescent's own personality interacts with cultural factors and the reactions of others. Adolescents who already feel unacceptable or who have low self-esteem may become anxious about their body image even though their development is well within the normal range (Petersen and Taylor, 1980).

Girls' Concerns

Although girls have traditionally been more concerned than boys with the failure of their developing bodies to match the culture's body ideal, there is no gender-based difference in self-esteem among American adolescents (Lerner et al., 1980). Despite shifts in sex roles, the pervasive advertising of cosmetics, hair products, clothing, and fad diets continues to testify to the importance of a woman's appearance. As a result, many girls perceive that boys prefer the slender figures, long legs, and well-developed breasts of the stereotypical women in television commercials and programs, and are concerned when their own bodies do not measure up to this

OBESITY: THE SEARCH FOR ITS CAUSE

As many as 30 to 35 percent of American adolescents are overweight (Hathaway and Sargent, 1962), and obesity puts the adolescent at a personal and social disadvantage. Reactions to being overweight vary with sex. Girls are much more disturbed than boys by obesity, and girls are inclined to label excess weight as "fat," whereas boys are likely to view it as desirable bone and muscle.

Several factors can contribute to obesity in the adolescent, but only about 5 out of every 100 adolescents can blame such medical problems as glandular dysfunction (for example, improper functioning of the hypothalamus or thyroid glands) or hereditary disease (Rodin, 1978). Most teen-agers eat more calories than they burn. But since some people burn calories more rapidly than others, a diet that makes one teen-ager fat will keep another of the same height trim (Harvard Medical School, 1981).

Obesity is probably due to the interaction of genetic, metabolic, psychological, and environmental factors (Rodin, 1981). Studies (e.g., Schachter and Rodin, 1974) that look for clues to obesity in the environment have shown that overweight people are especially responsive to stimuli around them. The sight, smell, or taste of food impels them to eat, even when they are not hungry. Richard Nisbett (1972), who believes that obesity is determined by physiology (some people were "meant to be fat"), proposes that this heightened responsiveness to food develops after a person becomes obese. He reasons that because fat people are always on diets, they continually eat less than their bodies were designed to consume, so their responsiveness to the sight or smell of food is to be expected.

Other studies, however, have shown that many people who are not overweight are also responsive to food cues. In an attempt to discover more about the relationship between heightened responsiveness and obesity, Judith Rodin and Joyce Slochower (1976) studied girls between the ages of nine and fifteen at a summer camp. At the beginning of camp, they gave each girl a test to determine her responsiveness to external stimuli. During the eight weeks of camp, most girls who showed a heightened responsiveness to food gained weight—even if their weight was normal when they arrived. In fact, the more responsive a girl was to external stimuli, the more weight she gained during camp.

Why do some externally responsive adolescents become obese when others do not? Rodin and Slochower believe that part of the answer may lie in the body's long-term regulatory mechanisms. When people of normal weight are placed in an environment that makes food especially noticeable, as at a summer camp abounding with candy bars, cake, and ice cream or a Caribbean cruise with its lavish four meals a day, those with heightened responsiveness will overeat. But as the novelty of the food-rich environment wears off, some people's regulatory mechanism causes them to cut back on their intake, and these people return to normal weight. Those whose regulatory mechanism does not function in this fashion keep on eating and put on weight.

This position was supported by the behavior of the girls at summer camp. Among normal-weight but externally responsive girls, 70 percent reached their highest weight during the session and began losing weight during the last week or so. But among those who were overweight when they came to camp, 86 percent reached their highest weight during the last week of camp. They were still continuing to eat more calories than they burned. It may be that to the excessively obese adolescent, the sight of food always has the effect of the first few days of a Caribbean cruise.

ideal (Wiggins, Wiggins, and Conger, 1968). In one large study (Offer, Ostrov, and Howard, 1981), more than 40 percent said they often felt ugly and unattractive, perhaps because most girls view their appearance as affecting their marital prospects (Walster et al., 1966).

The marked physical changes of adolescence lead most boys and girls to become concerned with their own bodies and how they appear to the opposite sex. ***(top: Richard Kalvar/Magnum Photos; bottom: Abigail Heyman/Magnum Photos)***

Girls are also concerned if they exhibit any characteristics they consider unfeminine, such as large hands and feet, a figure that is too full or too thin, pigmented facial hair, and a large body. Thus, many of the normal, temporary changes of adolescence may seem "unfeminine" to a girl. She grows body hair, her voice becomes lower, her hands and feet grow, and so forth. Eventually, however, a girl may be comforted by the fact that her friends are experiencing the same changes.

Because breast development is an obvious indicator of sexual maturity in women, it is often the focus of attention from others and of concern to the individual. The development of a girl's breasts, including size and contour, plays an important role in her evaluation of herself as a female. The emphasis of the popular media (in advertisements for brassieres and the dimensions of the playmate of the month) and the behavior of many American men add considerably to her concern.

Most adolescent girls are likely to have ambivalent feelings about their developing breasts. For example, they may be proud of their new femininity yet be embarrassed by the sudden attention that they receive from boys. They may worry that tight blouses or sweaters are too revealing and may try to hide their new shape by wearing loose-fitting clothes or by hunching slightly. Many girls complain that their breasts are too large or too small. Extremely large breasts can embarrass a girl because they draw attention to her and cause her to feel different from her peers. Extremely small breasts can make a girl worry whether she will ever reach sexual maturity or be attractive to men. In most cases, as a girl reaches her adult body proportions, the worries fade; breasts that seemed too large or too small during adolescence appear more appropriate to her mature stature.

Boys' Concerns

Boys are not so constantly confronted by the ideal physical stereotype as girls are, and less than a quarter of them say that they often feel ugly or unattractive (Offer, Ostrov, and Howard, 1981). Yet adolescent boys are particularly concerned about such characteristics as a circle of fat around the hips and thighs, underdeveloped external genitalia, or the development of subcutaneous tissue in the breast region. Although such developments as fatty hips and breast growth are normal and usually soon disappear, they are often a source of great embarrassment to a boy.

The size of his genital organs, especially the penis, can have profound significance for a boy. Boys' genitalia change in both size and contour more than girls' do. Because a boy can compare his genitals with those of his peers, they may become a primary source of concern. Men's rooms, showers, and gymnasiums provide ample opportunity for a boy to judge his development against that of other boys and men.

A boy with a small penis may feel particularly distressed. He may be a victim of widely held beliefs that the size of a man's penis is related to his physical strength, his virility, and his ability to satisfy a woman sexually. Sometimes a boy may consider his penis to be particularly small because he is ignorant about the wide range of penis size among normal men.

The belief that a large penis is related to masculinity and virility showed up in a study by John Verinis and Samuel Roll (1970). They found that men and women aged eighteen to twenty rated such traits as a large penis and hairy arms and chest as indications of virility and masculinity. There is, however, no empirical support for the belief that the size of a man's genitals is related to his masculinity and strength. William Masters and Virginia Johnson (1966) found that penis size is less consistently related to general physical development than any other organ of the body is. They found that the largest penis (5.5 inches in the flacid state) in a sampling of 312 men was displayed by a man who was 5 feet 7 inches tall, whereas the smallest (2.36 inches) belonged to a man 5 feet 11 inches tall. Masters and Johnson also noted that a small penis, when fully erect, shows a relatively greater increase in size than a large penis.

Masters and Johnson and others have also reported that the ability to provide sexual gratification for a female partner during intercourse bears little relation to the size of the erect penis. The vagina is flexible and elastic, contracting to the insertion of small objects and distending during the birth process to allow the passage of a baby. The vagina of a normally responsive woman therefore is readily able to adjust to a wide range of variation in penis size, and penis size is only a minor factor in sexual stimulation of the female.

Early and Late Maturing

Some children enter puberty earlier or later than their peers, and the timing of this physiological event can have social and psychological consequences, depending upon an individual's gender, social class, or cohort (Clausen, 1975). Developmental psychologists Mary Cover Jones and Nancy Bayley (1950) and their colleagues followed groups of early- and late-maturing boys from early adolescence through the fourth decade of life. The groups differed markedly in social and physical characteristics during the years from thirteen to fifteen. At the same chronological age, the early maturers were taller, stronger, more attractive, and better coordinated than the late maturers, and they tended to have well-muscled bodies. The late maturers tended to be thin and were more talkative, active, busy, and uninhibited, yet they also tended to be tenser and bossier than the early maturers. These findings suggest that late maturers possess less social maturity and that they use negative behavior to get attention, thereby compensating for their physical disadvantages. Additional studies support this interpretation. Compared with the early maturer, the late maturer shows a greater need for social acceptance, greater anticipation of rejection, heightened dependence, and a more negative self-concept (Mussen and Jones, 1957).

Many of the physical characteristics of late-maturing boys, which the boys themselves may regard as evidence of inadequate masculinity, fall within the normal range of development (Schonfeld, 1964). When such is the case, a late-maturing boy need only wait until he catches up with his peers. But in the meantime, the values placed on athletic prowess and manly appearance (by boys and girls alike) may make him feel inferior to those who mature early.

The early maturer is more active in athletics and student government and has greater visibility in the school social system. The social advantages of early maturity appear to continue into adulthood, when differences in physique no longer exist. Among the groups studied by Jones (1957), early maturers in their thirties tended to have higher occupational status than late maturers, they were more likely to work in supervisory or managerial positions, and they reported more active social lives in clubs, organizations, and business. The differences that appeared when the groups were in their late thirties suggest that early maturers achieve in a conforming way, whereas later maturers' achievements are more likely to be idiosyncratic. Early maturers are likely to be conventional in both thought and attitude; they continue to have social poise and to show responsibility. Late maturers appear to be more flexible and adaptive; they tolerate ambiguity better than early maturers (Jones, 1965). As Harvey Peskin (1967) suggests, the greater social advantage of early maturers may lead them to fix on their identity early in life, thereby producing conventionality.

Studies of early- and late-maturing girls suggest that the early-maturing girl has less prestige in early adolescence but that as the growth process continues, she comes to enjoy the social advantages of the early-maturing boy (Faust, 1960). At first, the early-maturing girl is somewhat conspicuous and is likely to be far out of step developmentally with boys of her own age. However, early maturity may be a source of satisfaction if a girl's favorite companions are also early maturers. A girl's social class affects her reaction to early maturity; middle-class girls who mature early tend to be self-confident, but working-class girls who mature early generally lack confidence (Clausen, 1975). At seventeen, girls who have matured early may have a more favorable view of themselves and may rate higher in popularity than they rated earlier in their teens. Studies that follow early- and late-maturing girls into adulthood have not been especially revealing, presumably because in the past a woman's social life, status, and opportunities for achievement have depended on the status of her husband (Eichorn, 1963). However, by the time the girls in one study reached the age of thirty, those who had matured early showed better psychological health than did those who had matured late (Peskin, 1973).

SOCIAL CHANGE AND SEXUAL BEHAVIOR

The three-year decrease in the average age at the onset of puberty represents a radical change in the timetable of development. Childhood has been shortened, and the social demands and urges associated with sexual maturity now occur earlier in life. This early sexual maturity, coupled with cultural changes in social conditioning, have led to great differences in sexual attitudes and behavior.

The Kinsey Reports

Much of our knowledge about the sexual behavior of Americans during the first half of this century comes from the pioneering work of Alfred Kinsey. The Kinsey reports (Kinsey, Pomeroy, and Martin, 1948; Kinsey et al., 1953) on the incidence and variety of sexual outlets were milestones in the open exchange of information about sexuality. Kinsey's sample was far from perfect; for example, there were too few rural people and too few data on blacks to analyze statistically. Nonetheless, his studies yielded a great deal of in-depth information.

One of Kinsey's major findings was that premarital virginity was much rarer than people thought. Before 1915, three-fourths of all first-time brides were virgins, but by the 1920s, the figure had dropped to a little more than half. Among the unmarried sixteen- to twenty-year-olds in the sample, 20 percent of the females and 71 percent of the males were "sexually active"—that is, were having sexual intercourse. Apparently a major shift in American sexual values had occurred during the "roaring twenties."

By the end of their teens, practically all boys and girls had had some heterosexual contact, ranging from holding hands to petting of the genitals. Furthermore, Kinsey's data indicated that by age twenty, over half of all girls had experienced orgasm, and nearly all boys. A majority of these orgasms occurred during masturbation, which, like premarital intercourse, was more common than people realized. About two-thirds of all boys experienced their first orgasm through masturbation. By the age of fifteen, 82 percent of all boys had masturbated, and by age twenty, 92 percent had done so.

For girls, the figures were lower: by age fifteen, 20 percent had masturbated, and by age twenty, 33 percent had done so. The figures continued to climb, so that in the sample as a whole, 66 percent of all females had masturbated. Masturbation was also the most common source of first orgasm for girls, accounting for 40 percent of the sample.

Social-class differences were related to the sexual behavior of men in Kinsey's study. For example, 98 percent of those with only a grade-school education had experienced premarital intercourse. For those with a high-school diploma, the figure was 85 percent, and for men with some college education, it was 68 percent. For women, however, the link between social factors and premarital sex was more apparent than real. Although it appeared at first that the more educated a woman, the more likely she was eventually to have premarital sex, this tendency could be accounted for almost entirely by the fact that less-educated women tended to marry younger.

The Changing Sixties

Had this section been written twenty years ago, we could have said that sexual behavior in the United States had changed little since the 1920s. During the second half of the 1960s, however, a second major change in sexual behavior appeared, one that seems to be continuing to the present.

During the 1960s, there was a general liberalization of attitudes toward sex (Tavris and

More than a third of the girls who become sexually active face the physical, social, and economic hazards that accompany adolescent pregnancy. ***(Elinor S. Beckwith/Taurus Photos)***

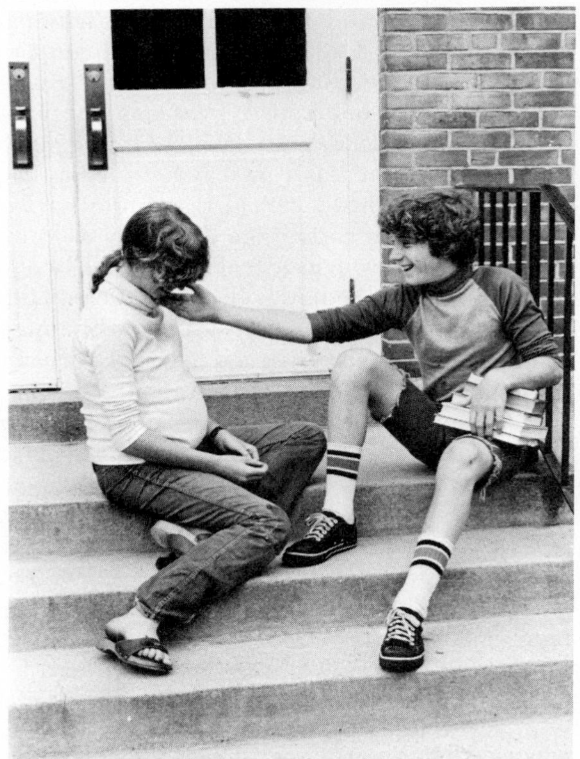

Offir, 1977; Feather, 1980). Behavior that once was considered unfit for public discussion began to appear in movies, television programs, books, magazines, and newspapers—perhaps in part because, as sociologist John Gagnon (1978) has put it, although the Kinsey reports had no direct effect on sexual conduct, they provided a basis for public and private talk about sexual matters. At the same time, attitudes toward authority in general began to change—in part, perhaps, because of opposition to the Vietnam War. As a result, the social climate in which young people became sexually mature altered considerably.

Contemporary surveys show that Kinsey's figures are now out of date, especially for teenagers and people in their twenties. For example, although the exact figures vary somewhat from study to study, nearly all studies find that premarital activity has become much more widespread since Kinsey's day. While Kinsey's figures showed that 17 to 19 percent of college women were sexually active, more recent figures range from 29 percent (Lewis and Burr, 1975) to 85 percent (Jessor and Jessor, 1975). A national study in 1971 of 4,600 girls between fifteen and nineteen indicated that 46 percent of all female adolescents had intercourse by the age of nineteen (Zelnik and Kantner, 1972). An update of this study by the same researchers using the same methods shows that girls are now having intercourse at an earlier age than they used to, and the number who have had intercourse by age nineteen has climbed from 46 to 55 percent (Zelnik and Kantner, 1977). Girls are also beginning to masturbate at an earlier age, and with greater frequency (Hunt, 1974).

Changes have taken place among young men as well, particularly among those headed for college. One survey found that by age seventeen, 50 percent of the males who are going on to college have had premarital intercourse, more than double the figure in Kinsey's study. For those who did not plan to go to college, the figure was 75 percent, compared with a little over 66 percent in Kinsey's study (Hunt, 1974).

These substantial increases in premarital intercourse for both sexes have taken place in a relatively short period of time, and are dramatic when one considers the almost fifty-year plateau of unchanged behavior prior to the 1960s.

Although the incidence of premarital intercourse has risen sharply in the United States, American college students appear to be no more experienced than students in other countries and tend to look inhibited alongside English college students (Luckey and Nass, 1969). Tables 17.1 and 17.2 present the results of surveys among college men and women in five countries. However, these surveys, which were taken more than a decade ago, give the lowest figure (58 percent) for sexual intercourse among American college men to come out of post-Kinsey studies. One subsequent study (Jessor and Jessor, 1975) indicates that 82 percent of American college men have engaged in intercourse, although the figure in other studies ranges from 60 percent (Lewis and Burr, 1975) to 73 percent (Baumann and Wilson, 1974). In any case, there has been a sharp increase since Kinsey reported that 49 percent of college-educated males had had premarital intercourse before they were twenty-one.

Along with a rise in sexual experience has come a drop in the proportion of males who visit prostitutes. As Table 17.2 (see page 430) shows, only 4.2 percent of American college men have been involved with prostitutes (Luckey and Nass, 1969), whereas earlier studies had reported that 20 to 25 percent had visited prostitutes (Kinsey, Pomeroy, and Martin, 1948).

SEXUALITY AND INTIMACY

Along with a new openness about sexual matters has come a tendency to see sexual behavior as a matter of personal choice rather than of law or morality, and an emphasis on interpersonal norms and values.

Sex Differences

Kinsey and his colleagues tended to explain differences in male and female sexual behavior in biological terms, by assuming, for example, a more urgent male sex drive—although by the

TABLE 17.1
COLLEGE WOMEN'S SEXUAL EXPERIENCE

Type	*United States*	*Canada*	*England*	*Germany*	*Norway*
Light embracing or fond holding of hands	97.5%	96.5%	91.9%	94.8%	89.3%
Casual goodnight kissing	96.8	91.8	93.0	74.0	75.0
Deep kissing	96.5	91.8	93.0	90.6	89.3
Horizontal embrace with some petting but not undressed	83.3	81.2	79.1	77.1	75.0
Petting of breast area from outside woman's clothing	78.3	78.8	82.6	76.0	64.3
Petting of breast area without clothes intervening	67.8	64.7	70.9	66.7	58.9
Petting below the waist under woman's clothing	61.2	64.7	70.9	63.5	53.6
Petting below the waist of both man and woman, under clothing	57.8	50.6	61.6	56.3	42.9
Nude embrace	49.6	47.6	64.0	62.1	51.8
Coitus	43.2	35.3	62.8	59.4	53.6
One-night affair involving coitus; did not date person again	7.2	5.9	33.7	4.2	12.5
Whipping or spanking before petting or other intimacy	4.5	5.9	17.4	1.0	7.1

Source: Adapted from Eleanore Luckey and Gilbert Nass, "A Comparison of Sexual Attitudes and Behavior in an International Sample," *Journal of Marriage and the Family,* 31 (1969), p. 375.

time the volume on female sexuality was published, Kinsey had come to believe that male sexuality and female sexuality were much closer than had been commonly assumed (Gagnon, 1978). The differences that do exist are the result of a complex interaction among neurological, hormonal, psychological, and cultural factors. It seems clear that male and female sexual behavior is influenced by sex-role stereotypes and expectations, just as much other behavior is (Miller and Simon, 1980). When each plays out the stereotypical role, the girl acts a passive part in sexual relations, with the boy taking the initiative in petting. The girl accedes, and, if the approach threatens to go beyond the limits she allows, she is expected to serve as a calming conscience for both. In courtship, it is the man who is supposed to propose. With wider acceptance of sexual activity, however, these stereotypes are changing, and the distinctions between acceptable sexual behavior for boys and girls have blurred (Miller and Simon, 1980).

In all studies, certain differences in sexual behavior have consistently appeared. Boys reach the peak of their sexual powers earlier than girls, even though girls reach menarche earlier than boys reach a corresponding level of development. Boys desire orgasm more often than girls;

TABLE 17.2
COLLEGE MEN'S SEXUAL EXPERIENCE

Type	*United States*	*Canada*	*England*	*Germany*	*Norway*
Light embracing or fond holding of hands	98.6%	98.9%	93.5%	93.8%	93.7%
Casual goodnight kissing	96.7	97.7	93.5	78.6	86.1
Deep kissing	96.0	97.7	91.9	91.1	96.2
Horizontal embrace with some petting but not undressed	89.9	92.0	85.4	68.8	93.6
Petting of woman's breast area from outside her clothing	89.9	93.2	87.0	80.4	83.5
Petting of woman's breast area without clothes intervening	83.4	92.0	82.8	69.6	83.5
Petting below the waist of the woman under her clothing	81.1	85.2	84.6	70.5	83.5
Petting below the waist of both man and woman, under clothing	62.9	64.8	68.3	52.7	55.1
Nude embrace	65.6	69.3	70.5	50.0	69.6
Coitus	58.2	56.8	74.8	54.5	66.7
One-night affair involving coitus; did not date person again	29.9	21.6	43.1	17.0	32.9
Whipping or spanking before petting or other intimacy	8.2	5.7	17.1	0.9	5.1
Sex on pay-as-you-go-basis	4.2	4.5	13.8	9.8	2.5

Source: Adapted from Eleanore Luckey and Gilbert Nass, "A Comparison of Sexual Attitudes and Behavior in an International Sample," *Journal of Marriage and the Family,* 31 (1969), p. 374.

they resort more than girls to sexual fantasies; they are more responsive to sexual symbols; they reach a sexual climax in dreams more often; they require less constant physical stimulation to remain aroused; they more often have had sexual relations with more than one partner; they do not tend to insist, as many girls do, that there be some affection between sexual partners; and they prefer to go steady less often than girls.

This pattern of sex differences is strongly influenced by the world around adolescents. Girls' childhood and early adolescent socialization generally make them more competent than boys in interpersonal relationships. For most girls, sexual behavior involves incorporating sexuality into a social role and identity that already included capacities for tenderness and sensitivity. For most boys, on the other hand, the pathway to mature heterosexual behavior involves sexuality first, and only secondarily does the capacity for concerned, tender, and loving sexual relationships develop. Thus cultural stereotypes and parental and peer socialization emphasize, to use Ira Reiss's (1973) terms, "body-centered" sexuality for the male and "person-centered" sexuality for the female.

Dating allows boys to train girls and girls to train boys in the meaning of each sex's commitment to the heterosexual relationship. *(© Glenn Cruickshank 1981/West Stock Inc.)*

Experiences among their peers further increase differences between the sexes. Groups of girls are likely to support and encourage one another for interpersonal competence and romantic interests, whereas groups of boys are likely to support and encourage one another for erotic interests, responsiveness to erotic stimuli, and proclaimed erotic activity. In addition, adolescent peer groups generally reward popularity with the opposite sex with status (Schwartz and Merten, 1967). Thus during adolescence, both boys and girls learn to incorporate sexual behavior into their gender roles, but the experiences each brings to his or her relationships are likely to be different. And each sex affects the other. As William Simon and John Gagnon (1969) suggest, adolescent dating and courtship serves as a process in which boys train girls and girls train boys in the meaning and context of each sex's commitment to the heterosexual relationship.

Promiscuity

It would be a mistake to interpret the data reported on sexual activity or on changing sexual attitudes as evidence of widespread promiscuity. In one national survey of female sexual behavior among college students, 60 percent of the girls who reported premarital intercourse had had only one partner, and half indicated that they planned to marry him (Zelnik and Kantner, 1972). In Robert Sorensen's (1973) study of thirteen- to nineteen-year-olds, 84 percent of the girls' first experiences with intercourse were with boys whom they knew well, liked a lot, went steady with, or were "engaged to be engaged to." Among boys, 56 percent of the first coital experiences were with partners whom they described in the same way. Among these adolescents, although 24 percent of those with coital experience had had more than six partners before they were nineteen, 47 percent had had only one partner.

From the evidence gathered in the last decade, we can conclude that, particularly among females, there has been a change in the direction of earlier premarital sexuality but that the frequency has not increased much. Indeed, the openness seems to make many adolescents feel that their own sexual activities are below normal; between the 1960s and the end of the 1970s, the proportion of American adolescents who believed they were "way behind" their peers sexually rose from 7 percent to 21 percent (Offer, Ostrov, and Howard, 1981). It also appears that changing attitudes have led more people to judge sexual behavior as acceptable or unacceptable on the basis of the affection in the overall relationship.

Personal Choice

Even young adolescents seem to be aware of alternatives and to value personal choice in sexual matters. In Sorensen's study, 39 percent of all adolescents agreed that sexual intercourse is immoral unless it is between two people who like each other and who have something in common, and 69 percent agreed with the assertion that "Anything two people want to do sexually is moral, as long as they both want to do it and it doesn't hurt either one of them." There was no difference between younger and older adolescents on this point. Further, both high-school and college students see kissing, petting, and coitus as most acceptable when a couple is engaged and least acceptable outside an affectionate relationship (Reiss, 1967). Like most adults, most adolescents do not condone promiscuity. Unlike the average adult, however, the average adolescent evaluates a specific sexual behavior within the framework of the relationship of which it is a part. Adolescents believe that premarital intercourse between loving partners is more acceptable than petting without affection, but adults are more likely to condemn premarital intercourse and accept petting without affection.

This difference in judgment may help explain why most adolescents between thirteen and nineteen (72 percent of the boys and 70 percent of the girls) told Sorensen (1973) that they and their parents still do not talk freely about sex. Many said that any conversation about sex was general and not specifically directed toward the boy's or girl's own behavior or problems. Only 18 percent reported talking with parents about masturbation or birth control; 24 percent had talked about venereal disease. Many of the adolescents suggested that parents delude themselves about their child's sexual behavior by refusing to acknowledge the youngster's sexual nature or by simply ignoring blatant violations of their own sexual standards. Sorensen found that 51 percent of the boys and 44 percent of the girls agreed with the statement "I wish my parents could overcome their own early training so that they could realize that sex is natural and beautiful." Traditional parental evasiveness in the face of new public openness about sex no doubt contributes to adolescent charges of parental hypocrisy. Only 28 percent of the boys and 44 percent of the girls believed that their own sexual attitudes were the same as those of their parents. Among adolescent girls, 60 percent claimed that they did not talk with parents about their sex lives as they thought sex to be a personal matter that is nobody's business but their own.

In general, studies confirm an apparent difference between the generations concerning both premarital sexuality and the affectionate relationship in which behavior occurs. However, this apparent generational difference is not as great as it may seem. Adults are becoming more permissive themselves, and single adults are likely to approve of premarital intercourse. Ira Reiss (1973) found that, in 1963, 44 percent of single adults were highly permissive of premarital intercourse but that only 18 percent of married adults were permissive. By 1973 the figures had risen to 74 percent and 50 percent. Thus, differences in marital status are at least as important as generational differences in attitudes toward premarital sexuality.

It also appears that assuming the role of a parent affects a person's attitudes toward sexual behavior, generally leading to a decrease in permissiveness. For example, childless couples are more permissive than couples with adolescent children. Sexual stereotypes, or the fear of a daughter's pregnancy, also seem to affect a parent's attitudes. The more sons a parent has, the more likely he or she is to be permissive, but the more daughters a parent has, the more likely he or she is to condemn premarital intercourse (Reiss, 1970). As might be expected, the number of adults who approve of premarital intercourse is considerably smaller than the number who themselves have engaged in it (Conger, 1973).

The evolutionary changes in American sexual behavior and attitudes can be seen as part of a more general movement toward equalitarianism and, therefore, may affect traditional gender roles. For example, after surveying these changes, Reiss (1973) concludes that the human sexual relationship is changing from an occasion for male satisfaction of body-centered sexuality to an equalitarian relationship that involves more than physical attraction. He notes that, although people will continue to pursue sexuality for pleasure, the pleasure is more likely to be mutual and equalitarian.

SUMMARY

1. Adolescence begins as a biological phenomenon centered around sexual maturation. The first incidence of menstruation in girls and the appearance of pubic hair, nocturnal emissions, and enlarging sex organs in boys are among the signs most often used to mark the attainment of sexual maturity. With the later release of ova and sperm, adolescents achieve the capability of biological reproduction.
2. The physical and maturational changes that indicate increased hormone production are dramatically reflected in the adolescent growth spurt and are apparently accompanied by changes in the structure and functioning of the brain. Trends over the decades indicate an earlier onset of puberty, increases in size and weight, and the earlier attainment of final adult height.
3. Through the mass media, individuals are constantly exposed to, and quickly learn, the mythical standards that make up the culture's ideal body type. Deviations from this body ideal—whether in height or weight, the timing of maturation, or the size and contour of body parts—are likely to influence the developing adolescent's self-concept and peer relationships. Early-maturing boys are likely to be taller, stronger, more attractive, more poised, and better coordinated than late-maturing boys. Early-maturing girls may have less prestige in early adolescence but later enjoy the same social advantages as early-maturing boys.
4. Sexual attitudes and behavior have generally become more open in the last twenty years. As a result, more adolescents today engage in a greater variety of sexual behavior at an earlier age than was once the case.
5. Male and female sexual behavior is influenced by cultural expectations, but the distinction between acceptable behavior for boys and girls has blurred. In the stereotypical relationship, sex is "body-centered" for males and "person-centered" for females. However, sexual relationships appear to be changing and are beginning to approach an equalitarian relationship that involves more than physical gratification.

VAL

18 COGNITION, IDENTITY, AND SOCIAL RELATIONS

Matt is sixteen years old, six feet tall, shaves three times a week, is second baseman on the softball team, and tries to be independent and self-sufficient. As a team member, he finds easy acceptance among his friends, whose dress, hair style, and speech patterns are nearly identical with his. But Matt is not sure what he wants to do with his life, is afraid his girl friend doesn't truly love him, finds his parents unreasonable, and—after behaving like an adult in a difficult situation—suddenly acts younger than his twelve-year-old sister Susan. In short, Matt is an adolescent.

The view that adolescence is only a recapitulation and working out of the themes of childhood does scant justice to its possibilities. To be sure, the preadolescent years are important in defining where Susan and Matt begin, how much they have to work with, and what they must work on. Human development is cumulative and layered. Adolescence is built on the early phases of life but at the same time has its own tasks. Whether adolescents accomplish these tasks depends not only on their past but on their present as well, on what they are offered and on what they can make of it.

It is impossible to discuss adolescent behavior and development without taking note of the wide variety of life styles and commitments that exist in our society. In a pluralistic society, adolescence takes many forms, and adolescents share the diverse values, beliefs, and attitudes characteristic of their elders.

In this chapter, we will discuss the adolescent's search for a sense of identity. We will see how the cognitive changes of adolescence and the development of formal thought affect a person's moral reasoning and self-concept. We will look at self-esteem and the role it plays in developing a secure sense of identity. We will see how adolescents decide on a career, how that choice relates to their sense of identity, and how it is shaped by their socialization. We will describe the course of friendship in adolescence and the function of the peer group. We will examine the family's influence on adolescents' autonomy and their choice of occupation, noting how socioeconomic class affects attitudes toward life and work. Finally, after a look at adolescent conformity and the generation gap, we will discuss the possibility that the life span in this society is developing a new phase, that of youth.

COGNITIVE CHANGE

It is not accidental that adolescence is the first phase of life in which people begin to think carefully about themselves, their roles in life, their plans, and the validity and integrity of their beliefs. Unlike the younger child, who deals largely with the present, the adolescent often is concerned with the hypothetical, the future, the remote. An adolescent remarked, "I found myself thinking about my future and then I began to think about why I was thinking about my future, and then I began to think about why I was thinking about why I was thinking about my future." This preoccupation with thinking is characteristic of formal thought.

Formal Thought

The adolescent who develops formal thought can achieve a new range and flexibility of mental processes. If encouraged and supported by her environment, Lauren can develop an increased capacity for planning, for the mental rehearsal of alternative plans of action, and for guiding her behavior according to long-range purposes.

The central feature of formal thought is the conception of possibilities that lie outside the immediate environment, and Jean Piaget (1952b) called this ability to deal with logical possibilities the stage of **formal operations.** The adolescent who has moved into this stage can also generate and test hypotheses, think ahead, and think about thought itself. Some children enter this stage as early as eleven, but Piaget (Inhelder and Piaget, 1958) believed that the abstract, scientific thought that characterizes the period and that he regarded as the culmination of cognitive development is not firmly established until children are about fifteen years old. Some people never develop formal thought, and it is neither required nor used in many aspects of life. In most studies, formal-operational thought is shown by from 40 to 60 percent of college students and adults (Keating, 1980).

Testing for Formal Thought Formal thought is a generalized orientation toward problem solving that involves isolating elements of a problem and systematically exploring all the possible solutions. A look at the pendulum-problem experiment, which was conducted by Bärbel Inhelder and Piaget (1958), illustrates the difference between problem-solving approaches based on formal and on concrete thought. The two investigators presented elementary- and high-school students with strings of different lengths and objects of different weights, which the children could attach to a rod so that they swung like pendulums. Inhelder and Piaget pointed out to the children that each of the various possible pendulums would swing through its arc at a different speed. The problem before each child was to determine the factor or factors that account for the speed with which a pendulum traverses its arc.

The four intuitively plausible causes are (1) the weight of the object, (2) the length of the string, (3) the height from which the object is released, and (4) the force of the initial push. Of the four possible factors, only the length of the string affects the speed of the pendulum. A child can discover this solution either by methodically trying all possible combinations of the four factors (varying a single factor with each trial) or by imagining trials of all possible combinations of factors.

Children between eight and thirteen, who were in the concrete-operational period, approached the problem in a somewhat systematic manner but were not methodical enough to solve it. At first they varied some but not all of the factors, having particular difficulty with weight. They also accurately judged the differences in the pendulum's movements. But not until the experimenter showed the way could they isolate the effect of one factor from the effect of others.

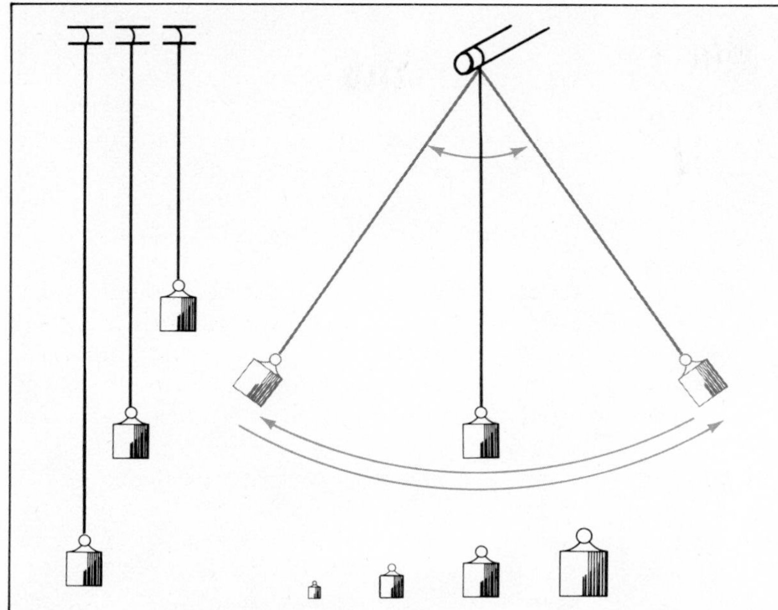

FIGURE 18.1 Illustration of a pendulum problem. The child is given a set of weights *(bottom)* and a string that can be shortened or lengthened *(left)*. His task is to determine which factor or factors account for the speed with which a pendulum traverses its arc. *(After Inhelder and Piaget, 1958)*

They did not generate on their own a set of procedures that specified all possible combinations of the four factors. As a result of these limitations, they concluded that length of the string is one determining factor but not that it is the only relevant one. They found it particularly difficult to exclude factors.

Only the fourteen- or fifteen-year-old anticipated all possible combinations, tested them experimentally, and deduced not only what affects a pendulum's speed but also what factors are irrelevant. On the basis of experiments like this, Inhelder and Piaget concluded that adolescent thought is characterized by the ability to hypothesize and to deduce.

Although Inhelder and Piaget found that eleven- and twelve-year-olds usually fail to solve the pendulum problem, Robert Siegler, Diane Liebert, and Robert Liebert (1973) have developed a training procedure that successfully taught even ten-year-olds the skills that enabled them to solve it. They conclude that Piaget is correct in stating that ten- and eleven-year-olds do not usually solve such problems on their own but that this does not mean that such problems are beyond children's intellectual grasp. Just as four-year-olds can be taught to understand conservation, a ten-year-old can learn to perform some of the mental activities that generally do not develop until adolescence.

Prevalence of Formal Thought A growing body of research suggests that formal thought is neither as inevitable nor as universal a step in development as is the concrete thought of childhood (Neimark, 1975; Moshman, 1979; Keating and Clark, 1980). Studies in other countries indicate that abstract categorization and reasoning may be not an inevitable outcome of growing up but the direct result of living in a highly technological Western society or of formal education (Super, 1980). In some societies, apparently few people develop the ability to reason from hypotheses. In Turkey, for example, formal thought appears in city dwellers but not in residents of primitive villages (Kohlberg and Gilligan, 1971).

On the basis of numerous studies in Africa

Using abstract categories and logical hypotheses to solve problems is probably the direct result of formal education, which appears to change the mind in several ways. ***(Ken Heyman)***

and Latin America, Michael Cole (1978) has concluded that formal education itself changes the mind in several ways: people group things into general classes according to formal rules (cow, horse, dog) instead of according to their function (cow, pasture, milk); they use these classes to solve problems and to organize their recall; and they treat problems in logic as hypothetical puzzles instead of as questions of fact or interpretation. Although literacy does not guarantee the development of formal thought, some children show these changes after as few as three years of schooling. Nine years of formal education, Cole discovered, will bring about the changes in most children.

Patricia Greenfield and Jerome Bruner (1966) attribute the greater evidence of formal thought in societies with schools to the fact that schooling provides training in written language, a view that is similar to Cole's. Writing forces a child to separate thought from objects and thus may encourage children to let their symbolic processes run ahead of concrete fact, allowing them to develop the capacity to think in terms of possibility rather than actuality. In modern societies with widespread school systems, more middle- and upper-middle-class adolescents show formal thought than adolescents from working- and lower-class backgrounds, and adolescents in the upper socioeconomic classes develop this thought earlier (Dulit, 1972; Peel, 1971).

Although formal thought is by no means a universal characteristic of adolescence, its development constitutes a change of primary importance for the individual. Because adolescents may see the world and the people in it, including themselves, in such a different way, speculating about what might be instead of accepting what is, it follows that profound changes can occur in their identities and in their social relations.

Moral Reasoning

The intensity with which some adolescents espouse moral attitudes and values may bear little relation to what they feel or do in situations they face. After all, adolescents are subject to the same kinds of powerful social influences as other people; they are also often aware of the radical discrepancies between what others tell them to do and what others actually do. Like the rest of us, they tend to model their conduct on others' deeds and not on their words. These modeling influences can bring about changes in the moral reasoning of adolescents (Prentice, 1972) as well as in their self-regulation and moral conduct (Thoresen and Mahoney, 1974).

As noted in Chapter 16, an individual's moral development does not necessarily follow a consistent, age-graded pattern. Adolescents can range from the lowest to the highest levels of moral reasoning, and the further they go in school, the higher they are likely to progress up Kohlberg's scale. In most adults, moral reasoning seems to stop developing when they leave school. No more than a third of high-school graduates reason at the principled level; but a majority of those who continue with advanced study in philosophy, political science, and theology reason on that level (Rest, Davison, and Robbins, 1978).

Some evidence suggests that the failure to develop a high level of moral reasoning is in part the result of a failure to develop formal thought. Lawrence Kohlberg and Carol Gilligan (1971) found that a majority (60 percent) of people above sixteen showed advanced formal thought but that only a small proportion (10 percent) of them also showed a principled level of moral reasoning. On the other hand, every individual who showed principled reasoning was also capable of formal thought. Such results suggest that the development of formal thought is a necessary condition for principled moral reasoning, but that formal thought does not ensure the development of such reasoning.

Adolescents who have developed both formal thought and a principled level of moral reasoning are most likely to show a high degree of both morality and consistency in what they think and do. For example, significantly fewer college students at a principled level of moral reasoning cheated in situations that required them to resist temptation than did those at a conventional or premoral level (Kohlberg, 1969). The adolescents at a principled level seemed to define the tempting situations as ones that involved an implicit contract based on trust, whereas those at lower levels seemed to respond to the looseness and permissiveness of unsupervised situations.

College students at a principled level of moral reasoning showed a higher, more consistent level of moral conduct than other students in an experiment conducted by Stanley Milgram (1963). In this study, undergraduates were ordered to administer what they thought were increasingly severe electric shocks to a "victim," who was supposed to be a subject in a learning experiment but who was actually a stooge. Only thinking characteristic of a principled level of reasoning clearly defines the situation as one in which the experimenter has no moral right to insist that pain be inflicted on another person. Accordingly, 75 percent of the students who had been judged to be at a principled level refused to shock the victim, but only 13 percent of those judged to be at lower levels refused to administer the shock (Kohlberg, 1970).

Finally, a study by Norma Haan, M. Brewster Smith, and Jeanne Block (1968) examined the possible relationship between moral reasoning and civil disobedience. They studied University of California students in Berkely at the time of the original Free Speech Movement sit-in. Among these students, 80 percent of those who were at a principled level sat in as compared with only 10 percent of those who were at a conventional level. But 60 percent of those students who were at a premoral level also sat in. However, the premoral students reported different reasons for their actions from those given by the principled students. Consistent with their level of moral reasoning, the principled students reported concern with the basic issues of civil liberties and civil rights, and of the relationship of students as citizens within the university community, whereas the premoral students focused on the issue of their individual rights in a conflict with power. As the actions of these students show, similar conduct can result from widely varied moral reasoning.

IDENTITY: SELF AND SOCIETY

Although self-definition and self-esteem are important throughout the life cycle, during adolescence these matters become paramount. Developmental change often brings about a disruption of the concept of self. As Erik Erikson (1968) has pointed out, an adolescent's body goes through marked physical changes and is flooded with sexual impulses; the young person confronts both imminent intimacy with the other sex and an immediate future filled with conflicting possibilities and choices.

Before adolescents can regain a sense of unity with themselves and with the world about them, they must incorporate their new physical and sexual attributes and the opportunities they present into a new self-concept. A society that universally recognizes these changes and attaches meaning to them makes reworking self-concepts a relatively uncomplicated task. In a pluralistic society like our own, however, the prolongation of adolescence and its bewildering variety of choices can make the process difficult. In either case, Erikson has postulated a "developmental crisis," a moment when development must move one way or the other.

Erikson's concept of identity has two facets. It refers to feelings about one's self, or self-esteem, and to the relationship between self-concept and descriptions of the self by significant others.

Defining the Self

The childhood self reflects the immediate world of persons crucial to the child and is based on relatively simple identification with these people. Adolescents often must reexamine this self-concept, integrating it with their emerging cognitive and behavioral abilities and their new values and purposes.

There are wide individual differences in the methods that adolescents use to consolidate their self-concepts or to attain new ones (Newman, 1979; Marcia, 1980). One youthful solution involves a determined attempt to change society so as to bring it into line with the adolescent's principles and needs. Another solution is a systematic attempt to change the self so as to fit into the existing system with less anxiety or discomfort. A third approach is the effort to carve out some special niche within society where the qualities of one's self can be preserved, enhanced, or acted on.

Some developmental changes, however, can threaten the adolescent's integration of his or her childhood self-concept and lead to what Erikson (1968) called **totalism,** an organization of one's self-concept that has rigid, absolute, and arbitrary boundaries. Totalism makes adolescents particularly susceptible to totalitarian movements and to ideologies of the left and the right. According to Erikson, if adolescents feel their emerging identities severely threatened by historical or technological development, they become ready to support doctrines that allow them to immerse themselves in a synthetic identity, such as extreme nationalism, racism, or class consciousness, and to condemn the stereotyped enemy of their new identities. This tendency toward total immersion in a synthetic identity can take other forms, and it characterized the participation of many American adolescents in the civil rights movement of two decades ago and, more recently, in opposition to nuclear power and resistance to registration for the draft.

A similar immersion in the peer group can

By accepting the norms of the peer group as infallible, adolescents are able to break away from dependence on the family. *(Marion Bernstein)*

play a major role in regulating feelings and in emancipating the adolescent from childhood dependence. What Peter Blos (1962) has called **uniformism,** or immersion in the peer group and acceptance of its norms as infallible, may help an adolescent to move away from dependence on the family at a time when she or he still needs some external source of control. Sometimes an adolescent clings to this source of control long after the need for it has passed, and conformity to peer-group norms merely replaces conformity to parental norms. When this happens, development is foreclosed before the adolescent can achieve real self-regulation and independence.

Self-Esteem

Erikson (1968) has suggested that, at its best, identity is experienced as a sense of well-being. People with secure identities feel at home in their bodies, know where they are going, and feel assured of recognition from people who count (Marcia, 1980).

People with low self-esteem generally have an unstable self-concept, which means that they lack a consistent frame of reference within which to assimilate their experiences of self and others. Such a situation provokes anxiety, a state intensified by the strain of putting on a front. Persons with low self-esteem are more likely than others to be lonely. They tend to be vulnerable, sensitive to criticism, and bothered if others have a low opinion of them. Poor performance on a task disturbs them, and any awareness of a personal fault or inadequacy upsets them. Others may describe them as touchy or easily hurt.

As a result, adolescents with low self-esteem are awkward with others, assume that others do not like them, have little faith in human nature, and are submissive and nonassertive. They are unlikely to participate in extracurricular activities and are rarely selected for leadership positions. They tend to be unpopular and avoid participating in class discussions and informal conversations. Enmeshed in this pattern, adolescents with extremely low self-esteem become caught in a trap in which their isolation keeps them from developing a positive view of themselves. Their anxiety and vulnerability often keeps them from entering any social situation that might raise their self-esteem and thereby open the trap.

Links between self-esteem, social class, and ethnic status showed clearly in a survey that Morris Rosenberg (1965) made of 5,000 adolescents in New York State. He found that adolescents from upper socioeconomic groups were more likely than other adolescents to accept themselves, the class difference being greater for boys than for girls. Although adolescents from some sociocultural groups showed greater self-esteem than others, the general prestige of an adolescent's social group was not the major influence. Instead, self-esteem had more to do with the adolescent's experiences in family and peer groups. The social-class effect seemed connected to the support many fathers in upper socioeconomic groups extend to their sons.

Rosenberg found the lowest self-esteem among minorities within a single neighborhood. That is, being a Catholic in a predominantly Catholic neighborhood leads to higher self-esteem than being a Catholic in a predominantly Protestant neighborhood. This result helps to

PERSONALITY IN ADOLESCENCE

PSYCHODYNAMIC VIEWS

Sigmund Freud considered adolescence as the time when the last identifiable stage of psychosexual development, the genital stage, emerged. During this stage, the individual's identity takes its final form and, in place of narcissistic self-love, love for others and altruistic behavior develop. Although the influence of peers and parents is not as strong as it was during earlier stages, both continue to play an important role in providing love and realistic direction for the individual.

Erik Erikson sees self-definition and self-esteem as central concerns during adolescence. As several forces (physical changes, powerful sexual impulses, conflicting choices and possibilities, and confusion in the roles expected of them by parents and peers) converge, adolescents are confronted with an identity crisis. They must incorporate new physical and sexual attributes into a fresh self-concept. They also must develop an orientation and a goal that will give them a sense of unity and purpose so that they can make vocational choices that match their views of themselves. Finally, they must integrate into their self-understanding the expectations and perceptions that others have of them.

SOCIAL-LEARNING VIEW

Walter Mischel takes the view that as adolescents move out of childhood, they encounter a multiplicity of adult roles and expectations and that each of them requires the adolescent to learn new discriminations and make new responses. Physical and hormonal changes require the adolescent to learn patterns of socially appropriate sexual behavior. Social expectations and consequences also change during this time, forcing the adolescent to confront the responsibility of choosing a career. As agents of socialization, parents and peers continue to exert a strong influence on the adolescent's behavior.

explain the self-esteem of black adolescents from predominantly black inner-city neighborhoods, who generally escape the low self-esteem that might be anticipated on the basis of their group's low social prestige (Rosenberg, 1975). Cases of low self-esteem among black adolescents appear to relate more to their experiences in family, peer, and neighborhood groups than to their group's general level of prestige.

Concepts of Self and Others

Adolescents take a far less simplistic view of themselves and of others than they did as youngsters (Livesley and Bromley, 1973; Montemayor and Eisen, 1977), and their ability to consider possibilities enables them to think of themselves in terms of what might be. Indeed, Inhelder and Piaget (1958) point out that formal thought makes it possible for people to appreciate abstract ideals (such as honesty, courage, and love) and consequently to attach value to them. Thus as they proceed to form an identity, adolescents must consider their own impressions of self and the impressions of others about them, using formal thought to integrate their self-concepts.

Self-Concept An effective integration of self-concept requires adolescents to monitor their own mental activity; they must think about their thought. Such reflective thought appeared in a study by W. J. Livesley and D. B. Bromley (1973), which detected a qualitative change in self-descriptions around the age of thirteen or fourteen. Adolescents used descriptive terms more flexibly and precisely than younger children did, often adding subtle qualifying and connecting terms.

Most impressive in the self-descriptions written by adolescents was the change in organization. Younger children's impressions were like beads on a string, but adolescents selected and organized their ideas in a coherent and complex fashion. They tended to refer to ambitions, aspirations, wants, needs, expectations, fear, wishes, self-reproaches, beliefs, attitudes, values, and comparisons with others. Some of these attributes clearly appear in a fourteen-year-old girl's description of herself:

> I am a very temperamental person, sometimes, well *most* of the time, I am happy. Then now and again I just go moody for no reason at all. I enjoy being different from everybody else, and like to think of myself as being fairly modern. Up till I was about 11, I was a pretty regular churchgoer (R.C.) but since then I have been thinking about religion and sometimes I do not believe in God. When I am nervous I talk a lot, and this gives some important new acquaintances a bad impression, when I am trying to make a good one. I worry a lot about getting married and having a family, because I am frightened that I will make a mess of it. (p. 239–240)

Self-Consciousness As the concept of self develops, so does an adolescent's self-consciousness—a concern with what others think of one. This heightened self-consciousness, suggests David Elkind (1980), is the result of the young adolescent's belief that other people share the adolescent's own preoccupation with him or herself and hence are always noticing the young person's appearance, behavior, and actions.

Elkind and Robert Bowen (1979) studied children and adolescents and found that self-consciousness shows a developmental trend, peaking in early adolescence and then subsiding. The investigators asked young people to imagine themselves in a number of situations in which they would have to reveal either their "transient selves" (momentary appearance or behavior, such as soiled clothing or inadvertent acts, which people do not regard as reflecting their true selves) or their "abiding selves" (mental ability or personality traits that people regard as permanent aspects of the self). These two concepts of self, believe Elkind and Bowen, are at first fused, and they separate only when children reach the concrete-operational stage.

Except for ten-year-old boys, both children and adolescents were more reluctant to reveal their "real" selves than their transient selves, perhaps because only aspects of the abiding self were linked with self-esteem on another test. Young adolescents were the most self-conscious about revealing either their abiding or their transient selves in all situations—again except for ten-year-old boys, who were just as reluctant to expose their transient selves as were fourteen- and fifteen-year-old boys. Thus, a fourteen-year-old who had discovered a split side seam in his or her jeans might agree to work a problem at the blackboard in front of the class, but the youngster would either hold a hand over the gaping seam or else try to turn it away from the class. Children and older adolescents were both likely to say the split seam would not bother them. Girls were more self-conscious than boys in every age group, and a fourteen-year-old girl might say that she would refuse to get up in front of the class wearing split jeans.

Concepts of Others Our interpretations of others come from our knowledge of how they have acted in the past, from cues in the immediate environment, and from what we know about ourselves. For in the last instance, we can only know about others' feelings and intentions by making inferences based on our own perceptions, emotions, and knowledge (Barenboim, 1981). Most adolescents have become increasingly proficient at these skills and see subtleties and complexities that were missing in their earlier views. They not only infer another's reactions but often attempt to explain them as well.

Although adolescents' descriptions of others may take the same egocentric-sounding form as the eight-year-old's "We play together" or "She sits with me," they are likely to have a different conceptual base. According to Terry Honess (1980), the adolescent often qualifies his or her description ("We *try* to wear the same clothes") or indicates an interpersonal involvement ("We share our troubles"). Such descriptions apparently reflect interpersonal closeness and understanding, not egocentrism.

In other studies (Livesley and Bromley,

1973), adolescents' analyses and interpretations of another's behavior showed an increased concern with making the description convincing. That is, in describing another person, only adolescents would report an impression of the person and hastily add a qualifier to prevent an inaccurate conclusion. For example, a fifteen-year-old might say of a friend, "He is daring—but not reckless." In order to make such a statement, the adolescent had to engage in reflective thought, considering other people's possible misinterpretations of the description.

Sex-Role Stereotypes As children develop, their conformity to traditional sex-role stereotypes does not remain stable. The stereotypes of "boy" and "girl" held by four-year-olds loosen during middle childhood, only to tighten again during early adolescence (Ullian, 1976).

It appears that during certain periods of life, most people find it useful to live within the confines of traditional sex roles, and in these same periods, there is accompanying social pressure to conform. Since adolescents are uncertain about their sex roles, conformity helps ease the uncertainty, leading most of them to retreat to the safety of sex-role stereotypes.

One place where the retreat to stereotypes shows clearly is in adolescents' responses to babies. Shirley Feldman, Sharon Nash, and Carolyn Cutrona (1977) watched children and adolescents react to a baby who was playing on the floor near them. Younger girls and boys showed a similar degree of interest, but adolescent girls paid more attention to the baby than did adolescent boys. Similar studies of adults have shown that this sex difference soon disappears.

When Ann Frodi and Michael Lamb (1978) measured children's reactions to crying and smiling babies, they found no difference between the sexes, whether at eight or fourteen years. Children and adolescents of both sexes showed the same increased heart rate and skin conductance when the baby cried. They felt distressed, irritated, unhappy, and sorry for the infant. When the baby smiled, their heart rates slowed and they felt good about it. Yet when these same young people were sitting near a baby, the adolescent boys interacted less with the baby than did the younger boys, and the adolescent girls interacted more than did the younger girls. The lack of sex differences on the physiological measures, coupled with strong sex differences in behavior, suggest that these behavior differences are largely a matter of learning, not biology.

Despite their changed behavior, individual adolescents see themselves as being less stereotypical than the rest of the world. In Katheryn Urberg's (1979) study of sex-role development, when twelfth graders described themselves, there was only one significant difference between the self-portrayals of boys and of girls. Girls saw themselves as more dependent than boys did. But when adolescents described the ideal person, stereotypes swarmed in for both sexes, and their descriptions of the opposite gender were always more stereotypical than their descriptions of their own gender. Seventh graders and adults (whether aged twenty or sixty-five) had similar and much less stereotypical views of males and females than did twelfth graders.

Vocational Identity

During adolescence, gender-role concepts, self-concepts, and future occupational possibilities combine to narrow a person's vocational alternatives and orientations (Sommer, 1978). For the male in our society, competence in a vocational role is as fundamental a dimension of his identity as is his masculinity in the sex role. For a majority of adolescent girls, at least at the present time, occupation is not the predominant concern; instead, they focus on the establishment and maintenance of interpersonal relationships (Marcia, 1980). As a result, marriage plays a dominant role in the identity formation and achievement of girls, with occupational plans viewed as optional or secondary (Tavris and Offir, 1977).

Cognition and Choice Adolescents' capacity to generate possibilities and to reason from them means that their vocational thinking need not be restricted by their personal exposure to the world of work and the people in it, and that they can match their personal attributes to future vocational possibilities. One factor that affects adolescents' choice of an occupation is the prestige they attribute to it, although as we will see, family and socioeconomic factors heavily influence the selection.

Developmental studies of occupational preferences provide an excellent example of the effects of cognitive organizational ability on career choice. Before children are eleven, their thinking about a vocation appears to be primarily subjective. Their preferences are based on occupational stereotypes and are unrelated to any assessment of their aptitude or other personal characteristics. They also seem unaware of the opportunities before them or the barriers that may stand in the way of their goals (Jordaan and Heyde, 1978).

Most adolescents being to crystallize their occupational choices when they are about thirteen or fourteen. But even fourteen-year-olds know little about the choices that they soon must face, about the decision pathways any alternative might lead to, or about the irreversibility of some choices. An individual's appreciation of the role played by his or her personal opportunities and by harsh economic realities in vocational choice continues to grow throughout adolescence. High-school seniors, for example, are more likely than younger adolescents to say they understand the necessity for choosing an occupation, and they are also more able to consider relevant factors when making that choice (Jordaan and Heyde, 1978).

An increasing stability of occupational choice is also characteristic of adolescence. Among fifteen-year-olds, the occupation named by a student on one occasion is likely to change by the next time he or she is asked about a chosen career. Only in later adolescence do more stable choices emerge. In one study, as few as 17 percent of the boys and 26 percent of the girls had the same vocational plans a year after graduation that they had had in the ninth grade (Project Talent, 1966). Individual differences in stability of occupational choice continue throughout adolescence; as many as half of young people in college change their career goals before graduation (D. Super, 1976). However, many of these changes remain within the same general family of occupations, because the process of career choice soon becomes nearly irreversible. Each choice adolescents make increasingly limits their range of remaining choices and absolutely precludes some careers.

Gender Differences Charting the identity of the adolescent girl remains difficult, since most adolescent psychology has been devoted to the psychology of the male adolescent. Despite the fact that during adolescence sex differences are more pronounced than at any other period of life, little research has been done on the adolescent girl (Adelson, 1980). We do know that many girls are still traditionally socialized, which means that they focus on interpersonal skills and the capacity for intimacy. For such girls, prior gender learning has pointed them directly toward marriage. A dependence on the marital role can teach a girl to derive her sense of esteem from her relationship to loved ones and from their achievements rather than her own. This kind of socialization has led Judith Bardwick (1971) to suggest that fear of the loss of love is a major motive for most women in our society and that such fear tends to result in emotional dependence among women who fail to develop any sense of vocational identity beyond that of wife and mother. Among males, on the other hand, identity is a far more active issue in adolescence and tends to center around the interrelated themes of autonomy, achievement, and vocational choice (Marcia, 1980).

As yet, no data contradict the assertion that most girls continue to be socialized in the traditional feminine gender role and that many of them prefer it (e.g., Bush et al., 1977–1978; Feather, 1980). However, investigators (Bardwick, 1971; Douvan, 1975; Frieze et al., 1978; Marcia, 1980) have detected a new feminine pattern in which achievement is as important as interpersonal success and traditional feminine behavior. Indeed, some investigators have pro-

FEAR OF SUCCESS

Achievement appears to develop differently in boys than in girls, and adolescent girls may feel an ambivalence about surpassing boys or succeeding in traditional male pursuits. This ambivalence, according to Matina Horner (1969), develops into a "fear of success." Girls learn early that achievement in the world is "aggressive" and therefore masculine (Tavris and Offir, 1977), and that if they defeat males in competition, they may be punished. When girls or women discover that aversive social consequences follow when they expend effort, persist in the face of obstacles, or compete and actually succeed, they may learn to withdraw from achievement situations or avoid them. At the very least, they may learn to play down their accomplishments. They withdraw, then, not because they are afraid of failing but because they are afraid of succeeding.

Subsequent research has shown that the situation is not quite that simple. Men and boys frequently show as much fear of success as girls and women do; and male college students who feel threatened by female competence score high on tests that measure fear of success, whereas their girl friends do not (Tresemer, 1974). The standard test requires a person to complete a story that begins with a male or female in a moment of high success. If that success is followed in the person's story with images of failure, "fear of success" has been demonstrated. Males tend to show an increased fear of success when writing about a female in a nontraditional situation ("Ann finds herself at the top of her medical-school class").

The developmental course of this impulse appeared when John Condry and Sharon Dyer (1977) studied it in a competitive situation. Fifth- to ninth-grade boys and girls, working by themselves but seated in pairs opposite each other, unscrambled anagrams as part of an "intelligence test." Afterward, they were taken to another room, one at a time, ostensibly for another test but actually to be told that they had "won" over their partner of the opposite sex. Then they returned to the testing room, where they were seated opposite the same partner and asked to unscramble more anagrams. If they feared success, they would not do so well on their second try with anagrams.

On the second test, fifth-grade girls and boys both improved—and by about the same amount. Among adolescents the picture was very different. The scores of seventh-grade girls plummeted while the scores of seventh-grade boys improved. The scores of ninth-grade boys went up substantially, and the girls' average scores also improved, but only by a slight amount. Placed in direct competition, neither girls nor boys in the fifth or ninth grades nor boys in the seventh grade showed any fear of success. But told they were outperforming a male, seventh-grade girls retreated. Their achievement was severely affected, despite the fact that they understood they were taking an intelligence test that might be expected to affect their academic futures. These girls simply withdrew from competition. In addition, when Condry and Dyer analyzed individual scores, they found a curious pattern among ninth-grade girls. Half of these older adolescents improved as much as the boys did, and half showed disastrous declines.

Condry and Dyer believe their study of actual behavior is in line with traditional sex-role development, in which adolescents show increased adherence to stereotypical views of appropriate gender behavior. By the time girls are in the ninth grade, many are in the stage of formal-operational thought, and those that have reached that cognitive level are able to break the restriction of stereotypes. Yet given a standard story-completion test, fifth-grade girls fear success more than do fifth-grade boys, but ninth-grade girls show less fear than boys of the same age. The discrepancy between behavior and performance on tests purporting to measure fear of success indicates that such tests may, as Condry and Dyer (1976) have suggested, be contaminated by knowledge of the social consequences that can befall a girl or woman who steps too far outside the boundaries of accepted female behavior. So when asked to predict the results of nontraditional behavior in others, people foretell unpopularity, loneliness, failure, lack of a husband, and loss of femininity.

posed that women are afraid to achieve, as the accompanying box indicates. Most girls who fit this new pattern come from upwardly mobile middle- and upper-middle-class families. The pattern appeared as early as 1966 among several thousand adolescents interviewed by Elizabeth Douvan and Joseph Adelson (1966), who found a group of girls with aspirations directed toward their own achievements rather than the status of their future husbands. These girls showed a greater interest in assuming adult roles and responsibilities than did traditional girls, and their perspective extended further into the future. Girls in this group more often dreamed of individual achievement, and they tended to judge prospective jobs by success criteria. As society provides greater support for dual family and career roles, and as girls who choose careers and reject motherhood come to be less frequently stigmatized, the number of girls who show this kind of feminine pattern will undoubtedly grow.

PEER RELATIONS AND THEIR INFLUENCE

The peer group can be a major influence in resolving an identity crisis (Erikson, 1968). For instance, in assuming the badges of clique membership, the fads of dress and appearance, an adolescent is borrowing a stereotypic identity as a temporary defense against the loss of his or her own identity. This sort of behavior is an example of adolescent uniformism. By their clannishness, intolerance, and cruelty toward outsiders, adolescents can temporarily clarify who they are by affirming who they are not. But the peer group also offers positive opportunities and rewards that are crucial to identity formation. With peers, the adolescent can try on new roles, using the reactions of others to judge how well the roles fit his or her self-concept. As peer relationships are transformed during adolescence, friendship also changes, moving from the congenial sharing of activities to psychological sharing and intimacy.

Friendship

In terms of what they expect of friends and what they like best about them, children are likely to mention play and to expect their friends to be fun or entertaining. But like adults, adolescents generally expect their friends to be useful—someone to do things with or to provide help when it is needed (Reisman and Schorr, 1978).

Although usefulness is a prime quality in the choice of friends, similar personal characteristics are a major determinant of whether any two people will form a friendship (Byrne, 1971). Studies suggest that obvious similarities are most important in the early stages of friendship, when people tend to assess others on the basis of such categories as physical characteristics, roles, or activities. But in friendships that last, the persons involved discover that they see the world of psychological intentions, motives, causes, and characteristics in the same way. In lasting friendships, the friends describe each other in terms of psychological categories such as "sly" or "tries hard," sharing a way of perceiving and thinking about the less obvious attributes of self and others (Duck, 1973; 1977).

This trend increases during adolescence. For example, Stephen Duck (1973) found that only 5 percent of the twelve-year-olds he studied used psychological constructs to describe others and that the number rose to 25 percent among fourteen- and fifteen-year-olds. Among college students, 63 percent described others in terms of psychological characteristics.

The developmental course of friendship parallels this view. Friendships among girls appear to progress from the activity-centered pairs of late childhood and preadolescence to the interdependent, emotional, and conflict-resolving relationships of middle adolescence, finally becoming relationships that are less emotional, less an instrument for reducing conflict, and more a sharing of personalities, talents, and interests (Douvan and Adelson, 1966). Friendships between two adolescent girls are more intimate than those between boys, with girls showing stronger attachment, greater sharing, and deeper trust and loyalty than boys (Sharabany,

Friendships among adolescent girls tend to be intense, emotional, and reciprocal, with each friend meeting the other's needs. *(Marion Bernstein)*

Gershoni, and Hofman, 1981).

As a result, junior-high and high-school boys appear to be less concerned with the personal relationship involved in friendship. Their friendships are more like those found among preadolescent girls and involve a congenial companion with whom one shares the same reality-oriented activities (Fine, 1981). Males are also more likely than females to spend their adolescent social lives in cliques and gangs instead of in pairs. This gender difference is part of a larger pattern of gender-role differences that make interpersonal relationships a major factor in the formation of identity among most females in this society.

Cliques

Because many young adolescents believe that everyone admires a person who belongs to a special group, acceptance into a clique enhances their self-esteem (Elkind, 1980). Being a clique member indicates to adolescents that they are indeed special, and unpopular adolescents are often shut out of these special groups.

Popularity Children who are popular with their peers are likely to be popular adolescents as well; popularity rankings generally remain stable throughout childhood and adolescence (Roff, Sells, and Golden, 1972). Popularity is highly related to conformity to peer-group norms, customs, and fads. During adolescence, as in childhood, the characteristics having most to do with peer acceptance are those that define appropriate sex-typed behavior in our society. Athletic participation and skill, standing up for one's rights, sexual prowess, and sometimes drinking prowess are valued in the adolescent boy. The popular girl is one who is fun to be with and who has interpersonal skills. Because these characteristics bring with them the positive consequences of peer acceptance, they are in turn strengthened, so that participation in peer activities reinforces childhood sex-role learning. This continuity in socialization may be largely responsible for the general stability of popularity ratings.

Another factor that has an important impact on popularity is physical attractiveness (Cavior and Dokecki, 1973). Although adolescents and young adults often say that they are looking for honesty and sincerity in the opposite sex, when it comes to dating, they forget what they have said about personal characteristics and pursue the most attractive members of the opposite sex.

Attractiveness may affect friendship and dating patterns differently, as Dennis Krebs and Allen Adinolfi (1975) discovered when they investigated friendship and dating choices of sixty male and sixty female residents of a student dormitory. Each resident chose the persons they liked and disliked most. The most liked persons were students who were attractive but not stunning. The most attractive students were rejected most frequently by members of their own sex, and the least attractive students were chosen neither as most nor as least liked—they were simply ignored.

Dating itself is powerfully influenced by peer pressure. When adolescents fail to date, they may be dropped by their peer group and later readmitted when they begin to date. As a result, chronological age, which is related to peer patterns of behavior, is a better predictor of the onset of dating than is sexual maturation (Dornbusch et al., 1981).

Structural Changes in the Peer Group Adolescence brings a new element to peer relations: sexual maturation and heterosexual behavior. And the structure of the peer group changes to accommodate these developments. At first, the peer group is similar to the preadolescent gang; it is a clique of adolescents of the same sex. Then, about midadolescence, it becomes heterosexual, and each member generally establishes a significant relationship with a member of the opposite sex. Once the basic role characteristics underlying these relationships are thoroughly acquired, the group breaks up into cliques of loosely associated couples, as members approach marriage (Dunphy, 1963).

Dexter Dunphy and other observers have found that group members generally deny the existence of a hierarchy within the group. However, this is not always the case, as Ritch Savin-Williams (1979) found in a study of twelve- to fourteen-year-olds at a summer camp. Dominance hierarchies in the boys' cabins were frankly recognized, but in only two of the four girls' cabins did the girls agree on the ranking of leaders and followers. Leaders among both sexes were self-confident, "cool," mature, athletic, intelligent, and popular. Boy leaders asserted themselves physically, argued with others, and tended to threaten and displace their cabinmates. Girls controlled by recognizing the status of their cabinmates, giving unsolicited advice and information to some and shunning or ignoring others. Leaders took the biggest pieces of cake at dinner, the preferred seats at discussions, and the best sleeping sites near the campfire at campouts. The rankings, says Savin-Williams, appeared to add stability and predictability to social relationships and to reduce group friction and overt aggression. Leaders took on group obligations; dominant girls, for example, often intervened in squabbles and patched interpersonal relationships.

Leaders are useful to their groups, and often their status depends on some combination of personal attributes and material resources. In male cliques, high status generally goes to the assertive, actively sociable, and intellectually able boy (Hartup, 1970). In some groups, however, an adolescent may win status by virtue of

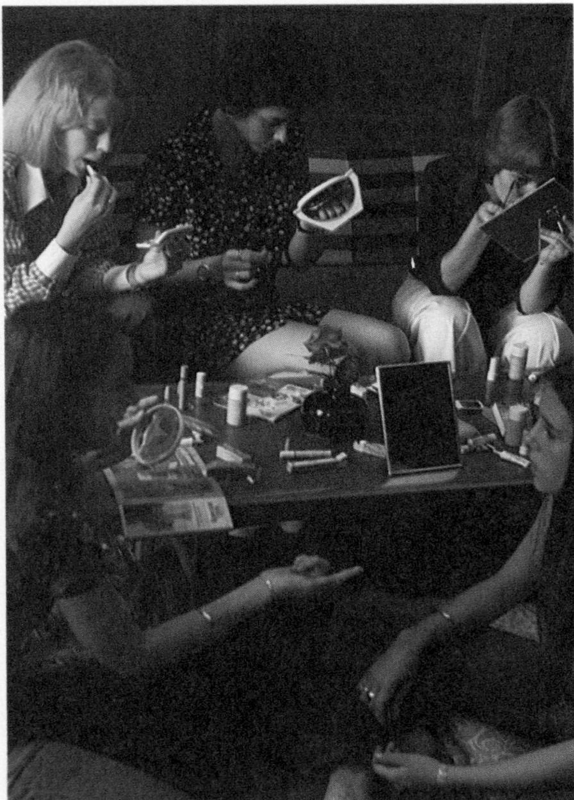

Leaders in the adolescent peer group tend to be self-confident, "cool," mature, athletic, intelligent, and popular. *(© Leonard Speier)*

unique social or athletic skills or by the possession of a car or money or access to a suitable place for the group's activities. Changes in group goals are likely to lead to fluctuations in the hierarchy; as activities change, the resources of different members may become important. Thus, status rankings over the months and years are less stable than popularity ratings. The relationship between leadership in adolescence and success in adulthood is not clear; in fact, a repeated finding is that the rate of skeletal maturity in adolescence (i.e., early or late maturing) is a better predictor of adult leadership and occupational success than is leadership in the peer group (Livson and Peskin, 1980).

FAMILY RELATIONS AND THEIR INFLUENCE

For some young people, the gradual move from childhood dependence toward ever greater involvement with the wider world is fraught with tension and conflict, but others move away from their families with only minor internal turmoil (Rutter, 1979). Most young adolescents feel some ambivalence about their state of dependence or independence, and the provocativeness of adolescents toward parents often can be understood in the context of this ambivalence. Indeed, it is by alternating between provocative self-assertion and childlike requests for help that many adolescents gradually become able to emerge from their families.

Despite ambivalent family relations, parents and the home environment have lasting influences on such basic decisions as the adolescent's choice of occupation. In addition, adolescents whose parents have fostered a high level of self-esteem look forward to the world of work with high aspirations and confidence; adolescents with low self-esteem place the same importance on occupational success but believe that they are unlikely to attain it (Rosenberg and Simmons, 1972). As they did during childhood, parents model and reinforce attitudes and values about work in general and about particular kinds of jobs. They also may provide support when their children show high levels of educational and occupational aspiration.

Social-Class Differences

Investigators have repeatedly discovered that adolescents from low-status families select high-status occupations less often than might be expected, whereas adolescents from high-status families select high-status occupations more often than chance would suggest (e.g., Elder, 1968). Some developmentalists have suggested that the difference comes about because higher- and lower-status families ascribe different levels of prestige to various occupations. Other researchers suggest that the difference reflects differing perceptions as to the accessibility of occupations (Caro and Pihlblad, 1965).

Middle-Class Families Most middle-class adolescents have been encouraged from childhood to act independently and to take personal responsibility (Kohn, 1977). When children misbehave, their parents reason with them, teaching them that they can and should control their own behavior on the basis of an internalized set of standards. The development of self-control is often the conscious goal of middle-class parents.

As middle-class children grow into adolescence, they increasingly participate in decisions that affect them. By late adolescence they will make many of their own decisions about peers, jobs, and money, either by themselves or in consultation with their parents. As a result, the middle-class adolescent is trained for the sort of autonomy that most can later exercise in a job or career.

Adolescents from upper-middle-class families (professional and managerial occupations) and from lower-middle-class families (semiprofessional, semimanagerial, white-collar, and skilled-crafts occupations) generally learn as children that their lives are under their own control and that they can achieve occupational status and other external symbols of success through their personal efforts (Kohn, 1979). But the two groups differ in an important respect. The experiences of upper-middle-class adolescents are likely to have prepared them for careers, and they grow up believing in the importance of delaying gratification in the interest of future success (Mischel and Mischel, 1976). They are also likely to value their cognitive competencies, because the future roles they are being socialized for involve using the head more than the hands (R. Hess, 1970).

For the most part, lower-middle-class adolescents' experiences make them look forward to *jobs,* not careers (Kohn, 1977). They will value individualism and take an activistic stance toward the world and their future in it. However, lower-middle-class adolescents and their parents are likely to see that future in terms of the security, stability, and respectability that jobs bring, rather than as opportunities for development, intrinsic satisfaction, or self-actualization.

Middle-class adolescents have developed attitudes that lead them to accept prolonged schooling, a delay of gratification that is less likely to be embraced by working- and lower-class adolescents. *(© Frank Siteman 1981/Taurus Photos)*

Whether from professional or white-collar families, most upper- and lower-middle-class young people share attitudes and beliefs that correspond to those demanded by schools and colleges (Feather, 1980). The idea of prolonged schooling, therefore, is more likely to make sense to them than it does to youths from other social strata.

Working- and Lower-Class Families Working-class parents seem to begin later than middle-class parents to train their children for independence, and they are less likely to permit their offspring to help establish the rules for appropriate behavior (Kohn, 1979). They are likely to value obedience instead of self-control and may often teach their children conformity to authority. On the other hand, working-class parents are less likely than middle-class parents to monitor an adolescent's activities outside the family circle (Blau, 1972). Although working-class adolescents are, therefore, freer from parental supervision than are middle-class adolescents, when questions of obedience do arise, parent-child conflict is likely to be greater.

Going to college, and thereby delaying immediate gratification in the interest of future success, is not likely to make much sense to many adolescents from lower-class families that depend on irregular employment in marginal work roles or on welfare funds. Nor is it likely to be appealing to the children of regularly employed working-class parents (semiskilled or unskilled blue-collar workers). Although working-class parents take pride in their regular employment, they rarely move up; the tasks that they perform are simple, specialized, circumscribed, and repetitive. If they work in a factory, the pace and rhythm of work is imposed from above by supervisors and technicians. The worker on an assembly line is rewarded for following orders and coordinating his or her work with the rest of the line, not for showing self-direction, individuality, or innovative techniques (Blau, 1972). It is not difficult to see how conforming to authority becomes an important aspect of working-class life, and this conformity is reflected in the socialization of working-class children and adolescents (Kohn, 1977).

Among many working-class families, employment is valued primarily as a means of providing the goods and services that lead to satisfaction in the extended family. A collectivistic orientation is likely to prevail, so that loyalty to the family may stand in the way of the decisions that would permit an adolescent to move out of the working class. Actions that are taken for granted by middle-class adolescents, such as moving away, going to school in another city or state, and taking advantage of opportunities that may weaken bonds with family members, are usually less possible for working-class youth.

Lower-class adolescents tend to adjust their job desires to what they think they can reasonably hope to achieve. When black youths from the lower class look around them, they are unlikely to expect much from life. The unemployment rate among black youths runs about 40 percent, and some inner-city blacks may live their entire lives without ever securing a regular job. The only choices they may believe are open to them are welfare, odd jobs, or hustling.

As a result of socioeconomic factors, the adolescent from a lower-class inner-city background is likely to have an external locus of control, characterized by a passive, even fatalistic attitude. "Luck" is a frequent explanation for both accomplishments and setbacks. In such an environment, children and adolescents have few experiences that lead them to believe in a rewarding world. The strategies that seem appropriate are those directed not toward careers but toward survival (Rainwater, 1966; Sharff, 1981). In a survival-oriented economy, gratifications of the present are important. The child or adolescent has few opportunities to learn that active individual effort might pay off in the interest of some long-term goal, whether that effort means studying now for a good report card or earning money to save for a car.

Adolescent Conformity

Some accounts of adolescent development assume that as a child reaches adolescence, conformity to parents' wishes decreases and conformity to peer wishes increases. Other discussions assume that conflict between peer and parental standards inevitably accompanies adolescence. Yet no evidence has demonstrated that the onset of adolescence necessarily means any decrease in conformity to parental demands (J. C. Coleman, 1980). Studies reviewed by Willard Hartup (1970) suggest that conformity to peer wishes increases in childhood, reaches its maximum around puberty, and then decreases in later adolescence. This same trend appeared in a more recent study by Thomas Berndt (1979), who found conflict between parental standards and those of the peer group strong among fourteen-year-olds, especially with respect to antisocial behavior. But among sixteen- and seventeen-year-olds, the conflict had lessened; they no longer felt compelled to conform to their peers' wishes. In addition, they were beginning to accept conventional adult standards for their behavior.

Studies of adolescent drug use illustrate the continuing link between adult and adolescent standards. Every study of alcohol use has found that the drinking patterns of teen-agers directly reflect those of their parents and the community in which they live. About two-thirds of all adults in the United States drink on occasion, and drinking is more prevalent among persons of higher social status than among those of lower social status. Margaret Bacon and Mary Brush Jones (1968) found that most adolescents who drink tend to drink moderately, begin drinking at home with their parents, and follow the rules of alcohol consumption that their parents set. They also found that drinking among adolescents varies from 86 percent in Nassau County, New York, to 44 percent in rural Kansas. Other studies (e.g., Maddox and McCall, 1964) also show that teen-age drinking patterns imitate adult drinking patterns: boys drink more than girls; city adolescents drink more than country adolescents; middle- and upper-middle-class adolescents drink more than working- or lower-class adolescents.

Because adolescents have learned from their parents and other adults to perceive drinking as an explicitly social affair, peer-group norms for acceptable drinking behavior tend to keep such behavior in line. Thus when adolescents drink in the secrecy of the peer group, social control remains present.

Smoking is one area where parental admonitions appear to have little effect, and most psychologists believe that peer pressure is a primary cause of adolescent smoking. Adolescents know about the risks connected with cigarettes, but since the effects do not appear for decades, young people are not gravely concerned about

When adolescents drink, they are likely to follow the adult drinking patterns prevalent in their own social class, sex, and area. *(© Lawrence Frank)*

the personal consequences (Evans, 1976). As a result, 20 percent of girls and 21 percent of boys have established regular smoking patterns by the time they enter high school (U.S. Department of Health, Education, and Welfare, 1976).

If peer pressure is indeed an important factor in adolescent smoking, then self-confident individuals should be the most resistant and, therefore, the least likely to smoke. A study sponsored by the American Cancer Society showed that this was true among boys but not among girls. Boys who smoked were less self-confident than boys who did not smoke, but girls who smoked were more self-confident than girls who did not. The girl smokers were also heavier smokers and more socially outgoing than the boys, but the girls did not regard smoking as a social asset. Many girls and women believe, however, that by keeping them from eating, smoking helps control their weight.

Adolescent use of other drugs alarms parents, but as with alcohol and tobacco, adult behavior serves as a model. Adolescents have had more than a decade of exposure to adults whose behavior—whether legal or illegal—has been a model for their own experimentation and for the

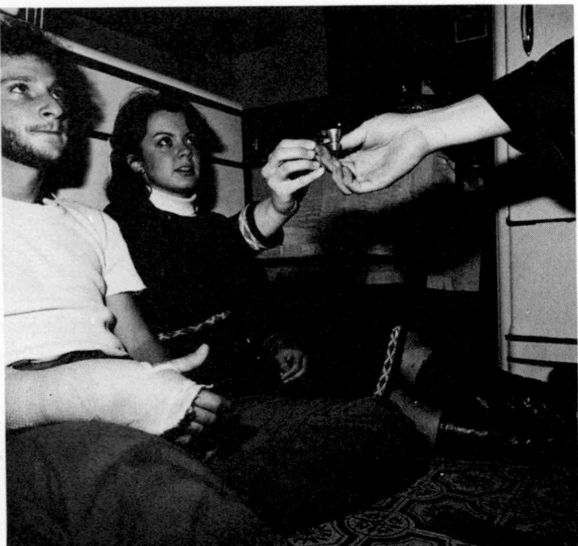

Although heavy drug-users tend to be male, more than a third of all high school seniors use marijuana at least once a month. *(Judy Herzl/The Picture Cube)*

control of group behavior. But adults who smoke, drink alcohol, or take tranquilizers or barbiturates tend to ignore these connections and consider drugs as a purely adolescent problem.

Despite press reports that alcohol consumption by young people was increasing rapidly while marijuana usage was falling off, a national survey of high-school seniors found no such trend (Johnston, Bachman, and O'Malley, 1977). High-school seniors were polled in 1975 and again in 1977, and daily use of alcohol remained constant (6 percent) while daily use of marijuana increased (from 6 percent in 1975 to 9 percent in 1977). When asked whether they had taken either drug within the past thirty days, 68 percent of the 1975 high-school seniors had drunk alcohol and 27 percent had used marijuana; in 1977, 71 percent of the seniors had drunk alcohol within the last thirty days and 35 percent of them had used marijuana. The study notes that heavy drug users tend to be male: 12 percent of male high-school seniors use marijuana daily as compared with 6 percent of the females; and 9 percent of males use alcohol daily as compared with 4 percent of the females.

Although marijuana is considered by some as "the first step" on the path to illicit drug usage, two longitudinal surveys by Denise Kandel (1975) among New York State high-school students indicate that it is better considered as a second or third step along the path. Other research supports this view (Huba, Wingard, and Bentler, 1981). Legal drugs, such as beer, wine, distilled beverages, and cigarettes, nearly always precede use of marijuana. For example, 27 percent of high-school students who both smoke and drink hard liquor progress to marijuana, but only 2 percent of those who neither smoke nor drink do so (Kandel, 1975). Among high-school marijuana users, 26 percent go on to LSD, amphetamines, or heroin; only 1 percent of students who use no drugs at all make the progression to hard drugs, and only 4 percent of those who use tobacco or alcohol make the jump. Using a particular drug does not mean that a student will invariably move on to the next drug in the path (Rutter, 1979).

The Generation Gap

The generation gap has been overstated and oversold by the mass media, bewildered parents, and the community. Manifestations of rebelliousness are by no means universal among the young, and adolescence is frequently a more peaceful and less conflict-filled period than it is generally held to be (Offer, Ostrow, and Howard, 1981). Some exaggerations of the generation gap go back to the activism of a few students in the 1960s and the sensationalized counterculture that developed in the country's elite colleges and universities (Feather, 1980). Other exaggerations come from earlier studies of adolescents that, after demonstrating the negative impacts of peer standards on school achievement and on the self-esteem of high achievers, concluded not only that a powerful adolescent society existed but also that adolescents' families progressively lost any ability to influence them.

Since that time, many studies of adolescents have documented the existence of an adolescent society, yet they have always found its connections to adult society to be far more robust than earlier conclusions would lead one to believe (J. C. Coleman, 1980). A number of studies (Brittain, 1963; Young and Ferguson, 1979) suggest that adolescents conform to peers in matters pertaining to choice of friends, language fads, and clothes but conform to parental values in matters pertaining to moral behavior and achievement, including academic performance and job or career aspirations. Similarly, numerous studies of political attitudes have shown close agreement between parents and adolescents, the generations parting sharply only over such matters as sex and drugs (Gallatin, 1980).

Studies by Denise Kandel and Gerald Lesser (1972) compared adolescents and their parents in the United States and in Denmark. They found that in both countries parental influence on an adolescent's life goals is much stronger than is peer influence. Although they confirmed earlier findings that adolescents rarely reward intellectual achievement in their peers, they also found that peers have less influence than parents on adolescents' future educational goals. This finding of close and harmonious relationships with parents is supported by research conducted by Daniel Offer, Eric Ostrow, and Kenneth Howard (1981) among adolescents in the United States, Australia, Ireland, and Israel. Most adolescents believe their parents are patient and supportive and that they are proud of their offspring. In none of the societies was there evidence of a generation gap.

Kandel and Lesser concluded that interactions with peers often support parental values and that the adolescent subculture is coordinated with the culture of the larger society. Their work, along with the research on drinking patterns and later studies (Timpane et al., 1976), suggests that the specter of the generation gap arises because the young openly express the divisions that exist within society. When they can attribute social problems to a generation gap, adults may find differences that come from race, class, or conflict of interest less threatening.

Despite frequent disagreements between parents and their adolescent children over behavior, most adolescents believe that their parents are patient and supportive and that they are proud of their offspring. *(Thomas Hopker/Woodfin Camp & Assoc.)*

Of course, adolescent social behavior varies widely from situation to situation. As Chapters 13 and 15 indicated, children learn very early, from parental reinforcement of their behavior, how to behave at different times and in different places. By adolescence, they have become expert discrimination learners and respond on the basis of the cues built into each situation. Thus differences in the adolescent's behavior within the family and in the peer group should be expected.

Parents and their adolescent children frequently disagree, and each often feels that the other simply does not understand. Friction over choices of friends, clothes, hair styles, use of the family car or telephone, family responsibilities, attitudes toward parents, grades, study habits, drugs, drinking, smoking, sex, and staying out of trouble may arise. But as long as adolescents live at home, their parents continue to exert a major influence on their behavior. As they have done for years, parents grant, withdraw, and reinstate

FAMILY RELATIONSHIPS IN ADOLESCENCE				
Item	Americans	Australian	Irish	Israeli
My parents will be disappointed with me in the future.	7%	11%	12%	8%
Understanding my parents is beyond me.	19%	23%	19%	17%
I can count on my parents most of the time.	76%	74%	79%	68%
When my parents are strict, I feel that they are right even if I get angry.	56%	69%	63%	64%
I feel that I have a part in making family decisions.	71%	63%	69%	24%
My parents are usually patient with me.	80%	81%	86%	85%
Usually, I feel that I am a bother at home.	23%	31%	28%	11%
Most of the time my parents are satisfied with me.	87%	87%	83%	87%
I have been carrying a grudge against my parents for years.	10%	11%	6%	9%
I try to stay away from home most of the time.	28%	23%	23%	30%

FIGURE 18.2 The generation gap failed to appear in a study that tapped the feelings and attitudes of adolescents in four cultures. Answers from 13- to 18-year-olds indicate that the typical family is a smoothly functioning social system. *(Adapted from Offer, Ostrov, and Howard, 1981)*

privileges; provide and withdraw attention, approval, affection, and money; and even use coercive techniques. Thus, much adolescent behavior, whether prized or detested by parents, is maintained by the consequences that the parents themselves provide for such behavior.

The primary changes of adolescence do, however, result in a radically changed organism, and parents who do not realize this may fail to appreciate greater autonomy in their son or daughter (Steinberg, 1981). It is tempting to speculate that what is so commonly reported as adolescent negativism may be the son's or daughter's reaction to the parents' failure to modify their expectations in relation to the adolescent's new capabilities and sexual maturity. In most cases, the problems are momentary and minor; the gap between generations appears to be a crack rather than a chasm.

FROM YOUTH TO ADULTHOOD

In the past decade or so, a constellation of factors has created a concept of "youth" as a possible phase of life and has created a consciousness of it similar to that associated with the concept of adolescence more than a century ago (J. Coleman et al., 1974; Braungart, 1980). Extended

ADOLESCENT DEVIANCE

When adolescents engage in deviant behavior as a way of establishing or renewing their identity, suggest Martin Gold and Richard Petronio (1980), the kind of behavior they choose is generally extreme enough to upset parents and other adults but not so extreme as to generate total rejection. In support of this speculation, Gold and Petronio review findings from several different areas.

During the years from 1967 to 1972, for example, the use of marijuana by adolescents from thirteen to sixteen years of age increased, while the frequency of other deviant acts decreased. In 1967, there was also a negative correlation between the closeness of the parent-child relationship and an adolescent's use of marijuana, so that pot smoking was most prevalent among adolescents who felt distant from their parents. At first, parents were upset over their children's use of marijuana, but by 1972 they seemed much less disapproving and the negative correlation disappeared, with no correlation between marijuana use and parent-child relationships. Presumably, as smoking pot became less upsetting to parents, its attractiveness as a form of deviant behavior decreased (Gold and Reimer, 1975).

Although religious conversion may not sound like deviant behavior, when the religion adopted is vastly different from parental beliefs, the behavior is a form of deviance. At the turn of the century, religious conversion was most likely to occur in early adolescence, perhaps because "being saved" helped the new believer to handle "sinful" sexual impulses that were condemned by most religious denominations. Even if the born-again adolescent did sin (think sexual thoughts, masturbate, become sexually aroused), abiding faith washed away the sin, restoring self-respect. Because sexual impulses and masturbation are no longer considered sinful among most fundamentalists, religious conversion in early adolescence is now less common.

Today, most adolescents who become religious converts are near the end of adolescence, but instead of "coming to God," say Gold and Petronio, they appear to be joining youth movements. Those who become converts appear to have reached the end of adolescence without constructing a sense of their own identity, are not sure who they are or where they are going, and perhaps feel desperate, since time is running out. Not knowing where they fit, but looking for "truth," floundering adolescents are ready to listen to and believe those peers who claim to have discovered the truth, and who behave as if they were convinced of it (Heirich, 1977). As a cult member, the adolescent receives the support and confirmation of the sect's active participants (Adams and Fox, 1976).

When their sons and daughters join the Jesus Movement, Pentecostal Catholicism, or Orthodox Judaism, parents consider their children strange and may be upset, but they believe their offspring will outgrow their choices. However, when children join such sects as the Children of God or the Unification Church, parents become dismayed or outraged. By joining any of these movements, adolescents are engaging in deviant behavior and espousing a "negative identity" with respect to parents and society in general. But the behavior is still not so deviant as to cause total rejection—as parents' attempts at bribery, kidnapping, or deprogramming of their errant offspring indicate.

According to Gold and Petronio, the attraction of ultrareligious sects as an expression of deviance may lie in the extreme expression they give to such parental values as faith, hope, charity, obedience, and so forth. By adopting these beliefs, adolescents can feel better than their parents, reproving both parents and adult society for failing the younger generation—for sending youths to a bad war, for not anticipating young people's need for jobs, for letting the energy supply run out, for despoiling the environment. Through their extreme religious behavior, adolescents tell their parents that adults have not lived up to the ideals they profess.

education has been largely responsible for the growing consciousness of youth: at least two-thirds of all young people in this country finish high school and over one-fourth of those between twenty-one and twenty-five are still in school. This means that substantial portions of young people are segregated into concentrated settlements with their peers—mostly in universities and colleges but also, as Richard Flacks (1971) has pointed out, in urban, often black, ghettos inhabited by those whom the educational system has not prepared for jobs. Such segregation no longer is restricted to members of the male upper-middle class who are being educated for elite roles; today most young people live separately from their families. This means that conditions exist that encourage the transformation of an *age grade* into an *age group,* and the mass media and business have encouraged this growth of self-consciousness of youth.

The concept has been defined in restrictive social-psychological terms by Kenneth Keniston (1968), who popularized the notion of a period of youth. Those whom Keniston considers youths have accomplished the traditional tasks of adolescence. They are emancipated from the family; relatively tranquil concerning sexuality; have a stable and relatively integrated self-concept; show a capacity for commitment, intimacy, and play; display synthesis in moral and ethical areas; and have passed through and beyond any adolescent rebellion. Despite their accomplishments, these young men and women continue to emphasize remaining open, fluid, and in motion, not foreclosing their development in any way, and not being prematurely integrated into the established society.

In view of the foreclosure of identity, the gender-related difficulties in integrating sexuality and intimacy, and the low incidence of principled morality among many adolescents, it is apparent that Keniston's definition of youth probably applies to only a small and privileged minority. Indeed, it must be noted that interest in youth grew out of the study of youthful dissent of the 1960s, in itself a phenomenon of the upper-middle class.

It is not certain whether youth as a separate phase of life will find its way firmly into public consciousness or formal developmental theory (Elder, 1980). At present, when the word is defined in social-psychological terms, the incidence of youth is quite low. Given the decline in dissent, the social definition of the period may decrease in the future.

Finally, it is misleading to separate adolescence drastically from early adulthood, for in most men and women these two phases of life merge and blur. Adolescence does not end; it fades away—either into youth or into early adulthood. This fading away of adolescence marks not the end of psychological development but the beginning of a lifetime of further development, as we will see in the following chapters.

SUMMARY

1. During adolescence, many young people enter Piaget's stage of formal operations, in which they can generate and test hypotheses, deal with logical possibilities, think ahead, and think about thought itself. Formal-operational thought may be the direct result of living in a highly technological Western society or of formal education, because in some societies this level of thought does not appear to develop. Formal thought is necessary if adolescents are to develop principled moral reasoning, as defined by Kohlberg, although the presence of formal thought does not guarantee the development of principled reasoning.
2. The adolescent's self-concept is generally disrupted by the physical, psychological, and social changes that accompany puberty, so that many go through a developmental crisis in the process of reestablishing an identity—a major developmental task of adolescence. During the

process, self-concept (a basic component of identity as defined by Erikson) is sometimes threatened, and adolescents may fall into totalism, in which they develop a rigid self-concept and become susceptible to totalitarian movements. Uniformism, an immersion in the peer group, can help free an adolescent from childhood dependence. An unstable self-concept can lead to low self-esteem (the second component of identity), making the individual awkward, submissive, and nonassertive.

3. As self-concept develops, so does an adolescent's self-consciousness, a concern with what others think of one. Self-consciousness peaks in early adolescence and then subsides. Adolescents' concepts of others change in the same way as their concept of self changes; young people now see complexities in others and attempt to explain the actions of others.

4. Sex-role stereotypes intensify during early adolescence, because conformity helps ease the uncertainty engendered by the changes of puberty. Sex roles also affect vocational identity, with males socialized to see competence in a vocational role as essential and females socialized to establish and maintain interpersonal relationships, thereby pushing vocational roles into second place. However, with an increasing number of girls being socialized in the direction of individual achievement, girls who form their vocational identities around occupational roles are likely to become more prevalent.

5. Social class affects an adolescent's choice of work, either because of the social-class related prestige attached to various occupations or because social class affects an adolescent's perceptions of the accessibility of an occupation. Adolescent conformity to the peer group peaks in early adolescence, especially in regard to antisocial behavior, then subsides as older adolescents begin to accept adult standards. Adolescents conform to peers in choice of friends, language, and clothes but ultimately conform to parental values in academic performance, moral behavior, job aspirations, and political attitudes. Despite parent-adolescent disagreement over sex and drugs, adolescent patterns of drug and alcohol usage show links between adult and adolescent standards. And despite the sometimes troubled interpersonal relationships, the generation gap between adolescents and adults is highly exaggerated.

6. Since prolonged education now allows many young people to go through an extended period of life before assuming adult responsibilities, it has been suggested that a new phase of life, called youth, may be developing. At present, however, the period is limited to a small number of young people.

MOSES

UNIT SEVEN

ADULTHOOD: FUNCTIONING IN SOCIETY

Our society has no rite or social ceremony to mark the passage from adolescence to adulthood. Although one may become a legal adult at eighteen or twenty-one, there is no one age at which a person becomes mature. We will, therefore, arbitrarily define adulthood as the years from twenty until death. To look more closely at this phase of development, we will further divide adulthood into three periods: (1) early adulthood, from twenty to forty; (2) middle adulthood, from forty to sixty; and (3) later adulthood, from sixty until death. Most people assume that growth and development halt once an individual reaches adulthood. However, as these chapters will show, adulthood is a time of change, of growth, and of development. Although the child does make the adult, the experiences of a lifetime make the citizen of sixty the same and yet very different from the adult of twenty-five.

19 EARLY ADULTHOOD: SELECTING THE OPTIONS

As she enters the adult world, Lauren has many more choices to make than her grandmother faced. Her grandmother knew that women married and became mothers, and her goals were simply and clearly set. Lauren, too, may choose a traditional marriage and devote the major part of her adult life to being a wife and mother. But, unlike her grandmother, she may also choose to marry and remain childless or to reject marriage altogether without feeling that she has failed as a human being. Lauren also has a third choice, one that more and more young women are selecting. She can marry and have both a family and a career, perhaps choosing a contract marriage, in which both she and her husband share in the obligations of making a home and rearing a family.

The choices that face Lauren show that early adulthood, the years between nineteen or twenty and forty, is a time when individuals are confronted with the tasks of becoming mature. During this period, adults generally become independent, choose a vocation or career, and select a marriage partner and begin a family. Adolescents see an adult as someone who no longer plays and who is no longer playful; nevertheless, adolescents generally anticipate becoming adults themselves. Perhaps one reason that adolescents look forward to entering the adult world of commitments and responsibility is that they look forward, not to adulthood itself, but to the freedom and social respect associated with it.

In this chapter we will describe the developmental and psychological characteristics that are typical of early adulthood, discovering that the achievement of independence and self-sufficiency is the central developmental task. We will find that identity seems to remain fairly stable from adolescence into early adulthood and that younger adults are generally at their peak of physical ability and performance. We will look at marriage and parenthood, divorce and remarriage, as transition points in development that challenge individuals to change and adjust. Throughout the chapter, we will emphasize that there are important differences in the ways individuals experience and cope with the tasks of early adulthood and that some of these differences depend on gender, on concepts of appropriate sex-role behavior, on social class, on education, and on each person's unique developmental history. Finally, we will see that there is no longer a single model for these early adult years and no one best road to maturity.

THE CONCEPT OF MATURITY

Almost all personality theories describe the development of maturity in early adulthood. Each theory offers a unique perspective, yet there are some characteristics of maturity that are common to all of them. All regard the ability to be intimate, to give and accept love, and to be affectionate and sexually responsive as necessary to the attainment of maturity. All stress the ability to be sociable, to have friends, to be devoted to others and to nurture them. All agree that some clear sense of who one is, of what one's aims and powers are, and of what is best for oneself typifies a mature individual. One probable result of these characteristics is an interest in productive work and an ability to do it.

One way to look at maturity is to think of it in terms of being able to cope successfully with the events and decisions that most people face at characteristic times in their lives. A mature adult, then, would be one who successfully deals with the demands to grow, develop, and change throughout adult life. In terms of Erik Erikson's (1963) concept of developmental stages, a mature individual has successfully resolved the crisis at each stage of development in the ideal direction. Thus maturity in early adulthood includes (1) a successful resolution of the developmental crises of childhood and adolescence, (2) the ability to commit the self to a close relationship with another (intimacy), and (3) a concern with guiding the next generation and with productive work (generativity) (Whitbourne and Waterman, 1979).

A second, related way of looking at maturity is in terms of feeling good about oneself. In this view, maturity is determined more by a person's subjective assessment of how things are going than by society's judgment that the person is doing things appropriate to his or her age. Adulthood is a time when the individual looks critically at him- or herself, at the direction life is taking, and at the way other people see him or her. James Birren and Jayne Renner (1980) have suggested that there is often a fairly close fit between the way mature people see themselves, the way they would ideally like to be, and the way they believe other people see them. A young man like Matt, for example, may have unrealistic career goals for himself. He may also perceive himself to be much more aggressive with women than he actually is. In the process of maturing, he will bring his career expectations and ideals more in line with career goals that he can realistically hope to achieve. For Matt, maturing will also involve becoming aware of his own shyness and caution in approaching women.

No matter how it is defined, maturity in adulthood is cumulative and changing. It involves continuing adjustment to constantly changing expectations and responsibilities. Although maturity does not require marriage, parenthood, and hard work at a career, it does demand that people become aware of who they are, of where they want to go, and that they work toward those goals. The phrase "getting it all together" is an accurate summation of the young adult's struggle to become mature.

PHYSICAL CHARACTERISTICS

In the two decades of early adulthood, most people are at the peak of their physical agility, speed, and strength. These are the years when their bodies, inside and out, are at their best. Despite this sense of physical perfection, many of the physical hallmarks of aging begin, almost imperceptibly, in early adulthood. Around the age of twenty, slow, continuing changes affect the workings of the human body (Weg, 1981). Muscle tone and strength, which generally peak between the ages of twenty and thirty, decline after that. Height begins to decrease slowly but measurably around twenty-five. Visual acuity and hearing decline after twenty.

Changes also occur deep inside the body. Even if weight remains constant, the proportion of fatty tissue to muscle begins to increase. In addition, on a number of measures—such as cardiac output and vital capacity—the functioning of many physiological systems appears to decrease by about 1 percent per year beginning in the twenties (deVries, 1981). Atherosclerotic changes in the arteries also are evident by the time an individual enters young adulthood, and poor diet and lack of exercise contribute to the development of chronic diseases that may become apparent only two or three decades later.

Considering society's overwhelming focus on youth and beauty, it might be expected that these small but noticeable changes in body appearance would have a negative effect on the way that young adults feel about themselves. However, this does not appear to be the case. A survey by Ellen Berscheid, Elaine Walster, and George Bohrnstedt (1973), which investigated Americans' attitudes toward their bodies, found that there was no difference between people under twenty-five years old and people twenty-five to forty-four years old in their overall liking for their bodies. Despite our focus on youth, young adults apparently seem not to be bothered much by these small changes in their physical appearance.

One reason for the lack of concern over the physical changes of early adulthood may be that, despite the occasional gray hair or wrinkle beside the eyes, people are enjoying their peak physical fitness and performance. Reaction times generally improve from childhood until the age of nineteen and then remain constant until around twenty-six. In any competitive situation or in any situation that demands a fast response, young adults usually come out ahead. This speed, together with the small but measurable declines that accumulate over the years, explain why the young excel in some sports. In competitive sports, such as basketball, boxing, tennis, skiing, and baseball, it takes early-adulthood strength and speed to stay on top. Other sports, such as bowling or golf, depend on concentration and experience, and not at all on speed or strength, so that adults can excel in these activities well into the later years.

These young women who serve as hospital volunteers have begun to assume responsibilities and to develop independence. ***(Michael Weisbrot and Family/Stock, Boston)***

NEW DEVELOPMENTAL TASKS

Each phase of life presents people with new tasks of development, and early adulthood is the first time in most people's lives when no one else makes their decisions for them. If adolescence is a time for pulling up roots, young adulthood is a time for making commitments, taking on responsibilities, and making plans come true. During adolescence, concerns are on inner tasks: becoming independent, discovering a personal and sexual identity, and developing a set of values. For young adults in their twenties, the tasks are more external and oriented to the world: deciding where to live, finding a job, choosing a sexual or marriage partner, beginning a family. According to George Vaillant (1977), a main focus in these years among the well-educated, middle-class males he studied is achieving intimacy, both in romantic, sexual relationships and in platonic relationships with both sexes.

As adults move into their thirties, the quality of life changes. Many alter commitments they made earlier and expand and deepen other longstanding commitments. Whereas individuals in their twenties feel their course of life is set and try hard to fill the role established by themselves and their culture, during the thirties people often question themselves, their goals, and their values.

When Roger Gould (1978) studied the concerns of adults, he found that life in the thirties was more painful and difficult and less certain than it had been in the twenties. In their thirties, many question their earlier decisions concerning their personal lives. For some, the thirties are a time of tearing up what was put together in the twenties. If David is single, he may try to find a lifelong partner. If Matt married early, he may decide to get a divorce. If Susan has been happy as a mother, she may now want to go back to school or work. If Lauren and her husband have been childless, they may decide to start a family.

The thirties are also a time for settling down. According to Daniel Levinson and his associates (1978), among men there are three aspects to settling down. The first involves getting one's life in order and achieving stability, security, and control. Career consolidation becomes a major goal, and adults concentrate on developing their skills and deepening their bases of experience. A second aspect of settling down concerns the attempt to reach major goals according to an inner timetable. For example, a manager may set forty as the age to become a corporate executive, or a truckdriver aim at becoming a union official by thirty-five. The third aspect contrasts with the first two, for people in their thirties often want to be free, unattached, and not tied down to any structure, no matter how satisfying it may be. According to Levinson, the thirties may also be a time for wanting to be "open to new possibilities, ready to soar, wander, quest in all directions as the spirit moves one."

Not all people get married, and not all people settle into careers or have children at approximately the same age. What is considered appropriate behavior at a particular age depends to some extent on a person's gender, social class, and historical era (Neugarten, 1968, 1979b). Each person perceives certain behavior as appropriate at a certain age. Bernice Neugarten (1968) once suggested that men and women have "social clocks" in their heads to help them judge their own and other people's behavior as being early, late, or on time. She noted that what constitutes the appropriate time for a particular developmental event may change with the passing of generations. In 1940, the young woman who was not married by the age of twenty-five faced the threat of spinsterhood. By 1966 it was the twenty-one-year-old who faced such a fate. In the 1970s, the appropriate age for marriage again became older, and young women who wanted to marry could postpone fears of spinsterhood. By the end of the decade, spinsterhood was no longer a general threat, because most Americans now agreed that women who chose to remain single were neither "neurotic" nor "immoral" (Yankelovich, 1981).

According to Neugarten, early adulthood is both quantitatively and qualitatively different for people in different socioeconomic classes. Early adulthood lasts longer for a person in the upper-middle class than for a member of the working class. The upper-middle class regards forty as the end of early adulthood, whereas the working class believes that it ends at thirty-five. Further, the upper-middle-class person sees young adulthood as a time of exploration and groping, of "feeling one's way" and trying out jobs and careers, marriage and adulthood. Among the working class, young adulthood is not a time of experimentation; it is a time when issues are settled. Sometimes this is explained as an obligation and there is some regret: "The responsibility is hung on you." Others in the working class see these decisions as necessary for independence; it is time to "be a man." People in the working class are likely to regard young adulthood as a time when youth is gone and when it is time to get down to the business of living—of job, marriage, children, and responsibility.

There is widespread agreement within each social class on the answers to such questions as "When is the best time to marry?" or "When is the best time to finish school?" Most people in the middle class, Neugarten found, say that the best age for a man to marry is between twenty-five and thirty-five. By contrast, working-class people believe that a man should marry at a somewhat younger age. The ages at which such major events as marriage actually occur also show a great deal of regularity within social classes. The higher the social class, the older people are likely to be when they leave school, get their first job, get married, and have children.

More recently, Neugarten (1979b) and others (e.g., Hirschhorn, 1977) have noted that the life cycle in our society appears to be becoming more fluid, as traditional norms and expectations are changing, and appropriate times for such events as marriage, careers, and parenthood are becoming less tied to chronological age. As a result, we may be witnessing the development of what Neugarten has called an "age-irrelevant society," in which there is no single appropriate age to take on the role of parent, student, worker, grandparent, and so forth. As Neugarten writes, "Our society is becoming accustomed to the 28-year-old mayor, the 30-year-old college president, the 35-year-old grandmother, the 50-year-old retiree, the 65-year-old father of a preschooler, and the 70-year-old student, and even the 85-year-old mother caring for a 65-year-old son." In an age-irrelevant society, developmental tasks would remain the same but adults would not feel that their social clocks were early or late if they postponed or accelerated the social roles of adulthood.

IDENTITY AND INTERPERSONAL BEHAVIOR

The direction in which a young adult's personal and interpersonal skills grow and develop is primarily the result of experience and not simply the product of growing older. In general, gradual stabilization rather than radical change seems to be the rule. Many of the changes that occur begin in adolescence and tend toward emotional maturity.

After studying personality development during young adulthood, Robert White (1975) discerned five different growth trends: the stabilizing of identity, the freeing of personal relationships, the deepening of interests, the humanizing of values, and the expansion of caring.

Under favorable circumstances, White found, *a person's identity stabilizes.* The individual's sense of who she or he is becomes sharper, clearer, more consistent, and freer of transient influences. Accumulated personal experience increasingly determines identity, and individuals are less affected by the social judgments of others and by their own single successes and failures.

In the second trend, *personal relationships become freer,* in that an adult becomes increasingly able to respond to other people as they are instead of reacting to them as if they were figures from his or her own past, as when a child reacts to a teacher as if he or she were the parent. As adults grow in this direction, they become flexible and find it easier to make allowances for the characteristics of others.

A third growth trend discovered by White is in the direction of *deepening interests.* Lifelong interests often develop early in life, but young adults tend to become fully engaged with their interests, which become ends in themselves rather than means to other ends. This deepening of interests is often accompanied by heightened self-confidence and increased effectiveness in a chosen occupation.

A fourth growth trend, *the humanizing of values,* describes an increased awareness of the human—as opposed to the abstract—meaning of values. It may result in the development of a personal value system, so that even values that do not change from childhood increasingly reflect personal experiences and purpose.

Finally, *the expansion of caring* leads individuals to outgrow the self-centeredness of their childhood and adolescence and to value the welfare of another person, a group, or some other aspect of life such as community or humanity as highly as their own. This caring is marked by an emotional involvement in the welfare of others, not simply an intellectual interest in them. As these trends develop, they affect self-concept, self-esteem, attitudes toward sex roles, and the way adults express their sexuality.

Self-Concept and Self-Esteem

As people move from adolescence to young adulthood, they rarely experience a sharp discontinuity between their adolescent and adult selves. But since an individual's self-concept is so closely related to physical appearance and to social roles and abilities, and since all these change in adulthood, it would seem likely that self-concept would change as well. In fact, when Jack Block (1971) looked at changes in personality from adolescence to young adulthood, he found both continuity and change in young people. Women and men tended to show less self-centered impulsiveness than adolescents and an increased ability to cope with problems. Young adults' sense of self-control, confidence, and mastery over the environment become evident when they are shown pictures and asked to tell stories about them. A majority of young adults studied by David Gutmann (1970) and Bernice Neugarten (Neugarten et al., 1964) told stories that reflected feelings of being in control of their own lives and destinies, and confidence that they could get what they wanted by their own actions.

Adults' sense of increasing power and control over their own lives, which is part of their self-concept, also shows in their self-portraits. When asked to draw themselves, men's drawings get bigger and bigger until they are about thirty years old, and women's self-portraits increase in size until they are forty (Birren, 1964).

This sense of mastery and self-control may be stronger for a man than for a woman. As we have seen in earlier discussions of personality, learning what it means to think, act, and feel male or female is a critical part of adolescent and childhood development. The concepts men and women have about themselves clearly indicate that our social stereotypes about male and female roles have a profound impact on the kinds of adults that boys and girls are likely to become. Traditionally, girls are socialized to be dependent, passive, emotionally expressive, and warm, whereas boys learn to be assertive, independent, and to think rationally. Brought up in this way, young women are less likely than men to have a sense of control over their lives, successes, and failures. Young men believe in their power to control their fate, but women are more likely to believe that outside powers are in control. As Kay Deaux (1976) found, when a man and a woman perform equally well on some task, particularly a traditionally masculine task such as playing darts, women tend to attribute their success to luck, but men tend to attribute their success to their own skill. This difference is reflected in unexpected aspects of life. For example, Deaux found that at state and county fairs, men seek out games of skill (tossing coins into dishes) but women seek out games of chance (bingo). When they begin to play a game of chance, men and women have similar expectations of success, but when they start to play a game that requires skill, men's expectations rise and women's drop.

Women and men generally express their needs for self-control and mastery in different ways. For example, men who have a high need for achievement typically express the need directly in their jobs; but women who are highly achievement-oriented may express the need directly or indirectly. In expressing this need directly, a woman might pursue a career or become involved in politics, in community work, or in gourmet cooking. She may, however, meet her need for achievement indirectly, deriving satisfaction from the successes of her husband and children. Women who choose to work in the home are not necessarily less achievement-oriented than women who work outside the home. In an investigation of self-concept and self-esteem, Carol Erdwins, Zita Tyer, and Jeanne Mellinger (1980) found that women who choose to remain full-time homemakers and those who return to school while rearing their children are similar in their ambitiousness, self-confidence, and achievement orientation. The homemakers, however, described themselves as more feminine than the students did.

As young adults develop an increasing sense of control over their lives, their self-esteem also becomes greater than it was when they were adolescents (Lowenthal and Chiriboga, 1973). Young men and women have similar levels of self-esteem (Frieze et al., 1978). Those whose personalities do not fit traditional stereotypes for either gender show the highest self-esteem, followed by men and women whose personality characteristics fall near the traditionally masculine end of the scale. Lowest of all in self-esteem are those adults—either men or women—whose personality characteristics reflect traditional femininity (Spence, 1979). This result probably reflects the fact that self-esteem based on personal accomplishment is considered masculine, whereas self-esteem based on being highly regarded by others is considered feminine. Because in most cases society values accomplishment over interpersonal success, those whose self-esteem depends on being liked and admired by others tend to have lower self-esteem than the rest of the population.

The sense of control also affects a person's general satisfaction with life, and one survey of young adults (Shaver and Freedman, 1976) showed that the happiest individuals were those who felt in control of their own lives and evaluated their progress by their own standards. As one woman put it, "Happiness is driving your own truck." At this time of life, increasing self-satisfaction means either increasing one's successes or lowering one's goals and aspirations.

As this young man expresses his need for achievement in his first job, he will develop an increasing sense of control over his life and a greater sense of self-esteem. *(© Hazel Hankin)*

Changing Sex Roles

Perhaps as a result of the women's movement in this country, young men and women are changing their concepts of masculinity and femininity; among young adults, sex-role stereotypes are breaking down. In a recent survey of more than 28,000 highly educated young adults, Carol Tavris (1977) found that neither sex saw the ideal man as being tough, strong, and aggressive, with many sexual conquests. Instead, he is seen as able to love, self-confident, ready to stand by his beliefs, and—especially by women—as warm and gentle. Among both sexes, the ideal woman, like the ideal man, is seen as able to love, ready to stand by her beliefs, self-confident, intelligent, and warm.

This tendency toward **androgyny**—having both feminine and masculine characteristics in one's self-image—appears to be a relatively recent phenomenon (Urberg, 1979; Leahy and Eiter, 1980); but as we have seen, it is associated with high levels of self-esteem. When today's adolescents and young adults are asked to describe their ideal male, ideal female, and own self-image, young adult men and women respond with less traditionally stereotyped views than adolescents do. Although many young men and women have abandoned traditional sex-role ideals for themselves, they continue to engage in stereotyping when describing their ideal of the opposite sex (Urberg, 1979). The discrepancy between this finding and the survey by Tavris may be due to the nature of the sample. The people who responded to Tavris's survey were highly educated readers of a national magazine who voluntarily returned a printed questionnaire; the people in Urberg's sample were se-

FINDING A JOB: NO HOPE IN THE INNER CITY

Finding a job, a major task for many young adults, becomes a source of enduring bitterness for many black young adults in the inner city, and long-term unemployment among young blacks leads to low self-esteem and alienation, and to crime and other antisocial behavior. This conclusion was drawn by sociologist Elijah Anderson (1980) after conducting a series of in-depth interviews with young black men and employers in Philadelphia.

The problem is serious, and it arises from a combination of new racial pride, mutual distrust, and a lack of job skills. According to Anderson, black identity and self-concept have changed over the past two decades, and the racial pride and self-assertiveness of today's young blacks makes it difficult for them to accept the menial jobs they are offered. Although most young whites and most middle-class blacks gladly accept entry-level jobs, inner-city blacks find them both demeaning and hopeless. This disparity in attitude, says Anderson, is due to the fact that whites and middle-class blacks view entry-level jobs as temporary and look forward to moving up in the labor market, whereas inner-city blacks, who tend to move from one entry-level job to another, regard such jobs as a sign of failure. Job mobility is vertical for the first group but is horizontal for the second.

With the development of a new black self-concept, says Anderson, young black males ceased to follow establishment dress and conduct codes. When a young black male appears for a job interview, he generally carries his portable radio and wears sneakers, "gangster cap," shades, and chain necklace. Potential employers (including middle-class blacks) immediately see him as a symbol of danger. Because employers have learned from the media that such blacks are angry, militant, insolent, and violent, and hear frequent reports of black urban street criminals, employers fear the stereotypical black. Thus the relationship begins in an atmosphere of employer distrust. Distrust on the part of the employer is matched by distrust on the part of the black employee, who regards dress codes, conduct standards, and the disparagement of his language as attempts to "get the black in line." Again, black experience leads to misunderstanding. When asked to conform to dress or behavior codes on the job, young white males assume they are simply being asked to follow universal work standards, but blacks assume such requests are displays of racial prejudice.

Finally, says Anderson, young blacks are not interested in dead-end jobs that provide only enough money to get by. They want "good" jobs—white-collar jobs in air-conditioned offices with "big money." Yet many, reports Anderson, have come through the urban segregated high-school system, and although they have high-school diplomas, they lack basic skills in reading, writing, and elementary arithmetic.

The resulting problem is enormous. Failed by the labor market and the schools, lacking skills, distrusted by employers, and often unwilling to adapt to demeaning jobs, many young blacks move into the underground economy—the network of informal connections and established means by which people gain money illegally. Willing to work (at good jobs) but denied employment, they turn to pimping, picking pockets, drug dealing, fencing, confidence games, and robbery. Some move back and forth between the underground and the legitimate economy; but because of mutual distrust, they rarely stay long at the legitimate entry-level jobs they do find—in fast-food restaurants, ghetto grocery stores, or day labor. Their sense of hopelessness, says Anderson, makes young blacks unable to recognize opportunities in the legitimate economy when such opportunities present themselves. Many young blacks feel they have no stake in society and therefore nothing to lose by breaking the law.

Unless the larger society wants to see civilized urban society undermined, warns Anderson, it must provide meaningful employment to young blacks—jobs that teach useful, money-making skills that will enable these young adults to enter a vertical pattern of job mobility. Without such employment, there will be a permanent under class of socially and spiritually alienated black Americans.

Type of Power	More Associated With
Helplessness	Female
Nagging	Female
Sexuality	Female
False Information	Female
Indirect Information (presented unobtrusively)	Female
Appeal to a Common Identity ("because we are friends")	Female
Expert	Male
Direct Information	Male
Legitimate (inherent in sex role)	Male
Coercion	Male
Reward	Male

FIGURE 19.1 Stereotypical perceptions of power use. Sex role stereotypes have produced our expectations concerning the appropriate uses of power by women and men. As a result when one gender uses methods perceived as being the province of the other, people who hold stereotypical notions of power use often react in a negative manner. ***(After Frieze, Parsons, Johnson, Ruble, and Zellman. 1978, page 317. Based on Johnson, 1976)***

lected scientifically, but all were connected with the same midwestern school system.

Young adults are going beyond thinking about maleness and femaleness in a new manner; a good many are behaving in less traditional ways. In a three-generation study, Lillian Troll (1975) found that less than a handful of grandmothers had had any higher education, but a quarter of their daughters were either planning to attend college, were in college, or had finished college. The young adult granddaughters, in contrast to the older two generations, wanted to be successful themselves instead of achieving vicariously through the successes of their husbands or children, and they believed more strongly than their mothers or grandmothers that they could control their own lives.

Women who had less traditional, more egalitarian life styles were the happiest women in a study by Helena Lopata (1971). Women who had become involved in community and educational programs were the most satisfied, and they felt that taking time off from child care and family responsibilities for personal development was important.

When Margaret Reedy (1977) looked at the personal needs of young, middle-aged, and older men and women, she also found that today young men and women define their roles and themselves less traditionally than earlier generations did. She found that in the middle-aged and older groups, men needed to be dominant and independent and women needed to be nurturing, friendly, and moral. These traditional sex differences did not characterize the young men and women; young men were comfortable with their "feminine" qualities, and young women were able to express their "masculine" side. Both young men and young women would like to see themselves as self-confident, intelligent, independent, loving, and understanding.

In the past decade, not only have more young women begun to enter professional and executive careers, but many young men have begun to question an overwhelming devotion to work and have shown an increased unwillingness to relocate if it will cause family or personal stress (Knox, 1980). In fact, nearly 80 percent of all adult workers have become concerned with self-fulfillment, seeking to expand the area of choice and flexibility in their lives (Yankelovich, 1981).

Sexuality

Sexual relationships and sexual performance continue to be important concerns during early adulthood. The data presented in the Kinsey reports indicated that the average American male establishes a pattern of orgasm and ejaculation that remains fairly consistent from adolescence through later adulthood and that is relatively independent of marital status. However, the relative frequency of various kinds of sexual behavior does change over the years. Masturbation is

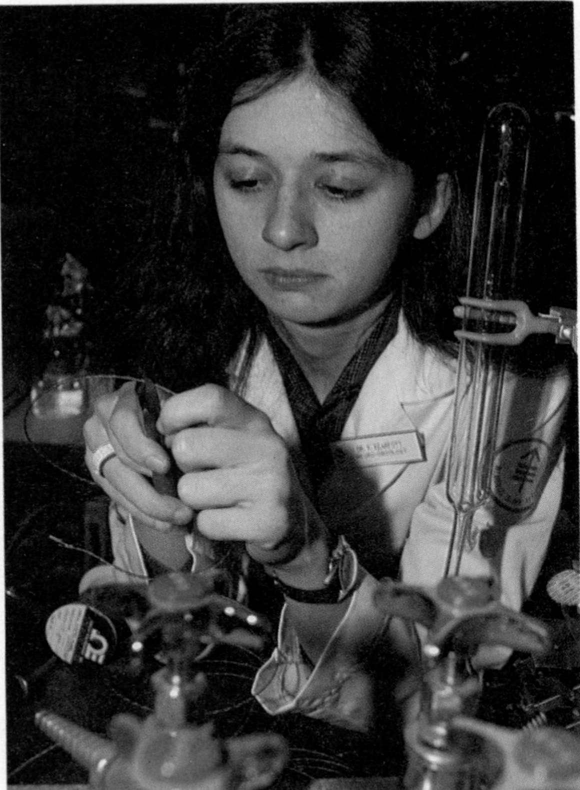

Women who have less traditional careers, such as this nuclear physicist, are likely to be happier than traditional women. *(© Leonard Speier)*

the dominant type of male sexual behavior before puberty and in early adolescence but sexual intercourse becomes more prominent in early adulthood (Kinsey, Pomeroy, and Martin, 1948; Masters and Johnson, 1966).

By the time a person reaches young adulthood, she or he is likely to be sexually experienced. For example, the results of a recent large survey of sexuality among women between the ages of eighteen and thirty-four revealed that today's young adult women have had sexual intercourse with more men compared with women a decade ago (Wolfe, 1980). In this survey, 25 percent of the women had had two to five partners and another 21 percent reported having had six to ten partners. Not all women were comfortable about the extent of their sexual freedom. Many reported that they found it difficult to say no to men, or that sexual relationships were no longer as meaningful as they once had been.

A survey by Philip Sarrel and Lorna Sarrel (1980) of the sexual practices and attitudes of more than 26,000 moderately well educated American men and women revealed that most young adults enjoy a high level of sexual pleasure in their relationships. Seventy-five percent said their sexual relationship with their partner was "good" or "excellent." The majority of these young men and women also reported having orgasm "every time" or "almost every time."

Especially during the first years of marriage, a young couple is likely to have intercourse frequently. In addition to its physiological benefit and its value as one of life's great pleasures, sexuality can be an affirmation of closeness, caring, and affection. In the Sarrel study, a large majority of the men and women reported having intercourse one to three times each week, and about a third said they made love four or more times each week. Those who said they had sex at least four times a week were four times as likely as those who had intercourse less frequently to say their sexual relationship was good or excellent. It is not clear whether frequent sexual intercourse leads to increased sexual satisfaction or whether good sexual relations result in frequent sex. Among women, reactions at the failure to reach orgasm were related to sexual satisfaction. Women who did not become upset over intercourse without orgasm were more likely to be satisfied with their sex lives than women who felt angry or frustrated or women who perceived their partners to be upset when the women did not reach orgasm.

Men and women who reported being highly satisfied with their sex lives also tended to talk more with their partners about their sexual relationship. Eight out of ten who rated their sexual relationship as good or excellent said that communication about sex with their partners was excellent. A majority also felt that talking out a sexual problem was the best way to resolve it. In general, communicating feelings, specific preferences, and likes and dislikes about sex were highly related to a satisfying sex life. Being able to communicate feelings and assert one's needs and being willing to talk out differences were also found to be highly related to sexual satisfaction. For example, 58 percent of the women who said it was easy for them to assert their rights or feelings in an argument with their partners described their sexual relationship as good or excellent, but only 16 percent of the women who said it was difficult to be assertive felt sexually satisfied. Finally, 75 percent of the women who reported they tried to make up with their partner after an argument were satisfied with their sex lives. By contrast, among women who said that they withdrew emotionally after an argument, only 17 percent were satisfied with their sex lives.

Intellectual Skills

People's intellectual skills, or at least their own perception of them, are likely to affect both their self-concept and their self-esteem. In the areas of verbal skills, stored facts, and information processing, young adults do better than they ever have before. Young adults also reach their peak performance on tests involving psychomotor skills, especially speed and coordination.

According to Paul Baltes and K. Warner Schaie (1974), young adults are better than they ever have been, but not necessarily better than they ever will be, in three major areas of intellectual functioning: (1) verbal comprehension and number skills, which are acquired through education and socialization; (2) the ability to shift easily from one way of thinking to another, as when a person must provide an antonym or a synonym to a given word, depending on whether the word is printed in upper- or lower-case letters; and (3) the ability to organize and process visual materials, such as finding a simple figure in a complex one or identifying a picture that is incomplete.

However, age is not the only factor that affects intellectual skills during adulthood. For example, our species is becoming smarter with each new generation (Schaie, 1980). We are also better educated and healthier, and both education and health are at least as important as age in determining an individual's intellectual ability (Botwinick, 1978).

Intellectual skills include learning and memory, thinking, problem solving, and creativity. In young adulthood, the ability to learn and remember is generally at its peak. On any kind of learning or memory task, young adults usually perform better than they ever did in childhood or adolescence. In addition, if success at a task depends on how quickly they complete it, they probably do better than they will ever do again.

In the case of thinking, early adulthood is likely to be the time when people have the maximum flexibility to form new concepts and find it easiest to shift the way they think in order to solve problems. This ability to shift an approach to a problem is most likely to be shown when the solution involves discovering the details of categories and using the information at hand. Compared with middle-aged and older people, young adults are also less likely to be distracted by irrelevant or uninformative information in solving a problem (Botwinick, 1978). Again, age is not the only determinant in efficient thinking; intelligence, education, and memory contribute heavily to the ability.

As for creativity, which involves finding original and unique solutions, the early adult years often provide the most fertile ground for creative thought. For example, maximum creativity in the arts and sciences may occur during the thirties (Lehman, 1953). Harvey Lehman found that the most influential books tend to be produced by writers in their late thirties, that many popular children's books and short stories are written by people in their early thirties, and that outstanding drama seems to be written by people in their thirties. The twenties are the time when poetry flourishes. Outstanding inventions and discoveries tend to be made by people in their thirties.

However, the fact that the production of outstanding novels, paintings, poetry, plays, and inventions reaches a peak during these years does not mean that creativity ends with the fortieth birthday. Lehman looked only at great con-

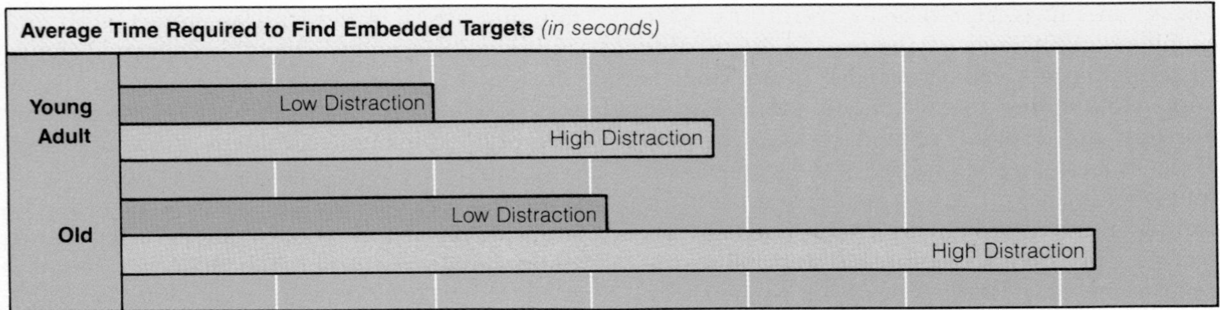

FIGURE 19.2 Information processing. The speed of information processing among young adults and their relative resistance to distraction was demonstrated when individuals were asked to detect visual symbols embedded among other symbols. As the distraction of the background increased, the superiority of the young adults' performance over that of older adults climbed sharply. ***(Table from Cerella, Poon, and Williams, 1974. Based on data collected by Arnold and Farkas)***

tributions and did not allow for the fact that with the passage of time, fewer artists, scholars, musicians, writers, and scientists are alive, hence a smaller group was being examined. A longitudinal study by Wayne Dennis (1968) of creative people who lived at least eighty years indicates that most creative individuals continue to produce works of high quality throughout their lives.

MARRIAGE

Nearly everyone gets married. In the United States, more than 90 percent of the population makes such a legal commitment (Stevens-Long, 1979). The age at which people first marry has been increasing over the past twenty years, but this major developmental decision generally takes place during the early adult years. In 1977, the median age of marriage was 24.0 for men and 21.6 for women (U.S. Bureau of the Census, 1978). Although people live and die, marry and divorce in the name of love, other factors are also important in determining whom a person marries and how long that marriage lasts.

Choosing a Mate

Choosing a mate, or choosing not to choose one, is one of the most significant decisions a person will ever make. The chosen person will have a great influence on his or her spouse's way of life, lifetime experiences, and happiness. Despite the importance of marriage and its impact on life, the decision to marry is often made quickly, easily, and rather casually. Most decisions to marry, however, do consider social level, temperamental compatibility, and similarity of outlook on life.

People tend to marry people who are like themselves. Individuals look for mates who have a suitable background; that is, a background that matches their own ethnically, religiously, and socially (Murstein, 1971). Although interracial and interfaith marriages and some forms of interclass marriages are more likely to be accepted today, in the past society has condemned, if not outlawed, such marriages.

People also tend to choose marriage partners who share their interests, values, and ways of behaving. This kind of selectivity reflects a human tendency to seek out persons who validate us as human beings and who approve of the way we live. If engaged couples are questioned separately, a striking agreement between the partners appears on such issues as smoking and drinking, and in their attitudes toward working women, the number of children they want, and where they should live (Burgess and Wallin, 1953).

Residential proximity and similarity of background are often important in starting a relationship, although the ways in which men and women meet are changing. The traditional approach, in which a man takes a woman out on a date, is giving way to a new pattern of "hanging out" and "getting together" (Libby, 1977). This informal method of acquaintance has led to the burgeoning of singles' bars and clubs. Once a relationship has begun, whether it stands the test of time and marriage depends in part on a similarity in values, attitudes, and interests (Z. Rubin, 1973). The course of choosing a mate follows a pattern somewhat like the course of friendship discussed in Chapter 18.

When we look at young adults' attitudes toward love and the person they would like to marry, interesting sex differences appear. A series of studies that followed nearly 200 Boston couples for two years found that men are likely to fall in love more quickly than women, to be more easily satisfied with the woman's qualities, to be more romantic, and to fall out of love less easily (Hill, Rubin, and Peplau, 1976). Women, in general, tend to be more practical about whom they marry. To put it succinctly, young adult women are picky. But those who enter a traditional relationship in which the wife does not plan to be the major wage earner must consider such aspects of marriage as economic security and social status, which are traditionally less important in men's selection of a mate.

The economic significance of the woman's choice in traditional marriage was once a major focus of researchers. In the past decade, sociologist Jessie Bernard (1972) has argued that the gains of marriage for women fail to outweigh the costs and that marriage benefits men more than it does women. Married men live longer and have better mental health than single men, and men tend to be more satisfied with married life than women are. In addition, married women have more neurosis and depression than do single women or married men. With more women working outside the home and more men involved in household responsibilities, the emotional and physical costs and benefits of married life may one day be equally shared (Bernard, 1981; Knox, 1980).

The choice of a marriage partner is more likely to be successful when husband and wife share values, attitudes, and interests. *(Suzanne Szasz)*

The State of Being Married

For couples who do not live together before marriage, and they remain in the majority, marriage means adjusting to all the social roles associated with marriage. To a considerable degree, people learn how to act as married people long before they become adult. In the process of socialization, they develop concepts of what it means to be a husband or a wife and their ideas about the way husbands and wives are "supposed" to act (Ahammer, 1973). Parents, family, and early heroes and heroines provide models of married people and show growing children how wives and husbands behave. Later, children and adolescents learn from friends, from experiences in intimate relationships, and from the mass media. The concepts of masculinity and femininity that are absorbed as children learn male and female roles also affect the characteristics of marriage relationships.

In addition to presenting new roles, marriage also requires couples to adjust to living with another person. The honeymoon may be over once the dirty dishes and laundry have to be washed and the bathroom scrubbed. The smallest things can have a profound impact on a marriage: Susan may roll the toothpaste tube from the bottom; her husband may just squish it out and leave the top uncapped. The romance and sexual attraction of dating and courtship are not enough to hold a relationship together through the realities of everyday living. If young adults have had good parental models to help them learn what a good relationship is like, they are at an advantage. If they also have the willingness and the patience to develop emotional intimacy and to communicate their feelings, the relationship will have more potential for enduring growth (C. Rogers, 1972).

New marriages can be described in terms of a few general characteristics (Cox, 1968). Newly married couples soon discover that their individual freedom is reduced, that they must make financial adjustments, and that they face problems involving the maturity or lack of maturity of their partners. By marrying in early adulthood, at a time when this freedom may still be critical to one's individual growth, people often find the restrictions of marriage difficult to handle. Adding children to the marriage generally exaggerates whatever problems already exist.

A new marriage confronts a couple with the problem of power. In the traditional, male-dominated relationship, the husband holds the power, and the wife either accepts his superior decision-making abilities or attempts to assert her power in less direct, more subtle ways (Bernard, 1981; Falbo and Peplau, 1980). Another kind of relationship is becoming common today, one in which the power is divided more equally between the man and the woman. Susan Kaplan (1976) looked at power in intimate relationships and found that both men and women strongly supported an egalitarian relationship. Asked to describe an ideal relationship, 95 percent of the women and 87 percent of the men indicated that both the partners should have an equal say. In their own relationships, however, only 49 percent of the women and 42 percent of the men perceived their current relationships as equal in power. When the relationship was unequal, the male was generally more powerful than the female. Male-dominated relationships tended to be those in which males and females had traditional sex-role attitudes, the male was less involved in the relationship, and the woman's educational plans were limited to high school or to a bachelor's degree.

It is common for the young wife to work during the early years of a marriage, at least until the couple decides to start a family. Today, the period between marriage and parenthood is becoming longer, as couples devote more time to getting to know each other and to enjoying life together. In addition, a growing number of women are continuing to work even after they begin a family (Alpert and Richardson, 1980). Some work because their income is necessary, but the majority of working wives now say that self-fulfillment also plays a part in their decision to work (Yankelovich, 1981). Among couples in which the working wife is well educated, more and more are choosing not to have children at all or to divide the responsibilities of child care more evenly between the husband and wife.

There no longer seems to be a single model for a good marriage (C. Rogers, 1972). Instead, the trend is toward establishing a relationship that optimizes the personal satisfaction and growth of each individual. A study of happily married couples by Margaret Reedy, James Birren, and Warner Schaie (1981) indicates that men and women seem to derive different satisfactions from the marital relationship. Asked about the characteristics of their marriage, women said that emotional security and intimacy were extremely important, whereas men emphasized loyalty and a sense of commitment to the future of the relationship. Young couples who were happily married placed a high value on their ability to communicate honestly and openly with each other and to express sexual feelings freely, a finding that concurs with the Sarrel study of sexual attitudes.

Parenthood

Although most young married couples become parents, a number of changes in planning families and in rearing children have occurred in the last ten years. The trend toward population control, together with inflation and the prevalence of dual-career families, has led many young married couples to reject the ideal of the two-child family and to stop with a single child (Hawke and Knox, 1977). As family size has declined, couples are spending fewer years of their lives actively engaged in child rearing.

Whether a couple has one or several children, becoming a parent requires learning new roles and making adjustments (Nash and Feldman, 1981). Many women claim that the greatest change in their lives came about not as a result of their marriage but with the birth of their first child. Adjustments are even greater for women who are professionally trained and who have had working experience, because the changes in their lives are more extensive. Adjustments tend to be easier when parents are older and have been married several years before conception (Belsky, 1981).

The demands and responsibilities of parenthood alter the marriage relationship. Children can, and frequently do, detract from the happiness of marriage (Schram, 1979). The birth of a first child is often a "moderately stressful" transition (Hobbs and Cole, 1976). Among marriages based on romance, the stress is likely to be much greater than among marriages based on the idea of partnership (Belsky, 1981). Couples with children communicate less than childless couples; and in many relationships, the division of labor becomes more traditional, with women doing most of the child care and homemaking, and men assuming responsibility for tasks outside the home. Perhaps as a result, more couples are choosing to remain childless, yet 90 percent of all parents would still have children if they "had to do it over again" (Yankelovich, 1981).

Although many people persist in pitying people who are childless by choice (Jamison Franzini, and Kaplan, 1979), the decision not to have children does not destine a couple to unhappiness, misery, and loneliness. Couples without children appear to be no different from couples with children in their self-esteem, life satisfaction, or maturity (Silka and Kiesler, 1977). In fact, young childless couples, especially husbands, report greater satisfaction with their lives than do couples with young children.

The transition to parenthood and the resulting experience have been heavily influenced by recent social changes. Since there is now less cultural pressure on women to assume the traditional role of mother (Yankelovich, 1981), motherhood can be a more voluntary and pleasurable experience than it used to be. In addition, the increased time between marriage and parenthood, when the wife generally works, and the tendency for more mothers to continue working give an egalitarian marital relationship a chance to develop, so that decisions and household responsibilities are shared by the spouses. This sharing of responsibilities is likely to carry over into child rearing, giving the woman more autonomy and the man more responsibility. Not all men are ready to participate in child rearing, however; not even those who are experimenting with new forms of marriage. In a study of parents in communal and contract marriages, the mother was the primary caretaker of the child in 95 percent of the families (*Science News,* 1977).

When people become parents, traditional sex roles tend to assert themselves, with mothers of young children rating higher than other women on tenderness, and fathers of young children rating higher than other men on autonomy (Feldman, Biringen, and Nash, 1981). Further modifications in sex roles appeared in a study by Shirley Feldman and Sharon Nash (1978), in which adults in their twenties and thirties were asked to wait in a room where a baby was playing. Mothers of babies showed a high interest in the baby and later spent a lot of time looking at baby pictures, but fathers did not. In fact, mothers were more interested in the baby than were women who were expecting their first child, childless married women, or childless women who were cohabiting. In addition, when tested on a sex-role inventory (which measures a person's degree of masculinity or femininity), mothers scored higher in femininity than did any childless women, and fathers scored higher in masculinity than did childless men.

The course of parenthood does not always run smoothly. Some women find that motherhood does not help them grow and mature; instead, they like themselves less than they did before their children were born (Bradburn and Caplovitz, 1965). This situation may come about because the process of rearing young children is full of unpleasant situations, with major mother-child conflicts occurring about three times each hour (Patterson, 1980). When mothers are inept at handling these conflicts, they are likely to feel overwhelmed, angry, and depressed. Such reactions are less common among mothers who are happy with their roles. Mothers who like what they are doing, whether as homemakers or as career women, are apt to like their children and themselves more than do women who dislike what they are doing (Ferree, 1976).

Fathers have traditionally been thought of as simply providing the paycheck so that the child has food to eat and clothes to wear. Although economic responsibility does fall heavily on most new fathers, fathers also play an important role in the child's emotional and social development. As earlier discussions have stressed, fathers can play a major role in caregiving, and more and more fathers are becoming active and involved in their children's growth and development (Knox, 1980).

In recent years there has been a dramatic increase in the number of single-parent households. In a single year, the number of one-parent homes in the United States increased by 9 percent (Alpert and Richardson, 1980); and in 1978, 19 percent of all children under eighteen were living in one-parent homes. The primary cause of the increase in one-parent households is the increased incidence of separation and divorce, although the growing tendency to postpone or forgo marriage, coupled with the increase in the number of unmarried women who keep their babies, has also contributed to the increase. Most single-parent families are headed by divorced or separated women (Stevens-Long, 1979), but the incidence of single-parent households headed by males is steadily increasing (Hoult, Henze, and Hudson, 1978). Divorced or separated men often feel badly prepared for child-rearing responsibilities, but the evidence indicates that they can successfully rear children alone. Many of their problems are similar to those faced by divorced mothers such as "understaffing," the need to rely on outside sources, and loneliness. Among the major concerns of single fathers are juggling work with child care and providing their daughters with adequate sex education (Orthner, Brown, and Ferguson, 1977).

Divorce and Remarriage

When a marriage is unhappy, divorce offers a way out. As divorce has become less stigmatized, increasing numbers of young adults have found themselves deciding to end their marriages and perhaps to remarry. Such major changes place additional demands on a person's ability to change and develop.

A number of factors tend to make marriages unhappy but do not necessarily lead to divorce. In general, unhappy marriages are found where occupational status, educational level, and income are low, and where differences exist between husband and wife in socioeconomic status, age, and religion. When a man and woman do not accurately see what the other is like, there is apt to be a great deal of marital discord and dissatisfaction. In addition, the less the husband and wife agree about their roles, the lower their marital satisfaction will be. The less emotional involvement in the relationship and the less communication between the partners, the less likely that couples will be satisfied with their marriages. Finally, an unwillingness to adapt to the demands, roles, and responsibilities of marriage usually accompanies an unsatisfactory relationship (Murstein, 1971).

Some relationships seem to last in spite of it all; others quickly break apart. In the young adult years, marriages seem especially subject to failure. Beyond the fact that marriage tends to be less stable among poorly paid blue-collar workers and less stable in the nonwhite population, divorce is most likely to occur early in a marriage. More divorces occur in the third or fourth year of marriage than any other, and the divorce rate drops steadily after that (Hicks and Platt, 1971). Age at marriage is also related to the probability of divorce, and adolescent marriages are the most likely to fail. Men who marry before they are twenty-one and women who marry before they are nineteen are least likely to stay married, whereas men who marry after they are thirty tend to stay married (Troll, 1975).

Increasingly, and this is especially true for young adults, couples who are unhappy in marriage are less likely to persist in a dismal relationship. The United States has the highest divorce rate in the world; about 40 percent of all American marriages end in divorce. However, these statistics include divorces among remarried couples; the initial divorce rate is lower: about 25 percent of first marriages end in divorce (Stevens-Long, 1979).

Being divorced changes a person's role and status and causes a reexamination of identity. Since there are no norms or expectations for the "once-married," divorced people are likely to feel cast adrift, rootless, and anxious. A survey of more than 2,000 adults showed that those who were divorced were less satisfied with their lives than the married, the never-married, or the widowed (Campbell, Converse, and Rogers, 1975). The dissatisfaction may come from several factors. Divorced people often regard the breakup of their marriages as evidence of personal failure. In addition, they often find themselves in serious financial straits; and they lose many friends, as people who related to them as part of a couple drift away.

When Mavis Hetherington, Martha Cox, and Roger Cox (1979) looked at the problems faced by newly divorced parents, they found that both men and women had difficulty handling their affairs, at least at first. Men found the practical problems of daily life particularly difficult, especially if their wives had not worked and they were used to having a full-time homemaker. Money problems often caused disagreements between divorced parents, who found it difficult to support two households on one salary.

The effects of divorce on self-concept were different for men and for women. Divorced mothers said they felt helpless and unattractive, and complained of a loss of identity because they were no longer linked to their husbands' status. Divorced fathers often said they no longer knew who they were and that they felt rootless and homeless. Both parents, but especially fathers, plunged into social activities; many tried self-improvement and took courses in photography, Eastern religions, or physical fitness. Men who had dressed conservatively often changed to flashy, fashionable clothing.

Divorced men and women generally tend to be less active socially than their married counterparts. Since American social life is centered around couples, divorced people tend to see less and less of their married friends, although they do begin to share time with divorced, separated, or never-married people. Divorced mothers who have primary custody of their children have less contact with adults than their ex-husbands do, and often report feeling "trapped" or "locked into a child's world."

Two years after divorce, couples in Hetherington's study were having sexual intercourse about as frequently as married couples, but the married people were happier with their lives. Some of the divorced men and women had a variety of sex partners, especially in the first year after divorce. Neither the men nor the women were satisfied with a series of superficial encounters, however, and both said they wanted sustained, meaningful relationships.

Most people do learn from failure, at least in marriage. Second marriages generally are as happy as first marriages that endure. Statistics show that 75 percent of divorced people remarry within five years of their decrees (Kimmel, 1974). Apparently, people are not disillusioned with marriage but only with the relationship they were in. As a result, a trend has developed toward serial or sequential marriages. The chances for remarriage vary by sex and age. Women under thirty are the most likely of all divorced people to remarry; after thirty, the tables turn and divorced men become the most likely to find another spouse.

People generally remarry for the same reasons they married in the first place. Men and women marry for love; and when they marry again they seem to work hard at making the relationship work.

Remarrying does not guarantee living happily the second time round, however. A second marriage has different problems from the first, and past experience usually has not prepared people to handle them. When Lillian Messinger (1976) interviewed seventy remarried couples, she found that they, like divorced persons who had not remarried, ranked their previous spouses' immaturity, sexual problems, and personal lack of motivation and readiness for marriage as the biggest problems in their broken marriages. Problems in the second marriages were different; whereas children and money were at the bottom of the list in the first marriages, they were at the top of the list in the second marriages.

Remarried people with children often find it difficult to maintain a comfortable relationship with their former spouses and to develop new households. Some partners find themselves caught between loyalty to their own children and their desire to please their new mates, whereas others feel guilty for not loving their new children. Financial responsibilities remaining from the first marriages create problems for the second. Some women reported feeling guilty about the burden their children placed on their new husbands, and some men felt uncertain about revising their insurance policies and wills.

ALTERNATIVES TO MARRIAGE

In the view of some younger adults, traditional marriage has failed and must be replaced with other styles of intimacy. Contemporary alternatives, such as singlehood, cohabitation, mate sharing, contract marriage, communal living, and group marriage are not new forms of human relationships. What is new about these alternatives is their openness to human sexuality and their ways of expressing intimacy and affection.

Singlehood

Singlehood is becoming increasingly common in Western societies as women and men remain unmarried longer than in past years. In 1960, 53 percent of American males and 28 percent of American females between the ages of 20 and 24 were unmarried; by 1976 these percentages had increased to 62 percent for males and 43 percent for females (Billingham, 1980). In the United States today, at any one time about a third of all adults are unmarried, separated, or in some way unattached (Libby, 1977). Although most divorced people remarry, the number of persons under thirty-five who have divorced but not remarried has doubled in the past ten years.

Increasing numbers of people are choosing singlehood as an alternative way of life. In interviews with young adults who had been involved in some type of exclusive sexual relationship before they chose a nonexclusive single life, Peter Stein (1975) found that men and women agreed that, although marriage offered economic, emotional, and sexual security, singlehood was attractive because it offered personal freedom, career opportunities, sexual availability and diversity, and a chance for self-improvement.

Cohabitation

Living together without a marriage contract, or **cohabitation,** is not a new phenomenon. Never before, however, has it been so visible, has the frequency of these relationships among college-educated individuals been so high, or has the relationship tended to be emotionally rather than financially based. Between 1960 and 1977, the number of cohabiting couples more than doubled (Yankelovich, 1981), and about 25 percent of young adults on college campuses have cohabited (Macklin, 1978).

Most couples do not make a conscious decision to live together. Instead, it happens gradually as the couple spend increasing amounts of time together. Although only a minority of cohabitants are committed to marrying their partners (Cole, 1977), most see living together

Increasing numbers of men and women are choosing to remain single because they believe that the unmarried state offers them freedom, career opportunities, sexual diversity, and opportunities for self-improvement. *(Eric Kroll/Taurus Photos)*

as a kind of trial marriage, a time for getting to know each other and for seeing whether the relationship can bear the closeness and realities of everyday life. The characteristics of cohabitating relationships are similar to those of marital relationships. Cohabitants, as do marrieds, frequently divide labor along sex-role lines and agree to be sexually monogamous (Bernard, 1977).

Sometimes partners become dissatisfied with this kind of arrangement because it lacks the apparent stability, security, and futurity of the married relationship. If the relationship does not work out, the partners are legally free, although generally not emotionally free, to leave. When cohabitation ends, the emotional, social, financial, and physical adjustments the partners must make are like those faced by divorcing couples.

Open Marriages and Mate Sharing

A growing number of couples in this country have chosen not to confine their sexual activities to the marital relationship. In 1948, 8 percent of the young wives interviewed by Alfred Kinsey acknowledged having had extramarital affairs; but by 1980, 41 percent of young American wives reported having had an extramarital affair (Wolfe, 1980). This large increase may indicate that the double standard for fidelity is giving way and that women are now about as likely as men to engage in extramarital affairs.

Some couples place extramarital sex on a formal basis, entering open marriages or seeking out opportunities for mate sharing.

Most people who enter sexually open marriages seek complexity, novelty, excitement, and increased personal awareness. According to Jacquelyn Knapp and Robert Whitehurst (1977), this sort of marital arrangement attracts two kinds of couples: (1) those who have a strong, affectionate, and respectful marriage and agree on the importance of expanding their interpersonal experiences, and (2) those who have unhappy marriages and are searching for an alternative to divorce. For couples in a shaky relationship, the sexually open marriage is rarely an effective Band-aid. According to Knapp and Whitehurst, couples with strong marriages who adopt the principle of sexual openness report improved personal awareness and fulfillment and increased self-esteem. They say that their sexual freedom strengthens their marital bond. According to these couples, the uncertainty, anxiety, and emotional pain of the open relationship generate high levels of communication, mutual problem solving, and continual excitement in their marital relationship.

Mate sharing, also called "swinging," refers to a mutual sexual exchange of partners between legally married couples. Few Americans are involved in mate sharing—only about 2 percent of all married couples, or 900,000 couples (Hunt, 1974). Couples who have tried mate sharing are likely to be well-educated and not particularly religious. Comparing swinging and nonswinging couples, Brian Gilmartin (1977) found that swingers had less emotionally satisfying relationships with their parents, saw their friends more often and depended on them more, and were less likely to become involved in conventional political or religious institutions. When he compared their sexual histories, Gilmartin found swingers had very early strong romantic interests and that they married earlier and had had sex with more partners than had nonswingers.

Husbands usually introduce the idea of mate sharing to their wives, and most men report learning about mate sharing by reading about it in newspapers, magazines, and books. People who support this way of life say that it enriches their marriage, provides variety, and contributes to individual growth, which makes marriage mutually satisfying. People who disapprove of mate sharing say that it is immoral, that it makes sex too impersonal, or that it violates the marital vows. Because mate sharing requires the consent of both partners, advocates of swinging claim that it is not adultery.

Commune members may be single or married, egalitarian or traditional, but nearly all seek intimacy within the extended family. ***(Dennis Stock/Magnum Photos)***

Contract Marriages

Among young couples who try to keep their relationships open and flexible, contract marriages are becoming popular. In this form of marriage, the couple draws up a contract or statement that specifies their values and communicates their expectations for the relationship. Many of the contracts emphasize an egalitarian rather than a traditional, male-dominated relationship. Common provisions in the contracts concern division of household responsibilities, division of assets held before marriage and income after marriage, caring for and support of children, and rules regarding career decisions and relationships with others—including sexual relationships. Many contracts also have clauses that cover changes, renewals, and termination of the agreement.

Groups

Group living arrangements fall into two general categories: communes and group marriages. Communal living is generally associated with the young and unmarried. There are, however, a number of communes made up of married couples who feel that only this style of living can make marriage and families satisfying. One thing most communes seem to have in common is the desire to achieve intimacy within the context of an extended family unit (Kanter, 1973). As we saw in Chapter 9, communes may have egalitarian or traditional sex-role arrangements, and communal life appears to vary from commune to commune.

Group marriage, which may involve any number of married couples, is a relatively rare alternative relationship in American society. Larry Constantine and Joan Constantine (1973; 1977) found that the average group consisted of four adult partners and three children and that personal growth was the most important reason for entering a group marriage. Other reasons for group marriage were similar to those given for entering a monogamous relationship: love, security, sex, child rearing, and companionship. As with sexually open marriages, couples who believed that multiple intimacy would solve their marital problems usually found that group marriages aggravated the problems.

Among the group marriages the Constantines studied, 80 percent of the participants regarded jealousy as a problem, and especially early in the history of most groups, the exchange of partners was fixed by a schedule of rotation in order to minimize the destructive emotion. By the conclusion of their research, the Constantines found that most group marriages had broken up and that monogamous marriages that predated the group's formation generally survived the dissolution.

SOCIAL-LIFE CHANGES

Career, marriage, and family are not the only concerns of young adulthood. These years are also a time for making friends and for developing new leisure interests, as well as for deepening old interests and friendships.

Friendships

Many of the factors important to the development of relationships that lead to marriage also loom large in the development of friendships. Friends are likely to live close together and to share similar interests, attitudes, and values. Not much else is known about the friendship patterns of adults, although most adults say they have only a few close friends and that the lack of more close relationships is felt as a serious void in their lives (Yankelovich, 1981). Studies have shown that most married couples have two close friends who live nearby and that, at any age in adulthood, men are more likely than women to initiate friendships for the couple (Babchuk, 1965). In addition, it is especially characteristic of young-married friendships that all the friends tend to be of the same age.

Because opportunities for vocational advancement may require well-educated younger couples to be highly mobile, the friendships they make in this period of life are not likely to be lasting. In contrast, less well-educated couples are more likely to have permanent friendships that revolve around the husband's job and that involve old high-school or even elementary-school friends.

Married individuals are more likely to have same-sex friends than friends of the opposite sex. One reason for this arrangement is that society generally regards opposite-sex friends as a threat to a marriage. In a survey of friendship (Parlee, 1979), about two-thirds of adults agreed that same-sex friendships are different from friendships with people of the opposite sex, primarily because opposite-sex friendships are often complicated by sexual feelings.

It has been proposed that friendships among males are stronger than friendships among females. However, in a study of 139 college students, Margaret Gibbs, Doris Auerback, and Margery Fox (1980) discovered that although both sexes valued empathy more than altruism or companionship in friends of the same gender, men were typically less friendly than women. On the basis of his review of studies exploring male friendship and intimacy, Jerome Tognoli (1980) concluded that men have more same-sex friendships than women, but that male friendships are generally not as deep and involve less self-disclosure than friendships among women. Similarly, a study of men at an Ivy League college showed than men are more likely to confide in female than in male friends (Komarovsky, 1976). Drawing on such findings, Tognoli suggests that fear of being considered homosexual, competition among men, overdependence on one woman for emotional self-disclosure, and socialization that stifles emotional expressiveness can act as barriers to the development of intimate friendships between men.

Leisure Activities

The fact that much of the young adult's life is bound up with his or her work has major implications for leisure activity. Ideally, work should be play, but since most people's work does not match their ideals, they must find other outlets for recreation and play. In Chapter 10, we saw the importance of recreation and play for the developing child and adolescent. Time for recreation and play is also important to adults; it helps them use up their surplus energy and meet their

The person who works at a sedentary job is likely to find relaxation in strenuous physical activities. *(© Leonard Spier 1981)*

needs for relaxation, creativity, and self-expression. Depending on their particular needs, adults may choose either physical or passive recreation. For example, a man who has been lifting beams all day on a housing project may prefer to spend a leisurely evening relaxing with a beer in front of the television. On the other hand, a man who has been trying to develop a series of equations to solve a complex engineering problem may look forward to playing tennis with a friend or to jogging along the beach.

Although leisure interests and activities in young adulthood are influenced by childhood experiences within families, marriage and parenthood also have their impact on the use of leisure time (Wilson, 1980). Among married adults, leisure time is likely to be spent in joint activities that encourage interaction between husband and wife and the development of shared commitments. As in later years, leisure activities are shaped by occupational choice, family roles, health, available time, financial resources, and personality (Kelly, 1974; 1975). During their thirties, when husbands and wives may be heading at full speed in different directions—men focusing on their careers and women on their families and often on their own careers as well—leisure time spent together is important for sustaining marital and family closeness as well as for expressing personal interests and needs.

As Chad Gordon, Charles Gaitz, and Judith Scott (1976) point out, the most popular leisure activities in young adulthood are centered on home and family: visiting with family and friends, watching television, gardening, pursuing hobbies, reading, and walking. Younger adults who read as a leisure activity often seek amusement instead of education in their reading, and they generally read on diverse topics. The young adult years are often filled with physically strenuous leisure activities: fishing, hunting, camping, swimming, skiing, and tennis. At this time, as in later years, men often prefer physical activity and activities away from home, whereas women spend much of their leisure time reading, cooking, and improving their homes.

Young adults do not spend all their leisure in play. Some go back to school, some work in the garden, and others spend long hours practicing musical instruments or developing skills in some sport. It is often difficult to categorize leisure activities, because one adult's play seems like hard work to another. Since it has been estimated that adults have twice as many free hours as were had in 1900, the kind of leisure activity they choose becomes more important in determining self-concept and satisfaction with life.

SUMMARY

1. Early adulthood is a time when individuals are confronted with the tasks of being adult, independent, and self-sufficient, and of becoming mature. Becoming mature in turn means becoming aware of who one is now and of where one wants to go in life, and it means working toward one's goals.
2. In these years an individual typically reaches the peak of physical agility, speed, and strength. Although physical aging begins dur-

ing these years, its effects generally are not noticed and are relatively inconsequential for most people.

3. During their twenties, many young adults make choices in such matters as a vocation or marriage, which give them social identity. During their thirties, they turn their attention to deepening and expanding their skills and bases of experience. For some, these years may involve questioning commitments made during the twenties. The way these early adult years are perceived and the kinds of choices that are considered possible are likely to vary, depending on an individual's gender and socioeconomic level and on cultural standards.

4. As adults develop an increasing sense of control over their lives, their self-esteem also becomes greater than it was during adolescence. The loosening of sex-role stereotypes has lead to the rise of androgyny (a self-image that includes both male and female characteristics) and to less traditional behavior. As young women have become involved in careers, young men have begun to question an overwhelming dedication to work, and most adult workers have become concerned with self-fulfillment.

5. Sexual relationships are most satisfactory when couples can communicate freely about sex. In young adulthood, the ability to learn and to remember is generally at its peak, as is the ability to think flexibly. Creativity is also high among young adults, especially in the arts and sciences.

6. Marriage is a major developmental decision that is often made during early adulthood. Once married, people must adjust to new social roles and to living with another individual. With the birth of a child, further—and even greater—adjustments must be made, and traditional sex roles reassert themselves. Divorce has increased, but most divorced people remarry, giving rise to serial, or sequential, marriages. Second or serial marriages have different problems from first marriages.

7. Singlehood is becoming increasingly common, with about a third of all adults unattached at any one time. Cohabitation, or living together without legal marriage, has more than doubled, and the characteristics and emotional adjustments involved in such a relationship are similar to those of marriage. Some marriages are now "contract marriages," in which all the obligations of both parties are spelled out. Open marriages, mate sharing, and group living arrangements are much less common than other forms of marriage and living arrangement.

8. Young adulthood is usually a time of experimentation and expansion in making friends and developing new leisure interests, as well as a time for deepening old interests and friendships. People's friends are likely to live close by and to share similar interests, attitudes, and values, and married individuals' friends are likely to be of the same sex. Young adults may choose either physical or passive recreation and play, but whatever its form, leisure activity is important as a way to use up surplus energy and to meet one's needs for relaxation, creativity, and self-expression.

MANUFACTURERS
11202
HANOVER

20 MIDDLE ADULTHOOD: MAKING THE MOST OF IT

Our uncertainty about middle age is reflected in the jokes we tell. When the middle-aged woman is an object of humor, we hear, "Middle age is when a woman's youth changes from present tense to pretense." Even presidents poke fun at the middle-aged. President Reagan once told a gathering, "Middle age is when you are offered two temptations and take the one that gets you home by nine o'clock." Because youth has been regarded as the most promising time of life in our society, many young people seem to believe that once they reach forty, they may as well sit in a rocking chair during their remaining days.

Although our society may be oriented toward youth, it is controlled by the middle-aged adult. In fact, the term "the command generation" has been coined to describe middle age and the position of the forty- to sixty-year-old in American society. Middle-aged adults hold positions in business and personal life that make them responsible not only for themselves but also for the young and the old. The advantage of all this responsibility is that it brings rewards in terms of power, prestige, and money. The middle adult years are generally a period of maximum productivity and maximum rewards.

One change that marks the middle adult years is that instead of using chronological age as markers of change and progress, people use their positions within various life contexts: self, career, family, community. In this chapter we will examine what it means to be middle-aged and focus on those characteristics that differentiate midlife from other periods of development. After discussing the meaning of maturity in middle adulthood, we will look at the physical changes that affect the middle-aged person and the new developmental tasks that must be confronted. We will examine change and stability in self-concept and self-esteem, in sexuality and intellectual processes. We will discuss the adjustments parents must make as their children leave home and as they become grandparents. Finally, we will examine social life in the middle years and its changing patterns of friendship and leisure.

MATURITY IN MIDDLE ADULTHOOD

Mature individuals in middle adulthood accept the new demands of these years and adjust to them. Mature individuals also become aware of and realistic about the changes occurring inside and outside themselves and about their ideals and goals in life.

Depending upon the person, awareness of middle age may be triggered by biological, psychological, or social events. A heightened awareness of personal mortality, a life-threatening illness, or stressful or unanticipated events, such as the illness or death of a parent, spouse, or friend may precipitate the realization that one is middle-aged. In addition, fewer child-rearing responsibilities, the feeling of decreased job mobility, and the sense that one has advanced as far as possible in a career may bring about an awareness of midlife (Cytrynbaum et al., 1980).

Men and women generally become aware of middle age for different reasons. Women tend to define their place in the life cycle by events within the family (Neugarten, 1968). For a married woman, middle age is closely linked to the time that she sends her children out into the world. An unmarried woman often becomes aware of middle age as she reflects on the kind of family she might have had. Men, by contrast, tend to become aware of middle age because of cues outside the family setting. For example, a man may find himself deferred to or treated ceremoniously by others for the first time in his life. Because middle age is generally thought of as the time of achieving occupational goals, men whose success has not matched their expectations generally have a heightened awareness of middle age (Kay, 1974).

Social class also has an important influence on a person's awareness of middle age (Neugarten and Hagestad, 1976). Middle age typically occurs later for middle-class men and women than for working-class people. An upper-middle-class business executive, for example, is in "the prime of life" at forty and considers middle age as beginning around fifty. By contrast, life goes more quickly for a blue-collar worker, whose occupation is often linked to physical strength and endurance. To the working class, people are in their prime at thirty-five and middle-aged at forty (Neugarten and Peterson, 1957).

Middle age is frequently marked by a change in life values and in the way that time is perceived. Instead of looking at life in terms of time-since-birth, as the young generally do, most individuals begin to look at life in terms of time-left-to-live. Aware that there is only a certain amount of time left, mature adults begin to structure their lives, their ideals, and their aspirations in terms of priorities.

Maturity in the middle years also refers to the individual's ability to deal effectively with the complexities and competing demands typical of this period (Pearlin, 1980). Having learned to handle past developmental demands, mature individuals have developed strategies that usually enable them to respond effectively to stress and change and to make judgments and decisions. A mature individual in the middle years seems to know when to pull back from a situation. Men and women are more likely than they were at twenty-five to be aware of the signs that tell them they are doing too much: the headaches, the stomach aches, the quick temper, the fact that nothing looks good to eat. A mature person is likely to say, "I cool myself down by accepting the fact that other people around me have to do their own learning and make their own mistakes. I stand back and simply don't let my insides get as involved as they used to . . ." (Birren, 1975). Thus, one effective strategy that mature individuals use is to be less emotionally involved in a stressful situation.

Maturity in middle age also tends to be characterized by a sense of self-confidence and competence. This I-know-I-can-handle-it attitude helps individuals deal effectively with the demands and events in their lives. Because expectations are important in determining the outcome of events, people who feel they can respond successfully increase the chance that they will. Mature individuals are characteristically less self-conscious about the impression that they are making on others, more sensitive to their

Item	Appropriate Age Range	Percent Agreeing on Age Range	
		Men	Women
A young woman	18–24	89	88
A young man	18–22	84	83
When a woman has the most responsibilities	25–40	93	91
When a man has the most responsibilities	35–50	79	75
When a woman accomplishes most	30–45	94	92
When a man accomplishes most	40–50	82	71
A middle-aged man	40–50	86	75
A middle-aged woman	40–50	87	77
When most people should become grandparents	45–50	84	70
When most people should be ready to retire	60–65	83	86
An old woman	60–75	83	87
An old man	60–75	75	57

FIGURE 20.1 Middle-class view of appropriate age ranges. People tend to judge their own and other people's behavior as being early, late, or on time. Although the timing of social clocks shifts with changes in culture, at any one time people within a social class generally agree on the appropriate age for certain tasks, as shown by the responses of middle-class, middle-aged adults in 1965. ***(Condensed from Neugarten, Moore, and Lowe, (1965)***

strengths as well as their limitations, and more confident about their ability to control and direct their lives than they were when they were younger.

PHYSICAL CHANGES

Adolescents look forward to the social strength and power that adulthood brings, but middle-aged adults begin to look backward, wishing they could recapture their youthful appearance and vigor (Nowak, 1977). The middle adult years are characterized by noticeable changes in the way the body looks and works. All the little changes that began in early adulthood progress steadily. Muscles do not work as strongly, as quickly, or as long as they used to. A less active life results in morning aches and pains and in middle-aged spread. The skin no longer stretches so tightly over the body, the face has a few wrinkles, and laugh lines lurk at the corners of the eyes. The hair does not grow as fast as it once did, and it may become thinner and begin to gray.

However, middle-aged declines in muscle strength and speed of reaction are likely to be of only marginal significance in a person's everyday life. Middle-aged people are not likely to be bothered much by these losses, because they have learned to compensate for them (Belbin, 1967). That is, people learn to pay attention to the features of a task in order to determine what they must do to maintain or even improve their performance in view of their changing physical abilities. David may begin to carry only two bags of groceries at a time instead of four and, at work, try to avoid jobs where speed is an important factor and instead look for jobs where he can work at his own pace.

Although the shadow of cardiovascular disease may darken the lives of middle-aged adults, many —like this man recovering from a stroke—are able to follow active lives. *(© Ira Berger 1982)*

For Susan as for other women, menopause is the medical marker of middle age. During menopause, which typically occurs between the ages of forty-five and fifty-five, ovulation, menstruation, and reproductive capacity cease. It has long been a popular notion that women experience the onset of menopause as a psychological crisis because it signals the end of reproductive capacity and youth. It is also commonly believed that menopausal women are irritable, nervous, and depressed. However, hot flashes and sweating are the only symptoms that have been found to be consistently associated with menopause (Notman, 1980), and although some studies find that 50 to 75 percent of menopausal women experience psychological symptoms, only a very few women seek psychological treatment (Resnick, 1979). In an earlier study, only 4 percent of menopausal women found their loss of reproductive capacity to be an important concern, and many said they were happy to be through with the menstrual cycle and the mothering of small children (Neugarten et al., 1963). Postmenopausal women typically feel better, more confident, calmer, and freer than before. Thus from a developmental standpoint, menopause is far from being "the change of life." Most middle-aged women do not see menopause as creating a major discontinuity in their lives. Instead, they feel that "You get what you are looking for." Women who expect to have difficulty during menopause are most likely to experience uncomfortable symptoms. But most middle-aged women tend to view menopause as a temporarily unpleasant period that is followed by increased happiness and health.

With menopause, the body's production of sex hormones (estrogen and progesterone) drops off to a negligible level. Until recently, estrogen, or hormone-replacement therapy, was widely used by women in an attempt to eliminate such menopausal symptoms as hot flashes, loss of hair, loss of skin elasticity, and changes in the breasts and genitals. Although estrogen therapy increases the physical comfort of menopausal and postmenopausal women, studies have shown that it also increases a woman's risk of developing uterine cancer (Finch and Flurkey, 1977). As a result, estrogen therapy has become less common.

Among middle-aged men, there is no similar cessation of reproductive ability. Instead, in some men the level of the male hormone (testosterone) drops off gradually during the middle years (Corby and Solnick, 1980). In later middle age, sperm are not produced as quickly and fewer of them are viable.

During middle age, men often become concerned about their health and tend to spend more time than women engaged in "body monitoring." This worry has some basis, since an increased incidence of chronic and life-threatening illness begins in the middle years, especially among men. The most common major disorders in otherwise healthy middle-aged Americans are overweight (16 percent), hypertension (8 percent), and arthritis (4 percent) (Weg, 1981). The death rate begins to increase in the middle adult years, accelerating during the late fifties. The most common cause of death in these years is cardiovascular disease; the second most common cause of death is cancer; and the third, hy-

THE EFFECT OF TYPE-A BEHAVIOR ON ACHIEVEMENT

Heart disease, which shows up with increasing frequency during middle adulthood, has been strongly linked to a pattern of behavior known as Type A, which appears to at least double a person's chance of developing heart disease. Type-A behavior is competitive, forceful, speeded-up, and sometimes hostile. The Type-A person is "aggressively involved in a chronic, incessant struggle to achieve more and more in less and less time, and if required to do so, against the opposing efforts of other things or persons" (Friedman and Rosenman, 1974). Because of the health risks connected with the Type-A pattern, most researchers try to tease out its precise link with cardiovascular disease (Matthews, 1982) or teach Type-A individuals to slow down and become calmer, to keep disease from developing.

One team of researchers has looked at Type A in a different manner. Since Type-A individuals are concerned about the esteem of significant others in their lives, and since they receive more academic honors than people who do not show Type-A behavior (Glass, 1977), Karen Matthews, Robert Helmreich, and their colleagues (1980) studied a group of successful men in midcareer to see if this competitive pattern had an effect on occupational achievement. They chose 118 male members of the Society of Experimental Social Psychology who were in their mid-forties and administered a series of tests.

Among this group of successful psychologists, Type-A behavior rating was strongly associated with scores on another scale that measured motivations connected with work. The more intense a man's Type-A behavior pattern, the more likely he was to prefer challenging tasks, to like work, and to be competitive in interpersonal situations.

All these men were successful, so the investigators judged their professional work in two ways: meritorious work (how often their research was cited by other researchers in the social sciences during a three-year period) and productivity (how many books and research articles they published during the same three-year period). Judging from their typical "struggle to achieve more and more in less and less time," we might expect Type As to score high on productivity and less high on meritorious work, since we learn early that haste makes waste and that we should do things slowly and do them right. But the results told a different story.

Type-A behavior was related to both measures, but psychologists who produced more career-related publications than the average society member had only slightly higher ratings on the Type-A behavior scale. However, meritorious work showed a strong connection to the Type-A pattern. Psychologists who were cited more often than the average society member were significantly higher on the Type-A scale; they also scored significantly higher on "hard-driving competitiveness." So despite its doubled risk of heart disease, the Type-A pattern gives an edge to researchers—or at least to male researchers.

pertension (American Heart Association, 1977).

There are, however, great individual differences in the rates of aging and in the way that people age. Not all the physical changes we connect with middle age are either necessary or due to the normal processes of aging; some may be the result of pathology, others, of disuse (deVries, 1981). There are a number of things that a person can do to decrease susceptibility to the common changes of middle age (Weg, 1981). For example, good nutrition, exercise, avoiding cigarettes and too much direct sunlight, and minimizing emotional stress can retard many of the expected changes in health and appearance.

Because American society stresses the importance of a youthful appearance, especially for women, making fading men and women feel and look young is big business. For those who can afford it, cosmetic surgery, health spas, gymnasiums, and weight-control centers offer youthful rejuvenation. Make-up techniques, hair creams and dyes, treatments for balding, wigs, ointments, creams, and vitamin therapies all promise to make the middle-aged look young again.

The cultural emphasis on looking and feeling young would make it seem likely that middle-aged men and women would be less happy about themselves and their physical appearance than younger adults are. Body image appears to be stable, however, because people over forty-five report just as much overall satisfaction with their bodies as do people under forty-five (Berscheid, Walster, and Bohrnstedt, 1973). Facial attractiveness does become a concern for women. Carol Nowak (1977) found that middle-aged women are more concerned with their facial appearance than are older or younger women, and are more likely to see traces of aging as affecting their general attractiveness. Physical appearance tends to be less important for men; both men and women report that age enhances a man's attractiveness.

Paul Gaugin, who in 1883 switched from stockbroker to painter, is a famous example of the radical career change that may come when an adult realizes that life will end. ***(New York Public Library)***

NEW DEVELOPMENTAL TASKS

Being middle-aged means being part of the age group that runs society and therefore means being in power, in command, and responsible. The middle years are characterized by a concern with expanding and asserting one's adulthood and, perhaps, with developing a new way of life. Some of the developmental tasks unique to these years include maintaining or reorienting oneself as an effective worker; realizing and accepting physical limitations and the prospect of mortality; assisting teen-age children to become responsible adults; relating to aging parents; establishing and maintaining a comfortable standard of living; achieving adult civic and social responsibility; maintaining friendships and social ties; and sustaining and developing leisure activities (Havighurst, 1972; Cytrynbaum et al., 1980).

During the forties and fifties, people reevaluate the past. As we saw in Chapter 18, an adolescent engages in introspection and tries to find a sense of personal identity. During the middle years, there is a return to introspection in an attempt to reassess goals and to develop increased self-awareness. After studying a group of middle-aged men, Daniel Levinson and his associates (1978) called the early forties a period of "mid-life transition" and suggested that self-evaluation occurs whether or not life goals are achieved. The central issue in this period is discovering "what I really want."

As individuals become aware that their future is finite, they develop an increasing sense of not having enough time to do most of the things they want to do (R. Gould, 1978). One task of the middle years, then, is to deal with the realization that life will end. The acceptance that remaining time is short leads many people to restructure their lives in terms of their priorities. For some, this may mean becoming more realistic about their goals. In his interviews with more than 500 white, middle-class people, Roger Gould found that, beginning in the forties, men and women increasingly agree that "I try to be satisfied with what I have and not to think so much about the things I probably won't be able to get." Middle-aged people also increasingly feel that "It's too late to make any major change in my career," that "Life doesn't change much from year to year," and that "My personality is pretty well set."

Becoming more realistic about goals doesn't necessarily mean becoming resigned. The realization that life will end leads some people to make radical changes. Some may try to make old dreams come true. Others, realizing that old dreams no longer offer satisfaction, may develop new ones. A study of middle-aged middle-class men who gave up their prosaic professions for new careers in the creative arts indicates that such switches entail a struggle in which the wish to preserve the past battles with the urge to discard it and rush into the future (Osherson, 1980). Midlife career changes have become more prevalent as the quest for self-fulfillment has taken precedence over the pursuit of worldly success among a majority of Americans; but among those who are past forty, only a small proportion of the working population are so deeply committed to the quest that they take such radical action (Yankelovich, 1981).

During the middle years, individuals become increasingly concerned for the growth and development of others. Some entered Erikson's stage of generativity during their thirties. But generativity, which involves caring for the next generation and becoming more concerned for their productivity, is especially characteristic of middle adulthood. For some, generativity may be achieved by helping children grow into independent, capable, competent, and loving adults. For others, it may mean helping younger workers become successful and competent in their jobs.

Additional tasks in the middle years include adjusting to new family roles. Adults often must assume the responsibility of being the child of aging parents and the task of establishing new boundaries of authority between themselves, their parents, and their children. Men and women face different tasks. Men face illness and increasing problems with their health and many women now begin to prepare themselves for the deaths of their husbands (Neugarten, 1977).

Other tasks that generally have to be dealt with during the fifties are the accelerating changes in body appearance and health, as well as changes in feelings of sexual potency and in sexual relationships. As William Masters and Virginia Johnson (1974) note, this decade is characteristically a time of tenderness, contentment, and tranquility in sexual relationships, and some individuals find this change disturbing when compared with the sexual fires of youth.

There may be personal turmoil in the middle years; but when life changes are expected and occur on time (Fiske, 1980), middle adulthood is a fairly stable period in terms of an individual's identity, coping capacities, influence, and productivity. If people can resolve their own uncertainties about their past and future, life is likely to become mellow. During the fifties, according to Gould (1978), parents are no longer seen as the cause of personal problems, children become a potential source of warmth and satisfaction, a spouse provides valued companionship, and there is increased self-acceptance and a heightened desire for friendship.

As at any age, approaching developmental tasks successfully in middle adulthood can sometimes be quite different from handling them successfully. For example, an adult may achieve occupational success in the middle years but be unable to deal with it. Some people turn to alcohol just at the moment of success and ruin what they had worked so hard and long to achieve. Others who had been successful at finding a spouse discover that once the children are gone, their marriage falls apart.

IDENTITY AND INTERPERSONAL BEHAVIOR

The way an individual characteristically responds to life's changes and challenges and to success and failure affects his or her sense of identity. Successful middle-aged adults tend to show both continuity and change in their sense of self (Giele, 1980). As new occupational and family roles are assumed, people incorporate these new aspects of themselves into their identities. For example, when a man at last starts his own business after twenty years of working for others, he will have a new image of himself as an entrepreneur. On the other hand, people's sense of who they are guides their life choices and decisions, and most individuals behave in ways that maintain their sense of self. If a woman views herself as having an eye for color and design, she is more likely to look for a job as an interior decorator than as a plumber.

Self-Concept and Self-Esteem

As individuals move into middle adulthood, they are likely to feel that they have changed greatly over the years; yet studies indicate that large changes are uncommon. This underlying consistency appeared when Diana Woodruff and James Birren (1972) asked a group of middle-aged people to fill out the same personality test they had taken as adolescents but to answer it twice: once to describe themselves now and once to duplicate the way they thought they had answered it twenty-five years earlier. There was almost no change between people's earlier scores as adolescents and their scores in middle age; both times they took the test they described themselves in almost the same terms.

However, the second test, in which middle-aged adults gave a retrospective picture of their adolescent selves, showed a relatively negative picture that disagreed with their own adolescent self-concepts. Most adults viewed their past selves as much less competent and as handling life much less well than they actually had done as adolescents. There was a subjective, but apparently nonexistent, discontinuity between their adolescent and adult views of themselves, suggesting that as these adults grew older, they may have manufactured a kind of identity gap.

Adults do get better as they get older. The sense of self-control and confidence that grows in the twenties and thirties continues to increase during the forties. George Vaillant (1977) found that men in their forties tend to use more mature strategies in coping with personal problems and to assume greater responsibility for them than they did as adolescents and young adults. They also show a more realistic sense of their strengths and weaknesses. Instead of assuming the young adult's attitude of "I can handle anything" or "I want to do it all myself," middle-aged adults have a growing awareness that other people can be relied on for advice and help.

Occupation, religious attitude, and self-concept interact to affect people's sense of control over their own lives, as Vira Kivett, Allen Watson, and Christian Busch (1977) found in a study of more than 300 middle-aged men and women in North Carolina. Individuals who had positive self-concepts and who saw themselves as active, optimistic, and autonomous felt that they were in control of their lives. This was especially true of men and women whose jobs gave them control over people or machines or who found a personal meaning in religion. By contrast, laborers or service workers, especially if they had high ideal self-concepts or used religion for status or prestige, were likely to feel at the mercy of their environment.

This sense of mastery over the environment shifts some time in the middle years, perhaps when people realize that life is finite. Although many young adults are confident that they can get what they want by their own actions and believe that boldness and risk taking bring rewards, attitudes change at some point in midlife. According to David Gutmann (1975) and Bernice Neugarten (1977), people start to focus on thoughts and feelings instead of on actions and events, and begin to be less confident that they can control their lives by their own actions.

Despite a lessened sense of mastery, self-esteem tends to increase into the middle years.

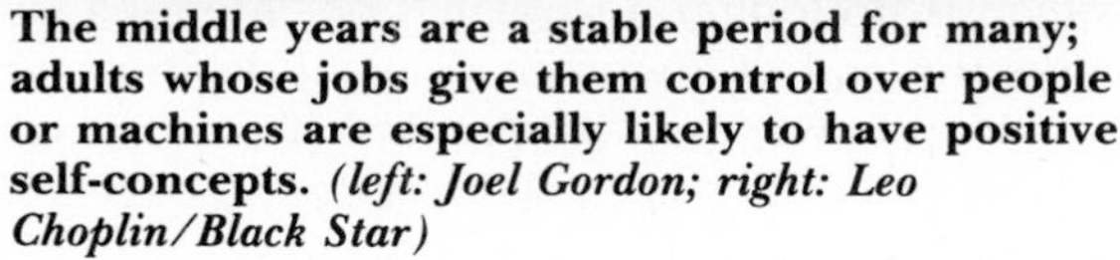

The middle years are a stable period for many; adults whose jobs give them control over people or machines are especially likely to have positive self-concepts. *(left: Joel Gordon; right: Leo Choplin/Black Star)*

Most middle-aged men continue to see themselves as being worthy (or unworthy) in terms of their careers or work achievement. By contrast, women split into traditional and independent groups. Florence Livson (1977) has found that both groups function successfully during their fifties; both groups develop stable personality styles by adolescence but each group follows a different path of psychological development. At fifty, "traditional" women are conventional, sociable, and nurturing; they are wives and mothers and move easily into middle age, finding satisfaction in interpersonal relationships even as their children grow up and away. "Independent" women at fifty are intellectual, achievement-oriented, and unconventional; they have been doers, not socializers, from adolescence. As forty-year-old wives and mothers, they are depressed and irritable, but by fifty, their crises are resolved. Their children leave home and relieve them of the mothering role, allowing them to revive their intellectual and career interests.

Changing Sex Roles

Although the historical period in which men and women live certainly influences their concepts of masculinity and femininity, the experience of parenthood appears to encourage the development of traditional sex differences, as we saw in

Chapter 19. According to David Gutmann (1975), as children grow up and leave home, and parents no longer feel the responsibility of child care, the strictures of traditional sex roles relax. Women generally become more autonomous, independent, assertive, and competitive ("masculine" traits), and men begin to develop the tender, sensuous, and dependent ("feminine" traits) aspects of themselves. This tendency has appeared in every culture Gutmann has studied: Americans in Kansas City, Navajos in Arizona, Maya in Mexico, and Druze in the Middle East. In addition, he reports that in fourteen out of twenty-six cultures studied by other anthropologists, a shift appeared in later life toward greater dominance among females. As middle-aged women and men begin to live out the behavioral and emotional potentials that have been suppressed by parenthood, Gutmann conjectures, both sexes tend to become androgynous.

However, it may be the birth of grandchildren and not simply the passage of children into adulthood that causes a shift in sex roles (Nash and Feldman, 1981). In one study, parents whose children had left home showed traditional gender differences, but among those who were grandparents, grandmothers were more autonomous than other women and grandfathers were more compassionate and tender than other men (Feldman, Biringen, and Nash, 1981).

In a study of blue-collar workers by Margorie Fiske and her colleagues, middle-aged women showed increasing mastery and self-assertion, and middle-aged men tended to show decreased commitment to mastery, curiosity, and creativity (Fiske, 1980). A study by Janet Hyde and Diane Phillis (1979), however, suggests that this tendency toward androgyny in midlife, and the expression of characteristics traditionally linked with the opposite sex, may be more easily accomplished by men than by women. Hyde and Phillis studied sex roles in 289 males and females whose ages ranged from thirteen to eighty-five. Only a few young adult males were classified as androgynous, but the percentage climbed among men between the ages of forty-one and sixty, many of whom had incorporated such characteristics as "gentleness" and "love for children" into their self-concepts. Although a tendency toward androgyny did not appear among the women, some traditionally "masculine" traits, such as "athletic" and "ambitious," may simply be irrelevant for middle-aged women.

Changes in Sexuality

Until middle age, the relationship of a woman's youthful beauty or a man's strength and virility to sexual ability is taken for granted. Consequently, as youthful beauty and strength fade, many men and women begin to question their adequacy in sexual performance (Rubin, 1968). Telling middle-aged people that youth and strength have little relationship to the ability to give and receive sexual pleasure does not stop them from worrying about it.

Historically, menopause has been thought of as the time when a woman loses not only her ability to reproduce but her sex drive and her femininity as well. Myths about the relationship of menopause to sexuality saturate our society. Old wives' tales warn: "After menopause a woman is no longer a woman," or "Menopause marks the end of a woman's sexual desires and sexual attractiveness." The reality of menopause is altogether different. One survey of 500 women (Boston Women's Health Book Collective, 1977) found that although younger women are likely to fear menopause, middle-aged women, who have experienced it, are positive and matter-of-fact about it. Many women report that after menopause their relationships with their husbands improve. Most middle-aged women feel that menopause has no effect on sexual relations, and some report that sexual intercourse becomes more important and more enjoyable (Neugarten et al., 1963).

Psychologically, a man's sexuality is more likely to be affected by age than a woman's. Changes in health, strength, appearance, and sexual responsiveness may threaten a man's sense of himself as "virile" or "manly." As we have seen, there are real changes in strength and appearance in the middle years. There are also real changes in sexual response. Men are slower to be aroused, slower to climax, and do not necessarily feel the urge to climax at every sexual encounter. Slowness in physical signs of arousal was characteristic of middle-aged men in a study by Robert Solnick and James Birren (1977), who measured penile responsiveness while men watched erotic movies. Among fifty-year-olds, penile diameter increased about six times slower than among men in their twenties.

Middle-aged men find that they need more direct stimulation to become aroused and that, after a climax, they require more time before they can become aroused again. These changes in sexual response in the middle years affect the nature of sexual experiences but do not decrease their pleasure. According to William Masters and Virginia Johnson (1970), how well a man copes with changes in his sexual responsiveness depends not only on his general ability to adapt to changes in his life but also on his past sexual relationships, his attitude toward aging, and his self-concept.

Thus, in the absence of major health problems, loss of sexual responsiveness is likely to be due to psychological factors, not physiological ones. Nevertheless, the incidence of sexual inadequacy in the human male increases sharply after the age of fifty. According to Masters and Johnson (1974), the single most important factor in reduced sexual responsiveness among middle-aged men appears to be the monotony of a repetitious sexual relationship. Other factors that may have a negative effect on a man's sexual responsiveness are preoccupation with his career or with economic pursuits, mental or physical fatigue, overindulgence in food or drink, or fear of impotence.

The majority of middle-aged men and women continue to be both interested in sex and sexually active. For example, Eric Pfeiffer and Glenn Davis (1972) found that among adults between the ages of forty-six and fifty, 90 percent of the men and 70 percent of the women expressed moderate to strong sexual interest. In general, the richer and the more regular an individual's sexual life has been, the more likely it is that his or her sexual interest and activity will be maintained throughout the middle years.

Intellectual Skills

Small signs in daily life lead many middle-aged men and women to fear the loss of their mental abilities. Often their memory for little things does not seem to be as good as it once was. It sometimes takes them longer to finish a task or solve a problem because they become distracted. As we will see, these common changes in intellectual skills are no reason for a person to believe that his or her mind is slipping.

Instead, if a person is healthy, many intellectual abilities show no change through the middle years and some continue to improve. Well-learned bits of information, knowledge of social rules, arithmetic skills, abstract reasoning, and vocabulary show no appreciable change over the midlife period (Schaie, 1980). People continue to store new information, and during the middle years there can be considerable increases in vocabulary (Birren, 1976). On intellectual tasks that demand speed, however, people begin to experience a modest decrease in performance beginning in the fifties (Schaie, 1980). For example, a fifty-year-old is slower than a twenty-year-old at tasks that require the coordination of eye-hand movements, such as solving a puzzle.

The results of long-term, longitudinal research confirm the absence of any large decline in intellectual abilities during the middle years. Since 1956, Warner Schaie and his colleagues have been studying the relationship between age and intellectual performance (Schaie and Labouvie-Vief, 1974). At seven-year intervals, people whose ages range from twenty to past eighty have taken Thurstone's Primary Mental Abilities Test. The results show no significant age changes in performance on any of the five primary mental abilities—verbal meaning, reasoning, space, number, and word fluency—until people reach their late sixties.

Individual differences in intellectual functioning that have existed since childhood are likely to become even more marked throughout middle adulthood, primarily because of the importance of environment on intelligence. Education, social class, health, activity, and the level of environmental stimulation continue their strong influence and are generally more important than age in determining just how efficiently people function intellectually (Kohn, 1980).

Although many middle-aged people fear that they can no longer learn new skills easily, the ability to learn and to remember shows little decline in middle age. If middle-aged people are given as much time as they need, they do about as well as young adults on tests of learning and memory. In addition to the factors affecting individual differences, the degree of a person's motivation to learn, the level of interest the information or skill has for an individual, and whether she or he has had recent educational experience are likely to have a strong influence on learning and memory abilities—as they do at any age.

Many people assume that middle-aged adults are more rigid than younger adults and that a middle-aged person holds tightly to a point of view, resisting change when the situation calls for it. This assumption appears to be strengthened by the finding that people over fifty-five are more likely than younger adults and adolescents to agree with clichés (Riegel and Riegel, 1960). However, the ability to think flexibly, to shift the set of the mind to solve a problem, is generally as good during middle age as it was in young adulthood. What seems to be a rigid approach to problem solving is less likely to be due to "rigidity" or "caution" than to the way that the middle-aged adult's abilities have been affected by past experiences. The accumulation of past associations and experiences can interfere with how flexibly a middle-aged adult solves problems. Long-established ways of solving problems, which tend to look rigid in laboratory situations, may serve individuals well as they confront the problems of everyday life.

Like other intellectual skills, creativity is not the exclusive possession of the young. Adults in their middle years are often equally creative. In fact, when creativity is measured in terms of total productivity rather than in terms of quality, creativity peaks in the middle and later years. For example, the forties are generally the most productive period of life in the humanities, sciences, and arts—and the fifties are not far behind (Dennis, 1966). Although individual productivity in the arts declines slightly during the middle years (except for novelists), the productivity of persons working in the sciences and humanities remains fairly stable. This discrepancy in productivity is probably due in part to the fact that scholarly or scientific creativity requires more years of study than artistic genius does, so that scholars and scientists may not begin to produce until a decade or more after musicians, poets, or painters have launched their careers.

MARRIAGE AND FAMILY LIFE

The life cycle of the family begins in the early adult years with marriage followed by a time of bearing and rearing children. Now, as couples enter their middle years, they face the tasks of relating to adolescent children, encouraging them to become independent and responsible adults, and adjusting to being alone together once the children have left home. As Evelyn Duvall (1971) points out, in many ways the family cycle resembles the life cycle of individual development. In each phase of the family cycle, changes occur that require individuals to adjust to new roles and to develop new ways of seeing themselves in the context of changing interpersonal relationships.

Historically, the postparental period of family life is new. At the turn of the century it was rare for both parents to live to see their last child marry and leave home. Today, because people are living longer and having smaller families, marital partners can expect to have a life together for a decade or two after their children leave home. On the average, men are fifty-four and women are fifty-one when their last child is married for the first time (Norton, 1974). This postparental period is characterized by its own unique set of psychological and social challenges.

Parental and Postparental Life

Although the middle years of parental life are a time of relative stability, there is also considerable stress. The tension in many middle-aged marriages is reflected in the divorce rate. From 1970 to 1974, the biggest rise in divorce occurred among women approaching forty (Bernard, 1975). It is, however, still true that the incidence of divorce declines with years of marriage.

Couples are less likely to divorce after twenty years of marriage, but their satisfaction with marriage often continues to decline until their children are grown. Adolescent children generally put a considerable emotional and financial strain on the marital relationship. In a study of over 800 married couples, Boyd Rollins and Harold Feldman (1970) found that marital satisfaction, especially for women, decreased during the early adult years of childbearing and child rearing and reached its lowest point just before adolescent sons and daughters left home for good. Couples in midlife generally report less communication, companionship, and affection than in their early years of marriage.

Although many couples experience a disenchantment with love and marriage, not all do. Middle-aged couples who have never considered divorce fall into several kinds of relationships (Cuber and Harroff, 1965). On the negative side, some marriages are characterized by continual tension and others by unsatisfying relationships between people with happy memories of their early years together. A third group of couples expect little from their relationship and get their satisfaction from material possessions and children. But a considerable proportion of midlife marriages are highly satisfying and are characterized by genuine sharing, companionship, and affection.

Once the children have gone, the majority of middle-aged couples enter a new era of freedom: freedom from financial responsibilities, freedom to be mobile, freedom from household responsibilities and chores, and freedom to be the people they want to be (Deutscher, 1968). Most couples report that after the children have left, they laugh more together, have more discussions, and work together more often on projects. Wives, especially, are likely to feel much more satisfied with their marriage once the children have left home. Apparently, companionship in the relationship, which tends to be reduced when children are growing up, is critical to a woman's satisfaction with her marriage.

Although the newly childless home presents an important transition point in the lives of middle-aged men and women, it does not mark the end of family involvement; instead, involvement with sons and daughters enters a new phase.

Parenthood Family conflicts are inevitable between generations because each generation is at a different point in its developmental agenda and faces different developmental tasks. Middle-aged parents and their almost-grown children often argue over their changing roles, their various responsibilities, the children's strivings for autonomy, and what the parents may see as the disintegration of family ties.

The adolescent's search for identity and independence is a developmental issue not only for the adolescent but for his or her middle-aged parent as well. Conflicts between parents and their adolescent children are likely to arise over sexuality, achievement, the setting of limits, values, and problems in communication (Rapoport, Rapoport, and Strelitz, 1977). Parents must also deal with the task of letting their children go. This can be an especially difficult issue for a mother who has defined her own identity in terms of her parental role. Some women are reluctant to encourage their offspring to leave home because once the children are gone, the women must redefine themselves. The transition to postparental life is, however, neither as abrupt nor as difficult as is generally assumed. Most parents gradually prepare for the day when their offspring will get married or leave home, and the preparation for and anticipation of postparental life is often the most stressful point in a marriage relationship. By the time the event arrives, many parents have already handled the problem.

Parents prepare themselves in a number of ways. First, an important American value, the belief that change is both inevitable and good, lessens the impact of this transition. As one father put it: "Of course you hate to give up your

State of Marriage	Wives		Husbands	
	Very Satisfied	Less Satisfied	Very Satisfied	Less Satisfied
New Marriage	74	4	55	6
New Parents	76	6	699	8
Preschool Children	50	17	61	8
School-Age Children	35	21	39	16
Adolescent Children	17	15	44	15
Launching Children	8	76	9	66
Postparental Parents	17	70	24	63
Aging Marriage	82	4	66	4

FIGURE 20.2 Marital satisfaction over the life span. The average person's satisfaction with the married state generally declines until the children leave home, with satisfaction returning among older adults. ***(Based on Rollins and Feldman, 1970)***

daughter, but I think we all understand that it is the way of life. You can't stand still; you can't be the same forever. Life moves on and that is the more natural thing" (Deutscher, 1973). Second, many middle-class parents have a chance to try out the postparental role when their sons and daughters go away to college (Sullivan and Sullivan, 1980). Other parents get the opportunity when a son or daughter enters military service. College and the military not only wean young adults away from their parents but also wean parents away from their offspring. Finally, in some families, young people spend so little time at home that the adjustment to postparental life is gradual.

The transition to the childless home is likely to be easier for women who perceive their sons and daughters as "on time" in such developmental events as college entrance and marriage. If a woman thinks that her offspring are well on the way to being educated, married, and fully developed as individuals, she is likely to feel free to pursue goals for herself. As Donald Spence and Thomas Lonner (1971) note, this means that the fewer long-range goals a mother has for her offspring, the sooner she will perceive herself as having completed the parental phase of her life. Fathers, especially those who work long hours, who are heavily involved in their careers, or who travel extensively, are likely to find the transition less difficult than mothers. Thus, parents who take advantage of their periodic opportunities to experience what postparental life will be like generally find it easier to be alone with each other.

When the young adult leaves home, the parent-child bond does not end. In fact, young adults are likely to be in contact with their parents more often than with their siblings. According to Judith Stevens-Long (1979), 70 percent of young married men and women visit their parents once a week. Contrary to popular belief, young married people also seem to get along with their in-laws, often spending more time with them than with their friends or neighbors (Stinnett and Walters, 1977). When tension exists, it is most likely to occur between a young wife and her middle-aged mother-in-law. When children are born and the mother-in-law assumes the role of grandmother, the tension frequently melts away.

Middle-aged parents generally continue giving financial and emotional support to their grown children. If the two generations live near each other, parents often provide direct services to their children, shopping, baby-sitting, or caring for sick family members.

Relating to Aging Parents Middle-aged adults often find themselves responsible for two generations. They have their own children to care for and they also may become responsible for their aging parents. As longevity increases, this situation becomes more common. Approximately 25

Parents who prepare in advance for the time when their grown children leave find the transition to a childless home is eased. *(Ken Heyman)*

percent of fifty-eight and fifty-nine-year-olds have one living parent, and among men and women aged fifty-eight to sixty-three, 10 percent have both parents living (Brody, 1979).

In one large survey, more than a thousand adults were asked about major changes in their lives over the past four years. The second most frequently reported change had to do with a parent or parent-in-law. Adults were deeply concerned about aging parents, whether or not the adult child lived near the parent or they were emotionally close. Although women are generally considered to be the most concerned about family relations, these women were only slightly more concerned about their aging parents than were the men (Neugarten, 1979a). Vern Bengston and Judith Treas (1980) suggest that as more women pursue careers outside the family, fewer may be willing to assume the primary responsibility for their aging parents.

Middle-aged adult children assist their parents in a number of ways, varying from economic support to personal care, from help with transportation to sharing of outings and holidays, from gifts of money and food to help with housekeeping and home chores (Sussman and Burchinal, 1968). This assistance takes place against the background of a parent-child relationship that can be positive or immensely trying. The relationship is generally most satisfac-

Adult children and their parents often share outings and holidays, and the children assist their parents in many ways. *(© Leonard Speier 1979)*

tory when it is characterized by independence and friendship rather than by dependence and authority (Adams, 1970). Health plays an important role in making independence possible. After interviewing adult children and their aging parents, Elizabeth Johnson and Barbara Bursk (1977) found that the more favorably the aging parents rated their own health and the more positive their attitude toward aging, the better the parent-child relationship. The healthy older parent also can serve as a positive role model, showing the adult child how aging can be handled well.

The attitude of the aging adult parent affects the relationship in other ways. In a study of middle-aged daughters and their mothers, Sylvia Weishaus (1979) found that neither the daughter's nor the mother's current situation (work, marital status, social class, education, or mother's age) had much effect on the quality of the relationship. Instead, middle-aged daughters felt warmly toward their mothers when the mothers approved of them, were interested in them, and tended not to criticize them.

When aging parents are ill or frail, have waning mental powers, face financial problems or the death of a spouse, or must be hospitalized or placed in a nursing home, the relationship with their adult children often becomes strained. Psychological problems appear to strain the parent-child relationship more than do physical problems. For example, Bertha Simos (1973) found that middle-aged children felt they could handle their parents' physical problems without much difficulty, even though attending to these problems required considerable time and energy. The psychological and interpersonal problems and the problems of social isolation were viewed as the most difficult to deal with. These adult children regarded their parents' interpersonal problems as the result of increasing psychological rigidity, and the children often urged their parents to become more socially active and were unwilling to accept the fact that their parents found it difficult to make new friends.

The mental problems of aging parents also were found to be most distressing in a study by Betty Robinson and Majda Thurnher (1976). The more severe a parent's mental problems or the more involved an adult child was in helping the parent, the lower the morale of the child. In addition, as the parent's health deteriorated, these middle-aged adult children tended to disengage from their parents, apparently as a way of protecting themselves from the pain of watching the parent decline in physical or mental health.

Parental incapacity is likely to pose the greatest crisis for the middle-aged child. The child may have to decide whether to take the parent into his or her own home or to place the parent in institutional care. The older and the sicker the aging parent, the greater the probability that adult children will take him or her into their homes. According to Bernice Neugarten (1979a), one in five women and one in ten men over the age of seventy-five live with one of their children. Three times as many elderly parents live with an adult child as reside in an institution, and the ability of middle-aged adults to adjust to having an aging parent living in their home depends greatly on the middle-aged adult's expectations as to whether the adjustment will be easy or difficult.

As Sandra Newman (1976) points out, either living arrangement has disadvantages for the middle-aged adult child. When aging parents live in the home, adult children generally feel that their freedom and privacy are limited; in addition, interpersonal conflicts become a problem. When aging parents live in an institution, the adult children generally find visiting a problem because of the distance between the family home and the facility, feel guilty about the decision to institutionalize the parent, and worry about the parent. Newman found that adult children who had decided to place their parents in some sort of institutional care were less certain than those who took parents into their homes that they had made the correct decision. Regardless of the decision, the more satisfied the aging parent was with the living arrangement, the more satisfied the adult children were with it.

Grandparenthood Besides concern for the previous generation, the middle-aged adult often has responsibilities that develop when his or her children become parents. Becoming a grandparent is more likely to occur in middle-age than in later adulthood, and many grandparents today are in their early forties. Middle-aged grandparents are likely to be working, married, and vigorous. Although most men and women enjoy being grandparents, not all do. Lillian Troll (1980) found that forty-year-olds tend to be less positive about their status as grandparent than those in their fifties, sixties, or seventies. She suggests that forty-year-olds may be uncomfortable with grandparenthood because they have been made grandparents early—before their social clocks reached the time for the grandparent role.

Grandmothers and grandfathers generally relate to their grandchildren in different ways. Gunhild Hagestad (1978) studied eighty grandparent-grandchild pairs and found that grandmothers' relationships with the grandchild were warmer than grandfathers' but that both grandmothers and grandfathers reported that they influenced their grandchildren. In extending their influence, grandfathers said they focused on the areas of work and education with their grandsons. Grandmothers' influence spread wider, including values and way of looking at life, interpersonal relationships, coping strategies, and style of life. Both grandfathers and grandmothers avoided arguments with their grandchildren by shunning topics of conversation where disagreement lurked, such as sexual and religious practices.

In an earlier study of grandparents, Bernice Neugarten and Karol Weinstein (1968) found five different styles of relating to grandchildren. Three of the styles are fairly traditional. First is the formal grandparent, who tends to leave the role of parent to the child's parent but likes to offer special treats. The second type, the surrogate parent (typically a grandmother), takes care of the child at the parent's request and is most likely to be found in a home where the mother works. The third kind of traditional grandparent is the repository of family wisdom, who sees him- or herself as an authority and teaches special skills.

There are two less traditional ways in which grandparents relate to grandchildren. The fun seeker is the grandparent who plays with the child simply to have fun. This style of grandparenthood is informal, and both the grandparent and the grandchild derive pleasure from the relationship. Finally, there is the distant-figure style, which characterizes the grandparent who relates to the child only on special occasions such as birthdays or religious holidays. These less traditional styles of grandparenthood occur more often today than in the past and are more commonly found among younger grandparents; older grandparents generally adopt one of the three traditional styles.

Neugarten and Weinstein went beyond styles of grandparenthood and explored the meaning of being a grandparent. Most of the seventy grandparents in their study expressed comfort, satisfaction, and pleasure with their role. As few as one-third reported that being a grandparent was uncomfortable, disappointing, or unrewarding. When asked specifically what being a grandparent meant to them, some said that they felt a sense of biological renewal ("It's through my grandchildren that I feel young again") or biological continuity with future generations. This aspect of grandparenthood

Grandfathers say they try to influence their grandchildren in choices concerning work and education. (© *Mead Powers 1980/West Stock Inc.*)

tended to be more important for grandmothers than for grandfathers.

Some found that grandparenthood provided emotional self-fulfillment in a way that being a parent did not. This aspect of grandparenthood was likely to be especially important for men, who felt that they were better grandfathers than they had been fathers. To some individuals, being a grandparent meant being a teacher or a resource person. In this role, grandparents saw themselves as contributing to their grandchild's welfare by giving money or emotional support. Some people regarded grandparenthood as an extension of the self, so that the grandchild was expected to accomplish what the grandparent had always dreamed of doing.

Finally, there were some grandparents for whom the existence of grandchildren had little meaning or effect on their lives. These grandparents tended to feel a psychological distance from their grandchildren. Sometimes the distance developed because they were too busy themselves to cultivate the relationship; at other times it was because they disapproved of their own child's marriage or the younger couple's decision to have a child. Some grandparents who reported a psychological distance, however, said that it was physical distance that minimized the meaning of grandparenthood.

Divorce and Remarriage

Some middle-aged couples wait until their children grow up and leave home and then end their marriage. Although the divorce rate is not quite so high in middle adulthood as it is in early adulthood, it remains substantial throughout the years just after the children are likely to have left home (U.S. Bureau of the Census, 1972a). As in the young adult years, the divorce rate is higher for blacks and for low-income individuals without a college education. Less wealthy people often separate instead of getting a legal divorce, because separation is not so financially devastating as divorce. In middle age, the demands on the newly divorced individual to adjust and change, as well as the impact of divorce on individual development, are like those faced by the young adult.

Divorce can be especially difficult for middle-aged people. Neither women nor men may have had recent practice in developing new intimate relationships with the opposite sex, and the process is likely to be lengthier and more stressful for them than it is for young adults. A middle-aged woman who has depended on her husband's position for her own identity and for her financial security is likely to find divorce particularly stressful. The recent passage of no-fault divorce laws has led to a trend away from permanent alimony, placing an additional burden on the middle-aged woman who has no job skills or profession.

In middle age, as in the early adult years, most people who get a divorce remarry. The rate of marriage remains higher for divorced men and women than for single persons at any age. The major change in the middle years is that marriage rates among women drop below those for men. That is, in the early adult years women are most likely to remarry, but in the middle years it is the men who marry again. This situation comes about partly because death rates for men begin to increase and partly because women traditionally marry older men. The result is that middle-aged women have an increasingly limited pool of marriageable men, whereas men can choose from an expanding group of marriageable women.

ALTERNATIVES TO MARRIAGE

Middle-aged adults are less likely than young adults to adopt a nontraditional way of life as a conscious choice. Some may simply continue the nontraditional lives they adopted years before. A single adult becomes the "never-married" adult of the middle years. Although some middle-aged single people would prefer to be married, death or divorce leaves a considerable number of people without partners. Finally, a few middle-aged people actively seek such alternatives to traditional marriage as extramarital relationships.

Most people who marry do so by the time they are forty. Among those who choose not to marry are a number of homosexual men and women. Others who stay single may be people who have rejected the idea of marriage or who simply have been unable to find permanent partners. For whatever reason, about 4 to 5 percent of middle-aged men and women have never been married. The unmarried men tend to have lower incomes and occupations than their married counterparts, but never-married women are likely to have good incomes and to be well-educated. This disparity adds to the problem of the single woman who wants to marry, because most people tend to marry people who are like themselves.

During the middle years, a good many people find themselves alone after the unexpected death of a spouse. Living through the death may be more stressful for the middle-aged than for the old, simply because the death occurs "too soon" and has not been anticipated (Fiske, 1980). Older widows seem to adjust more easily to their new role than younger widows, in part because there are more older companions available. A middle-aged woman who loses her husband often feels isolated, since most of her friends are occupied with their husbands and move in a society of couples. But at any age, the death of a spouse is so stressful that for a year or so afterward, death and suicide rates are substantially higher among the widowed than among married people.

The death of a spouse not only ends a man's role as a husband and a woman's role as a wife but also changes relationships with in-laws, the surviving spouse's friends, friends made as a couple, co-workers, and even with the widow's or widower's own family. The more dependent an individual has been on a spouse, the more life is disrupted by the partner's death. Like the newly divorced person, the wife finds she is missing a handyman and the husband discovers he is without a cook and housekeeper. Beyond such practical matters is the loss of a friend, companion, or lover; and as we will see in Chapter 21, the sense of personal loss is acutely painful. As among the divorced, middle-aged widowers have a higher chance of remarriage than do widows. Widows who lose their husbands suddenly, with no warning, seem least likely to remarry (Bowlby, 1980), and both widows and widowers remarry less often than their divorced counterparts.

Although extramarital relationships are becoming increasingly common among young adults (Libby, 1977), not much is known about extramarital activity among adults in midlife. The most reliable information regarding middle-aged people comes from Alfred Kinsey (1948; 1953). He found that males in lower socioeco-

The death of a spouse is always stressful, but when it occurs in middle age, women feel isolated and have a difficult time adjusting to their single status. *(Charles Harbutt/Magnum Photos)*

nomic classes had the most extramarital intercourse as young adults, and that the frequency of their extramarital relationships dropped off steadily until they reached fifty. However, college-educated males tended to have more extramarital affairs as they grew older. Kinsey found that education had no effect on the incidence of extramarital relationships among women, but society has changed radically since his survey. Now that women increasingly occupy the same kinds of positions in business and industry that were filled primarily by males in 1948, added prestige, freedom, and money may lead them to adopt the sexual practices of college-educated males.

The midlife extramarital relationship is not necessarily associated with marital unhappiness. In a study of middle-aged midwestern couples, Ralph Johnson (1970) found that 30 percent of the husbands with extramarital experience and 60 percent of the wives with such experience had high levels of marital adjustment. According to John Cuber (1969), middle-aged people seek extramarital intimacy for three reasons: to compensate for a disappointing marriage; to cope with long separations from a spouse caused by the demands of one's occupation or by war; or because they believe in an open marriage in which extramarital intimacy is fully sanctioned.

SOCIAL-LIFE CHANGES

As adults move into their middle years, social interaction tends to differ in both type and extent. Adolescents generally use leisure activities to assert their autonomy from parents and to form closely knit groups with their peers. In young adulthood, peer-group involvement loses its intensity and leisure interests and social activities become family centered. Over the adult years of development, individuals tend to become more involved in organizational activities, and they also increase their civic and political participation. For example, middle-aged people are more interested in political issues, are more politically active, and are more likely to vote in national elections than are young adults (Hudson and Binstock, 1976); during the middle years, 75 percent of men and 73 percent of women vote in national elections, as compared with 53 percent of men and women between eighteen and twenty-four (Wolfinger and Rosenstone, 1980). Throughout the middle adult years, individuals participate actively in politics by making contributions, circulating petitions, and occupying positions of political leadership.

Friendships

Roger Gould (1978) found that people in their forties and fifties show an increased interest in organizations and friends. Most men and women agree that they "like a very active social life" during their forties and that they would "feel lost without [their] friends" during their fifties.

In the middle years, similar interests and activities are more important than similarity of age in the choice of friends. The friends of most married couples are other couples whose children are close in age to their own; divorced people make friends with other divorced people; newly married middle-aged couples are likely to find friendships with others like themselves. Occupations provide another basis of friendship: plumbers generally make friends with plumbers, physicians with other physicians. Friendships developed in earlier years frequently endure despite physical separation. When Beth Hess (1972) talked to middle-aged people who had moved within the last five years, she found that they named as best friends women and men who lived in their previous communities.

When a divorced person remarries, she or he finds many new friendships, not only because the spouse has friends but also because married people tend to have more friends than single people do. But friendship is important to single people; middle-aged adults who have never married must meet their need for companionship with friends. Thus most middle-aged women who have never married have a close friend or confidant with whom they travel and party and to whom they turn for help and emotional support.

Leisure Activities

While a married couple's children live at home, the social activities of both mother and father are usually determined by their children's activities: Boy Scouts, Campfire Girls, Parent-Teacher Association, Sunday School, Little League. When their offspring marry, however, parents are free to develop their own circle of friends, and leisure activities generally become less home-centered. Couples tend to spend evenings out, to travel, and to develop their personal interests. With fewer financial responsibilities, many middle-aged individuals find they have more money to spend on their leisure activities. The transition from activities and attachments inside the home to activities outside tends to be easier for women who develop outside interests before their offspring leave home (Deutscher, 1973).

As a result of life's many changes, middle-aged people often have more time on their hands than ever before (Wilson, 1980). People who never had trouble finding some pleasurable activity to occupy their free time now have time to do what they want to do. But people who had been too busy with their careers to develop interests outside of work find learning to use leisure a difficult adjustment. Some people look at their new leisure as a freedom that challenges them to develop a different, more satisfying life style.

When Chad Gordon, Charles Gaitz, and Judith Scott (1976) examined the leisure interests of nearly 1,500 men and women who ranged in age from twenty to ninety-four, they found that activities in the middle adult years tended to become more sedentary than in young adulthood. Middle-aged men and women infrequently participated in activities or hobbies that required quick adjustment, produced excitement, or involved danger. Middle-aged people said they got the most pleasure out of watching sports, discussing important issues, participating in organizations, and improving their homes. Home-bound activities, such as entertaining friends, cooking, and watching television, were enjoyed as much in the middle years as in young adulthood. Men were more likely to use their leisure time for watching sports events and engaging in outdoor activities, whereas women were more likely to use their time for cooking, improving their homes, and going to plays, concerts, or museums.

Thus a youthful mountain climber may become a backpacker in his or her middle years. And those who enjoyed hang-gliding or motorcycling as young adults may switch to watching others do it after they have turned forty. But not all middle-aged people become less active. Increasing numbers of middle-class men and women have become concerned about the unhealthful effects of sedentary life, and have begun jogging, playing tennis, and engaging in other strenuous activities (deVries, 1981), and there are some indications that the resulting physical fitness improves mood and self-concept (Folkins and Sime, 1981). Such exercise can also be relaxing. Although middle-aged people may find that watching television or sipping a glass of wine relaxes them after a hard day's work, they are also likely to note that they feel sleepy. By contrast, after jogging or swimming they are likely to feel more relaxed, but also more alert.

Americans apparently have trouble separating recreation and leisure from their work. As John Kelly (1977) has pointed out, a close look at the choices of leisure activity makes it clear that most recreational activities are related to work. For example, an auto mechanic may read a copy of *Car and Driver* magazine, a physician may read a medical journal, an office worker may go to school during the evenings to get a better job.

This preference for work is deeply rooted in the history of our society and is especially likely to be reflected in the values of middle-class men and women in midlife. For example, when Eric Pfeiffer and Glenn Davis (1971) asked people if they would continue to work if they did not require the money, 80 percent of the women and 90 percent of the men said they would still work. Most reported that they got more satisfaction from work than from leisure and that they did not want more free time. People who were employed also said that they had had "more fun" lately than those who had not worked. It appears that many middle-aged people have little interest in using their free time for pure recreation.

Leisure or recreational activities tend to be more related to social class and to personal adjustment than to age or to sex (Gordon, Gaitz, and Scott, 1976). People in low socioeconomic groups generally use their leisure time for relaxing diversions: watching television, visiting their families, pursuing their hobbies, hunting, or fishing. They are especially likely to spend their free time with friends or relatives of the same sex. People in high socioeconomic groups are likely to use their free time to engage in cultural and educational activities: going to plays and concerts, taking an active role in clubs and organizations, traveling, and going to parties. The more education and income people have, the more they tend to participate in activities that are unconnected with work and the more they enjoy leisure. Presumably money frees people to do what they want to do where they want to do it, and education tends to make them aware of more varied ways of passing leisure time.

SUMMARY

1. A person's awareness of middle age may be triggered by biological, psychological, or social events, with social class affecting the perceived date of its onset. During middle age, an individual's values and the way time is perceived often change. Mature individuals have developed effective strategies to deal with changes, responsibilities, and demands.
2. Middle adulthood is characterized by noticeable changes in the appearance and functioning of the body. Menopause is the medical marker of middle age for women, but there is no known comparable marker for men. Most middle-aged people learn to compensate for any declines or losses in physical abilities and show as much satisfaction with their bodies as do younger adults.
3. Middle adulthood is a fairly stable period, and its developmental tasks revolve around expanding and deepening skills, goals, productivity, and social relations. For many, it may also require adjusting to new family roles as children grow up and leave home.
4. Many middle-aged people feel they have changed greatly over the years, but research indicates that large changes in self-concept or self-esteem are uncommon. There appears to be a tendency toward androgyny, in which women become more autonomous and men more compassionate and tender. Although there may be some decline in the frequency of sexual activity and the speed with which intellectual tasks are completed, such changes have little effect on psychological well-being.
5. During the middle adult years, many married couples must face such tasks as encouraging their adolescent children to become adults and caring for aging parents. The postparental years can bring new pleasure and fulfillment (as in becoming a grandparent) or dissatisfaction and disappointment (if there is friction with children or spouse). Although divorce is especially stressful in middle adulthood, an increasing number of people are divorcing, and most remarry.
6. Middle-aged men who have never married tend to have below-average incomes and occupations, but women who have remained single tend to be well educated and have good incomes. Middle-aged widows and widowers have a high suicide and death rate during the first year after a spouse's death, and widowed people are less likely than the divorced to remarry.
7. As adults move through the middle years, their social life tends to change in both type and extent. Friendship patterns often move from attachments inside the home to activities and friendships outside the family. Individuals tend to become more involved in organizational activities and to increase civic and political participation. Frequently there is also an increase in leisure time, allowing the individual to participate in new activities and to gain new satisfactions. These activities are more closely related to social class and personal adjustment than they are to either a person's age or gender.

21 LATER ADULTHOOD: LIVING SUCCESSFULLY

Human development continues into the last years of life, and the years after sixty place their own unique demands on the individual to grow, develop, and change. Although Matt is different now from the child, the adolescent, and the adult we have followed throughout this book, he remains the same person, and he continues to develop and change. He has more memories and a longer history than he once did, but he still lives in the present. At seventy-three, Matt's physical abilities are somewhat diminished, but he retains the human capacity and desire to control his environment. He has lost some of those close to him, but he still needs to love and to be loved. His friends are fewer, but he retains the capacity for friendship. He depends on other people more, but he values his independence.

Until recently, most people never worried about growing old. They simply did not live that long. In the Middle Ages, a person was old at forty. Continuous improvements in health care, diet, and the physical environment over the past century have allowed an increasing number of people to reach their seventies, eighties, and nineties. The twentieth century's gift of years is a welcome present to those who learn to manage and exploit them, but for those who cannot meet the developmental tasks of aging or whose health fails, they can be a nightmare. One thing is certain: America is graying. In 1900, only 4 percent of the total population was sixty-five or older; but today 25.5 million people, or 11 percent of the total population, are over the age of sixty-five (New York Times News Service, 1981). From 1953 to 1978, this group grew at twice the rate of the general population, increasing 76 percent. In addition, the number of people at the upper end of the group, those who are eighty-five or older, has tripled in the last twenty-five years; by 1978 they numbered more than 2 million (Rice, 1980).

Although we continue to learn more about older adults, much of our information is subject to change. Most studies of aging are cross-sectional, confined to an examination of only one age group. For this reason, it is often impossible to distinguish the effects of aging from cohort effects (Neugarten, 1977). Since each cohort encounters different social events and conditions, as was pointed out in Chapter 2, studies of older persons conducted in the 1970s and 1980s may sometimes produce different results from similar studies conducted twenty or thirty years earlier or later.

In this chapter, we will see that the major developmental tasks of later adulthood are to clarify, deepen, and accept one's own life and to use life's experiences to manage personal change. We will examine the various approaches people take toward aging and discover that continuity prevails: the later years generally accentuate early- and middle-life characteristics and abilities. A look at the changes of later life will reveal that the stereotypes of aging apply to a minority of the elderly; reasonably healthy older people have rich sexual lives and those who use their minds and memories continue to think, learn, and remember. Our examination of family life will explore the effects of a husband's retirement, the death of a spouse, remarriage, single life, and less conventional arrangements. Finally, we will discuss changes in friendships and leisure activities, finding that some curtailment of activities does not mean social isolation.

We are only as old as we feel, and many vigorous and healthy people who are in their seventies still regard themselves as middle-aged. (© *Ira Berger 1982*)

MATURITY IN LATER ADULTHOOD

What growing and being older means to a person in the later years is largely determined by the culture she or he lives in. In Asia, the older people are, the wiser they are thought to be and the more they are respected, esteemed, and listened to by those around them. According to Eastern philosophy, both life and death are part of the life cycle and within human experience. In Western societies, by contrast, death is regarded as being outside of life. Because this culture emphasizes individuality and control and because aging and death are not under personal control, most people in Western societies are inclined to look at aging and death as an outrage. Far from believing that older means wiser, we too often think of growing old as placing one foot in the grave.

Many popular stereotypes reinforce our fears about growing older. As Robert Butler and Myrna Lewis (1977) have pointed out, these stereotypes are more myth than reality, as demonstrated by the study in the accompanying box. One myth is that chronological age determines physical age. A better guide to aging is the adage that we are only as old as we feel. People who say that they feel young at seventy tend to age more slowly and more gracefully than people who say that they feel old. Another myth is that older people inevitably become senile. In truth, senility has nothing to do with the normal process of development and aging. Healthy older people have active, inquiring minds. A third related myth is that older people are unproductive. The fact is that about one-third of older people have some income from employment, and a good number are still active in a variety of civic affairs. A final myth is that older people resist change. The ability and willingness to change in later years has more to do with lifelong habits and behavior patterns than with age. People who challenged themselves to change and adapt earlier in life continue to do so in their later years; those who never did will not.

In an attempt to dispel the myths of aging, Bernice Neugarten (1980), who points out that some people over seventy regard themselves as middle-aged, suggests that we drop the term "old" for people in the later years. She recommends that we call vigorous and healthy older citizens "young-old," no matter what their age, and use the term "old-old" for those who are frail and ill.

Whether "young-old" or "old-old," people in later years who have attained maturity have achieved "ego integrity," the final stage of Erik Erikson's (1963) theory of development, which is described in Chapter 2. Because mature individuals have had a great deal of experience with change, they know when to accept change and when to oppose it, when to sit quietly and when to fight; they are able to accept their own limitations. As Erikson notes, the mature person can accept his or her own death. Failure to achieve integrity can leave people in a state of despair; they would like to live their lives over again, but time is running out.

A person's expectations about growing older seem to affect strongly how successfully he or she handles the stresses and changes of later life (Birren, 1975). Men who look forward to retirement adjust to it more easily and enjoy it more than men who find the idea distasteful. Those few who look forward to growing older also tend to grow old more gracefully than those who fear old age.

Maturity in later adulthood, as in the middle years, means relying on others for help and a willingness to depend on others when necessary (Giele, 1980). Hopefulness, as opposed to helplessness, characterizes the mature adult. Hope helps mobilize a person's energies and increases the ability to cope with change. When people feel that all hope is gone, they often lose the will to live. If an individual reacts to a major stress (such as the death of a loved one, the sudden loss of power, status, or purpose in life, or the loss of physical abilities) with hopelessness and helplessness, he or she may soon die (Seligman, 1974). People who continue to hope and to believe that they have some control over the direction of their lives are not only likely to handle the events of later life successfully but also to live longer.

PHYSICAL CHANGES

To most people, getting older means the continued loss of beauty, strength, and vigor. Although physical changes characterize the entire phase of adulthood, they rarely have much effect on daily life in the early and middle adult years. It is only in later life, and often not until the seventies or eighties, that cumulative changes tend to catch up with people and begin to interfere with their effectiveness and daily habits (Weg, 1981).

Although there are great individual differences in the rates of aging, it is relatively easy to estimate most people's ages, give or take a few years, just by looking at them. During later adulthood, hair turns white and becomes sparse. As hair gets thinner on top of the head, it starts to grow for the first time on the chins of older women. The skin loses its natural moisture and elasticity, and it becomes more and more wrinkled. Changes in the structure of the jaw cause the lower part of the face to become shortened and bring the nose, which lengthens as the skin's elasticity decreases, nearer to the chin. Eyelids thicken, and hollows develop beneath the eyes. As the skeletal structure changes, people in their sixties become shorter. The chests of men and women are no longer as full or as broad as they were thirty years before. Shoulders narrow, and

As people age, their senses become less acute; hearing, vision, touch, taste, and smell deliver less information about the environment than they once did. *(Abigail Heyman/Magnum Photos)*

the pelvis broadens. If they are not exercised, muscles atrophy and joints become stiff, so that a person's strength and movement become impaired. The dense part of the bone becomes spongy and fragile, so that bones break more easily in the later years.

Within the older adult's body, other changes take place. Although these changes leave few traces on appearance, they have a profound effect on a person's ability to function and to adapt to stress and change. Although the heart works as well as it ever did when people are resting, when they are exposed to the stress of exercise or emotional upset, their hearts do not react as fast or as well as they once did. The older heart takes longer to return to its normal level of beating and pumping (Shock, 1977). This inefficiency sometimes leads older people to complain that they feel hot or cold in a room where younger adults are perfectly comfortable.

Many other gradual changes begin to make a difference in later years. The circulatory system no longer carries the blood as well as it did. As circulation becomes slowed by thickening artery walls, blood pressure rises. In addition, by the time a person is eighty-five, the lungs can hold only about three-fifths of the volume of oxygen that they held when the person was twenty-five. Because the lungs hold less oxygen, an older adult generally has less energy for activity and less reserve to deal with stresses. Because signals travel more slowly along the motor nerves, the individual's reactions become slower. Digestion is no longer as good, and neither is the process of eliminating body waste.

All five senses are less acute. In the later years, vision, hearing, touch, taste, and smell are much less sensitive than they once were. Older people are more bothered by glare, see less well in the dark, require more light to see clearly, and have more trouble seeing than they did when they were younger (Botwinick, 1978). Glasses help compensate for visual losses in acuity and increase the ability of the eye to accommodate to close objects; increased and diffused light can also aid vision among older people.

Hearing loss is generally greater among men than among women, and the loss is greatest for high tones. This loss can be partially overcome when people speak slowly and distinctly and directly to an older person's face, providing visual cues. The gradual deterioration of hearing, so that normal conversations are perceived as clandestine whispers, may even lead to paranoia in some older people. This speculation is based on a study by Philip Zimbardo and his colleagues (1981), who used hypnosis to induce temporary deafness in college students. Those students who did not know why they could not hear showed changes in thought, emotions, and behavior. They realized that they had become irritable, hostile, and unfriendly, and their scores on tests of paranoia climbed. However, students who had been made temporarily deaf but who knew that the condition was hypnotically induced showed no such changes. Thus the cumulative loss of hearing may lead to psychological reactions in the elderly similar to those of the students who could not explain their deafness.

Older people get less sensory information of all kinds from the environment, so that they are more isolated from the world around them than when they were younger. Although paranoia rarely results, some older people become irritable, moody, and temperamental because they can not perceive and interpret their surroundings as acutely and rapidly as they once did.

Sleep patterns also change, and older people frequently complain that they sleep badly. They generally report that they take a long time to go to sleep, awaken more often during the night, sleep less deeply, and wake up early (Zarit, 1980). Especially in very old age, it is normal for people to make up for the lost sleep at night by taking cat naps during the day (Pfeiffer, 1977).

As physical changes become noticeable, alterations in body appearance tend to be more disturbing for women than for men. Older women complain more than men about their bodies, and they also worry more about their bodies (Plutchik, Weiner, and Conte, 1971). Despite physical changes, some people retain robust health and a zest for living into their eighties and nineties. A number of the distressing physical changes that plague old people are unnecessary; many are not the inevitable result of aging but come from lack of exercise and lack of preventive health care. Regular exercise is especially effective in preventing some of the effects of aging. Although older adults fall far behind in sprints, their endurance remains high; champion marathon runners in their seventies regularly run about 70 percent as fast as Olympic finalists who are in the prime of physical condition (P. Riegel, 1981). In the rest of this chapter, we will consider in detail other factors that contribute to health and vigor in late adulthood.

Regular exercise can enable many older adults to escape some of the distressing physical changes that often plague old people. *(David M. Grossman)*

NEW DEVELOPMENTAL TASKS

The developmental tasks of the later years are much more personal than the tasks of earlier life phases. Early phases of life were spent gathering and increasing strength and experience, which were put to productive social use during middle adulthood. By contrast, the major developmental task of older people is to understand and accept their life and to use their lifetime of experience to deal with personal changes or loss (Fiske, 1980). During late adulthood, a person must adjust to decreasing physical strength and health, to retirement and reduced income, and perhaps to the death of a spouse; they must establish satisfactory but often reduced physical living arrangements.

Erdman Palmore and his colleagues (1979) studied the way 375 older men and women adapted to five common events of later life: their own retirement, a spouse's retirement, major medical events, widowhood, and departure of the last child from home. Of these single life events, personal retirement generally had the most negative social and psychological effects. However, a lowering of life satisfaction was most likely to occur when several of these events happened together. People with greater resources—in terms of intelligence, income, education, and a social network—had less difficulty than others in adapting to major changes.

Once people reach their sixties, most begin to reduce their level of activity, but some refuse to slow down (Havighurst, Neugarten, and Tobin, 1968). For example, a man confronted with retirement may find new jobs and activities. A woman who is widowed may seek out new friendships and a new life style with other widows. Some people find that the sixties are full of conflict: they want to stay active, but their bodies and their friends pressure them to slow down. Other people may be ready and willing to give up social activities and roles, but they are likely to be people who have never really wanted to be socially active.

When people reach their seventies, many achieve a new and satisfying outlook on life. "Self-fulfillment," "integrity," and "self-actualization" are the ways that various theories have characterized the older individual who deals with developmental tasks in the best possible way. Although some people withdraw completely from social participation, most prefer to remain active, even if their activities are curtailed (Havighurst, 1972). Apparently, activity or the lack of it does not affect an older individual's ability to handle change. Instead, success in handling the social aspects of aging seems to depend on how the adult feels about his or her level of activity. Some older people are "active" and doing quite well; others are "disengaged" and also doing fine.

IDENTITY AND INTERPERSONAL BEHAVIOR

The Romans described the relationship between body and mind as "Sound mind, sound body." The connection is especially true in the later years of life. Older people who take no pleasure in life typically make little effort to adjust to changes in bodily functions. On the other hand, as long as people have their health, they are likely to maintain their emotional, social, and intellectual skills and curiosity. Changes in a person's views of self, in interpersonal relationships, and in intellectual skills are less related to age than to health and the amount of stress and social change that he or she experiences.

Self-Concept and Self-Esteem

Throughout the adult years, most people keep their personal style of relating to the world. The social aspects of identity remain stable as an individual moves from middle age into later adulthood. As Bernice Neugarten (1977) points out, people stay themselves and their characteristics generally deepen. If people are quick-tempered in middle age, for example, their tempers are likely to flare even more quickly in their later years. People who lean heavily on others in middle age will tend to be even more dependent as they grow older. When major changes in behavior suddenly appear, they are likely to be reactions to illness or to loss, such as the death of a spouse (Alpaugh and Hickey, 1977).

Although the young often fail to realize it, the old are as much like their younger counterparts as they are different from them. When Inge Ahammer and Paul Baltes (1972) asked people of all ages to rate the desirability of being affiliative, achieving, nurturant, and autonomous at their own ages, both adolescents and older people put a higher value on being affiliative than did middle-aged people. Middle-aged adults were more concerned about achievement than were the other two generations. All three generations thought it was desirable to be nurturant and autonomous. When each generation was asked to report what other generations are like, misperceptions were consistent. Older adults were regularly misjudged by others on aspects of self-concept that remain the same across generations. That is, both adolescents and middle-aged people saw older adults as wanting to be more nurturant and less autonomous than the old actually wanted to be. Clearly, an older person's ideal self-concept as an autonomous and fairly independent person is quite different from the view that the young and the middle-aged have of him or her.

Both men's and women's ideas about appropriate sex-role behavior generally change in later adulthood, continuing the androgynous trend that begins when people become grandparents (Nash and Feldman, 1981). Bernice Neugarten and David Gutmann (1968) found that, regardless of their social class, older men and women see the sexes as reversing their dominance roles in old age. Most people over sixty-five think of an older man as submissive, whereas they regard an older woman as being dominant and an authority figure. The behavior of some older men and women changes in a way that is consistent with this reversed image of sex roles. Some older men become more accepting and open about their needs to nurture and be nurtured. Older women sometimes become more tolerant of their own needs to be assertive and selfish.

In later life, both men and women often take a less active, less aggressive approach to life, and many view themselves as passive characters dominated by forces in the world. For others, the belief that they can actively control the direction of their own lives has simply diminished. They may be right. Most older people experience changes that are beyond their control: forced retirement, loss of income, death of a loved one, a disabling stroke.

Perhaps as a result of such changes, older men and women emphasize accomplishment, freedom, and happiness, whereas middle-aged men and women emphasize more active personality traits, such as ambition, competence, and courage (Ryff and Baltes, 1976). This increased passivity and decreased sense of personal control and competence may be related to the fact that older people tend to be more cautious and conforming than young adults (Botwinick, 1978). In a study of social conformity, Ron Klein (1972) found that older adults were more likely than younger adults to be swayed by the opinion of others in making perceptual and attitudinal judgments, especially as the judgments became more difficult. When the situation was rearranged to increase the older adults' sense of competence, however, they were less likely to conform to outside opinion.

As Robert Atchley (1972) points out, two factors make it possible for older adults to keep their middle-aged self-concepts: their own judgment and their persistence in thinking in terms of old roles. Older people tend to depend less on feedback from others and more on their own judgment in daily life. They frequently pay no attention to cues from other people that signal their age or dependence, and some older people simply reject the image of old age. In addition, despite the changes in social roles that older individuals may have experienced, they generally continue to think of themselves in terms of former roles. A widow may think of herself as Mrs. So-and-So, and a retired man may think of himself as a carpenter or lawyer. Being able to maintain this consistent sense of self in the face of change and loss is important. When Morton Lieberman (1975) studied older people who were moving from their homes into institutions,

Although some older people slow down, others refuse to curtail their physical activities. Many switch from paid to volunteer work, like this foster grandmother. (© *Timothy Eagan/Woodfin Camp & Assoc.*)

As long as people refuse to see themselves as old and feel they are managing their own lives, they can maintain their middle-aged self-concepts. ***(Jeff Albertson/Stock, Boston)***

he found that those who maintained their self-images during this radical change coped best with the move.

Because our society seldom regards the later years as desirable, it might be expected that older people would have lowered self-esteem. However, the same processes that help preserve older individuals' self-concepts help them maintain their self-esteem. For example, as long as people refuse to see themselves as "old," they do not have to accept the negative status that is often associated with age, and many people over seventy tend to identify themselves as "middle-aged" (Bengtson, Cuellar, and Ragan, 1977). Self-deception in the later years, then, can serve a purpose, making it possible for an individual to sense a continuity with the rest of life that is not supported by either the reality of the body or by others' views.

As in earlier life, older adults who feel they are managing their own lives generally have a greater sense of self-esteem than those who sense that others are making the decisions for them. In a study of nursing-home residents, for example, Ellen Langer and Judith Rodin (1977) found that residents who could decide how they wanted their rooms arranged, how they wanted to spend their time, and who could suggest changes in the nursing-home routine were happier and more alert than residents who were given no choice. Clearly, a sense of self-control and competence is important to a person's sense of well-being and self-esteem at any age.

Sexuality

Older people are not supposed to be sexy, interested in sex, or sexually active. American humor reinforces the notion that the years past sixty are sexless: "Definition of old age: The time of life when a man flirts with women but can't remember why"; "Description of the sexual life cycle of a man: Tri-weekly. Try weekly. Try weakly"; "Young men want to be faithful and are not. Old men want to be faithless and cannot" (Puner, 1974).

Because society teaches us that sexual interest disappears as we grow old, some older people give up sexual activity. For these people, the sexless older years are the result of a self-fulfilling prophecy; they lose their desire for sex because they are "supposed to." Other people, those who have thought of sex as a duty or as unpleasant, look forward to growing older because age gives them an acceptable excuse for ending sexual relations.

However, people are sexual beings throughout life. A majority of older people retain their interest in sex, and many continue to be sexually active well into their later years. In a study of fifty couples who had been married an average of fifty-five years, William Roberts (1979–1980) found that 40 percent of the men and 34 percent of the women reported having moderate to strong sexual feelings. Over half of the couples, whose average age was seventy-nine, were either still sexually active or had been active within the past five years. Clearly, sexual intercourse remains important and pleasurable.

In addition, sexuality often takes on an added dimension. When asked to describe changes in their love relationships, older people often say that tenderness, a gentle touch, an affectionate embrace, or just the physical presence of the person they love has become increasingly important (Reedy, 1978).

Some changes do occur in the sexual organs and in sexual performance during later adulthood. William Masters and Virginia Johnson (1966) found that these changes lead to differences in the experience of sexuality and sex but need not lead to impotence. During later adulthood, physical changes that began in the middle years become increasingly evident. Among women, vaginal tissues gradually atrophy, vaginal lubrication decreases, and the uterus and cervix get smaller. Among men, there is a steady decline in the production of testosterone. It may take an older man two or three times longer to achieve an erection, but he can preserve it without ejaculating much longer than he could in earlier years. Older men usually experience less intense orgasms, and it takes longer for them to be restimulated after an ejaculation.

Men and women show different patterns of sexual activity in their later years. When Adriann Verwoerdt, Eric Pfeiffer, and Hsioh-Shan Wang (1969) asked about sexual activity and interest over a ten-year period, older men generally reported more sexual activity than older women. The reason for this may lie in the fact that older women are less likely than older men to have a spouse, so women are more likely to be without a sex partner. Men in their eighties and nineties frequently reported continued sexual activity. Although the degree of sexual interest declined with age, nearly one half of those in their eighties and nineties reported mild or moderate sexual interest. Men and women agreed that their interest was generally higher than their activity.

Gender is not the only factor that influences sexual activity. Studies indicate that the more sexually active men or women are during youth, the more likely they are to continue sexual activity into the later years (Corby and Solnick, 1980). The rule "Use it or you'll lose it" describes the nature of sexuality across the life span. According to Masters and Johnson (1968), continued sexual activity requires several elements: an interesting and receptive partner, regular sexual activity, reasonably good physical health, and a healthy mental attitude toward aging. If these criteria are met, active and satisfying sex can last as long as life itself.

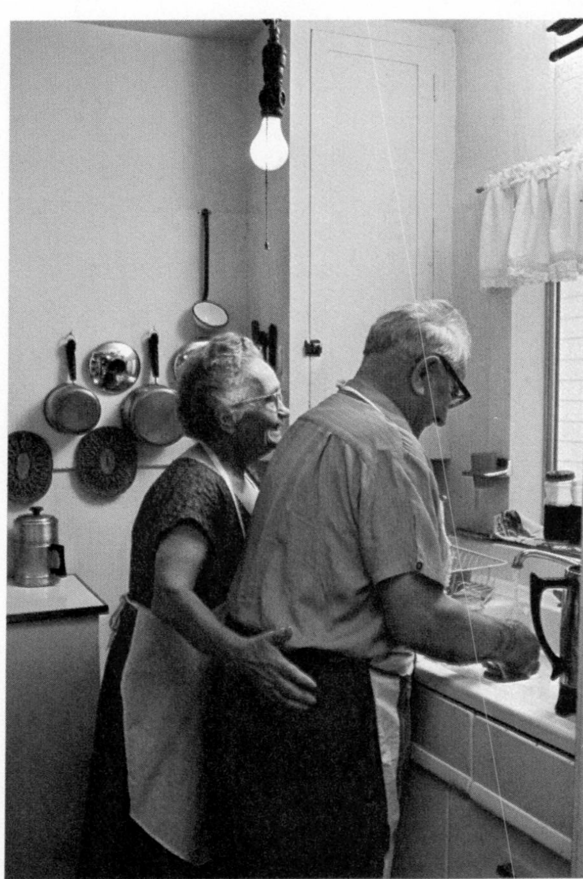

Contrary to popular belief, sexual interest and activity can continue as long as life itself; all that's required is an interested—and interesting—partner. *(Wayne Miller/Magnum Photos)*

Intellectual Skills

Although the idea that senility is the inevitable result of aging is pure myth, some intellectual skills do show declines in later years. According to Warner Schaie (1980), declines in some abilities are normal from the early sixties through the mid seventies, but declines in overall intellectual ability are generally reserved for individuals who are past eighty. When adults between the ages of sixty-seven and seventy-nine were tested every four years, their IQ scores showed little, if any, meaningful decline over the twelve-year period (Botwinick and Siegler, 1980). In some areas of

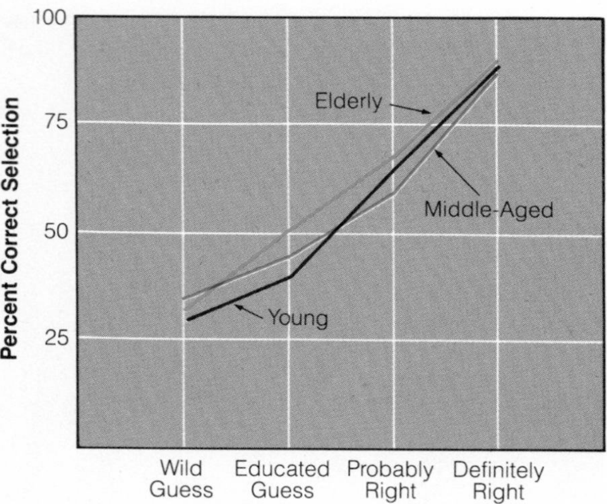

FIGURE 21.1 Aging and recognition memory. When adults were given a multiple-choice test, the efficiency of recognition memory remained constant across the life span as did the percentage of correct answers in relation to people's confidence in their choices. *(From Fozad, in Poon 1980,)* [*Data from Lachman, Lachman, in Poon, et al. (eds.), 1980*]

intellectual functioning, individuals often improve well into their later years. Verbal skills, in terms of word use and comprehension, for example, are better at sixty-five than they were at forty or at twenty-five. Similarly, visual skills, such as finding a simple figure in a complex one, keep on getting better right into old age (Baltes and Schaie, 1974).

In later adulthood, people also are generally about as flexible and as proficient at shifting from one way of thinking to another as they were in middle age. On tasks that involve eye-hand coordination, such as solving a puzzle or copying words, however, older people generally do progressively worse over the years.

Information processing tends to slow with age, and a number of studies have shown that older people generally do worse on any task where speed is important (e.g., Madden and Nebes, 1980). Being slower is perhaps the most characteristic thing about being older. As speed of processing diminishes, older adults may find it difficult to handle intellectual tasks that require them to do several things at once. When Gillian Cohen (1979) asked retired professional men and women and young graduate students to listen to a recorded message and then answer questions about it, she found that the two groups were equally good at answering simple questions of fact. When the questions required the drawing of inferences, however, the retired people did significantly worse. As a result of her study, Cohen suggests that the memory of older adults remains good, but because of their slowness, they find it hard both to register surface meaning and to reorganize its elements (a task that requires processing at a deeper level).

Other studies (Burke and Light, 1981) have revealed some changes in memory with age. The amount of information that can be held in immediate memory does not appear to change, so older people are likely to be as good as younger people in remembering, for example, a phone number they have looked up long enough to dial it. Long-term memory, however, shows changes in recall but not in recognition. For example, in experimental studies, older adults are often as good as young people at recognizing information that was presented earlier, but poorer at recalling such information. These differences in recall ability appear to result from the fact that older adults tend to use less efficient memory strategies. When Raymond Sanders and his colleagues (1980) studied the memory strategies used by adults, they found that young adults generally used active rehearsal and categorization of items to help them remember a list of words, but that older adults showed little use of such strategies in order to assist them in their remembering.

Memorizing word lists is not a regular part of daily life, and other research has shown that older adults can recall old, naturally learned information as well as younger adults. For example, Jack Botwinick and Martha Storandt (1980) studied recall and recognition memory in 120 women, whose ages ranged from twenty to seventy-nine. When the women were asked to recall or recognize historical events and events from the entertainment world, little decline appeared in either recall or recognition before the age of seventy. As might be expected, older women recalled more about very old events, whereas younger women knew more about recent events.

The meaningfulness of material also affects how well older people learn and remember it. Younger people, especially those who are well educated, are willing to learn almost anything, no matter how irrelevant it seems. Older people, by contrast, are often unwilling or unable to learn material they judge to be meaningless, irrelevant, or trivial. At any age, motivation affects memory. There may be fewer natural incentives (such as the hope of a raise or promotion) to motivate older adults to remember events in their lives. When Ellen Langer, Judith Rodin, and their associates (1979) introduced incentives to remember into the lives of nursing-home residents, the older men and women showed marked improvement in their memory abilities. Incentives were either social (a young interviewer who shared details of her life in regular conversations with the older person) or tangible (chips that could be exchanged for gifts). In addition to a marked increase in recall, ratings for alertness, activity, and social initiative as judged by the nurses were higher for residents who received incentives than for residents who did not.

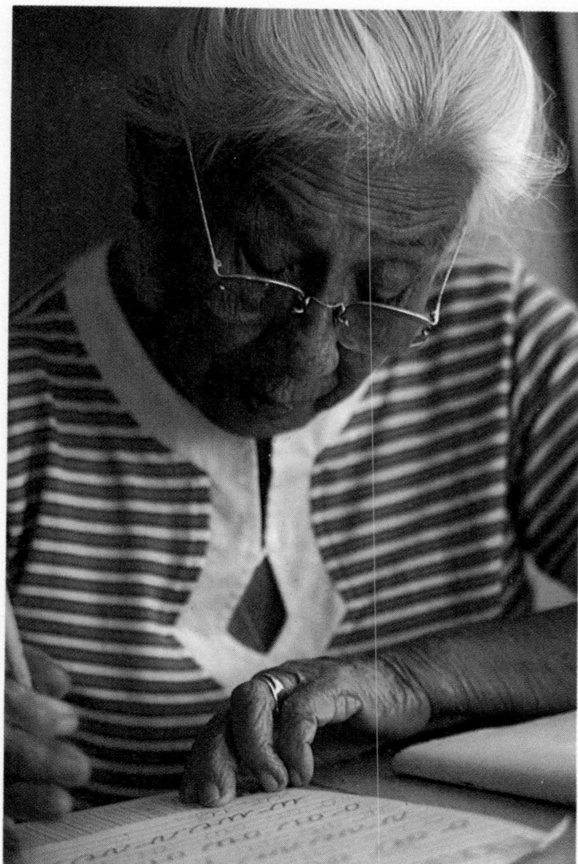

When they have an incentive and are given plenty of time, older people are efficient learners. This woman, who was never taught to read or write, is now on the road to literacy. *(© Mark Mittelman)*

Since information processing is slowed, older persons also learn more slowly than they once did. But given enough time, older people generally learn and remember as well as the young (Monge and Hultsch, 1971).

Just as having more time increases an older person's ability to learn, so the opportunity to practice helps. As Harvey Taub and Margaret Long (1972) found, older people typically benefit as much from practice as younger people do. When older individuals are allowed to go at their own speed and when they are given the opportunity to do a task themselves instead of watching others do it, they also learn better (Canestrari, 1963).

The capacity for creative thought and creative work persists into the later years. People who are creative in youth are likely to be creative throughout their lives. Tolstoy, Voltaire, Marc Chagall, Pablo Casals, and Pablo Picasso are outstanding examples of older people who continued to produce literature, art, and music of high quality into their seventies, eighties, or beyond. Creativity and productivity profit from accumulated experience and knowledge, as well as from a perspective that comes from having lived so many years. Wayne Dennis (1966) found that historians and philosophers tend to be most productive during their sixties. Supreme Court justices and political leaders tend to be older adults.

Creative people, like painter Georgia O'Keeffe, produce literature, art, and music of high quality into their eighties and beyond. *(Dennis Brack/Black Star)*

Even strenuous creative activities are within the ability of healthy old people; at eighty-five Maestro Vincenzo Celli continues to work with aspiring dancers. *(© Ira Berger 1981)*

Some people become creative only in their later years. The paintings of Grandma Moses are an outstanding example of late-blooming artistic talent, but new creative interests are not exceptional. Many retired older men and women develop new talents; some take up painting, some learn silvercrafting, and others start to write for the first time in their lives. According to Alex Comfort (1976), a creative person at any age is characterized by curiosity, flexibility, and a joy for life.

The more stimulating an individual's life has been and continues to be, the more likely she or he is to make intellectual gains during the later years. In one study, men who had been bright as children showed considerable increases in intellectual abilities during their adult years, whereas women who had been bright as children made fewer gains as they grew older. The difference seems to have come about because most of the men had stimulating jobs that forced them to think, but most of the women became housewives and had fewer opportunities for intellectual growth and stimulation (Correll, Rokosz, and Blanchard, 1966; Kangas and Bradway, 1971).

Individuals generally become the kind of older person they expect; those who assume that mental life after sixty is a downhill trip usually find that their assumptions are correct. As long as people expect to be alert, are healthy, put themselves in stimulating learning situations, and use their minds and memories, the myths of intellectual decline, fading memory, and worn-out genius are likely to remain just that.

The most important overall measure of older people's abilities is how well they function in daily life. As long as their abilities meet their needs, small declines in intellectual skills make little difference. This point is exemplified by an eighty-two-year-old woman who operated a small business for her absent-minded and unreliable middle-aged boss. She opened and closed the shop, waited on customers, kept the accounts, took inventories, placed orders, and completed tax forms. In addition, she maintained her own apartment and never failed to remember the birthdays of her relatives and close friends. Everyone counted on her to help organize the scheduled events at her church. On the other hand, when asked as part of an adult intelligence test "How are north and west alike?" she received no credit for her reply: "Well, I don't know how it is up your way, but around here the coldest winds come out of the north."

Family life continues to change; some older people enjoy their grandchildren and great-grandchildren; others move into retirement communities in distant towns where they live among new people. *(© Walter Hodges 1980/West Stock Inc.)*

FAMILY LIFE

Each person experiences an individual cycle of development and at the same time participates in a family with its own collective life cycle. The family grows and contracts with the births, deaths, and marriages of brothers, sisters, sons, daughters, nieces, and nephews. An older person who has never had children will experience a very different kind of family life and sense of family integrity and continuity from that known by a woman who has watched her children grow up to have their own children. Grandparents become great-grandparents; the death of a spouse leads to remarriage or to life as a single person.

With retirement, a couple may sell the house that has become too large for them and move into a retirement community. As Frederick Brand and Richard Smith (1974) have noted, these communities, made up of houses, condominiums, or apartments inhabited exclusively by older people, require new adjustments. A couple may find themselves far from grown children and grandchildren and far from old friends. They must learn to live in a new town, in a new climate, and among new people. Some appear to thrive in these new communities, where planned activities may fill every minute of what might have been vacant hours. Others find that the lack of younger people cuts off an important source of intellectual stimulation. However, the fact that so many older people adjust so readily to such an abrupt change in life style makes it apparent that their intellectual and personal skills are in good working order.

Marital Life

Being married is a demanding state at any age, and the later years are no exception. The most significant transition in later marital life is often the husband's retirement. The man finds himself suddenly without his occupation and shorn of daily contacts with his fellow workers. If the wife

In later life, marriage may be better than ever. For the first time, a couple can enjoy each other's companionship at their own pace. *(Guy Gillette/Photo Researchers)*

works and continues with her occupation for several years, the couple face a role reversal that can create additional problems.

Despite these problems, husbands typically look forward to retirement more than their wives do (Kerckhoff, 1966), and women who do not work outside the home must adjust to having their husbands home all day. Norah Keating and Priscilla Cole (1980) studied the impact of husbands' retirement on the relationships of four hundred retired male teachers and their wives. They found that whereas 42 percent of the men found that retirement had created problems in their marriage, 78 percent of the women reported problems, including decreased personal freedom, too much togetherness, and too many demands on their time.

A wife's reaction depends on how she views marriage. Alan Kerckhoff (1966) found that wives who look upon "home maintenance" as their primary marital responsibility have a more difficult time adjusting to their husbands' retirement than do women who regard "affection and caring" as their primary responsibilities. Women who are "home maintainers" find it disconcerting to have their husbands around the house all day, and such feelings were voiced by former First Lady Betty Ford, who said, "I'm glad we will have more time to spend together, dear. But don't come home to lunch." Most current studies of retirement look at couples in which the wife has not worked steadily; when working wives retire, they face the same loss of income and social contacts as husbands do, but they lose independence as well. However, contemporary increases in the proportion of working wives could eventually make husbands' and wives' reactions to retirement more nearly similar.

Regardless of the situation, retirement brings new demands to adjust. Among them are worries over money, disagreements over relationships with children, disagreements about moving into a smaller house or apartment, and health problems (Stinnett, Carter, and Montgomery, 1972). Yet, most married couples who reach the later adulthood years together have probably lived through enough stress to weather this period.

More older persons are married and living with their spouses than ever before. Because of sex differences in survival, men are more likely to be married than women: 36 percent of women over sixty-five are married, compared with 72 percent of men (Bengston and Treas, 1980). Once the immediate stress of retirement is over, most older couples describe their relationships as happy or very happy. The upswing in satisfaction that begins after the children leave home continues into the later years (Rollins and Feldman, 1970). The divorce rate among older couples is very low, partly because unhappy couples are likely to have divorced or separated years before and partly because older people usually find marriage is preferable to living alone.

Happy older marriages are those that meet both partners' needs for love, fulfillment, respect, communication, meaning in life, and the sense of continuity with the past. In a study of age differences in satisfying marital relationships, Margaret Reedy, James Birren, and Warner Schaie (1981) found that emotional security (concern, caring, trust, and dependability) takes on increased importance in old age. Older couples attributed a greater importance to emotional security and loyalty than did young and middle-aged couples. Older couples with happy marriages also tend to have a positive outlook on life and to be more active than those individuals who are either single or are unhappily married.

Older adults are likely to remain in close contact with at least one child. In a national survey (Harris and Associates, 1975), 80 percent of those over sixty-five who had children reported seeing at least one child during the past week, and 75 percent of those with grandchildren reported visiting a grandchild during the preceding week. Older parents not only see their children frequently but—perhaps most characteristically in the middle classes—also continue to help their children. As long as older parents are in relatively good health and financially secure, the exchange of goods and services between parents and children is mutual (Atchley and Miller, 1980).

When emotional bonds between older adults and their children are examined, relations seem warm and close, with parents emphasizing positive sentiments somewhat more than their offspring. The Harris survey (1975) revealed that the older people become, the more likely they are to feel close enough to their children to talk about "things that really bothered them." Only 25 percent of people from fifty-five to sixty-five years old felt this way; but among people over eighty, 43 percent felt this close.

Although most older people live near their children and other family members, about 10 to 20 percent of the aged have no relatives or family alive or living close to them. These people also tend to have inadequate financial resources. Thus older individuals who most need emotional and financial support are least likely to have them.

Widowhood

Three times as many women as men experience the trauma of losing a spouse, which marks a transition to a new role in the human life cycle. More than half of women over sixty-five are widowed (U.S. Bureau of the Census, 1976), and more than half of widows who are sixty-five will live another fifteen years. One-third have at least twenty more years of life ahead of them. Widows are much more likely than widowers to remain single; widowers over sixty-five are eight times as likely to remarry (Treas and Van Hilst, 1976).

Dealing with the loss of a spouse places heavy demands on the older person; once they manage their grief, many widows and widowers find themselves socially isolated. *(© Paul Fusco/Magnum Photos)*

Symptom	Percent reporting
Crying	84
Depressed	84
Disturbed Sleep	80
Difficulty Concentrating/ Poor Memory	56
Loss of Appetite or Weight	53
Tired	45
Loss of Interest	33
Self-Condemnation	27
Irritability	16
Life Viewed as Hopeless/ Wish for Death	12

FIGURE 21.2 Bereavement among widows. *(Based on Clayton, Halikes, and Maurice, (1971)*

Dealing with the loss of a spouse is a major developmental task and it places heavy demands on the older individual to adjust. Paula Clayton and her associates (1971) interviewed more than one hundred recently widowed women and found that their physical symptoms included changed sleep patterns, lack of appetite or weight loss, headaches, blurred vision, and general body pains. Common psychological reactions included anger, guilt, depression and crying, restlessness, lack of zest, and preoccupation with the image of the deceased.

Grieving over a spouse's death is a critical and necessary part of handling the crisis. As Marjorie Lowenthal and Clayton Haven (1968) have noted, the intensity of grief that follows the loss of a spouse and the amount of time required to complete the grief process can be somewhat reduced if the widowed person has at least one close friend during the adjustment period. If the grieving person is supported by a warm and loving family, if he or she has been able to anticipate and prepare for the loss, and if there is something left to live for, the grieving process will be shorter and easier. In addition, if the individual can rationalize the loss or make it meaningful through some religious or philosophical belief, or if the bereaved person has a confidant, the adjustment will be easier and the loneliness will not be so profound.

Like the divorced person, the widowed person must develop a new social identity. Most individuals learn to see themselves in a new way and learn to relate to other people differently, especially to people of the opposite sex (Morgan, Powers, and Bultena, 1979). Widowhood often means learning to live alone, perhaps for the first time. Many widows and widowers find themselves socially marooned. Friends and relatives are likely to avoid the widowed person because they do not know how to act or what to say or because contact is painful or because they need to deny the reality that they, too, are aging. Although the adjustment is difficult, once the grieving is over and they learn to deal with their new status, many widows and widowers find a new sense of freedom.

Remarriage

Older widows seek out other widows, but older widowers remarry. After the death of his wife, an older man generally finds many women his age to choose from, whereas the widowed woman has little choice. In addition, society approves when an older man marries a younger woman but frowns on the reverse. Although 20 percent of grooms who are more than sixty-five years old attract brides younger than forty-five, only 3 percent of older brides wed men who are younger than forty-five (Treas, 1981).

According to Walter McKain (1972), in many ways the courtship experiences of older adults resemble those of younger and middle-aged people. Older couples tend to have similar incomes and social and religious backgrounds. The older man is generally a little older than his bride. However, there is one major difference: among older people who remarry, half have known their new spouses since long before they were widowed—many for most of their lives. Some are related by marriage, some are childhood sweethearts, others are neighbors or old friends. The courtship usually is short and the marriage simple. Widowers rarely wait more than a year or two before remarrying, but widows take their time, usually about seven years.

Remarriage makes it possible to avoid living alone, living with a friend or friends, or moving in with children. Equally important, most couples who marry late in life have highly successful marriages. Widows who remarry generally say they are "very satisfied" or "satisfied" with their new lives. They give companionship as the most important reason for marrying, followed by the need to take care of someone. Most couples adopt traditional roles; the wives cook and clean, and the husbands do the heavy work around the house. Remarried widows tend to describe their marriages as calmer and more serene than their earlier marriages, and those who adapt easiest to married life are women who make no major changes in their way of life or their geographic location.

ALTERNATIVES TO MARRIAGE

Not all older couples who are in love and who get pleasure from each other's company marry. Like the young, increasing numbers of older people seek alternatives to marriage. Living together is becoming more common among older people, because marriage often means a reduction in social security benefits or in a widow's pension. According to census reports (U.S. Bureau of the Census, 1973), of the unmarried men over sixty-five who share living quarters with an unrelated person, one in five has a female roommate. Beyond necessity, there is the desire to be with each other that draws older men and women together outside of wedlock, although most who are cohabiting do not advertise their way of life.

Marvin Sussman (1976) found that an increasing number of older people are forming group marriages and are finding communes an attractive way of life. One such communal family is Share-A-Home group, which was formed by eleven persons from sixty-four to ninety-four years old who moved into a twenty-seven-room mansion in Winter Park, Florida, and hired a staff to run the household. Although neighbors contended that the group violated the single-dwelling zoning ordinance, the court ruled that the communal group was indeed a single family, noting that the residents were bound together for comfort, companionship, and ease of living.

Not all older people live with members of the opposite sex. Some cannot find a partner. About one-third of older women in the United States live alone, compared with only about one-sixth of older men. Since women live longer than men, the actual number of lone women is much larger than the proportional statistics indicate. Unmarried women frequently choose to live together. On the basis of her own experience, Faith Conklin (1974) concluded that it is a good idea for older women to share quarters, because it guarantees them companionship and because it is cheaper than living alone.

An increasing, but small, percentage of men and women who live alone remain single by choice. Up to 8 percent of people over the age of sixty-five have never married, and these older singles tend to be more isolated than their married counterparts. The single adult generally prefers solitary pursuits and independence. In a study of the consequences of singlehood, Russell Ward (1979) interviewed 162 single people over the age of fifty. He found that, like their younger counterparts, older singles were not as happy as married people of the same age. Nor was their outlook as positive. Although young and middle-aged singles saw their lives as more exciting than the lives of married people, older singles viewed their lives as less exciting—perhaps because poor health and lowered income narrow the possibilities of singlehood.

SOCIAL-LIFE CHANGES

The major characteristic of social life among older people is that there is less of it. Yet most older people are not completely isolated, and their satisfaction with life seems to depend more on the quality than on the quantity of social interaction (Beckman, 1981; Conner, Powers, and Baltena, 1979). Once people pass the age of seventy-five, however, they often become increasingly isolated, with older women generally being more isolated than men.

People over sixty continue to participate in the political process. Older people vote about as often as the middle-aged until they are eighty; but once they reach that age, participation drops off, with 62 percent of men and 46 percent of women over eighty voting in national elections, compared with 76 percent of men and 62 percent of women in their seventies (Wolfinger and Rosenstone, 1980). Most older adults actively discuss political issues and are well informed, because they watch the news on television and read newspapers (Glenn, 1969). Because there are more older people than ever before, if they were organized, they could wield considerable political power. Recently, groups like the Gray Panthers and the National Council of Senior Citizens have begun to exert sophisticated political pressure, primarily on specific issues that affect them directly, such as mandatory retirement, social security benefits, and local taxes.

Friendships

Most older people report having fewer friends than when they were younger; they also see them less often. When friends die or move away, many old people find it difficult to make new ones. According to Marjorie Lowenthal and her associates (1975), the same qualities that are important in sustaining friendships early in life play a major role in friendships between older adults—compatibility and companionship, shared experiences, and most of all, being able to depend on each other for help and support. There are some differences. Older adults are more likely than young and middle-aged adults to enjoy friendships with people who have different interests and backgrounds. They are also more likely to report having friends who are younger than themselves.

In recent years, retirement communities have become increasingly popular with older people in the middle class. Such communities provide physical security and, by providing recreation centers and various organized activities, make it easy for older people to find new friends. People who live in this kind of housing are more likely than those who live in areas where all ages reside to have neighbors who are also friends.

Some older people are more likely than others to have a close friend. When Nicholas Babchuk (1978) asked 800 people over the age of forty-five to list their close friends and confidants, about 15 percent reported they had no primary friendship ties. On the average, people said they had four close friends, with two of them serving as confidants. Age was significantly related to friendship patterns, and people who were over seventy were less likely than others to report having a close friend. Only about 10 percent of those under seventy had no close friends, but nearly 20 percent of those over seventy had none. Social class was strongly related to friendship patterns: people with extensive formal schooling and prestigious occupations reported a larger number of close friends and confidants. Finally, single people were more likely than married people to be without a close friend, and women were more likely than men to have confidants. The fact that women are more likely than men to have confidants during the later years may help explain why they live longer and adapt better to life than do men.

Retirement

Major changes in people's social life are ushered in by retirement (Glick, 1980), but money is a more important influence than retirement in determining what older people do with their time. Retirement generally cuts a couple's income in half, so that a greater proportion must go for food, housing, and medical expenses. If they can afford leisure activities, people now have the time to follow them. As might be expected, compared to older people of low socioeconomic status, older people of higher socioeconomic status tend to be more active, to have more leisure activities outside the home, to participate more in community activities, to have more friends, and to be more concerned citizens (Havighurst and Feigenbaum, 1968). They also tend to travel widely, and a good many in the upper-middle class spend the winters in Florida, Arizona, or California and the rest of the year near their families. Lack of money, not lack of interest, keeps many older people at home.

The idea of retirement, which means that people have as much free time as they choose, makes many adults anxious. Without their occupation, some men feel useless and begin to question who they are, in a kind of identity crisis. Although this is more likely to happen to men whose lives have centered around their work (Vogel and Schell, 1968), well-educated professional women may be even more reluctant than their male counterparts to retire.

Retirement has long been considered a crisis because work occupies so much time and provides so many rewards, including income, self-esteem, friendships, physical activities, outside interests, and intellectual challenge. Since most people have identities other than their work roles, only about 30 percent of older adults report difficulty in adjusting to their own retirement. People who look forward to retirement, who choose to retire early, and who have many roles tend to adjust most easily to retired life (Chown, 1977). Similarly, people who have many friends and are actively involved in family, church, and other social organizations generally find the transition to retirement an easy one.

Recreation centers and organized activities, such as this bridge group, make it easy for older people who move into retirement communities to find new friends. *(L. L. T. Rhodes/Taurus Photos)*

Leisure Activities

Despite decreasing opportunities for social participation, older people maintain an active role in organizational life. A recent study by Babchuk and his colleagues (1979) found no sharp drop in organizational affiliation, even among those beyond the age of eighty. The very old, however, generally belonged to fewer organizations than other older people and tended to be less active participants. Although men and women were equally likely to belong to groups, gender affected the type of affiliation: women generally tended to belong to church organizations and men to service clubs and groups related to their occupations.

The interests and activities of middle age heavily influence leisure activities in later life. If older adults developed many ways to spend their free time during middle age, they will probably continue these activities as long as their health

People who have developed interesting ways to spend their time are likely to continue their activities as long as they remain healthy. (© *Marty Heitner 1981/Taurus Photos*)

remains good. With increased leisure, some older people are returning to college, even if they already have degrees. In an Elders in Residence program at a branch of the University of California, a half dozen women in their sixties lived in student housing while they attended college (Stix, 1981). There was a considerable amount of social interaction between young and old, and the older women participated in extracurricular activities.

During later years, the tendency to participate in active, physically demanding forms of activity gradually decreases. Chad Gordon, Charles Gaitz, and Judith Scott (1976) report that older people engage in solitary relaxing activities, such as thinking, planning, or daydreaming, more often than do young and middle-aged adults. Other forms of leisure are enjoyed equally from youth to later maturity (Wilson, 1980). Home and family-centered forms of leisure, such as cooking and watching television, are equally popular throughout the adult years.

Life after sixty-five, then, does not have to be a period of isolation and failing physical and intellectual powers. Some curtailment of activities is necessary—no eighty-year-old is likely to run a four-minute mile, although at eighty, King Gustav of Sweden often played a good game of tennis—but many older people live satisfying lives. Health, money, and their own expectations appear to be major determinants of the quality of most old people's lives.

SUMMARY

1. What growing and being older means to people in the later years is largely determined by the culture or time they live in. In America today, many popular stereotypes reinforce our fears about growing older. In reality, productive living and functioning in later adulthood depend as much on life-long habits and behavior patterns as on anything else.
2. Although aging goes on throughout life, it is often only in later life that the cumulative effects of aging tend to catch up with people and begin to interfere with their everyday effectiveness. Many distressing physical changes in older people are the unnecessary result of inactivity and lack of preventive health care.
3. The major developmental task of the later years is to clarify, deepen, and accept one's own life and to use a lifetime of experience to deal with personal changes or loss. This often includes adjusting to retirement and reduced income, the death of a spouse, and new social roles and living arrangements.
4. An individual's style of relating to the world is likely to be retained, if not accentuated, during later adulthood. Self-concept and self-esteem are maintained by thinking in terms of old roles. When large changes do appear in self-concept, interpersonal relationships, or sexual or intellectual behavior, the shifts are likely to be due to changes in health or to social or psychological loss. Although information processing slows with age, meaningful material is learned and remembered efficiently, and creative thought and work often persist past the eighties.
5. When family life meets an individual's needs for fulfillment, meaning in life, and a sense of continuity with the past, the later years are likely to be satisfying. Retirement requires a major adjustment on the part of both retiree and spouse. The loss of a spouse is a major developmental crisis that is handled best if the widowed person has a close friend. Many widowed people remarry, finding it a satisfying alternative to living alone.
6. Among the unmarried, some older people live alone, some live with friends of the same sex, and others share their living quarters with unrelated members of the opposite sex. The never-married are more isolated and not as happy as their married counterparts.
7. Although their social life may decrease in form and extent, few older people become completely isolated. Most actively discuss politics, vote, enjoy the company of others, belong to organizations, and are likely to have a close friend with whom they can talk about their lives.

22 THE END OF LIFE

One of the things that gives life its urgency and meaning is the fact that it ends. For some, death comes too soon and interrupts a busy life, filled with plans and projects. For others, death comes too late or too slowly, making a dignified and appropriate end impossible. But no matter when the end comes, dealing with one's own death is life's last developmental task.

As far as we know, human beings are unique in their ability to contemplate their own deaths—although it is difficult for most people to conceive of their own lives ending. Our culture encourages us to avoid thinking about the end: people pass on, pass away, or depart—but they seldom die. As our reluctance to put death into words indicates, the fear and denial of death are common human experiences.

In this chapter, we will examine the factors that contribute to longevity and the prospect of personal control over them. We will look at the way the meaning of death has altered over the centuries, how it changes from youth to old age, and how it differs from culture to culture. In a discussion of terminally ill patients, we will explore the psychological changes that develop as well as how people react when they learn they are about to die. We will see that at any age, death comes easiest when others continue to show concern and affection and when the person is allowed to die with dignity. Finally, we will look at the ways people face the deaths of others and the role of mourning in coping with the grief that follows the death of a loved one.

LIFE EXPECTANCY

Only in recent times has death been associated primarily with advanced age. In earlier times, youth afforded little protection from death, and parents expected that some of their young children would die. Sanitation, improved nutrition, and medical advances have sharply reduced the death rate among the young, so that today the best predictor of approaching death is advanced age.

Historical Trends

Life expectancy has increased considerably over the centuries. In ancient Greece, life expectancy was about twenty years; by the Middle Ages, it had climbed to about thirty-three years. The big leap in life expectancy in the United States occurred in this century. In 1900, life expectancy was only forty-seven years; but babies born today in the United States can expect to live until they are seventy-three (U.S. National Center for Health Statistics, 1974b), and 75 percent of Americans already born will survive until they are sixty-five (Brotman, 1977).

This dramatic increase in life expectancy does not mean that the human life span has lengthened, but that more people are reaching old age. The real increase in life expectancy has occurred in infancy and childhood. In the eighteenth century only three out of every ten newborns lived past the age of twenty-five. Today, at least nineteen out of every twenty live to become adults. Although medical science has almost eliminated deaths from smallpox and diphtheria, sanitation and improved nutrition have been responsible for the major decreases in infant and early childhood mortality (McKeown, 1977). The pasteurization of milk has probably saved more babies than any other single advance.

Today, degenerative diseases such as heart disease, cancer, and strokes have replaced infectious diseases such as pneumonia, tuberculosis, and smallpox as the leading causes of death. Heart disease ranked fourth as the cause of death in 1900; today it is the most common cause of death. The mortality rate from heart disease has, however, declined slightly since 1968, probably because of changes in diet and smoking habits. Cancer, which ranked eighth in 1900, is the second most common cause of death in the United States. And strokes, which ranked fifth in 1900, are now the third most common cause of death (U.S. National Center for Health Statistics, 1974b). In addition to being associated with old age, the causes of death vary with sex and socioeconomic status. Men, for example, are more likely than women to die from heart disease and cancer, but women are more likely to die from a stroke. People who are poor are the most likely of any to die in youth or from an infectious disease, whereas white-collar middle-class men are most likely to die from a degenerative disease at midlife or in old age (Lerner, 1976).

Although many old people have chronic health problems, only 5 percent are institutionalized. Many are active and independent throughout their later years, despite the changes that aging brings about in their bodies. *(Michael Weisbrot and Family)*

Disease, Age, and Stress

Age tends to make older people more susceptible to disease, and disease tends to make people age faster. The circle is a vicious one: the processes work together and result in the loss of health and finally in death. Thus, the saying "Nobody ever dies of old age" has more than a glimmer of truth in it. In fact, when the causes of death were determined for some 12,000 individuals, the examiner found no cases of natural death; there was always a pathological condition responsible for death (Zur Aschoff, 1937). The connection between fatal disease and age is illustrated by mortality statistics: half the people who die from heart disease and stroke are more than seventy-six, and half of those who die from cancer are more than sixty-eight (U.S. National Center for Health Statistics, 1974b).

Even if disease does not kill them, old people are ill more frequently than the young. Because 80 percent have chronic health problems of one kind or another, they visit the doctor more frequently than the young do, go to the hospital more often and stay there longer, and spend more days each year sick at home (Weg, 1981). Older people chiefly complain of some ill-defined discomfort, rheumatism, arthritis, and digestive problems. Despite this ill health, 81 percent of older adults move around on their own, and only 5 percent live in institutions.

Older people are particularly affected by the close relationship between stress and disease. Life changes create stress, which involves physiological and psychological responses to environmental demands or threats, and the more changes that a person of any age undergoes in a short period of time, the more likely he or she is to experience a serious illness. Thomas Holmes and Richard Rahe (1967) have found that this relationship between stress and disease holds in spite of education, wealth, intellectual skills, or social class. They note that six of the thirteen most stressful life changes are characteristic of later life: death of a spouse, death of a close family member, personal injury or illness, retirement, change in the health of a family member, and sex difficulties. Because major life stresses tend to pile up in the later adult years, the older individual's abilities to handle change may be tested beyond his or her limits, and a serious and even terminal illness may result.

LONGEVITY

Some people appear to sail through their later years active, vigorous, and the picture of robust health. Others seem to spend those years in physicians' offices and in hospitals. To judge by the healthy, old age is merely a different period of life; to judge by the ill, it is a dismal period. Researchers interested in developmental changes over the life span are beginning to concentrate on this final period and to advance a number of different ideas as to why some people seem to age faster and die sooner than others.

Aging refers to the increasing inability of a person's body to maintain itself and to perform its operations as it once did. The result is that with the passing of time, the probability of dying by natural causes increases. Although this definition describes the biological process, it does not explain why people age.

A number of theories have attempted to explain why aging occurs (Shock, 1977), but none has yet been accepted as the primary cause of aging by scientists who study these processes. The first is the "wear and tear" theory, which maintains that the human body simply wears out with constant use, as a complex machine would. The "waste product" theory proposes that damaging substances build up within the cells and interfere with their function. The "homeostatic imbalance theory" supposes that the mechanisms that maintain vital physiological balances in the body do not work as well in times of stress. The "auto-immune" theory maintains that, as an individual ages, the body's immune system, which is normally directed against foreign substances, begins to attack normal body cells. The body ages because it can no longer distinguish between its own cells and germs or viruses. According to the "free radical" theory, the aging process is related to the presence of fragments of molecules whose original bonds have become unstuck from other molecules. These fragments seek new substances to latch onto, thereby throwing body functions out of order.

The "cellular" or "error in copying" theory is based on the fact that during a person's life span, most cells in the body reproduce themselves again and again. According to this theory, errors build up during the repeated copying of the cells' genetic message, in the way that nicks build up on a frequently played phonograph record. As a result, the messages that control the

Many factors affect longevity; in this society, a white woman whose grandparents all lived to a healthy old age is likely to outlive other people. *(Burk Uzzle/Magnum Photos)*

orderly behavior of the cells gradually become so full of errors that the cells no longer function normally. The "genetic" theory supposes that the program spelled out at conception in the genetic material eventually runs out, simply ending cell function. The "pacemaker" theory proposes that aging is controlled by specific pacemakers in the body, probably located in the brain.

Each of these theories assumes that human beings have a natural life span, which is the maximum number of years a person can expect to live under the best of conditions. Most researchers have set the human life span at one hundred years (Neugarten, 1980). If our natural life span is one hundred, we still have a long way to go before the average citizen can expect to live that long. Despite increases in life expectancy among the young, life expectancy for adults has not increased much since the turn of the century. An American who was sixty-five in 1900 could expect to live for thirteen more years. Today's life expectancy for sixty-five-year-olds is fifteen years, only an additional two years.

Factors in Longevity

Although we have no consensus on a theory of aging, we can agree on factors that play a role in determining how long a person can expect to

Ages	Females per 100 Males
14–24	98
25–44	103
45–64	108
65–74	132
75+	135

FIGURE 22.1 The longevity of women. Data are for 1976. *(U.S. Bureau of the Census, 1977)*

live. Genes, gender, the environment, the food we eat, how active we are, the stability of our social roles, our marital status, our attitude toward aging, and how long we expect to live affect our chances of living a long life.

Heredity is an important factor in determining how long an individual lives. Longevity tends to run in families, and children of long-lived parents tend to live longer than children of short-lived parents. One of the best predictors of longevity is having four grandparents who lived long and healthy lives. People with such a heritage live longer because tendencies toward heart disease, hypertension, and some kinds of cancer appear to run in families. In other words, placed in the environmental conditions that encourage one of these diseases, a person who has inherited a tendency to develop the ailment is likely to do so.

Gender is also important; women generally outlive men in societies where women no longer perform hard physical labor, where their chances of dying in childbirth are small, and where sanitation is adequate. In our society, although more boy babies are born than girl babies, girls begin to outnumber boys after age eighteen. In the later adulthood years, there are 135 women for every 100 men. The life expectancy of an American baby boy born today is sixty-nine years, and for a baby girl it is seventy-seven years (Rice, 1980).

In this country, a person's ethnic background also affects the length of time that he or she can expect to live. Black men and women have a lower life expectancy than white men and women (U.S. National Center for Health Statistics, 1974a). Black men generally live six years less than white men, or sixty-one years. Once black men reach the age of sixty-five, however, their survival rate surpasses that of white men. Black women live almost five years less than white women.

In terms of life expectancy, Hispanics fare even worse than blacks (R. Butler and Lewis, 1977). Life expectancy for Hispanics is around 56.7 years. In comparison with American Indians, however, Hispanics do well. The average American Indian can expect to live for forty-four years. Obviously, poverty, poor housing and sanitation, and lack of medical care and education have profound effects not only on the physical and intellectual development of blacks, Hispanics, and American Indians but also on their life expectancy.

Increasing Longevity

Heredity, gender, and ethnic background are beyond our control, but many environmental factors that affect longevity are not. In an attempt to discover those factors, researchers study groups of long-lived people.

From time to time, stories appear about communities where most people live past one hundred and a few live decades beyond that age. In every instance, careful studies have exploded the reports (Neugarten, 1980). In some places, a number of baptismal records carried the same names, so that birth dates were confused. In others, young men took the names of older brothers who had died in order to escape military service. In others, the age distribution as reported to investigators was skewed, so that many people claimed to be one hundred or one hundred and ten, but almost no one said she or he was seventy or eighty. This abnormal age distribution aroused misgivings, and when researchers returned to these communities after a lapse of several years, they found that people were claiming to be ten years older than they had been four years previously. In a study of Vilcabamba, an Ecuadorian community noted for longevity, a systematic exaggeration of age was found in peo-

People in Soviet Georgia remain healthy and active throughout life. Their diets are high in fiber and low in saturated fats, and they retain their social roles and responsibilities. *(Eve Arnold/Magnum Photos)*

In all parts of the world, long-lived people tend to be married. It appears that a happy marriage may add five years to the life span. *(Sepp Seitz/Woodfin Camp & Assoc.)*

ple who were more than seventy years old, and not one of the community's reputed centenarians had reached the age of one hundred, with many exaggerating their ages by more than twenty years (Mazess and Forman, 1979). Older people in these societies, although they may not be past one hundred, do seem vigorous and remain active throughout life. In their agrarian communities, there is no retirement and people retain their social roles and responsibilities, thus facing few stressful transition points (Leaf and Launois, 1973).

In our own country, people who live long and well have a number of common characteristics (Woodruff, 1977). Findings from interviews with people between the ages of eighty-seven and one hundred and three indicate that these individuals have parents who lived a long time, that they are happily married, and that they are sexually active. In fact, a good marriage appears to add five years to life.

Another characteristic of long-lived Americans is that their physical abilities and reaction times tend to remain above those considered normal for the later years, as do their intellectual skills and abilities. These people are physically and socially active. They refuse to give in to social or physical change. If they are widowed, they remarry; they develop hobbies, and they take long walks and get plenty of exercise (Palmore and Jeffers, 1971). Long-lived Americans are rarely anxious, they generally have always been independent, and they have a joy for living. All are religious but not extremely orthodox. They

tend to be moderate eaters of normal weight, and they have never slept long hours. Some drink, and some never have. Some smoke occasionally (C. Rose and Bell, 1971). By necessity, they tend to be highly adaptable, and all prefer to live in the present, with all its problems, rather than in the past (Jewett, 1973).

These examples of long-lived people demonstrate that living a healthy, long life is a matter over which people have some control. As other research shows, overweight people are predisposed to develop life-shortening diseases such as diabetes, hypertension, arteriosclerosis, or cardiovascular disease. Some investigators believe that a prevalence of fiber in the diet protects the body against cardiovascular disease and some cancers (Burkitt, Walker, and Painter, 1974). In addition, low levels of saturated fat may delay the progress of arteriosclerosis and the incidence of cardiovascular disease. Smoking is a major factor in heart disease and lung cancer. It has been estimated that if all men in the United States stopped smoking, the sex difference in longevity would be cut in half.

Physiologists argue that many of the bodily changes associated with aging may be due more to lack of activity than to the aging process itself, a contention that is supported by the vigorous old people in the supposedly long-lived communities. This position is further bolstered by Bengt Saltin and his associates' (1968) findings that when young people are kept in bed for a number of weeks, their bodies undergo physiological changes that mimic those that occur with

Long-lived Americans are physically and socially active; they refuse to give in to social or physical change. (© *Leonard Speier*)

aging. In addition, it is generally agreed that a moderately vigorous program of exercise can reverse some of the physiological changes associated with aging. Regular exercise—that is, about ten to fifteen minutes, three times each week, and strenuous enough to raise the heart rate—can improve cardiovascular and respiratory functions, lower blood pressure, decrease the amount of body fat, and improve muscle tone (deVries, 1981).

Although the freedom and competition of modern life may be exciting and challenging, its chronic stress and unpredictability may not only be hard on the health of some people, but may also shorten their lives. As we saw in Chapter 20, the sort of person who is tension-ridden, time-pressured, hostile, and competitive (Type-A behavior) is particularly prone to coronary heart disease and early death from heart failure (Friedman and Rosenman, 1974).

Having a hopeful attitude toward life and the future, even in the face of stress, appears to contribute to a long life (Woodruff, 1977). When there is something to live for, people live longer. How long people live, however, may be less important than the quality of their lives. Perhaps a more reasonable goal than avoiding aging is stretching out the productive middle years of life into later adulthood.

THE MEANING OF DEATH

When we experience the death of someone close to us or when we contemplate our own deaths, we feel many different emotions—fear, anger, sadness, loneliness, helplessness, resentment, inevitability, finality. Our attitudes toward death and the meaning it has for us change over the life span, and twentieth-century Western attitudes toward death are very different from those of past centuries.

Historical Views of Death

Today, we tend to believe that people in Western cultures have always felt about death as we do; but an intensive study of records has convinced Philippe Ariès (1981) that people in the nineteenth and early twentieth centuries created myths about death, attributing recently developed ideas to remote origins. Ariès believes that there is a relationship between general attitudes toward death and feelings of self-awareness and individuality, and that these attitudes continue to shift. According to Ariès, the experience of death in a predominantly Christian society has changed since the Middle Ages, progressing through five stages: the tame death, the death of the self, the remote death, the death of the other, and the invisible death.

During the era of the *tame death,* which characterized the Middle Ages, death was regarded as a misfortune, a frightening necessity, but one that was both expected and accepted. Only sudden death, whether in sleep or by violence, was truly fearful, and people calmly contemplated their own imminent deaths. The dead merely slept until the Second Coming of Christ, when all would be redeemed. Moreover, life was lived in the midst of death. The graveyard, which was attached to the church, was the center of public activity, serving as fairground, public meeting place, and site of the administrative tribunal. Except for the wealthy, people were buried in common pits, and once the bodies decayed, the skeletons were dug up to make room for more bodies. The disinterred bones were placed around the graveyard in ossuaries, so that all social activities took place in sight of the remains of the village ancestors.

As growing awareness of the self developed, death was no longer accepted; it became the *death of the self,* the personal extinction of the individual. This trend began in the late Middle Ages, and by the fifteenth century, the dead no longer slept peacefully until an assured redemption but were judged at the moment of death, making that moment feared, and the deathbed a time of conversion. The idea of an immortal soul, separate from the body, gained acceptance. As this occurred, the dead body became unbearable; it was sewn into a shroud and enclosed in a coffin. However, the graveyard retained its social function and the display of bones and skulls remained visible.

During the seventeenth and eighteenth centuries, death became *remote* and was seen as a moment of sorrow, like the sorrow of a broken friendship. Deathbed repentance was now seen as hopeless, so preparation for death switched from setting one's affairs in order just before death to living well, making all of life a preparation for death. With a devaluation of the moment of death arose a calm acceptance of mortality; death was kept at a distance, but at the same time the thought of personal death made people anxious. This anxiety was ignored in favor of meditations on the brevity of life. Perhaps because of a suppressed fear of death, the dead body was believed to have some kind of personality and to retain some sort of sensibility—a remnant of life. Along with the idea of the sensibility of the dead there developed a macabre eroticism, in which sex and death were mingled.

At the beginning of the nineteenth century, there arose a new attitude toward death, the *death of the other.* Death came to others, to loved ones with whom there would be a happy reunion in paradise. Since the self maintained its existence after death, death was neither ugly nor fearful but beautiful. The souls of the dead were seen as disembodied spirits that roamed the earth, and the room of the dying person was thronged with the souls of deceased friends who had come to assist the passage to the next world. The belief in hell began to disappear—or was at least reserved for enemies and strangers.

Toward the end of the nineteenth century began what Ariès calls "the lie"—the denial of death. As this tendency progressed, terminally ill people were encouraged to believe that they could recover and many were given no opportunity to set their affairs in order. At the same time, the custom of sending the dying to the hospital so that they would not die at home began to grow. Visible death was regarded as unsuitable and morbid, and families were eager accomplices in the transfer of death to the hospital. The *invisible death* had taken over, and death became as taboo as sex had been during the Victorian era. For the first time, children were excluded from participation in the deaths of their relatives, and the public show of mourning was discontinued. The management of grief was handed over to the undertaker, who removed it from daily life and concentrated it at the funeral. Instead of being regarded as a natural phenomenon, death had become a failure of medicine or a terrible accident. The good death was death during sleep, the very death that was regarded during the Middle Ages as the accursed death.

In the past two decades, a revolt against the denial of death has arisen, a revolt born of pity for the alienated dying who were shunted into hospitals. According to Ariès, the taboos surrounding death have been violated not because people are consciously concerned about their own deaths but because they are appalled by the image of another human being alone in a hospital, breathing artificially amid a tangle of tubes, slowly sinking into a solitary death.

Children's Views of Death

Although cultural attitudes deeply affect children's views of death, the two-year-old appears to have no understanding of the process. When Maria Nagy (1948) studied 378 children in Budapest, Hungary, she found that their concepts of death fell into three phases. In the first phase, which characterized children between three and five, the child saw death as a sleep or a journey, and as only a temporary separation. In the sec-

The concept of death changes as children grow. Although most nine- and ten-year-olds believe that death comes to everyone, less than half of them understand that death is irrevocable. *(© George W. Gardner/Stock, Boston)*

ond phase, between the ages of five and nine, death was personified. For some children, it was an angel; for others, an evil, frightening monster or a "death man." Although children now saw death as final, they still believed their own deaths could be avoided—all they had to do was to outrun the death man. In the final phase, beginning around the age of nine or ten, children developed a realistic, adult view of death. They realized that it is final and inevitable, a permanent biological process that happens to everyone.

The older children in Nagy's study had lived in war-torn Europe, when soldiers died in battles and civilians died in air raids. Their experiences might have influenced the rate at which they grasped death's irrevocable, universal nature. Children who grow up in a protected environment may develop the concept more slowly. More recently, Edward White, Bill Elson, and Richard Prawat (1978) examined suburban American schoolchildren's views of death. White and his associates read the story of an old woman's death to the children. In the first version of the story, Mrs. Wilson was a kind woman; she was nice to pets and children, and enjoyed reading newspaper comic strips. In the second, Mrs. Wilson was not kind; she was mean to her pets, never laughed, and yelled at children. After these five- to ten-year-olds had heard the story, they were asked questions that attempted to explore their understanding of death's finality and universality.

Children's understanding of the universal nature of death was strongly linked to their cognitive development. More than 60 percent of the children in this study who understood conservation believed that death came to everyone. But the idea that death was irrevocable and that it meant the end of bodily life showed no such connection. The big jump in understanding death's universality came between the first and second grades, just where Piaget places the transition from preoperational to concrete-operational thought (Koocher, 1981).

There was a relatively steady increase with age in the percentage of children who saw death as irrevocable and as involving the cessation of body processes, a finding that has appeared in other studies (Melear, 1973). Even among nine- and ten-year-olds, however, only about 40 percent of the children studied by White and his associates understood these two aspects of death. Nagy's children seemed to have a surer grasp of death's finality than did these American children. Since this aspect of the concept does not appear to be strongly linked to cognitive development, the difference may lie in the gulf that exists between the experiences of the two groups of children.

Although the nature of the story read to the children did not affect their views of death's nature, it did affect their belief in why the old woman died. Among children who heard of a mean woman's death, 22 percent said that she died because of her unkind acts; among those who heard about the death of a nice woman, less than 1 percent attributed her death to anything in her behavior.

Since the concept of death changes as children grow, what fatally ill children fear most about death varies, depending on their age. The three- to five-year-old seems to fear separation most; death means not being able to be with Mommy or Daddy, Grandma or Grandpa. The five- to nine-year-old is likely to be anxious about death as the end of life and is especially concerned about any accompanying physical injury or mutilation. Among six- to ten-year-olds, there is likely to be an awareness that their illnesses are life-threatening, even if they have not been told they are likely to die. In a study of sixty-three children, Eugenia Waechter (1971) found that when children with fatal illnesses were asked to make up stories about pictures, they were more likely to talk about death than were children with brief illnesses or healthy, nonhospitalized children. In a similar study, John Spinetta, David Rigler, and Myron Karon (1973) found that children who had leukemia were more anxious and more concerned with injury or interference with normal body functioning than were chronically but nonfatally ill children who had received the same number and duration of hospital-related treatments.

Adults' Attitudes toward Death

Most young Americans have grown up in a culture where the topic of death was taboo. In a survey of more than 30,000 young adults, for example, Edwin Shneidman (1973) found that one-third of them never recalled any discussion of death during their childhoods; one-third said it was discussed, but in an uncomfortable atmosphere; and only the remaining third said it was talked about openly. The majority reported first being aware of death between the ages of five and ten, and nearly half reported that the death of a grandparent marked their first personal involvement with mortality. For these young adults, death had a number of meanings: the end and final process of life; the termination of this life with the survival of the spirit; or the beginning of a new life after death. When contemplating their own ends, about a third were fearful or depressed, and over half felt either resolved to the prospect or pleased at being alive. The most distasteful aspect of death was that "one can no longer have any experiences" followed by the concern that "the process of dying might be painful."

Although young people are likely to have had few personal experiences with death, the middle years bring heightened awareness of it as a personal possibility. The middle-aged person often has experienced the death of one or both parents and may have had a friend die suddenly from a heart attack. As parents and friends begin to die with their goals and projects unfinished, men and women tend to become apprehensive about death arriving when they are least ready for it. Thus in a national survey of more than 1,500 adults, John Riley (1970) found that middle-aged adults were most fearful of death and more likely than the young or old to believe that "death always comes too soon."

Death is generally less frightening to older people, and compared with young adults and the middle-aged, they tend to think more often of death and to talk about it more. In Riley's survey, older people were least likely of any group to believe that "death always comes too soon" and were most likely to have made plans for it.

Among the reasons that have been suggested for the diminished fear of death among older persons are three put forth by Richard Kalish (1976). First, older people may place less value on life because they have finished many of their life projects, may be facing ill health, or may be having financial problems. Second, people who survive past their allotted span may feel that they are living on "borrowed time" and no longer regard death as unfair. Third, older people may become used to the idea of their own deaths since they have lived through the deaths of friends and relatives.

Death also has special meanings for older people. The fact that older people know themselves to be close to death alters their perception and use of time. Robert Kastenbaum (1966) found, for example, that when people were asked to tell about their plans for the future, older people did not plan as far ahead as did younger people. Many older people feel that they have completed what they set out to do with their lives, especially if they have achieved what Erik Erikson calls ego integrity. Thus when Richard Kalish and David Reynolds (1976) asked people what they would do if they had only six months left to live, older people were less likely than younger people to say they would change the way they lived and were more likely to say they would spend the time that remained to them in quiet contemplation.

In a recent study of more than 500 older men and women, Pat Keith (1979) found that their attitudes toward life and death divided them into four groups. About a third of them had positive attitudes toward their present activities and toward death. About a quarter had negative attitudes both toward their present life and toward death. The remaining people were about equally divided between those who were anxious about death because it promised to end the pleasure they found in life and those who viewed death as an end to life's disappointments.

The attitude of these older people toward life and death depended in good part on their previous experiences and their present status. Women were more likely than men to view death positively, as were both men and women with high incomes. Those who had achieved their goals and who were positive about life also tended to accept the prospect of death. And those whose lives were characterized by continuity were most likely either to have positive attitudes about death or to be concerned that death would end life's pleasures. In contrast, older men and women who had experienced discontinuities in their lives—through changes in marital status, health, or contacts with friends and family—usually had a negative view of death or saw it as a respite from life's disappointments.

What death means to people and how they view it also depends in part on their education. Individuals with little education generally think often of death and have negative views of it. The less education people have had, the more they tend to agree that "death always comes too soon" and that "to die is to suffer." Poorly educated people are also least likely to have made any plans for death. The more education people have, the more likely they are to have talked with others about death, to have made a will, and to have discussed funeral arrangements.

Understandably, people's views of death are likely to be strongly influenced by their religious beliefs. Dealing with death and dying is generally easier for those who are religious and are regular churchgoers (Bryer, 1979). But religion is not the only comfort. Being firm in one's beliefs, no matter what they are, is likely to ease the fear of death. People who are committed to religion or firm in their atheism are likely to fear death less than those who are less firmly religious and irregular churchgoers (Kalish, 1963).

Finally, once people are close to death, a stable living situation becomes particularly important. Morton Lieberman and Annie Coplan (1969) found that among people in institutions or those settled in the community, people who were near death could talk easily about dying and had come to terms with their own mortality. In contrast, those who were near death but were waiting to enter a nursing home or had just been admitted feared dying and had not come to terms with their own deaths.

Cross-Cultural Views of Death

As the historical discussion indicates, the culture in which people grow up influences their attitudes toward dying and death, their experience of dying, and the way they deal with the deaths of others. Most cultures offer philosophical or religious belief systems, traditions, or rituals that make it easier for individuals to deal with mortality. Death usually is not seen as the end of existence, and consciousness is believed to survive the death of the physical body; dead people are often believed to join their ancestors, spirits, or gods. Most frequently, the dead are seen as moving into a heaven or a hell. In some cultures, life is viewed as a time of separation, a prison for the spirit, and death as a reunion, a liberation, or a return home (Grof and Halifax, 1977).

In simple societies, people react to death with fear, anger, anguish, calm, or joyful acceptance, depending on the culture's belief system. Among the Murngin of Australia or the Gond of India, for example, death is believed to be caused by magic or demons, and the common reactions to death are fear and anger. In contrast, among the Tanala of Madagascar or the Tlingit of Alaska, death is believed to be due to natural causes, and the customary reaction is calm or even joyful acceptance. The Tanala believe that the afterlife is not much different from this one. They believe that their ancestors wait for them and that these ancestors can return to visit the living at any time (Grof and Halifax, 1977)

The idea of reincarnation is central to the concept of death in a number of religions, including Hinduism and Buddhism. In both, death is an integral part of life, a position on a constantly moving wheel, a temporary state in the continual cycle of births and deaths. Both religious traditions maintain that individuals can transcend the traumas of life and mortality by accepting death and by finding identity and unity with God. In these belief systems, the quality of an incarnation is influenced by a person's *karma*—his or her actions in previous lives. In Hinduism, individuals learn that the body passes through childhood, youth, and old age, and that at death the soul assumes another body (Long, 1975). Death is a normal part of life, not something that must be resisted. Among Hindus and Buddhists, an individual's frame of mind at the moment of death helps to determine the next state of existence.

Philosophical or religious belief systems make it easier to deal with death; when death is seen as an integral part of life or as a move to a new kind of existence, it can be contemplated without fear or anguish. *(© Leonard Speier 1981)*

In Western society, there are basically two views of death (R. Siegel, 1980). From the scientific perspective, death means the end of existence: the death of the physical body ends life, awareness, consciousness. From a religious perspective, the soul continues to exist after the death of the body. The religious perspective is more widely held than the scientific view. Among the people they surveyed, Richard Kalish and David Reynolds (1976) found that well over half believed that they would live on in some form after their deaths. This belief in an existence after death was held most widely among the elderly. The majority of those who believed in a life after death expected to find some kind of paradise.

Some Western philosophers see death as an extension of the developmental cycle, with the state varying from person to person, depending upon the level of development that had been reached in life (Kastenbaum, 1975). In this view of death, a future existence could be at worst total unawareness and at best a heightened experience beyond the imagination of the living.

In some parts of the world, cultures have developed manuals to ease the encounter with death. The Tibetan Book of the Dead, for example, reflects the Buddhist teaching on how to die well; it describes how to attain a state of mind, characterized by alertness and a focus on the experience of dying, that will be conducive to a "good rebirth" or to a liberation from the cycle of births and deaths.

Jewish tradition is directed toward easing the process of dying for the individual and for loved ones. The dying person is encouraged to put both worldly and spiritual houses in order through repentance, confession, blessings, and ethical instruction for the survivors. In this way, a dying person can express fears, find support, and communicate openly with loved ones. Jewish law also provides a structure that helps survivors mourn their loss and reaffirm their social ties. Customs like the bedside vigil, burial rituals, the tearing of clothes, the funeral eulogy, and the "meal of recuperation" encourage mourning and realism about death (Gordon, 1975). According to Jewish custom, the year of mourning is divided into three days of deep grief, seven days of mourning, thirty days of gradual readjustment, and eleven months of remembrance and healing. In this way, the mourners are gradually drawn back into community life.

Although we tend to view death as sudden and unexpected, in some societies the time of death is a matter of personal choice. Murray Trelease (1975), a priest who worked with Indians in the interior of Alaska, noted that these people had considerable control over the time, place, and manner of their deaths. When asked to give the sacrament to a dying person, Trelease often found that the person had spent the past few days making plans, telling stories of his or her life, and praying for all members of the family, an approach similar to the one prevalent in Europe during the Middle Ages. The person generally died shortly after receiving the sacrament. Individuals apparently have the power to take an active part in their own deaths, although studies in this society have been unable to establish the phenomenon.

THE PROCESS OF DYING

Some people die quickly and unexpectedly, perhaps from a heart attack or in an auto accident. For others, death comes more slowly and predictably. The older man with emphysema may find dying a slow, downhill process. But for some, as Barney Glaser and Anselm Strauss (1968) have pointed out, the process of dying can be charted in terms of ups and downs. For the woman with a disease like multiple sclerosis, dying may be a kind of staircase, with periods of remission during the course of a terminal illness.

How and Where

Given the choice, most young adults would prefer to die either a "sudden but not violent death" or a "quiet, dignified death," although one out of six believes there is "no appropriate kind of death" (Schneidman, 1973). Although one-third of the adults in Edwin Shneidman's survey were sure they would never commit suicide, one-half said that loneliness, illness, or physical pain might lead them to kill themselves. Men often said they might kill themselves because of failure or disgrace or to avoid pain and sickness, and as the accompanying box indicates, the suicide rate among older white males is fairly high. However, women are less likely to kill themselves, and the women in Shneidman's survey believed that loneliness, atomic war, or the loss of a loved one were more likely reasons for suicide. Few of these adults wanted a formal funeral, and one-third wanted no services of any kind.

Most adults want a painless death, but older people are more likely than the young to think that slow deaths are as tragic as unexpected deaths (Kalish and Reynolds, 1976). Older people generally want death to come quickly in order to avoid suffering; they believe that dying in one's sleep is the best possible end. Despite widespread fear of a lingering and painful death, few people spend many months being seriously ill before they die. Most people can expect no more than a few days or weeks of a final illness that requires special care.

A majority of terminally ill patients die without pain, and older people often die more easily than the young. In a sample of dying patients studied by John Hinton (1965), 45 percent of those under fifty had unrelieved pain; among patients between fifty and seventy, those with such pain dropped to 32 percent, and only 10 percent of those over seventy suffered in this way. As death approaches, people generally feel increasingly drowsy and are unaware of what is going on around them. Drugs, the disease, and the psychological distancing of the dying patient from the world as death approaches all tend to contribute to this drowsiness. Only about 6 percent of dying patients are conscious shortly before death, and the moment of death is rarely distressful (Hinton, 1965). There is evidence that, as death approaches, the brain releases a chemical that makes the moment of death pleasant instead of painful (Thomas, 1976). For most, then, death comes as it is desired—quickly, painlessly, and peacefully.

Age Range	Suicides per 100,000	
	Males	Females
25–34	24	9
35–44	25	13
45–54	30	13
55–64	32	12
65+	39	9

FIGURE 22.2 U.S. suicide rates for white adults. *(U.S. Public Health Service, 1977)*

The Experience of Dying

Individuals who have narrowly escaped death say that the experience can be peaceful, even blissful. On the basis of more than 35,000 deathbed observations reported by doctors and nurses, Karlis Osis (1961) concluded that fear was not common among dying patients who were conscious just before their deaths, and that a great many reported seeing visions of heaven, beautiful pastures, or lush vegetation.

A considerable similarity has been found in the reports of people who have been resuscitated after having been pronounced dead or who have narrowly escaped death by accident. Raymond Moody (1975) interviewed more than fifty such survivors and found similarities, although no one had all the reported experiences, and no single aspect was experienced by everyone. Many said it was difficult to talk about their brush with death because language was inadequate to describe it. Common elements of the experience included overhearing a doctor pronounce one dead; pleasant sensations; noises; the feeling of being drawn quickly through a dark, enclosed space; the feeling of watching one's body from some point outside it; encounters with close relatives or friends who had died; visions of a radiant and benevolent being of light; a partial or total review of one's life; and the feeling of approaching a border or limit. As Ronald Siegel (1980) points out, these reports are quite similar to those describing drug-induced experiences and hallucinations.

In the process of dying, Moody reports, attitudes toward life often changed. Although many made desperate attempts to get back into their bodies and felt sadness at the approach of death, they soon felt a sense of timelessness, peace, and tranquillity, and were unwilling to return to life. Most had difficulty telling others what had happened and reported that as a result of their experience, they were no longer afraid of death. They also valued and enjoyed life more and had become philosophical about existence.

Russell Noyes (1972) reviewed the accounts of people who had faced death and found that the experience has three phases: resistance, life review, and transcendence. In the first phase, individuals recognize they are in extreme danger, react with fear, and struggle, but finally accept the certainty of death with calmness. Their mental activity and senses may become enhanced and quickened, and time may seem greatly expanded. In the phase of life review, people often have the sensation of being outside their physical bodies and watch themselves approach death with detached interest. The past passes before them, and this experience is typically pleasant. In the final phase, they feel a cosmic consciousness, characterized by a sense of unity with other people, nature, and the universe; a feeling of being outside time and space; and extraordinary feelings of contentment or ecstasy.

Phases in Dying

Unless death comes by violence, most people do not suddenly move from being the same person they always were to a corpse. Although they may not be aware of subtle changes in their moods, their mental abilities, or the way their bodies function, shortly before they die people often begin to behave differently.

One change that may occur is a decline in intellectual abilities, which researchers have called "terminal drop" or "terminal decline" (Kleemeier, 1962; Riegel, Riegel, and Meyer, 1967). Robert Kleemeier was the first to study this decline. After he had tested older men on four occasions over a twelve-year period, he found that the men who died shortly after the last testing had declined more rapidly in their intellectual abilities than had the surviving men.

The decline may be connected with a tendency for the individual who is close to death to withdraw from the world and become distant. When Morton Lieberman (1965) spent two and one-half years studying people in a home for the aged, he found that those who died shortly after they had completed a series of psychological tests had less energy, were less able to organize information from their surroundings, and had less complex views of themselves and the world than did residents who were still alive a year afterward. According to Lieberman, people approaching death pull away from those around them, because they are struggling to deal with the changes going on within their minds and bodies. This psychological withdrawal and reduced effectiveness in dealing with the world was not the result of physical illness, but of nearness to death. Residents in the same home who became seriously ill, but who recovered, showed none of these changes.

As children approach death, they also tend to become isolated from their parents and surroundings. When John Spinetta, David Rigler, and Myron Karon (1974) studied six- to ten-year-old children with leukemia, they found that the children placed figures of their mothers, nurses, and doctors farther from themselves in a dollhouselike hospital room than did chronically ill hospitalized children. Like adults, children who are near death may feel a growing psychological distance from the people around them.

The reverse may also be true. It appears that one's surroundings can lead to psychological withdrawal from life. When Judith Rodin and Ellen Langer (1978) studied a home for the aged in which one group of old people was given some control over their lives and another group was not, they discovered psychological differences between the two groups. The group that had been given some control was happier, more active, and more alert than the other group. What is more, eighteen months later, 15 percent of the group that had control over their lives had died compared with 30 percent of the group that had no control. The normal death rate in the home was 25 percent.

Whether death comes quickly or slowly, according to Elisabeth Kübler-Ross (1969), most people pass through succeeding phases as they deal with it. At first the dying person denies the possibility of his or her death, saying "No, not me" and refusing to believe that the diagnosis is true. In the next phase, the person becomes filled with rage; the dominant reaction changes to "Why me?" and he or she feels anger at healthy people, envying their good fortune. In the third phase, the dying person attempts to bargain for life, trying to buy time from God, the doctor or nurse, or loved ones. At this time, the person believes that if one does the right thing, death can be postponed. The fourth phase is one of depression. Part of the depression may be a reaction to past losses, for example, the loss of physical health or of one's job because of illness. Another part is a preparation that enables the dying person to give up things of the world and relationships with loved ones. The final phase is acceptance, characterized by quiet expectation, peacefulness, and a sense of distance from the world. On the basis of her experiences with hundreds of dying patients, Kübler-Ross believes that acceptance is the healthiest way to face death. Once it is accepted, a person can await the end quietly and look back over the years, accepting life for what it has been.

There are, however, individual differences that can affect the way a person deals with death. As Robert Kastenbaum (1975) points out, the patient's gender, cultural background, personality, developmental level, and surroundings (e.g., home, intensive-care unit, nursing home) as well as the nature of the terminal illness interact so as to make deaths different. Some dying people may experience only some of the phases described by Kübler-Ross; others may experience them in a different order, or may rapidly move back and forth between the phases in a period of hours or even minutes. In a matter of days, for example, a dying man may talk to a friend with complete honesty about his approaching death and then surprise that same friend with the declaration that he will leave the hospital the following week and begin a new job.

Some researchers believe that a more useful way to regard preparation for death is to see the dying person's death as twofold. Edwin Shneidman (1976) argues that in facing death, which he calls "death work," the dying person first deals with impending death at a psychological level, preparing to meet the end. Second, the dying person prepares for death in a way that helps prepare loved ones to be survivors. Shneidman suggests that the way people face death reflects their total personalities—their "philosophy of life." In this sense, people are likely to face death in much the same way they have faced life's other developmental tasks.

No matter how preparation for death is regarded, acceptance is one of its important features, and the tendency of the dying person to reminisce is one way to come to terms with his or her own life. At any age, a person enjoys looking back at his or her past and telling stories about it, but for people who are approaching death, this life review helps them integrate their lives as they have been lived in relation to how they might have been (Butler, 1963). In this sense, the storytelling and reminiscing not only enable older people to recall facts but also to weave the past into an acceptable and meaningful perspective.

Easing the End

At any age, people want to die at home. Over the past few decades, however, fewer people have been dying there. In New York City, for example, the proportion of deaths in institutions rose from 66 percent in 1955 to 73 percent in 1967 (Lerner, 1976). Most hospital deaths are due to stroke, heart disease, cancer, and chronic diseases like diabetes. Although only about 5 percent of older people are institutionalized at any one time, 80 percent die in hospitals or nursing homes (Kastenbaum, 1980).

In the past few years, people have begun to emphasize their need to have some control over the time and place of their deaths. One response to this demand has been the establishment of hospices, where people can die gracefully, without the indignity of extraordinary measures to prolong life, such as intravenous feeding, transfusions, and respirators. The aim of the hospice is to provide a humane, dignified environment for the dying. St. Christopher's, the first hospice, was established in England by Cicely Saunders; others now exist in England, Canada, and the United States. Medical treatment eases discomfort and relieves pain, and friends and family can visit at any hour. Hospices offer dying people a warm, homelike atmosphere in which they can face death without placing the burden of care on their families.

In some places, physicians are releasing patients from the hospital so they can die at home. In Minneapolis, for example, children who are dying of cancer are allowed to go home. It has been reported that the parents of these children feel less guilty than parents of children who die in hospitals, and parents are pleased that they can satisfy their children's wishes to be at home. When a family member dies at home, death can become less mysterious and frightening for the whole family. Among people who had experienced the death of a family member at home,

One way people prepare for death is by reviewing their past; this often takes the form of storytelling, which helps them weave the past into a meaningful perspective. ***(Cornell Capa/Magnum Photos)***

most were glad that their loved ones had died among relatives (Cartwright, Hockey, and Anderson, 1973). Colin Murray Parkes (1978) compared the experiences of sixty-five cancer victims who died at home with one hundred who died in the hospital. According to their surviving spouses, the hospitalized cancer patients had less pain before death than those dying at home. However, the hospitalized patients were more likely to be confused than those who died at home and were also more likely to be confined to bed.

Many dying people believe they should have the right to choose death when the circumstances of their lives are no longer acceptable. They believe that death is better than a life filled with pain or considerable physical or mental incapacity. Because the granting of this right can entail suicide or murder, the proposal is a matter of sharp controversy.

The practice of euthanasia, or encouraging a "good" or "easy" death, takes two forms, passive and active (Morison, 1971). In passive euthanasia, everything possible is done to ease pain and discomfort, but extraordinary life-prolonging measures are eliminated. One's life is not extended by the use of machines, drugs, transfusions, or intravenous feedings. Hospices are an example of this passive approach, which has aroused little controversy.

In active euthanasia, death is hastened by the use of drugs or some other simple procedure. A growing number of people have begun to favor active euthanasia. In 1977, Russel Ward

(1980) asked 1,530 American adults, "When a person has a disease that cannot be cured, do you think doctors should be allowed by law to end the patient's life by some painless means if the patient and his family request it?" Nearly 63 percent agreed to this proposal, a steady increase from earlier surveys, in which 36 percent in 1950 and 53 percent in 1973 endorsed the same statement. Women were less likely than men to favor euthanasia, apparently on religious grounds. Nonwhites and older people also tended to reject the idea, and their rejection generally accompanied religious feelings and less education. The survey also found that older people who were dissatisfied with life and felt alienated were more likely than others to favor euthanasia.

Because many people would like to have some control over the manner of their deaths, an increasing number have begun to write "living wills," documents that give them an opportunity to decide how they will die by setting forth the circumstances at a time when they can make reasonable decisions. A living will specifies when the writer would choose death over life and expresses a preference for active or passive euthanasia. Although the will is not legally binding, it gives physicians and families some guidance at a time when their decisions can affect the quality of a loved one's death.

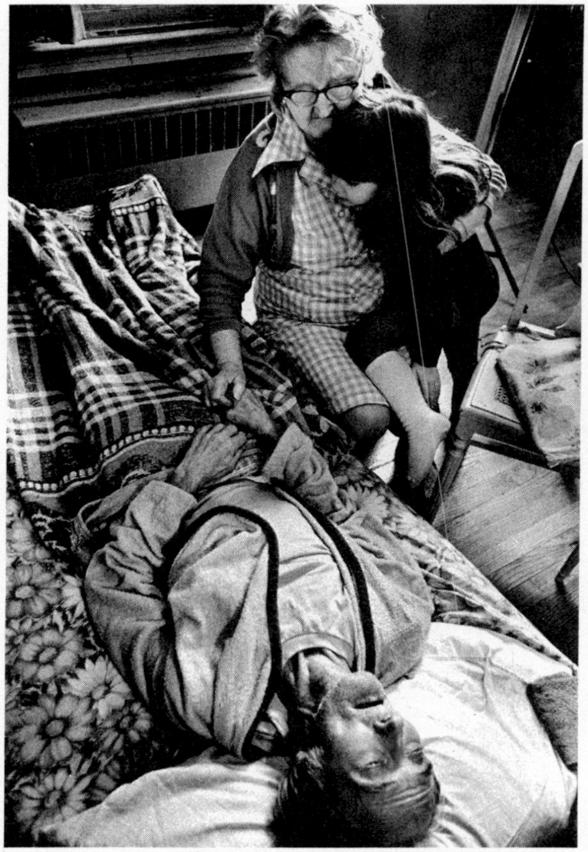

People want to die at home; 81-year-old Frank Tugend, who died at home after a three-year slide into senility, had the comfort of family life around him until the very end. ***(Mark and Dan Jury)***

COPING WITH DEATH

If the death of a loved one does not come quickly and unexpectedly, coping with it requires us to deal with our own feelings and reactions while we maintain a relationship with the dying person. The task differs according to the length of the preceding illness, the openness of communication, and our relationship to the dying person.

Anticipatory Grief

When people learn that a loved one is dying, they often begin to prepare themselves for the impending death. In this anticipatory grieving, people deal with their feelings about a death before the person dies. Thus during a prolonged terminal illness, survivors may have completed much of their mourning before the death occurs. When this happens, mourning after the loved one dies may be shorter and easier.

According to Elisabeth Kübler-Ross (1976), when family members anticipate the death of a loved one, their reactions go through a sequence similar to that felt by the dying person. The first response is denial, when family members cannot believe that the loved one will actually die. At this point, the family may shop

Dealing with death involves maintaining a warm and loving relationship with the dying person. When death can be talked about openly, the process is easier for both patient and family. ***(Michael Weisbrot and Family)***

around for a physician who will offer a more optimistic diagnosis. The second likely reaction is anger, commonly expressed toward the doctor, the hospital staff, or even toward the dying person. Family members often feel guilty and want to make up for past mistakes and lost opportunities. As they anticipate the impending death, they become sad and depressed. Kübler-Ross believes that the most difficult time for the family is likely to be when the dying person is becoming detached from the world. Although this detachment is a normal way for a person to deal with his or her own death, it tends to make the family feel rejected.

Communication

Dealing with the death of another involves maintaining a warm and loving relationship with the dying person and communicating in a satisfying way with that person. Since people find it hard to think about death, and even harder to talk about it, communicating with the dying can be difficult.

People frequently ask if dying people should be told of their condition. The answer depends on the person's wishes. In one study, 80 percent of cancer patients said they wanted to be told if their illness was fatal (Gilbertsen and Wangensteen, 1961). These patients felt that knowledge of impending death helped them understand their illness and gave them peace of mind. It also permitted them to plan for their deaths and to get their affairs in order. But not all people who say they want such information actually mean what they say (Cappon, 1962). Closeness to death may make some people less eager to know the truth. Even if people are not directly told they are dying, however, most become aware that their illness is no ordinary type of ailment.

Many doctors prefer not to tell patients that they are dying, and when the patient, the physician, the hospital staff, and the family all know that a person is dying but are unwilling to discuss it, a problem exists. Barney Glaser and Anselm Strauss (1965) have called this situation "the ritual drama of mutual pretense." Although the pretense may offer dignity and privacy to the dying person, it also keeps him or her from having warm and supportive relationships with the family and from being able to deal openly with concerns about death. The dying person may wish to talk about death at some times and not at others, but when the need to talk arises, it is important that someone who cares be nearby and willing to listen.

When illness and death can be talked about openly, people find it easier to face death, and families find it easier to cope with a patient's condition. This is especially true in the case of dying children. When John Spinetta (1977) studied families with dying children, he found that children who belonged to families that talked openly were the most willing to express their anxiety and anger about their illnesses, were the most willing to accept negative feelings expressed by their families, were the most able to express their desires for more affection and love from their families, and had the most positive self-concepts.

Grieving is a normal way of adjusting to the death of a loved one; survivors progress from numbness through yearning to despair, and at last are finally able to reorganize their lives. *(© Leonard Speier) (© Costa Manos 1964/Magnum Photos)*

Bereavement

The more closely a death affects the daily lives of the survivors, the more disruptive its impact is likely to be. Adjusting to the death of a spouse, a child, or a parent involves dealing with different kinds of grief.

Grieving is a normal way of adjusting to the death of a loved one, and Colin Murray Parkes (1972) has identified four phases of the emotion: a period of numbness; a time of yearning, characterized by the desire to recover the lost loved one; a period of despair, when the reality of the loss sets in; and a period of reorganizing one's way of life to adjust to the loss. For many, this grief lasts a year or two. For some, however, the loss of a loved one is overwhelmingly stressful. Death rates among widows, for example, are higher during the first year of widowhood than among married people of the same age. The suicide rate among the widowed, especially among older men, is also higher than among married people, as is the incidence of psychological and physiological disorders.

Some people find that they cannot talk to other family members about the death of a loved one, and others have no family or friends with whom they can discuss their feelings. To meet such needs, community bereavement centers and mutual-help groups have been started in many American cities. Most centers are professionally staffed and offer counseling designed to help people cope with their bereavement. Many of the mutual-help groups focus on a particular type of loss. For example, Compassionate Friends, which has almost two hundred chapters in thirty-eight states, offers help and services to parents who have lost a child; in some cases, the chapters schedule sessions for surviving siblings. Similarly, a group known as Widowed to Widowed, in Somerville, Massachusetts, offers surviving spouses an opportunity to talk about their experience with others who have suffered the same loss.

For parents, the death of a child is understandably painful and traumatic. At various points, we have emphasized the fact that developmental tasks are easier to handle when they occur on schedule. The death of a child is especially traumatic because it is untimely. Kübler-Ross (1976) points out that if parents are to cope with the death of a child, they need to express their feelings of shock, grief, anger, and anguish, to hold their dead child, to be encouraged to go

The relationships of young and old, present and past, symbolize the continuity of human development. *(Elliott Erwitt/Magnum Photos)*

back to the hospital several weeks after the child's death to ask questions that give them details that make their child's death real to them.

The death of a parent is equally difficult for children, and each year over three million American children under the age of nineteen lose one or both parents. The grief of children is made more difficult because they are rarely given any information about the death and are not helped to mourn by being encouraged to express their feelings (J. Bernstein, 1977). When children are not told how a parent died, they may feel that their own anger or resentment caused the death. But when children are encouraged to express their feelings about a parent's death, later emotional difficulties may be prevented (Koch, 1977).

In many cases, the death of a parent is hidden from a child. The child may not be permitted to go to the funeral, to visit the cemetery, or to see the parent's body. This void can make it hard for a child to realize that the parent has died. When they compared children who had made a good adjustment to the loss of a father with children who had developed psychological problems after such a loss, Josephine Hilgard and Martha Newman (1959) found that children who adjusted successfully to the loss came from a home where there was a good relationship between the parents before the death and where family and community resources were used by the surviving parent. These children also had an ability to tolerate separations, losses, and endings, and their surviving parent was able to cope with the demands and new roles after the death.

All of us are survivors, but all survivors eventually die. By objective standards, people have successfully prepared themselves for a developmental task if they handle it well. The problem with death is that it is impossible to determine whether anyone has dealt with it successfully. Dying is a personal and unique experience, and birth and death are the only two events in life that every individual must experience alone. Perhaps the most sensible preparation for the end of life, then, is a life well lived from its beginning.

SUMMARY

1. Life expectancy has increased dramatically in this century, primarily because more people survive infancy and childhood. In older people, disease and aging tend to go together,

forming a vicious circle that tends to result in faster aging, loss of health, and finally death.
2. A number of theories have been advanced to explain the precise mechanisms of aging, but none has yet been accepted as the primary cause of the process. Researchers agree that longevity involves both genetic and environmental factors, with longevity running in families, women outliving men, and members of the majority culture outliving blacks, Hispanics, and American Indians. Long-lived people share common characteristics, including sexual, physical, and social activity, moderate habits, independence, adaptability, and a tendency to live in the present rather than the past.
3. The meaning of death varies historically, from youth to old age, and from culture to culture. In Western societies, the acceptance of death changed gradually to a denial of death, an attitude that only now is beginning to alter. Children's views of death are linked with cognitive development, and the concept of death's universality seems linked to an understanding of conservation. Death is generally less frightening to the old than to young or middle-aged adults.
4. Most people who are facing death pass through similar phases: denial, rage, bargaining for life, depression, and acceptance. At any age, death comes easiest when the person is allowed to die with dignity. For most people, the moment of death is quick, painless, and peaceful.
5. Grieving is a normal way of coping with the death of a loved one, and survivors go through a sequence of emotions like that passed through by the dying person. Adjusting to the death of a spouse, a child, or a parent involves dealing with different kinds of grief. The death of a child is particularly traumatic, and the death of a parent is especially difficult for children because they are rarely given information about the death or encouraged to express their feelings.

GLOSSARY

accommodation. In Piaget's theory, the modification of schemes to incorporate new knowledge that previously did not fit them. In terms of visual perception, the change in the lens of the eye to keep an image in sharp focus.

acuity. The ability to see objects clearly and to resolve detail.

adolescence. The fourth of five chronological phases of development; it begins at puberty, around age twelve, and lasts until the late teens and early twenties, when an adolescent acquires adult economic and social status.

adulthood. The fifth and longest of five chronological phases of development; it begins in the late teens or early twenties and continues until death.

afterbirth. The placenta, its membranes, and the remainder of the umbilical cord, expelled in the final state of labor.

aggressiveness. Goal-directed verbal or physical behavior that is inappropriate or harmful to others.

alleles. The alternative forms of a gene found at a given site on a chromosome.

altruism. An unselfish concern for the welfare of others.

amniocentesis. A procedure used to detect fetal abnormalities; a sample of amniotic fluid is drawn out and chromosomal analyses performed on fetal cells within it.

amnion. The inner membrane of the sac that surrounds and protects the developing fertilized ovum.

anal stage. The second of Freud's stages of psychosexual development, covering the second and third years of life. During this period, a child's primary sensual pleasure is in expelling and retaining feces.

androgens. Male hormones.

androgyny. A development characterized by a self-concept that incorporates both feminine and masculine characteristics.

Apgar score. A common scoring system, developed in 1962 by Apgar and James; it assesses the newborn's physiological condition, rating color, heart rate, reflex irritability, activity, muscle tone, and respiratory effort.

artificialism. A kind of precausal thinking that refers to explanations involving either God or human beings as the artisans of all natural things.

assertiveness. Goal-directed verbal or physical behavior that is appropriate and not harmful to others.

assimilation. In Piaget's theory, the incorporating of new knowledge into existing schemes.

asynchrony. The maturation of different body parts at different rates, a growth characteristic typical of adolescence.

attachment. The primary social bond that develops between infant and caregiver.

autonomy. A feeling of self-control and self-determination.

baseline. Behavior in an experimentally unaltered situation that serves as a control condition in experiments.

behavior. An observable act that can be described or measured reliably.

body ideal. The body type defined by a culture as ideally attractive and sex-appropriate.

canalization. The temporary deviation from and subsequent return to a child's normal growth curve.

central learning. Relevant information acquired during the completion of a task.

cephalocaudal growth. The progression of physical growth from head to foot; a baby's head develops and grows before the torso, arms, and legs.

cerebral dominance. The greater proficiency of one hemisphere of the brain over the other in the control of body movements, as in handedness.

cervix. The pinhead-sized opening that separates the vagina from the uterus.

child advocacy. The movement to define and guarantee the rights of children and adolescents.

childhood. The third of five chronological phases of development; it begins around age two and continues until puberty, around age twelve.

chorion. The outer membrane of the sac that surrounds and protects the developing fertilized ovum.

chromosomes. Beadlike strings of genes present in every cell of the body. Except in the gametes, they occur in pairs that reproduce and split during cell formation. The appearance of enlarged segments of chromosomes, called puffs, is related to genetic activity.

classical conditioning. The association of one stimulus with another, so that the first evokes the response that normally follows the second stimulus. It is a simple form of learning, sometimes called respondent conditioning.

clinical study. A study consisting of in-depth interviews and observations, sometimes supplemented by questionnaires and tests.

cognition. All intellectual processes, including sensing, perceiving, remembering, using symbols, thinking, and imagining.

cohabitation. Couples living together without a legal marriage.

cohort. Individuals within the same age group; a group of people of the same age.

concrete-operational. A subdivision of Piaget's second major period of cognitive development, the representational stage. At about age seven or eight, children enter the concrete-operational stage, when they are capable of logical thought, but only in regard to concrete objects and situations.

conditioned reflex. A response to a formerly neutral stimulas that has been transformed by association with an unconditioned stimulus so that the formerly neutral stimulus evokes the same response as the unconditioned stimulus.

conservation. The understanding that irrelevant changes in the physical appearance of objects do not affect their quantity, mass, weight, or volume. Conservation is one of Piaget's concrete operations.

constructionist. Piaget's term that describes a child's understanding of reality. By acting on objects, the child discovers the effects of his or her actions and the properties of the objects; this knowledge leads to a construction of an understanding of the world.

conventional level. The third and fourth developmental stages of moral reasoning occur at this level, in which value is placed on maintaining the conventional social order and expectations of others.

convergence. The mechanism by which the slightly different objects seen by each eye come together to form a single image.

correlation coefficients. A numerical representation that describes how closely two sets of measurements correspond. Correlation coefficients range from +1.00 (perfect positive correlation) to −1.00 (perfect negative correlation).

cortex. A mantle of neural cells that covers the brain and comprises 99 percent of the cerebral hemispheres. The cortex is the seat of language, attention, memory, spatial understanding, and motor skills.

cross-sectional study. A study that compares the performance of different age groups.

deoxyribonucleic acid (DNA). The complex chemical containing the genetic code that guides development.

dependence. Reliance on others for comfort, nurturance, or assistance in accomplishing a task.

developmental dyslexia. A condition characterized by a child's extreme difficulty in learning to read, write, or spell; a major obstacle seems to be the child's inability to connect written symbols with their representative sounds.

dialectical psychology. A psychological approach that sees human development as proceeding in a dialectic between the individual and society, with each interaction leading to a higher level of functioning.

differentiation. The developmental trend in which an infant's abilities become increasingly distinct and specific.

discrepant stimuli. Stimuli that are related to but somewhat different from those that have been previously encountered.

displacement. The ability to communicate information about objects in another place or another time; one of language's three formal properties.

dominant gene. The gene whose corresponding trait appears in an individual when the gene is paired with a different gene for the same trait.

Down's syndrome. A condition that results when an extra Chromosome 21 is present in the fertilized egg, or when extra material from Chromosome 21 becomes attached to another chromosome. Formerly called mongolism, it produces various physical abnormalities and mental retardation in the afflicted child.

ecological approach. A view of human development that sees the growing individual as influenced not only by genes and the immediate physical and social settings, but also by the relationship among the settings and by the influence of the entire society.

ectoderm. The layer of cells in the embryo from which the skin, sense organs, and nervous system will develop.

ego. The conscious self, which in Freudian theory guides behavior and mediates the perpetual conflict between id and superego.

egocentric. Among babies, the inability to distinguish between the self and the external world; among older infants and young children, the belief that everyone sees the world and responds to it exactly as the child does.

embryonic period. The six weeks after the germinal period; during this period the organism begins to take shape, and organ systems begin to form.

emotional dependence. Dependence that aims at obtaining the affection and support of others.

encoding. Registering information in memory.

endoderm. The layer of cells in the embryo from which the visceral organs and the digestive tract develop.

equilibration. Piaget's developmental principle stating that the organism always tends toward biological and psychological balance and that development consists of progressive approximations to an ideal state of balance between assimilation and accommodation that is never fully achieved.

erythroblastosis. An abnormal condition that can develop in an Rh-positive fetus if substances from the mother's Rh-negative blood cross the placenta.

estrogens. Female hormones.

executive dependence. A type of dependence in which the parent acts as an executive arm, instrumental to the baby's needs.

executive independence. Autonomy; an infant's desire to act upon his or her own initiative.

experiment. A form of study designed to control the arrangement and manipulation of conditions in order to systematically observe particular phenomena.

extinction. The elimination of a response that is not reinforced.

Fallopian tube. The passage leading from an ovary to the uterus.

fetal alcohol syndrome. A condition that afflicts many babies born to alcoholic mothers. These infants may be small-for-dates, have abnormal head and facial features, and be mentally retarded.

fetus. The developing organism from eight weeks after conception until birth.

field study. An observational study in which the investigator introduces some factor into a natural setting that changes that setting.

formal operational stage. The final and major stage in Piaget's theory of cognitive development; it begins around age eleven and represents the culmination of cognitive development. Thought is logical and fully abstract and can be applied to hypothetical situations.

games. Piaget's third form of play, characterized by intricate rules that are accepted by all of its participants.

gametes. Mature reproductive cells —the spermatozoa and the ova.

gender constancy. The understanding that gender will never change, that boys always become men and girls always become women.

gender identity. The inner experience of gender—the unchanging sense of self as male or female.

genes. Microscopic particles that are carried by the chromosomes. Genes contain instructions that guide the development of physical traits and behavioral dispositions.

genetic epistemology. Piaget's basic approach to development, focusing on the development of intelligence (genetic = developmental; epistemology = how we know the world).

genital herpes simplex. An acute viral infection of the genital tract usually transmitted through sexual contact.

genital stage. The final stage in Freud's theory of psychosexual development; it begins at puberty. Primary sensual pleasure transfers to mature sexual relationships with members of the opposite sex.

genotype. The specific combination of alleles that characterizes an individual's genetic inheritance.

germinal period. The first two weeks after conception; during this period the fertilized ovum is primarily engaged in cell division.

gestational age. The age of the fetus as calculated from the date of conception.

gestation period. The period of prenatal development, calculated from fertilization (thirty-eight weeks) or from the date of the last menstruation (forty weeks).

glial cells. Supporting and connecting cells in the brain that play an essential role in the nourishment of neurons and in the formation of myelin.

gonococcus. The bacterium that produces gonorrhea.

gonorrhea. A venereal disease.

grasping reflex. A reflex that is strong during the first month of life; it consists of the baby's tendency to clutch any small object placed in his or her hand.

guilt. A negative feeling that arises when a person deviates from his or her own internalized moral standards.

habituation. Reduced response to a stimulus after repeated or continuous encounters with it—analogous to becoming bored with the stimulus.

heritability. An estimate, based upon a sample of individuals, of the relative contribution of genetics to any trait in that group.

heterozygous. The condition in which the alleles at a given chromosome site are different. In such cases, the dominant gene generally determines the appearance of the affected trait.

hierarchic integration. The tendency, in Werner's view, for the child's developing responses and skills to become increasingly organized into hierarchies.

homozygous. The condition in which the alleles at a given chromosome site are identical.

hostile aggression. Aggression aimed at hurting another person. (See instrumental aggression.)

hypothesis. A testable proposition or belief that derives from a theory.

id. That aspect of the personality that, in Freudian theory, contains all the unconscious impulses or drives.

identification. A developmental process through which a child tries to resemble specific people whom he or she respects, admires, or loves.

imagery. An encoding strategy in which a person associates visual images with items to be remembered.

imitation. Copying or reproducing observed behavior.

immanent justice. The perception of punishment as an inevitable consequence of transgressing rules. It is characteristic of Piaget's first stage of moral judgment, objective morality.

imprinting. The phenomenon occurring during a sensitive period of an animal's infancy; the young animal follows a moving object (generally the mother) and forms a strong, enduring attachment to it.

incidental learning. Irrelevant information acquired during completion of a task.

induced abortion. The premature removal of a fetus by deliberate interference.

infancy. The second of five chronological phases of development; it spans the period from birth to approximately age two.

inflection. A grammatical marker, such as the past tense "-ed" that is added to words to change their meaning.

instrumental aggression. Aggression aimed at retrieving or acquiring an object, territory, or privilege. (See hostile aggression.)

instrumental dependence. Dependence that involves seeking assistance as a means of accomplishing some task or activity.

intelligence. A disposition broadly defined as adaptive behavior in the face of environmental demands.

kwashiorkor. A serious, often fatal disease caused by severe, prolonged protein deficiency.

lanugo. Fine hair appearing on some newborns' bodies; it disappears within a few weeks.

latency period. In Freudian theory, the fourth period of psychosexual development; it lasts from about age six until puberty. Libidinal pleasures become less important, and children discover moral and aesthetic interests.

learned helplessness. A condition in which repeated failure in situations over which a person has no control leads to his or her refusal to try.

locus of control. The perceived location of control over an individual's life. If the locus is internal, individuals believe they control their own lives; if the locus is external, individuals believe their lives are controlled by forces outside themselves.

longitudinal study. A study that follows the behavior of certain subjects over time, comparing their performance at different ages.

long-term store. Permanent memory —where information is held indefinitely.

meiosis. The form of cell division [followed by gametes,] in which four cells, each containing twenty-three chromosomes, are produced.

menarche. The first incidence of menstruation.

menstrual age. The age of the fetus when calculated from the beginning of the mother's last menstrual period.

menstrual cycle. The discharge of blood and tissue from the uterus; it occurs monthly from puberty to menopause, except during pregnancy and lactation.

mesoderm. The layer of cells in the embryo from which the muscular, circulatory, and skeletal systems will develop.

metamemory. An understanding of the workings of the memory system.

miscarriage. A spontaneous abortion; the expulsion from the uterus of a fetus less than twenty-eight weeks old.

Moro reflex. A reflex present during the first three months of life; it consists of the baby's tendency to thrust out the arms and curl the hands when support for the neck and head is removed.

myelin. A fatty substance that keeps nerve impulses channeled along neural fibers and reduces the random spread of impulses from one fiber to another.

naturalistic observation. A form of study in which behavior is observed in natural settings with no interference from the investigator.

neonate. The technical term for a newborn baby, applicable through the first month of independent life.

neuron. A neural cell in the central nervous system.

novelty. Different or unique aspects of a stimulus, a factor in selective attention.

objective morality. The first stage of Piaget's theory of moral judgment; virtuous conduct is based on obedience to authority.

operant conditioning. A form of learning in which a response is strengthened or changed as a result of rewards or punishments (the consequences of the response)—sometimes called instrumental conditioning.

oral stage. According to Freud, the earliest stage in psychosexual development. It consists of the first year of life, when the lips and mouth are the focus of sensual pleasure.

organization. An encoding strategy in which a person groups items to be remembered around a common element.

orthogenetic principle. The major theme of Werner's developmental theory; it holds that the child moves from a global, undifferentiated state to one of high differentiation and integration.

ovaries. The female reproductive glands, which release ova.

overextension. A generalization in the child's meaning for a word so that the meaning includes a number of dissimilar objects or events.

ovum. The female reproductive cell —an egg.

perception. An important cognitive process involving the transformation of sensations into information.

perspectivism. A sense of the self as separate from the world and the realization that one's perceptions, reactions, and feelings are not identical to those of others.

phallic stage. The third, highly critical stage in Freud's theory of psychosexual development; it spans the ages from three to six. During this period the genitals are the focus of sensual pleasure.

phenotype. The nature of a trait as it appears in the individual; it reflects the influence of both genetic and environmental factors.

phenylketonuria (PKU). An inherited inability to metabolize phenylalanine, a component of some foods.

phonology. The study of the production and comprehension of speech sounds.

placenta. A pliable structure of tissue and blood vessels that transmits nourishment and waste between mother and fetus.

placing response. A reflex present during the first few months of life, in which the infant lifts up the foot and places it on top of a surface.

polygenic. Characteristic of most

traits, indicating that several genes have an equal and cumulative effect in producing a trait.

practice play. In Piaget's theory, activity within the primary circular reactions of the sensorimotor period, when a baby assimilates actions to existing schemes.

pragmatics. The study of language's social purposes.

precausal reasoning. A type of thinking found in young children who do not believe in accidents and who do believe that inanimate objects have thoughts or feelings.

premature delivery. The spontaneous termination of a pregnancy in which the fetus is more than twenty weeks but less than thirty-eight weeks old.

premoral level. The level encompassing the first two developmental stages of moral reasoning, in which value is placed on physical acts and needs, not on persons or social standards.

prenatal. The first of five chronological phases of development; it begins at conception and ends at birth.

preoperational stage. A subdivision of Piaget's second major period of cognitive development, the representational stage. Children in this stage, which covers the preschool period, record their experiences symbolically and use language, but their thought is intuitive, not logical.

primary circular reactions. Any unlearned behavior that the baby tends to repeat because of the stimulation it provides. These actions characterize the second substage of the sensorimotor period, which covers approximately the second to fourth months of life.

principled level. The level encompassing the final two developmental stages of moral reasoning, in which value resides in self-chosen principles and standards that have a universal logical validity and can therefore be shared.

productivity. The ability to combine a finite number of words into an infinite number of sentences; one of language's three formal properties.

proximodistal development. The progression of physical and motor growth from the center of the body to the periphery. For example, a baby learns to control shoulder movements before arm or finger movements.

puberty. The attainment of biological sexual maturity.

rapid eye movement (REM). A type of eye movement that occurs during a particular period of sleep and that is accompanied by changes in respiratory, muscle, and brain-wave activity.

reaction range. The range of possible responses within which a genetic trait can express itself.

reaction time. The interval of time between the instant a stimulus is presented and the individual's reaction to it.

recessive gene. The gene whose corresponding trait fails to appear in an individual who carries the gene; the subordinate member of a pair of genes.

reflex. An unlearned or naturally occurring reaction to a stimulus.

rehearsal. An encoding strategy in which a person repeats information that is to be remembered.

reinforcement. The presentation or withdrawal of an event following a response; it increases the likelihood of that response occurring again.

releasing stimuli. Events that regularly evoke certain behavior in all members of a species and help to explain regularities in typical behavior.

reliability. The dependability and consistency of a measure, observation, or finding.

replication. The repetition of an investigation's essential features and its findings.

representational stage. The second major stage in Piaget's theory of cognitive development; it begins around the age of two and continues until approximately age twelve. It is subdivided into preoperational and concrete-operational periods.

respiratory distress syndrome. A lung condition (formerly called hyaline membrane disease) in which the premature infant cannot maintain necessary surfactin levels.

retrieval. Removing information from long-term storage to short-term storage where it can be used; also called decoding.

reversibility. The understanding that irrelevant changes in appearance can be reversed and that such changes tend to compensate one another. Reversibility is one of Piaget's concrete operations.

rubella. Commonly called German measles, this disease can cause abnormalities in the developing fetus if contracted by the mother during her first trimester of pregnancy.

schedules of reinforcement. Timetables for reinforcing behavior, based either on intervals of time or on the number of responses.

schemes. Piaget's term for patterns of action (banging, sucking) or mental structures (classification of objects) that are involved in the acquisition and structuring of knowledge. For infants, schemes are like concepts without words.

secondary circular reactions. Any learned behavior that the baby tends to repeat because of the stimulation it provides. These actions appear in babies of four to eight months, and characterize the third and fourth substages of the sensorimotor period.

self-esteem. The way a person evaluates himself or herself.

semanticity. The ability to transmit meaning—one of language's three formal properties.

semantics. The study of meaning in language.

sensation. The reception through the sense organs of stimulation from the external world.

sensitive period. A period of development during which an organism is most likely to be susceptible to a particular influence.

sensorimotor. The first major stage in Piaget's theory of cognitive development; it lasts through most of the first two years of life. During this stage knowledge derives from the infant's sensations (sensori) and physical actions (motor).

sensory register. The first form of storage in the memory system, which holds a fleeting record of all stimuli received by the sense organs.

separation distress. A baby's negative reaction to being parted from an attachment figure.

sex role. The socially prescribed pattern of behavior and attributes considered appropriate for each gender.

sex-role stereotypes. Simplified, fixed concepts about the behavior and traits typical of each sex.

shame. A negative feeling that results from the disapproval of others.

short-term store. Temporary, working memory—holds active information in a person's awareness.

single-subject experiment. An experiment that focuses on the behavior of only one person, usually through the comparison of baseline and experimental behavior.

small-for-dates. The condition in which a baby is underweight for his or her gestational age.

socialization. The process by which an individual acquires the behavior, attitudes, values, and roles expected from its members by a society.

social-learning theory. A view of development in which behavioral change results from conditioning, observation, and imitation. Cognitive social-learning theorists believe that cognition also plays an important role, since a person's interpretation of the stimulus—not the stimulus itself—regulates behavior.

sociobiology. The systematic study of the biological basis of social behavior.

sociometric analysis. A method for charting how often a child is chosen by peers as a friend or preferred companion.

sonogram. A picture produced by bouncing sound waves off an object. Sonograms are used to detect the presence of twins, fetal abnormalities, and other visible complications of pregnancy.

spermatozoan. The male reproductive cell—a sperm.

spontaneous abortion. See miscarriage.

state-dependent learning. A phenomenon in which details and events occurring while in a particular mood (e.g., happy, sad) or state (e.g., drug-altered) are difficult to recall unless the person returns to the same mood or state in which the material was learned.

stepping response. A reflex present during the first few months of life; it consists of the baby's tendency to straighten out the legs at the hip and knee as if to stand when he or she is held with feet touching a surface.

strabismus. Lack of coordination between the muscles of the eyeballs so that the two eyes fail to focus on exactly the same point.

subjective morality. The second stage of Piaget's theory of moral judgment; morality develops from cooperative peer relationships, and rules can be changed.

sublimation. Handling the conflict between social demands and instincts by altering behavior in socially acceptable ways.

successive approximation. Behavior that resembles more and more closely a desired response.

superego. The conscience, in Freudian theory. It develops in early childhood as a child internalizes parental values and standards of conduct.

surfactin. A liquid that coats the air sacs of the lungs, enabling infants to transmit oxygen from the air to the blood.

symbolic play. Play involving imagination and pretense, in which objects or people stand for something they are not.

syntax. The structural principles that determine the form of sentences.

syphilis. A chronic venereal disease that can affect almost any organ or tissue in the body.

teratogen. Any influence that can disrupt fetal growth or cause malformation in the developing organism.

term. The gestational age of 266 days from conception. Babies born before term were once considered premature.

tertiary circular reactions. Intentional, adaptive behavior, that the baby tends to repeat because of the stimulation it provides. These actions appear in babies of twelve–eighteen months, during the fifth substage of the sensorimotor period.

testes. The male reproductive glands, which release sperm.

totalism. An organization of self-concept that has rigid, absolute, and arbitrary boundaries.

transitivity. The making of logical inferences based on separate observations; it requires the joining of two or more abstract relations.

trimester. A period of approximately three months, often used when discussing pregnancy.

Turner's syndrome. A condition resulting from the absence in girls of one female sex chromosome (XO). The girls are generally of short stature, lack secondary sex characteristics, and have mild to moderate mental retardation.

unconditioned reflex. A response to a stimulus that occurs naturally, without any learning.

unconscious impulses. In Freud's theory, the irrational urges that reside in the id and that the individual lacks any awareness of.

underextension. A temporary period in which the child's meaning for a word includes only part of the meaning adults attribute to it, as when a child fails to include "catsup" in the meaning of "food."

uniformism. Immersion in a peer group and acceptance of its norms as infallible.

variable. A factor that can vary in quantity or degree and that may or may not affect the result of a study.

visual accommodation. The ability to alternate focus for objects at different distances.

BIBLIOGRAPHY

Abramovitch, R., C. Corter, and B. Lando. "Sibling Interaction in the Home," *Child Development,* 50 (1979), 997–1003.

Abramovitch, R., and J. E. Grusec. "Peer Imitation in a Neutral Setting," *Child Development,* 49 (1978), 60–65.

Acheson, R. M. "Effects of Nutrition and Disease on Human Growth," in J. M. Tanner (ed.), *Human Growth.* New York: Pergamon Press, 1960, pp. 73–92.

Acredolo, C., and L. P. Acredolo. "Identity, Compensation, and Conservation," *Child Development,* 50 (1979), 524–535.

Acredolo, L. "Laboratory versus Home: The Effect of Environment on the 9-Month-Old Infant's Choice of Spatial Reference System," *Developmental Psychology,* 15 (1979), 666–667.

Acredolo, L., and D. Evans. "Developmental Changes in the Effects of Landmarks on Infant Spatial Behavior," *Developmental Psychology,* 16 (1980), 312–318.

Adams, B. N. "Isolation, Function and Beyond. American Kinship in the 1960's," *Journal of Marriage and the Family,* 32 (1970), 575–597.

Adams, R. L., and R. J. Fox. "Mainlining Jesus: The New Trip," *Society,* 9 (1976), 50–56.

Adamsons, K., Jr. "The Role of Thermal Factors in Fetal and Neonatal Life," *Pediatric Clinics of North America,* 13 (1966), 599–619.

Adelson, J., interviewed by E. Hall. "Children and Other Political Naifs," *Psychology Today,* 14 (November 1980), 56–70.

Ahammer, I. M. "Social Learning Theory as a Framework for the Study of Adult Personality Development," in P. B. Baltes and K. Warner Schaie (eds.), *Life Span Developmental Psychology: Personality and Socialization.* New York: Academic Press, 1973, pp. 253–284.

Ahammer, I. M., and P. B. Baltes. "Objective Versus Perceived Age Differences in Personality: How Do Adolescents, Adults, and Older People View Themselves and Each Other?" *Journal of Gerontology,* 27 (1972), 46–51.

Ainsworth, M. D. S. *Infancy in Uganda: Infant Care and the Growth of Love.* Baltimore: Johns Hopkins University, 1967.

Ainsworth, M. D. S., S. M. Bell, and D. J. Stayton. "Infant-Mother Attachment and Social Development: Socialization as a Product of Reciprocal Responsiveness to Signals," in M. P. M. Richards (ed.), *The Integration of the Child into a Social World.* London: Cambridge University Press, 1974, pp. 99–135.

Ainsworth, M. D. S., M. C. Blehar, Everett Waters, and Sally Wall. *Patterns of Attachment: A Psychological Study of the Strange Situation.* Hillsdale, N.J.: Erlbaum, 1978.

Ainsworth, M. D. S., and B. A. Witting. "Attachment and Exploratory Behavior of One-year-olds in a Strange Situation," in B. M. Foss (ed.), *Determinants of Infant Behavior.* Vol. 4. London: Methuen, 1969, pp. 111–136.

Aldrich, C. A., and E. S. Hewitt. "A Self-Regulating Feeding Program for Infants," *Journal of the American Medical Association,* 135 (1947), 340–342.

Allen, E., et al. "Against Sociobiology," in A. L. Caplan (ed.), *The Sociobiology Debate.* New York: Harper & Row, 1978, pp. 259–264 (orig. pub. 1975).

Allinsmith, W. "The Learning of Moral Standards," in D. R. Miller and G. E. Swanson (eds.), *Inner Conflict and Defense.* New York: Holt, Rinehart and Winston, 1960, pp. 141–176.

Alpaugh, P., and M. Hickey. *Counseling the Older Adult: A Training Manual.* Los Angeles: University of Southern California Press, 1978.

Alpert, J. L., and M. S. Richardson. "Parenting," in L. W. Poon (ed.), *Aging in the 1980's: Psychological Issues.* Washington, D.C.: American Psychological Association, 1980, pp. 441–454.

Ambrose, A. (ed.). *Stimulation in Early Infancy.* New York: Academic Press, 1969.

American Psychological Association. "Ethical Standards for Research with Human Subjects," *APA Monitor,* May (1972) I–XIX.

Ammar, H. *Growing up in an Egyptian Village.* London: Routledge & Kegan Paul, 1954.

Anderson, C. N., R. J. Nagle, W. A. Roberts, and J. W. Smith. "Attachment to Substitute Caregivers as a Function of Center Quality and Caregiver Involvement," *Child Development,* 52 (1981), 53–61.

Anderson, D. R. "Active and Passive Processes in Children's Television Viewing," Paper presented at American Psychological Association meeting, New York, September 1979.

Anderson, D. R., L. F. Alwitt, E. P. Lorch, and S. R. Levin. "Watching Children Watch Television," in G. Hale and M. Lewis (eds.), *Attention and Cognitive Development.* New York: Plenum, 1980, pp. 331–361.

Anderson, E. "Some Observations of Black Youth Employment," in B. E. Anderson and I. V. Sawhill (eds.), *Youth Employment and Public Policy.* Englewood Cliffs, N.J.: Prentice-Hall, 1980, pp. 64–87.

Anglin, J. M. *Word, Object, and Conceptual Development.* New York: Norton, 1977.

———. "The Child's First Terms of Reference," in N. R. Smith and M. B. Franklin (eds.), *Symbolic Functioning in Childhood.* Hillsdale, N.J.: Erlbaum, 1979, pp. 167–184.

Anooshian, L. J., and L. Prilop. "Developmental Trends in Auditory Selective Attention: Dependence on Central-Incidental Word Relations," *Child Development,* 51 (1980), 45–54.

Apgar, V., and L. S. James. "Further Observations on the Newborn Scoring System," *American Journal of Diseases of Children,* 104 (1962), 419–428.

Ariès, P. *Centuries of Childhood: A Social History of Family Life.* R. Baldick (tr.). New York: Vintage Books, 1962.

Ariès, P. *The Hour of Our Death.* New York: Knopf, 1981.

Aronfreed, J. "The Concept of Internalization," in D. A. Goslin (ed.), *Handbook of Socialization Theory and Research.* Chicago: Rand McNally, 1969, pp. 263–323.

Asher, S. A., and P. D. Renshaw. "Children without Friends: Social Knowledge and Social Skill Training," in S. R. Asher and J. M. Gottman (eds.), *The Development of Children's Friendships.* New York: Cambridge University Press, 1981, pp. 273–296.

Asher, S. R. "Children's Peer Relations," in M. E. Lamb (ed.), *Social and Personality Development.* New York: Holt, Rinehart and Winston, 1978, pp. 91–113.

Ashmead, D. H., and M. Perlmutter. "Infant Memory in Everyday Life," in M. Perlmutter (ed.), *New Directions in Child Development.* No. 10. *Children's Memory.* San Francisco: Jossey-Bass, 1980, pp. 1–16.

Atchley, R. C. *The Social Forces in Later Life: An Introduction to Social Gerontology.* Belmont, Calif.: Wadsworth, 1972.

Atchley, R. C., and S. J. Miller. "Older People and Their Families," in C. Eisdorfer (ed.), *Annual Review of Gerontology and Geriatrics.* Vol. 1. New York: Springer, 1980, pp. 337–369.

Atkinson, R. C., and R. M. Shiffrin. "Human Memory: A Proposed System and Its Control Processes," in K. W. Spence and J. T. Spence (eds.), *The Psychology of Learning and Motivation.* Vol. 2. New York: 1968, pp. 89–195.

Ault, R. L. *Children's Cognitive Development.* New York: Oxford University Press, 1977.

Ausubel, D. P. *Theory and Problems of Child Development.* New York: Grune & Stratton, 1958.

———. *Educational Psychology: A Cognitive View.* New York: Holt, Rinehart and Winston, 1968.

Axline, V. M. *Play Therapy.* Rev. ed. New York: Ballantine, 1969.

Babchuk, N. "Primary Friends and Kin: A Study of the Associations of Middle Class Couples," *Social Forces,* 43 (1965), 483–493.

———. "Aging and Primary Relations," *International Journal of Aging and Human Development,* 9 (1978), 137–151.

Babchuk, N., G. R. Peters, D. R. Hoyt, and M. A. Kaiser. "The Voluntary Associations of the Aged," *Journal of Gerontology,* 34 (1979), 579–587.

Babson, S. G., M. L. Pernoll, G. I. Benda, and K. Simpson. *Diagnosis and Management of the Fetus and Neonate at Risk: A Guide for Team Care.* 4th ed. St. Louis: C. V. Mosby, 1980.

Bacharach, V. R., and M. A. Luszcz. "Communicative Competence in Young Children: The Use of Implicit Linguistic Information," *Child Development,* 50 (1979), 260–263.

Bacon, M., and M. B. Jones. *Teenage Drinking.* New York: T. Y. Crowell, 1968.

Baer, K. E. von. *De ovi mammalium et hominis genesi.* Lipsiae: Sumptibus Vossii, 1827.

Bakeman, R., and J. R. Brownlee. "The Strategic Use of Parallel Play: A Sequential Analysis," *Child Development,* 51 (1980), 873–878.

Baltes, P. B., and K. W. Schaie. "Aging and IQ: The Myth of the Twilight Years," *Psychology Today,* 7 (March 1974), 35–40.

Bandura, A. "Social-Learning Theory of Identificatory Processes," in D. A. Goslin (ed.), *Handbook of Socialization Theory and Research.* Chicago: Rand McNally, 1969, pp. 213–262.

———. *Aggression: A Social Learning Analysis.* Englewood Cliffs, N.J.: Prentice-Hall, 1973.

———. *Social Learning Theory.* Englewood Cliffs, N.J.: Prentice-Hall, 1977.

Bandura, A., and F. J. McDonald. "Influence of Social Reinforcement and the Behavior of Models in Shaping Children's Moral Judgments," *Journal of Abnormal and Social Psychology,* 67 (1963), 274–281.

Bandura, A., and R. H. Walters. *Social Learning and Personality Development.* New York: Holt, Rinehart and Winston, 1963.

Banks, M. S., and P. Salapatek. "Infant Pattern Vision: A New Approach Based on the Contrast Sensitivity Function," *Journal of Experimental Child Psychology,* 31 (1981), 1–45.

Bardwick, J. M. *Psychology of Women: A Study of Bio-Cultural Conflicts.* New York: Harper & Row, 1971.

Barenboim, C. "The Development of Person Perception in Childhood and Adolescence: From Behavioral Comparisons to Psychological Constructs to Psychological Comparisons," *Child Development,* 52 (1981), 129–144.

Barker, R. G., H. F. Wright, et al. *One Boy's Day: A Specimen Record of Behavior.* New York: Harper & Row, 1951.

Barnett, M. A., L. M. King, J. A. Howard, and G. A. Dino. "Empathy in Young Children: Relation to Parents' Empathy, Affection, and Emphasis on the Feelings of Others," *Developmental Psychology,* 16 (1980), 243–244.

Barry, H., III, M. K. Bacon, and I. L. Child. "A Cross-Cultural Survey of Some Sex Differences in Socialization," *Journal of Abnormal and Social Psychology,* 55 (1957), 327–332.

Bartlett, J. C., and J. W. Santrock. "Affect-Dependent Episodic Memory in Young Children," *Child Development,* 50 (1979), 513–518.

Baruch, D., with medical collaboration by H. Miller. *One Little Boy.* New York: Dell, 1964.

Bates, E. *The Emergence of Symbols: Cognition and Communication in Infancy.* New York: Academic Press, 1979.

Bauman, K. D., and R. R. Wilson. "Sexual Behavior of Unmarried University Students in 1968 and 1972, *Journal of Sex Research,* 10 (1974), 327–333.

Baumrind, D. "Authoritarian vs. Authoritative Parental Control," *Adolescence,* 3 (1968), 255–272.

———. "Socialization and Instrumental Competence in Young Children," in W. W. Hartup (ed.), *The Young Child: Reviews of Research.* Vol. 12. Washington, D.C.: National Association for the Education of Young Children, 1972, pp. 202–224.

———. "The Contribution of the Family to the Development of Competence in Children," *Schizophrenia Bulletin,* 14 (1975), 12–37.

———. "A Dialectical Materialist's Perspective on Knowing Social Reality," in W. Damon (ed.), *New Directions for Child Development.* No. 2. *Moral Development.* San Francisco: Jossey-Bass, 1978, pp. 61–82.

Bax, M. "Man the Player," in B. Tizard and D. Harvey (eds.), *Biology of Play.* Philadelphia: Lippincott, 1977, pp. 1–5.

Bayley, N. "On the Growth of Intelligence," *American Psychologist,* 10 (1955), 805–818.

Beatty, R. A., and S. Gluecksohn-Waelsch. *Edinburgh Symposium on the Genetics of the Spermatozoan.* Edinburgh/New York, 1972.

Becker, J. M. "A Learning Analysis of the Development of Peer-Oriented Behavior in Nine-Month-Old Infants," *Developmental Psychology,* 13 (1977), 481–491.

Beckman, L. J. "Effects of Social Interaction and Children's Relative Input on Older Women's Psychological Well-Being," *Journal of Personality and Social Psychology,* 41 (1981), 1075–1086.

Beit-Hallahmi, B., and A. I. Rabin. "The Kibbutz as a Social Experiment and a Child-rearing Laboratory," *American Psychologist,* 32 (1977), 532–541.

Belbin, R. M. "Middle-age: What Happens to Ability," in R. Owen (ed.), *Middle Age.* London: Cox and Wyman, 1967, pp. 98–106.

Bell, R. Q., and L. V. Harper. *Child Effects on Adults.* Hillsdale, N.J.: Erlbaum, 1977.

Bell, S. M. "The Development of the Concept of Object as Related to Infant-Mother Attachment," *Child Development,* 41 (1970), 291–311.

Bell, S. M., and M. D. S. Ainsworth. "Infant Crying and Maternal Responsiveness," *Child Development,* 43 (1972), 1171–1190.

Bellugi, U. "Learning the Language," *Psychology Today,* 4 (December 1970), 32–35+.

Belmont, L., and F. A. Marolla. "Birth Order, Family Size, and Intelligence," *Science,* 182 (1973), 1096–1101.

Belsky, J. "Early Human Experience: A Family Perspective," *Developmental Psychology,* 17 (1981), 3–23.

Belsky, J., and R. K. Most. "From Exploration to Play: A Cross-Sectional Study of Infant Free Play Behavior," *Developmental Psychology,* 17 (1981), 630–639.

Belsky, J., and L. D. Steinberg. "The Effects of Day Care: A Critical Review," *Child Development,* 49 (1978), 929–949.

Bengtson, V. L., J. B. Cuellar, and P. K.

Ragan. "Stratum Contrasts and Similarities in Attitudes Toward Death." *Journal of Gerontology*, 1977, 32(1), 76–88.

Bengston, V. L., and J. Treas. "The Changing Family Context of Mental Health and Aging," in J. E. Birren and R. B. Sloane (eds.), *Handbook of Mental Health and Aging*. Englewood Cliffs, N.J.: Prentice-Hall, 1980, pp. 400–428.

Bereiter, C., et al. "An Academically Oriented Pre-school for Culturally Deprived Children," in F. M. Hechinger (ed.), *Pre-School Education Today*. New York: Doubleday, 1966, pp. 105–137.

Bereiter, C., and S. Engelmann. *Teaching Disadvantaged Children in the Preschool.* Englewood Cliffs, N.J.: Prentice-Hall, 1966.

Berg, W. K., and K. M. Berg. "Psychophysiological Development in Infancy: State, Sensory Function, and Attention," in J. D. Osofsky (ed.), *Handbook of Infant Development*. New York: Wiley-Interscience, 1979, pp. 283–343.

Berg-Cross, L. G. "Intentionality, Degree of Damage, and Moral Judgments," *Child Development*, 46 (1975), 970–974.

Berko, J. "The Child's Learning of English Morphology," *Word*, 14 (1958), 150–177.

Bernal, J. F. "Crying During the First Ten Days of Life and Maternal Response," *Developmental Medicine and Child Neurology*, 14 (1972), 367–372.

Bernard, J. *The Future of Marriage*. New York: World Publishing, 1972.

______. "Notes on Changing Life Styles: 1970–1974," *Journal of Marriage and the Family*, 37 (1975), 582–593.

______. "Infidelity: Some Moral and Social Issues," in R. W. Libby and R. N. Whitehurst (eds.), *Marriage and Alternatives: Exploring Intimate Relationships*. Glenview, Ill.: Scott, Foresman, 1977, pp. 131–146.

______. "The Good-Provider Role: Its Rise and Fall," *American Psychologist*, 36 (1981), 1–12.

Berndt, T. J. "Developmental Changes in Conformity to Peers and Parents," *Developmental Psychology*, 15 (1979), 608–616.

Bernstein, B. "Linguistic Codes, Hesitation Phenomena and Intelligence," *Language and Speech*, 5 (1962), 31–47.

______. "Elaborated and Restricted Codes: Their Social Origins and Some Consequences," in A. G. Smith (ed.), *Communication and Culture*. New York: Holt, Rinehart and Winston, 1966, pp. 427–442.

Bernstein, J. E. "Helping Young Children Cope with Death," in L. G. Katz (ed.), *Current Topics in Early Childhood Education*. Vol. 1. Norwood, N.J.: Ablex, 1977, pp. 179–189.

Berscheid, E., E. Walster, and G. Bohrnstedt. "Body Image," *Psychology Today*, 7 (November 1973), 119–131.

Bertenthal, B. I., and K. W. Fischer. "Development of Self-Recognition in the Infant," *Developmental Psychology*, 14 (1978), 44–50.

Berzonsky, M. "The Role of Familiarity in Children's Explanations of Physical Causality," *Child Development*, 42 (1971), 705–715.

Bever, T. G. "The Cognitive Basis for Linguistic Structures," in J. R. Hayes (ed.), *Cognition and the Development of Language*. New York: Wiley, 1970, pp. 279–362.

Bever, T. G. (ed.), *Regressions in Mental Development*. Hillsdale, N.J.: Erlbaum, 1981.

Biller, H. B. "The Father and Personality Development. Paternal Deprivation and Sex-Role Development," in M. E. Lamb (ed.), *The Role of the Father in Child Development*. New York: Wiley, 1976, pp. 89–156.

Billingham, R. E. "Family Life Contacts among Married and Never Married Professionals," *Psychological Reports*. 46 (1980), 715–718.

Bijou, S. W. *Child Development: The Basic Stage of Early Childhood*. Englewood Cliffs, N.J.: Prentice-Hall, 1976.

Bijou, S. W., and D. M. Baer. *Child Development*. Vol. 1. *A Systematic and Empirical Theory*. New York: Appleton-Century-Crofts, 1961.

______. *Child Development*. Vol. 2. *Universal Stage of Infancy*. New York: Appleton Century-Crofts, 1965.

Birch, H. B. "Field Measurement in Nutrition, Learning, and Behavior," in N. S. Scrimshaw and J. E. Gordon (eds.), *Malnutrition, Learning, and Behavior*. Cambridge, Mass.: M.I.T. Press, 1968.

Birren, J. E. *The Psychology of Aging*. Englewood Cliffs, N.J.: Prentice-Hall, 1964.

______. *Coping with the Stresses of Aging: Blueprint for Health*. Chicago: Blue Cross Association, 1975.

______. "Aging: The Psychologist's Perspective," in R. H. Davis (ed.), *Aging: Prospects and Issues*. Los Angeles: University of Southern California Press, 1976, pp. 16–28.

Birren, J. E., and V. J. Renner. "Concepts and Issues of Mental Health and Aging," in J. E. Birren and R. Bruce Sloane (eds.), *Handbook of Mental Health and Aging*. Englewood Cliffs, N.J.: Prentice-Hall, 1980, pp. 3–33.

Blank, M., and W. H. Bridger. "Cross-Modal Transfer in Nursery-School Children," *Journal of Comparative and Physiological Psychology*, 58 (1964), 277–282.

Blatt, M., and L. Kohlberg. "Effects of Classroom Moral Discussions upon Children's Levels of Moral Judgment," *Journal of Moral Education*, 4 (1975), 129–162.

Blau, Z. S. "Maternal Aspirations, Socialization, and Achievement of Boys and Girls in the White Working Class," *Journal of Youth and Adolescence*, 1 (1972), 35, 57.

Blehar, M. C., A. F. Lieberman, and M. D. S. Ainsworth. "Early Face-to-Face Interaction and Its Relation to Later Infant-Mother Attachment," *Child Development*, 48 (1977), 182–194.

Block, J. *Lives Through Time*. Berkeley: Bancroft Books, 1971.

Block, J. H. "Issues, Problems, and Pitfalls in Assessing Sex Differences: A Critical Review of *The Psychology of Sex Differences*," *Merrill-Palmer Quarterly*, 22, no. 4 (1976), 283–308.

______. "Another Look at Sex Differences in Socialization Practices of Mothers and Fathers," in F. Denmark and J. Sherman (eds.), *Psychology of Women: Future Directions of Research*. New York: Psychological Dimensions, 1978.

Bloom, L. *Language Development: Form and Function in Emerging Grammars*. Cambridge, Mass.: M.I.T. Press, 1970.

______. *One Word at a Time: The Use of a Single Word Utterance Before Syntax*. Janua Linguarum, Series Minor, 154 (1973).

Bloom, L., P. Lightbown, and L. Hood. "Structure and Variation in Child Language," *Monographs of the Society for Research in Child Development*, 40 (1975), whole no. 160.

Blos, P. *On Adolescence, A Psychoanalytic Interpretation*. New York: Free Press, 1962.

Blurton-Jones, N. (ed.), *Ethological Studies of Child Behavior*. London: Cambridge University Press, 1972.

Blurton-Jones, N. "Rough-and-Tumble Play among Nursery School Children," in J. Bruner, A. Jolly and K. Sylva (eds.), *Play: Its Role in Development and Evolution*. New York: Basic Books, 1976, pp. 352–363.

Blurton-Jones, N., and M. J. Konner. "Sex Differences in Behaviour of London and Bushmen Children," in R. P. Michael and J. H. Crook (eds.), *Comparative Ecology and Behaviour of Primates*. London: Academic Press, 1973, p. 689.

Boismier, J. D. "Visual Stimulation and Wake-Sleep Behavior in Human Neonates," *Developmental Psychobiology*, 10 (1977), 219–227.

Bolton, F. G., Jr. *The Pregnant Adolescent: Problems of Premature Parenthood*. Beverly Hills, Calif.: Sage Publications, 1980.

Bornstein, M. H. "Qualities of Color Vision in Infancy," *Journal of Experimental Child Psychology*, 19 (1975), 401–419.

______. "Infants' Recognition Memory for Hue," *Developmental Psychology*, 12 (1976), 185–191.

Boston Women's Health Book Collective. "Menopause," in S. H. Zarit (ed.), *Readings in Aging and Death: Contemporary Perspectives*. New York: Harper & Row, 1977, pp. 156–164.

Botvin, G. J., and F. B. Murray. "The Efficacy of Peer Modeling and Social Conflict in the Acquisition of Conservation," *Child Development*, 46 (1975), 796–799.

Botwinick, J. *Aging and Behavior*. 2nd ed. New York: Springer, 1978.

Botwinick, J., and I. C. Siegler. "Intellectual Ability among the Elderly: Simultaneous Cross-Sectional and Longitudinal Comparisons," *Developmental Psychology*, 16 (1980), 49–53.

Botwinick, J., and M. Storandt. "Recall and Recognition of Old Information in

Relation to Age and Sex," *Journal of Gerontology,* 35 (1980), 70–76.

Bouvier, L., E. Atlee, and F. McVeigh. "The Elderly in America," in S. H. Zarit (ed.), *Readings in Aging and Death: Contemporary Perspectives.* New York: Harper & Row, 1977, pp. 28–36.

Bower, G. H. "Mood and Memory," *American Psychologist,* 36 (1981), 129–148.

Bower, T. G. R. "The Visual World of Infants," *Scientific American,* 215 (December 1966), 80–92.

———. "The Object in the World of the Infant," *Scientific American,* 225 (October 1971), 30–38.

Bowerman, M. "Systematizing Semantic Knowledge: Changes over Time in the Child's Organization of Word Meaning," *Child Development,* 49 (1978), 977–987.

Bowlby, J. *Attachment: Attachment and Loss.* Vol. 1. New York: Basic Books, 1969.

———. *Separation: Attachment and Loss.* Vol. 2. New York: Basic Books, 1973.

———. *Loss: Attachment and Loss.* Vol. 3. New York: Basic Books, 1980a.

———. *Loss: Sadness and Depression.* New York: Basic Books, 1980b.

Brackbill, Y. "Cumulative Effects of Continuous Stimulation on Arousal Level in Infants," *Child Development,* 42 (1971), 17–26.

———. "Obstetrical Medication and Infant Behavior," in J. D. Osofsky (ed.), *Handbook of Infant Development.* New York: Wiley-Interscience, 1979, pp. 76–125.

Bradburn, N. M., and D. Caplovitz. *Reports on Happiness: A Pilot Study of Behavior Related to Mental Health.* Chicago: Aldine, 1965.

Braine, M. D. S. "Children's First Word Combination," *Monographs of the Society for Research in Child Development,* 41 (1976), whole no. 164.

Brainerd, C. J. "Feedback, Rule Knowledge, and Conservation Learning," *Child Development,* 48 (1977), 404–411.

———. *Piaget's Theory of Intelligence.* Englewood Cliffs, N.J.: Prentice-Hall, 1978.

Brand, F., and R. Smith. "Life Adjustment and Relocation of the Elderly," *Journal of Gerontology,* 29 (1974), 336–340.

Brandt, M. M. "Relations between Cognitive Role-Taking Performance and Age, Task Presentation, and Response Requirements," *Developmental Psychology,* 14 (1978), 206–213.

Brandt, M. M., and M. J. Strattner-Gregory. "Effect of Highlighting Intention on Intentionality and Restitutive Justice," *Developmental Psychology,* 16 (1980), 147–148.

Braungart, R. C. "Youth Movements," in J. Adelson (ed.), *Handbook of Adolescent Psychology.* New York: Wiley-Interscience, 1980, pp. 560–597.

Brazelton, T. B. *Neonatal Behavioral Assessment Scale.* Philadelphia: Lippincott, 1973.

Bremner, J. G., and P. E. Bryant. "Place versus Response as the Basis of Spatial Errors Made by Young Infants," *Journal of Experimental Child Psychology,* 23 (1977), 162–171.

Bretherton, I., and E. Bates. "The Emergence of Intentional Communication," in I. C. Uzgiris (ed.), *New Directions for Child Development.* No. 4. *Social Interaction and Communication during Infancy.* San Francisco: Jossey-Bass, 1979, pp. 81–100.

Bridger, W. H. "Sensory Habituation and Discrimination in the Human Neonate," *American Journal of Psychiatry,* 117 (1961), 991–996.

Brittain, C. V. "Adolescent Choices and Parent-Peer Cross Pressures," *American Sociological Review,* 28 (1963), 385–391.

Brody, E. M. "Aged Parents and Aging Children," in P. K. Ragan (ed.), *Aging Parents.* Los Angeles: University of Southern California Press, 1979, pp. 267–287.

Bronfenbrenner, U. *Two Worlds of Childhood: U.S. and U.S.S.R.* New York: Russell Sage Foundation, 1970.

———. "An Emerging Theoretical Perspective on Research and Social Policy." Paper presented at the biennial meeting of the Society for Research in Child Development, March 31, 1973.

———. *The Ecology of Human Development: Experiments by Nature and Design.* Cambridge, Mass.: Harvard University Press, 1979.

Bronson, G. "Aversive Reactions to Strangers: A Dual Process Interpretation," *Child Development,* 49 (1978), 495–499.

Bronstein, I. P., S. Wexler, A. W. Brown, and L. J. Halpern. "Obesity in Childhood: Psychologic Studies," *American Journal of the Disturbed Child,* 63 (1942), 238–251.

Brooks, J., and M. Lewis. "Infant's Response to Strangers: Midget, Adult and Child," *Child Development,* 47 (1976), 323–332.

Brotman, H. "Life Expectancy: Comparison of National Levels in 1900 and 1974 and Variations in State Levels, 1969–1971," *Gerontologist,* 17 (1977), 12–22.

Broverman, D. M., I. K. Broverman, W. Vogel, R. D. Palmer, and E. L. Klaiber. "Physique and Growth in Adolescence," *Child Development,* 35 (1964), 857–870.

Brown, A. L. "The Development of Memory: Knowing, Knowing About Knowing, and Knowing How to Know," in H. W. Reese (ed.), *Advances in Child Development and Behavior.* Vol. 10. New York: Academic Press, 1975, pp. 104–152.

———. "The Construction of Temporal Succession by Preoperational Children," in A. D. Pick (ed.), *Minnesota Symposium on Child Psychology,* Vol. 10, 1976, pp. 28–83.

Brown, P., and R. Elliott. "Control of Aggression in a Nursery School Class," *Journal of Experimental Child Psychology,* 2 (1965), 103–107.

Brown, R. *A First Language: The Early Stages.* Cambridge, Mass.: Harvard University Press, 1973.

———. "Introduction," in C. Snow and C. Ferguson (eds.), *Talking to Children: Language Input and Acquisition.* New York: Academic Press, 1977.

———. "The Maintenance of Conversation," in D. R. Olson (ed.), *The Social Foundations of Language and Thought.* New York: Norton, 1980, pp. 187–210.

Brown, R., C. Cazden, and U. Bellugi-Klima. "The Child's Grammar from I to III," in J. P. Hill (ed.), *Minnesota Symposia on Child Psychology.* Vol. 2. Minneapolis: University of Minnesota Press, 1968, pp. 28–73.

Bruch, H. *The Importance of Overweight.* New York: Norton, 1957.

Brück, K. "Temperature Regulation in the Newborn Infant," *Biologia neonatorum,* 3 (1961), 65–119.

Bruner, J. *Under Five in Britain.* London: Grant McIntire, 1980.

Bruner, J. S. "Nature and Uses of Immaturity," *American Psychologist,* 27 (1972), 687–708.

———. "The Beginnings of Intellectual Skill: 2," *New Behaviour,* October 9, 1975, pp. 58–61.

———. "From Communication to Language: A Psychological Perspective," *Cognition,* 3 (1976), 255–287.

———. "Learning the Mother Tongue," *Human Nature,* 1 (September 1978), 42–49.

———. "The Social Context of Language Acquisition." The Witkin Memorial Lecture. Educational Testing Service, Princeton, N.J., 1980.

Bruner, J. S., A. Jolly, and K. Sylva (eds.). *Play: Its Role in Development and Evolution.* New York: Basic Books, 1976.

Bryan, J. H. "Children's Cooperation and Helping Behaviors," in E. M. Hetherington (ed.), *Review of Child Development Research.* Vol. 5. Chicago: University of Chicago Press, 1975, pp. 127–182.

Bryan, J. H., and N. H. Walbek. "Preaching and Practicing Generosity: Children's Actions and Reactions," *Child Development,* 41 (1970), 329–353.

Bryant, P. E., P. Jones, V. C. Claxton, and G. M. Perkins. "Recognition of Shapes Across Modalities by Infants," *Nature,* 240 (1972), 303–304.

Bryant, P. E., and T. Trabasso. "Transitive Inferences and Memory in Young Children," *Nature,* 232 (1971), 456–458.

Bryer, K. B. "The Amish Way of Death," *American Psychologist,* 34 (1979), 255–261.

Bullock, T. H., R. Orkand, and A. Grinnell. *Introduction to Nervous Systems.* San Francisco: Freeman, 1977.

Burgess, A. Language Made Plain. Rev. ed. London: Fontana/Collins, 1975.

Burgess, E. W., and P. Wallin. *Engagement and Marriage.* Philadelphia: Lippincott, 1953.

Buriel, R. "The Relation of Anglo- and Mexican-American Children's Locus of Control Beliefs to Parents' and Teachers' Socialization Practices," *Child Development,* 52 (1981), 104–113.

Burke, D. B., and L. L. Light. "Memory

and Aging: The Role of Retrieval Processes," *Psychological Bulletin,* 90 (1981), 513–546.

Burkitt, D. P., A. R. P. Walker, and N. S. Painter. "Dietary Fiber and Disease," *Journal of the American Medical Association,* 229 (1974), 1068–1074.

Burridge, K. O. L. "A Tangu Game," in J. S. Bruner, A. Jolly, and K. Sylva (eds.), *Play: Its Role in Development and Evolution.* New York: Basic Books, 1976, pp. 364–366.

Burton, R. V. "Honesty and Dishonesty," in T. Lickona (ed.), *Moral Development and Behavior: Theory, Research, and Social Issues.* New York: Holt, Rinehart and Winston, 1976, pp. 173–197.

Bush, D. E., R. G. Simmons, B. Hutchinson, and D. A. Blyth. "Adolescent Perception of Sex-Roles in 1968 and 1975," *Public Opinion Quarterly,* 41 (1977–1978), 459–474.

Butler, R. N. "The Life Review: An Interpretation of Reminiscence in the Aged," *Psychiatry,* 26 (1963), 65–76.

Butler, R. N., and M. Lewis. *Aging and Mental Health.* 2nd ed. St. Louis: Mosby, 1977.

Butterfield, E. C., and G. N. Siperstein. "Influence of Contingent Auditory Stimulation upon Non-Nutritional Suckle," in *Proceedings of the Third Symposium on Oral Sensation and Perception: The Mouth of the Infant.* Springfield, Ill.: Charles C Thomas, 1974.

Butterworth, G. "Object Disappearance and Error in Piaget's Stage IV Task," *Journal of Experimental Child Psychology,* 23 (1977), 391–401.

Butterworth, G., and L. Hicks. "Visual Proprioception and Postural Stability in Infancy: A Developmental Study," *Perception,* 6 (1977), 255–262.

Byrne, D. *The Attraction Paradigm.* New York: Academic Press, 1971.

Caldwell, B. M. "The Rationale for Early Intervention," *Exceptional Children,"* 36 (1970), 717.

Callard, E. "Achievement Motive in the Four-Year-Old and Its Relationship to Achievement Expectations of the Mother." Doctoral dissertation, University of Michigan, 1964.

Campbell, A., P. E. Converse, and W. L. Rogers. *The Quality of American Life.* New York: The Russell Sage Foundation, 1975.

Campbell, J. D., and M. R. Yarrow. "Perceptual and Behavioral Correlates of Social Effectiveness," *Sociometry,* 24 (1961), 1–20.

Campbell, W. J. "US Rebuffed, Infant Formula Code Adopted," *The Boston Globe,* May 21, 1981, p. 3.

Campos, J. Heart Rate: A Sensitive Tool for the Study of Emotional Development," in L. Lipsitt (ed.), *Developmental Psychobiology: The Significance of Infancy,* Hillsdale, N.J.: Erlbaum, 1976.

Campos, J. J., S. Hiatt, D. Ramsay, C. Henderson, and M. Svejda. "The Emergence of Fear on the Visual Cliff," in M. Lewis and L. Rosenblum (eds.), *The Origins of Affect.* New York: Plenum, 1978.

Canestrari, R. E. "Paced and Self-paced Learning in Young and Elderly Adults," *Journal of Gerontology,* 18 (1963), 165–168.

Cantor, J. H., and C. C. Spiker. "The Effects of Introtacts on Hypothesis Testing in Kindergarten and First-Grade Children," *Child Development,* 50 (1979), 1110–1120.

Cappella, J. N. "Mutual Influence in Expressive Behavior: Adult-Adult and Infant-Adult Dyadic Interaction," 89 (1981), 101–132.

Cappon, D. "Attitudes of and Toward the Dying," *Canadian Medical Association Journal,* 87 (1962), 693–700.

Carew, J. V. "Experience and the Development of Intelligence in Young Children at Home and in Day Care," *Monographs of the Society for Research in Child Development,* 45 (1980), whole no. 187.

Carey, S. "Cognitive Competence," in K. Connolly and J. Bruner (eds.), *The Growth of Competence.* New York: Academic Press, 1974, pp. 169–193.

Carlsson, S. G., H. Fagerberg, G. Horneman, C. Hwang, K. Larsson, M. Rodhold, J. Schaller, B. Danielsson, and C. Gundewall. "Effects of Various Amounts of Contact between Mother and Child on the Mother's Nursing Behavior: A Follow-up Study," *Infant Behavior and Development,* 2 (1979), 209–214.

Caro, G., and C. T. Pihlblad. "Aspirations and Expectations: A Reexamination of the Bases for Social Class Differences in the Occupational Orientations of Male High School Students," *Sociology and Social Research,* 49 (1965), 465–475.

Carter, G. L., and M. Kinsbourne. "The Ontogeny of Right Cerebral Lateralization of Spatial Mental Set," *Developmental Psychology,* 15 (1979), 241–245.

Carter-Saltzman, L. "Biological and Sociocultural Effects on Handedness: Comparison between Biological and Adoptive Families," *Science,* 209 (1980), 1263–1265.

Cartwright, A., L. Hockey, and J. L. Anderson. *Life Before Death.* London: Routledge & Kegan Paul, 1973.

Cattell, P. *The Measurements of Intelligence of Infants and Young Children.* New York: Psychological Corporation, 1940.

Cavior, N., and P. R. Dokecki. "Physical Attractiveness, Perceived Attitude Similarity, and Academic Achievement as Contributors to Interpersonal Attraction among Adolescents," *Developmental Psychology,* 9 (1973), 44–54.

Cermak, L. S., and F. I. M. Craik (eds.). *Levels of Processing in Human Memory.* Hillsdale, N.J.: Erlbaum, 1979.

Chabon, I. *Awake and Aware: Participating in Childbirth through Psychoprophylaxis.* New York: Delacorte Press, 1966.

Chall, J. S. *Learning to Read: The Great Debate.* New York: McGraw-Hill, 1967.

Chance, P. *Learning through Play.* New York: Gardner Press, 1979.

Chaplin, J. P., and T. S. Krawiec. *Systems and Theories of Psychology.* 3rd ed. New York: Holt, Rinehart and Winston, 1974.

Chernoff, G. "The Fetal Alcohol Syndrome in Mice: An Animal Model," *Teratology,* 15 (1977), 223–230.

Chilman, C. *Adolescent Sexuality in a Changing American Society—Social and Psychological Perspectives.* Bethesda, Md.: DHEW Public Health Service, National Institutes of Health, No (NIH) 79-1426, 1979.

Chomsky, C. *Acquisition of Syntax in Children from 5 to 10.* Cambridge, Mass.: M.I.T. Press, 1969.

Chomsky, N. *Language and Mind.* Enl. ed. New York: Harcourt Brace Jovanovich, 1972.

———. *Reflections on Language.* New York: Pantheon, 1975.

———. *Language and Responsibility.* New York: Pantheon, 1979.

Chown, S. M. "Morale, Careers and Personal Potentials," in J. E. Birren and K. W. Schaie (eds.), *Handbook of the Psychology of Aging.* New York: Van Nostrand Reinhold, 1977, pp. 672–691.

Clark, E. V. "What's in a Word? On the Child's Acquisition of Semantics in His First Language," in T. E. Moore (ed.), *Cognitive Development and the Acquisition of Language.* New York: Academic Press, 1973, pp. 65–110.

———. "Awareness of Language: Some Evidence from What Children Say and Do," in A. Sinclair, R. J. Jarvella, and W. J. M. Levelt (eds.), *The Child's Conception of Language.* New York: Springer-Verlag, 1978, pp. 17–44.

Clark, H. H., and E. V. Clark. *Psychology and Language.* New York: Harcourt Brace Jovanovich, 1977.

Clarke, A. M., and A. D. B. Clarke. *Early Experience: Myth and Evidence.* New York: Free Press, 1977.

Clarke-Stewart, K. A. "Recasting the Lone Stranger," in J. Glick and K. A. Clarke-Stewart (eds.), *The Development of Social Understanding.* New York: Gardner Press, 1978, pp. 109–176.

Clarke-Stewart, K. A., and C. M. Hevey, "Longitudinal Relations in Repeated Observations of Mother-Child Interaction from 1 to 2½ Years," *Developmental Psychology,* 17 (1981), 127–145.

Clausen, J. A. "The Social Meaning of Differential Physical and Sexual Maturation," in S. E. Dragastin and G. H. Elder (eds.), *Adolescence in the Life Cycle.* New York: Halstead, 1975.

Clayton, P. J., J. A. Halikes, and W. L. Maurice. "The Bereavement of the Widowed," *Diseases of the Nervous System,* 32 (1971), 597–604.

Coates, B., and W. W. Hartup. "Age and Verbalization in Observational Learning," *Developmental Psychology,* 1 (1969), 556–562.

Cobb, W., and C. Mozociotti, (eds.). "The Evoked Potentials," *Electroencephalography and Clinical Neurophysiology* (Supplement No. 26). Amsterdam: Elsevier, 1967.

Cohen, E., M. Perlmutter, and N. A. Myers. "Memory for Location of Multiple Stimuli by 2- to 4-Year-Olds," Unpublished manuscript, University of Minnesota, 1977.

Cohen, E. A., D. M. Gelfand, and D. P. Hartmann. "Causal Reasoning as a Function of Behavioral Consequences," *Child Development,* 52 (1981), 514–522.

Cohen, G. "Language Comprehension in Old Age," *Cognitive Psychology,* 11 (1979), 412–429.

Cohen, L. B. "Habituation of Infant Visual Attention," in T. J. Tighe and R. N. Leaton (eds.), *Habituation: Perspectives from Child Development, Animal Behavior, and Neurophysiology.* Hillsdale, N.J.: Erlbaum, 1976, pp. 207–238.

Cohen, L. B., J. S. DeLoache, and M. S. Strauss. "Infant Visual Perception," in J. D. Osofsky (ed.), *Handbook of Infant Development.* New York: Wiley, 1979, pp. 393–438.

Cohen, S., D. C. Glass, and J. E. Singer. "Apartment Noise, Auditory Discrimination and Reading Ability," *Journal of Experimental Social Psychology,* 9 (1973), 407–422.

Colby, A. "Evolution of a Moral-Developmental Theory," in W. Damon (ed.), *New Directions for Child Development.* No. 2. *Moral Development.* San Francisco: Jossey-Bass, 1978, pp. 89–104.

Cole, C. L. "Cohabitation in Social Context," in R. W. Libby and R. N. Whitehurst (eds.), *Marriage and Alternatives: Exploring Intimate Relationships.* Glenview, Ill.: Scott, Foresman, 1977, pp. 62–79.

Cole, M. "How Education Affects the Mind," *Human Nature,* 1, no. 4 (1978), 50–58.

Cole, M., and S. Scribner. "Introduction," in L. S. Vygotsky, *Mind in Society.* Cambridge, Mass.: Harvard University Press, 1978, pp. 1–14.

Coleman, J. C. "Friendship and the Peer Group in Adolescence," in J. Adelson (ed.), *Handbook of Adolescent Psychology.* New York: Wiley-Interscience, 1980, pp. 408–431.

Coleman, J. S., *Youth: Transition to Adulthood.* Chicago: University of Chicago Press, 1974.

Collins, W. A. "Schemata for Understanding Television," in H. Kelly and H. Gardner (eds.), *New Directions for Child Development.* No. 13. *Viewing Children Through Television.* San Francisco: Jossey-Bass, 1981, pp. 31–45.

Colman, N., N. Hettiarachchy, and V. Herbert. "Detection of a Milk Factor That Facilitates Folate Uptake by Intestinal Cells," *Science,* 211 (1981), 1427–1429.

Colombio, J. "The Critical Period Concept: Research, Methodology, and Theoretical Issues," *Psychological Bulletin,* 91 (1982), 260–275.

Columbia Broadcasting System. *A Study of Messages Received by Children Who Viewed an Episode of Fat Albert and the Cosby Kids.* New York: CBS, 1974.

Comfort, A. *A Good Age.* New York: Crown, 1976.

Comstock, G., S. Chaffee, N. Katzman, M. McCombs, and D. Roberts. *Television and Human Behavior.* New York: Columbia University Press, 1978.

Condry, J. C., and S. L. Dyer. "Fear of Success: Attribution of Cause to the Victim," *Journal of Social Issues,* 32, no. 3 (1976), 63–83.

———. "Behavioral and Fantasy Measures of Fear of Success in Children," *Child Development,* 48 (1977), 1417–1425.

Conel, J. L. R. *The Cortex of the Four-Year Child.* Vol. 7. *The Postnatal Development of the Human Cerebral Cortex.* 7 vols., 1939–1963. Cambridge, Mass.: Harvard University Press, 1963.

Conger, J. J. *Adolescence and Youth: Psychological Development in a Changing World.* New York: Harper & Row, 1973.

Conklin, F. "Should Retired Women Live Together?" *NRTA Journal,* 25 (November–December, 1974), 19–20.

Connell, D. B., J. I. Layzer, and B. D. Goodson. "National Study of Day Care Centers for Infants: Findings and Implications," Paper presented at the American Psychological Association meeting. New York, September 1979.

Conner, K. A., E. A. Powers, and G. L. Bultena. "Social Interaction and Life Satisfaction: An Empirical Assessment of Late-Life Patterns," *Journal of Gerontology,* 34 (1979), 116–121.

Connor, J. M., L. A. Serbin, and M. Schackman. "Sex Differences in Children's Response to Training on a Visual-Spatial Test," *Developmental Psychology,* 13 (1977), 293–294.

Constantine, L., and J. M. Constantine. "The Group Marriage," in M. E. Lasswell and T. E. Lasswell (eds.), *Love, Marriage, Family: A Developmental Approach.* Glenview, Ill.: Scott, Foresman, 1973, pp. 446–454.

———. "Sexual Aspects of Group Marriage, in R. W. Libby and R. N. Whitehurst (eds.), *Marriage and Alternatives: Exploring Intimate Relationships.* Glenview, Ill.: Scott, Foresman, 1977, pp. 186–194.

Cook, M., J. Field, and K. Griffiths, "The Perception of Solid Form in Early Infancy," *Child Development,* 49 (1978), 866–869.

Coopersmith, S. *The Antecedents of Self-Esteem.* San Francisco: Freeman, 1967.

Corballis, M. C. "Laterality and Myth," *American Psychologist,* 35 (1980), 284–295.

Corby, N., and R. L. Solnick. "Psychosocial and Physiological Influences on Sexuality in the Older Adult," in J. E. Birren and R. B. Sloane (eds.), *Handbook of Mental Health and Aging.* Englewood Clifs, N.J.: Prentice-Hall, 1980, pp. 893–921.

Corcoran, D. W. J. *Pattern Recognition.* Baltimore: Penguin Books, 1971.

Coren, S. "Development of Ocular Dominance," *Developmental Psychology,* 10 (1974), 302.

Cornell, E. H. "Infants' Visual Attention to Pattern Arrangement and Orientation," *Child Development,* 46 (1975), 229–232.

Correll, R., S. Rokosz, and B. Blanchard. "Some Correlates of WAIS Performance in the Elderly," *Journal of Gerontology,* 21 (1966), 544–549.

Corsale, K., and P. A. Ornstein. "Developmental Changes in Children's Use of Semantic Information in Recall," *Journal of Experimental Child Psychology,* 30 (1980), 231–245.

Cosentino, F., and A. B. Heilbrun, Jr. "Anxiety Correlates of Sex-Role Identity in College Students," *Psychological Reports,* 14 (1964), 729–730.

Costanzo, P. R., and M. E. Shaw. "Conformity as a Function of Age Level," *Child Development,* 37 (1966), 967–975.

Cowan, W. M. "The Developing Brain," *Scientific American,* 241 (1979), 88–133.

Cox, F. D. *Youth, Marriage, and the Seductive Society.* Rev. ed. Dubuque, Iowa: William C. Brown, 1968.

Crandall, V. "Differences in Parental Antecedents of Internal-External Control in Children and in Young Adulthood," Paper presented at American Psychological Association meeting, Montreal, 1973.

Cratty, B. J. *Movement Behavior and Motor Learning.* 2nd ed. London: Kimpton, 1967.

Cravioto, J., and E. Delicarde. "Mental Performance in School Age Children," *American Journal of Diseases of Children,* 120 (1970), 404.

Crook, C. K. "The Organization and Control of Infant Sucking," in H. W. Reese and L. P. Lipsitt (eds.), *Advances in Child Development and Behavior.* Vol. 14. New York: Academic Press, 1979, pp. 209–253.

Crook, K. C., and L. P. Lipsitt. "Neonatal Nutritive Sucking: Effects of Taste Stimulation Upon Sucking Rhythm and Heart Rate," *Child Development,* 47 (1976), 518–522.

Cruise, M. O. "A Longitudinal Study of the Growth of Low Birth Weight Infants: 1. Velocity and Distance Growth, Birth to 3 Years," *Pediatrics,* 51 (1973), 620–628.

Cuber, J. F. "Adultery: Reality versus Stereotype," in G. Neubeck (ed.), *Extramarital Relations.* Englewood Cliffs, N.J.: Prentice-Hall, 1969, pp. 190–196.

Cuber, J. F., and P. B. Harroff. *The Significant Americans.* New York: Appleton-Century-Crofts, 1965.

Cummins, R. A., P. J. Livesey, J. G. M. Evans, and R. N. Walsh. "Mechanism of Brain Growth by Environmental Stimulation," *Science,* 205 (1979), 522.

Curtiss, S. R. *Genie: A Psycholinguistic Study of a Modern-Day 'Wild Child.'* " New York: Academic Press, 1977.

Cytrynbaum, S., L. Blum, R. Patrick, J. Stein, D. Wades, and C. Wilk. "Midlife Development: A Personality and Social Systems Perspective," in L. W. Poon (ed.), *Aging in the 1980's: Psychological Issues.* Washington, D.C.: American Psychological Association, 1980, pp. 463–474.

Daehler, M. W., and M. P. O'Connor. "Recognition Memory for Objects in Very Young Children: The Effect of Shape and Label Similarity on Preference for Novel Stimuli," *Journal of Experimental Child Psychology,* 29 (1980), 306–321.

Damon, W. *The Social World of the Child.* San Francisco: Jossey-Bass, 1977.

Darlington, R. B., J. M. Royce, A. S. Snipper, H. W. Murray, and I. Lazar. "Preschool Programs and Later School Competence of Children from Low-Income Families," *Science,* 208 (1980), 202–204.

Darwin, C. *The Expression of the Emotions in Man and Animals.* New York: The Philosophical Library, 1955 (orig. pub. 1872).

Dawe, H. C. "An Analysis of Two Hundred Quarrels of Preschool Children," *Child Development,* 5 (1934), 139–157.

Day, M. C. "Developmental Trends in Visual Scanning," in H. W. Reese (ed.), *Advances in Child Development and Behavior.* Vol. 10. New York: Academic Press, 1975, pp. 154–193.

Deaux, K. *The Behavior of Men and Women.* Belmont, Calif.: Brooks-Cole, 1976.

Debakan, A. *Neurology of Infancy.* Baltimore: Williams & Wilkins, 1959.

DeCasper, A. J., and W. P. Fifer. "Of Human Bonding: Newborns Prefer Their Mothers' Voices," *Science,* 208 (1980), 1174–1176.

DeChateau, P. "Neonatal Care Routines: Influences on Maternal and Infant Behavior and on Breastfeeding" (Thesis). Umea University (Sweden) Medical Dissertations, N. S. No. 20, 1976.

Deci, E. L., J. Nezlek, and L. Sheinman. "Characteristics of the Rewarder and Intrinsic Motivation of the Rewardee," *Journal of Personality and Social Psychology,* 40 (1981), 1–10.

DeLoache, J. S. "Naturalistic Studies of Memory for Object Location in Very Young Children," in M. Perlmutter (ed.), *New Directions in Child Development.* No. 10. *Children's Memory.* San Francisco: Jossey-Bass, 1980, pp. 17–32.

deMause, L. (ed.). *The History of Childhood.* New York: Harper & Row, 1975.

Denney, D. R., N. W. Denney, and M. J. Ziobrowski. "Alterations in the Information-Processing Strategies of Young Children Following Observation of Adult Models," *Developmental Psychology,* 8 (1973), 202–208.

Dennis, W. "Infant Development Under Conditions of Restricted Practice and of Minimum Social Stimulation," *Genetic Psychology Monographs,* 23 (1941), 143–191.

———. "Causes of Retardation Among Institutional Children: Iran," *Journal of Genetic Psychology,* 96 (1960), 47–59.

———. "Creative Productivity between the Ages of 20 and 80 Years," *Journal of Gerontology,* 21 (1966), 1–8.

Dennis, W. "Creative Productivity between the Ages of 20 and 80 Years," in B. L. Neugarten (ed.), *Middle Age and Aging.* Chicago: University of Chicago Press, 1968, pp. 106–114.

Dennis, W., and M. G. Dennis. "The Effect of Cradling Practices upon the Onset of Walking in Hopi Children," *Journal of Genetic Psychology,* 56 (1940), 77–86.

Dennis, W., and P. Najarian. "Infant Development Under Environmental Handicap," *Psychological Monographs,* 71 (1957), 436.

Dennis, W., and Y. Sayegh. "The Effect of Supplementary Experiences upon the Behavioral Development of Infants in Institutions," *Child Development,* 36 (1965), 81–90.

Deutscher, I. "The Quality of Postparental Life," in B. L. Neugarten (ed.), *Middle Age and Aging.* Chicago: University of Chicago Press, 1968, pp. 263–268.

———. "Socialization for Post-parental Life," in M. E. Lasswell and T. E. Lasswell (eds.), *Love, Marriage, Family: A Developmental Approach.* Glenview, Ill.: Scott, Foresman, 1973, pp. 510–517.

deVilliers, J. G., and P. A. deVilliers. "Development of the Use of Word Order in Comprehension," *Journal of Psycholinguistic Research,* 2 (1973), 331–341.

———. *Language Acquisition.* Cambridge, Mass.: Harvard University Press, 1978.

deVries, H. A. "Physiology of Exercise and Aging," in D. S. Woodruff and J. E. Birren (eds.), *Aging: Scientific Perspectives and Social Issues.* New York: Van Nostrand Reinhold, 1981.

DeVries, R. "Constancy of Generic Identity in the Years Three to Six," *Society for Research in Child Development,* Vol. 34, no. 3, Serial no. 127 (1969).

Dick-Read, G. *Childbirth without Fear: The Principles and Practice of Natural Childbirth.* New York: Harper & Bros., 1944.

Dion, K. K. "Young Children's Stereotyping of Facial Attractiveness," *Developmental Psychology,* 9 (1973), 183–188.

DiPietro, J. A. "Rough and Tumble Play: A Function of Gender," *Developmental Psychology,* 17 (1981), 50–58.

Dobbing, J., and J. L. Smart. "Vulnerability of the Developing Brain and Behavior," *British Medical Bulletin,* 30 (1974), 164–168.

Donaldson, M. *Children's Minds.* New York: Norton, 1979.

Dornbusch, S. M., J. M. Carlsmith, R. T. Gross, J. A. Martin, D. Jennings, A. Rosenberg, and P. Drake. "Sexual Development, Age, and Dating: A Comparison of Biological and Social Influences upon One Set of Behaviors," *Child Development,* 52 (1981), 179–185.

Douglas, J. W. B. "The Age at Which Premature Children Walk," *Medical Officer,* 95 (1956), 33–35.

Douvan, E. "Sex Differences in the Opportunities, Demands, and Developments of Youth," in R. J. Havighurst and P. H. Dreyer (eds.), *Youth* (74th Yearbook: National Society for the Study of Education). Chicago: University of Chicago Press, 1975.

Douvan, E., and J. Adelson. *The Adolescent Experience.* New York: Wiley, 1966.

Douvan, E., and M. Gold. "Modal Patterns in American Adolescence," in L. W. Hoffman and M. L. Hoffman (eds.), *Review of Child Development Research.* Vol. 2. New York: Russell Sage Foundation, 1966.

Doyle, A., J. Connolly, and L. Rivest. "The Effect of Playmate Familiarity on the Social Interactions of Children," *Child Development,* 51 (1980), 217–223.

Dragastin, S. E., and G. H. Elder, Jr. (eds.). *Adolescence in the Life Cycle.* New York: Halstead Press, 1975.

Duck, S. W. *Personal Relationships and Personal Constructs: A Study of Friendship Formation.* New York: Wiley-Interscience, 1973.

———. *Theory and Practice in Interpersonal Attraction.* New York: Academic Press, 1977.

Dulit, E. "Adolescent Thinking *à la* Piaget: The Formal Stage," *Journal of Youth and Adolescence,* 1 (1972), 281–301.

Dunn, J. *Distress and Comfort.* Cambridge, Mass.: Harvard University Press, 1977.

Dunphy, D. C. "The Social Structure of Urban Adolescent Peer Groups," *Sociometry,* 26 (1963), 230–246.

Dustman, R. E., and E. C. Beck. "Visually Evoked Potentials: Amplitude Changes with Age," *Science,* 151 (1966), 1013–1015.

Duvall, E. M. *Family Development.* 4th ed. Philadelphia: Lippincott, 1971.

Dweck, C. S. "Social-Cognitive Processes in Children's Friendships," in S. R. Asher and J. M. Gottman (eds.), *The Development of Children's Friendships.* New York: Cambridge University Press, 1981, pp. 322–333.

Dweck, C. S., and E. S. Bush. "Sex Differences in Learned Helplessness: I. Differential Debilitation with Peer and Adult Evaluators." *Developmental Psychology,* 12 (1976), 147–156.

Dweck, C. S., W. Davidson, S. Nelson, and B. Enna. "Sex Differences in Learned Helplessness: II. The Contingencies of Evaluative Feedback in the Classroom, and III. An Experimental Analysis," *Developmental Psychology,* 14 (1978), 268–276.

Dweck, C. S., and T. E. Goetz. "Attributions and Learned Helplessness," in J. W. Harvey, W. Ickes, and R. F. Kidd (eds.), *New Directions in Attribution Research.* Vol. 2. Hillsdale, N.J.: Erlbaum, 1977.

Dwyer, J., and J. Mayer. "Psychological Effects of Variations in Physical Appearance During Adolescence," *Adolescence,* 3 (Winter 1968–1969), 353–380.

———. "Overfeeding and Obesity in Infants and Children," *Bibliotheca Nutritio et Dieta,* 18 (1973), pp. 123–152.

Dziadosz, G. M., and M. J. Schaller. "Acuity and Sighting Dominance in Children and Adults," *Developmental Psychology,* 13 (1977), 288.

Easterbrooks, M. A., and M. E. Lamb. "Mother Attachment and Infant Competence in Initial Encounters with Peers," *Child Development,* 50 (1979), 380–387.

Eckerman, C. O., and H. L. Rheingold. "Infants' Exploratory Responses to Toys and People," *Developmental Psychology,* 10 (1974), 255–259.

Edwards, C. P., and B. B. Whiting. "Differential Socialization of Girls and Boys in the Light of Cross-Cultural Research," in C. M. Super and S. Harkness (eds.), *New Directions for Child Development.* No. 8. *Anthropological Perspectives on Child Development.* San Francisco: Jossey-Bass, 1980, pp. 45–57.

Egeland, B., and L. A. Sroufe. "Attachment and Early Maltreatment," *Child Development,* 52 (1981), 44–52.

Eibl-Eibesfeldt, I. *Ethology: The Biology of Behavior.* E. Klinghammer (tr.). New York: Holt, Rinehart and Winston, 1970.

Eich, J. E., H. Weingartner, R. C. Stillman, and J. C. Gillin. "State-Dependent Accessibility of Retrieval Cues in the Retention of a Categorized List," *Journal of Verbal Learning and Verbal Behavior,* 14 (1975), 408–417.

Eichorn, D. *Biological Correlates of Behavior.* Chicago: National Society for the Study of Education, 1963.

Eiduson, B. T. "Emergent Families of the 1970s: Values, Practices and Impacts upon Children," in D. Reiss and H. A. Hoffman (eds.), *The American Family: Dying or Developing?* New York: Plenum, 1979, pp. 157–201.

Eilers, R. E., W. R. Wilson, and J. M. Moore. "Developmental Changes in Speech Discrimination in Three-, Six-, and Twelve-Month-Old Infants," *Journal of Speech and Hearing Research,* 20 (1977), 766–780.

Eimas, P. D., and V. C. Tartter. "On the Development of Speech Perception: Mechanisms and Analogies," in H. W. Reese and L. P. Lipsitt (eds.), *Advances in Child Development and Behavior.* Vol. 13. New York: Academic Press, 1979, pp. 155–193.

Eisenberg, R. B. "The Development of Hearing in Man: An Assessment of Current Status," *Journal of the American Speech and Hearing Association,* 12 (1970), 119–123.

Eisenberg, R. B., E. J. Griffin, D. B. Coursin, and M. A. Hunter. "Auditory Behavior in the Human Neonate: A Preliminary Report," *Journal of Speech and Hearing Research,* 7 (1964), 245–269.

Eisenberg-Berg, N., and E. Geisheker. "Content of Preachings and Power of the Model/Preacher: The Effect on Children's Generosity," *Developmental Psychology,* 15 (1979), 168–175.

Elder, G. H., Jr. *Adolescent Socialization and Personality Development.* Chicago: Rand McNally, 1968.

———. "Adolescence in Historical Perspective," in J. Adelson (ed.), *Handbook of Adolescent Psychology.* New York: Wiley-Interscience, 1980, pp. 3–46.

Elder, J. L., and D. R. Pederson. "Preschool Children's Use of Objects in Symbolic Play," *Child Development,* 49 (1978), 500–504.

Elkind, D. "Strategic Interactions in Early Adolescence," in J. Adelson (ed.), *Handbook of Adolescent Psychology.* New York: Wiley-Interscience, 1980, pp. 432–446.

Elkind, D., and R. Bowen. "Imaginary Audience Behavior in Children and Adolescents," *Developmental Psychology,* 15 (1979), 38–44.

Elkind, D., and R. F. Dabek. "Personal Injury and Property Damage in Moral Judgments of Children," *Child Development,* 48 (1977), 518–522.

Elliott, V. "Impact of Day Care on Economic Status of the Family," in D. Peters (ed.), *A Summary of the Pennsylvania Day Care Study.* University Park: Pennsylvania State University, 1973.

Emde, R. N., T. J. Gaensbauer, and R. J. Harmon. *Emotional Expression in Infancy: A Biobehavioral Study.* New York: International Universities Press, 1976.

Emmerich, W. "Continuity and Stability in Early Social Development: II. Teacher Ratings," *Child Development,* 37 (1966), 17–27.

Engen, T., and L. P. Lipsitt. "Decrement and Recovery of Responses to Olfactory Stimuli in the Human Neonate," *Journal of Comparative and Physiological Psychology,* 59 (1965), 312–316.

Entwisle, D. R., and L. A. Hayduk. *Too Great Expectations.* Baltimore: Johns Hopkins University Press, 1978.

Epstein, R., R. P. Lanza, and B. F. Skinner. "Symbolic Communication between Two Pigeons (Columbia livia domestica)," *Science,* 207 (1980), 543–545.

Erdwins, C. J., Z. E. Tyer, and J. C. Mellinger. "Personality Traits of Mature Women in Student versus Homemaker Roles," *Journal of Psychology* 105 (1980), 189–195.

Erikson, E. H. *Childhood and Society.* 2nd rev. ed. New York: Norton, 1963.

———. *Identity, Youth, and Crisis.* New York: Norton, 1968.

Eron, L. D. "Prescription for Reduction of Aggression," *American Psychologist,"* 35 (1980), 244–252.

Ervin-Tripp, S. "Language Development," in *Master Lecture Series,* American Psychological Association, 1976.

Etaugh, C. "Effects of Nonmaternal Care on Children," *American Psychologist,* 35 (1980), 309–319.

Evans, G. W. "Environmental Cognition," *Psychological Bulletin,* 88 (1980), 259–287.

Evans, R. I. "Smoking in Children: Developing a Social Psychological Strategy of Deterrence," *Journal of Preventive Medicine,* 5 (1976), 122–127.

Evans, W. F., and G. Gratch. "The Stage IV Error in Piaget's Theory of Object Concept Development: Difficulties in Object Conceptualization or Spatial Localization?" *Child Development,* 43 (1972), 682–688.

Evers, W. L., and J. C. Schwartz. "Modifying Social Withdrawal in Pre-Schoolers: The Effects of Filmed Modeling and Teacher Praise," *Journal of Abnormal Child Psychology,* 1 (1973), 248–256.

Fagan, J. F., III. "Infants' Recognition Memory for a Series of Visual Stimuli," *Journal of Experimental Child Psychology,* 11 (1971), 244–250.

———. "Infants' Recognition of Invariant Features of Faces," *Child Development,* 47 (1976), 627–638.

Fagan, J. F., III, R. L. Fantz, and S. B. Miranda. "Infants' Attention to Novel Stimuli as a Function of Postnatal and Conceptual Age," Paper presented at the biennial meeting of Society for Research in Child Development, Minneapolis, Minnesota, 1971.

Fagen, J. W. "Stimulus Preference, Reinforcer Effectiveness, and Relational Responding in Infants," *Child Development,* 51 (1980), 372–378.

Fagot, B. I. "Sex Differences in Toddler's Behavior and Parental Reaction," *Developmental Psychology,* 10 (1974), 554–558.

———. "Consequences of Moderate Cross-Gender Behavior in Preschool Children," *Child Development,* 48 (1977), 902–907.

———. "The Influence of Sex of Child on Parental Reactions to Toddler Children," *Child Development,* 49 (1978a), 459–465.

———. "Reinforcing Contingencies for Sex-Role Behaviors: Effect of Experience with Children," *Child Development,* 49 (1978b), 30–36.

Falbo, T. "Achievement Attributions of Kindergartners," *Developmental Psychology,* 11 (1975), 529–530.

———. "A Social Psychological Model of Human Sexuality," in J. E. Parsons (ed.), *The Psychobiology of Sex Differences and Sex Roles.* New York: McGraw-Hill, 1980, pp. 131–142.

Falbo, T., and L. A. Peplau. "Power Strategies in Intimate Relationships," *Journal of Personality and Social Psychology,* 38 (1980), 618–628.

Falkner, F. T. (ed.). *Human Development.* Philadelphia: Saunders, 1966.

Fantz, R. L. "The Origin of Form Perception," *Scientific American,* 204 (May 1961), 66–72.

———. "Visual Perception from Birth as Shown by Pattern Selectivity," *Annals of the New York Academy of Sciences,* 118 (1965), 793–814.

Farb, P. *Word Play: What Happens When People Talk.* New York: Knopf, 1974.

Farnham-Diggory, S. *Learning Disabilities.* Cambridge, Mass.: Harvard University Press, 1978.

Farrington, D. P. "Experiments on Deviance with Special Reference to Dishonesty," in L. Berkowitz (ed.), *Advances in Experimental Social Psychology,* Vol. 12. New York: Academic Press, 1979, pp. 207–252.

Faust, M. S. "Developmental Maturity as a Determinant in Prestige of Adolescent Girls," *Child Development,* 31 (1960), 173–184.

Feather, N. T. "Values in Adolescence," in J. Adelson (ed.), *Handbook of Adolescent*

Psychology. New York: Wiley-Interscience, 1980, pp. 247–294.

Fein, G. G. "Pretend Play in Childhood: An Integrative Review," *Child Development*, 52 (1981), 1095–1118.

Feitelson, D. "Developing Imaginative Play in Preschool Children as a Possible Approach to Fostering Creativity," *Early Child Development and Care*, 1 (1972), 181.

———. "Cross-Cultural Studies of Representational Play," in B. Tizard and D. Harvey (eds.), *Biology of Play*. Philadelphia: Lippincott, 1977, pp. 6–14.

Feldman, S. S., Z. D. Biringen, and S. C. Nash. "Fluctuations of Sex-Related Self-Attributions as a Function of Stage of Family Life Cycle," *Developmental Psychology*, 17 (1981), 24–35.

Feldman, S. S., and S. C. Nash. "Interest in Babies during Young Adulthood," *Child Development*, 49 (1978), 617–622.

Feldman, S. S., S. C. Nash, and C. Cutrona. "The Influence of Age and Sex on Responsiveness to Babies," *Developmental Psychology*, 13 (1977), 675–676.

Fenson, L., J. Kagan, R. B. Kearsley, and P. R. Zelazo. "The Developmental Progression of Manipulative Play in the First Two Years," *Child Development*, 47 (1976), 232–236.

Fenson, L., and D. S. Ramsay. "Decentration and Integration of Children's Play in the Second Year," *Child Development*, 51 (1980), 171–178.

———. "Effects of Modeling Action Sequences on the Play of Twelve-, Fifteen-, and Nineteen-Month-Old Children," *Child Development*, 52 (1981), 1028–1036.

Ferguson, C. A. "Baby Talk as a Simplified Register," in C. E. Snow and C. A. Ferguson (eds.), *Talking to Children: Language Input and Acquisition*. New York: Cambridge University Press, 1977, pp. 219–236.

Ferguson, C. A., and C. Farwell. "Words and Sounds in Early Language Acquisition: English Consonants in the First 50 Words," *Language*, 51 (1975), 419–439.

Ferree, M. M. "Working Class Jobs: Housework and Paid Work as Sources of Satisfaction," *Social Problems*, 23 (1976) 431–441.

Feshbach, S. "Aggression," in P. H. Mussen (ed.), *Carmichael's Manual of Child Psychology*. Vol. 2. New York: Wiley, 1970, pp. 159–259.

Feshbach, S., and A. Fraczek (eds.). *Aggression and Behavior Change*. New York: Praeger, 1979.

Field, J., D. Muir, R. Pilon, M. Sinclair, and P. Dodwell. "Infants' Orientation to Lateral Sounds from Birth to Three Months," *Child Development*, 51 (1980), 295–298.

Field, T. M. "Interaction Behaviors of Primary versus Secondary Caretaker Fathers," *Developmental Psychology*, 14 (1978), 183–184.

Field, T. M., S. M. Widmayer, S. Stringer, and E. Ignatoff. "Teenage, Lower-Class, Black Mothers and Their Preterm Infants: An Intervention and Developmental Follow-up," *Child Development*, 51 (1980), 426–436.

Finch, C. E., and K. Flurkey. "The Molecular Biology of Estrogen Replacement," *Contemporary Obstetrics and Gynecology*, 9 (1977), 97–106.

Fine, G. A. "Friends, Impression Management, and Preadolescent Behavior," in S. R. Asher and J. M. Gottman (eds.), *The Development of Children's Friendships*. New York: Cambridge University Press, 1981, pp. 29–52.

Fiske, M. "Tasks and Crises of the Second Half of Life: The Interrelationship of Commitment, Coping, and Adaptation," in J. E. Birren and R. B. Sloane (eds.), *Handbook of Mental Health and Aging*. Englewood Cliffs, N.J.: Prentice-Hall, 1980, pp. 337–373.

Fitzgerald, H., and Y. Brackbill. "Classical Conditioning in Infancy: Development and Constraints," *Psychological Bulletin*, 83 (1976), 353–376.

Flacks, R. *Youth and Social Change*. Chicago: Markham, 1971.

Flavell, J. H. "Role-taking and Communication Skills in Children," *Young Children*, 21 (1966), 164–177.

———. *Cognitive Development*. Englewood Cliffs, N.J.: Prentice-Hall, 1977.

Flavell, J. H., et al. The Development of Role-taking Communication Skills in Children. New York: Wiley, 1968.

Flavell, J. H., D. R. Beach, and J. M. Chinsky. "Spontaneous Verbal Rehearsal in a Memory Task as a Function of Age," *Child Development*, 37 (1966), 283–299.

Flavell, J. H., S. G. Shipstead, and K. Croft. "Young Children's Knowledge about Visual Perception: Hiding Objects from Others," *Child Development*, 49 (1978), 1208–1211.

Flavell, J. H., and H. M. Wellman. "Metamemory," in R. V. Kail, Jr., and J. W. Hagen (eds.), *Perspectives on the Development of Memory and Cognition*. Hillsdale, N.J.: Erlbaum, 1977, pp. 3–33.

Floyd, J. M. "Effects of Amount of Reward and Friendship Status of the Other on the Frequency of Sharing in Children," *Dissertation Abstracts*, 25 (1965), 5396–5397.

Folkins, C. H., and W. E. Sime. "Physical Fitness Training and Mental Health," *American Psychologist*, 36 (1981), 373–389.

Fortes, M. "Social and Psychological Aspects of Education in Taleland," in J. S. Bruner, A. Jolly, and K. Sylva (eds.), *Play: Its Role in Development and Evolution*. New York: Basic Books, 1976, pp. 474–483 (orig. pub. 1938).

Fox, N. "Attachment of Kibbutz Infants to Mother and Metapelet," *Child Development*, 48 (1977), 1228–1239.

Frank, L. K. *On the Importance of Infancy*. New York: Random House, 1966.

Franzini, L. R., A. L. Litrownik, and F. H. Blanchard. "Modeling of Sex-Typed Behaviors: Effects on Boys and Girls," *Developmental Psychology*, 14 (1978), 313–314.

Freda, V. J., J. G. Gorman, W. Pollack, and E. Bowe. "Prevention of Rh Hemolytic Disease—Ten Years' Clinical Experience with Rh Immune Globulin," *New England Journal of Medicine*, 282 (1975), 19.

Freedman, D. G. "Constitutional and Environmental Interactions in Rearing of Four Breeds of Dogs," *Science*, 127 (1958), 585–586.

———. *Human Infancy, an Evolutionary Perspective*. Hillsdale, N.J.: Erlbaum, 1974.

French, D. C., C. A. Brownell, W. G. Graziano, and W. W. Hartup. "Effects of Cooperative, Competitive, and Individualistic Sets on Performance in Children's Groups," *Journal of Experimental Child Psychology*, 24 (1977), 1–10.

Freud, S. *Psychopathology of Everyday Life*. New York: Macmillan, 1917.

———. "Three Essays on the Theory of Sexuality," in *The Standard Edition of the Complete Psychological Works of Sigmund Freud*. Vol. 7. London: Hogarth, 1953, pp. 125–245 (orig. pub. 1905).

Frias, J. L. "Prenatal Diagnosis of Genetic Abnormalities," *Clinical Obstetrics and Gynecology*, 18 (1975), 221–236.

Friedman, M., and R. H. Rosenman. *Type A Behavior and Your Heart*. New York: Knopf, 1974.

Friedman, S. "Habituation and Recovery of Visual Response in the Alert Human Newborn," *Journal of Experimental Child Psychology*, 13 (1972), 339–349.

Friedman, S., L. A. Bruno, and P. Vietze. "Newborn Habituation to Visual Stimuli: A Sex Difference in Novelty Detection," *Journal of Experimental Child Psychology*, 18 (1974), 242–251.

Fries, M. E. "Some Hypotheses on the Role of the Congenital Activity Type in Personality Development," *International Journal of Psychoanalysis*, 35 (1954), 206–207.

Friesen, D. "Academic-Athletic- Popularity Syndrome in the Candian High School Society: 1967," *Adolescence*, 3 (1968), 39–52.

Frieze, I. H., J. E. Parsons, P. B. Johnson, D. N. Ruble, and G. L. Zellman. *Women and Sex Roles: A Social Psychological Perspective*. New York: Norton, 1978.

Frisch, H. L. "Sex Stereotypes in Adult-Infant Play," *Child Development*, 48 (1977), 1671–1675.

Frodi, A. M., and M. E. Lamb. "Sex Differences in Responsiveness to Infants: A Developmental Study of Psychophysiological and Behavioral Responses," *Child Development*, 49 (1978), 1182–1188.

Frodi, A. M., M. E. Lamb, L. A. Leavitt, and W. L. Donovan. "Fathers' and Mothers' Responses to Infant Smiles and Cries," *Infant Behavior and Development*, 1 (1978), 187–198.

Frodi, A. M., J. Macaulay, and P. R. Thome. "Are Women Always Less Aggressive Than Men? A Review of the Experimental Literature," *Psychological Bulletin*, 84 (1977), 634–660.

Frueh, T., and P. E. McGhee. "Traditional Sex Role Development and

Amount of Time Spent Watching Television," *Developmental Psychology,* 11 (1975), 109.

Fryer, J. G., and J. R. Ashford. "Trends in Perinatal and Neonatal Mortality in England and Wales 1960–69," *British Journal of Preventive and Social Medicine,* 26 (1972), 1–9.

Furman, W., and J. C. Masters. "Peer Interactions, Sociometric Status, and Resistance to Deviation in Young Children," *Developmental Psychology,* 16 (1980), 229–236.

Furth, H. G. "Research with the Deaf: Implications for Language and Cognition," *Psychological Bulletin,* 62 (1964), 145–164.

———. *Piaget and Knowledge.* Englewood Cliffs, N.J.: Prentice-Hall, 1969.

———. *The World of Grown-Ups: Children's Conceptions of Society.* New York: Elsevier, 1980.

Furth, H. G., B. M. Ross, and J. Youniss. "Operative Understanding in Reproductions of Drawings," *Child Development,* 45 (1974), 63–70.

Gagnon, J. H. "Reconsiderations: Sexual Behavior in the Human Male; Sexual Behavior in the Human Female," *Human Nature,* 1 (October 1978), 92–95.

Galin, D., J. Johnstone, L. Nakell, and J. Herron. "Development of the Capacity for Tactile Information Transfer between Hemispheres in Normal Children," *Science,* 204 (1979), 1330–1332.

Gallatin, J. "Political Thinking in Adolescence," in J. Adelson (ed.), *Handbook of Adolescent Psychology.* New York: Wiley-Interscience, 1980, pp. 344–382.

Galton, F. *Inquiries into Human Faculty and Its Development.* London: Macmillan, 1883.

Garbarino, J. "A Preliminary Study of Some Ecological Correlates of Child Abuse: The Impact of Socioeconomic Stress on Mothers," *Child Development,* 47 (1976), 178–185.

Garbarino, J., and A. Crouter. "Defining the Community Context for Parent-Child Relations: The Correlates of Child Maltreatment," *Child Development,* 49 (1978), 604–616.

Garbarino, J., and D. Sherman. "High-Risk Neighborhoods and High-Risk Families: The Human Ecology of Child Maltreatment," *Child Development,* 51 (1980), 188–198.

Gardner, H. "Metaphors and Modalities: How Children Project Polar Adjectives Onto Diverse Domains," *Child Development,* 45 (1974), 84–91.

———. *The Shattered Mind.* New York: Knopf, 1975.

Gardner, H., and E. Winner. "The Child Is Father to the Metaphor," *Psychology Today,* 12 (May 1979), 81–91.

Gardner, R. A., and B. T. Gardner. "Teaching Sign Language to a Chimpanzee," *Science,* 165 (1969), 664–672.

Garnica, O. K. "The Development of Phonemic Speech Perception," in T. E. Moore (ed.), *Cognitive Development and the Acquisition of Language.* New York: Academic Press, 1973, pp. 215–222.

Garvey, C. *Play.* Cambridge, Mass.: Harvard University Press, 1977.

———. "Communicational Controls in Social Play," in B. Sutton-Smith (ed.), *Play and Learning.* New York: Gardner Press, 1979, pp. 109–126.

Garwood, S. G. "First-Name Stereotypes as a Factor in Self-Concept and School Achievement," *Journal of Educational Psychology,* 68 (1976), pp. 482–487.

Geis, F. L., V. Brown, J. Jennings (Walstedt), and N. Porter. "Do Stereotyped TV Commercials Depress Women's Achievement Aspirations?" Paper presented at annual meeting of American Psychological Association, New York, September 1979.

Gelman, R. "The Nature and Development of Early Number Concepts," in H. W. Reese (ed.), *Advances in Child Development and Behavior.* Vol. 7. New York: Academic Press, 1972, pp. 115–167.

———. "How Young Children Reason about Small Numbers," in W. J. Castellan, D. P. Pisoni, and G. R. Potts (eds.), *Cognitive Theory.* Hillsdale, N.J.: Erlbaum, 1977, pp. 219–238.

———. "Cognitive Development," *Annual Review of Psychology,* 29 (1978), 297–332.

Gelman, R., and C. R. Gallistel. *The Child's Understanding of Number.* Cambridge, Mass.: Harvard University Press, 1978.

Gelman, R., and M. Shatz. "Appropriate Speech Adjustments: The Operation of Conversational Constraints on Talk to Two-Year-Olds," in M. Lewis and L. A. Rosenblum (eds.), *Interaction, Conversation and the Development of Language.* New York: Wiley, 1977, 27–61.

Gentner, D. "On Relational Meaning: The Acquisition of Verb Meaning, *Child Development,* 49 (1978), 988–998.

Gerbner, G., and L. Gross. "Living with Television: The Violence Profile," *Journal of Communication,* 26 (1976), 173–199.

Gerson, R. P., and W. Damon. "Moral Understanding and Children's Conduct," in W. Damon (ed.), *New Directions for Child Development.* No. 2. *Moral Development.* San Francisco: Jossey-Bass, 1978, pp. 41–59.

Geschwind, N. "Specialization of the Human Brain," *Scientific American,* 241 (September 1979), 180–201.

Gesell, A. L. *The Mental Growth of the Pre-School Child: A Psychological Outline of Normal Development from Birth to the Sixth Year, Including a System of Developmental Diagnosis.* New York: Macmillan, 1925.

———. *Infancy and Human Growth.* New York: Macmillan, 1928.

———. "Maturation and Infant Behavior Patterns," *Psychological Review,* 36 (1929), 307–319.

Gholson, B. *The Cognitive-Developmental Basis of Human Learning: Studies in Hypothesis Testing.* New York: Academic Press, 1980.

Gibbs, F. A., and E. L. Gibbs. *Atlas of Electroencephalography.* Vol. III. Reading, Mass.: Addison-Wesley, 1964.

Gibbs, M., E. Auerbach, and M. Fox. "A Comparison of Male and Female Same-Sex Friendships," *International Journal of Women's Studies,* 3 (1980), 261–272.

Gibson, E. J. *Principles of Perceptual Learning and Development.* New York: Appleton-Century-Crofts, 1969.

———. "Trends in Perceptual Development: Implications for the Reading Process," in A. D. Pick (ed.), *Minnesota Symposia on Child Psychology.* Vol. 8. Minneapolis: University of Minnesota Press, 1974, pp. 24–54.

Gibson, E. J., C. J. Owsley, and J. Johnston. "Perception of Invariants by Five-Month-Old Infants: Differentiation of Two Types of Motion," *Developmental Psychology,* 14 (1978), 407–415.

Gibson, E. J., J. Y. Tenney, and M. Zaslow. "Is Discovery of Structure Reinforcing? The Effect of Categorizable Context on Scanning for Visual Targets," in *The Relationship between Perceptual Development and the Acquisition of Reading Skill,* Final Report. Project No. 90046, Cornell University and the United States Office of Education, 1971.

Gibson, E. J., and R. D. Walk. "The Visual Cliff," *Scientific American,* 202 (April 1960), 64–71.

Giele, J. Z. "Adulthood as Transcendence of Age and Sex," in N. J. Smelser and E. H. Erikson (eds.), *Themes of Work and Love in Adulthood.* Cambridge, Mass.: Harvard University Press, 1980, pp. 151–173.

Gilbertsen, V. A., and O. H. Wangensteen. "Should the Doctor Tell the Patient That the Disease Is Cancer?" in *The Physician and the Total Care of the Cancer Patient.* New York: American Cancer Society, 1961.

Gilligan, C. "In a Different Voice: Women's Conceptions of Self and of Morality," *Harvard Educational Review,* 47, no. 4 (1977), 481–517.

Gilmartin, B. G. "Swinging: Who Gets Involved and How?" in R. W. Libby and R. N. Whitehurst (eds.), *Marriage and Alternatives: Exploring Intimate Relationships.* Glenview, Ill.: Scott, Foresman, 1977, pp. 161–185.

Glaser, B. G., and A. L. Strauss. *Awareness of Dying.* Chicago: Aldine, 1965.

———. *Time for Dying.* Chicago: Aldine, 1968.

Glass, D. C. *Behavior Patterns, Stress, and Coronary Disease.* Hillsdale, N.J.: Erlbaum, 1977.

Gleason, J. "Do Children Imitate?" *Proceedings of the International Conference on Oral Education of the Deaf,* 2 (1967), 1441-1448.

Gleason, J. B., and S. Weintraub. "Input Language and the Acquisition of Communicative Competence," in K. E. Nelson (ed.), *Children's Language,* Vol. 1. New York: Gardner Press, 1978, pp. 171–222.

Glenn, N. "Aging, Disengagement, and Opinionation," *Public Opinion Quarterly,* 33 (1969), 17–33.

Glick, P. G., and A. J. Norton. "Marrying, Divorcing, and Living Together in the U.S. Today," *Population Bulletin,* 32 (1978), 3–38.

Glick, R. "Promoting Competence and Coping through Retirement Planning," in L. A. Bond and J. C. Rosen (eds.), *Competence and Coping during Adulthood.* Hanover, N.H.: University Press of New England, 1980, pp. 288–303.

Gluck, L., and M. V. Kulovich. "Fetal Lung Development: Current Concepts," *Pediatric Clinics of North America,* 20 (1973), 367–379.

Gold, D., and D. Andres. "Developmental Comparisons between Ten-Year-Old Children with Employed and Unemployed Mothers," *Child Development,* 49 (1978), 75–84.

Gold, M., and R. J. Petronio. "Delinquent Behavior in Adolescence," in J. Adelson (ed.), *Handbook of Adolescent Psychology.* New York: Wiley-Interscience, 1980, pp. 495–535.

Gold, M., and D. J. Reimer. "Changing Patterns of Delinquent Behavior among Americans 13 through 16 Years Old: 1967–72," *Crime and Delinquency Literature,* 7 (1975), 483–517.

Goldberg, S. "Social Competence in Infancy: A Model of Parent-Infant Interaction," *Merrill-Palmer Quarterly,* 23 (1977), 163–177.

Goldberg, S., and M. Lewis. "Play Behavior in the Year-Old Infant: Early Sex Differences," *Child Development,* 40 (1969), 21–31.

Golden, M., and B. Birns. "Social Class and Infant Intelligence," in M. Lewis (ed.), *Origins of Intelligence: Infancy and Early Childhood.* New York: Plenum, 1976, pp. 299–352.

Goldenberg, H. *Abnormal Psychology: A Social Community Approach.* Monterey, Calif.: Brooks-Cole, 1979.

Goldsmith, H. H., and I. I. Gottesman. "Origin of Variation in Behavioral Style: A Longitudinal Study of Temperament in Young Twins," *Child Development,* 52 (1981), 91–103.

Goldstein, J., A. Freud, and A. J. Solnit. *Beyond the Best Interests of the Child.* New ed. New York: Free Press, 1979.

Golinkoff, R. M. "Children's Discrimination of English Spelling Patterns with Redundant Auditory Information," Paper presented at American Educational Research Association meeting, 1974.

Golomb, C. "Children's Representation of the Human Figure: The Effects of Models, Media, and Instruction," *Genetic Psychology Monographs,* 87 (1973), 197–251.

Goodenough, F. L. *Anger in Young Children.* Minneapolis: University of Minnesota Press, 1931.

Goodnow, J. *Children Drawing.* Cambridge, Mass.: Harvard University Press, 1977.

Gordon, A. "The Jewish View of Death: Guidelines for Mourning," in E. Kübler-Ross (ed.), *Death: The Final Stage of Growth.* Englewood Cliffs, N.J.: Prentice-Hall, 1975, pp. 38–43.

Gordon, C., C. M. Gaitz, J. Scott. "Leisure and Lives: Personal Expressivity Across the Life Span," in R. H. Binstock and E. Shanas (eds.), *Handbook of Aging and the Social Sciences.* New York: Van Nostrand Reinhold, 1976, pp. 310–341.

Gottesman, I. I. "Developmental Genetics and Ontogenetic Psychology," in A. D. Pick (ed.), *Minnesota Symposia on Child Psychology.* Vol. 8. Minneapolis: University of Minnesota Press, 1974, pp. 55–80.

Gottlieb, D. E., S. E. Taylor, and A. Ruderman. "Cognitive Bases of Children's Moral Judgments," *Developmental Psychology,* 13 (1977), 547–556.

Gottman, J., J. Gonso, and B. Rasmussen. "Social Interaction, Social Competence, and Friendship in Children," *Child Development,* 46 (1975), 709–718.

Gouin-Décarie, T. *Intelligence and Affectivity in Early Childhood.* E. P. Brandt and L. W. Brandt (trs.), New York: International Universities Press, 1965.

Gould, R. *Transformations: Growth and Change in Adult Life.* New York: Simon and Schuster, 1978.

Govatos, L. A. "Relationships and Age Differences in Growth Measures and Motor Skills," *Child Development,* 30 (1959), 333–340.

Gove, F. L., and D. P. Keating. "Empathic Role-Taking Precursors," *Developmental Psychology,* 14 (1979), 594–600.

Graham, D. *Moral Learning and Development: Theory and Research.* New York: Wiley, 1972.

Gratch, G. "Recent Studies Based on Piaget's View of Object Concept Development," in L. B. Cohen and P. Salapatek (eds.), *Infant Perception: From Sensation to Cognition.* Vol.2. *Perception of Space, Speech, and Sound.* New York: Academic Press, 1975, pp. 51–99.

Gratch, G., K. J. Appel, W. F. Evans, G. K. LeCompte, and N. A. Wright. "Piaget's Stage IV Object Concept Error: Evidence of Forgetting or Object Conception?" *Child Development,* 45 (1974), 71–77.

Greenberg, M. T. "Social Interaction between Deaf Preschoolers and Their Mothers: The Effects of Communication Method and Communication Competence," *Developmental Psychology,* 16 (1980), 465–474.

Greenfield, P. M. "Informativeness, Presupposition, and Semantic Choice in Single-Word Utterances," in E. Ochs and B. B. Schieffelin (eds.), *Developmental Pragmatics.* New York: Academic Press, 1979, pp. 159–166.

Greenfield, P. M., and J. Bruner. "Culture and Cognitive Growth," *International Journal of Psychology,* 1 (1966), 89–107.

Greenough, W. T. "Enduring Brain Effects of Differential Experience and Training," in M. R. Rosenzweig and E. L. Bennett (eds.), *Neural Mechanisms of Learning and Memory.* Cambridge, Mass.: M.I.T. Press, 1976, pp. 255–278.

Griffiths, R. *The Abilities of Babies.* New York: McGraw-Hill, 1954.

Grof, S., and J. Halifax. *The Human Encounter with Death.* New York: E. P. Dutton, 1977.

Grosser, D., N. Polansky, and R. Lippitt. "A Laboratory Study of Behavioral Contagion," *Human Relations,* 4 (1951), 115–142.

Gruendel, J. M. "Referential Overextension in Early Language Development," *Child Development,* 48 (1977), 1567–1576.

Grusec, J. E., L. Kuczynski, J. P. Rushton, and Z. M. Simutis. "Modeling, Direct Instruction, and Attributions: Effects on Altruism," *Developmental Psychology,* 14 (1978), 51–57.

———. "Learning Resistance to Temptation through Observation," *Developmental Psychology,* 15 (1979), 233–240.

Grusec, J. E., and E. Redler. "Attribution, Reinforcement, and Altruism: A Developmental Analysis," *Developmental Psychology,* 16 (1980), 525–534.

Grusec, J. E., and S. L. Skubiski. "Model Nurturance, Demand Characteristics of the Modeling Experiment, and Altruism," *Journal of Personality and Sosial Psychology,* 14 (1970), 352–359.

Guinaugh, B. J., and I. J. Gordon. "School Performance as a Function of Early Stimulation," Final Report to Office of Child Development, 1976.

Gump, P. V. "School Environments," in I. Altman and J. F. Wohlwill (eds.), *Children and the Environment.* New York: Plenum, 1978, pp. 131–174.

———. "The School as a Social Situation," in *Annual Review of Psychology,* 1980. Palo Alto, Calif.: Annual Reviews, 1980, pp. 335–582.

Gusinow, J. F., and L. E. Price. "Modification of Form and Color Responding in Young Children as a Function of Differential Reinforcement and Verbalization," *Journal of Experimental Child Psychology,* 13 (1972), 145–153.

Gutmann, D. "Female Ego Styles and Generational Conflict," in J. Bardwick and Associates, *Feminine Personality and Conflict.* Belmont, Calif.: Brooks-Cole, 1970.

———. "Parenthood: A Key to the Comparative Study of the Life Cycle," in N. Datan and L. H. Ginsberg (eds.), *Life Span Developmental Psychology: Normative Life Crises.* New York: Academic Press, 1975, pp. 167–184.

Haaf, R. A. "Visual Response to Complex Facelike Patterns by 15- and 20-Week-Old Infants," *Developmental Psychology,* 13 (1977), 77–78.

Haan, N., M. B. Smith, and J. Block. "Moral Reasoning of Young Adults: Political-Social Behavior, Family Background, and Personality Correlates," *Journal of Personality and Social Psychology,* 10 (1968), 183–201.

Haber, R. N., and M. Hershenson. *The Psychology of Visual Perception.* New York: Holt, Rinehart and Winston, 1973.

Hagen, J. W., and G. H. Hale. "The Development of Attention in Children," in A. D. Pick (ed.), *Minnesota Symposia on Child Psychology.* Vol. 7. Minneapolis:

University of Minnesota Press, 1973, pp. 117–140.

Hagestad, G. "Patterns of Communication and Influence between Grandparents and Grandchildren in a Changing Society," Paper presented at the World Congress of Sociology, Sweden, 1978.

Hahn, S. R., and K. E. Paige. "American Birth Practices: A Critical Review," in J. E. Parsons (ed.), *The Psychobiology of Sex Differences.* New York: McGraw-Hill, 1980, pp. 145–175.

Hainline, L. "Developmental Changes in Visual Scanning of Face and Nonface Patterns by Infants," *Journal of Experimental Child Psychology,* 25 (1978), 90–115.

Hainline, L., and E. Feig. "The Correlates of Father Absence in College-Aged Women," *Child Development,* 49 (1978), 37–42.

Haith, M. M. "The Response of the Human Newborn to Visual Movement," *Journal of Experimental Child Psychology,* 3 (1966), 235–243.

______. *Rules That Newborns Look By.* Hillsdale, N. J.: Erlbaum, 1980.

Haith, M. M., T. Bergman, and M. J. Moore. "Eye Contact and Face Scanning in Early Infancy," *Science,* 198 (1977), 853–855.

Hale, G. A., and J. S. Morgan. "Developmental Trends in Children's Component Selection," *Journal of Experimental Child Psychology,* 15 (1973), 302–314.

Hall, E. "Will Success Spoil B. F. Skinner?" *Psychology Today,* 6 (November 1972), 65–72+.

Hall, E. T. *Beyond Culture.* New York: Anchor/Doubleday, 1976.

Hall, G. S. "Notes on the Study of Infants," *The Pedagogical Seminary,* 1 (1891), 127–138.

______. *Adolescence: Its Psychology and Its Relations to Physiology, Anthropology, Sociology, Sex, Crime, Religion, and Education.* 2 vols. New York: Appleton-Century-Crofts, 1904.

Hall, J. W., J. Murphy, M. S. Humphreys, and K. P. Wilson. "Children's Cued Recall: Developmental Differences in Retrieval Operations," *Journal of Experimental Child Psychology,* 27 (1979), 501–511.

Hamburg, B. "Early Adolescence: A Specific and Stressful Stage of the Life Cycle," in G. Coelho, D. A. Hamburg, and J. E. Adams (eds.), *Coping and Adaptation.* New York: Basic Books, 1974.

Hamill, P. V., F. E. Johnston, and S. Lemeshow. "Height and Weight of Children: Socio-Economic Status: United States," Rockville, Md.: U.S. Department of Health, Education and Welfare. Pub. No. HRA 74-1608, 1973.

Harari, H., and J. W. McDavid. "Situational Influence on Moral Justice: A Study of 'Finking,'" *Journal of Personality and Social Psychology,* 3 (1969), 240–244.

______. "Teachers' Expectations and Name Stereotypes," *Journal of Educational Psychology,* 65 (1973), 222–225.

Hardyck, C., and F. Petrinovich. "Left-Handedness," *Psychological Bulletin,* 84 (1977), 385–404.

Harkness, S. "The Cultural Context of Child Development," in C. M. Super and S. Harkness (eds.), *New Directions for Child Development.* No. 8. *Anthropological Perspectives on Child Development.* San Francisco: Jossey-Bass, 1980, pp. 7–13.

Harlow, H. F., and M. K. Harlow. "Learning to Love," *American Scientist,* 54 (1966), 244–272.

______. "Effects of Various Mother-Infant Relationships on Rhesus Monkey Behaviors," in B. M. Foss (ed.), *Determinants of Infant Behavior.* Vol. 4. London: Methuen, 1969, pp. 15–36.

Harlow, H. F., and R. R. Zimmermann. "Affectional Responses in the Infant Monkey," *Science,* 130 (1959), 421–432.

Harper, L. V. "The Scope of Offspring Effects: From Caregiver to Culture," *Psychological Bulletin,* 82 (1975), 784–801.

Harris, L., and Associates. *The Myth and Reality of Aging in America.* Washington, D.C.: National Council on the Aging, 1975.

Harris, P. L. "Perseverative Search at a Visibly Empty Place by Young Infants," *Journal of Experimental Child Psychology,* 18 (1974), 535–542.

Harrison, C. W., J. R. Rawls, and D. J. Rawls. "Difference between Leaders and Nonleaders in Six- to Eleven-Year-Old Children," *Journal of Social Psychology,* 84 (1971), 269–272.

Hartshorne, H., and M. A. May. *Studies in Deceit.* New York: Macmillan, 1928.

Hartup, W. W. "Friendship Status and the Effectiveness of Peers as Reinforcing Agents," *Journal of Experimental Child Psychology,* 1 (1964a), 154–162.

______. "Patterns of Imitative Behavior in Young Children," *Child Development,* 35 (1964b), 183–191.

______. "Peer Interaction and Social Organization," in P. H. Mussen (ed.), *Carmichael's Manual of Child Psychology.* Vol. 2. New York: Wiley, 1970, pp. 361–456.

______. "Aggression in Childhood: Developmental Perspectives," *American Psychologist,* 29 (1974), 336–341.

______. "The Social Worlds of Childhood," *American Psychologist,* 34 (1979), 944–950.

Hartup, W. W., and B. Coates. "Imitation of a Peer as a Function of Reinforcement from the Peer Group and Rewardingness of the Model," *Child Development,* 38 (1967), 1003–1016.

Harvard Medical School. "Further Insight into Fat," *Harvard Medical School Letter,* 6, no. 4 (1981), 5.

Harvey, S. E., and R. M. Liebert. "Abstraction, Inference, and Acceptance in Children's Processing of an Adult Model's Moral Judgments," *Developmental Psychology,* 15 (1979), 552–558.

Hathaway, M. L., and D. W. Sargent. "Overweight in Children," *Journal of the American Dietetic Association,* 40 (1962), 511–515.

Havighurst, R. J. *Developmental Tasks and Education.* 3rd ed. New York: McKay, 1972.

Havighurst, R. J., and K. Feigenbaum. "Leisure and Life-Style," in B. L. Neugarten (ed.), *Middle Age and Aging: A Reader in Social Psychology.* Chicago: University of Chicago Press, 1968, pp. 347–353.

Havighurst, R. J., B. L. Neugarten, and S. S. Tobin. "Disengagement and Patterns of Aging," in B. L. Neugarten (ed.), *Middle Age and Aging: A Reader in Social Psychology.* Chicago: University of Chicago Press, 1968, pp. 58–71.

Hawke, S., and D. Knox. *One Child by Choice.* Englewood Cliffs, N.J.: Prentice-Hall, 1977.

Haynes, H., B. L. White, and R. Held. "Visual Accommodation in Human Infants," *Science,* 148 (1965), 528–530.

Hebb, D. O. *Organization of Behavior.* New York: Wiley, 1949.

______. "Age and the Brain: Not Quite Senile, Yet," Paper presented at American Psychological Association meeting, Toronto, September 1978.

Hécaen, H., and J. de Ajuriaguerra. *Left-Handedness.* New York: Grune & Stratton, 1964.

Heider, E. R. "Universals in Color Naming and Memory," *Journal of Experimental Child Psychology,* 93 (1972), 10–20.

Heirich, M. "Change of Heart: A Test of Some Widely Held Theories about Religious Conversion," *American Journal of Sociology,* 83 (1977), 653–680.

Hershenson, M. "Visual Discrimination in the Human Newborn," *Journal of Comparative and Physiological Psychology,* 58 (1964), 270–276.

Herzog, E., and C. E. Sudia. "Children in Fatherless Families," in B. M. Caldwell and H. N. Ricciuti (eds.), *Review of Child Development Research.* Vol. 3. Chicago: University of Chicago Press, 1973, pp. 141–232.

Hess, B. "Friendship," in M. W. Riley, M. Johnson, and A. Foner (eds.), *Aging and Society:* Vol. 3. *A Sociology of Age Stratification.* New York: Russell Sage Foundation, 1972, pp. 357–396.

Hess, E. H. "Imprinting in a Natural Laboratory," *Scientific American,* 227 (1972), 24–31.

______. *Imprinting: Early Experience and the Developmental Psychobiology of Attachment.* New York: Van Nostrand, 1973.

Hess, R. D. "Social Class and Ethnic Influences on Socialization," in P. H. Mussen (ed.), *Carmichael's Manual of Child Psychology.* Vol. 2. 3rd ed. New York: Wiley, 1970, pp. 457–557.

Hetherington, E. M. "Effects of Paternal Absence on Sex-Typed Behaviors in Negro and White Preadolescent Males," *Journal of Personality and Social Psychology,* 4 (1966), 87–91.

______. "Effects of Father Absence on Personality Development in Adolescent Daughters," *Developmental Psychology,* 7 (1972), 313–326.

______. "Divorce: A Child's Perspective," *American Psychologist,* 34 (1979), 859–865.

Hetherington, E. M., M. Cox, and R. Cox. "Stress and Coping in Divorce: A

Focus on Women," in J. E. Gullahorn (ed.), *Psychology and Women: In Transition.* New York: Wiley, 1979, pp. 95–128.

Hetherington, E. M., and J. Deur. "The Effects of Father Absence on Child Development," in W. W. Hartup and N. L. Smothergill (eds.), *The Young Child: Reviews of Research.* Vol. 2. Washington, D.C.: National Association for the Education of Young Children, 1972, pp. 303–319.

Hicks, D. J. "Imitation and Retention of Film-Mediated Aggressive Peer and Adult Models," *Journal of Personality and Social Psychology,* 2 (1965), 97–100.

______. "Girls' Attitudes Toward Modeled Behaviors and the Content of Imitative Private Play," *Child Development,* 42 (1971), 139–147.

Hicks, M. W., and M. Platt. "Marital Happiness and Stability: A Review of the Research in the 60s," *Journal of Marriage and the Family,* 32 (1971), 553–573.

Higgins, E. T. "Social Class Differences in Verbal Communication Accuracy: A Question of 'Which Question?' " *Psychological Bulletin,* 83 (1976), 695–714.

Hilgard, J. R., and M. F. Newman. "Anniversaries in Mental Illness," *Psychiatry,* 22 (1959), 113–121.

Hill, C. T., Z. Rubin, and L. A. Peplau. "Breakups Before Marriage: The End of 103 Affairs," *Journal of Social Issues,* 32 (1976), 147–168.

Hill, R. B. *Strengths of Black Families.* New York: Emerson Hall, 1971.

Hinton, J. M. "Distress in the Dying," in J. N. Agate (ed.), *Medicine in Old Age.* London: Pitman, 1965.

Hirsch, H. V. B., and M. Jacobson. "The Perfectible Brain: Principles of Neuronal Development," in M. S. Gazzaniga and C. Blakemore (eds.), *Handbook of Psychobiology.* New York: Academic Press, 1975.

Hirschhorn, L. "Social Policy and the Life Cycle: A Developmental Perspective," *Social Service Review,* 51 (1977), 434–450.

Hiscock, M., and M. Kinsbourne. "Selective Listening Asymmetry in Preschool Children," *Developmental Psychology,* 13 (1977), 217–224.

Hobbs, D. F., Jr., and S. P. Cole. "Transition to Parenthood: A Decade of Replication," *Journal of Marriage and the Family,* 38 (1976), 723–731.

Hoffman, L. W. "Early Childhood Experiences and Women's Achievement Motives," *Journal of Social Issues,* 28 (1972), 129–155.

Hoffman, M. L. "Moral Internalization: Current Theory and Research," in L. Berkowitz (ed.), *Advances in Experimental Social Psychology,* Vol. 10. New York: Academic Press, 1977a, pp. 85–133.

______. "Sex Differences in Empathy and Related Behaviors," *Psychological Bulletin,* 84 (1977b), 712–722.

______. "Toward a Theory of Empathic Arousal and Development," in M. Lewis and L. A. Rosenblum (eds.), *The Development of Affect.* New York: Plenum, 1978, pp. 227–256.

______. "Development of Moral Thought, Feeling, and Behavior," *American Psychologist,* 34 (1979), 958–966.

______. "Moral Development in Adolescence," in J. Adelson (ed.), *Handbook of Adolescent Psychology.* New York: Wiley-Interscience, 1980, pp. 295–343.

______. "Is Altruism Part of Human Nature?" *Journal of Personality and Social Psychology,* 40 (1981), 121–137.

Hoffman, M. L., and H. D. Saltzstein. "Parent Discipline and the Child's Moral Development," *Journal of Personality and Social Psychology,* 5 (1967), 45–57.

Hoffman, R. F. "Developmental Changes in Human Infant Visual-Evoked Potentials to Patterned Stimuli Recorded at Different Scalp Locations," *Child Development,* 49 (1978), 110–118.

Hogan, R., and N. P. Emler. "Moral Development," in M. E. Lamb (ed.), *Social and Personality Development.* New York: Holt, Rinehart and Winston, 1978, pp. 200–223.

Hollos, M., and P. A. Cowan. "Social Isolation and Cognitive Development: Logical Operations and Role-Taking Abilities in Three Norwegian Social Settings," *Child Development,* 44 (1973), 630–641.

Holmberg, M. C. "The Development of Social Interchange Patterns from 12 to 42 Months," *Child Development,* 51 (1980), 448–456.

Holmes, L. "How Fathers Can Cause the Down's Syndrome," *Human Nature,* 1 (October 1978), 70–72.

Holmes, T. H., and R. H. Rahe. "The Social Readjustment Rating Scale," *Journal of Psychosomatic Research,* 11 (1967), 213–218.

Holstein, C. B. "The Relation of Children's Moral Judgment Level to That of Their Parents and to Communication Patterns in the Family," in R. C. Smart and M. S. Smart (eds.), *Readings in Child Development and Relationship.* New York: Macmillan, 1972, pp. 484–494.

______. "Irreversible, Stepwise Sequence in the Development of Moral Judgment: A Longitudinal Study of Males and Females," *Child Development,* 47 (1976), 51–61.

Honess, T. "Self-Reference in Children's Descriptions of Peers: Egocentricity or Collaboration?" *Child Development,* 51 (1980), 476–480.

Honzik, M. P. "Developmental Studies of Parent-Child Resemblance in Intelligence," *Child Development,* 28 (1957), 215–228.

Hooker, D. *The Prenatal Origin of Behavior.* Lawrence: University of Kansas Press, 1952.

Horner, M. "Fail: Bright Women," *Psychology Today,* 3 (November 1969), 36–38.

Horowitz, M. J., and N. Wilner. "Life Events, Stress, and Coping," in L. Poon (ed.), *Aging in the 1980s.* Washington, D.C.: American Psychological Association, 1980, pp. 361–374.

Hoult, T. F., L. F. Henze, and J. W. Hudson. *Courtship and Marriage in America.* Boston: Little, Brown, 1978.

Huba, G. J., J. A. Wingard, and P. M. Bentler. "A Comparison of Two Latent Variable Causal Models for Adolescent Drug Use," *Journal of Personality and Social Psychology,* 40 (1981), 180–193.

Hudson, R. B., and R. H. Binstock. "Political Systems and Aging," in R. H. Binstock and E. Shanas (eds.), *Handbook of Aging and the Social Sciences.* New York: Van Nostrand Reinhold, 1976, pp. 369–400.

Humphrey, N. K. "The Origins of Human Intelligence," *Human Nature,* 1 (December 1978), 42–47.

Hunt, E. "Varieties of Cognitive Power," in L. B. Resnick (ed.), *The Nature of Intelligence.* Hillsdale, N.J.: Erlbaum, 1976, pp. 13–26.

Hunt, J. McV. "Psychological Development: Early Experience," *Annual Review of Psychology,* 30 (1979), 103–143.

Hunt, M. M. *Sexual Behavior in the 1970s.* Chicago: Playboy Press, 1974.

Hutt, C. *Males and Females.* Baltimore: Penguin, 1972.

______."Exploration and Play in Children," in J. S. Bruner, A. Jolly, and K. Sylva (eds.), *Play: Its Role in Development and Evolution.* New York: Basic Books, 1976, pp. 202–215.

______. "Exploration and Play," in B. Sutton-Smith (ed.), *Play and Learning.* New York: Gardner Press, 1979, pp. 175–194.

Huttenlocher, J., and C. C. Presson. "The Coding and Transformation of Spatial Information," *Cognitive Psychology,* 11 (1979), 375–394.

Huxley, A. *Brave New World.* New York: Harper, 1932.

Hyde, J. S., and D. E. Phillis. "Androgyny across the Life Span," *Developmental Psychology,* 15 (1979), 334–336.

Hyman, I. A. "Psychology, Education, and Schooling," *American Psychologist,* 34 (1979), 1024–1029.

Iannotti, R. J. "Effect of Role-Taking Experiences on Role-Taking, Empathy, Altruism, and Aggression," *Developmental Psychology,* 14 (1978), 119–124.

Ingram, D. "Motor Asymmetries in Young Children," *Neuropsychologia,* 13 (1975a), 95–102.

______. "Cerebral Speech Lateralization in Young Children," *Neuropyschologia,* 13 (1975b), 103–105.

Inhelder, B. "Memory and Intelligence in the Child," in B. Inhelder and H. H. Chipman (eds.), *Piaget and His School.* New York: Springer-Verlag, 1976, pp. 100–120.

Inhelder, B., and J. Piaget. *The Growth of Logical Thinking from Childhood to Adolescence: An Essay on the Construction of Formal Operational Structures.* A. Parsons and S. Milgram (trs.). New York: Basic Books, 1958.

Interprofessional Task Force on Health Care of Women and Children. *The Development of Family-Centered Maternity/*

Newborn Care in Hospitals. Chicago: Interprofessional Task Force, 1978.

Jackowitz, E. R., and M. W. Watson. "Development of Object Transformation in Early Pretend Play," *Developmental Psychology,* 16 (1980), 543–549.

Jackson, E., J. J. Campos, and K. W. Fischer. "The Question of Decalage between Object Permananence and Person Permanence," *Developmental Psychology,* 14 (1978), 1–10.

Jackson, J. M., and B. Latané. "All Alone in Front of All Those People: Stage Fright as a Function of Number and Type of Co-Performer and Audience," *Journal of Personality and Social Psychology,* 40 (1981), 73–85.

Jacobson, S. W. "Matching Behavior in the Young Infant," *Child Development,* 50 (1979), 425–430.

Jacobson, S. W., and J. Kagan. "Interpreting 'Imitative' Responses in Early Infancy," *Science,* 205 (1979), 215–217.

James, W. *The Principles of Psychology.* Vol. 1. New York: Dover, 1950 (orig. pub. 1890).

Jamison, P. H., L. R. Franzini, and R. M. Kaplan. "Some Assumed Characteristics of Voluntarily Child Free Women and Men," *Psychology of Women Quarterly,* 4 (1979), 266–273.

Jarvik, L. F., and D. Cohen. "A Biobehavioral Approach to Intellectual Changes with Aging," in C. Eisdorfer and M. P. Lawton (eds.), *The Psychology of Adult Development and Aging.* Washington, D.C.: American Psychological Association, 1973, pp. 220–280.

Jelliffe, D. B., and E. F. P. Jelliffe. *Human Milk in the Modern World.* New York: Oxford University Press, 1978.

Jensen, A. R. "How Much Can We Boost IQ and Scholastic Achievement?" *Harvard Educational Review,* 39 (1969), 1–123.

Jensen, A. R., and W. D. Rohwer, Jr. "Syntactical Mediation of Serial and Paired-Associate Learning as a Function of Age," *Child Development,* 36 (1965), 601–608.

Jensen, R. E., and S. G. Moore. "The Effect of Attribute Statements on Cooperativeness and Competitiveness in School-Age Boys," *Child Development,* 48 (1977), 305–307.

Jersild, A., and F. B. Holmes. *Children's Fears.* New York: Columbia University Press, 1935.

Jessor, S., and R. Jessor. "Transition from Virginity to Nonvirginity among Youth: A Social-Psychological Study over Time," *Developmental Psychology,* 11 (1975), 473–484.

Jewett, S. "Longevity and the Longevity Syndrome," *Gerontologist,* 13 (1973), 91–99.

Joffe, J. M. "Genotype and Prenatal and Premating Stress Interact to Affect Adult Behavior in Rats," *Science,* 150 (1965), 1844–1845.

Johnson, D. W., G. Maruyama, R. Johnson, D. Nelson, and L. Skon. "Effects of Cooperative, Competitive, and Individualistic Goal Structures on Achievement: A Meta-Analysis," *Psychological Bulletin,* 89 (1981), 47–62.

Johnson, E., and B. Bursk. "Relationships between the Elderly and Their Adult Children," *Gerontologist,* 17 (1977), 90–96.

Johnson, J. E., J. Ershler, and C. Bell. "Play Behavior in a Discovery-Based and a Formal-Educational Preschool Program," *Child Development,* 51 (1980), 275–278.

Johnson, P., and D. M. Salisbury. "Breathing and Sucking During Feeding in the Newborn," in *Parent-Infant Interaction.* Amsterdam: CIBA Foundation Symposium 33, new series, ASP, 1975.

Johnson, R. "Some Correlates of Extramarital Coitus," *Journal of Marriage and Family,* 32 (1970), 449–456.

Johnston, L. D., J. G. Bachman, and P. M. O'Malley. "Drug Use Among American High School Students, 1975–1977." National Institute on Drug Abuse, U.S. Department of Health, Education and Welfare, 1977.

Jones, K. L., D. W. Smith, A. P. Streissguth, and N. C. Myrianthopoulos. "Outcome in Offspring of Chronic Alcoholic Women," *Lancet,* 1 (1974), 1076–1078.

Jones, M. C. "The Later Careers of Boys Who Were Early- or Late-Maturing," *Child Development,* 28 (1957), 113–128.

———. "Psychological Correlates of Somatic Development," *Child Development,* 36 (1965), 899–911.

Jones, M. C., and N. Bayley. "Physical Maturing among Boys as Related to Behavior," *Journal of Educational Psychology,* 41 (1950), 129–248.

Jordaan, J. P., and M. B. Heyde. *Vocational Development During the High School Years.* New York: Teachers College Press, 1978.

Jurkovic, G. J. "The Juvenile Delinquent as a Moral Philosopher: A Structural-Developmental Perspective," *Psychological Bulletin,* 88 (1980), 709–727.

Jusczyk, P. W. "Perception of Syllable-Final Stop Consonants by 2-Month-Old Infants," *Perception and Psychophysics,* 21 (1977), 450–454.

Kagan, J. "The Concept of Identification," *Psychological Review,* 65 (1958), 296–305.

———. "Cognitive Development," in *Master Lecture Series,* American Psychological Association, 1976.

———. "The Baby's Elastic Mind," *Human Nature,* 1 (January 1978), 66–78.

———. *The Growth of the Child.* New York: Norton, 1978.

Kagan, J., et al. *Change and Continuity in Infancy.* New York: Wiley, 1971.

Kagan, J., R. B. Kearsley, and P. R. Zelazo. *Infancy: Its Place in Human Development.* Cambridge, Mass.: Harvard University Press, 1978.

Kagan, J., and H. A. Moss. *Birth to Maturity, A Study in Psychological Development.* New York: Wiley, 1962.

Kagan, J., and S. R. Tulkin. "Social Class Differences in Child Rearing During the First Year," in H. R. Schaffer (ed.), *The Origins of Human Social Relations: Proceedings. Centre for Advanced Study in the Developmental Sciences Study Group.* New York: Academic Press, 1971, pp. 165–186.

Kagan, S., and M. C. Madsen. "Cooperation and Competition of Mexican, Mexican-American, and Anglo-American Children of Two Ages Under Four Instructional Sets," *Developmental Psychology,* 5 (1971), 32–39.

Kail, R. V., Jr., and A. W. Siegel. "The Development of Mnemonic Encoding in Children: From Perception to Abstraction," in R. V. Kail, Jr., and J. W. Hagen (eds.), *Perspectives on the Development of Memory and Cognition.* Hillsdale, N. J.: Erlbaum, 1976.

Kakar, S. "Images of the Life Cycle and Adulthood in Hindu India," in E. J. Anthony and C. Chiland (eds.), *The Child in His Family:* Vol. 4. *Children and Their Parents in a Changing World.* New York: Wiley-Interscience, 1978, pp. 319–332.

Kalish, R. A. "An Approach to the Study of Death Attitudes," *American Behavioral Scientist,* 6 (1963), 68–70.

———. "Death and Dying in a Social Context," in R. H. Binstock and M. E. Shanas (eds.), *The Handbook of Aging and the Social Sciences.* New York: Van Nostrand Reinhold, 1976, pp. 483–509.

Kalish, R. A., and D. K. Reynolds. *Death and Ethnicity: A Psychocultural Study.* Los Angeles: University of Southern California Press, 1976.

Kamin, L. J. "Heredity, Intelligence, Politics, and Psychology," Invited address, Eastern Psychological Association, Washington, D.C., March 1973.

Kandel, D. "Stages in Adolescent Involvement in Drug Use," *Science,* 190 (1975), 912–914.

Kandel, D. B., and G. S. Lesser. *Youth in Two Worlds.* San Francisco: Jossey-Bass, 1972.

Kane, F. J. "Adolescent Pregnancy: A Study of Aborters and Nonaborters," *American Journal of Orthopsychiatry,* 43 (1973), 796–803.

Kangas, J., and K. Bradway. "Intelligence at Middle Age: A Thirty-Eight Year Follow-Up," *Developmental Psychology,* 5 (1971), 333–337.

Kanter, R. M. *Communes: Creating and Managing the Collective Life.* New York: Harper & Row, 1973.

Kaplan, S. L. "The Assertion of Power: Ideals, Perceptions and Styles," Paper presented at American Psychological Association meeting, Washington, D.C., September 6, 1976.

Karniol, R. "Children's Use of Intention Cues in Evaluating Behavior," *Psychological Bulletin,* 85 (1978), 76–85.

———. "A Conceptual Analysis of Immanent Justice Responses in Children," *Child Development,* 51 (1980), 118–130.

Kastenbaum, R. "On the Meaning of Time in Later Life," *Journal of Genetic Psychology,* 109 (1966), 9–25.

———. "Is Death a Life Crisis? On the

Confrontation with Death in Theory and Practice," in N. Datan and L. H. Ginsberg (eds.), *Life-Span Developmental Psychology: Normative Life Crises.* New York: Academic Press, 1975, pp. 19–50.

———. "Death, Dying, and Bereavement in Old Age: New Developments and Their Possible Implications for Psychosocial Care," in H. Cox (ed.), *Aging.* 2nd ed. Guilford, Conn.: Dushkin Publishing, 1980, pp. 200–207.

Kay, E. "The World of Work: Its Promises, Conflicts and Reality," in American Medical Association, *The Quality of Life: The Middle Years.* Acton, Mass.: Publishing Sciences Group, 1974, pp. 63–69.

Kaye, K., and A. J. Wells. "Mothers' Jiggling and the Burst-Pause Pattern in Neonatal Feeding," *Infant Behavior and Development,* 3 (1980), 29–46.

Keasey, C. B. "Social Participation as a Factor in the Moral Development of Preadolescents," *Developmental Psychology.* 5 (1971), 216–220.

Keating, D. P. "Thinking Processes in Adolescence," in J. Adelson (ed.), *Handbook of Adolescent Psychology.* New York: Wiley-Interscience, 1980, pp. 211–246.

Keating, D. P., and L. V. Clark. "Development of Physical and Social Reasoning in Adolescents," *Developmental Psychology,* 16 (1980), 23–30.

Keating, N. C., and P. Cole. "What Do I Do with Him 24 Hours a Day? Changes in the Housewife Role after Retirement," *Gerontologist,* 20 (1980), 84–89.

Keeney, T. J., S. R. Cannizzo, and J. H. Flavell. "Spontaneous and Induced Verbal Rehearsal in a Recall Task," *Child Development,* 38 (1967), 953–965.

Keith, P. M. "Life Changes and Perceptions of Life and Death among Older Men and Women," *Journal of Gerontology,* 34 (1979), 870–878.

Keller, A., L. H. Ford, Jr., and J. A. Meacham. "Dimensions of Self-Concept in Preschool Children," *Developmental Psychology,* 14 (1978), 483–489.

Keller, B. B., and R. Q. Bell. "Child Effects on Adult's Method of Eliciting Altruistic Behavior," *Child Development,* 50 (1979), 1004–1009.

Kelly, H., and H. Gardner (eds.), *New Directions in Child Development.* No. 13. *Viewing Children through Television.* San Francisco: Jossey-Bass, 1981.

Kelly, J. "Leisure Socialization: Replication and Extension," *Journal of Leisure Research,* 9 (1977), 121–132.

Kelly, J. R. "Work and Leisure: A Simplified Paradigm," *Journal of Leisure Research,* 4 (1972), 50–62.

———. "Socialization Toward Leisure: A Developmental Approach," *Journal of Leisure Research,* 6 (1974), 181–193.

———. "Life Styles and Leisure Choices," *Family Coordinator,* 24(1975), 190–195.

Kendler, T. S. "An Ontogeny of Mediational Deficiency," *Child Development,* 43 (1972), 1–19.

———. "The Development of Discrimination Learning: A Levels-of-Functioning Explanation," in H. W. Reese and L. P. Lipsitt (eds.), *Advances in Child Behavior and Development.* Vol. 13. New York: Academic Press, 1979, pp. 83–117.

Kendrick, C., and J. Dunn. "Caring for a Second Baby: Effects on Interaction between Mother and Firstborn," *Developmental Psychology,* 16 (1980), 303–311.

Keniston, K. *Young Radicals: Notes on Committed Youth.* New York: Harcourt Brace Jovanovich, 1968.

Kennell, J. H., R. Jerauld, H. Wolfe, D. Chesler, N. C. Kreger, W. McAlpine, N. Steffa, and M. H. Klaus. "Maternal Behavior One Year after Early and Extended Post-Partum Contact," *Developmental Medicine and Child Neurology,* 16 (1974), 172–179.

Kennell, J. H., D. K. Voos, and M. H. Klaus. "Parent-Infant Bonding," in J. D. Osofsky (ed.), *Handbook of Infant Development.* New York: Wiley-Interscience, 1979, pp. 786–798.

Kerckhoff, A. "Husband-Wife Expectations and Reactions to Retirement," in I. H. Simpson and J. C. McKinney (eds.), *Social Aspects of Aging.* Durham, N.C.: Duke University Press, 1966, pp. 160–172.

Kershner, J. R. "Ocular-Manual Laterality and Dual Hemisphere Specialization," *Cortex,* 10 (1974), 293–302.

Kessen, W., M. M. Haith, and P. H. Salapatek. "Human Infancy: A Bibliography and Guide," in P. H. Mussen (ed.), *Carmichael's Manual of Child Psychology.* Vol. 1. 3rd ed. New York: Wiley, 1970, pp. 287–445.

Kessen, W., J. Levine, and K. A. Wendich. "The Imitation of Pitch in Infants," *Infant Behavior and Development,* 2 (1979), 93–100.

Kilmer, S. "Infant-Toddler Group Day Care: A Review of Research," in L. G. Katz (ed.), *Current Topics in Early Childhood Education.* Vol. 2. Norwood, N.J.: Ablex, 1979, pp. 69–115.

Kimmel, D. C. *Adulthood and Aging: An Interdisciplinary Developmental View.* New York: Wiley, 1980.

Kinsbourne, M., and J. M. Swanson. "Developmental Aspects of Selective Orientation," in G. A. Hale and M. Lewis (eds.), *Attention and Cognitive Development.* New York: Plenum, 1979, pp. 119–134.

Kinsey, A. C., W. B. Pomeroy, and C. E. Martin. *Sexual Behavior in the Human Male.* Philadelphia: Saunders, 1948.

Kinsey, A. C., W. B. Pomeroy, C. E. Martin, and P. H. Gebhard. *Sexual Behavior in the Human Female.* Philadelphia: Saunders, 1953.

Kirschenblatt-Gimblett, B. "Speech Play and Verbal Art," in B. Sutton-Smith (ed.), *Play and Learning.* New York: Gardner Press, 1979, pp. 219–238.

Kivett, V. R., J. A. Watson, and J. C. Busch. "The Relative Importance of Physical, Psychological, and Social Variables of Locus of Control Orientation in Middle Age," *Journal of Gerontology,* 32 (1977), 203–210.

Klarh, D., and J. G. Wallace. *Cognitive Development: An Information-Processing View.* Hillsdale, N.J.: Erlbaum, 1976.

Kleemeier, R. W. "Intellectual Change in the Senium," *Proceedings of the Social Statistics Section of the American Statistical Association,* 1962, pp. 290–295.

Klein, M. *The Psycho-Analysis of Children.* London: Hogarth, 1932.

Klein, R. "Age, Sex, and Task Difficulty as Predictors of Social Conformity," *Journal of Gerontology,* 27 (1972), 229–236.

Klima, E. S., and U. Bellugi. "Teaching Apes to Communicate," in G. A. Miller (ed.), *Communication, Language, and Meaning: Psychological Perspectives.* New York: Basic Books, 1973, pp. 95–106.

Knapp, J. J., and R. N. Whitehurst. "Sexually Open Marriage and Relationships: Issues and Prospects," in R. W. Libby and R. N. Whitehurst (eds.), *Marriage and Alternatives: Exploring Intimate Relationships.* Glenview, Ill.: Scott, Foresman, 1977, pp. 147–160.

Knight, G. P., S. Kagan, and R. Buriel. "Confounding Effects of Individualism in Children's Cooperation-Competition Social Motive Measures," *Motivation and Emotion,* 5 (1981), 167–178.

Knox, D. "Trends in Marriage and Family, the 1980's," *Family Relations,* 29 (1980), 145–160.

Kobasigawa, A. "Retrieval Strategies in the Development of Memory," in R. V. Kail, Jr., and J. W. Hagen (eds.), *Perspectives on the Development of Memory and Cognition.* Hillsdale, N.J.: Erlbaum, 1977, pp. 177–201.

Koch, H. L. *Twins and Twin Relations.* Chicago: University of Chicago Press, 1966.

Koch, J. "When Children Meet Death," *Psychology Today* (August 1977), 64, 66, 79.

Kogan, N., K. Connor, A. Gross, and D. Fava. "Understanding Visual Metaphor: Developmental and Individual Differences," *Monographs of the Society for Research in Child Development* 45, no. 1, Serial no. 183 (1980).

Kohlberg, L. "The Development of Children's Orientations Toward a Moral Order: I. Sequence in the Development of Moral Thought," *Vita Humana,* 6 (1963), 11–33.

———. "A Cognitive-Developmental Analysis of Children's Sex-Role Concepts and Attitudes," in E. E. Maccoby (ed.), *The Development of Sex Differences.* Stanford, Calif.: Stanford University Press, 1966, pp. 82–173.

———. "The Child as a Moral Philosopher," *Psychology Today,* 2 (1968), 25–30.

———. "Stage and Sequence: The Cognitive-Developmental Approach to Socialization," in D. A. Goslin (ed.), *Handbook of Socialization Theory and Research.* Chicago: Rand McNally, 1969, pp. 347–480.

———. "Education for Justice: A Modern Statement of the Platonic View," in Nancy F. Sizer and Theodore R. Sizer (eds.), *Moral Education: Five Lectures.*

Cambridge, Mass.: Harvard University Press, 1970, pp. 57–84.

______. "Moral Stages and Moralization: The Cognitive-Developmental Approach," in T. Lickona (ed.), *Moral Development and Behavior*, New York: Holt, Rinehart and Winston, 1976, pp. 31–53.

______. "Revisions in the Theory and Practice of Moral Development," in W. Damon (ed.), *New Directions for Child Development*. No. 2. *Moral Development*. San Francisco: Jossey-Bass, 1978, pp. 83–87.

______. *The Meaning and Measurement of Moral Development*. Worcester, Mass.: Clark University Press, 1981.

Kohlberg, L., and C. Gilligan. "The Adolescent as a Philosopher: The Discovery of the Self in a Postconventional World," *Daedalus*, 100 (1971), 1051–1086.

Kohlberg, L., and R. B. Kramer. "Continuities and Discontinuities in Childhood and Adult Moral Development," *Human Development*, 12 (1969), 93–120.

Kohn, M. L. *Class and Conformity: A Study in Values*. 2nd ed. Chicago: University of Chicago Press, 1977.

______. "The Effects of Social Class on Parental Values and Practices," in D. Reiss and H. A. Hoffman (eds.), *The American Family: Dying or Developing*. New York: Plenum, 1979, pp. 45–68.

______. "Job Complexity and Adult Personality," in N. J. Smelser and E. H. Erikson (eds.), *Themes of Work and Love in Adulthood*. Cambridge, Mass.: Harvard University Press, 1980, pp. 193–210.

Kolata, G. B. "Behavioral Teratology: Birth Defects of the Mind," *Science*, 202 (1978), 732–734.

______. "Prenatal Diagnosis of Neural Tube Defects," *Science*, 209 (1980), 1216–1218.

Komarovsky, M. *Dilemma of Masculinity: A Study of College Youth*. New York, Norton, 1976.

Konner, M. "Infancy among the Kalahri San," in P. H. Leiderman, S. R. Tulkin, and A. Rosenfeld (eds.), *Culture and Infancy: Variations in the Human Experience*. New York: Academic Press, 1977, pp. 287–328.

Koocher, G. P. "Children's Conceptions of Death," in R. Bibace and M. E. Walsh (eds.), *New Directions for Child Development*. No. 14. *Children's Conceptions of Health, Illness, and Bodily Functions*. San Francisco: Jossey-Bass, 1981, pp. 85–99.

Kopp, C. B., and A. H. Parmalee. "Prenatal and Perinatal Influence on Infant Behavior," in J. D. Osofsky (ed.), *Handbook of Infant Development*. New York: Wiley-Interscience, 1979, pp. 29–75.

Kornfeld, J. R. "Theoretical Issues in Child Phonology," in *Proceedings of the Seventh Annual Meeting of the Chicago Linguistic Society (CLS 7)*, University of Chicago, 1971, pp. 454–468.

Krebs, D., and A. A. Adinolfi. "Physical Attractiveness, Social Relations, and Personality Style," *Journal of Personality and Social Psychology*, 31 (1975), 245–253.

Krebs, R. L. "Some Relationships Between Moral Judgment, Attention, and Resistance to Temptation," Unpublished doctoral dissertation, University of Chicago, 1968.

Kremnitzer, J. P., H. G. Vaughan, Jr., D. Kurtzberg, and K. Dowling. "Smooth-Pursuit Eye Movements in the Newborn Infant," *Child Development*, 50 (1979), 442–448.

Kreutzer, M. A., C. Leonard, and J. H. Flavell. "An Interview Study of Children's Knowledge about Memory," *Monographs of the Society for Research in Child Development*, 40 (1975), whole no. 159.

Kübler-Ross, E. *On Death and Dying*. New York: Macmillan, 1969.

______. "Coping with the Reality of Terminal Illness in the Family," in E. S. Shneidman (ed.), *Death: Current Perspectives*. Palo Alto, Calif.: Mayfield, 1976, pp. 138–162.

Kuczaj, S. A. "Children's Judgments of Grammatical and Ungrammatical Irregular Past-Tense Verbs," *Child Development*, 49 (1978), 319–326.

______. "Evidence for a Language Learning Strategy. On the Relative Ease of Acquisition of Prefixes and Suffixes," *Child Development*, 50 (1979), 1–13.

Kuczaj, S. A., and N. Brannick. "Children's Use of the *Wh-* Question Modal Auxiliary Placement Rule," *Journal of Experimental Child Psychology*, 28 (1979), 43–67.

Kuhn, D., S. C. Nash, and L. Brucken. "Sex Role Concepts of Two- and Three-Year-Olds," *Child Development*, 49 (1978), 445–451.

Kumaresan, P., G. S. Han, P. B. Anandarangam, and A. Vasicka. "Oxytocin in Maternal and Fetal Blood," *Journal of Obstetrics and Gynecology*, 46, no. 3 (1975), 272–274.

Kun, A. "Evidence for Preschoolers' Understanding of Causal Direction in Extended Causal Sequences," *Child Development*, 49 (1978), 218–222.

______. "Structural Components and Intellectual Correlates of Cognitive Perspective Taking in First- through Fourth-Grade Children," *Child Development*, 48 (1977), 1503–1511.

Kurdek, L. A. "Perspective Taking as the Cognitive Basis of Children's Moral Development: A Review of the Literature," *Merrill-Palmer Quarterly*, 24 (1978), 3–28.

Kurtines, W., and E. B. Greif. "The Development of Moral Thought: Review and Evaluation of Kohlberg's Approach," *Psychological Bulletin*, 8 (1974), 453–470.

Labov, W. "Contraction, Deletion, and Inherent Variability of the English Copula," *Language*, 45 (1969a), 715–762.

______. "The Logic of Nonstandard English," *Georgetown Monographs on Language and Linguistics*, 22 (1969b), 1–31.

______. *Language in the Inner City: Studies in the Black English Vernacular*. Philadelphia: University of Pennsylvania Press, 1973.

Ladd, G. W., and S. L. Oden. "The Relationship between Peer Acceptance and Children's Ideas about Helpfulness," *Child Development*, 50 (1979), 402–408.

Lamb, M. E. "Effects of Stress and Cohort on Mother- and Father-Interaction," *Developmental Psychology*, 12 (1976a), 435–443.

______. "Interactions between Eight-Month-Old Children and Their Fathers and Mothers," in M. E. Lamb (ed.), *The Role of the Father in Child Development*. New York: Wiley, 1976b, pp. 307–328.

______. "Twelve-Month-Olds and Their Parents: Interactions in a Laboratory Playroom," *Developmental Psychology*, 12 (1976c), 237–244.

______. "Father-Infant and Mother-Infant Interaction in the First Year of Life," *Child Development*, 48 (1977a), 167–181.

______. "The Development of Mother-Infant and Father-Infant Interaction in the First Year of Life," *Child Development*, 48 (1977b), 167–181.

______. "Interactions between Eighteen-Month-Olds and Their Preschool-Aged Siblings," *Child Development*, 49 (1978a), 51–59.

______. "The Development of Sibling Relationships in Infancy: A Short-Term Longitudinal Study," *Child Development*, 49 (1978b), 1189–1196.

Lamb, M. E., and D. Baumrind. "Socialization and Personality Development in the Preschool Years," in M. E. Lamb (ed.), *Social and Personality Development*. New York: Holt, Rinehart and Winston, 1978c, pp. 50–69.

Lamb, M. E., M. A. Easterbrooks, and G. W. Holden. "Reinforcement and Punishment among Preschoolers: Characteristics, Effects, and Correlates," *Child Development*, 51 (1980), 1230–1236.

Lamb, M. E., A. Frodi, C. P. Hwang, and M. Frodi. "Varying Degrees of Paternal Involvement in Infant Care: Correlates and Effects," in M. E. Lamb (ed.), *Nontraditional Families*. Hillsdale, N.J.: Erlbaum, 1982.

Lamb, M. E., and J. L. Roopnarine. "Peer Influences on Sex-Role Development in Preschoolers," *Child Development*, 50 (1979), 1219–1222.

Lamb, M. E., and K. A. Urberg. "The Development of Gender Role and Gender Identity," in M. E. Lamb (ed.), *Social and Personality Development*. New York: Holt, Rinehart and Winston, 1978, pp. 178–199.

Lancioni, G. E. "Infant Operant Conditioning and Its Implications for Early Intervention," *Psychological Bulletin*, 88 (1980), 516–534.

Landry, M. O., and K. Lyons-Ruth. "Recursive Structure in Cognitive Perspective Taking," *Child Development*, 51 (1980), 386–394.

Lane, H. "A Chronology of the Oppression of Sign Language: France and the United States," in H. Lane and F. Grosjean (eds.), *Recent Perspectives on Ameri-*

can Sign Language. Hillsdale, N.J.: Erlbaum, 1980, pp. 119–161.

Langer, E. and J. Rodin. "The Effects of Choice and Enhanced Personal Responsibility for the Aged: A Field Experiment in an Institutionalized Setting," *Journal of Personality and Social Psychology,* 34 (1977), 191–198.

Langer, E. J., J. Rodin, P. Beck, C. Weinman, and L. Spitzer. "Environmental Determinants of Memory Improvement in Late Adulthood," *Journal of Personality and Social Psychology,* 37 (1979), 2003–2013.

Langlois, J. H., and C. F. Stephan. "The Effects of Physical Attractiveness and Ethnicity on Children's Behavioral Attributions and Peer Preferences," *Child Development,* 48 (1977), 1694–1698.

Laosa, L. M. "Maternal Behavior: Sociocultural Diversity in Modes of Family Interaction," in R. W. Henderson (ed.), *Parent-Child Interaction.* New York: Academic Press, 1981, pp. 125–267.

Lasky, R. E., R. E. Klein, C. Yarbrough, P. L. Engle, A. Lechtig, and R. Martorell. "The Relationship between Physical Growth and Infant Behavioral Development in Rural Guatemala," *Child Development,* 52 (1981), 219–226.

Laurendeau, M., and A. Pinard. *Casual Thinking in the Child: A Genetic and Experimental Approach.* New York: International Universities Press, 1962.

———. *The Development of the Concept of Space in the Child.* New York: International Universities Press, 1970.

LaVoie, J. C. "Type of Punishment as a Determinant of Resistance to Deviation." *Developmental Psychology,* 10 (1974), 181–189.

LaVoie, J. C., K. Anderson, B. Fraze, and K. Johnson. "Modeling, Tuition, and Sanction Effects on Self-Control at Different Ages," *Journal of Experimental Child Psychology,* 31 (1981), 446–455.

Leacock, E. "At Play in African Villages," in J. S. Bruner, A. Jolly, and K. Sylva (eds.), *Play: Its Role in Development and Evolution.* New York: Basic Books, 1976, pp. 466–473.

Leaf, A., and J. Launois. "Every Day Is a Gift When You Are Over 100," *National Geographic,* 143 (1973), 93–119.

Leahy, R. L., and M. Eiter. "Moral Judgment and the Development of Real and Ideal Androgynous Self-Image during Adolescence and Young Adulthood," *Developmental Psychology,* 16 (1980), 362–370.

Leboyer, F. *Birth without Violence.* New York: Knopf, 1975.

Lee, D. N., and E. Aronson. "Visual Proprioceptive Control of Standing in Human Infants," *Perception & Psychophysics,* 15 (1974), 529–532.

Lee, P. C., and G. R. Voivodas. "Sex-Role and Pupil Role in Early Childhood Education," in L. G. Katz (ed.), *Current Topics in Early Childhood Education.* Vol. 1. Norwood, N.J.: Ablex, 1977, pp. 105–118.

Lefcourt, H. M. *Locus of Control: Current Trends in Theory and Research.* New Jersey: Halsted Press, 1976.

Lefkowitz, M. M., L. D. Eron, L. O. Walder, and L. R. Huesman. *Growing Up to Be Violent.* New York: Pergamon, 1977.

Lehman, H. C. *Age and Achievement.* Princeton, N.J.: Princeton University Press, 1973.

Leiderman, P. H., and G. F. Leiderman. "Economic Change and Infant Care in an East African Agricultural Community," in P. H. Leiderman, S. R. Tulkin, and A. Rosenfeld (eds.), *Culture and Infancy: Variations in the Human Experience.* New York: Academic Press, 1977, pp. 405–438.

Leiter, M. P. "A Study of Reciprocity in Preschool Play Groups," *Child Development,* 48 (1977), 1288–1295.

Lempert, H. "Extrasyntactic Factors Affecting Passive Sentence Comprehension by Young Children," *Child Development,* 49 (1978), 694–699.

Lenneberg, E. H. "Understanding Language Without Ability to Speak: A Case Report," *Journal of Abnormal and Social Psychology,* 65 (1962), 419–425.

———. *Biological Foundations of Language.* New York: Wiley, 1967.

———. "Biological Aspects of Language," in G. A. Miller (ed.), *Communication, Language, and Meaning: Psychological Perspectives.* New York: Basic Books, 1973, pp. 49–60.

Leopold, W. F. *Speech Development of a Bilingual Child: A Linguist's Record.* Vol. 3. *Grammar and General Problems in the First Two Years.* Evanston, Ill.: Northwestern University Press, 1949.

Lerner, M. "When, Why and Where People Die," in E. S. Shneidman (ed.), *Death: Current Perspectives.* Palo Alto, Calif.: Mayfield, 1976, pp. 138–162.

Lerner, M. J. *The Belief in a Just World.* New York: Plenum, 1980.

Lerner, R. M., S. Iwawaki, T. Chihara, and G. T. Sorell, "Self-Concept, Self-Esteem, and Body Attitudes among Japanese Male and Female Adolescents," *Child Development,* 51 (1980), 847–855.

Lerner, R. M., and G. B. Spanier. *Adolescent Development: A Life-Span Perspective.* New York: McGraw-Hill, 1980.

Lesser, G. S. *Children and Television: Lessons From Sesame Street.* New York: Random House, 1974.

Lester, B. M., M. Kotelchuck, E. Spelke, M. J. Sellers, and R. E. Klein. "Separation Protest in Guatemalan Infants: Cross Cultural and Cognitive Findings," *Developmental Psychology,* 10 (1974), 79–85.

Leung, E. H., and H. L. Rheingold. "Development of Pointing as a Social Gesture," *Developmental Psychology,* 17 (1981), 215–220.

Leventhal, A. S., and L. P. Lipsitt. "Adaptation, Pitch Discrimination, and Sound Localization in the Neonate," *Child Development,* 35 (1964), 759–767.

Levine, E. S. *The Psychology of Deafness.* New York: Columbia University Press, 1960.

Levine, R. A. "Anthropology and Child Development," in C. M. Super and S. Harkness (eds.), *New Directions for Child Development.* No. 8. *Anthropological Perspectives on Child Development.* San Francisco: Jossey-Bass, 1980, pp. 71–86.

Levine, R. A., and B. B. Levine. "Nyansongo: A Gusii Community in Kenya," in B. B. Whiting (ed.), *Six Cultures: Studies of Child-Rearing.* New York: Wiley, 1963, pp. 19–202.

Levinson, D. J. *The Seasons of a Man's Life.* New York: Knopf, 1978.

Levy, S. M., L. R. Derogatis, D. Gallagher, and M. Gatz. "Intervention with Older Adults and the Evaluation of Outcome," in L. W. Poon (ed.), *Aging in the 1980's: Psychological Issues.* Washington, D.C.: American Psychological Association, 1980, pp. 41–61.

Lewis, M. "Social Interaction in the First Days of Life: Discussion," in H. R. Schaffer (ed.), *The Origins of Human Social Relations.* New York: Academic Press, 1971.

———. "The Social Determination of Play," in B. Sutton-Smith (ed.), *Play and Learning.* New York: Gardner Press, 1979, pp. 23–34.

Lewis, M., and Brooks-Gunn, J. *Social Cognition and the Acquisition of Self.* New York: Plenum, 1979a.

———. "Toward a Theory of Social Cognition: The Development of Self," in I. C. Uzgiris (ed.), *New Directions for Child Development.* No. 4. *Social Interaction and Communication during Infancy.* San Francisco: Jossey-Bass, 1979b, pp. 1–20.

Lewis, M., and R. Freedle. "Mother-Infant Dyad: The Cradle of Meaning," in P. Pliner, L. Kranes, and T. Alloway (eds.), *Communication and Affect: Language and Thought.* New York: Academic Press, 1973, pp. 127–155.

Lewis, M., with the collaboration of S. Goldberg and H. Campbell. "A Developmental Study of Information Processing Within the First Three Years of Life: Response Decrement to a Redundant Signal," *Monographs of the Society for Research in Child Development,* 34 (1969), whole no. 133.

Lewis, M., and L. A. Rosenblum (eds.), *The Effect of an Infant on Its Caregiver.* New York: Wiley-Interscience, 1974.

Lewis, R. A., and W. R. Burr. "Premarital Coitus and Commitment among College Students," *Archives of Sexual Behavior,* 4 (1975), 73–79.

Libby, R. W. "Creative Singlehood as a Sexual Life-Style: Beyond Marriage as a Rite of Passage," in R. W. Libby and R. N. Whitehurst (eds.), *Marriage and Alternatives: Exploring Intimate Relationships.* Glenview, Ill.: Scott, Foresman, 1977a, pp. 37–61.

———. "Extramarital and Comarital Sex: A Critique of the Literature," in R. W. Libby and R. W. Whitehurst (eds.), *Marriage and Alternatives: Exploring Intimate Relationships.* Glenview, Ill.: Scott, Foresman, 1977b, pp. 80–111.

Liben, L. S. "Memory in the Context of Cognitive Development: The Piagetian

Approach," in R. V. Kail, Jr., and J. W. Hagen (eds.), *Perspectives on the Development of Memory and Cognition.* Hillsdale, N.J.: Erlbaum, 1977, pp. 297–332.

______. "Perspective-Taking Skills in Young Children: Seeing the World through Rose-Colored Glasses," *Developmental Psychology,* 14 (1978), 87–92.

Liben, L. S., and B. Belknap. "Intellectual Realism: Implications for Investigations of Perceptual Perspective Taking in Young Children," *Child Development,* 52 (1981), 921–924.

Lickona, T. "Research on Piaget's Theory of Moral Development," in T. Lickona (ed.), *Moral Development and Behavior.* New York: Holt, Rinehart and Winston, 1976, pp. 219–240.

Lieberman, A. F. "Preschoolers' Competence with a Peer: Relations with Attachment and Peer Experience," *Child Development,* 48 (1977), 1277–1287.

Lieberman, M. "Adaptive Processes in Late Life," in N. Datan and L. H. Ginsberg (eds.), *Life Span Developmental Psychology: Normative Life Crises.* New York: Academic Press, 1975, pp. 135–160.

Lieberman, M. A., and A. S. Coplan. "Distance from Death as a Variable in the Study of Aging," *Developmental Psychology,* 2 (1969), 71–84.

Liebert, R. M., and R. A. Baron. "Some Immediate Effects of Televised Violence on Children's Behavior," *Developmental Psychology,* 6 (1972), 469–475.

Lind, J. "The Infant Cry," *Proceedings of the Royal Society of Medicine,* 64 (1971), 468.

Lind, J., V. Vuorenkoski, and O. Wasz-Höckert, in N. Morris (ed.), *Psychosomatic Medicine in Obstetrics and Gynaecology.* Basel: Karger, 1973.

Lindberg, M. A. "Is Knowledge Base Development a Necessary and Sufficient Condition for Memory Development?" *Journal of Experimental Child Psychology,* 30 (1980), 401–410.

Livesley, W. J., and D. B. Bromley. *Person Perception in Childhood and Adolescence.* New York: Wiley, 1973.

Livson, F. B. "Coming Out of the Closet: Marriage and Other Crises of Middle Age," in L. E. Troll, J. Israel, and K. Israel (eds.), *Looking Ahead: A Woman's Guide to the Problems and Joys of Growing Older.* Englewood Cliffs, N.J.: Prentice-Hall, 1977, pp. 81–92.

Livson, N., and H. Peskin. "Perspectives on Adolescence from Longitudinal Research," in J. Adelson (ed.), *Handbook of Adolescent Psychology.* New York: Wiley-Interscience, 1980, pp. 47–98.

Locke, J. *An Essay Concerning Human Understanding.* Collated and annotated by Alexander Campbell Fraser. Oxford: Clarendon Press, 1894 (orig. pub. 1690).

Locke, J. L. "The Child's Processing of Phonology," in W. A. Collins (ed.), *Minnesota Symposia on Child Psychology.* Vol. 12. *Children's Language and Communication.* Hillsdale, N.J.: Erlbaum, 1979, pp. 83–120.

Locke, J. L., and K. J. Kutz. "Memory for Speech and Speech for Memory," *Journal of Speech and Hearing Research,* 18 (1975), 176–191.

Loeb, R. C. "Concomitants of Boys' Locus of Control Examined in Parent-Child Interactions," *Developmental Psychology,* 11 (1975), pp. 353–358.

Loehlin, J. C., G. Lindzey, and J. N. Spuhler. *Race Differences in Intelligence.* San Francisco: Freeman, 1975.

Long, J. B. "The Death That Ends Death in Hinduism and Buddhism," in E. Kübler-Ross (ed.), *Death: The Final Stage of Growth.* Englewood Cliffs, N.J.: Prentice-Hall, 1975, pp. 52–72.

Lopata, H. Z. *Occupation: Housewife.* New York: Oxford University Press, 1971.

Lorch, E. P., D. R. Anderson, and S. R. Levin. "The Relation of Visual Attention to Children's Comprehension of Television," *Child Development,* 50 (1979), 722–727.

Lorenz, K. "Die Angeborenen Formen Möglicher Erfahrung," *Zeitschrift Für Tierpsychologie,* 5 (1942–1943), 235–409.

Lovitt, T., D. Smith, J. Kidder, and R. Evison. "Using Arranged and Programmed Events to Alter Subtraction Performance of Children with Learning Disabilities," in F. S. Keller and E. Ribes-Inesta (eds.), *Behavior Modification: Applications to Education.* New York: Academic Press, 1974, pp. 27–62.

Lowenthal, M., and D. Chiriboga. "Social Stress and Adaptation: Toward a Life Course Perspective," in C. Eisdorfer and M. P. Lawton (eds.), *The Psychology of Adult Developing and Aging.* Washington, D.C.: American Psychological Association, 1973, pp. 281–310.

Lowenthal, M. F., and C. Haven. "Interaction and Adaptation: Intimacy as a Critical Variable," *American Sociological Review,* 33 (1968), 20–30.

Lowenthal, M. F., M. Thurnher, and D. Chiraboga. *Four Stages of Life.* San Francisco: Jossey-Bass, 1975.

Luckey, E. B., and G. D. Nass. "A Comparison of Sexual Attitudes and Behavior in an International Sample," *Journal of Mariage and the Family,* 31 (1969), 364–379.

Luria, A. R. *Cognitive Development: Its Cultural and Social Foundations.* Cambridge, Mass.: Harvard University Press, 1976.

Maccoby, E. E. "Sex Differentiation during Childhood Development," in *Master Lecture Series,* American Psychological Association, 1976.

Maccoby, E. E., and C. N. Jacklin. *The Psychology of Sex Differences.* Stanford, Calif.: Stanford University Press, 1974.

______. "Sex Differences in Aggression: A Rejoinder and a Reprise," *Child Development,* 51 (1980), 964–980.

Macfarlane, A. *The Psychology of Childbirth.* Cambridge, Mass.: Harvard University Press, 1977.

Macfarlane, A., P. Harris, and I. Barnes. "Central and Peripheral Vision in Early Infancy," *Journal of Experimental Child Psychology,* 21 (1976), 532–538.

Macklin, E. D. "Review of Research on Non-Marital Cohabitation in the United States," in B. Murstein (ed.), *Exploring Intimate Life Styles.* New York: Springer, 1978, pp. 197–243.

Madden, D. J., and R. D. Nebes. "Aging and the Development of Automaticity in Visual Search," *Developmental Psychology,* 16 (1980), 377–384.

Maddox, G., and B. McCall. *Drinking among Teenagers.* New Brunswick, N.J. Rutgers Center for Alcohol Studies, 1964.

Main, M., and D. R. Weston. "The Quality of the Toddler's Relationship to Mother and to Father: Related to Conflict Behavior and the Readiness to Establish New Relationships," *Child Development,* 52 (1981), 932–940.

Mandler, J. M., S. Scribner, M. Cole, and M. DeForest. "Cross-Cultural Invariance in Story Recall," *Child Development,* 51 (1980), 19–26.

Maratos, O. "The Origin and Development of Imitation in the First Six Months of Life," Unpublished doctoral dissertation, University of Geneva, 1973.

Maratsos, M., S. A. Kuczaj II, D. E. C. Fox, and M. A. Chalkley. "Some Empirical Studies in the Acquisition of Transformational Relations: Passives, Negatives, and the Past Tense," in W. A. Collins (ed.), *Minnesota Symposia on Child Psychology.* Vol. 12. *Children's Language and Communication.* Hillsdale, N.J.: Erlbaum, 1979, pp. 1–46.

Maratsos, M. P. "Nonegocentric Communication Abilities in Preschool Children," *Child Development,* 44 (1973), 697–700.

Marcia, J. E. "Identity in Adolescence," in J. Adelson (ed.), *Handbook of Adolescent Psychology.* New York: Wiley-Interscience, 1980, pp. 159–187.

Marcus, D. E., and W. F. Overton. "The Development of Cognitive Gender Constancy and Sex Role Preference," *Child Development,* 49 (1978), 434–444.

Marcus, T. L., and D. A. Corsini. "Parental Expectations of Preschool Children as Related to Child Gender and Socioeconomic Status," *Child Development,* 49 (1978), 243–246.

Maretzki, T., and H. Maretzki. "Taira: An Okinawan Village," in B. B. Whiting (ed.), *Six Cultures: Studies of Child-Rearing.* New York: Wiley, 1963, pp. 363–539.

Markman, E., and J. Seibert. "Classes and Collections: Internal Organization and Resulting Holistic Properties," *Cognitive Psychology,* 8 (1976), 561–577.

Markman, E. M. *Factors Affecting the Young Child's Ability to Monitor His Memory.* Doctoral dissertation, University of Pennsylvania, Philadelphia, 1973.

Martin, C. L., and C. F. Halverson, Jr. "A Schematic Processing Model of Sex Typing and Stereotyping in Children," *Child Development,* 52 (1981), 1119–1134.

Martin, M. F., D. M. Gelfand, and D. P. Hartmann. "Effects of Adult and Peer Observers on Boys' and Girls' Responses to an Aggressive Model," *Child Development,* 42 (1971), 1271–1275.

Martin, R. M. "Effects of Familiar and Complex Stimuli on Infant Attention," *Developmental Psychology,* 11 (1975), 178–185.

Maslow, A. H. *Toward a Psychology of Being.* 2nd ed. Princeton, N.J.: Van Nostrand, 1968.

Mason, W. A., and M. D. Kenney. "Redirection of Filial Attachments in Rhesus Monkeys: Dogs as Mother Surrogates," *Science,* 183 (1974), 1209–1211.

Masters, J. C., and W. Furman. "Popularity, Individual Friendship Selection, and Specific Peer Interaction among Children," *Developmental Psychology,* 17 (1981), 344–350.

Masters, W. H., and V. E. Johnson. *Human Sexual Response.* Boston: Little, Brown, 1966.

———. "Human Sexual Response: The Aging Female and the Aging Male," in B. L. Neugarten (ed.), *Middle Age and Aging.* Chicago: Chicago University Press, 1968, pp. 269–279.

———. *Human Sexual Inadequacy.* Boston: Little, Brown, 1970.

———. "Emotional Poverty, A Marriage Crisis of the Middle Years," in American Medical Association, *The Quality of Life: The Middle Years.* Acton, Mass.: Publishing Sciences Group, 1974, pp. 101–108.

Matas, L., R. Arend, and L. A. Sroufe. "Continuity of Adaptation in the Second Year: The Relation between Quality of Attachment and Later Competence," *Child Development,* 49 (1978), 547–556.

Matthews, K. A. "Psychological Perspectives on the Type A Behavior Pattern," *Psychological Bulletin,* 91 (1982), 293–323.

Matthews, K. A., R. L. Helmreich, W. E. Beane, and G. W. Lucker. "Pattern A, Achievement Striving, and Scientific Merit: Does Pattern A Help or Hinder?" *Journal of Personality and Social Psychology,* 39 (1980), 962–967.

Maurer, D. "Infant Visual Perception: Methods of Study," in L. B. Cohen and P. Salapatek (eds.), *Infant Perception: From Sensation to Cognition.* Vol. 2. New York: Academic Press, 1975, 3–31.

Maurer, D., and T. L. Lewis. "Peripheral Discrimination by Three-Month-Old Infants," *Child Development,* 50 (1979), 276–279.

Maurer, D., and P. Salapatek. "Developmental Changes in the Scanning of Faces by Infants," *Child Development,* 47 (1976), 523–527.

Mazess, R. B., and S. H. Forman. "Longevity and Age Exaggeration in Vilcabamba, Ecuador," *Journal of Gerontology,* 34 (1979), 94–98.

McCall, R. B. "Attention in the Infant: Avenue to the Study of Cognitive Development," in D. N. Walcher and D. L. Peters (eds.), *Early Childhood: The Development of Self-Regulatory Mechanism.* New York: Academic Press, 1971, pp. 107–140.

———. "The Development of Intellectual Functioning in Infancy and the Prediction of Later IQ," in J. D. Osofsky (ed.), *Handbook of Infant Development.* New York: Wiley, 1979a, pp. 707–741.

———. "Stages of Play Development between Zero and Two Years of Age," in B. Sutton-Smith (ed.), *Play and Learning.* New York: Gardner Press, 1979b, pp. 35–44.

McCall, R. B., M. I. Appelbaum, and P. S. Hogarty. "Developmental Changes in Mental Performance," *Monographs of the Society for Research in Child Development,* 38 (1973), whole no. 150.

McCarthy, D. "Language Development in Children," in L. Carmichael (ed.), *Manual of Child Psychology.* 2nd ed. New York: Wiley, 1954, pp. 492–630.

McClearn, G. E. "Genetic Influences on Behavior and Development," in P. H. Mussen (ed.), *Carmichael's Manual of Child Psychology.* Vol. 1. 3rd ed. New York: Wiley, 1970, pp. 39–76.

McDavid, J. W., and H. Harari. "Stereotyping of Names and Popularity in Grade School Children," *Child Development,* 37 (1966), pp. 453–459.

McGhee, P. E. "The Role of Operational Thinking in Children's Comprehension and Appreciation of Humor," *Child Development,* 42 (1971), 733–744.

———. *Humor: Its Origin and Development.* San Francisco: Freeman, 1979.

McGraw, M. B. *Growth, A Study of Johnny and Jimmy.* New York: Appleton-Century-Crofts, 1935.

———. "Later Development of Children Specially Trained During Infancy: Johnny and Jimmy at School Age," *Child Development,* 10 (1939), 1–19.

McKain, W. "A New Look at Older Marriages," *Family Coordinator,* 21 (1972), 61–69.

McKenzie, B. E., and R. H. Day. "Object Distance as a Determinant of Visual Fixation in Early Infancy," *Science,* 178 (1972), 1108–1110.

McKenzie, B. E., H. E. Tootell, and R. H. Day. "Development of Visual Size Constancy during the 1st Year of Human Infancy," *Developmental Psychology,* 16 (1980), 163–174.

McKeown, T. *The Modern Rise of Population.* New York: Academic Press, 1977.

McLaughlin, L. J., and J. F. Brinley. "Age and Observational Learning of a Multiple-Classification Task," *Developmental Psychology,* 9 (1973), 9–15.

McLoyd, V. C. "Verbally Expressed Modes of Transformation in the Fantasy Play of Black Preschool Children," *Child Development,* 51 (1980), 1133–1139.

McMichael, R. E., and R. E. Grinder. "Children's Guilt After Transgression: Combined Effect of Exposure to American Culture and Ethnic Background," *Child Development,* 37 (1966), 425–431.

McNeill, D. *The Acquisition of Language: The Study of Developmental Psycholinguistics.* New York: Harper & Row, 1970a.

———. "The Development of Language," in P. H. Mussen (ed.), *Carmichael's Manual of Child Psychology.* Vol. 1. 3rd ed. New York: Wiley, 1970b, pp. 1061–1161.

McQueen, A. J. "The Adaptation of Urban Black Families: Trends, Problems, and Issues," in D. Reiss and H. A. Hoffman (eds.), *The American Family: Dying or Developing?* New York: Plenum, 1979, pp. 79–101.

Meacham, J. A. "Soviet Investigations of Memory Development," in R. V. Kail, Jr., and J. W. Hagen (eds.), *Perspectives on the Development of Memory and Cognition.* Hillsdale, N.J.: Erlbaum, 1977, pp. 273–295.

Mead, M. *Coming of Age in Samoa: A Psychological Study in Primitive Youth for Western Civilisation.* New York: Dell, 1968.

Mead, M., and N. Newton. "Cultural Patterning of Perinatal Behavior," in S. A. Richardson and A. F. Guttmacher (eds.), *Childbearing: Its Social and Psychological Factors.* Baltimore: Williams & Wilkins, 1967.

Meadow, K. P. "The Development of Deaf Children," in E. M. Hetherington (ed.), *Review of Child Development Research.* Vol. 5. Chicago: University of Chicago Press, 1975.

Meece, J. L., J. E. Parsons, C. H. Kaczala, F. B. Goff, and R. Futterman. "Sex Differences in Math Achievement: Toward a Model of Academic Choice," *Psychological Bulletin,* 91 (1982), 324–328.

Meichenbaum, D. H., and J. Goodman. "Training Impulsive Children to Talk to Themselves: A Means of Developing Self-Control," *Journal of Abnormal Psychology,* 77 (1971), 115–126.

Melear, J. D. "Children's Conception of Death," *Journal of Genetic Psychology,* 123 (1973), 359–360.

Meltzoff, A. N., and M. K. Moore. "Imitation of Facial and Manual Gestures by Human Neonates," *Science,* 198 (1977), 75–78.

Mendelson, M. J., and M. M. Haith. "The Relation Between Audition and Vision in the Human Newborn," *Monographs of the Society for Research in Child Development,* 41 (1976), whole no. 167.

Menyuk, P. *The Acquisition and Development of Language.* Englewood Cliffs, N.J.: Prentice-Hall, 1971.

Menyuk, P., and N. Bernholtz. "Prosodic Features and Children's Language Production," *M.I.T. Research Laboratory of Electronics Quarterly Progress Reports,* no. 93 (1969), 216–219.

Menzel, E. W., Jr., R. K. Davenport, Jr., and C. M. Rogers. "The Effects of Environmental Restriction upon the Chimpanzee's Responsiveness to Objects," *Journal of Comparative and Physiological Psychology,* 56 (1963), 78–85.

Mercer, J. R. "IQ: The Lethal Label," *Psychology Today,* 6 (September 1972), 44–47+.

Meredith, H. V. "Change in the Stature and Body Weight of North American Boys During the Last 80 Years," in L. P. Lipsitt and C. C. Spiker (eds.), *Advances in Child Development and Behavior.* Vol.

1. New York: Academic Press, 1963, pp. 69–114.

———. "A Synopsis of Pubertal Changes in Youth," *Journal of School Health,* 37 (1967), 171–176.

Messinger, L. "Remarriage Between Divorced People with Children from Previous Marriages: A Proposal for Preparation for Remarriage," *Journal of Marriage and Family Counseling,* 2 (1976), 193–200.

Michaels, R. H., and G. W. Mellin. "Prospective Experience with Maternal Rubella and the Associated Congenital Malformations," *Pediatrics,* 26 (1960), 200–209.

Michel, G. F. "Right-Handedness: A Consequence of Infant Supine Head-Orientation Preference?" *Science,* 212 (1981), 685–687.

Midlarsky, E., and J. H. Bryan. "Training Charity in Children," *Journal of Personality and Social Psychology,* 5 (1967), 408–415.

Milgram, S. "Behavioral Study of Obedience," *Journal of Abnormal and Social Psychology,* 67 (1963), 371–378.

———. *Obedience to Authority.* New York: Harper & Row, 1974.

Millar, S. The Psychology of Play. New York: Penguin, 1968.

Millar, W. S. "A Study of Operant Conditioning Under Delayed Reinforcement in Early Infancy," *Monographs of the Society for Research in Child Development,* 37 (1972), whole no. 147.

Millar, W. S., and J. S. Watson. "The Effect of Delayed Feedback on Infant Learning Reexamined," *Child Development,* 50 (1979), 747–751.

Miller, D. R., and G. E. Swanson. *Inner Conflict and Defense.* New York: Holt, Rinehart and Winston, 1966.

Miller, D. T., and C. D. McCann. "Children's Reactions to the Perpetrators and Victims of Injustices," *Child Development,* 50 (1980), 861–868.

Miller, G. A. "The Acquisition of Word Meaning," *Child Development,* 49 (1978), 999–1004.

Miller, M. "Geriatric Suicide: The Arizona Study," *Gerontologist,* 18 (1978), 488–496.

Miller, N. E., and J. Dollard. *Social Learning and Imitation.* New Haven, Conn.: Yale University Press, 1941.

Miller, P. Y., and W. Simon. "The Development of Sexuality in Adolescence," in J. Adelson (ed.), *Handbook of Adolescent Psychology.* New York: Wiley-Interscience, 1980, pp. 383–407.

Miller, W., and S. Ervin. "The Development of Grammar in Child Language," in *Cognitive Development in Children.* Chicago: University of Chicago Press, 1970, pp. 309–334.

Milstein, R. M. "Responsiveness in Newborn Infants of Overweight and Normal Weight Parents," *Appetite,* 1 (1980), 65–74.

Minkowski, A. *Regional Development of the Brain in Early Life.* Oxford: Blackwell, 1967.

Mischel, W. *Personality and Assessment.* New York: Wiley, 1968.

———. "Sex-Typing and Socialization," in P. H. Mussen (ed.), *Carmichael's Manual of Child Psychology.* Vol. 2. New York: Wiley, 1970, pp. 3–72.

Mischel, W., and N. Baker. "Cognitive Appraisals and Transformations in Delay Behavior," *Journal of Personality and Social Psychology,* 31 (1975), 254–261.

Mischel, W., and H. Mischel. "A Cognitive Social-Learning Approach to Morality and Self-Regulation," in T. Lickona (ed.), *Moral Development and Behavior.* New York: Holt, Rinehart and Winston, 1976, pp. 84–107.

Miscione, J. L., R. S. Marvin, R. G. O'-Brien, and M. T. Greenberg. "A Developmental Study of Preschool Children's Understanding of the Words "Know" and "Guess," *Child Development,* 49 (1978), 1107–1113.

Modahl, C., and N. Newton. "Mood State Differences between Breast and Bottle-Feeding Mothers," in L. Carenza and L. Zichella (eds.), *Emotion and Reproduction.* New York: Academic Press, 1979, pp. 819–822.

Moely, B. E. "Organizational Factors in the Development of Memory," in R. V. Kail, Jr., and J. W. Hagen (eds.), *Perspectives on the Development of Memory and Cognition.* Hillsdale, N.J.: Erlbaum, 1977, pp. 203–236.

Mohr, D. M. "Development of Attributes of Personal Identity," *Developmental Psychology,* 14 (1978), 427–428.

Molfese, D. L., R. B. Freeman, Jr., and D. S. Palermo. "The Ontogeny of Brain Lateralization for Speech and Nonspeech Stimuli," *Brain and Language,* 2 (1975), 356–368.

Molfese, D. L., and V. J. Molfese. "Hemisphere and Stimulus Differences as Reflected in the Cortical Responses of Newborn Infants to Speech Stimuli," *Developmental Psychology,* 15 (1979), 505–511.

Money, J., and A. A. Ehrhardt. *Man and Woman, Boy and Girl: The Differentiation and Dimorphism of Gender Identity from Conception to Maturity.* Baltimore: Johns Hopkins University Press, 1972.

Montemayor, R., and M. Eisen. "The Development of Self-Conceptions from Childhood to Adolescence," *Developmental Psychology,* 13 (1977), 314–319.

Moody, R. *Life after Life.* Atlanta, Ga.: Mockingbird Books, 1975.

Moore, B. S., A. Clyburn, and B. Underwood. "The Role of Affect in Delay of Gratification," *Child Development,* 47 (1976), 273–276.

Moore, S. G. "Correlates of Peer Acceptance in Nursery School Children," in W. W. Hartup and N. L. Smothergill (eds.), *The Young Child.* Washington, D.C.: National Association for the Education of Young Children, 1967, pp. 229–247.

Moore, T. "Exclusive Early Mothering and Its Alternatives: The Outcome to Adolescence," *Scandinavian Journal of Psychology,* 16 (1975), 255–272.

Morgan, G. A., and H. N. Ricciuti. "Infants' Responses to Strangers During the First Year," in B. M. Foss (ed.), *Determinants of Infant Behavior.* Vol. 4. London: Methuen, 1969, pp. 253–272.

Morgan, L. A., E. A. Powers, and G. L. Bultena. "Social Interaction and Life Satisfaction: An Empirical Assessment of Late-Life Patterns," *Journal of Gerontology,* 34 (1979), 116–121.

Morison, R. S. "Death: Process or Event?" *Science,* 173 (1971), 694–702.

Moro, E. *"Das Erste Trimenon," Münchener Medizinische Wochenschrift,* 65 (1918), 1147–1150.

Morsbach, G., and C. Bunting. "Maternal Recognition of Their Neonates' Cries," *Developmental Medicine and Child Neurology,* 21 (1979), 178–185.

Mosatche, H. S., and P. Bragonier. "An Observational Study of Social Comparison in Preschoolers," *Child Development,* 52 (1981), 376–378.

Moshman, D. "Development of Formal Hypothesis-Testing Ability," *Developmental Psychology,* 15 (1979), 104–112.

Mueller, E. C., and D. Vandell. "Infant-Infant Interaction," in J. D. Osofsky (ed.), *Handbook of Infant Development.* New York: Wiley-Interscience, 1979, pp. 591–622.

Muir, D., and J. Field. "Newborn Infants Orient to Sounds," *Child Development,* 50 (1979), 431–436.

Mundy-Castle, A. "Perception and Communication in Infancy: A Cross-Cultural Study," in D. R. Olson (ed.), *The Social Foundations of Language and Thought: Essays in Honor of Jerome S. Bruner.* New York: Norton, 1980, pp. 231–253.

Mundy-Castle, A. C., and J. Anglin. "The Development of Looking in Infancy," Unpublished paper presented at Society for Research in Child Development, Santa Monica, Calif., 1969.

Murphy, L. B. "Infants' Play and Cognitive Development," in M. W. Piers (ed.), *Play and Cognitive Development.* New York: Norton, 1972.

Murray, J. P., and S. Kippax. "From the Early Window to the Late Night Show: International Trends in the Study of Television's Impact on Children and Adults," in L. Berkowitz (ed.), *Advances in Experimental Psychology.* Vol. 12. New York: Academic Press, 1979, pp. 322–352.

Murstein, B. I. "A Theory of Marital Choice," in B. I. Murstein (ed.), *Theories of Attraction and Love.* New York: Springer, 1971, pp. 100–151.

Muson, H. "Moral Thinking: Can It Be Taught?" *Psychology Today,* 12 (February 1979), 48–68, 92.

Mussen, P., and N. Eisenberg-Berg. *Roots of Caring, Sharing, and Helping: The Development of Prosocial Behavior in Children.* San Francisco: Freeman, 1977.

Mussen, P. H., and M. C. Jones. "Self-Conceptions, Motivations, and Interpersonal Attitudes of Late and Early-Maturing Boys," *Child Development,* 28 (1957), 243–256.

Muuss, R. E. "Adolescent Development and the Secular Trend," *Adolescence,* 5 (1970), 267–284.

Myers, N. A., and M. Perlmutter. "Memory in the Years from Two to Five," in P. A. Ornstein (ed.), *Memory Development in Children.* Hillsdale, N.J.: Erlbaum, 1978, pp. 191–218.

Nagy, M. "The Child's View of Death," *Journal of Genetic Psychology,* 73 (1948), 3–27.

Nakamura, C. Y., and D. N. Finck. "Relative Effectiveness of Socially Oriented and Task-Oriented Children and Predictability of Their Behaviors, *Monographs of the Society for Research in Child Development,* 45 (1980), whole no. 185.

Nash, S. C., and S. S. Feldman. "Sex-Role and Sex-Related Attributions: Constancy and Change across the Family Life Cycle," in M. E. Lamb and A. L. Brown (eds.), *Advances in Developmental Psychology.* Vol. 1. Hillsdale, N.J.: Erlbaum, 1981, pp. 1–35.

National Childcare Consumer Study (contract 105-74-1107). Washington, D.C.: Office of Child Development, Department of Health, Education and Welfare, 1975.

Needham, J. *A History of Embryology,* 2nd rev. ed., with the assistance of A. Hughes. Cambridge: Cambridge University Press, 1959.

Neimark, E. D. "Intellectual Development during Adolescence," in F. D. Horowitz (ed.), *Review of Child Development Research.* Vol. 4. Chicago: University of Chicago Press, 1975, pp. 541–594.

Nelsen, E. A., R. E. Grinder, and R. L. Flack. "Incentive Conditions and Social Desirability as Determinants of Behavioral Variance on a Temptation Task," *Child Development,* 51 (1980), 1260–1267.

Nelson, K. "Structure and Strategy in Learning to Talk," *Monographs of the Society for Research in Child Development,* 38 (February, April 1973), whole nos. 1 and 2.

———. "Semantic Development and the Development of Semantic Memory," in K. E. Nelson (ed.), *Children's Language.* Vol. 1. New York: Gardner Press, 1978, pp. 39–80.

———. "Individual Differences in Language Development," *Developmental Psychology,* 17 (1981), 170–187.

Nelson, K., L. Rescorla, J. Gruendel, and H. Benedict. "Early Lexicons: What Do They Mean?" *Child Development,* 49 (1978), 960–968.

Nelson, K. E., and S. M. Kosslyn. "Recognition of Previously Labeled or Unlabeled Pictures by 5-Year-Olds and Adults," *Journal of Experimental Child Psychology,* 21 (1976), 40–45.

Nelson, K. E., and K. Nelson. "Cognitive Pendulums and Their Linguistic Realization," in K. Nelson (ed.), *Children's Language.* Vol. 1. New York: Gardner Press, 1978, pp. 223–286.

Nelson, S. A. "Factors Influencing Young Children's Use of Motives and Outcomes as Moral Criteria," *Child Development,* 51 (1980), 823–829.

Neugarten, B. L., "Adult Personality: Toward a Psychology of the Life Cycle," in B. L. Neugarten (ed.), *Middle Age and Aging: A Reader in Social Psychology.* Chicago: University of Chicago Press, 1968, pp. 137–147.

———. "Age: Grow Old Along with Me! The Best Is Yet to Be," *Psychology Today,* 5 (December 1971), 42–45+.

———. "Personality and Aging," in J. E. Birren and K. W. Schaie (eds.), *Handbook of the Psychology of Aging.* New York: Van Nostrand Reinhold, 1977, pp. 626–649.

———. "The Middle Generation," in P. K. Ragan (ed.), *Aging Parents.* Los Angeles: University of Southern California Press, 1979a, pp. 258–266.

———. "Time, Age, and the Life Cycle," *American Journal of Psychiatry,* 136 (1979b), 887–894.

———. interviewed by E. Hall. "Acting One's Age: New Rules for Old," *Psychology Today,* 13 (April 1980), 66–80.

Neugarten, B. L., and associates (eds.). *Personality in Middle and Late Life.* New York: Atherton, 1964.

Neugarten, B. L., and L. Brown-Rezanka. "A Midlife Woman in the 1980's," in *Women in Midlife—Security and Fulfillment.* Part 1. Select Committee on Aging and Subcommittee on Retirement Income and Employment. U.S. House of Representatives, 95th Congress, 2nd session. Committee Publication No. 95-170. 1978.

Neugarten, B. L., and D. L. Gutmann. "Age-Sex Roles and Personality in Middle Age: A Thematic Apperception Study," in B. L. Neugarten (ed.), *Middle Age and Aging: A Reader in Social Psychology.* Chicago: University of Chicago Press, 1968, pp. 58–71.

Neugarten, B. L., and G. O. Hagestad. "Age and the Life Course," in R. H. Binstock and E. Shanas (eds.), *Handbook of Aging and the Social Sciences.* New York: Van Nostrand Reinhold, 1976, pp. 35–55.

Neugarten, B. L., and W. A. Peterson. "A Study of the American Age-Grade System," *Proceedings of the Fourth Congress of the International Association of Gerontology,* 3 (1957), 497–502.

Neugarten, B. L., and K. K. Weinstein. "The Changing American Grandparent," in B. L. Neugarten (ed.), *Middle Age and Aging: A Reader in Social Psychology.* Chicago: University of Chicago Press, 1968, pp. 280–286.

Neugarten, B. L., V. Wood, R. J. Kraines, and B. Loomis. "Women's Attitudes Toward the Menopause," *Vita Humana,* 6 (1963), 140–151.

Newcomb, A. F., and W. A. Collins. "Children's Comprehension of Family Role Portrayals in Televised Dramas: Effects of Socioeconomic Status, Ethnicity, and Age," *Developmental Psychology,* 15 (1979), 417–423.

Newman, B. M. "Coping and Adaptation in Adolescence," *Human Development,* 22 (1979), 255–262.

Newman, O. *Defensible Space: Crime Prevention through Urban Design.* New York: Macmillan, 1973.

Newman, S. *Housing Adjustments of Older People: A Report from the Second Phase.* Ann Arbor: Institute for Social Research, University of Michigan, 1976.

Newton, N. "Psychologic Differences between Breast and Bottle Feeding," *American Journal of Clinical Nutrition,*" 24 (1971), 993–1004.

———. "Key Psychological Issues in Human Lactation," in L. R. Waletzky (ed.), *Symposium on Human Lactation,* No. HSA 79-5107. Rockville, Md.: Department of Health, Education and Welfare, 1979, pp. 25–37.

Newton, N., N. Paschall, A. Melamed, and F. Ryan. "Psychological and Behavioral Correlates of Mother's Choice of Postpartum Nearness to Infant," *The Family: Fourth International Congress on Psychosomatic Obstetrics and Gynecology.* Basel: Karger, 1975.

New York Times. "Babyfood Industry Agrees to Curb Promotion of Infant Formulas," October 13, 1979, p. 46.

New York Times News Service. "America Aging: 25.5 Million Are over 65," *New York Times,* May 24, 1981, pp. A-1, 9.

Nisbett, R. E. "Hunger, Obesity, and the Ventromedial Hypothalamus," *Psychological Review,* 79 (1972), 433–453.

Norman, D. K. "A Comparison of Children's Spatial Reasoning: Rural Appalachia, Suburban, and Urban New England," *Child Development,* 51 (1980), 288–291.

Norton, A. J. "The Family Life Cycle Updated: Components and Uses," in R. F. Winch and G. B. Spanier (eds.), *Selected Studies in Marriage and the Family.* New York: Holt, Rinehart and Winston, 1974, pp. 162–170.

Notman, M. "Adult Life Cycles: Changing Roles and Changing Hormones," in J. E. Parsons (eds.), *The Psychobiology of Sex Differences and Sex Roles.* New York: McGraw-Hill, 1980, pp. 209–224.

Nowak, C. A. "Does Youthfulness Equal Attractiveness?" in L. E. Troll, J. Israel, and K. Israel (eds.), *Looking Ahead: A Woman's Guide to the Problems and Joys of Growing Older.* Englewood Cliffs, N.J.: Prentice-Hall, 1977, pp. 59–64.

Noyes, R. "The Experience of Dying," *Psychiatry,* 35 (1972), 174–183.

Ochs, E. "Introduction: What Child Language Can Contribute to Pragmatics," in E. Ochs and B. B. Schieffelin (eds.), *Developmental Pragmatics.* New York: Academic Press, 1979, pp. 1–17.

Oden, S., and S. R. Asher. "Coaching Children in Social Skills for Friendship Making," *Child Development,* 48 (1977), 495–506.

Offer, D., E. Ostrov, and K. I. Howard. *The Adolescent: A Psychological Self-Portrait.* New York: Basic Books, 1981.

Office of the Surgeon General. *Television and Growing Up: The Impact of Televised Violence.* Washington, D.C.: U.S. Government Printing Office, 1972.

Olejnik, A. B. "Adults' Moral Reasoning with Children," *Child Development,* 51 (1980), 1285–1288.

Olson, D. R. "Some Social Aspects of Meaning in Oral and Written Language," in D. R. Olson (ed.), *The Social Foundations of Language and Thought.* New York: Norton, 1980, pp. 90–108.

Orlando Sentinel, July 21 and August 20, 1971.

Ornstein, P. A., and K. Corsale. "Process and Structure in Children's Memory," in G. J. Whitehurst and B. Zimmerman (eds.), *The Functions of Language and Cognition.* New York: Academic Press, 1979, pp. 199–228.

Orthner, D. K., T. Brown, and D. Ferguson. "Single-Parent Fatherhood: An Emerging Life Style," *Family Coordinator,* 24 (1977), 489–505.

Osborn, D. K., and R. C. Endsley. "Emotional Reactions of Young Children to TV Violence," *Child Development,* 41 (1971), 321–331.

Osherson, S. D. *Holding On or Letting Go: Men and Career Change at Midlife.* New York: Free Press, 1980.

Osis, K. *Deathbed Observations by Physicians and Nurses.* New York: Parapsychology Foundation, 1961.

Osler, S. F., and E. Kofsky. "Stimulus Uncertainty as a Variable in the Development of Conceptual Ability," *Journal of Experimental Child Psychology,* 2 (1965), 264–279.

Osofsky, J. D., and K. Connors. "Mother-Infant Interaction: An Integrative View of a Complex System," in J. D. Osofsky (ed.), *Handbook of Infant Development.* New York: Wiley-Interscience, 1979, pp. 519–548.

Palmore, E., W. P. Cleveland, J. B. Nowlin, D. Ramm, and I. C. Siegler. "Stress and Adaptation in Later Life," *Journal of Gerontology,* 34 (1979), 841–851.

Palmore, E., and F. C. Jeffers (eds.). *Prediction of Life Span: Recent Findings.* Lexington, Mass.: Heath, 1971.

Pannor, R., F. Massarik, and B. Evans. *The Unwed Father: New Approaches for Helping Unmarried Young Parents.* New York: Springer, 1971.

Papoušek, H. "Conditioning During Early Postnatal Development," in Y. Brackbill and G. G. Thompson (eds.), *Behavior in Infancy and Early Childhood: A Book of Readings.* New York: Free Press, 1967, pp. 259–274.

Papoušek, H., and M. Papoušek. "Interdisciplinary Parallels in Studies of Early Human Behavior: From Physical to Cognitive Needs, from Attachment to Dyadic Education," *International Journal of Behavioral Development,* 1 (1978), 37–49.

Parikh, B. "Development of Moral Judgment and Its Relation to Family Environmental Factors in Indian and American Families," *Child Development,* 51 (1980), 1030–1039.

Parke, R. D. *Fathers.* Cambridge, Mass.: Harvard University Press, 1981.

Parke, R. D., and D. B. Sawin. "The Father's Role in Infancy: A Re-evaluation," *Family Coordinator,* 25 (1976), 365–371.

Parkes, C. M. *Bereavement: Studies of Grief in Adult Life.* New York: International Universities Press, 1972.

———. "Home or Hospital? Terminal Care as Seen by Surviving Spouses," *Journal of the Royal College of General Practitioners,* 28 (1978), 19–30.

Parlee, M. B. "The Friendship Bond," *Psychology Today,* 13 (1979), 43–54+.

Parry, M. H. "Infants' Responses to Novelty in Familiar and Unfamiliar Settings," *Child Development,* 43 (1972), 233–237.

Patterson, G. R. "Mothers: The Unacknowledged Victims," *Monographs of the Society for Research in Child Development,* 45 (1980), whole No. 186.

Patterson, G. R., R. A. Littman, and W. Bricker. "Assertive Behavior in Children: A Step Toward a Theory of Aggression," *Monographs of the Society for Research in Child Development,* 32 (1967), whole no. 113.

Pavlov, I. P. *Conditioned Reflexes: An Investigation of the Physiological Activity of the Cerebral Cortex.* G. V. Anrep (ed. and tr.). London: Oxford University Press, 1927.

Pearlin, L. I. "Life Strains and Psychological Distress," in N. J. Smelser and E. H. Erikson (eds.), *Themes of Work and Love in Adulthood.* Cambridge, Mass.: Harvard University Press, 1980, pp. 174–192.

Peck, R. F., and R. J. Havighurst. *The Psychology of Character Development.* New York: Wiley, 1960.

Peel, E. A. *The Nature of Adolescent Judgment.* New York: Wiley-Interscience, 1971.

Perlmutter, M. "Development of Memory in the Preschool Year," in R. Greene and T. D. Yawkey (eds.), *Childhood Development.* Westport, Conn.: Technemic Publishing, 1980.

Perry, D. G., and K. Bussey. "The Social Learning Theory of Sex Differences: Imitation Is Alive and Well," *Journal of Personality and Social Psychology,* 37 (1979), 1699–1712.

Peskin, H. "Pubertal Onset and Ego Functioning," *Journal of Abnormal Psychology,* 72 (1967), 1–15.

———. "Influence of the Developmental Schedule of Puberty on Learning and Ego Development," *Journal of Youth and Adolescence,* 2 (1973), 273–290.

Petersen, A. C., and B. Taylor. "The Biological Approach to Adolescence: Biological Change and Psychological Adaptation," in J. Adelson (ed.), *Handbook of Adolescent Psychology.* New York: Wiley-Interscience, 1980, pp. 117–155.

Pfeifer, W. D., R. Rotundo, M. Myers, and V. H. Dennenberg, "Stimulation in Infancy: Unique Effects of Handling," *Physiological Behavior,* 17 (1976), pp. 781–784.

Pfeiffer, E. "Psychopathology and Social-pathology," in J. E. Birren and K. W. Schaie (eds.), *Handbook of the Psychology of Aging.* New York: Van Nostrand Reinhold, 1977, pp. 650–671.

Pfeiffer, E., and G. C. Davis. "The Use of Leisure Time in Middle Life," *Gerontologist,* 11 (1971) 187–195.

———. "Determinants of Sexual Behavior in Middle and Old Age," *Journal of the American Geriatrics Society,* 20 (1972), 151–158.

Phillips, D. P. "Deathday and Birthday: An Unexpected Connection," in J. M. Tanner (ed.), *Statistics: A Guide to the Unknown.* San Francisco: Holden-Day, 1972.

Piaget, J. *The Language of the Child.* M. Warden (tr.). New York: Harcourt, 1926.

———. *Judgment and Reasoning in the Child.* M. Warden (tr.). New York: Harcourt, 1928.

———. *The Moral Judgment of the Child.* M. Gabain (tr.). Boston: Routledge & Kegan Paul, 1932.

———. *Play, Dreams and Imitation in Childhood.* C. Gattegno and F. M. Hodgson (trs.). New York: Norton, 1951.

———. *The Child's Conception of Number.* C. Gattegno and F. H. Hodgson (trs.). Boston: Routledge & Kegan Paul, 1952a.

———. *The Origins of Intelligence in Children.* M. Cook (tr.). New York: International Universities Press, 1952b.

———. *Logic and Psychology.* Manchester: Manchester University Press, 1953.

———. *The Construction of Reality in the Child.* M. Cook (tr.). New York: Basic Books, 1954.

———. *Six Psychological Studies.* New York: Random House, 1967.

———. *On the Development of Memory and Identity.* Barre, Mass.: Clark University Press, 1968.

———. *The Child's Conception of Time.* London: Routledge & Kegan Paul, 1969.

———. *Genetic Epistemology.* New York: Columbia University Press, 1970a.

———. "Piaget's Theory," in P. H. Mussen (ed.), *Carmichael's Manual of Child Psychology.* Vol. 1. 3rd ed. New York: Wiley, 1970b, pp. 703–732.

———. *The Science of Education and the Psychology of the Child.* D. Coltman (tr.). New York: Viking, 1972.

———. *The Grasp of Consciousness: Action and Concept in the Young Child.* Cambridge, Mass: Harvard University Press, 1976.

———. *Success and Understanding.* Cambridge, Mass.: Harvard University Press, 1978.

Piaget, J., and B. Inhelder. *Le Développement des quantités chez l'enfant; Conservation et atomisme.* Neuchatel: Delachaux et Niestlé, 1941.

———. *Mémoire et intelligence.* Paris: Presses Universitaires de France, 1968.

———. *The Psychology of the Child.* Boston: Routledge & Kegan Paul, 1969a.

———. *The Psychology of the Child.* New York: Basic Books, 1969b.

———. *Memory and Intelligence.* New York: Basic Books, 1973.

Piaget, J., B. Inhelder, and A. Szeminska. *The Child's Conception of Geometry.* New York: Basic Books, 1960.

Pick, A. D., D. G. Frankel, and V. L. Hess.

"Children's Attention: The Development of Selectivity," in E. M. Hetherington (ed.), *Review of Child Development Research.* Vol. 5. Chicago: University of Chicago Press, 1975, pp. 325–383.

Pickert, S. M., and H. G. Furth. "How Children Maintain a Conversation with Adults," *Human Development,* 23 (1980), 162–176.

Pien, D., and M. K. Rothbart. "Incongruity and Resolution in Children's Humor: A Reexamination," *Child Development,* 47 (1976), 966–971.

Pitkin, R. M. "Nutritional Support in Obstetrics and Gynecology," *Clinical Obstetrics and Gynecology* 19, (1976), 489.

Plutchik, R., M. B. Weiner, and H. Conte. "Studies of Body Image: I. Body Worries and Body Discomforts," *Journal of Gerontology,* 26 (1971), 344–350.

Powell, G. F., J. A. Brasel, and R. M. Blizzard. "Emotional Deprivation and Growth Retardation Simulating Idiopathic Hypopituitarism. I. Clinical Evaluation of the Syndrome," *New England Journal of Medicine,* 276 (1967), 1271–1278.

Pratt, K. C. "The Neonate," in L. Carmichael (ed.), *Manual of Child Psychology.* 2nd ed. New York: Wiley, 1954, pp. 215–291.

Prechtl, H. F. R. "Problems of Behavioral Studies in the Newborn Infant," in D. S. Lehrman, R. A. Hinde, and E. Shaw (eds.), *Advances in the Study of Behavior.* Vol. 1. New York: Academic Press, 1965, pp. 75–98.

Premack, D. "Discussion," in S. R. Harnad, H. D. Steklis, and J. Lancaster (eds.), *Origins and Evolution of Language and Speech.* New York: New York Academy of Sciences, 1976.

Prentice, N. M. "The Influence of Live and Symbolic Modeling on Promoting Moral Judgment of Adolescent Delinquents," *Journal of Abnormal Psychology,* 80 (1972), 157–161.

Pressley, M., and J. R. Levin. "The Development of Mental Imagery Retrieval," *Child Development,* 51 (1980), 558–560.

Pritchard, J. A., and P. C. MacDonald. *Williams Obstetrics.* 15th edition. New York: Appleton-Century-Crofts, 1976.

Project Talent Office, University of Pittsburgh. "One Year Follow-Up Study," *Bulletin #5,* Washington D.C.: U.S. Government Printing Office, 1966.

Pulaski, M. "The Rich Rewards of Make-Believe," *Psychology Today,* 7 (January 1974), 68–74.

Puner, M. *To the Good Long Life: What We Know About Growing Old.* New York: Universe Books, 1974.

Putallaz, M., and J. M. Gottman. "Social Skills and Group Acceptance," in S. R. Asher and J. M. Gottman (eds.), *The Development of Children's Friendships.* New York: Cambridge University Press, 1981, pp. 116–149.

Rainwater, L. "Crucible of Identity: The Negro Lower-Class Family," *Daedalus,* 95 (1966), 172–216.

Ramey, C. T., and L. L. Ourth. "Delayed Reinforcement and Vocalization Rates of Infants," *Child Development,* 42 (1971), 291–298.

______. "Beginnings of Bimanual Handedness and Speech in Infants," *Infant Behavior and Development,* 3 (1980a), 67–78.

______. "Onset of Unimanual Handedness in Infants," *Infant Behavior and Development,* 3 (1980b), 377–386.

Ramsay, D. S., J. J. Campos, and L. Fenson. "Onset of Bimanual Handedness in Children," *Infant Behavior and Development,* 2 (1979), 69–76.

Rapoport, R., R. N. Rapoport, and Z. Strelitz. *Fathers, Mothers, and Society.* New York: Basic Books, 1977.

Redl, F. "The Impact of Game Ingredients on Children's Play Behavior," in B. Schaffner (ed.), *Group Processes: Transactions of the Fourth Conference.* New York: Josiah Macy Jr. Foundation, 1959.

Reedy, M. N. "Age and Sex Differences in Personal Needs and the Nature of Love: A Study of Happily Married Young, Middle-aged and Older Couples," Unpublished doctoral dissertation, University of Southern California, 1977.

______. "Love, Sexuality, and Aging," in I. N. Burnside and R. Solnick (eds.), *Sexuality and Aging.* Los Angeles: University of Southern California Press, 1978.

Reedy, M. N., J. E. Birren, and K. W. Schaie. "Age and Sex Differences in Satisfying Love Relationships across the Adult Life Span," *Human Development,* 24 (1981).

Reese, H. W. "Imagery and Associative Memory," in R. V. Kail, Jr., and J. W. Hagen (eds.), *Perspectives on the Development of Memory and Cognition.* Hillsdale, N.J.: Erlbaum, 1977, pp. 113–175.

Reinisch, J. M., N. G. Simon, W. G. Karow, and R. Gandelman. "Prednisone Therapy and Birth Weight," *Science,* 206 (1979), 97.

Reisman, J. M., and S. I. Shorr. "Friendship Claims and Expectations among Children and Adults," *Child Development,* 49 (1978), 913–916.

Reiss, I. L. *The Social Context of Premarital Sexual Permissiveness.* New York: Holt, Rinehart and Winston, 1967.

______. "How and Why Americans' Sex Standards Are Changing," in J. H. Gagnon and W. Simon (eds.), *The Sexual Scene.* Chicago: Aldine, 1970, pp. 43–57.

______. *Heterosexual Relationships Inside and Outside Marriage.* Morristown, N.J.: General Learning Press, 1973.

Resnick, J. L. "Women and Aging," *Counseling Psychologist,* 8 (1979), 29–30.

Rest, J. "The Hierarchical Nature of Moral Judgment: A Study of Patterns of Comprehension and Preference of Moral Stages," *Journal of Personality,* 41 (1973), 86–109.

______. "New Approaches in the Assessment of Moral Judgment," in T. Lickona (ed.), *Moral Development and Behavior.* New York: Holt, Rinehart and Winston, 1976, pp. 198–218.

Rest, J., M. L. Davison, and S. Robbins. "Age Trends in Judging Moral Issues: A Review of Cross-Sectional, Longitudinal, and Sequential Studies of the Defining Issues Test," *Child Development,* 49 (1978), 263–279.

Rest, J., E. Turiel, and L. Kohlberg. "Level of Moral Development as a Determinant of Preference and Comprehension of Moral Judgments Made by Others," *Journal of Personality,* 37 (1969), 225–252.

Rheingold, H. L. "The Social and Socializing Agent," in D. A. Goslin (ed.), *Handbook of Socialization Theory and Research.* Chicago: Rand McNally, 1969, pp. 779–791.

Rheingold, H. L., and C. O. Eckerman. "The Infant Separates Himself from His Mother," *Science,* 168 (1970), 78–83.

Rheingold, H. L., J. L. Gewirtz, and H. W. Ross. "Social Conditioning of Vocalizations in the Infant," *Journal of Comparative and Physiological Psychology,* 52 (1959), 68–73.

Rice, D. P. "Long Life to You," in H. Cox (ed.), *Aging.* 2nd ed. Guilford, Conn.: Dushkin Publishing, 1980, pp. 4–7.

Richards, C. S., and L. J. Siegel. "Behavioral Treatment of Anxiety States and Avoidance Behaviors in Children," in D. Marholin II (ed.), *Child Behavior Therapy.* New York: Gardner Press, 1978, pp. 274–338.

Richards, J. E., and N. Rader. "Crawling-Onset Age Predicts Visual Cliff Avoidance in Infants," *Journal of Experimental Psychology: Human Perception and Performance,* 7 (1981), 382–387.

Richards, M. "Early Separation," in R. Lewin (ed.), *Child Alive!* Garden City, N.Y.: Anchor Press/Doubleday, 1975, pp. 13–21.

Riegel, K. F. "Adult Life Crises: A Dialectical Interpretation of Development," in N. Datan and L. H. Ginsberg (eds.), *Life-Span Developmental Psychology: Normative Life Crises.* New York: Academic Press, 1975a, pp. 99–128.

______. "Toward a Dialectical Theory of Development," *Human Development,* 18 (1975b), 50–64.

______. "The Dialectics of Human Development," *American Psychologist,* 31 (1976), 689–699.

Riegel, K. F., and R. M. Riegel. "A Study on Changes of Attitudes and Interests During Later Years of Life," *Vita Humana,* 3 (1960), 177–206.

Riegel, K. F., R. M. Riegel, and M. Meyer. "A Study of the Dropout Rate in the Longitudinal Research on Aging and the Prediction of Deaths," *Journal of Personality and Social Psychology,* 5 (1967), 342–348.

Riegel, P. S. "Athletic Records and Human Endurance," *American Scientist,* 69 (1981), 285–290.

Riesen, A. H. *The Developmental Neuropsychology of Sensory Deprivation.* New York: Academic Press, 1975.

Riley, J. W., Jr. "What People Think About Death," in O. B. Brim, Jr., H. E.

Freeman, S. Levine, and N. A. Scotch (eds.), *The Dying Patient.* New York: Russell Sage Foundation, 1970, pp. 30–41.

Roberts, D. F., C. Herold, M. Hornby, S. King, D. Sterne, S. Whiteley, and T. Silverman. "Earth's a Big Blue Marble: A Report of the Impact of a Television Series on Children's Opinions," Unpublished manuscript, Stanford University, 1974.

Roberts, W. L. "Significant Elements in the Relationship of Long-Married Couples," *International Journal of Aging and Human Development,* 10 (1979–1980), 265–271.

Robinson, B., and M. Thurnher. "Parental Care-Taking: A Family Transition," Paper presented at Gerontological Society meeting, New York, October 1976.

Robinson, E. J., and W. P. Robinson. "Development in the Understanding of Causes of Success and Failure in Verbal Communication," *Cognition,* 5 (1977), 363–378.

Robinson, H. B., and N. M. Robinson. *The Mentally Retarded Child: A Psychological Approach.* New York: McGraw-Hill, 1965.

Rodin, J. "The Puzzle of Obesity," *Human Nature,* 1 (February 1978), 38–47.

______. "Current Status of the Internal-External Hypothesis for Obesity: What Went Wrong?" *American Psychologist,* 36 (1981), 361–372.

Rodin, J., and E. J. Langer. "Long-Term Effects of a Control-Relevant Intervention with Institutionalized Aged," *Journal of Personality and Social Psychology, (1978; in press).*

Rodin, J., and J. Slochower. "Externality in the Nonobese: Effects of Environmental Responsiveness on Weight," *Journal of Personality and Social Psychology,* 33 (1976), 338–344.

Roeper, T. "Connecting Children's Language and Linguistic Theory," in T. E. Moore (ed.), *Cognitive Development and the Acquisition of Language.* New York: Academic Press, 1973, pp. 187–196.

Roff, N., S. B. Sells, and M. M. Golden. *Social Adjustment and Personality Development in Children.* Minneapolis: University of Minnesota Press, 1972.

Roffwarg, H. P., J. N. Muzio, and W. C. Dement. "Ontogenic Development of the Human Sleep-Dream Cycle," *Science,* 152 (1966), 604–619.

Rogers, C. R. *Becoming Partners: Marriage and Its Alternatives.* New York: Delacorte, 1972.

Rohwer, W. D., Jr. "Learning, Race, and School Success," *Review of Educational Research,* 41 (1971), 191–210.

Rollings, B. C., and H. Feldman. "Marital Satisfaction Over the Family Life Cycle," *Journal of Marriage and the Family,* 32 (1970), 20–28.

Rose, C. L., and B. Bell. *Predicting Longevity: Methodology and Critique.* Lexington, Mass.: Heath, 1971.

Rose, S. A. and M. Blank. "The Potency of Context in Children's Cognition: An Illustration through Conservation." *Child Development,* 45 (1974) 499–502.

Rose, S. A., K. Schmidt, M. L. Riese, and W. H. Bridger. "Effects of Prematurity and Early Intervention on Responsivity to Tactual Stimuli: A Comparison of Preterm and Full-Term Infants," *Child Development,* 51 (1980), 416–425.

Rose, S. P. R. *The Conscious Brain.* New York: Knopf, 1973.

Rosen, B. C. "The Achievement Syndrome: A Psychocultural Dimension of Social Stratification," *American Sociological Review,* 21 (1956), 203–211.

Rosen, B. C., and R. D'Andrade. "The Psychological Origins of Achievement Motivation," *Sociometry,* 22 (1959), 185–218.

Rosenberg, M. *Society and the Adolescent Self-Image.* Princeton, N.J.: Princeton University Press, 1965.

______. "The Dissonant Context and the Adolescent Self-Concept," in S. E. Dragastin and G. H. Elder, Jr., *Adolescence in the Life Cycle,* New York: Wiley, 1975, pp. 97–116.

Rosenberg, M., and R. Simmons. *Black and White Self-Esteem: The Urban School Child.* Washington, D.C.: American Sociological Association, 1972.

Rosenhan, D. L. "The Natural Socialization of Altruistic Autonomy," in J. R. Macaulay and L. Berkowitz (eds.), *Altruism and Helping Behavior: Social Psychological Studies of Some Antecedents and Consequences.* New York: Academic Press, 1970, pp. 251–268.

Rosenthal, R. "Self-Fulfilling Prophecy," *Psychology Today,* 2 (1968), 44–51.

______. "The Pygmalion Effect Lives," *Psychology Today,* 7 (September 1973), 56–63.

Rosenthal, T. L., and B. J. Zimmerman. *Social Learning and Cognition.* New York: Academic Press, 1978.

Rosenzweig, M. R., and E. L. Bennett (eds.). *Neural Mechanisms of Learning and Memory.* Cambridge, Mass.: M.I.T. Press, 1976.

Ross, H. S., and D. A. Kay. "The Origins of Social Games," in K. H. Rubin (ed.), *New Directions for Child Development.* No. 9. *Children's Play.* San Francisco: Jossey-Bass, 1980, pp. 17–31.

Ross, H. S., H. L. Rheingold, and C. O. Eckerman. "Approach and Exploration of a Novel Alternative by 12-Month-Old Infants," *Journal of Experimental Child Psychology,* 13 (1972), 85–93.

Rossman, E., M. Golden, B. Birns, A. Moss, and A. Montare. "Mother-Child Interaction, IQ, and Social Class," Paper presented at the biennial meeting of the Society for Research in Child Development, Philadelphia, March 1973.

Rotter, J. B. "Interpersonal Trust, Trustworthiness, and Gullibility," *American Psychologist,* 35 (1980), 1–7.

Rousseau, J. J. *Emile.* New York: Dutton, 1911 (orig. pub. 1762).

Rovee-Collier, C. K., M. W. Sullivan, M. Enright, D. Lucan, and J. W. Fagen. "Reactivation of Infant Memory," *Science,* 208 (1980), 1159–1161.

Rozin, P. "The Evolution of Intelligence and Access to the Cognitive Unconscious," in J. M. Sprague and A. N. Epstein (eds.), *Progress in Psychobiology and Physiological Psychology.* Vol. 6. New York: Academic Press, 1976, pp. 245–280.

Rubenstein, E. A. "Television and the Young Viewer," *American Scientist,* 66 (1978), 685–693.

Rubenstein, E. A., R. M. Liebert, J. M. Neale, and R. W. Poulos. *Assessing Television's Influence on Children's Prosocial Behavior.* Stony Brook, N.Y.: Brookdale International Institute, 1974.

Rubenstein, J., and C. Howes. "The Effects of Peers on Toddler Interaction with Mother and Toys," *Child Development,* 47 (1976), 597–605.

Rubin, I. "The 'Sexless Older Years'—A Socially Harmful Stereotype," *Annals of the American Academy of Political and Social Science,* 376 (1968), 86–95.

Rubin, K. H. "Fantasy Play: Its Role in the Development of Social Skills and Social Cognition," in K. H. Rubin (ed.), *New Directions for Child Development.* No. 9. *Children's Play.* San Francisco: Jossey-Bass, 1980, pp. 69–84.

Rubin, K. H., and F. W. Schneider. "The Relationship between Moral Judgment, Egocentrism, and Altruistic Behavior," *Child Development,* 44 (1973), 661–665.

Rubin, Z. *Liking and Loving.* New York: Holt, Rinehart and Winston, 1973.

______. *Children's Friendships.* Cambridge, Mass.: Harvard University Press, 1980.

Ruble, D. N., A. K. Boggiano, N. S. Feldman, and J. H. Loebl. "Developmental Analysis of the Role of Social Comparison in Self-Evaluation," *Developmental Psychology,* 16 (1980), 105–115.

Ruble, D. N., J. E. Parsons, and J. Ross. "Self-Evaluative Responses of Children in an Achievement Setting," *Child Development,* 47 (1976), 990–997.

Rumbaugh, D. M., and T. V. Gill. "The Mastery of Language-Type Skills by Chimpanzees (Pan)," in S. R. Harnard, H. D. Steklis, and J. Lancaster, (eds.), *Origins and Evolution of Language and Speech.* New York: New York Academy of Sciences, 1976.

Rushton, J. P. "Effects of Prosocial Television and Film Material on the Behavior of Viewers," in L. Berkowitz (ed.), *Advances in Experimental Social Psychology."* Vol. 12. New York: Academic Press, 1979, pp. 321–351.

______. *Altruism, Socialization, and Society.* Englewood Cliffs, N.J.: Prentice-Hall, 1980.

Rutter, M. "Parent-Child Separation: Psychological Effects on the Children," *Journal of Child Psychology and Psychiatry and Allied Disciplines,* 12 (1971), 233–260.

______. "Maternal Deprivation, 1972–1978: New Findings, New Concepts, New Approaches," *Child Development,* 50 (1979), 283–305.

Ryff, C., and P. B. Baltes. "Value Transition and Adult Development in Women: The Instrumentality-Terminality Sequence Hypothesis," *Developmental Psychology,* 12 (1976), 567–568.

Sachs, J. S., and M. Johnson. "Language Development in a Hearing Child of Deaf Parents," in W. von Raffler Engel and Y. LeBrun (eds.), *Baby Talk and Infant Speech.* Amsterdam: Swets and Zweitlinger, 1976, pp. 246–252.

Saegert, S., and R. Hart. "The Development of Sex Differences in the Environmental Competence of Children," in P. Burnett (ed.), *Women in Society.* Chicago: Maaroufa Press, 1976.

Sagi, A., and M. L. Hoffman. "Emphathic Distress in Newborns," *Developmental Psychology,* 12 (1976), 175–176.

Salapatek, P. H., and W. Kessen. "Visual Scanning of Triangles by the Human Newborn," *Journal of Experimental Child Psychology,* 3 (1966), 155–167.

Salk, L. "Mothers' Heartbeat as an Imprinting Stimulus," *Transactions of the New York Academy of Sciences,* 24 (1962), 753–763.

Saltin, B., G. Bloomquist, J. H. Mitchell, R. L. Johnson, K. Wildenthal, and C. B. Chapman. "Response to Exercise after Bed Rest and after Training," *American Heart Association Monograph,* 23 (1968).

Sander, L. W. "The Regulation of Exchange in the Infant-Caretaker System and Some Aspects of the Context-Content Relationship," in M. Lewis and L. Rosenblum (eds.), *Interaction, Conversation, and the Development of Language.* New York: Wiley, 1977, pp. 133–156.

Sanders, R. E., M. D. Murphy, F. A. Schmitt, and K. K. Walsh. "Age Differences in Free Recall Rehearsal Strategies," *Journal of Gerontology,* 15 (1980), 550–558.

Sarrel, P., and L. Sarrel. "The Redbook Report on Sexual Relationships," *Redbook,* 150 (October 1980), 73–80.

Savage-Rumbaugh, E. S., D. M. Rumbaugh, and S. Boysen. "Do Apes Use Language?" *American Scientist,* 68 (1980), 49–61.

Savage-Rumbaugh, E. S., D. M. Rumbaugh, S. T. Smith, and J. Lawson. "Reference: The Linguistic Essential," *Science,* 210 (1980), 922–924.

Savin-Williams, R. C. "Dominance Hierarchies in Groups of Early Adolescents," *Child Development,* 50 (1979), 923–935.

Scaife, M., and J. S. Bruner. "The Capacity for Joint Visual Attention in the Infant," *Nature,* 253, no. 5489 (1975), 265–266.

Scarr, S., and P. Salapatek. "Patterns of Fear Development During Infancy," *Merrill-Palmer Quarterly,* 16 (1970), 53–90.

Scarr, S., and R. A. Weinberg. "IQ Test Performance of Black Children Adopted by White Families," *American Psychologist,* 31 (October 1976), 726–739.

______. "Attitudes, Interests, and IQ," *Human Nature,* 1, no. 4 (1978), 29–36.

Scarr-Salapatek, S. "Genetics and the Development of Intelligence," in F. D. Horowitz et al. (eds.), *Review of Child Development Research.* Vol. 4. Chicago: University of Chicago Press, 1975.

______. "An Evolutionary Perspective on Infant Intelligence," in M. Lewis (ed.), *Origins of Intelligence: Infancy and Early Childhood.* New York: Plenum, 1976, pp. 165–198.

Schachter, S., and J. Rodin. *Obese Humans and Rats.* Washington, D.C.: Erlbaum/Halstead, 1974.

Schaffer, H. R. *The Growth of Sociability,* Baltimore: Penguin, 1971.

______. *Mothering.* Cambridge, Mass.: Harvard University Press, 1977.

Schaffer, H. R., and P. E. Emerson. "The Development of Social Attachments in Infancy," *Monographs of the Society for Research in Child Development,* 29 (1964a), whole no. 94.

______. "Patterns of Response to Physical Contact in Early Human Development," *Journal of Child Psychology and Psychiatry,* 5 (1964b), 1–13.

Schaie, K. W. "A General Model for the Study of Developmental Problems," *Psychological Bulletin,* 64 (1965), 92–107.

______. "Intelligence and Problem Solving," in J. E. Birren and R. B. Sloane (eds.), *Handbook of Mental Health and Aging.* Englewood Cliffs, N.J.: Prentice-Hall, 1980, pp. 262–284.

Schaie, K. W., and G. Labouvie-Vief. "Generational versus Ontogenetic Components of Change in Adult Cognitive Behavior: A Fourteen-Year Cross Sequential Study," *Developmental Psychology,* 10 (1974), 305–320.

Schaller, J., S. G. Carlsson, and K. Larsson. "Effects of Extended Post-Partum Mother-Child Contact on the Mother's Behavior during Nursing," *Infant Behavior and Development,* 2 (1979), 319–324.

Schein, J. D., and M. T. Delt. *The Deaf Population of the United States.* Silver Spring, Md.: National Association of the Deaf, 1974.

Schlesinger, H. S., and K. P. Meadow. *Sound and Sign: Childhood Deafness and Mental Health.* Berkeley: University of California Press, 1972.

Schonbuch, S. S., and R. E. Schell. "Judgments of Body Appearance by Fat and Skinny Male College Students," *Perceptual and Motor Skills,* 24 (1967), 999–1002.

Schonfeld, W. A. "Body-Image in Adolescents: A Psychiatric Concept for the Pediatrician," *Pediatrics,* 31 (1963), 845–855.

______. "Body-Image Disturbances in Adolescents with Inappropriate Sexual Development," *American Journal of Orthopsychiatry,* 34 (1964), 493–502.

Schram, R. W. "Marital Satisfaction over the Family Life Cycle: A Critique and Proposal. *Journal of Marriage and the Family,* 41 (1979), 7–40.

Schulz, R., and M. Bazerman. "Ceremonial Occasions and Mortality: A Second Look," *American Psychologist,* 35 (1980), 253–261.

Schwartz, G., and D. Merten. "The Language of Adolescence: An Anthropological Approach to the Youth Culture," *American Journal of Sociology,* 72 (1967), 453–468.

Schwartz, J. C., R. G. Strickland, and G. Krolick. "Infant Day Care: Behavioral Effects at Preschool Age," *Developmental Psychology,* 10 (1974), 502–506.

Schwartz, M., and J. Schwartz. "Evidence Against a Genetical Component to Performance on IQ Tests," *Nature,* 248 (March 1974), 84–85.

Science News, "Avant Garde Parents: Traditional Infants," 3, 1977, 262.

Scollan, R. "A Real Early Stage: An Unzippered Condensation of a Dissertation on Child Language," in E. Ochs and B. B. Schieffelin (eds.), *Developmental Pragmatics.* New York: Academic Press, 1979, pp. 215–227.

Scott, E. M., R. Illsby, and A. M. Thomson. "A Psychological Investigation of Primigravidae. II. Maternal Social Class, Age, Physique, and Intelligence," *Journal of Obstetrics and Gynaecology of the British Empire,* 63 (1956), 338–343.

Scott, J. P. "The Development of Social Motivation," *Nebraska Symposium on Motivation,* 15 (1967), 111–132.

Scott, K. G., T. Field, and E. G. Robertson (eds.), *Teenage Parents and Their Offspring.* New York: Grune & Stratton, 1981.

Scrimshaw, N. S. "Early Malnutrition and Central Nervous System Function," *Merrill-Palmer Quarterly,* 15 (1969), 375–388.

Scrimshaw, N. S., and J. E. Gordon (eds.). *Malnutrition, Learning, and Behavior,* Cambridge, Mass.: M.I.T. Press, 1968.

Searleman, A. "A Review of Right Hemisphere Linguistic Capabilities," *Psychological Bulletin,* 84 (1977), 503–528.

Sears, R. R. "Relation of Early Socialization Experiences to Self-Concepts and Gender Role in Middle Childhood," *Child Development,* 41 (1970), 267–290.

______. "Your Ancients Revisited: A History of Child Development," in E. M. Hetherington (ed.), *Review of Child Development Research.* Vol. 5. Chicago: University of Chicago Press, 1975, pp. 1–73.

______. "Sources of Life Satisfaction of the Terman Gifted Men," *American Psychologist,* 32 (1977), 119–128.

Sears, R. R., E. E. Maccoby, and H. Levin. *Patterns of Child Rearing.* Evanston, Ill.: Row, Peterson, 1957.

Sears, R. R., L. Rau, and R. Alpert. *Identification and Childrearing.* Stanford, Calif.: Stanford University Press, 1965.

Self, P. A., and F. D. Horowitz. "The Behavioral Assessment of the Neonate: An Overview," in J. D. Osofsky (ed.), *The Handbook of Infant Development.* New York: Wiley-Interscience, 1980, pp. 126–164.

Seligman, M. E. P. Submissive Death: Giving Up on Life," *Psychology Today,* 7 (May 1974), 80–85.

______. *Helplessness: On Depression, Development, and Death.* San Francisco: Freeman, 1975.

Selman, R. L. "The Relation of Role Taking to the Development of Moral Judgment in Children," *Child Development,* 42 (1971), 79–91.

Semb, G. (ed.). *Behavior Analysis and Education.* Lawrence: University of Kansas Press, 1972.

Serbin, L. A., K. D. O'Leary, R. N. Kent, and I. J. Tonick. "A Comparison of Teacher Response to the Pre-academic and Problem Behavior of Boys and Girls," *Child Development,* 44 (1973), 796–804.

Shaffer, D. R., and G. H. Brody. "Parental and Peer Influences on Moral Development," in R. W. Henderson (ed.), *Parent-Child Interaction.* New York: Academic Press, 1981, pp. 83–124.

Shanab, M. E., and K. A. Yahya. "A Behavioral Study of Obedience," *Journal of Personality and Social Psychology,* 35 (1977), 550–586.

Shantz, C. U. "The Development of Social Cognition," in E. M. Hetherington (ed.), *Review of Child Development Research.* Vol. 5. Chicago: University of Chicago Press, 1975, pp. 257–324.

Sharabany, R., R. Gershoni, and J. E. Hofman. "Girlfriend, Boyfriend: Age and Sex Differences in Intimate Friendship," *Developmental Psychology,* 17 (1981), 800–808.

Sharff, J. G. "Free Enterprise and the Ghetto Family," *Psychology Today,* 15 (March 1981), 41–48.

Shatz, M. "On the Development of Communicative Understandings: An Early Strategy for Interpreting and Responding to Messages," *Cognitive Psychology,* 10 (1978), 271–301.

Shaver, P., and J. Freedman. "Your Pursuit of Happiness," *Psychology Today,* 10 (1976), pp. 26–32, 75.

Shelton, L. A. "A Comparative Study of Educational Achievement in One-Parent and Two-Parent Families," *Dissertation Abstracts,* 29 (8-A), 1969, 2535–2536.

Sherif, M., and C. W. S. Sherif. *Groups in Harmony and Tension: An Integration of Studies on Intergroup Relations.* New York: Harper & Row, 1953.

———. *Reference Groups: Explorations into Conformity and Deviation of Adolescents.* New York: Harper & Row, 1964.

Sherman, L. W. "An Ecological Study of Glee in Small Groups of Preschool Children," *Child Development,* 46 (1975), 53–61.

Shigetoni, C. C., D. P. Hartmann, and D. M. Gelfand. "Sex Differences in Children's Altruistic Behavior and Reputations for Helpfulness," *Developmental Psychology,* 17 (1981), 434–438.

Shneidman, E. S. *Deaths of Man.* New York: Quadrangle, 1973.

———. "Death Work and Stages of Dying," in E. S. Shneidman (ed.), *Death: Current Perspectives.* Palo Alto, Calif.: Mayfield, 1976, pp. 443–451.

Shock, N. W. "The Physiology of Aging," *Scientific American,* 206 (January 1962), 100–110.

———. "Biological Theories of Aging," in J. E. Birren and K. W. Schaie (eds.), *Handbook of the Psychology of Aging.* New York: Van Nostrand Reinhold, 1977, pp. 103–115.

Shore, M. F. "Legislation, Advocacy, and the Rights of Children and Youth," *American Psychologist,* 34 (1979), 1017–1019.

Shotwell, J. M., D. Wolf, and H. Gardner. "Exploring Early Symbolization: Styles of Achievement," in B. Sutton-Smith (ed.), *Play and Learning.* New York: Gardner Press, 1979, pp. 127–156.

Shultz, T. "A Cognitive-Developmental Analysis of Humor," in A. J. Chapman and H. C. Foot (eds.), *Humour and Laughter: Theory, Research, and Applications.* London: Wiley, 1976.

———. "Development of the Concept of Intention," in W. A. Collins (ed.), *Minnesota Symposia on Child Psychology.* Vol. 13. Hillsdale, N.J.: Erlbaum, 1980, pp. 131–164.

———. "Development of the Appreciation of Riddles," *Child Development,* 45 (1974), 100–105.

Siegel, A. W., G. L. Allen, and K. L. Kirasic. "Children's Ability to Make Bidirectional Distance Comparisons: The Advantage of Thinking Ahead," *Developmental Psychology,* 15 (1979), 656–657.

Siegel, A. W., and S. H. White. "The Development of Spatial Representations of Large-Scale Environments," in H. W. Reese (ed.), *Advances in Child Development and Behavior.* Vol. 10. New York: Academic Press, 1975, pp. 10–56.

Siegel, R. K. "The Psychology of Life after Death," *American Psychologist,* 35 (1980), 911–931.

Siegler, R. S., D. E. Liebert, and R. M. Liebert. "Inhelder and Piaget's Pendulum Problem: Teaching Preadolescents to Act as Scientists," *Developmental Psychology,* 9 (1973), 97–101.

Sigel, I. E., and E. Mermelstein. "Effects of Nonschooling on Piagetian Tasks of Conservation," Unpublished paper, 1966. (Cited in J. H. Flavell, "Concept Development," in P. H. Mussen (ed.), *Carmichael's Manual of Child Psychology.* 3rd ed. New York: Wiley, 1970.

Silka, L., and S. Kiesler. "Couples Who Choose to Remain Childless," *Family Planning Perspectives,* 9 (1977), 16–35.

Simner, M. L. "Newborn's Response to the Cry of Another Infant," *Developmental Psychology,* 5 (1971), 136–150.

Simon, W., and J. H. Gagnon. "On Psychological Development," in D. A. Goslin (ed.), *Handbook of Socialization Theory and Research.* Chicago: Rand McNally, 1969, pp. 733–752.

Simos, B. F. "Adult Children and Their Aging Parents," *Social Work,* 18 (1973), 78–85.

Simpson, E. L. "Moral Development Research: A Case Study of Scientific Cultural Bias," *Human Development,* 17, no. 2 (1974), 81–106.

Sinclair, C. B. *Movement of the Young Child: Ages Two to Six.* Columbus, Ohio: Merrill, 1973.

Singer, J. L., and D. G. Singer. "The Values of the Imagination," in B. Sutton-Smith (ed.), *Play and Learning.* New York: Gardner Press, 1979, pp. 195–218.

———. *Television, Imagination, and Aggression: A Study of Preschoolers.* Hillsdale, N.J.: Erlbaum, 1981.

Siqueland, E., and C. A. Delucia. "Visual Reinforcement of Non-Nutritive Sucking in Human Infants," *Science,* 165 (1969), 1144–1146.

Skinner, B. F. *The Behavior of Organisms: An Experimental Analysis.* New York: Appleton-Century-Crofts, 1938.

———. *Verbal Behavior.* New York: Appleton-Century-Crofts, 1957.

———. "Pigeons in a Pelican," *American Psychologist,* 15 (1960), 28–37.

———. *Cumulative Record: A Selection of Papers.* 3rd ed. New York: Appleton-Century-Crofts, 1972.

Skodak, M., and H. M. Skeels. "A Final Follow-Up Study of One Hundred Adopted Children," *Journal of Genetic Psychology,* 75 (1949), 85–125.

Slaby, R. G., and K. S. Frey. "Development of Gender Constancy and Selective Attention to Same-Sex Models," *Child Development,* 46 (1975), 849–856.

Slobin, D. I. "Children and Language: They Learn the Same Way All Around the World," *Psychology Today,* 6 (July 1972), 71–74+.

———. "Cognitive Prerequisites for the Development of Grammar," in C. A. Ferguson and D. I. Slobin (eds.), *Studies of Child Language Development.* New York: Holt, Rinehart and Winston, 1973, pp. 175–208.

———. "On the Nature of Talk to Children," in E. H. Lenneberg and E. Lenneberg (eds.), *Foundations of Language Development: A Multidisciplinary Approach.* UNESCO-IBRO, 1975.

———. "A Case Study of Early Language Awareness," in A. Sinclair, R. J. Jarvella and W. J. M. Levelt (eds.), *The Child's Conception of Language.* New York: Springer-Verlag, 1978, pp. 45–54.

Smith, C. "Effects of Maternal Undernutrition upon the Newborn Infant in Holland (1944–45)," *Journal of Pediatrics,* 30 (1947), 229–243.

Smith, C., and B. Lloyd. "Maternal Behavior and Perceived Sex of Infant: Revisited," *Child Development,* 49 (1978), 1263–1265.

Smith, P. K. "Aspects of the Playgroup Environment," in D. Canter and T. Lee (eds.) *Psychology and the Built Environment.* London: Architectural Press, 1974, 56–64.

———. "Social and Fantasy Play in Young Children," in B. Tizard and D. Harvey (eds.), *Biology of Play.* Philadelphia: Lippincott, 1977, pp. 123–145.

———. "A Longitudinal Study of Social Participation in Preschool Children: Solitary and Parallel Play Reexamined," *Developmental Psychology,* 14 (1978), 517–523.

Smith, P. K., and S. Dutton. "Play and Training in Direct and Innovative Problem Solving," *Child Development,* 50 (1979), 830–836.

Snow, C. E. "The Development of Conversation Between Mothers and Babies," *Journal of Child Language,* 4 (1977), 1–22.

Snow, C. E., A. Arlman-Rupp, Y. Hassing, J. Jobse, J. Jootsen, and J. Vorster. "Mothers' Speech in Three Social Classes," *Journal of Psycholinguistic Research,* 5 (1976), 1–20.

Snow, C. E., and M. Hoefnagel-Hohle. "The Critical Period for Language Acquisition: Evidence from Second Language Learning," *Child Development,* 49 (1978), 1114–1128.

Snow, M. E., C. N. Jacklin, and E. E. Maccoby. "Cry Episodes and Sleep-Wakefulness Transitions in the First 26 Months of Life," *Infant Behavior and Development,* 3 (1980), 387–394.

Solnick, R. L., and J. E. Birren. "Age and Male Erectile Responsiveness," *Archives of Sexual Behavior,* 6 (1977), 1–9.

Sommer, B. B. *Puberty and Adolescence.* New York: Oxford University Press, 1978.

Sonnenschein, S., and G. J. Whitehurst. "The Development of Communication: When a Bad Model Makes a Good Teacher," *Journal of Experimental Child Psychology,* 29 (1980), 371–390.

Sontag, L. W. "Implications of Fetal Behavior and Environment for Adult Personalities," *Annals of the New York Academy of Sciences,* 134 (1966), 782.

Sontag, L. W., and H. Newbery. "Normal Variations of Fetal Heart Rate During Pregnancy," *American Journal of Obstetrics and Gynecology,* 40 (1940), 449–452.

Sorensen, R. C. *Adolescent Sexuality in Contemporary America: Personal Values and Sexual Behavior, Ages Thirteen to Nineteen.* New York: World Press, 1973.

Soroka, S. M., C. M. Corter, and R. Abramovitch. "Infants' Tactual Discrimination of Novel and Familiar Stimuli," *Child Development,* 50 (1979), 1251–1253.

Spelke, E. S. "Perceiving Bimodally Specified Events in Infancy," *Developmental Psychology,* 15 (1979), 626–636.

Spelt, D. K. "The Conditioning of the Human Fetus *in utera,*" *Journal of Experimental Psychology,* 38 (1948), 338–346.

Spence, D., and T. Lonner. "The 'Empty Nest': A Transition Within Motherhood," *Family Coordinator,* 20 (October 1971), 369–375.

Spence, J. T. "Traits, Roles, and the Concept of Androgyny," in J. F. Gullahorn (ed.), *Psychology and Women in Transition.* New York: Wiley, 1979, pp. 167–187.

Spence, J. T., and R. L. Helmreich. *Masculinity and Feminity.* Austin, Texas: University of Texas Press, 1978.

Spinetta, J. J. "The Child with Cancer: Patterns of Communication," Paper presented at the Western Psychological Association, 1977.

Spinetta, J. J., D. Rigler, and M. Karon. "Anxiety in the Dying Child," *Pediatrics,* 52 (1973), 841–845.

———. "Peronal Space as a Measure of a Dying Child's Sense of Isolation." *Journal of Consulting and Clinical Psychology,* 42 (1974), 751–756.

Spring, C., and C. Capps. "Encoding Speed, Rehearsal, and Probed Recall of Dyslexic Boys," *Journal of Educational Psychology,* 66 (1974), 780–786.

Springer, S. P., and G. Deutsch. *Left Brain, Right Brain.* San Francisco: Freeman, 1981.

Sroufe, L. A. "Wariness of Strangers and the Study of Infant Development," *Child Development,* 48 (1977), 731–746.

Sroufe, L. A., and J. P. Wunsch. "The Development of Laughter in the First Year of Life," *Child Development,* 43 (1972), 1326–1344.

Staffieri, J. R. "A Study of Social Stereotype of Body Image in Children," *Journal of Personality and Social Psychology,* 7 (1967), 101–104.

Starkey, P., and R. G. Cooper, Jr. "Perception of Numbers by Human Infants," *Science,* 210 (1980), 1033–1035.

Starr, R. H., Jr. "Child Abuse," *American Psychologist,* 34 (1979), 872–878.

Staub, E. *The Development of Prosocial Behavior in Children.* New York: General Learning Press, 1975.

———. *Positive Social Behavior and Morality.* Vol. 2. New York: Academic Press, 1979.

Staub, E., and H. Noerenberg. "Property Rights, Deservingness, Reciprocity, Friendship: The Transactional Character of Children's Sharing Behavior," *Journal of Personality and Social Psychology,* 40 (1981), 271–289.

Stein, A. H., S. R. Pohly, and E. Mueller. "The Influence of Masculine, Feminine, and Neutral Tasks on Children's Achievement Behavior, Expectancies of Success, and Attainment Values," *Child Development,* 42 (1971), 195–207.

Stein, N. L., and C. G. Glenn. "An Analysis of Story Comprehension in Elementary School Children," in R. O. Freedle (ed.), *Discourse Processing: Multi-Disciplinary Perspectives.* Norwood, N.J.: Ablex, 1979.

Stein, P. "Singlehood: An Alternative to Marriage," *Family Coordinator,* 24 (1975), 489–505.

Steinberg, L. D. "Transformations in Family Relations at Puberty," *Developmental Psychology,* 17 (1981), 833–840.

Steiner, J. E. "Facial Expressions in Response to Taste and Smell Stimulation," in H. W. Reese and L. P. Lipsitt (eds.), *Advances in Child Development and Behavior.* Vol. 13. New York: Academic Press, 1979, pp. 257–296.

Stephens, M. W., and P. Delys. "External Control Expectancies Among Disadvantaged Children at Preschool Age," *Child Development,* 44 (1973), 670–674.

Stern, D. N. *The First Relationship: Infant and Mother.* Cambridge, Mass.: Harvard University Press, 1977.

Sternglanz, S. H., and L. A. Serbin. "Sex Role Stereotyping in Children's Television Programs," *Developmental Psychology,* 10 (1974), 710–715.

Stevens-Long, J. *Adult Life: Development Processes.* Palo Alto, Calif.: Mayfield, 1979.

Stevenson, H. W. *Children's Learning.* New York: Appleton-Century-Crofts, 1972.

Stinnett, N., L. Carter, and J. Montgomery. "Older Persons' Perceptions of Their Marriages," *Journal of Marriage and the Family,* 34 (1972), 665–670.

Stinnett, N., and J. Walters. *Relationships in Marriage and Family.* New York: Macmillan, 1977.

Stirnimann, F. Über das Farbempfinden Neugeborener," *Annales Paediatrici,* 163 (1944), 1–25.

Stix, H. "Elders in Residence—Bridging the Generation Gap on Campus," *Los Angeles Times,* March 16, 1981, V 1, 8.

Stolz, H. R., and L. H. Stolz. *Somatic Development of Adolescent Boys: A Study of the Growth in Boys During the Second Decade of Life.* New York: Macmillan, 1951.

Strayer, F. F., and J. Strayer. "An Ethological Analysis of Social Agonism and Dominance Relations among Preschool Children," *Child Development,* 47 (1976), 980–989.

Strayer, J. "Social Conflict and Peer-Group Status," Paper presented at the biennial meeting of the Society for Research in Child Development. New Orleans, March 1977.

Streissguth, A. P., S. Landesman-Dwyer, J. C. Martin, and D. W. Smith. "Teratogenic Effects of Alcohol in Humans and Laboratory Animals," *Science,* 209 (1980), 353–361.

Sullivan, K., and A. Sullivan. "Adolescent-Parent Separation," *Developmental Psychology,* 16 (1980), 93–99.

Suls, J., and R. J. Kalle. "Children's Moral Judgments as a Function of Intention, Damage, and an Actor's Physical Harm," *Developmental Psychology,* 15 (1979), 93–94.

Suomi, S. J. "Development of Attachment and Other Social Behaviors in Rhesus Monkeys," in T. Alloway, P. Pliner, and L. Kranes (eds.), *Attachment Behavior.* Vol.3. New York: Plenum, 1977.

———. "Peers, Play, and Primary Prevention in Primates," in M. W. Kent and J. E. Rolf (eds.), *Social Competence in Children.* Hanover, N.H.: University Press of New England, 1979, pp. 127–149.

Suomi, S. J., and H. F. Harlow. "The Role and Reason of Peer Relationships in Rhesus Monkeys," in M. Lewis and L. A. Rosenblum (eds.), *Friendship and Peer Relations.* New York: Wiley, 1975, pp. 153–185.

Super, C. M. "Cognitive Development: Looking Across at Growing Up," in C. M. Super and S. Harkness (eds.), *New Directions for Child Development.* No. 8. *Anthropological Perspectives on Child Development.* San Francisco: Jossey-Bass, 1980, pp. 59–69.

Super, C. M., J. Kagan, F. J. Morrison, M. M. Haith, and J. Weiffenbach. "Discrepancy and Attention in the Five-

Month Infant," *Genetic Psychology Monographs,* 85 (1972), 305–331.

Surber, C. F. "Developmental Processes in Social Inference: Averaging of Intentions and Consequences in Moral Judgment," *Developmental Psychology,* 13 (1977), 654–665.

Susman, E. J. "Visual and Verbal Attributes of Television and Selective Attention in Preschool Children," *Developmental Psychology,* 14 (1978), 565–566.

Sussman, M. B. "The Family Life of Old People," in R. H. Binstock and E. Shanas (eds.), *The Handbook of Aging and the Social Sciences.* New York: Van Nostrand Reinhold, 1976, pp. 218–243.

Sussman, M. B., and L. Burchinal. "Kin Family Network: Unheralded Structure in Current Conceptualizations of Family Functioning." in M. Sussman (ed.), *Marriage and the Family.* 3rd ed. Boston: Houghton Mifflin, 1968, pp. 72–81.

Sutton-Smith, B. "Children's Play: Some Sources of Play Theorizing," in K. H. Rubin (ed.), *New Directions for Child Development.* No. 9. *Children's Play.* San Francisco: Jossey-Bass, 1980, pp. 1–16.

Sutton-Smith, B., and J. M. Roberts. "Rubrics of Competitive Behavior, *Journal of Genetic Psychology,* 105 (1964), 13–37.

Sutton-Smith, B., and B. G. Rosenberg. *The Sibling.* New York: Holt, Rinehart and Winston, 1970.

Swanson, J. M., and M. Kinsbourne. "The Cognitive Effect of Stimulant Drugs on Hyperactive Children," in G. A. Hale and M. Lewis (eds.), *Attention and Cognitive Development.* New York: Plenum, 1979, pp. 249–296.

Sylva, K., J. S. Bruner, and P. Genova. "The Role of Play in the Problem-Solving of Children 3–5 Years Old," in J. S. Bruner, A. Jolly, and K. Sylva (eds.), *Play: Its Role in Development and Evolution.* New York: Basic Books, 1976, pp. 244–257.

Tanner, J. M. *Education and Physical Growth: Implications of the Study of Children's Growth for Educational Theory and Practice.* London: University of London Press, 1961.

______. *Growth of Adolescence, with a General Consideration of the Effects of Hereditary and Environmental Factors upon Growth and Maturation from Birth to Maturity.* 2nd ed. Oxford: Blackwell, 1962.

______. "Sequence, Tempo and Individual Variation in Growth and Development of Boys and Girls Aged Twelve to Sixteen," in J. Kagan and R. Coles (eds.), *Twelve to Sixteen: Early Adolescence.* New York: Norton, 1972, pp. 1–24.

______. *Fetus into Man.* Cambridge, Mass.: Harvard University Press, 1978.

______. "Ceremonial Occasions and Mortality: A Third Look," *American Psychologist,* 36 (1981), 315–316.

Taub, H. A., and M. K. Long. "The Effects of Practice on Short-Term Memory of Young and Old Subjects," *Journal of Gerontology,* 27 (1972), 494–499.

Tavris, C. "Men and Women Report Their Views on Masculinity," *Psychology Today,* 10 (January 1977), 34–42, 82.

Tavris, C., and C. Offir. *The Longest War: Sex Differences in Perspective.* New York: Harcourt Brace Jovanovich, 1977.

Taylor, D. C. "Differential Rates of Cerebral Maturation between Sexes and between Hemispheres," *Lancet,* 2 (1969), 140–142.

Terman, L. M., and M. Oden. *The Gifted Group at Mid-Life.* (Genetic Studies of Genius, Vol. V.) Stanford, Calif.: Stanford University Press, 1959.

Terrace, H. S. *Nim: A Chimpanzee Who Learned Sign Language.* New York: Knopf, 1979.

Thomas, A., S. Chess, and H. G. Birch. "The Origin of Personality," *Scientific American,* 223 (August 1970), 102–109.

Thomas, A., S. Chess, H. G. Birch, M. E. Hertzig, and S. Korn. *Behavioral Individuality in Early Childhood.* New York: New York University Press, 1963.

Thomas, L. "A Meliorist View of Disease and Dying," *Journal of Medicine and Philosophy,* 1 (1976), 212–221.

Thompson, R. A., and M. L. Hoffman. "Empathy and the Development of Guilt in Children," *Developmental Psychology,* 16 (1980), 155–156.

Thompson, S. K. "Gender Labels and Early Sex Role Development," *Child Development,* 46 (1975), 339–347.

Thompson, W. R. "Influence of Prenatal Maternal Anxiety on Emotionality in Young Rats," *Science,* 125 (1957), 698–699.

Thomson, A. M. "Historical Perspectives of Nutrition, Reproduction and Growth," in N. S. Scrimshaw and J. E. Gordon (eds.), *Malnutrition, Learning, and Behavior.* Cambridge, Mass.: M.I.T. Press, 1968, pp. 17–28.

Thoresen, C. E., and M. Mahoney. *Behavioral Self-Control.* New York: Holt, Rinehart and Winston, 1974.

Thornburg, H. *Teenage Pregnancies: Have They Reached Epidemic Proportions?* Phoenix: Arizona Governor's Council on Children, Youth, and Families, 1979.

Timpane, M., S. Abramowitz, S. B. Brobow, and A. Pascal. *Youth Policy in Transition.* Santa Monica, Calif.: Rand Corporation, 1976.

Tinbergen, N. *The Study of Instinct.* Oxford: Clarendon Press, 1951.

______. *The Animal in Its World: Explorations of an Ethologist, 1932–1972.* Field Studies, vol. 1. Cambridge, Mass.: Harvard University Press, 1972.

Todd, C. M., and M. Perlmutter. "Reality Recalled by Preschool Children," in M. Perlmutter (ed.), *New Directions in Child Development.* No. 10. *Children's Memory.* San Francisco: Jossey-Bass, 1980, pp. 69–85.

Tognoli, J. "Male Friendship and Intimacy across the Life Span," *Family Relations,* 29 (1980), 273–279.

Trabasso, T. "The Role of Memory as a System in Making Transitive Inferences," in R. V. Kail, Jr., and J. W. Hagen (eds.), *Perspectives on the Development of Memory and Cognition.* Hillsdale, N.J.: Erlbaum, 1977, pp. 333–366.

Trabasso, T., A. G. McLanahan, A. M. Isen, C. A. Riley, P. Dolecki, and T. Tucker. "How Do Children Solve Class Inclusion Problems?" in R. S. Siegler (ed.), *Children's Thinking: What Develops?* Hillsdale, N.J.: Erlbaum, 1978, pp. 151–180.

Tracy, R. L., M. E. Lamb, and M. D. Ainsworth. "Infant Approach Behavior as Related to Attachment," *Child Development,* 47 (1976), 571–578.

Trause, M. A. "Stranger Responses: Effects of Familiarity, Strangers' Approach, and Sex of Infant," *Child Development,* 48 (1977), 1657–1661.

Treas, J. "Aging and the Family," in D. S. Woodruff and J. E. Birren (eds.), *Aging: Scientific Perspectives and Social Issues.* New York: Van Nostrand, 1981.

Treas, J., and A. Van Hilst. "Marriage and Remarriage Rates Among Older Americans," *Gerontologist,* 16 (1976), 132–136.

Trelease, M. L. "Dying Among Alaskan Indians: A Matter of Choice," in E. Kübler-Ross (ed.), *Death: The Final State of Growth.* Englewood Cliffs, N. J.: Prentice-Hall, 1975, pp. 33–37.

Tresemer, D. "Fear of Success: Popular But Unproven," *Psychology Today,* 7 (March 1974), 82–85.

Trivers, R. L. *Early and Middle Adulthood.* Belmont, Calif.: Wadsworth, 1975.

Troll, L. E. "Grandparenting," in L. W. Poon (ed.), *Aging in the 1980's: Psychological Issues.* Washington, D.C.: American Psychological Association, 1980, pp. 475–481.

Tryon, R. C. "Genetic Differences in Maze Learning in Rats," *Thirty-Ninth Yearbook: National Society for the Study of Education.* Part 1. Bloomington, Ill.: Public School Publishing, 1940, pp. 111–119.

Tuchman-Duplessis, H. *Drug Effects on the Fetus.* Sydney: ADIS Press, 1975.

Tulkin, S. R., and J. Kagan. "Mother-Child Interaction in the First Year of Life," *Child Development,* 43 (1972), 31–41.

Tumblin, A., B. Gholson, T. L. Rosenthal, and J. E. Kelley. "The Effects of Gestural Demonstration, Verbal Narration, and Their Combination on the Acquisition of Hypothesis-Testing Behavior by First-Grade Children," *Child Development,* 50 (1979), 254–256.

Tyler, L. E. "The Intelligence We Test—An Evolving Concept," in L. B. Resnick (ed.), *The Nature of Intelligence.* Hillsdale, N. J.: Erlbaum, 1976, pp. 13–26.

Udwin, O., and D. Shmukler. "The Influence of Sociocultural, Economic, and Home Background Factors on Children's Ability to Engage in Imaginative Play," *Developmental Psychology,* 17 (1981), 66–72.

Uguroglu, M., and H. Walberg. "Motivation and Achievement: A Quantitative

Synthesis," *American Educational Research Journal,* 16 (1979), 375–389.

Ullian, D. Z. "The Development of Conceptions of Masculinity and Feminity," in B. Lloyd and J. Archer (eds.), *Exploring Sex Differences.* New York: Academic Press, 1976, pp. 25–48.

Underwood, B., and B. Moore. "Perspective-Taking and Altruism," *Psychological Bulletin,* 91 (1982), 143–173.

U.S. Bureau of the Census. "Marital Status and Living Arrangements: March 1972," *Current Population Reports.* Series P-20, no. 242. Washington, D.C.: U.S. Government Printing Office, 1972.

______. *Census of Population, 1970: Persons by Family Characteristics.* Vol. II, 4B, U.S. Government Printing Office, 1973.

______. "Demographic Aspects of Aging and the Older Population in the United States," *Current Population Reports.* Series P-23, no. 59. Washington, D. C.: U.S. Government Printing Office, 1976.

______. Marital Status and Living Arrangements: March 1977." *Current Population Reports,* Series P-20, No. 323. Washington, D.C.: U.S. Government Printing Office, 1978.

U.S. National Center for Health Statistics. *Vital Statistics of the United States, 1970.* Vol. 2, Part A: Mortality. Washington, D.C.: U.S. Government Printing Office, 1974a.

______. *Vital Statistics of the United States, 1973.* Vol. 2, Part A: Mortality. Rockville, Md.: U.S. Department of Health, Education and Welfare, 1974b.

______. *Teenage Smoking: National Patterns of Cigarette Smoking, Age 12 through 18, in 1972 and 1974.* Publication No. (NIH) 76-931. Rockville, Md.: U.S. Department of Health, Education, and Welfare 1976.

Urberg, K. A. "Sex Role Conceptualizations in Adolescents and Adults," *Developmental Psychology,* 15 (1979), 90–92.

Uzgiris, I. C. "Situational Generality of Conservation," *Child Development,* 35 (1964), 831–841.

______. "Organization of Sensorimotor Intelligence," in M. Lewis (ed.), *Origins of Intelligence.* New York: Plenum, 1976, pp. 123–163.

Vaillant, G. E. *Adaptation to Life.* Boston: Little, Brown, 1977.

Verinis, J. S., and S. Roll. "Primary and Secondary Male Characteristics: The Hairiness and Large Penis Stereotypes," *Psychological Reports,* 26 (1970), 123–126.

Verne, G. B. "The Effects of Four-Hour Delay of Punishment under Two Conditions of Verbal Instructions," *Child Development,* 48 (1977), 621–624.

Verwoerdt, A., E. Pfeiffer, and H. Wang. "Sexual Behavior in Senescence. II. Patterns of Sexual Activity and Interest," *Geriatrics,* 24 (1969), 137–154.

Vincent, C. *Unmarried Mothers.* New York: Free Press, 1961.

Vlietstra, A. G., and J. C. Wright. "Sensory Modality and Transmodal Stimulus Properties in Children's Discrimination Learning and Transfer," *Annual Report, Kansas Center for Research in Early Childhood Education.* Lawrence: University of Kansas, 1971.

Vogel, B. S., and R. E. Schell. "Vocational Interest Patterns in Late Maturity and Retirement," *Journal of Gerontology,* 23 (1968), 66–70.

Volkmar, F. R., E. L. Hoder, and A. E. Siegel. "Discrepant Social Communications," *Developmental Psychology,* 16 (1980), 495–505.

Von Frisch, K. *The Dance Language and Orientation of Bees.* L. E. Chadwick (tr.). Cambridge, Mass.: Belknap Press of Harvard University Press, 1967.

Vurpillot, E. "The Development of Scanning Strategies and Their Relation to Visual Differentiation," *Journal of Experimental Child Psychology,* 6 (1968), 622–650.

Vygotsky, L. S. *Mind in Society.* Cambridge, Mass.: Harvard University Press, 1978.

Waber, D. P. "Sex Differences in Cognition: A Function of Maturation Rate?" *Science,* 192 (1976), 572–573.

______. "Sex Differences in Mental Abilities, Hemisphere Lateralization, and Rate of Physical Growth at Adolescence," *Developmental Psychology,* 13 (1977), 29–38.

Waechter, E. H. "Children's Awareness of Fatal Illness," *American Journal of Nursing,* 71 (1971), 1168–1172.

Wahler, R. G. "Child-Child Interactions in Free Field Settings: Some Experimental Analyses," *Journal of Experimental Child Psychology,* 5 (1967), 278–293.

Walsh, R. P., and C. L. Connor. "Old Men and Young Women: How Objectively Are Their Skills Assessed?" *Journal of Gerontology,* 34 (1979), 561–568.

Walster, E., V. Aronson, D. Abrahams, and L. Rottmann. "Importance of Physical Attractiveness in Dating Behavior," *Journal of Personality and Social Psychology,* 4 (1966), 508–516.

Walters, C. E. "Prediction of Postnatal Development from Fetal Activity." *Child Development,* 36 (1965), 801–808.

Walters, G. C., and J. E. Grusec. *Punishment.* San Francisco: Freeman, 1977.

Walters, R. H., M. Leat, and L. Mezei. "Response Inhibition and Disinhibition through Empathetic Learning," *Canadian Journal of Psychology,* 17 (1968), 235–243.

Walters, R. H., and R. D. Parke. "Influence of Response Consequences to a Social Model on Resistance to Deviation," *Journal of Experimental Child Psychology,* 1 (1964), 260–280.

Walters, R. H., R. D. Parke, and V. A. Cane. "Timing of Punishment and the Observation of Consequences to Others as Determinants of Response Inhibition," *Journal of Experimental Child Psychology,* 2 (1965), 10–30.

Ward, R. A. "The Never-Married in Later Life," *Journal of Gerontology,* 34 (1979), 861–869.

______. "Age and Acceptance of Euthanasia," *Journal of Gerontology,* 35 (1980), 911–931.

Waterlow, J. C. "Note on the Assessment and Classification of Protein-Energy Malnutrition in Children," *Lancet,* 2 (1973), 87–89.

Waterlow, J. C., and P. R. Payne. "The Protein Gap," *Nature,* 258 (1975), 113–117.

Waters, E., J. Wippman, and L. A. Sroufe. "Attachment, Positive Affect, and Competence in the Peer Group: Two Studies in Construct Validation," *Child Development,* 50 (1979), 821–829.

Waters, H. S. "Memory Development in Adolescence: Relationships Between Metamemory, Strategy Use, and Performance," *Journal of Experimental Child Psychology,* 33 (1982), 183–195.

Watson, J. B. "Psychology as the Behaviorist Views It," *Psychological Review,* 20 (1913), 158–177.

______. *Behaviorism.* New York: People's Institute, 1924.

Watson, J. S. "The Development and Generalization of 'Contingency Awareness' in Early Infancy: Some Hypotheses," *Merrill-Palmer Quarterly,* 12 (1966), 123–135.

______. "Cognitive-Perceptual Development in Infancy: Setting for the Seventies," *Merrill-Palmer Quarterly,* 17 (1971), 139–152.

______. "Smiling, Cooing, and 'the Game,'" *Merrill-Palmer Quarterly,* 18 (1972), 323–339.

Watson, J. S., L. A. Hayes, L. Dorman, and P. Vietze. "Infant Sex Differences in Operant Fixation with Visual and Auditory Reinforcement," *Infant Behavior and Development,* 3 (1980), 107–114.

Watt, J. H., and R. Krull. "An Examination of Three Models of Television Viewing and Aggression," *Human Communications Research,* 3 (1977), 99–112.

Weg, R. B. "The Changing Physiology of Aging," *American Journal of Occupational Therapy,* 27 (1937), 213–217.

______. "Changing Physiology of Aging: Normal and Pathological," in D. S. Woodruff and J. E. Birren (eds.), *Aging: Scientific Perspectives and Social Issues.* New York: Van Nostrand Reinhold, 1981.

Weinberg, J., and S. Levine. "Early Handling Influences on Behavioral and Physiological Responses during Active Avoidance," *Developmental Psychobiology,* 10 (1977), 161–169.

Weinrott, M. R., J. A. Corson, and M. Wilchesky. "Teacher-Mediated Treatment of Social Withdrawal," *Behavior Therapy,* 10 (1979), 280–294.

Weishaus, S. "Aging Is a Family Affair," in P. K. Ragan (ed.), *Aging Parents.* Los Angeles: University of Southern California, 1979, pp. 154–174.

Weiss, R. S. *Going It Alone: The Family Life and Social Situation of the Single Parent.* New York: Basic Books, 1979.

Weisz, J. R. "Autonomy, Control, and

Other Reasons Why 'Mom Is the Greatest': A Content Analysis of Children's Mother's Day Letters," *Child Development,* 51 (1980), 801–807.

Wellman, H. M. "Preschoolers' Understanding of Memory—Relevant Variables," *Child Development,* 48 (1977), 1720–1723.

Wellman, H. M., J. Collins, and J. Glieberman. "Understanding the Combination of Memory Variables: Developing Conceptions of Memory Limitations," *Child Development,* 52 (1981), 1313–1317.

Werker, J. F., J. H. V. Gilbert, K. Humphrey, and R. C. Tees, "Developmental Aspects of Cross-Language Speech Perception," *Child Development,* 52 (1981), 349–355.

Werner, E. *Cross-Cultural Child Development.* Monterey, Calif.: Brooks-Cole, 1979.

Werner, H. *Comparative Psychology of Mental Development.* E. B. Garside (tr.). New York: International Universities Press, 1948.

———. "The Concept of Development from a Comparative and Organismic Point of View," in D. B. Harris (ed.), *The Concept of Development: An Issue in the Study of Human Behavior.* Minneapolis: University of Minnesota Press, 1957, pp. 125–148.

Werner, J. S., and M. Perlmutter. "Development of Visual Memory in Infants, in H. W. Reese and L. P. Lipsitt (eds.), *Advances in Child Development and Behavior.* Vol. 14. New York: Academic Press, 1979, pp. 2–56.

Whitbourne, S. K., and A. S. Waterman. "Psychosocial Development during the Adult Years: Age and Cohort Comparisons," *Developmental Psychology,* 15 (1979), 373–378.

White, B. L. *Human Infants: Experience and Psychological Development.* Englewood Cliffs, N. J.: Prentice-Hall, 1971.

———. *The First Three Years of Life.* Englewood Cliffs, N. J.: Prentice-Hall, 1975.

White, B. L., and R. Held. "Plasticity of Sensorimotor Development in the Human Infant," in J. F. Rosenblith and W. Allinsmith (eds.), *The Causes of Behavior. II: Readings in Child Development and Educational Psychology.* 2nd ed. Boston: Allyn & Bacon, 1966, pp. 60–70.

White, C. B., N. Bushnell, and J. L. Regnemer. "Moral Development in Bahamian School Children: A 3-Year Examination of Kohlberg's Stages of Moral Development," *Developmental Psychology,* 14 (1978), 58–65.

White, E., B. Elson, and R. Prawat. "Children's Conceptions of Death," *Child Development,* 49 (1978), 307–310.

White, R. *Lives in Progress: A Study of the Natural Growth of Personality.* 3rd ed. New York: Holt, Rinehart and Winston, 1975.

White, S. "Age Differences in Reaction to Stimulus Variation," in O. J. Harvey (ed.), *Experience Structure and Adaptability.* New York: Springer, 1966 pp. 95–122.

White, T. G. "Naming Practices, Typicality, and Underextension in Child Language," *Journal of Experimental Child Psychology,* 33 (1982), 324–346.

Whitehurst, G. J. "The Role of Comprehension Training in the Generative Production of Direct-Indirect Object Sentences by Preschool Children, Unpublished paper, State University of New York at Stony Brook, 1974.

Whitehurst, G. J., and R. Vasta. "Is Language Acquired through Imitation?" *Journal of Psycholinguistic Research,* 4 (1975), 37–59.

Whiting, B. B. *Six Cultures: Studies of Child Rearing.* New York: Wiley, 1963.

Whiting, B. B., and J. W. M. Whiting. *Children of Six Cultures: A Psycho-Cultural Analysis.* Cambridge, Mass.: Harvard University Press, 1975.

Whiting, J. W. M. "Resource Meditation and Learning by Identification," in I. Iscoe and H. W. Stevenson (eds.), *Personality Development in Children.* Austin: University of Texas Press, 1960, pp. 112–126.

Wichern, F., and S. Nowicki, Jr. "Independent Training Practices and Locus of Control Orientation in Children and Adolescence," *Developmental Psychology,* 12 (1976), 77.

Wickelgren, L. W. "Convergence in the Human Newborn," *Journal of Experimental Child Psychology,* 5 (1967), 74–85.

Widdowson, E. M. "Mental Contentment and Physical Growth," *Lancet,* 260 (1951), 1316–1318.

Wilson, E. O. *Sociobiology.* Cambridge, Mass.: Harvard University Press, 1975.

———. *On Human Nature.* Cambridge, Mass.: Harvard University Press, 1978a.

———. "For Sociobiology," in A. L. Caplan (ed.), *The Sociobiological Debate.* New York: Harper & Row, 1978b, pp. 265–268.

Wilson, J. "Sociology of Leisure," in *Annual Review of Sociology.* Vol. 6. Palo Alto, Calif.: Annual Reviews, 1980, pp. 21–40.

Wimmer, H. "Children's Understanding of Stories: Assimilation by a General Schema for Actions or Coordination of Temporal Relations?" in F. Wilkening, J. Becker, and T. Trabasso (eds.), *Information Integration by Children.* Hillsdale, N. J.: Erlbaum, 1980, pp. 267–290.

Winer, G. A. "Class-Inclusion Reasoning in Children: A Review of the Empirical Literature," *Child Development,* 51 (1980), 309–328.

Winnicott, D. W. *Therapeutic Consultations in Child Psychiatry.* London: Hogarth, 1971.

Winterbottom, M. "The Relation of Need for Achievement to Learning Experiences in Independence and Mastery," in J. Atkinson (ed.), *Motives in Fantasy, Action, and Society.* Princeton, N.J.: Van Nostrand, 1958, pp. 453–478.

Witelson, S. F. "Sex and the Single Hemisphere: Specialization of the Right Hemisphere for Spatial Processing," *Science,* 193 (1976), 425–427.

Wittig, M. A., and A. C. Petersen (eds.). *Sex Differences in Cognitive Performance.* New York: Academic Press, 1979.

Wittrock, M. C. (ed.). *The Brain and Psychology.* New York: Academic Press, 1980.

Wolf, T. M. "A Developmental Investigation of Televised Modeled Verbalizations on Resistance to Temptation," *Developmental Psychology,* 6 (1972), 537.

Wolfe, L. "The Sexual Profile of That Cosmopolitan Girl," *Cosmopolitan,* 189 (1980), 254–265.

Wolff, G. "Increased Bodily Growth of School-Children Since the War," *Lancet,* 228 (1935), 1006–1011.

Wolff, P. H. "The Role of Biological Rhythms in Early Psychological Development," *Bulletin of the Menninger Clinic,* 31 (1967), 197–218.

———. "The Natural History of Crying and Other Vocalizations in Early Infancy," in B. M. Foss (ed.), *Determinants of Infant Behavior.* Vol. 4. London: Methuen, 1969, pp. 81–109.

Wolfinger, R. E., and S. J. Rosenstone. *Who Votes?* New Haven, Conn.: Yale University Press, 1980.

Woodruff, D. C. *Can You Live to Be 100?* New York: Chatham Square, 1977.

Woodruff, D. S., and J. E. Birren. "Age Changes and Cohort Difference in Personality," *Developmental Psychology,* 6 (March 1972), 252–259.

Wright, J. C., and A. G. Vlietstra. "The Development of Selective Attention: From Perceptual Exploration to Logical Search," H. W. Reese (ed.), *Advances in Child Development and Behavior.* Vol. 10. New York: Academic Press, 1975, pp. 195–239.

Yalisove, D. "The Effect of Riddle Structure on Children's Comprehension of Riddles," *Developmental Psychology,* 14 (1978), 173–180.

Yankelovich, D. *New Rules.* New York: Random House, 1981.

Yarrow, L. J. "Maternal Deprivation: Toward an Empirical and Conceptual Reevaluation," *Psychological Bulletin,* 58 (1961), 459–490.

Yarrow, M. R., P. M. Scott, and C. Z. Waxler. "Learning Concern for Others," *Developmental Psychology,* 8 (1973), 240–260.

Yates, B. T., and W. Mischel. "Young Children's Preferred Attentional Strategies for Delaying Gratification," *Journal of Personality and Social Psychology,* 37 (1979), 286–300.

Yonas, A., C. Oberg, and A. Norcia. "Development of Sensitivity to Binocular Information for the Approach of an Object," *Developmental Psychology,* 14 (1978), 147–152.

Yonas, A., and H. L. Pick, Jr. "An Approach to the Study of Infant Space Perception," in L. B. Cohen and P. Salapatek (eds.), *Infant Perception: From Sensation *to Cognition.* Vol. 2. New York: Academic Press, 1975, 3–31.

Young, J. W., and L. R. Ferguson. "Developmental Changes through Adolescence in the Spontaneous Nomination of Reference Groups as a Function of Decision Content," *Journal of Youth and Adolescence,* 8 (1979), 239–252.

Youniss, J. *Parents and Peers in Social Development.* Chicago: University of Chicago Press, 1980.

Youniss, J., and J. Volpe. "A Relational Analysis of Children's Friendship," in W. Damon (ed.), *New Directions for Child Development.* No. 1. *Social Cognition.* San Francisco: Jossey-Bass, 1978, pp. 1–22.

Yussen, S. R., S. R. Mathews II, R. R. Buss, and P. T. Kane. "Developmental Change in Judging Importance and Critical Elements of Stories," *Developmental Psychology,* 16 (1980), 213–219.

Zahn-Waxler, C., M. Radke-Yarrow, and R. A. King. "Child Rearing and Children's Prosocial Initiations toward Victims of Distress," *Child Development,* 50 (1979), 319–330.

Zaporozhets, A. V. "The Development of Perception in the Preschool Child," in P. H. Mussen (ed.), "European Research in Cognitive Development," *Monographs of the Society for Research in Child Development,* 30 (1965), 82–101.

Zarit, S. H. *Aging and Mental Disorders: Psychological Approaches to Assessment and Treatment.* New York: Free Press, 1980.

Zelazo, N. A., P. R. Zelazo, and S. Kolb. "Walking in the Newborn," *Science,* 176 (1972), 314–315.

Zelnik, M., and J. F. Kantner. *Sexuality, Contraception, and Pregnancy Among Young Unmarried Females in the U. S.,* Unpublished manuscript, 1972. (Cited in I. L. Reiss, *Heterosexual Relationships Inside and Outside Marriage.* Morristown, N.J.: General Learning Press, 1973, p. 15.)

______. "Sexual and Contraceptive Experience of Young Unmarried Women in the United States, 1976 and 1971," *Family Planning Perspectives,* 9 (1977), 55–71.

______. "Contraceptive Patterns and Premarital Pregnancy among Women Aged 15–19 in 1976," *Family Planning Perspectives,* 10 (1978), 135–142.

Zelnik, M., J. Y. Kim, and J. F. Kantner. "Probabilities of Intercourse and Contraception among U.S. Teenage Women, 1971 and 1976," *Family Planning Perspectives,* 11 (1979).

Zigler, E., and P. K. Trickett. "IQ, Social Competence, and Evaluation of Early Childhood Intervention Programs," *American Psychologist,* 33 (1978), 789–798.

Zill, N. *National Survey of Children: Preliminary Results.* New York: Foundation for Child Development, 1977.

Zimbardo, P. G., S. M. Andersen, and L. G. Kabat. "Induced Hearing Deficit Generates Experimental Paranoia," *Science,* 212 (1981), 1529–1531.

Zur Aschoff, L. "Normalen und Pathologischen Anatomie des Criesenalters," *Medisinische Klinik,* 33 (1937), 257–291.

INDEX

ABOUT THE AUTHORS

Robert E. Schell received his Ph.D. from the University of Illinois and has held academic appointments at Michigan State University, Dartmouth College, and the Merrill-Palmer Institute. He has published articles in various journals, including *Child Development, Journal of Comparative and Physiological Psychology, Journal of Speech and Hearing Disorders,* and *Journal of Abnormal and Social Psychology.* He is the author of *Letters and Sounds* and has been a contributing author and consultant on several CRM/Random House texts, including *Abnormal Psychology: Current Perspectives, Readings in Developmental Psychology,* and *Educational Psychology: A Contemporary View.* He is currently lecturer in the psychology department at San Diego State University, and a clinical and consulting psychologist in California.

Elizabeth Hall has been Editor-in-Chief of *Human Nature* magazine and Managing Editor of *Psychology Today* magazine. She is also the author of *Child Psychology Today,* which was published by Random House last year, as well as several popular psychology books, two of which were honored by the American Psychological Foundation's National Merit Award: *Why We Do What We Do: A Look at Psychology,* and *From Pigeons to People: A Look at Behavior Shaping.*